Fodor's 2011

ENGLAND

Where to Stay and Eat for All Budgets

Must-See Sights and Local Secrets

Ratings You Can Trust

Fodor's Travel Publications   New York, Toronto, London, Sydney, Auckland
www.fodors.com

FODOR'S ENGLAND 2011
Editor: Linda Cabasin

Editorial Contributor: Mark Sullivan
Writers: Robert Andrews, Paul Cannon, Christi Daugherty, Kiki Deere, Jan Fuscoe, Julius Honnor, Kate Hughes, Jack Jewers, Michelle Rosenberg, Ellin Stein, Roger Thomas, Alex Wijeratna

Production Editor: Carrie Parker
Maps & Illustrations: David Lindroth, Inc., Ed Jacobus, *cartographers;* Bob Blake, Rebecca Baer, *map editors;* William Wu, *information graphics*
Design: Fabrizio La Rocca, *creative director;* Guido Caroti, Siobhan O'Hare, *art directors;* Tina Malaney, Chie Ushio, Ann McBride, Jessica Walsh, *designers;* Melanie Marin, *senior picture editor*
Cover Photo: Yellow Dog Productions/The Image Bank/Getty Images
Production Manager: Angela L. McLean

COPYRIGHT

ISBN 978-1-4000-0483-6

ISSN 1558–870X

SPECIAL SALES
This book is available at special discounts for bulk purchases for sales promotions or premiums. Special editions, including personalized covers, excerpts of existing books, and corporate imprints, can be created in large quantities for special needs. For more information, write to Special Markets/Premium Sales, 1745 Broadway, MD 6-2, New York, New York 10019, or e-mail specialmarkets@randomhouse.com.

AN IMPORTANT TIP & AN INVITATION
Although all prices, opening times, and other details in this book are based on information supplied to us at press time, changes occur all the time in the travel world, and Fodor's cannot accept responsibility for facts that become outdated or for inadvertent errors or omissions. So **always confirm information when it matters,** especially if you're making a detour to visit a specific place. Your experiences—positive and negative— matter to us. If we have missed or misstated something, **please write to us.** We follow up on all suggestions. Contact the England editor at editors@fodors.com or c/o Fodor's at 1745 Broadway, New York, NY 10019.

PRINTED IN THE UNITED STATES OF AMERICA

10 9 8 7 6 5 4 3 2 1

Be a Fodor's Correspondent

Your opinion matters. It matters to us. It matters to your fellow Fodor's travelers, too. And we'd like to hear it. In fact, we need to hear it.

When you share your experiences and opinions, you become an active member of the Fodor's community. That means we'll not only use your feedback to make our books better, but we'll publish your names and comments whenever possible. Throughout our guides, look for "Word of Mouth," excerpts of your unvarnished feedback.

Here's how you can help improve Fodor's for all of us.

Tell us when we're right. We rely on local writers to give you an insider's perspective. But our writers and staff editors—who are the best in the business—depend on you. Your positive feedback is a vote to renew our recommendations for the next edition.

Tell us when we're wrong. We're proud that we update most of our guides every year. But we're not perfect. Things change. Hotels cut services. Museums change hours. Charming cafés lose charm. If our writer didn't quite capture the essence of a place, tell us how you'd do it differently. If any of our descriptions are inaccurate or inadequate, we'll incorporate your changes in the next edition and will correct factual errors at fodors.com immediately.

Tell us what to include. You probably have had fantastic travel experiences that aren't yet in Fodor's. Why not share them with a community of like-minded travelers? Maybe you chanced upon a beach or bistro or B&B that you don't want to keep to yourself. Tell us why we should include it. And share your discoveries and experiences with everyone directly at fodors.com. Your input may lead us to add a new listing or highlight a place we cover with a "Highly Recommended" star or with our highest rating, "Fodor's Choice."

Give us your opinion instantly at our feedback center at www.fodors.com/feedback. You may also e-mail editors@fodors.com with the subject line "England Editor." Or send your nominations, comments, and complaints by mail to England Editor, Fodor's, 1745 Broadway, New York, NY 10019.

You and travelers like you are the heart of the Fodor's community. Make our community richer by sharing your experiences. Be a Fodor's correspondent.

Happy traveling!

Tim Jarrell, Publisher

CONTENTS

ABOUT THIS BOOK

Our Ratings

Sometimes you find terrific travel experiences and sometimes they just find you. But usually the burden is on you to select the right combination of experiences. That's where our ratings come in.

As travelers we've all discovered a place so wonderful that its worthiness is obvious. And sometimes superlatives don't do that place justice: you just have to be there to know. These sights, properties, and experiences get our highest rating, **Fodor's Choice** indicated by orange stars throughout this book.

Black stars highlight sights and properties we deem **Highly Recommended** places that our writers, editors, and readers praise again and again for consistency and excellence.

There's another category: any place we include in this book is by definition worth your time, unless we say otherwise. And we will.

Disagree with any of our choices? Care to nominate a place or suggest that we rate one more highly? Visit our feedback center at www.fodors.com/feedback.

Budget Well

Hotel and restaurant price categories from £ to £££££ are defined in the opening pages of each chapter. For attractions, we always give standard adult admission fees; reductions are usually available for children, students, and senior citizens. Want to pay with plastic? **AE, DC, MC, V** following restaurant and hotel listings indicate whether American Express, Diners Club, MasterCard, and Visa are accepted.

Restaurants

Unless we state otherwise, restaurants are open for lunch and dinner daily. We mention dress only when there's a specific requirement and reservations only when they're essential or not accepted—it's always best to book ahead.

Hotels

Hotels have private bath, phone, and TV and operate on the European Plan (aka EP, meaning without meals), unless we specify that they use the Continental Plan (CP, with a continental breakfast), Breakfast Plan (BP, with a full breakfast), or Modified American Plan (MAP, with breakfast and dinner). We always list facilities but not whether you'll be charged an extra fee to use them,

so when pricing accommodations, find out what's included.

Many Listings
- ★ Fodor's Choice
- ★ Highly recommended
- ⊠ Physical address
- ✛ Directions or Map coordinates
- ⬧ Mailing address
- ☎ Telephone
- ⊟ Fax
- ⊕ On the Web
- ✉ E-mail
- ⊡ Admission fee
- ☉ Open/closed times
- Ⓤ Metro stations
- ⊟ Credit cards

Hotels & Restaurants
- ⬚ Hotel
- ⇌ Number of rooms
- ⚲ Facilities
- ⑪ Meal plans
- ✕ Restaurant
- ⚲ Reservations
- ⚱ Dress code
- ⚲ Smoking
- ⚱ BYOB

Outdoors
- ⚑ Golf
- ⚑ Camping

Other
- ⚈ Family-friendly
- ⇨ See also
- ⊠ Branch address
- ☞ Take note

1

Experience England

WORD OF MOUTH

"England, I shall miss the charm and vibrant nature of many of your towns, the incredible frequency and scope of your public transportation, the millennia of continuous history that you give to your people, the accessibility and beauty of countryside within a short walk of your busy Hampshire and Wiltshire town centers. Thanks for all those lovely visuals I have to keep with me."

—Daniel_Williams

WHAT'S WHERE

The following numbers refer to chapters.

2 London. Not only Britain's financial and governmental center but also one of the world's great cities, London has mammoth museums, posh palaces, double-decker buses, and iconic sights such as Big Ben. Intriguing villagelike neighborhoods from Notting Hill to Bloomsbury call out to be explored; when you need a break, pop into a pub or relax in one of the city's sprawling parks.

3 The Southeast. This compact green and pleasant region within day-trip distance of London takes in Canterbury and its cathedral, funky seaside Brighton, the appealing towns of Rye and Lewes, Dover's white cliffs, and castles such as Bodiam, Leeds, and Hever. Noted gardens as different as smaller, romantic Sissinghurst and large-scale Wisley add to the mix.

4 The South. Hampshire, Dorset, and Wiltshire are quintessential English countryside, with gentle hills and green pastures. Explore the stone circles at Stonehenge and Avebury, and take in Winchester (Jane Austen country) and Salisbury, and Lyme Regis and the fossil-rich Jurassic Coast.

5 The West Country. Somerset, Devon, and Cornwall are sunnier and warmer than the rest of the country, with sandy beaches. Cornwall has lush gardens and stunning coast, Bristol is a vibrant city, and Wells and Exeter are pretty towns. Take in the brooding heaths and moors of Exmoor and Dartmoor, too.

6 The Thames Valley. London's commuter belt takes in Windsor, where the Queen spends time. Then there are the spires of Oxford, peaceful river towns such as Henley and Marlow, and stately homes such as over-the-top Blenheim Palace.

7 Shakespeare Country. Stratford-upon-Avon, a leafy, literary, theatrical town 100 mi north of London, is the place to see Shakespeare's birthplace and watch his plays. Warwickshire has gentle landscapes as well as noble Warwick and Kenilworth castles.

8 Bath and the Cotswolds. The grand Georgian town of Bath is one of England's highlights, with the Roman Baths and golden-stone 18th- and 19th-century architecture. Nearby, pretty as a picture, the Cotswolds region is justly famous for its tranquil villages, stone cottages, and gardens.

Belfast

NORTHERN IRELAND

Isle of Man

Douglas

Irish Sea

Dublin

Isle of Anglesey

Holyhead

IRELAND

Caernarfon

Aberystwyth

WALES

Swansea

Bristol Chan.

Barnstaple

0   30 miles

0   30 kilometers

5

Plymouth

Penzance

Falmouth

SCOTLAND

Berwick-upon-Tweed

Carlisle

Newcastle
Gateshead
Penrith
Keswick
Durham
Sunderland
Hartlepool

Kendal
Darlington
Middlesbrough

Barrow-
in-Furness
Lancaster
Scarborough

Blackpool
Harrogate
York

Preston
Bradford
Leeds
Kingston-
upon-Hull

Bolton
Blackburn
M62
M1
M62

Liverpool
M54
Manchester
Stockport
M180
Grimsby

Birkenhead
M56
Sheffield

Chester
Doncaster

Newcastle
Stoke-on-Trent
Lincoln
Skegness

Shrewsbury
Derby
Nottingham
Boston
The Wash

M54
Stafford
M1
Grantham

Wolverhampton
Leicester
King's
Lynn
Norwich

Birmingham
M6
Peterborough
Lowestoft

Stratford-upon-Avon
Coventry
Northampton
Newmarket
Bury St. Edmunds

7

Worcester
M40
M1
Bedford
Cambridge
Ipswich

Cheltenham
Oxford
A1
M11
Harwich

Gloucester
M40
M25
Colchester

M4
Severn
Thames
Swindon
Reading
6
2
M25
Southend-on-Sea

8
Cardiff
Bristol
Bath
M4
Guildford
LONDON
*Isle of
Sheppey*

M5
Reigate
Maidstone
M20
Canterbury

Taunton
M3
Salisbury
Winchester
M23
Royal
Tunbridge
Wells
Folkestone
Dover

M5
4
Southampton
Rye
*Channel
Tunnel*
Calais

Exeter
Bournemouth
Portsmouth
Brighton
3

Lyme Regis
Weymouth
*Isle of
Wight*

*North
Sea*

E n g l i s h   C h a n n e l

FRANCE

TO JERSEY
AND GUERNSEY

WHAT'S WHERE

9 The Welsh Borders. This lovely rural area bordering Wales has few real sights except the Industrial Revolution museums of Ironbridge Gorge; it's a good place to relax. Ludlow has half-timber buildings, and medieval Shrewsbury is a fine excursion; Chester draws the tourists. Birmingham offers a modern urban experience.

10 Lancashire and the Peaks. Liverpool rides the Beatles' coattails but, like Manchester, has transformed its warehouses and docks into sleek hotels, restaurants, and shops. Buzzing nightlife and museums are highlights in both cities. The Peak District has great walking and stately homes such as Chatsworth and Haddon Hall.

11 The Lake District. A popular national park, this is a startlingly beautiful area of craggy hills, wild moorland, stone cottages, and glittering silvery lakes. Nature lovers and hikers crowd the area in summer. Among the literary high points are Wordsworth's homes.

12 East Anglia. The biggest lure in this green, flat, low-key region is Cambridge, with its medieval halls of learning. The countryside is dominated by the cathedrals of Ely and Norwich and by time-warp

towns such as Lavenham. Coastal spots from Aldeburgh to Wells-next-the-Sea add a salty flavor.

13 Yorkshire. This wilder part of England has great appeal for lovers of the outdoors, but ancient walled York is also a center of attention. To York's west are the moors and dales that inspired the Brontës, and in east Yorkshire the moors collide with the sea at salty towns such as Whitby. Leeds is a reviving urban center worth a look.

14 The Northeast. Travelers can walk in the footsteps of Roman soldiers along Hadrian's Wall in this remote northern region. Bamburgh and Dunstanburgh castles guard the coast; Alnwick Castle has stunning gardens. The small city of Durham is a medieval gem, a contrast to modern Newcastle.

15 Wales. Clinging to the western edge of England, Wales is green and ruggedly beautiful, with mountainous inland scenery reaching out to a magnificent coastline. Except for Cardiff and Swansea, this is a rural country, with three national parks. Wales is justly famous for castles, including Conwy and Caernarfon.

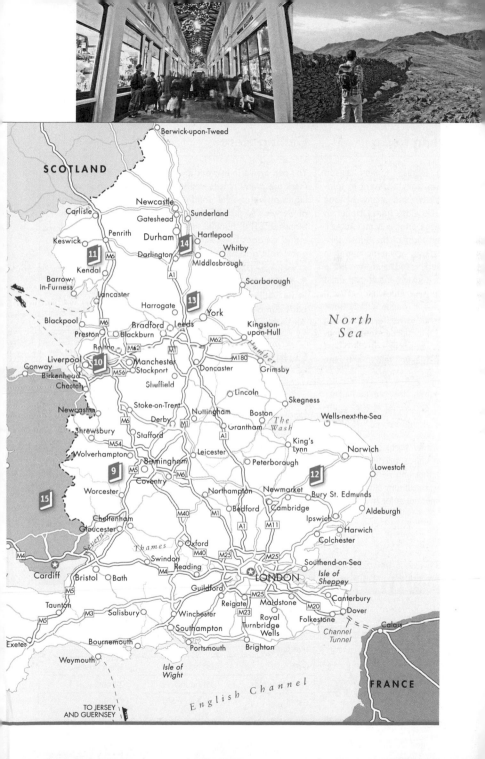

ENGLAND PLANNER

When to Go

The English tourist season peaks from mid-April to mid-October, and many historic houses close from October to Easter. During July and August, when most of the British take vacations, accommodations in popular resorts and areas are in high demand and at their most expensive. The winter cultural season in London is lively. Hotel rates are lower then, too. Spring and fall can be good alternatives, as prices are still below high-season rates, and the crowds are thinner.

Generally, the climate in England and Wales is mild. Summer temperatures can reach the 90s, with high humidity. In winter there can be heavy frost, thin snow, thick fog, and rain, rain, rain. Here are average daily maximum and minimum temperatures for two cities.

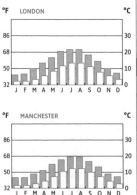

Getting Here

You can arrive in England by plane, train, or boat, and there are many places to disembark. Most international flights arrive at either London's Heathrow Airport (LHR) or at Gatwick Airport (LGW). A third, much smaller airport, Stansted (STN), handles mainly European and domestic traffic, as does Luton Airport (LLA). These airports have good train and bus options for getting into London.

Manchester (MAN) in northwest England handles some flights from the United States, as does Birmingham (BHX) in the Midlands. Most people fly into London, but other airports can be useful. *For more details, see Getting Here and Around in Travel Smart England.*

Getting Around

England is not a large country: the entire United Kingdom (including England, Scotland, Wales, and Northern Ireland) is about the size of Oregon, so you're less likely to fly. The country's train and bus systems are extensive and relatively well maintained; for major towns and cities, there is generally no need to rent a car. To see castles and historic houses—which may be far from towns—you may have to rent a car or join a tour. Driving is on the left, and gas (petrol) is expensive at about $7 a gallon.

Train tickets tend to be two to three times more expensive than bus fares, but train journeys are at least twice as fast as bus journeys. *For more details, see Getting Here and Around in Travel Smart England.*

FROM LONDON TO	BY CAR	BY TRAIN
Newquay, Cornwall	5½ hours	5 hours
The Lake District	5½ hours	4 hours
York	4 hours	2–3 hours
Liverpool	4 hours	3 hours
Bath	1½ hours	1½–2 hours
The Cotswolds	1½ hours	2 hours
Oxford	1½ hours	1 hour

Restaurants: The Basics

What you should eat in England depends on where you are, as food is surprisingly regional. Fresh seafood dominates the coastal areas, but lamb and beef lead the way in the inland regions. Local cuisine is also affected by ethnic communities. Although England is increasingly a foodie country with a good restaurant scene, the strongest food culture is limited to major cities and a few regions, most notably London and the Southeast.

In the rural north—Cumbria, Yorkshire, and Northumberland—you'll get hearty meals in family-friendly pubs and inns. York and Harrogate have better options, and Leeds has a burgeoning food subscene. Look for local lamb and beef. Birmingham, in the Midlands, is famous for its Indian restaurants serving spicy curries. In Cornwall, Devon, and Dorset, it's all about fresh seafood that is some of the country's best. However, don't overlook Cornish pasties (hand-size meat-and-potato pies), sold everywhere. *For details and a price-category chart, see Eating Out in Travel Smart England.*

Lodging: The Basics

London is in part about sleek, modern hotels, where enormous amounts of money get you relatively small amounts of space. One way to get a good deal is to book a chain—such as Millennium or Premier—online well in advance. Check for off-season deals, too. Budget hotels in London can be so unattractive that it's better to look for a special offer at a better chain.

In major towns, you have more options than in rural areas. Hotels are harder to come by in the countryside, and you may stay in a small bed-and-breakfast in a family's home. Prices may be half or less of what you'll pay in London. Some B&Bs are gorgeous, and many are in handy locations; others are neither, so be careful. B&Bs are popular with British travelers and can be a great way to meet locals.

You might also stay in an old coaching inn from the stagecoach era. There are modern twists on the theme, with chains operating cheap modern hotels with bland pub-restaurants. Some older hotels can be old-fashioned but also less pricey. House and apartment rentals can be a good, sometimes cheaper alternative to hotels. ⇨ *For details and a price-category chart, see the Lodging Primer in this chapter and Accommodations in Travel Smart England.*

Saving Money

Here are ways to start pinching your pence.

■ Take advantage of free breakfasts if your hotel or B&B offers them. Or grab a croissant at a coffee shop.

■ Many pubs serve lunches for less than £10; most restaurants offer cheap lunch deals.

■ Make one meal a prepared sandwich from a grocery store or sandwich shop.

■ In London, consider staying in a house or apartment. Outside of London, stay in a B&B or small guesthouse.

■ Check the Web sites of major chains for deals, especially in the off-season.

■ Buy a prepaid Oyster Card in London to save on the Tube and buses.

■ Ask about family tickets at major sights.

■ Get your culture kicks in free national museums.

■ Check out a sightseeing pass such as the Great British Heritage Pass.

■ Purchase a BritRail train pass or regional passes.

Visitor Information

These sites have information useful for planning.

Contacts VisitEngland (⊕ *www.enjoyengland. com*). **VisitBritain** (⊕ *www. visitbritain.us*).

ENGLAND'S TOP ATTRACTIONS

Houses of Parliament and Big Ben

(A) One of the world's most famous sights, the gold-tipped towers of Parliament and the famous clock tower stand at the center of British power, and at the heart of London. The facade is glorious when flood-lighted at night, especially when viewed from the south side of the Thames. *(⇨ See Chapter 2.)*

Hampton Court Palace

(B) This Thames-side redbrick palace was built by and for Cardinal Wolsey, Henry VIII's religious adviser. But Henry coveted it, so it became a splendid royal home. Hampton Court, a half hour from London by train, has grand Tudor kitchens, sprawling gardens, and a tricky maze. *(⇨ See Chapter 2.)*

Bath

(C) Exquisitely preserved but entertaining, this Georgian town still centers on the hot mineral springs that made it the fashionable spa for the wealthy in the 18th and early 19th centuries. Streets lined with Palladian buildings made of golden limestone, an ancient abbey, tea shops, boutiques, and ruined Roman baths combine to give Bath real character. *(⇨ See Chapter 8.)*

The Tower of London

(D) The scene of much blood and gore since the 11th century, this extraordinary minicity of 20 towers has sturdy outer walls and a deep, drained moat. The Yeoman Wardens, known as Beefeaters, wear colorful Tudor clothes and give magnificent tours. All this, and the Crown Jewels are here, too. *(⇨ See Chapter 2.)*

British Museum

(E) The self-appointed protector of global treasures, this vast and varied museum in London is packed to bursting with antiquities and alluring objects. Among the greatest hits are the Parthenon Marbles, the Rosetta Stone, and Egyptian mummies. *(⇨ See Chapter 2.)*

Hadrian's Wall

(F) Begun in AD 122, the thick stone wall built by the Emperor Hadrian across the rugged far north of the country is a remarkable survivor from Roman Britain, where it protected Roman soldiers from invading tribes. Biking, hiking, and horseback riding are wonderful ways to explore. (⇨ *See Chapter 14.*)

Oxford

(G) Dubbed "the city of dreaming spires" for its fairy-tale cityscape formed by the steeples, towers, and domes of hundreds of university buildings and churches, Oxford is an ancient, atmospheric university town. You can stroll through the colleges, visit the university's museum, and relax in the city's pubs. (⇨ *See Chapter 6.*)

Coastal Cornwall

(H) The coasts of Cornwall, in England's far southwest corner, are beloved by many (too many, in summer) for different reasons. The more rugged northern coast has cliffs that drop to tiny coves and beaches; ruined, cliff-top Tintagel Castle is here. The south coast has sandy beaches and resort towns such as Penzance and arty St. Ives. (⇨ *See Chapter 5.*)

Cotswold Villages

(I) Marked by rolling hills, green fields, and limestone cottages with prim flower beds, the Cotswolds, 100 mi west of London, make a peaceful getaway. There's little to do in idyllic villages except to stroll and pile clotted cream on your scone, but that's the point. Gardens and stately homes add to the charm. (⇨ *See Chapter 8.*)

Lake District

(J) Sprawling across northwest England, this area of 16 major lakes and jagged mountains inspired Romantic poets to write sweeping verse. You can hike the trails or view the mountains from a boat, or seek out the retreats of writers in towns such as Grasmere, Hawkshead, and Coniston. (⇨ *See Chapter 11.*)

QUINTESSENTIAL ENGLAND

Pints and Pubs

Pop in for a pint at a pub to encounter what has been the center—literally the "public house"—of English social life for centuries. The basic pub recipe calls for a variety of beers on draft—dark creamy stouts like Guinness; bitter, including brews such as Tetley's and Bass; and lager, the blondest and blandest of the trio—a dartboard, oak paneling, and paisley carpets. Throw in a bunch of young suits in London, a generous dash of undergrads in places such as Oxford or Cambridge, and, in rural areas, a healthy helping of blokes around the television and ladies in the corner sipping their *halves* (half pints) and having a *natter* (gossip). In smaller pubs, listen in and enjoy the banter among the regulars—you may even be privy to the occasional *barney* (harmless argument). Join in if you care to, but remember not to take anything too seriously—a severe breach of pub etiquette. Make your visit soon: the encroachment of gastro-pubs (bar-restaurant hybrids) is just one of the forces challenging traditional pub culture.

Daily Rags

To blend in with the English, stash your street map, slide a folded newspaper under your arm, and head for the nearest park bench or café. Lose yourself in any one of the national dailies for often well-written insight into Britain's worldview. For a dose of tabloid melodrama, choose the *Sun,* Britain's most popular newspaper. The sensational headlines are hard to miss—"Prince's Cheating Scandal" and "Empire Strikes Bark: Dogs Dress Up as Vader"—and you can assume that the topless model on Page 3 has helped rather than hindered the paper's success. The biweekly *Private Eye* offers British wit at its best, specializing in political cartoons, parodies, and satirical reporting.

If you want to get a sense of contemporary England culture, and indulge in some of its pleasures, start by familiarizing yourself with the rituals of daily life. Here are a few highlights—things you can take part in with relative ease.

A Lovely Cuppa

For almost four centuries, the English and tea have been immersed in a love affair passionate enough to survive revolutions, rations, tariffs, and lattes, but also soothing, as whistling kettles across the nation mark moments of quiet comfort in public places and in homes and offices. The ritual known as "afternoon tea" had its beginnings in the early 19th century, in the private chambers of the duchess of Bedford, where she and her "ladies of leisure" indulged in afternoons of pastries and fragrant blends. But you don't need to dress up to lift your pinky to sip the steamy brew. Department stores and tearooms across the nation offer everything from simple tea and biscuits to shockingly overpriced spreads with sandwiches and cakes that would impress even the duchess herself. And if tea is not your cup of tea, don't worry; there's no shame for those who prefer coffee with their scones and clotted cream.

Sports Fever

Whoever says England is not an overtly religious country has not considered the sports mania that has descended here, and not merely because of the approaching 2012 Olympic Games in London. Whether water events (such as Henley, Cowes, and the Head of the River Race) or a land competition (the Grand National steeplechase, the Virgin London Marathon, a good football match), most bring people to the edge of their seats— or more often the living room couch. To partake in the rite, you'll need Pimm's (the drink for swank spectators of the Henley Royal Regatta) or beer (the drink for most everything else). You may experience the exhilaration yourself—which, you'll probably sense, is not for the love of *a* sport, but for the love of *sport* itself.

IF YOU LIKE

Castles and Stately Homes

Exploring the diversity and magnificence of England's castles and stately homes, from Norman towers to Palladian palaces, can occupy most of a blissful vacation. Whether world famous or less visited, owned by royalty, aristocratic families, or the National Trust, each abode has tales to tell about history or domestic life. Castles and houses are spread around the nation (with fewer stately homes in Cornwall and the Lake District), but certain clusters may help your planning. Note that most stately homes are open only from spring through fall. England's southeastern coast is lined with sturdy castles; nearby but inland, around Royal Tunbridge Wells, are treasure houses such as Hever Castle and Knole. West of Salisbury are Wilton House, Stourhead, and Longleat, and the Cotswolds have a rich assortment. England's north has gems from Peak District manors to castles on the remote northeastern coast. London visitors won't miss out, either: Buckingham and Kensington palaces, the Tower of London, and Hampton Court Palace and Windsor Castle lie within easy reach. If your itinerary extends to Wales, look for Edward I's "iron ring" of castles, including Harlech and Conwy.

Blenheim Palace, Thames Valley. This baroque extravaganza is touted as England's only rival to Versailles.

Holkham Hall, East Anglia. A splendid 60-foot-tall marble entryway and salons filled with old masters distinguish this Palladian palace.

Petworth House, the Southeast. One of the National Trust's glories is known for art from J. M. W. Turner.

Charming Villages

Year after year, armies of tourists with images of green meadows, thatched roofs, and colorful flower beds flock to England's countryside, for good reason. Most will find their way to famously adorable towns along the Thames, magical seaside resorts in the West Country, and a smattering of fairy-tale hamlets in the Cotswolds—a hilly area in west-central England renowned for its golden and gray stone cottages. However, torrential tourist traffic has made these once-quintessentially quaint areas a little *too* accessible for some. Steer clear of busy Cotswolds towns such as Broadway in summer (especially on weekends); Winchcombe and Snowshill are more unspoiled options. Choose a weekday to visit the Thames Valley towns, which attract Londoners. To avoid some crowds, consider the pastoral flatlands of East Anglia beyond Cambridge, where historic villages remain relatively undiscovered, or explore the Norfolk coast. The rural Welsh Borders region has tranquil landscapes and towns, or head to Wales, with its mountainside hamlets and sleepy seaside resorts.

Lavenham, East Anglia. This village is full of Tudor buildings, the former houses of wool merchants and weavers.

Ludlow, Welsh Borders. Medieval and Georgian buildings cluster below a castle in this town, whose restaurants that have made it a foodie favorite.

Whitby, Yorkshire. A ruined abbey and a cliff-lined harbor combine with a rich fishing and whaling legacy to enhance this coastal gem.

Glorious Gardens

Despite being cursed with impertinent weather and short summers, English gardeners will gladly grab a gardening tool and attack a misbehaving rose garden for just a few short months of enjoyment. The Tudors were the first to produce gardens that were more than strictly utilitarian, and since then French, Italian, Dutch, and even Japanese ideas have been imported and adapted to suit the national aesthetic. A pilgrimage to a garden is an essential part of any spring or summer trip, whether you visit a large educational garden such as Kew Gardens near London or the West Country's Eden Project; a period gem such as Arts and Crafts Hidcote Manor in the Cotswolds; or gardens that are part of a stately home and as lovely as the house. Green havens thrive all over England, but perhaps the most fertile hunting grounds are in Oxfordshire, Gloucestershire (including the Cotswolds), and Kent (the "Garden of England"). Some of these visions of paradise have limited hours, and most close in winter; they're all worth the trip.

Sissinghurst Castle Garden, Southeast. Vita Sackville-West's masterpiece, set within the remains of a Tudor castle, is busy in summer but also spectacular in autumn.

Stourhead, South. One of the country's most impressive house-and-garden combinations is an artful 18th-century sanctuary with a tranquil lake, colorful shrubs, and grottoes.

Wisley, Southeast. The Royal Horticultural Society's garden splendidly blends the pretty and the practical in its inspirational displays.

Urban Action

London has everything a world capital should have—rich culture and history, thrilling art and theater scenes, world-class restaurants and sensational shopping—along with crowds, traffic, and high prices. It shouldn't be missed, but if you appreciate modern cities, fall out of the tourist trap and spend time in some of England's reviving urban centers, including those in its former industrial heartland, where blossoming multiculturalism has paved the way for a unique vibe. Football (soccer) fans might take in a match in Manchester or Liverpool, two bitter sporting rivals in the Northwest, or join hordes of fans to watch the game at a local pub. Manchester's museums are excellent, and its downtown (rebuilt after a 1996 IRA bombing) is worth a look, as are its famous clubs. Liverpool claims the Beatles sites and the stellar museums of the Albert Dock; its stint as the European Union's Capital of Culture in 2008 produced dramatic changes. See what's gentrifying in Birmingham, the country's second-largest city and a cultural force in England.

Brighton, Southeast. Bold, bright, and boisterous are the words to describe a seaside charmer that has everything from the dazzling Royal Pavilion to the trendy shops of the Lanes.

Bristol, West Country. With its lively waterfront and homegrown music talent, this youthful city has vibrant nightlife as well as a long history.

Leeds, Yorkshire. Another northern, former industrial city polishing its Victorian buildings, Leeds is known for its shopping arcades and youthful music scene.

Ancient Mysteries

Stone circles as well as ancient stone and earthen forts and mounds offer tantalizing hints about Britain's mysterious prehistoric inhabitants. The country's southwestern landscape, particularly the Salisbury Plain, Dorset, and the eastern side of Cornwall, has a notably rich concentration of these sites, perplexing mysteries that human nature compels us to try to solve. Stonehenge, the stone circle begun 5,000 years ago, stands on the wide Salisbury Plain; crowds detract from the magic, so arrive early or late to appreciate the monument's timeless power. Hypotheses about its purpose range from the scientific (ancient calendar) to the fantastic (a gift from extinct giants). Other relics—chambered tombs and mounds—dot the Avebury area to the north. Equally enigmatic are Maiden Castle, a colossal prehistoric hill fort near Dorchester, and the nearby figure of a giant carved into the hillside overlooking Cerne Abbas. Sometimes the setting of these ancient creations, such as Castlerigg Stone Circle in the Lake District, is as awesome as the surviving remains.

Avebury Stone Circles, South. Large and marvelously evocative, these circles surround part of the village of Avebury.

Stanton Drew Circles, West Country. Use your imagination to visualize the vast size of the two avenues of standing stones, three rings, and burial chamber that now lie in a field.

Vale of the White Horse, Thames Valley. The gigantic horse here was actually carved into the chalky hillside around 1750 BC.

Wonderful Walks

England seems to be designed with walking in mind—footpaths wind through the contours of the landscape, and popular routes are well endowed with cozy bed-and-breakfasts and pubs. Your decisions will be what kind of landscape you prefer (coast or countryside, flat or mountainous) and how long a hike you want, though you can often do just part of a long-distance trail such as the Thames Path. Ramble through one of England's national parks (which are sprinkled with towns), and you'll generally find well-maintained trails and handy maps at local tourist information centers. The country's most famous walking spots are in the Lake District, from a short meander to a major mountain trek—but beware of summer congestion. Yorkshire's dales and moors are also popular. Cross the border to Wales, where the Brecon Beacons offer windswept uplands with easy paths, and ferocious peaks in Snowdonia National Park promise challenging hikes. Wherever you hike, always be prepared for storms or fogs. Check out ⊕ *www.nationaltrail.co.uk* for inspiration and advice.

Borrowdale, Lake District. Have a color-pencil kit handy to capture the beauty of the dramatically verdant valleys and jagged peaks.

Peak District, Lancashire and the Peaks. Its rocky outcrops and vaulting meadows make some people say this is the country's most beautiful national park.

South West Coast Path, West Country. Spectacular is the word for the 630-mi trail that winds from Minehead in Somerset to Poole Harbour in Dorset.

Thrilling Theater

There's no better antidote to an overdose of stately homes and glorious gardens than a face-to-face encounter with another British specialty, the theater. London is the heart and soul of the action: here companies famous and lesser known consistently churn out superb productions, from musicals and monologues to comedies and avant-garde dramas. Be sure to sample theater outside London, wherever you travel. Previews of the capital's productions often take place in Lincoln's Theatre Royal, and the Stephen Joseph Theatre in Yorkshire premieres many of Alan Ayckbourn's plays. Stratford-upon-Avon may be the Bard's hometown, but festivals all over the country celebrate Shakespeare's work—the best are the Ludlow Festival in the Welsh Borders and London's Shakespeare Under the Stars at Regent's Park. Brighton Dome and Windsor's Theatre Royal specialize in pantomime—theatrical entertainment with puppetry, slapstick, and music. Theatrical arts are often a major component of English festivals: see musicals at the Exeter Festival (West Country) and street theater at the Harrogate International Festival (Yorkshire). Try a university production; you may see the next big star.

Minack Theatre, West Country. This open-air theater in coastal Cornwall, near Land's End and Penzance, nuzzles the slope of a sandy cliff.

Royal Shakespeare Company, Shakespeare Country. Seeing any play by the Bard performed in Stratford is a treat.

Yvonne Arnaud Theatre, Guildford, the Southeast. The productions at this theater on an island often travel to London.

Country-House Hotels

In all their luxurious glory, country-house hotels are an essential part of the English landscape, particularly in the southern part of the country. Whether you choose a converted castle, Elizabethan manor, or neoclassical retreat, these are places to indulge yourself and escape, however briefly (most are pricey), most realities of modern life. Some hotels are traditional in style, with flowery fabrics and polished wood furniture, a newer breed juxtaposes modern design with the traditional architecture. At some hotels, spas and sports—and even, alas, meeting facilities—are becoming more elaborate, but service is less stuffy. If you can't spend a night, consider just having dinner; notable chefs are turning up in more hotel kitchens. In the Thames Valley, dress up for dinner at Hartwell House or indulge in French cuisine at Le Manoir aux Quat' Saisons. The West Country's concentration includes Bovey Castle and Gidleigh Park in Dartmoor National Park, and the Cotswolds are prime ground for these retreats. One tip: before you reserve, ask if a wedding party will be using the hotel during your stay; these can take over a smaller establishment.

Cliveden, Thames Valley. Live like Lord Astor for a night (and pay accordingly), taking in his palatial parlors and riverfront gardens.

Miller Howe, Lake District. Stunning views of Windermere, Arts and Crafts touches, and superior service are part of the appeal at this retreat.

Victoria at Holkham, East Anglia. In the shadow of stately Holkham Hall, this Eastern-inspired hideaway provides a colorful seaside escape.

ENGLAND LODGING PRIMER

If your England dreams involve staying in a cozy cottage with a tidy garden, here's some good news: you won't have to break the budget. Throughout the country, you'll find stylish lodging options—from good-value hotels and intimate bed-and-breakfasts to chic apartments and historic houses—in all price ranges.

Hotels

England is a popular vacation destination, so be sure to reserve hotel rooms weeks (months for London) in advance. The country has everything from budget chain hotels to luxurious retreats in converted country houses. In many towns and cities you will find old inns that are former coaching inns, which served travelers as they journeyed around the country in horse-drawn carriages and stagecoaches.

Apartments and House Rentals

For a home base with cooking facilities and roomy enough for a family, consider renting furnished "flats" (the word for apartments in England) or houses. These are popular throughout the country and can save you money, especially if you're traveling with a group, and provide more privacy than a hotel or B&B.

Bed-and-Breakfasts

A special English tradition, and the backbone of budget travel, B&Bs are usually in a family home. Typical prices (outside of London) range from £45 to £100 a night. They vary in style and grace, but these days most have private bathrooms. B&Bs range from the ordinary to the truly elegant. Guesthouses are a slightly larger and sometimes more luxurious version of the same thing.

Some Tourist Information Centres in cities and towns can help you find and book a B&B even on the day you show up in town. There are also many private services. ⇨ *For reservation services in London, see the Where to Stay section in Chapter 2.*

Cottages

Cottages and other houses are available for weekly rental in all areas of the country. These vary from quaint older homes to brand-new buildings in scenic surroundings. For families and large groups, they offer the best value-for-money accommodations, but because they are often in isolated locations, a car is vital. Lists of rental properties are available free of charge from VisitBritain. You may find discounts of up to 50% on rentals during the off-season (October through March).

Farmhouses

Farmhouses have become increasingly popular; their special appeal is the rural experience, whether in Cornwall or Yorkshire. Consider this option only if you are touring by car, since farmhouses may be in remote locations. Prices are generally reasonable. Ask VisitBritain for the booklet "Stay on a Farm" or contact Farm Stay UK. Regional tourist boards may have information as well.

Historic Buildings

Looking for a unique experience and want to spend your vacation in a Gothic banqueting house, an old lighthouse, or maybe in an apartment at Hampton Court Palace? Several organizations, such as the Landmark Trust, National Trust, English Heritage, and Vivat Trust, have specially adapted historic buildings to rent. Many of these have kitchens.

⇨ *For a price chart, resources and contacts, and information on hotel grading and booking, see Essentials in Travel Smart England.*

GREAT ITINERARIES

BEST OF ENGLAND: UNFORGETTABLE IMAGES

12 days

London

Day 1. The capital is just the jumping-off point for this trip, so choose a few highlights that grab your interest. If it's the Changing of the Guard at Buckingham Palace, check the time to be sure you catch the pageantry. If Westminster Abbey appeals to your sense of history, arrive as early as you can. Pick a museum (many are free, so you needn't linger if you don't want to), whether it's the National Gallery on Trafalgar Square, the British Museum in Bloomsbury, or a smaller gem like the Queen's Gallery. Stroll Hyde Park or take a boat ride on the Thames before you find a pub or Indian restaurant for dinner. End with a play; the experience of theatergoing may be as interesting as whatever work you see.

Windsor

Day 2. Resplendent with centuries of treasures, Windsor Castle is favored by the Queen, and has been by rulers for centuries. Tour it to appreciate the history and wealth of the monarchy. The State Apartments are open if the Queen is not in residence, and 10 kings and queens are buried in magnificent St. George's Chapel. Time permitting, take a walk in the adjacent Great Park. If you can splurge for a luxurious stay, head up the valley to Cliveden, the Thames Valley's most spectacular hotel.

Logistics: Trains from Paddington and Waterloo stations leave about twice hourly and take less than one hour. Green Line buses depart from the Colonnades opposite London's Victoria Coach Station.

Salisbury and Stourhead

Day 3. Visible for miles around, Salisbury Cathedral's soaring spire is an unforgettable image of rural England. See the Magna Carta in the cathedral's Chapter House as you explore this marvel of medieval engineering, and walk the town path to get the view John Constable painted. Pay an afternoon visit to Stourhead to experience the finest example of the naturalistic 18th-century landscaping for which England is famous; the grand Palladian mansion here is a bonus.

Logistics: For trains to Salisbury, head back to London's Clapham Junction to catch a train on the Portsmouth line.

Bath and Stonehenge

Day 4. Bath's immaculately preserved, golden-stone Georgian architecture helps you recapture the late 18th century. Take time to stroll; don't miss the Royal Crescent (No. 1 may be open, allowing you to view a period interior), and sip the Pump Room's vile-tasting water as Jane Austen's characters might have. The Roman Baths are an amazing survivor of the ancient empire, complete with curses left by soldiers. Today you can do as the Romans did as you relax in the warm mineral waters at the Thermae Bath Spa. There's plenty to do in Bath (museums, shopping, theater), but you might make an excursion to Stonehenge (by car or tour bus). Go early or late to avoid the worst crowds at Stonehenge, and use your imagination to appreciate this enigma.

Logistics: Trains and buses leave hourly from Salisbury to Bath.

TIPS

❶ Train travelers should keep in mind that regional "Rovers" and "Rangers" offer unlimited train travel in one-day, three-day, or weeklong increments. See ⊕ *www. nationalrail.co.uk/promotions/* for details. Also check out BritRail passes, which must be purchased before your trip.

❷ Buses are time-consuming, but more scenic and cheaper than train travel. National Express offers discounts including funfares—fares to and from London to various cities (including Cambridge) as low as £1 if booked more than 24 hours in advance. Or check out low-cost Megabus.

❸ To cut the tour short, consider skipping Chester and Shrewsbury and proceed to the Lake District from Stratford-upon-Avon on Day 8. Likewise, you can consider passing up a visit to Cambridge if you opt for Oxford. You can add the time to your London stay.

❹ It's easy to visit Stonehenge from Salisbury, as well as from Bath, whether you have a car or want a guided excursion.

❺ Buy theater tickets well in advance for Stratford-upon-Avon.

The Cotswolds

Day 5. Antiques-shop in fairy-tale Stow-on-the-Wold and feed the ducks at the brook in Lower Slaughter for a taste of the mellow stone villages and dreamy green landscapes for which the area is beloved. Choose a rainy or off-season day to visit Broadway or risk jams of tourist traffic. Another great experience is a walk on the Cotswold Way or any local path.

Logistics: Drive to make the best of the beautiful scenery. Alternatively, opt for a guided tour bus.

Oxford and Blenheim Palace

Day 6. Join a guided tour of Oxford's glorious quadrangles, chapels, and gardens to get the best access to these centuries-old academic treasures. This leaves time for a jaunt to Blenheim, a unique combination of baroque opulence (inside and out) and gorgeous parkland. For a classic Oxford experience, join students in pub-crawling around Jericho, the hopping nightlife district.

Logistics: Hourly trains depart from Bath for Oxford. Buses frequently depart from Oxford's Gloucester Green for Blenheim Palace.

Stratford-upon-Avon

Day 7. Skip this stop if you don't care about you-know-who. Fans of Shakespeare can see his birthplace and Anne Hathaway's Cottage (walking there is a delight), and then finish with a memorable performance at the Courtyard Theater or, after February 2011, at the Royal Shakespeare Company's renovated main stage. Start the day early and be prepared for crowds.

Logistics: From Oxford there are direct trains and more frequent Stagecoach bus service.

Shrewsbury to Chester

Day 8. Head north to see the half-timber buildings of Shrewsbury, one of the best-preserved of England's Tudor towns. Strolling is the best way to experience it. In Chester the architecture is more or less the same (though not always authentic), but the Rows, a series of two-story shops with medieval crypts beneath, and the fine city walls are sights you can't pass by.

Logistics: For Shrewsbury, change trains at Birmingham. The train ride to Chester is 55 minutes.

The Lake District

Days 9 and 10. In the area extending north beyond Kendal and Windermere, explore the English lakes on foot. This area is jam packed with hikers in summer and on weekends, so rent a car to seek out the more isolated routes. Take a cruise on Windermere or Coniston Water, or rent a boat. If you have time for one Wordsworth-linked site, head to Dove Cottage; you can even have afternoon tea there.

Logistics: Train to Liverpool, with a switch in either Windermere or Oxenholme.

York

Day 11. This historic cathedral city is crammed with 15th- and 16th-century buildings, but don't miss magnificent York Minster and the medieval streets of the Shambles. Take in the Castle Museum; have tea at Betty's or unwind at a pub. The energetic can take a walk along the top of the several miles of city walls.

Logistics: By train, switch in Carlisle and Newcastle for the four-hour journey. Buses take twice as long.

Cambridge

Day 12. Spend the afternoon touring King's College Chapel and the Backs—gardens and sprawling meadows—and refining your punting skills on the River Cam. Join the students for a pint at one of the many pubs.

Logistics. For train service, switch at Leeds and again at Peterborough or Stevenage. Trains leave Cambridge for London frequently.

GREAT ITINERARIES

STATELY HOMES AND LANDSCAPES TOUR

11 days
Hampton Court Palace

Day 1. Start your trip royally at this palace a half hour from London by train. It's two treasures in one: a Tudor palace with magnificent baroque additions by Christopher Wren. As you walk through cobbled courtyards, Henry VIII's State Apartments, and the enormous kitchens, you may feel like you've been whisked back to the days of the Tudors and William and Mary. A quiet stroll through the 60 acres of immaculate gardens—the sculpted yews look like green gumdrops—is recommended. Be sure to get lost in the 18th-century maze—if it's open (diligent maintenance leads to occasional closures). It's easy to spend a whole day here, so start early.

Logistics: Tube to Richmond, then Bus R68; or catch the train from Waterloo to Hampton Court Station.

Knole and Ightham Mote

Days 2 and 3. Clustered around Royal Tunbridge Wells south of London is the highest concentration of stately homes in England, and, as if that weren't enough, the surrounding fields and colorful orchards are often wrapped in clouds of mist, creating a picture-perfect scene. We've picked two very different homes to visit, leaving you plenty of time to tour at a leisurely pace. Knole, Vita Sackville-West's sprawling childhood home, has dark, baroque rooms and a famous set of silver furniture. Ightham Mote, a smaller, moated house, is a vision from the Middle Ages. Its rooms are an ideal guide to style changes from the Tudor to Victorian eras. Spend the

evening at one of the many good restaurants in Royal Tunbridge Wells.

Logistics: Take the Hastings-bound train from London's Charing Cross to Tunbridge Wells, then the bus to Knole. There is no public transportation to Ightham Mote.

Petworth House

Day 4. Priceless paintings by Gainsborough, Reynolds, and Turner (19 by Turner alone) embellish the august rooms of Petworth House, present-day home to Lord and Lady Egremont and one of the National Trust's treasures. Check out Capability Brown's 700-acre deer park or the Victorian kitchens, and for the perfect lunch, peruse the offerings in the winding lanes of Petworth town. Head to Chichester for the evening, along a route passing through the rolling grasslands and deep valleys of the South Downs.

Logistics: Train to Chichester, switching in Redhill, then bus to Petworth.

Wilton House

Day 5. Base yourself in Salisbury for two days, taking time to see the famous cathedral with its tall spire and to walk the town path for the best view of it. Visit neoclassical Wilton House first, where the exquisite Double Cube Room contains a spectacular family portrait by Van Dyck and gilded furniture that accommodated Eisenhower when he contemplated the Normandy invasion here. On your way back make a detour to Stonehenge to view the wide-open Salisbury Plain and ponder the enigmatic stones.

Logistics: Take a train from Chichester to Salisbury, with a switch in Cosham; then bus it to Wilton House.

Stourhead to Longleat House

Day 6. Day-trip west to Stourhead, to experience perhaps the most stunning house-garden combination in the country, and either spend the day here (climb Alfred's Tower for a grand view of the house) or leave some time for nearby Longleat House—a vast, treasure-stuffed Italian Renaissance palace complete with safari park and a devilish maze. If you want to see the safari park, you'll need plenty of time here. Once back in Salisbury, relax in one of New Street's many cafés.

Logistics: Bus to Warminster for Longleat; for Stourhead, take the train to Gillingham from Salisbury.

Blenheim Palace

Day 7. Home of the dukes of Marlborough and birthplace of Winston Churchill, Blenheim Palace uniquely combines exquisitely designed parklands (save time to walk) and one of the most ornate baroque structures in the world. After your visit, have afternoon tea at Blenheim Tea Rooms in the adorable village of Woodstock. Overnight in Oxford; do your own pub crawl.

Logistics: From Salisbury, change at Bath or Basingstoke for Oxford, then catch a bus to Blenheim.

Snowshill Manor and Sudeley Castle

Days 8 and 9. Here you can take in the idyllic Cotswold landscape, a magical mix of greenery and mellow stone cottages and ancient churches (built with wool-trade money), along with some famous buildings. Spend the first night in Broadway to explore nearby Snowshill Manor—with its delightfully eccentric collection of Tibetan scrolls, Persian lamps, and samurai armor—in the unspoiled village of Snowshill. If you have a car, don't linger in busy Broadway. Instead, head to Chipping Campden, one of the best-preserved Cotswolds villages, which nestles in a secluded valley. Move to another charming town, Winchcombe, on the second day. Take a stroll past honey-color stone cottages and impeccably well-kept gardens. Visit Sudeley Castle, once home to Catherine Parr (Henry VIII's last wife), a Tudor-era palace with romantic gardens (only a few rooms are now open to the public). Another option near Winchombe is Stanway House, a Jacobean manor owned by Lord Neidpath; hours are limited, but this timeworn home and its gabled gatehouse is typically English.

Logistics: Take a train from Oxford to Moreton-in-Marsh for Broadway; from

gardens, grounds, shops, and farmyard exhibits make it easy to spend a day here. If you have any time left over, get out of Bakewell and take a walk in the hills of the Peak District National Park (maps are available at the town's tourist information center).

On the second day, devote the morning to the crenellations and boxy roofs of medieval Haddon Hall, a quintessentially English house. Give your afternoon to Hardwick Hall, an Elizabethan stone mansion with a facade that is "more glass than wall"—a truly innovative idea in the 16th century. Its collections of period tapestries and embroideries are remarkable reminders of the splendor of the age.

Logistics: Take a train back to Oxford and then up to Manchester for the connection to Buxton; then catch a bus to Bakewell.

TIPS

❶   All stately homes in this itinerary, with the exception of Hampton Court Palace and Longleat House, are closed for the winter, though gardens may remain open. Even homes open April through October may not be open every day. It's best to confirm all hours before visiting.

❷   A car is best for this itinerary, as some houses are remote. Have good maps or use a GPS.

❸   Country roads around the Peak District are hard to negotiate; be especially careful when driving to Chatsworth House, Haddon Hall, and Hardwick Hall. Drives will take longer than you expect.

❹   Look into discount passes, such as the Great British Heritage Pass (⇨ *see Sightseeing Passes in Essentials in Travel Smart England*), which save you money on visits to multiple sites.

Broadway, walk to Snowshill Manor; for Sudeley Castle, take a bus from Broadway to Winchcombe, then walk.

Chatsworth House, Haddon Hall, and Hardwick Hall

Days 10 and 11. For the final stops, head north, east of Manchester, to a more dramatic landscape. In or near the craggy Peak District, where the gentle slopes of the Pennine Hills begin their ascent to Scotland, are three of England's most renowned historic homes. Base yourself in Bakewell, and spend your first day taking in the art treasures amassed by the dukes of Devonshire at Chatsworth House. The

ON THE
CALENDAR

ONGOING Late May– mid-September	**Regent's Park Open Air Theatre** gives you the chance to see Shakespeare's plays and other works. ✉ *Inner Circle, London* ☎ *0844/826–4242* ⊕ *www.openairtheatre.org.*
Mid-July–mid-September	**The Proms** is a celebrated series of classical-music concerts that take place largely in London, but a few events are held in cities across the country. ✉ *Royal Albert Hall, Kensington Gore, London* ☎ *020/7589–8212* ⊕ *www.bbc.co.uk/proms.*
WINTER December 31	**New Year's Eve at Trafalgar Square** in London is a huge, freezing, sometimes drunken slosh through the fountains to celebrate the new year. Not organized by any official body, it is held in the ceremonial heart of London under an enormous Christmas tree.
SPRING Mid-March	The **Head of the River Boat Race** offers the spectacle of up to 420 eight-man crews dipping their oars in the Thames as they race from Mortlake to Putney. The best view is from Surrey Bank above Chiswick Bridge (Tube to Chiswick); the starting time depends on the tide. ⊕ *www.horr.co.uk.* The **Oxford versus Cambridge University Boat Race** takes place a week or two after the Head of the River Boat Race, in the opposite direction but over the same 4½-mi course, carrying on a tradition going back to 1829. Around a quarter of a million people watch from the banks of the river.
April 21	The **Queen's Birthday** earns a showy 41-gun salute at Hyde Park in London. In June, Elizabeth II's ceremonial birthday is celebrated by Trooping the Colour.
Mid–late May	The **Chelsea Flower Show**, a prestigious four-day floral extravaganza, covers 22 acres on the Royal Hospital grounds in London's Chelsea neighborhood. Tickets can sell out well in advance. ✉ *Royal Horticultural Society, Royal Hospital Rd., London* ☎ *0870/906–3781* ⊕ *www.rhs.org.uk/chelsea.*
SUMMER Early June	**Trooping the Colour** is Queen Elizabeth's official birthday show at Horse Guards Parade, Whitehall, London. (Her actual birthday is in April.) Note that on the two previous Saturdays there are Queenless rehearsals—the Colonel's Review and the Major General's Review. You can stand; seats require tickets. *Write for tickets in the seated stands from January 1 to February 28 (enclose SASE or International Reply Coupon):*

	Ticket Office, Headquarters Household Division, Horse Guards, London SW1 2AX ☎ 020/7414–2479.
Mid-June	**Royal Ascot** is the most glamorous date in British horse racing. Usually held during the third week of June, the four-day event in the Thames Valley is graced by the Queen. Reserve months in advance for tickets. ✉ *Ascot Racecourse, Ascot, Berkshire* ☎ *0870/727–1234* ⊕ *www.ascot.co.uk*.
Late June	**Glastonbury Festival,** the biggest musical event in England, sprawls across Somerset farmland, where hundreds of bands (rock, pop, folk, and world music) perform on a half-dozen stages for three days and nights. Note: tickets sell out as soon as they go on sale. ☎ *0844/412–4626* ⊕ *www.glastonburyfestivals.co.uk*.
Late June–early July	**Wimbledon Lawn Tennis Championships** get bigger every year. Applications for the ticket lottery for the two-week tournament are available October through December of the preceding year, but you can also line up early each morning for tickets for that day. *All-England Lawn Tennis & Croquet Club, Church Rd., Wimbledon, London SW19 5AE* ☎ *020/8971–2473* ⊕ *www.wimbledon.org*. **Royal Henley Regatta** attracts premier rowers from around the world on the first weekend in July. High society lines the banks of the Thames during this four-day event. ✉ *Henley-on-Thames* ☎ *01491/572153* ⊕ *www.hrr.co.uk*.
Early July	**Hampton Court Palace Flower Show,** a five-day event on the grounds of the palace, nearly rivals the Chelsea Flower Show for glamour. ✉ *Hampton Court Palace, East Molesey, Surrey* ☎ *020/7649–1885* ⊕ *www.rhs.org.uk/hamptoncourt*.
Late August	**Beatles Week Festival** sees hundreds of Beatles tribute bands descend on Liverpool for a week to play to fans. Other events add to the fun. ✉ *Liverpool* ⊕ *www.beatlesfestival.co.uk*. **Notting Hill Carnival,** one of the largest street festivals in London, includes Caribbean foods, reggae music, and street parades. ✉ *Notting Hill, London* ☎ *020/8964–0544* ⊕ *www.thenottinghillcarnival.com*.
FALL November 5	**Guy Fawkes Day** commemorates a foiled 1605 attempt to blow up Parliament. Fireworks shows and bonfires are held all over the country, with the biggest celebrations in Lewes in Sussex.

London

WORD OF MOUTH

"I loved the Portobello Road market, Saturday mornings, divided into three sections—the first is near all the permanent antique and craft shops, so it is crafts and jewelry, shawls, trinkets; the second is the food, fruit & veg and flower market; the third is shops and stalls with trendy youthful clothes. Go early!"

—ninastdream

"I really, really recommend taking a verger's tour at Westminster Abbey—our guide really made history come alive. If you get to the Abbey when it opens, just sign up for the first tour of the day or you can sign up in advance the previous day."

—azzure

Updated
by Christi
Daugherty, Kiki
Deere, Jan Fus-
coe, Jack Jew-
ers, Michelle
Rosenberg,
Ellin Stein, and
Alex Wijeratna

London is an ancient city whose history greets you at every turn; it's also one of the coolest cities in the world. If the city contained only its famous landmarks—the Tower of London, Big Ben, Westminster Abbey, Buckingham Palace—it would still rank as one of the world's top cities. But London is so much more.

To gain a sense of its continuity, stand on Waterloo Bridge at sunset. To the east, the great globe of St. Paul's Cathedral glows golden in the fading sunlight as it has since the 17th century, still majestic amid the modern glass towers. To the west stand the mock-medieval ramparts of Westminster, home to the "Mother of Parliaments," which has met here or hereabouts since the 1250s. Past them both snakes the swift, dark Thames, which flowed past the Roman settlement of Londinium nearly 2,000 years ago.

The city beckons with great museums, royal pageantry, and history-steeped houses. There's no other place like it in its medley of styles, in its mixture of the green loveliness of parks and the modern gleam of neon. Modern-day London largely reflects its medieval layout, a will-fully difficult tangle of streets. Even Londoners, most of whom own a dog-eared copy of an indispensable A–Z street finder, get lost in their own city. But the bewildering street patterns will be a plus for anyone who likes to get lost in atmosphere. London is a walker's city, and will repay every moment you spend exploring on foot.

To penetrate beyond the crust of popular knowledge, you should not only visit St. Paul's Cathedral and the Tower of London, but also set aside some time for random wandering. Walk in the city's backstreets and mews, around Park Lane and Kensington. Pass up Buckingham Palace for Kensington Palace. Take in the National Gallery, but don't forget London's "time machine" museums, such as the 19th-century home of Sir John Soane. Abandon the city's standard-issue chain stores for its wonderful markets.

Today the city's art, style, fashion, and dining scenes make headlines around the world. London's chefs have become superstars. Its fashion designers have conquered Paris, avant-garde artists have caused waves at the august Royal Academy of Arts, the raging after-hours scene is packed with music mavens ready to catch the Next Big Thing, and the theater continues its tradition of radical, shocking productions. And the city is now looking forward to hosting the 2012 Olympics.

Although the outward shapes may alter and the inner spirit may be warmer, the base-rocks of London's character and tradition remain the same. The British bobby is alive and well. The tall, red, double-decker buses (in an updated model) still lumber from stop to stop. Then there's that greatest living link with the past—the Royal Family. Don't let the tag of "typical tourist destination" stop you from enjoying the pageantry of the Windsors: the Changing of the Guard, at

2

TOP REASONS TO GO

Westminster Abbey: Steeped in history, the pillars of this great vaulted hall stand on the final resting place for the men and women who built Britain.

Buckingham Palace: Not the prettiest royal residence, but a must-see for the glimpse it affords of modern royal life. The Queen's Gallery is next door.

St. Paul's Cathedral: No matter how many times you have been here, the scale and elegance of Sir Christopher Wren's masterpiece take the breath away.

Tower of London: The Tower is London at its majestic, idiosyncratic best. This is the heart of the kingdom, with foundations dating back nine centuries.

British Museum: A visit to the British Museum has hours of eye-catching artifacts from the world's greatest civilizations.

Shakespeare's Globe Theatre: Watching an offering from the Bard in a re-created version of the galleried Tudor theater for which he wrote is a special thrill.

Hampton Court Palace: These buildings won over Henry VIII and became his favorite royal residence. Tudor charm, grand gardens, and a wing designed by Sir Christopher Wren make Hampton Court a great day out.

Tate Modern: A visit here is more of an event than the average museum stop. Tate Modern, housed in a striking 1930s power station, is a hip, immensely successful addition to the London gallery landscape.

National Gallery: Whatever the collective noun is for a set of old masters—a palette? a canvas?—there are enough here to have the most casual art enthusiast cooing with admiration. Enjoy pedestrianized Trafalgar Square on the doorstep.

Buckingham Palace and at Whitehall, is one of the greatest free shows in the world.

The London you discover may include some enthusiastic recommendations from this guide, but be prepared to be taken by surprise. The best that a great city has to offer often comes in unexpected ways. The great 18th-century author Samuel Johnson said that a man who is tired of London is tired of life. Armed with energy and curiosity, you can find, to quote Dr. Johnson again, "in London all that life can afford."

ORIENTATION AND PLANNING

GETTING ORIENTED

London grew from a wooden bridge built over the Thames in the year AD 43 to its current 600 square mi and 7 million souls in haphazard fashion, meandering from its two official centers: Westminster, seat of government and royalty, to the west, and the City, site of finance and commerce, to the east. In this city of urban villages, the neighborhoods continue to evolve. If the city's great parks such as Hyde Park are, in

Lord Chatham's phrase, "the lungs of London," then the River Thames remains its backbone. Here are some key areas to explore.

Westminster and Royal London. This is the place to embrace the "tourist" label. Snap pictures of the mounted Horse Guards, play with the pigeons in Trafalgar Square, and visit stacks of art in the national galleries. It's well worth braving the crowds to wander ancient Westminster Abbey and its historic bounty.

Soho and Covent Garden. More sophisticated than seedy these days, the heart of London puts Theaterland, strip joints, Chinatown, and the trendiest of film studios side by side. Nearby Charing Cross Road is a bibliophile's dream, but steer clear of the hectic hordes in Leicester Square, London's answer to Times Square.

Bloomsbury and Legal London. The literary and left-wing set that made Bloomsbury world famous has left its mark, and the area remains the heart of brainy London. The University of London and the Law Courts are worth a passing glance; stop for a good while in the incomparable British Museum.

The City. London's Wall Street might be the oldest part of the capital, but thanks to futuristic skyscrapers and a sleek Millennium Bridge, it looks like the newest. Fans of ages gone by won't be disappointed, however: head for the dome of St. Paul's Cathedral, the storybook Tower Bridge, and grisly tales from the Tower of London.

The South Bank. Diehard culture vultures could spend a lifetime here. The South Bank Arts Complex—including the Royal National Theatre and Royal Festival Hall, the National Film Theatre, Shakespeare's Globe, the Design Museum, and the Tate Modern—pretty much seals the artistic deal. Or take it all in from high up on the London Eye.

Kensington, Knightsbridge, and Mayfair. The museums are as awe-inspiring as ever. The Science Museum and the Natural History Museum are the most fun for children. Flash your cash at the capital's snazziest department stores, Harrods and Harvey Nichols. You might not have the wallet for London's most prestigious district, but the window-shopping in Mayfair is free.

Up and Down the Thames. The quaint Thameside streets of Greenwich are an excellent rummaging ground for trendy antiques. Throw in some brilliant sights, Christopher Wren architecture, and the Greenwich Meridian Line, and you have a great day out. Other excursions include lovely Kew Gardens and Hampton Court Palace, England's version of Versailles.

LONDON PLANNER

WHEN TO GO

The heaviest tourist season runs mid-April through mid-October, with another peak around Christmas—though the tide never really ebbs. Spring is the time to see the countryside and the royal London parks and gardens at their freshest; fall to enjoy near-ideal exploring conditions. In late summer, be warned: air-conditioning is rarely found in places other than department stores, modern restaurants, hotels, and cinemas in London. Winter can be rather dismal, but all the theaters, concerts, and exhibitions go full speed ahead.

One good time to avoid is the October "half-term" when schools in the capital take a break for a week and nearly all attractions are flooded by children. Arriving at the start of August can be a very busy time, and the weather makes Tube travel a nightmare.

GETTING HERE AND AROUND
ADDRESSES

Central London and its surrounding districts are divided into 32 boroughs—33, counting the City of London. More useful for finding your way around, however, are the subdivisions of London into postal districts. The first one or two letters give the location: N means north, NW means northwest, etc.

AIR TRAVEL

For information about airports and airport transfers, see Getting Here and Around in Travel Smart England.

BUS TRAVEL

Buses, or "coaches," as privately-operated bus services are known here, operate mainly from London's Victoria Coach Station to more than 1,200 major towns and cities. Buses are about half as expensive as the train, but trips take twice as long. *For information, see Getting Here and Around in Travel Smart England.*

In central London, Transport for London (TfL) buses are traditionally bright red double- and single-deckers. Not all buses run the full length of their route at all times, so check with the driver. In central London you must purchase tickets from machines at bus stops along the routes before you board. Bus stops are clearly indicated: the main stops have a red TfL symbol on a white background. When the word REQUEST is written across the sign, you must flag the bus down. Buses are a good way to see the town, but don't take one if you're in a hurry.

A flat-rate fare of £2 applies for all bus fares. If you buy a one-day Travelcard for tube, bus and train, it covers all journeys. You can also get an Oystercard, an electronic smart card that you load with money, which is then deducted each time you use the card on buses or the tube: a single fare is £1.20 or £1.50. A 7-Day Bus Pass for zones 1 through 4 is £16.60 but must be bought before boarding from one of the machines at bus stops, most newsagents, or underground stations. Children ages 11–15 travel free on buses as long as they order an Oystercard at least four weeks before they travel.

Traveling without a valid ticket makes you liable for an on-the-spot fine (£20), or you can be charged with a criminal offense. For more information, there are Transport for London Travel Information Centres at the following tube stations: Euston, Liverpool Street, Piccadilly Circus, Victoria, and Heathrow. Most are open in daytime only.

Night Buses can prove helpful when traveling in London from 11 PM to 5 AM—these buses add the prefix "N" to their route numbers. You may have to transfer at one of the Night Bus nexuses: Victoria, Westminster,

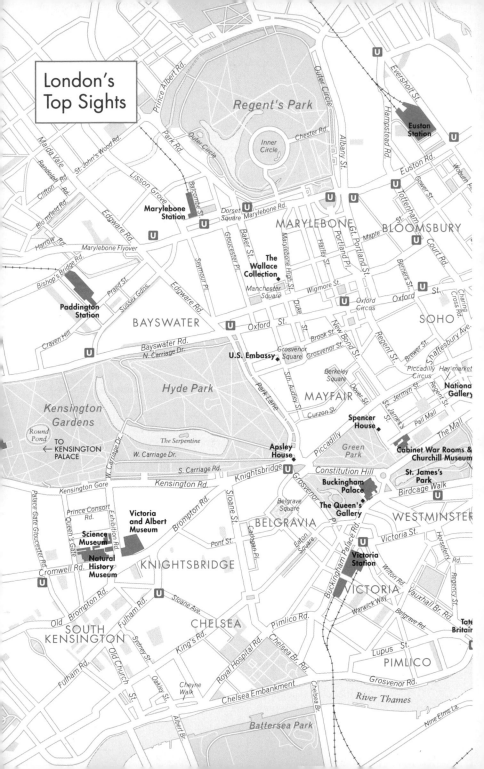

London's Top Sights

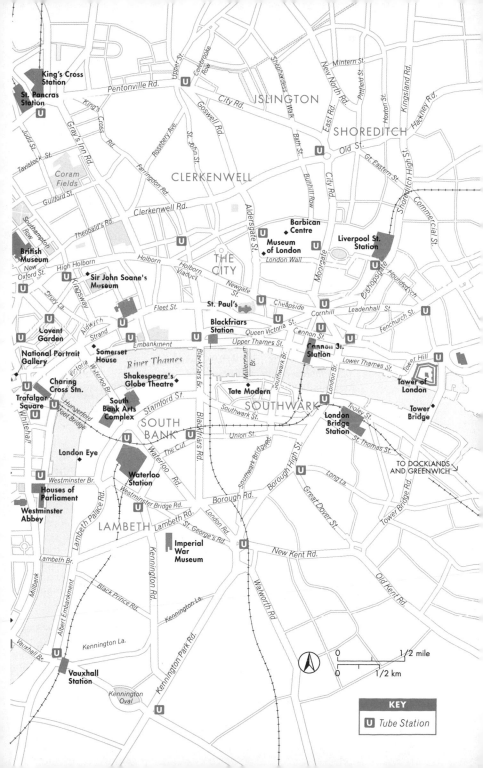

and either Piccadilly Circus or Trafalgar Square. For safety reasons, avoid sitting alone on the top deck of a Night Bus.

Contact Transport for London (☎ *020/7222–1234* ⊕ *www.tfl.gov.uk*).

CAR TRAVEL

The major approach roads to London are six-lane motorways. Motorways (from Heathrow, M4; from Gatwick, M23 to M25, then M3; Stansted, M11) are usually the faster option for getting in and out of town, although rush-hour traffic is horrendous. Stay tuned to local radio stations for updates.

The simple advice about driving in London is: don't. The city never had a central street plan, and the result is a chaotic winding mass, made no easier by the one-way street systems. If you must drive, remember to drive on the left and stick to the speed limit (30 MPH on most city streets, 20 MPH near schools and in some residential areas).

A "congestion charge" is levied on all vehicles entering central London (bounded by the Inner Ring Road except to the west, where the charging zone has been extended to encompass Notting Hill, Kensington, and Chelsea; street signs and "C" road markings note the area) on weekdays from 7 AM to 6 PM, excluding bank holidays. (However, as of this writing a proposal to return the zone to its original size in 2011 is under consideration.) You can pay up to 90 days in advance, or by midnight on the day of travel (£8) or by midnight on the following day (£10). A £2 price increase is being discussed at time of writing. You can pay by phone, mail, or Internet, or at retail outlets (look for signs), except for following day payments, which can only be paid via the Web site or call center. There are no tollbooths; cameras monitor the area. The penalty for not paying is stiff: £120. For current information, check ⊕ *www.cclondon.com*.

TAXI TRAVEL

Taxis are expensive, but if you're with several people they can be practical. Hotels and main tourist areas have taxi ranks; you can also hail taxis on the street. If the yellow FOR HIRE sign is lighted on top, the taxi is available. Drivers often cruise at night with their signs unlighted, so if you see an unlighted cab, keep your hand up. Generally fares start at £2.20 for the first minute and increase by units of 20p, and then increase at varying amounts depending on time of day, distance traveled, and taxi speed. Surcharges are added around Christmas and New Year's days. Fares also go up between 10 PM and 6 AM. Tips are extra, usually 10% to 15% per ride. The average cost for a journey within central London is £10.

TRAIN TRAVEL

London has eight major train stations, each serving a different area of the country, all accessible by Underground or bus. Trains are operated by a number of private companies, but National Rail Enquiries acts as a central rail information number. *For further information on train travel, see Getting Here and Around in Travel Smart England.*

Contact National Rail Enquiries (☎ *0845/748–4950* ⊕ *www.nationalrail.co.uk*).

UNDERGROUND (TUBE) TRAVEL

London's extensive Underground (tube) system has color-coded routes, clear signs, and extensive connections. Trains run out into the suburbs, and all stations are marked with the London Underground circular symbol. (In Britain, the word "subway" means "pedestrian underpass.") Some lines have branches (Central, District, Northern, Metropolitan, and Piccadilly), so be sure to note which branch is needed for your destination. Electronic platform signs tell you the final stop and route of the next train and how many minutes until it arrives.

London is divided into six concentric zones (ask at Underground ticket booths for a map and booklet, which give details of the ticket options). Tube fares are determined by how many zones the journey covers and whether it includes the most expensive central Zone 1. The more zones your trip crosses, the higher the fare. Most tourist sights are within Zone 1, but some are not—Kew Gardens, for example, is in Zone 4. If you inadvertently travel into a zone for which you do not have the right ticket, you can purchase an "extension" to your own ticket at the ticket office by the barriers. This usually costs a pound, and merely equalizes your fare. Buy an Oystercard (*see Bus Travel*) for fare reductions; it can be a huge money-saver, since for single fares a flat fee of £4 applies across all six zones, even if you're traveling one stop.

If you're traveling on the tube as well as the bus, consider an off-peak one-day Travelcard (£5.60 for zones 1 and 2, more for farther zones), which allows unrestricted travel on buses *and* tubes after 9:30 AM and all day on weekends and national holidays. "Peak" travelcards—those for use before 9:30 AM—are more expensive (£7.40 for zones 1 and 2, more for farther zones). Children under 11 travel free on the tube and buses after 9:30 AM.

The tube begins running just after 5 AM Monday through Saturday; the last services leave central London between midnight and 12:30 AM. On Sunday, trains start two hours later and finish about an hour earlier. Normally you should not have to wait more than 10 minutes in central areas. Lines may be closed or partially suspended for engineering works on weekends—check the TfL Website or boards in stations. Most tube stations are not accessible for people with disabilities. Travelers with disabilities should get the free leaflet "Access to the Underground," which lists the stations that are.

Contact Transport for London (☎ 020/7222–1234 ⊕ www.tfl.gov.uk).

DISCOUNTS AND DEALS

All national collections (such as the Natural History Museum, Science Museum, Victoria & Albert Museum) are free, a real bargain for museumgoers. The London Pass, a smart card, offers entry to more than 50 top attractions, such as museums and tours on boats and buses. The charge is £40 for one day, which drops to £15 per day for those with weekly passes. The London Pass is available by phone, online, or from the Britain Visitor Centre and Tourist Information Centre branches. *For other discounts, see Sightseeing Passes in Essentials in Travel Smart England.*

Contact London Pass (☎ 0870/242–9988 ⊕ www.londonpass.com).

TOUR OPTIONS
BOAT TOURS

The Thames Clippers commuter river service stops at 10 piers between the London Eye/Waterloo and Greenwich, with peak-time extensions to Putney in the west and Woolwich Arsenal in the east. The Waterloo–Woolwich commuter service runs every 20 minutes from 6 AM–1 AM on weekdays, 8:30 AM–midnight on weekends. Tickets are £5.30, with discounts for Oystercard and Travelcard holders (full integration into the Oyster card system is expected in 2011). There is also a special Tate-to-Tate express, a 20-minute trip between Tate Modern and Tate Britain that costs £5. Boats run every 40 minutes from 10 to 5. A £12 River Roamer ticket offers unlimited river travel from 10 to 10 weekdays and 8 AM–10 PM on weekends.

Year-round, but more frequently from April to October, sightseeing cruises leave from Westminster Pier, the London Eye Pier, Greenwich Pier, and Tower Pier. Downstream routes go to the Tower of London, Greenwich, and the Thames Barrier via Canary Wharf. Upstream destinations include Kew, Richmond, and Hampton Court (mainly in summer). Most of the launches seat between 100 and 250 passengers, and provide a running commentary on passing points of interest. Depending upon the destination, river trips may last from one to four hours.

A River Red Rover ticket (about £13.50) permits unlimited "hop-on, hop-off" travel on the City Cruise line between Westminster, Waterloo, Tower, and Greenwich piers. For £14.50 it can be combined with a DLR Rail ticket to allow one day's travel on the Docklands Light Railway to Canary Wharf as well. Tickets are available year-round from the piers on the route, Tower Gateway station, or DLR stations; ticket holders also get discounted tickets to the London Aquarium in Westminster and the National Maritime Museum in Greenwich.

The tranquil side of London can be found on narrow boats that cruise the city's two canals, the Grand Union and Regent's Canal; most vessels operate on the latter, which runs between Little Venice in the west (nearest Tube: Warwick Avenue on the Bakerloo Line) and Camden Lock (about 200 yards north of Camden Town Tube station). Fares start at £8.50 for 1½-hour round-trip cruises.

Contacts Bateaux London (☎ 020/7695–1800 ⊕ www.bateauxlondon.com). **Canal Cruises** (☎ 020/8440–8962 ⊕ www.londoncanalcruises.com). **Jason's Trip (canal)** (☎ 020/7286–3428 ⊕ www.jasons.co.uk).**London Duck Tours** (☎ 020/7928–3132 ⊕ www.londonducktours.co.uk). **London River Services** (☎ 020/7941–2400 ⊕ www.tfl.gov.uk). **Thames Clippers** (☎ 020/7781–5049 ⊕ www.thamesclippers.com). **Thames Cruises** (☎ 020/7930–3373 ⊕ www. thamescruises.com). **Westminster Passenger Service Association** (☎ 020/7930–2062 ⊕ www.wpsa.co.uk).

BUS TOURS

Guided sightseeing tours from the top of double-decker buses, which are open-top in summer, are a good introduction to the city, as they cover all the main central sights. Numerous companies run daily bus tours that depart (usually between 8:30 and 9 AM) from central points. You may board or alight at any of the numerous stops to view the sights, and reboard on the next bus. Tickets can be bought from the driver and are good all day. Prices vary according to the type of tour, although £22 is the benchmark.

Green Line, Evan Evans, and National Express offer day excursions by bus to places within easy reach of London, such as Hampton Court, Oxford, Stratford, and Bath.

Contacts Big Bus Company (☎ 020/7233–9533 ⊕ www.bigbustours.com). **Evan Evans** (☎ 020/7950–1777, 800/422–9022 in U.S. ⊕ www.evanevans.co.uk). **Green Line** (☎ 0844/801–7261 ⊕ www.greenline.co.uk). **National Express** (☎ 0871/781–8181 ⊕ www.nationalexpress.com). **Original London Sightseeing Tour** (☎ 020/8877–1722 ⊕ www.theoriginaltour.com).

PRIVATE GUIDES

Black Taxi Tour of London is a personal tour by cab direct from your hotel. The price is per cab, so the fare can be shared among as many as five people. An introductory two-hour tour is £100 by day, £110 by night. You can hire a Blue Badge–accredited guide (trained by the tourist board) for walking or driving tours.

Contacts Black Taxi Tour of London (☎ 020/7935–9363 ⊕ www. blacktaxitours.co.uk). **Blue Badge tour guides** (☎ 020/7403–1115 ⊕ www.blue-badge-guides.com).

WALKING TOURS

One of the best ways to get to know London is on foot. If horror and mystery are your interest, try walks with a Jack the Ripper or ghost theme, or Blood and Tears walks (not suitable for younger children). Other themed tours include Secret London, The Beatles, Sherlock Holmes, Gandhi, Dickens—you name it. Context London's expert docents lead small groups on walks with art, architecture, and similar themes. London Walks hosts more than 100 walks every week on themes, including a Thames pub walk, Literary Bloomsbury, and Spies and Spycatchers.

Contacts Blood and Tears Walk (☎ 07905/746733 ⊕ www.shockinglondon. com). **Blue Badge** (☎ 020/7403–1115 ⊕ www.blue-badge-guides.com). **Context London** (☎ 020/193–9158, 800/691–6036 in U.S. ⊕ www.contexttravel.com/london). **Richard Jones's London Walking Tours** (☎ 020/7928–2627 ⊕ www.walksoflondon.co.uk). **London Walks** (☎ 020/7624–3978 ⊕ www.walks.com). **Shakespeare City Walk** (☎ 07905/746733 ⊕ www.shakespeareguide.com).

VISITOR INFORMATION

When you arrive in London, you can get good information at the Travel Information Centres at Victoria Station and St. Pancras International train station. These are helpful if you're looking for brochures for London sights, or if something's gone horribly wrong with your hotel reservation—as they have a useful reservations service. There are also Travel Information Centres at Euston and Liverpool Street train stations, Heathrow Airport, and Piccadilly Circus. The Britain and London Visitor Centre is a worthwhile stop for travel, hotel, and entertainment information, but you need to visit in person. There are Tourist Information Centres for the City of London, Greenwich, and various outer boroughs of London. VisitLondon, the city's tourist board, has a helpful

Web site, ⊕ *www.visitlondon.com*, with links to other sites; you can also book a hotel on the site.

Information Britain and London Visitor Centre (⊠ *1 Regent St., Piccadilly Circle, Piccadilly* ☎ *No phone* ⊕ *www.visitbritain.com*). **King's Cross/St. Pancras Travel Information Centre** (⊠ *LUL Western Ticket Hall, Euston Rd., King's Cross* ☎ *No phone*). **Victoria Station Travel Information Centre** (⊠ *Opposite Platform 8, Victoria Station Forecourt, Victoria* ☎ *No phone*). **VisitLondon** (⊕ *www.visitlondon.com*).

EXPLORING LONDON

Westminster and the City contain many of the grand buildings that have played a central role in British history: the Tower of London and St. Paul's Cathedral, Westminster Abbey and the Houses of Parliament, Buckingham Palace, and the older royal palace of St. James's.

London's *un*official centers multiply and mutate year after year. But life is not lived in monuments, as the patrician patrons of the great Georgian architects understood when they commissioned the city's elegant squares and town houses. Within a few minutes' walk of Buckingham Palace, for instance, lie St. James's and Mayfair, neighboring quarters of elegant town houses built for the nobility during the 17th and early 18th centuries and now notable for shopping opportunities. Westminster Abbey's original vegetable patch (or convent garden), which became the site of London's first square, Covent Garden, is now a popular stop.

Hyde Park and Kensington Gardens, preserved by past kings and queens for their own hunting and relaxation, create a swath of parkland across the city center. A walk across Hyde Park brings you to the museum district of South Kensington, with the Natural History Museum, the Science Museum, and the Victoria & Albert Museum. The South Bank has many cultural highlights: the theaters of the South Bank Centre, the Tate Modern, and the reconstruction of Shakespeare's Globe theater. The London Eye observation wheel here gives stunning city views, or you can walk across the Millennium or Hungerford Bridge. Farther downstream is the gorgeous 17th- and 18th-century symmetry of Greenwich, and its maritime attractions.

WESTMINSTER AND ROYAL LONDON

If you have time to visit only one part of London, this is it. Westminster and Royal London might be called "London for Beginners." If you went no farther than these few acres, you would have seen many of the famous sights, from the Houses of Parliament, Big Ben, Westminster Abbey, and Buckingham Palace, to two of the world's greatest art collections, in the National and Tate Britain galleries. You can truly call this area Royal London, since it is bounded by the triangle of streets that make up the route that the Queen usually takes when journeying from Buckingham Palace to Westminster Abbey or to the Houses of Parliament on state occasions. The three points on this royal triangle are Trafalgar Square, Westminster, and Buckingham Palace. Naturally, in an area that regularly sees the pomp and pageantry of royal occasions, the streets are wide and the vistas long. St. James's Park lies at the heart of the triangle, which has a feeling of timeless dignity—flowerbeds bursting with color, long avenues of trees framing classically proportioned buildings, glimpses of pinnacles and towers over the treetops, the distant *bong!* of Big Ben counting off the hours. This is concentrated sightseeing, so pace yourself. For a large part of the year, much of Royal London is floodlighted at night, adding to the theatricality of the experience.

GETTING HERE Trafalgar Square—easy to access and smack dab in the center of the action—is a good place to start. Take the Tube to Embankment (District and Circle lines) and walk north until you cross the Strand, or alight at Charing Cross (Bakerloo, Jubilee, and Northern lines), where the Northumberland Avenue exit deposits you on the southeast corner of the Square.

PLANNING YOUR TIME You could spend a lifetime absorbing the rich history of this part of London. More practically, try to leave at least two days if you want to dip into the full gamut of attractions without feeling horribly rushed. If Royal London is what you want, make a day of Buckingham Palace or Westminster Abbey, the Queen's Gallery, and the Guards Museum at Wellington Barracks. If you've a more constitutional bent, visit the Houses of Parliament and the Cabinet War Rooms.

Numbers in the margin correspond to numbers on the Westminster and Royal London map.

TOP ATTRACTIONS

❾ **Buckingham Palace.** It's rare to get a chance to see how the other half—

Fodor's Choice ★ well, other minute fraction—lives and works. But when the Queen heads off to Scotland on her annual summer holiday (you can tell because the Union Jack flies above the palace instead of the Royal Standard), the palace's 19 State Rooms open up to visitors (although the north wing's private apartments remain behind closed doors). With fabulous gilt moldings and walls adorned with masterpieces by Rembrandt, Rubens, and other old masters, the State Rooms are the grandest of the palace's 775 rooms.

Inside the palace, the **Grand Hall,** followed by the **Grand Staircase** and **Guard Room,** gives a taste of what's to follow: marble, gold leaf galore, and massive, twinkling chandeliers. Don't miss the theatrical **Throne Room,** with the original 1953 coronation throne, or the sword in **The Ballroom,** used by the Queen to bestow knighthoods and other honors. Royal portraits line the **State Dining Room,** and the **Blue Drawing Room** is splendor in overdrive. The alabaster-and-gold plasterwork of the **White Drawing Room** is a suitable crescendo on which to end the tour.

The **Changing the Guard,** also known as **Guard Mounting,** remains one of London's best free shows and culminates in front of the palace. Marching to live bands, the old guard proceeds up the Mall from St. James's Palace to Buckingham Palace. Shortly afterward, the new guard approaches from Wellington Barracks. Then within the forecourt, the captains of the old and new guards symbolically transfer the keys to the palace. ■TIP→ **Get there by 10:30** AM **to grab a spot in**

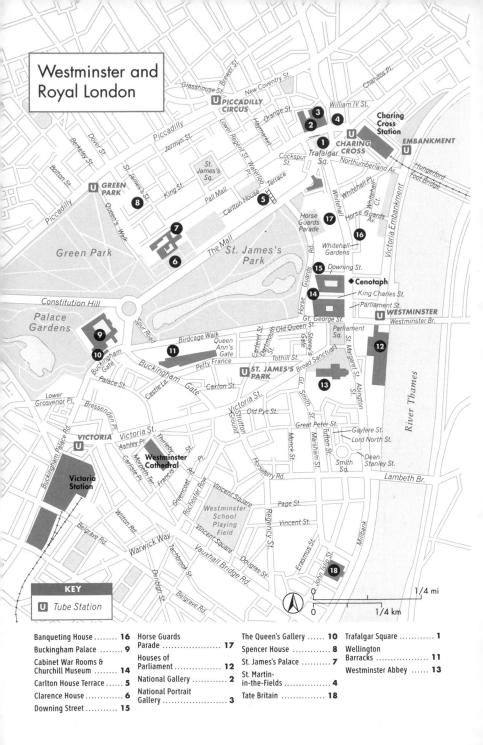

Westminster and Royal London

KEY
Ⓤ Tube Station

the best viewing section at the gate facing the palace, since most of the hoopla takes place behind the railings in the forecourt. ✉ *Buckingham Palace Rd., St. James* ☎ *020/7766–7300* ⊕ *www.royalcollection.org.uk* 🎫 *£16.50* ⊗ *Late July–late Sept., daily 9:45–6 (last admission 3:45); times subject to change; check Web site before visiting* Ⓤ *Victoria, St. James's Park, Green Park.*

2

🔟 **Cabinet War Rooms & Churchill Museum.** It was from this small warren of underground rooms—beneath the vast government buildings of the Treasury—that Winston Churchill and his team directed troops in World War II. Designed to be bombproof, the whole complex has been preserved almost exactly as it was when the last light was turned off at the end of the war. Every clock shows almost 5 PM, and the furniture, fittings, and paraphernalia of a busy, round-the-clock war office are in situ, down to the colored map pins. During air raids, the leading government ministers met here, and the Cabinet Room is still arranged as if a meeting were about to convene. In the Map Room, the Allied campaign is charted on wall-to-wall maps with a rash of pinholes showing the movements of convoys.

An exciting addition to the Cabinet War Rooms is the **Churchill Museum,** which opened in 2005 on the 40th anniversary of his death. Different zones explore his life and achievements—and failures, too—through objects and documents, many of which, such as his personal papers, had never previously been made public. Central to the exhibition is an interactive timeline, with layers of facts, figures, and tales. ✉ *Clive Steps, King Charles St., Westminster* ☎ *020/7930–6961* ⊕ *cwr.iwm.org.uk* 🎫 *£12.95, includes audio tour* ⊗ *Daily 9:30–6; last admission 5* Ⓤ *Westminster.*

🔟 **Horse Guards Parade.** Once the tiltyard of Whitehall Palace, where jousting tournaments were held, the Horse Guards Parade is now notable mainly for the annual Trooping the Colour ceremony, in which the Queen takes the salute, her official birthday tribute, on the second Saturday in June. (Like Paddington Bear, the Queen has two birthdays; her real one is on April 21.) There is pageantry galore, with marching bands and throngs of onlookers. Covering the vast expanse of the square that faces Horse Guards Road, opposite St. James's Park at one end and Whitehall at the other, the ceremony is televised. At the Whitehall facade of Horse Guards, the changing of two mounted sentries known as the **Sovereign's Life Guards** provides what may be London's most popular photo opportunity. ✉ *Whitehall, Whitehall* ☎ *020/7930–4832* ⊗ *Queen's mounted guard ceremony Mon.–Sat. 11* AM *and 4* PM, *Sun. 10* AM *and 4* PM Ⓤ *Westminster.*

🔟 **Houses of Parliament.** If you want to understand some of the centuries-old traditions and arcane idiosyncrasies that make up constitutionless British parliamentary democracy, the Palace of Westminster, as the complex is still properly called, is the place to come. The architecture in this 1,100-room labyrinth impresses, but the real excitement lies in stalking the corridors of power. A palace was first established on the site by Edward the Confessor in the 11th century. William II started building a new palace in 1087, and this gradually became the seat of English administrative power. However, the current building dates from the

Fodor's Choice
★

GREAT ITINERARIES

London overflows with choices: from exploring local pubs and tearooms to taking in great theater and concerts, it's easy to fill a day. A stroll through a quiet neighborhood or a ride on the Thames may be as satisfying as seeing a world-famous museum. Below are suggestions for different experiences.

CROWNING GLORIES

This regal runaround packs more into a day than most cities can offer in a week. Hit Westminster Abbey early to avoid the crowds, then cut through St. James's Park to catch the Changing of the Guard at 11:20 at Buckingham Palace. Take a quick detour of the Tudor delights of St. James's Palace, before a promenade down the Mall past the Regency glory of Carlton House Terrace and through Admiralty Arch to Trafalgar Square. Choose from the treasures of the National Gallery, the Who's Who of the National Portrait Gallery, or a brass rubbing in the crypt of St. Martin's-in-the-Fields. This leaves a stroll down Whitehall—past Downing Street, Horse Guards Parade, and Banqueting House—to the Houses of Parliament, where you have the option of prebooking a tour, or trying to get in to see a debate. If you have any time or energy left, stroll through Hyde Park to Kensington Palace, childhood home of Queen Victoria, and (for aspiring princesses everywhere) the Royal Dress Collection.

MUSEUM MAGIC

London has one of the finest collections of museums in the world, and many are free. Some resemble hands-on playgrounds that will keep children and adults amused for hours; others take a more classical approach. One of the latter is the British Museum in Bloomsbury, an Aladdin's cave of treasures from across the world. While in the area, pop into the nearby museum of architect Sir John Soane.

Alternatively, South Kensington's "Museum Mile" on Cromwell Road houses a triple-whammy that makes for a substantial day's-worth of diversion: the Victoria & Albert Museum, the Natural History Museum, and the Science Museum.

RETAIL THERAPY

It's not hard to shop 'til you drop in London's West End. Start with the upscale on New Bond Street, an awesome sweep of expense and elegance. In the afternoon, head to Oxford Street, which encompasses four Tube stations and is unbeatable for mass-market shopping. Run the gauntlet of designers, cheap odds and ends, department stores, and ferocious pedestrians: it's seriously busy.

A more sedate but utterly fashionable experience can be found in Knightsbridge, wandering between Harvey Nichols and Harrods department stores. Head south down Sloane Street to Sloane Square and head out along King's Road, with boutiques galore. To dip into the ever-expanding world of urban chic, try an afternoon in the lively Portobello street market in Notting Hill, where you can pick up remnants of various bygone ages: glassware, furniture, art, and clothes.

19th century, when fire destroyed the rest of the complex in 1834.

Visitors aren't allowed to snoop too much, but the **Visitors' Galleries** of the House of Commons do afford a view of democracy in process when the banks of green-leather benches are filled by opposing MPs (members of Parliament). When they speak, it's not directly to each other but through the Speaker, who also decides who will get time on the floor. Elaborate procedures

> **A VIEW TO REMEMBER**
>
> The most romantic view of the Houses of Parliament is from the opposite (south) side of the river, especially dramatic at night when the spires, pinnacles, and towers are floodlighted green and gold— a fairy-tale vision only missing the presence of Peter Pan and Wendy on their way to Never-Never Land.

notwithstanding, debate is often drowned out by raucous jeers. When MPs vote, they exit by the "Aye" or the "No" corridor, thus being counted by the party "tellers."

Westminster Hall, with its remarkable hammer-beam roof, was the work of William the Conqueror's son William Rufus. It's one of the largest remaining Norman halls in Europe, and its dramatic interior was the scene of the trial of Charles I.

After the 1834 fire, the **Clock Tower** was completed in 1858, and contains the 13-ton bell known as **Big Ben.** At the southwest end of the main Parliament building is the 323-foot-high Victoria Tower. ■ **TIP →** The only tour nonresidents can go on is the £12 tour offered when Parliament is in recess, midweek during July, August, September, and October through www.ticketmaster.co.uk. ⊠ *St. Stephen's Entrance, St. Margaret St., Westminster* ☎ *020/7219–4272 or 0870/906–3773* ⊕ *www. parliament.uk* ⊠ *Free; £12 summer tours (must book ahead)* ⊙ *Call to confirm hrs* Ⓤ *Westminster.*

QUICK BITES

The **Wesley Café** (⊠ *Storey's Gate, Westminster* ☎ *020/7222–8010)* is a popular daytime haunt for office workers around Westminster, and a good stopping point if you don't want to go farther along Victoria Street in search of food. It's almost opposite Westminster Abbey, in the crypt of Central Hall, a former Methodist church.

Fodor's Choice
★

❷ National Gallery. Standing proudly at the top of Trafalgar Square is one of the world's best art collections. The gallery fills the north side of the square, with Nelson's column in the center, with more than 2,300 masterpieces on show, for free.

This brief selection is your jumping-off point, but there are hundreds more, enough to fill a full day. In chronological order: (1) **Van Eyck** (circa 1395–1441), *The Arolfini Portrait*—a solemn couple holds hands, the fish-eye mirror behind them mysteriously illuminating what can't be seen from the front view. (2) **Holbein** (1497–1543), *The Ambassadors*— two wealthy visitors from France are depicted surrounded by what were considered luxury goods at the time, such as musical instruments, a book of mathematics, and items for studying astronomy. (3) **Botticelli** (1445–1510), *Venus and Mars*—Mars sleeps, exhausted by the love goddess, oblivious to the lance wielded by mischievous cherubs. (4)

Leonardo da Vinci (1452–1519), *The Virgin and Child*—this haunting black-chalk cartoon is partly famous for having been attacked at gunpoint, and it now gets extra protection behing glass. (5) **Caravaggio** (1573–1610), *The Supper at Emmaus*—a cinematically lightened, freshly resurrected Christ blesses bread in an astonishingly domestic vision from the master of chiaroscuro. (6) **Constable** (1776–1837), *The Hay Wain*—rendered overfamiliar by too many greeting cards, this is the definitive image of golden-age rural England. (7) **Turner** (1775–1851), *The Fighting Téméraire*—the final voyage of the great French bettleship into a livid, hazy sunset. (8) **Seurat** (1859–91), *Bathers at Asnières*—this static summer day's idyll is one of the pointillist extraordinaire's best-known works. ■TIP➜ **One-hour free, guided tours start at the Sainsbury Wing daily at 11:30 and 2:30. Or print out your own free personal tour map at one of the computers in the Art Start multimedia room in the Sainsbury Wing or East Wing Espresso Bar.** ✉ *Trafalgar Sq.* ☎ *020/7747–2885* ⊕ *www.nationalgallery.org.uk* ⊠ *Free, charge for special exhibitions* ☉ *Sun.–Thurs. 10–6, Fri. 10–9* Ⓤ *Charing Cross, Embankment, Leicester Square.*

❸ **National Portrait Gallery.** A suitably idiosyncratic collection that presents
★ a potted history of Britain through its people, past and present, this museum is an essential stop for all history and literature buffs, where you can choose to take in a little or a lot. The spacious, bright galleries are accessible via a state-of-the-art escalator, which lets you view the paintings as you ascend to a skylighted space displaying the oldest works in the Tudor Gallery. At the summit, the Portrait Restaurant, open beyond gallery hours, will delight skyline aficionados. ■TIP➜ **Here you'll see one of the best landscapes for real: a panoramic view of Nelson's Column and the backdrop along Whitehall to the Houses of Parliament.** In the Tudor Gallery—a modern update on a Tudor long hall—is a Holbein cartoon of Henry VIII; Joshua Reynolds's self-portrait hangs in the refurbished 17th-century rooms, and portraits of notables, including Shakespeare, the Brontë sisters, Jane Austen, and the Queen, are always on display. ✉ *St. Martin's Pl., Covent Garden* ☎ *020/7312–2463, 020/730–0555 recorded switchboard information* ⊕ *www.npg.org.uk* ⊠ *Free, charge for special exhibitions* ☉ *Mon.–Wed. and weekends 10–6, Thurs. and Fri. 10–9, last admission 45 mins before closing* Ⓤ *Charing Cross, Leicester Sq.*

❿ **The Queen's Gallery.** The former chapel at the south side of Buckingham
★ Palace is now a temple of art and rare and exquisite objects, acquired by kings and queens over the centuries. Although Her Majesty herself is not the personal owner, she has the privilege of holding these works for the nation. Step through the splendid portico (designed by John Simpson) into elegantly restrained, spacious galleries whose walls are hung with some truly great works. An excellent audio guide takes you through the treasures. ■TIP➜ **The E-gallery provides an interactive electronic version of the collection, allowing the user to open lockets, remove a sword from its scabbard, or take apart the tulip vases.** ✉ *Buckingham Palace, Buckingham Palace Rd., St. James's* ☎ *020/7766–7301* ⊕ *www.royal.gov.uk* ⊠ *£8.50 with free audio guide, joint ticket with Royal*

Where to See the Royals

CLOSE UP

The Queen and the Royal Family attend approximately 400 functions a year, and if you want to know what they are doing on any given date, turn to the *Court Circular,* printed in the major London dailies, or check out the Royal Family Web site, ⊕ *www. royal.gov.uk,* for the latest pictures and events. Trooping the Colour is usually held on the second Saturday in June, to celebrate the Queen's official birthday. This spectacular parade begins when she leaves Buckingham Palace in her carriage and rides down the Mall to arrive at Horse Guards Parade at 11 exactly. To watch, just line up along the Mall with your binoculars!

Another time you can catch the Queen in all her regalia is when she and the Duke of Edinburgh ride in state to Westminster to open the Houses of Parliament. The famous gilded coach, such an icon of fairytale glamour, parades from Buckingham Palace, escorted by the brilliantly uniformed Household Cavalry—on a clear day, it's to be hoped, for this ceremony takes place in late October or early November, depending on the exigencies of Parliament.

But perhaps the most relaxed, least formal time to see the Queen is during Royal Ascot, held at the racetrack near Windsor Castle—a short train ride out of London—usually during the third week of June (Tuesday–Friday). After several races, the Queen invariably walks down to the paddock on a special path, greeting race goers as she proceeds.

2

Mews £14.50 ⊗ Daily 10–5:30; last admission 4:30 Ⓤ Victoria, St. James's Park, Green Park.

ⓒ **St. James's Park.** With three palaces at its borders (the Palace of Westminster, the Tudor **St. James's Palace,** and Buckingham Palace), St. James's Park is acclaimed as the most royal of the royal parks. It's London's smallest, most ornamental park, as well as the oldest; it was acquired by Henry VIII in 1532 for a deer park. Henry VIII built the palace next to the park, which was used for hunting only—dueling and sword fights were forbidden. James I improved the land and installed an aviary and zoo (complete with crocodiles). Charles II (after his exile in France, where he admired Louis XIV's formal Versailles Palace landscapes) had formal gardens laid out, with avenues, fruit orchards, and a canal. ✉ *The Mall or Horse Guards approach, or Birdcage Walk, St. James's* ⊕ *www.royalparks.gov.uk ⊗ Daily 5 AM–midnight Ⓤ St. James's Park, Westminster.*

⑱ **Tate Britain.** Although the building is not quite as awe-inspiring as Tate
★ Modern, its younger sister on the south bank of the Thames, Tate Britain's lovely, bright galleries hold only a fraction of the Modern's crowds, making it a pleasant, hands-on place to explore great British art from 1500 to the present. It also hosts the annual Turner Prize exhibition, with its accompanying furor about the state of contemporary art, from about October to January each year. First opened in 1897, funded by the sugar magnate Sir Henry Tate, the museum includes the Linbury Galleries on the lower floors, which stage temporary exhibitions (they

can get busy), whereas the upper floors show the permanent collection. Each room has a theme and displays key works by major British artists: Van Dyck, Hogarth, and Reynolds rub shoulders with Rossetti, Sickert, Hockney, and Bacon. Not to be missed are the selection of Constable landscapes and, especially, magnificent works by J.M.W. Turner in the Clore Gallery. ⊠ *Millbank, Westminster* ☎ *020/7887–8888, 020/7887– 8008 recorded information* ⊕ *www.tate.org.uk/britain* ✉ *Free, exhibitions £3–£10* ☉ *Daily 10–5:50, last entry at 5* Ⓤ *Pimlico (signposted 5-min walk).*

❶ Trafalgar Square. This is literally the center of London: a plaque on the corner of the Strand and Charing Cross Road marks the spot from which distances on U.K. signposts are measured. **Nelson's Column** stands at the heart of the square (which is named after the great admiral's most important victory), guarded by haughty lions designed by Sir Edwin Landseer and flanked by statues of two generals who helped establish the British Empire in India, **Charles Napier** and **Henry Havelock.** The fourth plinth is given over to rotating works by contemporary sculptors. Great events, such as New Year's Eve celebrations, political protests, and sporting triumphs always see the crowds gathering in the city's most famous square. ⊠ *Trafalgar Sq., Westminster* Ⓤ *Charing Cross.*

⓭ Westminster Abbey. A monument to the nation's rich—and often bloody— and scandalous—history, the abbey rises on the Thames skyline as one of London's most iconic sites. The mysterious gloom of the lofty medieval interior is home to more than 600 statues, tombs, and commemorative tablets. About 3,300 people, from kings to composers to wordsmiths, are buried in the abbey. It has been the scene of 14 royal weddings and no fewer than 38 coronations—the first in 1066, when William the Conqueror was made king here.

Fodor's Choice ★

There's only one way around the abbey, and as there will almost certainly be a long stream of shuffling tourists at your heels, you'll need to be alert to catch the highlights. Enter by the north door then, turn around and look up to see the **painted-glass rose window,** the largest of its kind.

As you walk east towards the apse you'll see the **Coronation Chair,** at the foot of the Henry VII Chapel, which has been briefly graced by nearly every regal posterior since Edward I ordered it in 1301. Look for the graffiti on the back of the Coronation chair. It's the work of 18th- and 19th-century visitors and Westminster schoolboys who carved their names there. Further along, the **Chapel of Henry VII** contains the tombs of Henry VII and his queen, Elizabeth of York. Close by are monuments to the young daughters of James I, and an urn purported to hold the remains of the so-called Princes in the Tower—Edward V and Richard. Interestingly, arch enemies Elizabeth I and her half-sister Mary Tudor share a tomb here. An inscription reads: "Partners both in throne and grave, here rest two sisters, Elizabeth and Mary, in the hope of the Resurrection." In front of the **High Altar,** which was used for the funerals of Princess Diana and the Queen Mother, is a black-and-white marble pavement laid in 1268. The intricate Italian Cosmati work contains

three Latin inscriptions, one of
which states that the world will last
for 19,683 years.

Continue through the South Ambulatory to the **Chapel of St. Edward
the Confessor,** which contains the
shrine to the pre-Norman king.
Because of its great age, you must
join a tour with the verger to be
admitted to the chapel. (Details are
available at the admission desk;
there is a small extra charge.)

> **IN A HURRY?**
>
> If you're pressed for time, concen-
> trate on these four Westminster
> Abbey highlights: the Corona-
> tion Chair; tombs of Elizabeth
> I and Mary, Queen of Scots, in
> the Chapel of Henry VII; Poets'
> Corner; and Tomb of the Unknown
> Warrior.

To the left, you'll find **Poets' Corner.** Geoffrey Chaucer was the first
poet to be buried here in 1400. Other memorials include: William
Shakespeare, William Blake, John Milton, Jane Austen, Samuel Taylor Coleridge, William Wordsworth, and Charles Dickens. A door
from the south transept and south choir aisle leads to the calm of the
Great Cloisters.

The nearby medieval **Chapter House** is adorned with 14th-century frescoes. The King's Council met here between 1257 and 1547. Be sure to
look at the floor, one of the finest surviving tiled floors in the country.
Take a left out of the Chapter House to visit the **Abbey Museum,** which
houses a collection of deliciously macabre effigies made from the death
masks and actual clothing of Charles II and Admiral Lord Nelson (complete with eye patch). Past the museum, the **Little Cloister** is a quiet
haven, and just beyond, the **College Garden** is a delightful diversion.
Filled with medicinal herbs, it has been tended by monks for more than
900 years. On the west side of the abbey, the **Dean's Yard** is the best
spot for a fine view of the massive flying buttresses above.

Continue back to the nave of the abbey. In the choir screen, north of
the entrance to the choir, is a marble **monument to Sir Isaac Newton.** If you walk towards the West Entrance, you'll see **a plaque to
Franklin D. Roosevelt**—one of the Abbey's very few tributes to a for-
eigner. The **Grave of the Unknown Warrior,** in memory of the soldiers
who lost their lives in both world wars, is near the exit of the abbey.
■ TIP→ **Arrive early if possible, but be prepared to wait in line to tour the
abbey.** ✉ *Broad Sanctuary, Westminster* ☎ *020/7222–5152* ⊕ *www.
westminster-abbey.org* 🖰 *Abbey and museum £15* ☉ *Abbey, weekdays 9:30–3:45, Wed. until 6, Saturday 9:30–1:45; closes 1 hr after
last admission. Museum, daily 10:30–4. Cloisters daily 8–6. College
Garden, Apr.–Sept., Tues.–Thurs., 10–6; Oct.–Mar., Tues.–Thurs. 10–4.
Chapter House, daily 10–4. Services may cause changes to hrs, so call
ahead* Ⓤ *Westminster.*

WORTH NOTING

16 Banqueting House. Built on the site of the original Tudor Palace of Whitehall, which was (according to one foreign visitor) "ill-built, and nothing but a heap of houses," James I commissioned Inigo Jones, one of
England's great architects, to undertake a grand building. Influenced
during a sojourn in Italy by Andrea Palladio's work, Jones brought

Palladian sophistication and purity back to London with him. The resulting graceful and disciplined classical style of Banqueting House, completed in 1622, must have stunned its early occupants. In the quiet vaults beneath, James would escape the stresses of being a sovereign with a glass or two. ✉ *Whitehall, Westminster* ☎ *020/3166–6154 or 020/3166–6155, 020/3166–6153 concert information* ⊕ *www.hrp.org. uk* ✍ *£4.80, includes audio guide, concerts from £17.50* ⊙ *Mon.–Sat. 10–5, last admission 4:30. Closed Christmas wk. Liable to close at short notice for events so calling first is advisable* Ⓤ *Charing Cross, Embankment, Westminster.*

❺ **Carlton House Terrace.** A glorious example of Regency architect John Nash's genius, Carlton House Terrace was built between 1812 and 1830, under the patronage of George IV (Prince Regent until George III's death in 1820). Today Carlton House Terrace houses the Royal College of Pathologists (No. 2), the Royal Society (No. 6), whose members included Isaac Newton and Charles Darwin, the Turf Club (No. 5), and, at No. 12, the **Institute of Contemporary Arts,** better known as the ICA. ✉ *The Mall, St. James's* Ⓤ *Charing Cross.*

❻ **Clarence House.** The London home of Queen Elizabeth the Queen Mother for nearly 50 years, Clarence House is now the Prince of Wales' and the Duchess of Cornwall's residence. The Regency mansion was built by John Nash for the Duke of Clarence, who found living in St. James's Palace quite unsuitable. The rooms have been sensitively preserved to reflect the Queen Mother's taste, with the addition of many works of art from the Royal Collection. You'll find it less palace and more home (for the Prince and his sons William and Harry), with informal family pictures and comfortable sofas. Like Buckingham Palace, Clarence House is open only in August and September and tickets must be booked in advance. ✉ *Clarence House, St. James's Palace, St. James's* ☎ *020/7766–7303* ⊕ *www.royalcollection.org.uk* ✍ *£8* ⊙ *Aug. and Sept.* Ⓤ *Green Park.*

⓯ **Downing Street.** Looking like an unassuming alley but for the iron gates at both its Whitehall and Horse Guards Road approaches, this is the location of the famous **No. 10,** London's modest version equivalent of the White House. The Georgian entrance is deceptive, though, since the old house now leads to a large mansion behind it, overlooking the Horse Guards Parade. ✉ *Whitehall, Whitehall* Ⓤ *Westminster.*

❼ **St. James's Palace.** With its solitary sentry posted at the gate, this surprisingly small palace of Tudor brick was once a home for many British sovereigns, including the first Elizabeth and Charles I, who spent his last night here before his execution. Today it's the working office of another Charles—the Prince of Wales. ✉ *Friary Court, St. James's* ⊕ *www.royal. gov.uk* Ⓤ *Green Park.*

❹ **St. Martin-in-the-Fields.** One of London's best-loved and most welcoming
♋ of churches, has been enhanced both inside and out by expensive and time-consuming refurbishment work and the building's array of functions continues unabated. The crypt is a hive of lively activity, with a café and shop, plus the **London Brass-Rubbing Centre,** where you can make your own life-size souvenir knight, lady, or monarch from replica

tomb brasses, with metallic waxes, paper, and instructions provided from about £5; and the **Gallery in the Crypt,** showing an exhibition on the history of the church. ✉ *Trafalgar Sq., Covent Garden* ☎ *020/7766–1100, 020/7839–8362 evening-concert credit-card bookings* ⊕ *www. smitf.org* ✒ *Concerts £6–£22* ⊙ *Mon.–Sat. 8–6, Sun. 8–6 for worship; café Mon.–Wed. 8–8, open until 9 Thurs.–Sat., Sun. 11–6* Ⓤ *Charing Cross, Leicester Sq.*

8 **Spencer House.** Ancestral abode of the Spencers—Diana, Princess of Wales's family—this is perhaps the finest example of an elegant 18th-century town house extant in London. Reflecting his passion for the Grand Tour and classical antiquities, the first Earl Spencer commissioned architect John Vardy to adapt designs from ancient Rome for a magnificent private palace. Vardy was responsible for gorgeous west-facing Palladian facade, its pediment adorned with classical statues, and the ground-floor interiors, notably the lavish Palm Room, which boasts a spectacular screen of columns covered in gilded carvings that resemble gold palm trees. The house is open only on Sunday (closed January and August), and only to guided tours. ✉ *27 St. James's Pl., St. James's* ☎ *020/7499–8620* ⊕ *www.spencerhouse.co.uk* ✒ *£9* ⊙ *Sept.–Dec. and Feb.–July, Sun. 10:30–5:45, last tour 4:45; tour leaves approx. every 25 mins; tickets on sale Sun. at 10:30* Ⓤ *Green Park.*

⑪ **Wellington Barracks.** These are the headquarters of the Guards Division, the Queen's five regiments of elite foot guards (Grenadier, Coldstream, Scots, Irish, and Welsh) who protect the sovereign and patrol her palaces dressed in tunics of gold-purled scarlet and tall bearskin caps. Guardsmen alternate these ceremonial postings with serving in current conflicts, for which they wear more practical uniforms. If you want to learn more about the guards, visit the **Guards Museum.** ✉ *Wellington Barracks, Birdcage Walk, Westminster* ☎ *020/7414–3428* ⊕ *www. theguardsmuseum.com* ✒ *£3* ⊙ *Daily 10–4; last admission 3:30* Ⓤ *St. James's Park.*

SOHO AND COVENT GARDEN

Once a red-light district, the Soho of today delivers more "grown-up" than "adult" entertainment. Its theaters, restaurants, pubs, and clubs merge with the first-run cinemas of Leicester Square and the venerable venues (Royal and English National Operas) of Covent Garden to create the mega-entertainment district known as the West End. During the day Covent Garden's historic piazza is packed with shoppers and sightseers, while Soho reverts to the business side of its lively, late-night scene—ad agencies, media, film distributors, actors, agents, and casting agents all looking for each other.

A quadrilateral bounded by Regent Street, Coventry and Cranbourn streets, Charing Cross Road, and the eastern half of Oxford Street encloses Soho. This appellation, unlike the New York City neighborhood's similar one, is not an abbreviation of anything, but a blast from the past—derived from the shouts of "So-ho!" that royal huntsmen in Whitehall Palace's parklands were once heard to cry. For many years Soho was London's peep show–sex shop–brothel center. Legislation in the mid-1980s granted expensive licenses to a few such establishments and closed down the rest. Today Soho remains the address of wonderful ethnic restaurants, including those of London's Chinatown.

The Covent Garden Market became the Covent Garden Piazza in 1980. It was originally the "convent garden" belonging to the Abbey of St. Peter at Westminster (later Westminster Abbey), and still functions as the center of a neighborhood—one that has always been alluded to as "colorful." After centuries of magnificence and misery, Covent Garden became London's vegetable and flower market in the 19th century. When the produce moved to the Nine Elms Market in Vauxhall in 1974, the glass-covered market halls took on new life with stores and entertainment. Today it bustles with tourists and shoppers.

GETTING HERE Take any train to the Piccadilly Circus station (on the Piccadilly and Bakerloo lines or Leicester Square and Northern lines for Soho). Get off at Covent Garden on the Piccadilly Line for Covent Garden and Embankment (Bakerloo, Northern, District, and Circle lines) or Charing Cross (Northern, Bakerloo, and main railway lines) for the area south of the Strand.

PLANNING You can comfortably tour all the sights in Covent Garden in a day. Visit
YOUR TIME the small but perfect Courtauld Institute Gallery on Monday before 2 PM when it's free. That leaves plenty of time to visit the marketplace, watch the street entertainment, and do a bit of shopping, with energy left over for a night on the town (or "on the tiles," as the British say) in Soho.

Numbers in the margin correspond to numbers on the Soho and Covent Garden map.

TOP ATTRACTIONS

7 **Courtauld Institute Gallery.** One of London's most beloved art collections, the Courtauld is to your left as you pass through the archway into the grounds of the beautifully restored, grand 18th-century classical **Somerset House.** Founded in 1931 by the textile magnate Samuel Courtauld to house his remarkable private collection, this is one of the world's finest impressionist and postimpressionist galleries, with artists ranging from Bonnard to van Gogh. A déjà-vu moment with Cézanne, Degas, Seurat, or Monet awaits on every wall (Manet's *Bar at the Folies-Bergère* is the star), with bonus post-Renaissance works thrown in. ⊠ *Somerset House, Strand, Covent Garden* ☎ *020/7848–2526* ⊕ *www.courtauld. ac.uk* ☑ *£5, free Mon. 10–2, except bank holidays* ⊗ *Daily 10–6; last admission 5:30* Ⓤ *Covent Garden, Holborn, Temple.*

3 **Covent Garden Piazza.** The 1840 market building around which Cov-
Ċ ent Garden pivots is known as the Piazza. Inside, the shops are mostly higher-class clothing chains, plus a couple of cafés and some knick-knack stores that are good for gifts. One particular gem is Benjamin Pollock's Toyshop at No. 44 in the market. Established in the 1880s, it sells delightful toy theaters. There's the superior **Apple Market** for crafts on most days, too. If you turn right, you'll reach the indoor **Jubilee Market,** which, with its stalls of clothing, army-surplus gear, and more crafts and knickknacks, is disappointingly ordinary. In summer it may seem that everyone you see around the Piazza (and the crowds

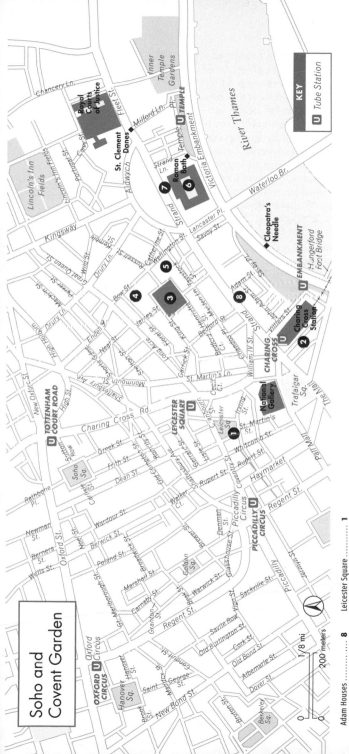

Soho and Covent Garden

KEY

U Tube Station

Adam Houses **8**

Benjamin Franklin
House **2**

Courtauld Institute
Gallery **7**

Covent Garden Piazza ... **3**

Leicester Square **1**

London's Transport
Museum **5**

Royal Opera House **4**

Somerset House **6**

0   1/8 mi

0   200 meters

are legion) is a fellow tourist, but there's still plenty of office life in the area. Londoners who shop here tend to head for Neal Street and the area to the left of the subway entrance rather than the touristy market itself. By the church in the square, street performers—from global musicians to jugglers and mimes—play to the crowds, as they have done since the first English Punch and Judy Show, staged here in the 17th century. ⊠ *Covent Garden* Ⓤ *Covent Garden.*

> **FEELING PECKISH?**
>
> Although they may set out a few tables, the coffee shops and snack bars along the Covent Garden market buildings are better for takeout than for comfortable coffee breaks or lunches. They can be overpriced and of iffy quality. Head for Soho when the munchies strike.

❻ **Somerset House.** An old royal palace once stood on the site, but it was ★ eventually replaced by this 18th-century building, the work of Sir William Chambers (1726–96), during the reign of George III. It was built to house government offices, principally those of the navy. Now, for the first time in more than 100 years, these gracious rooms are on view, including the Seamen's Waiting Hall and the Nelson Stair. In addition, the Navy Commissioners' Barge has returned to dry dock at the Water Gate. The rooms are on the south side of the building, by the river. The **Courtauld Institute Gallery** occupies most of the north building, facing the busy Strand. ⊠ *The Strand, Covent Garden* ☏ *020/7845–4600* ⊕ *www.somerset-house.org.uk* ✉ *Embankment Gallery £5, Courtauld Gallery £5, other areas free* ☉ *Daily 10–6; last admission 5:30* Ⓤ *Charing Cross, Waterloo, Blackfriars.*

WORTH NOTING

❽ **Adam Houses.** All that remains of what was once a regal riverfront row of houses on a 3-acre site, connected by arches and streets below grade, are a few of the structures, but such is their quality that they are worth a detour off the Strand to see. The work of 18th-century Scottish architects and interior designers (John, Robert, James, and William Adam, known collectively as the Adam brothers), the original development was damaged in the 19th century during the building of the embankment, and mostly demolished in 1936 to be replaced by an art deco tower. The original houses still standing are protected, and give a glimpse of their former grandeur. Nos. 1–4 Robert Street and Nos. 7 and 10 Adam Street are the best. At the **Royal Society of Arts** (⊠ *8 John Adam St.* ☏ *020/7930–5115* ⊕ *www.thersa.org* ✉ *Free* ☉ *1st Sun. of month, 10–1*), you can see a suite of Adam rooms; no reservations are required. ⊠ *The Strand, Covent Garden* Ⓤ *Charing Cross, Embankment.*

❷ **Benjamin Franklin House.** Opened to the public for the first time in 2006, this architecturally significant 1730 house is the only surviving residence of American statesman, scientist, writer, and inventor Benjamin Franklin, who lived and worked there for 16 years preceding the American Revolution. The restored Georgian town house has been left unfurnished, the better to show off the original features—18th-century paneling, stoves, beams, bricks, and windows. Older children (under 16 admitted free) particularly enjoy the "Historical Experience," an interactive biography of the Founding Father that is offered on the hour from noon to 4. ⊠ *36 Craven St., Covent Garden* ☎ *020/7839–2006, 020/7925–1405 booking line* ⊕ *www.benjaminfranklinhouse.org* 🖃 *£7* 🕑 *Wed.–Sun. noon–5.*

➊ **Leicester Square.** Looking at the neon of the major movie houses, the fast-food outlets, and the disco entrances, you'd never guess that this square (pronounced Lester) was a model of formality and refinement when it was first laid out around 1630. By the 19th century it was already bustling and disreputable, and although today it's not a threatening place, you should still be on your guard, especially at night—any space so full of tourists and people a little the worse for wear is bound to attract pickpockets, and Leicester Square certainly does. Londoners generally tend to avoid this windswept pedestrianized plaza, crowded as it is with suburban teenagers, wandering backpackers, and mimes. That said, the liveliness can be quite cheering. In the middle is a statue of a sulking Shakespeare, clearly wishing he were somewhere else. ■ TIP➜ One landmark worth visiting is TKTS, the Society of London Theatre ticket kiosk, which sells half-price tickets for many of that evening's performances. ⊠ *Covent Garden* Ⓤ *Leicester Sq.*

➌ **London's Transport Museum.** Housed in the old flower market at the southeast corner of the Covent Garden Piazza, the recently refurbished museum includes the interactive space "Green Futures" that focuses on the challenge of meeting London's growth in partnership with the environment. Food and drink are available at the aptly named Upper Deck café. ⊠ *Covent Garden Piazza* ☎ *020/7379–6344* ⊕ *www.ltmuseum. co.uk* 🖃 *£10* 🕑 *Sat.–Thurs. 10–6 (last admission 5:15), Fri. 11–6 (last admission 5:15)* Ⓤ *Leicester Sq., Covent Garden.*

➍ **Royal Opera House.** London's premier opera and ballet venue was designed in 1858 by E.M. Barry, son of Sir Charles, the House of Commons architect, and is the third theater on the site. The first theater opened in 1732 and burned down in 1808; the second opened a year later, only to succumb to fire in 1856. The entire building, which has been given a spectacular overhaul, retains the magic of the grand Victorian theater but is now more accessible. ⊠ *Bow St., Covent Garden* ☎ *020/7240–1200* ⊕ *www.royalopera.org* Ⓤ *Covent Garden.*

BLOOMSBURY AND LEGAL LONDON

The hub of intellectual London, Bloomsbury is anchored by the British Museum and the University of London, which houses—among other institutions—the internationally ranked London School of Economics and the School of Oriental and African Studies. As a result, the streets and cafés around Bloomsbury's Russell Square are often crawling with students and professors engaged in heated conversation, while literary agents and academics surf the shelves of the antiquarian bookstores nearby.

The character of an area of London can change visibly from one street to the next. Nowhere is this so clear as in the contrast between fun-loving Soho and intellectual Bloomsbury, a mere 100 yards to the northeast, or between arty, trendy Covent Garden and—on the other side of Kingsway—sober Holborn (pronounced *hoe*-bun). Bloomsbury is known for its famous flowering of literary-arty bohemia, personified during the first three decades of the 20th century by the clique known as the Bloomsbury Group, including Virginia Woolf, E. M. Forster, Vanessa Bell, and Lytton Strachey. The second, filled with ancient buildings of the legal profession, is more interesting and beautiful than you might suppose. The Great Fire of 1666 razed most of the city but spared the buildings of legal London, and all of Holborn oozes history. Leading landmarks here are the Inns of Court, where the country's top solicitors and barristers have had their chambers for centuries.

GETTING HERE   You can easily get to where you need to be on foot in Bloomsbury, and the Russell Square Tube stop on the Piccadilly Line leaves you right at the corner of Russell Square. The best Tube stops for the Inns of Court are Holborn on the Central and Piccadilly lines or Chancery Lane on the Central Line. Tottenham Court Road on the Northern and Central lines or Russell Square (Piccadilly Line) are best for the British Museum.

PLANNING   Bloomsbury can be seen in a day, or in half a day, depending on your
YOUR TIME   interests. If you plan to visit the Inns of Court as well as the British Museum, and you'd also like to get a feel for the neighborhood, then you may devote an entire day to this literary and legal enclave, or come back on another day to visit the vast British Museum. Avoid Bloomsbury in mid-September, when the streets around Russell Square are filled with students moving into housing for the upcoming school session. At other times it's a pleasure to wander through the quiet, leafy squares, examining Blue Plaques or relaxing at a street-side café. You can also pick up a "Museum Mile" map, which marks all the museums in this area, and use it to plan your path.

Numbers in the margin correspond to numbers on the Bloomsbury and Legal London map.

TOP ATTRACTIONS

① **British Museum.** With a facade like a great temple, this celebrated trea-
Fodor'sChoice   sure house, filled with plunder of incalculable value and beauty from
★   around the globe, occupies an immense Greco-Victorian building that makes a suitably grand impression. Inside are some of the greatest relics of humankind: the Parthenon Sculptures (Elgin Marbles), the Rosetta Stone, the Sutton Hoo Treasure—almost everything, it seems, but the Ark of the Covenant. The three rooms that comprise the **Sainsbury African** Galleries are a must-see in the Lower Gallery—together they present 200,000 objects, highlighting such ancient kingdoms as the Benin and Asante. The museum's focal point is the **Great Court**, a brilliant modern design with a vast glass roof that reveals the museum's covered courtyard. The revered **Reading Room** has a blue-and-gold dome and hosts temporary exhibitions until its more than 104,000 ancient tomes return from the British Library in 2012. If you want to navigate the highlights of the almost 100 galleries, join the free **eyeOpener** 30- to 40-minute tours by museum guides.

The collection began when Sir Hans Sloane, physician to Queen Anne and George II, bequeathed his personal collection of antiquities to the nation. It grew quickly, thanks to enthusiastic kleptomaniacs after the Napoleonic Wars—most notoriously the seventh Earl of Elgin, who

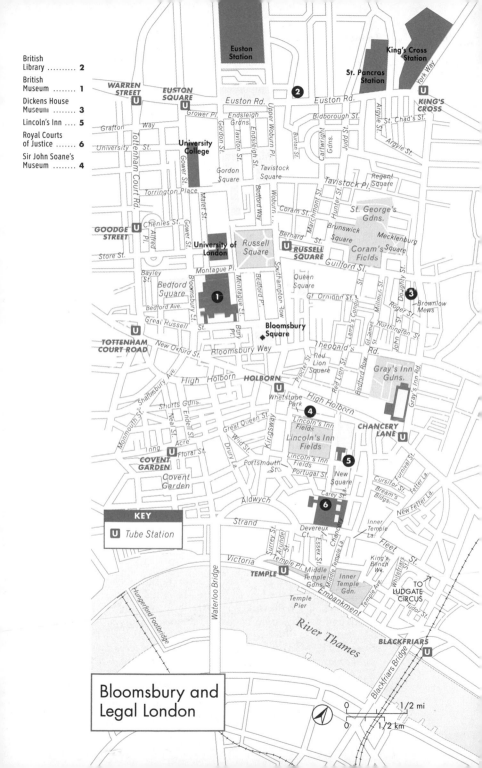

KEY

U *Tube Station*

Bloomsbury and Legal London

0   1/2 mi

0   1/2 km

acquired the marbles from the Parthenon and Erechtheion in Athens during his term as British ambassador in Constantinople. Here follows a highly edited résumé (in order of encounter) of the British Museum's greatest hits: close to the entrance hall, in Room 4, is the **Rosetta Stone**, found by French soldiers in 1799, and carved in 196 BC by decree of Ptolemy V in Egyptian hieroglyphics, demotic (a cursive script developed in Egypt), and Greek. This inscription provided the French Egyptologist Jean-François Champollion with the key to deciphering hieroglyphics. Also in Room 4 is the Colossal statue of Ramesses II, a 7-ton likeness of this member of the 19th dynasty's (ca. 1270 BC) upper half. Maybe the **Parthenon Sculptures** should be back in Greece, but while the debate rages on, you can steal your own moment with the Elgin Marbles in Room 18. Carved in about 400 BC, these graceful decorations are displayed along with a high-tech exhibit of the Acropolis.

Upstairs are some of the most popular galleries, especially beloved by children: Rooms 62–63, where the **Egyptian mummies** live. Nearby are the glittering 4th-century **Mildenhall Treasure** and the equally splendid 8th-century Anglo-Saxon **Sutton Hoo Treasure** (with magnificent helmets and jewelry). A more prosaic exhibit is that of Pete Marsh, sentimentally named by the archaeologists who unearthed the **Lindow Man** from a Cheshire peat marsh; poor Pete was ritually slain in the 1st century, and lay perfectly pickled in his bog until 1984. The **Korean Foundation Gallery** (Room 67) delves into the art and archaeology of the country, including a reconstruction of a sarangbang, a traditional scholar's study. ⊠ *Great Russell St., Bloomsbury* ☎ *020/7323–8000* ⊕ *www.britishmuseum.org* ⊡ *Free; donations encouraged* ⊙ *Museum Sat.–Wed. 10–5:30, Thurs. and Fri. 10–8:30. Great Court Sun.–Wed. 9–6, Thurs.–Sat. 9 AM–11 PM* Ⓤ *Russell Square.*

❸ **Dickens House Museum.** This is the only one of the many London houses
ⓒ Charles Dickens (1812–70) inhabited that's still standing, and it would have had a real claim to his fame in any case because he wrote *Oliver Twist* and *Nicholas Nickleby* and finished *Pickwick Papers* here between 1837 and 1839. The house looks exactly as it would have in Dickens's day, complete with a tall clerk's desk (where the master wrote standing up, often while chatting with visiting friends and relatives). ⊠ *48 Doughty St., Bloomsbury* ☎ *020/7405–2127* ⊕ *www. dickensmuseum.com* ⊡ *£5* ⊙ *Mon.–Sat. 10–5, Sun. 11–5; last admission 4:30* Ⓤ *Chancery La., Russell Sq.*

❺ **Lincoln's Inn.** There's plenty to see at one of the oldest, best preserved, and
★ most attractive of the Inns of Court—from the Chancery Lane Tudor brick gatehouse to the wide-open, tree-lined, atmospheric Lincoln's Inn Fields and the 15th-century chapel remodeled by Inigo Jones in 1620. ⊠ *Chancery La., Bloomsbury* ☎ *020/7405–1393* ⊕ *www.lincolnsinn. org.uk* ⊡ *Free* ⊙ *Gardens weekdays 7–7, chapel weekdays noon–2:30; public may also attend Sun. service in chapel at 11:30 during legal terms* Ⓤ *Chancery La.*

❹ **Sir John Soane's Museum.** Sir John (1753–1837), architect of the Bank of
★ England, bequeathed his house to the nation on condition that nothing be changed. He obviously had enormous fun with his home: in the

Picture Room, for instance, two of Hogarth's *Rake's Progress* series are among the paintings on panels that swing away to reveal secret gallery pockets with even more paintings. Everywhere mirrors and colors play tricks with light and space, and split-level floors worthy of a fairground fun house disorient you. In a basement chamber sits the vast 1300 BC sarcophagus of Seti I, lit by a domed skylight two stories above. (When Sir John acquired this priceless object for £2,000, after it was rejected by the British Museum, he celebrated with a three-day party.) ⊠ *13 Lincoln's Inn Fields, Bloomsbury* ☎ *020/7440–4263* ⊕ *www.soane. org* ✉ *Free, Sat. tour £5* ⊙ *Tues.–Sat. 10–5; also 6–9 on 1st Tues. of month* Ⓤ *Holborn.*

WORTH NOTING

❷ British Library. Formerly in the British Museum, the collection of around 18 million volumes now has a home in state-of-the-art surroundings, and if you're a researcher, it's a wonderful place to work (special passes are required). The library's treasures are on view to the general public: the Magna Carta, a Gutenberg Bible, Jane Austen's writings, Shakespeare's First Folio, and musical manuscripts by Handel as well as Sir Paul McCartney are on show in the Sir John Ritblat Gallery. ⊠ *96 Euston Rd., Bloomsbury* ☎ *0870/7412–7332* ⊕ *www.bl.uk* ✉ *Free, donations appreciated, charge for special exhibitions* ⊙ *Mon. and Wed.–Fri. 9:30–6, Tues. 9:30–8, Sat. 9:30–5, Sun. and bank holidays Mon. 11–5* Ⓤ *Euston, Euston Sq., King's Cross.*

❻ Royal Courts of Justice. Here is the vast Victorian Gothic pile of 35 million bricks containing the nation's principal law courts, with 1,000-odd rooms running off 3½ mi of corridor. And here are heard the most important civil law cases—that's everything from divorce to fraud, with libel in between. You can sit in the viewing gallery to watch any trial you like, for a live version of Court TV. The more dramatic criminal cases are heard at the Old Bailey. ⊠ *The Strand, Bloomsbury* ☎ *020/7947–6000* ⊕ *www.hmcourts-service.gov.uk* ✉ *Free* ⊙ *Weekdays 9–4:30; during Aug. there are no sittings and public areas close at 2:30* Ⓤ *Temple.*

THE CITY

The City, as opposed to the city, is the capital's fast-beating financial heart. Behind a host of imposing neoclassical facades lie the banks and exchanges whose frantic trade determines the fortunes that underpin London—and the country. But the "Square Mile" is much more than London's Wall Street—the capital's economic engine room also has currency as a religious and political center. St. Paul's Cathedral has looked after Londoners' souls since the 7th century, and the Tower of London—that moat-surrounded royal fortress, prison, and jewel house—has taken care of beheading them. The City's maze of backstreets is also home to a host of old churches, marketplaces, and cozy pubs.

Twice the City has been nearly wiped off the face of the earth. The Great Fire of 1666 necessitated a total reconstruction, in which Sir Christopher Wren had a big hand, contributing not only his masterpiece, St. Paul's Cathedral, but 49 additional parish churches. The second wave of destruction was dealt by the German bombers of World War II. The ruins were rebuilt, but slowly, and with no overall plan, leaving the City a patchwork of the old and the new, the interesting and the flagrantly awful. Since a mere 8,000 or so people call it home, the nation's financial center is deserted on weekends, with restaurants shuttered.

Crossing the Millennium Bridge from the Tate Modern to St. Paul's is one of the finest walks in London for views of the river and the cathedral that towers over it. Dubbed the "blade of light," this shiny aluminum-and-steel construction was the result of a collaboration between architect Norman Foster and sculptor Anthony Caro.

GETTING HERE　The City is well served by a concentrated selection of underground stops. St Paul's and Bank, on the Central Line, and Mansion House, Cannon Street, and Monument, on the District and Circle lines, deliver visitors to the heart of the City. Liverpool Street and Aldgate border the City's eastern edge, while Chancery Lane and Farringdon lie to the west. Barbican and Moorgate provide easy access to the theaters and galleries of the Barbican, while Blackfriars, to the south, leads to Ludgate Circus and Fleet Street.

PLANNING YOUR TIME　The "Square Mile" is as compact as the nickname suggests, with very little distance between points of interest, making it easy to dip into the City for an afternoon stroll. For full immersion in the Tower of London, however, set aside half a day, especially if seeing the Crown Jewels is a priority. Allow an hour minimum each for the Museum of London, St. Paul's Cathedral, and the Tower Bridge. On weekends, without the scurrying suits, the City is nearly deserted, making it hard to find lunch—and yet this is when the major attractions are at their busiest. So if you can manage to come on a weekday, do so.

Numbers in the margin correspond to numbers on the City map.

TOP ATTRACTIONS

⓫ **Monument.** Commemorating the "dreadful visitation" of the Great Fire
☾ of 1666, this is the world's tallest isolated stone column. It is the work of Sir Christopher Wren and Dr. Robert Hooke, who were asked to erect it "on or as neere unto the place where the said Fire soe unhappily began as conveniently may be." ✉ *Monument St., The City* ☎ *020/7626–2717* ⊕ *www.themonument.info* ⛃ *£2* ☉ *Daily 9:30–5:30, last admission 5* Ⓤ *Monument.*

❺ **Museum of London.** If there's one place to get the history of London sorted
☾ out, right from 450,000 BC to the present day, it's here—although there's
★ a great deal to sort out: Oliver Cromwell's death mask, Queen Victoria's crinoline gowns, Selfridges' art deco elevators, and the London's Burning exhibition are just some of the goodies. The museum appropriately shelters a section of the 2nd- to 4th-century London wall, which you can view from a window inside. Permanent displays include "London Before London," "Roman London," "Medieval London," and "Tudor London." The lower galleries, dealing with London's history from 1666 until the 21st century, have undergone extensive modernization. ✉ *London Wall, The City* ☎ *0870/444–3851* ⊕ *www.museumoflondon.org.uk* ⛃ *Free* ☉ *Mon.–Sat. 10–5:50, Sun. noon–5:50; last admission 5:30* Ⓤ *Barbican, St. Paul's.*

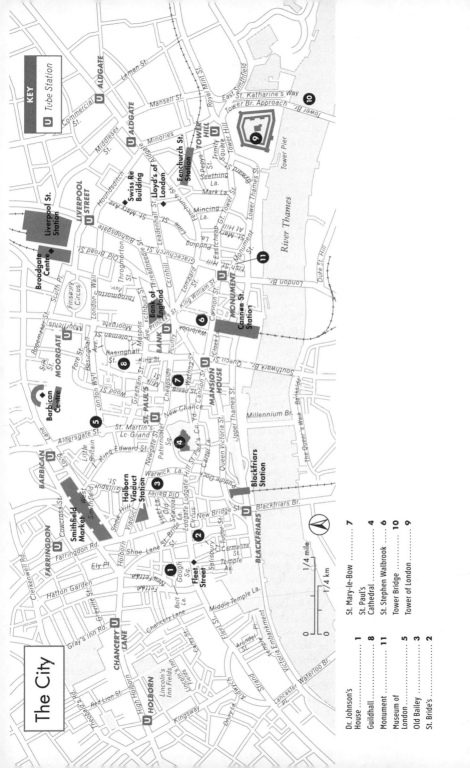

The City

KEY

U Tube Station

Dr. Johnson's House **1**
Guildhall **8**
Monument **11**
Museum of London **5**
Old Bailey **3**
St. Bride's **2**
St. Mary-le-Bow **7**
St. Paul's Cathedral **4**
St. Stephen Walbrook **6**
Tower Bridge **10**
Tower of London **9**

2 St. Bride's. According to legend, the distinctively tiered steeple of this Christopher Wren–designed church gave rise to the shape of the traditional wedding cake. As St. Paul's (in Covent Garden) is the actors' church, so St. Bride's belongs to journalists, many of whom have been buried or memorialized here. ⊠ *Fleet St., The City* ☎ *020/7427–0133* ⊕ *www.stbrides.com* ⊡ *Free* ☉ *Weekdays 8–6, Sat. 11–3, Sun for services only 10–1 and 5–7:30* Ⓤ *St. Paul's, Blackfriars.*

> **MUSICAL FRICTION**
>
> The organ at St. Paul's, with its cherubs and angels, was not installed without controversy. The mighty instrument proved a tight fit, and the maker, known as Father Schmidt, and Wren nearly came to blows. Wren was reputed to have said he would not adapt his cathedral for a mere "box of whistles."

7 St. Mary-le-Bow. This church is another classic City survivor; various versions have stood on the site since the 11th century. In 1284 a local goldsmith took refuge here after committing a murder, only to be killed inside the church by enraged relatives of his victim. The church was rebuilt in its current form after the Great Fire. ⊠ *Cheapside, The City* ☎ *020/7248–5139* ⊕ *www.stmarylebow.co.uk* ☉ *Mon.–Thurs. 7–6, Fri. 7–4* Ⓤ *Mansion House, St. Paul's.*

QUICK BITES

The **Place Below** (☎ *020/7329–0789*), in St. Mary-le-Bow's Norman crypt, is packed with City workers weekdays from 7:30 until 3 for a vegetarian menu covering breakfasts and scrumptious light lunches.

4 St. Paul's Cathedral. The symbolic heart of London, St. Paul's may take your breath away, even more so now that it's been spruced up for its 300th anniversary. The dome—the world's third largest—peeps through the skyline from many an angle around London. The structure is Sir Christopher Wren's masterpiece, completed in 1710 after 35 years of building, and, much later, miraculously spared (mostly) by World War II bombs. Wren's first plan, known as the New Model, did not make it past the drawing board. The second, known as the Great Model, got as far as the 20-foot oak rendering you can see here before it also was rejected. The third was accepted, with the fortunate coda that the architect be allowed to make changes as he saw fit. Without that, there would be no dome, since the approved design had a steeple. When you enter and see the dome from the inside, it may seem smaller than you expected. It *is* smaller, and 60 feet lower than the lead-covered outer dome. Beneath the lantern is Wren's famous epitaph, which his son composed and had set into the pavement, and which reads succinctly: LECTOR, SI MONUMENTUM REQUIRIS, CIRCUMSPICE—"Reader, if you seek his monument, look around you." The epitaph also appears on Wren's memorial in the Crypt. Up 259 spiral steps is the **Whispering Gallery,** an acoustic phenomenon; you whisper something to the wall on one side, and a second later it transmits clearly to the other side, 107 feet away. Ascend to the **Stone Gallery,** which encircles the base of the dome. Farther up (280 feet from ground level) is the small **Golden Gallery,** around the dome's highest point. From both these galleries (if you have

Fodor's Choice
★

a head for heights) you can walk outside for a spectacular panorama of London. The climb up the spiraling steps can be fun for older kids.

The remains of the poet John Donne, who was dean of St. Paul's for his final 10 years (he died in 1631), are in the south choir aisle. The vivacious choir-stall carvings nearby are the work of Grinling Gibbons, as are those on the organ, which Wren designed and Handel played. Behind the high altar is the **American Memorial Chapel,** dedicated in 1958 to the 28,000 GIs stationed in the United Kingdom who lost their lives in World War II. Among the famous whose remains lie in the **Crypt** are the duke of Wellington and Admiral Lord Nelson. The Crypt also has a gift shop and a café. ⊠ *St. Paul's Churchyard, The City* ☎ *020/7236–4128* ⊕ *www.stpauls.co.uk* ⌦ *£11, audio tour £4, guided tour £3* ⊙ *Cathedral Mon.–Sat. 8:30–4:30 (last admission at 4), Shop Mon.–Sat. 8:30–5, Sun. 10–4:30, Crypt Café Mon.–Sat. 9–5, Sun. 12–4* Ⓤ *St. Paul's.*

🔟 **Tower Bridge.** Despite its medieval, fairy-tale appearance, this is a Victo-
☾ rian youngster. Constructed of steel, then clothed in Portland stone, the
★ Horace Jones masterpiece was deliberately styled in the Gothic persua-
sion to complement the Tower next door. The **Tower Bridge Exhibition** is a child-friendly tour where you can discover how one of the world's most famous bridges actually works. ⊠ *Tower Bridge Rd., The City* ☎ *020/7403–3761* ⊕ *www.towerbridge.org.uk* ⌦ *£6* ⊙ *Daily Apr.–Sept., 10–6:30; Oct.–Mar. 9:30–5:30; last admission 30 mins before closing time* Ⓤ *Tower Hill.*

❾ **Tower of London.** Nowhere else does London's history come to life so
☾ vividly as in this minicity of 20 towers filled with heraldry and trea-
★ sure, the intimate details of lords and dukes and princes and sovereigns etched in the walls (literally, in some places), and quite a few pints of royal blood spilled on the stones. ■ **TIP→ This is one of Britain's most popular sights—the Crown Jewels are here—and you can avoid lines by buying a ticket in advance on the Web site, by phone, at any tube station, or at an on-site kiosk. Arriving before 11 can also help at busy times.** The visitor center provides an introduction to the Tower. Allow at least three hours for exploring, and take time to stroll along the battlements for a wonderful overview.

The Tower holds the royal gems because it's still one of the royal pal-aces, although no monarch since Henry VII has called it home. It has also housed the Royal Mint, the Public Records, the Royal Menagerie (which formed the basis of the London Zoo), and the Royal Observa-tory, although its most renowned and titillating function has been as a jail and place of torture and execution. A person was mighty privileged to be beheaded in the peace and seclusion of **Tower Green** instead of before the mob at Tower Hill. In fact, only seven people were ever impor-tant enough—among them Anne Boleyn and Catherine Howard, wives two and five of Henry VIII's six; Elizabeth I's friend Robert Devereux, earl of Essex; and the nine-day queen, Lady Jane Grey, age 17.

Free tours depart every half hour or so from the Middle Tower. They are conducted by the 39 Yeoman Warders, better known as Beefeaters—ex-servicemen dressed in resplendent navy-and-red (scarlet-and-gold on special occasions) Tudor outfits. Beefeaters have been guarding the Tower since Henry VII appointed them in 1485. One of them, the Yeoman Ravenmaster, is responsible for making life comfortable for the Tower ravens (six birds plus reserves)—an important duty, because if the ravens were to desert the Tower, goes the legend, the kingdom would fall.

In prime position stands the oldest part of the Tower and the most conspicuous of its buildings, the **White Tower;** the other towers were built in the next few centuries. This central keep was begun in 1078 by William the Conqueror; Henry III (1207–72) had it whitewashed, which is where the name comes from. The spiral staircase is the only way up, and here are the **Royal Armouries,** with a collection of arms and armor. The **Chapel of St. John the Evangelist,** downstairs from the armories, is a pure example of 11th-century Norman style—very rare, very simple, and very beautiful. Across the moat, **Traitors' Gate** lies to the right. Opposite Traitors' Gate is the former Garden Tower, better known since about 1570 as the **Bloody Tower.** Its name comes from one of the most famous unsolved murders in history, the saga of the "little princes in the Tower." In 1483 the uncrowned boy king, Edward V, and his brother Richard were left here by their uncle, Richard of Gloucester, after the death of their father, Edward IV. They were never seen again, Gloucester was crowned Richard III, and in 1674 two little skeletons were found under the stairs to the White Tower. The obvious conclusions have always been drawn.

The most famous exhibits are the **Crown Jewels,** in the Jewel House, Waterloo Block. Moving walkways on either side of the jewels hasten progress at the busiest times. You get so close to the fabled gems you feel you could polish them (there are, however, wafers of bulletproof glass), if your eyes weren't so dazzled by the sparkle of the gems, enhanced with special lighting. Before you see them, you view a short film that includes scenes from Elizabeth's 1953 coronation.

The little chapel of **St. Peter ad Vincula** is the second church on the site, and it conceals the remains of some 2,000 people executed at the Tower, Anne Boleyn and Catherine Howard among them.

Evocative **Beauchamp Tower** was built west of Tower Green by Edward I (1272–1307). It was soon designated as a jail for the higher class of miscreant, including Lady Jane Grey, who is thought to have added her Latin graffiti to the many inscriptions carved by prisoners here.

For tickets to the Ceremony of the Keys (locking of main gates, nightly between 9:30 and 10), write well in advance. ⊠ *H. M. Tower of London, Tower Hill, The City* ☎ *0844/482–7777* ⊕ *www.hrp.org.uk* ✆ *£17* ☺ *Mar.–Oct., Tues.–Sat. 9–5:30, Sun. and Mon. 10–5:30; last admission at 5. Nov.–Feb., Tues.–Sat. 9–4:30, Sun. and Mon. 10–4:30, last admission at 4* Ⓤ *Tower Hill.*

WORTH NOTING

 Dr. Johnson's House. This is where Samuel Johnson lived between 1748 and 1759, compiling his famous dictionary in the attic as his health deteriorated. Built in 1700, the elegant Georgian residence, with its paneled rooms and period furniture, is where the Great Bear (as he was known) compiled his *Dictionary of the English Language*—two early editions of which are among the mementos of Johnson and his friend, diarist, and later, his biographer, James Boswell. ⊠ *17 Gough Sq., The City* ☎ *020/7353–3745* ⊕ *www.drjohnsonshouse.org* ☞ *£4.50* ⊙ *May–Sept., Mon.–Sat. 11–5:30; Oct.–Apr., Mon.–Sat. 11–5; closed bank holidays* Ⓤ *Holborn, Chancery La.*

❽ **Guildhall.** The Corporation of London, which oversees The City, has ceremonially elected and installed its lord mayor here for the last 800 years. The Guildhall was built in 1411, and though it failed to avoid either the 1666 or 1940 flames, its core survived. To the right of Guildhall Yard is the **Guildhall Art Gallery,** which includes portraits of the great and the good, cityscapes, famous battles, and a slightly cloying pre-Raphaelite section. The **Clockmakers' Museum** has more than 600 timepieces on show, including a skull-faced watch that belonged to Mary, Queen of Scots. ⊠ *Aldermanbury, The City* ☎ *020/7606–3030, 020/7332–3700 gallery* ⊕ *www.cityoflondon.gov.uk* ☞ *Free; gallery and amphitheater £2.50* ⊙ *Mon.–Sat. 9:30–5; clockmaker museum Mon.–Sat. 9:30–4:45; gallery Mon.–Sat. 10–5, Sun. noon–4, last admission 4:30 or 3:30* Ⓤ *St. Paul's, Moorgate, Bank, Mansion House.*

Museum of London Docklands. Beside the tower of Canary Wharf, this museum is worth a visit for its warehouse building alone. With uneven wood floors, beams, and pillars, the museum used to be a storehouse for coffee, tea, sugar, and rum from the West Indies—hence the name West India Quay. The fascinating story of the old port and the river is told using films, together with interactive displays and reconstructions. ⊠ *No. 1 Warehouse, West India Quay, Hertsmere Rd., East End* ☎ *020/7001–9844* ⊕ *www.museumindocklands.org.uk* ☞ *£5* ⊙ *Daily 10–6; last admission 5:30* Ⓤ *Canary Wharf; DLR: West India Quay.*

OFF THE BEATEN PATH

❸ **Old Bailey.** This is the place to watch the real-life drama of justice in action in one of the 16 courtrooms that are open to the public. The day's hearings are posted on the sign outside, but your best bet is to consult the previous day's tabloid newspapers. The present-day **Central Criminal Court** is where Newgate Prison stood from the 12th century right until the beginning of the 20th century. The most famous feature of the solid Edwardian building is the 12-foot gilded statue of Justice perched on top; she was intended to mirror the dome of St. Paul's. ⊠ *Newgate St., The City* ☎ *020/7248–3277 information* ⊕ *www.cityoflondon.gov. uk* ⊙ *Public Gallery weekdays 10–1 and 2–4:30 (approx.); line forms at Newgate St. entrance or in Warwick St. Passage; closed bank holidays and day after* Ⓤ *St. Paul's.*

❻ **St. Stephen Walbrook.** This is the parish church many think is Wren's best, by virtue of its practice dome, which predates the one at St. Paul's by some 30 years, and its celestial atmosphere inside. Yet there's far more to the history of the church than as a dry run for its next-door big brother. There has been a church here since the 7th century, built on the site of an older Roman shrine. ⊠ *39 Walbrook, The City* ☎ *020/7626–9000* ⊕ *www.ststephenwalbrook.net* ⊙ *Weekdays 10–4* Ⓤ *Bank, Cannon St.*

THE SOUTH BANK

Culture, history, sights: the South Bank has it all. Stretching from the Imperial War Museum in the southwest as far as the Design Museum in the east, high-caliber art, music, film, and theater venues sit alongside the likes of an aquarium, historic warships, and Borough Market, a foodie favorite. Pedestrians cross between the north and south banks using the futuristic Hungerford Bridge and the curvaceous Millennium Bridge, as they take in the compelling views of the Thames.

There's an old North London quip about needing a passport to cross the Thames, but times have changed dramatically. The Tate Modern is the star attraction, installed in a 1930s power station, with the eye-catching Millennium Bridge linking its main door across the river to the City. Near the theaters of the South Bank Centre, the London Eye observation wheel gives you a flight over the city. The South Bank of the Thames isn't beautiful, but this area of theaters and museums has Culture with a capital C.

It's fitting that so much of London's artistic life should once again be centered on the South Bank—in the past, Southwark was the location of theaters, taverns, and cockfighting arenas. The Globe Theatre, in which Shakespeare acted and held shares, was one of several here. In truth the Globe was as likely to stage bear-baiting as Shakespeare, but today, at the reconstructed "Wooden O," you can see only the latter. Be sure to take a walk along Bankside, the embankment along the Thames from Southwark to Blackfriars Bridge.

GETTING HERE   For the South Bank use Westminster station on the Jubilee or Northern line, from where you can walk across Westminster Bridge; Embankment on District, Circle, Northern, and Bakerloo lines, where you can walk across Hungerford Bridge; or Waterloo on the Jubilee, Northern, and Bakerloo lines, where it's a five-minute walk to the Royal Festival Hall. In the east, alternatively, use Tower Gateway on the Docklands Light Railway (DLR). London Bridge on the Northern and Jubilee lines is but a five-minute stroll from Borough Market and Southwark Cathedral.

PLANNING   The South Bank sprawls; block out visiting times based on locations
YOUR TIME   and your interests. The Imperial War Museum demands a couple of hours, with the nearby Museum of Garden History worth an hour. The Tate Modern deserves a whole morning or afternoon to do justice to temporary exhibitions and the permanent collection. The Globe Theatre requires about two hours for the exhibition theater tour and two to three hours for a performance. Finish with drinks or dinner at the Oxo Tower or a stroll west along the riverbank and then across Hungerford Bridge.

Numbers in the margin correspond to numbers on the South Bank map.

TOP ATTRACTIONS

🔟 **Design Museum.** This was the first museum in the world to elevate everyday design and design classics to the status of art by placing them in their social and cultural context. Fashion, creative technology, and architecture are explored with thematic displays from the museum's permanent collection, and temporary exhibitions provide an in-depth focus on such subjects as the work of great designers such as Charles Eames and Isamu Noguchi. ✉ *28 Shad Thames, South Bank* ☎ *0870/7403–6933* ⊕ *www.designmuseum.org* ✍ *£8.50* ⊙ *Daily 10–5:45, last admission 5:15* Ⓤ *London Bridge; Tower Hill; DLR: Tower Gateway.*

➊ **Imperial War Museum.** Despite its title, this museum of 20th-century warfare does not glorify bloodshed but emphasizes understanding through evoking what life was like for citizens and soldiers alike through the two world wars and beyond. Sights, sounds, and smells are used to recreate the very uncomfortable Trench Experience in the World War I gallery, which is just as effective as The Blitz Experience in the World War II gallery: a 10-minute taste of an air raid in a street of acrid smoke with sirens blaring and searchlights glaring. ✉ *Lambeth Rd., South Bank* ☎ *020/7416–5320* ⊕ *www.iwm.org.uk* ✍ *Free (charge for special exhibits)* ⊙ *Daily 10–6* Ⓤ *Lambeth North.*

➌ **London Eye.** The London Eye is the largest observation wheel ever built and among the tallest structures in London. The 25-minute slow-motion ride inside one of the enclosed passenger capsules is so smooth you'd hardly know you were suspended over the Thames, moving slowly around. ■ TIP➔ **Buy your ticket online, over the phone, or at the ticket office in advance to avoid the long lines.** The London Eye sightseeing cruise also departs here for a 40-minute cruise of the Thames. ✉ *Jubilee Gardens, South Bank* ☎ *0870/990–8883* ⊕ *www.londoneye.com* ✍ *£17.50, cruise £12.50* ⊙ *June and Sept., daily 10–9; July and Aug., daily 10–9:30; Oct.–Apr., daily 10–8* Ⓤ *Waterloo.*

➍ **OXO Tower.** Long a London landmark to the insider, the art deco–era Oxo building has graduated from its former incarnations as a power-generating station and warehouse into a vibrant community of artists' and designers' workshops, a pair of restaurants, and five floors of community homes. ✉ *Bargehouse St., South Bank* ☎ *020/7021–1686* ⊕ *www.oxotower.co.uk* ✍ *Free* ⊙ *Studios and shops Tues.–Sun. 11–6* Ⓤ *Blackfriars, Waterloo.*

➏ **Shakespeare's Globe Theatre.** A spectacular theater, this is a replica of Shakespeare's open-roof, wood-and-thatch Globe Playhouse (built in 1599 and burned down in 1613), where most of the Bard's great plays premiered. For several decades, American actor and director Sam Wanamaker worked ceaselessly to raise funds for the theater's reconstruction, 200 yards from its original site, using authentic materials and techniques. His dream was realized in 1997. At the plays, "groundlings"— those with £5 standing-only tickets—are not allowed to sit during the performance. You can reserve an actual seat, though, on any one of the theater's three levels, but you will want to rent a cushion for £1 (or bring your own) to soften the backless wooden benches. The show must go on, rain or shine, warm or chilly—so come prepared for anything. Umbrellas are banned, but you can bring a raincoat or buy a cheap Globe rain poncho, which doubles as a great souvenir. Throughout the year, you can tour the theater as part of the **Shakespeare's Globe Exhibition,** a museum under the theater (the entry is adjacent) that provides background material on the Elizabethan theater and the construction

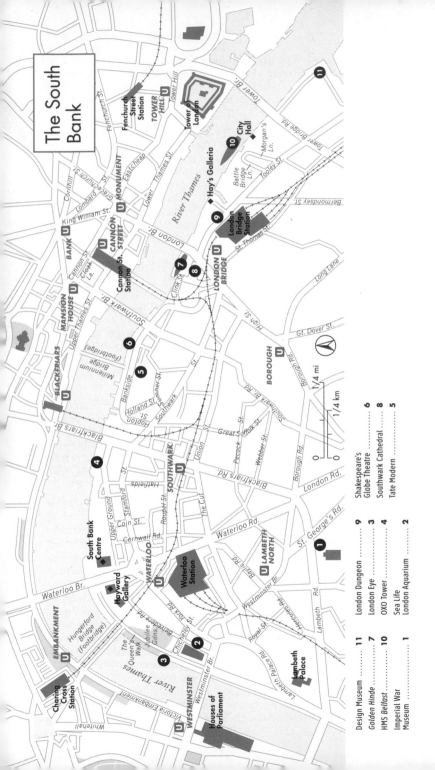

The South Bank

River Thames

Fenchurch Street Station

TOWER HILL **U**

Tower of London

10 City Hall

Morgan's Ln.

◆ Hay's Galleria

Battle Bridge Ln.

Tooley St.

9 London Bridge Station

Bermondsey St.

Tower Bridge Rd.

11

(Tower Br.)

Fenchurch St.

Tower Hill

Eastcheap

Lower Thames St.

MONUMENT **U**

Gracechurch St.

Lombard St.

Cornhill

King William St.

BANK **U**

CANNON STREET **U**

Cannon St.

Cloak La.

Cannon St. Station

MANSION HOUSE **U**

Upper Thames St.

London Br.

7 **U** LONDON BRIDGE

8

Clink St.

St. Thomas St.

Long Lane

Southwark Br.

BLACKFRIARS **U**

Millennium Bridge (Footbridge)

6

Bankside

5

Holland St.

Hopton St.

Summer St.

Southwark St.

BOROUGH **U**

High St.

Gt. Dover St.

Blackfriars Br.

Southwark Br. Rd.

Great Suffolk St.

Union St.

SOUTHWARK **U**

Peacock St.

Webber St.

Borough Rd.

London Rd.

Blackfriars Rd.

Hatfields

Stamford St.

The Cut

St. George's Rd.

4

Upper Ground

Coin St.

Cornwall Rd.

Roupell St.

South Bank Centre ◆

Hayward Gallery ◆

EMBANKMENT **U**

Hungerford Bridge (Footbridge)

Jubilee Gdns.

The Queen's Walk

WATERLOO **U**

Waterloo Station

Waterloo Rd.

LAMBETH NORTH **U**

Baylis Rd.

1

Charing Cross Station

WESTMINSTER **U**

Victoria Embankment

Whitehall

River Thames

Westminster Br.

Houses of Parliament

Belvedere Rd.

Chicheley St.

York Rd.

2

3

Westminster Br.

Royal St.

Hercules Rd.

Lambeth Rd.

Lambeth Palace Rd.

Lambeth Palace

Waterloo Br.

1/4 mi

1/4 km

0   0

of the modern-day Globe. Admission also includes a tour of the theater. On matinee days, the tour visits the archaeological site of the nearby (and older) Rose Theatre. ✉ *21 New Globe Walk, Bankside, South Bank* ☎ *020/7401–9919 box office; 020/7902–1500 New Shakespeare's Globe Exhibition* ⊕ *www.shakespeares-globe.org* ✉ *Exhi-*

WHEN TO GO

Avoid going to the Tate Modern on weekends, when visitor numbers are at their greatest. Visit during the week or join the cool crowd on Friday evenings, when it's open until 10.

bition & Globe Theatre Tour £10.50 (£2 reduction with valid performance ticket); ticket prices for plays vary (£5–£33) ⊗ *Exhibition May–early Oct., daily 10–5; mid-Oct.–Apr., daily 9–12:30 and 1–5; plays May–early Oct., call for performance schedule* Ⓤ *Southwark, then walk to Blackfriars Bridge and descend the steps; Mansion House, then cross Southwark Bridge; Blackfriars, then walk across Blackfriars Bridge; St. Paul's, then cross Millennium Bridge.*

❽ **Southwark Cathedral.** Pronounced "Suth-uck," this is the second-oldest Gothic church in London, after Westminster Abbey, with parts dating back to the 12th century. Although it houses some remarkable memorials, not to mention a program of lunchtime concerts, it's seldom visited. ■**TIP**➡ **The Refectory serves full English breakfasts, light lunches, and tea daily 10 6.** ✉ *London Bridge, South Bank* ☎ *020/7367–6700* ⊕ *www.southwark.anglican.org* ✉ *Free, suggested donation £4* ⊗ *Daily 8–6* Ⓤ *London Bridge.*

❺ **Tate Modern.** A working power station from 1947 to 1981, this hulking monolith of a building was all but derelict when the Tate adopted it as the home for their modern art collection in the late '90s. And what a magnificent transformation it has been. On permanent display in the galleries are classic works from 1900 to the present day, by Matisse, Picasso, Dalí, Moore, Bacon, Warhol, and the most-talked-about British upstarts.

FodorśChoice
★

The vast **Turbine Hall** is a dramatic entrance point used to showcase big, audacious installations that tend to generate a lot of publicity. Past highlights include a massive glowing sun, a working spiral slide, and, perhaps most bizarrely, a long crack in the floor. The **Material Gestures** galleries on Level 3 feature an impressive offering of post–World War II painting and sculpture. Room 7 contains a breathtaking collection of Rothkos and Monets.

Head to the Restaurant on Level 7 or the Espresso Bar on Level 4 for stunning vistas of the Thames. The view of St. Paul's from the Espresso Bar's balcony is one of the best in London. ■**TIP**➡ **Don't know where to start? Join one of the free, 45-minute guided tours.** ✉ *Bankside, South Bank* ☎ *020/7887–8888* ⊕ *www.tate.org.uk/modern* ✉ *Free, charge for special exhibitions* ⊗ *Sun.–Thurs. 10–6, Fri. and Sat. 10–10 (last admission to exhibitions 45 mins before close)* Ⓤ *Blackfriars, Southwark.*

WORTH NOTING

❼ Golden Hinde. Sir Francis Drake circumnavigated the globe in this little
☼ galleon, or one just like it. This exact replica made a 23-year round-
the-world voyage—much of it spent along U.S. coasts, both Pacific
and Atlantic—and has settled here to continue its educational purpose.
✉ *Unit 1 & 2, Pickfords Wharf, Clink St., South Bank* ☎ *0870/011–
8700 or 0870/7403–0123* ⊕ *www.goldenhinde.com* ✉ *£6* ◷ *Daily
10–6* Ⓤ *London Bridge, Mansion House.*

❿ HMS Belfast. At 613 feet, this is one of the largest and most powerful
☼ cruisers the Royal Navy has ever had. It played an important role in
the D-Day landings off Normandy, left for the Far East after the war,
and has been moored in the relative calm of the Thames since 1971.
✉ *Morgan's La., Tooley St., South Bank* ☎ *020/7940–6300* ⊕ *www.
iwm.org.uk* ✉ *£10.70* ◷ *Mar.–Oct., daily 10–6; Nov.–Feb., daily 10–5;
last admission 1 hr before closing* Ⓤ *London Bridge.*

❾ London Dungeon. Here's the goriest, grisliest, most gruesome attraction
☼ in town. Tableaux depict famous bloody moments—like Anne Boleyn's
decapitation and the martyrdom of St. George—alongside the torture,
murder, and ritual slaughter of lesser-known victims, all to a sound
track of screaming, wailing, and agonized moaning. ■ TIP→ **Expect long
lines on weekends and during school holidays. Booking online will save at
least £5.** ✉ *28–34 Tooley St., South Bank* ☎ *0871/7403–7221* ⊕ *www.
thedungeons.com* ✉ *£21.95* ◷ *Daily; opening times vary slightly, week
by week, but generally Sept.–Mar. 10–5; Apr.–July 9:30–6; Aug. 9:30–7;
phone to confirm times* Ⓤ *London Bridge.*

❷ Sea Life London Aquarium. The curved, colonnaded, neoclassic hulk
☼ of County Hall once housed London's local government administration. Now it's where you can catch a dark and thrilling glimpse of the
waters of the world, focused around a superb three-level aquarium
full of sharks and stingrays, among other common and rarer breeds.
✉ *County Hall, Riverside Bldg., Westminster Bridge Rd., South Bank*
☎ *0871/663–1678* ⊕ *www.sealife.co.uk* ✉ *£16* ◷ *Daily 10–6; last
admission 5; mid-July–early Sept. 10–7; last admission 6* Ⓤ *Westminster, Waterloo.*

KENSINGTON, KNIGHTSBRIDGE, AND MAYFAIR

Splendid houses with pillared porches, as well as fascinating museums,
stylish squares, and glittering antiques shops, line the streets of this
elegant area of the Royal Borough of Kensington. Also here is Kensington Palace (the former home of both Diana, Princess of Wales, and
Queen Victoria), which put the district literally on the map back in
the 17th century. To Kensington's east is one of the highest concentrations of important artifacts anywhere, the "museum mile" of South
Kensington. Kensington first became the *Royal* Borough of Kensington
(and Chelsea) when William III, who suffered terribly from the Thames
mists over Whitehall, decided in 1689 to buy Nottingham House in the
rural village of Kensington. By the time Queen Anne was on the throne
(1702–14), Kensington was overflowing. In a way, it still is, since most

of its grand houses have been divided into apartments, or are serving as embassies.

Hyde Park and Kensington Gardens together form by far the biggest of central London's royal parks. It's probably been centuries since any major royal had a casual stroll here, but the parks remain the property of the Crown, and it was the Crown that saved them from being devoured by the city's late-18th-century growth spurt.

Around the borders of Hyde Park are several of London's most beautiful and posh neighborhoods. To the south of the park and a short carriage ride from Buckingham Palace is the splendidly aristocratic enclave of Belgravia. Its white-stucco buildings and grand squares—particularly Belgrave Square—are Regency-era jewels. On the eastern border of Hyde Park is Mayfair, which gives Belgravia a run for its money as London's wealthiest district. Two mansions here allow you to get a peek into the lifestyles of London's rich and famous: Apsley House, the home of the duke of Wellington, and the Wallace Collection, a mansion on Manchester Square stuffed with great art treasures.

GETTING HERE There's good tube service to these areas. On the Central Line, Marble Arch and Bond Street (also Jubilee Line) take you to the heart of Mayfair; the Hyde Park Corner stop on the Piccadilly line is at the southeast corner of the park, near Apsley House. South Kensington and Gloucester Road on the District, Circle, and Piccadilly lines are convenient stops for the South Kensington museums; Knightsbridge on the Piccadilly line leaves you close to Harrods and many retail temptations.

PLANNING YOUR TIME The best way to approach these neighborhoods is to treat Knightsbridge shopping and the South Kensington museums as separate days out, although the three vast museums may be too much to take in at once. The parks are best in the growing seasons and during fall, when the foliage is turning; the summer roses in Regent's Park are stunning. On Sunday the Hyde Park and Kensington Gardens railings all along the Bayswater Road are hung with mediocre art, which may slow your progress; this is prime perambulation day for locals.

Numbers in the margin correspond to numbers on the Kensington, Knightsbridge, and Mayfair map.

TOP ATTRACTIONS

❼ ★ Apsley House (Wellington Museum). Once popularly known as No. 1, London, because it was the first and grandest house at the old tollgate from Knightsbridge village, this was long celebrated as the best address in town. Built by Robert Adam and later refaced and extended, it housed the Duke of Wellington from 1817 until his death in 1852. As the Wellington Museum, it has been faithfully restored, down to Wellesley's uniforms, weapons, a fine collection of paintings, and his porcelain and plate collections acquired as a result of his military success, such as a Sévres dessert service commissioned by Napoléon for his empress, Josephine. ⊠ *149 Piccadilly, Hyde Park Corner, Mayfair* ☎ *020/7499–5676* ⊕ *www.english-heritage.org.uk* ⊘ *Mar.–Oct., Wed.–Sun. and bank holiday Mon. 11–5; Nov.–Feb., Wed.–Sun. 11–4* ▱ *£5.70, joint ticket with Wellington Arch £6.80* Ⓤ *Hyde Park Corner.*

6 Harrods. Just in case you don't notice it, this well-known shopping destination frames its domed terra-cotta Edwardian outline in thousands of white lights each night (or pink, or green, or pretty much however the mood takes its famously eccentric owner, Mohammed al Fayed). The 4.5-acre store's sales weeks are world-class, and inside it's as frenetic as a stock-market floor. ⊠ *87–135 Brompton Rd., Knightsbridge* ☎ *020/7730–1234* ⊕ *www.harrods.com* ☉ *Mon.–Sat. 10–8, Sun. 11:30–6* Ⓤ *Knightsbridge.*

☺ Hyde Park. Along with the smaller St. James's and Green parks to the east, Hyde Park started as Henry VIII's hunting grounds. Along its south side runs Rotten Row, once Henry's royal path to the hunt—the name is a corruption of *route du roi* (route of the king). It's still used by the Household Cavalry, who live at the Hyde Park Barracks—a high-rise and a low, ugly, red block—to the left. This is where the brigade that mounts the guard at Buckingham Palace resides, and you can see them leave to perform their duty, in full regalia, at about 10:30, or await the return of the guard about noon. Hyde Park is wonderful for strolling, watching the locals, or just relaxing by the Serpentine, the long body of water near its southern border. On the south side, by the 1930s Serpentine Lido, is the site of the Diana Princess of Wales Memorial Fountain, which opened in 2003 and is a good spot to refuel at one of the cafés. On Sunday, Speakers' Corner, in the park near Marble Arch, is an unmissable spectacle of vehement, sometimes comical, and always entertaining orators. ⊠ *Mayfair* ☎ *020/7298–2100* ⊕ *www.royalparks. gov.uk* ☉ *Daily 5* AM*–midnight* Ⓤ *Hyde Park Corner, Knightsbridge, Lancaster Gate, Marble Arch.*

15 Jewish Museum. After a £10 million refurbishment, the Jewish Museum reopened in March 2010. Here you can follow the history of the Jewish people in Britain from medieval times to the present day, although most of the exhibits date from the 17th century—when Cromwell repealed the laws against Jewish settlement—and later. The collection is spread over four galleries. History: A British Story provides a general overview of British Jewish people over the centuries, through a mix of rare artifacts and interactive displays, including a re-creation of a Victorian street from what was then the Jewish Quarter of East London. ⊠ *Raymond Burton House, 129–131 Albert St., Camden Town* ☎ *020/7284–7384* ⊕ *www.jewishmuseum.org.uk* ☒ *£7* ☉ *Sun.–Thurs. 10–5, Fri. 10–2* Ⓤ *Camden Town.*

13 Keats House. Here you can see the plum tree under which the young Romantic poet composed "Ode to a Nightingale," many of his original manuscripts, his library, and other possessions he managed to acquire in his short life. A major refurbishment in 2009 saw the house decorated to match its original Regency Style. ■**TIP➔ Picnics can be taken into the grounds during the summer.** ⊠ *Wentworth Pl., Keats Grove, Hampstead* ☎ *020/7332–3868* ⊕ *www.keatshouse.cityoflondon.gov.uk* ☒ *£5* ☉ *Apr.–Oct., Tues.–Sun. 10–5; Nov.–Apr., Fri.–Sun. 1–5* Ⓤ *Hampstead; North London Line overground: Hampstead Heath from Highbury & Islington.*

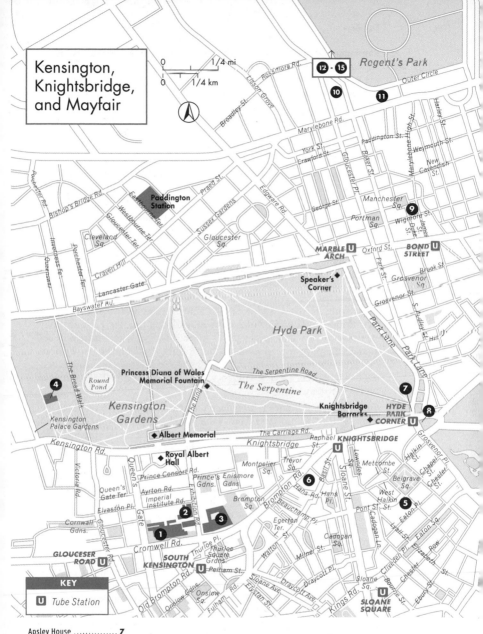

Kensington,
Knightsbridge,
and Mayfair

0 ___ 1/4 mi
0 ___ 1/4 km

Regent's Park

Outer Circle

12 - 15

10

11

Rossmore Rd.

Lisson Grove

Broadley St.

Marylebone Rd.

York St.
Crawford St.

Paddington St.

Gloucester Pl.

Baker St.

Marylebone High St.

Harley St.

Weymouth St.

New Cavendish St.

Manchester Sq.

George St.

Wigmore St.

James St.

BOND STREET U

Portman Sq.

Porchester Rd.

Bishop's Bridge Rd.

Eastbourne Ter.

Paddington Station

Praed St.

Sussex Gardens

Westbourne Ter.

Gloucester Ter.

Edgware Rd.

Cleveland Sq.

Gloucester Sq.

MARBLE ARCH U

Oxford St.

Inverness Ter.

Porchester Ter.

Queensway

Craven Hill

Lancaster Gate

Brook St.

Grosvenor Sq.

Grosvenor St.

Bayswater Rd.

Speaker's Corner

S. Audley St.

Park Lane

Hill St.

Hyde Park

Park Lane

The Broad Walk

Round Pond

Princess Diana of Wales Memorial Fountain

The Ring

The Serpentine Road

The Serpentine

7

Kensington Gardens

Kensington Palace Gardens

4

Knightsbridge Barracks

HYDE PARK CORNER U

8

Grosvenor Pl.

Albert Memorial

The Carriage Rd.

Knightsbridge

Raphael St.

KNIGHTSBRIDGE U

Halkin St.

Chapel St.

Chester St.

Kensington Rd.

Royal Albert Hall

Montpelier Sq.

Trevor Sq.

Basil St.

Sloane St.

Lowndes St.

Metcombe St.

Belgrave Sq.

Victoria Rd.

Queen's Gate

Prince Consort Rd.

Prince's Gdns.

Ennismore Gdns.

6

Brompton Rd.

Hans Rd.

Hans Pl.

West Halkin St.

5

Queen's Gate Ter.

Ayrton Rd.

Imperial Institute Rd.

Brompton Sq.

Beauchamp Pl.

Pont St.

Cadogan Ln.

Eaton Pl.

Eaton Sq.

GLOUCESER ROAD U

Elvaston Pl.

Exhibition Rd.

2

3

Egerton Ter.

Cadogan Sq.

Cliveden Pl.

Chester Row.

Eaton Sq.

Eaton Ter.

Eaton Pl.

Cornwall Gdns.

Gloucester Rd.

Cromwell Rd.

Thurloe Pl.

Thurloe Square Gdns.

Walton St.

Milner St.

Draycott Pl.

Elizabeth St.

Ebury St.

1

SOUTH KENSINGTON U

Pelham St.

Brompton Rd.

Old Brompton Rd.

Onslow Gdns.

Onslow Sq.

Fulham Rd.

Sloane Ave.

Draycott Ave.

Sloane Sq.

King's Rd.

SLOANE SQUARE U

Elystan St.

Bourne St.

Chester Sq.

KEY

U Tube Station

⟳ **Kensington Gardens.** More formal than neighboring Hyde Park, Kensington Gardens was first laid out as palace grounds for William III. He was attracted to the location for its clean air and tranquility, and subsequently commissioned Sir Christopher Wren for the splendid **Kensington Palace.** To the north of the palace complex is the early-20th-century **Sunken Garden.** Nearby is George Frampton's beloved 1912 *Peter Pan.* The **Round Pond** is a magnet for model-boat enthusiasts and duck feeders. The fabulous **Diana Princess of Wales Memorial Playground** has specially designed structures and areas on the theme of Barrie's Neverland. ✉ *Kensington* ⊕ *www.royalparks.gov.uk* ☽ *Daily 6 AM–dusk* Ⓤ *Kensington High Street, Lancaster Gate, Queensway, South Kensington.*

④ **Kensington Palace.** Not as splendid as Buckingham Palace, or as famous
★ as Hampton Court, Kensington Palace is the most intimate of London's great royal residences. Originally a more modest dwelling called Nottingham House, it was bought in 1689 by King William III, whose acute asthma made it necessary for him to live outside the city (Kensington was, in those days, a small countryside village). He commissioned Wren and Hawksmoor to turn the building into a palace, and royals have been living here in grand style ever since. It was at Kensington Palace that Princess Victoria awoke in 1837, shortly after her 18th birthday, to discover that she had become Queen. In 1997, the world watched as the funeral procession for another former resident, the late Princess Diana, made its way out of the front gates. Today, the Duke and Duchess of Gloucester as well as Prince and Princess Michael of Kent have private apartments here.

On the Garden Floor is the palace's visitor entrance, which takes you into the Red Saloon and Teck Saloon, where the **Royal Ceremonial Dress Collection** displays garments dating to the 18th century. State and occasional dresses, hats, shoes, and gloves from the present Queen's wardrobe are showcased, as are some incredible evening gowns worn by Princess Diana. The **King's Staircase** is overlooked by a vast, panoramic trompe l'oeil painting, covering the walls and ceiling with a burst of color. The **King's Gallery** was built to display some of the monarch's personal art collection. Many of the paintings here now are copies, but no matter; the room itself is a work of art, with rich red damask walls, intricate gilding, and a beautiful painted ceiling.

The grounds are almost as lovely as the palace itself. Highlights include the Sunken Garden with its fountains and Tudor design that echoes Hampton Court. Unmissable—especially in the spring, when tulips bloom in a riot of color. ■ TIP→ **If you also plan to visit the Tower of London, Hampton Court Palace, Banqueting House, or Kew Palace, consider becoming a member of Historic Royal Palaces. It costs £39 per person, or £77 for a family, and gives you free entry to all five sites for a year.** ✉ *The Broad Walk, Kensington Gardens, Kensington* ☎ *0844/482–7799 advance booking, 0844/482–7777 information* ⊕ *www.hrp.org.uk* ☞ *£12.50* ☽ *Mar.–Oct., daily 10–6; Nov.–Feb., daily 10–5; last admission 1 hr before closing* Ⓤ *Queensway, Kensington High Street.*

⑭ Kenwood House. This gracious Georgian villa was first built in 1616 and
ℭ remodeled by Robert Adam between 1764 and 1779. Adam refaced
★ most of the exterior and added the splendid library, which, with its
curved painted ceiling, rather garish coloring, and gilded detailing, is
the sole highlight of the house for decorative arts and interior design
buffs. What is unmissable here is the **Iveagh Bequest,** a collection of
paintings that the Earl of Iveagh gave the nation in 1927, including a
wonderful Rembrandt self-portrait and works by Reynolds, Van Dyck,
Hals, Gainsborough, and Turner. Top billing goes to Vermeer's *Guitar
Player.* In front of the house, a graceful lawn slopes down to a little lake
crossed by a trompe-l'oeil bridge; the rest of the grounds are skirted by
Hampstead Heath. A popular café, the Brew House, has outdoor tables
in the courtyard and terraced garden. ⊠ *Hampstead La., Hampstead*
☎ *020/8348–1286* ⊕ *www.english-heritage.org.uk* ☝ *Free* ☉ *House
daily except Dec. 24–26 and Jan. 1, 11:30–4. Gardens daily dawn–
dusk* Ⓤ *Golders Green, then Bus 210.*

① Natural History Museum. The outrageously ornate terra-cotta facade of
ℭ this enormous Victorian museum is strewn with relief panels, depicting
★ living creatures to the left of the entrance and extinct ones to the right.
It's an appropriate design, for within these walls lie more than 70 million
different specimens. The museum is full of cutting-edge exhibits, with
all the wow power and interactives necessary to secure interest from
younger visitors. The **Dinosaur Gallery** contains plenty of real-life dino
bones, fossils—and some extremely long teeth. A dizzyingly tall escalator takes you into a giant globe in the **Earth Galleries,** where there's a
choice of levels—and Earth surfaces—to explore. Don't leave without
checking out the earthquake simulation in Gallery 61. ⊠ *Cromwell
Rd., South Kensington* ☎ *020/7942–5000* ⊕ *www.nhm.ac.uk* ☝ *Free*
☉ *Daily 10–5:50, last admission at 5:30* Ⓤ *South Kensington.*

ℭ **Regent's Park.** Cultivated and formal—compared with the relative wild-
★ ness of Hampstead Heath—Regent's Park was laid out in 1812 by
John Nash, in honor of the Prince Regent (hence the name), who was
later crowned George IV. The idea was to re-create the feel of a grand
country residence close to the center of town, with all those magnificent white-stucco terraces facing in on the park. Your nostrils should
lead you to **Queen Mary's Gardens,** a fragrant 17-acre circle that riots
with 400 different varieties of roses in summer. ⊠ *Marylebone Rd.,
Regent's Park* ☎ *020/7486–7905* ⊕ *www.royalparks.gov.uk* ☝ *Free* ☉ *5
AM–dusk* Ⓤ *Baker St., Regent's Park, Great Portland St.*

② Science Museum. This, the third of the great South Kensington museums,
ℭ stands next to the Natural History Museum in a far plainer building.
★ Highlights include the Launch Pad gallery, which demonstrates basic
scientific principles; *Puffing Billy,* the oldest steam locomotive in the
world; and the actual *Apollo 10* capsule. The six floors are devoted
to subjects as diverse as the history of flight, space exploration, steam
power, medicine, and a sublime exhibition on science in the 18th century. ⊠ *Exhibition Rd., South Kensington* ☎ *0870/870–4868* ⊕ *www.
sciencemuseum.org.uk* ☝ *Free* ☉ *Daily 10–6* Ⓤ *South Kensington.*

3 Victoria and Albert Museum. Always referred to as the V&A, this huge museum is devoted to the applied arts of all disciplines, all periods, and all nationalities. Full of innovation, it's a wonderful, generous place to get lost in. First opened as the South Kensington Museum in 1857, it was renamed in 1899, in honor of Queen Victoria's late husband and has since grown to become one of the country's best-loved cultural institutions.

The **British Galleries** (Rooms 52–58), devoted to British art and design from 1500 to 1900, are full of beautiful diversions—among them the Great Bed of Ware (immortalized in Shakespeare's *Twelfth Night*). The **Asian Galleries** (Rooms 44–47) are full of treasures, but among the most striking items on display is a remarkable collection of ornate samurai armor in the **Japanese Gallery** (Room 44). There are also galleries devoted to China, Korea, and the Islamic Middle East. ■ **TIP→ The V&A is a notoriously difficult building to navigate, so be sure to pick up a free map. There are stacks of them at each entrance.** ⊠ *Cromwell Rd., South Kensington* ☎ *020/7942–2000* ⊕ *www.vam.ac.uk* ☻ *Free* ☉ *Sat.–Tues. 10:45–5:45, Fri. 10–10* Ⓤ *South Kensington.*

9 Wallace Collection. Assembled by four generations of marquesses of Hertford and given to the nation by the widow of Sir Richard Wallace, illegitimate son of the fourth, this collection of art and artifacts is important, exciting, undervisited—and free. Look for Rembrandt's portrait of his son, the Rubens landscape, Gainsborough and Romney portraits, the Van Dycks and Canalettos, the French rooms, and of course the porcelain. The highlight is Fragonard's *The Swing,* which conjures up the 18th century's let-them-eat-cake frivolity better than any other painting around. ⊠ *Hertford House, Manchester Sq., Marylebone* ☎ *020/7563–9500* ⊕ *www.wallacecollection.org* ☻ *Free* ☉ *Daily 10–5* Ⓤ *Bond St.*

WORTH NOTING

Albert Memorial. This gleaming, neo-Gothic shrine to Prince Albert created by George Gilbert Scott epitomizes the Victorian era. Albert's grieving widow, Queen Victoria, had this elaborate confection (including a 14-foot bronze statue of the prince) erected on the spot where his Great Exhibition had stood a decade before his early death, from typhoid, in 1861. ⊠ *Kensington Gore, Hyde Park, Kensington, Knightsbridge.*

5 Belgrave Square. The square, as well as the streets leading off it, are genuine grand territory and have been since they were built in the mid-1800s. The grand, porticoed mansions were created as town residences for courtiers, conveniently close to Buckingham Palace, just around the corner.

12 London Zoo. The zoo, owned by the Zoological Society of London, opened in 1828 and peaked in popularity during the 1950s, when more than 3 million people passed through its turnstiles every year. A recent modernization program has seen several big new attractions open up. By far the biggest new arrival is Gorilla Kingdom, where you can watch the four resident gorillas—Effie, Mjukuu, Bobby, and Zaire—at close range. Also popular is the Clore Rainforest Lookout, home to tiny primates such as marmosets and golden lion tamarins. ⊠ *Regent's Park*

A TRIP TO ABBEY ROAD

For countless Beatlemaniacs and baby boomers, No. 3 Abbey Road is one of the most beloved spots in London. Here, outside the legendary Abbey Road Studios, is the most famous zebra crossing in the world, immortalized on the Beatles' 1969 *Abbey Road* album. The studios are closed to the public, but tourists like to Beatle-ize themselves by taking the same sort of photo. One of the best—and safer—ways Beatle lovers can enjoy the history of the group is to take one of the smashing walking tours offered by the **Original London Walks** (☎ *020/7624-3978* ⊕ *www.walks.com*), including **The Beatles In-My-Life Walk** (11:20 AM at the Marylebone Underground on Saturday and Tuesday) and **The Beatles Magical Mystery Tour** (Wednesday at 2 PM, Thursday at 11 AM, and Sunday at 10:55 AM at Underground Exit 3, Tottenham Court Road), which cover nostalgic landmark Beatles spots in the city.

☎ *020/7722-3333* ⊕ *www.zsl.org* ⌂ *£16.90* ☉ *Nov.–Feb., daily 10–4; Mar.–Oct., daily 10–5:30, last week in Oct. 10–4:30; last admission 1 hr before closing* Ⓤ *Camden Town, then Bus 274.*

⑪ **Madame Tussauds.** One of London's busiest sights, this is nothing more
☾ and nothing less than the world's premier exhibition of lifelike waxwork models of celebrities. Madame T. learned her craft while making death masks of French Revolution victims, and in 1835 set up her first show of the famous ones near this spot. Top billing still goes to the murderers in the Chamber of Horrors, who stare glassy-eyed at visitors—one from an electric chair, one sitting next to the tin bath where he dissolved several wives in quicklime. ✉ *Marylebone Rd., Regent's Park* ☎ *0870/400–3000 for timed entry tickets* ⊕ *www.madame-tussauds. com* ⌂ *From £12.50* ☉ *Daily 9–6* Ⓤ *Baker St.*

⑩ **Sherlock Holmes Museum.** Outside Baker Street station, by the Marylebone Road exit, is a 9-foot-high bronze statue of the celebrated detective. Keep your eyes peeled for close by his image, "Holmes" himself, in his familiar deerstalker hat, will escort you to his abode at 221B Baker Street, the address of Arthur Conan Doyle's fictional detective. Inside, Mrs. Hudson, "Holmes's housekeeper," conducts you into a series of Victorian rooms full of Sherlock-abilia. ✉ *221B Baker St., Regent's Park* ☎ *020/7935–8866* ⊕ *www.sherlock-holmes.co.uk* ⌂ *£6* ☉ *Daily 9:30–6* Ⓤ *Baker St.*

⑧ **Wellington Arch.** Opposite the Duke of Wellington's mansion, Apsley House, this majestic stone arch surveys the busy traffic rushing around Hyde Park Corner. Designed by Decimus Burton and built in 1828, it was created as a grand entrance to the west side of London and echoes the design of that other landmark gate, Marble Arch. ✉ *Hyde Park Corner, Mayfair* ☎ *020/7930–2726* ⊕ *www.english-heritage.org. uk* ⌂ *£3.50* ☉ *Apr.–Oct., Wed.–Sun. 10–5; Nov.–Mar., Wed.–Sun. 10–4* Ⓤ *Hyde Park Corner.*

UP AND DOWN THE THAMES

Downstream—meaning seaward, or east—from central London, Greenwich has enough riches, especially if the maritime theme is your thing, that you should allow a very full day to see them. Upstream, the royal palaces and grand houses that dot the area were built not as town houses but as country residences with easy access to London by river; Hampton Court Palace is the best and biggest of all.

GREENWICH
8 mi east of central London.

Greenwich makes an ideal day out from central London, thanks to its historic and maritime attractions. Sir Christopher Wren's Royal Naval College and Inigo Jones's Queen's House reach architectural heights; the Old Royal Observatory measured time for the entire planet; and the Greenwich Meridian divides the world in two. You can stand astride it with one foot in either hemisphere. The National Maritime Museum will appeal to seafaring types, and landlubbers can stroll the parkland that surrounds the buildings, the pretty 19th-century houses, and the weekend crafts and antiques markets.

Once, Greenwich was considered remote by Londoners, with only the river as a direct route. With transportation links in the form of the Docklands Light Railway (DLR) and the tube's Jubilee Line, getting here is easy and inexpensive. The quickest route to maritime Greenwich is the tube to Canary Wharf and the Docklands Light Rail to the Greenwich stop. However, river connections to Greenwich make the journey memorable. On the way, the boat glides past famous London sights and the ever-changing Docklands.

🕓 ★ **National Maritime Museum.** Following a millennial face-lift, one of Greenwich's star attractions has been completely updated to make it one of London's most enjoyable museums. Its glass-covered courtyard of grand stone, dominated by a revolving propeller from a powerful frigate, is reminiscent of the British Museum. The collection spans seascape paintings to scientific instruments, interspersed with the heroes of the waves. A permanent Nelson gallery contains the uniform he wore, complete with bloodstain, when he met his end in 1805. Allow at least two hours in this absorbing, adventurous place; if you're in need of refreshment, the museum has a good café with views over Greenwich Park. ⊠ *Romney Rd., Greenwich* ☎ *020/8858–4422* ⊕ *www.nmm.ac.uk* 🎟 *Free* 🕓 *Daily 10–5; last admission 30 mins before closing* Ⓤ *DLR: Greenwich.*

QUICK BITES

For the best pub in Greenwich, head to the Trafalgar Tavern (⊠ Park Row ☎ 020/8858-2909 ⊕ www.trafalgartavern.co.uk), with excellent views of the Thames. It's a grand place to have a pint and some upscale grub.

Old Royal Naval College. Begun by Christopher Wren in 1694 as a rest home for ancient mariners, it became instead a school for young ones in 1873. Today the University of Greenwich and Trinity College of Music have classes here. Architecturally, you'll notice how the structures part to reveal the **Queen's House** across the central lawns. Behind the college are two more buildings you can visit: the **Painted Hall,**

the college's dining hall, derives its name from the baroque murals of William and Mary (reigned 1689–95; William alone 1695–1702) and assorted allegorical figures. ⊠ *Old Royal Naval College, King William Walk, Greenwich* ☎ *020/8269–4747* ⊕ *www.oldroyalnavalcollege.org* ⊠ *Free, guided tours £5* ☉ *Painted Hall and chapel daily 10–5; grounds 8–6* Ⓤ *DLR: Greenwich.*

★ **Ranger's House.** This handsome, early-18th-century villa, which was the Greenwich Park ranger's official residence during the 19th century, is hung with Stuart and Jacobean portraits. But the most interesting diversion is the Wernher Collection, more than 650 works of art with a northern European flavor, amassed by diamond millionaire Julius Wernher at the turn of the 20th century. ⊠ *Chesterfield Walk, Blackheath, Greenwich* ☎ *020/8853–0035* ⊕ *www.english-heritage.org.uk* ⊠ *£5.70* ☉ *Apr.–Sept., Mon.–Wed. guided tours only, 11:30 and 2:30, Sun. 11–5; call ahead to confirm* Ⓤ *DLR: Greenwich; no direct bus access, only to Vanbrugh Hill (from east) and Blackheath Hill (from west).*

☾ **Royal Observatory.** Since 1884, the ultimate standard for time around
★ the world has been set here; Greenwich is on the prime meridian at 0° longitude. The honor was because of its importance as a site for study of the stars and of the passing of time. Since a redesign in 2007, the observatory has been split into two sites a short walk apart, one dedicated to the wonders of space, the other to mankind's cataloguing of moments.

If you come with children, don't miss the high-technology rooms of the **Astronomy Galleries,** where cutting-edge touch screens and interactive programs give young explorers the chance to run their own space missions to Ganymede, one of Jupiter's moons. ⊠ *Romney Rd., Greenwich* ☎ *020/8858–4422* ⊕ *www.rog.nmm.ac.uk* ⊠ *Free, planetarium shows £6* ☉ *July and Aug., daily 10–6; Sept.–June, daily 10–5; last entry 30 mins before closing* Ⓤ *DLR: Greenwich.*

HAMPTON COURT PALACE
20 mi southwest of central London.

☾ **Hampton Court Palace.** Today the royal palace that sits beside the slow-
FodorsChoice moving Thames gives you two palaces for the price of one: The mag-
★ nificent Tudor redbrick mansion that was begun in 1514 by Cardinal Wolsey to impress the young Henry, and the larger 17th-century baroque offering, for which the graceful south wing was designed by Christopher Wren of St. Paul's fame. The first buildings of Hampton Court belonged to a religious order founded in the 11th century and were expanded over the years by its many subsequent residents, none more important than Henry VIII and his six wives. Henry spent a king's ransom (today's equivalent of £18 million or $27.5 million) expanding and refurbishing the palace.

If Tudor takes your fancy, wander through the **State Apartments,** hung with priceless paintings, and on to the wood-beamed magnificence of **Henry's Great Hall,** lined with tapestries and the mustiness of old, before taking in the strikingly azure ceiling of the **Chapel Royal.** Topping it all is the Great House of Easement, a lavatory that could sit 28 people at a time.

Feel a chill in the air? Watch out for the ghost of Henry VIII's doomed fifth wife, Catherine Howard, who literally lost her head yet apparently still screams her way along the **Haunted Gallery**. The latter-day baroque transformers of the palace, William and Mary, maintained beautiful **King's and Queen's Apartments, Georgian Rooms**, and fine collections of porcelain.

The gardens here are lovely, and don't miss the famous maze, its ½ mi of pathways among clipped hedgerows still fiendish to negotiate. There's a trick, but we won't give it away here: it's much more fun to go and lose yourself.

■TIP→ Avoid the queue and save by buying your tickets online. ⊠ *Hampton Court Palace, East Molesley, Surrey* ☎ *0844/482–7799* ⊕ *www.hrp. org.uk/hamptoncourtpalace* 🎫 *£14* ☯ *Apr.–Oct., daily 10–6 (last ticket sold at 5); Nov.–Mar., daily 10–4:30 (last ticket sold at 3:30); check Web site before visiting* Ⓤ *Richmond, then Bus R68; National Rail, South West: Hampton Court Station, 35 mins from Waterloo.*

KEW GARDENS

6 mi southwest of central London.

Fodor's Choice
★
Kew Gardens. Enter Kew Gardens and you are enveloped by blazes of color, extraordinary blooms, hidden trails, magnificent buildings, and centuries of endeavor aimed at getting to grips with the mysteries of plants that entrance, medicate, and excite. Even today academics are hard at work on more than 300 scientific projects across as many acres, researching everything from the cacti of eastern Brazil to the yams of Madagascar. Two great 19th-century greenhouses—the **Palm House** and the **Temperate House**—are filled with exotic blooms, and many of the plants have been there since the final glass panel was fixed into place. The crazy 50-story **Pagoda**, visible for miles around, is the star turn. ■TIP→ Guided tours with nature-loving volunteers leave at 11 and 2. ⊠ *Royal Botanic Gardens, Kew, Richmond, Surrey, TW9 3AB (main entrance is between Richmond Circus and the traffic circle at Mortlake Rd.)* ☎ *020/8332–5655* ⊕ *www.kew.org* 🎫 *£13* ☯ *Feb. and Mar., daily 9:30–5:30; Apr.–Aug., weekdays 9:30–6:30, weekends 9:30–7:30; Sept. and Oct., 9:30–6; Nov.–Feb. 9:30–4:15* Ⓤ *Kew Gardens.*

Kew Palace and Queen Charlotte's Cottage. To this day quietly domestic Kew Palace remains the smallest royal palace in the land. The house and gardens offer a glimpse into the 17th century. Originally known as the Dutch House, it was bought by King George II to provide more room in addition to the White House (another royal residence that used to exist on the grounds) for the extended Royal Family. In spring there's a romantic haze of bluebells. ⊠ *Kew Gardens, Kew* ⊕ *www.hrp.org.uk* 🎫 *£5, in addition to ticket for Kew Gardens* ☯ *Apr.–Sept., Tues.–Sun. 10–5, Mon. 11–5* Ⓤ *Kew Gardens.*

QUICK
BITES

Maids of Honour (⊠ *288 Kew Rd., Kew* ☎ *020/8940–2752*), the most traditional of Old English tearooms, is named for the famous tarts invented here and still baked by hand on the premises. Tea is served Tuesday–Saturday 2:30–5:30. If you want to take some of the lovely cakes and pastries to

eat at Kew Gardens or on Kew Green, the shop is open Tuesday–Saturday
9:30–6 and Monday until 1.

WHERE TO EAT

2

*Use the coordinate (✛ B2) at the end of each listing to locate a site on
the corresponding map.*

London rivals New York, Paris, and Tokyo as one of the best places
to eat in the world right now. The sheer diversity of restaurants here is
unparalleled. Among the city's 6,700 restaurants are see-and-be-seen
hot spots, casual ethnic eateries, innovative gastro-pubs, and shrines
to haute cuisine.

To measure London's spectacular culinary rise, note that it was once a
common dictum that the British ate to live, whereas the French lived to
eat. The best of British food—local, regional, seasonal, and meticulously
sourced—is now all the rage and appears on more smart menus by the
day. "Nose-to-tail" eating—where every scrap of meat is deemed fair
game for the plate—has made a spectacular comeback at St. John in
Clerkenwell, and fits perfectly with the new mood of austerity.

Meanwhile, the much-lauded haute cuisine scene is dominated by
world-class masters. Marcus Wareing roars up on his mentor Gordon
Ramsay's shoulder at Wareing's self-named place at the Berkeley, Michel
Roux Jr. rules the roost at Le Gavroche in Mayfair, Hélène Darroze
does it for the girls at the Connaught, and Claude Bosi bosses things
at Hibiscus.

For cheap eats, don't miss the city's unofficial dish, the ubiquitous
Indian curry. The quality of other international cuisines also has grown
in recent years, with London becoming known for its Spanish, Italian,
Turkish, Thai, and North African restaurants. With all of the choices,
traditional British food, when you track it down, appears as just one
more exotic cuisine in the pantheon.

Whatever eating experience you seek, London can likely deliver. From
dirt-cheap street food to posh multi-course meals, the city has become a
destination for gustatory adventurers. In this chapter, we've uncovered
the best of the best. Dig in, and enjoy!

PRICES AND SAVING MONEY

London is not an inexpensive city. A modest lunch for two can cost
£40 (about $60) and the £100-a-head dinner is not so taboo. Damage-
control strategies include making lunch your main meal—the top places
have bargain lunch menus, halving the price of evening à la carte—and
ordering a second appetizer instead of an entrée, to which few places
object. Note that an appetizer, usually known as a "starter" or "first
course," is sometimes called an "entrée," as it is in France, and an entrée
in England is dubbed the "main course" or simply "mains."

Indian and other international restaurants have always been a good
money-saving bet here. Sandwich shops and chains proliferate. *See
Local Chains Worth a Taste box for the best bets.* Seek out fixed-price
menus, and watch for hidden extras on the check: cover, bread, or

vegetables charged separately, and service. Many restaurants exclude service charges from the menu (which the law obliges them to display outside), then add 10% to 12.5% to the check, or else stamp SERVICE NOT INCLUDED along the bottom, in which case you should add the 10% to 12.5% yourself. Don't pay twice for service.

WHAT IT COSTS IN POUNDS					
	£	££	£££	££££	£££££
AT DINNER	under £10	£10–£16	£17–£23	£24–£32	over £32

Prices are per person for a main course, excluding drinks, service, and V.A.T.

BAYSWATER

£££
FRENCH

✗**Angelus.** Owner, sommelier, and former pro rugby player Thierry Tomasin scores a converted try at this distinctive French brasserie in Lancaster Gate. Styled with art deco mirrors and button-back banquettes in a 200-year-old converted former pub, Angelus has a reputation for unrivaled Paris-style brasserie cuisine. The foie gras crème brûlée, egg cocotte, sole, or quail with bacon are as good as they get. Light bites, such as beef tartare or banana bread, are served at the bar. Tomasin is sure to select a classy bottle from the wine list focused mainly on France. ⊠ *4 Bathurst St., Bayswater* ☎ *020/402–0083* ⊕ *www. angelusrestaurant.co.uk* ⊟ *AE, MC, V* Ⓤ *Lancaster Gate* ✛ *B3.*

£££
MODERN BRITISH
Fodor'sChoice
★

✗**Hereford Road.** Bespectacled chef–co-owner Tom Pemberton mans the front-of-house grill at this Bayswater favorite, which specializes in pared-back best-of-British fare. With an accent on well-sourced regional and seasonal ingredients, many dishes are as uncluttered as you'll find. Slide into a stylish booth, and gorge on cockles and leeks, brill with peashoots, or ox cheeks with pickled walnuts. Expect to see the well-heeled Tory-leaning Notting Hill set. ⊠ *3 Hereford Rd., Bayswater* ☎ *020/7727–1144* ⊕ *www.herefordroad.org* ⊟ *AE, MC, V* Ⓤ *Bayswater, Queensway* ✛ *A3.*

££
CHINESE
☾

✗**Royal China.** The black-and-gold '70s Biba-style decor is half the fun at this flagship dim sum palace on Queensway. Expect queues and mirrored ceilings at this longtime favorite that churns out stacks of dim sum at a furious pace. Start with dumplings stuffed with pork, squid, duck, prawns, scallops, or crab, and follow up with spareribs and greens, and pots of Chinese tea. ⊠ *13 Queensway, Bayswater* ☎ *020/7221–2535* ⊕ *www.royalchinagroup.co.uk* ⚠ *Reservations not accepted* ⊟ *AE, MC, V* Ⓤ *Queensway, Bayswater* ✛ *A3.*

CHELSEA

££
MODERN BRITISH

✗**The Pig's Ear.** Heir to the throne Prince William once came with friends and split the bill in the first-floor dining room at this classic gastropub off the King's Road. Elbow in at the crowded ground-floor pub area, or choose a more formal vibe in the dark wood-paneled salon upstairs. You'll find creative dishes on a short menu, like pig's ear, Cornish crab, and braised pork belly, which are all typical, and

BEST BETS FOR LONDON DINING

Where can I find the best food London has to offer? Fodor's writers and editors have selected their favorite restaurants by price, cuisine, and experience in the lists below. In the first column, the Fodor's Choice properties represent the "best of the best" across price categories. You can also search by neighborhood for excellent eating experiences—just peruse our complete reviews on the following pages.

2

Marcus Wareing at the Berkeley, £££££ p. 96

INDIAN

Lahore Kebab House, £ p. 90

Rasoi Restaurant, ££££ p. 97

Tayyabs, £ p. 92

ITALIAN

Bocca di Lupo, £££ p. 93

Cecconi's, £££ p. 97

L'Anima, £££ p. 91

River Café, ££££ p. 96

SEAFOOD

Golden Hind, £ p. 97

J Sheekey, £££ p. 95

Scott's, ££££ p. 99

Sweetings, £££ p. 92

Fodor's Choice ★

Anchor & Hope, ££–£££ p. 100

Busaba Eathai, £ p. 94

Giaconda Dining Room, ££ p. 94

Great Queen Street, £££ p. 94

Hélène Darroze at the Connaught, £££££ p. 98

Hereford Road, £££ p. 86

J Sheekey, £££ p. 95

La Petite Maison, £££ p. 98

Le Gavroche, £££££ p. 98

Marcus Wareing at the Berkeley, £££££ p. 96

Moro, £££ p. 91

Scott's, ££££ p. 99

St. John, £££ p. 91

Wild Honey, £££ p. 99

By Price

£

Busabe Eathai, p. 94

Tayyabs, p. 92

Wahaca, p. 96

££

Anchor & Hope, p. 100

Côte, p. 94

Giaconda Dining Room, p. 94

£££

Arbutus, p. 92

Barrafina, p. 93

Boundary, p. 90

Corrigan's Mayfair, p. 97

Great Queen Street, p. 94

Hereford Road, p. 86

Hibiscus, p. 98

J Sheekey, p. 95

La Petite Maison, p. 98

Moro, p. 91

Wild Honey, p. 99

The Wolseley, p. 99

££££

Rasoi Restaurant, p. 97

River Café, p. 96

Scott's, p. 99

£££££

Hélène Darroze at the Connaught, p. 98

Le Gavroche, p. 98

Marcus Wareing at the Berkeley, p. 96

Nobu Berkeley Street, p. 98

By Cuisine

MODERN BRITISH

Anchor & Hope, ££–£££ p. 100

Great Queen Street, £££ p. 94

Hereford Road, £££ p. 86

Magdalen, ££ p. 101

St. John, £££ p. 91

FRENCH

Hélène Darroze at the Connaught, £££££ p. 98

Hibiscus, £££ p. 98

Le Gavroche, £££££ p. 98

La Petite Maison, £££ p. 98

By Experience

KID-FRIENDLY

Busaba Eathai, £ p. 94

Royal China, ££ p. 86

HOT SPOTS

Bocca di Lupo, £££ p. 93

Boundary, £££ p. 90

Cecconi's, £££ p. 97

Nobu Berkeley Street, ££££–£££££ p. 98

Scott's, ££££ p. 99

BEST PRETHEATER EATS

Arbutus, £££ p. 92

Busaba Eathai, £ p. 94

Giaconda Dining Room, ££ p. 94

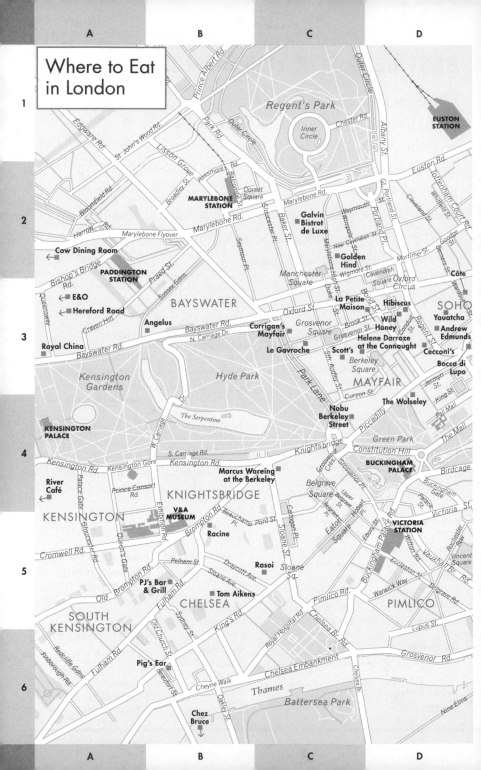

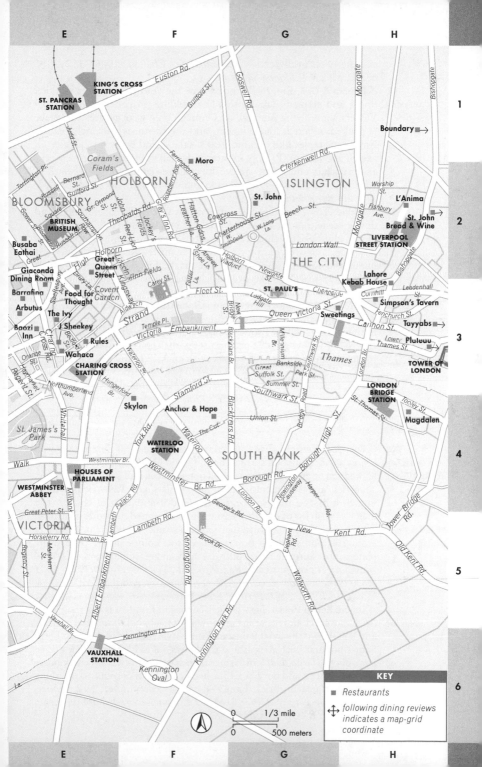

executed . . . royally. ⊠ *35 Old Church St., Chelsea* ☎ *020/7352–2908* ▭ *AE, MC, V* Ⓤ *Sloane Sq.* ✛ *B6.*

££ ✕ **PJ's Bar & Grill.** Enter PJ's and assume the Polo Joe lifestyle: wooden
AMERICAN floors and stained glass, a slowly revolving propeller from a 1919 Vickers Vimy flying bomber, and vintage polo gear galore. The place is packed, relaxed, and efficient, and the menu, which includes all-American staples like organic steaks, salads, and brownies, pleases all except vegetarians. PJ's opens late, and the bartenders are pros. Weekend brunch is a must with the wealthy Chelsea jet set. ⊠ *52 Fulham Rd., Chelsea* ☎ *020/7581–0025* ⊕ *www.pjsbarandgrill.co.uk* ▭ *AE, MC, V* Ⓤ *South Kensington* ✛ *B5.*

££ ✕ **Racine.** There's an upscale buzz at this star of the Brompton Road
BRASSERIE dining scene, not far from the V&A, Harrods, and Holy Trinity Brompton church. This chic French brasserie excels in doing simple things well—and not overcharging. Classics like melted Raclette cheese, roast quail, and rack of lamb all hit the mark. The £17.50 set lunch or early dinners (6–7:30 PM) are popular. ⊠ *239 Brompton Rd., Chelsea* ☎ *020/7584–4477* ▭ *AE, MC, V* Ⓤ *South Kensington* ✛ *B5.*

£££££ ✕ **Tom Aikens.** Wonder chef Tom Aikens trained under French stars
FRENCH Pierre Koffman and Joël Robuchon and excels at his eponymous place in upmarket Chelsea. Prone to flights of fancy, his food is technically superb. You'll swoon over his foie gras with Sauternes jelly, pollack with truffle scrambled eggs, John Dory with couscous, and pear-and-ginger mousse. There's an expert sommelier to help with the wine. ⊠ *43 Elystan St., Kensington* ☎ *020/7584–2003* ⊕ *www.tomaikens.co.uk* ⌲ *Reservations essential* ▭ *AE, MC, V* Ⓤ *South Kensington* ✛ *B5.*

THE CITY

£££ ✕ **Boundary.** Design guru and veteran restaurateur Sir Terence Conran
FRENCH scores an absolute bull's-eye at Boundary in über-fashionable Hoxton–
Fodor'sChoice Shoreditch. A spangly glass-fronted open kitchen and sparkling lighting,
★ acoustics, and Technicolor seats, make this smart 124-seat basement French brasserie the *glamorati's* east-end destination of choice. The menu's a wish list of crowd-pleasing dishes designed to impress: shellfish bisque, escargots à la Bourguignonne, cassoulet Toulousain, lapin à la moutarde, and steak au poivre. Dover sole comes simply on a white plate, and desserts like tarte tatin are tasty and reasonably priced. ⊠ *2–4 Boundary St., entrance at 9 Redchurch St., The City* ☎ *020/7729–1051* ⊕ *www.theboundary.co.uk* ⌲ *Reservations essential* ▭ *AE, MC, V* ⊘ *No lunch Mon.* Ⓜ *Liverpool St.* ✛ *H1.*

£ ✕ **Lahore Kebab House.** Best budget curries in London is the mantra at
PAKISTANI the Lahore Kebab House in run-down Whitechapel. It may be no-frills and BYOB, but the halal Pakistani home-style cooking is cheap and brilliant—popular with Asians and City boys alike. Mutton *tikka*, grilled lamb chops, *tarka daal* lentils, masala fish curry, and *karahi* chicken are all super-spiced and fiery. A £15-a-head meal knocks spots off anything on offer in nearby Brick Lane's so-called "curry mile." ⊠ *2 Umberston St., The City* ☎ *020/7481–9737* ⊕ *www.lahore-kebabhouse.com* ▭ *MC, V* 𝓨*BYOB* Ⓤ *Aldgate* ✛ *H3.*

£££ ✕ **L'Anima.** Brilliant Southern Italian cuisine in a love-it-or-loathe-it
ITALIAN glass-fronted box of a restaurant characterizes the scene at L'Anima.
Chef Francesco Mazzei draws inspiration from Sicily, Sardinia, and
Calabria, and works the floor, bar, and clear-fronted kitchen like the
proud owner that he is. Simple, modern dishes like wild mushroom and
black truffle tagliolini are near perfection, as is the baked sea bass—as
succulent as you could wish. Dessert puddings, like peach and Ama-
retto, are *belissimo*, and the wines are mainly Italian. ⊠ *1 Snowden
St., City* ☎ *020/7422–7000* ⊕ *www.lanima.co.uk* ▤ *AE, DC, MC, V*
☉ *Closed Sun.* Ⓤ *Liverpool St.* ✛ *H2.*

£££ ✕ **Moro.** Up from The City, near Clerkenwell and Sadler's Wells con-
MEDITERRANEAN temporary dance theater, is Exmouth Market, a cluster of cute shops,
Fodor's Choice a few delis, an Italian church, and more fine restaurants like Moro.
★ The menu includes a mélange of Spanish and North African flavors.
Spiced meats, Serrano hams, salt cod, and wood-fired and char-grilled
offerings are the secret to Moro's success. Grilled lamb with marrow
and yogurt stands out. Sidle up to the zinc bar, or squeeze into a tiny
table and lean in—it's noisy here. But then again, that's part of the
buzz. ⊠ *34–36 Exmouth Market, The City* ☎ *020/7833–8336* ⊕ *www.
moro.co.uk* ⟡ *Reservations essential* ▤ *AE, DC, MC, V* ☉ *Closed Sun.*
Ⓤ *Farringdon* ✛ *F1.*

£££ ✕ **Plateau.** Credit crunch or no, Plateau's an excellent venue for a Canary
MODERN FRENCH Wharf business meal. In an all-white space, with tulip-shaped chairs
and floor-to-ceiling glass windows overlooking Canada Square, Plateau
houses a restaurant, rotisserie, two bars, private dining, and outdoor terraces. Food like baked monkfish, wood pigeon with gnocchi, and lamb
with sweetbreads are all pricey, but executed well. ⊠ *4th fl., Canada
Pl., Canada Sq., The City* ☎ *020/7715–7100* ⊕ *www.plateaurestaurant.
co.uk* ▤ *AE, DC, MC, V* Ⓤ *Canary Wharf* ✛ *H3.*

££ ✕ **Simpson's Tavern.** This historic back-alley City chophouse was founded
BRITISH in 1757 and is as raucous and atmospheric as you'll find. It draws pin-
striped City folk, who love the boardinghouse scene and old-school
grub: oxtail stew, steak-and-kidney pie, chump chops, potted shrimp,
or "stewed cheese" house special (cheese on toast with Béchamel sauce).
Brusque service and shared oak bench stalls are part of the charm. Note
it's only open weekdays from noon until 3. ⊠ *38½ Cornhill, at Ball Ct.,
The City* ☎ *020/7626–9985* ⊕ *www.simpsonstavern.co.uk* ▤ *AE, DC,
MC, V* ☉ *Closed weekends. No dinner* Ⓤ *Bank* ✛ *H3.*

£££ ✕ **St. John.** Fans travel the world for Fergus Henderson's ultra-Brit-
BRITISH ish nose-to-tail cooking at this stark-white converted smokehouse in
Fodor's Choice Clerkenwell. His chutzpah is galling: one appetizer is pigskin, and oth-
★ ers, like ox heart or pig nose and tail, are marginally less extreme.
Dishes like bone marrow and parsley, or chitterlings and dandelion
appear stark on the plate but arrive with aplomb. Expect an all-French
wine list, plus port. Finish with strawberry trifle and Madeleines. ⊠ *26
St. John St., Clerkenwell* ☎ *020/7251–0848* ⊕ *www.stjohnrestaurant.
co.uk* ▤ *AE, DC, MC, V* ☉ *Closed Sun.* Ⓤ *Farringdon* ✛ *G2.*

££ ✕ **St. John Bread & Wine.** The canteen cousin of St. John in Clerkenwell
MODERN BRITISH is a winner no matter what meal of the day: have porridge, prunes, and
pikelets for breakfast, seed cake and Madeira for "elevenses," beetroot

and pickled walnuts for lunch, and smoked sprats for dinner. It's similar to St. John in that you'll find ox heart, pigskin, "blood cake," and duck egg on the menu. You can feast on a whole roast suckling pig that feeds 14. Note it's a handy spot before or after visits to nearby Brick Lane or Old Spitalfields markets. ⊠ *94–96 Commercial St., The City* ☎ *020/7251–0848* ⊕ *www.stjohnrestaurant.co.uk* ⊟ *AE, MC, V* Ⓤ *Aldgate East, Liverpool St.* ✛ *H2*

£££ ✕**Sweetings.** Established in 1889, Sweetings is a remnant from the
SEAFOOD old imperial City of London heyday. There are some things Sweetings *doesn't* do: reservations, dinner, coffee, weekends. It does, however, do seafood. Not far from St. Paul's cathedral, it's patronized by City gents who drink tankards of Black Velvet (Guinness and champagne) and eat soused herrings, roe on toast, and skate wings with black butter at linen-covered raised counters. The oysters are fresh, and desserts like spotted dick are classic favorites. ⊠ *39 Queen Victoria St., The City* ☎ *020/7248–3062* ⊛ *Reservations not accepted* ⊟ *AE, MC, V* ☾ *Closed weekends. No dinner* Ⓤ *Mansion House* ✛ *G3.*

£ ✕**Tayyabs.** Reckless City financiers, Asians, and medics from the
PAKISTANI Royal London Hospital swamp this high-turnover Pakistani halal curry canteen in Whitechapel. Expect queues after dark, and bear in mind it's BYOB, jam-packed, noisy, and mildly chaotic. Nonetheless, prices are cheap and you can gorge for £15 on minced meat kebabs, karahi chicken, or marinated lamb chops. ⊠ *83 Fieldgate St., The City* ☎ *020/7247–9543* ⊕ *www.tayyabs.co.uk* ⊛ *Reservations not accepted* ⊟ *AE, MC, V* ⌴ *BYOB* Ⓤ *Aldgate East* ✛ *H3.*

COVENT GARDEN AND SOHO

££ ✕**Andrew Edmunds.** Rustic food at realistic prices defines this perpetually
MEDITERRANEAN jammed, Dickensian, softly lighted romantic Soho restaurant—though it could be larger and the wooden bench seats more forgiving. Tucked away behind Carnaby Street, it's a favorite with the media crowd that come for daily changing, fixed-price lunch menus. Starters and main courses draw on the taste of Ireland, the Mediterranean, and Middle East. Pigeon breast (£5.75), Roquefort soufflé (£6.50), and swordfish with basil mayonnaise (£15) are all hale and hearty. ⊠ *46 Lexington St., Soho* ☎ *020/7437–5708* ⊛ *Reservations essential* ⊟ *MC, V* Ⓤ *Oxford Circus, Piccadilly Circus* ✛ *D3.*

£££ ✕**Arbutus.** Serious cuisine at midrange prices has established Arbutus
MODERN BRITISH in the winners' enclosure of favorite Soho eateries. The £15.50 three-course lunch or £17.50 pretheater special are bargains of the year. Chef Anthony Demetre might surprise with squid-and-mackerel burger, rabbit cottage pie, or pollack and tomato jam, and finishes off with English trifle. All wines are offered in third-of-a-bottle carafes—a great way to sample new delights. ⊠ *63–64 Frith St., Soho* ☎ *020/7734–4545* ⊕ *www.arbutusrestaurant.co.uk* ⊟ *AE, MC, V* Ⓤ *Tottenham Court Rd.* ✛ *E3.*

£ ✕**Baozi Inn.** Chairman Mao paraphernalia decorates the walls of this
CHINESE handy Sichuan café on a busy side street in Chinatown. Baozi steamed buns—pork and onion or shrimp and radish—are house specials (£1.50), and there's dragon wonton broth or Chengdu pork dumplings

British Food Decoder

In London, local could mean any global flavor, but for pure Britishness, roast beef and Yorkshire pudding top the list. If you want the best-value traditional Sunday lunch, go to a pub. Gastro-pubs, where Sunday roasts are generally made with top-quality ingredients, are a good bet. The meat is usually served with crisp roast potatoes and carrots, and with Yorkshire pudding, a savory batter baked in the oven until crisp. A rich, dark, meaty gravy is poured on top.

Other tummy liners include shepherd's pie, made with stewed minced lamb and a mashed-potato topping and baked until lightly browned on top; cottage pie is a similar dish, but made with minced beef instead of lamb. Steak-and-kidney pie is a delight when done properly: with chunks of lean beef and ox kidneys, braised with onions and mushrooms in a thick gravy, and topped with a light puff-pastry crust.

Fish-and-chips, usually battered deep-fried cod or haddock, comes with thick chips, or french fries, as we call them in the States. A ploughman's lunch in a pub is crusty bread, a strong-flavored English cheese with bite (cheddar, blue Stilton, crumbly white Cheshire, or smooth red Leicester), and tangy pickles with a side-salad garnish. For a hot, comforting dessert, seek out a sweet bread-and-butter pudding, made from layers of bread and dried currants baked in cream until crisp. And one can't forgo English cream tea, which consists of scones served with jam and clotted cream, and sandwiches made with wafer-thin slices of cucumber—served as an accompaniment to properly brewed tea.

---

with chili oil (£5.20). Try "ginger juice" spinach (£4.50), or "peace and happiness" noodle soup, topped with duck, garlic, and Chinese toon tree shoots (£6.50). Tables are cramped, and service is bang, bang, bang! ⊠ *25 Newport Ct., Soho* ☎ *020/7287–6877* ⊛ *Reservations not accepted* ⊟ *AE, MC, V* Ⓤ *Leicester Sq.* ✥ *E3.*

£££   ✕ **Barrafina.** London's top tapas bar on Frith Street in Soho is mod-
SPANISH   eled on Cal Pep in Barcelona and similarly has only a few (23) raised counter seats. It doesn't take bookings and you're likely to queue, but staff are past masters, and the tapas are supreme. Pick at gambas or chorizo, quail, sardines, and octopus, or classics like Jabugo ham and tortilla. You can check out the scene—or who's in the queue—at the live webcam. ⊠ *54 Frith St., Soho* ☎ *020/7813–8016* ⊕ *www.barrafina. co.uk* ⊛ *Reservations not accepted* ⊟ *AE, MC, V* Ⓤ *Tottenham Court Rd.* ✥ *E3.*

£££   ✕ **Bocca di Lupo.** The place is always packed, the tables are jammed too
ITALIAN   close together, and the acoustics are lousy, but everyone loves the buzz and the brilliant regional Italian cuisine. Set in an unlikely street off Soho's red-light district, pile into a succession of small plates and dishes from Bologna to Venato. Try fried anchovies, grilled red prawns, lamb *prosciutto*, cannellini beans, or rustic pork and foie gras sausages. You may not be able to hear your dining companions speak, but at least the amazing milk-free espresso ice cream makes up for the loss. ⊠ *12 Archer*

St., Soho ☎ *020/7734–2223* ⊕ *www.boccadilupo.com* ⌕ *Reservations essential* ⊟ *AE, DC, MC, V* ⊘ *Closed Sun.* Ⓤ *Piccadilly Circus* ✛ *D3*

£   ✕ **Busaba Eathai.** It's top Thai nosh for little moolah at this superior
THAI   no-bookings canteen in the heart of Soho. Fitted with bench seats and
Fodor's Choice   hardwood tables, it's no less seductive for the communal dining, rapid
★   service, and fast-moving queue out the front. The menu includes noodles, curries, soups, juices, and stir-fries. Try the chicken with shiitake, cuttlefish curry, or vermicelli with prawns, squid, and scallops. ⊠ *106–110 Wardour St., Soho* ☎ *020/7255–8686* ⊕ *www.busaba.com* ⌕ *Reservations not accepted* ⊟ *AE, MC, V* Ⓤ *Tottenham Court Rd.* ✛ *E2.*

££   ✕ **Côte.** Where else can you get a surprisingly good three-course
FRENCH   French meal for £11.70? The Côte French brasserie—softly lighted and smoothly decked out with banquettes and Parisian-style round tables—does just the trick, and offers these deals weekdays from 3 until 7. With four choices per course, you'll find all your favorites: Bayonne ham, Les Landes chicken, moules marinière, tuna Niçoise and steak haché. ⊠ *124–126 Wardour St., Soho* ☎ *020/7287–9280* ⊕ *www.cote-restaurants.co.uk* ⊟ *AE, MC, V* Ⓤ *Tottenham Court Rd.* ✛ *D3.*

£   ✕ **Food for Thought.** It may only be an unfussy '70s-style subterranean
VEGETARIAN   vegetarian café with no liquor license (but BYOB without a corkage fee) on Neal Street, but it's got a cult following, so be prepared to queue down the stairs here in the heart of Covent Garden. You'll find wooden communal tables and a crunchy daily menu of soups, salads, stews, quiches, stir-fries, bakes, and casseroles. Wheat-free, gluten-free, genetically modified–free, and vegan options are available, but note that it closes at 8:30 PM daily, and 5 PM Sunday. ⊠ *31 Neal St., Covent Garden* ☎ *020/7836–9072* ⌕ *Reservations not accepted* ⊟ *No credit cards* ⌁ *BYOB* Ⓤ *Covent Garden* ✛ *E3.*

££   ✕ **Giaconda Dining Room.** A real find on Denmark Street's "Tin Pan
MODERN   Alley" (think David Bowie, Bob Marley, and the Clash), the Australian-
EUROPEAN   run two-room dining room may seat only 35, but the menu is inspired.
Fodor's Choice   Chef Paul Merrony sends out starters—pumpkin risotto, crispy pigs'
★   trotters—and a full range of main entrées for a reasonable cost. Try the fish cakes, salmon and fennel, or hearty dishes like veal kidneys, Italian pork sausage stew, or ham-hock hash with a fried egg on top. Popular puddings such as apricot compote and whipped cream come in at a tasty £6. ⊠ *9 Denmark St., Soho* ☎ *020/7240–3334* ⊕ *www.giacondadining.com* ⊟ *AE, MC, V* ⊘ *Closed weekends* Ⓤ *Tottenham Court Rd.* ✛ *E3.*

£££   ✕ **Great Queen Street.** Expect crowds and a buzz at Covent Garden's
MODERN BRITISH   leading gastropub that showcases classic British dishes in a burgundy
Fodor's Choice   and bare oak-floor-and-table setting. Old-fashioned dishes like pressed
★   tongue, mackerel, and gooseberry, and mussels and chips may be revived from a bygone era, but Londoners adore them. Dishes for the whole table—like seven-hour shoulder of lamb—are highly convivial. There's little for nonmeat eaters, and no dinner Sunday. ⊠ *32 Great Queen St., Covent Garden* ☎ *020/7242–0622* ⌕ *Reservations essential* ⊟ *MC, V* ⊘ *No dinner Sun.* Ⓤ *Covent Garden, Holborn* ✛ *E2.*

£££–££££   ✕ **The Ivy.** The A-list spurn the Ivy for Scott's and J Sheekey, but it's
BRITISH   still hard to bag a table. A mix of daytime TV stars and gawkers dine

2

GREAT LONDON CURRIES

The East End's Brick Lane is famous for its numerous Bangladeshi curry houses and dodgy sidewalk "curry touts" who encourage you to come inside and dine, but there are other places around town to grab great curries.

✕ **Aladin** is a local Brick Lane BYOB favorite. Legend has it that HRH Prince Charles stopped by for a chicken tikka masala once. Though lacking in ambience, Aladin makes up for it with low prices and its aromatic curries. Average price of dinner for two: £22. ⊠ *132 Brick La.* ☎ *020/7247–8210* ⌂♈ *BYOB* Ⓤ *Aldgate East.*

✕ **Hot Stuff** in Vauxhall offers some of the best-loved and best-priced curries in London. Run by the Dawood family, it's just a BYOB café with two tables. Home-cooked specials include king prawn biryani, chicken bhuna, and chili paneer. There's wonderful rice, bhagis, naan bread, and creamy dal (spiced lentils). Average price of dinner for two:

£24. ⊠ *19 Wilcox Rd.* ☎ *020/7720–1480* ⊕ *www.eathotstuff.com* ⌂♈ *BYOB* Ⓤ *Vauxhall.*

✕ **Rooburoo** is popular throughout north London's Islington neighborhood. It has a reputation for modern spins on classic dishes and is liked by young professionals. Dishes include classic chicken jalfrezi, plus specialties such as Indian wraps and sea-bass fillet in banana leaves. Average price of dinner for two: £30. ⊠ *21 Chapel Market* ☎ *020/7278–8100* ⊕ *www.rooburoo.com* Ⓤ *Angel.*

✕ **Vama's** upscale, stylish setting on the King's Road makes it a favorite among Chelsea's trendy crowd. The place has won countless awards and offers its own take on coconut prawn curry, as well as other dishes such as scallop masala and tandoori lamb chops. Average price of dinner for two: £80. ⊠ *438 King's Rd.* ☎ *020/7351 4118* ⊕ *www.vama.co.uk* Ⓤ *Sloane Sq., South Kensington.*

on bang bang chicken, salmon fish cakes, and English classics like shepherd's pie in a handsome wood-paneled salon. For midrange star-spotting and daytime stars this is a prime spot. If you can't score a reservation, try walking in for a table at the last moment. ⊠ *1–5 West St., Covent Garden* ☎ *020/7836–4751* ⊕ *www.the-ivy.co.uk* ⌂ *Reservations essential* ▭ *AE, DC, MC, V* Ⓤ *Covent Garden* ⊕ *E3.*

£££   ✕ **J Sheekey.** Theater and film stars slip in here as an alternative to Scott's
SEAFOOD   or Nobu Berkeley Street. Linked with nearby Theaterland, J Sheekey
Fodor's Choice is one of Londoners' favorite West End haunts. It charms with warm
★   wood paneling, showbiz monochromes, alcove tables, and lava-rock
          bar tops. Opt for Arctic herrings, Dover sole, oysters, monkfish, or
          famous Sheekey fish pie. Dine at the mirrored bar for the ultimate in
          true romance, or enjoy the £24.50 weekend lunch. ⊠ *28–32 St. Martin's Ct., Covent Garden* ☎ *020/7240–2565* ⊕ *www.j-sheekey.co.uk* ▭ *AE, DC, MC, V* Ⓤ *Leicester Sq.* ⊕ *E3.*

£££–££££ ✕ **Rules.** Come, escape from the 21st century. Opened by Thomas Rule
BRITISH   in 1798, London's oldest restaurant has hosted everyone from Charles
          Dickens to Laurence Olivier and the Prince of Wales. This traditional
          English dining salon has plush red banquettes and lacquered yellow

walls crammed with engravings, oil paintings, and Victorian cartoons. Try historic British dishes—steak-and-kidney pie or roast beef and Yorkshire pudding—for a taste of the 18th century. In season, daily specials include game from the restaurant's High Pennines estate. ⊠ *35 Maiden La., Covent Garden* ☎ *020/7836–5314* ⊕ *www.rules.co.uk* ⊟ *AE, MC, V* Ⓤ *Covent Garden* ✛ *E3.*

£
MEXICAN

✕ **Wahaca.** Expect a wait for the fab-value Mexican street food at this brightly colored Covent Garden favorite. Mud walls and bench seats make for buzzy basement surroundings, but it's the cheap £3.75–£8.50 tacos, enchiladas, quesadillas, and burritos that pull in the studenty crowds. A £19.50 spread for two will produce a feast of chorizo quesadillas, tacos, slaw, and guacamole, but note that bookings aren't taken and that it's often full by 6:30 PM. ⊠ *66 Chandos Pl., Covent Garden* ☎ *020/7240–1883* ⊕ *www.wahaca.co.uk* ⚒ *Reservations not accepted* ⊟ *AE, MC, V* Ⓤ *Charing Cross* ✛ *E3.*

££££
CHINESE

✕ **Yauatcha.** It's all-day dim sum at this superbly lighted slinky Soho classic. Well designed by Christian Liaigre—with black granite floors, aquarium, candles, and a starry ceiling—the food is a match for the seductive setting. There's wicked dim sum (try prawns or scallops), crispy duck rolls, silver cod, fancy cocktails, and tea and colorful cakes in the first-floor tearoom. Note the quick table turns, and ask to dine in the more romantic basement at night. ⊠ *15 Broadwick St., Soho* ☎ *020/7494–8888* ⊕ *www.yauatcha.com* ⚒ *Reservations essential* ⊟ *AE, MC, V* Ⓤ *Oxford Circus* ✛ *D3.*

HAMMERSMITH

££££
ITALIAN

✕ **River Café.** This open-kitchen Italian restaurant sets the standard with its simple roasts, fresh salads, pastas, and char-grilled meats. The chefs source ultrafresh, impeccable seasonal ingredients, so expect Tuscan bread soup, handmade nettle-and-ricotta pasta, and and veal shin with lemon and sage—plus one of London's highest bills. This is in distant Hammersmith, so if you bag an evening table, remember that you'll need to book a cab ahead or walk about 10 minutes to the closest Tube. Note that tables are cleared by 11 PM on weekdays, and 11:20 PM Friday and Saturday. ⊠ *Thames Wharf, Rainville Rd., Hammersmith* ☎ *020/7386–4200* ⊕ *www.rivercafe.co.uk* ⚒ *Reservations essential* ⊟ *AE, DC, MC, V* Ⓤ *Hammersmith* ✛ *A4.*

KNIGHTSBRIDGE

£££££
MODERN
EUROPEAN
Fodor'sChoice
★

✕ **Marcus Wareing at the Berkeley.** Wonder chef Marcus Wareing vies to be the best in London at his eponymous restaurant at the Berkeley. Opulently designed by David Collins—all clarets, carpet, and burgundy leather seats—Wareing pulls out all the haute cuisine stops with a succession of world-class dishes. Standouts include roast quail with hispi cabbage; a fine chunk of Scottish halibut with charred leeks or Anjou pigeon with amaretti. Chocolate moëlleux with banana jelly or orange crème with spiced brioche are absolutely faultless, and the wine list includes page after page of famous names. ⊠ *The Berkeley, Wilton Pl., Knightsbridge* ☎ *020/7235–1200* ⊕ *www.the-berkeley.co.uk*

⚲ *Reservations essential* = *AE, DC, MC, V* ☭ *Closed Sun. No lunch Sat.* ⍳ *Knightsbridge* ⍓ *C4.*

££££   ✗ **Rasoi Restaurant.** Chef-proprietor Vineet Bhatia showcases the finest
INDIAN   new Indian cuisine in London at this tony town-house venue off the
King's Road. Super-seductive and decked with Indian silks, prints, masks,
bells, and ornaments, Bhatia pushes the boundaries with signatures like
wild mushroom rice with tomato ice cream or grilled lobster dusted
with cocoa and sour spices. Don't leave without sampling the warm
chocolate samosas. ⌂ *10 Lincoln St., Knightsbridge* ☎ *020/7225–1881*
⊕ *www.rasoirestaurant.co.uk* = *AE, DC, MC* ⍳ *Sloane Sq.* ⍓ *C5.*

MARYLEBONE AND MAYFAIR

£££   ✗ **Cecconi's.** Enjoy all-day buzz at this fashionable Italian brasserie oppo-
ITALIAN   site the Royal Academy on Burlington Gardens. Between Savile Row
and New Bond Street, the jet set pitch up for breakfast, brunch, and
Italian tapas (*cicchetti*) and return for something more substantial later
on. Ilse Crawford's green-and-brown interior is a stylish backdrop for
classics like veal Milanese, Venetian calves' liver, and tiramisu. Note:
It's a cool pit stop during a shopping spree. ⌂ *5A Burlington Gardens,
Mayfair* ☎ *020/7434–1500* ⊕ *www.cecconis.co.uk* = *AE, DC, MC, V*
⍳ *Green Park, Piccadilly Circus* ⍓ *D3.*

£££   ✗ **Corrigan's Mayfair.** The nearby streets may be a touch quiet but there's
MODERN BRITISH   a warm welcome and a lively scene at Richard Corrigan's flagship haute
cuisine venture off Park Lane. This 2008 addition to the Mayfair scene
is self-assured and on top of its game. Dark blue banquettes and crisp
Irish linen provide a handsome setting for a high-powered clientele who
love the lobster Waldorf salad, black bream and spinach, and heartier
dishes like rabbit cutlet with dandelion and carrots. There's a chef's
table and private dining, and you might see chef Richard Corrigan
knocking around. ⌂ *28 Upper Grosvenor St., Mayfair* ☎ *020/7499–
9943* ⊕ *www.corriganmayfair.com* ⚲ *Reservations essential* = *AE,
MC, V* ⍳ *Marble Arch* ⍓ *C3.*

£££   ✗ **Galvin Bistrot de Luxe.** The Galvin brothers blaze a trail for the deluxe
BISTRO   bistro concept on a no-man's-land stretch of Baker Street. Feted chefs
Chris and Jeff forsake Michelin stars and cut loose under the brasserie
banner. A more mature crowd enjoys impeccable service in a handsome
slate floor and mahogany-paneled salon. There's no finer crab lasagna
around, and mains punch above their weight: gilthead bream, stuffed
pig's trotter, and the Landaise chicken are all a triumph. The £15.50
set lunch or £17.50 dinners (6–7 PM) are unbeatable. ⌂ *66 Baker St.,
Marylebone* ☎ *020/7935–4007* ⊕ *www.galvinrestaurants.com* = *AE,
MC, V* ⍳ *Baker St.* ⍓ *C2.*

£   ✗ **Golden Hind.** You'll find some of the best fish-and-chips in London at
SEAFOOD   the Golden Hind, a British chippy run by Greek Cypriots in a 1914 art
deco café, off Marylebone High Street. Locals and tourists alike love the
calamari, skate wings, and fish cakes, but it's the perfect—nongreasy—
deep-fried or steamed battered cod, plaice, and haddock, the classic
Maris Piper chips, and mushy peas that are the big draw. Note it's
open noon–3 PM weekdays and 6–10 PM Monday through Saturday.

✉ *73 Marylebone La., Marylebone* ☎ *020/7486–3644* ▭ *AE, MC, V* 🍷 *BYOB* ☾ *Closed Sun.* Ⓤ *Bond St.* ✛ *C2.*

£££££
FRENCH
Fodor's Choice
★

✕ **Hélène Darroze at the Connaught.** London's crème de la crème flock to Hélène Darroze at the Connaught for exemplary regional French haute cuisine, served in a quintessentially Edwardian wood-paneled hotel dining room. Taking inspiration from Les Landes in southwest France, Darroze sallies forth with a procession of magical dishes. Caviar d'Acquitaine wows with oyster tartare in a stylish martini glass, topped with black caviar jelly and white haricot bean velouté. Spit-roasted and flambéed grouse is served delightfully pink, with duck foie gras, and mini–Brussels sprouts. To finish, enjoy Madagascar chocolate ganache with raspberry sorbet. Note that the prices are high: £32 for lunch, and £85 or £95 for the set dinners. ✉ *The Connaught, Carlos Pl., Mayfair* ☎ *020/3147–7200* ⊕ *www.the-connaught.co.uk* ✍ *Reservations essential* 🎩 *Jacket required* ☾ *Closed Sun. and Mon.* ▭ *AE, DC, MC, V* Ⓤ *Green Park* ✛ *C3.*

£££
MODERN FRENCH

✕ **Hibiscus.** Chef and front-of-house Claude and Claire Bosi excel at one of London's finest Modern French restaurants, tucked away on Maddox Street in Mayfair. Wood-paneled and kitted in muted gray and green, gastronomes swoon at the fireworks on the plate. Bosi's effortless cuisine might impress with frogs' leg fricassée, Goosnargh duck breast with wonton, or Lyonnaise tripe with cuttlefish and pig's ear. Lime and olive oil mille-feuille (puff pastry) is bound to send you home happy. ✉ *29 Maddox St., Mayfair* ☎ *020/7629–2999* ⊕ *www. hibiscusrestaurant.co.uk* ▭ *AE, MC, V* ☾ *No lunch Sat. Closed Sun. and Mon.* Ⓤ *Oxford Circus, Piccadilly* ✛ *D3.*

£££
FRENCH
Fodor's Choice
★

✕ **La Petite Maison.** Gwyneth Paltrow blogs that this is her all-time favorite London restaurant, and no wonder—there's nothing on the impeccably well-sourced French Mediterranean and Provençale menu that fails to deliver. Try a crab and lobster salad, a soft Burrata cheese, Datterini tomato and basil spread, or an aromatic baked turbot with artichokes, or chorizo and white wine sauce. Based on the style of the original La Petite Maison in Nice in France, dishes come to the table when they're ready, and friendly staff make for a convivial vibe. ✉ *53–54 Brook's Mews, Mayfair* ☎ *020/7495–4774* ⊕ *www.lpmlondon.co.uk* ▭ *AE, MC, V* Ⓤ *Bond St.* ✛ *D3.*

£££££
FRENCH
Fodor's Choice
★

✕ **Le Gavroche.** Michel Roux Jr. thrives at this 43-year-old clubby basement haven in Mayfair, which some rate the best formal dining in London. With silver domes and unpriced ladies' menus, Roux's mastery of classic French cuisine dazzles with signatures like foie gras with cinnamon-scented crispy duck pancake, langoustine with Hollandaise sauce, or lamb with flageolets. Desserts, like roast pineapple with white-pepper ice cream, are delightful, too. Weekday set lunch is a relatively affordable treat at £48.60—with a half bottle of wine, water, coffee, and petits fours. ✉ *43 Upper Brook St., Mayfair* ☎ *020/7408–0881* ⊕ *www.le-gavroche. co.uk* ✍ *Reservations essential* 🎩 *Jacket required* ▭ *AE, DC, MC, V* ☾ *Closed Sun. and 10 days at Christmas* Ⓤ *Marble Arch* ✛ *C3.*

££££–£££££
JAPANESE

✕ **Nobu Berkeley Street.** Supermodels, football (soccer) stars, and the Formula One crowd pay silly money for new-style sashimi with Peruvian flair at this so-hip-it-hurts Nobu spin-off near Piccadilly. The beautiful people go bonkers for miso black cod, California sushi rolls, tuna teriyaki, yellowtail, and Wagyu beef. Prices are extreme, but the people-watching is just *so* good. ⊠ *15 Berkeley St., Mayfair* ☎ *020/7290–9222* ⊕ *www.noburestaurants.com* ⊟ *AE, MC, V* Ⓤ *Green Park* ✛ *C4.*

££££
SEAFOOD
Fodor'sChoice
★

✕ **Scott's.** Scott's is so hot that it's where the A-list go to dine. Founded in 1851, and renovated and reborn as a glamorous seafood haven and oyster bar, it draws beautiful people who pick at Cumbrae oysters, Red Sea prawns, and Stargazy pie. Standouts like cod with chorizo and padron peppers are to die for. Prices are high, but don't worry: this really is *the* hottest joint in town. ⊠ *20 Mount St., Mayfair* ☎ *020/7495–7309* ⊕ *www.scotts-restaurant.com* ⌣ *Reservations essential* ⊟ *AE, DC, MC, V* Ⓤ *Bond St.* ✛ *C3.*

£££
MODERN
EUROPEAN
Fodor'sChoice
★

✕ **Wild Honey.** Wild Honey's amazing set lunch or early evening deals (£18.95–£21.95) are wildly popular. Book ahead at this wood-paneled clublike salon, with modern pictures and comfy booths, in swanky Mayfair. Try the tasty Exmouth crab and white peach, Icelandic cod, panna cotta, or signature warm chocolate soup with milk ice cream. All 50-odd wines are available in third-of-a-bottle carafes. ⊠ *12 St. George St., Mayfair* ☎ *020/7758–9160* ⊕ *www.wildhoneyrestaurant.co.uk* ⊟ *AE, MC, V* ⊘ *No lunch Sun.* Ⓤ *Oxford Circus* ✛ *D3.*

NOTTING HILL

£££
MODERN BRITISH

✕ **The Cow Dining Rooms.** A boho-chic gastropub, the Cow comprises a faux-Dublin '50s backroom saloon bar that serves Fines de Claires oysters, whelks and winkles, and Dorset crab. Upstairs the chef whips up Brit specialties like Welsh lamb cutlets, English summer salad, black bream, and sea trout and shrimp. Post-recession or millionaire Notting Hill locals love the house special in the packed bar: draft Guinness with a pint of prawns and mayonnaise. ⊠ *89 Westbourne Park Rd., Notting Hill* ☎ *020/7221–0021* ⊕ *www.thecowlondon.co.uk* ⊟ *MC, V* Ⓤ *Westbourne Park* ✛ *A2.*

£££
ASIAN

✕ **E&O.** The jet set hang at E&O, one of London's hip scene bars and restaurants, off Portobello Road. E&O means "Eastern and Oriental," and the mix of Chinese, Japanese, Vietnamese, and Thai dishes includes a slew of vegetarian options. Don't skip the lychee martinis, miso black cod, chili tofu, Thai rare beef, or papaya salad. ⊠ *14 Blenheim Crescent, Notting Hill* ☎ *020/7229–5454* ⊕ *www.rickerrestaurants.com/eando* ⊟ *AE, DC, MC, V* Ⓤ *Ladbroke Grove* ✛ *A3.*

ST. JAMES'S

£££
AUSTRIAN

✕ **The Wolseley.** The whole of London seems to enjoy the grand elegance at this Viennese-style grand café on Piccadilly. Framed with black lacquerware, the brasserie begins its long decadent days with breakfast at 7 AM and stays opens until midnight. Linger for beef Tafelspitz, kippers, and kedgeree, or Matjes herrings and Wiener Holstein. For dessert, go for apple strudel or *kaiserschmarren*—a pancake with stewed fruit and raisins. It's known for Viennoiserie pastries and sinful afternoon tea. ⊠ *160 Piccadilly, St. James's* ☎ *020/7499–6996* ⊕ *www.thewolseley.com* ⊟ *AE, DC, MC, V* Ⓤ *Green Park* ✛ *D4.*

LOCAL CHAINS WORTH A TASTE

When you're on the go or don't have time for a leisurely meal—and Starbucks won't cut it—you might want to try a local chain restaurant or sandwich bar. The ones listed below are well priced and are the best in their category.

✕ **Byron Hamburgers:** Bright and child-friendly, this six-strong line of burger joins storms the market with its delicious Aberdeen Angus Scotch hamburgers and fries. ⊕ *www.byronhamburgers.com.*

✕ **Café Rouge:** A classic 28-strong French bistro chain that's been around for eons and does great prix-fixe deals—so "uncool" that it's now almost fashionable. ⊕ *www.caferouge.co.uk.*

✕ **Carluccio's Caffè:** The Carluccio's chain of 11 all-day Italian café/bar/food shops are freshly sourced, family-friendly, and make brilliant pasta and salad stops on a shopping spree. ⊕ *www.carluccios.com.*

✕ **Ed's Easy Diner:** Overdose on shakes and made-to-order hamburgers at this chain of shiny, retro '50s-theme American diners. ⊕ *www.edseasydiner.co.uk.*

✕ **Le Pain Quotidien:** Try tartine open sandwiches or baguettes and salads at the communal tables. There are 12 branches, including at Eurostar's stunning St. Pancras station. ⊕ *www.lepainquotidien.co.uk.*

✕ **Pizza Express:** Serving classic thin-crust pizzas, Pizza Express is everywhere (there are nearly 100 in London). The Soho branch has a live jazz program. ⊕ *www.pizzaexpress.com.*

✕ **Pret A Manger:** London's high-street take-out supremo isn't just for store-made sandwiches: there are wraps, noodles, baguettes, sushi, salads, fruit, juices, and tea cakes, too. ⊕ *www.pret.com.*

✕ **Ranoush Juice Bar:** Shawarma kebabs are the draw at these mirrored late-night kebab and juice bars (open 8 AM to 3 AM daily). They also serve falafel, meze, and tabbouleh. ⊕ *www.maroush.com.*

✕ **Strada:** Stop at this 27-strong chain for authentic hand-stretched pizzas baked over a wood fire, plus classic pastas, steaks, and risottos. It's cheap, stylish, and packed. ⊕ *www.strada.co.uk.*

✕ **Tootsies:** This superior burger joint does yummy grilled burgers, fries, salads, steaks, BLTs, and chicken spreads. It's family-friendly, with a children's meal for £5.95. ⊕ *www.tootsiesrestaurants.com.*

✕ **Wagamama:** Londoners drain bowls of noodle soup at this child-friendly chain of high-tech, high-turnover, high-volume Japanese communal canteens. ⊕ *www.wagamama.com.*

SOUTH BANK

££–£££
MODERN BRITISH
Fodor's Choice
★

✕ **Anchor & Hope.** Great things at friendly prices come from the open kitchen at this permanently packed, no-reservations, leading gastropub on the Cut in Waterloo: pot-roast duck stands out. It's cramped, informal, and highly original, and there are great dishes for groups, like slow-roasted leg of lamb. Expect to share a table, too. ✉ *36 The Cut,*

South Bank ☎ *020/7928–9898* ⌾ *Reservations not accepted* ⊏ *MC, V* Ⓤ *Waterloo, Southwark* ✛ *F4.*

£££
MODERN FRENCH
✕ **Chez Bruce**. Gutsy French cuisine, perfect service, and a neighborhood vibe make for one of London's favorite restaurants. Take the overland train south of the river to this cozy haunt overlooking Wandsworth Common and expect wonders ranging from old-fashioned braises and daubes to delicious offal and lighter, simply grilled fish dishes. Saddle of rabbit or roast cod and gremolata are immaculately done. The wines are great, the sommelier is superb, and all in all it's hard to beat. ⊠ *2 Bellevue Rd., Wandsworth* ☎ *020/8672–0114* ⊕ *www.chezbruce.co.uk* ⌾ *Reservations essential* ⊟ *AE, DC, MC, V* ✛ *B6.*

££
MODERN BRITISH
✕ **Magdalen**. South of the river between London and Tower bridges, and a hop from the London Assembly headquarters, Magdalen is a beacon of class in an otherwise dowdy part of town. It majors in inventive Modern British cuisine at keen prices; grilled venison (£8), Welsh lamb and chard (£16), lemon sole (£18), and Eton Mess (£5.50) will hardly break the bank. With civilized dark-wood and aubergine surroundings, sit back with a clever 70 bottle wine list that carries 11 by the carafe. ⊠ *152 Tooley St., South Bank* ☎ *020/7403–1342* ⊕ *www.magdalenrestaurant.co.uk* ⊟ *AE, MC, V* ⊘ *No lunch Sat. Closed Sun.* Ⓤ *London Bridge* ✛ *H4.*

PUBS AND AFTERNOON TEA

PUBS

The city's pubs, public houses, or "locals" dispense beer, good cheer, and casual grub in settings that range from ancient wood-beam rooms to ornate Victorian interiors to utilitarian modern rooms. Pubs in the capital are changing: 90-year-old licensing laws have finally been modernized, gastro-pub fever is sweeping London, and smoking in all pubs has been illegal since 2007. At many places, char-grills are being installed in the kitchen out back, and up front the faded wallpapers are being replaced by abstract paintings. The best of these luxe pubs are reviewed above. Some of the following also showcase nouveau pub grub, but whether you have Moroccan chicken or the usually dismal ploughman's special, do order a pint. Note that American-style beer is called "lager" in Britain, whereas the real British brew is "bitter" (usually served warm). Order up your choice in two sizes—pints or half pints. Some London pubs also sell "real ale," which is less gassy than bitters and, many would argue, has a better flavor.

The list below offers a few pubs selected for central location, historical interest, a pleasant garden, music, or good food, but you might just as happily adopt your own temporary local.

✕ **Black Friar**. A step from Blackfriars Tube stop, this spectacular pub has an Arts-and-Crafts interior that is entertainingly, satirically ecclesiastical, with inlaid mother-of-pearl, wood carvings, stained glass, and marble pillars all over the place. In spite of the finely lettered temperance tracts on view just below the reliefs of monks, fairies, and friars, there is a nice group of ales on tap from independent brewers. ✉ *174 Queen Victoria St., The City* ☎ *020/7236–5474* Ⓤ *Blackfriars.*

Fodor's Choice ★ ✕ **Jerusalem Tavern.** Owned by the well-respected St. Peter's Brewery from Suffolk, the Jerusalem Tavern is one-of-a-kind, small and endearingly eccentric. Ancient Delft-style tiles meld with wood and concrete in a converted watchmaker and jeweler's shop dating back to the 18th century. The beer, both bottled and on tap, is some of the best available anywhere in London. It's often busy, especially after work. ✉ *55 Britton St., Clerkenwell* ☎ *020/7490–4281* Ⓤ *Farringdon.*

★ ✕ **The Lamb.** Charles Dickens and his contemporaries drank here, but today's enthusiastic clientele make sure this intimate pub avoids the pitfalls of feeling too old-fashioned. For private chats at the bar, you can close the delicate etched-glass "snob screen" to the bar staff, opening it only when you fancy another pint. ✉ *94 Lamb's Conduit St., Bloomsbury* ☎ *020/7405–0713* Ⓤ *Russell Sq.*

✕ **Lamb & Flag.** This refreshingly un-gentrified 17th-century pub was once known as the Bucket of Blood because the upstairs room was used as a ring for bare-knuckle boxing. Now it's a friendly—and bloodless—pub, serving food (lunch only) and real ale. It's on the edge of Covent Garden, off Garrick Street. ✉ *33 Rose St., Covent Garden* ☎ *020/7497–9504* Ⓤ *Covent Garden.*

✕ **Mayflower.** An atmospheric 17th-century riverside inn with exposed beams and a terrace, this is practically the very place from which the Pilgrims set sail for Plymouth Rock. ✉ *117 Rotherhithe St., South Bank* ☎ *020/7237–4088* Ⓤ *Rotherhithe.*

★ ✕ **Museum Tavern.** Across the street from the British Museum, this friendly and classy Victorian pub makes an ideal resting place after the rigors of the culture trail. Karl Marx unwound here after a hard day in the Library. He could have spent his *Kapital* on any of seven well-kept beers available on tap. ✉ *49 Great Russell St., Bloomsbury* ☎ *020/7242–8987* Ⓤ *Tottenham Court Rd.*

✕ **Prospect of Whitby.** Named after a ship, this is London's oldest riverside pub, dating from around 1520. Once upon a time it was called the Devil's Tavern because of the lowlife criminals—thieves and smugglers—who congregated here. Ornamented with pewter ware and nautical objects, this much-loved "boozer" is often pointed out from boat trips up the Thames. ✉ *57 Wapping Wall, East End* ☎ *020/7481–1095* Ⓤ *Wapping.*

✕ **Sherlock Holmes.** This pub used to be known as the Northumberland Arms, and Arthur Conan Doyle popped in regularly for a pint, in the days before old black-and-white Basil Rathbone films played on loop on the pub's television. It figures in *The Hound of the Baskervilles,* and you can see the hound's supposed head and plaster casts of its huge paws among other Holmes "memorabilia" in the bar. Even if you're not a Conan Doyle fan, the beer is excellent. ✉ *10 Northumberland St., Trafalgar Square* ☎ *020/7930–2644* Ⓤ *Charing Cross.*

★ ✕ **White Hart.** This elegant, family-owned pub on Drury Lane is one of the best places to mix with cast and crew of the stage. A female-friendly environment, a cheery skylight above the lounge area, a late license, and above-average pub fare make the White Hart a particularly sociable spot for a drink. ⌧ *191 Drury La., Covent Garden* ☎ *020/7242–2317* Ⓤ *Holborn.*

Fodor's Choice   ✕ **White Horse.** This pub in well-to-do Parson's Green has a superb menu
★   with a beer or wine chosen to match each dish. Open early for weekend
brunch, the "Sloaney Pony" (named for its wealthy Sloane Square clientele) is enormously popular and a place to find many a Hugh Grant and
Liz Hurley look-alike. In the summer delicious barbecues are rustled up
on the patio. The owner is an expert on cask-conditioned ale, with as
many as 20 on tap, and there are more than 70 wines. ⌧ *1–3 Parson's
Green, Parson's Green* ☎ *020/7736–2115* Ⓤ *Parson's Green.*

✕ **Ye Olde Cheshire Cheese.** Yes, it's a tourist trap, but it's also an extremely
historic pub (it dates from 1667, the year after the Great Fire of London), and it deserves a visit for its sawdust-covered floors, low woodbeam ceilings, and the 14th-century crypt of Whitefriars' monastery
under the cellar bar. But if you want to see the set of 17th-century pornographic tiles that once adorned the upstairs, go to Blacks Museum.
This was the most regular of Dr. Johnson's and Dickens's *many* locals.
⌧ *145 Fleet St., The City* ☎ *020/7353–6170* Ⓤ *Blackfriars.*

AFTERNOON TEA

The English afternoon tea ritual has been quietly brewing among London polite society. Perhaps it's an anti-Starbucks thing, but nevertheless,
it is now ever so fashionable to take afternoon tea—and preferably in
the warm embrace of an established hotel tea salon.

So, what is afternoon tea, exactly? Well, it means real tea (English
Breakfast, Ceylon, Indian, or Chinese—and preferably loose leaf)
brewed in a china pot, and usually served with china cups and saucers
and silver spoons any time between 3 and 5:30 PM daily. In particularly
grand places—such as some bigger hotels—there should be elegant finger foods on a three-tier silver tea stand: bread and butter, and crustless
cucumber, watercress, and egg sandwiches on the bottom; scones with
clotted cream and strawberry preserve in the middle; and rich fruitcake
and fancies on top.

Dress is smart casual in posh hotels. Make reservations for all these
below.

✕ **Brown's Hotel.** This classic Mayfair town-house hotel sets the standard at the English Tea Room, where one of London's best-known
afternoon teas is served (£35–£48). ⌧ *33 Albermarle St., Mayfair*
☎ *020/7493–6020* ▭ *AE, DC, MC, V* ⊙ *Tea weekdays 3–6, weekends 1–6* Ⓤ *Green Park.*

✕ **Café at Sotheby's.** What could be better than perusing the famous
Mayfair auction house before afternoon tea? It's open from 9:30 AM
and tends to book up days in advance. Teas are available from £6.50
to £18.75, including toasted tea cakes, scones, and Welsh rarebit. ⌧ *Sotheby's, 34 New Bond St., Mayfair* ☎ *020/7293–5077* ⚲ *Reservations
essential* ▭ *AE, DC, MC, V* ⊙ *Tea weekdays 3–4:45* Ⓤ *Green Park.*

✕ **The Dorchester.** Amid a maze of marble and gold leaf, afternoon tea in
the Promenade is best taken on comfy sofas and to the sound of the resident pianist. Teas are £33.50, £48.50, or £60 for high tea—with light

bites like salmon and Cromer crab. Book well ahead. ⊠ *53 Park La.* ☎ *020/7629–8888* ⌕ *Reservations essential* ▤ *AE, DC, MC, V* ⊙ *Tea daily 2:30 and 4:45* Ⓤ *Hyde Park Corner.*

✕ **Fortnum & Mason.** Upstairs at the revamped 300-year-old Queen's grocers, three set teas are ceremoniously served: afternoon tea (sandwiches, scones, and cakes: £32), old-fashioned high tea (the traditional nursery meal, with scrambled eggs and salmon: £34), and champagne tea (£42). ⊠ *St. James's Restaurant, 4th fl., 181 Piccadilly, St. James's* ☎ *020/7734–8040* ▤ *AE, DC, MC, V* ⊙ *Tea Mon.–Sat. 2–7, Sun. noon–5* Ⓤ *Green Park.*

✕ **The Ritz.** At the Ritz tea is served in the impressive Palm Court, with marble tables and Louis XIV chaises complete with musical accompaniment, giving the last morsel of Edwardian London. Afternoon tea is £37 and champagne tea £48. Reserve at least four weeks ahead and remember to wear a jacket and tie. ⊠ *150 Piccadilly, St. James's* ☎ *020/7300–2309* ⌕ *Reservations essential* ▤ *AE, MC, V* ⊙ *Tea daily 11:30, 1:30, 3:30, 5:30, 7:30* Ⓤ *Green Park.*

✕ **The Wolsely.** This bustling art deco tea salon was inspired by the grand Viennese cafés. Cream teas are well priced at £9.75 or £19.75; you'll find Vienna opera cake and mini-mousse fancies. ⊠ *160 Piccadilly, St. James's* ☎ *020/7499–6996* ⌕ *Reservations essential* ▤ *AE, DC, MC, V* ⊙ *Tea Mon.–Sat. 3:30–5:30, Sun. 3:30–6:30* Ⓤ *Green Park.*

WHERE TO STAY

Use the coordinate (⊹ B2) at the end of each listing to locate a site on the corresponding map.

You'll find many things in London hotels: luxury, extraordinary service, and incredible views. But rooms have traditionally been expensive, and the wild swings of the exchange rate make it hard to predict just how much you'll end up paying. Meanwhile, five-star hotels close, renovate, and reopen with increased prices. If it's any consolation, London does luxury better than just about any city, so you'll get your money's worth.

For those on more moderate budgets, the situation is in transition. The city is still struggling to develop a solid base of moderately priced high-quality hotels. Two places that have opened in recent years—the Hoxton and Guesthouse West—are great options in this category. A newly attractive alternative are hotels in the Premier and Millennium chains, which offer sleek, modern rooms, modern conveniences, and sales that frequently bring room prices well below £100 a night. The Best Western Premier Shaftesbury Kensington and Millennium Gloucester are both good examples.

At the budget level, small bed-and-breakfasts still dominate, although most are quite battered and basic. An alternative to that is the easyHotel chain, with its tiny, bright orange "pod" rooms. There's also the more sophisticated base2stay, which falls somewhere between budget and not so much. And even at the very bottom of the price scale, accommodations can be unexpectedly trendy—just look at the slick simplicity of the Generator hostel.

Wherever you decide to stay, do reserve in advance. London is popular, and special events can fill hotels suddenly.

WHICH NEIGHBORHOOD?

Where you stay can affect your experience. The West End is equivalent to downtown, but there's a big difference between, say, posh Park Lane and bustling, touristy Leicester Square. Hotels in Mayfair and St. James's are central and yet distant in both mileage and sensibility from funky, youthful neighborhoods such as Notting Hill and from major tourist sights such as the Tower of London, St. Paul's Cathedral, and the Kensington museums. On the edges of the West End, Soho and Covent Garden are crammed with eateries and entertainment options. South Kensington, Kensington, Chelsea, and Knightsbridge are patrician and peaceful, which will give you a more homey feeling than anything in the West End; Belgravia is super elegant. From Bloomsbury it's a stroll to the shops and restaurants of Covent Garden, to Theatreland, and to the British Museum; Hampstead and Islington are close enough to explore easily, too. Bayswater is an affordable haven north of Hyde Park. The South Bank, with all its cultural attractions, is an affordable option.

PRICES AND MONEY-SAVING OPTIONS

London is expensive, and in the £££££ category you can often pay considerably more than £300 per room. Finding a cheap but tolerable double room is a real coup. Look around Russell Square in Bloomsbury, around Victoria and King's Cross stations, on the South Bank, in Bayswater or Earl's Court, or farther out in Shepherd's Bush. Your cheapest option is a pod hotel, a B&B, or a dorm bed in a hostel; but apartments are an increasingly popular choice. *For other suggestions, see Accommodations in Travel Smart England.*

University residence halls offer a cheap alternative during university vacation periods. Whatever the price, *don't* expect a room that's large by American standards. **City University Hall of Residence: Walter Sickert Hall** (✉ *Graham St.* ☎ *020/7040–8822* ⊕ *www.city.ac.uk/ems*) starts at £20 per person year-round, and gives you access to kitchen facilities. **London School of Economics Vacations** (☎ *020/7955–7575* ⊕ *www.lsevacations. co.uk*) starts at £45 for a double without a private bathroom and £53 for a double with one. You can choose from a variety of rooms in their five halls of residence around London. **University College London** (✉ *Residence Manager, Campbell House, 5–10 Taviton St.* ☎ *020/7679–1479* ⊕ *www.ucl.ac.uk*) starts at £45 for a double and is open from mid-June to mid-September.

In any event, you should confirm *exactly* what your room costs before checking in. British hotels are obliged by law to display a price chart at the reception desk; study it carefully. In January and February you can often find reduced rates, and large hotels with a business clientele have frequent weekend packages. The usual practice these days in all but the cheaper hotels is for quoted prices to cover room alone; breakfast, whether continental or "full English," costs extra. V.A.T. (Value Added Tax—sales tax) follows the same rule, with the most expensive hotels excluding a hefty 17.5%; middle-of-the-range and budget places include it in the initial quote.

BEST BETS FOR LONDON LODGING

Fodor's offers a selective listing of quality lodging experiences at every price range, from the city's best budget motel to its most sophisticated luxury hotel. Here, we've compiled our top recommendations by price and experience. The very best properties—in other words, those that provide a particularly remarkable experience in their price range—are designated in the listings with the Fodor's Choice logo.

Fodor's Choice ★

Mandarin Oriental Hyde Park, £££££ p. 121
One Aldwych, £££££ p. 113
Zetter Rooms, £££–££££ p. 113

Best by Price

£

easyHotel, p. 118
The Generator, p. 109

££

B&B Belgravia, p. 124
base2stay, p. 118
Premier Travel Inn County Hall, p. 123

£££

Athenaeum Hotel and Apartments, p. 121
Best Western Premier Shaftesbury Kensington, p. 118

Guesthouse West, p. 107
The Hoxton, p. 114
Millennium Gloucester, p. 119
Number Sixteen, p. 119
Zetter Rooms, p. 113

££££

Claridge's, p. 122
The Levin, p. 120
The Rookery, p. 115

£££££

Covent Garden Hotel, p. 113
The Dorchester, p. 122
Mandarin Oriental Hyde Park, p. 121
One Aldwych, p. 113

Best by Experience

BEST SPAS

One Aldwych, £££££ p. 113

Claridge's, ££££–£££££ p. 122
Mandarin Oriental, £££££ p. 121

BEST HISTORIC HOTELS

Claridge's, ££££–£££££ p. 122
The Dorchester, £££££ p. 122
The Rookery, ££££ p. 115

BUSINESS TRAVELERS

Ramada Hotel and Suites Docklands, £££ p. 115
Millennium Gloucester, £££ p. 119
Zetter Rooms, £££–££££ p. 113

BEST CONCIERGE

The Dorchester, £££££ p. 122
Mandarin Oriental Hyde Park, £££££ p. 121

Claridge's, ££££–£££££ p. 122

MOST ROMANTIC

Number Sixteen, £££–££££ p. 119
The Rookery, ££££ p. 115
The Gore, ££££–£££££ p. 118

MOST KID-FRIENDLY

Astons Apartments, ££–£££ p. 115
City Inn Westminster, ££££ p. 124
Trafalgar Hilton, ££££ p. 114
Premier Travel Inn County Hall, ££ p. 123

	WHAT IT COSTS IN POUNDS				
	£	££	£££	££££	£££££
FOR TWO PEOPLE	under £80	£80–£140	£141–£200	£201–£300	over £300

Prices are for a standard double room in high season, including V.A.T., with no meals or, if indicated, CP (with Continental breakfast), BP (Breakfast Plan, with full breakfast), or MAP (Modified American Plan, with breakfast and dinner).

BAYSWATER, NOTTING HILL, AND SHEPHERD'S BUSH

£££ **Guesthouse West.** This hip hotel offers high-class chic at moderate prices. They almost get it right. The minimalist decor and technology—cool black-and-white photos and flat-screen TVs—are stylish. Rooms, however, are truly tiny, and there's no room service. The child-friendly restaurant is packed with locals, and the bar is a beautiful homage to the 1930s. The hotel's relationship with a local spa provides guests with discounts, and there are guaranteed seats for shows at the small Gate Theatre. **Pros:** sophisticated decor; lots of gadgets. **Cons:** a bit out of the way; tiny rooms; no room service. ✉ *163–165 Westbourne Grove, Notting Hill* ☎ *020/7792–9800* 🌐 *www.guesthousewest.com* *20 rooms* *In-room: a/c, DVD, Wi-Fi. In-hotel: restaurant, bar, parking (paid)* *AE, MC, V* Ⓤ *Notting Hill Gate* ✣ *A3.*

£££–££££ **K West.** The proudly edgy K West is hidden away inside a featureless glass-and-steel building near the Shepherd's Bush Tube stop, just outside Notting Hill. This is a grown-up place popular with business types and young couples, and *not* geared toward families with kids. Suites have two-person baths and drawers with "adult entertainment" supplies. Dark wood, soft suede, and sleek beige walls combine to create a designer look in the bedrooms. And the minimalist style extends to the all-white hotel bar, dubbed the K Lounge, and the hotel restaurant "Kanteen." **Pros:** sleek, modern decor; funky attitude. **Cons:** a bit off the tourist track; not for kids. ✉ *Richmond Way, Shepherd's Bush* ☎ *020/8008–6600* 🌐 *www.k-west.co.uk* *216 rooms, 6 suites* *In-room: a/c, safe, DVD, Wi-Fi. In-hotel: restaurant, room service, bar, gym, spa, laundry service, Internet terminals (free), parking (paid)* *AE, DC, MC, V* *CP* Ⓤ *Shepherd's Bush* ✣ *A4.*

££–£££ **Main House.** A brass lion door knocker marks Main House's Victorian front door, typical of Notting Hill. With just four rooms, this hotel offers nothing but a good night's sleep in a Victorian home. Furnished with clean white linens, polished wood floors, modern furniture, and Asian art, it is uncluttered and delightfully spacious. The tiny urban terrace is a great place for stargazing or reading the morning paper. A day rate at the local health club is available, too. **Pros:** unusual option; great location. **Cons:** few rooms mean it books up far in advance; no room service. ✉ *6 Colvile Rd., Notting Hill* ☎ *020/7221–9691* 🌐 *www.themainhouse.com* *4 rooms* *In-room: a/c (some), Wi-Fi (some). In-hotel: bicycles, laundry service, parking (paid)* *MC, V* *CP* Ⓤ *Notting Hill Gate* ✣ *A3.*

££–£££ ⊡ **Portobello Gold.** This no-frills B&B in the heart of the Portobello Road antiques area is on the floor above the pub and restaurant of the same name. Flat-screen TVs are mounted on the wall, and the beds take up almost the entire tiny room in the doubles. The best of the bunch is the split-level apartment (£££—sleeps six) with roof terrace, small kitchen, and soothing aquarium. The casual restaurant serves international food and has a great wine list, all at reasonable prices. There's free Wi-Fi in guest rooms as well as an Internet café that charges £1 per half hour. **Pros:** great location; free Internet access in rooms. **Cons:** rooms are tiny; no elevator. ⊠ *95–97 Portobello Rd., Notting Hill* ☎ *020/7460–4910* ⊕ *www.portobellogold.com* ↻ *6 rooms, 1 apartment* ⅗ *In-room: a/c, Wi-Fi. In-hotel: restaurant, room service, bar* ▭ *MC, V* ⅞ *CP* Ⓤ *Notting Hill Gate* ✛ *A3.*

££–£££ ⊡ **Space Apart.** This Georgian hotel near Hyde Park is a great find. Its 30 studio apartments have all been recently renovated in stellar style. Each is done in soothing tones of white and gray, with polished wood floors and attractive modern kitchenettes equipped with all you need to make small meals. The standard rooms are quite small, but premium rooms cost only £20 more and give you much more space to play with. Bathrooms are new and modern, although they are not big. The location is handy, and the value for money here is really impressive. **Pros:** the price is right; the larger suites have space for four people. **Cons:** no in-house restaurant or bar; minimum two-night stay required. ⊠ *32–37 Kensington Gardens Square, Bayswater* ☎ *0207/908–1340* ⊕ *www. aparthotel-london.co.uk* ↻ *30 rooms* ⅗ *In-room: a/c, no phone, kitchen, refrigerator, Internet* ▭ *MC, V* Ⓜ *Bayswater* ✛ *A3.*

££ ⊡ **Vancouver Studios.** This little hotel in a heritage-listed Victorian town house is perfect for those wanting a home away from home. All rooms are like efficiency apartments, with mini-kitchens and microwaves, and you can even preorder groceries, which are stocked in your mini-refrigerator upon arrival. Each studio has daily maid service as well as room service. Some rooms have working fireplaces, and one opens onto the leafy, paved garden. **Pros:** more space than a hotel room; unique little apartments. **Cons:** a bit out of the way; a bargain only if several people share the space. ⊠ *30 Prince's Sq., Bayswater* ☎ *020/7243–1270* ⊕ *www.vancouverstudios.co.uk* ↻ *45 studios* ⅗ *In-room: no a/c, kitchen, refrigerator, DVD, Wi-Fi. In-hotel: room service, bar, laundry facilities, laundry service, parking (paid)* ▭ *AE, DC, MC, V* Ⓤ *Bayswater, Queensway* ✛ *A3.*

BLOOMSBURY, HAMPSTEAD, AND HOLBORN

£ ⊡ **Alhambra Hotel.** One of the best bargains in Bloomsbury, this family-run hotel has singles as low as £50 and doubles as low as £60. Rooms are small and the look is dated, but they're definitely good value. All rooms have a TV, all guests have access to free Wi-Fi, and tea/coffee-makers are available on request. It's not fancy, but it certainly is cheap. **Pros:** low price; great location. **Cons:** decor's a bit old-fashioned; no frills here. ⊠ *17–19 Argyle St., Bloomsbury* ☎ *020/7837–9575* ⊕ *www. alhambrahotel.com* ↻ *52 rooms* ⅗ *In-room: no a/c, no phone, Wi-Fi. In-hotel: parking (paid)* ▭ *AE, MC, V* ⅞ *BP* Ⓤ *King's Cross* ✛ *G1.*

££–£££   ⊡ **The Buckingham.** This Georgian town house near Russell Square is a great bargain for the money. Its spacious, well-designed rooms are all studios and suites. Each has its own tiny kitchenette, giving you an alternative to eating in restaurants every night. All have marble-and-granite bathrooms and plenty of amenities. Staff are friendly, and the location is an easy walk from the British Museum and Covent Garden. **Pros:** great location; small kitchens free you from restaurants. **Cons:** no room service. ⊠ *11–13 Bayley St., Bedford Sq., Bloomsbury* ☎ *020/7636–2474* ⊕ *www.grangehotels.com* ⇆ *17 rooms* ♿ *In-room: no a/c, Internet. In-hotel: bar* ☰ *MC, V* Ⓤ *Tottenham Court Rd.* ✛ *F2.*

££££–£££££   ⊡ **Charlotte Street Hotel.** On a busy street in the media hub around Soho, this hotel fuses the modern and traditional with real style. Bedrooms are beautifully decorated with unique printed fabrics by designer and owner Kit Kemp. Each bathroom is lined with gleaming granite and oak, with walk-in showers and deep baths, and a flat-screen TV so you can catch up on the news while you soak with exclusive products by London perfumer Miller Harris. The restaurant, Oscar, is excellent for European cuisine, and the bar is a trendy local hangout. There's a public screening room for the Sunday-night dinner-and-film club or you might want to read a paper by the fire in the spacious drawing room. **Pros:** elegant, luxurious; great location. **Cons:** the popular bar can be noisy; reservations are necessary for the restaurant. ⊠ *15 Charlotte St., Bloomsbury* ☎ *020/7806–2000; 800/553–6674 in U.S.* ⊕ *www.charlottestreethotel. com* ⇆ *44 rooms, 8 suites* ♿ *In-room: safe, refrigerator, DVD, Wi-Fi. In-hotel: restaurant, room service, bar, gym, laundry service* ☰ *AE, DC, MC, V* Ⓤ *Goodge St.* ✛ *E2.*

££   ⊡ **Crescent Hotel.** Located on one of Bloomsbury's grand old squares, the Crescent is a friendly, attractive B&B. Rooms are small and simply decorated in cheery colors, and breakfast is big and hearty. Bathrooms are tiny and utilitarian—some have a bath and shower, others only a bath, so if you have a preference, ask when you book. You can use the tennis courts and private gardens in the square—great for picnics on a sunny day. **Pros:** lovely, convenient location; friendly staff. **Cons:** basic decor; no elevator. ⊠ *49–50 Cartright Gardens, Bloomsbury* ☎ *020/7383–2054* ⊕ *www.crescenthoteloflondon.com* ⇆ *27 rooms, 10 with bath* ♿ *In-room: no a/c, Internet. In-hotel: tennis court* ☰ *MC, V* ⊠ *BP* Ⓤ *Russell Sq.* ✛ *F1.*

£   ⊡ **The Generator.** This is where the young, enthusiastic traveler comes to find fellow partyers. It's also the cleverest youth hostel in town. Set in a former police barracks, the decor makes the most of the bunk beds and dim lighting. The Internet café provides handy brochures. The Generator Bar has cheap drinks and a rowdy crowd, and the Fuel Stop cafeteria provides inexpensive meals. There are singles, twins, and dormitory rooms, each with a washbasin, locker, and free bed linens. Prices run from £20 to £35 per person. **Pros:** funky, youthful attitude; great location. **Cons:** bar is crowded and noisy; party atmosphere is not for everyone. ⊠ *MacNaghten House, Compton Pl. off 37 Tavistock Pl., Bloomsbury* ☎ *020/7388–7666* ⊕ *www.generatorhostels.com* ⇆ *214 beds* ♿ *In-room: no a/c, no phone, no TV. In-hotel: restaurant, bars, Internet terminal, parking (paid)* ☰ *MC, V* ⊠ *CP* Ⓤ *Russell Sq.* ✛ *F1.*

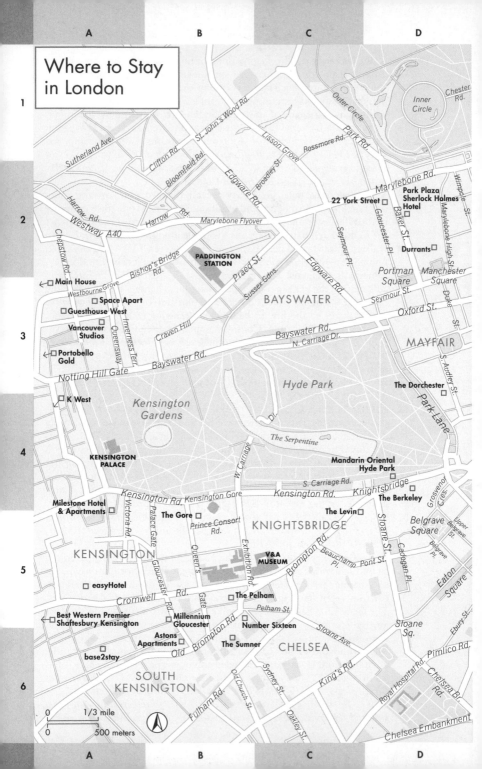

Where to Stay in London

A   **B**   **C**   **D**

1

Inner Circle

Chester Rd.

Outer Circle

St. John's Wood Rd.

Sutherland Ave.

Clifton Rd.

Bloomfield Rd.

Broadley St.

Lisson Grove

Rossmore Rd.

Park Rd.

Wimpole St.

Marylebone Rd.

Park Plaza Sherlock Holmes Hotel □

22 York Street □

Baker St.

Gloucester Pl.

Seymour Pl.

Marylebone High St.

2

Harrow Rd.

Westway A40

Harrow Rd.

Marylebone Flyover

Edgware Rd.

Durrants □

Portman Square

Manchester Square

Chepstow Rd.

Bishop's Bridge Rd.

PADDINGTON STATION

Praed St.

Sussex Gdns.

Edgware Rd.

Seymour St.

Oxford St.

Duke St.

← □ **Main House**

Westbourne Grove

□ **Space Apart**

□ **Guesthouse West**

□ **Vancouver Studios**

Inverness Terr.

Queensway

Craven Hill

BAYSWATER

MAYFAIR

3

← □ **Portobello Gold**

Notting Hill Gate

Bayswater Rd.

Bayswater Rd.

N. Carriage Dr.

Hyde Park

The Dorchester □

S. Audley St.

Park Lane

□ **K West**

Kensington Gardens

The Serpentine

4

KENSINGTON PALACE

W. Carriage Dr.

Mandarin Oriental Hyde Park □

S. Carriage Rd.

Kensington Rd.

Knightsbridge

Grosvenor Cres.

Belgrave Square

Upper Belgrave St.

Milestone Hotel & Apartments □

Kensington Rd.

Kensington Gore

The Gore □

Prince Consort Rd.

Victoria Rd.

Palace Gate

The Berkeley □

The Levin □

KNIGHTSBRIDGE

Sloane St.

Belgrave Pl.

Cadogan Pl.

Eaton Square

5

KENSINGTON

Gloucester Rd.

Queen's Gate

Exhibition Rd.

V&A MUSEUM

Brompton Rd.

Beauchamp Pl.

Pont St.

Sloane Sq.

Ebury St.

□ **easyHotel**

Cromwell Rd.

□ **The Pelham**

Pelham St.

Best Western Premier Shaftesbury Kensington □

□ **Millennium Gloucester**

□ **Number Sixteen**

Sloane Ave.

Astons Apartments □

Brompton Rd.

□ **The Sumner**

CHELSEA

Pimlico Rd.

Royal Hospital Rd.

Chelsea Br. Rd.

6

□ **base2stay**

Old Brompton Rd.

SOUTH KENSINGTON

Fulham Rd.

Old Church St.

Sydney St.

King's Rd.

Oakley St.

Chelsea Embankment

0   1/3 mile

0   500 meters

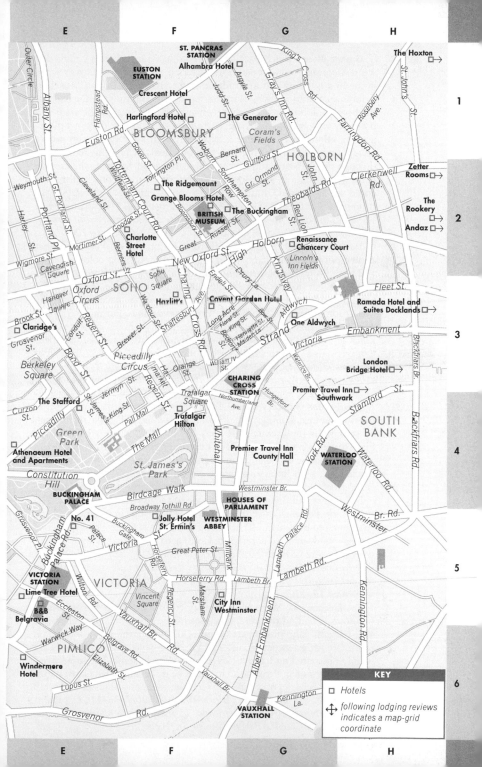

££–£££ 🖫 **Grange Blooms Hotel.** Part of the reliable Grange hotels chain, this white Georgian town-house hotel offers a pleasant home away from home in a building just around the corner from the British Museum. Rooms are not too tiny by London standards, and those in the back of the hotel look out onto a leafy green garden. Decor in public areas is a bit stuffy with bright carpeting, curtains, and sofas, but only in a pleasant, traditional way. Service is excellent, with a concierge and porter always on hand to help. You can get good deals by booking in advance through the Web site, and on the whole, it's good value for the money. **Pros:** great location; good prices if you book early. **Cons:** bathrooms could use an upgrade; outdated decor; no elevator. ⊠ *7 Montague St., Bloomsbury* ☎ *020/7323–1717* ⊕ *www.grangehotels.com* ⤳ *26 rooms, 1 suite* ⚿ *In-room: no a/c, Internet. In-hotel: restaurant, room service, bar, some pets allowed* ☰ *AE, DC, MC, V* Ⓤ *Russell Sq.* ✛ *F2.*

££ 🖫 **Harlingford Hotel.** The Harlingford is by far the sleekest and most contemporary of the Cartwright Gardens hotels. Bold color schemes and beautifully tiled bathrooms enliven the family-run place. Bedrooms aren't big, but they're attractive, quiet, and comfortable. Public rooms are similarly small but perfectly appointed. With space for four, the quad rooms are a good choice for traveling families. For those who tire of eggs and sausage every morning, the hotel promises a choice of 10 kinds of cereal. **Pros:** good location; friendly staff; breakfast included. **Cons:** rooms are quite small; bathrooms are tiny. ⊠ *61–63 Cartwright Gardens, Bloomsbury* ☎ *020/7387–1551* ⊕ *www.harlingfordhotel.com* ⤳ *43 rooms* ⚿ *In-room: no a/c, Internet. In-hotel: bar, tennis court* ☰ *AE, DC, MC, V* ⦿*BP* Ⓤ *Russell Sq.* ✛ *F1.*

£££££ 🖫 **Renaissance Chancery Court.** This landmark structure, built by the Pearl Assurance Company in 1914, houses a beautiful Marriott hotel. So striking is the architecture that the building was featured in the film *Howards End.* The spacious bedrooms are popular with business travelers and the decor has a masculine edge—lots of leather and dark-red fabrics, with luxurious mattresses. The day spa in the basement is a peaceful cocoon. There's marble everywhere, from the floors in public spaces and the massive staircase to the in-room bathrooms. The restaurant, Pearl, is known for its Modern European cuisine, and the bar, in an old banking hall, has elegant soaring ceilings. **Pros:** gorgeous space; your every need catered to. **Cons:** area is deserted at night and on weekends. ⊠ *252 High Holborn, Holborn* ☎ *020/7829–9888* ⊕ *www.marriott.com* ⤳ *343 rooms, 14 suites* ⚿ *In-room: a/c, safe, refrigerator, Internet. In-hotel: restaurant, room service, bar, gym, spa, laundry service* ☰ *AE, MC, V* Ⓤ *Holborn* ✛ *G2.*

£ 🖫 **The Ridgemount.** Mere blocks away from the British Museum and London's West End theaters, this guesthouse has clean and neat rooms at a bargain. The public areas, especially the family-style breakfast room, are rather sweetly cluttered Victorian-style parlors. Rooms are plainly decorated and not all have private bathrooms, but some overlook a leafy garden. **Pros:** good location near the museums. **Cons:** guest-room decor is basic; no customer services; cheapest rooms have shared bathrooms. ⊠ *65 Gower St., Bloomsbury* ☎ *020/7636–1141* ⊕ *www.ridgemounthotel.co.uk* ⤳ *32 rooms, 15 with bath* ⚿ *In-room: no a/c, no phone* ☰ *MC, V* ⦿*BP* Ⓤ *Goodge St.* ✛ *F2.*

£££–££££ ⊞ **Zetter Rooms.** By day, nothing but business suits buzz through the
Fodor's Choice area between Holborn and Clerkenwell. By night, though, the ties are
★ loosened and it's all oh-so-trendy. One of London's latest "it" hotels,
Zetter reflects both personalities. The dizzying five-story atrium, art
deco staircase, and slick European restaurant are your first indications
of what to expect at this converted warehouse: a breath of fresh air
(and a little space) in London's mostly Victorian hotel scene. Rooms are
smoothly done up in soft dove gray and vanilla fabrics, and the views
of the city from the higher floors are wonderful. **Pros:** big rooms; lots
of gadgets; free broadband in rooms. **Cons:** recently increased prices
mean this place is no longer a bargain; rooms with good views cost
more. ⊠ *86–88 Clerkenwell Rd., Holborn* ☎ *020/7324–4444* ⊕ *www.
thezetter.com* ⇄ *59 rooms* ☾ *In-room: a/c, safe, refrigerator, DVD,
Internet. In-hotel: restaurant, room service, bar, laundry service* ⊟ *AE,
MC, V* Ⓤ *Farringdon* ⊹ *H2.*

COVENT GARDEN, PICCADILLY, AND SOHO

£££££ ⊞ **Covent Garden Hotel.** In the midst of boisterous Covent Garden, this
hotel is now the London home-away-from-home for a mélange of off-
duty celebrities, actors, and style mavens. With painted silks, *style
anglais* ottomans, and 19th-century Romantic oils, the public salons are
perfect places to decompress over a glass of sherry from the bar. Guest
rooms are *World of Interiors* stylish, each showcasing matching-but-
mixed couture fabrics to stunning effect. For £35, the popular Saturday-
night film club includes dinner in the brasserie and a film in the deluxe
in-house cinema. **Pros:** great for star-spotting, and movie buffs. **Cons:**
you can feel you don't matter if you're not a film star. ⊠ *10 Monmouth
St., Covent Garden* ☎ *020/7806–1000, 800/553–6674 in U.S.* ⊕ *www.
firmdale.com* ⇄ *55 rooms, 3 suites* ☾ *In-room: a/c, safe, DVD, Wi-Fi.
In-hotel: restaurant, room service, gym, spa, laundry service* ⊟ *AE, MC,
V* Ⓤ *Covent Garden* ⊹ *F3.*

££££ ⊞ **Hazlitt's.** Three connected early-18th-century houses, one of which
was the last home of essayist William Hazlitt (1778–1830), make up
this charming Soho hotel. It's a disarmingly friendly place, full of personality but devoid of certain modern amenities (as the owners say, "In
1718 there were no elevators, and there still aren't"). Robust antiques
are everywhere, most beds are four-posters, and every bathroom has
a Victorian claw-foot tub. There are tiny sitting rooms, wooden staircases, and more restaurants nearby than you could visit in a year. **Pros:**
great for art and antiques lovers; truly beautiful and relaxed. **Cons:**
no in-house restaurant; no elevators. ⊠ *6 Frith St., Soho* ☎ *020/7434–
1771* ⊕ *www.hazlittshotel.com* ⇄ *20 rooms, 3 suites* ☾ *In-room: a/c,
Wi-Fi. In-hotel: room service, laundry service, parking (paid), some pets
allowed* ⊟ *AE, DC, MC, V* Ⓤ *Tottenham Court Rd.* ⊹ *F3.*

£££££ ⊞ **One Aldwych.** An understated blend of contemporary and classic
Fodor's Choice results in pure, modern luxury here. Flawlessly designed inside an
★ Edwardian building, One Aldwych is coolly eclectic, with an artsy
lobby, feather duvets, Italian linen sheets, and ample elegance. It's the
ultimate in 21st-century style, from the free, hotel-wide Wi-Fi, down to
the gorgeous swimming pool in the health club. Suites have amenities

such as a private gym, a kitchen, and a terrace. Breakfast is made with organic ingredients. The pool at One Aldwych has underwater speakers that play music you can hear only when you dive in. **Pros:** understated (and underwater) luxury. **Cons:** all this luxury doesn't come cheap. ⊠ *1 Aldwych, Covent Garden* 🕿 *020/7300–1000* ⊕ *www.onealdwych.co.uk* ✑ *93 rooms, 12 suites* ⌂ *In-room: a/c, safe, kitchen (some), refrigerator, Wi-Fi. In-hotel: 2 restaurants, room service, bars, pool, gym, spa, laundry service, parking (paid)* ☰ *AE, MC, V* Ⓤ *Charing Cross, Covent Garden* ✛ *G3.*

££££   ⊡ **Trafalgar Hilton.** This fresh, contemporary hotel defies the Hilton norm. The rooms here, in either sky-blue or beige color schemes, keep many of the 19th-century office building's original features, and some have floor-to-ceiling windows with extraordinary views of Trafalgar Square and the city. Twenty-one rooms are split-level, with upstairs space for chilling out with a CD or DVD and sleeping space below. Bathrooms have deep baths, full-size toiletries, eye masks, and mini-TVs. Go up to the roof garden for spectacular views of the Houses of Parliament, Westminster Abbey, and the London Eye. Better yet, ask for Room 303 to enjoy these exquisite views in privacy. **Pros:** amazing views; spacious rooms. **Cons:** prices never seem to drop, even in the off-season. ⊠ *2 Spring Gardens, Covent Garden* 🕿 *020/7870–2900* ⊕ *www.hilton.co.uk* ✑ *127 rooms, 2 suites* ⌂ *In-room: a/c, safe, DVD, Internet. In-hotel: restaurant, room service, bar, laundry service, parking (paid)* ☰ *AE, DC, MC, V* Ⓤ *Charing Cross* ✛ *F4.*

THE CITY AND EAST LONDON

£££   ⊡ **Andaz.** This swanky, upscale hotel owned by the Hyatt group opened in late 2007 and has been making headlines for its modern, masculine design and unconventional approach. Instead of checking in at a desk, guests sit in a lounge while a staff member with a handheld computer takes their information. Rooms are sparsely decorated with designer furniture, and most important, intensely comfortable beds. Most have white walls, charcoal floors, and ruby-red touches. Rooms have Wi-Fi, MP3 docking stations, and "healthy minibars" stocked with nuts, fruit, and yogurt. The 1901 restaurant is exquisite, with marble floors and modern chandeliers, and the champagne bar is popular with city workers. **Pros:** nice attention to detail; guests can borrow an iPod from the front desk; no standing in line to check in. **Cons:** sparse decor is not for all. ⊠ *40 Liverpool St., East London* 🕿 *020/7961–1234* ⊕ *london. liverpoolstreet.andaz.hyatt.com* ✑ *267 rooms* ⌂ *In-room: a/c, safe, Wi-Fi. In-hotel: restaurant, room service, bar, gym, laundry service, parking (paid)* ☰ *MC, V* Ⓤ *Liverpool St.* ✛ *H2.*

£££   ⊡ **The Hoxton.** This trendy, East London hotel sits in the eponymous neighborhood and is designed to reflect the funky galleries and small boutiques for which the area is known. It claims to combine a country-lodge lifestyle with true urban living, and to that end its lobby has both crackling fires and cool cocktails, and the comfortable guest rooms have Frette linen sheets, down comforters, and free Wi-Fi. The design throughout is contemporary—but not so modern as to be absurd. There's still wood furniture and soft carpets. The bar is popular with

2

local office workers, and the Hoxton Grille restaurant combines American steak-house style with French bistro chic. All rooms come with a free healthful breakfast of yogurt and fruit. **Pros:** cool-looking place; every night five rooms in this hotel are priced at £1, but you'll need to join the mailing list. **Cons:** restaurant and bar can be crowded in the evening; area is a bit off the beaten tourist track. ⊠ *81 Great Eastern St., East London* ☎ *020/7550–1000* ⊕ *www.hoxtonhotels.com* ⇨ *205 rooms* ⚭ *In-room: a/c, safe, Internet, Wi-Fi. In-hotel: restaurant, room service, bar* ⊟ *AE, MC, V* ⎰ *BP* Ⓤ *Old St.* ✢ *H1.*

£££ ⊡ **Ramada Hotel and Suites Docklands.** Built in a dramatic waterfront location, this modern hotel is in the rejuvenated London Docklands in East London. Many rooms have water views, and others have views of the city. Rooms are sleek and modern, geared at business travelers, with Wi-Fi, large desks, data ports, and personal voice mail. The hotel's restaurants and bars are handy, although there's plenty to choose from these days in Docklands. **Pros:** waterfront views; big discounts for weekend bookings. **Cons:** area is very quiet on weekends; about a 20-minute Tube ride to central London. ⊠ *ExCel, 2 Festoon Way, Royal Victoria Dock, East London* ☎ *020/7540–4820* ⊕ *www.ramadadocklands.co.uk* ⇨ *224 rooms* ⚭ *In-room: a/c, safe, Internet. In-hotel: restaurant, room service, bar, gym* ⊟ *AE, MC, V* ⎰ *BP* Ⓤ *Old St.* ✢ *H3.*

££££ ⊡ **The Rookery.** This is an extraordinary hotel, where each beautiful double room is decorated with a lavish, theatrical flair and an eye for history. Many have four-poster beds, and each has a claw-foot bathtub, antique carved wooden headboard, and period furnishings, including exquisite salvaged pieces. In the Rook's Nest, the hotel's duplex suite, you can relax in an antique bath in the corner of the bedroom or enjoy a magnificent view of The City's historic buildings. The conservatory, with its small patio garden, is a relaxing place to unwind. Great deals are available here in the winter. **Pros:** beautiful, quirky space; helpful staff. **Cons:** area is quiet at night and busy during the day. ⊠ *12 Peter's La., at Cowcross St., The City* ☎ *020/7336–0931* ⊕ *www.rookeryhotel. com* ⇨ *30 rooms, 3 suites* ⚭ *In-room: a/c, safe, refrigerator, Internet. In-hotel: room service, bar, laundry service, parking (paid)* ⊟ *AE, DC, MC, V* Ⓤ *Farringdon* ✢ *H2.*

KENSINGTON AND SOUTH KENSINGTON

££–£££ ⊡ **Astons Apartments.** Three redbrick Victorian town houses on a quiet residential street hold Astons' comfortable studios and apartments. All are simple and small but well designed with tiny kitchenettes, and the apartments (£££) have marble bathrooms and other extra touches as well. Some sleep families of four; others are barely big enough for two people. The decor has a modern, blond-wood look, and it all makes a nice alternative to normal hotel rooms. **Pros:** kitchenettes free you from restaurant tyranny; rooms are well designed. **Cons:** furnishings look a bit cheap; few customer services. ⊠ *31 Rosary Gardens, South Kensington* ☎ *020/7590–6000, 800/525–2810 in U.S.* ⊕ *www.astons-apartments.com* ⇨ *43 rooms, 12 suites* ⚭ *In-room: no a/c, safe, kitchen, refrigerator, Internet. In-hotel: parking (paid), some pets allowed* ⊟ *AE, MC, V* Ⓤ *Gloucester Rd.* ✢ *B6.*

RENTALS, B&BS, AND HOME EXCHANGES

APARTMENT RENTALS

For a home base that's roomy enough for a family and that comes with cooking facilities, consider renting furnished "flats" (what apartments are called in Britain). These can save you money, especially if you're traveling with a group. If you're interested in home exchange, but don't feel like sharing, some home-exchange directories list rentals as well. If you want to deal directly with local agents, get a personal recommendation from someone who has used the company; there's no accredited rating system for apartment-rental standards like the one for hotels.

International Agents

Interhome (✉ *1990 N.E. 163rd St., Suite 110, North Miami Beach, FL* ☎ *305/940–2299 or 800/882–6864* ⊕ *www.interhome.us*) has dozens of rather pricey, but luxurious, flats all over London with £3,000 per week being a not unusual price.

Villanet (✉ *1251 N.W. 116th St., Seattle, WA* ☎ *206/417–3444 or 877/250–4366* ⊕ *www.rentavilla.com*) has hundreds of flats in residential neighborhoods all over London, with prices starting at £75 per person per night.

The **Villas International** (✉ *4340 Redwood Hwy., Suite D309, San Rafael, CA* ☎ *415/499–9490 or 800/221–2260* ⊕ *www.villasintl.com*) agency has exclusively priced flats all over London that start around £1,800 per week—some sleep up to 10 people.

Local Agents

Acorn Apartments (✉ *Ground Fl., 19 Bedford Pl.* ☎ *020/7636–8325* ⊕ *www.acornapartments.co.uk*) offers attractive small central apartments starting at around £90; however, the Web site is not very good and it may be easier to call for information.

The **Apartment Service** (✉ *5 Francis Grove, Wimbledon* ☎ *020/8944–1444* ⊕ *www.apartmentservice.com*) specializes in executive apartments for business travelers in and around the City, so prices are high, but so

is the level of quality. Prices start at around £80 per night, although most apartments are around £180.

At Home in London (✉ *70 Black Lion La., Hammersmith* ☎ *020/8748–1943* ⊕ *www.athomeinlondon.co.uk* 🖃 *MC, V*) has rooms in private homes in Knightsbridge, Kensington, Mayfair, Chelsea, and West London. Prices average around £75 a night per room, making this a great alternative to budget hotels.

Bulldog Club (✉ *14 Dewhurst Rd., Kensington* ☎ *0870/803–4414, 877/727–3004 in U.S.* ⊕ *www.bulldogclub.com* 🖃 *AE, MC, V* ☞ *There's a 2.5% fee for using a credit card; debit cards incur no fees; the full price of the room must be paid in advance. Check their cancellation policies carefully*) offers delightful little London flats in Knightsbridge, Kensington, and Chelsea. Many properties are available for about £100 per night with full English breakfasts.

Stay in the properties of Londoners who are temporarily away with **Coach House London Vacation Rentals** (✉ *2 Tunley Rd., Balham* ☎ *020/8133–8332* ⊕ *www.rentals.chslondon.com* 🖃 *AE, MC, V* ☞ *Payment by credit card only; 10% deposit required*). Attractive apartments and houses are primarily in Notting Hill, Kensington, and Chelsea, and most cost around £115 per night. The minimum booking of three nights is a bit limiting, though, and you must make a substantial security deposit (usually between £200 and £1,000), which is returned after your stay.

Landmark Trust (☎ *01628/825–925* ⊕ *www.landmarktrust.org.uk*) has London apartments in unusual and historic buildings, prices start at around £100 a night, but many buildings require a minimum stay of seven days.

Uptown Reservations (☎ 020/7937–2001 ⊕ www.uptownres.co.uk) accepts only upscale addresses, and specializes in hosted homes or apartments for Americans, often business executives. Nearly all the homes on its register are in Knightsbridge, Belgravia, Kensington, and Chelsea. Prices start at £550 per week. There's limited information on their Web site; bookings must be made over the phone. A nonrefundable deposit is required.

Additionally, travelers at Fodors.com recommend these rental services:

"I've used **London Guest Suites** (⊕ www.londonguestsuites.com) many times and like them. They have rentals of all lengths. I also just booked a flat at **A Place Like Home** (⊕ www.aplacelikehome.co.uk)." —carrybean

"We stayed in 1 Sloane Ave. and were extremely happy and pleased with the apartment and the company **The Apartments** (⊕ www.theapartments.co.uk)." —jrecm

"Try the biggest rental site in Europe: **Holiday-Rentals from Home Away** (⊕ www.holiday-rentals.co.uk)" —travel_tomato

"Check out **VRBO** (⊕ www.vrbo.com), lots of London listings, and **Farnum-Christ** (⊕ www.farnum-christ.com), which is a high-ish end agency with some wonderful flats." —janisj

"I've used **London Connections** (⊕ www.londonconnections.com) several times and I've been very pleased." —Tinathread

BED-AND-BREAKFASTS
You can stay in small, homey B&Bs for an up-close-and-personal brush with city life, or find yourself in what is really a modern guesthouse, where you never meet the owners. The main benefit of staying in a B&B is that the price is usually cheaper than a hotel room of comparable quality, and you receive more personal service. The limitations may be few in number, but can be off-putting for some: although you can sometimes arrange for daily maid service, there is no restaurant

or bar, and no concierge should you have a question. If you book a room in a privately owned house through an agency, prices start as low as £70 a night, and go up for more central neighborhoods and larger and more luxurious homes. It's a nice option, both for seasoned travelers and for those trying to travel well without busting their budgets. Search the Web and call around to find the place that's right for you.

Contacts Host & Guest Service (✉ 103 Dawes Rd., Fulham ☎ 0870/220–2640 ⊕ www.host-guest.co.uk ▤ MC, V ✧ Full payment in advance) can find you a room in London as well as the rest of the United Kingdom. It's a great way to find bargains, knowing that all have been vetted by the agency, but the Web site functionality is a bit creaky. The long-established family-run agency **London B&B** (✉ 437 J St., Suite 210, San Diego, CA ☎ 800/872–2632 ⊕ www.londonbandb.com ✧ 30% deposit required) has some truly spectacular—and some more modest—homes in central London. Most cost $130–$150 per night. You can check many of them out online, but you still have to call even to find out prices.

HOME EXCHANGES
If you would like to exchange your home for someone else's, join a home-exchange organization, which will send you its updated listings of available exchanges for a year and will include your own listing in at least one of them. It's up to you to make specific arrangements.

Exchange Clubs

HomeLink International (⌂ Box 47747, Tampa, FL 33647 ☎ 954/566–2687 or 800/638–3841 ⊕ www.homelink.org); $115 yearly for a listing and online access.

Intervac U.S (⌂ Box 590504, San Franciso, CA 94159 ☎ 800/756–4663 ⊕ www.intervacus.com); $95 yearly for a listing and online access.

££–£££   ⊡ **base2stay.** In a creamy white Georgian town house in chic Kensington, this hotel promises a new approach—a near-budget hotel. Prices are just above budget and just below moderate. Rooms are mostly comfortable doubles, but some have bunk beds, for traveling friends or children. Bathrooms are small but well designed. The air-conditioned rooms are not big, but have a stylish, modern look with white walls and bedding, and dark throws and pillows. Tiny kitchenettes give you alternatives to another restaurant meal. Its "arrival base" system allows you to use a room before your check-in time for £15 an hour. **Pros:** attractive rooms; handy mini-kitchens; good location. **Cons:** prices are a bit high for what you get; bathrooms are very tiny. ⊠ *25 Courtfield Gardens, South Kensington* ☎ *020/7244–2255, 800/511–9821 in U.S.* ⊕ *www.base2stay.com* ⇄ *67 rooms* ♿ *In-room: a/c, kitchen, Internet* ▤ *MC, V* Ⓤ *Earls Court Station* ✛ *A6.*

£££   ⊡ **Best Western Premier Shaftesbury Kensington.** Just steps from Earl's Court Tube station at the edge of Kensington, this hotel offers a lot for your money. Its look is fresh and relaxing, with cool grays and earth tones in the guest rooms, and firm queen-size beds. Bathrooms are small but handsome, with modern bowl sinks, towel warmers, and big walk-in showers. Staff are friendly and helpful. **Pros:** rates are as low as half price in the off-season and for early bookings; free Wi-Fi. **Cons:** rooms are quite small; reservations do get lost here, so bring your confirmation number. ⊠ *33–37 Hogarth Rd., Kensington* ☎ *020/7370–6831* ⊕ *www.bestwestern.co.uk* ⇄ *133 rooms* ♿ *In-room: a/c, safe, refrigerator, Wi-Fi. In-hotel: restaurant, room service* ▤ *AE, MC, V* ⓘⓄⓘ *BP* Ⓤ *Earl's Court* ✛ *A5.*

£   ⊡ **easyHotel.** This budget hotel opened in 2005 as London's first "pod hotel." Crammed into a big white town house are 34 tiny rooms, all with a double bed, private bathroom, and little else. Each is brightly decorated in the trademark orange and white of the easyGroup (which includes the budget airline easyJet). The idea behind the hotel is to provide high-quality basics (bed, sink, shower, and toilet) for little money. The small reception desk can't offer much in terms of service, and if you want your room cleaned while you stay, it's an additional £10 a day. The concept continues to be a huge hit—easyHotel is fully booked months in advance and has opened additional branches at Heathrow Airport, as well as near Victoria and Paddington stations and elsewhere in Kensington. Check the Web site for all locations. **Pros:** amazing price; safe and pleasant space. **Cons:** not for the claustrophobic; six floors, no lift; everything costs extra, from a TV in your room to fresh towels; no customer services. ⊠ *14 Lexham Gardens, Kensington* ☎ *020/7216–1717* ⊕ *www.easyhotel.com* ⇄ *34 rooms* ♿ *In-room: no a/c, no phone* ▤ *MC, V* Ⓤ *Gloucester Rd.* ✛ *A5.*

££££–£££££   ⊡ **The Gore.** Just down the road from the Albert Hall, this gorgeous, friendly hotel has a luxurious mixture of the comfortable and the extraordinary. The lobby evokes a wealthy estate from centuries past, and upstairs most rooms are spacious and decorated in calming neutral tones with rich fabrics. A handful of rooms are spectacular: one is a Tudor fantasy with minstrel gallery, stained glass, and four-poster bed, another—the "Judy Garland"—is done up in over-the-top Hollywood style. **Pros:** small scale means the staff can lavish attention on you; spacious rooms. **Cons:** price has gone up in recent years, making this only for those with deep pockets. ☒ *189 Queen's Gate, Kensington* ☎ *020/7584–6601* ⊕ *www.gorehotel.com* ↻ *50 rooms* ⅋ *In-room: no a/c, safe, refrigerator, Wi-Fi. In-hotel: restaurant, room service, bar, laundry service* ⊟ *AE, DC, MC, V* Ⓤ *Gloucester Rd.* ✛ *B5.*

2

£££££ 📷 **Milestone Hotel & Apartments.** This pair of intricately decorated Victorian town houses overlooking Kensington Palace and Gardens is an intimate, luxurious alternative to the city's more famous high-end hotels. Great thoughtfulness goes into the hospitality, and everything is possible in this special place. You'll be offered a drink upon arrival and, if you so desire, you can return to a post-theater midnight snack in your room or leave with a picnic basket for the park across the street. Each sumptuous room is full of antiques; many have canopied beds. A favorite is the Ascot Room, which is filled with elegant hats of the kind worn at the famous races. **Pros:** beautiful space; big rooms. **Cons:** service can be a bit stuffy (it seems you're not expected to do anything for yourself). ☒ *1 Kensington Ct., Kensington* ☎ *020/7917–1000* ⊕ *www.milestonehotel. com* ↻ *45 rooms, 12 suites, 6 apartments* ⅋ *In-room: a/c, safe, kitchen (some), refrigerator, DVD, Wi-Fi. In-hotel: 2 restaurants, room service, bar, gym, laundry service, some pets allowed* ⊟ *AE, DC, MC, V* Ⓤ *High Street Kensington* ✛ *A4.*

£££ 📷 **Millennium Gloucester.** Refurbished in 2007, the hotel has a sleek lobby with polished wood columns, a warming fireplace, and glittering chandeliers. Guest rooms are done in neutral creams and earth tones, and blond-wood desks and leather chairs have a blandly masculine look. The hotel is popular with business travelers, so rooms come equipped with satellite TV and broadband. Bathrooms are relatively small but have all you need. There are two bars and several restaurants, which means you don't have to go out if you'd prefer to stay in. **Pros:** good deals available if you book in advance. **Cons:** public areas and restaurant can get crowded. ☒ *4–18 Harrington Gardens, Kensington* ☎ *020/7373–6030* ⊕ *www.millenniumhotels.co.uk/millenniumgloucester* ↻ *143 rooms* ⅋ *In-room: a/c, safe, refrigerator, Wi-Fi. In-hotel: restaurant, room service* ⊟ *AE, MC, V* ⅋⊙⅋ *BP* Ⓤ *Gloucester Rd.* ✛ *B5.*

£££–££££ 📷 **Number Sixteen.** In a white-portico row of Victorian houses, close to the South Kensington Tube and a short walk from the Victoria & Albert Museum, Number Sixteen is a lovely luxury guesthouse. Rooms are spacious and have marble- and oak-clad bathrooms. The style is not so much interior-designed as understated—new furniture and modern prints are juxtaposed with weighty oil paintings and antiques. The staff is friendly, so lingering in the drawing rooms is a pleasure, and drinks are served in the leafy garden in summer. **Pros:** just the right level of helpful service; decor is gorgeous. **Cons:** there's no restaurant; very small elevator. ☒ *16 Sumner Pl., South Kensington* ☎ *020/7589–5232, 800/553–6674 in U.S.* ⊕ *www.firmdale.com* ↻ *42 rooms* ⅋ *In-room: no a/c (some), safe, refrigerator, Wi-Fi. In-hotel: room service, bar, laundry service* ⊟ *AE, MC, V* ⅋⊙⅋ *CP* Ⓤ *South Kensington* ✛ *B5.*

££££–£££££ 📷 **The Pelham.** Museum lovers flock to this sweet hotel across the street from the South Kensington Tube station. The Natural History, Science, and V&A museums are all a short stroll away, as is the King's Road. At the end of a day's sightseeing, settle down in front of the fireplace in one of the two snug drawing rooms with their honor bars. The stylish, contemporary rooms by designer Kit Kemp have sash windows and marble bathrooms. Some top-floor rooms have sloping ceilings and casement windows. Downstairs, the Bistro Fifteen offers a contemporary take on British cuisine. **Pros:** great location for museum-hopping; gorgeous bathrooms. **Cons:** top-floor rooms are not for the tall! ⊠ *15 Cromwell Pl., South Kensington* ☎ *020/7589–8288, 888/757–5587 in U.S.* ⊕ *www.pelhamhotel.co.uk* ⟲ *47 rooms, 4 suites* ⚹ *In-room: a/c, safe (some), refrigerator, Wi-Fi. In-hotel: restaurant, room service, bar, parking (paid)* ▤ *AE, MC, V* Ⓤ *South Kensington* ✛ *B5.*

£££ ⊞ **The Sumner.** This elegant Georgian town house on a quiet residential street is the kind of place where you can feel yourself relaxing the minute you enter. Guest rooms are painted in neutral tones with splashes of rich color, and the interior design has a modern flair—even the fruit bowl is arranged creatively. There's plenty here for the gadget lover, including flat-screen TVs and free broadband. If the weather is good, relax in the small garden; in winter, warm your feet by the fire. In the morning, take breakfast in the sunny conservatory. **Pros:** small enough that the staff know your name. **Cons:** services are limited but prices high. ⊠ *5 Sumner Pl., South Kensington* ☎ *020/7723–2244* ⊕ *www. thesumner.com* ⟲ *20 rooms* ⚹ *In-room: a/c, refrigerator, Internet. In-hotel: room service, parking (paid)* ▤ *AE, MC, V* ❑⃝ *BP* Ⓤ *South Kensington* ✛ *B6.*

KNIGHTSBRIDGE, CHELSEA, AND BELGRAVIA

£££££ ⊞ **The Berkeley.** The elegant Berkeley is increasingly known for its luxurious, modern approach, which culminates in its splendid penthouse swimming pool. The big bedrooms have either swags of William Morris prints or art deco touches. All have sitting areas and ample luxury, including CD/DVD players, and Floris toiletries in the big marble bathrooms. Dining venues include Marcus Wareing's high-class Pétrus restaurant, Gordon Ramsay's excellent and extremely popular Boxwood Café, the eclectic and sumptuous Blue Bar (popular with celebrities), and the whimsical Caramel Room where morning coffee and decadent doughnuts are served to slim ladies who look as if they've never eaten such a thing in their lives. **Pros:** lavish luxury; attentive service; handy location for shopping. **Cons:** stratospheric prices; you'll need designer clothes to fit in here. ⊠ *Wilton Pl., Belgravia* ☎ *020/7235– 6000, 800/637–2869 in U.S.* ⊕ *www.the-berkeley.com* ⟲ *103 rooms, 55 suites* ⚹ *In-room: a/c, safe, refrigerator, DVD, Internet. In-hotel: restaurant, room service, bar, pool, gym, spa, laundry service, parking (paid)* ▤ *AE, DC, MC, V* Ⓤ *Knightsbridge* ✛ *D4.*

££££ ⊞ **The Levin.** This posh boutique hotel created by the people behind the Capital Hotel is owned by luxury-loving oenophiles. Expect smooth, duck-egg-blue walls, hyper-modern furnishings, and a champagne bar in every room. Yes, that's right—each room has its own selection of pricey splits of bubbly, along with all the mixings (and directions) for making champagne cocktails. Downstairs, the relaxed Le Metro Bar

& Brasserie serves French and English classics (steak frites, sausages and mash) paired with an outstanding wine list. Located next door to Harrods, shopping locations don't get any more prime than this. **Pros:** your own champagne bar; sauntering to Harrods. **Cons:** no elevator; no bargains here. ⊠ *28 Basil St., Knightsbridge* ☎ *020/7589–6286* ⊕ *www. thelevinhotel.co.uk* ↻ *12 rooms, 1 suite* ⌂ *In-room: a/c, DVD, Internet. In-hotel: restaurant, bar, parking (paid)* ⊟ *AE, V* ⎮◯⎮ *CP* Ⓤ *Knightsbridge* ✛ *C5.*

££££ **⊡ Mandarin Oriental Hyde Park.** Stay here, and the three greats of
Fodor's Choice   Knightsbridge—Hyde Park, Harrods, and Harvey Nichols—are on your
★   doorstep. Built in 1880, the Mandarin Oriental is one of London's most elegant hotels. Bedrooms are Victorian but with hidden high-tech gadgets and luxurious touches like Frette linen duvets, fresh orchids, and delicate chocolates. Miles of marble were used to fill the grand entrance. The Park restaurant, glittering Foliage restaurant, and quirky Mandarin Bar all attract Europe's jet setters. The service here is legendary and there's a butler on every floor, should you, for example, need a bit of help with the pillow menu. **Pros:** amazing views of Hyde Park; excellent service. **Cons:** nothing here comes cheap; you must dress for dinner (and lunch and breakfast). ⊠ *66 Knightsbridge, Knightsbridge* ☎ *020/7235–2000* ⊕ *www.mandarinoriental.com* ↻ *177 rooms, 23 suites* ⌂ *In-room: a/c, safe, refrigerator, DVD (some), Wi-Fi. In-hotel: 2 restaurants, room service, bar, gym, spa, laundry service, parking (paid)* ⊟ *AE, DC, MC, V* Ⓤ *Knightsbridge* ✛ *D4.*

MAYFAIR, MARYLEBONE, AND ST. JAMES'S

££ **⊡ 22 York Street.** This Georgian town house has a cozy, family feel with polished pine floors and plenty of quilts and antiques. Pride of place goes to the central, communal dining table where guests share a varied Continental breakfast. A living room with tea/coffeemaker is at your disposal as well. The homey bedrooms are individually furnished in charming white and cream tones. Triples and family rooms for four are available. **Pros:** handy guesthouse in a great location for shoppers. **Cons:** price is a bit steep for what is, in the end, a glorified B&B. ⊠ *22 York St., Mayfair* ☎ *020/7224–2990* ⊕ *www.22yorkstreet.co.uk* ↻ *10 rooms* ⌂ *In-room: no a/c. In-hotel: bar* ⊟ *AE, MC, V* ⎮◯⎮ *CP* Ⓤ *Baker St.* ✛ *D2.*

£££–££££ **⊡ Athenaeum Hotel and Apartments.** This grand hotel overlooking Green Park offers plenty for the money. Rooms are both comfortable and lavishly decorated, with deeply comfortable Hypnos beds, plasma-screen television systems, luxurious fabrics, and original contemporary artworks. If you need more space, you can choose one of its apartments instead. (These occupy a row of Georgian town houses next to the main hotel buildings, and each has separate living, dining, and sleeping spaces; and tiny, fully equipped kitchenettes.) The spa downstairs is available only to guests, ensuring you can always get an appointment. The elegant restaurant serves butter-rich European cuisine, and a full afternoon tea here (£26) is an elegant experience. Breakfasts are luxurious and varied, with endless Continental and cooked options. **Pros:** peaceful park views; handy for Buckingham Palace and Piccadilly; great value for elegant setting. **Cons:** some rooms could use a decor update; bathrooms are almost all small. ⊠ *116 Piccadilly, Mayfair* ☏ *020/7640–3333* ⊕ *www. athenaeumhotel.com* ⮐ *111 rooms, 46 suites and apartments* ♿ *In-room: a/c, safe, kitchen (some), DVD, Wi-Fi. In-hotel: restaurant, room service, bar, gym, spa* ⊟ *AE, MC, V* ⏚ *BP* Ⓤ *Green Park* ✛ *E4.*

££££–£££££   ☷ **Claridge's.** Stay here, and you're staying at a hotel legend with one of the world's classiest guest lists, founded in 1812. The friendly, liveried staff is not in the least condescending, and the rooms are never less than luxurious. Enjoy a cup of tea in the lounge, or retreat to the stylish bar for cocktails—or, better, to Gordon Ramsay's inimitable restaurant. The bathrooms are spacious (with enormous showerheads), as are the bedrooms (with soothing, modern decor in tones of taupe and cream). The grand staircase and magnificent elevator complete with sofa and driver are equally glamorous. Perhaps Spencer Tracy said it best when he remarked that, when he died, he wanted to go not to heaven, but to Claridge's. **Pros:** serious luxury everywhere—this is an old-money hotel. **Cons:** it's a bit pretentious—the guests in the hotel bar can be almost cartoonishly snobbish. ⊠ *Brook St., St. James's* ☏ *020/7629–8860, 866/599–6991 in U.S.* ⊕ *www.claridges.co.uk* ⮐ *203 rooms* ♿ *In-room: a/c, safe, DVD, Wi-Fi. In-hotel: restaurant, bar, gym, spa, laundry service, parking (paid)* ⊟ *AE, DC, MC, V* Ⓤ *Bond St.* ✛ *E3.*

£££££   ☷ **The Dorchester.** Few hotels this opulent manage to be as personable. The glamour level is off the scale: 1,500 square yards of gold leaf and 1,100 square yards of marble. Bedrooms (some not as spacious as you might expect) have Irish linen sheets on canopied beds, brocades, velvets, and Italian marble and etched-glass bathrooms with exclusive toiletries created by Floris. Furnishings throughout are English country-house style, with more than a hint of art deco, in keeping with the original 1930s building. The hotel has embraced modern technology, and employs "e-butlers" to help guests figure out the advanced Web TVs in the rooms. There are three elegant-to-the-point-of-fussy restaurants, including one helmed by Alain Ducasse, which is always making headlines. **Pros:** historic luxury; lovely views of Hyde Park; top-notch star-spotting. **Cons:** traditional look is not to all tastes; prices are high. ⊠ *Park Lane, Mayfair* ☏ *020/7629–8888* ⊕ *www.thedorchester.com* ⮐ *195 rooms, 55 suites* ♿ *In-room: a/c, safe, DVD, Internet. In-hotel: 3 restaurants, bar, gym, spa, laundry service, parking (paid)* ⊟ *AE, DC, MC, V* Ⓤ *Marble Arch, Hyde Park Corner* ✛ *D3.*

£££   ☷ **Durrants.** A stone's throw from Oxford Street and the smaller, posher shops of Marylebone High Street, Durrants sits on a quiet corner not far from the Wallace Collection. It's a tasteful option, with old-English wood paneling, leather armchairs, and patterned carpet. Note: bedrooms at the back of the hotel are smaller than those at the front, but also quieter and air-conditioned. The building has served as a hotel since the late 18th century. **Pros:** comfortable; relaxed base for exploring. **Cons:** not all rooms are air-conditioned; some rooms are quite small. ⊠ *26–32 George St., Mayfair* ☏ *020/7935–8131* ⊕ *www. durrantshotel.co.uk* ⮐ *87 rooms, 5 suites* ♿ *In-room: no a/c (some), Internet. In-hotel: restaurant, room service, bar, laundry service* ⊟ *AE, MC, V* Ⓤ *Bond St.* ✛ *D2.*

£££ ⌂ **Park Plaza Sherlock Holmes Hotel.** This was once a rather ordinary Hilton, until somebody noticed its location and had the idea of making it a boutique hotel. Add a beautiful bar for a bit of local buzz, and—presto!—the place took off like a rocket. You might say it was elementary. With wood floors and leather furniture, the bar is relaxing; rooms have a masculine edge with lots of earth tones, pinstripe sheets, and hyper-modern bathrooms stocked with fluffy bathrobes. Still, overall, it's a handsome option near the good shopping of Marylebone High Street. Rooms are equipped with international electrical outlets, including those that work with American equipment. **Pros:** nicely decorated; good location for fans of shopping and Holmes. **Cons:** have to walk through the bar to get to reception; not well soundproofed from noisy street. ✉ *108 Baker St., Marylebone* ☎ *020/7486–6161* ⊕ *www. sherlockholmeshotel.com* ⌨ *119 rooms* ♿ *In-room: a/c, safe, refrigerator, Wi-Fi. In-hotel: restaurant, room service, bar, gym, spa* ▤ *AE, DC, MC, V* Ⓤ *Baker St.* ✛ *D2.*

£££££ ⌂ **The Stafford.** This is a rare find: a posh hotel that is equal parts elegance and friendliness. It's hard to check in without meeting the gregarious manager, and his unshakable cheeriness must be infectious, for the staff are also upbeat and helpful. The location is one of the few peaceful spots in the area, down a small lane behind Piccadilly. Its 13 adorable carriage-house rooms are installed in the 18th-century stable block; each individually decorated room has a cobbled mews entrance and gas-fueled fireplace, exposed beams, iPod dock, and CD player. The popular little American Bar has ties, baseball caps, and toy planes hanging from the ceiling. **Pros:** great staff; big, luxurious rooms; quiet location. **Cons:** traditional decor is not to all tastes; men must wear jackets in the bar. ✉ *St. James's Pl., St. James's* ☎ *020/7493–0111* ⊕ *www. thestaffordhotel.co.uk* ⌨ *81 rooms* ♿ *In-room: a/c, Internet. In-hotel: restaurant, bar* ▤ *AE, DC, MC, V* Ⓤ *Green Park* ✛ *E4.*

SOUTH BANK

£££–££££ ⌂ **London Bridge Hotel.** Just steps away from the London Bridge rail and Tube station, this thoroughly modern, stylish hotel is popular with business travelers, but leisure travelers find it just as handy. Most of the South Bank's attractions are within easy walking distance, and it's a short stroll to London Bridge station to catch the Tube. Each diminutive but sleek room is understated and contemporary, with a calming, neutral decor. Three spacious two-bedroom apartments (£££££) come with kitchen, living room, and dining room. **Pros:** great for the arty South Bank; good deals available on its Web site in the off-season. **Cons:** small rooms, even smaller bathrooms. ✉ *8–18 London Bridge St., South Bank* ☎ *020/7855–2200* ⊕ *www.london-bridge-hotel.co.uk* ⌨ *138 rooms, 3 apartments* ♿ *In-room: a/c, safe, kitchen (some), refrigerator, Wi-Fi (free). In-hotel: restaurant, room service, bar, gym, laundry service, parking (paid)* ▤ *AE, DC, MC, V* Ⓤ *London Bridge* ✛ *H3.*

££ ⌂ **Premier Travel Inn County Hall.** It might be near the riverfront, but any ⟳ view of the Thames from this hotel is blocked by the nearby Marriott. Still, it's got a handy location near the London Eye, and you get a decent value here. Rooms are not very big, but they're nicely decorated, and the staff are helpful. Best of all for families on a budget are the foldout beds that let you accommodate two kids at no extra charge. **Pros:** good location for the South Bank; bargains to be had if you book in advance. **Cons:** denied great views by other buildings nearby; limited services. ⊠ *Belvedere Rd., South Bank* ☎ *0870/238–3300* ⊕ *www. premiertravelinn.com* ↩ *313 rooms* ♨ *In-room: no a/c, Internet. In-hotel: 2 restaurants, bar, parking (paid)* ⊟ *AE, DC, MC, V* Ⓤ *Westminster* ✛ *G4.*

££ ⊡ **Premier Travel Inn Southwark.** This excellent branch of the Premier Travel Inn chain is a bit out of the way on the South Bank, but it sits on a quiet cobbled lane, and is ideally located for visiting the Tate Modern or the Globe Theatre. Rooms are simply decorated, and all have the chain's signature 6-foot-wide beds (really two 3-foot-wide beds zipped together). Ask for a room away from the elevators, which can be a little noisy. **Pros:** great location for the South Bank; quiet street. **Cons:** small rooms; limited customer services. ⊠ *34 Park St., South Bank* ☎ *020/7089–2580 or 0870/990–6402* ⊕ *www.premiertravelinn.com* ↩ *56 rooms* ♨ *In-room: a/c, Internet. In-hotel: parking (paid)* ⊟ *AE, DC, MC, V* Ⓤ *London Bridge* ✛ *H3.*

WESTMINSTER AND VICTORIA

££ ⊡ **B&B Belgravia.** This modern guesthouse a short walk from Victoria Station has cool all-white decor—white chairs and walls, white pillars and desks, white linens and towels. It all looks a bit ethereal, which is what they're aiming for. Rooms are small but beds are comfortable, and at least nothing you're wearing will clash. There's a modern, open-plan lounge where a fire crackles away in the winter. It's a good place to grab a cup of tea (always available) and check your e-mail on the free computer. **Pros:** free Wi-Fi; nice extras like free use of a laptop in the hotel lounge; coffee and tea always available. **Cons:** bathrooms and rooms are small; no hotel restaurant or bar. ⊠ *64–66 Ebury St., Victoria* ☎ *020/7259–8570* ⊕ *www.bb-belgravia.com* ↩ *17 rooms* ♨ *In-room: no a/c, Wi-Fi* ⊟ *AE, DC, MC, V* ⵙ *CP* Ⓤ *Knightsbridge* ✛ *E5.*

££££ ⊡ **City Inn Westminster.** In a rather stark steel-and-glass building steps
⊙ from the Tate Britain, this member of a small U.K. chain has some rooms with spectacular views of Big Ben and the London Eye. Extras like floor-to-ceiling windows and flat-screen TVs complement the contemporary, monochrome guest rooms. Cots, baby baths, Nickelodeon, special menus, and baby food are all on tap for kids. The restaurant and bar serve Modern British cooking. **Pros:** amazing views; lots of high-tech toys including iMac computers. **Cons:** with more than 400 rooms, you're just a number. ⊠ *30 John Islip St., Westminster* ☎ *020/7630–1000* ⊕ *www.cityinn.com* ↩ *444 rooms, 16 suites* ♨ *In-room: a/c, safe, DVD, Wi-Fi. In-hotel: restaurant, room service, bar, gym, laundry service, parking (paid)* ⊟ *AE, MC, V* Ⓤ *Pimlico* ✛ *F5.*

££–£££ ⊡ **Jolly Hotel St. Ermin's.** The hotel is just a short stroll from Westminster Abbey, Buckingham Palace, and the Houses of Parliament. An Edwardian anomaly in the shadow of modern skyscrapers, it's set on a tiny cul-de-sac courtyard. The lobby is an extravaganza of Victorian stylings like cake-frosting stuccowork in shades of baby blue and creamy white.

Sadly, guest rooms are much more ordinary and not likely to be much to write home about. The hotel's restaurant is an ornately carved 19th-century Jacobean-style salon, and one of the most magnificent rooms in which to dine in London. **Pros:** amazing lobby; great location near Buckingham Palace. **Cons:** rooms are a bit small and plain. ⊠ *2 Caxton St., Westminster* ☎ *020/7222–7888* ⊕ *www.jollyhotels.it* ⮌ *277 rooms, 8 suites* ⚹ *In-room: a/c, safe (some), refrigerator, Internet. In-hotel: restaurant, room service, bar, laundry service, parking (paid)* ⊟ *AE, DC, MC, V* Ⓤ *St. James's Park* ✛ *F5.*

££–£££   🖽 **Lime Tree Hotel.** On a street filled with budget hotels, the homey Lime Tree stands out for its gracious proprietors, the Davies family, who also act as concierges. The flowery, comfortable rooms include tea/coffeemakers. The triples and quads are suitable for families, but children under five are not allowed. The simple breakfast room covered with notes and gifts from former guests opens onto a garden. **Pros:** friendly and cheap; great location. **Cons:** some rooms are up several flights of stairs, and there's no elevator. ⊠ *135–137 Ebury St., Victoria* ☎ *020/7730–8191* ⊕ *www.limetreehotel.co.uk* ⮌ *25 rooms* ⚹ *In-room: no a/c, safe, Wi-Fi. In-hotel: no kids under 5* ⊟ *MC, V* ⍾ *BP* Ⓤ *Victoria* ✛ *E5.*

£££££   🖽 **No. 41.** This luxurious abode's designer credentials are everywhere, from the unusual tiled floors to the extraordinary furnishings drawn from every corner of the globe. Even the entrance is unique: you walk into a guests-only elevator and are swept up to the fifth-floor lobby. Rooms, some of them split-level, are complete with high-tech gadgets to keep you in touch with the office back home. When you're not working, you can relax on the butter-soft leather sofa in front of the fireplace, recline on the exquisite bed linens and feather duvets, or luxuriate in the marble bath. A "whatever, whenever" button on the telephone connects you with the helpful, amiable staff who provide exactly that. **Pros:** unique place; lots of technology in gorgeous rooms; great service. **Cons:** the unusual design is not for everyone. ⊠ *41 Buckingham Palace Rd., Victoria* ☎ *020/7300–0041* ⊕ *www.41hotel.com* ⮌ *14 rooms, 4 suites* ⚹ *In-room: a/c, safe, Internet. In-hotel: room service, bar, laundry service, parking (paid)* ⊟ *AE, DC, MC, V* ⍾ *CP* Ⓤ *Victoria* ✛ *5E.*

££   🖽 **Windermere Hotel.** This sweet little hotel will not let you forget that it stands on the site of London's first B&B, which opened here in 1881. It's draped in charmingly sunny floral fabrics, which look appropriate on the antique beds. Bathrooms are thoroughly modern, and the attached restaurant, small though it may be, is actually quite good. It's a decent option if you can't get a discount rate at a plusher hotel for the same price. **Pros:** attractive rooms; good location. **Cons:** price is a bit high for what you get; rooms and bathrooms are tiny; there's no elevator. ⊠ *142–144 Warwick Way, Victoria* ☎ *020/7834–5163* ⊕ *www.windermere-hotel.co.uk* ⮌ *22 rooms* ⚹ *In-room: a/c, Internet. In-hotel: room service, bar, Wi-Fi* ⊟ *MC, V* Ⓤ *Victoria* ✛ *E6.*

NIGHTLIFE AND THE ARTS

London is a veritable utopia for excitement junkies, culture fiends, and those who like to party. Most who visit London will be mesmerized by the city's energy, which reveals itself in layers. Whether you prefer a romantic evening at the opera, rhythm and blues with fine French food, the gritty guitar riffs of east London, a pint and gourmet pizza at a local gastro-pub, or swanky cocktails and sushi at London's sexiest lair, the U.K. capital is sure to feed your fancy. Admission prices are not always bargain-basement, but when you consider how much a London hotel room costs, the city's arts and nightlife diversions are a bargain.

NIGHTLIFE

As with nearly all cosmopolitan centers, the pace with which bars and clubs go in and out of fashion is mind-boggling. The phenomenon of absinthe has been replaced by bourbon's bite and the frenzy for the perfect cocktail recipe, and the dreaded velvet rope has been usurped by the doorbell-ringing mystique of members-only drinking clubs. The understated glamour of North London's Primrose Hill, which makes movie stars feel so at ease might be considered dull by the über-trendy clubgoers of London's West End, whereas the price of a pint in Chelsea would be dubbed blasphemous by the musicians and poets of racially diverse Brixton. Meanwhile, some of the city's most talked-about nightlife spots are turning out to be those attached to some of its best restaurants and hotels—no wonder when you consider the increased popularity of London cuisine in international circles.

BARS

Time was, bars were just a stopover in an evening full of fun—perhaps the pub first, then a bar, and then it's off to boogie the night away at the nearest dance club. These days, however, bars have become less pit stops and more destinations in themselves. With the addition of dinner menus, DJs, dance floors, and the still-new later opening hours, people now stay into the wee hours of the morning at many fashionable bars.

American Bar. Festooned with a chin-dropping array of club ties, signed celebrity photographs, sporting mementos, and baseball caps, this sensational hotel cocktail bar has superb martinis. ■ TIP→ **Jacket required.** ⊠ *Stafford Hotel, 16–18 St. James's Pl., St. James's* ☎ *020/7493–0111* ☉ *Weekdays 11:30–11, weekends noon–11* Ⓤ *Green Park.*

★ **The Blue Bar at the Berkeley Hotel.** With low-slung gray-blue walls this hotel bar is ever so slightly sexy. Immaculate service, an excellent cocktail list—try the Sex in the City—and a trendy David Collins design make this an ideal spot for a secretive tête-à-tête, complete with jazzy music in the background. ⊠ *Wilton Pl., Knightsbridge* ☎ *020/7235–6000* ☉ *Mon.–Sat. 4 PM–1 AM, Sun. 4–11 PM* Ⓤ *Knightsbridge.*

Cafe des Amis. This relaxed basement wine bar near the Royal Opera House is the perfect pre- or post-theater spot, popular among musicians and performers alike—and a friendly enough place to go on your own. More than 30 wines are served by the glass, along with a good selection of cheeses. Opera buffs will enjoy the performance and production prints on the walls. ⊠ *11–14 Hanover Pl., Covent Garden* ☎ *020/7379–3444* ☽ *Mon.–Sat. 11:30* AM*–1* AM Ⓤ *Covent Garden.*

Fodor's Choice ★ **Claridge's Bar.** This elegant Mayfair meeting place remains unpretentious even when it brims with beautiful people. A library of rare champagnes and brandies as well as a delicious choice of traditional and exotic cocktails—try The Flapper or the Black Pearl—will occupy your taste buds. Request a glass of vintage Cristal in the Macanudo Fumoir. ⊠ *55 Brook St., Mayfair* ☎ *020/7629–8860* ☽ *Mon.–Sat. noon–1* AM*, Sun. noon–midnight* Ⓤ *Bond St.*

Fodor's Choice ★ **Cocoon.** Pan-Asian restaurant Cocoon transforms itself into a sophisticated lounge bar (with DJ) Thursday through Saturday until 3 AM. Soft curves give the tastefully modern place a bubbly feel, and contrasting levels of lighting blend intimacy with a vibrant atmosphere. Nibble away on one of chef Ricky Pang's original dishes while you sip on some of London's best cocktails, all with an Asian twist—try the Love & Rockets. ⊠ *65 Regent St., St. James's* ☎ *020/7494–7600* ☽ *Thurs.–Sat. 11* PM*–3* AM Ⓤ *Piccadilly.*

★ **Crazy Bear.** This sexy basement bar with cowhide stools and croc-skin tables feels like Casablanca in Fitzrovia. As you enter Crazy Bear, a spiral staircase leads to a mirrored parlor over which presides a 1947 Murano chandelier. But don't let the opulence fool you: waitstaff here are warm and welcoming to an all-ages international crowd abuzz with chatter. ⊠ *26–28 Whitfield St., Fitzrovia* ☎ *020/7631–0088* ☽ *Mon.–Wed. noon–midnight, Thurs.–Sat. 6* PM*–1* AM Ⓤ *Goodge St.*

★ **Dogstar.** This popular South London hangout is frequented by local hipsters and counterculture types. The vibe is unpretentious, and the Mexican cuisine is a treat. This "surrealist boudoir" space hosts top-name DJs playing cutting-edge sounds every night (free Monday–Thursday). ⊠ *389 Coldharbour La., Brixton* ☎ *020/7733–7515* ▦ *Free–£5* ☽ *Mon.–Thurs. 4* PM*–2* AM*, Fri. and Sat. noon–4* AM*, Sun. noon–2* AM Ⓤ *Brixton.*

Nordic. With shooters called "Husky Poo" and "Danish Bacon Surprise" and crayfish tails and meatballs on the smorgasbord menu, Nordic takes its Scandinavian feel the whole way. This secluded, shabby-chic bar serves many couples cozied up among travel brochures promoting the Viking lands. If you can't decide what to drink, the cocktail roulette wheel on the wall may help. ⊠ *25 Newman St., Soho* ☎ *020/7631–3174* ⊕ *www.nordicbar.com* ☽ *Mon.–Thurs. noon–11* PM*, Fri. noon–midnight, Sat. 6* PM*–midnight* Ⓤ *Tottenham Court Rd.*

COMEDY

Amused Moose. This Soho basement/retro nightclub is widely considered the best place to see breaking talent as well as household names doing "secret" shows. Ricky Gervais, Eddie Izzard, and Russel Brand are among those who have graced this stage, and every summer a handful of the Edinburgh Fringe comedians preview here. The bar is open late, and there's a DJ and dancing until 5 AM after the show. Tickets are often discounted with a printout from their Web site. ⊠ *Moonlighting, 17 Greek St., Soho* ☎ *020/7287–3727* ⊕ *www.amusedmoose.com* ▦ *£9 and up* ☽ *Showtimes vary; call for details* Ⓤ *Tottenham Court Rd.*

★ **Comedy Store.** Known as the birthplace of alternative comedy, this is where the United Kingdom's funniest stand-ups have cut their teeth before being launched onto prime-time TV. Comedy Store Players entertain audiences on Wednesday and Sunday; the Cutting Edge team steps in every Tuesday; and on the last Monday of every month the King Gong show (£5) hits the stage, where amateur comedians try their luck. Thursday, Friday, and Saturday have the best stand-up acts. There's a bar with food also available. ■ **TIP→ Tickets can be booked through Ticketmaster or over the phone.** Note that children under 18 are not admitted to this venue. ✉ *1A Oxendon St., Soho* ☎ *0844/847–1728* ⊕ *www. thecomedystore.co.uk* ✉ *£13–£18* ☉ *Shows daily 8* PM*, with extra shows Fri. and Sat. at midnight* Ⓤ *Piccadilly Circus, Leicester Sq.*

Fodor'sChoice **Soho Theatre.** This theater's programs include comedy shows by estab-
★ lished acts and up-and-coming comedians. The bar downstairs, Café Lazeez, stays open until 11:30 Sunday through Thursday, and until 1 AM on Friday and Saturday. Check local listings or the Web site for what's on, and book tickets in advance. ✉ *21 Dean St., Soho* ☎ *020/7478– 0100* ⊕ *www.sohotheatre.com* ✉ *£10–£22.50* ☉ *Mon.–Sat. usually 9:30–11, although show times vary* Ⓤ *Tottenham Court Rd.*

DANCE CLUBS

The club scene ranges from mammoth-size playgrounds to more intimate venues where you can actually hear your friends talk. Check the daily listings in *Time Out* for "club nights," which are theme nights that take place the same night every week. Another good way to learn about club nights is by picking up fliers in your favorite bar.

Fabric. This sprawling subterranean club is now a firm fixture on the London scene. "Fabric Live" hosts drum 'n' bass and hip-hop crews and live acts on Friday; international big-name DJs play slow, sexy bass lines and cutting-edge music on Saturday. Sunday is "Polysexual Night." The devastating sound system and "bodysonic" dance floor ensure that bass riffs vibrate through your entire body. ■ **TIP→ Get there early to avoid a lengthy queue, and don't wear a suit.** ✉ *77A Charterhouse St., East End* ☎ *020/7336–8898* ⊕ *www.fabriclondon.com* ✉ *£13–£16* ☉ *Fri. 10* PM*–6* AM*, Sat. 10* PM*–7* AM Ⓤ *Farringdon.*

★ **KOKO.** This Victorian theater, formerly known as Camden Palace, has seen acts from Charlie Chaplin to Madonna, and genres from punk to rave. Updated with lush reds not unlike a cockney Moulin Rouge, this is still one of London's most stunning venues. Sounds of live indie rock, cabaret, funky house, and club classics keep the big dance floor moving, even when it's not heaving. ✉ *1A Camden High St., Camden Town* ☎ *0870/432–5527* ⊕ *www.koko.uk.com* ✉ *£3–£20* ☉ *Fri. and Sat. 10* PM*–4* AM*, also some Wed.* Ⓤ *Mornington Crescent.*

Fodor'sChoice **Vendome Mayfair.** This recently opened classy club draws a trendy crowd
★ for house music, colorful furnishings, and futuristic designs with '70s retro disco decor. The revolving DJ booth at the center of the club, the Renaissance-like entrance, the individually themed booths, and the faux snakeskin banisters shout out pure decadence. ✉ *85 Piccadilly, Mayfair* ☎ *020/7581–8609* ⊕ *www.vendomemayfair.com* ✉ *£20* ☉ *Wed. and Thurs. 10* PM*–3* AM*, Fri. and Sat. 10* PM*–4* AM*.*

ECLECTIC MUSIC

The Borderline. This important small venue has a solid reputation for booking everything from metal to country and beyond. Oasis, Pearl Jam, Blur, Sheryl Crow, PJ Harvey, Ben Harper, Jeff Buckley, and Counting Crows have all played live here. ⊠ *Orange Yard off Manette St., Soho* ☎ *020/7734–5547* ⊕ *www.meanfiddler.com* ⊠ *£6–£25* ☉ *Mon.– Sat. 7 PM–3 AM, Sun. 7–10:30* Ⓤ *Tottenham Court Rd.*

Fodor's Choice ★
O2 Academy Brixton. This legendary Brixton venue has seen it all—mods and rockers, hippies and punks. Despite a capacity for almost 5,000 people, this refurbished Victorian hall with original art deco fixtures retains a clublike charm; it has plenty of bars and upstairs seating. ⊠ *211 Stockwell Rd., Brixton* ☎ *020/7771–3000* ⊕ *www.brixton-academy.co.uk* ⊠ *£10–£50* ☉ *Opening hrs vary* Ⓤ *Brixton.*

★ **Union Chapel.** This beautiful old chapel has excellent acoustics and sublime architecture. The beauty of the space and its impressive multicultural programming have made it one of London's best musical venues, especially for acoustic shows. Performers have included Björk, Beck, and Goldfrapp, though now you're more likely to hear lower-key alternative country, world music, and jazz. ⊠ *Compton Terr., Islington* ☎ *020/7226–1686* ⊕ *www.unionchapel.org.uk* ⊠ *Free–£25* ☉ *Opening hrs vary* Ⓤ *Highbury and Islington.*

JAZZ

Dover Street Restaurant & Jazz Bar. Put on your blue-suede shoes and prepare to dance the night away—that is, after you've feasted from the French Mediterranean menu. Fun for dates as well as groups, Dover Street Restaurant has three bars, a DJ, and a stage with the latest live bands performing everything from jazz to soul to R&B, all this encircling linen-covered tables with a friendly staff catering to your every whim. ⊠ *8–10 Dover St., Mayfair* ☎ *020/7491–7509* ⊕ *www.doverst. co.uk* ⊠ *Free–£15* ☉ *Mon.–Thurs. noon–3 PM and 5:30 PM–3 AM, Fri. noon–3 PM and 7 PM–3 AM, Sat. 7 PM–3 AM* Ⓤ *Green Park.*

Jazz Café. A palace of high-tech cool in bohemian Camden—it remains an essential hangout for fans of both the mainstream end of the repertoire and hip-hop, funk, rap, and Latin fusion. Book ahead if you want a prime table overlooking the stage, in the balcony restaurant. ⊠ *5 Pkwy., Camden Town* ☎ *020/7688–8899 restaurant reservations, 0870/060–3777 standing tickets* ⊕ *www.jazzcafe.co.uk* ⊠ *£10–£25* ☉ *Daily 7 PM–2 AM* Ⓤ *Camden Town.*

★ **Pizza Express Jazz Club Soho.** One of the capital's most ubiquitous pizza chains also runs a great Soho jazz venue. The dimly lighted restaurant hosts top-quality international jazz acts every night. The Italian-style thin-crust pizzas are good, too, though on the small side. ⊠ *10 Dean St., Soho* ☎ *020/7439–8722* ⊕ *www.pizzaexpresslive.com* ⊠ *£10–£25* ☉ *Daily from 11:30 AM for food; music 7:30 PM–11 PM* Ⓤ *Tottenham Court Rd.*

Ronnie Scott's. Since the '60s, this legendary jazz club has attracted big names. It's usually crowded and hot, the food isn't great, and service is slow—but the mood can't be beat, even since the sad departure of its eponymous founder and saxophonist. Reservations are recommended.

⊠ *47 Frith St., Soho* ☎ *020/7439–0747* ⊕ *www.ronniescotts.co.uk* ✉ *£15–£25 nonmembers, £5–£15 members, annual membership £165* ⊗ *Mon.–Sat.* 6 PM–3 AM, *Sun.* 6:30 PM–11 PM Ⓤ *Leicester Sq.*

ROCK

★ **Barfly Club.** At one of the finest small clubs in the capital, punk, indie guitar bands, and new metal rock attract a nonmainstream crowd. Weekend club nights upstairs host DJs (and live bands) who rock the decks. ⊠ *49 Chalk Farm Rd., Camden Town* ☎ *020/7424–0800* ⊕ *www.barflyclub.com* ✉ *£5–£8* ⊗ *Mon.–Wed.* 7–midnight, *Thurs.* 7 PM–2 AM, *Fri. and Sat.* 7 PM–3 AM, *Sun.* 7–11 Ⓤ *Camden Town, Chalk Farm.*

The HMV Forum. The best medium-to-big-name rock performers consistently play at the 2,000-capacity club. It's a converted 1920 art deco cinema, with a balcony overlooking the dance floor. Consult the Web site for current listings. ⊠ *9–17 Highgate Rd., Kentish Town* ☎ *020/7428–4099* ⊕ *www.kentishtownforum.com* ✉ *£12–£25* ⊗ *Opening hrs vary, depending on concert schedule* Ⓤ *Kentish Town.*

THE ARTS

London's arts scene pushes the boundaries, whether you prefer your art classical or modern, or as a contemporary twist on a time-honored classic. Celebrity divas sing original-language librettos at the Royal Opera House; the Almeida Opera focuses on radical productions of new opera and musical theater. Shakespeare's plays are brought to life at the reconstructed Globe Theatre, and challenging new writing is produced at the Royal Court.

To find out what's showing now, the weekly magazine *Time Out* (£2.99, issued every Tuesday) is invaluable. The *Evening Standard* carries listings, many of which are available online at ⊕ *www.thisislondon.co.uk*. London's widely available free newspapers are also worth checking out, as are many Sunday papers, and the Saturday *Independent, Guardian,* and *Times.* You can pick up the free fortnightly *London Theatre Guide* from hotels and tourist-information centers.

CLASSICAL MUSIC

Whether it's a concert by cellist Yo-Yo Ma or a Mozart requiem by candlelight, it's possible to hear first-rate musicians in world-class venues almost every day of the year. The London Symphony Orchestra is in residence at the Barbican Centre, although other top orchestras—including the Philharmonia and the Royal Philharmonic—also perform here. The Barbican also hosts chamber-music concerts, with celebrated orchestras such as the City of London Sinfonia. Wigmore Hall, a lovely venue for chamber music, is renowned for its song recitals by up-and-coming young singers. The Southbank Centre has an impressive international music season, held in the Queen Elizabeth Hall and the small Purcell Room as well as in the Royal Festival Hall, now completely refurbished. Full houses are rare, so even at the biggest concert halls you should be able to get a ticket for £12. If you can't book in advance, arrive at the hall an hour before the performance for a chance at returns.

2

■TIP➔ Lunchtime concerts take place all over the city in smaller concert halls, the big arts-center foyers, and churches; they usually cost less than £5 or are free, and feature string quartets, singers, jazz ensembles, or gospel choirs. St. John's, Smith Square, and St. Martin-in-the-Fields are popular locations. Performances usually begin about 1 PM and last one hour.

A great British tradition since 1895, the **Henry Wood Promenade Concerts** (more commonly known as the "Proms" ⊕ *www.bbc.co.uk/proms*) run eight weeks, from July to September, at the Royal Albert Hall. Despite an extraordinary quantity of high-quality concerts, it's renowned for its (atypical) last night: a madly jingoistic display of singing "Land of Hope and Glory," Union Jack–waving, and general madness. Demand for last-night tickets is so high that you must enter a lottery. For regular Proms, tickets run £5–£90, with hundreds of standing tickets for £5 available at the hall on the night of the concert. ■TIP➔ **The last night is broadcast in Hyde Park on a jumbo screen, but even here a seat on the grass requires a paid ticket that can set you back around £25.**

Barbican Centre. Home to the London Symphony Orchestra (⊕ *www.lso.co.uk*) and frequent host of the English Chamber Orchestra and the BBC Symphony Orchestra, the Barbican has an excellent season of big-name virtuosos. ⊠ *Silk St., East End* ☎ *020/7638–8891 box office* ⊕ *www.barbican.org.uk* Ⓤ *Barbican, Moorgate.*

★ **Royal Albert Hall.** Built in 1871, this splendid iron-and-glass–dome auditorium hosts music programs in a wide range of genres, including top-flight pop artists, as well as being the home of Europe's most democratic music festival, the Proms. The hall is also open daily for daytime guided tours (£6). ⊠ *Kensington Gore, Kensington* ☎ *020/7589–8212* ⊕ *www.royalalberthall.com* Ⓤ *South Kensington.*

St. John's, Smith Square. This baroque church behind Westminster Abbey offers chamber music and organ recitals as well as orchestral concerts September through July. There are occasional lunchtime recitals for £7. ⊠ *Smith Sq., Westminster* ☎ *020/7222–1061* ⊕ *www.sjss.org.uk* Ⓤ *Westminster.*

★ **St. Martin-in-the-Fields.** Popular lunchtime concerts (free but £3.50 donation suggested) are held in this lovely 1726 church, as are regular evening concerts. You can sit in on many rehearsals for free. ■TIP➔ **Stop for a snack at the Café in the Crypt.** ⊠ *Trafalgar Sq., Covent Garden* ☎ *020/7766–1100* ⊕ *www.stmartin-in-the-fields.org* Ⓤ *Charing Cross.*

Southbank Centre. Both the Philharmonia and the London Philharmonic orchestras are based here, and other venues host smaller-scale music performances; the Queen Elizabeth Hall has chamber orchestras and top-tier soloists, and in the intimate Purcell Room you can listen to chamber music and solo recitals. ⊠ *Belvedere Rd., South Bank* ☎ *0844/847–9910* ⊕ *www.southbankcentre.org.uk* Ⓤ *Waterloo.*

Fodor's Choice **Wigmore Hall.** Hear chamber music and song recitals in this charming ★ hall with near-perfect acoustics. Don't miss the midmorning Sunday concerts. ⊠ *36 Wigmore St., Marylebone* ☎ *020/7935–2141* ⊕ *www.wigmore-hall.org.uk* Ⓤ *Bond St.*

CONTEMPORARY ART

In the 21st century, the focus of the city's art scene has shifted from the past to the future. Helped by the prominence of the Tate Modern, London's contemporary art scene has never been so high profile. In publicly funded exhibition spaces like the Barbican Gallery, the Hayward Gallery, the Institute of Contemporary Arts, and the Serpentine Gallery, London now has a modern-art environment on a par with Bilbao and New York. Young British Artists (YBAs, though no longer as young as they once were) Damien Hirst, Tracey Emin, and others are firmly planted in the public imagination. The celebrity status of British artists is in part thanks to the annual Turner Prize, which always stirs up controversy in the media during a monthlong display of the work, usually at Tate Britain.

The South Bank's Tate Modern may house the giants of modern art, but East London is where the innovative action is. There are dozens of galleries in the fashionable spaces around Old Street, and the truly hip have already moved even farther east, to areas such as Bethnal Green. The Whitechapel Art Gallery and Jay Jopling's influential White Cube in Hoxton Square remain at the epicenter of the new art establishment and continue to show exciting work by emerging British artists.

Barbican Centre. Innovative exhibitions of 20th-century and current art and design are shown in the Barbican Gallery and the **Curve** (✉ *Usually free* ⊙ *Mon., Thurs.–Sun. 11–8, Tues. and Wed. 11–6).* ⊠ *Silk St., The City* ☎ *020/7638–8891* ⊕ *www.barbican.org.uk* ✉ *Prices vary with exhibition (some free), tickets cheaper if booked online in advance* ⊙ *Mon., Thurs.–Sun. 11–8, Tues. and Wed. 11–6* Ⓤ *Barbican.*

★ **Hayward Gallery.** This modern art gallery is a classic example of 1960s Brutalist architecture. It's part of the Southbank Centre and is one of London's major venues for contemporary art exhibitions. ⊠ *Belvedere Rd., Southbank Centre, South Bank* ☎ *08703/800–400* ⊕ *www. hayward.org.uk* ✉ *Prices vary with exhibition (some free)* ⊙ *Sat.– Thurs. 10–6, Fri. 10–10* Ⓤ *Waterloo.*

Institute of Contemporary Arts. Housed in an elegant John Nash–designed Regency terrace, the ICA's three galleries have changing exhibitions of contemporary visual art. The ICA also programs performance, film, new media, literary talks, and photography. There's an arts bookstore, cafeteria, and bar. ⊠ *Nash House, The Mall, St. James's* ☎ *020/7930– 3647 or 020/7930–0493* ⊕ *www.ica.org.uk* ✉ *Free* ⊙ *Daily noon–7:30, Thurs. noon–9* Ⓤ *Charing Cross.*

Lisson. Owner Nicholas Logsdail represents about 40 blue-chip artists, including minimalist Sol Lewitt and Dan Graham, at arguably the most respected gallery in London. The gallery is most associated with New Object sculptors like Anish Kapoor and Richard Deacon, many of whom have won the Turner Prize. A branch down the road at 29 Bell Street features work by younger, up-and-coming artists. ⊠ *52–54 Bell St., Marylebone* ☎ *020/7724–2739* ⊕ *www.lissongallery.com* ✉ *Free* ⊙ *Weekdays 10–6, Sat. 11–5* Ⓤ *Edgware Rd., Marylebone.*

Royal Academy. Housed in an aristocratic mansion and home to Britain's first art school (founded in 1768), the academy is best known for its blockbuster special exhibitions—like the record-breaking Monet, and the controversial Sensation drawn from the Saatchi collection. The annual Summer Exhibition has been a popular London tradition since 1769. ⊠ *Burlington House, Mayfair* ☎ *020/7300–8000* ⊕ *www. royalacademy.org.uk* ✉ *From £8, prices vary with exhibition* ☉ *Daily 10–6, except Fri. 10–10* Ⓤ *Piccadilly Circus.*

Saatchi Gallery. Charles Saatchi's ultramodern gallery devoted to leading contemporary artists occupies all 70,000 square feet of the duke of York's HQ building in Chelsea and has a bookshop and café-bar. ⊠ *Duke of York's HQ, Sloane Sq., Chelsea* ☎ *020/7823–2332* ⊕ *www. saatchi-gallery.co.uk* ✉ *Free* Ⓤ *Sloane Sq.*

Serpentine Gallery. Built in 1934 as a tea pavilion in Kensington Gardens, the Serpentine has an international reputation for exhibitions of modern and contemporary art. Man Ray, Henry Moore, Andy Warhol, Bridget Riley, Damien Hirst, and Rachel Whiteread are a few of the artists who have had exhibits here. The annual Summer Pavilion, designed by a different leading architect every year, is always worth catching. ⊠ *Kensington Gardens, South Kensington* ☎ *020/7402–6075* ⊕ *www.serpentinegallery.org* ✉ *Free* ☉ *Daily 10–6* Ⓤ *South Kensington, Knightsbridge.*

Fodor's Choice ★ **Tate Modern.** This converted power station is one of the largest modernart galleries in the world, so give yourself ample time to take it all in. The permanent collection includes work by all the major 20th-century artists, though only a fraction is shown at any one time. There are also blockbuster touring shows and solo exhibitions of international artists. ■ TIP→ The bar on the top floor has gorgeous views overlooking the Thames and St. Paul's Cathedral. ⊠ *Bankside, South Bank* ☎ *020/7887–8888* ⊕ *www.tate.org.uk* ✉ *Free–£12.50* ☉ *Sun.–Thurs. 10–6, Fri. and Sat. 10–10* Ⓤ *Southwark.*

Victoria Miro Gallery. This important commercial gallery has exhibited some of the biggest names on the British contemporary art scene—Chris Ofili, the Chapman brothers, Peter Doig, to name a few. ⊠ *16 Wharf Rd., Islington* ☎ *020/7336–8109* ⊕ *www.victoria-miro.com* ✉ *Free* ☉ *Tues.–Sat. 10–6* Ⓤ *Old St., Angel.*

★ **White Cube.** Jay Joplin's influential gallery is housed in a 1920s light-industrial building on Hoxton Square. Many of its artists are Turner Prize stars—Hirst, Emin, Hume, et al.—and many live in the East End, which supposedly has the highest concentration of artists in Europe. Farther west, White Cube has a second gallery in a striking building in Mason's Yard, St. James's. ⊠ *48 Hoxton Sq., Hoxton* ☎ *020/7930–5373* ⊕ *www.whitecube.com* ✉ *Free* ☉ *Tues.–Sat. 10–6* Ⓤ *Old St.*

★ **Whitechapel Art Gallery.** Established in 1897, this independent East End gallery is one of London's most innovative and consistently interesting. Jeff Wall, Bill Viola, Gary Hume, and Janet Cardiff have exhibited here. In spring 2009 the gallery will complete its expansion into what was previously a library next door; confirm opening hours in advance. ⊠ *80–82 Whitechapel High St., Shoreditch* ☎ *020/7522–7888* ⊕ *www. whitechapel.org* ✉ *Free–£8* ☉ *Wed.–Sun. 11–6* Ⓤ *Aldgate East.*

DANCE

The **English National Ballet** and visiting international companies usually perform at the London Coliseum and at Sadler's Wells. The **Royal Ballet**, world renowned for its classical excellence, as well as innovative contemporary dance from several companies and scores of independent choreographers, can be seen at the Royal Opera House. Encompassing the newly refurbished **Royal Festival Hall**, the Southbank Centre has a seriously good contemporary dance program that hosts top international companies and important U.K. choreographers, as well as multicultural offerings from Japanese Butoh and Indian Kathak to hip-hop. The **Place** and the **Lilian Bayliss Theatre** at Sadler's Wells are where you'll find the most daring, cutting-edge performances.

The biggest annual event is **Dance Umbrella** (☎ *0844/412–4312* ⊕ *www.danceumbrella.co.uk*), a seven-week season from September to November that hosts international and British-based artists at various venues across the city.

The following theaters are the key dance venues. Check weekly listings or ⊕ *www.londondance.com* for current performances and fringe venues.

DANCE BOX OFFICES **London Coliseum** (✉ *St. Martin's La., Covent Garden* ☎ *020/7632–8300* Ⓤ *Leicester Sq.*).

The **Place** (✉ *17 Duke's Rd., Bloomsbury* ☎ *020/7121–1000* ⊕ *www.theplace.org.uk* Ⓤ *Euston*).

Fodor'sChoice ★ **Royal Opera House** (✉ *Bow St., Covent Garden* ☎ *020/7304–4000* ⊕ *www.roh.org.uk* Ⓤ *Covent Garden*).

Fodor'sChoice ★ **Sadler's Wells** (✉ *Rosebery Ave., Islington* ☎ *0844/412–4322* ⊕ *www.sadlers-wells.com* Ⓤ *Angel*).

Southbank Centre (✉ *Belvedere Rd., South Bank* ☎ *0844/875–0073* ⊕ *www.southbankcentre.co.uk* Ⓤ *Waterloo, Embankment*).

FILM

There are many lovely movie theaters in London and several that are committed to nonmainstream cinema, notably the National Film Theatre. Most of the major houses, such as the Odeon Leicester Square and the Empire, are in the Leicester Square–Piccadilly Circus area, where tickets average £12. Monday and matinees are often cheaper, at around £6–£10, and there are also fewer crowds.

Ⓒ ★ **BFI Southbank.** With easily the best repertory programming in London, the three cinemas at what was previously known as the National Film Theatre are effectively a national film center run by the British Film Institute. They show more than 1,000 titles each year, favoring art-house, foreign, silent, overlooked, classic, noir, and short films over Hollywood blockbusters. After a recent rejuvenation and expansion, the center also has a gallery, bookshop, and "mediatheque," where visitors can watch film and television from the National Archive. ■TIP→ **The London Film Festival is based here at BFI Southbank; throughout the year there are minifestivals, seminars, and guest speakers. Members (£35) get priority bookings (useful for special events) and £1 off each screening.** ✉ *Belvedere*

Rd., South Bank ☎ *020/7633–0274 information, 020/7928–3232 box office* ⊕ *www.bfi.org.uk* Ⓤ *Waterloo.*

★ **Curzon Soho.** This comfortable cinema runs an artsy program of mixed repertoire and mainstream films. There are also branches in Mayfair, Bloomsbury, Chelsea, and Richmond. Members (£25) get discounts. ✉ *99 Shaftesbury Ave., Soho* ☎ *0871/703–3988* Ⓤ *Piccadilly Circus, Leicester Sq.* ✉ *38 Curzon St., Mayfair* ☎ *0871/703–3989* ⊕ *www. curzoncinemas.com* Ⓤ *Green Park.*

☺ **The Electric Cinema.** This refurbished Portobello Road art house screens mainstream and international movies. The emphasis is on comfort, with leather sofas, armchairs, footstools, and mini–coffee tables for your popcorn. Saturday matinees for kids are popular. ✉ *191 Portobello Rd., Notting Hill* ☎ *020/7908–9696* ⊕ *www.electriccinema.co.uk* Ⓤ *Ladbroke Grove, Notting Hill Gate.*

OPERA

The two key players in London's opera scene are the Royal Opera House (which ranks with the Metropolitan Opera House in New York) and the more innovative English National Opera (ENO), which presents English-language productions at the London Coliseum. Only the Theatre Royal, Drury Lane, has a longer theatrical history than the Royal Opera House—the third theater to be built on the site since 1858.

Despite occasional performances by the likes of Björk, the Royal Opera House struggles to shrug off its reputation for elitism and ticket prices that can rise to £190. It is more accessible than it used to be—the cheapest tickets are just £4. Conditions of purchase vary; call for information. Prices for the ENO are generally lower, ranging from around £12 to £80. You can get same-day balcony seats for as little as £5.

Almeida Opera is a festival that often showcases cutting-edge opera. In summer, the increasingly adventurous Opera Holland Park presents the usual chestnuts alongside some obscure works under a newly enlarged canopy in leafy Holland Park.

OPERA BOX OFFICES **Almeida Theatre** (✉ *Almeida St., Islington* ☎ *020/7359–4404* ⊕ *www. almeida.co.uk* Ⓤ *Angel*).

English National Opera (✉ *St. Martin's La., Covent Garden* ☎ *0871/911–0200* ⊕ *www.eno.org* Ⓤ *Leicester Sq.*).

Opera Holland Park (✉ *Holland Park, Kensington High St., Kensington* ☎ *0845/230–9769* ⊕ *www.operahollandpark.com* Ⓤ *Kensington High St.*).

Fodor'sChoice ★ **Royal Opera House** (✉ *Bow St., Covent Garden* ☎ *020/7304–4000* ⊕ *www.royalopera.org* Ⓤ *Covent Garden*).

THEATER

In London the play really *is* the thing, ranging from a long-running popular musical like *Mamma Mia!*, a groundbreaking reworking of Pinter, imaginative physical theater from an experimental company like *Complicite,* a lavish Disney spectacle, or a small fringe production above a pub. West End glitz and glamour continue to pull in the audiences, and so do the more innovative productions. Only in London will a Tuesday matinee of the Royal Shakespeare Company's *Henry IV* sell out a 1,200-seat theater.

The **Royal Shakespeare Company** (⊕ *www.rsc.org.uk*) and the **Royal National Theatre Company** (⊕ *www.nationaltheatre.org.uk*) often stage contemporary versions of the classics. The Almeida, Battersea Arts Centre (BAC), Donmar Warehouse, Royal Court Theatre, Soho Theatre, and the Old Vic attract famous actors and have excellent reputations for new writing and innovative theatrical approaches. These are the venues where you'll see an original production before it becomes a hit in the West End or on Broadway (and for a fraction of the cost). From mid-May through mid-September you can see the Bard served up at the open-air reconstruction of Shakespeare's Globe Theatre on the South Bank.

Theatergoing isn't cheap. Tickets less than £10 are a rarity, although designated productions at the National Theatre have seats at this price. At the commercial theaters you should expect to pay from £15 for a seat in the upper balcony to at least £25 for a good one in the stalls (orchestra) or dress circle (mezzanine). However, last-minute returns available on the night may provide some good deals. Tickets may be booked through ticket agents, at individual theater box offices, or over the phone by credit card. Be sure to inquire about any extra fees—prices can vary enormously, but agents are legally obliged to reveal the face value of the ticket if you ask. All the larger hotels offer theater bookings, but they tack on a hefty service charge.

Be very wary of ticket touts (scalpers) and unscrupulous ticket agents outside theaters and working the line at TKTS (a half-price ticket booth)—they try to sell tickets at five times the price of the ticket at legitimate box offices, and you pay a stiff fine if caught buying a scalped ticket.

Ticketmaster (☎ *0870/534–4444* ☎ *161/385–1420 from outside U.K.* ⊕ *www.ticketmaster.co.uk*) sells tickets to a number of different theaters, although they charge a booking fee. For discount tickets, **Society of London Theatre** (☎ *020/7557–6700*) operates TKTS, a half-price ticket booth (⊕ *www.tkts.co.uk*) on the southwest corner of Leicester Square, and sells the best available seats to performances at about 25 theaters. It's open Monday–Saturday 10–7, Sunday noon–3; there's a £2.50 service charge (included in the price). Major credit cards are accepted.

THEATERS

★ **Almeida Theatre.** This Off–West End venue premieres excellent new plays and exciting twists on the classics. Hollywood stars often perform here. ⊠ *Almeida St., Islington* ☎ *020/7359–4404* ⊕ *www.almeida. co.uk* Ⓤ *Angel, Highbury, and Islington.*

★ **BAC.** Battersea Arts Centre has a reputation for producing innovative new work. Check out Scratch, a monthly, pay-what-you-can night of low-tech cabaret theater by emerging artists where the audience provides feedback on works-in-progress. Tuesday shows also have pay-what-you-can entry. ⊠ *176 Lavender Hill, Battersea* ☎ *020/7223–2223* ⊕ *www.bac.org.uk* Ⓤ *British Rail: Clapham Junction.*

Barbican Centre. Built in 1982, the Barbican Centre puts on a number of performances by British and international theater companies as part of its year-round **B.I.T.E.** (Barbican International Theatre Events), which also features groundbreaking performance, dance, drama, and musical theater. ✉ *Silk St., The City* ☎ *020/7638–8891* ⊕ *www.barbican.org. uk* Ⓤ *Barbican.*

Fodor's Choice ★ **Donmar Warehouse.** Hollywood stars often perform here in diverse and daring new works, bold interpretations of the classics, and small-scale musicals. It works both ways, too—former director Sam Mendes went straight from here to directing *American Beauty.* ✉ *41 Earlham St., Covent Garden* ☎ *0870/060–6624* ⊕ *www.donmarwarehouse.com* Ⓤ *Covent Garden.*

National Theatre. Opened in 1976, the National Theatre has three venues: the 1,120-seat Olivier, the 890-seat Lyttelton, and the 300-seat Cottesloe. Musicals, classics, and new plays are in repertoire. ■**TIP➜ An adventurous ticketing scheme means some performances can be seen for as little as £10.** ✉ *Southbank Centre, Belvedere Rd., South Bank* ☎ *020/7452–3000* ⊕ *www.nationaltheatre.org.uk* ⚑ *Tour £5* ⊙ *Foyer Mon.–Sat. 10 AM–11 PM; 75-min tour backstage up to 6 times daily weekdays, twice on Sat.* Ⓤ *Waterloo.*

The Old Vic. American actor Kevin Spacey is the artistic director of this grand 1818 Victorian theater. Legends of the stage have performed here, including John Gielgud, Vivien Leigh, Peter O'Toole, Richard Burton, Judi Dench, and Laurence Olivier, who called it his favorite theater. ✉ *The Cut, Southwark* ☎ *0870/060–6628* ⊕ *www.oldvictheatre.com* Ⓤ *Waterloo.*

Fodor's Choice ★ **Open Air Theatre.** On a warm summer evening, classical theater in the pastoral and royal Regent's Park is hard to beat for magical adventure. Enjoy a supper before the performance, a bite during the intermission on the picnic lawn, or drinks in the spacious bar. ✉ *Inner Circle, Regent's Park* ☎ *0844/826–4242* ⊕ *www.openairtheatre.org* Ⓤ *Baker St., Regent's Park.*

★ **Royal Court Theatre.** Britain's undisputed epicenter of new writing, the RCT is now 50 years old and continues to produce gritty British and international drama. ■**TIP➜ Don't miss the best deal in town–£10 tickets on Monday.** ✉ *Sloane Sq., Chelsea* ☎ *020/7565–5000* ⊕ *www. royalcourttheatre.com* Ⓤ *Sloane Sq.*

Fodor's Choice ★ **Shakespeare's Globe Theatre.** This faithful reconstruction of the open-air playhouse where Shakespeare worked and wrote many of his greatest plays re-creates the 16th-century theatergoing experience. Standing room in the "pit" right in front of the stage costs £5. The season runs May through September. ✉ *21 New Globe Walk, Bankside, South Bank* ☎ *020/7401–9919* ⊕ *www.shakespeares-globe.org* Ⓤ *Southwark, Mansion House, walk across Southwark Bridge; London Bridge.*

Soho Theatre. This sleek theater in the heart of Soho is devoted to fostering new writing and is a prolific presenter of work by emerging writers and comedy performance. ✉ *21 Dean St., Soho* ☎ *0870/429–6883* ⊕ *www.sohotheatre.com* Ⓤ *Tottenham Court Rd.*

THE SPORTS SCENE

London will host the 2012 Olympics, but don't expect to see many city inhabitants practicing their javelin throws in Hyde Park. Sport in the capital comes into its own when it's watched, rather than participated in. You'll most easily witness London's fervent sporting passions in front of a screen in a pub with a pint in hand. And those passions run deep.

CRICKET

★ Lord's (✉ St. John's Wood Rd., St. John's Wood ☎ 020/7432–1000 ⊕ www.lords.org Ⓤ St. John's Wood) has been hallowed turf for worshippers of England's summer game since 1811. Tickets are hard to come by: obtain an application form and enter the ballot (lottery) to purchase tickets. Forms are sent out in early December or you can apply online. Test Match tickets cost between £25 and £95. Cheaper county matches (Middlesex plays here) can usually be seen by lining up on match day.

FOOTBALL

Three of London's football (soccer) clubs competing in the **Premier League** and the Football Association's FA Cup are particularly popular, though not always correspondingly successful: **Arsenal** (✉ Emirates Stadium, Ashburton Grove, Islington ☎ 020/7704–4040 ⊕ www.arsenal.com Ⓤ Arsenal), **Chelsea** (✉ Stamford Bridge, Fulham Rd., Fulham ☎ 0871/984–1905 ⊕ www.chelseafc.co.uk Ⓤ Fulham Broadway), and **Tottenham Hotspur** ("Spurs" ✉ White Hart La., 748 High Rd., Tottenham ☎ 0844/499–5000 ⊕ www.tottenhamhotspur.com Ⓤ National Rail: White Hart La.). Try to buy tickets in advance, and don't get too carried away by the excitement a vast football crowd can generate.

TENNIS

The **Wimbledon Lawn Tennis Championships** (☎ 020/8946–2244 ⊕ www.wimbledon.org), the most prestigious of the four Grand Slam tournaments, is also one of London's most eagerly awaited annual events. There's a lottery system for advance purchse; check the Web site. You can purchase tickets online for the next day's matches throughout the tournament.

↺ **Tricycle Theatre.** The Tricycle is committed to the best in Irish, African-Caribbean, Asian, and political drama, and the promotion of new plays. ✉ 269 Kilburn High Rd., Kilburn ☎ 020/7328–1000 ⊕ www.tricycle. co.uk Ⓤ Kilburn.

Young Vic. Ensconced in a new home near Waterloo, big names perform here alongside young talent, often in daring, innovative productions of classic plays. ✉ 66 The Cut, Waterloo, South Bank ☎ 020/7928–6363 ⊕ www.youngvic.org Ⓤ Waterloo.

SHOPPING

Napoléon was being scornful when he called Britain a nation of shopkeepers, but Londoners have had the last laugh. The finest emporiums are in London, still. You can shop like royalty at Her Majesty's glove maker, discover an uncommon Toby jug in a Kensington antiques shop, or find a leather-bound edition of *Wuthering Heights* on Charing Cross Road. If you have a yen to keep up with the Windsors, head for stores proclaiming they are "By Appointment" to H. M. the Queen— or to Prince Philip or the Prince of Wales. The fashion-forward crowd favors places such as Harvey Nichols or Browns of South Molton Street, whereas the most ardent fashion victims will shoot to Notting Hill, London's prime fashion location. If you have limited time, zoom in on one of the city's grand department stores, such as Harrods, Marks & Spencer, or Selfridges, where you can find enough booty for your entire gift list. Below is a brief introduction to the major shopping areas.

Apart from bankrupting yourself, the only problem you may encounter is exhaustion. London is a town of many far-flung shopping areas. ■TIP→ **Real shophounds plan their excursions with military precision, taking in only one or two shopping districts in a day, with fortifying stops for lunch, tea, and a pint or glass of wine in the pub.**

CAMDEN TOWN
: Every kind of alternative style—retro, Goth, New Romantic, New Age, punk, hippie, "Annie Hall"—is catered to in the crafts and vintage-clothing markets spreading out from Camden Town Underground Station.

CHELSEA
: Chelsea centers on King's Road, once synonymous with ultrahigh fashion; it still harbors some designer boutiques, plus antiques and home-furnishings stores.

COVENT GARDEN
: This neighborhood has chain clothing stores and top designers, stalls selling crafts, and shops selling gifts of every type—bikes, kites, tea, herbs, beads, hats—you name it.

FULHAM
: Fulham is divided into two postal districts, SW6 (farther away from the center of town) and SW10 (which is the closer, beyond Chelsea) on the high-fashion King's Road.

KENSINGTON
: Kensington's main drag, Kensington High Street, houses some small, classy shops, with a few larger stores at the eastern end. Try Kensington Church Street for expensive antiques, plus a little fashion.

KNIGHTS-BRIDGE
: Knightsbridge, east of Kensington, has Harrods but also Harvey Nichols, the top clothes stop, and many expensive designers' boutiques along Sloane Street, Walton Street, and Beauchamp Place.

MARYLEBONE
: Behind Oxford Street lies this village-like spot, with Marylebone High Street as its main artery. There are restaurants, upscale delis, and designer furniture stores; chic boutiques spill over onto satellite streets.

MAYFAIR
: In Mayfair are the two Bond streets, Old and New, with desirable dress designers, jewelers, and fine art. South Molton Street has high-price, high-style fashion, and the tailors of Savile Row have worldwide reputations.

NOTTING HILL
: Go westward from the famous Portobello Road market and explore the Ledbury Road–Westbourne Grove axis, Clarendon Cross, and Kensington Park Road for a mix of antiques and up-to-the-minute must-haves for body and lifestyle. Toward the more bohemian foot of Portobello are Ladbroke Grove and Golborne Road, where, in among the tatty stores, Portuguese cafés, and patisseries, you can bag bargains.

PIMLICO AND VICTORIA
Not quite Belgravia, not quite anywhere really, this odd little corner of London, bounded by Lower Sloane Street, Pimlico Road, Ebury Street, and Elizabeth Street, is a center for quirky and individual antiques, home decor, fashion, and food shops.

REGENT STREET
At right angles to Oxford Street is Regent Street, with possibly London's most pleasant department store, Liberty, plus Hamleys, the capital's favorite toy store. Shops around once-famous Carnaby Street stock designer youth paraphernalia and 57 varieties of the T-shirt.

ST. JAMES'S
Here the English gentleman buys everything but the suit (which is from Savile Row): handmade hats, shirts and shoes, silver shaving kits, and hip flasks. Nothing in this neighborhood is cheap, in any sense.

DEPARTMENT STORES

Browns (⌂ *24–27 South Molton St., Mayfair* ☎ *020/7514–0016* Ⓤ *Bond St.*) caters to the very label-conscious customer in a mini-department store setting. You will find men's and women's fashion from Alexander McQueen and Marni and Chloe, as well as lesser-known designers.

Fodor'sChoice
★
Harrods (⌂ *87–135 Brompton Rd., Knightsbridge* ☎ *020/7730–1234* Ⓤ *Knightsbridge*), one of the world's most famous department stores, can be forgiven its immodest motto, *Omnia, omnibus, ubique* ("everything, for everyone, everywhere"), because it has more than 300 well-stocked departments. If you approach Harrods as a tourist attraction rather than a fashion store, you won't be disappointed: focus on the spectacular food halls, the huge ground-floor perfumery, the marble-clad accessory rooms, and the theme park–like Egyptian Room.

Harvey Nichols (⌂ *109–125 Knightsbridge, Knightsbridge* ☎ *020/7235–5000* Ⓤ *Knightsbridge*) is famed for five floors of ultimate fashion; every label any chic, well-bred London lady covets is here, as well as a home-furnishings department. It's also known for the restaurant, Fifth Floor.

Fodor'sChoice
★
Liberty (⌂ *Regent St., Mayfair* ☎ *020/7734–1234* Ⓤ *Oxford Circus*), full of nooks and crannies, is famous principally for its fabulous fabrics. It also carries Eastern and exotic goods, menswear, womenswear, fragrances, soaps, and accessories.

Marks & Spencer (⌂ *458 Oxford St., Oxford Street* ☎ *020/7935–7954* Ⓤ *Marble Arch*) is a major chain that's an integral part of the British way of life—sturdy, practical clothes and good materials. What it *is* renowned for is underwear; the English all buy theirs here. The food department at M&S is consistently superb. (Look for their M&S Simply Food stores all over town.)

★
Selfridges (⌂ *400 Oxford St., Oxford Street* ☎ *0870/837–7377* Ⓤ *Bond St.*), huge and hip, is giving Harvey Nicks a run as London's leading fashion department store. It's packed with high-profile, popular designer clothes for everyone in the family. There's a globe-spanning Food Hall on the ground floor, and a ground-floor Wonder Room, which showcases extravagant jewelry and unusual gifts.

SPECIALTY STORES

ANTIQUES

★ **Alfie's Antique Market** (✉ *13–25 Church St., Marylebone* ☎ *020/7723–6066* ✆ *Closed Sun. and Mon.* Ⓤ *Edgware Rd.*), a huge labyrinth on several floors, has dealers specializing in anything and everything but particularly in vintage clothing, decorative accessories, and furniture. **Antiquarius** (✉ *131–145 King's Rd., Chelsea* ☎ *020/7823–3900* ✆ *Closed Sun.* Ⓤ *Sloane Sq.*), near Sloane Square, is an indoor antiques market with around 100 stalls selling collectibles, art deco brooches, vintage costume jewelry, old pocket watches, and silver salt cellars. **Grays Antique Market** (✉ *58 Davies St., Mayfair* ☎ *020/7629–7034* ✆ *Closed Sun.; open Sat. in Dec. only* Ⓤ *Bond St.*) assembles dealers specializing in everything from Sheffield plates to Asian antiquities. Bargains are not impossible, and proper pedigrees are guaranteed. It's closed Saturday (except December) and Sunday.

★ **London Silver Vaults** (✉ *53–64 Chancery La., Holborn* ☎ *020/7242–3844* ✆ *Closed Sat. after 1, and Sun.* Ⓤ *Chancery La.*) has more than 30 dealers specializing in antique silver and jewelry.

APPLIED ARTS AND HANDICRAFTS

★ The **Lesley Craze Gallery** (✉ *33–35A Clerkenwell Green, East End* ☎ *020/7608–0393* ✆ *Closed Sun.; open Mon. in Nov. and Dec. only* Ⓤ *Farringdon*) carries exquisite jewelry by some 100 young designers from around the world, with a strong British bias, featuring both precious and semiprecious stones. There's also a textiles room showcasing unusual and colorful handmade scarves, bags, and cushions. **OXO Tower** (✉ *Bargehouse St., South Bank* ☎ *020/7401–2255* ✆ *Some studios closed Mon. or Sun.* Ⓤ *Southwark*) holds around 30 glass walled workshops that sell excellent handmade goods.

BOOKS, CDS, AND RECORDS

BOOKS Charing Cross Road is London's "booksville," with a couple of dozen antiquarian booksellers and many mainstream bookshops, too. Cecil Court, off Charing Cross Road, is a pedestrian-only lane filled with specialty bookstores (⊕ *www.cecilcourt.co.uk*).

Books for Cooks (✉ *4 Blenheim Crescent, Notting Hill* ☎ *020/7221–1992* Ⓤ *Notting Hill Gate*) is hard to resist. Just about every world cuisine is represented on its shelves, along with the complete lineup of celebrity-chef editions.

Fodor'sChoice **Foyles** (✉ *113–119 Charing Cross Rd., Soho* ☎ *020/7437–5660* Ⓤ *Tottenham Court Rd.*) is so vast you can find almost anything. Store-within-a-store Ray's Jazz has a cool café, and there's even a piranha tank on the children's floor.

Fodor'sChoice **Hatchards** (✉ *187 Piccadilly, St. James's* ☎ *020/7439–9921* Ⓤ *Piccadilly Circus*) has a huge stock and a well-informed staff. **John Sandoe Books, Ltd.** (✉ *10 Blacklands Terr., Chelsea* ☎ *020/7589–9473* Ⓤ *Sloane Sq.*) has more than 25,000 titles that fill three dollhouse-size floors of an 18th-century house. **Maggs Brothers Ltd.** (✉ *50 Berkeley Sq., Mayfair* ☎ *020/7493–7160* ✆ *Closed weekends* Ⓤ *Green Park*), with a deliciously Dickensian name, is in a Georgian town house in one of

GREAT SPOTS TO SHOP

Portobello Road Market. Whether you are a serious antiques buyer or just want to browse the stalls and people-watch, Portobello Road is London's most dynamic market.

Liberty. In a Tudor-style building, Liberty has an outstanding collection of clothing crafted from its famous prints and furniture, as well as cutting-edge fashion.

Dover Street Market. This concept store is a combination art gallery and department store, and also hosts design retrospectives.

Hamleys. With floor after floor of treasures for every child on your list, this is *the* London toy shop.

Rellik. Celebs love Rellik for its superb collection of vintage clothing, ranging from classic Dior to Vivienne Westwood.

Mint. Fans of contemporary furniture and housewares should head to Mint, which showcases the work of both leading and up-and-coming designers.

Mayfair's elegant squares. Maggs was established in 1853, and is one of the world's oldest and largest rare-book dealers. **Stanfords** (⊠ *12–14 Long Acre, Covent Garden* ☎ *020/7836–1321* Ⓤ *Covent Garden*) specializes in travel books and maps. **Waterstone's** (⊠ *203–206 Piccadilly, St. James's* ☎ *020/7851–2400* Ⓤ *Piccadilly Circus*) is part of an admirable chain with long hours and a program of author readings and signings. Their most upscale branch is book buying as hedonistic leisure activity, with five floors, a studio cocktail lounge with a view, and a café in the basement.

CDS AND RECORDS   The place for house, drum 'n' bass, electro, and dubstep, **BM Soho** (⊠ *25 D'Arblay St., Soho* ☎ *020/7437–0478* ☉ *Closed Sun.* Ⓤ *Oxford Circus*) stocks the hottest club music around. There are some CDs, but this is really a shop for vinyl lovers. **MDC Music & Movies** (⊠ *Festival Riverside, Royal Festival Hall, South Bank* ☎ *020/7620–0198* Ⓤ *Waterloo*) is a classical music specialist that has branched out into jazz and world music. **Music & Video Exchange** (⊠ *38 Notting Hill Gate, Notting Hill* ☎ *020/7243–8573* Ⓤ *Notting Hill Gate*) is a convenient destination for seekers of unusual and mainstream chart music as well as classical and pop.

★ **Rough Trade East** (⊠ *Dray Walk, Old Truman Brewery, 91 Brick La., East End* ☎ *020/7392–7788* Ⓤ *Liverpool St.*)is a veteran indie-music specialist that seems to have gotten the formula right—in 2007 it opened this spacious new East End branch that's as much a hangout as a shop, complete with a stage for live gigs, a café, and even free Internet access.

CLOTHING

Agent Provocateur (⊠ *16 Pont St., Knightsbridge* ☎ *020/7235–0229* ☉ *Open Sun. in Dec. only* Ⓤ *Knightsbridge, Sloane Sq.*) is the place to go for sexy, naughty-but-nice lingerie in gorgeous fabrics and lace. **Aquascutum** (⊠ *100 Regent St., Soho* ☎ *020/7675–8200* Ⓤ *Piccadilly Circus*) is known for its classic raincoats but also stocks clothing for men and women in classic British style. The men's suits and sweaters are timeless, and the women's collection has become surprisingly funky, offering fresh takes on overcoats and items like tunics and jersey dresses. Up-to-the-minute **b Store** (✉ *24A Savile Row, Mayfair* ☎ *020/7734–6846* ✆ *Closed Sun.* Ⓤ *Bond St.*, *Oxford Circus*) couldn't be farther away in terms of style from the traditional tailors down the street. Head here for cutting-edge pieces from avant-garde London designers such as Diana Brinks and Ute Ploeir, plus the store's quirky own-label shoes. **Burberry** (✉ *21–23 New Bond St.*, *Mayfair* ☎ *020/7968–0000* Ⓤ *Piccadilly Circus*) has gone for a more rock and roll image of late but still evokes English tradition, with mahogany closets and merchandise with the trademark "Burberry Check" tartan—scarves, umbrellas, shortbread tins, and those famous raincoats.

Fodor'sChoice **Dover Street Market** (✉ *17–18 Dover St.*, *Mayfair* ☎ *020/7518–0680*
★ Ⓤ *Green Park*) isn't just about buying; with its arty displays, it's as fascinating as any gallery. The creation of Comme des Garçons' Rei Kawakubo, it showcases the label's collections alongside other designers such as Lanvin, Alaïa, and exclusive Japanese lines, plus curiosities including antique medical specimens. ■**TIP➔ An outpost of the Rose Bakery on the top floor makes a handy pit stop.**

James Lock & Co. Ltd. (✉ *6 St. James's St.*, *St. James's* ☎ *020/7930–5849* ✆ *Closed Sun.* Ⓤ *Green Park, Piccadilly Circus*) is a cozy shop with a full selection of classic and traditional hats. **Margaret Howell** (✉ *34 Wigmore St.*, *Soho* ☎ *020/7009–9009* ✆ *Closed Sun.* Ⓤ *Oxford Circus*) makes quintessentially English clothes that have a nostalgic feel while managing to look contemporary. Howell mixes impeccable British tailoring and traditional fabrics (linen, cashmere, tweed) with relaxed modern cuts. **Nicole Farhi** (✉ *158 New Bond St.*, *Mayfair* ☎ *020/7499–8368* Ⓤ *Bond St.*) makes contemporary yet timeless quality clothes that are standbys in many a working woman's wardrobe; the men's collection is available at a branch in Covent Garden.

Fodor'sChoice **Rellik** (✉ *8 Golborne Rd.*, *Ladbroke Grove* ☎ *020/8962–0089* Ⓤ *West-*
★ *bourne Park*) is favored by the likes of Kate Moss and began as a street stall on Portobello Road. Today vintage hunters looking to splurge can find a selection of YSL, Chanel, and Dior, as well as items from lesser-known designers. Prices start at £30 and go up well over £1,000.

Fodor'sChoice **Topshop** (✉ *214 Oxford St.*, *Soho* ☎ *020/7636–7700* Ⓤ *Oxford Circus*)
★ is a genuine fashion hot spot with affordable prices. Clothing and accessories are geared to the younger end of the market, and the aim is to copy runway trends as fast as possible—although the store also has its own catwalk line, and a changing array of front-of-the-pack designers create small collections for the in-store Boutique. Topman is the male version of the chain.

MENSWEAR **Bamford & Sons** (✉ *31 Sloane Sq.*, *Chelsea* ☎ *020/7881–8010* Ⓤ *Sloane Sq.*) combines the British heritage of tailoring and fabrics with suave modernity. Dashing city wear, romantically nonchalant country clothes, plus fine leather and cashmere accessories are all available.

★ **Ozwald Boateng** (✉ *12A Savile Row, Mayfair* ☎ *0870/777–1377* ✆ *Closed Sun* Ⓤ *Piccadilly Circus*), pronounced Bwa-teng, is one of the funkiest tailors working on Savile Row. His made-to-measure suits are sought after by rock luminaries for their shock-color linings as well as great classic cuts.

★ **Turnbull & Asser** (✉ 71–72 Jermyn St., St. James's ☎ 020/7808–3000 ⊘ Closed Sun. Ⓤ Piccadilly Circus) is the custom shirtmaker. Alas, the first order must be for a minimum of six shirts, from about £150 each. There are less expensive, still exquisite ready-to-wear shirts, too.

WOMENSWEAR **Browns** (✉ 23–27 S. Molton St., Mayfair ☎ 020/7514–0000 ⊘ Open
★ Sun. in Dec. only Ⓤ Bond St.) was a pioneer designer boutique in the 1970s and continues to talent-spot the newest and best around. You may find the windows showcasing the work of top graduates from this year's student shows or displaying well-established designers such as Marni, Chloé, Juyna Watanabe, Yves Saint Laurent, Dries Van Noten, or Anne Demeulemeester.

Jigsaw (✉ 126–127 New Bond St., Mayfair ☎ 020/7491–4484 Ⓤ Bond St.) wins points for its reasonably priced separates, which don't sacrifice quality for fashion and suit women in their 20s through 40s.

Koh Samui (✉ 65–67 Monmouth St., Covent Garden ☎ 020/7240–4280 Ⓤ Covent Garden) stocks the clothing of about 40 hot young designers. Discover the next fashion wave before Vogue gets there. **Rigby & Peller** (✉ 2 Hans Rd., Knightsbridge ☎ 020/7589–9293 ⊘ Closed Sun. Ⓤ Knightsbridge) is a magnet for those who love luxury lingerie. The quality and service are excellent and much friendlier than you might expect. **Vivienne Westwood** (✉ 44 Conduit St., Mayfair ☎ 020/7439–1109 Ⓤ Bond St.), one of the top British designers, produces pompadour-punk ball gowns, Lady Hamilton vest coats, and foppish landmark getups that still represent the apex of high-style British couture.

GIFTS

Fodor's Choice **Floris** (✉ 89 Jermyn St., St. James's ☎ 020/7930–2885 ⊘ Closed Sun.
★ Ⓤ Piccadilly Circus) is one of London's most beautiful shops, with 19th-century glass and mahogany showcases filled with beautifully packaged soaps, perfumes, and its famous rose-scented mouthwash, gift possibilities include goose-down powder puffs and cut-glass atomizers.

Fodor's Choice **Fortnum & Mason** (✉ 181 Piccadilly, St. James's ☎ 020/7734–8040 Ⓤ Pic-
★ cadilly Circus), the Queen's grocer, is, paradoxically, the most egalitarian of gift stores, with plenty of luxury foods, stamped with the gold BY APPOINTMENT crest, for less than £5. Try the teas, preserves, tins of pâté, or or a box of Duchy Originals oatcakes.

Fodor's Choice **Hamleys** (✉ 188–196 Regent St., Soho ☎ 0870/333–2455 Ⓤ Oxford
★ Circus) is at the top of every London childs' wish list. A Regent Street institution, the shop has demonstrations, a play area, a café, and every cool toy on the planet.

Jo Malone, London's own passionate perfumer and cosmetician, began blending scents and creams in the 1990s, and now has shops around the world. In addition to selling heavenly scented products in elegantly simple, modern packaging, the shop also does facials and Fragrance Combining consultations. ✉ 150 Sloane St., Chelsea ☎ 0870/192–5121 Ⓤ Sloane Sq.

HOME DECOR

Fodor'sChoice
★
Mint (✉ *30 Wigmore St., Marylebone* ☎ *020/7224–4406* Ⓤ *Bond St.*) stocks an eclectic mix of furniture, art, ceramics, and home accessories. Mint also showcases works by up-and-coming designers and sells plenty of limited edition and one-off pieces.

CHINA AND
GLASS
Emma Bridgewater (✉ *81A Marylebone High St., Marylebone* ☎ *020/7486–6897* Ⓤ *Baker St., Regents Park*) is the home of fun and funky casual plates, mugs, jugs, and breakfast tableware for country-style designer kitchens. **Thomas Goode** (✉ *19 S. Audley St., Mayfair* ☎ *020/7499–2823* ☽ *Closed Sun.* Ⓤ *Green Park*) stocks lead crystal and formal china, including English Wedgwood and Minton, and is one of the world's top shops for these items.

JEWELRY

Asprey (✉ *167 New Bond St., Mayfair* ☎ *020/7493–6767* ☽ *Closed Sun.* Ⓤ *Bond St.*) displays exquisite jewelry and gifts, both antique and modern, in a discreet and very British environment

★ **Butler & Wilson** (✉ *189 Fulham Rd., Chelsea* ☎ *020/7352–3045* Ⓤ *S. Kensington*) has been marketing the diamanté, colored rhinestones, and crystal look—long before anybody ever heard the word bling. You can also find nostalgic gowns here. There's another branch at 20 South Molton Street. **Garrard** (✉ *24 Albemarle St., Mayfair* ☎ *020/7758–8520* ☽ *Closed Sun.* Ⓤ *Bond St.*) sets precious gems in simple, classic settings. Tradition rules, so you can still drop in to pick up a jeweled tiara.

★ **Kabiri** (✉ *37 Marylebone High St., Marylebone* ☎ *020/7224–1808* Ⓤ *Baker St., Bond St.*) is a dazzling array of exciting contemporary jewelry by emerging and established designers from around the world is packed into this small shop. There is something to suit most budgets and tastes.

PRINTS

Besides print stores, browse around the gallery shops, such as those at the Tate Britain and Tate Modern. In the open air, try hunting around Waterloo Bridge along the Riverside Walk Market, at St. James's Craft Market at St. James's Church in Piccadilly, and at the Apple Market near the Piazza, Covent Garden.

Grosvenor Prints (✉ *19 Shelton St., Covent Garden* ☎ *020/7836–1979* ☽ *Closed Sun.* Ⓤ *Covent Garden*) sells antiquarian prints, with an emphasis on London views and architecture as well as sporting and decorative prints

STREET MARKETS

★ **Bermondsey** is the market the dealers frequent for small antiques, which gives you an idea of its scope. The real bargains start going at 4 AM, but there'll be a few left if you arrive later. Take Bus 15 or 25 to Aldgate, then Bus 42 over Tower Bridge to Bermondsey Square; or take the tube to London Bridge and walk. ✉ *Long La. and Bermondsey Sq., South Bank* ☽ *Fri. 4* AM*–1* Ⓤ *London Bridge.*

★ **Borough Market,** a foodie's delight, carries whole-grain, organic everything, mainly from Britain but with an international flavor. ✉ *Borough*

*High St., South Bank ⊙ Thurs.
11–5, Fri. noon–6, Sat. 8–5 ⓤ London Bridge, Borough.*

The **Camden Markets** area is actually several markets gathered around a pair of locks in the Regent's Canal. The markets on Camden High Street mainly sell cheap T-shirts, second-hand clothes, and tacky pop-culture paraphernalia; it's best to head to Camden Lock and Stable Markets. Though much of the merchandise is youth oriented, the markets have

a lively appeal to aging hippies, fashion designers, and anyone with a taste for the bohemian who doesn't mind crowds and a bit of a madhouse scene. ⊠ *Camden Town ⊙ Camden Market, daily 9–6; Camden Lock Market, Stables Market, and Canal Market, daily 10–6; Electric Market, Sun. 10–5 ⓤ Camden Town, Chalk Farm.*

Covent Garden has craft stalls, jewelry designers, clothes makers, potters, and other artisans who congregate in the undercover central area known as the Apple Market. The Jubilee Market, toward Southampton Street, is less classy (printed T-shirts and the like), but on Monday the selection of vintage collectibles is worthwhile. This is more of a tourist magnet than other markets, and prices may reflect this. ⊠ *The Piazza, Covent Garden ⊙ Daily 9–5 ⓤ Covent Garden.*

Fodor'sChoice
★
Portobello Market, London's most famous market, still wins the prize for the all-round best. There are 1,500 antiques dealers here, so bargains are still possible. Nearer Notting Hill Gate, prices and quality are highest; the middle is where locals buy fruit and vegetables and hang out in trendy restaurants. Under the Westway elevated highway is a great flea market, and more bric-a-brac and bargains appear as you walk toward Golborne Road. Take Bus 52 or the tube here, and arrive early to beat the crowds. ⊠ *Portobello Rd., Notting Hill ⊙ Fruit and vegetables Mon.–Wed. and Fri. 8–5, Thurs. 8–1; antiques Fri. 8–3; food market and antiques Sat. 6–4:30 ⓤ Ladbroke Grove, Notting Hill Gate.*

Spitalfields, the covered market (once London's wholesale meat market), is at the center of this area's boho revival. The original building has been restored to its Victorian splendor, and a modern shopping complex that respects its character has been developed around it, with a covered area housing additional stalls. Wares include crafts, retro clothing, handmade rugs, soap, and cakes. And, from Spanish tapas to Thai satays, it's possible to eat your way around the world. ⊠ *Brushfield St., East End ⊙ Stalls Thurs. and Fri. 10–4, Sun. 9–5; restaurants weekdays 11–11, Sun. 9–5; retail shops daily 11–7 ⓤ Liverpool St., Aldgate, Aldgate East.*

The Southeast

CANTERBURY, DOVER, BRIGHTON, TUNBRIDGE WELLS

WORD OF MOUTH

"Dover Castle is massive. It takes much of a day by itself. There is everything from a Roman lighthouse to World War II tunnels. It isn't just a castle on top of a hill; it is a huge complex. Even driving and parking right at the top of the cliff without having to travel up from the town, I have usually spent about 5 hours there."

—janisj

"I think that your family might enjoy a day in Brighton—cool shops, some history and the beach, pier, etc."

—alihutch

Updated
by Christi
Daugherty

Once you are away from the highways and commuter tract housing near London, the Southeast—including Surrey, Kent, and Sussex, East and West—reveals some of England's loveliest countryside. Farms and storybook villages rooted in history punctuate gentle hills and woodlands, and the area's cathedral cities, including ancient Canterbury, wait patiently to be explored. Rivers wind down to a coast that is alternately sweeping chalk cliff and bustling seaside resort.

Where ancient hedgerows have been allowed to stand, this is still a landscape of small-scale features and pleasant hills. Viewed from the air, the tiny fields, neatly hedged, form a patchwork quilt. On the ground, fruit trees and even vineyards flourish in archetypal English landscapes and, often, atypical English sunshine.

Although it is close to London (both Surrey and Kent reach all the way to London's suburbs) and is one of the most densely populated areas of Britain, the Southeast includes Kent, the "Garden of England." Acre upon acre of orchards burst into a mass of pink-and-white blossoms in spring, though even here large-scale modern farming has done much to homogenize the landscape. In the Southeast, too, is Dover, whose chalky white cliffs and brooding castle have become symbols of Britain. Castles and stately homes, such as Petworth House and Knole, are major draws for travelers. Lovely gardens such as Vita Sackville-West's Sissinghurst and the Royal Horticultural Society's Wisley are also popular.

Famous seaside towns and resorts dot Sussex and Kent, the most famous being that eccentric combination of carnival and culture, Brighton. The busy ports of Newhaven, Folkestone, Dover, and Ramsgate have long been gateways to continental Europe. The Channel Tunnel, linking Britain to France by rail, runs from near Folkestone.

Indeed, because the English Channel is at its narrowest here, a great deal of British history has been forged in the Southeast. The Romans landed in this area and stayed to rule Britain for four centuries. So did the Saxons—Sussex means "the land of the South Saxons." The biggest invasion of them all took place here when William ("the Conqueror") of Normandy defeated the Saxons at a battle near Hastings in 1066, changing the island forever.

TOP REASONS TO GO

Bodiam, Dover, Hever, and Herstmonceux castles: Take your pick: the most evocative castles in a region filled with them dazzle you with their fortitude and fascinate you with their histories.

Brighton: With its nightclubs, sunbathing, and funky, relaxed atmosphere, this is the quintessential English seaside city. From the arcades of Brighton Pier to the fanciful rooms of the Royal Pavilion, there's something for everyone.

Canterbury Cathedral: This massive building, a textbook of medieval architecture, inspires awe with its soaring towers and flagstone corridors. The past seems very near in such places as Trinity Chapel, where ancient stained-glass windows celebrate Thomas à Becket's miracles.

Rye: Wandering the cobbled streets of this medieval town is a pleasure, and rummaging through its antiques stores is an adventure in itself. Reward yourself afterward as the English do, with tea and scones.

Treasure houses: Here is one of England's richest concentrations of historic homes: among the superlatives are Petworth House, with its luminous paintings by Turner; sprawling Knole, with its set of silver furniture; Ightham Mote, with its Tudor chapel; and Chartwell, home of Winston Churchill.

Amazing gardens: Gardens of all kinds are an English specialty, and at Sissinghurst and Wisley, as well as in the gardens of Hever Castle and Chartwell, you can easily spend an entire afternoon wandering through acres of floral exotica.

ORIENTATION AND PLANNING

GETTING ORIENTED

For sightseeing purposes, the Southeast can be divided into four sections. The eastern part of the region takes in the cathedral town of Canterbury, as well as the port city of Dover. The next section stretches along the southern coast from the medieval hill town of Rye to picturesque Lewes. A third area reaches from the coastal city of Brighton inward to Chichester and to sprawling Guildford. The fourth section takes in the spa town of Royal Tunbridge Wells and western Kent, where stately homes and castles dot the farmland. Larger towns in the area can be easily reached by train or bus from London for a day trip. To visit most castles, grand country homes, or quiet villages, though, you need to rent a car or join a tour.

Canterbury to Dover. Dover's distinctive white chalk cliffs plunging hundreds of feet into the sea are just a part of this region's dramatic coastal scenery. Don't miss Canterbury's medieval town center, dominated by its massive cathedral.

Rye to Lewes. Medieval villages dot the hills along this stretch of Sussex coastline. The centerpiece is Rye, a pretty hill town of cobbled streets lined with timbered homes. Lewes, with its crumbling castle, is another gem.

Brighton to Guildford. Funky, lively Brighton perfectly melds Victorian architecture with a modern vibe that includes the best shopping and dining on the coast. Outside of town are beautiful old homes such as Petworth House and even a Roman villa.

Castles and Houses Near Tunbridge Wells. From Anne Boleyn's regal childhood abode at Hever Castle to the medieval manor at Ightham Mote, this area is rich with grand houses. Spend a couple of days exploring them; Tunbridge Wells is a comfortable base.

PLANNING

WHEN TO GO

The counties of Kent, Surrey, and Sussex offer marvelous scenic landscapes, and you'll want to get your fill of the many outdoor attractions. It's best to visit in the spring, summer, or early fall. Many privately owned castles and mansions are open only between April and September or October. Failing that, the great parks surrounding the stately houses are often open all year. If crowds tend to spoil your fun, avoid August, Sunday, and national holidays, particularly in Canterbury and the seaside towns.

PLANNING YOUR TIME

With the exception of Brighton, you can easily see the highlights of most of the towns in less than a day. Brighton has more to offer, and you should allot at least two days to take it all in. Consider basing yourself in one town while exploring a region. For example, you could stay in Brighton and take in Lewes on a day trip. Base yourself in Rye for a couple of days while exploring Winchelsea, Battle, Hastings, and Herstmonceux Castle. Tunbridge Wells is a great place to overnight if you plan on exploring stately homes and castles like Hever and Ightham Mote.

GETTING HERE AND AROUND

AIR TRAVEL

Heathrow is very convenient for Surrey, but Gatwick Airport is a more convenient gateway for Kent. The rail station inside Gatwick has trains to Brighton and other major towns, and you can take a taxi from Heathrow to Guildford for around £40.

BUS TRAVEL

National Express buses serve the region from London's Victoria Coach Station. Trips to Brighton and Canterbury take two hours; to Chichester, about three hours. Megabus runs buses at budget prices from Victoria Coach Station to many of the same destinations as National Express and can be cheaper, although luggage limits are strict.

Bus service between towns can be useful but is often intermittent. Out in the country, don't expect buses more often than once every half hour or hour. Sometimes trains are a better option; sometimes they're much worse. Traveline is the best central place to call for bus information, and local Tourist Information Centres can help. Because more than

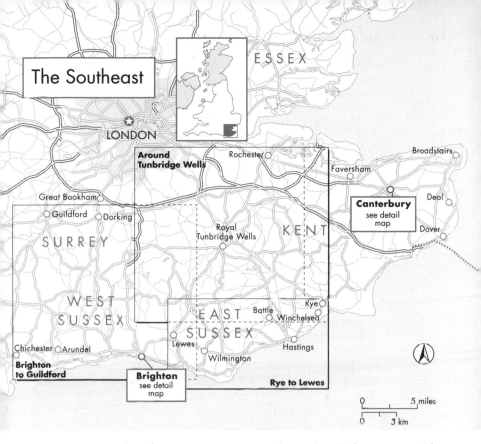

The Southeast

one private bus company can operate in a region, it's best to start with Traveline.

Contacts Megabus (⊕ *www.megabus.co.uk*). **National Express** (☏ *0871/781–8181* ⊕ *www.nationalexpress.com*). **Traveline** (☏ *0871/200–2233* ⊕ *www.traveline.org.uk*).

CAR TRAVEL

Traveling by car is the best way to get to the stately homes and castles in the region. Having a car in Canterbury or Brighton, however, is a nuisance; you'll need to park and walk. Major routes radiating outward from London to the Southeast are, from west to east, M23/A23 to Brighton (52 mi); A21, passing by Royal Tunbridge Wells to Hastings (65 mi); A20/M20 to Folkestone (58 mi); and A2/M2 via Canterbury (56 mi) to Dover (71 mi).

TRAIN TRAVEL

Trains are the fastest and most efficient way to travel to major cities in the region, but they do not stop in many small towns. From London, Southeastern trains serve Sussex and Kent from Victoria and Charing Cross stations, and South West trains travel to Surrey from Waterloo station. Getting to Brighton takes about one hour, to Canterbury about 1½ hours, and to Dover almost two hours. A Network Railcard costing £26, valid throughout the southern and southeastern regions for a year, entitles you and three companions to one-third off many off-peak fares.

Contacts National Rail Enquiries (☎ *0845/748–4950* ⊕ *www.nationalrail. co.uk*). **Network Railcard** (⊕ *www.railcard.co.uk*).

RESTAURANTS

If you're in a seaside town, look for that great British staple, fish-and-chips. Perhaps "look" isn't the word—just follow your nose. On the coast, seafood, much of it locally caught, is a specialty. Try local smoked fish (haddock and mackerel), or the succulent local oysters. Inland, sample fresh local lamb and beef. In cities such as Brighton and Tunbridge Wells there are numerous restaurants and cafés, but out in the countryside your options will be limited largely to pubs.

HOTELS

All around the coast, resort towns stretch along beaches, their hotels standing cheek by jowl. Of the smaller hotels and guesthouses only a few remain open year-round; most do business only from mid-April to September or October. Some hotels have all-inclusive rates for a week's stay. Prices rise in July and August, when the seaside resorts can get solidly booked, especially Brighton. (On the other hand, hotels may drop rates by up to 40% off season.) Places in Brighton may not take a booking for a single night in summer or on weekends.

WHAT IT COSTS IN POUNDS				
£	££	£££	££££	£££££
Restaurants	under £10	£10–£14	£15–£19	£20–£25	over £25
Hotels	under £70	£70–£120	£121–£160	£161–£220	over £220

Restaurant prices are for a main course at dinner. Hotel prices are for two people in a standard double room in high season, including V.A.T., with no meals or, if indicated, CP (with Continental breakfast), BP (Breakfast Plan, with full breakfast), or MAP (Modified American Plan, with breakfast and dinner).

VISITOR INFORMATION

Local Tourist Information Centres in the main towns can help with information and accommodations.

Contacts Southeast England Tourist Board (☎ *023/8062–5400* ⊕ *www. visitsoutheastengland.com*).

CANTERBURY TO DOVER

The cathedral city of Canterbury is an ancient place that has attracted travelers since the 12th century. Its magnificent cathedral, the Mother Church of England, remains a powerful draw. Even in prehistoric times, this part of England was relatively well settled. Saxon settlers, Norman conquerors, and the folk who lived here in late-medieval times all left their mark. From Canterbury there's rewarding wandering to be done in the gentle Kentish countryside between the city and the busy port of Dover. Here the landscape ravishes the eye in spring with apple blossoms, and in the autumn with lush fields ready for harvest. It is a county of orchards, market gardens, and round oasthouses with their tilted, pointed roofs; they were once used for drying hops, but now many are pricey homes.

CANTERBURY

56 mi southeast of London.

Just mention Canterbury, and most people are taken back to memories of high-school English classes and Geoffrey Chaucer's *Canterbury Tales*, about medieval pilgrims making their way to Canterbury Cathedral. Judging from the tales, however, in those days Canterbury was as much a party for people on horses as it was a spiritual center.

The city has been the seat of the Primate of All England, the Archbishop of Canterbury, since Pope Gregory the Great dispatched St. Augustine to convert the heathen hordes of Britain in 597. The height of Canterbury's popularity came in the 12th century, when thousands of pilgrims flocked here to see the shrine of the murdered archbishop St. Thomas à Becket. This southeastern town became one of the most visited in England, if not Europe. Buildings that served as pilgrims' inns (and that survived World War II bombing of the city) still dominate the streets of Canterbury's center, though it's tourists who flock to this city of about 40,000 people today.

Check with the Canterbury Roman Museum, the West Gate Museum, and the Museum of Canterbury before you visit; budget concerns mean that opening hours may be shorter (or museums may close).

GETTING HERE AND AROUND

The fastest way to reach Canterbury from London is by train. Southeastern trains to Canterbury run every half hour in peak times from London's Charing Cross station. The journey takes around 1½ hours. Canterbury has two centrally located train stations, Canterbury East Station (a five-minute walk from the cathedral square) and Canterbury West Station (a 10-minute walk from the cathedral).

National Express and Megabus buses bound for Canterbury depart several times a day from London's Victoria Coach Station. Trips to Canterbury take around two hours, and drop passengers near the train stations. If you're driving, take the A2/M2 to Canterbury from London (56 mi). Park in one of the signposted parking lots at the edge of the town center.

Canterbury has a small, walkable town center. Although the town has good local bus service, you're unlikely to need it. Most major tourist sites are on one street that changes name three times—beginning as St. George's Street and then becoming High Street and St. Peter's Street.

Canterbury Guild of Guides provides walking guides who have a specialized knowledge of the city and its surrounding area. Tours (£5) are at 11 every day between Easter and October, with an additional tour at 2 during July and August. VisitBritain offers an MP3 tour of Canterbury (£5) that you can download from its Web site.

TIMING

The town tends to get crowded around religious holidays—particularly Easter weekend—and on other national holiday weekends. If you'd rather avoid the tour buses, try visiting midweek.

ESSENTIALS

Visitor and Tour Information Canterbury (⊠ *12–13 Sun St.* ☎ *01227/378100* ⊕ *www.canterbury.co.uk).* **Canterbury Guild of Guides** (⊠ *Arnett House, Hawks La.* ☎ *01227/459779* ⊕ *www.canterbury-walks.co.uk).* **VisitBritain** (⊕ *www. visitbritainshop.com).*

EXPLORING

TOP ATTRACTIONS

❸ Canterbury Cathedral. The focal point of the city was the first of England's great Norman cathedrals. Nucleus of worldwide Anglicanism, the Cathedral Church of Christ Canterbury (its formal name) is a living textbook of medieval architecture. The building was begun in 1070, demolished, begun anew in 1096, and then systematically expanded over the next three centuries. When the original choir section burned to the ground in 1174, another replaced it, designed in the new Gothic style, with tall, pointed arches. The cathedral is very popular, so arrive early or late in the day to avoid the worst crowds. You can just walk around, or you can buy a guidebook with an overview of the building's history, use an audio guide for the most detail, or take a tour for the personal touch. Classical concerts are often held in the cathedral.

Fodor's Choice
★

The cathedral was only a century old, and still relatively small, when Thomas à Becket, the archbishop of Canterbury, was murdered here in 1170. Becket, a defender of ecclesiastical interests, had angered his friend Henry II, who was heard to exclaim, "Who will rid me of this troublesome priest?" Thinking they were carrying out the king's wishes, four knights burst in on Becket in one of the side chapels and killed him. Two years later Becket was canonized, and Henry II's subsequent submission to the authority of the church and his penitence helped establish the cathedral as the center of English Christianity.

Becket's tomb, destroyed by Henry VIII in 1538 as part of his campaign to reduce the power of the church and confiscate its treasures, was one of the most extravagant shrines in Christendom. In **Trinity Chapel,** which held the shrine, you can still see a series of 13th-century stained-glass windows illustrating Becket's miracles. So hallowed was this spot that in 1376, Edward, the Black Prince, warrior son of Edward III and a national hero, was buried near it. The actual site of Becket's murder is down a flight of steps just to the left of the nave. In the corner, a second flight of steps leads down to the enormous Norman **undercroft,** or vaulted cellarage, built in the early 12th century. A row of squat pillars whose capitals dance with animals and monsters supports the roof.

If time permits, explore the **cloisters** and the small monastic buildings to the north of the cathedral. The 12th-century octagonal water tower is still part of the cathedral's water supply. The Norman staircase in the northwest corner of the Green Court dates from 1167 and is a unique example of the architecture of the times. ⊠ *Cathedral Precincts* ☎ *01227/762862* ⊕ *www.canterbury-cathedral.org* ⊠ *£7.50,*

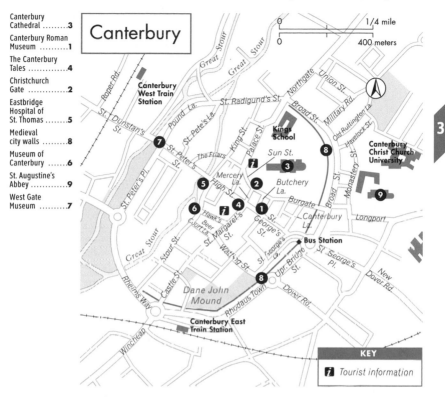

Canterbury

KEY

🛈 Tourist information

free for services and ½ hr before closing; £5 for tour, £3.50 for audio guide ⊙ Easter–Sept., Mon.–Sat. 9–5:30, Sun. 12:30–2:30; Oct.–Easter, Mon.–Sat. 9–5, Sun. 12:30–2:30. Last entry ½ hr before closing. Restricted access during services.

**QUICK
BITES**

The Custard Tart (⊠ *35A St. Margaret's St.* ☎ *01227/785178*), a short walk from the cathedral, serves freshly made sandwiches, pies, tarts, and cakes, along with steaming cups of tea and coffee. You can take your choice upstairs to the seating area. It's not open for dinner.

❶ Canterbury Roman Museum. Belowground, at the level of the remnants of Roman Canterbury, this museum features colorful mosaic Roman pavement and a hypocaust—the Roman version of central heating. Displays of excavated objects (some of which you can hold in the Touch the Past area) and computer-generated reconstructions of Roman buildings and the marketplace help re-create the past. ⊠ *Butchery La.* ☎ *01227/785575* ⊕ *www.canterbury.co.uk* ☞ *£3.10; £6.40 combined ticket includes Museum of Canterbury and West Gate Museum ⊙ June–Oct., Mon.–Sat. 10–5, Sun. 1:30–5; Nov.–May, Mon.–Sat. 10–5; last admission at 4. Closed last wk in Dec.*

❽ Medieval city walls. For an essential Canterbury experience, follow the circuit of the 13th- and 14th-century walls, built on the line of the

Roman walls. Those to the east survive intact, towering some 20 feet high and offering a sweeping view of the town. You can access these from a number of places, including Castle Street and Broad Street.

WORTH NOTING

❹ **The Canterbury Tales.** It's a kitschy audiovisual (and occasionally olfac-
☷ tory) dramatization of 14th-century English life—touristy but popular. You'll "meet" Chaucer's pilgrims at the Tabard Inn near London and view tableaus illustrating five tales. In the summer, actors in period costume play out scenes from the town's history. ⊠ *St. Margaret's St.* ☎ *01227/479227* ⊕ *www.canterburytales.org.uk* ⊡ *£7.75* ☉ *Nov.– Feb., daily 10–4:30; Mar.–June, Sept., and Oct., daily 10–5; July and Aug., daily 9:30–5.*

❷ **Christchurch Gate.** This immense gate, built in 1517, leads into the cathe-dral close. As you pass through, look up at the sculpted heads of two young figures: Prince Arthur, elder brother of Henry VIII, and the young Catherine of Aragon, to whom Arthur was betrothed. After Arthur's death, Catherine married Henry. Her failure to produce a male heir after 25 years of marriage led to Henry's decision to divorce her, creating an irrevocable breach with the Roman Catholic Church and altering the course of English history.

❺ **Eastbridge Hospital of St. Thomas.** The 12th-century building (which would now be called a hostel) lodged pilgrims who came to pray at the tomb of Thomas à Becket. It's a tiny place, fascinating in its simplicity. The refectory, the chapel, and the crypt are open to the public. ⊠ *25 High St.* ☎ *01227/471668* ⊕ *www.eastbridgehospital.org.uk* ⊡ *£1* ☉ *Mon.– Sat. 10–5; last admission at 4:30.*

❻ **Museum of Canterbury.** The medieval Poor Priests' Hospital is the site of
☷ this local museum, where exhibits provide an overview of the city's his-tory and architecture from Roman times to World War II. It's a quirky place that covers everything and everyone associated with the town, including the Blitz, the mysterious death of the 16th-century writer Christopher Marlowe, and the British cartoon characters Bagpuss and Rupert Bear. ⊠ *20 Stour St.* ☎ *01227/475202* ⊕ *www.canterbury.co.uk* ⊡ *£3.60; £6.40 combined ticket includes Canterbury Roman Museum and West Gate Museum* ☉ *Jan.–May and Oct.–Dec., Mon.–Sat. 11–4; June–Sept., Mon.–Sat. 11–4, Sun. 1:30–4.*

❾ **St. Augustine's Abbey.** Augustine, England's first Christian missionary, was buried here in 597, at one of the oldest monastic sites in the country. The site remained intact for nearly 1,000 years, until Henry VIII seized the abbey in the 16th century, destroying some of the original buildings and converting others into a royal manor for his fourth wife, Anne of Cleves. It's now made up of beautiful ruins that give a good idea of what it must have looked like when it was intact. A free interactive audio tour vividly puts events into context. ⊠ *Longport* ☎ *01227/378100* ⊕ *www. english-heritage.org.uk* ⊡ *£4.50* ☉ *Apr.–June, Wed.–Sun. 10–5; July and Aug., daily 10–6; Sept.–Mar., Sun. 11–5.*

❼ **West Gate Museum.** Only one of the city's seven medieval gatehouses
☷ survives, complete with twin castellated towers; it now contains this museum. Inside are medieval bric-a-brac and armaments used by the

city guard, as well as more contemporary weaponry. The building became a jail in the 14th century, and you can view the prison cells. ■ **TIP→ Climb to the roof for a panoramic view of the city.** ⊠ *St. Peter's St.* ☎ *01227/789576* ⊕ *www.canterbury.co.uk* ⊠ *£1.30; £6.40 combined ticket includes Canterbury Roman Museum and Museum of Canterbury* ☉ *Sat. 11–12:30 and 1:30–3:30; last admission 3:15.*

WHERE TO EAT

£ ✕ **City Fish Bar.** Long lines and lots of satisfied finger-licking attest to
BRITISH the deserved popularity of this excellent fish-and-chips outlet in the center of town. Everything is freshly fried, the batter crisp and the fish tasty; the fried mushrooms are also surprisingly good. There's no seating, so your fish is wrapped up in paper and you eat it where you want, perhaps in the park. This place closes at 7. ⊠ *30 St. Margaret's St.* ☎ *01227/760873* ☰ *No credit cards.*

£££ ✕ **The Goods Shed.** Next to Canterbury West station, this vaulted wooden
BRITISH space with exposed stone-and-brick walls was a storage shed in Victorian times. Now it's a farmers' market with a restaurant that has wooden tables and huge curved windows overlooking the market and a butchers' stall. It's well known for offering fresh Kentish food—from locally caught fish and smoked meats to local cider and bread baked in-house. The menu changes every day and usually includes four or five main courses, a handful of starters, and a few deserts. Whatever is fresh that day appears on the menu, whether it's grilled bass with brown shrimp or roasted goose with turnips and prunes. The food is reliably good, but service is slow. ⊠ *Station Rd.* W ☎ *01227/459153* ⊕ *www. thegoodsshed.net* ☰ *MC, V* ☉ *Closed Mon. No dinner Sun.*

££££ ✕ **Michael Caines.** Canterbury's most sought-after tables are at Michael
MODERN FRENCH Caines (named not for the actor, but for the chef with a similar name). This
Fodor's Choice light-filled eatery in the trendy Abode Canterbury, with its pine tables,
★ white walls, and sophisticated country style, packs in the foodies. Modern French cuisine is the main attraction—true aficionados will reserve the chef's table in the kitchen to watch the staff in action. Dishes change weekly but look for treats such as wild sea bass with baby Mediterranean vegetables, or English lamb with tapenade jus. The seven-course tasting menu (£55) is great for special occasions. There's a glass-enclosed wine room and an adjoining champagne bar, ensuring that the wine is as good as the food. ⊠ *30–33 High St.* ☎ *01227/766266* ⊕ *www.michaelcaines. com* ⌖ *Reservations essential* ☰ *AE, DC, MC, V.*

££ ✕ **Old Brewery Tavern.** Although it's part of a hotel, this pub has a sepa-
BRITISH rate entrance leading to a room with polished floors, wooden tables, and whitewashed stone. The menu and kitchen are overseen by top chef Michael Caines, so it's a good place to try his food without paying as much as you would at his flagship restaurant in the hotel (a two-course lunch is £10). The atmosphere is relaxed and casual, except on weekend nights when the music gets turned up for the party crowd. Expect reliably good comfort food—juicy burgers, crispy fish-and-chips, or sirloin steak grilled to order. Sandwiches and salads, and a roast on Sunday round out the menu. The courtyard is perfect for alfresco dining. ⊠ *Abode Canterbury, High St.* ☎ *01227/826682* ⊕ *www.michaelcaines. com* ☰ *AE, MC, V.*

££ ✕**Old Buttermarket.** A colorful, friendly old pub near the cathedral, the
BRITISH Buttermarket is a great place to grab a hearty lunch, including consistently tasty meat pies. There's been a pub on this site for more than
500 years, so although the current building is a few hundred years
younger than that, it's carrying on a fine tradition. You can indulge in
a fresh English ale from the changing selection while sampling a creamy
chicken and leek pie or a steaming steak and ale pie. Other choices
are fish-and-chips and wild mushroom–and-pea risotto. ⊠ *39 Burgate*
☎ *01227/462170* ⊕ *www.nicholsonspubs.co.uk* ⊟ *MC, V.*

WHERE TO STAY

££–£££ ⊡ **Abode Canterbury.** This glossy boutique hotel inside the old city walls
brought an up-to-date style to traditional Canterbury. The good-size
rooms, modern but not minimal, are classed as Comfortable, Desirable,
and Enviable. Enviable rooms have the most space and extras like wood
floors, sitting areas, and nibbles. Even Comfortable rooms are nicely
designed with soft bedding in neutral colors, although most have no
view. Michael Caines is one of the town's top restaurants because of
its elegant atmosphere and French-influenced cuisine. The Old Brewery Tavern, an upscale pub, serves less expensive meals, and there's a
champagne bar. **Pros:** central location; luxurious handmade beds; great
restaurants and bars. **Cons:** one of the priciest hotels in town; bar gets
quite crowded. ⊠ *High St.* ☎ *01227/766266* ⊕ *www.abodehotels.co.uk*
⤵ *73 rooms* ⅄ *In-room: a/c, DVD (some), Internet. In-hotel: 2 restaurants, bar, laundry service, parking (paid)* ⊟ *AE, DC, MC, V.*

££ ⊡ **Canterbury Cathedral Lodge.** Small and modern, this hotel is tucked
away within the grounds of the cathedral. Inside are quiet, pleasantly
designed guest rooms with white walls and exposed oak trim. All guests
have free access to the cathedral and receive a precious extra: they
get to stay inside the cathedral grounds when the gates close at night.
There is no more peaceful place to stay in Canterbury. The hotel acts
as a conference center for events at the cathedral, and during those
events it will be fully booked. There's limited free parking; ask when
you book. **Pros:** outstanding location; incredible views; free access to
the cathedral. **Cons:** no hot breakfast option or restaurant; few services.
⊠ *The Precincts* ☎ *01227/865350* ⊕ *www.canterburycathedrallodge.
org* ⤵ *35 rooms* ⅄ *In-room: no a/c, Wi-Fi. In-hotel: Wi-Fi hotspot*
⊟ *AE, DC, MC, V* ⍾ *CP.*

££ ⊡ **Ebury Hotel.** Family-run, this hotel earns raves for its laid-back attitude and comfortable rooms. Made up of two big Victorian buildings
a 10-minute walk from central Canterbury, it has been sympathetically
converted. Rooms are simply decorated but good size (bathrooms can
be a bit tiny), and beds are firm. The cozy lounge has a wood-burning
fireplace, and the indoor pool is perfect for hot days. Maybe the hotel's
old-fashioned look is not for everyone, but if you like the kind of inn
that has a house Labradoodle, it's perfect. **Pros:** cozy lounge; comfortable rooms. **Cons:** a bit of a walk to the town center; no elevator.
⊠ *65–67 New Dover Rd.* ☎ *01227/768433* ⊕ *www.ebury-hotel.co.uk*
⤵ *15 rooms* ⅄ *In-room: no a/c. In-hotel: restaurant, bar, pool* ⊟ *MC,
V* ⍾ *BP.*

££–£££   🏠 **Magnolia House.** A lovely walled garden enhances this bed-and-breakfast in a Georgian house. Bedrooms have floral motifs and traditional furnishings; one has a four-poster. The quiet location is a 10-minute walk from the center of town. To get here, follow St. Dunstan's Street until London Road and take a left; it will be three blocks on the right side. **Pros:** adorable house; friendly atmosphere. **Cons:** a bit of a walk to the town center; some rooms are smaller than others; no elevator. ⊠ *36 St. Dunstan's Terr.* 🕾🕾 *01227/765121* ⊕ *www.magnoliahousecanterbury. co.uk* ➷ *7 rooms* ♿ *In-room: no a/c, no phone, Wi-Fi. In-hotel: no kids under 12* ⊟ *AE, DC, MC, V* ❙○❙ *BP.*

££   🏠 **The White House.** Reputed to have been the place in which Queen Victoria's head coachman came to live upon retirement, this handsome Regency building on a quiet road off St. Peter's Street sits between the city center and Canterbury West train station. Guest rooms are decorated in pastel shades with antiques, and a few are large enough for four people. **Pros:** historic house; spacious rooms; family-friendly atmosphere. **Cons:** a bit outside the center; no restaurant; no elevator. ⊠ *6 St. Peter's La.* 🕾 *01227/761836* ⊕ *www.canterburybreaks.co.uk* ➷ *9 rooms* ♿ *In-room: no a/c; no phone. In-hotel: bar* ⊟ *No credit cards* ❙○❙ *BP.*

NIGHTLIFE AND THE ARTS

NIGHTLIFE   Canterbury is home to a popular university, and the town's many pubs and bars are busy, often crowded with college-age folks. **Alberry's Wine Bar** (⊠ *St. Margaret's St.* 🕾 *01227/452378*), with late-night jazz and hip-hop and a trendy crowd, is the coolest place in town. The **Parrot** (⊠ *3–9 Church La.* 🕾 *01227/762355*) is a pub known for its real ales—at least six kinds are available at any time—and its convivial setting in an old wood-beam building. **Thomas Becket** (⊠ *21 Best La.* 🕾 *01227/464384*), a traditional English pub, has a fire crackling in the winter, copper pots hanging from the ceiling, and a friendly crowd.

THE ARTS   The two-week-long, mixed-arts **Canterbury Festival** (🕾 *01227/452853* ⊕ *www.canterburyfestival.co.uk*) is held every October. The **Gulbenkian Theatre** (⊠ *Giles La.* 🕾 *01227/769075*), outside the town center at the University of Kent, mounts all kinds of plays, particularly experimental works, and is a venue for dance performances, concerts, comedy shows, and films. The **New Marlowe** (⊠ *St. Margaret's St.* 🕾 *01227/787787*) reopens in fall 2011, though productions are still being staged around town. Expect popular and innovative theater and music.

SHOPPING

Canterbury's medieval streets are lined with shops, perfect for an afternoon of rummaging. The best are in the district just around the cathedral. The King's Mile, which stretches past the cathedral and down Palace Street and Northgate, is a good place to start. **925** (⊠ *57 Palace St.* 🕾 *01227/785699*) has a great selection of handmade silver jewelry. **Burgate Antiques** (⊠ *23 Palace St.* 🕾 *01227/456500*) is a rambling shop full of fine British and French antiques, mostly Georgian and Victorian, with high-end and less expensive selections. It's a great place to nose around on a rainy day. **Crowthers of Canterbury** (⊠ *1 The Borough* 🕾 *01227/763965*) is for music lovers, as it carries an extensive selection of musical instruments, gifts, and sheet music. **Hawkin's Bazaar** (✉ *34 Burgate* ☏ *01227/785809*) carries an exceptional selection of traditional and modern toys and games.

BROADSTAIRS

17 mi east of Canterbury.

Like other Victorian seaside towns such as Margate and Ramsgate on this stretch of coast, Broadstairs was once the playground of vacationing Londoners. Charles Dickens spent many summers here between 1837 and 1851 and wrote glowingly of its bracing freshness. Today grand 19th-century houses line the waterfront. In the off-season Broadstairs is peaceful, but day-trippers pack the town in July and August.

Park your car in one of the town lots, and strike out for the crescent beach or wander down the residential Victorian streets. Make your way down to the amusement pier and try your hand in one of the game arcades. You can grab fish-and-chips to go and eat it on the beach.

GETTING HERE AND AROUND

By car, Broadstairs is about a two-hour drive (78 mi) from London, off A256 on the southeast tip of England. Trains run from London's St. Pancras station to Broadstairs once an hour; it's a 90-minute trip. Broadstairs Station is off The Broadway in the town center. National Express buses travel to Broadstairs from London several times a day; the journey takes about three hours.

ESSENTIALS

Visitor Information Broadstairs (✉ *6B High St.* ☏ *01843/862242* ⊕ *www. broadstairs.gov.uk*).

EXPLORING

The cliff overlooking Viking Bay is dominated by a stern structure long known as **Bleak House**. One of Dickens's homes, it was here that he wrote *David Copperfield* and drafted the novel *Bleak House*. A fire tore through the privately owned building in 2006; since then the interior has been closed to visitors. ✉ *Fort Rd.* ⊕ *www.bleakhouse.info.*

What is now the **Dickens House Museum** was originally the home of Mary Pearson Strong, on whom Dickens based the character of Betsey Trotwood, David Copperfield's aunt. It's a funny little place, with a reconstruction of Miss Trotwood's room as described by Dickens, a few objects that once belonged to the Dickens family, and prints and photographs commemorating the author's association with Broadstairs. ✉ *2 Victoria Parade* ☏ *01843/861232 or 01843/863453* ⊕ *www. dickensfellowship.org* ⌑ *£3.50* ☉ *Apr.–Oct., daily 2–5.*

WHERE TO STAY

£–££ ⊡ **Number 68.** Charming decor and a friendly atmosphere are the pluses of this sweet Edwardian house a five-minute walk from central Broadstairs. The three guest rooms are individually decorated with unobtrusive themes (French, Seaside, Chinese), and puffy white comforters top the comfortable beds. Breakfasts, made to order, range from the meaty English variety to lighter croissants and fruit. In high season a minimum two-night stay is required, and there is a minimum 50% penalty for any cancellation. **Pros:** close to the sea; tasty breakfasts; free Wi-Fi. **Cons:** minimum stay required; tough cancellation policy. ⊠ *68 West Cliff Rd.* ☎ *01843/609459* ⊕ *www.number68.co.uk* ⌨*3 rooms* ⬩ *In-room: no a/c, no phone, Wi-Fi. In-hotel: no kids under 11* ⊟ *No credit cards* ⦿| *BP.*

NIGHTLIFE AND THE ARTS

Each June Broadstairs holds a **Dickens Festival** (☎ *01843/861827* ⊕ *www. broadstairsdickensfestival.co.uk*), lasting about a week, with readings, people in Dickensian costume, a Dickensian cricket match, a Victorian bathing party, and vaudeville, among other entertainments.

DEAL

18 mi south of Broadstairs.

The large seaside town of Deal, known for its castle, is famous in history books as the place where Caesar's legions landed in 55 BC, and it was from here that William Penn set sail in 1682 on his first journey to the American colony he founded, Pennsylvania.

EXPLORING

Deal Castle, erected in 1540 and intricately built to the shape of a Tudor rose, is the largest of the coastal defenses constructed by Henry VIII. A moat surrounds its gloomy passages and austere walls. The castle museum has exhibits about prehistoric, Roman, and Saxon Britain. ⊠ *Victoria Rd.* ☎ *01304/372762* ⊕ *www.english-heritage.org.uk* ⬩*£4.50* ⊗ *Apr.–Sept., daily 10–6.*

Walmer Castle and Gardens, one of Henry VIII's fortifications, was converted in 1708 into a residence for the lord warden. Made up of four round towers around a circular keep, the castle has sprawling lavender gardens and a croquet lawn. Among its famous lord wardens were William Pitt the Younger; the duke of Wellington, hero of the Battle of Waterloo, who lived here from 1829 until his death here in 1852 (a small museum contains memorabilia); and Sir Winston Churchill. Except for when the lord warden is in residence, the drawing and dining rooms are open to the public, and pretty gardens and a grassy walk fill what was the moat. ⊠ *A258, 1 mi south of Deal* ☎ *01304/364288* ⊕ *www.english-heritage.org.uk* ⬩*£7* ⊗ *Mar. and Oct., Wed.–Sun. 10–4; Apr.–Sept., daily 10–6.*

DOVER

8 mi south of Deal, 78 mi east of London.

The busy passenger port of Dover has for centuries been Britain's gateway to Europe and is known for the famous White Cliffs. You may find the town itself disappointing; the savage bombardments of World War II and the shortsightedness of postwar developers left the city center an unattractive place. Roman legacies include a lighthouse adjoining a stout Anglo-Saxon church.

GETTING HERE AND AROUND

National Express buses depart from London's Victoria Coach Station for Dover every hour and a half. The journey takes about two hours and 40 minutes. Drivers from London take the M20, which makes a straight line south to Dover. The 76-mi journey should take around two hours. Southeastern trains leave London's Charing Cross station every 20 minutes or so for Dover Priory station in Dover. The trip is an hour and 45 minutes.

> ### HENRY VIII'S CASTLES
>
> Why did Henry VIII rapidly (1539–42) build sturdy forts along the southern coast? After enraging the pope and Europe's Catholic monarchs with his marriages and by seizing control of the wealthy monasteries, he prepared for a possible invasion. It did not come. Today you can bike or walk along the beachfront between Deal and Walmer castles.

For the best views of the cliffs, you need a car or taxi; it's a long way to walk from town.

ESSENTIALS

Visitor Information Dover (⊠ *The Old Town Gaol, Biggin St.* ☎ *01304/205108*).

EXPLORING

★ Plunging hundreds of feet into the sea, Dover's chalk **White Cliffs** are an inspirational site and a symbol of England. They stay white because of the natural process of erosion. Because of this, you must be cautious when walking along the cliffs—experts recommend staying at least 20 feet from the edge. The best places to see the cliffs are at Samphire Hoe, St. Margaret's Bay, or East Cliff & Warren Country Park. Signs will direct you from the roads to scenic spots. ■TIP➔ **The visitor center at Langdon Cliffs on Upper Road introduces you to the area and has 5 mi of walking trails with some spectacular views.**

☾ Spectacular and with plenty to explore, **Dover Castle**, towering high ★ above the ramparts of the White Cliffs, is a mighty medieval castle that has served as an important strategic center over the centuries, even in World War II. Most of the castle, including the keep, dates to Norman times. It was begun by Henry II in 1181 but incorporates additions from almost every succeeding century. There's a lot to see besides the castle rooms: among the exhibits, many of which will appeal to kids, are the Siege of 1216, the Princess of Wales Regimental Museum, and Castle Fit for a King. ■TIP➔ **Take time to tour the secret wartime tunnels (timed ticket needed), a medieval and Napoleonic-era system that was used as a World War II command center during the evacuation of Dunkirk in 1940.** ⊠ *Castle Rd.* ☎ *01304/211067* ⊕ *www.english-heritage.org.uk* ☞ *£13.40* ☾ *Feb. and Mar., daily 10–4; Apr.–Sept., daily 10–6; Oct., daily 10–5; Nov.–Jan., Thurs.–Mon. 10–4.*

The **Roman Painted House,** believed to have been a hotel, includes some Roman wall paintings, along with the remnants of an ingenious heating system. ⊠ *New St.* ☎ *01304/203279* ⊕ *www.theromanpaintedhouse. co.uk* ☞ *£3.80* ☾ *Apr.–Sept., Tues.–Sat. 10–5, Sun. 1–5.*

WHERE TO STAY

£ **Number One Guest House.** One of the best bargains in the area is this family-run guesthouse. Wallpapers and porcelain collections decorate the cozy corner terrace home built in the early 19th century, and you can even have breakfast in your room. The walled garden has a fine view of the castle. Pros: affordable rates; breakfast in bed. Cons: rooms are small. ⊠ *1 Castle St.* ☎ *01304/202007* ⊕ *www.number1guesthouse. co.uk* ⇨ *4 rooms* ⚲ *In-room: no a/c, no phone. In-hotel: parking (paid)* ▭ *No credit cards* ⏀ *BP.*

RYE TO LEWES

From Dover the coast road winds west through Folkestone (a genteel resort, small port, and Channel Tunnel terminal), across Romney Marsh (reclaimed from the sea and famous for its sheep and, at one time, its ruthless smugglers), and on to the delightful medieval town of Rye. The region along the coast is noted for Winchelsea, the history-rich sites of Hastings and Herstmonceux, and the Glyndebourne Opera House festival, based outside Lewes, a town celebrated for its architectural heritage. One of the three steam railroads in the Southeast services part of the area: the Romney, Hythe, and Dymchurch Railway.

RYE

★ *68 mi southeast of London, 34 mi southwest of Dover.*

With cobbled streets and ancient timbered dwellings, Rye is an artist's dream. It was an important port town until the harbor silted up and the waters retreated more than 150 years ago; now the nearest harbor is 2 mi away. The village of Rye begins where the sea once lapped at its ankles, and winds its way to the top of a low hill that overlooks the Romney Marshes and the old seabed. Virtually every building in the little town center is intriguingly old. Rye is known for its many antiques stores and also for its sheer pleasantness. This place can be easily walked without a map, but the local tourist office has an interesting audio tour of the town as well as maps.

GETTING HERE AND AROUND

If you're driving to Rye, take the M20 to A2070. There's no direct route by train; take a Southeastern train from Charing Cross or Victoria Station to Ashford and change for the Rye train, which runs every hour or so.

ESSENTIALS

Visitor Information Rye (⊠ *The Heritage Centre, Strand Quay* ☎ *01797/226696* ⊕ *www.rye-tourism.co.uk*).

EXPLORING
TOP ATTRACTIONS
Church of St. Mary the Virgin. At the top of the hill at the center of Rye, this classic English village church is more than 900 years old and encompasses a number of architectural styles. The turret clock dates to 1561 and still keeps excellent time. Its huge pendulum swings inside the

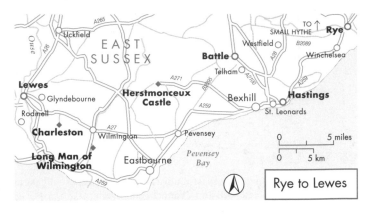

church nave. ■ TIP→ **You can climb the tower to see amazing views of the town and surrounding area.** ⊠ *Church Sq.* ☉ *Daily 10–4.*

Mermaid Street. One of the town's original cobbled streets heads steeply from the top of the hill to the former harbor. Its name, according to local lore, came from the night a sailor who had sipped a few too many walked down it. He swore he heard a mermaid call him down to the sea. Do take a stroll here to see the many ancient buildings that make it one of the town's most scenic streets.

Ypres Tower. Down the hill past Church Square, Ypres Tower was originally built as part of the town's fortifications (now largely gone) in 1249; it later served as a prison. The stone chambers hold a rather random collection of local items, such as smuggling bric-a-brac and shipbuilding mementos. ⊠ *Gungarden* ☎ *01797/226728* ⊠ *£1.95, £2.95 includes Rye Castle Museum* ☉ *Apr.–Oct., Thurs.–Mon. 10:30–1 and 2–5; Nov.–Mar., weekends 10:30–3:30; last admission 30 mins before closing.*

WORTH NOTING

Chapel Down Winery. English wine? Indeed, the English wine industry is beginning to be taken more seriously. For a change of pace, head several miles north of Rye to see one of Britain's leading wine producers. The Chapel Down wines have won awards, including one for a sparkling wine. You must join a one-hour guided tour to view the grounds, after which you are free to peruse the herb garden, plant center, shop, and the restaurant, the Grapevine Bistro. ⊠ *Off B2082, Small Hythe* ☎ *01580/766111* ⊕ *www.englishwinesgroup.co.uk* ⊠ *£7 tour* ☉ *June–Sept., daily 10–5; May and Oct., weekends 10–5.*

Lamb House. Something about Lamb House, an early-18th-century dwelling, attracts writers. The novelist Henry James lived here from 1898 to 1916. E. F. Benson, onetime mayor of Rye and author of the witty *Lucia* novels (written in the 1920s and 1930s, with some set in a town based on Rye; worth a read), was a later resident. The ground-floor rooms contain some of James's furniture and personal belongings. ⊠ *West St.* ☎ *01580/762334* ⊕ *www.nationaltrust.org.uk* ⊠ *£4* ☉ *Apr.–Oct., Thurs. and Sat. 2–6; last admission at 5:30.*

Rye Castle Museum. The diminutive Rye Castle Museum, below the remains of the castle wall, displays watercolors and examples of Rye pottery, for which the town was famous. ⊠ *3 East St.* ☎ *01797/226728* ⊕ *www.ryemuseum.co.uk* ✉ *£1.95, £2.95 includes Ypres Tower* ⊙ *Apr.– Oct., Thurs.–Mon. 2–5, weekends 10:30–1 and 2–5; last admission 30 mins before closing.*

Winchelsea. Like Rye, Winchelsea perches prettily atop its own small hill amid farmland. The town's historic houses, some with clapboards, are surrounded with gardens. Look for the splendid (though damaged) church built in the 14th century with Caen stone from Normandy. This was once a walled town, and some original town gates still stand. Winchelsea was built on a grid system devised in 1283, after the sea destroyed an earlier settlement at the foot of the hill. The sea later receded, leaving the town high and dry. The town is 2 mi southwest of Rye.

WHERE TO EAT

£££   ✗ **Fish Café.** One of Rye's most popular restaurants occupies a brick
SEAFOOD   building that dates to 1907, but the interior has been redone in a sleek, modern style. The ground-floor café has a relaxed atmosphere, and upstairs is a more formal dining room. Most of the seafood here is caught nearby, so it's very fresh. Sample the shellfish platter with oysters, welks, winkles, shrimp, and crab claws, or try the sesame-crusted tuna. Reservations are recommended for dinner. ⊠ *17 Tower St.* ☎ *01797/222226* ⊕ *www.webbesrestaurants.co.uk* ⊟ *DC, MC, V* ⊙ *Closed Mon. Oct.–Apr. No dinner Sun.*

£   ✗ **Simply Italian.** In a prime location near the marina, this popular local
ITALIAN   Italian chain restaurant packs in the crowds on weekend nights with its inexpensive classic pasta and pizza dishes. The atmosphere is cheerful and bright, and the food is straightforward and unfussy. Try tagliatelle with salmon in a creamy sauce, or king prawns and penne. Good pizza picks are the *quarto stagioni*, with mushrooms, salami, and peppers on a crisp crust, and pizza *reale* with red peppers, spinach, goat cheese, and red onion. ⊠ *The Strand* ☎ *01797//226024* ⊕ *www.simplyitalian. co.uk* ⊟ *MC, V.*

WHERE TO STAY

£££–££££   ⊞ **The George.** One of the newest options in Rye takes a boutique approach, mixing modern pieces cleverly with antiques in a sprawling Georgian building. Rooms are individually decorated but many have bedding in shades of caramel and coffee; touches such as red lamps, bookshelves, and dramatic prints add variety. All room have handmade Vi-Spring beds, Italian Frette linens, and covetable REN toiletries. Standard rooms are quite small, but deluxe rooms give you more space. The restaurant and bar downstairs are both popular with locals as well as visitors. **Pros:** elegant room design; amazingly comfortable beds; very central. **Cons:** main-street location makes street noise unavoidable; bar can get crowded and a bit raucous. ⊠ *98 High St.* ☎ *01797/222114* ⊕ *www.thegeorgeinrye.com* ⇨ *24 rooms* ᐃ *In-room: no a/c, Internet. In-hotel: restaurant, bar* ⊟ *AE, MC, V* ⦿l *BP.*

££ ⛺ **Jeake's House.** Antiques fill the cozy bedrooms of this rambling 1689 house, where the snug, painted-and-paneled parlor has a wood-burning stove for cold days. The breakfast menu includes buttered kippers and smoked haddock alongside more traditional egg-and-bacon options, and it's served in a galleried room formerly used for Quaker meetings. Rooms are 20% cheaper from November to March. **Pros:** pleasant atmosphere; delicious breakfasts; winter discounts. **Cons:** Mermaid Street is steep and cobbled; books up far in advance. ⊠ *Mermaid St.* ☎ *01797/222828* ⊕ *www.jeakeshouse.com* ⤶ *11 rooms, 10 with bath* ⅛ *In-room: no a/c. In-hotel: bar, some pets allowed, no kids under 8* ⊟ *MC, V* ⦿ *BP.*

££££ ⛺ **The Mermaid.** Once the headquarters of a smuggling gang, this classic half-timber inn has been in business for nearly six centuries. Sloping floors, oak beams, low ceilings, and a huge open hearth in the bar testify to its roots in the 15th century (some parts date back to the 12th century). Rooms vary in size; the most expensive rooms have four-posters. The decor is a bit dated for the price, but the history keeps the crowds coming in. In the main restaurant, you can soak up period details while choosing from an extensive British menu. **Pros:** city's most historic hotel; full of period charm; good restaurant. **Cons:** some parts need refurbishment; price is high for what's on offer; it's allegedly haunted. ⊠ *Mermaid St.* ☎ *01797/223065* ⊕ *www.mermaidinn.com* ⤶ *31 rooms* ⅛ *In-room: no a/c. In-hotel: restaurant, bar* ⊟ *AE, MC, V* ⦿ *BP.*

£££ ⛺ **White Vine House Hotel.** Occupying a building from the late 1500s (although the cellar is two centuries older), this small guesthouse shows a traditional approach in features such as wood-paneled lounges with warming fireplaces. Bedrooms pleasantly mix antiques and reproductions; some have four-poster beds, others have pretty headboards. In the downstairs restaurant (no dinner Monday and Tuesday) you can sample excellent British cuisine from local sources, including lamb and Rye bay scallops. Two-night stays are expected on weekends in high season. **Pros:** beautiful building; soothing neutral-tone decor; a fireplace to warm your toes; pampering touches such as organic toiletries. **Cons:** main street location can be a bit noisy; price is high for so few services; minimum stay on weekends. ⊠ *24 High St.* ☎ *01797/224748* ⊕ *www. whitevinehouse.co.uk* ⤶ *7 rooms* ⅛ *In-room: no a/c, no phone, DVD, Wi-Fi. In-hotel: restaurant* ⊟ *MC, V* ⦿ *BP.*

SHOPPING

Rye has great antiques shops, perfect for an afternoon of rummaging, with the biggest cluster at the foot of the hill near the tourist information center. **Black Sheep Antiques** (⊠ *72 The Mint* ☎ *01797/224508*) has a superior selection of antique crystal and silver. **Collectors Corner** (⊠ *2 Market Rd.* ☎ *01797/225796*) sells a good mix of furniture, art, and silver. **David Sharp Pottery** (⊠ *55 The Mint* ☎ *01797/222620*) specializes in the ceramic name plaques that are a feature of the town.

HASTINGS

9 mi southwest of Winchelsea, 68 mi southeast of London.

Big and sprawling, this Victorian seaside town will always be associated with the 1066 Norman invasion, when William, duke of Normandy, landed his troops at Pevensey Bay and was met by King Harold's army. A vicious battle ensued. Though it was called the Battle of Hastings, the skirmish actually took place 6 mi away at a town now called, well, Battle. Harold's troops had just successfully fended off the Vikings near York and marched across the country to take on the Normans. Utterly exhausted, Harold never stood a chance, and William became known as William the Conqueror.

In the 19th century Hastings became one of England's many popular spa resorts. Tall Victorian row houses painted in lemony hues still cover the cliffs around the deep blue sea, and the views from the hilltops are extraordinary. The old town, east of the amusement pier, offers a glimpse into the city's 16th-century past. Hastings has been through difficult times in recent decades, and the town developed a reputation as a rough place. However, gentrification has encouraged a climb back toward respectability. All visitors may notice, though, is that it's a handsome place, and the seafront has all the usual English accoutrements—fish-and-chips shops, candy stores, shops selling junk, miniature golf, and rocky beaches that stretch for miles.

BEACH HUTS

As English as clotted cream, rows of tiny, cheerfully painted, one-room wooden beach huts brighten the shoreline in Sussex (look for them at the edges of Hastings and Brighton) and elsewhere. The huts originated in the Victorian wheeled bathing machines that were rolled into the water so that women could swim modestly behind them. Eventually the wheels came off, and they and similar structures became favored for storage and as a windbreak. Most huts lack electricity or plumbing but are beloved for their adorableness. Some are rented; others are owned, and prices can be quite high.

GETTING HERE AND AROUND

If you're driving to Hastings from London (70 mi), take A21. Trains travel to Hastings every 30 minutes or so from London's Charing Cross and St. Pancras stations; the journey takes just under two hours. The station is in the town center, within easy walking distance of most sights. National Express buses travel from London to Hastings about twice a day in about 3½ hours.

ESSENTIALS

Visitor Information Hastings (✉ *Queens Sq., Priory Meadow* ☎ *01424/781111* ✉ *2 The Stade* ☎ *01424/781111* ⊕ *www.visit1066country.com*).

EXPLORING

☺ Take the West Hill Cliff Railway from George Street precinct to the atmospheric ruins of the Norman fortress now known as **Hastings Castle**, built by William the Conqueror in 1069. All that remains are fragments of the fortifications, some ancient walls, and a number of gloomy dungeons. Nevertheless, you get an excellent view of the chalky cliffs, the rocky coast, and the town below. The 1066 Story retells the Norman invasion in a film and display aimed largely at kids. ✉ *West Hill* ☎ *01424/781112* ⊕ *www.discoverhastings.co.uk* 🏷 *£3.75* ⊙ *Easter–Sept., daily 10–5; Oct.–Easter, daily 11–3; last admission 30 mins before closing.*

🅲 Waxworks and exhibits recall the history of smuggling at **Smuggler's Adventure**, in a labyrinth of caves and passages a 5- or 10-minute walk above Hastings Castle. You can spend about an hour here. ✉ *St. Clement Caves* ☎ *01424/422964* ⊕ *www.smugglersadventure.co.uk* 🏷 *£7.20* ⊙ *Easter–Sept., daily 10–5:30; Oct.–Easter, daily 11–4:30; last admission 30 mins before closing.*

Below the East Cliff in the Stade, tall, black wooden towers called **net shops**, unique to the town, are still used for drying fishermen's nets and for selling fresh seafood.

Carr Taylor Vineyards is well known locally for its traditional methods of bottled fermentation, known as *Méthode Champenoise*. The store also stocks fruit wines, ranging from strawberry to apricot, and mead—a wine of medieval origin—made following the *very* sweet Carr Taylor recipe with fermented grapes, apple juice, and honey. Take the A21 north from Hastings for 3 mi, turn onto the A28, and follow the signs. ✉ *Westfield, Hastings* ☎ *01424/752501* ⊕ *www.carr-taylor.co.uk* 🏷 *£1.50* ⊙ *Daily 10–5; closed last wk of Dec.*

WHERE TO EAT AND STAY

£ ✗ **Blue Dolphin.** The crowds line up all day to make their way into this

SEAFOOD small fish-and-chips shop just off the seafront, down near the fish shacks. Although the atmosphere is humble, reviewers consistently rank the battered fresh cod and haddock and huge plates of fries as among the best in the country. Everything is steaming fresh, and it's all cheaper if you get it to take out. ✉ *61 High St.* ☎ *01424/425778* ⊟ No credit cards ⊙ No dinner.

£ 🛏 **Eagle House Hotel.** This guesthouse in St. Leonards, just west of Hastings's city center, is in a large Victorian building with a lovely garden. It's a quirky place with somewhat dated decor, but the guest rooms have Victorian touches. The restaurant uses fresh produce from local farms. **Pros:** quiet neighborhood; historic house. **Cons:** furnishings are a bit worn; service is hit or miss. ✉ *12 Pevensey Rd., St. Leonards* ☎ *01424/430535* ⊕ *www.eaglehousehotel.co.uk* ⇆ *18 rooms* ⚤ *In-room: no a/c. In-hotel: restaurant* ⊟ *AE, DC, MC, V* ⧖ *BP.*

££–£££ 🛏 **Hastings House.** In Warrior Square at the edge of Hastings near St. Leonards-on-Sea, this renovated boutique guesthouse in a Victorian house is livening up the local hotel scene. Its individually styled guest rooms are chic and modern, with big, comfortable beds and bright splashes of color. Marble bathrooms are small, but just big enough. Rooms 3, 5, and 7 have sea views but are also the priciest in the house. Dinner is available if you let the owners know in advance, as is afternoon tea. **Pros:** spacious rooms; near the sea. **Cons:** no restaurant; few services. ✉ *9 Warrior Sq., St. Leonards-on-Sea* ☎ *01424/422709*

⊕ *www.hastingshouse.co.uk* ⬎ *8 rooms* 🛇 *In-room: no a/c, DVD, Wi-Fi. In-hotel: Wi-Fi hotspot* ▤ *MC, V* ¶◯| *BP.*

££££–££££ 🔲 **Zanzibar International Hotel.** New on the scene, this quirky hotel pays homage to exotic destinations with large, themed guest rooms. The Morocco room is exotic, textile-filled, and colorful, while the Manhattan suite is a streamlined, modern, white penthouse. Several rooms (including the South America) have whirlpool baths in the bedroom; the Antarctic has a sea-view sauna. A seafront location means that rooms at the front of the house have extraordinary water views, especially the Manhattan. **Pros:** spacious rooms; water views; breakfasts begin with a glass of champagne. **Cons:** a bit over the top; high prices for this town. ⊠ *9 Everfield Pl., St. Leonards-on-Sea* ☎ *01424/460109* ⊕ *www. zanzibarhotel.co.uk* ⬎ *9 rooms* 🛇 *In-room: no a/c, DVD, Internet. In-hotel: bar, no kids under 14* ▤ *MC, V* ¶◯| *BP.*

BATTLE

7 mi northwest of Hastings, 61 mi southeast of London.

Battle is the actual site of the crucial Battle of Hastings, at which, on October 14, 1066, William of Normandy and his army trounced King Harold's Anglo-Saxon army. Today it's a sweet, quiet town, and a favorite of history buffs.

ESSENTIALS

Visitor Information Battle (⊠ *High St.* ☎ *01424/773721*).

EXPLORING

The ruins of **Battle Abbey**, the great Benedictine abbey William the Conqueror erected after his victory, still convey the sense of past conflict. A memorial stone marks the high altar, which stood on the spot where Harold II was killed. Despite its historical significance, this abbey was not spared Henry VIII's wrath, and it was largely destroyed during his dissolution of the monasteries. The visitor center shows filmed explanations of the battle and its impact on England, and interactive exhibits engage kids and adults. You can also take the 1-mi-long walk around the edge of the battlefield and see the remains of many of the abbey's buildings. ⊠ *High St.* ☎ *01424/775705* ⊕ *www.english-heritage.org.uk* 🎟 *£7* ⊙ *Apr.–Sept., daily 10–6; Oct.–Mar., daily 10–4.*

WHERE TO STAY

£ 🔲 **Fox Hole Farm.** About 2 mi outside Battle, this pretty wood-and-brick bed-and-breakfast sits in farm country. The owners are a friendly couple, and the house is spacious with sturdy beamed ceilings, colorful bedspreads, a handful of antiques, and lots of homey touches. It's a working farm, so things can be a bit rough around the edges. Still, there's a wood-burning stove for chilly nights, and on sunny days you can sit in the garden and look out over the hills as sheep nibble the grass nearby. **Pros:** peaceful views; relaxing atmosphere. **Cons:** outside of town; small, so tends to book up. ⊠ *Kane Hythe Rd.* ☎ *07801/668669* ⬎ *3 rooms* 🛇 *In-room: no a/c, no phone. In-hotel: parking (free)* ▤ *No credit cards* ⊙ *Closed Jan.–Mar.* ¶◯| *BP.*

££   ⌐ **Little Hemingfold Hotel.** Forty acres of fields and woodlands, including a lake full of trout, provide the main enticement of this early-Victorian farmhouse. Guest rooms, done in simple country style, are bright and serene, and there's a piano in one of the sitting rooms. The fixed-price dinner in the candlelighted restaurant uses homegrown fruit and vegetables; the menu changes daily. The hotel is 2 mi south of Battle off the A2100. **Pros:** peace and quiet; fishing galore; great food. **Cons:** outside of town; not close to the sights. ✉ *Hastings Rd., Telham* ☎ *01424/774338* ⌐ *12 rooms* ⌖ *In-room: no a/c. In-hotel: restaurant, bar, tennis court, some pets allowed, no kids under 7* ⊙ *Closed Jan.– mid-Feb.* ⊟ *AE, MC, V* ⦿ *BP.*

HERSTMONCEUX CASTLE

11 mi southwest of Battle, 61 mi southeast of London.

EXPLORING

★   A banner waving from one tower and a glassy moat crossed by what was, surely, once a drawbridge—this fairy-tale castle has everything except knights in shining armor. For true castle lovers, **Herstmonceux** is a fabled name. The redbrick structure was originally built by Sir Roger Fiennes (ancestor of actor Ralph Fiennes) in 1444, although it was altered in the Elizabethan age and again early in the 20th century, after it had largely fallen to ruin. Canada's Queen's University owns the castle, so only part of it is open for guided tours once or twice a day (except Saturday). Highlights include the magnificent ballroom, a medieval room, and the stunning Elizabethan-era staircase. When school is not in session, the castle rents out its small, plain guest rooms for £75 per night. ■ **TIP→** Explore the formal walled garden, lily-covered lakes, and miles of woodland—the perfect place for a picnic on a sunny afternoon. Try the scones in the castle's tea shop and watch the outside from within. ✉ *Off A271, Hailsham* ☎ *01323/834481* ⊕ *www.herstmonceux-castle. com* ⌐ *Castle tours £2.50, grounds £6* ⊙ *Mid-Apr.–Sept., daily 10–6; Oct., daily 10–5; last admission 1 hr before closing.*

WHERE TO EAT AND STAY

£££   ✕ **The Sundial.** This 17th-century brick farmhouse with views of the
MODERN FRENCH   South Downs is home to a popular Modern French restaurant run by chef Vincent Rongier and his wife, Mary. Wood-beamed rooms and white tablecloths provide a backdrop for the imaginative choices on the changing menu, such as poached Dover sole with crayfish tails and lobster sauce, and roast rack of lamb with rosemary cream. Chocolate fondant with berry milk shake merits credit as one of the memorable desserts. The fixed-price options are a better value. ✉ *Gardner St., Herstmonceux* ☎ *01323/832217* ⊕ *www.sundialrestaurant.co.uk* ⊟ *DC, MC, V* ⊙ *Closed Mon. No dinner Sun.*

£££   ⌐ **Crossways Hotel.** Near the Long Man of Wilmington, this small hotel in a whitewashed house with 2 acres of gardens is under the hills of the South Downs by the river Cuckmere. The interior is decorated in warm, upbeat colors that contrast with the antiques the owners have collected. Convenient for walking, the hotel is also only a 15-minute drive from the Glyndebourne Opera House near Lewes. The cottage here offers more privacy and a kitchen (prices start at £110 for two nights in the off-season). ✉ *Lewes Rd., Polegate* ☎ *01323/482455* ⊕ *www. crosswayshotel.co.uk* ➲ *7 rooms, 1 cottage* ⚏ *In-room: no a/c. In-hotel: restaurant* ☰ *AE, MC, V* ❙◯❙ *BP.*

EN ROUTE

Wilmington, 9 mi southwest of Herstmonceux Castle on A27, has a famous landmark that people drive for miles to see. High on the downs to the south of the village (signposted off A27), a 226-foot-tall white figure, known as the **Long Man of Wilmington**, is carved into the chalk; he has a staff in each hand. His age is a subject of great debate, but some researchers think he might have originated in Roman times.

LEWES

★ *10 mi northwest of Wilmington, 8 mi northeast of Brighton, 54 mi south of London.*

The town nearest to the celebrated Glyndebourne Opera House, Lewes is so rich in architectural history that the Council for British Archaeology has named it one of the 50 most important English towns. A walk is the best way to appreciate its appealing jumble of building styles and materials—flint, stone, brick, tile—and the secret lanes (called "twittens") behind the castle, with their huge beeches. Here and there are smart antiques shops and secondhand-book dealers. Most of the buildings in the center date to the 18th and 19th centuries.

Something about this town has always attracted rebels. It was once the home of Thomas Paine (1737–1809), whose pamphlet *Common Sense* advocated that the American colonies break with Britain, and was also favored by Virginia Woolf and the Bloomsbury Group, early-20th-century countercultural artistic innovators.

Today Lewes's beauty and proximity to London mean that the counterculture crew can't really afford to live here anymore, but its rebel soul still peeks through, particularly on Guy Fawkes Night (November 5), the anniversary of Fawkes's foiled attempt to blow up the Houses of Parliament in 1605. Flaming tar barrels are rolled down High Street and into the River Ouse; costumed processions fill the streets. The night here is enthusiastically anti-Catholic (Fawkes was a Catholic fanatic), if a bit tongue-in-cheek. Although the pope is burned in effigy, figures from popular culture are also burned, in the spirit of (dark-humored) fun.

GETTING HERE AND AROUND

If you're driving to Lewes from London, take the M23 south. The 57-mi journey takes around an hour and 45 minutes. Southern trains run direct to Lewes from Victoria Station every 30 minutes or so on the Brighton line. It may be faster to take a train to Brighton and change to the regional service for Lewes. There's no easy way to get to Lewes by bus; you need to take a National Express or Megabus to Brighton and change to a regional bus line.

ESSENTIALS

Visitor Information Lewes (✉ *187 High St.* ☎ *01273/483448* ⊕ *www.lewes. gov.uk*).

EXPLORING

High above the valley of the River Ouse stand the majestic ruins of **Lewes Castle,** begun in 1100 by one of the country's Norman conquerors; it took 300 years to complete. The castle's barbican holds a small museum with archaeology collections, a changing temporary exhibition gallery, and a bookshop. There are panoramic views of the town and countryside. ⊠ *169 High St.* ☎ *01273/486290* ⊕ *www.sussexpast.co.uk* ⌨ *£6, £8.80 includes Anne of Cleves House* ☉ *Tues.–Sat. 10–5:30 or dusk; Sun., Mon., and holidays 11–5:30 or dusk; last admission 30 mins before closing; closed Mon. in Jan.*

The 16th-century **Anne of Cleves House,** a fragile-looking, timber-frame building, holds a notable collection of Sussex ironwork and other items of local interest, such as Sussex pottery. A famous painting of the local Guy Fawkes procession is also here. The house was part of Anne of Cleves's divorce settlement from Henry VIII, but she never lived in it. To get to the house, walk down steep, cobbled Keere Street, past lovely Grange Gardens, to Southover High Street. ⊠ *52 Southover High St.* ☎ *01273/474610* ⊕ *www.sussexpast.co.uk* ⌨ *£4.20, £8.80 includes Lewes Castle* ☉ *Mar.–Oct., Tues.–Thurs. 10–5, Sun., Mon., and holidays 11–5; Nov.–Feb., weekends 11–5; last admission at 4.*

Of interest to Bloomsbury fans, **Monk's House** was the home of novelist Virginia Woolf and her husband, Leonard Woolf, who purchased it in 1919. Leonard lived here until his death in 1969. Rooms in the small cottage include Virginia's study and her bedroom. Artists Vanessa Bell (Virginia's sister) and Duncan Grant helped decorate the house. ⊠ *C7, off A27, 3 mi south of Lewes, Rodmell* ☎ *01323/870001 (c/o Alfriston Clergy House)* ⊕ *www.nationaltrust.org.uk* ⌨ *£4* ☉ *Apr.–Oct., Wed. and Sat. 2–5:30.*

Art and life mixed at **Charleston,** the farmhouse Vanessa Bell—sister of Virginia Woolf—bought in 1916 and decorated with Duncan Grant (who resided here until 1978), fancifully painting the walls, doors, and furniture. The house became a refuge for writers and artists of the Bloomsbury Group and displays colorful ceramics and textiles of the Omega Workshop—in which Bell and Grant participated—and paintings by Picasso and Renoir as well as by Bell and Grant. You view the house on a guided tour (there may be a wait) except on Sunday. Bloomsbury fans will not want to miss this. ⊠ *Off A27, 7 mi east of Lewes, Firle* ☎ *01323/811265* ⊕ *www.charleston.org.uk* ⌨ *£9; gardens only, £3.50* ☉ *Apr.–June, Sept., and Oct., Wed.–Sun. 1–5; July and Aug., Wed.–Sat. noon–5, Sun. 1–5.*

WHERE TO EAT AND STAY

£ ✕**Robson's of Lewes.** Good coffee, fresh produce, and delicious pastries
CAFÉ have made this coffee shop very popular with locals. A light-filled space with wood floors and simple tables creates a pleasant, casual spot to enjoy a cup of joe with breakfast, a scone, or a light sandwich or salad lunch. You can also order to go. ⊠ *22A High St.* ☎ *01273/480654* ⊕ *www.robsonsoflewes.co.uk* ▭ *AE, MC, V* ☉ *No dinner.*

££ 🏨 **Berkeley House.** A smart town house in one of Lewes's Georgian terraces now serves as a cozy B&B. Rooms are spacious and homey, if
somewhat tired looking, and a roof terrace and guest lounge provide
room to unwind. The full English breakfasts use free-range eggs from
a local farmer. **Pros:** warm atmosphere; great breakfast. **Cons:** rooms
are a bit bland; nothing fancy here. ⊠ *2 Albion St.* ☎ *01273/476057*
⊕ *www.berkeleyhousehotel.co.uk* ⇆ *3 rooms* ᕦ *In-room: no a/c, DVD,
Wi-Fi. In-hotel: Wi-Fi hotspot* ⊟ *AE, DC, MC, V* ⚭ *BP.*

££££ 🏨 **Horsted Place.** On 1,100 acres, this luxurious Victorian manor-house
hotel is a few minutes' drive from Glyndebourne Opera House. Built
as a private home in 1850 with Gothic Revival elements by Augustus-
Charles Pugin, it was owned by a friend of the Queen's until the 1980s,
and Elizabeth was a regular visitor. Today it is richly furnished in traditional country-house style and has a magnificent Victorian staircase and
a Gothic library with a secret door that leads to a courtyard. The dining
room, also Gothic, prepares such elegant fare as venison with spaetzle
noodles. Golfers get a special rate at a nearby course. **Pros:** historic building; amazing architecture; lovely gardens. **Cons:** too formal for some;
creaky floors bother light sleepers. ⊠ *Little Horsted* ✛ *2½ mi south of
Uckfield, 6 mi north of Lewes* ☎ *01825/750581* ⊕ *www.horstedplace.
co.uk* ⇆ *15 rooms, 5 suites* ᕦ *In-room: no a/c, Wi-Fi. In-hotel: restaurant, Wi-Fi hotspot, tennis court* ⊟ *AE, DC, MC, V* ⚭ *BP.*

££££ 🏨 **The Shelleys.** A 17th-century building, this hotel on the hilly main road
is a longtime overnight stop for Glyndebourne operagoers. Public rooms
are on the grand scale, furnished with antiques; the garden is a joy.
Prints and floral fabrics pair with antiques in the guest rooms, which
have comfortable beds. The hotel is known for its old-fashioned but
friendly service and its excellent restaurant. **Pros:** historic atmosphere;
good, French-influenced cuisine. **Cons:** service a bit spotty; securing
a table at the restaurant can be tough. ⊠ *High St.* ☎ *01273/472361*
⊕ *www.the-shelleys.co.uk* ⇆ *19 rooms* ᕦ *In-room: no a/c, Wi-Fi. In-
hotel: restaurant, bar* ⊟ *AE, DC, MC, V* ⚭ *BP.*

NIGHTLIFE AND THE ARTS

NIGHTLIFE Lewes has a relatively young population and a nightlife scene to match;
there are also many lovely old pubs. Try the **Brewers' Arms** (⊠ *91 High
St.* ☎ *01273/475524*), a good pub with a friendly crowd. The **King's
Head** (⊠ *9 Southover High St.* ☎ *01273/474628*), a traditional pub, has
a good menu with game and fish dishes.

THE ARTS **Glyndebourne Opera House** (⊠ *Off A26, Glyndebourne* ✛ *Near Lewes*
☎ *01273/813813* ⊕ *www.glyndebourne.com*) is one of the world's leading opera venues. Nestled beneath the downs, Glyndebourne combines
first-class productions, a state-of-the-art auditorium, and a beautiful setting. Seats are *very* expensive (£25–£140) and often difficult to acquire,
but they're worth every penny to aficionados, some of whom wear
evening dress and bring a hamper for a picnic in the gardens. The main
season runs from mid-May to the end of August. The Glyndebourne
Touring Company performs here in October, when seats are cheaper
and slightly easier to obtain.

SHOPPING

Antiques shops offer temptation along the busy High Street. Lewes also has plenty of tiny boutiques and independent clothing stores vying for your pounds. **Adamczewski** (⊠ *88 High St.* ☎ *01273/470105*) is a marvelous throwback to the days when everything was made by hand. Its homemade soaps, scents, and even hand-hewn brooms are works of art. **Cliffe Antiques Centre** (⊠ *47 Cliffe High St.* ☎ *01273/473266*), a great place for one-stop antiques shopping, carries a fine mix of vintage English prints, estate jewelry, and art at reasonable prices. Classic bone china and antique glass are the center of attention at **Louis Potts & Co.** (⊠ *43 Cliffe High St.* ☎ *01273/472240*).

BRIGHTON TO GUILDFORD

The self-proclaimed belle of the coast, Brighton is upbeat, funky, and endlessly entertaining. Outside of town the soft green downs of Sussex and Surrey hold stately homes you can visit, including Arundel Castle and Petworth House. Along the way, you'll discover the largest Roman villa in Britain, the bustling city of Guildford, and Chichester, whose cathedral is a poem in stone.

BRIGHTON

9 mi southwest of Lewes, 54 mi south of London.

For more than 200 years, Brighton has been England's most interesting seaside city, and today it is more vibrant, eccentric, and cosmopolitan than ever. A rich cultural mix—Regency architecture, specialty shops, sidewalk cafés, lively arts, and a flourishing gay scene—makes it unique and unpredictable.

In 1750 physician Richard Russell published a book recommending seawater treatment for glandular diseases. The fashionable world flocked to Brighton to take Dr. Russell's "cure," and sea bathing became a popular pastime. Few places in the south of England were better for it, since Brighton's broad beach of smooth pebbles stretches as far as the eye can see. It has been popular with sunbathers ever since.

The next windfall for the town was the arrival of the Prince of Wales (later George IV). "Prinny," as he was called, created the Royal Pavilion, a mock-Asian pleasure palace that attracted London society. Visitors followed, triggering a wave of villa-building, and today the elegant terraces of Regency houses are among the town's greatest attractions. The coming of the railroad set the seal on Brighton's popularity: the *Brighton Belle* brought Londoners to the coast within an hour.

Londoners still flock to Brighton. Add them to the many local university students, and you have a trendy, young, laid-back city that does, occasionally, burst at its own seams. Property values have skyrocketed, but all visitors may notice is the good shopping and restaurants, attractive (if pebbly) beach, and wild nightlife. Brighton is also the place to go if you're looking for hotels with offbeat design and party nights.

GETTING HERE AND AROUND

Brighton-bound National Express and Megabus buses depart from London's Victoria Coach Station. The trip takes about two hours. Southeastern trains leave from London's Victoria and Charing Cross stations every 30 minutes. The journey takes just under an hour, and the trains stop at Gatwick Airport. By car from London, head to Brighton on the M23/A23. The journey should take about 1½ hours.

Brighton (and the adjacent Hove) sprawls in all directions, but the part of interest to travelers is fairly compact. None of the sights is more than a 10-minute walk from the train station. You can pick up a town map at the station. City Sightseeing has a hop-on, hop-off tour bus that leaves Brighton Pier every 20 to 30 minutes. It operates May through mid-September and costs £8.

TIMING

On summer weekends, the town is packed with Londoners looking for a day by the sea. Oceanfront bars can be rowdy, especially on national holidays when concerts and events bring in people. But summer is also when Brighton looks its best, and revelers pack the shops, restaurants, and bars. At other times, the town is much quieter. The Brighton Festival in May fills the town with music and other performances.

ESSENTIALS

Visitor and Tour Information Brighton (✉ *10 Bartholomew Sq.* ☎ *0906/7112255* ⊕ *www.visitbrighton.com*). **City Sightseeing** (☎ *01789/294466* ⊕ *www.city-sightseeing.com*).

EXPLORING
TOP ATTRACTIONS

Beach. The foundation of everything in Brighton is its broad beach, which spreads smoothly from one end of town to the other. In the summer sunbathers, swimmers, and hawkers selling ice cream and toys pack the shore; in the winter people stroll at the water's stormy edge, walking their dogs and searching for seashells. The water is bracingly cold, and the beach is covered in a thick blanket of large, smooth pebbles.
■TIP➜ **If you plan on swimming, bring a pair of rubber swimming shoes, as the stones are hard on bare feet.**

❶ **Brighton Museum and Art Gallery.** The grounds of the Royal Pavilion contain this museum, whose buildings were designed as a stable block for the prince regent's horses. The museum, looking great after a £10 million face-lift, has particularly interesting art nouveau and art deco collections. Look out for Salvador Dalí's famous sofa in the shape of Mae West's lips, and pause at the Balcony Café for its bird's-eye view over the 20th-century Art and Design Gallery. ✉ *Church St.* ☎ *03000/290900* ⊕ *www.brighton.virtualmuseum.info* ⊠ *Free* ☉ *Tues.–Sun. 10–5.*

❺ **Brighton Pier.** Opened in 1899, the pier is an amusement park set above
☺ the sea. In the early 20th century it had a music hall and entertainment;
★ today it has carnival rides and game arcades, along with clairvoyants, henna tattoo artists, and greasy food stalls. In the summer it is packed with children by day and teenagers by night. The skeletal shadow of a pier you can see off in the water is all that's left of the old West Pier. Long-term plans call for construction by 2012 of an observation tower,

i360, where that pier once touched the shore. ☎ *01273/609361* ⊕ *www.brightonpier.co.uk* ⊙ *Mid-Sept.–June, daily 10 AM–midnight; July–mid-Sept., daily 9 AM–2 AM.*

❹ **The Lanes.** This maze of tiny alleys and passageways was once the home of fishermen and their families. Closed to vehicular traffic, the area's narrow cobbled streets are filled with interesting restaurants, boutiques, and antiques shops. Fish and seafood restaurants line the

heart of the Lanes, at Market Street and Market Square. ✉ *Bordered by West, North, East, and Prince Albert Sts.*

❷ **Royal Pavilion.** The city's most remarkable building is this delightfully
★ over-the-top domed and pinnacled fantasy. Planned as a simple seaside villa and built in the fashionable classical style of 1787 by architect Henry Holland, the Pavilion was rebuilt between 1815 and 1822 by John Nash for the prince regent (later George IV), who wanted an exotic, Eastern design with opulent Chinese interiors. Today period furniture and ornaments, some given or lent by the current Royal Family, fill the interior. The two great set pieces are the **Music Room,** styled in the form of a Chinese pavilion, and the **Banqueting Room,** with its enormous flying-dragon "gasolier," or gaslight chandelier, a revolutionary invention in the early 19th century. The gardens, too, have been restored to Regency splendor, following John Nash's naturalistic design of 1826. ■ TIP→ **For an elegant time-out, retire to one of the Pavilion's bedrooms, where a tearoom serves snacks and light meals.** ✉ *Old Steine* ☎ *03000/290900* ⊕ *www.royalpavilion.org.uk* ▦ *£9.50* ⊙ *Oct.–Mar., daily 10–5:15; Apr.–Sept., daily 9:30–5:45; last admission 45 mins before closing.*

▐ QUICK
BITES

On the street adjacent to the bus station, and less than a five-minute walk from the Royal Pavilion, the **Mock Turtle** (✉ **4 Pool Valley** ☎ **01273/328380**) is a great old-fashioned, homey café. Alongside a decent selection of teas and coffees are four types of rarebit, soups, and scones. It's closed Monday.

❸ **Steine.** One of the centers of Brighton's action is the Steine (pronounced steen), a large open area close to the seafront. This was a river mouth until the Prince of Wales had it drained in 1793.

WORTH NOTING

❻ **Sea Life Centre.** Near Brighton Pier, this aquarium has many sea-dwelling
 creatures—from sharks to sea horses—in more than 30 marine habitats. It also has a giant-turtle convalescence center. Allow two hours for your visit. ■ TIP→ **Buy tickets online in advance to get a discount.** ✉ *Marine Parade* ☎ *0871/423–2110* ⊕ *www.sealifeeurope.com* ▦ *£15.50* ⊙ *Apr.–Oct., daily 10–5; Nov.–Mar., daily 10–4.*

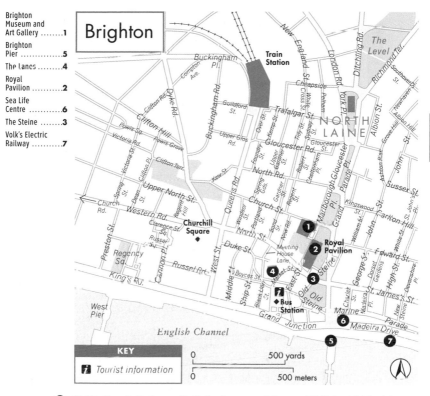

Brighton

7 **Volk's Electric Railway** Built by inventor Magnus Volk in 1883, this was the first public electric railroad in Britain. In summer you can take the 1¼-mi trip along Marine Parade. ✉ *Marine Parade* ☎ *01273/292718* ⊕ *www.volkselectricrailway.co.uk* 🎫 *£1.70 one way, £2.70 round-trip* ⊗ *Apr.–Sept., weekdays 10:30–5, weekends 10:30–6.*

WHERE TO EAT

£ **✗ Bill's Produce.** Even groceries manage to seem attractive at this casual,

CAFÉ pleasant coffee shop–restaurant–deli. On tall shelves all around the light-filled dining room, bottles of olive oil and vinegars glisten alongside stacks of fresh fruit, vegetables, baskets, and flowers. Blackboards near the counter list the day's specials: these usually include a variety of salads, sandwiches (your choice of fresh breads), and a few hot dishes. For mains, consider Thai spiced pumpkin curry or pepper steak with horseradish and a leafy salad. Breakfast is great here too, but on weekends expect a line of hungry diners. ✉ *The Depot, 100 North Rd.* ☎ *01273/692894* ⊕ *www.billsproducestore.co.uk* ▭ *MC, V.*

£££ **✗ Due South.** Arguably the highest-quality dining option on Brighton's

SEAFOOD seafront, this beachfront place is making waves on the local food scene, drawing young professionals who also appreciate its celebratory atmosphere. Big windows overlook the sea and let in plenty of light. The menu changes monthly and showcases clever, classic seafood dishes,

Brighton and the Regent

The term "Regency" comes from the last 10 years of the reign of George III (1811–20), who was deemed unfit to rule because of his mental problems. Real power was officially given to the Prince of Wales, also known as the prince regent, who became King George IV and ruled until his death in 1830.

Throughout his regency, George spent grand sums indulging his flamboyant tastes in architecture and interior decorating—while failing in affairs of state.

The distinctive architecture of the Royal Pavilion is a prime, if extreme, example of the Regency style, popularized by architect John Nash (1752–1835) in the early part of the 19th century. The style is characterized by a diversity of influences—French, Greek, Italian, Persian, Japanese, Chinese, Roman, Indian—you name it. Nash was George IV's favorite architect, beloved for his interest in Indian and Asian designs and for his neoclassical designs, as evidenced in his plans for Regent's Park and its terraces in London.

with everything from the grilled catch of the day to local oysters on the half shell, to vegetables sourced locally and organically. Desserts are decadent. ⊠ *139 King's Road Arches* ☎ *01273/821218* ⊕ *www. duesouth.co.uk* ⊟ *AE, MC, V.*

££   ✕ **Nia Café.** In the funky North Laine area, Nia has views down Trafal-
CAFÉ   gar Street from its outdoor tables. Besides good coffees and leaf teas, excellent café food is available all day, from simple (but freshly made) sandwiches at lunch to more sophisticated dinners like goat cheese and vegetable strudel or duck breast with spiced chutney. The decor is coffee-shop chic, with wood tables, chairs, and floors; large windows flood the room with light. Nia is near the station, which is handy if you have time to kill before a train or need to reenergize before sightseeing. ⊠ *87–88 Trafalgar St.* ☎ *01273/671371* ⊕ *www.nia-brighton. co.uk* ⊟ *MC, V.*

££   ✕ **Pomegranate.** A contemporary Kurdish restaurant, Pomegranate takes
MIDDLE EASTERN   a light-hearted, fun approach to Middle Eastern cuisine. Its small dining area spreads over two floors and has large windows and exposed brick walls; the staff creates a friendly, relaxed atmosphere. The menu sprawls and includes slow-roasted lamb with phyllo parcels stuffed with nuts and apricots, beef stewed with pomegranates, and salmon on grape leaves with cream sauce. For dessert, try the figs stuffed with walnuts and pomegranate. ⊠ *10 Manchester St.* ☎ *01273/628386* ⊕ *www. eatpomegranates.com* ⊟ *MC, V.*

££££   ✕ **Riddle and Finns.** A sparse, white-tiled room and metal tables without
SEAFOOD   cloths greet you when you walk in this restaurant, but the sparkling chandeliers overhead indicate that all is not as it seems. The latest critics' darling in Brighton calls itself a "Champagne oyster bar," and the elegant simplicity of its approach is impressive. Freshness and the sustainable sourcing of the seafood on the menu are the calling cards. The house specialty is oysters, offered eight different ways, hot or cold; a sampler plate lets you try them all. Other options include mixed shellfish

marinière, boiled crab and lobster served cold, and smoked local mackerel with fennel and poached egg. The Champagne selection is pricey and interesting. ⊠ *12B Meeting House La.* ☎ *01273/323008* ⊕ *www. riddleandfinns.co.uk* ⚏ *Reservations essential* ▤ *AE, MC, V.*

££££ ✕ **Seven Dials.** A former bank houses a restaurant that's undeniably
MODERN BRITISH striking and surprisingly laid-back, given the elegance of the cooking. Sophisticated Modern British cuisine rules the menu, with main dishes including panfried rib-eye steak served with "proper chips" (well-cooked, hand-cut, chunky fries), and braised rabbit leg with carrot and buttered Savoy cabbage. For dessert? Treacle tart, of course. ⊠ *1 Buckingham Pl.* ☎ *01273/885555* ⊕ *www.sevendialsrestaurant.co.uk* ⚏ *Reservations essential* ▤ *AE, MC, V.*

££ ✕ **Terre à Terre.** This inspiring vegetarian restaurant is incredibly popular,
VEGETARIAN so come early for a light lunch or later for a more sophisticated evening meal. The wood tables are modern but simple; it's the food that shines. Dishes span the globe in terms of their influences, so choose from Jamaican Jonny maize cakes stuffed with coconut spinach in a black bean sauce, or shredded phyllo lemon baklava layered with feta, pine nuts, and oregano and served with hot lemon soup. The "terre à tapas" option offers small bites of several dishes. All wines served here are organic. ⊠ *71 East St.* ☎ *01273/729051* ⊕ *www.terreaterre.co.uk* ▤ *AE, DC, MC, V* ⊗ *Closed Mon. No lunch Tues. and Wed. in winter.*

WHERE TO STAY

£££–££££ ⊡ **Blanch House.** A theatrical experience as much as a night's rest, this boutique hotel off the seafront sets itself apart with eclectic, clever theme rooms, including a '70s-style Boogie Nights room (with animal-print wallpaper) and elaborate Moroccan and Renaissance rooms. As you'd expect, the bathrooms are stylish and have the latest amenities. The hip cocktail bar (the owner is a former manager of London's Groucho Club) and sleek modern restaurant complete the picture. **Pros:** quirky approach; popular bar; good restaurant. **Cons:** may be far too theatrical for some; restaurant books up fast. ⊠ *17 Atlingworth St.* ☎ *01273/603504* ⊕ *www.blanchhouse.co.uk* ⇥ *9 rooms, 3 suites* ⚙ *In-room: no a/c, Internet. In-hotel: restaurant, bar* ▤ *MC, V* ⍾ *BP.*

££–£££ ⊡ **Brighton Wave.** Sleekly designed, this hotel off the seafront but near the Brighton Pier is all about relaxation. Beds are big and covered in soft, white linens; rooms are painted in restful, pale shades of blue and white; and breakfast is served in bed. The look is minimal without being cold, and service hits just the right note of friendliness and helpfulness. **Pros:** big, comfy beds; soothing decor; breakfast in bed. **Cons:** not a lot of privacy. ⊠ *10 Madeira Pl.* ☎ *01273/676794* ⊕ *www.brightonwave. com* ⇥ *8 rooms* ⚙ *In-room: DVD. In-hotel: Wi-Fi hotspot* ▤ *AE, DC, MC, V* ⍾ *BP.*

£££–££££ ⊡ **Drakes.** It's easy to miss the low-key sign for this elegant, modern hotel, tucked away amid the frilly houses on Marine Parade on the seafront. Inside, everything is cool, calm, and sleekly designed. The lobby is dark and sophisticated, and each guest room has its own style, with handmade wallpaper, firm beds covered in luxurious linens, well-designed bathrooms, and art everywhere. Some "feature" rooms have quirky touches, including claw-foot tubs in front of the bedroom windows. Rooms with sea views are more expensive than other rooms. Gingerman, the hotel restaurant, has a huge local following for its Modern British cuisine. **Pros:** cool atmosphere; great attention to detail; excellent restaurant. **Cons:** can feel a bit cold; too trendy for some. ☒ *43–44 Marine Parade* ☏ *01273/696934* ⊕ *www.drakesofbrighton. com* ⇆ *20 rooms* ☖ *In-room: DVD, Internet. In-hotel: restaurant, bar* ⊟ *AE, DC, MC, V.*

££££ **Grand Hotel.** The city's most famous hotel and a Brighton landmark,
★ the Grand sits on the seafront, a huge, creamy Victorian wedding cake of a building dating from 1864. It's both imposing and elegant, with high-ceiling public rooms richly decorated with enormous chandeliers and plenty of marble. Having tea here is a Brighton tradition, and highly recommended. The spacious bedrooms are traditional in style, with luxurious fabrics and large bathrooms. The Grand is famous in Britain for having survived an IRA bombing attack in 1984 that targeted Prime Minister Margaret Thatcher. **Pros:** as grand as its name; lovely sea views. **Cons:** a bit impersonal; lobby can be crowded with people taking tea. ☒ *King's Rd.* ☏ *01273/224300* ⊕ *www.grandbrighton.co.uk* ⇆ *200 rooms, 3 suites* ☖ *In-room: no a/c (some), Internet. In-hotel: restaurant, bar, pool, gym, some pets allowed* ⊟ *AE, DC, MC, V* ⦿ *BP.*

££–£££ **Granville Hotel.** Three grand Victorian buildings facing the sea make up this hotel. Guest rooms, heavily decorated with a theme (themed rooms are a Brighton fad), include the pink-and-white Brighton Rock and the art deco Noël Coward rooms. You'll pay the highest price for rooms with sea views. **Pros:** creative design; friendly staff; rambunctious atmosphere. **Cons:** rooms are a bit too quirky; can get noisy. ☒ *124 King's Rd.* ☏ *01273/326302* ⊕ *www.granvillehotel.co.uk* ⇆ *24 rooms* ☖ *In-room: no a/c, Internet. In-hotel: restaurant, bar, some pets allowed* ⊟ *AE, DC, MC, V* ⦿ *BP.*

££££ **Hotel du Vin.** In the Lanes area, this outpost of a stylish chain has crisply modern rooms. Pampering touches include Egyptian linens and large "monsoon" showers. The bistro restaurant offers classic fare that makes use of local seafood, and the extensive wine list includes many good values. Even connoisseurs will be satisfied by the wine bar (special events take place throughout the year), and you can have a cigar from the cigar gallery before you play billiards. **Pros:** gorgeous rooms; comfortable beds; excellent eatery. **Cons:** bar can get crowded; restaurant books up fast. ☒ *Ship St.* ☏ *01273/718588* ⊕ *www.hotelduvin.com* ⇆ *40 rooms, 3 suites* ☖ *In-room: no a/c, Wi-Fi. In-hotel: restaurant, bar* ⊟ *AE, DC, MC, V.*

£££–££££ **Nineteen.** A calm oasis of white, this guesthouse is filled with contemporary art and chic designer accessories. Beds are supported on platforms of glass bricks that filter an ocean-blue light. Massages, yoga sessions, and manicures are pampering amenities, and the basement kitchen stocks snacks for guests. **Pros:** relaxing rooms; innovative design. **Cons:** not on the nicest street in town; a bit New Agey. ☒ *19 Broad St.* ☏ *01273/675529* ⊕ *www.hotelnineteen.co.uk* ⇆ *8 rooms* ☖ *In-room: no a/c, DVD, Wi-Fi. In-hotel: Wi-Fi hotspot, some pets allowed* ⊟ *MC, V* ⦿ *BP.*

££–£££ ☲ **Pelirocco.** Here the imaginations of designers have been given free rein, and the result is a vicarious romp through pop culture and rock and roll. Rooms have themes: there's the leopard-print pin-up parlor, a boxing ring, and the futuristic Bubble Suite with a plunge bath and mirrored ceiling. It's way over the top, so you'll either love this place or hate it. **Pros:** quirky design; laid-back atmosphere; near the beach. **Cons:** a bit too form-over-function; no hotel restaurant. ⊠ *10 Regency Sq.* ☎ *01273/327055* ⊕ *www.hotelpelirocco.co.uk* ⇌ *18 rooms, 1 suite* ⚭ *In-room: no a/c, Internet. In-hotel: bar, no kids under 12 on weekends* ⊟ *AE, MC, V* |⊙| *BP.*

NIGHTLIFE AND THE ARTS
NIGHTLIFE
Brighton is a techno hub, largely because so many DJs have moved here from London. Clubs and bars present live music most nights, and on weekends the entire place can be a bit too raucous for some tastes. There's a large gay scene. The popular **Above Audio** (⊠ *10 Marine Parade* ☎ *01273/606906*), in an art deco building east of Brighton Pier, has a mix of house and underground music. Specialty nights at the **Funky Buddha Lounge** (⊠ *169 King's Road Arches* ☎ *01273/725541*) are at the forefront of Brighton's underground, with funk and acid disco blasting out to a fairly sophisticated crowd. Small, friendly, and unfailingly funky, the **Jazz Place** (⊠ *10 Ship St.* ☎ *01273/328439*), in the basement of Smugglers bar, can get a little cramped but makes up for it with cool, jazzy attitude. The **Pussycat Club** (⊠ *189–192 King's Road Arches* ☎ *08455/191909*), under the arches right on the beach, is currently one of Brighton's hottest clubs, having replaced the tired Zap Club. Paint your face with glitter and dance, dance, dance.

THE ARTS
★ The three-week-long **Brighton Festival** (☎ *01273/706771* ⊕ *www. brightonfestival.org*), one of England's biggest and liveliest arts festivals, takes place every May in venues around town. The more than 600 events include drama, music, dance, and visual arts.

The **Brighton Dome** (⊠ *New Rd.* ☎ *01273/709709*), just west of the Royal Pavilion, was converted from the prince regent's stables in the 1930s. It includes a theater and a concert hall that stage pantomime (a British theatrical entertainment with songs and dance) and classical and pop concerts. The **Theatre Royal** (⊠ *New Rd.* ☎ *0844/871–7627*), close to the Royal Pavilion, has a gem of an auditorium that is a favorite venue for shows on their way to or fresh from London's West End.

The **Cinematheque** (⊠ *9–12 Middle St.* ☎ *01273/384300*) screens sub-art-house oddities, obscurities, and rarities. The elegant 1910 **Duke of York's Picture House** (⊠ *Preston Circus* ☎ *01273/626261*), a 10-minute walk north of the main train station, shows art-house movies.

SHOPPING
The main shopping area to head for is **the Lanes**, especially for antiques or jewelry. It also has clothing boutiques, coffee shops, and pubs. Across North Street from the Lanes lies the **North Laine**, a network of narrow streets full of little stores, less glossy than those in the Lanes, but fun, funky, and exotic.

The **Antique House** (✉ 43 Meeting House La. ☎ 01273/321684) has a mix of pricey and affordable antiques spread over two floors. **Colin Page** (✉ 36 Duke St. ☎ 01273/325954), at the western edge of the Lanes, stocks a wealth of antiquarian and secondhand books at all prices. **Curiouser & Curiouser** (✉ 2 Sydney St. ☎ 01273/673120) is filled with unique, handmade jewelry, mostly sterling silver pieces with semiprecious stones. **The Lavender Room** (✉ 16 Bond St. ☎ 01273/220380), a relaxing boutique, tempts with scented calendars, glittery handmade jewelry, and little things you just can't live without.

The **Pavilion Shop** (✉ 4–5 Pavilion Bldgs. ☎ 01273/292798), next door to the Royal Pavilion, carries well-designed toys, trinkets, books, and cards—all with a loose Regency theme—and high-quality fabrics, wallpapers, and ceramics based on material in the Pavilion itself. The old-fashioned **Pecksniff's Bespoke Perfumery** (✉ 45–46 Meeting House La. ☎ 01273/723292) mixes and matches ingredients to suit your wishes. **Simultane** (✉ 52 Ship St. ☎ 01273/777535), a boutique near the waterfront, displays women's fashions from its own label—contemporary looks inspired by the styles of the 1940s and '50s—and clothing from other designers.

ARUNDEL

23 mi west of Brighton, 60 mi south of London.

The little hilltop town of Arundel is dominated by its great castle, the much-restored home of the dukes of Norfolk for more than 700 years, and an imposing neo-Gothic Roman Catholic cathedral—the duke is Britain's leading Catholic peer. The town itself is full of interesting old buildings and well worth a stroll.

GETTING HERE AND AROUND

Arundel is on the A27, about a two-hour drive south of central London. There are no direct trains from London, but you can take a Southern train from London Bridge station and change at Three Bridges to an Arundel train. The trip takes about 90 minutes, and trains run every 30 minutes or so. No direct buses run from London, but you can take a National Express bus to Worthing or Chichester and change to a local bus to Arundel; that journey could easily take five hours, though.

ESSENTIALS

Visitor Information Arundel (✉ 1–3 Crown Yard Mews, River Rd. ☎ 01903/882419 ⊕ www.sussex-by-the-sea.co.uk).

EXPLORING

Begun in the 11th century, vast **Arundel Castle** remains rich with the history of the Fitzalan and Howard families and with paintings by Van Dyck, Gainsborough, and Reynolds. It suffered destruction during the Civil War and was remodeled during the 18th century and in the Victorian era, when it was reconstructed in the fashionable Gothic style. The keep, rising from its conical mound, is as old as the original castle (you can climb its 130 steps for great views of the River Arun and the area), and the barbican and the Barons' Hall date from the 13th century. Among the treasures are the rosary beads and prayer book used

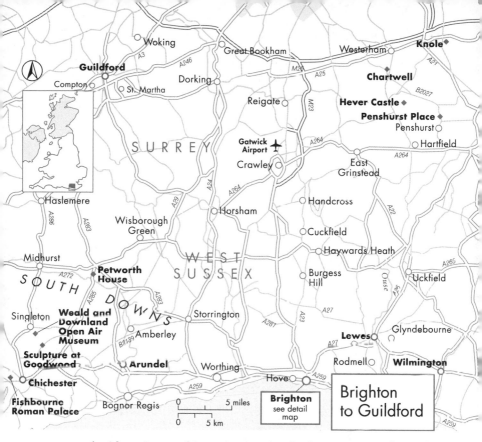

by Mary, Queen of Scots, in preparing for her execution. The newly redesigned formal garden is a triumph of order and beauty. Although the castle's ceremonial entrance is at the top of High Street, you enter at the bottom, close to the parking lot. ✉ *Mill Rd.* ☎ *01903/882173* ⊕ *www.arundelcastle.org* 🎫 *£16; grounds only, £7.50* ☉ *Apr.–Oct., Tues.–Sun. noon–5 (grounds open at 10); last admission at 4.*

WHERE TO EAT AND STAY

£   ✗ **Black Rabbit.** This renovated 18th-century pub outside Arundel is a
BRITISH   find, and you must persevere along Mill Road to find it. Its location by the River Arun, with views of the castle and a bird sanctuary, makes it ideal for a summer lunch. There's a good selection of real ales and an all-day restaurant. ✉ *Mill Rd., Offham* ☎ *01903/882828* 🟰 *DC, MC, V.*

££££–£££££   🏨 **Amberley Castle.** The lowering of the portcullis every night at midnight
★   is a sure sign that you're in a genuine medieval castle. Across the dry moat, present-day luxury dominates. Antiques and rich drapery furnish the individually designed bedrooms, and many have lattice windows, beamed ceilings, and curtained four-posters. You can dine in either the Queens restaurant, beneath a 12th-century barrel-vaulted ceiling, or amid suits of armor in the Great Room. **Pros:** sleep in a castle, with a moat; putting course for golfers; lovely gardens and grounds. **Cons:** a bit too formal; you have to dress for dinner. ✉ *5 mi north of Arundel,*

off B2139, Amberley ☎ *01798/831992* ⊕ *www.amberleycastle.co.uk* ⊅ *20 rooms* ♿ *In-room: no a/c, Internet. In-hotel: restaurant, bar, tennis court, no kids under 12* ☰ *AE, DC, MC, V* ⏺ *CP.*

££-£££ 🔅 **Norfolk Arms Hotel.** Like the cathedral and the castle in Arundel, this 18th-century coaching inn on the main street was built by one of the dukes of Norfolk. Some rooms are small (the hotel dubs them "cozy"), but those in an annex in the courtyard block are larger and more modern. Many are decorated in a frilly style. **Pros:** charming building; historic setting. **Cons:** many rooms are very small; decor is dated. ⊠ *22 High St.* ☎ *01903/882101* ⊕ *www.norfolkarmshotel.com* ⊅ *34 rooms* ♿ *In-room: no a/c, Wi-Fi. In-hotel: restaurant, bars, Wi-Fi hotspot, some pets allowed* ☰ *AE, DC, MC, V* ⏺ *BP.*

NIGHTLIFE AND THE ARTS
The **Arundel Festival** (☎ *01903/883690* ⊕ *www.arundelfestival.co.uk*) presents dramatic productions and classical and pop concerts in and around the castle grounds for 10 days in August or September.

CHICHESTER

10 mi west of Arundel, 66 mi southwest of London.

The Romans founded Chichester, the capital city of West Sussex, on the low-lying plains between the wooded South Downs and the sea. The city walls and major streets follow the original Roman plan. This cathedral town, a good base for exploring the area, is a well-respected theatrical hub, with a reputation for attracting good acting talent during its summer repertory season. North of town is Petworth House, a National Trust treasure house.

GETTING HERE AND AROUND
From London, take A3 south and follow exit signs for Chichester. The 67-mi journey takes slightly more than two hours; much of it is in on smaller highways. Southern trains run to Chichester every half hour from Victoria station, with a travel time of about 90 minutes. Bus service from London requires a trip to Brighton or Portsmouth and a change to a regional service; the train is faster.

ESSENTIALS
Visitor Information Chichester (⊠ *29A South St.* ☎ *01243/775888* ⊕ *www. visitchichester.org*).

EXPLORING
TOP ATTRACTIONS
Chichester Cathedral. Standing on Roman foundations, Norman Chichester Cathedral celebrated its 900th birthday in 2008. Inside, a glass panel reveals Roman mosaics uncovered during restoration. Other treasures are the wonderful Saxon limestone reliefs of the raising of Lazarus and Christ arriving in Bethany, both in the choir area. Among the outstanding contemporary artworks are a stained-glass window by Marc Chagall, a colorful tapestry by John Piper, and a painting by Graham Sutherland. ⊠ *West St.* ☎ *01243/782595* ⊕ *www.chichestercathedral. org.uk* 🎫 *£3 suggested donation* ☉ *Easter–Sept., daily 7:15–7; Oct.–Easter, daily 7:15–6. Tours Mon.–Sat. at 11:15 and 2:30.*

Fishbourne Roman Palace. In 1960, workers digging a water-main ditch uncovered a Roman wall; so began nine years of archaeological excavation of this site, the remains of the largest, grandest Roman villa in Britain. Intricate mosaics (including Cupid riding a dolphin) and painted walls lavishly decorate what is left of many of the 100 rooms of the palace, built in the 1st century AD, possibly for local chieftain Tiberius

Claudius Togidubnus. It's a glimpse of high living, Roman-leader style. You can explore the sophisticated bathing and heating systems, and the only example of a Roman garden in northern Europe. An expansion has added many modern attributes, including a video reconstruction of how the palace might have looked. The site is ½ mi west of Chichester. ⊠ *Salthill Rd., Fishbourne* ☎ *01243/785859* ⊕ *www.sussexpast.co.uk* 🖭 *£7.60* ◌ *Mar.–Nov., daily 10–4; Jan., Sun. 10–4.*

Fodor's Choice ★ **Petworth House.** One of the National Trust's greatest treasures, Petworth is the imposing 17th-century home of Lord and Lady Egremont and holds an outstanding collection of English paintings by Gainsborough, Reynolds, and Van Dyck, as well as 19 oil paintings by the great proponent of Romanticism J. M. W. Turner, who often visited Petworth and immortalized it in luminous drawings. A 13th-century chapel is all that remains of the original manor house. The celebrated landscape architect Capability Brown (1716–83) added a 700-acre deer park. Other highlights include Greek and Roman sculpture and Grinling Gibbons wood carvings, such as those in the spectacular Carved Room. Six rooms in the servants' quarters, among them the old kitchen, are also open to the public. A restaurant serves light lunches. You can reach the house off A272 and A283 (parking lots are off the latter); Petworth house is 13 mi northeast of Chichester and 54 mi south of London. Between 11 and 1 visits are by guided tour only. ⊠ *Petworth* ☎ *01798/342207* ⊕ *www.nationaltrust.org.uk* 🖭 *£9.90; gardens only, £4* ◌ *House mid-Mar.–early Nov., Sat.–Wed. 11–5; last admission at 4:30. Gardens Mar.–late Oct., Sat.–Wed. 11–6; Nov.–mid-Dec., Wed.–Sat. 10–3:30. Park daily 8–dusk.*

★ **Sculpture at Goodwood.** Twenty acres of woodland provide a backdrop for this collection of contemporary British sculpture specially commissioned by the Hat Hill Sculpture Foundation. A third of the approximately 40 exhibits change annually, and walks through green fields connect the pieces, sited to maximize their effect. It's a stimulating way to spend an afternoon. The park is 3 mi north of Chichester, signposted on the right off A286. Entrance fees are usually dropped in winter; wear appropriate footwear because the site gets muddy. ⊠ *Hat Hill Copse, Goodwood* ☎ *01243/538449* ⊕ *www.sculpture.org.uk* 🖭 *£10* ◌ *Jan.–Mar., weekdays 10:30–3; Apr.–Oct., Tues.–Sun. and national holidays 10:30–5.*

WORTH NOTING

Pallant House. Chichester's architecture is mainly Georgian, and its 18th-century stone houses give it a wonderful period appearance. One of the best is Pallant House, built in 1712 as a wine merchant's mansion. At that time its state-of-the-art design showed the latest in complicated brickwork and superb wood carving. Appropriate antiques and porcelains furnish the faithfully restored rooms. The **Pallant House Gallery,** attached to the house, showcases a small but important collection of mainly modern British art. Admission includes entry to the **Hans Fiebusch Studio,** nearby in St. Martin's Square, with an exact re-creation of the St. John's Wood (London) studio of this exiled German artist (1898–1998) who was the last member of the so-called degenerate art group. ☒ *9 N. Pallant* ☎ *01243/774557* ⊕ *www.pallant.org.uk* ☒ *£7.50* ☉ *Tues., Wed., Fri., and Sat. 10–5, Thurs. 10–8, Sun. and national holidays 12:30–5.*

Ⓒ **Weald and Downland Open Air Museum.** It's worth a stop in Singleton, a secluded village 5 mi north of Chichester, to see this excellent museum, a sanctuary for historical buildings dating from the 13th to 19th century. Among the 45 structures moved to 50 acres of wooded meadows are a cluster of medieval houses, a water mill, a Tudor market hall, and an ancient blacksmith's shop. ☒ *A286* ☎ *01243/811363* ⊕ *www.wealddown.co.uk* ☒ *£9* ☉ *Apr.–Oct., daily 10:30–6; Nov., Dec., and mid-Feb.–Mar., daily 10:30–4; Jan.–mid-Feb., weekends and Wed. 10:30–4:30; last admission 1 hr before closing.*

WHERE TO EAT AND STAY

£££
FRENCH ✕ **Comme Ça.** Its location, about a five-minute walk across the park from the Chichester Festival Theatre, makes this attractively converted pub a pleasant spot for a meal before a performance. Bunches of dried hops, suspended from the ceiling, and antique children's toys decorate the dining room. The owner, Michel Navet, is French, and his chef produces sophisticated, authentic French dishes such as duck with cassis jus or Dover sole fillet in phyllo with mushrooms. The fixed-price lunch menu offers two courses for £21; pre-theater and bar menus are other options. ☒ *67 Broyle Rd.* ☎ *01243/788724* ⊕ *www.commeca.co.uk* ☐ *AE, DC, MC, V* ☉ *Closed Mon. No dinner Sun. No lunch Tues.*

£££ ⊡ **Ship Hotel.** Built in 1790, this architecturally interesting hotel near the Chichester Festival Theatre was originally the home of Admiral Sir George Murray, one of Admiral Nelson's right-hand men. Among the outstanding elements are the flying (partially freestanding) staircase and colonnade. The house has been restored to its 18th-century elegance after spending time as a dental clinic and then an antiques shop. Reproduction period furniture fills the guest rooms, which have a simpler design than the grand public areas. Prices rise steeply during the Glorious Goodwood horse race in July. **Pros:** well-restored building; great for architecture buffs; good location. **Cons:** rooms are a little bland; not many amenities. ☒ *North St.* ☎ *01243/778000* ⊕ *www.theshiphotel.net* ⇨ *36 rooms* ⌂ *In-room: no a/c, Internet. In-hotel: restaurant, bar, some pets allowed* ☐ *MC, V* ⊚ *BP.*

NIGHTLIFE AND THE ARTS

The **Chichester Festival Theatre** (⊠ *Oaklands Park* ☎ *01243/781312* ⊕ *www.cft.org.uk*) presents classics and modern plays from May through September and is a venue for touring companies the rest of the year. Built in 1962, it has an international reputation for innovative performances and attracts theatergoers from across the country.

GUILDFORD

22 mi north of Petworth House, 35 mi north of Chichester, 28 mi southwest of London.

Guildford, the largest town in Surrey and the county's capital, is a busy commuter town with a noted theater, but its town center retains a faint 18th-century air. Gabled merchants' houses line the steep, pleasantly provincial High Street, filled with upscale household shops and restaurants. The remains of its old Norman castle are tucked away in a peaceful garden off High Street, and the large clock on the town's old guildhall adds charm. Wisley, one of the Royal Horticultural Society's display gardens, is 10 mi away.

GETTING HERE AND AROUND

From London, take A3 south and then exit onto the A31, following signs for Guildford. The 28-mi journey takes about an hour. Southwest trains run to Guildford every half hour from London's Waterloo station; the trip takes about 40 minutes. Guildford Station is a short walk from the town center, but the town's modern layout is confusing, with many busy roads. Follow signs for the High Street (the main street), or ask for directions. National Express buses travel from London to Guildford every couple of hours; the trip takes 75 minutes, and buses stop near the train station. The town has a good local bus service, but the main attractions are all accessible on foot, so there's little reason to use it. There's a taxi stand at the station, and another in the shopping district off the High Street.

ESSENTIALS

Visitor Information Guildford (⊠ *14 Tunsgate* ☎ *01483/444333* ⊕ *www. guildford.gov.uk*).

EXPLORING

Displays in the **Guildford Museum**, in the old castle building, include interesting exhibits on local history and archaeology, as well as memorabilia of Charles Dodgson, better known as Lewis Carroll, the author of *Alice in Wonderland*. Dodgson spent his last years in a house on nearby Castle Hill. He was buried in the Mount Cemetery, up the hill on High Street. **Castle Arch,** all that remains of the entrance of the old castle, displays a slot for a portcullis. ⊠ *Quarry St.* ☎ *01483/444751* ⊕ *www.guildfordmuseum.co.uk* ⊠ *Free* ☉ *Mon.–Sat. 11–5.*

Fodor'sChoice ★ In a nation of gardeners and garden goers, **Wisley** is the Royal Horticultural Society's innovative and inspirational 240-acre showpiece. Both an ornamental and scientific center, it claims to have greater horticultural diversity than any other garden in the world. The flower borders and displays in the central area, the rock garden and alpine meadow in

HIKING IN THE SOUTHEAST

For those who prefer to travel on their own two feet, the Southeast offers long sweeps of open terrain that makes walking a pleasure. Ardent walkers can explore all or part of the **North Downs Way** (153 mi) and the **South Downs Way** (106 mi), following ancient paths along the tops of the downs—the undulating treeless uplands typical of the area. Both trails give you wide views over the countryside.

The North Downs Way follows part of the old Pilgrim's Way to Canterbury that so fascinated Chaucer. The South Downs Way crosses the chalk landscape of Sussex Downs, with parts of the route going through deep woodland. Along the way, charming little villages serve the walkers cool ale in inns that have been doing precisely that for centuries. The 30-mi (north–south) **Downs Link** joins the two routes. Along the Kent coast, the Saxon Shore Way, 143 mi from Gravesend to Rye, passes four Roman forts. Guides to these walks are available from the **Southeast England Tourist Board** (⊕ *www.visitsoutheastengland.com*); also check the **National Trails** Web site (⊕ *www.nationaltrail.co.uk*).

spring, and the impressive conservatories are just a few highlights, along with a garden center that sells more than 10,000 types of plants and an impressive bookstore. Near Woking, the garden is 10 mi northeast of Guildford. It's very easy to spend half a day or more here. ⊠ *A3, Woking* ☎ *01483/224234* ⊕ *www.rhs.org.uk/gardens/wisley* ☜ *£9.50* ☉ *Mar.–Oct., weekdays 10–6, weekends and national holidays 9–6; Nov.–Feb., weekdays 10–4:30, weekends 9–4:30.*

WHERE TO EAT

££
FRENCH
✕ **Café Rouge.** Part of a British chain of inevitably charming and friendly French-style cafés, the Guildford branch is no exception. It's a great place to stop for a coffee, or to have a full lunch or dinner. Menu stalwarts include warming onion soup (with gooey Gruyère cheese) and the meltingly good croque monsieur sandwich, with ham and cheese. In the evening, steak frites with a pile of crisp french fries is a good choice. The decent wine list is pleasantly priced, and the coffee is excellent. ⊠ *8–9 Chapel St.* ☎ *01483/451221* ⊕ *www.caferouge.co.uk* ▭ *AE, MC, V.*

££
SEAFOOD
✕ **Loch Fyne.** Tucked away in one of Guildford's old buildings, this cleanly designed seafood restaurant has whitewashed walls and a casual atmosphere. Loch Fyne is a reliably good, innovative chain dedicated to using fresh, sustainable British seafood. Menu items change with the seasons, but oysters (in season) lead the way and are served several ways, although purists insists they are best on the half shell, on ice. Main courses can include poached smoked haddock with mashed potatoes in a whole-grain-mustard sauce, or char-grilled kiln-roasted salmon with whisky sauce. ⊠ *Centenary Hall, Chapel St.* ☎ *01483/230550* ⊕ *www. lochfyne.com* ▭ *AE, MC, V.*

£
THAI
✕ **Rumwong.** On the incredibly long menu, the Thai name of each dish appears with a clear English description. Good choices are the fisherman's soup, a spicy mass of delicious saltwater fish in a clear broth, or *yam pla muek*, a hot salad with squid. The restaurant runs an Asian

supermarket next door. ⊠ *16–18 London Rd.* ☎ *01483/536092* ⊕ *www. rumwong.co.uk*▤ *MC, V* ☉ *Closed Mon.*

WHERE TO STAY

££££   ☷ **Angel Posting House and Livery.** Guildford was once famous for its coaching inns, but this 500-year-old hotel is the last of them. The courtyard, where coaches and horses clattered to a stop, opens to the sky, and light lunches are offered here in summer. Individually designed guest rooms have luxurious fabrics, reproductions of antiques, and marble-lined bathrooms; 10 are in a modern annex. There's a salon with a fireplace and minstrels' gallery, and the 13th-century stone-vaulted crypt serves as the backdrop for fine Modern British food (£32 for fixed-price menu). **Pros:** historic building; lovely rooms. **Cons:** price is high for this area; books up far in advance. ⊠ *91 High St.* ☎ *01483/564555* ☞ *21 rooms* ⚭ *In-room: no a/c, Wi-Fi. In-hotel: restaurant, gym, spa, some pets allowed* ▤ *AE, DC, MC, V.*

££   ☷ **Old Great Halfpenny.** Surrounded by well-maintained grounds, this 16th-century half-timbered house looks like something out of a picture book. The owners are decorators and gardeners, so the place is impeccably done, from top to bottom. Rooms have comfortable antique beds, and you can have breakfast on the patio in the summertime. **Pros:** beautiful gardens; lovely old building; peace and quiet. **Cons:** a 15-minute drive out of town; small. ⊠ *Halfpenny La., St. Martha* ✛ *5 mi north of Guildford* ☎ *01483/567835* ☞ *2 rooms* ⚭ *In-room: no a/c, no phone. In-hotel: Wi-Fi hotspot* ▤ *No credit cards* ○ *CP.*

NIGHTLIFE AND THE ARTS

The **Yvonne Arnaud Theatre** (⊠ *Millbrook* ☎ *01483/440000*), a horseshoe-shaped building on an island in the River Wey, frequently previews West End productions; it also has a restaurant. The smaller Mill Studio showcases more intimate productions.

CASTLES AND HOUSES NEAR TUNBRIDGE WELLS

England is famous for its magnificent stately homes and castles, but many of them are scattered across the country, presenting a challenge for travelers. Within a 15-mi radius of Tunbridge Wells, however, in that area of hills and hidden dells known as the Weald, lies a wealth of architectural wonder in historic homes, castles, and gardens: Penshurst Place, Hever Castle, Chartwell, Knole, Ightham Mote, Leeds Castle, Sissinghurst Castle Garden, and Bodiam Castle.

ROYAL TUNBRIDGE WELLS

39 mi southeast of London.

Nobody much bothers with the "Royal" anymore, but Tunbridge Wells is no less regal because of it. Because of its wealth and political conservatism, this historic bedroom community has been the subject of (somewhat envious) British humor for years. Its restaurants and lodgings make it a convenient base for exploring the many homes and gardens nearby.

The city owes its prosperity to the 17th- and 18th-century passion for spas and mineral baths. In 1606 a mineral-water spring was discovered here, drawing legions of royal visitors looking for eternal health. Tunbridge Wells reached its zenith in the mid-18th century, when Richard "Beau" Nash presided over its social life. The buildings at the lower end of High Street are mostly 18th century, but as the street climbs the hill north, changing its name to Mount Pleasant Road, structures become more modern.

GETTING HERE AND AROUND

National Express buses headed to Kent and Tunbridge Wells depart from London's Victoria Coach Station several times a day. The trip takes about 90 minutes. Southeastern trains leave from London's Charing Cross station every 30 minutes. The journey to Tunbridge Wells takes just under an hour. If you're traveling by car from London, head here on the A21; travel time is about an hour.

Tunbridge Wells sprawls in all directions, but the historic center is compact. None of the sights is more than a 10-minute walk from the main train station. You can pick up a town map at the station.

ESSENTIALS

Visitor Information Royal Tunbridge Wells (✉ *The Old Fish Market, the Pantiles* ☎ *01892/515675* ⊕ *www.visittunbridgewells.com*).

EXPLORING

A good place to begin a visit is at the **Pantiles**, a famous promenade with colonnaded shops near the spring on one side of town. Its odd name derives from the Dutch "pan tiles" that originally paved the area. Now bordered on two sides by busy main roads, the Pantiles remains an elegant, tranquil oasis, and the site of the actual well. ■ TIP→ **You can still drink the waters when a "dipper" (the traditional water dispenser) is in attendance, from Easter through September.**

The **Church of King Charles the Martyr** (✉ *Chapel Pl.*), across the road from the Pantiles, dates from 1678, when it was dedicated to Charles I, who had been executed by Parliament in 1649. Its plain exterior belies its splendid interior; take special note of the beautifully plastered baroque ceiling.

OFF THE BEATEN PATH

All Saints Church. This modest 13th-century church holds one of the glories of 20th-century church art. The building is awash with the luminous yellows and blues of 12 windows by Marc Chagall (1887–1985), commissioned as a tribute by the family of a young girl who was drowned in a sailing accident in 1963. The church is 4 mi north of Tunbridge Wells; turn off A26 before Tonbridge and continue a mile or so east along B2017. ✉ *B2017, Tudeley* ☎ *0870/744–1456* ✉ *Free* ☉ *Daily 9–6 or dusk.*

WHERE TO EAT

£££
CHINESE

✕ **Gracelands Palace.** Weird and wonderful, this place is a temple to Chinese food and, well, Elvis. Owner Paul Chan is famous in the region for his cabaret of Elvis songs and two- or three-course fixed-price menus of

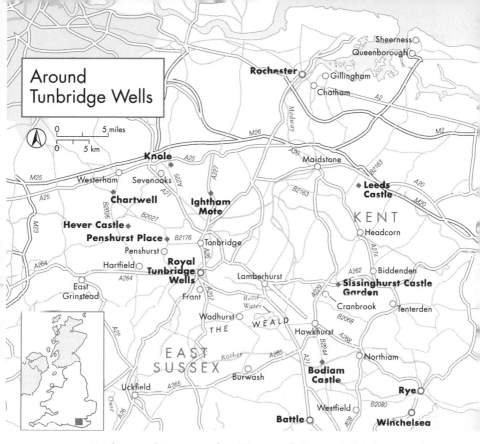

Around
Tunbridge Wells

KENT

EAST
SUSSEX

THE WEALD

Szechuan and Cantonese fare. Pictures of Chan and Elvis decorate the building; it's packed most nights with cheerful fans. The three-course prix-fixe menu is £19. ✉ *3 Cumberland Walk* ☎ *01892/540754* 🖃 *AE, MC, V* ⊘ *Closed Sun. No lunch Mon.*

£ ✕ **Himalayan Gurkha Restaurant.** It's not what you might expect to find

ASIAN in the cozy confines of Tunbridge Wells, but the Nepalese cuisine of this friendly spot is popular with locals. Spicy mountain dishes are cooked with care in traditional clay ovens or barbecued on flaming charcoal. Vegetarian options are appealing, too. ✉ *31 Church Rd.* ☎ *01892/527834* ⊕ *www.himalayangurkha.com* 🖃 *MC, V.*

£ ✕ **Mount Edgcumbe Restaurant and Bar.** To some degree, the attraction of

BRITISH this casual restaurant above the old town center is the fact that it's in a cave. Since it's carved out of the limestone foundation of the Mount Edgcumbe Hotel it's a nice cave, though. Service can be a bit shaky, but the food is pretty good. These days it's mostly straightforward pub grub: grilled steaks and french fries, sausage and mashed potatoes, or fried fish and fries. The bar has a good selection of cask ales and lagers. ✉ *The Common* ☎ *01892/526823* ⊕ *www.mountedgcumbe. com* 🖃 *MC, V.*

££££ ✕ **Thackeray's House.** Once the home of Victorian novelist William

FRENCH Makepeace Thackeray, this mid-17th-century tile-hung house is now

★ an elegant restaurant known for creative French cuisine. A terrace accommodates alfresco dining in season. The menu changes daily, but often lists dishes such as braised shoulder of Romney Marsh lamb, baked turbot with wild mushroom crust, and butter-poached lobster with cumin linguine. Desserts are butter-rich and delicious. The lunchtime menu du jour is a good value at £16.50 for two courses. ⊠ *85 London Rd.* ☎ *01892/511921* ⊕ *www.thackerays-restaurant.co.uk* ⊟ *AE, MC, V* ☺ *Closed Mon. and last wk in Dec. No dinner Sun.*

WHERE TO STAY

££££   **Hotel du Vin.** This elegant sandstone house dating from 1762 has been transformed into a chic boutique hotel with polished wood floors and luxurious armchairs and sofas. Oriental rugs give public rooms a warmth that is both intimate and grand, and guest rooms are minimalist modern, with pampering bathrooms. The Burgundy Bar stocks a fine selection of wines from the eponymous region of France. In the bistro, the contemporary menu changes daily but is strong on creamy soups and crisp salads. Book early online for good discounts. **Pros:** beautifully renovated historic building; luxurious linens. **Cons:** restaurant can get booked up; popular bar can be crowded. ⊠ *Crescent Rd. near Mount Pleasant Rd.* ☎ *01892/526455* ⊕ *www.hotelduvin.com* ⤶ *34 rooms* ⅃ *In-room: no a/c, Wi-Fi. In-hotel: restaurant, bars* ⊟ *AE, DC, MC, V* ⊺◎⫿ *BP.*

££   **Smart & Simple Hotel.** One of the city's best new budget hotels, this small place near the train station takes a modern, boutique approach. Rooms are small but nicely and minimally decorated, most with neutral colors. Bed linens are soft Egyptian cotton, and fluffy comforters top the beds. Bathrooms are unbelievably tiny but modern. A light Continental breakfast is included, and there's a Lilliputian in-house gym if you really must. **Pros:** handy location; free Wi-Fi. **Cons:** few services; no frills at all. ⊠ *54–57 London Rd.* ☎ *0845/4025744* ⊕ *www. smartandsimple.co.uk* ⤶ *40 rooms* ⅃ *In-room: no a/c, Wi-Fi. In-hotel: gym* ⊟ *MC, V* ⊺◎⫿ *CP.*

££££   **Spa Hotel.** Carefully chosen furnishings and details help maintain the country-house flavor of this 1766 Georgian mansion, although modern touches like wireless Internet connections in the guest rooms make it convenient. There are superb views from the 15-acre grounds across the town and into the Weald of Kent. Kids can take pony-riding lessons at the stables here. The traditional British fare of the Chandelier Restaurant is popular with locals. **Pros:** lap-of-luxury feel; gorgeous views. **Cons:** very formal atmosphere; can be a bit stuffy. ⊠ *Mount Ephraim* ☎ *01892/520331* ⊕ *www.spahotel.co.uk* ⤶ *69 rooms* ⅃ *In-room: no a/c (some), Wi-Fi. In-hotel: restaurant, bar, tennis court, pool, gym, spa, Wi-Fi hotspot, some pets allowed* ⊟ *AE, DC, MC, V.*

PENSHURST PLACE

7 mi northwest of Royal Tunbridge Wells, 33 mi southeast of London.

EXPLORING

★ At the center of the adorable hamlet of Penshurst stands **Penshurst Place**, one of England's finest medieval manor houses, hidden behind tall trees and walls. Although it has a 14th-century hall, Penshurst is mainly Elizabethan and has been the family home of the Sidneys since 1552, giving it particular historical interest. The most famous Sidney is the Elizabethan poet Sir Philip, author of *Arcadia*. The **Baron's Hall**, topped with a chestnut roof, is the oldest and one of the grandest halls to survive from the early Middle Ages. Family portraits, furniture, tapestries, and armor help tell the story of this house that was first inhabited in 1341 by Sir John de Pulteney, the very wealthy four-time London mayor. On the grounds are a toy museum, a gift shop, and the enchanting 11-acre walled Italian Garden, which displays tulips and daffodils in spring, roses in July, and mistletoe during the winter months. The house is off Leicester Square; take time to study the village's late-15th-century half-timber structures adorned with soaring brick chimneys. ✉ *Off B2188; from Tunbridge Wells, follow A26 and B2176* ☎ *01892/870307* ⊕ *www.penshurstplace.com* 🎫 *£9.50 for house and grounds; grounds only, £7.50* ☯ *Mar., weekends noon–4; Apr.–Oct., daily noon–4. Grounds daily 10:30–6. Last admission 30 mins before closing.*

WHERE TO EAT AND STAY

££ ✕ **Spotted Dog.** This pub first opened its doors in 1520 and hardly
BRITISH appears to have changed. Its big inglenook fireplace and heavy beams give it character, the views from the hilltop are lovely, and the good food and friendly crowd make it a pleasure. Cheeses, meats, and beer are locally sourced. The pub is 1.3 mi from Penshurst by the narrow B2188. ✉ *Smarts Hill* ☎ *01892/870253* ⊕ *www.spotteddogpub.co.uk* 💳 *MC, V.*

££ 🏨 **Best Western Rose and Crown Hotel.** Originally a 16th-century inn, this hotel on the main street in Tonbridge (5 mi east of Penshurst, 5 mi north of Tunbridge Wells) has low-beam ceilings and good Jacobean woodwork in the snug, inviting bar and the restaurant. Guest rooms in the main building are traditionally furnished, whereas rooms in the newer annex are more modern in style. There's a pretty bicycle route from Tonbridge to Penshurst. **Pros:** lovely old building; atmospheric setting; public pool nearby. **Cons:** older rooms are quite small; annex rooms have less charm. ✉ *125 High St., Tonbridge* ☎ *01732/357966* ⊕ *www.bestwestern.co.uk* 🛏 *56 rooms* ⅋ *In-room: no a/c, Wi-Fi. In-hotel: restaurant, bar, Wi-Fi hotspot, laundry service, parking (free)* 💳 *AE, MC, V* 🍽 *BP.*

HEVER CASTLE

3 mi west of Penshurst, 10 mi northwest of Royal Tunbridge Wells, 30 mi southeast of London.

EXPLORING

Fodor's Choice ★ For some, 13th-century **Hever Castle** fits the stereotype of what a castle should look like: all turrets and battlements, the whole encircled by a water lily–bound moat. For others, it's too squat in structure (and perhaps too renovated). Here, at her childhood home, the unfortunate Anne Boleyn, second wife of Henry VIII and mother of Elizabeth I, was courted and won by Henry. He loved her dearly for a time but had her beheaded in 1536 after she failed to give birth to a son. He then gave Boleyn's home to his fourth wife, Anne of Cleves, as a present. Famous though it was, the castle fell into disrepair in the 19th century. American millionaire William Waldorf Astor acquired Hever in 1903, and the Astor family owned it until 1983. Astor built a Tudor village to house his staff (it's now used for private functions) and created the stunning gardens, which include an excellent yew maze, a water maze, ponds, playgrounds, tea shops, gift shops, plant shops—you get the picture. There's a notable collection of Tudor portraits, and in summer activities are nonstop here, with jousting, falconry exhibitions, and country fairs, making this one of southern England's most rewarding castles to visit. ✉ *Off B2026, Hever* ☎ *01732/865224* 🌐 *www.hevercastle.co.uk* 🎫 *£13; grounds only, £10.50* ⏲ *Castle Apr.–Oct., daily noon–6; Mar., Wed.–Sun., noon–4; Nov. and Dec., Thurs.–Sun. noon–4. Grounds Apr.–Oct., daily 10:30–6; Mar., Wed.–Sun. 10:30–4; Nov. and Dec., Thurs.–Sun. 10:30–4. Last admission 1 hr before closing.*

CHARTWELL

9 mi north of Hever Castle, 12 mi northwest of Tunbridge Wells, 28 mi southeast of London.

EXPLORING

A grand Victorian mansion with views over the Weald, **Chartwell** was the home of Sir Winston Churchill from 1924 until his death in 1965. Virtually everything has been kept as it was when he lived here, with his pictures, books, photos, and maps. There's even a half-smoked cigar that the World War II prime minister never finished. Churchill was an amateur artist, and his paintings show a different side of the crusty politician. Admission to the house is by timed ticket, which can't be prebooked. The garden may be open year-round, weather permitting. ■ **TIP→ Be sure to explore Chartwell's rose gardens and take one of the country walks.** ✉ *Off B2026, Westerham* ☎ *01732/866368* 🌐 *www.nationaltrust.org.uk* 🎫 *£10.60, garden only £5.30* ⏲ *Mid-Mar.–June and early Sept.–late Oct., Wed.–Sun. 11–5; July–early Sept., Tues.–Sun. 11–5; last admission at 4:15.*

CLOSE UP

Tips for Visiting Treasure Houses

Throughout the Southeast you can wander through the gorgeous homes of the wealthy and the formerly wealthy. Some are privately owned; hundreds of other homes and castles are owned by the National Trust or English Heritage, organizations that raise part of the money needed to maintain them through entrance fees. Here are some things to keep in mind when you visit:

Houses and castles are unique. What you get for your entrance fee differs enormously. You may be free to wander at will, or you may be organized into groups like prisoners behind enemy lines. Sometimes the exterior of a building may be spectacular, but the interior dull. It's also true that the gardens and grounds may be just as interesting as (or moreso than) the house. Our individual reviews alert you to these instances. You can often pay separately for the house and grounds, so choose your admission ticket accordingly.

Passes may save you money. If you plan to see lots of houses and castles, it might be cheaper to buy a pass, such as VisitBritain's Great British Heritage Pass, or to join an organization such as the National Trust (⇨ Sightseeing Passes in Essentials in Travel Smart England) and thus get free entry. Check entrance fees

against your itinerary to be sure what you will save.

Opening hours are seasonal and change. Hours can change abruptly, so call the day before. Many houses are open only from April to October, and they may have extremely limited hours. In other cases the houses have celebrated parks and gardens that are open much of the year. Consider a trip in shoulder seasons if you can't take the crowds that inevitably pack the most popular houses; or explore lesser-known abodes. You'll still have a great time.

Transportation can be a challenge. If you don't have a car, plan transportation in advance. Some places are tucked deep in the countryside; others are more accessible.

Consider a stay at a property. To get even more up close and personal, you can rent a cottage from the **National Trust** (⊕ www.nationaltrustcottages.co.uk) or **English Heritage** (⊕ www.english-heritage.org.uk/holidaycottages). You could stay in the servants' quarters, a lodge, or even a lighthouse. Some privately owned houses have cottages for rent on their estates; their Web sites generally have this information. Also ⇨ See Accommodations in Travel Smart England.

KNOLE

8 mi east of Chartwell, 11 mi north of Royal Tunbridge Wells, 27 mi southeast of London.

EXPLORING

Fodor'sChoice ★ The town of Sevenoaks lies in London's commuter belt, a world away from the baronial air of its premier attraction, **Knole**, the grand, beloved home of the Sackville family since the 16th century. Begun in the 15th century and enlarged in 1603 by Thomas Sackville, Knole, with its complex of courtyards and buildings, resembles a small town. You'll need most of an afternoon to explore it thoroughly. The house is noted for its tapestries, embroidered furnishings, and the most famous set of 17th-century silver furniture to survive. Most of the salons are in the pre-baroque mode, rather dark and armorial. The magnificently florid staircase was a novelty in its Elizabethan heyday. Vita Sackville-West grew up at Knole and set her novel *The Edwardians,* a witty account of life among the gilded set, here. Encompassed by a 1,000-acre deer park, the house lies in the center of Sevenoaks, opposite St. Nicholas Church. To get here from Chartwell, drive north to Westerham, then pick up A25 and head east for 8 mi to A225. ⊠ *Off A225* ☎ *01732/450608* ⊕ *www.nationaltrust.org.uk* ⊠ *House £9.50, gardens £2.50* ⊗ *Mar., weekends noon–4; Apr.–June, Sept., and Oct., Wed.–Sun. noon–4; July and Aug., Tues.–Sun. 11–4:30. Gardens Apr.–Sept., Wed. 11–4. Last admission 30 mins before closing.*

IGHTHAM MOTE

7 mi southeast of Knole, 10 mi north of Royal Tunbridge Wells, 31 mi southeast of London.

EXPLORING

★ Finding **Ightham Mote** requires careful navigation, but it's worth the effort to see a vision right out of the Middle Ages. To enter this outstanding example of a small manor house, you cross a stone bridge over one of the dreamiest moats in England. This moat, however, does not relate to the "mote" in the name, which refers to the role of the house as a meeting place, or "moot." Ightham (pronounced *i*-tem) Mote's magical exterior has changed little since the 14th century, but within you'll find that it encompasses styles of several periods, Tudor to Victorian. The Great Hall is an antiquarian's delight, both comfy and grand, and the Tudor chapel, drawing room, and billiards room in the northwest quarter are highlights. To reach the house from Sevenoaks, follow A25 east to A227 (8 mi) and follow the signs. ⊠ *Off A227, Ivy Hatch, Sevenoaks* ☎ *01732/811145* ⊕ *www.nationaltrust.org.uk* ⊠ *£11* ⊗ *House Mid-Mar.–Oct., Thurs.–Mon. 11–5; Nov. and Dec., Thurs.–Sun. 11–3. Estate daily all yr, dawn–dusk.*

ROCHESTER

15 mi north of Ightham Mote, 28 mi southeast of London.

Positioned near the confluence of the Thames and the River Medway, this posh town has a history of Roman, Saxon, and Norman occupation, all of which have left architectural remains, including the vast castle at the town center. Novelist Charles Dickens called Rochester home for more than a decade, until his death in 1870. The Charles Dickens Centre in Eastgate House on High Street is closed, though you can still stroll through the garden and see the exterior of the Swiss-style chalet where he wrote. Across the river from Rochester is Chatham, with a noted maritime museum and the Dickens World theme park.

ESSENTIALS

Visitor Information Rochester (✉ *95 High St.* ☎ *01634/843666* 🌐 *www.cometorochester.co.uk*).

EXPLORING

The impressive ruins of **Rochester Castle** are a superb example of Norman military architecture. The keep, built in the 1100s using the old Roman city wall as a foundation, is 125 feet high, the tallest in England. It's been shored up but left without floors, so that from the bottom you can see to the open roof and study the complex structure. At the shop you can pick up well-researched guides to the building. ✉ *Boley Hill* ☎ *01634/402276* 🌐 *www.english-heritage.org.uk* 🎟 *£5* 🕑 *Apr.–Sept., daily 10–6; Oct.–Mar., daily 10–4; last admission 30 mins before closing.*

3

In AD 604 Augustine of Canterbury ordained the first English bishop in a small cathedral on the site of **Rochester Cathedral**. The current cathedral, England's second oldest, is a jumble of architectural styles. Much of the original Norman building (1077) remains, including the striking west front, the highly carved portal, and the tympanum above the doorway. Some medieval art survives, including a 13th-century Wheel of Fortune on the choir walls; it's a reminder of how difficult medieval life was. ✉ *Boley Hill* ☎ *01634/843366* 🌐 *www.rochestercathedral.org* 🎟 *£2 donation suggested* 🕑 *Mon.–Sat. 7:30–6, Sun. 7:30–5.*

Filling an aluminum-clad hangar in a giant shopping center, **Dickens World** is a literary theme park. Inside is a small but beautifully designed Victorian London scene. It not only introduces you to the author and his works but also allows you to walk down a Victorian alley and climb the stairs in Victorian houses. There's a schoolroom with a fierce headmaster; a haunted house; and a (silly but fun) boat ride down a narrow canal that is loosely based on the story of Pip and Magwitch in *Great Expectations*. A 3-D film about Dickens is actually pretty good. This curiosity is popular for families with young children and for local school field trips. ✉ *Leviathan Way, Chatham* ☎ *01634/890421* 🌐 *www.dickensworld.co.uk* 🎟 *£12.50* 🕑 *Daily 10–5:30; last admission at 5.*

The buildings and 47 retired ships at the 80-acre **Historic Dockyard** across the River Medway from Rochester constitute the country's most complete Georgian-to-early-Victorian dockyard. Fans of maritime history could easily spend a day at the exhibits and structures. The dockyard's origins go back to the time of Henry VIII; some 400 ships were built here over the centuries. There's a guided tour of the submarine HMS *Ocelot*, the last warship to be built for the Royal Navy at Chatham. ■ **TIP→ Each ticket is good for 12 months.** ✉ *Chatham* ☎ *01634/823807* 🌐 *www.chdt.org.uk* 🎟 *£14* 🕑 *Mid-Mar.–Oct., daily 10–6 (or dusk if earlier); Nov., weekends 10–4.*

WHERE TO STAY

££ **Gordon House Hotel**. Across from the cathedral, this friendly guesthouse in central Rochester is a well-priced option. Rooms are done in creamy colors, and some have Victorian architectural details; most have antiques. You can have a cup of tea and relax in the ground-floor lounge after a busy day of sightseeing. **Pros:** friendly staff; quiet rooms. **Cons:** some rooms are small; bathrooms are a bit old-fashioned. ⌧ *91 High St.* ☎ *01634/814769* ⊕ *www.gordonhousehotel.net* ⇩ *12 rooms* ⚭ *In-room: no a/c. In-hotel: restaurant, bar* ⊟ *MC, V* ⏀ *BP.*

NIGHTLIFE AND THE ARTS

Rochester sponsors a **Dickensian Christmas Festival** (☎ *01634/306000*) on the first weekend in December. Thousands of people in period dress participate in reenactments of scenes from the author's novel *A Christmas Carol.* A candlelight procession, mulled wine and roasted chestnuts, and Christmas carols at the cathedral add to the celebration. Another important Dickens festival takes place in Broadstairs (40 mi east).

LEEDS CASTLE

12 mi south of Rochester, 19 mi northwest of Royal Tunbridge Wells, 40 mi southeast of London.

EXPLORING

The bubbling River Medway runs through Maidstone, Kent's county seat, with its backdrop of chalky downs. Nearby, the fairy-tale stronghold of **Leeds Castle** commands two small islands on a peaceful lake. Dating to the 9th century and rebuilt by the Normans in 1119, Leeds (not to be confused with the city in the north of England) became a favorite home of many medieval English queens. Henry VIII liked it so much he had it converted from a fortress into a grand palace. The interior doesn't match the glories of the much-photographed exterior, although there are fine paintings and furniture, including many pieces from the 20th-century refurbishment by the castle's last private owner, Lady Baillie. The outside attractions are more impressive and include a maze, a grotto, an aviary of native and exotic birds, and woodland gardens. The castle is 5 mi east of Maidstone. ⌧ *A20* ☎ *01622/765400* ⊕ *www.leedscastle. uk* ⌸ *£17.50; grounds only, £11* ⊙ *Apr.–Oct., daily 10–5; Nov.–Mar., daily 10–3:30; last admission 30 mins before closing.*

SISSINGHURST CASTLE GARDEN

10 mi south of Leeds Castle, 53 mi southeast of London.

GETTING HERE AND AROUND

For those without a car, take a train from London's Charing Cross station and transfer to a bus in Staplehurst. Direct buses operate on Tuesday, Friday, and Sunday between May and August; at other times, take the bus to Sissinghurst village and walk the remaining 1¼ mi. From Leeds Castle, make your way south on B2163 and A274 through Headcorn, and then follow signs.

EXPLORING

Fodor's Choice ★ One of the most famous gardens in the world, **Sissinghurst Castle Garden** rests deep in the Kentish countryside, unpretentiously beautiful and quintessentially English. The gardens, 10 themed garden "rooms," were laid out in the 1930s around the remains of part of a moated Tudor castle by writer Vita Sackville-West (one of the Sackvilles of Knole; she grew up there) and her husband, the diplomat Harold Nicolson. Climb the tower to see Sackville-West's study and to get wonderful views of the garden and surrounding fields. You can also enter the house to see the library, with its echoes of Knole. ∎ **TIP→ Good times to visit the grounds are June and July, when the roses are in bloom. It's also less busy later in the afternoon.** The White Garden, with its white flowers and silver-gray foliage, is a classic, and the herb garden and cottage garden show Sackville-West's knowledge of plants. There are woodland and lake walks, too, making it easy to spend a half day or more here. Stop by the big tea shop for lunch or a snack; the property's farmland helps supply the restaurant with fruits and vegetables. ✉ *A262, Cranbrook* ☎ *01580/710701* ⊕ *www.nationaltrust.org.uk* ✉ *£9.50* ☉ *Mid-Mar.–Oct., Mon., Tues., and Fri. 11–6:30, weekends 10–6:30; last admission at 6.*

Biddenden Winery and Cider Works, 3½ mi east of Sissinghurst on the A262, cultivates nine types of grapes on 22 acres, with a focus on the German Ortega, Huxelrebe, Bacchus, and Reichensteiner varieties. There are free tours once a month or so; check the Web site or call. It also rents out a loft with a kitchen by the week (from £240 per week in winter to £420 in summer). ✉ *Biddenden* ☎ *01580/291726* ⊕ *www.biddendenvineyards.com* ✉ *Free* ☉ *Mar.–late Dec., Mon.–Sat. 10–5, Sun. 11–5; Jan. and Feb., Mon.–Sat. 10–5. Closed Christmas wk.*

WHERE TO EAT AND STAY

£ ✕ **Claris's Tea Shop.** Claris's, near Sissinghurst Castle Garden, serves tra-
CAFÉ ditional English teas in a handsome half-timber room. A cream tea includes scones and butter, clotted cream, preserves, and a pot of tea for £5.25, or choose from cakes and toasted sandwiches. The garden is pleasant on sunny summer days, and a gift shop stocks china and glass. ✉ *1–3 High St., Biddenden* ☎ *01580/291025* ⊕ *www.collectablegifts. net* ⊟ *No credit cards* ☉ *Closed Mon.–Wed. No dinner.*

££ ⊡ **Bishopsdale Oast.** This converted 18th-century double-kiln oasthouse (used for drying hops) makes an atmospheric place to stay in tiny Biddenden, near Sissinghurst. The sprawling redbrick house with its tiptilty roof has been elegantly renovated, with cream-color walls, dark furniture, and framed pictures of flowers on the walls. On cold days a fire burns in the spacious lounge, and on warm, sunny days you can breakfast outside on the terrace. Bedrooms vary in size: the more expensive rooms are quite spacious, but cheaper rooms are more of a squeeze. All are nicely decorated, and many have sweeping views of a nearby deer park. **Pros:** quiet and restful setting; owner is a chef so breakfasts are great (dinners can be arranged, too); nice garden. **Cons:** some rooms are small; car needed to get around. ✉ *Biddenden* ☎ *01580/291027* ✐ *www.bishopsdaleoast.co.uk* ⛌ *5 rooms* ⅋ *In-room: no a/c, no phone. In-hotel: parking (free)* ⅋⊙ *BP.*

As you leave Sissinghurst Castle Garden, continue south along A229 through Hawkhurst, a little village that was once the headquarters of a notorious gang of smugglers. Turn left onto the B2244 and left at the Curlew pub to arrive in the tiny Sussex village of Bodiam.

3

BODIAM CASTLE

9 mi south of Cranbrook (Sissinghurst), 15 mi southeast of Royal Tunbridge Wells, 57 mi southeast of London.

EXPLORING

Ⓒ Immortalized in paintings, postcards, and photographs, the ruins of
★ **Bodiam Castle** rise out of the distance like a piece of medieval legend. Its turrets, battlements, wooden portcullis, glassy moat, and 2-foot-thick walls survive, but all that was within them is long gone. Built in 1385 to withstand a threatened French invasion, it was "slighted" (partly demolished) during the English Civil War of 1642–46 and has been uninhabited ever since. Still, you can climb the towers to take in sweeping countryside views, and kids can run around the castle. The castle schedules organized activities for kids during school holidays. ⊠ *Off B2244, Bodiam* ☎ *01580/830196* ⊕ *www.nationaltrust.org. uk* ⊠ *£5.80* ⊙ *Mid-Feb.–Oct., daily 10:30–5; Nov. and Dec., Wed.– Sun. 11–4 or dusk; Jan.–mid-Feb., weekends 11–4; last admission 1 hr before closing.*

The South

WINCHESTER, SALISBURY, AND STONEHENGE

WORD OF MOUTH

"I found on two occasions that the audio gadget you carry around at Stonehenge is absolutely necessary if you want to get the most out of the experience. Just looking at these incredible ancient stones is not enough. It's far more interesting hearing which stone is which, about the direction of the sun, what the historians think happened here, etc. Don't take anyone along who is not enthralled by ancient monuments."

—tod

"You might consider going to Salisbury and staying the night before. It is a great little city with the cathedral, the Magna Carta, and everything, and close—less than 30 minutes—to Stonehenge."

—laurie_ann

www.fodors.com/community

Updated
by Robert
Andrews

Cathedrals, stately homes, stone circles—the South, made up of Hampshire, Dorset, and Wiltshire counties, holds all kinds of attractions, and not a few quiet pleasures. Two important cathedrals, Winchester and Salisbury (pronounced *sawls-bree*), are here, as are stately homes—Longleat, Stourhead, and Wilton House, among them—intriguing market towns, and hundreds of haunting prehistoric remains, two of which, Avebury and Stonehenge, should not be missed.

These are just the tourist-brochure superlatives. Anyone spending time in these parts should rent a bike or a car and set out to discover the back-road villages—*not* found in those brochures. After a drink in the village pub and a look at the cricket game on the village green, stretch out in a field for a nap. Close to London, the green fields of Hampshire divide the cliffs and coves of the West Country from the hustle and bustle of the big city. If you have a coastal destination in mind, you may see this as farmland to rush through, but hit the brakes—there's plenty to see.

One of the area's many historical highlights was when Alfred the Great, teaching religion and letters, made Winchester the capital of 9th-century England and helped lay plans for Britain's first navy, sowing the seeds of the Commonwealth. This well-preserved market town is dominated by its cathedral, an imposing edifice filled with the Gothic tombs of 15th-century bishops. Winchester is a good center from which to visit quiet villages where many of England's once great personages lived or died, including Jane Austen; the road to her home at Chawton has become a much-trodden path.

Beyond the gentle, gardenlike landscape of Hampshire, you can explore the somewhat harsher terrain of Salisbury Plain. Two monuments, millennia apart, stand sentinel over the plain. One is the 404-foot-tall stone spire of Salisbury Cathedral, which dominates the entire Salisbury valley and has been immortalized in oil by John Constable. Not far away is the most imposing and dramatic prehistoric structure in Europe: Stonehenge. The many theories about its construction and purpose only add to its mystical attraction.

Other districts have their own pleasures, and many have literary or historical associations. Turn your sights to the Dorset heathland, the countryside explored in the novels of Thomas Hardy. This district is spanned by grass-covered chalk hills—the downs—wooded valleys, and meadows through which course meandering rivers. Facing the sea are Lyme Regis, on the fossil-rich Jurassic Coast, and Cowes, on the Isle of Wight—Queen Victoria's favorite getaway—where colorful flags flutter from sleek yachts.

TOP REASONS TO GO

Salisbury Cathedral: You may be stunned by the sight of one of England's most spectacular cathedrals; try a tour around the roof and spire for a fascinating angle on this must-see monument.

Stonehenge: Despite mixed reports of just how impressive this greatest of all prehistoric stone circles actually is, don't put off a visit. At the right time of day (early or late is best), this mystical ring can still cast a memorable spell against the backdrop of Salisbury Plain.

House and garden at Stourhead: It's the perfect English combination. Acres of parkland, landscaped in the 18th century, induce feelings of Arcadian bliss. There are classical temples, a folly, and gorgeous vistas over the lake, as well as a Palladian mansion to explore.

The New Forest: Get away from it all in the South's most extensive wilderness—crisscrossed by myriad trails that are ideal for horseback riding, hiking, and biking.

Historic Dockyard, Portsmouth: Rule, Britannia! Immerse yourself in the country's seafaring history, including an informative and fascinating tour around Nelson's flagship, HMS *Victory*, conducted by naval personnel.

Literary trails: Jane Austen, Thomas Hardy, and John Fowles have all made this part of Britain a happy stomping ground for book buffs, with a concentration of sights in Chawton, Dorchester, and Lyme Regis. The Isle of Wight was particularly popular with Victorian literati, notably Tennyson.

4

The South has been quietly central to England's history for well over 4,000 years, occupied successively by prehistoric man, the Celts, the Romans, the Saxons, the Normans, and the modern British. History continues to be made here. On D-Day, Allied forces sailed for Normandy from this coast; nearly 40 years later, British forces set out to recover the Falklands.

ORIENTATION AND PLANNING

GETTING ORIENTED

The wide-open, wind-blown inland county of Wiltshire offers a sharp contrast to the tame, sequestered villages of Hampshire and Dorset and the self-important bustle of the ports of Southampton and Portsmouth. You may not want to spend much time in these two cities; instead, spend your nights in the more compelling towns of Salisbury and Winchester.

The obvious draw outside Salisbury is Stonehenge, but you're also within reach of an equally interesting prehistoric monument, Avebury. From there you can swing south to the cultivated woodlands of the New Forest. The southern coast of Dorset is another major area, with a couple of popular vacation resorts, Bournemouth and Weymouth, and a string of ancient sites: Corfe Castle, Maiden Castle, and Cerne

Abbas. Lyme Regis, on the Devon border at the center of the wide arc of Lyme Bay, is a favorite vacation destination in this area. It provides a gateway to the Jurassic Coast, a World Heritage Site that stretches between Swanage in the east and Exmouth in Devon.

Winchester to Southampton. One of the region's most compelling and historically rich towns, Winchester, lies a short distance from the well-heeled villages of New Alresford and Chawton and the great south-coast ports of Portsmouth and Southampton.

Isle of Wight. Osborne House, near Cowes, and Carisbrooke Castle, outside Newport, have much historic interest. The picturesque east-coast resorts of Ryde and Ventnor contrast with the dramatic Needles, the island's most iconic landmark, on the western tip.

Salisbury, Stonehenge, and Salisbury Plain. A tour of Wiltshire kicks off in the cathedral city of Salisbury, close to Wilton and Stonehenge. Farther afield are the market towns of Shaftesbury and Sherborne, and the great estates of Stourhead and Longleat.

New Forest to Lyme Regis. The sparsely populated New Forest stretches between Southampton and Bournemouth. The route west passes Wimborne Minster, dominated by its church, and ruined Corfe Castle. Historic Dorchester and Weymouth lead to Lyme Regis.

PLANNING

WHEN TO GO
Places such as Stonehenge and Longleat House attract plenty of people at all times; bypass such sights on weekends, public holidays, or school vacations. Don't plan to visit the cathedrals of Salisbury and Winchester on a Sunday, when your visit will be restricted, or during services, when it won't be appreciated by worshippers. In summer the coastal resorts of Bournemouth and Weymouth are crowded; it may be difficult to find the accommodations you want. The Isle of Wight gets its fair share of summer visitors, especially during the weeklong Cowes Regatta in late July or early August. Because ferries fill up to capacity, you may have to wait for the next one. The New Forest is most alluring in spring and early summer (for the foaling season) and fall (for the colorful foliage), whereas summer can be busy with walkers and campers. In all seasons, take waterproof boots for the mud and puddles.

PLANNING YOUR TIME
The South has no obvious hub, though many people base themselves in one or both of the cathedral cities of Winchester and Salisbury and make excursions to nearby destinations. The coastal cities of Portsmouth and Southampton have their charms, but neither of these large urban centers is particularly attractive as an overnight stop. Busy Bournemouth, whose major sight is a Victorian-era museum, has quieter areas that are more conducive for staying over.

To escape the bustle, the New Forest, southwest of Southampton, offers space and semi-wilderness. It's easy to take a morning or afternoon break to enjoy the activities it offers, whether on foot, by bike, or on

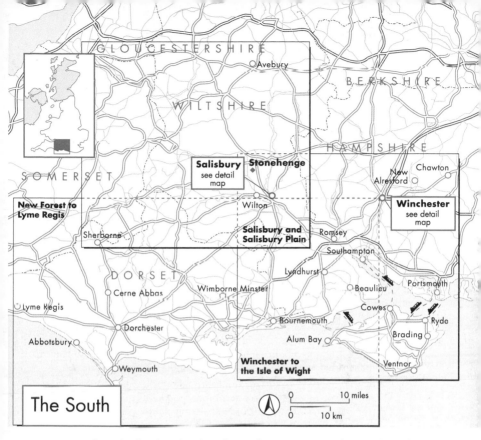

The South

0 ——— 10 miles
0 ——— 10 km

horseback. The Isle of Wight needs more time, and is worth exploring at leisure over at least a couple of days.

GETTING HERE AND AROUND
BUS TRAVEL

National Express buses at London's Victoria Coach Station on Buckingham Palace Road depart every one to two hours for Bournemouth (2½ hours), Southampton (two hours, 15 minutes), and Portsmouth (two hours), and every two to three hours for Winchester (one hour, 40 minutes). There are three buses daily to Salisbury (about three hours).

Bluestar and Stagecoach South operate a comprehensive service in the Portsmouth, Southampton, New Forest, Winchester, and Bournemouth areas. First and Wilts & Dorset serve Salisbury, Bournemouth, and Dorchester, and Southern Vectis covers the Isle of Wight. Greyhound operates a daily bus service between Bulleid Way, near Victoria Coach Station, and Portsmouth, Southampton, and Bournemouth.

Wilts & Dorset offers both one-day Dayrider and seven-day Network passes valid on all the company's bus routes. Ask about the Megarider tickets offered by Stagecoach, Rover and Freedom tickets offered by Southern Vectis, and Dayrider and Freedom tickets offered by Bluestar. Explorer tickets allow you unlimited travel on buses operated by different companies. Contact Traveline for all information on routes and tickets.

Bus Contacts Bluestar (☎ *01983/827005* ⊕ *www.bluestarbus.co.uk*). **First** (☎ *0870/010–6022* ⊕ *www.firstgroup.com*). **Greyhound** (☎ *0900/096–0000* ⊕ *www.greyhounduk.com*). **National Express** (☎ *0871/781–8178* ⊕ *www.nationalexpress.com*). **Southern Vectis** (☎ *01983/827000* ⊕ *www.islandbuses.info*). **Stagecoach South** (☎ *0845/121–0170* ⊕ *www.stagecoachbus.com*). **Traveline** (☎ *0871/200–2233* ⊕ *www.traveline.org.uk*). **Wilts (Wiltshire) & Dorset Bus Co.** (☎ *01722/336855* ⊕ *www.wdbus.co.uk*).

CAR TRAVEL

On the whole, the region is easily negotiable using public transportation. But for rural spots, especially the grand country estates, a car is most useful. The well-developed road network includes M3 to Winchester (70 mi from London) and Southampton (77 mi); A3 to Portsmouth (77 mi); and M27 along the coast, from the New Forest and Southampton to Portsmouth. For Salisbury, take M3 to A303, then A30. A35 connects Bournemouth to Dorchester and Lyme Regis, and A350 runs north to Dorset's inland destinations.

TRAIN TRAVEL

South West Trains serves the South from London's Waterloo Station. Travel times average one hour to Winchester, 1½ hours to Southampton, 1¾ hours to Bournemouth, and 2¾ hours to Weymouth. The trip to Salisbury takes 1½ hours, and Portsmouth about 1¾ hours.

A yearlong Network card, valid throughout the South and Southeast, entitles you and up to three accompanying adults to one-third off most train fares, and up to four accompanying children ages 5–15 to a 60% discount off the full fare. It costs £25.

Train Contacts National Rail Enquiries (☎ *0845/748–4950* ⊕ *www.nationalrail.co.uk*). **South West Trains** (☎ *0845/748–4950 or 0845/600–0650* ⊕ *www.southwesttrains.co.uk*).

TOURS

The Guild of Registered Tourist Guides maintains a directory of qualified Blue Badge guides who can meet you anywhere in the region for private tours. Local organizations such as Wessexplore can also arrange Blue Badge tours. On the Isle of Wight, Southern Vectis operates open-top bus tours.

Tour Information Guild of Registered Tourist Guides (☎ *020/7403–1115* ⊕ *www.blue-badge-guides.com*). **Wessexplore** (☎ *01722/326304* ⊕ *www.dmac.co.uk/wessexplore*).

RESTAURANTS

In summer, and especially on summer weekends, visitors can overrun the restaurants in small villages, so either book a table in advance or be prepared to wait. The more popular or upscale the restaurant, the more critical a reservation is. For local specialties, try fresh-grilled river trout or sea bass poached in brine, or dine like a king on the New Forest's renowned venison. Hampshire is noted for its pig and sheep farming, and you might zero in on pork and lamb dishes on local restaurant menus. The region places a strong accent on seasonal produce, so venison, for example, is best sampled between September and February.

HOTELS

Modern hotel chains are well represented, and in rural areas you can choose between elegant country-house hotels, traditional coaching inns (updated to different degrees), and modest guesthouses. Some seaside hotels do not accept one-night bookings in summer. If you plan to visit Cowes on the Isle of Wight during Cowes Week, the annual yachting jamboree in late July or early August, book well in advance.

WHAT IT COSTS IN POUNDS					
	£	££	£££	££££	£££££
Restaurants	under £10	£10–£14	£15–£19	£20–£25	over £25
Hotels	under £70	£70–£120	£121–£160	£161–£220	over £220

Restaurant prices are for a main course at dinner. Hotel prices are for two people in a standard double room in high season, including V.A.T., with no meals or, if indicated, CP (with Continental breakfast), BP (Breakfast Plan with full breakfast), or MAP (Modified American Plan, with breakfast and dinner).

VISITOR INFORMATION
Tourism South East (🌐 www.visitsoutheastengland.com).

WINCHESTER TO SOUTHAMPTON

From the cathedral city of Winchester, 70 mi southwest of London, you can meander southward to the coast, stopping at the bustling ports of Southampton and Portsmouth to explore their maritime heritage. From either port you can strike out for the restful shores of the Isle of Wight, vacation home of Queen Victoria and thousands of modern-day Britons.

WINCHESTER

70 mi southwest of London, 12 mi northeast of Southampton.

Winchester is among the most historic of English cities, and as you walk the graceful streets and wander the many gardens, a sense of the past envelops you. Although it is now merely the county seat of Hampshire, for more than four centuries Winchester served as England's capital. Here, in AD 827, Egbert was crowned first king of England, and his successor, Alfred the Great, held court until his death in 899. After the Norman Conquest in 1066, William I ("the Conqueror") had himself crowned in London, but took the precaution of repeating the ceremony in Winchester. William also commissioned the local monastery to produce the Domesday Book, a record of the general census begun in 1085. The city remained the center of ecclesiastical, commercial, and political power until the 13th century, when that power shifted to London. Winchester still preserves some of its past glory even if some fast-food outlets and retail chains have moved onto High Street.

GETTING HERE AND AROUND

On a main train line and on the M3 motorway, Winchester is easily accessible from London. The train station is a short walk from the sights; the bus station is in the center, opposite the tourist office. The one-way streets are notoriously confusing, so find a parking lot as soon as possible. The city center is very walkable, and most of High Street is closed to vehicular traffic. A walk down High Street and Broadway will bring you to St. Giles Hill, which has a panoramic view of the city.

TIMING

The city is busier than usual during the farmers' market, held on the second and the last Sunday of each month.

ESSENTIALS

Visitor and Tour Information Winchester (⊠ *The Guildhall, Broadway* ☎ *01962/840500* ⊕ *www.visitwinchester.co.uk*). **Winchester Tourist Guides** (⊕ *www.winchestertouristguides.com*).

EXPLORING
TOP ATTRACTIONS

❻ City Museum. Across from the cathedral, the museum interprets Winchester's past through displays of Celtic pottery, Saxon jewelry and coins, and reconstructed Victorian shops. It's an imaginative, well-presented collection that will appeal to children and adults alike—check out the Saxon costumes, local ceramics, and domestic and agricultural bits and pieces from the Middle Ages, and, on the top floor, some well-restored Roman mosaics. Pick up an audio guide at the entrance (£2) to get the most out of the museum. ⊠ *The Square* ☎ *01962/863064* ⊕ *www.winchester.gov.uk* ☜ *Free* ☉ *Apr.–Oct., Mon.–Sat. 10–5, Sun. noon–5; Nov.–Mar., Tues.–Sat. 10–4, Sun. noon–4.*

❺ Great Hall. A few blocks west of the cathedral, this hall is all that remains of the city's Norman castle. Here the English Parliament met for the first time in 1246; Sir Walter Raleigh was tried for conspiracy against King James I and condemned to death in 1603 (although he wasn't beheaded until 1618); and Dame Alice Lisle was sentenced to death by the brutal Judge Jeffreys for sheltering fugitives, after Monmouth's Rebellion in 1685. Occupying one corner of the Great Hall is a huge and gaudy sculpture of Queen Victoria, carved to mark her Golden Jubilee in 1887. But the hall's greatest relic hangs on its west wall: King Arthur's Round Table has places for 24 knights and a portrait of Arthur bearing a remarkable resemblance to King Henry VIII. In fact, the table dates back no farther than the 13th century and was repainted by order of Henry on the occasion of a visit by the Holy Roman Emperor Charles V; the real Arthur was probably a Celtic chieftain who held off the invading Saxons after the fall of the Roman Empire in the 5th or 6th century. The Tudor monarchs revived the Arthurian legend for political purposes. Take time to wander through Queen Eleanor's Garden—a re-creation of a medieval noblewoman's shady retreat. ⊠ *Castle Hill* ☎ *01962/846476* ⊕ *www.hants.gov.uk/greathall* ☜ *Free* ☉ *Daily 10–5 (but mid-July–Aug., Fri. 10–7).*

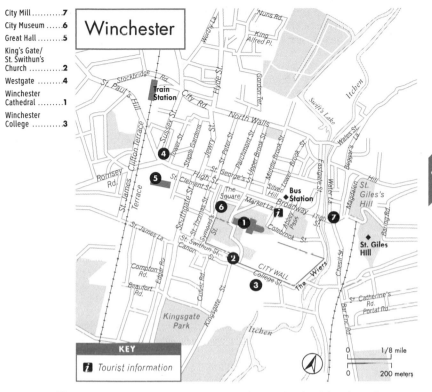

Winchester

KEY

ℹ️ *Tourist information*

0   1/8 mile

0   200 meters

---

② **King's Gate.** On St. Swithun Street on the south side of the Close, this structure was built in the 13th century and is one of two gates remaining from the original city wall. **St. Swithun's Church** is built over King's Gate.

① **Winchester Cathedral.** The city's greatest monument, begun in 1079 and
★ consecrated in 1093, presents a sturdy, chunky appearance in keeping with its Norman construction, so that the Gothic lightness within is even more breathtaking. Its tower, transepts, and crypt, and the inside core of the great Perpendicular nave, reveal some of the world's best surviving examples of Norman architecture. Other features, such as the arcades, the presbytery (behind the choir, holding the high altar), and the windows, are Gothic alterations carried out between the 12th and 14th century. Little of the original stained glass has survived, however, thanks to Cromwell's Puritan troops, who ransacked the cathedral in the 17th century during the English Civil War, but you can still see the sumptuously illuminated 12th-century Winchester Bible in the Library and Triforium Gallery.

Among the many well-known people buried in the cathedral are William the Conqueror's son, William II ("Rufus"), mysteriously murdered in the New Forest in 1100; Izaak Walton (1593–1683), author of *The Compleat Angler,* whose memorial window in Silkestede's Chapel was paid for by "the fishermen of England and America"; and Jane Austen, whose grave lies in the north aisle of the nave. The tombstone makes no mention of Austen's literary status, though a brass plaque in the wall, dating from 80 years after her death, celebrates her achievements, and modern panels provide an overview of her life and work.

Firmly in the 20th century, Antony Gormley's evocative statue *Sound II* (1986) looms in the crypt, as often as not standing in water (as it was designed to do), because of seasonal flooding. You can also explore the bell tower—with views as far as the Isle of Wight in fair weather—and other recesses of the building on a tour. Special services or ceremonies may mean the cathedral is closed to visits, so telephone first to avoid disappointment. Outside the cathedral, explore the Close, the area that nearly envelopes the

> **ST. SWITHUN WEATHER**
>
> St. Swithun (died AD 862) is interred in Winchester Cathedral, although he requested outdoor burial. Legend says that when his body was transferred inside from the cathedral's churchyard, it rained for 40 days. Since then, folk wisdom says that rain on St. Swithun's Day (July 15) means 40 more days of wet weather. (Elsewhere in England the name is usually spelled "Swithin.") Near St. Swithun's Church at King's Gate, at 8 College Street, is the house where Jane Austen died on July 18, 1817, three days after writing a comic poem about the legend of St. Swithun's Day (copies are usually available in the cathedral).

cathedral and contains neat lawns and the Deanery, Dome Alley, and Cheyney Court. ⊠ *The Close, Cathedral Precincts* ☏ *01962/857200* ⊕ *www.winchester-cathedral.org.uk* ⌑ *£6; Library and Triforium Gallery free; bell tower tour £6; combined entry to cathedral and bell tower tour £9* ☉ *Mon.–Sat. 9–5, Sun. 12:30–3, longer for services. Library and Triforium Gallery Apr.–Oct., Mon. 2–4, Tues.–Sat. and national holidays 10:30–4; Nov., Dec., and Mar., Wed. and Sat. 11–3:30; Jan. and Feb., Sat. 11–3:30. Free tours on the hr Mon.–Sat. 10–3, bell tower tours late May–Aug., Mon., Wed., and Fri. 2:15, Sat. 11:30 and 2:15; Sept.–late May, Wed. 2:15, Sat. 11:30 and 2:15.*

WORTH NOTING

❼ City Mill. Set over the River Itchen, this working 18th-century water mill, complete with small island garden, is at the east end of High Street. The medieval mill on the site was rebuilt in 1743, remaining in use until the early 20th century. Restored by the National Trust, it still operates as a working mill on weekends, and you can purchase flour produced here in the gift shop. ⊠ *Bridge St.* ☏ *01962/870057* ⊕ *www.nationaltrust. org.uk* ⌑ *£3.60* ☉ *Mid-Mar.–early Apr., late Apr.–May, mid-June–early July, and mid-Sept.–late Oct., Wed.–Sun. 10:30–5; mid-Apr., early June, mid-July–mid-Sept., and late Oct.–late Dec., daily 10:30–5.*

↺ Watercress Line. New Alresford, 8 mi northeast of Winchester by A31 and B3046, is the starting point of the Watercress Line, a 10-mi railroad reserved for steam locomotives that runs to Alton. The line (named for the watercress beds formerly in the area) takes you on a nostalgic tour through reminders of 19th-century England. New Alresford has a village green crossed by a stream and some Georgian houses and antiques shops. ⊠ *Railway Station* ☏ *01962/733810* ⊕ *www.watercressline.*

co.uk 🚌 *£12* ⓢ *May–Sept., departures most days; Oct. and Dec.–Apr., weekends and national holidays; call for details.*

④ Westgate. At the top of High Street, this fortified medieval structure was
ⓒ a debtor's prison for 150 years, and now holds a motley assortment of items relating to Tudor and Stuart times. Suits of armor—examples can be tried on—and the opportunity to make brass rubbings make it popular with kids, and you can take in a view of Winchester from the roof. ✉ *High St.* ☎ *01962/869864* 🚌 *Free* ⓢ *Apr.–Oct., Mon.–Sat. 10–5, Sun. noon–5; early Feb.–Mar., Tues.–Sat. 10–4, Sun. noon–4.*

❸ Winchester College. One of England's oldest "public" (i.e., private) schools was founded in 1382 by Bishop William of Wykcham, who has his own chapel in Winchester Cathedral. The school chapel is notable for its delicately vaulted ceiling. Among the buildings still in use is Chamber Court, center of college life for six centuries. Notice the "scholars"—students holding academic scholarships—clad in their traditional gowns. ✉ *College St.* ☎ *01962/621209* ⊕ *www.winchestercollege.co.uk* 🚌 *£4* ⓢ *1-hr tours Mon., Wed., Fri., and Sat. 10:45, noon, 2:15, and 3:30, Tues. and Thurs. 10:45 and noon, Sun. 2:15 and 3:30* ☞ *Tours may be canceled because of college events: call to check.*

WHERE TO EAT

£££ ✕ **The Bistro at Hotel du Vin.** Classic French and British fare is served
MODERN BRITISH with modern touches in this stylish bistro, converted from a redbrick Georgian town house. Dishes such as fillet of sea bass and char-grilled rib-eye steak are complemented by the many eclectic wine selections. In summer, food is served in the walled garden. The hotel's luxurious rooms (£££) are richly furnished in crisp modern style, with Oriental rugs enhancing the polished wooden floors. ✉ *14 Southgate St.* ☎ *01962/841414* ⊕ *www.hotelduvin.com* ▭ *AE, DC, MC, V.*

£ ✕ **Cathedral Refectory.** With a vaulted glass roof and steel supports, this
BRITISH self-service eatery next to the cathedral has a bold modern style that helps make it a refreshing lunch or snack stop. The menu ranges from traditional soups and panini to pork, apricot, and ginger hotpot, and chicken, leek, and Stilton stew. Food is served daily until 5, and there are tables outside for fair-weather eating. ✉ *Inner Close* ☎ *01962/857200* ▭ *MC, V* ⓢ *No dinner.*

£££ ✕ **Chesil Rectory.** The timbered and gabled building may be old English—
MODERN BRITISH 15th or 16th century—but the cuisine is contemporary, mixing classic recipes with local ingredients. Dishes might include seared Portland scallops, followed by braised shoulder of lamb or fish stew. Good-value fixed-price lunches and early-evening dinners are available. Service and the antique charm of the surroundings match the quality of the food. ✉ *1 Chesil St.* ☎ *01962/851555* ⊕ *www.chesilrectory.co.uk* ▭ *AE, DC, MC, V* ⓢ *No dinner Sun.*

£ ✕ **The Royal Oak.** Quaff a half pint of draft bitter or dry cider at this
BRITISH lively traditional pub, which claims to be England's oldest bar. The interior has been modernized, and there's plenty of space to find a comfortable spot, including a secluded cellar with the remains of a Saxon wall. Bar meals, including roasts and burgers, are served until 9 PM. ✉ *Royal Oak Passage, off High St.* ☎ *01962/842701* ⊕ *www. theroyaloakwinchester.com* ▭ *AE, MC, V.*

WHERE TO STAY

££   ⊡ **Enmill Barn.** Surrounded by gardens, this converted barn in peaceful
★   countryside 3 mi west of the center of Winchester makes a good base for
exploring villages and the South Downs. The ground-floor guest rooms
are freshly decorated in neutral tones and filled with personality—not
to mention refrigerators stocked with drinks and nibbles—and breakfast includes fresh fruit and free-range eggs (sometimes fresh duck eggs
are available). The large, beamed, and galleried sitting room holds a
snooker table. **Pros:** comfortable and spacious rooms; personal service;
top-quality snooker and tennis facilities. **Cons:** guests share one breakfast table; rather remote location. ⊠ *Enmill La., Pitt* ☎ *01962/856740*
⊕ *www.enmill-barn.co.uk* ⇄ *3 rooms* �⌂ *In-room: no a/c, no phone,*
refrigerator, Wi-Fi (some). In-hotel: tennis court, Wi-Fi hotspot ⊟ *No*
credit cards ¶⊙¶ *BP.*

£££££   ⊡ **Lainston House.** Dating from 1668, this elegant country-house hotel in
a 63-acre park is discreetly secluded, an obvious attraction for such eminent guests as Margaret Thatcher, who stayed here to write her memoirs.
Inside, cedar and oak paneling and other restored 17th-century details
adorn the public rooms. Bedrooms, many of which are beamed, are
done in warm colors and rich fabrics. Ground-floor suites have access
to the gardens, and a converted stable holds luxury rooms. The hotel is
2½ mi northwest of Winchester. **Pros:** beautiful setting; attentive staff;
sumptuous guest rooms and bathrooms. **Cons:** lower-priced rooms are
drab; food sometimes disappoints. ⊠ *Woodman La., off B3049, Spar-*
sholt ☎ *01962/776088* ⊕ *www.lainstonhouse.com* ⇄ *41 rooms, 9 suites*
�⌂ *In-room: no a/c (some), Wi-Fi. In-hotel: restaurant, tennis courts, gym,*
Wi-Fi hotspot, some pets allowed ⊟ *AE, DC, MC, V* ¶⊙¶ *BP.*

££–£££   ⊡ **Old Vine.** Blessed with an ideal location opposite the cathedral, this
18th-century inn has received a smart, modern makeover without losing
any of its character: no small achievement. Guest rooms are streamlined and have modern bathrooms but retain their period features
and traditional look, with fabrics from noted designers such as Nina
Campbell. Because of trees, few rooms have actual cathedral views,
though the top-floor Design House suite is an outstanding exception.
The restaurant and wine bar below offer superb food and drink, with
warming open fires in winter, and tables on the terrace in summer.
Permits are issued for street parking nearby. **Pros:** comfortable, elegant rooms; delicious food. **Cons:** some rooms are small with no view;
parking may be tricky to find. ⊠ *8 Great Minster St.* ☎ *01962/854616*
⊕ *www.oldvinewinchester.com* ⇄ *4 rooms, 1 suite* �⌂ *In-room: no a/c,*
no phone, refrigerator, safe, Internet. In-hotel: restaurant, bar, parking
(free) ⊟ *MC, V* ¶⊙¶ *BP.*

££   ⊡ **Wykeham Arms.** This old place is conveniently central, near the cathedral and the college. Bedrooms at the inn itself are cozy and full of quirky
knickknacks, with period touches; those across the road in the St. George
annex are slightly larger. The bars, happily cluttered with prints and
pewter, make use of old school desks for tables. A good wine list sets
off the French and British dishes at the restaurant, which is popular
with locals. **Pros:** central location; quirky charm; lively bar. **Cons:** rooms
above pub can be noisy; steep stairs; shabby in places. ⊠ *75 Kingsgate*

St. ☎ *01962/853834* ⊕ *www.fullershotels.com* ⇋ *13 rooms, 1 suite* ♿ *In-room: no a/c, Wi-Fi. In-hotel: restaurant, bars, Wi-Fi hotspot, parking (free), no kids under 14* ▤ *AE, MC, V* ⊠⦿ *BP.*

SHOPPING

A complete list of local antiques stores is available from the **Winchester Tourist Information Centre** (⊠ *The Guildhall, Broadway* ☎ *01962/840500*). **King's Walk**, off Friarsgate, has a number of stalls selling antiques, crafts, gift items, and bric-a-brac. **The Jays' Nest** (⊠ *King's Walk* ☎ *01962/865650*) specializes in jewelry, silver, and china. **Kingsgate Books and Prints** (⊠ *Kingsgate Arch, College St.* ☎ *01962/864710*) has a selection of secondhand books, maps, and prints. The oldest bookshop in town, **P&G Wells** (⊠ *11 College St.* ☎ *01962/852016*) has numerous books by and about Jane Austen, who took lodgings almost next door in 1817. It also has the region's largest selection of children's books.

> **OPEN-AIR MARKETS**
>
> Local markets provide a unique sense of place. Among the best is Winchester's, held in Middle Brook Street on the second and the last Sunday of each month. It specializes in local produce and goods. Also worth a look are Salisbury's traditional city market (Tuesday and Saturday); Southampton's Bargate Market for bric-a-brac (Friday), arts and crafts (first Saturday of each month), antiques (third Saturday), and local produce (second and fourth Saturday); Dorchester's massive market of more than 500 stalls (Wednesday); and a general country market at Ringwood, near the New Forest (Wednesday).

CHAWTON

16 mi northeast of Winchester.

In Chawton you can visit the home of Jane Austen (1775–1817), who lived the last eight years of her life in the village; she moved to Winchester only during her final illness. The site has always drawn literary pilgrims, but with the ongoing release of successful films based on her novels, the town's popularity among visitors has grown enormously.

GETTING HERE AND AROUND

Hourly Stagecoach bus X64 service connects Winchester and New Alresford with Chawton. It's a 10-minute walk from the bus stop to Jane Austen's House. By car, take A31.

EXPLORING

Here, in an unassuming redbrick house, Jane Austen wrote *Emma, Persuasion,* and *Mansfield Park,* and revised *Sense and Sensibility, Northanger Abbey,* and *Pride and Prejudice.* Now a museum, the rooms ★ of **Jane Austen's House** retain the atmosphere of restricted gentility suitable to the unmarried daughter of a clergyman. In the left-hand parlor, Jane would play her piano every morning, then repair to her mahogany writing desk in the family sitting room—leaving her sister, Cassandra, to do the household chores ("I find composition impossible with my head full of joints of mutton and doses of rhubarb," Jane wrote). In the early 19th century the road near the house was a bustling thoroughfare,

IN SEARCH OF JANE AUSTEN

A tour of "Jane Austen country" in the South of England and beyond can put you into the world of Austen's novels. Thanks to film adaptations of *Sense and Sensibility, Emma, Persuasion,* and *Pride and Prejudice,* the great author has captured another audience eager to peer into decorous 18th- and early-19th-century society. By visiting one or two main locales—such as Chawton and Winchester—it is possible to imagine hearing the tinkle of teacups raised by the likes of Elinor Dashwood and Mr. Darcy. Serious Janeites will want to retrace her life—starting out in the hamlet of Steventon, southwest of Basingstoke, where she spent her first 25 years, and then moving on to Bath, Southampton, Chawton, and Winchester.

Jane Austen country—a pleasant landscape filled with intimately scaled villages—is a perfectly civilized stage on which her characters organized visits to stately homes and husband-hunting expeditions. Entering that world, you find that its heart is the tiny Hampshire village of Chawton. Here, at a former bailiff's cottage on her brother's estate—now a museum—Austen produced three of her greatest novels. Her daily 6-mi walks often took her to Chawton

Manor—her brother's regal Jacobean mansion, now Chawton House Library, a center for the study of 16th- to 18th-century women's literature (for a consultation, call ☎ *01420/541010* or see ⊕ *www.chawton.org*)—or to nearby Lyards Farm, where her favorite niece, Anna Lefroy (thought to be the model for Emma Woodhouse), came to live in 1815.

Driving southwest from Chawton, take A31 for about 15 mi to Winchester, where you can visit Austen's austere grave within the cathedral and view an exhibit about her life; then take in No. 8 College Street, where her battle with Addison's disease ended with her death on July 18, 1817. Heading 110 mi southwest you can visit Lyme Regis, the 18th-century seaside resort on the Devon border where Austen spent the summers of 1804–05. Here, at the Cobb, the stone jetty that juts into Lyme Bay, Louisa Musgrove jumps off the steps known as Granny's Teeth—a turning point in Chapter 12 of *Persuasion.* Northwest of Winchester by some 60 mi is Bath, the elegant setting that served as the backdrop for some of Austen's razor-sharp observations. Bath's Jane Austen Centre explores the relationship between the city and the writer.

and one traveler reported that a window view proved that the Misses Austen were "looking very comfortable at breakfast." Jane was famous for working through interruptions, but one protection against the outside world was the famous door that creaked. She asked that its hinges remain unattended to because they gave her warning that someone was coming. ⊠ *Signed off A31/A32 roundabout* ☎ *01420/83262* ⊕ *www. jane-austens-house-museum.org.uk* ⌺ *£7* ⊙ *Jan.–mid-Feb., weekends 10:30–4:30; mid-Feb.–May and Sept.–Dec., daily 10:30–4:30; June–Aug., daily 10–5; last admission 30 mins before closing.*

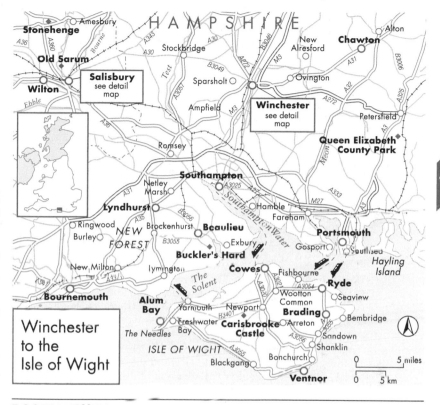

Winchester
to the
Isle of Wight

PORTSMOUTH

24 mi south of Chawton, 77 mi southwest of London.

Largely charmless, Portsmouth was England's naval capital and principal port of departure for centuries. The newly developed Gunwharf Quays and the soaring Spinnaker Tower reflect a recent upturn in the fortunes of this weary old coastal city. Along with these, the main attraction for many travelers is the extraordinary collection of maritime memorabilia, including well-preserved warships from the Napoleonic era, at the Portsmouth Historic Dockyard, and other museums. For others, Portsmouth is primarily of interest for the ferries that set off from here to the Isle of Wight and more distant destinations.

GETTING HERE AND AROUND

The M27 motorway from Southampton and the A3 from London take you to Portsmouth. There are also frequent buses and trains that drop you off at the Hard, the main transport terminus. It's near the tourist information center and a few steps from the Historic Dockyard and Gunwharf Quays. Regular passenger ferries cross Portsmouth Harbour from the Hard for Gosport's Submarine Museum. Attractions in Southsea are best reached by car or by buses departing from the Hard.

ESSENTIALS

Visitor Information Portsmouth
(✉ *The Hard* ☎ *023/9282–6722* ⊕ *www. visitportsmouth.co.uk* ✉ *Clarence Esplanade, Southsea* ☎ *023/9282–6722*).

EXPLORING

TOP ATTRACTIONS

🍃 **D-Day Museum.** In the absorbing
★ D-Day Museum, in nearby Southsea, an eclectic range of exhibits
illustrates the planning and logistics
involved in the D-Day landings, as
well as the actual invasion on June
6, 1944. The museum's centerpiece is the Overlord Embroidery
("Overlord" was the code name
for the invasion), a 272-foot-long
embroidered cloth with 34 panels
illustrating the history of World
War II, from the Battle of Britain

in 1940 to D-Day and the first days of the liberation. ✉ *Clarence Esplanade, Southsea* ☎ *023/9282–7261* ⊕ *www.ddaymuseum.co.uk* 🎟 *£6* ⊙ *Apr.–Sept., daily 10–5:30; Oct.–Mar., daily 10–5; last admission 30 mins before closing.*

Fodor's Choice **Portsmouth Historic Dockyard.** The city's most impressive attraction includes
★ an unrivaled collection of historic ships and the comprehensive Royal
Naval Museum (a great place to learn about British naval hero Admiral
Lord Horatio Nelson). The dockyard's youngest ship, **HMS *Warrior
1860*,** was England's first ironclad battleship. Admiral Nelson's flagship,
HMS *Victory*, has been painstakingly restored to appear as it did at the
battle at Trafalgar (1805). You can inspect the cramped gun decks, visit
the cabin where Nelson entertained his officers, and stand on the spot
where he was mortally wounded by a French sniper. Visits aboard the
Victory are by guided tour only and may require a long wait. The *Mary
Rose*, former flagship of the Tudor navy, which capsized and sank in the
harbor in 1545, was raised in 1982. Described in the 16th century as "the
flower of all the ships that ever sailed," the *Mary Rose* is now housed in a
special enclosure, where water continuously sprays her timbers to prevent
them from drying out and breaking up. Exhibits in the intriguing *Mary
Rose* Museum display more than 1,200 artifacts from the ship. Note that
although the ship cannot be viewed until 2012 because of work on the
premises, the museum remains open. The **Royal Naval Museum** has a fine
collection of painted figureheads, extensive exhibits about Nelson and
the battle of Trafalgar, and galleries of paintings and mementos recalling
naval history from King Alfred to the present. **Action Stations,** an interactive attraction, gives insight into life in the modern Royal Navy and tests
your sea legs with tasks such as piloting boats through gales. **Dockyard
Apprentice** showcases the skills of the shipbuilders and craftsmen who
constructed and maintained the naval vessels, with illustrations of rope
making, sail making, caulking, signals, and knots. You should allow

the best part of a day to tour all the attractions in the Historic Dock-yard. ⊠ *Historic Dockyard, Portsmouth Naval Base* ☎ *023/9272–8060* ⊕ *www.historicdockyard.co.uk* ✉ *£19.50 includes harbor tour; valid for return visits* ⊙ *Apr.–Oct., daily 10–6; Nov.–Mar., daily 10–5:30; last admission 90 mins before closing.*

QUICK BITES

After a slog around the Historic Dockyard you can find rest and replenishment, including seafood, at the harborside **Still & West Country House** (⊠ *Bath Sq.* ☎ *023/9282–1567*), a pub with plenty of outdoor seating. It faces the Spice Island Inn, another pub.

Spinnaker Tower. Newly erected on the lively Gunwharf Quays development of shops and bars, Spinnaker Tower provides a striking visual focus on Portsmouth's skyline. The slender structure, with the form of a mast and billowing sail, rises to a height of 541 feet. An elevator whisks you to three viewing platforms 330 feet high, for thrilling all-around views over the harbor and up to 20 mi beyond. ⊠ *Gunwharf Quays* ☎ *023/9285–7520* ⊕ *www.spinnakertower.co.uk* ✉ *£7.25* ⊙ *Sept.–July, daily 10–6; Aug., Sun.–Thurs. 10–7, Fri. and Sat. 10–6.*

WORTH NOTING

☺ **Explosion!** In a former arms depot near Submarine World, Explosion! (the name given to the Museum of Naval Firepower) gathers together munitions, mines, and missiles in relating the history of armaments used at sea. The museum also tells the story of the many locals who manufactured them. Interactive exhibits help you understand what it's like to do nautical things such as walk on a seabed. ⊠ *Priddy's Hard, Gosport* ☎ *023/9250–5600* ⊕ *www.explosion.org.uk* ✉ *£10* ⊙ *Apr.–Oct., daily 10–5; Nov.–Mar., weekends 10–4; last admission 1 hr before closing.*

Portchester Castle. Incorporating the walls of a Roman fort built more than 1,600 years ago, Portchester Castle claims the most complete set of Roman walls in northern Europe. In the 12th century a Norman castle (now in ruins) was built inside the impressive fortifications. From the keep's central tower you can take in a sweeping view of the harbor and coastline. ⊠ *Off A27, near Fareham* ☎ *023/9237–8291* ⊕ *www. english-heritage.org.uk* ✉ *£4.50* ⊙ *Apr.–Sept., daily 10–6; Oct.–Mar., daily 10–4.*

☺ **Submarine World.** The highlight at Submarine World is the tour of the World War II submarine HMS *Alliance,* from the cramped quarters to the engine room. The museum fills you in on submarine history and lets you view Portsmouth Harbour through a periscope. There are plenty of subs, weapons, and diving paraphernalia around the large site. From Portsmouth Harbour, take the ferry to Gosport and walk along Millennium Promenade past the huge sundial clock. ⊠ *Haslar Jetty Rd., Gosport* ☎ *023/9251–0354* ⊕ *www.rnsubmus.co.uk* ✉ *£10* ⊙ *Apr.–Oct., daily 10–5:30; Nov.–Mar., daily 10–4:30; last tour 1 hr before closing.*

WHERE TO EAT AND STAY

££
BISTRO

✗ **Abarbistro.** A relaxed, modern bistro midway between Old Portsmouth and Gunwharf Quays, this place is ideal for a snack, a full meal, or just a drink. Seafood dishes, mostly sourced from Portsmouth's fish market right opposite, include *moules marinière*, fish cakes, and salmon steak in a creamy dill sauce; alternatively, opt for the sirloin steak and fries, or an asparagus-and–wild mushroom tartlet. You can sit indoors, in a garden at the back, or at Continental-style tables on the pavement. ⊠ *58 White Hart Rd.* ☎ *023/9281–1585* ⊕ *www.abarbistro. co.uk* ⊟ *AE, MC, V.*

£££££ ✕ **Montparnasse.** Modern photographs on cinnamon walls add a con-
MEDITERRANEAN temporary touch to this relaxed but semiformal restaurant. The fixed-
★ price menus (£29.50 and £34.50) may list sautéed pigeon breast and roasted lamb fillet, and desserts such as Amaretto-and-mascarpone mousse with white coffee ice cream are to die for. Service is discreet but attentive and knowledgeable. Book a table downstairs for more atmosphere. ⊠ *103 Palmerston Rd., Southsea* ☎ *023/9281–6754* ⊕ *www. bistromontparnasse.co.uk* ⊟ *AE, MC, V* ⊗ *Closed Sun. and Mon.*

££ 🛏 **Fortitude Cottage.** With sleek modern bedrooms done in white and neutrals, this friendly B&B provides top-class accommodation in two buildings in the center of Old Portsmouth, just yards from the waterside. The best option here is the penthouse room—costing slightly more—offering stunning views over the harbor (binoculars are provided) as well as its own rooftop terrace. Across the road, a chain trail in the pavement leads alongside the harbor to Gunwharf Quays and the Historic Dockyard. The couple who run the guesthouse also rent an apartment in Southsea, available for one night or more. **Pros:** central but quiet location; immaculate, modern rooms. **Cons:** stairs; some rooms have poor view. ⊠ *47–51 Broad St.* ☎ *023/9282–3748* ⊕ *www.fortitudecottage.co.uk* ➥ *6 rooms* ⚴ *In-room: no a/c (some), Wi-Fi. In-hotel: Wi-Fi hotspot, parking (free), some pets allowed* ⊟ *MC, V* ⑩ *BP.*

££ 🛏 **Westfield Hall.** Portsmouth is well supplied with chain offerings, but this pleasant smaller establishment has personal service and character. It occupies two converted early-20th-century houses close to the water in the resort of Southsea. Rooms (seven are on the ground floor) have large bay windows and are restfully furnished in greens and creams; three sitting rooms provide a place to relax. **Pros:** reliably clean; hospitable staff; good breakfast. **Cons:** dated decor; thin walls; some smallish rooms. ⊠ *65 Festing Rd., off Eastern Parade* ☎ *023/9282–6971* ⊕ *www.whhotel.info* ➥ *26 rooms* ⚴ *In-room: no a/c, Internet, Wi-Fi. In-hotel: restaurant, parking (free)* ⊟ *AE, MC, V* ⑩ *BP.*

THE OUTDOORS

Queen Elizabeth Country Park, part of an Area of Outstanding Beauty in the South Downs, has 1,400 acres of chalk hills and shady beeches with 20 mi of scenic trails for hikers, cyclists, and horse riders. You can climb to the top of Butser Hill (888 feet) to take in a splendid view of the coast. The park lies 12 mi north of Portsmouth, and 4 mi south of the Georgian market town of Petersfield, in a wide valley between wooded hills and open downs. A visitor center has an audiovisual theater, café, and shop. ⊠ *A3* ☎ *023/9259–5040* ⊕ *www3.hants.gov.uk/ qecp* ⊠ *Free; parking £1, Sun. £1.50* ⊗ *Park open 24 hrs; visitor center Mar.–Oct., daily 10–5:30; Nov.–Feb., daily 10–4:30. Visitor center closed late Dec.–early Jan.*

SOUTHAMPTON

17 mi northwest of Portsmouth, 24 mi southeast of Salisbury, 77 mi southwest of London.

Seafaring Saxons and Romans used Southampton's harbor, Southampton Water, as a commercial trading port for centuries. The city thrived, becoming one of England's wealthiest. But Plymouth eventually supplanted it, and Southampton has been going downhill ever since. Still, it remains England's leading passenger port, and as the home port of Henry V's fleet bound for Agincourt, the *Mayflower,* the *Queen Mary,* and the ill-fated *Titanic,* along with countless other great ocean liners of the 20th century, Southampton has one of the richest maritime traditions in England.

Much of the city center is shoddy, having been hastily rebuilt after World War II bombing, but bits of the city's history peek out from between modern buildings. The Old Town retains its medieval air, and considerable parts of Southampton's castellated town walls remain. Other attractions include a decent art gallery, extensive parks, and a couple of good museums. The Southampton Boat Show, a 10-day event in mid-September, draws huge crowds.

GETTING HERE AND AROUND

Located on the M3 motorway from London and Winchester, and on the M27 from Portsmouth, Southampton is also easily accessed by bus or train from these cities. The bus and train stations are a few minutes' walk from the tourist office, and the main sights can be reached by foot.

ESSENTIALS

Visitor Information Southampton (✉ *9 Civic Centre Rd.* ☎ *023/8083–3333* ⊕ *www.visit-southampton.co.uk).*

EXPLORING

Incorporated in the town walls are a number of old buildings, including **God's House Tower**, originally a gunpowder factory and now an archaeology museum. Displays focus on the Roman, Saxon, and medieval periods of Southampton's history. ✉ *Winkle St.* ☎ *023/8063–5904* ⊕ *www.southampton.gov.uk* 🎫 *£2.50* ⊙ *Early May–late Sept., weekdays 10–6, weekends 11–6; late Sept.–early May, weekdays 10–4, weekends 11–4.*

Mayflower Park and the Pilgrim Fathers' Memorial (✉ *Western Esplanade*) commemorate the departure of 102 passengers on the North America–bound *Mayflower* from Southampton on August 15, 1620. A plaque also honors the 2 million U.S. troops who left Southampton in World War II.

Incongruously housed in a 14th-century wool warehouse, the **Southampton Maritime Museum** brings together models, mementos, and pieces of furniture from the age of the great clippers and cruise ships, including a wealth of memorabilia relating to the *Titanic*—footage, photos, crew lists, and so on. Boat buffs will relish plenty of vital statistics dealing with the history of commercial shipping. ✉ *Bugle St.* ☎ *023/8022–3941* ⊕ *www.southampton.gov.uk* 🎫 *£2.50* ⊙ *Early May–late Sept.,*

4

weekdays 10–6, weekends 11–6; late Sept.–early May, weekdays 10–4, weekends 11–4.

WHERE TO EAT AND STAY

££££ ✕**Oxford Brasserie.** Close to the docks, this informal place gets lively
BRASSERIE in the evening, but it's calmer at lunchtime. Fresh fish is always available (the fixed-price menus are a particularly good value), along with Mediterranean fare. The tile floor and cream-color walls hung with paintings are straightforward and not gimmicky. ⊠ *33–34 Oxford St.* ☎ *023/8063–5043* ⊕ *www.theoxfordbrasserie.co.uk* ⊟ *AE, MC, V* ⊙ *No dinner Sun.*

£££–££££ ⊡ **TerraVina Hotel.** Owned by two of the founders of the esteemed Hotel
Fodor's Choice du Vin group, this small and select boutique hotel outside the city shows
★ the same high standards. The public areas invite lingering with their mix of contemporary and period furnishings. Guest rooms—decorated in soothing tones with splashes of emerald green and burnt orange—are spacious and have thoughtful touches like espresso machines. The three ground-floor (and more expensive) rooms have private patios; four others have terraces. The California wine country–themed restaurant (£££) boasts an impressive wine cellar and uses organic ingredients in its Modern British cuisine. The hotel's location on the edge of the New Forest makes it well placed for excursions. **Pros:** chic, well-appointed rooms; fantastic food; attention to detail. **Cons:** some noise intrusion; a little remote from Southampton. ⊠ *174 Woodlands Rd., Woodlands, Netley Marsh* ☎ *023/8029–3784* ⊕ *www.hotelterravina.co.uk* ⤢ *11 rooms* & *In-room: safe, DVD, refrigerator, Wi-Fi. In-hotel: restaurant, bar, pool, Wi-Fi hotspot* ⊟ *AE, MC, V.*

NIGHTLIFE AND THE ARTS

The **Mayflower** (⊠ *Commercial Rd.* ☎ *023/8071–1811*) is among the larger theaters outside London; the Royal Shakespeare Company and Barnum on Ice are among the organizations that have packed the house. The **Nuffield** (⊠ *University Rd.* ☎ *023/8067–1771*), at Southampton University, has a repertory company and also hosts national touring groups.

ISLE OF WIGHT

A slightly tattered, slightly romantic place, this island sometimes gets so crowded it seems that it might sink beneath the weight of the throngs of summer visitors. Its appealingly dusty Victorian look comes courtesy of Queen Victoria, who put the Isle of Wight (pronounced white) on the map by choosing it for the site of Osborne House. She lived here as much as she could, and ultimately she died here. Perhaps understandably, islanders are chauvinistic; like Tennyson, who lived here until tourist harassment drove him away, they resent the crowds of tourists. But every season the day-trippers arrive—thanks to the ferries and hydrofoils that connect the island with Southampton, Portsmouth, Southsea, and Lymington.

People come to this 23-mi-long island for its vacation resorts—Ryde, Bembridge, Ventnor, Freshwater (stay away from tacky Sandown and

Shanklin)—its rich vegetation, narrow lanes, thatched cottages, curving bays, sandy beaches, and walking paths. The fabulous ocean air, to quote Tennyson, is "worth six pence a pint." All is not sea and sails, however. There is splendid driving to be done in the interior of the island, in such places as Brading Down, Ashley Down, and Mersely Down, and the occasional country house to visit, none more spectacular than Queen Vicky's Osborne House.

GETTING HERE AND AROUND

Wightlink operates a car ferry between the mainland and the Isle of Wight. The crossing takes about 30 minutes from Lymington to Yarmouth, 40 minutes from Portsmouth to Fishbourne. The company also operates catamaran service between Portsmouth and Ryde (20 minutes). Red Funnel runs a car ferry (one hour) and hydrofoil service (25 minutes) between Southampton and Cowes. Hovertravel runs a hovercraft shuttle between Southsea (Portsmouth) and Ryde (10 minutes). The island is covered by a good network of roads, and you can rely on a regular local bus service.

Southern Vectis, the local bus company, operates open-top tours between March and October. One goes to Dimbola Lodge, the Needles, and Alum Bay. You can board and disembark at different points for £10.

TIMING

Summer traffic slows things down considerably. Try to avoid Cowes Week in late July or early August and the two major rock festivals that take place in mid-June and mid-September.

ESSENTIALS

Bus and Tour Information Southern Vectis (☎ 01983/827000 ⊕ www.islandbuses.info).

Ferry Information Hovertravel (☎ 01983/811000 or 023/9281–1000 ⊕ www.hovertravel.co.uk). **Red Funnel** (☎ 0844/844–9988 ⊕ www.redfunnel.co.uk). **Wightlink** (☎ 0871/376–1000 ⊕ www.wightlink.co.uk).

COWES

7 mi northwest of Ryde.

If you embark from Southampton, your ferry will cross the Solent channel and dock at Cowes, which is near Queen Victoria's Osborne House. Cowes is a magic name in the sailing world because of the internationally known Cowes Week yachting festival (⊕ *www.cowesweek.co.uk*), held each July or August. Fifty years ago the Cowes Regatta was a supreme event; the world's most famous figures crowded the green lawns of the Royal Yacht Squadron. Although its elegance is a thing of the past, the Cowes Regatta remains an important yachting event. At the north end of High Street, on the Parade, a tablet commemorates the 1633 sailing from Cowes of two ships carrying the first English settlers of the state of Maryland.

ESSENTIALS

Visitor Information Cowes (✉ Fountain Quay ☎ 01983/813813 ⊕ www.islandbreaks.co.uk).

EXPLORING

Queen Victoria's **Osborne House,** designed by Prince Albert after a villa in the stodgiest Italian Renaissance style, holds enormous interest for anyone drawn to the domestic side of history. After Albert's death in 1861 the queen spent much of her time here, mourning her loss in relative seclusion. In this massive pile, one sees the engineer manqué in Prince Albert and his clever innovations—including a kind of central heating—as well as evidence of Victoria's desperate attempts to give her children a normal but disciplined upbringing. A carriage ride will take you to the Swiss Cottage, a superior version of a playhouse built for the children. The antique-filled rooms have scarcely been altered since Victoria's death here in 1901. The house and grounds—which can be quite crowded during July and August—were used as a location for the 1998 movie *Mrs. Brown.* ■TIP→ Ask about guided tours of the house and gardens, available throughout the year. Buses 4 (from Ryde) and 5 (from Cowes and Newport) stop outside. ⊠ *Off A3021, 1 mi southeast of Cowes* ☎ *01983/200022* ⊕ *www.english-heritage.org.uk* ⊠ *£10.90* ⊙ *Apr.–Sept., daily 10–6; Oct., daily 10–4; Nov.–Mar., Wed.–Sun. pre-booked guided tours only, last tour at 2:30.*

★ Standing above the village of Carisbrooke, **Carisbrooke Castle** was built by the Normans and enlarged in Elizabethan times. It had its moment of historical glory when King Charles I was imprisoned here during the English Civil War. Note the small window in the north curtain wall through which he tried unsuccessfully to escape. A museum holds items from his incarceration. You can stroll along the battlements and visit the well house, where donkeys draw water from a deep well. The castle is about a mile southwest of the Isle of Wight's modern-day capital, Newport. From Cowes, take Bus 1 or 5 (1 from West Cowes, near Holmwood Hotel; 5 from East Cowes, near Osborne House) to Newport, from where you can walk (about 30 min) or pick up the 7 or 38 buses— it's about a 10-minute walk from the bus stop in The Mall, Carisbrooke. ⊠ *Off B3401* ☎ *01983/522107* ⊕ *www.english-heritage. org.uk* ⊠ *£7* ⊙ *Apr.–Sept., daily 10–5; Oct.–Mar., daily 10–4.*

WHERE TO STAY

££ ⌂ **New Holmwood Hotel.** This Best Western hotel occupies an unrivaled location above the western end of the Esplanade—ideal for watching yachters in the Solent. The lounge area has an open fire on winter evenings, and the sun terrace and bijou pool take full advantage of fine weather. Patterned fabrics contrast with plain walls in the guest rooms. **Pros:** good sea views; friendly staff; within walking distance of passenger ferry. **Cons:** some rooms are small and dated; slightly run-down feel. ⊠ *Queens Rd., Egypt Point* ☎ *01983/292508* ⊕ *www. newholmwoodhotel.co.uk* ⇄ *24 rooms, 2 suites* ⋔ *In-room: no a/c, Wi-Fi. In-hotel: restaurant, bar, pool, Wi-Fi hotspot, some pets allowed* ▤ *AE, MC, V* ⋈ *BP.*

RYDE

7 mi southeast of Cowes.

The town of Ryde has long been one of the Isle of Wight's most popular summer resorts, with several family attractions. After the construction of Ryde Pier in 1814, elegant town houses sprang up along the seafront and on the slopes behind, commanding fine views of the harbor. In addition to its long, sandy beach, Ryde has a large lake (you can rent rowboats and pedal boats) and children's playgrounds. To get here from Cowes, leave on A3021, and then follow the signs on A3054.

ESSENTIALS

Visitor Information Ryde (⊠ *81–83 Union St.* ☎ *01983/813813* ⊕ *www. islandbreaks.co.uk*).

WHERE TO EAT

£££

MODERN BRITISH

Fodor'sChoice

★

✕ **Seaview.** A strong maritime flavor defines this outstanding restaurant, in the heart of a harbor village just outside Ryde. Choose between the two main dining areas, one a smaller Victorian room, the other bright and modern, with tables spilling out into a conservatory. The menu specializes in seafood and fresh island produce that includes everything from beef and chicken to vegetables, much of it raised on the Seaview's own farm. You might start with the chicken-liver parfait and then move on to roast salmon fillet or whatever the catch of the day may be. Plainer, less expensive fish dishes and snacks can be ordered in the two congenial bars, one modern, one traditional. Pale brown tones and luxurious fabrics characterize the chic guest rooms in the adjoining hotel (££££). ⊠ *Seaview Hotel, High St., Seaview* ☎ *01983/612711* ⊕ *www.seaviewhotel.co.uk* ⊟ *AE, DC, MC, V*

BRADING

3 mi south of Ryde on A3055.

In Brading, St. Mary's Church, dating from Norman times, contains monuments to the local Oglander family, whose ancestor from Normandy served William the Conqueror.

EXPLORING

☺ Housed within a striking wooden-walled, glass-roofed building, the remains of the substantial 3rd-century **Brading Roman Villa** include walls, splendid mosaic floors, and a well-preserved heating system. The mosaics, depicting peacocks (symbolizing eternal life), gods, gladiators, sea beasts, and reclining nymphs, are a rare example of this type of floor preserved in situ in a domestic building. There's also a café at the site, 1 mi south of Brading. ⊠ *Morton Old Rd., off A3055* ☎ *01983/406223* ⊕ *www.bradingromanvilla.co.uk* ⚏ *£6.50* ☉ *Daily 9:30–5; last entry at 4.*

4

VENTNOR

11 mi south of Ryde.

The south coast resorts are the sunniest and most sheltered on the Isle of Wight. Handsome Ventnor rises from such a steep slope that the ground floors of some of its houses are level with the roofs of those across the road.

EXPLORING

The **Ventnor Botanic Gardens,** laid out over 22 acres, contain more than 3,500 species of trees, plants, and shrubs. The impressive greenhouse includes banana trees and a waterfall, and a visitor center puts the subtropical and display gardens into context. ⊠ *Undercliff Dr.* ☎ *01983/855397* ⊕ *www.botanic.co.uk* 🎟 *Free* ☺ *Gardens always open. Visitor center Mar.–Oct., daily 10–5; Nov.–Feb., call to check.*

WHERE TO EAT

££££–£££££
MEDITERRANEAN
✕ **The Pond Café.** Overlooking a secluded, elongated pond in the hamlet of Bonchurch, a mile north of Ventnor, this quiet, understated restaurant is a good place to gently unwind. The simply furnished interior is compact and contemporary in style, and there are a few outdoor tables for eating alfresco when the weather permits. Come for a tea or coffee, or tuck in to a full meal. The set-price menus (£14–£19 at lunch, £24–£28 at dinner) include such dishes as sautéed squid with chorizo, followed by wild mushroom risotto with truffles or fillet of sea bass with salsify and champagne sauce. There are fresh-baked breads and homemade ice creams, among other toothsome desserts. The café is under the same ownership as the chic Hambrough hotel, a mile up the road at Ventnor. ⊠ *Bonchurch Village Rd., Bonchurch* ☎ *01983/855666* ⊕ *www. thehambrough.com* ➡ *MC, V* ☺ *Closed Tues. and Wed. Sept.–May.*

ALUM BAY AND THE NEEDLES

19 mi northwest of Ventnor, 18 mi southwest of Cowes.

At the western tip of the Isle of Wight is the island's most famous natural landmark, the **Needles,** a long line of jagged chalk stacks jutting out of the sea like monstrous teeth, with a lighthouse at the end. It's part of the Needles Pleasure Park, which has mostly child-oriented attractions. Adjacent is **Alum Bay,** accessed from the Needles by chairlift. Here you can catch a good view of the multicolor sand in the cliff strata or take a boat to view the lighthouse.

ESSENTIALS

Visitor Information Yarmouth (⊠ *The Quay* ☎ *01983/813813* ⊕ *www. islandbreaks.co.uk*).

EXPLORING

Dimbola Lodge was the home of Julia Margaret Cameron (1815–79), the eminent Victorian portrait photographer and friend of Lord Tennyson. A gallery includes more than 60 examples of her work, including striking images of Carlyle, Tennyson, and Browning. There's also a room devoted to the various Isle of Wight rock festivals, most famously the five-day event in 1970 that featured the Who, the Doors, Joni Mitchell, and Jimi

Hendrix. On the ground floor you'll find a bookshop and a good café for snacks and full meals. ✉ *Terrace La., Freshwater Bay* ☎ *01983/756814* ⊕ *www.dimbola.co.uk* 🖻 *Gallery £4* ⏱ *Mar.–Oct., Tues.–Sun. and national holiday Mon. 10–5; Nov.–Feb., Tues.–Sun. and national holiday Mon. 10–4; open daily during school summer vacation.*

SALISBURY, STONEHENGE, AND SALISBURY PLAIN

The roster of famous sights in this area begins in the attractive city of Salisbury, renowned for its glorious cathedral, and then loops west around Salisbury Plain, up to Avebury, and back to Stonehenge. A trio of stately homes reveals the ambitions and wealth of their builders—Wilton House with its Inigo Jones–designed state rooms, Stourhead and its exquisite gardens, and the Italian Renaissance pile of Longleat. Your own transportation is essential to see anything beyond Salisbury.

SALISBURY

24 mi northwest of Southampton, 44 mi southeast of Bristol, 79 mi southwest of London.

The silhouette of Salisbury Cathedral's majestic spire signals your approach to this historic city long before you arrive. Although the cathedral is the principal interest in the town, and the Cathedral Close one of the country's most atmospheric spots (best experienced on a foggy night), Salisbury has much more to see, not least its largely unspoiled—and relatively traffic-free—old center. Here are stone shops and houses that grew up in the shadow of the great church over the centuries. You're never far from any of the three rivers that meet here, or from the bucolic water meadows that stretch out to the west of the cathedral and provide the best views of it.

Salisbury did not become important until the early 13th century, when the seat of the diocese was transferred here from Old Sarum, the original settlement 2 mi to the north, of which only ruins remain. In the 19th century, novelist Anthony Trollope based his tales of ecclesiastical life, notably *Barchester Towers,* on life here, although his fictional city of Barchester is really an amalgam of Salisbury and Winchester. The local tourist office organizes walks—of differing lengths for varying stamina—to lead you to the treasures. And speaking of treasures, prehistoric Stonehenge is less than 10 mi away and easily visited from the city.

GETTING HERE AND AROUND

Salisbury is on main bus and train routes from London and Southampton; regular buses also connect Salisbury with Winchester. The bus station is centrally located on Endless Street. Trains stop west of the center. After negotiating a ring-road system, drivers will want to park as soon as possible. The largest of the central parking lots is by Salisbury Playhouse. The city center is compact, so you won't need to use local buses for most sights. For Wilton, take Bus 3 from New Canal, near Market Square.

TIMING
Market Square hosts general markets every Tuesday and Saturday and farmers' markets on the first and third Wednesday of the month. It's also the venue for other fairs and festivals during the year, notably the one-day Food & Drink Festival in mid-September and the three-day Charter Fair in October. Expect congestion during any of these events. The city gets busy during the arts festival in May and June, when accommodation may be scarce.

TOURS
The Stonehenge Tour has open-top buses leaving once or twice an hour all year from the train station and the bus station. Tickets cost £11, or £18 including admission to Stonehenge. Salisbury City Guides offers city tours, departing from the tourist office, every day from April through September and on weekends the rest of the year. The cost is £4. Wessexplore has everything from walking tours to trips in luxury cars to a helicopter ride over Stonehenge.

ESSENTIALS
Visitor and Tour Information Salisbury (⊠ *Fish Row off Market Sq.* ☎ *01722/334956* ⊕ *www.visitwiltshire.co.uk/salisbury).* **Salisbury City Guides** (☎ *01722/320349* ⊕ *www.salisburycityguides.co.uk).* **Stonehenge Tour** (☎ *01983/827005* ⊕ *www.thestonehengetour.info).* **Wessexplore** (☎ *01722/326304* ⊕ *www.dmac.co.uk/wessexplore).*

EXPLORING
TOP ATTRACTIONS
Cathedral Close. Salisbury's close forms probably the finest backdrop of any British cathedral, with its smooth lawns and splendid examples of architecture from many periods (except modern) creating a harmonious background. Some of the historic houses are open to the public.

❸ **Mompesson House.** One of Britain's most appealing Queen Anne houses, dating from 1701, sits on the north side of Cathedral Close. There are no treasures per se, but some fine original paneling and plasterwork, as well as a fascinating collection of 18th-century drinking glasses, are highlights. Tea and refreshments are served in a walled garden. ⊠ *The Close* ☎ *01722/335659* ⊕ *www.nationaltrust.org.uk* ☜ *£5* ☉ *Mid-Mar.–Oct., Sat.–Wed. 11–5; last admission 4:30.*

Old Sarum. Massive earthwork ramparts in a bare sweep of Wiltshire countryside are all that remain of this impressive Iron Age hill fort, which was successively taken over by Romans, Saxons, and Normans (who built a castle and cathedral within the earthworks). The site was still fortified in Tudor times, though the population had mostly decamped in the 13th century for the more amenable site of New Sarum, or Salisbury. You can clamber over the huge banks and ditches and take in the bracing views over the chalk downland. ⊠ *Off A345, 2 mi north of Salisbury* ☎ *01722/335398* ⊕ *www.english-heritage.org.uk* ☜ *£3.50* ☉ *Apr.–June and Sept., daily 10–5; July and Aug., daily 9–6; Oct. and Mar., daily 10–4; Nov.–Jan., daily 11–3; Feb., daily 11–4.*

❷ **Salisbury and South Wiltshire Museum.** Opposite the cathedral's west front, this excellent museum is in the King's House, parts of which date back to the 15th century (James I stayed here in 1610 and 1613). Models and

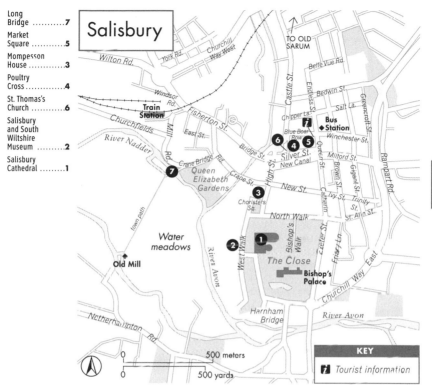

exhibits at the Stonehenge Gallery arm you with helpful background information for a visit to the famous stones. Also on view are skeletons, collections of costumes, lace, embroidery, and Wedgwood pottery, all dwarfed by the medieval pageant figure of St. Christopher, a 14-foot-tall giant, and his companion hobbyhorse, Hob Nob. A cozy café is in one of the oldest sections of the building. ⊠ *The King's House, 65 The Close* ☎ *01722/332151* ⊕ *www.salisburymuseum.org.uk* ⊡ *£5.45* ☉ *July and Aug., Mon.–Sat. 10–5, Sun. noon–5; Sept.–June, Mon.–Sat. 10–5.*

① **Salisbury Cathedral.** Salisbury is dominated by the towering cathedral,
Fodor'sChoice a soaring hymn in stone. It is unique among cathedrals in that it was
★ conceived and built as a whole, in the amazingly short span of 38 years (1220–58). The spire, added in 1320, is the tallest in England and a miraculous feat of medieval engineering—even though the point, 404 feet above the ground, is 2½ feet off vertical. For a fictional, keenly imaginative reconstruction of the drama underlying such an achievement, read William Golding's novel *The Spire.* The excellent model of the cathedral in the north transept, the "arm" of the church to your left as you look toward the altar, shows the building about 20 years into construction, and makes clear the ambition of Salisbury's medieval builders. For all their sophistication, the height and immense weight of the great spire have always posed structural problems. In the late

CLOSE UP

The South's Ancient Sites

Prehistoric monuments dot Britain's landscape, silent but tantalizing reminders of civilizations long vanished. Ceremonial stone circles, barrows used for burials, and Iron Age hill forts attract endless speculation about the motives and methods of their ancient builders.

TOP PLACES TO VISIT

The South contains not only 5,000-year-old Stonehenge, one of the great treasures of Britain and, indeed, Europe, but also an abundance of other sites, some of them overlaid with reminders of other eras. At Old Sarum, near Salisbury, the earthwork ramparts of an Iron Age hill fort survive, although Romans and Normans took over the site. The evocative Avebury Stone Circles surround part of a village; nearby is the West Kennett Long Barrow, a chambered tomb. Close to Dorchester, Maiden Castle is a stone-and-earth hill fort with ramparts that enclose 45 acres.

WHERE TO LEARN MORE

If all this fuels your imagination, the shop at Stonehenge sells plenty of books with plenty of theories, and the Salisbury and South Wiltshire Museum in Salisbury and the Alexander Keiller Museum in Avebury provide helpful background. Start by visiting one site, and you may find yourself rerouting your trip to seek out others.

17th century Sir Christopher Wren was summoned from London to strengthen the spire, and in the mid-19th century Sir George Gilbert Scott, a leading Victorian Gothicist, undertook a major program of restoration. He also initiated a clearing out of the interior and removed some less-than-sympathetic 18th-century alterations. Despite this, the interior seems spartan and a little gloomy, but check out the remarkable lancet windows and sculpted tombs of crusaders and other medieval heroes. The clock in the north aisle—probably the oldest working mechanism in Europe, if not the world—was made in 1386.

■TIP→ You can join a free 45-minute tour of the church leaving two or more times a day, and there are tours to the roof and spire at least once a day (except on Sunday from October through April). The cloisters are the largest in England, and the octagonal **Chapter House** contains a marvelous 13th-century frieze showing scenes from the Old Testament. In the Chapter House you can also see one of the four original copies of the **Magna Carta**, the charter of rights the English barons forced King John to accept in 1215; it was sent here for safekeeping in the 13th century. ⊠ *Cathedral Close* ☎ *01722/555120* ⊕ *www.salisburycathedral.org. uk* ▣ *Cathedral £5.50 requested donation, tower tour £8.50, Chapter House free* ☉ *Cathedral daily 7:15–6:15. Chapter House Apr.–Oct., Mon.–Sat. 9:30–5:30, Sun. 12:45–5:30; Nov.–Mar., Mon.–Sat. 10–4:30, Sun. 12:45–4:30. Access to cathedral restricted during services.*

WORTH NOTING

 Long Bridge. For a classic view of Salisbury, head to the Long Bridge and the town path. From High Street walk west to Mill Road, which leads you across Queen Elizabeth Gardens. Cross the bridge and continue on the town path through the water meadows along which you can find the very spot where John Constable set down his easel to create that 19th-century icon, *Salisbury Cathedral,* now hung in the Constable Room of London's National Gallery. Walk about 20 minutes on the path and you arrive at the Old Mill, now an atmospheric pub and a hotel.

❺ **Market Square.** One of southern England's most popular markets fills this square on Tuesday and Saturday. Permission to hold an annual fair here was granted in 1221, and that right is still exercised for three days every October, when the Charter Fair takes place. A narrow side street links Poultry Cross to Market Square.

❹ **Poultry Cross.** One of Salisbury's best-known landmarks, the hexagonal Poultry Cross is the last remaining of the four original medieval market crosses, and dealers still set up their stalls beside it. A cross on the site was first mentioned in 1307, and a poultry cross here was first named as such a century or so later. The canopy and flying buttresses were added in 1852. ⊠ *Silver St.*

❻ **St. Thomas's Church.** This church contains a rare medieval doom painting of Judgment Day, the best-preserved and most complete of the few such works left in Britain. Created around 1470 and covering the chancel arch, the scenes of heaven and hell served to instill the fear of damnation into the congregation. ■TIP➡ It's best seen on a spring or summer evening when the light through the west window illuminates the details. ⊠ *Silver St.* ☎ *01722/322537* ⊕ *www.stthomassalisbury.co.uk* ☜ *Free* ☉ *Apr.–Oct., Mon.–Sat. 8:30–5, Sun. noon–6; Nov.–Mar., Mon.–Sat. 8:30–3, Sun. noon–6.*

QUICK BITES
In a lively, central location but away from traffic, **Polly Tearooms** (⊠ *8 St. Thomas's Sq.* ☎ *01722/336037*) provides relief from sightseeing fatigue in the form of fruit meringues, Wiltshire cream teas, and freshly ground coffee.

WHERE TO EAT

££ ✗ **Anokaa.** For a refreshing, modern take on Indian cuisine, try this
INDIAN bustling eatery a few minutes' walk from the center. Classic recipes are taken as starting points for the artistically presented dishes, which include Goan beef marinated in yogurt and rum, cinnamon-glazed duck breast stuffed with garlicky spinach, and black tiger prawns in a South Indian sauce of curry leaves and coconut oil. At lunchtime, choose from the buffet selection. The setting is contemporary and cosmopolitan, and service by staff in traditional dress is friendly and prompt. ⊠ *60 Fisherton St.* ☎ *01722/414142* ⊕ *www.anokaa.com* ☰ *MC, V.*

££ ✗ **Charter 1227.** Casual and friendly but upscale, with regal blue carpets
BRITISH and cream leather seats, this second-floor restaurant enjoys a prime position overlooking Market Square. The menu blends traditional British and Mediterranean dishes, such as scallops wrapped in pancetta and slow-braised lamb shank. There are good-value fixed-price lunches. ⊠ *7 Ox Row, Market Sq.* ☎ *01722/333118* ☰ *MC, V* ☉ *Closed Sun. and Mon.*

££ ✗ **Haunch of Venison.** This wood-panel tavern opposite the Poultry Cross
BRITISH has been going strong for more than six centuries and brims with period details, such as the mummified hand of an 18th-century card player

still clutching his cards, found by workmen in 1903. You can fortify yourself with any of 80-odd malt whiskies, and choose between bar food or more substantial meals such as spiced fried salmon and haunch of venison (naturally). Sit in the bar area or the stylish upstairs restaurant. ⊠ *1 Minster St.* ☎ *01722/411313* ⊕ *www.haunchofvenison. uk.com* ⊟ *MC, V.*

££££ ✕ **Howard's House.** If you're after complete tranquillity, head for this
BRITISH early-17th-century house set on 2 acres of grounds in the Nadder Val-
★ ley. The style is traditional and smart, and a terrace provides alfresco dining overlooking the tidy lawns in summer. Sophisticated contemporary fare makes up most of what's on the set-price menus, such as fillet of wild turbot with goat cheese gnocchi, and breast of guinea fowl with seared foie gras. Nine luxuriously furnished guest rooms (££££) may tempt you into forgoing the 10-mi drive back to Salisbury. ⊠ *Off B3089, Teffont Evias* ☎ *01722/716392* ⊕ *www.howardshousehotel. co.uk* ⊟ *AE, MC, V.*

££ ✕ **Lemon Tree.** It's just a few steps from Cathedral Close and the High
BRITISH Street Gate to this light, airy café and bistro. Hot dishes range from spinach-and-ricotta pancakes to pork fillets panfried with apricots and pine nuts, and there are daily specials. You can also come here just for morning coffee or afternoon tea. Choose to sit in the conservatory or in the paved garden. ⊠ *92 Crane St.* ☎ *01722/333471* ⊕ *www.thelemontree. co.uk* ⊟ *AE, MC, V* ⊙ *No lunch Sun. Apr.–Sept. No dinner Sun.*

WHERE TO STAY

££ 🛏 **Cricket Field House.** As the name suggests, this ex-gamekeeper's cottage overlooks a cricket ground, allowing you to puzzle over the intricacies of the game at leisure. Some of the functional rooms are in the main house and others are in the annex. There is no restaurant, but evening snacks are available on weekdays. The hotel is on the main A36 road, a mile or so west of Salisbury's center. **Pros:** efficient, helpful management; quiet, well-maintained rooms. **Cons:** dated decor; on a busy road; lacks charm. ⊠ *Wilton Rd.* ☎ *01722/322595* ⊕ *www. cricketfieldhousehotel.co.uk* ⇥ *17 rooms* ⌂ *In-room: no a/c, no phone, Wi-Fi. In-hotel: Wi-Fi hotspot, parking (free), no kids under 14* ⊟ *MC, V* ⊙ *BP.*

££ 🛏 **Rokeby Guest House.** Easy to find on the east side of town, this fourstory Edwardian B&B has a spick-and-span, traditionally styled interior and a large, landscaped garden with a summerhouse and small gym. Despite its proximity to Salisbury's ring road, it's a peaceful spot, and less than a 15-minute walk from the town center. Bedrooms have private bathrooms, though some are separate from the room; family rooms are also available. In the split-level conservatory, breakfast choices include smoked salmon and pancakes. **Pros:** convenient location; helpful hosts; abundant and tasty breakfasts. **Cons:** not central; excess of patterned carpets and wallpaper. ⊠ *3 Wain-a-Long Rd.* ☎ *01722/329800* ⊕ *www. rokebyguesthouse.co.uk* ⇥ *8 rooms* ⌂ *In-room: no a/c, no phone, Wi-Fi. In-hotel: Internet terminal, no kids under 12, parking (free)* ⊟ *No credit cards* ⊙ *BP.*

££–£££   **Mercure Salisbury White Hart Hotel.** Behind the pillared portico and imposing classical facade of this 17th-century hotel (part of the Mercure chain) near the cathedral lie cozily old-fashioned yet spacious public rooms. The uncluttered bedrooms (of various sizes) have a muted cream-and-brown color scheme and are grouped around an inner courtyard or face onto the street. **Pros:** polite staff; cozy public areas; rooms are comfortable. **Cons:** some rooms are small; impersonal, corporate feel. ✉ *1 St. John St.* ☎ *01722/327476* ⊕ *www.mercure.com* 🛏 *67 rooms, 1 suite* ⚷ *In-room: safe, no a/c (some), Wi-Fi. In-hotel: restaurant, bar, parking (free), some pets allowed* ☰ *AE, DC, MC, V* ⦿*BP.*

£   **Wyndham Park Lodge.** This simple Victorian house in a quiet part of town (off Castle Street) provides an excellent place to rest and a delicious breakfast, as well as a garden. Furnishings are in keeping with the period, with antiques and elegant patterned wallpapers and drapes, and one room has its own patio. **Pros:** efficient and hospitable owners; convenient location; good breakfast. **Cons:** spotty Wi-Fi connection. ✉ *51 Wyndham Rd.* ☎ *01722/416517* ⊕ *www.wyndhamparklodge. co.uk* 🛏 *4 rooms* ⚷ *In-room: no a/c, no phone, DVD, Wi-Fi. In-hotel: Internet terminal, Wi-Fi hotspot, parking (free)* ☰ *MC, V* ⦿*BP.*

NIGHTLIFE AND THE ARTS

★   The **Salisbury International Arts Festival** (✉ *87 Crane St.* ☎ *0845/241–9651* ⊕ *www.salisburyfestival.co.uk*), held in May and June, has outstanding classical concerts, recitals, plays, and outdoor events.

The **Salisbury Playhouse** (✉ *Malthouse La.* ☎ *01722/320333*) presents high-caliber drama all year and is the main venue for the Salisbury Arts Festival.

SHOPPING

Most of the shops are gathered around Market Square, venue for twice-weekly markets and the annual Charter Fair, and along High Street, where chain stores predominate. **Dauwalders** (✉ *42 Fisherton St.* ☎ *01722/412100*) specializes in stamps, coins, medals, and models, including some quirky gift ideas. The **National Trust Shop** (✉ *41 High St.* ☎ *01722/331884*) has a range of traditional gifts, from pottery to books, bags, ornaments, and fragrances.

SPORTS

Hayball Cyclesport (✉ *26–30 Winchester St.* ☎ *01722/411378*) rents bikes for about £10 per day or £65 per week, with a £25 cash deposit.

FOOD AND DRINK FESTIVAL

Salisbury forces you to squeeze a lot in during its one-day **Food & Drink Festival** (☎ *01722/332241* ⊕ *www.salisburyfestival.co.uk*) in mid-September. There are wine and beer tents, a Waiters' Race, cooking demonstrations, barbecues, and festival menus in the restaurants. The main venue is Market Square.

4

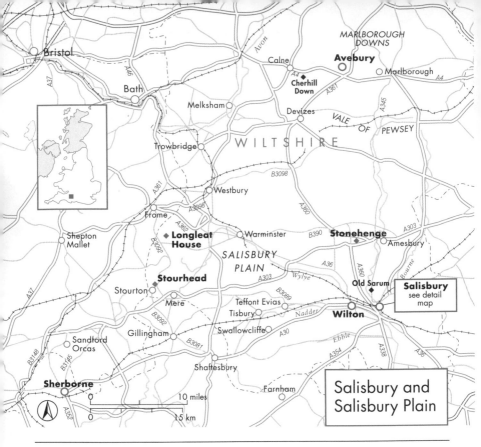

Salisbury and
Salisbury Plain

WILTON

4 mi west of Salisbury.

Five rivers—the Avon, the Bourne, the Nadder, the Wylye, and the
Ebble—wind from Salisbury into the rich heart of Wiltshire. Following
the valley of the Nadder will lead you to the ancient town of Wilton,
from which the county takes its name. A market is held here every
Thursday, and the Wilton Carpet Factory Shop draws visitors (Wilton
is renowned for its carpets), but the main attraction is Wilton House.

EXPLORING

★ The home of the 18th earl of Pembroke, **Wilton House** would be noteworthy if it contained no more than the magnificent 17th-century state
rooms designed by Inigo Jones, Ben Jonson's stage designer and the
architect of London's Banqueting House. John Webb rebuilt the house
in neoclassical style after fire damaged the original Tudor mansion in
1647. In fine weather the lordly expanse of sweeping lawns that surrounds the house, bisected by the River Avon and dotted with towering oaks and a gracious Palladian bridge, is a quintessential English
scene. Wilton House contains the Single Cube Room (built as a perfect
30-foot cube) and one of the most extravagantly beautiful rooms in the
history of interior decoration, the aptly named Double Cube Room.

The name refers to its proportions (60 feet long by 30 feet wide and 30 feet high), evidence of Jones's classically inspired belief that beauty in architecture derives from harmony and balance. The room's headliner is the spectacular Van Dyck portrait of the Pembroke family. Elsewhere at Wilton House, the art collection includes several other old master paintings, including works by Rembrandt and members of the Brueghel family. ■ TIP→ Be sure to explore the extensive gardens; children will appreciate the large playground. ✉ *Wilton* ☎ *01722/746714* ⊕ *www.wiltonhouse.co.uk* ⌨ *£12; grounds only, £5* ☉ *House Easter and May–Aug., Sun.–Thurs. 11:30–4:30, last admission 3:45, grounds Easter and May–Aug., daily 11–5; Sept., weekends 11–5, last admission 4:30.*

> **DOUBLE CUBE ROOM**
>
> Adorned with gilded furniture by William Kent, Wilton House's Double Cube was where Eisenhower prepared plans for the Normandy invasion during World War II. It has been used in many films, including *The Madness of King George, Mrs. Brown,* the 2005 version of *Pride and Prejudice,* Emma Thompson's adaptation of *Sense and Sensibility,* and *The Young Victoria.*

EN ROUTE Between Salisbury and Sherborne on the A30, **Shaftesbury** was the model for the town of Shaston in Thomas Hardy's *Jude the Obscure.* Shaftesbury lies on a ridge overlooking Blackmore Vale—you can catch a sweeping view of the surrounding countryside from the top of Gold Hill, a steep, relentlessly picturesque street lined with cottages. It has even appeared in TV commercials.

SHERBORNE

15 mi west of Shaftesbury, 40 mi west of Wilton, 43 mi west of Salisbury.

Once granted cathedral status, until deferring to Old Sarum in 1075, this unspoiled market town is awash with medieval buildings honed from the honey-color local stone. The focal point of the winding streets is the abbey church. Also worth visiting here are the ruins of the 12th-century Old Castle and Sherborne Castle with its grounds.

GETTING HERE AND AROUND

Hourly trains from Salisbury take 45 minutes to reach Sherborne. The station is at the bottom of Digby Road, near the abbey. Drivers should take A30, passing through Shaftesbury.

ESSENTIALS

Visitor Information Sherborne (✉ *3 Tilton Ct., Digby Rd.* ☎ *01935/815341* ⊕ *www.westdorset.com*).

EXPLORING

The glory of **Sherborne Abbey,** a warm, "old gold" stone church, is the delicate and graceful 15th-century fan vaulting that extends the length of the soaring nave and choir. ("I would pit Sherborne's roof against any contemporary work of the Italian Renaissance," enthused Simon Jenkins, in his *England's Thousand Best Churches.*) If you're lucky, you might hear "Great Tom," one of the heaviest bells in the world, pealing out from the bell tower. Guided tours are offered from April through September on Tuesday (10:30) and Friday (2:30), or by prior arrangement. ⊠ *Abbey Close* ☎ *01935/812452* ⊕ *www.sherborneabbey.com* 🖾 *Guided tour free Apr.–Sept., Tues. 10:30 and Fri. 2:30 (call first to check), or £3.50 suggested donation at other times by prior arrangement* ☉ *Apr.–Sept., daily 8–6; Oct.–Mar., daily 8–4.*

Sherborne Castle, built by Sir Walter Raleigh in 1594, remained his home for 10 years before it passed to the custodianship of the Digby family. The interior has been remodeled in 19th-century Gothic style, and ceilings have splendid plaster moldings. After admiring the extensive collections of Meissen and Asian porcelain, stroll around the lake and landscaped grounds, the work of Capability Brown. The house is a half mile southeast of town. ⊠ *Off A352* ☎ *01935/812072* ⊕ *www. sherbornecastle.com* 🖾 *£9.50; gardens only, £5* ☉ *Apr.–Oct., Tues.– Thurs., Sun., and national holiday Mon. 11–5, Sat. 2–5.*

WHERE TO STAY

£ 🌋 **The Alders.** A quiet, unspoiled village 3 mi north of Sherborne contains this B&B, an old stone house with a walled garden. The lounge has an inglenook fireplace, and the bedrooms are modern and cheerfully decorated. Massage therapies are offered, and the house displays the owner's watercolors and sleek pottery, which you can view while tasting homemade jam during breakfast at the farmhouse table. Nearby pubs provide evening meals. **Pros:** peaceful setting; relaxing massages; interesting artworks. **Cons:** a bit remote; nothing to do in evening. ⊠ *Off B3145, Sandford Orcas* ☎ *01963/220666* ⊕ *www.thealdersbb.com* ⇱ *3 rooms* ⚘ *In-room: no a/c, Wi-Fi* ⊟ *No credit cards* ⑩ *BP.*

STOURHEAD

15 mi northeast of Sherborne, 30 mi west of Salisbury.

ESSENTIALS

Visitor Information Frome (⊠ *2 Bridge St.* ☎ *01373/467271* ⊕ *www. frometouristinfo.co.uk*).

EXPLORING

Fodor's Choice Close to the village of Stourton lies one of Wiltshire's most breathtaking
★ sights—**Stourhead,** a country-house-and-garden combination that has few parallels for beauty anywhere in Europe. Most of Stourhead was built between 1721 and 1725 by Henry the Magnificent, the wealthy banker Henry Hoare. A fire gutted the center of the house in 1902, but it was reconstructed with only a few differences. Many rooms in the Palladian mansion contain Chinese and French porcelain, and some have furniture by Chippendale. The elegant library and floridly colored picture gallery were built for the cultural development of this exceedingly civilized family. Still, the house takes second place to the adjacent gardens designed by Hoare's son Henry Hoare II, which are the most celebrated example of the English 18th-century taste for "natural" landscaping. Temples, grottoes, and bridges have been placed among shrubs, trees, and flowers to make the grounds look like a three-dimensional oil

painting. A walk around the artificial lake (1½ mi) reveals changing vistas that conjure up the 17th-century landscapes of Claude Lorrain and Nicolas Poussin; walk counterclockwise for the best views. ■ TIP→ **The best time to visit is early summer, when the massive banks of rhododendrons (introduced in Victorian times) are in full bloom, but the gardens are beautiful at any time of year.** You can get a fine view of the estate from Alfred's Tower, a 1772 folly (a structure built for picturesque effect). In summer there are occasional concerts, sometimes accompanied by fireworks and gondoliers on the lake. A restaurant and plant shop are on the grounds. All in all, it's easy to spend half a day here. From London by train, get off at Gillingham and take a five-minute cab ride to Stourton. ⊠ *Off B3092, northwest of Mere, Stourton* ☎ *01747/841152* ⊕ *www.nationaltrust.org.uk* ⛱ *£11.60; house only, £7; gardens only, £7; Alfred's Tower £2.80* ⊘ *House and Alfred's Tower mid-Mar.–Oct., Fri.–Tues. 11–5 or dusk; last admission 30 mins before closing; gardens daily 9–6 or dusk.*

WHERE TO STAY

££ ⌨ **The Spread Eagle.** You can't stay at Stourhead, but this popular hostelry, built at the beginning of the 19th century at the entrance to the landscaped park (and inside the main entrance to Stourhead), is the next best thing. Guests are admitted free to the gardens at any time. Bedrooms are elegant and understated, with some period features. The restaurant specializes in seasonal and locally sourced fare, from mushroom-and-asparagus Stroganoff to brochette of Lyme Bay scallops, tiger prawns, and salmon. **Pros:** period character; easy and free access to Stourhead. **Cons:** needs some modernization; food can be disappointing. ⊠ *Off B3092, northwest of Mere, Stourton* ☎ *01747/840587* ⊕ *www. spreadeagleinn.com* ➦ *5 rooms* ⅄ *In-room: no a/c, DVD, Wi-Fi. In-hotel: restaurant, bar, Wi-Fi hotspot* ⊟ *MC, V* ⏀ *BP.*

LONGLEAT HOUSE

6 mi north of Stourhead, 19 mi south of Bath, 27 mi northwest of Salisbury.

ESSENTIALS

Visitor Information Warminster (⊠ *Central car park, off Station Rd.* ☎ *01985/218548* ⊕ *www.visitwiltshire.co.uk*).

EXPLORING

Ⓒ ★ Home of the marquess of Bath, **Longleat House** is one of southern England's most famous private estates, and possibly the most ambitiously, even eccentrically, commercialized, as evidenced by the presence of a drive-through safari park (open since 1966) with giraffes, zebras, monkeys, rhinos, and lions. The blocklike Italian Renaissance building was completed in 1580 (for just more than £8,000, an astronomical sum at the time) and contains outstanding tapestries, paintings, porcelain, and furniture, as well as notable period features such as the Victorian kitchens, the Elizabethan minstrels' gallery, and the great hall with its massive wooden beams. Giant antlers of the extinct Irish elk decorate the walls, and free tours of the present Lord Bath's occasionally raunchy murals—described as "keyhole glimpses into my psyche," ranging from philosophical subjects to depictions of the Kama Sutra— can be booked separately at the front desk. Besides the safari park, Longleat has a butterfly garden, a miniature railway, an extensive (and fairly fiendish) hedge maze, and an adventure castle, all of which make it extremely popular, particularly in summer and during school vacations. ■TIP➔ You can easily spend a whole day here, in which case it's best to visit the house in the morning, when tours are more relaxed, and the safari park in the afternoon. A safari bus service is available (£6) for those arriving without their own transport. ⊠ *Off A362, Warminster* ☎ *01985/844400* ⊕ *www.longleat.co.uk* ▢ *£24, house and grounds only £12, safari park only £12, gardens and grounds only £4* ۞ *House Jan.–mid-Feb., prebooked themed guided tours only; mid-Feb.–late Feb. and Oct., weekdays 10–5, weekends, school vacations, and national holiday Mon. 10–5:30; late Feb.–late Mar., weekdays guided tours at noon and 2, weekends 10–5:30; late Mar.–Sept., weekdays 10–5:30, weekends, school vacations, and national holiday Mon. 10–6; Nov.– mid-Dec., weekdays guided tour at noon, weekends guided tours at 11, noon, 1, and 2; mid-Dec.–end Dec., weekdays guided tours at noon and 2, weekends guided tours at 11, noon, 1, and 2; last entry 30 mins before closing. Safari park late Mar.–Oct., weekdays 10–5, weekends and school vacations 10–6; last entry 1 hr before closing.*

WHERE TO STAY

££££   ▦ **Bishopstrow House.** This ivy-covered Georgian house has been converted into a refreshingly relaxed hotel that combines well-chosen antiques with modern amenities such as DVD players. There's an airy conservatory and a spa where you can book pampering treatments. The lavish, classically styled guest rooms overlook either the 27-acre grounds or an interior courtyard. The Mulberry restaurant creates imaginative modern British meals with Mediterranean elements (fixed-price menus £14.50 and £19 at lunchtime, £34 and £42.50 in the evening). Bishopstrow House is 1½ mi east of town. **Pros:** country-house ambience; impressive suites; excellent leisure facilities. **Cons:** expensive extras; restaurant lacks charm. ⊠ *Boreham Rd., Warminster* ☎ *01985/212312* ⊕ *www.bishopstrow.co.uk* ⇌ *29 rooms, 2 suites* ☖ *In-room: no a/c, DVD, Internet, Wi-Fi (some). In-hotel: restaurant, bar, tennis courts, pools, gym, spa, Wi-Fi hotspot, some pets allowed* ⊟ *AE, DC, MC, V* ⊚| *BP.*

■ EN
ROUTE
Four miles west of Avebury, on A4, **Cherhill Down** is a prominent hill carved with a vivid white horse and topped with a towering obelisk. It's one of a number of hillside etchings in Wiltshire, none of which dates back farther than the late 18th century. This one was put there in 1780 to indicate the highest point of the downs between London and Bath. The views from the top are well worth the half-hour climb. (The best view of the horse is from A4, on the approach from Calne.)

AVEBURY

25 mi northeast of Longleat, 27 mi east of Bath, 34 mi north of Salisbury.

The village of Avebury was built much later than the stone circles that brought it fame; it has an informative museum.

GETTING HERE AND AROUND

To get here from Longleat House, drive north for about 12 mi along A36 and A350, then northeast on the A361 through Devizes to Avebury. From Salisbury, follow A345 north as far as Marlborough, then drive 7 mi west on A4, or take Wilts & Dorset bus 5 to Pewsey, changing there to number 96 for Avebury (by bus, travel time is over 90 min).

ESSENTIALS

Visitor Information Avebury (✉ *Avebury Chapel, Green St.* ☎ *01672/539179* ⊕ *www.visitwiltshire.co.uk*).

EXPLORING

★ The **Avebury Stone Circles**, which surround part of Avebury village, are one of England's most evocative prehistoric monuments—not so famous as Stonehenge, but all the more powerful for their lack of commercial exploitation. The stones were erected around 2500 BC, some 500 years after Stonehenge was started but about 500 years before that much smaller site assumed its present form. As with Stonehenge, the purpose of this stone circle has never been ascertained, although it most likely was used for similar ritual purposes. Unlike Stonehenge, however, there are no astronomical alignments at Avebury, at least none that have survived. The main site consists of a wide, circular ditch and bank, about 1,400 feet across and more than half a mile around. Entrances break the perimeter at roughly the four points of the compass, and inside stand the remains of three stone circles. The largest one originally had 98 stones, although only 27 remain. Many stones on the site were destroyed centuries ago, especially in the 17th century when they were the target of religious fanaticism. Some were pillaged to build the thatched cottages you see flanking the fields. You can walk around the circles at any time; early morning and early evening are recommended. Be sure to visit the nearby Alexander Keiller Museum. (✉ *1 mi north of A4* ☎ *No phone* ⊕ *www.english-heritage.org.uk* 🎟 *Free* ⊙ *Daily.*

☾ In the **Alexander Keiller Museum,** finds from the Avebury area, and charts, photos, models, and home movies taken by the archaeologist Keiller himself, put the Avebury Stone Circles and the site into context. Recent revelations suggest that Keiller, responsible for the excavation of Avebury in the 1930s, may have adapted the site's layout more in the interests of presentation than authenticity. The exhibits are divided between the **Stables Gallery,** showing excavated finds, and the more child-friendly, interactive **Barn Gallery.** (✉ *1 mi north of A4* ☎ *01672/539250* ⊕ *www. english-heritage.org.uk* 🎟 *£4.20* ⊙ *Apr.–Oct., daily 10–6; Nov.–Mar., daily 10–4:30.*

The Avebury monument lies at the end of **Kennett Stone Avenue,** a sort of prehistoric processional way leading to Avebury. The avenue's stones were spaced 80 feet apart, but only the half mile nearest the main monument survives intact. The lost stones are marked with concrete, and you can wander around the whole complex.

WHERE TO EAT AND STAY

£

BRITISH

✗ **Waggon and Horses.** A 16th-century thatched building created in part with stones taken from the Avebury site, this traditional inn and pub is beside the traffic circle linking A4 and A361, a two-minute drive from the prehistoric circle. Dickens mentioned the building in the *Pickwick Papers*. Excellent lunches and dinners are served beside a fire; homemade dishes include steak, kidney, and ale pie, baked Camembert, and a smoked fish platter, or you can opt for a baguette. In high season it's something of a tourist hub. ⊠ *Beckhampton* ☎ *01672/539418* 🖃 *AE, MC, V* ☉ *No dinner Sun. Oct.–May.*

££

☷ **Manor Farm.** Views of Avebury's monoliths straggling across the field greet you from the windows of this 18th-century farmhouse right in the heart of the village. Rooms, stocked with complimentary sherry, are spacious, light, and elegantly furnished, and you have your own sitting room. The bathroom is separate, but for your exclusive use, as only one room is rented at a time (unless the same party takes both rooms). Breakfast choices include Scotch pancakes with bacon, scrambled eggs with smoked salmon, and kippers. **Pros:** ideal location; cozy and comfortable rooms; good breakfasts. **Cons:** often booked up; young children not accepted. ⊠ *High St.* ☎ *01672/539294* ⊕ *www.manorfarmavebury. com* 🛏 *2 rooms without bath* ♿ *In-room: no a/c, refrigerator. In-hotel: no kids under 12* 🖃 *No credit cards* ⏍ *BP.*

▀▘
EN
ROUTE

Prehistoric relics dot the entire Avebury area; stop at the **West Kennett Long Barrow,** a chambered tomb dating from about 3250 BC, 1 mi east of Avebury on A4. You can explore all around the site and also enter the tomb.

As you turn right at the traffic circle onto A4, **Silbury Hill** rises on your right. This man-made mound, 130 feet high, dates from about 2500 BC and is the largest of its kind in Europe. Excavations over 200 years have provided no clue as to its original purpose, but the generally accepted notion is that it was a massive burial chamber. You can walk around the hill; at this writing maintenance work has meant that you can't climb the hill.

STONEHENGE

20 mi south of Avebury, 8 mi north of Salisbury.

GETTING HERE AND AROUND

Stonehenge Tour buses leave from Salisbury's train and bus stations every half hour from 9:30 from June to September and hourly from 10 from October to May. Tickets cost £11, or £18 with admission to Stonehenge. Other options are a taxi or an organized tour. Drivers will find the monument near the junction of A303 with A344.

ESSENTIALS

Visitor Information Amesbury (⊠ *The Library, Smithfield St.* ☎ *01980/622833* ⊕ *www.visitwiltshire.co.uk).*

EXPLORING

Fodor'sChoice Mysterious and ancient, **Stonehenge** has baffled archaeologists for cen-
★ turies. One of England's most visited monuments, the circle of giant
stones that sits in lonely isolation on the wide sweep of Salisbury Plain
still has the capacity to fascinate and move those who view it. Sadly,
though, this World Heritage Site is now enclosed by barriers after incidents of vandalism, and amid fears that its popularity could threaten
its existence. Visitors are kept on a paved path a short distance away
from the stones, so that you can no longer walk among the giant stones
or see up close the prehistoric carvings, some of which show axes and
daggers. But if you visit in the early morning, when the crowds have
not yet arrived, or in the evening, when the sky is heavy with scudding
clouds, you can experience Stonehenge as it once was: a mystical, awe-
inspiring place.

Stonehenge was begun about 3000 BC, enlarged between 2100 and
1900 BC, and altered yet again by 150 BC. It has been excavated and
rearranged several times over the centuries. The medieval term Stonehenge means "hanging stones." Many of the huge stones that ringed
the center were brought here from great distances, but it is not certain
by what ancient form of transportation they were moved. The original
80 bluestones (dolerite), which made up the two internal circles, originated in the Preseli mountains, on the Atlantic coast of Wales. They
may have been moved by raft over sea and river, and then dragged on
rollers across country—a total journey of 130 mi as the crow flies, but
closer to 240 by the practical route. Every time a reconstruction of the
journey has been attempted, though, it has failed. The labor involved
in quarrying, transporting, and carving these stones is astonishing, all
the more so when you realize that it was accomplished about the same
time that the major pyramids of Egypt were built.

Although some of the mysteries concerning the site have been solved,
the reason Stonehenge was built remains unknown. It is fairly certain
that it was a religious site, and that worship here involved the cycles
of the sun; the alignment of the stones to point to sunrise at midsummer and sunset in midwinter makes this clear. The druids certainly had
nothing to do with the construction: the monument had already been
in existence for nearly 2,000 years by the time they appeared. Some
historians have maintained that Stonehenge was a kind of neolithic
computer, with a sophisticated astronomical purpose—an observatory
of sorts—though evidence that emerged in 2007 may shed new light on
the matter. Excavations at Durrington Walls, another henge a couple
of miles northeast (off A345), have unearthed a substantial settlement
dating from around 2500 BC, which was probably built and occupied
by those who constructed Stonehenge. One other possibility is that this
neolithic village was home to those who performed the religious rites
at Stonehenge, where people gathered from far and wide to feast and
worship. The finds show Stonehenge not to be an isolated monument,
but part of a much larger complex of ceremonial structures.

Since the path for visitors skirts the stones, it's helpful to bring a pair of
binoculars to help make out the details of the monoliths more clearly. It
pays to walk all about the site, near and far, to get that magical photo

and to engage your imagination. Romantics may want to view Stonehenge at dawn or dusk, or by a full moon. Your ticket entitles you to an informative audio tour, but in general, visitor amenities at Stonehenge are limited, especially for such a major tourist attraction. ■TIP➜ **English Heritage, which manages the site, can arrange entrance to the inner circle outside of regular hours on Stone Circle Access tours. These require an application and payment of £14.50 well in advance.** ✉ *Junction of A303 and A344/A360, near Amesbury* ☎ *0870/333–1181, 01722/343830 for information about private access outside regular hrs* ⊕ *www.english-heritage.org.uk* ✆ *£6.90* ⊙ *Mid-Mar.–May and Sept.–mid-Oct., daily 9:30–6; June–Aug., daily 9–7; mid-Oct.–mid-Mar., daily 9:30–4.*

NEW FOREST TO LYME REGIS

Tucked southwest of Southampton, the New Forest was once the hunting preserve of William the Conqueror and his royal descendants. Thus protected from the deforestation that has befallen most of southern England's other forests, this wild, scenic expanse offers great possibilities for walking, riding, and biking.

West of here stretches the green, hilly, and largely unspoiled county of Dorset, the setting for most of the books of Thomas Hardy, author of *Far from the Madding Crowd* and other classic Victorian-era novels. "I am convinced that it is better for a writer to know a little bit of the world remarkably well than to know a great part of the world remarkably little," he wrote as he immortalized the towns, villages, and fields of this idyllically rural area, not least the country capital, Dorchester, an ancient agricultural center. Other places of historic interest such as Maiden Castle and the chalk-cut giant of Cerne Abbas are interspersed with the bustling seaside resorts of Bournemouth and Weymouth. You may find Lyme Regis (associated with another writer, John Fowles) and the villages along the route closer to your ideal of rural England. The Jurassic Coast is the place to search for fossils.

LYNDHURST

26 mi southeast of Stonehenge, 18 mi southeast of Salisbury, 9 mi west of Southampton.

Lyndhurst is famous as the capital of the New Forest. Although some popular spots can get crowded in summer, there are ample parking lots, picnic areas, and campgrounds. Miles of trails crisscross the region.

GETTING HERE AND AROUND

To get here from Stonehenge, head south along A360 to Salisbury, then follow A36, B3079, and continue along A337 another 4 mi or so. To explore the depths of the New Forest, take A35 out of Lyndhurst (the road continues southwest to Bournemouth) or A337 south. A hop-on, hop-off open-top bus runs a circular route through the New Forest between mid-June and mid-September (adults £9 per day, bikes carried free; tickets on board). There are 8 departures daily, and the bus will stop anywhere. Regular bus services are operated by Bluestar and Wilts & Dorset; see Traveline for details.

ESSENTIALS

Visitor and Tour Information Lyndhurst (✉ *Main Car Park, High St.* ☎ *023/8028–2269* ⊕ *www.thenewforest.co.uk*). **New Forest Tour** (⊕ *www. thenewforesttour.info*).

EXPLORING

The **New Forest** consists of 150 square mi of open countryside interspersed with dense woodland, a natural haven for herds of free-roaming deer, cattle, and, most famously, hardy New Forest ponies. The forest was "new" in 1079, when William the Conqueror cleared the area of farms and villages and turned it into his private hunting grounds. An extensive network of trails makes it a wonderful place for biking, walking, and horseback riding. ⊕ *www.thenewforest.co.uk*.

☾ The **New Forest Museum**, in the same building as the Visitor Information Centre, contains fascinating and informative background on the region. The exhibits focus on the area's fauna, flora, and social traditions and are linked by quizzes, and there are other interactive elements that will keep children engaged. ✉ *High St.* ☎ *023/8028–3444* ⊕ *www. newforestmuseum.org.uk* ₤3 ⊙ *Daily 10–5; last entry at 4.*

Lyndhurst's High Street is dominated by the redbrick, high Victorian church of **St. Michael and All Angels**, which holds stained glass from William Morris's studio and a large fresco of the parable of the virgins by Frederick Leighton. Fans of Lewis Carroll's *Alice in Wonderland* should note that Alice Hargreaves (née Liddell), the inspiration for the fictional Alice, is buried in the back of the churchyard here. ✉ *High St.* ☎ *023/8028–2154* ⊕ *www.newforestparishes.com*.

WHERE TO EAT AND STAY

££ ✕ **White Buck Inn.** This traditional forest lodge makes a welcome stop
BRITISH for refreshment. The extensive menu relies on local seasonal fare, such as pork belly with a cider and apple sauce, and venison. In summer you can sit in the spacious garden, where there are regular barbecues. Live Dixieland jazz plays on Thursday evenings. There are also seven guest rooms (££) ranging from functional to plush, all with garden views, and four of them themed along Elizabethan or Indian lines. ✉ *Bisterne Close, Burley, 7 mi west of Lyndhurst* ☎ *01425/402264* ⊕ *www.fullershotels.com* ☰ *AE, MC, V.*

£££££ ▢ **Chewton Glen.** Once the home of Captain Frederick Marryat, author
★ of *The Children of the New Forest*, this early-19th-century country house on extensive grounds is now a luxurious hotel that ranks among Britain's most acclaimed—and most expensive. All rooms are decorated in rich fabrics, with an eye to the minutest detail, and the plush spa provides the latest treatments. The restaurant, the Marryat Room (fixed-price evening menu £65), is worth a pilgrimage. It concentrates on classic meat and seafood dishes enlivened with contemporary touches, and there's a choice of more than 700 wines. Chewton Glen is 12 mi southwest of Lyndhurst on A35. **Pros:** classic English luxury; excellent restaurant; top-notch leisure facilities. **Cons:** dated in parts; patchy service in restaurant. ✉ *Christchurch Rd., New Milton* ☎ *01425/275341, 800/344–5087 in U.S.* ⊕ *www.chewtonglen.com* ⇨ *33 rooms, 25 suites* ₺ *In-room: safe, refrigerator, DVD, Wi-Fi. In-hotel: restaurant, golf*

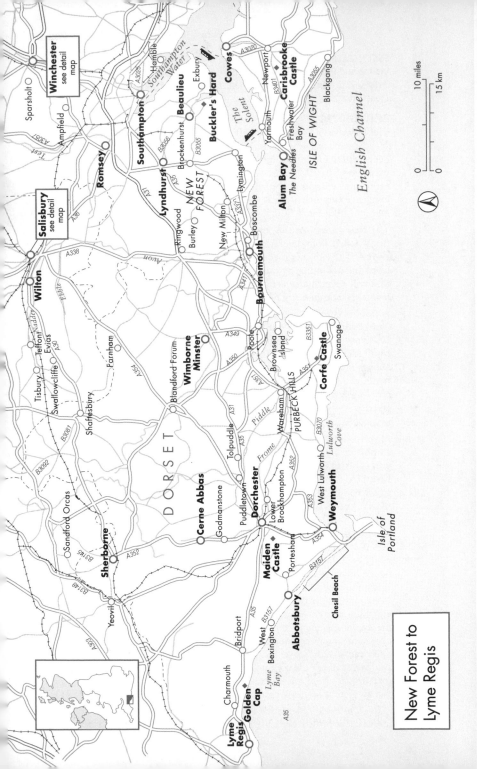

New Forest to Lyme Regis

course, tennis courts, pools, gym, spa, Internet terminal ⊟ *AE, DC, MC, V.*

££ ⊡ **The Rufus House.** If you're looking for personal service and easy access to the New Forest, book a room at this turreted Victorian house run by a Japanese-Italian couple, a short walk from Lyndhurst. The pastel-color rooms are bright, airy, and spotlessly clean—opt for one of the two suites in the turret, both with four-poster beds, if these are available. As you enjoy the nourishing breakfast you can gaze out over the gardens. **Pros:** friendly owners; delicious breakfasts; great location. **Cons:** traffic noise in front-facing rooms; some rooms and beds are small. ⊠ *Southampton Rd.* ☎ *023/8028–2930* ⊕ *www.rufushouse.co.uk* ➥ *8 rooms, 2 suites* ⏦ *In-room: no a/c, Wi-Fi. In-hotel: Wi-Fi hotspot, no kids under 5* ⊟ *MC, V* ⑩ *BP.*

SPORTS AND THE OUTDOORS
BIKING
The range of trails weaving through the New Forest makes this one of Britain's best terrains for off-road biking. For £14 per day you can rent bikes at **Cycle Experience** (⊠ *2–4 Brookley Rd., Brockenhurst* ☎ *01590/624204*).

HORSEBACK RIDING
The New Forest was created for riding, and there's no better way to enjoy it than on horseback. The **Burley Manor Riding Stables** (⊠ *Burley Manor Hotel, Ringwood Rd., Burley* ☎ *01425/403489*) caters to all levels. Hour-long rides are £30. You can arrange a ride at the **Forest Park Riding Centre** (⊠ *Rhinefield Rd., Brockenhurst* ☎ *01590/623429*). The cost is £30 per hour.

WALKING
The **New Forest** is fairly domesticated, and the walks it provides are not much more than easy strolls. For one such walk (about 4 mi), start from Lyndhurst and head directly south for Brockenhurst, a commuter village. The path goes through woods, pastureland, and heath—and you'll see plenty of New Forest ponies.

BEAULIEU

7 mi southeast of Lyndhurst.

The unspoiled village of Beaulieu (pronounced *byoo*-lee) has three major attractions in one at Beaulieu Abbey and is near the museum village of Buckler's Hard.

EXPLORING
☺ **Beaulieu,** with a ruined abbey, a stately home, and an automobile museum, can satisfy different interests. In 1204 King John established **Beaulieu Abbey** for the Cistercian monks, who gave their new home its name, which means "beautiful place" in French. It was badly damaged as part of the suppression of Catholicism during the reign of Henry VIII, leaving only the cloister, the doorway, the gatehouse, and two buildings. A well-planned exhibition in one building re-creates daily life in the monastery. **Palace House** incorporates the abbey's 14th-century gatehouse and has been the home of the Montagu family since they

purchased it in 1538, after the dissolution of the monasteries. Inside you can see drawing rooms, dining halls, and fine family portraits. The present Lord Montagu is noted for his work in establishing the **National Motor Museum**, which traces the development of motor transport from 1895 to the present. You can see more than 250 classic cars and motorcycles. Museum attractions include a monorail, audiovisual presentations, and a trip in a 1912 London bus. ⊠ *Off B3056* ☎ *01590/612345* ⊕ *www.beaulieu.co.uk* ⛾ *Abbey, Palace House, and Motor Museum £15.75–£16.75* ⊙ *Late May–late Sept., daily 10–6; late Sept.–late May, daily 10–5; last admission 30 mins before closing.*

Among the interesting places in the area is the museum village of **Buckler's Hard**, 2 mi south of Beaulieu. This restored 18th-century hamlet is home to a fascinating **Maritime Museum** that tells the story of Lord Nelson's favorite ship, HMS *Agamemnon*. Exhibits and model ships trace the town's shipbuilding history. Also part of the museum are four building interiors in the hamlet that re-create 18th-century village life. Easter through October, you can take a cruise on the Beaulieu River. The Master Builder's House Hotel has a bar and restaurant. ⊠ *Off B3056* ☎ *01590/616203* ⊕ *www.bucklershard.co.uk* ⛾ *£5.95* ⊙ *Mar.–June, Sept., and Oct., daily 10–5; July and Aug., daily 10–5:30; Nov.–Feb., daily 10–4:30; last entry 30 mins before closing.*

EN ROUTE   From Beaulieu, take any of the minor roads leading west through wide-open heathland to Lymington and pick up A337 for the popular seaside resort of Bournemouth, a journey of about 18 mi.

BOURNEMOUTH

26 mi southwest of Southampton, 26 mi south of Salisbury, 24 mi east of Dorchester.

Bournemouth has 7 mi of beaches, and the waters are said to be some of southern England's cleanest. The resort was founded in 1810 by Lewis Tregonwell, an ex-army officer who had taken a liking to the area. He settled near what is now the Square and planted the first pine trees in the distinctive steep little valleys—or chines—cutting through the cliffs to the Bournemouth sands. The scent of fir trees was said to be healing for consumption (tuberculosis) sufferers, and the town grew steadily. Today, the city has expanded to swallow up neighboring settlements, making it a somewhat amorphous sprawl on first view. Its stodgier, more traditional side is kept in check by the presence of a lively student population—partly made up of foreign-language students from abroad.

Gardens laid out with trees and lawns link the Square and the beach. This is an excellent spot to relax and listen to music wafting from the Pine Walk bandstand. Regular musical programs take place at the Pavilion and at the Winter Gardens (home of the Bournemouth Symphony Orchestra) nearby.

GETTING HERE AND AROUND

From the New Forest, take A35 or A31/A338 southwest to Bournemouth. The center of town is best explored on foot, but to reach East Cliff or Boscombe you'll need to drive or use the frequent local buses. Fast trains from London take about two hours.

ESSENTIALS

Visitor Information Bournemouth (✉ *Westover Rd., near bandstand* ☎ *0845/051–1701* ⊕ *www.bournemouth.co.uk*).

EXPLORING

Taking the zigzag paths through the leafy public gardens, you can descend to the seafront, where Bournemouth Pier juts into the channel from the pristine sandy **beach.** If you're not tempted to swim, you can stroll the promenade behind the beach. Europe's first artificial **surf reef** was constructed here in 2009. The goal is to attract surf fans as well as create an area of calm water that's perfect for children—surfers, however, have reported that the reef is more suitable for bodyboarding than standing up.

On the corner of Hinton Road stands **St. Peter's** parish church, easily recognizable by its 200-foot-high tower and spire. Lewis Tregonwell, founder and developer of Bournemouth, is buried in the churchyard. Here, too, is the elaborate tombstone of Mary Shelley, author of *Frankenstein* and wife of the great Romantic poet Percy Bysshe Shelley, whose heart is buried with her. ✉ *Hinton Rd.* ⊕ *www.stpetersbournemouth.org.*

★ The **Russell-Cotes Art Gallery and Museum,** a late-Victorian mansion perched on East Cliff, overflows with Victorian paintings and miniatures, cases of butterflies, and treasures from Asia, including an exquisite suit of Japanese armor. Members of the Russell-Cotes family, wealthy hoteliers who traveled widely, collected the items. Fine landscaped gardens surround the house. ✉ *East Cliff* ☎ *01202/451858* ⊕ *www.russell-cotes.bournemouth.gov.uk* ✒ *Free* ⊗ *Tues.–Sun. and national holiday Mon. 10–5.*

WHERE TO EAT AND STAY

£££
SEAFOOD
✕ **WestBeach.** Superbly positioned right on the marine promenade, close to Bournemouth Pier, this place has views over sand and sea. It also serves the best seafood in town, whether grilled, baked, or in fish pies and stews. The menu usually lists halibut, sea bass, plaice, and shellfish (oysters, mussels, lobster). Nonfish dishes may include rib-eye steak and sesame mille-feuille with grilled sweet potato and eggplant. The simple wooden tables and large glass front lend a modern, minimalist feel, and there's a narrow deck for eating alfresco. Live jazz bands serenade diners on Thursday evenings. In summer you can pick up baguettes, ice cream, and other snacks from the adjacent takeout. ✉ *Pier Approach* ☎ *01202/587785* ⊕ *www.west-beach.co.uk* ▤ *AE, MC, V.*

£££
▦ **The Urban Beach.** Once-sedate Bournemouth has been waiting a long time for the injection of contemporary style and energy provided by this funky boutique hotel. Though located in the slightly suburban setting of Boscombe (a 10-minute drive from Bournemouth's center), and resembling a B&B from the outside, the hotel is a short walk from

the seafront, and boasts a tastefully minimalist interior with muted tones and a slightly retro feel. Its youthful staff are simultaneously laid-back, enthusiastic, and professional. The buzzing downstairs bistro lays out a good spread, and you have access to a health club. **Pros:** modern designer decor; friendly staff. **Cons:** not central; occasional noise intrusion. ⊠ *23 Argyll Rd., Boscombe* ☎ *01202/301509* ⊕ *www. urbanbeachhotel.co.uk* ⊲ *12 rooms* ⟨ *In-room: no a/c, DVD, Wi-Fi. In-hotel: restaurant, bar, Wi-Fi hotspot, Internet terminal, parking (free)* ⊟ *AE, MC, V* ⊺⊙⊦ *BP.*

££ ⊺⊞⊦ **Wood Lodge Hotel.** Calm and sedate, this small hotel just 200 yards from the shore is a reliable choice. Bedrooms are clean and functional without being bland, and most are a good size, though those with showers instead of bathtubs are small. Kippers, croissants, and muffins are offered at breakfast, you can have a light lunch in the restaurant, and three-course evening meals are available for £18. The garden has a spacious lawn for coffees and cream teas in summer. You have access to a pool, spa bath, and sauna at a nearby health club. **Pros:** welcoming staff; close to beach. **Cons:** dated in places; some bathrooms need improving. ⊠ *10 Manor Rd., East Cliff* ☎ *01202/290891* ⊕ *www.woodlodgehotel. co.uk* ⊲ *15 rooms* ⟨ *In-room: no a/c, Wi-Fi (some). In-hotel: restaurant, bar, Wi-Fi hotspot* ⊟ *MC, V* ⊺⊙⊦ *BP.*

WIMBORNE MINSTER

7 mi northwest of Bournemouth via A341.

The impressive minster of this quiet market town makes it seem like a miniature cathedral city.

GETTING HERE AND AROUND

To reach Wimborne Minster from central Bournemouth, take any main road heading west, following signs for A341 or A349, or take advantage of the regular bus service.

ESSENTIALS

Visitor Information Wimborne Minster (⊠ *29 High St.* ☎ *01202/886116* ⊕ *www.ruraldorset.com*).

EXPLORING

The crenellated and pinnacled twin towers of **Wimborne Minster** present an attractive patchwork of gray and reddish-brown stone. The church's Norman nave has zigzag molding interspersed with carved heads, and the Gothic chancel has tall lancet windows. ■TIP➜ See the chained library (accessed via a spiral staircase), a survivor from the days when books were valuable enough to keep on chains. Look out for the 14th-century astronomical clock on the inside wall of the west tower. ⊠ *High St.* ☎ *01202/884753* ⊕ *www.wimborneminster.org.uk* ⊠ *£2 suggested donation for church, 50p suggested donation for chained library* ⊙ *Church Mar.–Dec., Mon.–Sat. 9:30–5:30, Sun. 2:30–5:30; Jan. and Feb., Mon.–Sat. 9:30–4, Sun. 2:30–4. Chained library Easter–Oct., weekdays 10:30–12:30 and 2–4, Sat. 10:30–12:30; Nov.–Easter, Sat. 10–12:30.*

The **Priest's House Museum**, on the main square in a Tudor building with a garden, includes rooms furnished in period styles and a Victorian kitchen. It also has Roman and Iron Age exhibits, including a cryptic, three-faced Celtic stone head. The garden displays agricultural and horticultural tools and holds a tearoom. ⊠ *23–27 High St.* ☎ *01202/882533* ⊕ *www.priest-house.co.uk* ▤ *£3.50, free in Dec.* ☉ *Apr.–Oct., Mon.– Sat. 10–4:30; also open for 10 days before Christmas, 3 days at the end of Dec., and 1 wk Feb.*

Kingston Lacy, a grand 17th-century house built for the Bankes family (who had lived in Corfe Castle), was altered in the 19th century by Sir Charles Barry, co-architect of the Houses of Parliament in London. It holds a choice picture collection with works by Titian, Rubens, Van Dyck, and Velásquez, as well as the fabulous Spanish Room, lined with gilded leather and topped with an ornate Venetian ceiling. There's also a fine collection of Egyptian artifacts. Parkland with walking paths surrounds the house. ⊠ *B3082, 1½ mi northwest of Wimborne Minster* ☎ *01202/883402* ⊕ *www.nationaltrust.org.uk* ▤ *£10.50; park and garden only, £5.25* ☉ *House mid-Mar.–Oct., Wed.–Sun. and national holiday Mon. 11–5, last admission 4. Garden and park early Feb.–early Mar., Fri.–Sun. 10:30–4; mid-Mar.–Oct., daily 10:30–6; Nov.–late Dec., daily 10:30–4.*

WHERE TO EAT AND STAY

££
MEDITERRANEAN

✕ **Primizia**. Its tangerine walls, low ceiling, and tile floor lend this popular bistro an intimate feel. The regularly changing menu, which shows French and Italian influences, may include marinated crayfish tails or roasted butternut squash risotto with sweet peppers, pesto, and Parmesan. ⊠ *26 West Borough* ☎ *01202/883518* ⊟ *MC, V* ☉ *Closed Sun. and Mon. No lunch Tues. and Sat.*

££–£££

⊞ **Museum Inn**. It's worth making the detour 10 mi north of Wimborne Minster to find this characterful inn known for fine contemporary British fare. Despite a stylish transformation, the building remains in harmony with its 17th-century beginnings, retaining its flagstone floors and inglenook fireplace. Bedrooms are rustic but smart. Good fresh food, from slow-roast pork belly to grilled seafood, is available daily in the bar, or, on Friday night, Saturday night, and Sunday afternoon in the more formal Shed restaurant (£££). **Pros:** pretty village location; great food. **Cons:** remote from Wimborne Minster. ⊠ *Farnham* ☎ *01725/516261* ⊕ *www.museuminn.co.uk* ➘ *8 rooms* ⚏ *In-room: no a/c, Wi-Fi (some), DVD (some). In-hotel: restaurant, bar, Wi-Fi hotspot, some pets allowed, no kids under 8* ⊟ *MC, V* ⚏ *BP.*

CORFE CASTLE

25 mi south of Wimborne Minster, 15 mi south of Poole, 5 mi southeast of Wareham.

ESSENTIALS

Visitor Information Wareham (⊠ *Holy Trinity Church, South St.* ☎ *01929/552740* ⊕ *www.visitswanageandpurbeck.com*).

EXPLORING

★ One of the most impressive ruins in Britain, Dorset's **Corfe Castle** overlooks the appealing gray limestone village also known as Corfe Castle. The castle site guards a gap in the surrounding Purbeck Hills and has been fortified since at least 900. The present ruins are of the castle built between 1105, when the great central keep was erected, and the 1270s, when the outer walls and towers were built. It owes its ramshackle state to Cromwell's soldiers, who blew up the castle in 1646 during the Civil War, after Lady Bankes led its defense during a long siege. ⊠ *A351* ☎ *01929/481294* ⊕ *www.nationaltrust.org.uk* ⊠*£5.63* ☉ *Mar. and Oct., daily 10–5; Apr.–Sept., daily 10–6; Nov.–Feb., daily 10–4.*

OFF THE BEATEN PATH

Clouds Hill. This brick-and-tile cottage served as the retreat of T.E. Lawrence (Lawrence of Arabia) before he was killed in a motorcycle accident on the road from Bovington in 1935. The house remains very much as he left it, with photos and memorabilia from the Middle East. It's particularly atmospheric on a gloomy day, as there's no electric light. ⊠ *8 mi northwest of Corfe, off B3390, Wareham* ☎ *01929/405616* ⊕ *www.nationaltrust.org.uk* ⊠*£4.50* ☉ *Mid-Mar.–Oct., Thurs.–Sun. and national holiday Mon. noon–5 or dusk.*

WHERE TO EAT AND STAY

££ ✕ **The Fox.** An age-old pub, the Fox has a fine view of Corfe Castle from
BRITISH   its flower garden. There's an ancient well in the lounge bar and more
★   timeworn stonework in an alcove, as well as a pre-1300 fireplace. The bar cheerfully doles out soups and sandwiches, as well as steaks and fish dishes. This place is popular, and can get uncomfortably congested in summer. ⊠ *West St., Corfe* ☎ *01929/480449* ▭ *MC, V.*

££   ☷ **Castle Inn.** This thatched hotel, 10 mi west of Corfe Castle, has a flagstone bar and other 15th-century features. Bedrooms are individually furnished, including one with a four-poster bed. There's an extensive garden to sit in, and the sea is a 10-minute walk away. A lengthy bar menu is available daily. The place is extremely dog-friendly, so anyone with an aversion to Fido should stay away. **Pros:** close to Lulworth Cove; historic vibe. **Cons:** shabby in places; some rooms are over the noisy bar. ⊠ *Main Rd., West Lulworth* ☎ *01929/400311* ⊕ *www. lulworthinn.com* ⋈ *10 rooms* & *In-room: no a/c, Wi-Fi. In-hotel: bar, Wi-Fi hotspot, some pets allowed* ▭ *MC, V* ☉*BP.*

DORCHESTER

21 mi west of Corfe on A351 and A352, 30 mi west of Bournemouth, 43 mi southwest of Salisbury.

In many ways Dorchester, the Casterbridge of Thomas Hardy's novel *The Mayor of Casterbridge,* is a traditional southern country town. The town owes much of its fame to its connection with Hardy, whose bronze statue looks westward from a bank on Colliton Walk. Born in a cottage in the hamlet of Higher Bockhampton, about 3 mi northeast of Dorchester, Hardy attended school in the town and was apprenticed to an architect here. Today Hardy-related sights and other nearby attractions are pleasant diversions.

Dorchester has many reminders of the Roman presence in the area. The Romans laid out the town about AD 70, and a stroll along Bowling Alley Walk, West Walk, and Colliton Walk follows the approximate line of the original Roman town walls. On the north side of Colliton Park lies an excavated Roman villa with a marvelously preserved mosaic floor.

High Street was tranquil in Hardy's day, but today it is usually busy with vehicle traffic. To appreciate the town's contemporary character, pick up a walking itinerary from the tourist office, which will take you past the main points of interest along quieter routes.

GETTING HERE AND AROUND
Dorchester can be reached from Corfe Castle via A351 and A352. From Salisbury take A354. Park wherever you can (pay parking lots are scattered around the center) and explore the town on foot.

ESSENTIALS
Visitor Information Dorchester (✉ *11 Antelope Walk* ☎ *01305/267992* ⊕ *www.westdorset.com*).

EXPLORING
TOP ATTRACTIONS
Athelhampton House and Gardens. Fine 19th-century gardens enhance an outstanding example of 15th-century domestic architecture at Athelhampton House and Gardens, 5 mi east of Dorchester and 1 mi east of Puddletown. Thomas Hardy called this place Athelhall in some of his writings, referring to the legendary King Aethelstan, who had a palace on this site. The current house includes the Great Hall, with much of its original timber roof intact, the King's Room, and the Library, with oak paneling and more than 3,000 books. The 10 acres of landscaped gardens contain water features and the Great Court with its 12 giant yew pyramids. ✉ *A35* ☎ *01305/848363* ⊕ *www.athelhampton.co.uk* 🎟 *£9.25, £6.25 if buying lunch in restaurant* ۞ *Mar.–Oct., Sun.–Thurs. 10:30–5; Nov.–Feb., Sun. 11–dusk.*

Dorset County Museum. This labyrinthine museum contains ancient Celtic remains from nearby Maiden Castle and Roman remains from town, a rural crafts gallery, and a local-history gallery. It's better known for its large collection of Hardy memorabilia, and there's a gallery focusing on the nearby Jurassic Coast. ✉ *High West St.* ☎ *01305/262735* ⊕ *www.dorsetcountymuseum.org* 🎟 *£6.50* ۞ *Apr.–Oct., Mon.–Sat. 10–5; Nov.–Mar., Tues.–Sat. 10–4.*

QUICK BITES Drop into **Potters Café** (✉ *19 Durngate St.* ☎ 01305/260312), occupying a 17th-century cottage, for teas and delicious cakes and pastries, as well as grilled ciabattas and lunches of fish pie or macaroni and cheese. The courtyard garden is pleasant in summer.

★ **Maiden Castle.** After Stonehenge, Maiden Castle, 2 mi southwest of Dorchester, is the most important pre-Roman archaeological site in England. It's not an actual castle but an enormous hill fort of stone and earth with ramparts that enclose about 45 acres. England's mysterious prehistoric inhabitants built the fort, and many centuries later it was a Celtic stronghold. In AD 43 invading Romans, under the general

CLOSE UP

Hardy's Dorset

Among this region's proudest claims is its connection with Thomas Hardy (1840–1928), one of England's most celebrated novelists. If you read some of Hardy's novels before visiting Dorset—re-created by Hardy as his part-fact, part-fiction county of Wessex—you may well recognize some places immediately from his descriptions. The tranquil countryside surrounding Dorchester is lovingly described in *Far from the Madding Crowd*, and Casterbridge, in *The Mayor of Casterbridge*, stands for Dorchester itself. Any pilgrimage to Hardy's Wessex begins at the author's birthplace in Higher Bockhampton, 3 mi east of Dorchester. Salisbury makes an appearance as "Melchester" in *Jude the Obscure*. Walk in the footsteps of Jude Fawley by climbing Shaftesbury—"Shaston"—and its steep Gold Hill, a street lined with cottages. Today many of these sights seem frozen in time, and Hardy's spirit is ever present.

(later emperor) Vespasian, stormed the fort. Finds from the site are on display in the Dorset County Museum in Dorchester. To experience an uncanny silence and sense of mystery, climb Maiden Castle early in the day (access to it is unrestricted). Leave your car at the lot at the end of Maiden Castle Way, a 1½-mi lane signposted off the A354. ⊠ *A354.*

WORTH NOTING

☾ **Dinosaur Museum.** The popular Dinosaur Museum has life-size models, interactive displays, and a hands-on Discovery Gallery. ⊠ *Icen Way, off High East St.* ☏ *01305/269880* ⊕ *www.thedinosaurmuseum.com* ⌨ *£6.95* ☾ *Apr.–Oct., daily 9:30–5:30; Nov.–Mar., daily 10–4:30.*

Hardy's Cottage. The small thatch-and-cob cottage, where the writer was born in 1840, was built by his grandfather and is little altered since that time. From here Thomas Hardy would make his daily 6-mi walk to school in Dorchester. Among other things, you can see the desk at which the author completed *Far from the Madding Crowd.* ⊠ *½ mi south of Blandford Rd. (A35), Higher Bockhampton* ☏ *01305/262366* ⊕ *www.nationaltrust.org.uk* ⌨ *£4* ☾ *Mid-Mar.–Oct., Thurs.–Mon. 11–5 or dusk.*

Maumbury Rings. These remains of a Roman amphitheater on the edge of town were built on a prehistoric site that later served as a place of execution. (Hardy's *Mayor of Casterbridge* contains a vivid evocation of the Rings.) As late as 1706 a girl was burned at the stake here. ⊠ *Maumbury Rd.*

Max Gate. Thomas Hardy lived in Max Gate from 1885 until his death in 1928. An architect by profession, Hardy designed the house, in which the dining room and the light, airy drawing room are open to the public. He wrote much of his poetry here and many of his novels, including *Tess of the d'Urbervilles* and *The Mayor of Casterbridge.* ⊠ *Allington Ave., 1 mi east of Dorchester on A352* ☏ *01305/262538* ⊕ *www.nationaltrust. org.uk* ⌨ *£3* ☾ *Apr.–Sept., Mon., Wed., and Sun. 2–5.*

OFF THE
BEATEN
PATH

Poundbury. Owned by the Duchy of Cornwall and under the aegis of the Prince of Wales, this model village a mile west of Dorchester on B3150 is a showcase of Prince Charles's vision of urban planning and community living. The emphasis is on conservation and energy efficiency; private houses coexist with shops, offices, small-scale factories, and leisure facilities. Central Pummery Square is dominated by the colonnaded Brownsword Hall. Here you'll find the pub and restaurant Poet Laureate (☎ *01305/251511*) and Dorchester's Farmer's Market, held the first Saturday of the month. For more information consult the **Duchy of Cornwall office** (✉ *Poundbury Farmhouse, Dorchester* ☎ *01305/250533* ⊕ *www.duchyofcornwall.org*).

WHERE TO EAT AND STAY

£
ITALIAN

✕ **Judge Jeffreys.** Relaxed and characterful, this eatery occupies the former residence of Judge Jeffreys, a 17th-century hanging judge. The restaurant serves a reliable menu of Italian classics. Alongside the risottos, pastas, and pizzas, you'll also find crab cakes and *pollo siciliana* (char-grilled chicken breast). Both dining areas are paneled (dark at street level, lighter upstairs), with beamed ceilings, antique fireplaces, and swords on the walls. ✉ *6 High West St.* ☎ *01305/259678* ⊕ *www. loveprezzo.co.uk* ▤ *MC, V*.

£££££
MODERN BRITISH

✕ **Yalbury Cottage.** A thatch roof and inglenook fireplaces add to the appeal of this 300-year-old cottage, 2½ mi east of Dorchester. The restaurant's three-course fixed-price menu (£34) of superior Modern British and European fare emphasizes seasonal local fare and might include seared Lyme Regis scallops, roast cannon (the lean eye of the loin of lamb), or glazed duck breast. There are eight functional but comfortable bedrooms (££) available in an extension overlooking gardens or adjacent fields. Lower Bockhampton is signposted off the A35, northeast of town. ✉ *Lower Bockhampton* ☎ *01305/262382* ⊕ *www. yalburycottage.com* ▤ *AE, MC, V* ⊗ *No dinner Sun. or Mon.*

££–£££
★

▦ **The Casterbridge.** Small but full of character, this Georgian building (1790) reflects its age with period furniture and elegance. Guest rooms—one with its own small patio—are individually and impeccably furnished in traditional style, and the conservatory overlooks a courtyard garden. The generous breakfast includes free-range eggs and fresh fruit. **Pros:** central location; elegant period setting; good breakfasts. **Cons:** traffic noise in front rooms; annex rooms are small and lack character; limited parking. ✉ *49 High East St.* ☎ *01305/264043* ⊕ *www. thecasterbridge.co.uk* ⬎ *14 rooms* ౮ *In-room: no a/c, Wi-Fi (some). In-hotel: bar, Wi-Fi hotspot, parking (free)* ▤ *AE, MC, V* ꙳⊙ *BP.*

SHOPPING

You can find Dorset delicacies such as Blue Vinney cheese (which some connoisseurs prefer to Blue Stilton) in the **Wednesday Market** (✉ *Fairfield parking lot, off Weymouth Ave.*).

THE OUTDOORS

From April through October the **Thomas Hardy Society** (⌂ *c/o Dorset County Museum, High West St., Dorchester DT1 1XA* ☎ *01305/251501* ⊕ *www.hardysociety.org*) organizes walks that follow in the steps of Hardy's novels. Readings and discussions accompany the walks, which take most of a day.

CERNE ABBAS

6 mi north of Dorchester.

The village of Cerne Abbas, worth a short exploration on foot, has some Tudor houses on the road beside the church. Nearby you can also see the original village stocks.

EXPLORING

Tenth-century **Cerne Abbey** is now a ruin, with little left to see except its old gateway, although the nearby Abbey House is still in use.

Cerne Abbas's main claim to fame is the colossal and unblushingly priapic **Cerne Abbas Giant,** a figure cut in chalk on a hillside overlooking the village. The 180-foot-long giant carries a huge club, and may have originated as a tribal fertility symbol long before Roman times; authorities disagree. His outlines are formed by 2-foot-wide trenches. The present giant is thought to have been carved in the chalk about AD 1200. The best place to view the figure is from the A352 itself, where you can park in any of numerous nearby turnouts. ⊠ *A352* ⊕ *www. nationaltrust.org.uk.*

WEYMOUTH

8 mi south of Dorchester.

Dorset's main coastal resort, Weymouth, is known for its wide, safe, sandy beaches and its royal connections. King George III took up sea bathing here for his health in 1789, setting a trend among the wealthy and fashionable people of the day. Popularity left Weymouth with many fine buildings, including the Georgian row houses lining the esplanade. Striking historical details clamor for attention: a wall on Maiden Street, for example, holds a cannonball that was embedded in it during the Civil War. Nearby, a column commemorates the launching of United States forces from Weymouth on D-Day.

GETTING HERE AND AROUND

You can reach Weymouth on frequent local buses and trains from Dorchester, or on less frequent services from Bournemouth. The bus and train stations are close to each other near King's Statue, on the Esplanade. Drivers can take A354 from Dorchester and should park on or near the Esplanade—an easy walk from the center—or in a parking lot near the harbor.

ESSENTIALS

Visitor Information Weymouth (⊠ *King's Statue, The Esplanade* ☎ *01305/785747* ⊕ *www.visitweymouth.co.uk*).

EXPLORING

A 5-mi-long peninsula jutting south from Weymouth leads to the Isle of Portland, well known for its limestone. The peninsula is the eastern end of the unique geological curiosity known as **Chesil Beach**—a 200-yard-wide, 30-foot-high bank of pebbles that decrease in size from east to west. The beach extends for 18 mi. A powerful undertow makes swimming dangerous, and tombstones in local churchyards attest to the many shipwrecks the beach has caused.

WHERE TO EAT

£££ ✕ **Perry's.** In a Georgian town house right by the harbor, this busy res-
SEAFOOD taurant specializes in simple dishes using the best local seafood. Try the lobster or scallops, or grilled fillet of sea bass with asparagus and a mussel, lemon, and vanilla sauce. Meat dishes, such as roast beef fillet and rump of lamb, are tasty, too. Set-price lunch menus are a good value. ☒ *The Harbourside, 4 Trinity Rd.* ☎ *01305/785799* ⊕ *www. perrysrestaurant.co.uk* ⊟ *MC, V* ☽ *Closed Mon. No lunch Sat.*

ABBOTSBURY

10 mi northwest of Weymouth.

Pretty Abbotsbury is at the western end of Chesil Beach and has a swannery. In other parts of the village, you can also visit a children's farm, housed in an impressive medieval barn, and subtropical gardens.

GETTING HERE AND AROUND

By car, take B3157 from Weymouth, or the steep and (very) minor road passing through Martinstown off A35 from Dorchester; the latter route brings you past the Hardy Monument and has marvelous views of the coast.

EXPLORING

A lagoon outside the village serves as the **Abbotsbury Swannery**, a famous breeding place for swans. Introduced by Benedictine monks as a source of meat in winter, the swans have remained for centuries, building new nests every year in the soft, moist eelgrass. Cygnets hatch between mid-May and late June. Try to visit during feeding time, at noon and 4 PM. ☒ *New Barn Rd.* ☎ *01305/871858* ⊕ *www.abbotsbury-tourism.co.uk* ⊠ *£9.50* ☽ *Apr.–Sept., daily 10–6; late Mar. and Oct., daily 10–5; last admission 1 hr before closing.*

On the hills above Abbotsbury stands the **Hardy Monument**—dedicated to Sir Thomas Masterman Hardy, Lord Nelson's flag captain at Trafalgar, to whom Nelson's dying words, "Kiss me, Hardy," were addressed. The monument lacks charm, but in clear weather you can scan the whole coastline between the Isle of Wight and Start Point in Devon. The monument may close after April 2011 for most of the year; check. ☒ *Black Down, Portesham* ☎ *01297/489481* ⊕ *www.nationaltrust.org.uk* ⊠ *£2* ☽ *Apr.–Sept., weekends 11–5. May close in bad weather.*

LYME REGIS

19 mi west of Abbotsbury.

"A very strange stranger it must be, who does not see the charms of the immediate environs of Lyme, to make him wish to know it better," wrote Jane Austen in *Persuasion*. Judging from the summer crowds, most people appear to be not at all strange. The ancient, scenic town of Lyme

Regis and the so-called Jurassic Coast are highlights of southwest Dorset. The crumbling seaside cliffs in this area are especially fossil rich.

GETTING HERE AND AROUND

Lyme Regis is off the A35, extending west from Bournemouth and Dorchester. Drivers should park as soon as possible—there are parking lots at the top of town, for example off Charmouth Road, on the eastern approach (A3052)—and explore the town on foot. First buses run here from Dorchester and Axminster, 6 mi northwest; the latter town is on the main rail route from London Waterloo and Salisbury.

ESSENTIALS

Visitor Information Lyme Regis (⊠ *Guildhall Cottage, Church St.* ☎ *01297/442138* ⊕ *www.lymeregis.org*).

EXPLORING

Lyme Regis is famous for its curving stone harbor breakwater, the **Cobb**, built by King Edward I in the 13th century to improve the harbor. The duke of Monmouth landed here in 1685 during his ill-fated attempt to overthrow his uncle James II. The Cobb figured prominently in the movie *The French Lieutenant's Woman*, based on John Fowles's novel set in Lyme Regis, as well as in the film version of Jane Austen's *Persuasion*. Fowles was a longtime resident of Lyme.

ⓒ The small but child-friendly **Marine Aquarium** offers the usual up-close look at creatures aquatic, from conger eels to spider crabs. ⊠ *End of the Cobb* ☎ *01297/444230* ⊕ *www.lymeregismarineaquarium.co.uk* ⊡ *£5* ⊘ *Mid-Mar.–Oct., daily 10–5.*

In a gabled and turreted Victorian building, the lively **Lyme Regis Museum** contains engaging items that illustrate the town's maritime and domestic history, as well as a section on local writers and a good selection of local fossils. ⊠ *Bridge St.* ☎ *01297/443370* ⊕ *www.lymeregismuseum. co.uk* ⊡ *£3.50* ⊘ *Easter–Oct., Mon.–Sat. 10–5, Sun. 11–5; Nov.–Easter, Wed.–Sun. 11–4, daily during school vacations.*

ⓒ The **Dinosaurland Fossil Museum**, in a former church, displays an excellent collection of local fossils and gives the background on regional geology and how fossils develop. Although the museum is aimed at children, most people find it informative. Ask here about guided fossil-hunting walks. The **shop** on the ground floor sells books and fascinating fossils from around the world as well as reproductions of fossils, some fashioned into jewelry or ornaments. ⊠ *Coombe St.* ☎ *01297/443541* ⊕ *www.dinosaurland.co.uk* ⊡ *£5* ⊘ *Mid-Feb.–mid-Oct., daily 10–5; mid-Oct.–mid-Feb., weekends 10–5, but call to check.*

WHERE TO EAT AND STAY

£ ✕ **Bell Cliff Restaurant.** This friendly little place at the bottom of Lyme's
BRITISH main street makes a great spot for a light lunch or tea, although it can get noisy and cramped. Apart from teas and coffees, you can order seafood, including salmon, cod, and breaded plaice stuffed with prawns and mushrooms, or a gammon steak (a thick slice of cured ham) or leek-and-mushroom crumble. ⊠ *5–6 Broad St.* ☎ *01297/442459* ▭ *AE, MC, V* ⊘ *No dinner during school terms.*

CLOSE UP

Fossil Hunting on the Jurassic Coast

Fossils and fossil hunting are the lure for visitors to the coast that stretches for 95 mi between Studland Bay in the east to Exmouth (Devon) in the west. This cliff-lined coast encompasses 185 million years of the Earth's geological history, for which it has been granted World Heritage Site status.

Fossils formed in the distant past are continuously being uncovered here as parts of the crumbly cliffs erode, and good examples of ammonites and dinosaur traces can be seen in museums in Dorchester and Lyme Regis. Though it is dubbed "Jurassic Coast," there are also examples of older Triassic and younger Cretaceous rocks. As a rule, the older rocks can be seen in the western parts of the coast, and younger rocks form the cliffs to the east.

FINDING FOSSILS

A good path that traces the whole coast allows you to explore the area at close quarters. Fossil hunters are free to pick and chip away at the rocks, the best stretch being within 6 mi on either side of Lyme Regis (the beach below Stonebarrow Hill, east of Charmouth, is especially fruitful). As signs along the seafront warn, the best place to find fossils is not at the

rock face but on the shore. Check weather conditions and tides—collecting on a falling tide is best, and the ideal time to do it is in winter, when heavy storms are continuously uncovering new areas.

To spot the most commonly found fossils, ammonites (chambered cephalopods from the Jurassic era, related to today's nautilus), just look down hard at the shingle (large gravel) on the beach and inspect the gaps between rocks and boulders. Ammonites are usually preserved in either calcite or iron pyrite ("fool's gold"); shinier, more fragile specimens may be found in aragonite. Visit the museums in Lyme to remind you what to look for: the lustrous spirals are similar in heft and size to a brass coin, most smaller than a 10p coin. Other fossils to be found include sea urchins, white oyster shells, and coiled worm tubes.

INFORMATION AND TOURS

If you want to leave nothing to chance, hook up with a pro: information on guided walks is available from the tourist office and the Lyme Regis Museum. Publications are also available for sale in the tourist offices of Lyme Regis, Weymouth, and Dorchester; they can also tell you about coastal boat trips.

£££
SEAFOOD

✕ **Hix Oyster & Fish House.** The finest oysters complement the grandest views at this trendy, white-walled bistro on a height overlooking the Cobb. Seafood rules here, simply cooked and beautifully presented, from Cornish hake with clams to wild sea trout with asparagus and pea shoots. Non-fish-eaters have limited choices, but the dessert menu is extensive, including cider brandy chocolate truffles, and buttermilk pudding. Book well ahead to sit by the panoramic floor-to-ceiling windows or on the small terrace. Coffees are served during the morning, and oysters and champagne in the afternoon. ⊠ *Cobb Rd.* ☎ *01297/446910* ⊕ *www.hixoysterandfishhouse.co.uk* ⚓ *Reservations essential* ▭ *AE, MC, V* ⊘ *Closed Mon. Oct.–June.*

£££–££££ ⊡ **Alexandra.** Magnificently sited above the Cobb, the Alexandra combines contemporary decor with an old-fashioned, genteel air. Depending on the cost, some guest rooms have a restrained elegance and others are purely functional, although most have a view over the garden and sea. Bathrooms are on the small side. Informal meals and teas are served in the Conservatory Restaurant that overlooks an expanse of lawn. The formal Alexandra Restaurant has an impressive wine list to complement the fixed-price, five-course dinners (£38), featuring such entrées as grilled gilthead bream with a Thai red-chili salsa, and Ruby Devon beef and kidney pie. **Pros:** great garden; lovely views; deck overlooking the sea; central location. **Cons:** cheaper rooms have no sea views; restricted parking. ✉ *Pound St.* ☎ *01297/442010* ⊕ *www.hotelalexandra.co.uk* ⇄ *24 rooms* ⅊ *In-room: no a/c, Wi-Fi (some), Internet. In-hotel: 2 restaurants, bar, Internet terminal, Wi-Fi hotspot, some pets allowed* ▭ *MC, V* ☺ *Closed late Dec.–late Jan.* ⏀ *BP.*

> **EVEN KIDS DIG IT**
>
> In 1811 a local child named Mary Anning dug out an ichthyosaur skeleton near Lyme Regis (it's on display in London's Natural History Museum). Anning's obsession with Jurassic remains left her labeled locally as the "fossil woman"; throughout her life she made many valuable discoveries that were sought by museums and collectors.

£ ⊡ **Coombe House.** Tucked away on one of the oldest lanes in Lyme (dating from the 16th century), this simple B&B has genial hosts and spacious, modern guest rooms in pastel shades. Breakfast, which includes homemade jams, is brought to your room. A delightful three-bedroom apartment is also available. **Pros:** friendly owners; pleasant rooms; central location. **Cons:** only two rooms; little parking. ✉ *41 Coombe St.* ☎ *01297/443849* ⊕ *www.coombe-house.co.uk* ⇄ *2 rooms* ⅊ *In-room: no a/c, no phone, Wi-Fi. In-hotel: Wi-Fi hotspot* ▭ *No credit cards* ⏀ *BP.*

SPORTS AND THE OUTDOORS

The 72-mi **Dorset Coast Path** (☎ *01392/383560* ⊕ *www.southwestcoastpath.com*) runs east from Lyme Regis to Poole, bypassing Weymouth and taking in the quiet bays, shingle beaches, and low chalk cliffs of the coast. Some highlights are Golden Cap, the highest point on the south coast; the Swannery at Abbotsbury; Chesil Beach; and Lulworth Cove (between Weymouth and Corfe Castle). Villages and isolated pubs dot the route, as do many rural B&Bs.

The West Country

SOMERSET, DEVON, CORNWALL

WORD OF MOUTH

"Driving from M5 to Wells is already a lovely thing—through pretty villages and countryside. Wells is a quaint little town with a pretty market, old gates, and bookshops everywhere. The cathedral is gorgeous and appears ridiculously oversized in such a small town, but this gives a proper impression how proportions were in the old times."

—traveller1959

"Clovelly: don't go there to get away from the crowds—it has become such an attraction that they now charge to enter it. That said, it is lovely and charming, and quaint; by all means go for an hour or two."

—annhig

Updated
by Robert
Andrews

Leafy, narrow country roads all around the southwest lead through miles of buttercup meadows and cider-apple orchards to heathery heights overlooking the sea and mellow villages of stone and thatch. This can be one of England's most relaxing regions to visit. The secret of exploring it is to ignore the main highways and just follow the signposts—or, even better, to let yourself get lost, which won't be difficult. The village names alone are music to the ears: there's Tintinhull, St. Endellion, and Huish Episcopi—just to name a few hamlets that *haven't* been covered here.

Somerset, Devon, and Cornwall are the three counties that make up the long, dangling peninsula known as the West Country. Each has its own distinct flavor, and each comes with a regionalism that borders on patriotism. Somerset is noted for its subtly rolling green countryside; Devon's wild and dramatic moors—bare, boggy, upland heath dominated by heathers and gorse—contrast with the restfulness of its many sandy beaches and coves; and Cornwall has managed to retain a touch of its old insularity, despite the annual invasion of thousands of people lured by the Atlantic waves or the ripples of the English Channel.

Bristol is where you come across the first unmistakable burrs of the western brogue. Its historic port retains a strong maritime air, and Georgian architecture and a dramatic gorge create a backdrop to what has become one of Britain's most dynamic cities. You might weave south through the lovely Chew Valley on your way to the cathedral city of Wells. The county's lush countryside is best seen in a cloak of summer heat when its orchards give ample shade and its old stone houses and inns welcome you with a breath of coolness. Abutting the north coast are the Quantock and Mendip hills, and heather-covered Exmoor National Park.

Devon, farther west, is famed for its wild moorland—especially Dartmoor, where ponies roam amid an assortment of strange tors: rocky outcroppings eroded into weird shapes. Devon's large coastal towns are as interesting for their cultural and historical appeal—many were smugglers' havens—as for their scenic beauty. Some propagandists of east Devon speak of the "red cliffs" of Devon in contrast to the more famous "white cliffs of Dover." Parts of south Devon, on the other hand, resemble some balmy Mediterranean shore—hence its soubriquet, the English Riviera.

Cornwall, England's southernmost county, has always regarded itself as separate from the rest of Britain, and the Arthurian legends really took root here, not least at Tintagel Castle, the legendary birthplace of Arthur. High, jagged cliffs line Cornwall's Atlantic coast and indeed

TOP REASONS TO GO

A coastal walk: Pick almost any stretch of coast in Devon and Cornwall for a close encounter with the sea. For high, dramatic cliff scenery, choose the Exmoor coast around Lynmouth or the coast around Tintagel. The South West Coast Path, one of Britain's national trails, is 630 mi long, but you can tackle a few miles of it for great walks around the region.

Riding or hiking on Dartmoor: Get away from it all in southern England's greatest wilderness—an empty, treeless expanse dotted with rocky outcrops called tors. Organized walks and pony trekking operations are advertised at visitor centers.

Seafood in Padstow: Celebrity chef Rick Stein rules the roost in this small Cornish port, and any of his establishments will strongly satisfy, though the Seafood Restaurant has the wow factor. A pre- or post-dinner stroll around the harbor will allow you to soak up the spirit of this congenial town.

Tate St. Ives: There's nowhere better to absorb the local arts scene than this offshoot of London's Tate in the pretty seaside town of St. Ives. A marvelous rooftop café claims views over Porthmeor Beach.

A visit to Eden: It's worth the journey west for Cornwall's Eden Project alone: a wonderland of plant life, magnificently sited in a former clay pit. Two gigantic geodesic "biomes" are filled with flora from around the world, and the elaborate outdoor plantations are equally engaging.

Wells Cathedral: A perfect example of medieval craftsmanship, the building is a stunning spectacle. Come at the end of the day when Evensong is performed to experience its lofty interior at its most evocative.

pose a menace to passing ships. The south coast, Janus-like, is filled with sunny beaches, delightful coves, and popular resorts. England's last outposts, the flower-filled Isles of Scilly, claim the most hours of sunshine in the country.

ORIENTATION AND PLANNING

GETTING ORIENTED

Going from east to west, the counties of Somerset, Devon, and Cornwall make up the West Country. A circular tour of the West Country peninsula covers stark contrasts, from the bustling city of Bristol in the east to the remote and rocky headlands of Devon and Cornwall to the west. On the whole, the northern coast is more rugged, the cliffs dropping dramatically to tiny coves and beaches, whereas the south coast shelters many more resorts and wider expanses of sand. The crowds gravitate to the southern shore, but there are many remote inlets and estuaries, and you don't need to go far to find a degree of seclusion. The national parks of Exmoor on the northern part of the peninsula and Dartmoor, with their wilder landscapes, add even more variety.

Bristol to North Devon. Bristol is filled with remnants of its long history, but you need to explore small towns like Wells and Glastonbury to get the full flavor of the region. West of here, Exmoor National Park has an unfettered, romantic appeal, with some entrancing coastline.

Cornwall. You're never more than 20 mi from the sea in this western outpost of Britain, and the maritime flavor imbues such port towns as Padstow and Falmouth. A string of good beaches and resort towns such as St. Ives pull in the summer crowds.

Plymouth and Dartmoor. Though modern in appearance, Plymouth has some important historical sights. To the northeast, the open heath and wild moorland of Dartmoor National Park invites walking and horseback riding; towns such as Chagford make a good base for exploring.

Dartmouth, Torbay, and Exeter. Bustling Dartmouth and relaxed Totnes lie close to the English Riviera resorts of Torquay and Brixham (both part of the Torbay district). North of here, Exeter's sturdy cathedral dominates the historic city, from which you can make easy forays to Topsham and Honiton.

PLANNING

WHEN TO GO

In July and August, traffic chokes the roads leading into the West Country. Somehow the region squeezes in all the "grockles," or tourists, and the chances of finding a remote oasis of peace and quiet are severely curtailed. The beaches and resort towns are either bubbling with zest or unbearably tacky, depending on your point of view. In summer, your best option is to find a secluded hotel and make brief excursions from there. Avoid traveling on Saturday, when weekly rentals start and finish and the roads are jammed. Most properties that don't accept business year-round open for Easter and close in late September or October. Those that remain open have reduced hours. Winter has its own appeal: the Atlantic waves crash dramatically against the coast, and the austere Cornish cliffs are at their most spectacular.

The most notable festivals are Padstow's Obby Oss, a traditional celebration of the arrival of summer that takes place around May 1; the Cornish-themed, weeklong Golowan Festival in Penzance in late June; the Exeter Festivals in June/July and October/November; and the St. Ives September Festival of music and art in mid-September. In addition, many West Country maritime towns host regattas over summer weekends. The best times to visit Devon are late summer and early fall, during the end-of-summer festivals, especially popular in the towns of eastern Dartmoor.

PLANNING YOUR TIME

The elongated shape of Britain's southwestern peninsula means that you may well spend more time traveling than seeing the sights. The key is to base yourself in one or two places and make day trips to the surrounding region. The cities of Bristol, Exeter, and Plymouth make handy bases from which to explore the region, but they can also swallow up a lot of time, at the expense of smaller, less demanding places. The same is true

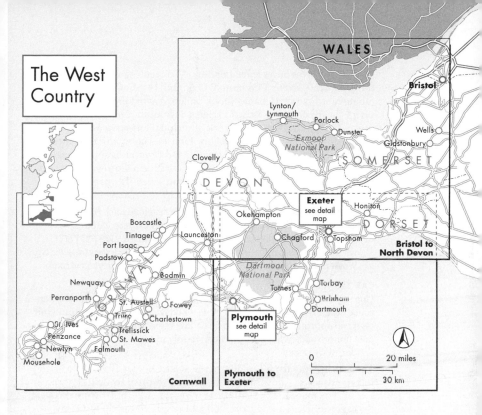

The West Country

of the resorts of Torquay, Newquay, and Falmouth, which can get very busy. Choose instead towns and villages such as Wells, Lynmouth, Port Isaac, St. Mawes, and Charlestown to soak up local atmosphere. Allow time for aimless rambling—the best way to explore the moors and the coast—and leave enough free time for doing nothing at all.

GETTING HERE AND AROUND

AIR TRAVEL

Bristol International Airport, a few miles southwest of the city, has flights from domestic and international cities. Plymouth has a small airport 4 mi north of the center. Exeter International Airport is 5 mi east of the city. Newquay Cornwall Airport, 5 mi northeast of town, has daily flights to London Stansted and London Gatwick.

Airport Information Bristol International Airport (⊠ Lulsgate Bottom ☎ 0871/334–4444 ⊕ www.bristolairport.co.uk). **Exeter International Airport** (⊠ Clyst Honiton ☎ 01392/367433 ⊕ www.exeter-airport.co.uk). **Plymouth City Airport** (⊠ Crownhill ☎ 01752/204090 ⊕ www.plymouthairport. com). **Newquay Cornwall Airport** (⊠ St. Mawgan ☎ 01637/860600 ⊕ www. newquaycornwallairport.com).

BUS TRAVEL

National Express buses leave London's Victoria Coach Station for Bristol (2½ hours), Exeter (4¼ hours), Plymouth (4¾ hours), and Penzance (about nine hours). Megabus (book online to avoid premium-line costs) offers cheap service to Bristol, Exeter, Plymouth, Newquay, and Penzance. There's also a good network of regional bus services. Stagecoach Devon covers mainly South Devon. First bus company runs most of the services in Somerset, North Devon, and Plymouth, and throughout Cornwall. Western Greyhound operates in North Cornwall. First and Stagecoach Devon money-saving one- and seven-day passes are good for unlimited bus travel. Traveline can help you plan your trip.

Bus Contacts First (☎ 0845/600–1420 ⊕ www.firstgroup.com). **Megabus** (☎ 0900/160–0900 ⊕ www.megabus.com). **National Express** (☎ 0871/781–8178 ⊕ www.nationalexpress.com). **Stagecoach Devon** (☎ 01392/427711 ⊕ www.stagecoachbus.com). **Traveline** (☎ 0871/200–2233 ⊕ www.traveline.org.uk). **Western Greyhound** (☎ 01637/871871 ⊕ www.westerngreyhound.com).

CAR TRAVEL

Unless you confine yourself to a few towns—for example, Exeter, Penzance, and Plymouth—you will be at a huge disadvantage without your own transportation. The region has a few main arteries, but you should take minor roads whenever possible, if only to see the real West Country at a leisurely pace.

The fastest route from London to the West Country is via the M4 and M5 motorways. Allow at least two hours to drive to Bristol, three to Exeter. The main roads heading west are the A30 (burrowing through the center of Devon and Cornwall all the way to the tip of Cornwall), the A39 (near the northern shore), and the A38 (near the southern shore, south of Dartmoor and taking in Plymouth).

TRAIN TRAVEL

Rail travelers can make use of a fast service connecting Exeter, Plymouth, and Penzance. First Great Western and South West Trains serve the region from London's Paddington and Waterloo stations. Average travel time to Exeter is 2½ hours, to Plymouth 3½ hours, and to Penzance about 5½ hours. Once you've arrived, however, you'll find trains to be of limited use in the West Country, as only a few branch lines leave the main line between Exeter and Penzance.

Regional Rail Rover tickets provide three days' unlimited travel throughout the West Country in any seven-day period, or eight days in any 15-day period; localized Rangers cover Devon or Cornwall.

Train Contacts National Rail Enquiries (☎ 0845/748–4950 ⊕ www.nationalrail.co.uk).

RESTAURANTS

The last few years have seen a food renaissance in England's West Country. In the top restaurants, the accent is firmly on local and seasonal products. Seafood is the number one choice along the coasts, from Atlantic pollock to Helford River oysters, and it's available in places from haute restaurants to harborside fish shacks. Celebrity chefs have marked their pitch all over the region, including Michael

Caines in Exeter and Dartmoor, the Tanner brothers in Plymouth, John Burton-Race in Dartmouth, Rick Stein in Padstow, and Jamie Oliver in Newquay. Better-known establishments are often completely booked on Friday or Saturday, so reserve well in advance.

HOTELS

Availability can be limited on the coasts during August, so book well ahead. Accommodations include national hotel chains, represented in all the region's principal centers, as well as ancient inns and ubiquitous bed-and-breakfast places. Many farmhouses also rent out rooms— offering tranquillity in rural surroundings—but these lodgings are often difficult to reach without a car. If you have a car, though, renting a house or cottage with a kitchen may be ideal. It's worth finding out about weekend and winter deals that many hotels offer.

WHAT IT COSTS IN POUNDS				
£	££	£££	££££	£££££
Restaurants	under £10	£10–£14	£15–£19	£20–£25	over £25
Hotels	under £70	£70–£120	£121–£160	£161–£220	over £220

Restaurant prices are for a main course at dinner. Hotel prices are for two people in a standard double room in high season, including V.A.T., with no meals or, if indicated, CP (with Continental breakfast), BP (Breakfast Plan, with full breakfast), or MAP (Modified American Plan, with breakfast and dinner).

VISITOR INFORMATION
Contacts Somerset Tourism (✉ Somerset County Council, County Hall, Taunton ☎ 01934/750833 ⊕ www.visitsomerset.co.uk). **South West Tourism** (⊕ www.visitsouthwest.co.uk). **VisitCornwall** (✉ Pydar House, Pydar St., Truro ☎ 01872/322900 ⊕ www.visitcornwall.com). **Visit Devon** (⊕ www.visitdevon. co.uk).

BRISTOL TO NORTH DEVON

On the eastern side of this region is the vibrant city of Bristol. From here, you might head south to the pretty cathedral city of Wells and continue on via Glastonbury, possibly the Avalon of Arthurian legend. Proceed west along the Somerset coast into Devon, skirting the moorlands of Exmoor and tracing the northern shore via Clovelly.

BRISTOL

120 mi west of London, 46 mi south of Birmingham, 13 mi northwest of Bath.

The West Country's biggest city (population 420,000), Bristol has in recent years become one of the country's most vibrant centers, with a thriving cultural scene encompassing some of the best contemporary art, theater, and music. Buzzing bars, cafés, and restaurants, and a largely youthful population make it an attractive place to spend time.

Now that the city's industries no longer rely on the docks, the historic harbor along the River Avon has been given over to recreation. Arts and entertainment complexes, museums, and galleries fill the quayside. The pubs and clubs here draw the under-25 set and make the area fairly boisterous (and best avoided) on Friday and Saturday nights.

Bristol also trails a great deal of history in its wake. It can be called the "birthplace of America" with some confidence, for John Cabot and his son Sebastian sailed from the old city docks in 1497 to touch down on the North American mainland, which he claimed for the English crown. The city had been a major center since medieval times, but in the 17th and 18th centuries it became the foremost port for trade with North America. Bristol was the home of William Penn, developer of Pennsylvania, and a haven for John Wesley, whose Methodist movement played an important role in colonial Georgia.

GETTING HERE AND AROUND

Bristol has good connections by bus and train to most cities in the country. From London, calculate about 2½ hours by bus, or 1¾ hours by train. By train, make sure you get tickets for Bristol Temple Meads station (not Bristol Parkway), which is a short bus or taxi ride (or a 20-minute walk) from the center. The bus station is more central, near the Broadmead shopping center. Most sights can be visited on foot, though a bus or a taxi is necessary to reach the Clifton neighborhood.

ESSENTIALS

Visitor Information Bristol (✉ *E Shed, Canon's Rd.* ☎ *0333/321–0101, 870/444–0654 from outside U.K.* ⊕ *www.visitbristol.co.uk*).

EXPLORING

TOP ATTRACTIONS

ℭ **At-Bristol.** In the Harbourside area, this multimedia attraction provides a "hands-on, minds-on" exploration of science and technology in more than 300 interactive exhibits and displays. A planetarium in a gleaming stainless-steel sphere takes you on a 25-minute voyage through the galaxy. There are five to ten shows a day, bookable when you buy your ticket. Allow two to three hours to see it all. ✉ *Anchor Rd.* ☎ *0845/345– 1235* ⊕ *www.at-bristol.org.uk* ✍ *£10.80* ☉ *Weekdays 10–5, weekends, national holiday Mon., and school vacations 10–6.*

The excellent café-restaurant upstairs at **Watershed** (✉ *1 Canon's Rd.* ☎ *0117/927–5100* ⊕ *www.watershed.co.uk*) overlooks part of the harborside. Sandwiches and hot snacks are served during the day, along with coffees and cakes.

★ **Church of St. Mary Redcliffe.** Built by Bristol merchants who wanted a place in which to pray for the safe (and profitable) voyages of their ships, the rib-vaulted, 14th-century church was called "the fairest in England" by Queen Elizabeth I. High up on the nave wall hang the arms and armor of Sir William Penn, father of the founder of Pennsylvania. The church is a five-minute walk from Temple Meads train station toward the docks. ✉ *Redcliffe Way* ☎ *0117/929–1487* ⊕ *www. stmaryredcliffe.co.uk* ✍ *Free* ☉ *Mon.–Sat. 9–5 (until 4 in winter), Sun. 8–7:30.*

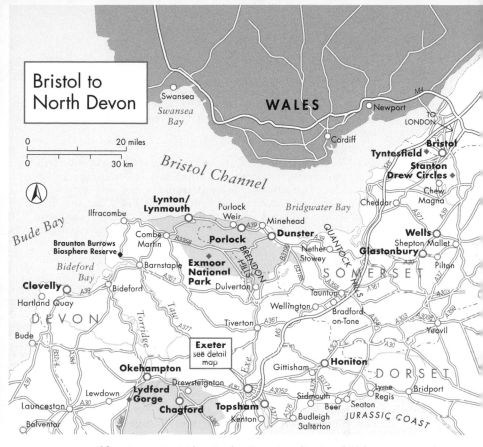

Exeter
see detail
map

Clifton Suspension Bridge. In the Georgian district of Clifton—a sort of Bath in miniature—you can take in a monument to Victorian engineering, the 702-foot-long bridge that spans the Avon Gorge. Work began on Isambard Kingdom Brunel's design in 1831, but the bridge was not completed until 1864. Free hour-long guided tours take place on summer Sundays, departing from the tollbooth at the Clifton end of the bridge. At the far end of the bridge, the **Clifton Suspension Bridge Interpretation Centre** (☎ 0117/974–4664 ⊕ *www.clifton-suspension-bridge.org.uk*) has a small exhibition on the bridge and its construction, including a 10-minute video. At the Bristol end of the bridge lies **Clifton Village**, which is studded with boutiques, antiques shops, and smart crafts shops in its lanes and squares. Bus number 8 from Bristol Temple Meads station stops near the bridge. ✉ *Bridge Rd., Leigh Woods* 🚆 *Free* ☉ *Daily 10–5. Tours Easter–mid-Sept., Sun. 3* PM.

★ **SS *Great Britain*.** On view in the harbor is the first iron ship to cross the Atlantic. Built by the great English engineer Isambard Kingdom Brunel in 1843, it remained in service until 1970, first as a transatlantic liner and ultimately as a coal storage hulk. On board, everything from the galley to the officers' quarters comes complete with sounds and smells of the time. You can descend into the ship's dry dock for a view of the hull and propeller. A replica of the *Matthew,* the tiny craft that carried

John Cabot to North America in 1497, may be moored alongside (when it's not sailing on the high seas). Your ticket admits you to the **Dockyard Museum,** which presents the history of the *Great Britain.* ✉ *Great Western Dockyard, Gas Ferry Rd.* ☎ *0117/926–0680* ⊕ *www.ssgreatbritain.org* 🖼 *£10.95* ☯ *Apr.–Oct., daily 10–5:30; Nov.–Mar., daily 10–4:30; last entry 1 hr before closing.*

WORTH NOTING

Ⓒ **Bristol Zoo Gardens.** Alongside the leafy expanse of Clifton Downs is one of the country's most famous zoos. More than 300 animal species live in 12 acres of gardens; the Seal and Penguin Coasts, with underwater viewing, are rival attractions for Gorilla Island, Bug World, and Twilight World. Take Bus 8 or 9 from the city center, or a train to Clifton Down. ✉ *Clifton Down* ☎ *0117/974–7399* ⊕ *www.bristolzoo.org.uk* 🖼 *£11.81* ☯ *Apr.–Oct., daily 9–5:30; Nov.–Mar., daily 9–5.*

New Room. John Wesley and Charles Wesley were among the Dissenters from the Church of England who found a home in Bristol, and in 1739 they built the New Room, a meeting place that became the first Methodist chapel. Its simplicity contrasts with the style of Anglican churches and with the modern shopping center hemming it in. Upstairs you can visit the Preachers' Rooms, now containing a small museum. ✉ *Broadmead* ☎ *0117/926–4740* ⊕ *www.newroombristol.org.uk* 🖼 *Free* ☯ *Mon.–Sat. and national holidays 10–4.*

▌OFF THE BEATEN PATH

Tyntesfield. The National Trust is gradually restoring this extravagant, 35-bedroom Victorian–Gothic Revival mansion. You can see the house, garden, and chapel at your own pace; entry, by timed ticket, can't be guaranteed on the busiest days. Every ornate detail of this decorative-arts showcase compels attention. Besides magnificent woodwork, stained glass, tiles, and original furniture and fabrics, the house contains the modern conveniences of the 1860s, such as a heated billiards table, and the servants' quarters are equally absorbing. Tyntesfield is 7 mi southwest of Bristol; there is bus service from the city. ✉ *B3128 Wraxall* ☎ *0844/800–4966* ⊕ *www.nationaltrust.org.uk* 🖼 *£10; gardens only, £5* ☯ *House late Mar.–Oct., Sat.–Wed. 11–5; gardens late Mar.–Oct., Sat.–Wed. 10:30–5:30.*

WHERE TO EAT

£££
MEDITERRANEAN

✕ **Bell's Diner.** A local institution, this bistro occupies a former grocery shop and has polished wood floors and pale gray walls lined with shelves. The inventive Mediterranean menu includes locally sourced poultry, rabbit, and seafood, as well as toothsome desserts such as crème brûlée with pear compote and shortbread. In the Montpelier area, Bell's is rather hard to find. To get here, take A38 north, then turn right on Ashley Road and immediately left at Picton Street, which will lead you to York Road. Alternatively, from Broadmead, take any bus heading up Gloucester Road, or board a taxi. ✉ *1 York Rd.* ☎ *0117/924–0357* ⊕ *www.bellsdiner.com* 🖃 *AE, MC, V* ☯ *Closed Sun. No lunch Sat. and Mon.*

£££
MODERN BRITISH

✕ **Bordeaux Quay.** This converted riverside warehouse is the place for modern, sophisticated dining in Bristol. In the more formal upstairs dining room, where a large skylight and harbor views set the scene, you

EATING WELL IN THE WEST COUNTRY

From cider to cream teas, many specialties tempt your palate in the West Country. Lamb, venison, and, in Devon and Cornwall, seafood are favored in restaurants, which have improved markedly, notably through the influence of Rick Stein's seafood-based culinary empire in Padstow, in Cornwall. In many towns the day's catch is unloaded from the harbor and transported directly to eateries. The catch varies by season, but lobster is available year-round, as is crab, stuffed into sandwiches at quayside stalls and in pubs.

Seafood is celebrated at fishy frolics that include the Newlyn Fish Festival (late August) and Falmouth's Oyster Festival (early or mid-October).

COUNTY SPECIALTIES

Somerset is the home of Britain's most famous cheese—the ubiquitous cheddar, originally from the Mendip Hills village of the same name. Make certain that you sample a real farmhouse cheddar, made in the traditional barrel shape known as a truckle.

Devon's caloric cream teas consist of a pot of tea, homemade scones, and lots of strawberry jam and thickened clotted cream (clotted, or specially thickened cream, is a regional specialty and is sometimes called Devonshire cream).

Cornwall's specialty is the pasty, a pastry shell filled with chopped meat, onions, and potatoes. The pasty was devised as a handy way for miners to carry their dinner to work; today's versions are generally pale imitations of the original, though you can still find delicious home-cooked pasties if you're willing to search a little.

WHAT TO DRINK

For liquid refreshment, try scrumpy, a homemade dry cider that is refreshing but carries a surprising kick. Look out, too, for perry, similar to cider but made from pears. English wine, similar to German wine, is made in all three counties (you may see it on local menus), and in Devon and Cornwall you can find a variant of age-old mead made from local honey.

can select from such dishes as roast pheasant breast with spelt risotto and kale, and desserts such as almond meringue parfait with poached Yorkshire rhubarb. Sharing the space downstairs with a delicatessen and bar is a rough-and-ready brasserie where tables are allocated on a first-come, first-served basis—recommended for Sunday brunch. ⊠ *Canon's Way* ☎ *0117/943–1200* ⊕ *www.bordeaux-quay.co.uk* ⊟ *AE, MC, V* ⊗ *Restaurant closed Mon. No lunch in restaurant Sat. No dinner in restaurant or brasserie Sun.*

£ ✕ **Boston Tea Party.** Despite the name, this laid-back and vaguely eccen-
BRITISH tric place is quintessentially English, and ideal for a relaxed lunch away from the nearby rigors of the Park Street shopping scene. Good sandwiches can be taken out or eaten in the terraced backyard or the upstairs sofa salon. Hot dishes like fish pie and generous salads are also available; the restaurant closes at 8 PM daily. The mini-chain has two other branches in Clifton. ⊠ *75 Park St.* ☎ *0117/929–8601* ⊕ *www. bostonteaparty.co.uk* ⊟ *MC, V.*

WHERE TO STAY

For a notable overture to your West Country excursion, you might book a night at Thornbury Castle, 12 mi north of Bristol in Thornbury *(See Berkeley Castle in Chapter 8).*

£　⊡ **Hotel24seven.** A functional stop, this is Bristol's best budget option and also offers self-catering facilities, either in the rooms or in a separate kitchen. Furnishings and decor are basic but modern and well maintained; the rooms—which come in a range of sizes—are well equipped, and a family apartment has its own patio. The hotel lies in the quiet Southville area of south Bristol, a 15-minute walk from the center. You must book online or by telephone before arriving. **Pros:** good value; clean rooms; self-catering. **Cons:** no reception; no breakfast. ⊠ *Dean La. and 15 Acramans Rd., Southville* ☎ *0844/770–9411* ⊕ *www.hotel24seven.com* ↪ *30 rooms* ☖ *In-room: no a/c, no phone, kitchen (some), refrigerator, DVD, Wi-Fi. In-hotel: Wi-Fi hotspot, parking (paid)* ▤ *MC, V.*

£££　⊡ **Hotel du Vin.** This hip chain has an ambitious outlet in the Sugar House—six former sugar-refining warehouses built in 1728 when the River Frome ran outside the front door—close to the docklands and the city center. Rooms are crisply contemporary, with high-tech gadgetry, but retain many original industrial features. The restaurant specializes in modern but robust French fare. **Pros:** tastefully restored old building; great bathrooms; excellent food. **Cons:** traffic-dominated location; some noise on weekends; service can be poor. ⊠ *Narrow Lewins Mead* ☎ *0117/925–5577* ⊕ *www.hotelduvin.com* ↪ *40 rooms* ☖ *In-room: a/c, DVD, Wi-Fi. In-hotel: restaurant, bar, Wi-Fi hotspot, parking (paid)* ▤ *AE, DC, MC, V.*

££　⊡ **Victoria Square Hotel.** In two mellow Victorian buildings overlooking one of Clifton's leafiest squares, this hotel makes an excellent base for exploring Bristol. Rooms are decorated in neutral colors and are well equipped, most with modern bathrooms; Rooms 229 and 247 open directly onto a small walled garden. Some rooms, however, are a bit cramped or are accessed via steep stairs. **Pros:** good advance-booking deals; pleasant location. **Cons:** numerous steps; needs sprucing up; occasional street noise. ⊠ *Victoria Sq., Clifton* ☎ *0843/357–1490* ⊕ *www.victoriasquarehotel. co.uk* ↪ *41 rooms* ☖ *In-room: no a/c, Wi-Fi. In-hotel: restaurant, bar, Wi-Fi hotspot, parking (paid)* ▤ *AE, MC, V* ⍰ *BP.*

NIGHTLIFE AND THE ARTS

The **Arnolfini**, in a prime waterfront position, is one of the country's most prestigious contemporary-art venues, known for uncovering innovative yet accessible art. There's a cinema and a lively bar and bistro. ⊠ *16 Narrow Quay* ☎ *0117/917–2300* ⊕ *www.arnolfini.org.uk* ⍜ *Free* ⊙ *Gallery Tues.–Sun. and national holiday Mon. 11–6.*

St. George's (⊠ *Great George St. off Park St.* ☎ *0845/402–4001*), a church built in the 18th century, now serves as one of the country's leading acoustic venues for classical, jazz, and world music. Stop by for lunchtime concerts. **Watershed** (⊠ *1 Canon's Rd.* ☎ *0117/927–5100*), a contemporary art center by the harbor, also has a movie theater that shows excellent international films.

STANTON DREW CIRCLES

6 mi south of Bristol, 10 mi west of Bath.

GETTING HERE AND AROUND

To get here from Bristol, head south on the A37 and turn right after about 5 mi onto the B3130, marked Stanton Drew. The circles are just east of the village.

EXPLORING

Three rings, two avenues of standing stones, and a burial chamber make up the **Stanton Drew Circles**, one of the grandest and most mysterious monuments in Britain, dating from 3000 to 2000 BC. It's far less well known than Stonehenge and other circles, however. The size of the circles suggests that the site was once as important as Stonehenge for its ceremonial functions, although little of great visual impact remains. ■ TIP→ You have to walk through a farmyard to reach the field where the site lies, so wear sturdy shoes. English Heritage supervises the stones, which stand on private land. Access is given at any reasonable time, and a small admission fee may be requested. ✉ B3130, Stanton Drew ☎ 0117/975-0700 ⊕ www.english-heritage.org.uk.

WELLS

16 mi south of Stanton Drew Circles, 22 mi south of Bristol, 132 mi west of London.

England's smallest cathedral city, with a population of 10,000, lies at the foot of the Mendip Hills. Although set in what feels like a quiet country town, the great cathedral is a masterpiece of Gothic architecture the first to be built in the Early English style. The city's name refers to the underground streams that bubble up into St. Andrew's Well within the grounds of the Bishop's Palace. Spring water has run through High Street since the 15th century. Seventeenth-century buildings surround the ancient marketplace, which hosts market days on Wednesday and Saturday.

GETTING HERE AND AROUND

Regular First buses from Bristol take an hour to reach Wells; the bus station is a few minutes' walk south of the cathedral. Drivers should take A37, and park outside the compact and eminently walkable center.

ESSENTIALS

Visitor Information Wells (✉ *Town Hall, Market Pl.* ☎ *01749/672552* ⊕ *www. wellstourism.com*).

EXPLORING

★ The great west towers of the medieval **Cathedral Church of St. Andrew**, the oldest surviving English Gothic church, can be seen for miles. Dating from the 12th century, the cathedral derives its beauty from the perfect harmony of all of its parts, the glowing colors of its original stained-glass windows, and its peaceful setting among stately trees and majestic lawns. To appreciate the elaborate west front facade, approach the building from the cathedral green, accessible from Market Place through a great medieval gate called "penniless porch" (named after the beggars who once waited here to collect alms from worshippers). The cathedral's west front is twice as wide as it is high, and some 300 statues of kings and saints adorn it. Inside, vast inverted arches—known as scissor arches—were added in 1338 to stop the central tower from sinking to one side. The cathedral also has a rare and beautiful medieval clock, the second-oldest working clock in the world, consisting of the seated figure of a man called Jack Blandifer, who strikes a bell on the quarter hour while mounted knights circle in a joust. Near the clock is the entrance to the Chapter House—a small wooden door opening onto a great sweep of stairs worn down on one side by the tread of pilgrims over the centuries. Free 45-minute guided tours begin at the back of the cathedral. A cloister restaurant serves tea cakes. ⊠ *Cathedral Green* ☎ *01749/674483* ⊕ *www.wellscathedral.org.uk* ⊠ *£5.50 suggested donation* ☉ *Apr.–Sept., daily 7–7; Oct.–Mar., daily 7–6. Tours Apr.– Sept. at 10, 11, 1, 2, and 3; Oct.–Mar. at 11 and 2. No tours Sun.*

QUICK BITES **Goodfellows Patisserie** (⊠ **5 Sadler St.** ☎ **01749/673866** ⊕ **www. goodfellowswells.co.uk**), a little French café near the cathedral, serves exquisite cakes and pastries, chocolate concoctions, and excellent coffee. Soups and sandwiches are also available, and there's a patio. The café offers a meat-based menu Wednesday–Saturday evenings, and a delicatessen and a good seafood restaurant share the premises. It's closed Sunday.

The Bishop's Eye gate leading from Market Place takes you to the magnificent, moat-ringed **Bishop's Palace**, which retains most parts of the original 12th- and 13th-century residence. You can also see the ruins of a late-13th-century great hall. The hall lost its roof in the 16th century because Edward VI needed the lead it contained. ⊠ *Market Pl.* ☎ *01749/677698* ⊕ *www.bishopspalacewells.co.uk* ⊠ *£5* ☉ *Mid-Feb.–Mar., daily 10:30–4:30; Apr.–Oct., daily 10:30–6; last admission 1 hr before closing.*

To the north of the cathedral, the cobbled **Vicar's Close**, one of Europe's oldest streets, has terraces of handsome 14th-century houses with strange, tall chimneys. A tiny medieval chapel here is still in use.

OFF THE BEATEN PATH **Wookey Hole Caves.** Signs in Wells's town center direct you 2 mi north to limestone caves in the Mendip Hills that may have been the home of Iron Age people. Here, according to ancient legend, the Witch of Wookey turned to stone. You can tour the caves, dip your fingers in an underground river (artful lighting keeps things lively), and visit a museum, a working paper mill (that once supplied banknotes for the Confederate States of America), and a penny arcade full of Victorian amusement machines. There's plenty for kids. ⊠ *Wookey Hole* ☎ *01749/672243* ⊕ *www.wookey.co.uk* ⊠ *£16* ☉ *Apr.–Oct., daily 10–6; Nov.–Mar., daily 10–5; last tour 1 hr before closing.*

WHERE TO EAT AND STAY

££££–£££££
MODERN BRITISH
✕ **The Old Spot.** For relaxed but top-notch dining in the heart of Wells, this sociable bistro with wood paneling and creamy white walls hits all the right notes. The Modern British and Mediterranean menu (£27.50 for three courses in the evening) varies seasonally, but might include wood pigeon salad with quince, hazelnuts, artichokes, and bacon for

starters, and a main course of braised shoulder of lamb, tapenade, and peperonata. Arrive early for a table at the back, where there are views of the west front of the cathedral. ⊠ *12 Sadler St.* ☎ *01749/689099* ☰ *AE, MC, V* ☺ *Closed Mon. No lunch Tues. No dinner Sun.*

££ ⑪ **Ancient Gate House.** This venerable hostelry makes a convenient base for exploring the area. The premises, dating to 1473, incorporate the Great West Gate and are full of character. There's an ancient stone staircase, and some rooms have four-posters. Rugantino's serves Italian and English dishes, made largely from local produce. Breakfast may be across the street at the White Hart. **Pros:** richly atmospheric; cathedral views. **Cons:** unsuitable for anyone with mobility problems; cramped rooms; traffic noise in front rooms. ⊠ *20 Sadler St.* ☎ *01749/672029* ⊕ *www.ancientgatehouse.co.uk* ⇱ *9 rooms* ☆ *In-room: no a/c, Wi-Fi. In-hotel: restaurant, bar, Wi-Fi hotspot, some pets allowed* ☰ *AE, MC, V* ¶◎¶ *BP.*

££-£££ ⑪ **Swan Hotel.** A former coaching inn built in the 15th century, the Swan faces the cathedral. Bedrooms, furnished with antiques, are done in subtle, restful colors; some have four-poster beds (including No. 40, which has a to-die-for view of the cathedral), and 15 are in an adjacent converted stable block, the Coach House. Check out the rooms first, as some are better than others. The award-winning restaurant, which is worth booking, prepares traditional English roasts and fish dishes. **Pros:** friendly, professional service; great views from some rooms; good restaurant. **Cons:** some rooms are small; some noise problems; parking lot a bit tricky. ⊠ *11 Sadler St.* ☎ *01749/836300* ⊕ *www.swanhotelwells. co.uk* ⇱ *49 rooms* ☆ *In-room: no a/c, Wi-Fi. In-hotel: restaurant, bar, Wi-Fi hotspot* ☰ *AE, DC, MC, V* ¶◎¶ *BP.*

GLASTONBURY

★ *5 mi southwest of Wells, 27 mi south of Bristol, 27 mi southwest of Bath.*

A town steeped in history, myth, and legend, Glastonbury lies in the lee of Glastonbury Tor, a grassy hill rising 520 feet above the drained marshes known as the Somerset Levels. The Tor is supposedly the site of crossing ley lines (hypothetical alignments of significant places), and, in legend, Glastonbury is identified with Avalon, the paradise into which King Arthur was reborn after his death. Partly because of these associations but also because of its world-class rock-music festival, the town has acquired renown as a New Age center, mixing crystal-gazers with druids, yogis, and hippies, variously in search of Arthur, Merlin, Jesus— and even Elvis. ■ **TIP→ Between April and September, a shuttle bus runs every half hour between all of Glastonbury's major sights, including the abbey, Rural Life Museum, and the base of Glastonbury Tor. Tickets (£2.50) are valid all day.**

GETTING HERE AND AROUND

Frequent buses link Glastonbury to Wells and Bristol, pulling in close to the Abbey. Drivers should take the A39. You can walk to all the sights or take the shuttle bus, though you'll need a stock of energy for ascending the Tor.

ESSENTIALS

Visitor Information Glastonbury (✉ *The Tribunal, 9 High St.* ☎ *01458/832954*
⊕ *www.glastonburytic.co.uk*).

EXPLORING

At the foot of **Glastonbury Tor** is **Chalice Well,** the legendary burial place
of the Grail. It's a stiff climb up the Tor, but your reward is the fabulous
view across the Vale of Avalon. At the top stands a ruined tower, all
that remains of **St. Michael's Church,** which collapsed after a landslide
in 1271. Take the Glastonbury Tor bus to the base of the hill.

The ruins of the great **Glastonbury Abbey,** in the center of town, are on
the site where, according to legend, Joseph of Arimathea built a church
in the 1st century. A monastery had certainly been erected here by the
9th century, and the site drew many pilgrims. The ruins are those of
the abbey completed in 1524 and destroyed in 1539, during Henry
VIII's dissolution of the monasteries. A sign south of the Lady Chapel
marks the sites where Arthur and Guinevere were supposedly buried.
The visitor center has a scale model of the abbey as well as carvings and
decorations salvaged from the ruins. ✉ *Magdalene St.* ☎ *01458/832267*
⊕ *www.glastonburyabbey.com* ⌦ *£5.50* ⊙ *Feb., daily 10–5; Mar., daily
9:30–5:30; Apr., May, and Sept., daily 9:30–6; June–Aug., daily 9–6;
Oct., daily 9:30–5; Nov., daily 9:30–4:30; Dec. and Jan., daily 10–4:30;
last admission 30 mins before closing.*

⟳   The **Somerset Rural Life Museum** occupies a Victorian farmhouse and the
large, 14th-century abbey tithe barn. More than 90 feet in length, the
barn once stored the one-tenth portion of the town's produce that was
owed to the church. Exhibits illustrate 19th-century farming practices,
and there's a cider-apple orchard nearby. Events designed for children
take place most weekends during school holidays. ■**TIP→ For a good
walk, take the scenic footpath from the museum that leads up to the Tor, a
half mile east.** ✉ *Chilkwell St.* ☎ *01458/831197* ⊕ *www.somerset.gov.
uk/museums* ⌦ *Free* ⊙ *Tues.–Sat. and national holiday Mon. 10–5.*

WHERE TO EAT AND STAY

££   ✗ **Who'd a Thought It.** As an antidote to the natural-food cafés of Glas-
BRITISH   tonbury's High Street, try this traditional backstreet inn for some more
down-to-earth food that doesn't compromise on quality. Bar classics
such as grilled gammon (cured ham) steak with eggs and fries appear
alongside more ambitious dishes like lamb with rosemary and red-
currant topping, and roast Gressingham duck on stir-fried vegetables.
The beers are local, and the pub's quirky decor—including ancient
radios, a red telephone box, and a bicycle on the ceiling—has a definite
entertainment quotient. ✉ *17 Northload St.* ☎ *01458/834460* ⊕ *www.
whodathoughtit.co.uk* ☰ *MC, V.*

££   ▥ **George and Pilgrim Hotel.** Pilgrims en route to Glastonbury Abbey
stayed here in the 15th century. Today the stone-front hotel is equipped
with modern comforts but retains its flagstone floors, wooden beams,
and antique furniture. The rooms come in different shapes and sizes,
and the better ones are spacious and furnished with antiques; three
rooms have four-posters. Rooms in the newer part of the building
lack character but are cheaper. **Pros:** historic surroundings; steps from

the abbey. **Cons:** limited parking; pub-with-rooms, not a hotel; some rooms and bathrooms are small. ✉ *1 High St.* ☎ *01458/831146* ⊕ *www. relaxinnz.co.uk* ⌁ *14 rooms* ♿ *In-room: no a/c. In-hotel: restaurant, bar* ▭ *AE, MC, V* ⍾ *BP.*

£ ⚍ **The White House.** You'll receive warm hospitality from the owners of this eco-friendly B&B a few minutes' walk from High Street. With its stripped wooden floors, brass beds, and freestanding Victorian baths, the house blends period character with smart, modern touches. If you take breakfast (it's optional and costs an extra £5 or £7.50 per person, and is served a time of your choosing), you'll be served the best organic and vegetarian ingredients in the comfort of your room.

TALE OF THE GRAIL

According to tradition, Glastonbury was where Joseph of Arimathea brought the Holy Grail, the chalice used by Jesus at the Last Supper. Centuries later, the Grail was said to be the objective of the quests of King Arthur and the Knights of the Round Table. When monks claimed to have found the bones of Arthur and Guinevere at Glastonbury in 1191, the popular association of the town with the mythical Avalon was sealed. Arthur and Guinevere's presumed remains were lost to history after Glastonbury Abbey was plundered for its riches in 1539.

Aromatherapy and reflexology treatments are offered. **Pros:** friendly hosts; flexible breakfasts. **Cons:** one room on the small side; separate bathrooms; not for families. ✉ *21 Manor House Rd.* ☎ *01458/830886* ⊕ *www.theglastonburywhitehouse.com* ⌁ *2 rooms* ♿ *In-room: no a/c, no phone, refrigerator, DVD, Wi-Fi. In-hotel: Wi-Fi hotspot, no kids under 16* ▭ *No credit cards.*

NIGHTLIFE AND THE ARTS

Held annually a few miles away in Pilton, the **Glastonbury Festival** (⊕ *www.glastonburyfestivals.co.uk*) is England's biggest and perhaps best rock festival. For five days over the last weekend in June, it hosts hundreds of bands—established and up-and-coming—on five stages. Tickets are steep—around £195—and sell out months in advance; they include entertainment, a camping area, and service facilities.

DUNSTER

35 mi west of Glastonbury, 43 mi north of Exeter.

Lying between the Somerset coast and the edge of Exmoor National Park, Dunster is a picture-book village with a broad main street. The eight-sided yarn-market building on High Street dates from 1589.

ESSENTIALS

Visitor Information Dunster (✉ *Dunster Steep* ☎ *01643/821835* ⊕ *www. exmoor-nationalpark.gov.uk* ⊗ *Closed Nov.–Easter except some weekends*).

EXPLORING

Dunster Castle, a 13th-century fortress remodeled in 1868, dominates the village from its site on a hill. Parkland and unusual gardens with subtropical plants surround the building, which has fine plaster ceilings, stacks of family portraits (including one by Joshua Reynolds),

17th-century Dutch leather hangings, and a magnificent 17th-century oak staircase. The climb to the castle from the parking lot is steep. ⊠ *Off A39* ☎ *01643/823004* ⊕ *www.nationaltrust.org.uk* 🖅 *£8.10; gardens only, £4.50* ☉ *Castle mid-Mar.–Oct., Fri.–Wed. 11–5. Gardens mid-Mar.–Oct., daily 10–5; Nov.–mid-Mar., daily 11–4.*

EXMOOR NATIONAL PARK

20 mi northwest of Taunton.

GETTING HERE AND AROUND

A car is necessary for getting around the inner reaches of Exmoor, though the coast is relatively well-connected by bus. The 300 bus route traces the coast between Minehead and Lynmouth. The summer-only 400 service—a vintage double-decker bus—also follows the coast between Minehead and Porlock then circles through Exmoor back to Minehead. Both services are open-top in fine weather and are run by Quantock Motor Services.

ESSENTIALS

Bus Contacts Quantock Motor Services (☎ *01823/430202* ⊕ *www. quantockmotorservices.co.uk*).

Visitor Information Combe Martin (⊠ *13 Cross St.* ☎ *01271/883319* ⊕ *www. visitcombemartin.co.uk*). **Dulverton** (⊠ *7–9 Fore St.* ☎ *01398/323841*). **Exmoor National Park Authority** (⊠ *Exmoor House, Dulverton* ☎ *01398/323665* ⊕ *www.exmoor-nationalpark.gov.uk*). **Lynmouth** (⊠ *Lyndale Car Park* ☎ *01598/752509*).

EXPLORING

Less wild and forbidding than Dartmoor to its south, 267-square-mi **Exmoor National Park** is no less majestic for its bare heath and lofty views. The park extends right up to the coast and straddles the county border between Somerset and Devon. Some walks offer spectacular views over the Bristol Channel. Although it is interwoven with cultivated farmland and pasturage, Exmoor can be desolate. Taking one of the more than 700 mi of paths and bridleways through the bracken and heather (at its best in the fall), you might glimpse the ponies and red deer for which the region is noted. ■TIP→ **Be careful: the proximity of the coast means that mists and squalls can descend with alarming suddenness.**

The national park visitor centers at Combe Martin, Dulverton, Dunster, and Lynmouth have information and maps. Guided walks, many of which have themes (archaeology or deer, for example), cost £3 to £5. If you're walking on your own, check

---

SOUTH WEST COAST PATH

Britain's longest national trail, the South West Coast Path, wraps around the coast of the peninsula for 630 mi from Minehead (near Dunster, Somerset) to South Haven Point, near Poole (Dorset). To complete the trail takes 50 to 60 days.

The **South West Coast Path Association** (☎ *01752/896237* ⊕ *www.swcp.org.uk*) has information about the trail. Another Web site, ⊕ *www.southwestcoastpath. com*, suggests short walks.

the weather, take water and a map, and tell someone where you're going. ✉ *Exmoor National Park Authority, Exmoor House, Dulverton* ☎ *01398/323665* ⊕ *www.exmoor-nationalpark.gov.uk.*

PORLOCK

6 mi west of Dunster, 45 mi north of Exeter.

Buried at the bottom of a valley, with the slopes of Exmoor all about, the small, unspoiled town of Porlock lies near "Doone Country," setting for R.D. Blackmore's swashbuckling saga *Lorna Doone*. Porlock had already achieved a place in literary history by the late 1790s, when Samuel Taylor Coleridge declared it was a "man from Porlock" who interrupted his opium trance while the poet was composing "Kubla Khan."

ESSENTIALS

Visitor Information Porlock (✉ *The Old School, High St.* ☎ *01643/863150* ⊕ *www.porlock.co.uk*).

EXPLORING

The 36-mi **Coleridge Way** (⊕ *www.coleridgeway.co.uk*) trail passes through the Quantock and Brendon hills and part of Exmoor, from Nether Stowey (site of Coleridge's home) to Porlock.

The small harbor in the town of **Porlock Weir** is the starting point for an undemanding 2-mi walk along the coast through chestnut and walnut trees to **Culbone church,** reputedly the smallest and most isolated church in England. Saxon in origin, it has a small Victorian spire and is lighted by candles. It would be hard to find a more enchanting spot.

WHERE TO EAT

£££ ✗ **Andrew's on the Weir.** Calling itself a restaurant with rooms, this water-
MODERN BRITISH front Georgian hotel is pure, relaxed, English country house with touches of glamour. The ambitious contemporary restaurant takes advantage of local specialties like Exmoor lamb and Somerset pork. You can expect unusual desserts, such as lemon posset (a mousse-like pudding) with rhubarb jelly and ginger cream, and excellent local cheeses. The five guest rooms (££–£££) have print drapes and patchwork quilts. ✉ *Porlock Weir* ☎ *01643/863300* ⊕ *www.andrewsontheweir.co.uk* ▤ MC, V ⊘ *Closed Mon. and Tues.*

■ EN
ROUTE
As you're heading west from Porlock to Lynton, the coast road A39 mounts **Porlock Hill,** an incline so steep that signs encourage drivers to "keep going." The views across Exmoor and north to the Bristol Channel and Wales are worth it. A less steep but quieter and equally scenic route up the hill on a toll road is accessed from Porlock Weir.

LYNTON AND LYNMOUTH

13 mi west of Porlock, 60 mi northwest of Exeter.

A steep hill separates this pretty pair of Devonshire villages, which are linked by a Victorian cliff railway you can still ride. Lynmouth, a fishing village at the bottom of the hill, crouches below 1,000-foot-high cliffs at the mouths of the East and West Lyn rivers; Lynton is higher up. The poet Percy Bysshe Shelley visited Lynmouth in 1812, in the company of his 16-year-old bride, Harriet Westbrook. During their nine-week sojourn, the poet found time to write his polemical *Queen Mab*. The grand landscape of Exmoor lies all about, with walks to local beauty spots: Watersmeet, the Valley of the Rocks, or Hollerday Hill, where rare feral goats graze.

ESSENTIALS

Visitor Information Lynton (✉ *Lee Rd.* ☎ *0845/660–3232* ⊕ *lynton-lynmouth-tourism.co.uk*).

DONKEYS AT WORK

Donkey stables, donkey rides for kids, and abundant donkey souvenirs in Clovelly recall the days when these animals played an essential role in town life, carrying food, packages, and more up and down the village streets. Even in the 1990s, donkeys helped carry bags from the hotels. Today sledges do the work, but the animals' labor is remembered.

EXPLORING

Water and a cable system power the 862-foot **cliff railway** that connects Lynton with Lynmouth by a ride up a rocky cliff; riders get fine views over the harbor. Inaugurated in 1890, it was the gift of publisher George Newnes, who also donated Lynton's imposing Town Hall, near the top station on Lee Road. ✉ *Lee Rd., Lynton* ☎ *01598/753908* ⊕ *www.cliffrailwaylynton.co.uk* ⌦ *£3 round-trip* ☉ *Mid-Feb.–Mar. and early Oct.–early Nov., daily 10–5; Apr.–mid-June and mid-Sept.–early Oct., daily 10–6; mid-June–late July and early Sept., daily 10–7; late July and Aug., daily 10–9.*

Exmoor Coast Boat Cruises runs boat trips around the dramatic Devon coast from Lynmouth Harbour. A one-hour excursion goes as far as Woody Bay, allowing you to experience the clamorous birdlife on the cliffs. Other cruises include mackerel-fishing trips (£10), between May and August. ☎ *01598/753207* ⌦ *£10* ☉ *Easter–Sept.*

OFF THE BEATEN PATH

Braunton Burrows Biosphere Reserve. Bird-watching and miles of trails through the dunes are the draws at this sanctuary on the north side of the Taw estuary, the core of a UNESCO-designated biosphere reserve. Empty stretches of sand dunes have vistas of marram grass and the sea, and bird-watching is first-class, especially in winter. The flora is most colorful between May and August. Talks are held in the **Countryside Centre** (✉ *Caen parking lot, Braunton* ☎ *01271/817171* ☉ *Apr.–Oct., Mon.–Sat. 10–4*). The reserve is 18 mi southwest of Lynton. ✉ *Off B3231, 2 mi west of Braunton* ⌦ *Free* ☉ *Daily 24 hrs.*

WHERE TO EAT AND STAY

£££

MODERN BRITISH

✗ **Rising Sun.** A 14th-century inn and a row of thatched cottages make up this restaurant and hotel with great views over the Bristol Channel. The kitchen specializes in local cuisine with European influences such as veal schnitzel with warm dill potato salad and roast shellfish with ginger and coriander, and there's a superb game menu December through February. Corridors and creaking staircases lead to cozy guest rooms (£££) decorated in stylish print or solid fabrics. ✉ *Harbourside, Lynmouth* ☎ *01598/753223* ⊕ *www.risingsunlynmouth.co.uk* ▭ *MC, V.*

££–£££   ⛝ **Shelley's Hotel.** Centrally located, this well-maintained hotel has bright
★   and spacious rooms with generous windows and great views. Hearty
breakfasts are served in the conservatory, and the service is genial and
efficient. Poet Percy Bysshe Shelley is said to have stayed here during
his honeymoon—and apparently left without paying the bill (he later
mailed £20 of the £30 owed). **Pros:** excellent harbor views from most
rooms; good breakfasts; hospitable owners. **Cons:** some rooms overlook
car park; no restaurant; Shelley link a little overplayed. ⊠ *8 Watersmeet
Rd., Lynmouth* ☎ *01598/753219* ⊕ *www.shelleyshotel.co.uk* ⥱ *11
rooms* ⸝ *In-room: no a/c, Wi-Fi (some). In-hotel: bar, Wi-Fi hotspot*
▤ *MC, V* ⵙ *BP.*

CLOVELLY

Fodor's Choice   *40 mi southwest of Lynton, 60 mi northwest of Exeter.*
★
Lovely Clovelly always seems to have the sun shining on its flower-
lined cottages and stepped and cobbled streets. Alas, its beauty is well
known, and day-trippers can overrun the village in summer. Perched
precariously among cliffs, a steep, cobbled road—tumbling down at
such an angle that it's closed to cars—leads to the toylike harbor with
its 14th-century quay. The climb back is steep, but, happily, from Easter through October a reasonably priced shuttle service takes you to
and from the parking lot at the top. Allow about two hours (more if
you stop for a drink or a meal) to take in the village. Hobby Drive, a
3-mi cliff-top carriageway laid out in 1829 through thick woods, gives
scintillating views over the village and coast.

EXPLORING

You pay £5.95 to park and use the **Clovelly Visitor Centre** (⊠ *Off A39*
☎ *01237/431781* ⊕ *www.clovelly.co.uk*); this is the only way to enter
the village. The fee includes admission to a fisherman's cottage in the
style of the 1930s and an exhibition about Victorian writer Charles
Kingsley, who lived here as a child. All the buildings in the village
are owned by the Clovelly Estate Company. ■**TIP→ To avoid the worst
crowds, visit before or after school summer vacation. If you must visit in
summer, arrive early or late in the day.**

WHERE TO STAY

£££   ⛝ **Red Lion Hotel.** One of only two hotels in this coastal village, the 18th-
century Red Lion sits right on the harbor. Guest rooms are decorated
with a nautical theme; all have sea or harbor views and modern bathrooms. The climb up through Clovelly is perilously steep, but guests
can bring cars via a back road to and from the hotel. The restaurant
specializes in seafood dishes. **Pros:** superb location; rooms are clean
and comfortable; good service. **Cons:** gets crowded at peak times; any
excursion requires steep ascent. ⊠ *The Quay* ☎ *01237/431237* ⊕ *www.
clovelly.co.uk* ⥱ *11 rooms* ⸝ *In-room: no a/c, Wi-Fi (some). In-hotel:
restaurant, bars, Wi-Fi hotspot* ▤ *AE, MC, V* ⵙ *BP.*

5

CORNWALL

Cornwall stretches west into the sea, with plenty of magnificent coastline to explore, along with tranquil towns and some bustling resorts. One way to discover it all is to travel southwest from Boscastle and the cliff-top ruins of Tintagel Castle, the legendary birthplace of Arthur, along the north Cornish coast to Land's End. This predominantly cliff-lined coast, interspersed with broad expanses of sand, has many tempting places to stop, including Padstow (for a seafood feast), Newquay (a surfing and tourist center), or St. Ives, a delightful artists' colony.

From Land's End, the westernmost tip of Britain, known for its savage land- and seascapes and panoramic views, turn northeast, stopping in the popular seaside resort of Penzance, the harbor city of Falmouth, and a string of fishing villages, including Charlestown and Fowey. The Channel coast is less rugged than the northern coast, with more sheltered beaches. Leave time to visit the excellent Eden Project, with its surrealistic-looking conservatories in an abandoned clay pit, and to explore the boggy, heath-covered expanse of Bodmin Moor.

BOSCASTLE

15 mi north of Bodmin, 30 mi south of Clovelly.

In tranquil Boscastle, some of the stone-and-slate cottages at the foot of the steep valley date from the 1300s. A good place to relax and walk, the town is centered on a little harbor and set snug within towering cliffs. Nearby, 2 mi up the valley of the Valency, is St. Juliot's, the "Endelstow" referred to in Thomas Hardy's *A Pair of Blue Eyes*—the young author was involved with the restoration of this church while he was working as an architect.

ESSENTIALS
Visitor Information Boscastle (⊠ *The Harbour* ☎ *01840/250010* ⊕ *www. visitboscastleandtintagel.com*).

WHERE TO STAY

££ ⊞ **The Old Rectory.** Thomas Hardy stayed here, in what is now a delightful B&B, while restoring St. Juliot's church, and this is where he first met his wife-to-be, Emma, the rector's sister-in-law. The stone house, set in 3 acres of lush grounds about 1½ mi from Boscastle, has been in the same family for five generations. The sensitive renovations are mainly in Victorian style. At the rear of the building, the Old Stable has a wood-burning stove and a separate entrance. Delicious breakfasts usually include organic produce from the kitchen garden, and evening meals can be arranged. **Pros:** secluded setting; romantic ambience; helpful hosts. **Cons:** a little hard to find; far from Boscastle; one-night reservations may not be possible on weekends and in high season. ⊠ *Off B3263, St. Juliot, Boscastle* ☎☎ *01840/250225* ⊕ *www.stjuliot. com* ⊊ *4 rooms* ⌂ *In-room: no a/c, no phone, Wi-Fi. In-hotel: Wi-Fi hotspot, some pets allowed, no kids under 12* ⊟ *MC, V* ☉ *Closed mid-Nov.–mid-Feb.* �ⓘ *BP.*

Fodor'sChoice
★

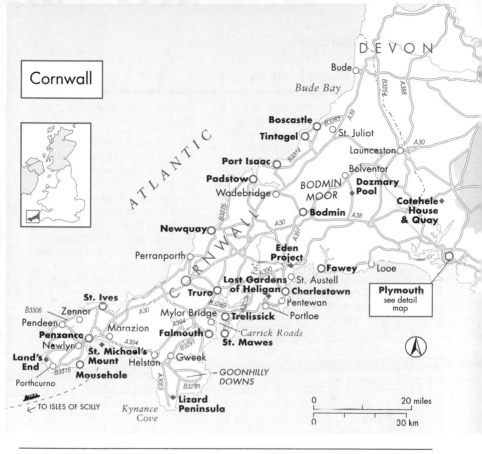

TINTAGEL

3 mi southwest of Boscastle.

The romance of Arthurian legend thrives around Tintagel's ruined castle on the coast. Ever since the somewhat unreliable 12th-century chronicler Geoffrey of Monmouth identified Tintagel as the home of Arthur, son of Uther Pendragon and Ygrayne, devotees of the legend cycle have revered the site. In the 19th century Alfred, Lord Tennyson described Tintagel's Arthurian connection in *The Idylls of the King.* Today the village has its share of tourist junk—including Excaliburgers. Never mind: the headland around Tintagel is splendidly scenic.

ESSENTIALS

Visitor Information Tintagel (✉ *Bossiney Rd.* ☎ *01840/779084* ⊕ *www.visitboscastleandtintagel.com*).

EXPLORING

The **Old Post Office**, a 14th-century stone manor house with yard-thick walls, smoke-blackened beams, and an undulating slate-tile roof, has been restored to its Victorian appearance, when one room served as a post office. ✉ *Fore St.* ☎ *01840/770024* ⊕ *www.nationaltrust.org.uk*

CLOSE UP

All About King Arthur

Legends about King Arthur have resonated through the centuries, enthusiastically taken up by writers and poets from 7th-century Welsh and Breton troubadours to Tennyson and Mark Twain in the 19th century and T.H. White in the 20th century.

WHO WAS ARTHUR?

The historical Arthur was probably a Christian Celtic chieftain battling against the heathen Saxons in the 6th century, although most of the tales surrounding him have a much later setting, thanks to the vivid but somewhat fanciful chronicles of his exploits by medieval scholars.

The virtuous warrior-hero of popular myth has always been treated with generous helpings of nostalgia for a golden age. For Sir Thomas Malory (circa 1408–71), author of *Le Morte d'Arthur*, the finest medieval prose collection of Arthurian romance, Arthur represented a lost era of chivalry and noble romance before the loosening of the traditional bonds of feudal society and the gradual collapse of the medieval social order.

FINDING KING ARTHUR

Places associated with Arthur and his consort, Guinevere, the wizard Merlin, the knights of the Round Table, and the related legends of Tristan and Isolde (or Iseult) can be found all over Europe, but the West Country claims the closest association. Arthur was said to have had his court of Camelot at Cadbury Castle (17 mi south of Wells) and to have been buried at Glastonbury.

Cornwall holds the greatest concentration of Arthurian links, notably his supposed birthplace, Tintagel, and the site of his last battle, on Bodmin Moor. However tenuous the links—and, barring the odd, somewhat ambiguous inscription, there is nothing in the way of hard evidence of Arthur's existence—the Cornish have taken the Once and Future King to their hearts, and his spirit is said to reside in the now-rare bird, the Cornish chough.

£3.20 ⊙ Mid-Mar.–early Apr. and Oct., daily 11–4; early Apr.–late May, daily 10:30–5; late May–Sept., daily 10:30–5:30.

Fodor's Choice Although all that remains of the ruined cliff-top **Tintagel Castle**, legendary
★ birthplace of King Arthur, is the outline of its walls, moats, and towers, it requires only a bit of imagination to conjure up a picture of Sir Lancelot and Sir Galahad riding out in search of the Holy Grail over the narrow causeway above the seething breakers. Archaeological evidence, however, suggests that the castle dates from much later—about 1150, when it was the stronghold of the earls of Cornwall. Long before that, Romans may have occupied the site. The earliest identified remains here are of Celtic (AD 5th century) origin, and these may have some connection with the legendary Arthur. Legends aside, nothing can detract from the castle ruins, dramatically set off by the wild, windswept Cornish coast, on an island joined to the mainland by a narrow isthmus. Paths lead down to the pebble beach and a cavern known as **Merlin's Cave.** Exploring Tintagel Castle involves some arduous climbing on steep steps, but even on a summer's day, when people swarm over the battlements and a westerly Atlantic wind sweeps through Tintagel, you can

FOUR DAYS IN CORNWALL

Here's a trip if you want to see some highlights of Cornwall. Traveling down along the North Devon coast, stop at the harbor village of **Boscastle** before steeping yourself in Arthurian legends at **Tintagel**, ideally taking a coastal walk here. Overnight in ⚅ **Padstow** and dine on excellent seafood (reserve ahead). The next day, head for **St. Ives**, popular with art lovers and beach fans, and push on to the dramatic scenery of the country's westernmost tip, **Land's End**. Stay In ⚅ **Penzance** for your second night; from here you can visit the island castle of **St. Michael's Mount**. Then either follow the coast around to tour the scenic **Lizard Peninsula**, or head straight for Pendennis Castle in **Falmouth**. Across the Carrick Roads estuary basin, explore the Roseland Peninsula, spending your third night in ⚅ **St. Mawes**, which has a fine castle. Start early the next day to visit the **Eden Project**, a must for anyone with even a passing interest in greenery, and then choose between two superb country piles: Victorian Lanhydrock, near **Bodmin**, and **Cotehele House**, a Tudor manor house.

feel the proximity of the distant past. ⊠ *Castle Rd., ½ mi west of village* ☎ *01840/770328* ⊕ *www.english-heritage.org.uk* 🎫 *£5.20* ☉ *Apr.– Sept., daily 10–6; Oct., daily 10–5; Nov.–Mar., daily 10–4.*

PORT ISAAC

6 mi southwest of Tintagel.

A mixture of granite, slate, and whitewashed cottages tumbles precipitously down the cliff to the tiny harbor at Port Isaac, still dedicated to the crab and lobster trade. Low tide reveals a pebbly beach and rock pools. Relatively unscathed by tourists, it makes for a peaceful and secluded stay. For an extra slice of authentic Cornwall life, you can hear the local choir sing shanties at the harborside on Friday nights in summer.

WHERE TO STAY

££–£££   ⚅ **Slipway Hotel.** This 16th-century inn on the harborfront has low ceilings, exposed timbers, and steep staircases that lead to rooms with simple but stylish modern furnishings. Check in at the bar. The split-level restaurant, with oak beams and pillars, serves supremely fresh fish, scallops, and crab dishes. **Pros:** casual atmosphere; great location; tasty restaurant. **Cons:** few facilities; steep staircases; remote parking. ⊠ *Harbourfront* ☎ *01208/880264* ⊕ *www.portisaachotel.com* 🛏 *8 rooms, 2 suites* ⚏ *In-room: no a/c. In-hotel: restaurant, bar, some pets allowed* ▭ *MC, V* ❧ *BP.*

PADSTOW

10 mi southwest of Port Isaac.

A small fishing port at the mouth of the Camel River, Padstow attracts attention and visitors as a center of culinary excellence, largely because of the presence here since 1975 of pioneering seafood chef Rick Stein. Stein's empire includes two restaurants, a café, a fish-and-chips joint, a delicatessen, a patisserie, and a cooking school where classes fill up months in advance.

Even if seafood is not your favorite fare, Padstow is worth visiting. The cries of seagulls fill its lively harbor, a string of fine beaches lies within a short ride—including some choice strands highly prized by surfers—and two scenic walking routes await: the Saints Way across the peninsula to Fowey, and the Camel Trail, a footpath and cycling path that follows the river as far as Bodmin Moor. If you can avoid peak visiting times—summer weekends—so much the better.

GETTING HERE AND AROUND

Regular buses connect Padstow with Bodmin, the main transportation hub hereabouts, and on the main Plymouth–Penzance train line. From Port Isaac, change buses at Wadebridge. There are numerous direct buses on the Newquay–Padstow route. Drivers should take A39/A389 and park in the waterside parking lot before reaching the harbor.

ESSENTIALS

Visitor Information Padstow (⊠ *North Quay* ☎ *01841/533449* ⊕ *www.padstowlive.com*).

WHERE TO EAT AND STAY

££££ ✕ **The Seafood Restaurant.** Rick Stein's flagship restaurant, just across from where the lobster boats and trawlers unload their catches, has built its reputation on the freshest fish and the highest culinary artistry. The exclusively fish and shellfish menu includes everything from bouillabaisse to Indonesian seafood curry. Choose between sitting formally at a table or grabbing a stool at the Seafood Bar in the center of the modern, airy restaurant (no reservations for bar). Don't want to move after your meal? Book one of the sunny, individually designed guest rooms (£££–££££) overlooking the harbor. ⊠ *Riverside* ☎ *01841/532700* ⊕ *www.rickstein.com* ⚲ *Reservations essential* ⊟ *MC, V.*

SEAFOOD

Fodor's Choice

★

£££ ✕ **St. Petroc's Bistro.** Part of chef Rick Stein's empire, this bistro with contemporary art adorning its walls serves French-inspired fare like rib-eye steak with béarnaise sauce and *pommes frites* (french fries). The food is simpler and cheaper than at his other restaurants, and in fine weather you can dine in the sunny walled garden. Also here are spacious bedrooms (£££–££££), which are individually decorated with stylish modern pieces. ⊠ *4 New St.* ☎ *01841/532700* ⊕ *www.rickstein.com* ⊟ *MC, V.*

FRENCH

££££ ▦ **St. Edmund's House.** The most luxurious Rick Stein venture has a sophisticated minimalist style. Excellently equipped, the bedrooms have polished oak floors and glass doors facing the harbor and estuary. Booking here guarantees a dinner table at the Seafood Restaurant, but you should reserve as far ahead as possible. There's a two-night minimum stay on weekends. **Pros:** stylish bedrooms; select ambience. **Cons:** inflated prices; variable service; absent staff. ⊠ *St. Edmund's La.* ☎ *01841/532700* ⊕ *www.rickstein.com* ⇱ *6 rooms* ⚙ *In-room: refrigerator, DVD, Wi-Fi. In-hotel: Internet, Wi-Fi hotspot* ⊟ *MC, V* ⟟⊙⟨ *BP.*

SPORTS AND THE OUTDOORS

BIKING Bikes of all shapes and sizes can be rented at **Trail Bike Hire** (⊠ *South Quay* ☎ *01841/532594* ⊕ *www.trailbikehire.co.uk*), at the start of the Camel Trail.

SURFING **Harlyn Surf School** (⊠ *23 Grenville Rd.* ☎ *01841/533076*) can arrange two-hour to four-day surfing courses.

WALKING The **Saints Way**, a 30-mi inland path between Padstow and the Camel Estuary on Cornwall's north coast to Fowey on the south coast, follows a Bronze Age trading route, later used by Celtic pilgrims to cross the peninsula. Several relics of such times can be seen along the way. Contact the tourist offices in Padstow or Fowey or VisitCornwall for information.

NEWQUAY

14 mi southwest of Padstow, 30 mi southwest of Tintagel.

The biggest, most developed resort on the north Cornwall coast is a fairly large town established in 1439. It was once the center of the trade in pilchards (a small herringlike fish), and on the headland you can still see a white hut where a lookout known as a "huer" watched for pilchard schools and directed the boats to the fishing grounds. Newquay has become Britain's surfing capital, and in summer young California-dreamin' devotees can pack the wide, cliff-backed beaches.

ESSENTIALS

Visitor Information Newquay (⊠ *Marcus Hill* ☎ *01637/854020* ⊕ *www.visitnewquay.org*).

WHERE TO EAT

£££££ ✕ **Fifteen Cornwall**. One of Britain's culinary heroes, Cockney chef Jamie

BRITISH Oliver has led campaigns to encourage healthful eating in schools and

★ to provide training in the catering arts to young people. This restaurant, part of the latter project, has won plaudits for execution, not just for its worthy intentions. To provide staff with the widest possible repertoire, the daily-changing sampling menu (£55) lists six courses that might include tortellini with duck and radicchio with chestnuts and balsamic butter sauce for a starter, followed by seared scallops, and baked yogurt cheesecake to finish. A fixed-price lunch is a cheaper option at £26. The dining area is modern and bright, with views over magnificent Watergate Bay—a broad beach much beloved of water-sports enthusiasts. Watergate Bay lies 3 mi east of Newquay. ⊠ *Watergate Bay* ☎ *01637/861000* ⊕ *www.fifteencornwall.co.uk* ▤ *AE, MC, V.*

ST. IVES

25 mi southwest of Newquay, 10 mi north of Penzance.

James McNeill Whistler came here to paint his landscapes, Barbara Hepworth to fashion her modernist sculptures, and Virginia Woolf to write her novels. Today sand, sun, and superb art continue to attract thousands of vacationers to the fishing village of St. Ives, named after Saint Ia, a 5th-century female Irish missionary said to have arrived on a

BEACH BASICS

The beaches lining parts of the peninsula have made the West Country one of England's main family vacation destinations. Even natives have to steel themselves for the water's chilly temperature, though, and foreigners, especially those pampered by the warm waves of the Mediterranean, are understandably reluctant to brave the elements. Fortunately, wet suits are available at most resorts, making the experience more pleasurable.

At most resorts, red-and-yellow flags show the limits of safe swimming. If you see a blue flag, you can be confident that the beach and sea are unpolluted. The Blue Flag plan, which rewards cleanliness, water quality, easy access, and facilities, is run by the Foundation for Environmental Education and is used across Europe, the Caribbean, South Africa, and parts of North America. This region of England has the biggest concentration of winners—20 beaches in 2009. There can be strong undertows, and beware of fast-moving tides.

The northern coast of the peninsula has the region's best surfing beaches, and Cornwall, especially Newquay, is the center of a thriving surfing industry. Go ahead and give it a try: it's easy to rent equipment, and plenty of places offer lessons.

floating leaf. The town has long played host to a well-established artists' colony, and there are plenty of craftspeople, too. ■TIP→ **Day-trippers often crowd St. Ives, so it's best to park away from the center.**

GETTING HERE AND AROUND
St. Ives has good bus and train connections with Bristol, Exeter, and Penzance. Train journeys usually involve a change at St. Erth (the brief St. Erth–St. Ives stretch is one of the West Country's most scenic train routes). The adjacent bus and train stations are within a few minutes' walk of the center. Drivers should avoid the center—parking lots are well marked in the higher parts of town.

ESSENTIALS
Visitor Information St. Ives (⊠ *The Guildhall, Street-an-Pol* ☎ *01736/796297* ⊕ *www.visit-westcornwall.com*).

EXPLORING
The studio and garden of Dame Barbara Hepworth (1903–75), who pioneered abstract sculpture in England, are now the **Barbara Hepworth Museum and Sculpture Garden**. London's prominent Tate gallery runs the museum. The artist lived here for 26 years. ⊠ *Trewyn Studio, Barnoon Hill* ☎ *01736/796226* ⊕ *www.tate.org.uk* 🖾 *£4.75, combined ticket with Tate St. Ives £8.75* ⊘ *Mar.–Oct., daily 10–5:20; Nov.–Feb., Tues.–Sun. 10–4:20.*

★ The spectacular **Tate St. Ives** displays the work of artists who lived and worked in St. Ives, mostly from 1925 to 1975, and has selections from the rich collection of the Tate in London. It occupies a modernist building—a fantasia of seaside deco-period architecture with a panoramic view of rippling ocean. The rooftop café is excellent, for the food and views. ⊠ *Porthmeor Beach* ☎ *01736/796226* ⊕ *www.tate.org.*

uk ✉ *£5.75, combined ticket with Barbara Hepworth Museum and Sculpture Garden £8.75* ⊗ *Mar.–Oct., daily 10–5:20; Nov.–Feb., Tues.–Sun. 10–4:20.*

QUICK BITES

One of Cornwall's oldest pubs (built in 1312), the harbor-front **Sloop Inn** (✉ *The Wharf* ☎ *01736/796584*) serves simple lunches as well as evening meals in wood-beam rooms that display the work of local artists. If the weather's good, you can eat at the tables outside.

At the **St. Ives Society of Artists Gallery,** local artists display selections of their current work for sale in the former Old Mariners' Church. The Mariners Gallery in the crypt is also used for private exhibitions. ✉ *Norway Sq.* ☎ *01736/795582* ⊕ *www.stisa.co.uk* ⊗ *Mar.–Easter and mid-Oct.–early Jan., Mon.–Sat. and national holidays 10:30–5:30; Easter–mid Oct., Mon.–Sat. 10:30–5:30, Sun. 2:30–5:30.*

The winding B3306 coastal road southwest from St. Ives passes through some of Cornwall's starkest yet most beautiful countryside. Barren hills crisscrossed by low stone walls drop abruptly to granite cliffs and wide bays. Evidence of the ancient tin-mining industry is everywhere. Now a fascinating mining heritage center, the early-20th-century **Geevor Tin Mine** employed 400 men, but in 1985 the collapse of the world tin market wiped Cornwall from the mining map. Wear sturdy footwear for the surface and underground tours. A museum, shop, and café are on the site. ✉ *B3306, Pendeen* ☎ *01736/788662* ⊕ *www.geevor.com* ✉ *£9.50* ⊗ *Mar.–Oct., Sun.–Fri. 9–5; Nov.–Feb., Sun.–Fri. 9–4; last admission 1 hr before closing.*

WHERE TO EAT

££££–£££££
MODERN BRITISH

✕ **Garrack Restaurant.** This family-run restaurant is known for the panoramic sea views from its hilltop location and for relaxed and undemanding fine dining. The set-price menus (£23 and £26.50) specialize in local fish and seafood, including steamed local mussels, as well as Cornish beef. Breads are made in-house, and the wine list features some Cornish vineyards. Some rooms (£££–££££) at the attached hotel are furnished in traditional style; others are more modern. ✉ *Burthallan La.* ☎ *01736/796199* ⊕ *www.garrack.com* ▭ *AE, DC, MC, V* ⊗ *No lunch Mon.–Sat.*

££
SEAFOOD

✕ **Gurnard's Head.** It's really in the middle of nowhere: this gastro-pub with bright, homey furnishings and a relaxed ambience sits near the coast road 8 curvy mi west of St. Ives, looking out over green fields and the Atlantic beyond. The daily-changing menu features fresh, inventively prepared seafood, and might include pilchards with pickled beets and horseradish ice cream, and the signature Gurnard's fish stew. A great way to arrive is to walk from St. Ives, a tough but exhilarating cliff-top walk along the coast path; it's also on a bus route. Seven smallish rooms provide guest accommodation (££–£££). ✉ *B3306, Treen, near Zennor* ☎ *01736/796928* ⊕ *www.gurnardshead.co.uk* ▭ *MC, V.*

5

£££
MODERN BRITISH
✗**Porthminster Café.** Unbeatable for its location alone—on the broad, golden sands of Porthminster Beach—this sleek, modern eatery prepares imaginative lunches, teas, and evening meals you can savor while you take in the marvelous vista across the bay. Typical choices are white crab risotto, monkfish curry, and plaice fillets. The sister Porthgwidden Beach Café, in the Downalong area of town, has a smaller and cheaper but equally varied menu. ⊠ *Porthminster Beach* ☎ *01736/795352* ⊕ *www. porthminstercafe.co.uk* ⬥ *Reservations essential* ⊟ *MC, V* ⊘ *Closed Mon. Nov.–Easter. No dinner Sun.–Thurs. Nov.–Easter.*

WHERE TO STAY

££
⊡**Cornerways.** Everything in St. Ives seems squeezed into the tiniest of spaces, and this cottage B&B in the quiet Downalong quarter is no exception. The light, tastefully converted rooms are pleasingly simple in design and enlivened by modern art; the more expensive have sea views. Most rooms are named after characters in Daphne du Maurier's novels (she once stayed in one of them). Fresh local fish is offered at breakfast, and guests can use complimentary tickets to visit the Tate, which is just minutes away. **Pros:** friendly owner; stylish decor; tasty breakfasts. **Cons:** rooms are small; narrow stairways to climb; very limited parking. ⊠ *1 Bethesda Pl.* ☎ *01736/796706* ⊕ *www.cornerwaysstives.com* ⬥ *6 rooms* ⚭ *In-room: no a/c, no phone, Wi-Fi. In-hotel: Wi-Fi hotspot, parking (free)* ⊟ *No credit cards* ⦿ *BP.*

£££
★
⊡**Primrose Valley Hotel.** Blending the elegance of an Edwardian villa with clean-lined modern style, this family-friendly hotel has the best of both worlds. Guest rooms are bright and contemporary, and the spacious common areas include a large lounge that opens onto the veranda. An easygoing management and a great location a few steps up from Porthminster Beach are other pluses. Freshly prepared "platters" of cold meats, seafood, and Cornish cheeses are available all day from the bar. There's an extra charge for sea-facing rooms with balconies, and minimums of three- or four-day stays are required in July and August, respectively. **Pros:** close to beach and train and bus stations; friendly atmosphere; attention to detail. **Cons:** difficult to find; some rooms lack views. ⊠ *Porthminster Beach* ☎ *01736/794939* ⊕ *www. primroseonline.co.uk* ⬥ *9 rooms, 1 suite* ⚭ *In-room: no a/c, no phone, Wi-Fi. In-hotel: bar, Wi-Fi hotspot, parking (free), no kids under 8* ⊟ *MC, V* ⦿ *BP.*

LAND'S END

17 mi southwest of St. Ives, 9 mi southwest of Penzance.

The coastal road, B3306, ends at the western tip of Britain at what is, quite literally, Land's End.

GETTING HERE AND AROUND
Frequent buses serve Land's End from St. Ives (taking around one hour, 40 minutes) and Penzance (around 50 minutes). In summer, an open-top double-decker tracks the coast between St. Ives and Penzance, taking in Land's End en route.

EXPLORING

★ The sea crashes against the rocks at **Land's End** and lashes ships battling their way around the point. ■**TIP**➔ **Approach from one of the coastal footpaths for the best panoramic view.** Over the years, sightseers have caused some erosion of the paths, but new ones are constantly being built, and Cornish "hedges" (granite walls covered with turf) have been planted to prevent erosion. The scenic grandeur of Land's End remains undiminished. The Land's End Hotel here is undistinguished, though the restaurant has good views.

A low-key theme park, **Land's End Experience** (☎ 0871/720–0044 ⊕ www.landsend-landmark.co.uk), runs a poor second to nature.

MOUSEHOLE

★ *7 mi east of Land's End, 3 mi south of Penzance.*

On B3315 between Land's End and Penzance, Mousehole (pronounced *mow*-zel, the first syllable rhyming with "cow") merits a stop—and plenty of people do stop—to see this archetypal Cornish fishing village of tiny stone cottages. It was the home of Dolly Pentreath, supposedly the last person to speak solely in Cornish, who died in 1777.

WHERE TO EAT

££–£££ ✕ **2 Fore Street.** Within view of Mousehole's tiny harbor, you can dine
MODERN BRITISH on the freshest seafood in this popular bistro. The seasonal, Mediterranean-inspired menu takes in everything from crab Florentine and lobster to wild sea bass in fennel and fish stew. Meat eaters are also well catered to. The bright, white-walled dining room has a maritime flavor, and there are tables in the sheltered back garden. ✉ *2 Fore St.* ☎ *01736/731164* ⊕ *www.2forestreet.co.uk* ⟁ *Reservations essential* ▭ *AE, MC, V* ☒ *Closed Jan.–mid-Feb.*

■ EN
ROUTE
About 2 mi north of Mousehole on B3315, **Newlyn** has long been Cornwall's most important fishing port. The annual Fish Festival takes over the town for a weekend at the end of August. Newlyn became the magnet for artists at the end of the 19th century, and today has a good gallery of contemporary works, but only a few of the fishermen's cottages that first attracted artists to the area remain.

PENZANCE

1½ mi north of Newlyn, 10 mi south of St. Ives.

Superb views over Mount's Bay are one lure of this popular, unpretentious seaside resort. Even though it does get very crowded in summer, Penzance makes a good base for exploring the area. The town's isolated position has always made it vulnerable to attack from the sea. During the 16th century, Spanish raiders destroyed most of the original town, and the majority of old buildings date from as late as the 18th century. The main street is Market Jew Street, a folk mistranslation of the Cornish expression Marghas Yow, which means "Thursday Market." Where Market Jew Street meets Causeway Head is Market House, constructed in 1837, an impressive, domed granite building that now serves as a bank.

In contrast to arty St. Ives, Penzance is a no-nonsense working town. Though lacking the traffic-free lanes and quaint cottages of St. Ives, Penzance preserves pockets of handsome Georgian architecture.

GETTING HERE AND AROUND
The main train line from Plymouth terminates at Penzance, which is also served by National Express buses. Bus and train stations are next to each other at the east end of town. A car is an encumbrance here, so use one of the parking lots near the tourist office and the bus and train stations.

ESSENTIALS
Visitor Information Penzance (⊠ *Station Approach* ☎ *01736/362207* ⊕ *www. visit-westcornwall.com*).

EXPLORING
The former main street and one of the prettiest thoroughfares in Penzance, **Chapel Street** winds down from Market House to the harbor. Its predominantly Georgian and Regency houses suddenly give way to the extraordinary **Egyptian House**, whose facade recalls the Middle East. Built around 1830 as a geological museum, today it houses vacation apartments. Across Chapel Street is the 17th-century **Union Hotel**, where in 1805 the death of Lord Nelson and the victory of Trafalgar were first announced. Near the Union Hotel on Chapel Street is the **Turk's Head**, an inn said to date from the 13th century.

The small collection at the **Penlee House Gallery and Museum**, in a gracious Victorian house in Penlee Park, focuses on paintings by members of the so-called Newlyn School from about 1880 to 1930. These works evoke the life of the inhabitants of Newlyn, mostly fisherfolk. The museum also covers 5,000 years of West Cornwall history through archaeology, decorative arts, costume, and photography exhibits. ⊠ *Morrab Rd.* ☎ *01736/363625* ⊕ *www.penleehouse.org.uk* ⊠ *£3, Sat. free* ☉ *Easter–Sept., Mon.–Sat. 10–5; Oct.–Easter, Mon.–Sat. 10:30–4:30; last admission 30 mins before closing.*

★ Rising out of Mount's Bay just off the coast, the spectacular granite-and-slate island of **St. Michael's Mount** is one of Cornwall's greatest natural attractions. The 14th-century castle perched at the highest point—200 feet above the sea—was built on the site of a Benedictine chapel founded by Edward the Confessor. In its time, the island has served as a church (Brittany's island abbey of Mont St. Michel was an inspiration), a fortress, and a private residence. The castle rooms you can tour include the Chevy Chase Room—a name probably associated with the Cheviot Hills or the French word *chevaux* (horses), after the hunting frieze that decorates the walls of this former monks' refectory. Don't miss the wonderful views from the battlements. Around the base of the rock are buildings from medieval to Victorian, but they appear harmonious. Fascinating gardens surround the Mount, and many kinds of plants flourish in its microclimate. To get to the island, walk the cobbled causeway from the village of Marazion or, when the tide is in during the summer, take the ferry. There are pubs and restaurants in the village, but the island also has a café and restaurant. ■TIP→ **Wear stout shoes for your visit to this site, which requires a steep climb.** Visits may be canceled in severe weather. ⊠ *A394, 3 mi east of Penzance, Marazion* 🕾 *01736/710507* ⊕ *www.stmichaelsmount.co.uk* ⌨ *Castle £7, garden £3.50, castle and garden £8.75, £1.50 for ferry each way* ☉ *Castle Apr.–June, Sept., and Oct., Sun.–Fri. 10:30–5; July and Aug., Sun.–Fri. 10:30–5:30; Nov.–Mar., tours Tues. and Fri. 11 and 2, call to check. Garden May and June, weekdays 10:30–5; July–Oct., Thurs. and Fri. 10:30–5; last admission 4:15.*

<table>
<tr><td>

**OFF THE
BEATEN
PATH**

</td><td>

Isles of Scilly. Fondly regarded in folklore as the lost land of Lyonesse, this compact group of more than 100 islands 30 mi southwest of Land's End is equally famed for the warm summer climate and ferocious winter storms. In fair weather you can find peace, flowers—wild, cultivated, and subtropical—swarms of seabirds, and unspoiled beaches galore. If you have time, take the 2½-hour ferry service from Penzance; otherwise, there's plane and helicopter service. These all arrive at the largest of the five inhabited islands, St. Mary's, which has the bulk of the lodgings, though the most palatial retreats are on the islands of Tresco and St Martin's.

</td></tr>
</table>

WHERE TO EAT

££

BRITISH

★

✕ Admiral Benbow. One of the town's most famous inns, the 17th-century Admiral Benbow was once a smugglers' pub—look for the figure of a smuggler on the roof. Seafaring memorabilia, a brass cannon, model ships, and figureheads fill the place. In the family-friendly restaurant area, decorated to resemble a ship's galley, you can dine on seafood or a steak-and-ale pie. ⊠ *46 Chapel St.* 🕾 *01736/363448* ⊟ *MC, V.*

£££

SEAFOOD

✕ Harris's. Seafood is the main event in the two small, boldly colored rooms of this restaurant off Market Jew Street. The menu showcases whatever the boats bring: crab Florentine, grilled on a bed of spinach with a cheese sauce, is usually available. Meat dishes might include guinea fowl stuffed with Cornish Brie or medallions of venison. The semiformal style is intimate, elegant, and traditional. ⊠ *46 New St.* 🕾 *01736/364408* ⊕ *www.harrissrestaurant.co.uk* ⊟ *MC, V* ☉ *Closed Sun. Closed Mon. Nov.–June and 4 wks Nov.–Mar.*

WHERE TO STAY

£££–££££

★

Abbey Hotel. Co-owned by former 1960s model-icon Jean Shrimpton, this Wedgwood-blue-color hotel off Chapel Street is marvelously homey. Books fill the 17th-century drawing room, and antiques and chintzes decorate many of the rooms, most of which have harbor views. If you need more space, there's also a pair of comfortable apartments. **Pros:** full of character; inspiring views; solicitous staff. **Cons:** some rooms slightly cramped; limited parking. ⊠ *Abbey St.* 🕾 *01736/366906* ⊕ *www.theabbeyonline.co.uk* ⌨ *6 rooms, 2 apartments* ⅙ *In-room: no a/c. In-hotel: Wi-Fi hotspot, parking (free), some pets allowed* ⊟ *AE, MC, V* ☉ *Closed late Dec.–mid-Feb.* ⦿*BP.*

££

Camilla House. This flower-bedecked Georgian house stands on a road parallel to the promenade, close to the harbor. Guest rooms are cheerfully decorated; those at the front have sea views. The owners are great sources of local information and loan out bicycles for touring West Cornwall. Evening meals are available on request. There's usually a three-night minimum stay from April to October. **Pros:** friendly management; quiet location near seafront; great breakfasts. **Cons:** some rooms are small; far from bus and train stations. ⊠ *12 Regent Terr.* 🕾 *01736/363771* ⊕ *www.camillahouse-hotel.co.uk* ⇥ *8 rooms* ⟨ *In-room: no a/c, no phone, DVD, Wi-Fi. In-hotel: restaurant, bar, bicycles, Internet terminal, Wi-Fi hotspot* ⊟ *AE, MC, V* ¹⊘¹ *BP.*

£   🖭 **Union Hotel.** Strong on historical and nautical details, this central lodging housed the town's assembly rooms, where news of Admiral Nelson's victory at Trafalgar and of the death of Nelson himself were first announced from the minstrels' gallery in 1805. The bar, lounge, and dining rooms retain their Georgian elegance. The guest rooms, in traditional style, could use updating; some have tired-looking carpets and old-fashioned prints. A number have window seats, with views over Mount's Bay. Breakfast is served in the restored assembly rooms. **Pros:** historic character; spacious rooms; good value for the money. **Cons:** feels dowdy; sparse staff; no elevator. ⊠ *Chapel St.* 🕾🖳 *01736/362319* ⊕ *www.unionhotel.co.uk* ⇥ *28 rooms* ⟨ *In-room: no a/c, no phone. In-hotel: restaurant, bars, Wi-Fi hotspot, parking (free)* ⊟ *MC, V* ¹⊘¹ *BP.*

NIGHTLIFE AND THE ARTS

★   The open-air **Minack Theatre** perches high above a beach 3 mi southeast of Land's End and about 6 mi southwest of Penzance. The slope of the cliff forms a natural amphitheater, with bench seats on the terraces and the sea as a magnificent backdrop. Different companies present plays from classic dramas to modern comedies afternoons and evenings in summer. An exhibition center tells the story of the theater's creation. ⊠ *Off B3315, Porthcurno* 🕾 *01736/810181* ⛴ *Exhibition center £3, performances £8–£9.50* ⊘ *Apr.–Oct., daily 9:30–5:30; Nov.–Mar., daily 10–4. Exhibition center closed during matinees, usually May–Sept., Wed. and Fri. noon–5:30.*

SPORTS AND THE OUTDOORS

Many ships have foundered on Cornwall's rocky coastline, resulting in an estimated 3,600 shipwrecks. The area around Land's End has some of the best diving in Europe, in part because the convergence of the Atlantic and the Gulf Stream here results in impressive visibility and unusual subtropical marine life. **Silver Dolphin** (⊠ *Trinity House, Wharf Rd., Penzance* 🕾 *01736/364860*) offers courses and guided dives for beginners and experts.

LIZARD PENINSULA

★   *23 mi southwest of Penzance.*

The southernmost point on mainland Britain, this peninsula is a government-designated Area of Outstanding Natural Beauty, named so for the rocky, dramatic coast rather than the flat and boring interior. The huge, eerily rotating dish antennae of the Goonhilly Satellite Communications Earth Station are visible from the road as it crosses Goonhilly Downs, the backbone of the peninsula. There's no coast road, unlike Land's End, so get out and explore on foot. The beaches are good. With no large town (Helston at the northern end is the biggest, and is not a tourist center), it's far less busy than the Land's End peninsula.

EXPLORING

A path close to the tip of the peninsula plunges down 200-foot cliffs to the tiny **Kynance Cove**, with its handful of pint-size islands. The sands here are reachable only during the 2½ hours before and after low tide. The peninsula's cliffs are made of greenish serpentine rock, interspersed with granite; souvenirs of the area are carved out of the stone.

FALMOUTH

8 mi northeast of Lizard Peninsula, 7 mi northeast of Gweek, 12 mi south of Truro.

The bustle of this resort town's fishing harbor, yachting center, and commercial port only adds to its charm. In the 18th century Falmouth was the main mail-boat port for North America, and in Flushing, a village across the inlet, you can see the slate-covered houses built by prosperous mail-boat captains. A ferry service now links the two towns. On Custom House Quay, off Arwenack Street, is the King's Pipe, an oven in which seized contraband was burned.

GETTING HERE AND AROUND

Falmouth can be reached from Truro on a branch rail line or on frequent buses, and it is also served by local and National Express buses from other centers. Running parallel to the seafront, the long, partly pedestrianized main drag links the town's main sights. Visitors to Pendennis Castle traveling by train should use Falmouth Docks station, from which it's a short walk. Alternatively, drive or take a local bus to the castle to save legwork.

ESSENTIALS

Visitor Information Falmouth (⊠ *11 Market Strand, Prince of Wales Pier* ☎ *01326/312300* ⊕ *www.discoverfalmouth.co.uk*).

EXPLORING

The granite and oak-clad **National Maritime Museum Cornwall** by the harbor is an excellent place to come to grips with Cornish maritime heritage, weather lore, and navigational science. You can view the collection of 140 or so boats, examine the tools associated with Cornish boatbuilders, and study the prospect across to Flushing from the lighthouse-like Look-out, which is equipped with maps, telescopes, and binoculars. In the glass-fronted Tidal Zone below sea level, you come face-to-face with the sea itself. ⊠ *Discovery Quay* ☎ *01326/313388* ⊕ *www.nmmc. co.uk* ⊠ *£9.50* ☉ *Daily 10–5.*

At the end of its own peninsula stands the formidable **Pendennis Castle**, built by Henry VIII in the 1540s and improved by his daughter Elizabeth I. You can explore the defenses developed over the centuries. In the Royal Artillery Barracks, the Key to Cornwall exhibit explores the castle's history and its connection to Cornwall and England. The castle has sweeping views over the English Channel and across to St. Mawes Castle, designed as a companion fortress to guard the roads. Call about events such as concerts, plays, jousting, and shows for kids. ⊠ *Pendennis Head* ☎ *01326/316594* ⊕ *www.english-heritage.org.uk*

🖬 *£6* ⊙ *Apr.–June and Sept., Sun.–Fri. 10–5, Sat. 10–4; July and Aug., Sun.–Fri. 10–6, Sat. 10–4; Oct.–Mar., daily 10–4.*

WHERE TO EAT AND STAY

££   ✕ **Gylly Beach Café.** For views and location, this beachside eatery with
SEAFOOD   a crisp, modern interior and deck seating cannot be beat. By day, it's a
breezy café and lunch spot for burgers, salads, and sandwiches, while
the fishy menu comes to the fore in the evening, featuring such items
as steamed mussels, grilled lemon sole, and mackerel fillets. There are
barbecues in summer, and live-music evenings. ⊠ *Cliff Rd., Gyllyngvase
Beach* ☎ *01326/312884* ⊕ *www.gyllybeach.com* ▭ *MC, V* ⊙ *No dinner Mon.–Wed.*

££   ✕ **Pandora Inn.** This thatched pub on a creek 4 mi north of Falmouth is a
SEAFOOD   great retreat, with both a patio and a moored pontoon for summer dining. Maritime memorabilia and fresh flowers provide decoration, and
you can eat in the bar, in the formal Upper Deck room upstairs, or outside. The menu highlight is fresh seafood—try the grilled sea bream—
though there's a good selection of game in winter. ⊠ *Restronguet Creek,
Mylor Bridge* ☎ *01326/372678* ⊕ *www.pandorainn.co.uk* ▭ *MC, V.*

£££   ✕ **Seafood Bar.** Head down an alley off the quay to get to this basement
SEAFOOD   bistro. Beyond the door is some of the best local seafood, with such
choices as thick crab soup, Helford River oysters, or scallops from Falmouth Bay. ⊠ *Quay St.* ☎ *01326/315129* ▭ *MC, V* ⊙ *Sept.–July, closed
Sun. and Mon. except national holiday weekends. No lunch.*

££££   🛏 **St. Michael's Hotel.** Colorful subtropical gardens front this seaside hotel
overlooking Falmouth Bay. The public areas and spacious guest rooms
are sleek and contemporary, and the young staff welcomes families. The
Flying Fish restaurant is worth sampling, and the treatments in the spa's
four rooms are state-of-the-art. **Pros:** excellent facilities; enthusiastic and
amiable staff. **Cons:** some rooms are small; poor soundproofing; uneven
service. ⊠ *Stracey Rd.* ☎ *01326/312707* ⊕ *www.stmichaelshotel.co.uk*
🛏 *57 rooms, 4 suites* ⚭ *In-room: a/c (some), Wi-Fi (some). In-hotel:
restaurant, bar, pool, gym, spa, Internet terminal, Wi-Fi hotspot* ▭ *AE,
MC, V* ¶◎¶ *BP.*

TRELISSICK

6 mi northeast of Falmouth.

Trelissick has a ferry terminal as well as colorful Trelissick Garden,
owned by the National Trust.

EXPLORING

The **King Harry Ferry** (☎ *01872/862312* ⊕ *www.kingharryscornwall.
co.uk*), a chain-drawn car ferry, runs to the scenically splendid Roseland
Peninsula three times hourly every day. From its decks you can see up
and down the Fal, a deep, narrow river with steep, wooded banks. The
river's great depth provides mooring for old ships waiting to be sold;
these mammoth shapes lend a surreal touch to the riverscape. On very
rare occasions, you may even spot deer swimming across.

Cornwall's mild climate has endowed it with some of the country's
most spectacular gardens, among which **Trelissick Garden**, on the banks

of the Fal river, is especially lovely. Famous for its camellias, azaras, and photinias, the terraced garden is set within 375 acres of wooded parkland, offering wonderful panoramic views and making this a paradise for walkers. Between May and October you can visit by river ferry from Falmouth, St. Mawes, and Truro. ⊠ *Feock* ☎ *01872/862090* ⊕ *www.nationaltrust.org.uk* ✉ *£7.40* ⊙ *Mid-Feb.–Oct., daily 10:30–5:30 or dusk; Nov.–mid-Feb., daily 11–4 or dusk; last admission 30 mins before closing.*

ST. MAWES

16 mi east of Falmouth by road, 1½ mi east by sea, 11 mi south of Truro by ferry.

At the tip of the Roseland Peninsula is the quiet, unspoiled village of St. Mawes, where subtropical plants thrive. The peninsula itself is a lovely backwater with old churches, a lighthouse, and good coast walking. One or two sailing and boating options are available in summer, but most companies operate from Falmouth.

EXPLORING

The well-preserved Tudor-era **St. Mawes Castle**, outside the village, has a cloverleaf shape that makes it seemingly impregnable, yet during the Civil War its Royalist commander surrendered without firing a shot. (In contrast, Pendennis Castle in Falmouth held out at this time for 23 weeks before submitting to a siege.) ⊠ *A3078* ☎ *01326/270526* ⊕ *www.english-heritage.org.uk* ✉ *£4.20* ⊙ *Apr.–June and Sept., Sun.–Fri. 10–5; July and Aug., Sun.–Fri. 10–6; Oct., daily 10–4; Nov.–Mar., Fri.–Mon. 10–4.*

★ North of St. Mawes on A3078 is **St. Just in Roseland**, one of the most beautiful spots in the West Country. This tiny hamlet made up of stone cottage terraces and a 13th-century church is set within a subtropical garden, often abloom with magnolias and rhododendrons on a summer's day. St. Just in Roseland is 9 mi south of Truro.

WHERE TO STAY

£££ 🏨 **Lugger Hotel.** It's worth the winding drive on some of Cornwall's narrowest roads to get to this waterfront hideaway in a tiny fishing village. Several 17th-century cottages have been transformed in an eclectic modern style with bleached Portuguese wood and subdued hues in the small bedrooms. Seafood is a good choice at the excellent restaurant overlooking the diminutive harbor. There's a terrace for drinks and sunbathing, and on either side of the hotel the rugged coastline tempts you with exhilarating walks. The Lugger is 8 mi east of St. Mawes and 12 mi southeast of Truro. **Pros:** unforgettable location; relaxing and comfortable rooms; attentive staff. **Cons:** some rooms are cramped; pricey restaurant. ⊠ *Portloe* ☎ *01872/501322* ⊕ *www.luggerhotel.co.uk* ⇌ *22 rooms ⌂ In-room: no a/c, Wi-Fi (some). In-hotel: restaurant, spa, Wi-Fi hotspot, Internet terminal* ▤ *AE, MC, V* ⏹ *BP.*

£££££ 🏨 **Tresanton Hotel.** It's the Cornish Riviera, Italian style: this former
★ yachtsman's club, owned by Olga Polizzi, daughter of grand hotelier Charles Forte, makes for a luxuriously relaxed stay. Decorated in sunny

whites, blues, and yellows, with terra-cotta pots on the terrace, the Tresanton seems distinctly Mediterranean, and the yacht and speedboat available in summer to guests reinforce the jet-set spirit. In the fixed-price restaurant (dinner £42), the Italian-inspired menu includes local scallops, crab, risotto, and honey-glazed pork. **Pros:** superb service; excellent restaurant; stylishly luxurious setting. **Cons:** some steps to climb; dispersed layout inconvenient in rainy weather; distant parking lot. ⊠ *Lower Castle Rd.* ☎ *01326/270055* ⊕ *www. tresanton.com* ⤴ *27 rooms, 2 suites* ⚄ *In-room: no a/c, DVD, Wi-Fi (some). In-hotel: restaurant, bar, Internet terminal, Wi-Fi hotspot* ⊟ *AE, MC, V* ⏣ *BP.*

> **RENT A COTTAGE**
>
> There are plenty of opportunities for experiencing rural peace in a rented cottage amid the meadows and moors of England's West Country. However, the best places are often booked up from year to year in the high season (school vacation). Ask at the information centers, or try any of the following specialist companies: **Classic Cottages** (☎ *01326/555555* ⊕ *www. classic.co.uk*). **Cornish Cottage Holidays** (☎ *01326/573808* ⊕ *www.cornishcottageholidays. co.uk*). **Cornish Traditional Cottages** (☎ *01208/821666* ⊕ *www. corncott.com*). **Helpful Holidays** (☎ *01647/433593* ⊕ *www. helpfulholidays.com*).

EN ROUTE The shortest route from St. Mawes to Truro is via the King Harry Ferry. The longer way swings in a circle on A3078 for 19 mi through countryside where subtropical shrubs thrive. It takes you past Portloe and the 123-foot-tall church tower in Probus, which flaunts gargoyles and pierced stonework.

TRURO

8 mi north of Falmouth, 8 mi north of St. Mawes.

The county seat and Cornwall's only real city, Truro is a good option mostly for food and shopping, and for cathedral and museum buffs. For an overview of the Georgian houses, take a stroll down steep, broad Lemon Street. The elegant 18th-century facades are of pale stone—unusual for Cornwall, where granite predominates. Like Lemon Street, Walsingham Place is a typical Georgian street, a curving, flower-lined pedestrian oasis. The city nestles in a crook of the River Truro.

GETTING HERE AND AROUND

Truro is on the main rail line between Penzance and Plymouth, and is served by local and National Express buses. The compact center can be easily walked from the bus and train stations.

ESSENTIALS

Visitor Information Truro (⊠ *City Hall, Boscawen St.* ☎ *01872/274555* ⊕ *tourism.truro.gov.uk*).

EXPLORING

The **Cathedral Church of St. Mary** dominates the city. Although built between 1880 and 1910, it evokes a medieval church, with an exterior in early English Gothic style. The interior is filled with relics from the

16th-century parish church that stood on this site, part of which has been incorporated into a side chapel. An open, cobbled area called High Cross lies in front of the west porch, and the city's main shopping streets fan out from here. ⊠ *14 St. Mary's St.* ☎ *01872/276782* ⊕ *www.trurocathedral.org.uk* ✉ *Free* ☉ *Mon.–Sat. 7:30–6, Sun. 9–7; tours Apr.–Oct., Mon.–Thurs. and Sat. at 11, Fri. at 11:30, also weekdays at 2 during school vacations.*

The **Royal Cornwall Museum**, in a Georgian building, displays some fine examples of Cornwall-inspired art, a sampling of Cornish archaeology, an absorbing hodgepodge of local history, and an extensive collection of minerals. There's a café and a shop. ⊠ *River St.* ☎ *01872/272205* ⊕ *www.royalcornwallmuseum.org.uk* ✉ *Free* ☉ *Mon.–Sat. 10–4:45.*

CHARLESTOWN

15 mi east of Truro.

Charlestown has managed to avoid overdevelopment since its heyday in the early 1800s, and its Georgian harbor often appears in period film and television productions. This port was built by a local merchant in 1791 to export the huge reserves of china clay from St. Austell, 1 mi to the north, and it became one of the ports from which 19th-century emigrants left for North America. Some spectacular gardens are nearby.

EXPLORING

★ The sprawling, popular **Lost Gardens of Heligan** have something for all garden lovers, as well as an intriguing history. Restored in the early 1990s by former rock music producer Tim Smit (the force behind the Eden Project garden) after decades of neglect, they were begun by the Tremayne family in the late 18th century. In Victorian times the gardens displayed plants from around the British Empire. The Jungle zone contains surviving plants from this era, including a lone Monterey pine, as well as giant redwood and clumps of bamboo. The Italian Garden and walled Flower Gardens are delightful, but don't overlook the fruit and vegetable gardens or Flora's Green, bordered by a ravine. It's easy to spend half a day here. ■TIP➔ **Travel via St. Austell to avoid confusing country lanes, then follow signs to Mevagissey.** ⊠ *B3273, Pentewan* ☎ *01726/845100* ⊕ *www.heligan.com* ✉ *£10* ☉ *Apr.–Sept., daily 10–6; Oct.–Mar., daily 10–5; last entry 1½ hrs before closing.*

☾ Spectacularly set in a former china-clay pit, the **Eden Project** garden pres-

Fodor'sChoice ents the world's major plant systems in microcosm. The crater contains

★ more than 70,000 plants—many of them rare or endangered species—from three climate zones. Plants from the temperate zone are outdoors, and those from other zones are housed in hexagonally paneled geodesic domes. In one dome, olive and citrus groves mix with cacti and other plants indigenous to warmer climates. The tropical dome steams with heat, resounds to the gushing of a waterfall, and blooms with exotic flora. The emphasis is on conservation and ecology, but is free of any editorializing. A free shuttle, the Land Train, helps the footsore, and well-informed guides provide information. An entertaining exhibition in the visitor center gives you the lowdown on the project, and the Core, an education center, provides amusement and instruction for

5

children. Extra attractions include open-air concerts in summer and an ice-skating rink in winter. The Eden Project is 3 mi northeast of Charleston. ■TIP→ To avoid the biggest crowds, visit on a Friday or Saturday, early in the morning, or after 2; you need at least half a day to see everything. ⊠ *Bodelva, signposted off A30, A390, and A391, St. Austell* ☎ *01726/811911* ⊕ *www.edenproject.com* ⊠ *£16, £12 if arriving by bike or on foot* ⊙ *Apr.–late Oct., daily 10–6; late Oct.–Mar., daily 10–4:30; last admission 1½ hrs before closing.*

FOWEY

7 mi northeast of the Eden Project, 10 mi northeast of Charlestown.

Nestled in the mouth of a wooded estuary, Fowey (pronounced Foy) is still very much a working china-clay port as well as a focal point for the sailing fraternity. Increasingly, it's also a favored home of the rich and famous. Good and varied dining and lodging options abound; these are most in demand during Regatta Week in mid-August and the annual Daphne du Maurier Festival in mid-May. The Bodinnick Ferry takes cars as well as foot passengers across the river for the coast road on to Looe.

GETTING HERE AND AROUND

Fowey is not on any train line, but the town is served by frequent buses from St. Austell. Don't attempt to drive into the steep and narrow-lane town center, which is ideal for strolling around. Parking lots are signposted on the approach roads.

ESSENTIALS

Visitor Information Fowey (⊠ *5 South St.* ☎ *01726/833616* ⊕ *www.fowey. co.uk*).

WHERE TO EAT AND STAY

££
SEAFOOD
✕ **Sam's.** Be prepared for a wait at this small and buzzing bistro with a rock-and-roll flavor. Diners squeeze onto benches and into booths to savor dishes made with local seafood, including a majestic bouillabaisse, or just a simple "Samburger." There's a slinky lounge-bar upstairs for a preprandial drink. ⊠ *20 Fore St.* ☎ *01726/832273* ⊕ *www.samsfowey. co.uk* ⌕ *Reservations not accepted* ⊟ *MC, V.*

£££££
⊡ **Fowey Hall.** A showy Victorian edifice, all turrets and elaborate plasterwork, this hotel with 5 acres of gardens is a great place for families. Most rooms are spacious enough for several people, and there are great facilities for the kids. You can dine in the sumptuously oak-paneled Hansons or in the less formal Conservatory, which opens onto the terrace. **Pros:** grand manorial setting; family-friendly atmosphere. **Cons:** could do with a revamp; erratic housekeeping and service. ⊠ *Hanson Dr.* ☎ *01726/833866* ⊕ *www.foweyhallhotel.co.uk* ⇝ *24 rooms, 12 suites* ⌕ *In-room: no a/c, DVD, Wi-Fi (some). In-hotel: 2 restaurants, bar, spa, pool, laundry service, Wi-Fi hotspot, some pets allowed* ⊟ *AE, MC, V* ⊺⊙⌐ *BP.*

SPORTS AND THE OUTDOORS

Between June and September, **Fowey River Expeditions** (✉ *17 Passage St.* ☎ *01726/833627*) runs daily canoe trips up the tranquil River Fowey, the best way to observe the abundant wildlife. Kayaks are also available to rent.

BODMIN

12 mi north of Fowey.

Bodmin was the only Cornish town recorded in the 11th-century Domesday Book, William the Conqueror's census. During World War I the Domesday Book and the Crown Jewels were sent to Bodmin Prison for safekeeping. From the Gilbert Memorial on Beacon Hill, you can see both of Cornwall's coasts. Lanhydrock, a stately home, is also near Bodmin.

ESSENTIALS

Visitor Information Bodmin (✉ *The Shire Hall, Mount Folly* ☎ *01208/76616* ⊕ *www.bodminlive.com*).

EXPLORING

Fodor'sChoice
★ One of Cornwall's greatest country piles, **Lanhydrock** gives a look into the lives of the upper classes in the 19th century. The former home of the powerful, wealthy Robartes family was originally constructed in the 17th century but was totally rebuilt after a fire in 1881. Its granite exterior remains true to the house's original form, however, and the long picture gallery in the north wing, with its barrel-vaulted plaster ceiling depicting 24 biblical scenes, survived the devastation. A small museum in the north wing shows photographs and letters relating to the family. The house's endless pantries, sculleries, dairies, nurseries, and linen cupboards bear witness to the immense amount of work involved in maintaining this lifestyle. About 900 acres of wooded parkland border the River Fowey, and in spring the gardens present an exquisite ensemble of magnolias, azaleas, and rhododendrons. Allow two hours to see the house and more time to stroll the grounds. ✉ *Signposted off A30, A38, and B3268, 3 mi southeast of Bodmin* ☎ *01208/265950* ⊕ *www. nationaltrust.org.uk* ✉ *£9.90; grounds only, £5.80* ☉ *House Mid-Mar.– Sept., Tues.–Sun. and national holidays 11–5:30; Oct., Tues.–Sun. 11–5; garden daily 10–6; last admission 30 mins before closing.*

For a taste of Arthurian legend, follow A30 northeast out of Bodmin across the boggy, heather-clad granite plateau of Bodmin Moor. After about 10 mi, turn right at Bolventor to get to **Dozmary Pool.** A lake rather than a pool, it was here that King Arthur's legendary magic sword, Excalibur, was supposedly returned to the Lady of the Lake after Arthur's final battle.

5

PLYMOUTH AND DARTMOOR

Just over the border from Cornwall is Plymouth, an unprepossessing city but one with a historic old core and splendid harbor that recall a rich maritime heritage. North of Plymouth, you can explore the vast, boggy reaches of hilly Dartmoor, the setting for the Sherlock Holmes classic *The Hound of the Baskervilles*. This national park is a great place to hike or go horseback riding away from the crowds.

PLYMOUTH

48 mi southwest of Exeter, 124 mi southwest of Bristol, 240 mi southwest of London.

Devon's largest city has long been linked with England's commercial and maritime history. The Pilgrims sailed from here to the New World in the *Mayflower* in 1620. Although much of the city center was destroyed by air raids in World War II and has been rebuilt in an uninspiring style, there are worthwhile sights. A harbor tour is also a good way to see the city.

GETTING HERE AND AROUND

Frequent trains arrive from Bodmin, Penzance, and Exeter. From London Paddington, trains take around three hours, 20 minues; National Express buses from London's Victoria Coach Station take five hours, 20 minutes. The train station is 1 mi north of the seafront, connected by frequent buses. Long-distance buses stop at the centrally located bus station off Royal Parade. Drivers can leave their cars in one of the numerous parking lots, including a couple right by the harbor. The seafront and central city areas are best explored on foot.

ESSENTIALS

Visitor Information Plymouth (⊠ *Plymouth Mayflower, 3–5 The Barbican* ☎ *01752/306330* ⊕ *www.visitplymouth.co.uk*).

EXPLORING
TOP ATTRACTIONS

❺ Barbican. East of the Royal Citadel is the Barbican, the oldest surviving section of Plymouth. Here Tudor houses and warehouses rise from a maze of narrow streets leading down to the fishing docks and harbor. Many of these buildings have become antiques shops, art shops, and bookstores. It's well worth a stroll for the atmosphere.

❹ Elizabethan House. In the heart of the Barbican section, this former sea captain's home offers a fascinating insight into how well-to-do Plymothians lived during the city's golden age. The three floors of the timber-frame house are filled with 16th- and 17th-century furnishings, and there's a spiral staircase built around a ship's mast. ⊠ *32 New St.* ☎ *01752/304774* 🗐 *£2* ⊙ *Apr.–Sept., Tues.–Sat. and national holidays 10–5.*

❶ Hoe. From the Hoe, a wide, grassy esplanade with crisscrossing walkways high above the city, you can take in a magnificent view of the inlets, bays, and harbors that make up Plymouth Sound.

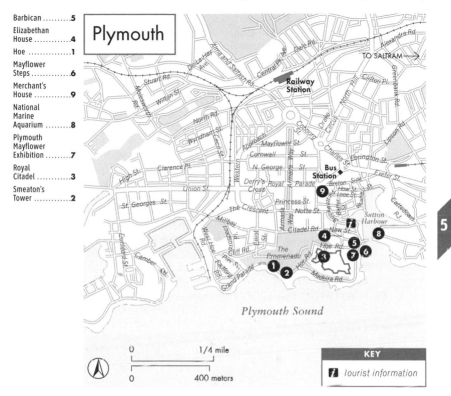

Plymouth

8 **National Marine Aquarium.** This excellent aquarium, on a central harborside site, presents aqueous environments, from a freshwater stream to a seawater wave tank and a huge "shark theater." Not to be missed is the extensive collection of sea horses, part of an important breeding program, and the chance to walk under sharks in the Mediterranean tank. Explorocean highlights undersea technology with demonstrations and hands-on gizmos, and there's a 3-D cinema. ⊠ *Rope Walk, Coxside* ☎ *01752/600301* ⊕ *www.national-aquarium.co.uk* ⊡ *£11* ⊙ *Apr.–Sept., daily 10–6; Oct.–Mar., daily 10–5; last admission 1 hr before closing.*

7 **Plymouth Mayflower Exhibition.** On three floors, this interactive exhibition narrates the story of Plymouth, from its beginnings as a fishing and trading port to the modern industrial city it is today. Along the way, you'll take in the stories of various expeditions that embarked from here to the New World, including the *Mayflower* itself. The city's tourist office is also in this building. ⊠ *3–5 The Barbican* ☎ *01752/306330* ⊕ *www.visitplymouth.co.uk* ⊡ *£2* ⊙ *Apr.–Oct., Mon.–Sat. 10–4, Sun. 11–3; Nov.–Mar., weekdays 10–4, Sat. 11–3; last admission 1 hr before closing.*

Saltram. An exquisite 18th-century home with many of its original furnishings, Saltram was built around the remains of a late-Tudor mansion.

Its jewel is one of Britain's grandest neoclassical rooms, a vast, double-cube salon designed by Robert Adam and adorned with paintings by Sir Joshua Reynolds, first president of the Royal Academy of Arts, who was born nearby in 1723. The Axminster carpet was created for the space. Fine plasterwork adorns many rooms, and three have original Chinese wallpaper. The outstanding garden includes rare trees and shrubs, and there's a restaurant and a cafeteria. Saltram is 3½ mi east of Plymouth city center. ⊠ *South of A38, Plympton* ☎ *01752/333503* ⊕ *www. nationaltrust.org.uk* ⊠ *£8.70; garden only, £4.50* ⊙ *House mid-Mar.– Oct., Sat.–Thurs. noon–4:30; last admission 3:45. Garden mid-Mar.– Oct., Sat.–Thurs. 11–5; Nov.–mid-Mar., Sat.–Thurs. 11–4.*

WORTH NOTING

❻ **Mayflower Steps.** By the harbor you can visit the Mayflower Steps, where the Pilgrims embarked in 1620; the **Mayflower Stone** marks the exact spot. They had sailed from Southampton but had to stop in Plymouth because of damage from a storm. ⊠ *In front of 3–5 The Barbican.*

❾ **Merchant's House.** Near the Barbican, just off the Royal Parade, this largely 17th-century house is a museum of local history. ⊠ *33 St. Andrew's St.* ☎ *01752/304774* ⊠ *£2* ⊙ *Apr.–Sept., Tues.–Sat. and national holidays 10–5.*

❸ **Royal Citadel.** This huge citadel was built by Charles II in 1666 and still operates as a military center. ⊠ *End of the Hoe* ⊕ *www.english-heritage.org.uk* ⊠ *£4* ⊙ *May–Sept., Tues. and Thurs. 1¼-hr guided tours at 2:30.*

❷ **Smeaton's Tower.** This lighthouse, transferred here at the end of the 19th century from its original site 14 mi out to sea, provides a sweeping vista over Plymouth Sound and the city as far as Dartmoor. ⊠ *Hoe Rd.* ☎ *01752/304774* ⊠ *£2* ⊙ *Apr.–Sept., Tues.–Fri. 10–noon and 1–4:30, Sat. 10–noon and 1–4; Oct.–Mar., Tues.–Sat. 10–noon and 1–3.*

WHERE TO EAT AND STAY

£££
SEAFOOD
✕ **Piermasters.** Fresh seafood landed at nearby piers, notably squid, mussels, and oysters, appears high on the menu at this Barbican eatery. Blending modern decor in a traditional setting, the downstairs dining area has a tile floor, wooden tables, and sails on the ceiling, and upstairs is wood paneled with contemporary art on the walls. There are excellent fixed-price lunchtime and early-evening menus. ⊠ *33 Southside St.* ☎ *01752/229345* ⊕ *www.piermastersrestaurant.com* ⊟ *AE, MC, V* ⊙ *Closed Sun. and 10 days over Christmas.*

£££££
MODERN BRITISH
✕ **Tanners.** One of the city's oldest buildings, the 15th-century Prysten House, is the setting for the highly regarded, inventive cuisine of brothers Chris and James Tanner. On the fixed-price menus are such lunch options as braised beef and fish pie; evening choices include roast Creedy Carver duck breast (from a high-quality Devon producer) with sweet potato mousseline. One of the two lattice-windowed rooms has a well in it, and the other is hung with tapestries. A canopied courtyard is ideal for alfresco dining. The brothers also operate the Barbican Kitchen, a more relaxed, less pricey offshoot of the restaurant at the Black Friars Distillery on Southside Street. ⊠ *Finewell St.* ☎ *01752/252001* ⊕ *www.*

tannersrestaurant.com ⚏ *Reservations essential* ▭ *AE, MC, V* ⊘ *Closed Sun. and Mon.*

££ ⚏ **The Bowling Green.** Friendly and unpretentious, this Georgian house overlooks Sir Francis Drake's bowling green on Plymouth Hoe. Guest rooms have pastel colors and creamy linens, and there's a sunny conservatory and garden. The B&B is a short stroll from shops, restaurants, and the central sights. **Pros:** convenient base for sightseeing; welcoming owner/manager. **Cons:** low shower pressure in some rooms. ⊠ *9–10 Osborne Pl., Lockyer St.* ☎ *01752/209090* ⊕ *www. thebowlingreenplymouth.com* ⇆ *12 rooms* ♿ *In-room: no a/c, Wi-Fi. In-hotel: Wi-Fi hotspot, parking (paid)* ▭ *MC, V* ⊗ *BP.*

££ ⚏ **Holiday Inn.** Grandly sited in a tall block overlooking Plymouth Hoe, this modern chain hotel has a businesslike tone but doesn't skimp on comforts. Rooms are spacious and uncluttered, with a brown-and-cream color scheme. One story is reserved for smokers. On the penthouse floor, Elliot's restaurant provides a panoramic dining area, which is also used for self-serve breakfasts. There's a good-size indoor pool. **Pros:** excellent location; fantastic views. **Cons:** impersonal feel; uninteresting food; occasionally shoddy housekeeping. ⊠ *Armada Way* ☎ *0871/423–4896* ⊕ *www.holidayinn.co.uk* ⇆ *211 rooms* ♿ *In-room: a/c, refrigerator (some), Wi-Fi. In-hotel: restaurant, room service, bar, pool, gym, Internet terminal, Wi-Fi hotspot, parking (paid)* ▭ *AE, DC, MC, V* ⊗ *BP.*

NIGHTLIFE AND THE ARTS

Plymouth's **Theatre Royal** (⊠ *Royal Parade* ☎ *01752/267222*) presents ballet, musicals, and plays by some of Britain's best companies.

HARBOR AND RIVER TOURS

Sound Cruising. This company runs harbor and river sightseeing trips all year; boats depart every 45 minutes in peak season from Phoenix Wharf (call to check November–March). ⊠ *Madeira Rd., Barbican* ☎ *01752/408590* ⊕ *www.soundcruising.com.*

Tamar Cruising. Harbor cruises and longer scenic trips on the Rivers Tamar and Yealm leave from the Mayflower Steps and Cremyll Quay between Easter and September. ⊠ *Cremyll Quay, Cremyll, Torpoint* ☎ *01752/822105* ⊕ *www.tamarcruising.com.*

SHOPPING

At the **Black Friars Distillery** (⊠ *60 Southside St.* ☎ *01752/665292*), where Plymouth's most famous export, gin, has been distilled since 1793, you can purchase bottles of sloe gin, damson liqueur, fruit cup, or the fiery "Navy Strength" gin that traditionally was issued to the Royal Navy.

EN ROUTE From Plymouth you have a choice of routes northeast to Exeter. If rugged, desolate, moorland scenery appeals to you, take A386 and B3212 northeast across Dartmoor. There is plenty to stir the imagination.

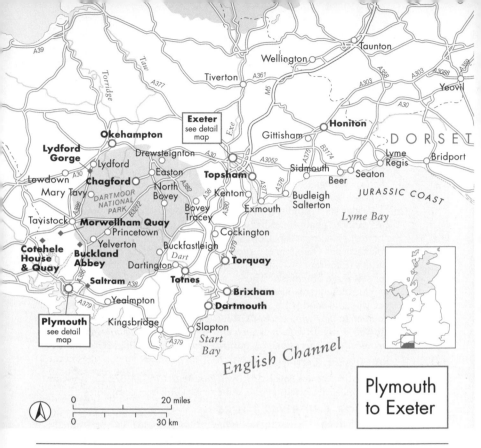

Plymouth
to Exeter

DARTMOOR NATIONAL PARK

10 mi north of Plymouth, 13 mi west of Exeter.

GETTING HERE AND AROUND

Public transport services are extremely sparse on Dartmoor, making a car indispensable for anywhere off the beaten track. The peripheral towns of Okehampton and Tavistock are well served by bus from Exeter and Plymouth, and Chagford also has direct connections to Exeter, but central Princetown has only sporadic links with the outside world.

EXPLORING

Even on a summer's day, the brooding hills of this sprawling wilderness appear a likely haunt for such monsters as the hound of the Baskervilles, and it seems entirely fitting that Sir Arthur Conan Doyle set his Sherlock Holmes thriller in this landscape.

Sometimes the wet, peaty wasteland of **Dartmoor National Park** vanishes in rain and mist, although in clear weather you can see north to Exmoor, south over the English Channel, and west far into Cornwall. Much of Dartmoor consists of open heath and moorland, unspoiled by roads—wonderful walking and horseback-riding territory but an easy place to lose your bearings. Dartmoor's earliest inhabitants left behind stone monuments and burial mounds that help you envision prehistoric man roaming these pastures. Ponies, sheep, and birds are the main animals to be seen.

Several villages scattered along the borders of this 368-square-mi reserve—one-third of which is owned by Prince Charles—make useful bases for hiking excursions. Accommodations include simple inns and some elegant havens. Okehampton is a main gateway, and **Chagford** is a good base for exploring North Dartmoor. Other scenic spots include **Buckland-in-the-Moor,** a hamlet with thatched-roof cottages, **Widecombe-in-the-Moor,** whose church is known as the Cathedral of the Moor, and **Grimspound,** the Bronze Age site featured in Conan Doyle's most famous tale. Transmoor Link buses connect most of Dartmoor's towns and villages. Park information centers include the main **High Moorland Visitor Centre** in Princetown and centers in Newbridge, Postbridge, and Haytor. The park also works with tourist information centers in Ivybridge, Okehampton, Tavistock, and Totnes. ⊠ *High Moorland Visitor Centre, Tavistock Rd., Princetown* ☎ *01822/890414* ⊕ *www.dartmoor-npa.gov.uk.*

SPORTS AND THE OUTDOORS

Tourist information centers can help you decide what to do here; another source is the **Dartmoor National Park Authority** (⊠ *Parke, Haytor Rd., Bovey Tracey, Newton Abbot* ☎ *01626/832093* ⊕ *www.dartmoor-npa.gov.uk*). This is a great area for horseback riding; many towns have stables for guided rides. Hiking is popular, but longer hikes in the bleak, unpeopled region of Dartmoor—for example, the tors south of Okehampton—are appropriate only for the most experienced walkers. The areas around Widgery Cross, Becky Falls, and the Bovey Valley, and the short but dramatic walk along Lydford Gorge, have wide appeal, as do the many valleys around the southern edge of the moors. Guided hikes (£3–£8) are available through the park; reservations are not needed for most, but you can check with the High Moorland Visitor Centre in Princetown.

BUCKLAND ABBEY

8 mi north of Plymouth.

ESSENTIALS

Visitor Information Tavistock (⊠ *The Archway, Bedford Sq.* ☎ *01822/612938* ⊕ *www.dartmoor.co.uk*).

EXPLORING

Buckland Abbey, a 13th-century Cistercian monastery, became the home of Sir Francis Drake in 1581. Today it is filled with mementos of Drake and the Spanish Armada and has a restaurant. From Tavistock, take A386 south to Crapstone and then head west. ⊠ *Yelverton* ☎ *01822/853607* ⊕ *www.nationaltrust.org.uk* ☑ *£7.80 (free with garden ticket in winter); grounds only, £4* ⊙ *Late Feb.–early Mar. and early Nov.–mid-Dec., Fri.–Sun. 11–4:30; mid-Mar.–Oct., daily 10:30–5:30; last admission 45 mins before closing.*

COTEHELE HOUSE AND QUAY

4 mi west of Buckland Abbey, 15 mi north of Plymouth.

ESSENTIALS

Visitor Information Tavistock (⊠ *The Archway, Bedford Sq.* ☎ *01822/612938* ⊕ *www.dartmoor.co.uk*).

EXPLORING

★ **Cotehele House and Quay** was formerly a busy port on the River Tamar, but it is now usually visited for the well-preserved, atmospheric late-medieval manor, home of the Edgcumbe family for centuries. The house has original furniture, tapestries, embroideries, and armor, and you can also visit the impressive gardens, a restored mill (in operation at 3 PM Tuesday, Thursday, and some Sundays), and a quay museum. A limited number of visitors are allowed per day, so arrive early and be prepared to wait during busy periods. Choose a bright day, because the rooms have no electric light. Shops, crafts studios, a gallery, and a restaurant provide other diversions. ■TIP→ **Take advantage of the shuttle bus that runs between the house, quay, and mill roughly every half hour.** ⊠ *St. Dominick, north of Saltash, signposted off A390* ☎ *01579/351346* ⊕ *www.nationaltrust. org.uk* ⊠ *£8.70; gardens and mill only, £5.20* ⊙ *House mid-Mar.–Oct., Sat.–Thurs. 11–4:30. Mill mid-Mar.–Sept., daily 11–5; Oct., daily 11–4:30. Gardens daily 10–dusk.*

> ### STAY ON A FARM
>
> Do you plan to travel by car and want to be far from resorts, traffic jams, and hubbub? One way to experience the authentic rural life in Somerset, Devon, and Cornwall is to stay on a farm. **Southwest Tourism's** Web site (⊕ *www. naturesouthwest.co.uk*) gives details about working farms that supply accommodation—including bed-and-breakfasts and house rentals—throughout the region. Other reference points are **Visit Devon** (⊕ *www.visitdevon.co.uk*), for farms in Devon, and **Cornish Farm Holidays** (⊕ *www.cornish-farms.co.uk*), for Cornwall.

MORWELLHAM QUAY

2 mi east of Cotehele House & Quay, 5 mi southwest of Tavistock, 18 mi north of Plymouth.

ESSENTIALS

Visitor Information Tavistock (⊠ *The Archway, Bedford Sq.* ☎ *01822/612938* ⊕ *www.dartmoor.co.uk*).

EXPLORING

☾ In the 19th century **Morwellham Quay** (pronounced More-*wel*-ham) was England's main copper-exporting port, and it has been carefully restored as a working museum, with quay workers and coachmen in costume. Visitors can board a special train that goes along the River Tamar and into the Charlotte and George Copper Mine. ⊠ *Off A390, on minor road off B3257* ☎ *01822/832766, 01822/833808 recorded information* ⊕ *www.morwellham-quay.co.uk* ⊠ *£6.95; mine train £3.50* ⊙ *July–mid-Sept., daily 10–6; mid-Sept.–June, daily 10–5.*

WHERE TO EAT

££££ ✕ **Horn of Plenty.** The restaurant within this Georgian house has magnifi-
MODERN BRITISH cent views across the wooded, rhododendron-filled Tamar Valley. Peter
★ Gorton's sophisticated cooking takes its inspiration from around the
world, but local ingredients are favored. Spiced duck breast with cherry
compote and port sauce is a typical main course. There are three-course,
fixed-price menus (lunch £26.50, dinner £47); the best value is Monday evening's potluck menu (£28). A converted coach house and the
main house contain 10 sumptuously furnished guest rooms (£££). ⊠ *3
mi west of Tavistock on A390, Gulworthy* ☎ *01822/832528* ⊕ *www.*
thehornofplenty.co.uk ⊟ *AE, MC, V.*

LYDFORD GORGE

12 mi north of Morwellham Quay, 7 mi north of Tavistock, 9 mi east
of Launceston, 24 mi north of Plymouth.

GETTING HERE AND AROUND

The gorge is easily accessed on Holsworthy buses from Tavistock (which
has frequent bus connections to Plymouth) and Okehampton (connected
to Exeter). By car, take A386 between Tavistock and Okehampton.

ESSENTIALS

Visitor Information Tavistock (⊠ *The Archway, Bedford Sq.* ☎ *01822/612938*
⊕ *www.dartmoor.co.uk*).

EXPLORING

The River Lyd has carved a spectacular 1½-mi-long chasm through the
★ rock at **Lydford Gorge**, outside the pretty village of Lydford, midway
between Okehampton and Tavistock on the edge of Dartmoor. Two
paths follow the gorge past gurgling whirlpools and waterfalls with
evocative names such as the Devil's Cauldron and the White Lady.
Sturdy footwear is recommended. Although the walk can be quite challenging, the paths can still get congested during busy periods. ⊠ *Off*
A386, Lydford ☎ *01822/820320* ⊕ *www.nationaltrust.org.uk* ⊠ *£5.50*
(£3 in winter) ☉ *Mid-Mar.–early Oct., daily 10–5; early–late Oct., daily*
10–4; Nov.–mid-Mar., daily 11–3:30 (check first in winter, when walk
is restricted to main waterfall and top of gorge).

WHERE TO EAT AND STAY

£££ ✕ **Dartmoor Inn.** Locals and visitors alike make a beeline for this gastro-
MODERN BRITISH pub in a 16th-century building with a number of small dining spaces
done in spare, contemporary country style. Dishes may include Devon
Red Ruby beef with shallots, or fillet of cod with creamed lemon lentils. There are inspired vegetarian choices as well as an "easy dining"
menu in which a grilled fish salad or asparagus risotto cost around £10.
The pub is at the Lydford junction. Three spacious guest rooms (££)
make it possible to linger. ⊠ *A386, Lydford* ☎ *01822/820221* ⊕ *www.*
dartmoorinn.com ⚓ *Reservations essential* ⊟ *MC, V* ☉ *No dinner Sun.*
No lunch Mon.

£–££ ⌂ **Castle Inn.** The heart of Lydford village, this 16th-century inn is next
to Lydford Castle. Rose trellises frame its rosy brick facade, and the
public rooms are snug, lamp-lighted, and full of period clutter. Vivid

5

colors are used in the guest rooms; one room has its own roof garden. A range of snacks and full bar meals is available. **Pros:** antique character; peaceful rural setting. **Cons:** shabby in places; substandard food. ⊠ *1 mi off A386, Lydford* ☎ *01822/820241* ⊕ *www.castleinnlydford. co.uk* ⇔ *8 rooms* ⌂ *In-room: no a/c, no phone, DVD, Wi-Fi. In-hotel: restaurant, bar, Wi-Fi hotspot, some pets allowed* ⊟ *MC, V* ⏅ *BP.*

SPORTS AND THE OUTDOORS

Cholwell Stables (⊠ *Mary Tavy* ☎ *01822/810526*) has one- and two-hour horseback rides through some of Dartmoor's wilder tracts. Riders of all abilities are escorted, and equipment is provided. The stables are about 6 mi south of Lydford; call for directions.

OKEHAMPTON

8 mi northeast of Lydford Gorge, 28 mi north of Plymouth, 23 mi west of Exeter.

This town at the confluence of the rivers East and West Okement is a good base for exploring North Dartmoor. It has numerous pubs and cottage tearooms—take time to indulge in a classic, rich Devon cream tea—as well as a helpful tourist office.

ESSENTIALS

Visitor Information Okehampton (⊠ *Okehampton Museum Yard, West St.* ☎ *01837/53020* ⊕ *www.okehamptondevon.co.uk*).

EXPLORING

On the riverbank a mile southwest of the town center, the jagged ruins of the Norman **Okehampton Castle** occupy a verdant site with a picnic area and woodland walks. ☎ *01837/52844* ⊕ *www.english-heritage. org.uk* ⊠ *£3.50* ☉ *Apr.–June and Sept., daily 10–5; July and Aug., daily 10–6.*

The three floors of the informative **Museum of Dartmoor Life** contain models, a working waterwheel, and photos of traditional farming methods. ⊠ *3 West St.* ☎ *01837/52295* ⊕ *www.museumofdartmoorlife.eclipse. co.uk* ⊠ *£3.50* ☉ *Easter–Oct., weekdays 10:15–4:30, Sat. 11–3; Nov.– mid-Dec., Mon.–Sat. 11–3.*

WHERE TO STAY

££££–£££££ ⊡ **Lewtrenchard Manor.** Paneled rooms, stone fireplaces, leaded-glass windows, and handsome gardens outfit this spacious 1620 manor, now a country-house hotel, on the northwestern edge of Dartmoor. Victorian hymn writer Sabine Baring Gould was responsible for the eclectic mix of architectural styles. Prints, chintzes, and upholstered furniture create comfort in the individually decorated guest rooms (where there may be a two-night minimum stay on summer weekends). The fixed-price restaurant, with its big log fire and family portraits, serves Modern British fare such as roast duck breast with salsify and bok choy. Serious foodies might sample the Purple Carrot (£95 per person), a sumptuous private dining room. **Pros:** beautiful Jacobean setting; conscientious service; outstanding food. **Cons:** dated in parts; not very child-friendly. ⊠ *Between Launceston and Okehampton, Lewdown* ☎ *01566/783222*

⊕ *www.lewtrenchard.co.uk* ⇥ *9 rooms, 5 suites* ⚲ *In-room: no a/c, DVD (some), Internet, Wi-Fi (some). In-hotel: restaurant, bar, Wi-Fi hotspot, some pets allowed* ═ *AE, MC, V* ⊚⎮ *BP.*

SPORTS AND THE OUTDOORS

Skaigh Stables Farm (⊠ *Skaigh La., Belstone, near Okehampton* ☎ *01837/ 840917* ⊕ *www.skaighstables.co.uk*) arranges horseback rides by the hour, half day, and full day from Easter through September.

CHAGFORD

9 mi southeast of Okehampton, 30 mi northeast of Plymouth.

Chagford, once a tin-weighing station, was an area of fierce fighting between the Roundheads and the Cavaliers during the Civil War. Although officially a "town" since 1305, Chagford is more of a village, with old taverns grouped around a seasoned old church and a curious "pepper-pot" market house on the site of the old Stannary Court. With a handful of cafés and shops to browse around, it makes a convenient base from which to explore North Dartmoor.

EXPLORING

The intriguing **Castle Drogo**, east of Chagford across A382 above the Teign Gorge, looks like a medieval fortress, complete with battlements, but construction actually took place between 1910 and 1930. Designed by noted architect Sir Edwin Lutyens for Julius Drewe, a wealthy grocer, the castle is only half finished (funds ran out). Inside, this magisterial pile combines medieval grandeur and early-20th-century comforts like the large bathrooms. ■ TIP➔ **Between June and September, you can play croquet on the lawn while taking in awesome views over Dartmoor.** Take the A30 Exeter–Okehampton road to reach the castle, which is 4 mi northeast of Chagford and 6 mi south of A30. ⊠ *Off A30 and A382, Drewsteignton* ☎ *01647/433306* ⊕ *www.nationaltrust.org.uk* ⊡ *£7.80, £5 in winter; grounds only, £5, £2.30 in winter* ☉ *Castle mid-Feb. and Apr.–early Sept., daily 11–5; early Mar., weekends 11–5; mid-Mar.– late Mar. and early Sept.–Oct., Wed.–Mon. 11–5; late Nov.–mid-Dec., weekends 11–4:30.*

★ The **Devon Guild of Craftsmen**, the southwest's most important contemporary arts-and-crafts center, is in a converted 19th-century coach house on the edge of Dartmoor in the town of Bovey Tracey, 10 mi southeast of Chagford and 14 mi southwest of Exeter. The center has excellent exhibitions of local, national, and international crafts as well as a crafts shop and café. ⊠ *Riverside Mill, B3344 (Fore St.), Bovey Tracey* ☎ *01626/832223* ⊕ *www.crafts.org.uk* ⊡ *Free* ☉ *Daily 10–5:30.*

QUICK BITES

The Old Cottage Tea Shop (⊠ *20 Fore St., Bovey Tracey* ☎ *01626/833430*) is the real deal, perfect for a light lunch or, even better, a cream tea served on bone china. Warm scones come in baskets, with black currant and other homemade jams and plenty of clotted cream. It's closed Wednesday afternoon and all day Sunday.

WHERE TO EAT AND STAY

££££ ✕ **Gidleigh Park.** One of England's foremost country-house hotels,
MODERN BRITISH lauded in poetry by Ted Hughes, occupies an enclave of landscaped
★ gardens and streams up a lengthy, winding private drive at the edge of
Dartmoor. The extremely pricey (£95 fixed-price dinner menu) contemporary restaurant, directed by chef Michael Caines, has been showered with culinary awards. You may see why when you dig into the turbot and scallops with leeks, wild mushrooms, and chive butter sauce. The locally pumped spring water is like no other. Antiques fill the long, half-timber building, built in 1928 in Tudor style; there are 24 luxurious guest rooms. ⊠ *Gidleigh Park* ☎ *01647/432367* ⊕ *www.gidleigh.com* ⚐ *Reservations essential* ▤ *AE, DC, MC, V.*

££££–£££££ ⚏ **Bovey Castle.** With the grandeur of a country estate and the amenities
★ of a modern hotel, Bovey Castle, built in 1906 for Viscount Hambledon, has it all. On its vast grounds are an outstanding golf course and 24 mi of riverbank that can be used for salmon fishing. There is a resident pianist, and children have a barn filled with activities. Enormous fireplaces and oak-panel rooms give a sense of early-20th-century pomp to the public rooms; bedrooms are luxurious, and even some of the bathrooms have great views across the valley. **Pros:** baronial splendor; efficient, friendly service; range of activities. **Cons:** costly extras. ⊠ *Off B3212, North Bovey* ☎ *01647/445000* ⊕ *www.boveycastle.com* ⚐ *63 rooms, 14 self-catering lodges* ⚇ *In-room: no a/c, Wi-Fi (some). In-hotel: 3 restaurants, bar, golf course, tennis courts, pool, spa, Internet terminal, Wi-Fi hotspot, some pets allowed* ▤ *AE, MC, V* ⚐ *BP.*

££ ⚏ **Easton Court.** Discerning travelers such as C.P. Snow, Margaret Mead, John Steinbeck, and Evelyn Waugh—who completed *Brideshead Revisited* here—made this their Dartmoor home-away-from-home. The Tudor thatched-roof house has a 3½-acre garden and simple but elegant cottage-style rooms in an adjoining wing; all rooms have views over the well-maintained garden. Breakfast choices include soufflé omelet. A two-night minimum stay is usually required on weekends in high season. **Pros:** helpful hosts; airy, spacious rooms; quiet environment. **Cons:** rooms lack much character; need to drive to get anywhere. ⊠ *A382, Easton Cross* ☎ *01647/433469* ⊕ *www.easton.co.uk* ⚐ *5 rooms* ⚇ *In-room: no a/c, DVD, Wi-Fi (some). In-hotel: Wi-Fi hotspot, some pets allowed, no kids under 10* ▤ *MC, V* ⚐ *BP.*

DARTMOUTH, TORBAY, AND EXETER

Sheltered by the high mass of Dartmoor to the west, the yachting center of Dartmouth and the coastal resort area known as the English Riviera, Torbay, enjoy a mild, warm climate. The Gulf Stream, too, makes possible subtropical vegetation, including palm trees. To the north is Exeter, Devon's county seat, an ancient city that has retained some of its medieval character despite wartime bombing. From Exeter you can explore south and east to Exmouth and Honiton.

DARTMOUTH

35 mi east of Plymouth, 35 mi south of Exeter.

An important port in the Middle Ages, Dartmouth is today a favorite haunt of yacht owners. Traces of its past include the old houses in Bayard's Cove near Lower Ferry, the 16th-century covered Butterwalk, and the two castles guarding the entrance to the River Dart. The Royal Naval College, built in 1905, dominates the town.

GETTING HERE AND AROUND

Frequent buses connect Dartmouth with Plymouth and Totnes. Drivers coming from the west should follow A381 and A3122. Approaching from the Torbay area, you can save mileage by using the passenger and car ferries crossing the Dart.

ESSENTIALS

Visitor Information Dartmouth (✉ *The Engine House, Mayors Ave.* ☎ *01803/834224* ⊕ *www.discoverdartmouth.com*).

EXPLORING

A rewarding way to experience the River Dart is to join a cruise from Dartmouth's quay to visit **Greenway**, the 16th century the riverside home of the Gilbert family (Sir Humphrey Gilbert claimed Newfoundland on behalf of Elizabeth I), more famous today for its association with the crime writer Agatha Christie. Mrs. Mallowan (Christie's married name) made it her holiday home in 1938 and the house displays collections of archaeological finds, china, and silver. The gorgeous gardens are thickly planted with magnolias, camellias, and rare shrubs, and richly endowed with panoramic views. Beware, however, that the grounds are steeply laid out, and those arriving by boat face a daunting uphill climb. Allow three hours to see everything; timed tickets for the house are given on arrival. **Greenway Cruises** (☎ *0845/489–0418* ⊕ *www.greenwayferry.co.uk*) runs ferries from Dartmouth; a round-trip ticket costs £8. Parking spaces here are restricted and must be booked in advance. Alternatively, ask at the tourist office about walking and cycling routes to reach the house (non-car-users get discounted entry). ✉ *Galmpton* ☎ *01803/842382* ⊕ *www.nationaltrust.org.uk* 🎫 *£8* ⊙ *Mar.–mid-July and Sept.–Oct., Wed.–Sun. 10:30–5; mid-July–Aug., Tues.–Sun. 10:30–5:30.*

WHERE TO EAT AND STAY

££££   ✕ **New Angel.** John Burton-Race, a celebrity chef, has a restaurant in
MODERN BRITISH   this prime waterfront spot; it's another sign of the region's ongoing food
★   revolution. The British and European menu offers good value for the quality, and emphasizes local fare such as ravioli of Dartmouth crab with cognac-and-cream-enriched bisque, and Devon Red Rub beef with smoked bacon and snails. Open in the mornings for coffee and croissants, and with a snazzy evening cocktail lounge on the top floor, this place is relaxed and family friendly. Six guest rooms are available (££–£££). ✉ *2 S. Embankment* ☎ *01803/839425* ⊕ *www.thenewangel.co.uk* ♣ *Reservations essential* ▬ *MC, V* ⊙ *Closed Sun., Mon., and Jan.*

£££–££££   🏨 **Royal Castle Hotel.** This hotel has truly earned the name "Royal"—several monarchs have slept here. Part of Dartmouth's historic waterfront (and consequently a hub of activity), it was built in the 17th century, reputedly of timber from wrecks of the Spanish Armada. Fireplaces and beamed ceilings are traditional features. Rooms come in different sizes and styles, but all are thoughtfully and richly furnished, with a liberal sprinkling of antiques. Number 6 has its own priest hole, a secret room used to hide Roman Catholic priests. Most of the pricier rooms facing the river have hot tubs. **Pros:** historical resonance; superb central location; great service. **Cons:** occasional noise; no elevator. ⊠ *11 The Quay* ☏ *01803/833033* ⊕ *www.royalcastle.co.uk* ⇘ *25 rooms* ⚭ *In-room: no a/c, Wi-Fi (some). In-hotel: restaurant, bars, Wi-Fi hotspot, parking (free), some pets allowed* ⊟ *AE, MC, V* ⎰◯⎱ *BP.*

■ **EN ROUTE** Two ferries cross the River Dart at Dartmouth; in summer, lines can be long, and you may want to try the inland route, heading west via A3122 to Halwell and then taking A381 north to Totnes. An attractive, relaxed approach to Dartmouth is by boat down the Dart from Totnes.

TOTNES

9 mi northwest of Dartmouth, 28 mi southwest of Exeter.

This busy market town on the banks of the River Dart preserves plenty of its medieval past, and on summer Tuesdays some shopkeepers dress in Elizabethan costume. Market days proper are Friday and Saturday, when the town's status as a center of alternative medicine and culture becomes especially clear, with an abundance of crafts stalls. The historic buildings include a guildhall and St. Mary's Church.

GETTING HERE AND AROUND

Totnes is on a regular fast bus route between Plymouth and Torbay, and is a stop for main-line trains between Plymouth and Exeter. Buses pull in the center, and the train station lies a few minutes' walk north of the center. Drivers should take A38 and A385 from Plymouth or A3122 and A381 from Dartmouth.

ESSENTIALS

Visitor Information Totnes (⊠ *The Town Mill, Coronation Rd.* ☏ *01803/863168* ⊕ *www.totnesinformation.co.uk*).

EXPLORING

You can climb up the hill in town to the ruins of **Totnes Castle**—a fine Norman motte and bailey design—for a wonderful view of Totnes and the River Dart. ☏ *01803/864406* ⊕ *www.english-heritage.org.uk* ⎘ *£3.20* ⊙ *Late Mar.–June and Sept., daily 10–5; July and Aug., daily 10–6; Oct., daily 10–4.*

☾ Steam trains of the **South Devon Railway** run through 7 mi of the wooded Dart Valley between Totnes and Buckfastleigh, on the edge of Dartmoor. There are often special trips around Christmas. ⊠ *Near Totnes, Littlehempston* ☏ *0845/345–1466* ⊕ *www.southdevonrailway.co.uk* ⎘ *£10 round-trip* ⊙ *Late Mar.–Oct., daily; call for winter operation.*

Brixham, at the southern point of Tor Bay, has kept much of its original charm, partly because it is still an active fishing village. Much of the catch goes straight to restaurants as far away as London. Sample fish-and-chips on the quayside, where there is a (surprisingly petite) full-scale reproduction of the vessel on which Sir Francis Drake circumnavigated the world. The village is 10 mi southeast of Totnes by A385 and A3022.

WHERE TO STAY

££ ⚑ **Royal Seven Stars Hotel.** Conveniently located at the bottom of the main street, this centuries-old coaching inn has counted Daniel Defoe and Edward VII among its former guests. A modern makeover has transformed the interior without sacrificing its period features and created well-equipped bedrooms that are clean and elegant (some have spa baths). You can order hot and cold snacks in the traditional Saloon Bar or the contemporary Bar 7, whereas the stylish TQ9 restaurant has more substantial fare. **Pros:** central location; friendly staff; spotless rooms. **Cons:** occasional noise; busy public areas. ⊠ *The Plains* ☎ *01803/862125* ⊕ *www.royalsevenstars.co.uk* ⟋ *16 rooms* ⚐ *In-room: no a/c, Wi-Fi. In-hotel: restaurant, bars, Wi-Fi hotspot, parking (free), some pets allowed* ▤ *AE, MC, V* |◯| *BP.*

NIGHTLIFE AND THE ARTS

★ One of the foremost arts centers of the West Country, **Dartington Hall** (⊠ *Off A384 and A385, Dartington* ☎ *01803/847070* ⊕ *www. dartington.org/arts*) lies 2 mi northwest of Totnes. The medieval estate was an experimental school before it evolved into an arts and education center. There are concerts, a respected summer school of classical music with master classes and performances, film screenings, and exhibitions, usually with a contemporary slant. The gardens, free year-round, are the setting for outdoor performances of Shakespeare in summer. There's a café, and you can stay overnight in some rooms in the hall.

SHOPPING

Near Dartington Hall, 15 stores and two restaurants in and around an old cider press make up the **Dartington Cider Press Centre** (⊠ *Shinners Bridge, Dartington* ☎ *01803/847500* ⊕ *www.dartington.org/ cider-press-centre*), open daily, which markets handmade Dartington crystal glassware, kitchenware, high-quality crafts, books, and toys from Devon and elsewhere. The farm shop sells fudge, ice cream, and cider, and Cranks is an excellent vegetarian restaurant.

TORQUAY

5 mi north of Brixham via A3022, 23 mi south of Exeter.

The most important resort area in South Devon, Torquay envisions itself as the center of the "English Riviera." Since 1968 the towns of Paignton and Torquay (pronounced tor-*kee*) have been amalgamated under the common moniker of Torbay. Torquay is the supposed site of the hotel in the popular British television comedy *Fawlty Towers* and was the home of mystery writer Agatha Christie. Fans should check out the exhibit devoted to Christie at the town museum. Torre Abbey Mansion holds one of Devon's best collections of 19th-century art.

The town has shed some of its old-fashioned image in recent years, with modern hotels, luxury villas, and apartments that climb the hillsides above the harbor. Still, Torquay is more like Brighton's maiden aunt in terms of energy and fizz, though a pubs-and-clubs culture makes an appearance on Friday and Saturday nights. Palm trees and other semitropical plants (a benefit of being near the warming Gulf Stream) flourish in the seafront gardens; the sea is a clear and intense blue.

GETTING HERE AND AROUND
Buses arrive near Torquay's harbor and the tourist office. The train station is close to Torre Abbey Mansion, but other points in town are best reached on local buses or by taxi. Drivers should take A385 from Totnes or A38 and A380 from Exeter.

ESSENTIALS
Visitor Information Torquay (⊠ *Vaughan Parade* ☎ *01803/211211* ⊕ *www. englishriviera.co.uk*).

EXPLORING
Torbay's **beaches**, a mixture of sand and shingle (coarse gravel), have won awards for their water quality and facilities, and can get very crowded in summer. Apart from the central Torre Abbey Sands, they are scattered around town, often separated by the crumbly red cliffs characteristic of the area. To sun and swim, head for Anstey's Cove, a favorite spot for scuba divers, with more beaches farther along at neighboring Babbacombe.

★ For lovers of fine things, Torquay's chief attraction is the **Torre Abbey Mansion**, surrounded by parkland but close to the seafront. It was built on the site of the abbey razed in 1539, and you can still see traces of the old construction. The artistic riches lie within the main building: marine paintings, Victorian sculptures, Pre-Raphaelite window designs, and drawings by William Blake. Children can have fun in the brass-rubbing center. ⊠ *King's Dr.* ☎ *01803/293593* ⊕ *www.torre-abbey.org. uk* ☜ *£5.75* ☉ *Mar.–Oct., daily 10–6; Nov., Dec., and Feb., Tues.–Sun. 10–5; last admission 1 hr before closing.*

Just a mile outside the heart of Torbay by bus or car lies a chocolate-box Devon village, **Cockington**, which has thatched cottages, a 14th-century forge, and the square-tower Church of St. George and St. Mary. Repair to the Old Mill for a café lunch or head to the Drum Inn, designed by Sir Edwin Lutyens to be an archetypal pub. On the village outskirts lies Cockington Court—a grand estate with crafts studios, shops, and an eatery. Cockington has, however, more than a touch of the faux: cottages that don't sell anything put up signs to this effect.

WHERE TO EAT AND STAY

££££
MODERN BRITISH
★

✕ **The Elephant.** Set back from Torquay's harbor, this elegant eatery offers sophisticated but relaxed dining, either in the dining room upstairs with views over Tor Bay or in the less formal street-level brasserie. In the latter, you can tuck into such dishes as steamed Brixham mussels, lemon sole with shellfish ragout, and slow-braised beef. Upstairs, with its high-back chairs, antique lighting fixtures, and polished floorboards, has more innovative concoctions, available on fixed-price tasting menus, which may include risotto of squid and cauliflower as a starter, and ray wing with parsnip puree for the main course. ⊠ *3–4 Beacon Terr.* ☎ *01803/200044* ⊕ *www.elephantrestaurant.co.uk* ☐ *AE,*

MC, V ⊘ *Closed Sun., Mon., and 2 wks early Jan; upstairs restaurant closed Oct.–mid-Apr. No lunch in upstairs restaurant.*

£££   ✕ **Number 7 Fish Bistro.** Seafood
SEAFOOD   fans can indulge their passion at this unpretentious, convivial spot near the harbor; wood floors, white walls, and plenty of maritime knick-knacks set the mood. Fresh, locally caught fish is brought to your table for inspection before being simply but imaginatively prepared. The extensive menu offers dishes ranging from humble—but abundant and beautifully cooked—fish-and-chips to lobster and crab grilled with garlic and brandy butter. ⊠ *7 Beacon Terr.* ☏ *01803/295055* ⊕ *www.no7-fish.com* ⚓ *Reservations essential* ▤ *AE, MC, V* ⊘ *Closed Sun. Oct.–June, Mon. Nov.–May. No lunch Sun.–Tues.*

> ### FAWLTY TOWERS
>
> John Cleese was inspired to write the TV series *Fawlty Towers* after he and the Monty Python team stayed at a hotel in Torquay while filming the series *Monty Python's Flying Circus* in the early 1970s. The "wonderfully rude" owner became the model for Basil Fawlty, the exasperated, accident-prone manager in the series. The owner died in 1981, but his hotel, the Gleneagles, is still going strong—though happily nothing like the chaotic Fawlty Towers.

££–££££   ▦ **Barceló Torquay Imperial Hotel.** This enormous pile perched above the sea, overlooking Torbay, exudes slightly faded Victorian splendor. Magnificent gardens surround the property, and the interior of the 1886 hotel is, well, imperial, with chandeliers, marble floors, and the general air of a bygone world. Most of the traditionally furnished bedrooms are large and comfortable—it's worth paying a bit extra for front-facing ones that have balconies and entrancing views across the bay. **Pros:** stunning location; great views. **Cons:** renovation overdue; inland-facing rooms overlook parking lot. ⊠ *Park Hill Rd.* ☏ *01803/294301* ⊕ *www.barcelo-hotels.co.uk* ⤴ *139 rooms, 13 suites* ⚭ *In-room: no a/c, refrigerator, Internet, Wi-Fi (some). In-hotel: 2 restaurants, bar, tennis court, pools, gym, spa, parking (paid), some pets allowed* ▤ *AE, DC, MC, V* � *BP.*

££   ▦ **Lanscombe House.** Located in the postcard-pretty village of Cockington, a rural hideaway within Torquay, this family-run Victorian guesthouse offers spacious bedrooms with Laura Ashley wallpaper and period furnishings, and a walled garden where you can try your hand at croquet. Though Cockington gets quite busy at peak periods, the place preserves a blissfully peaceful ambience in the morning and late afternoon, and the Country Park is just steps away. **Pros:** quiet, traditional setting; pleasant garden. **Cons:** touristy environment; car necessary for local sights. ⊠ *Cockington La., Cockington* ☏ *01803/606938* ⊕ *www.lanscombehouse.co.uk* ⤴ *8 rooms* ⚭ *In-room: no a/c, no phone. In-hotel: bar, parking (free)* ▤ *MC, V* ⊘ *Closed Nov.–Easter* ⡏ *BP.*

EXETER

23 mi north of Torbay, 48 mi northeast of Plymouth, 85 mi southwest of Bristol, 205 mi southwest of London.

Devon's county seat, Exeter, has been the capital of the region since the Romans established a fortress here 2,000 years ago. Evidence of the Roman occupation remains in the city walls. Although it was heavily bombed in 1942, Exeter retains much of its medieval character, as well as examples of the gracious architecture of the 18th and 19th centuries. It's convenient to both Torquay and Dartmoor.

GETTING HERE AND AROUND
Train service (leaving roughly hourly) from London Paddington takes about two hours, 15 minutes; Megatrain service takes three hours, 20 minutes and leaves London Waterloo four times daily. National Express buses depart every two hours from London's Victoria Coach Station and take around four hours, 30 minutes. Exeter is a major transportation hub for Devon. Trains from Bristol, Salisbury, and Plymouth stop at Exeter St. David's, and connect to the center by frequent buses. Some trains also stop at the more useful Exeter Central. The bus station is off Paris Street near the tourist office. Cars are unnecessary in town, so park yours as soon as possible—all the sights are within an easy walk.

TOURS   Free 90-minute walking tours of Exeter by Red Coat guides take place daily all year, focusing on different aspects of the city. See ⊕ *www.exeter. gov.uk/guidedtours* for details, or contact the tourist office. You can also pick up a leaflet on self-guided walks from here.

ESSENTIALS
Visitor Information Exeter (✉ *Dix's Field* ☎ *01392/665700* ⊕ *www. exeterandessentialdevon.com*).

EXPLORING
TOP ATTRACTIONS
❶ **Cathedral of St. Peter.** At the heart of Exeter, the great Gothic cathedral
★ was begun in 1275 and completed almost a century later. Its twin towers are even older survivors of an earlier Norman cathedral. Rising from a forest of ribbed columns, the nave's 300-foot stretch of unbroken Gothic vaulting is the longest in the world. Myriad statues, tombs, and memorial plaques adorn the interior. In the minstrels' gallery, high up on the left of the nave, stands a group of carved figures singing and playing musical instruments, including bagpipes. The **Close**, a pleasant green space for relaxing, surrounds the cathedral. Don't miss the 400-year-old door to No. 10, the bishop of Crediton's house, ornately carved with angels' and lions' heads. (✉ *Cathedral Close* ☎ *01392/285983* ⊕ *www. exeter-cathedral.org.uk* ⌨ *£5* ⊙ *Mon.–Sat. 9–4:45, Sun. open for services only. Guided tours Mar.–May and Oct., weekdays at 11 and 2:30, Sat. at 11; June–Sept., weekdays at 11, 12:30, and 2:30, Sat. at 11 and 12:30; Nov.–Feb., Mon.–Sat. various times.*

■
OFF THE   **Powderham Castle.** Seat of the earls of Devon, this notable stately home
BEATEN   8 mi south of Exeter is famed for its staircase hall, a soaring fantasia of
PATH   white stuccowork on a turquoise background, constructed in 1739–69. Other sumptuous rooms, adorned with family portraits by Sir Godfrey

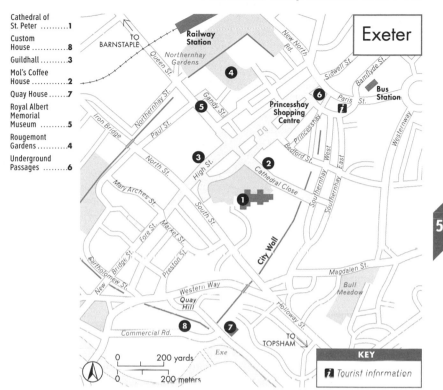

Kneller and Sir Joshua Reynolds, were used in the Merchant-Ivory film *Remains of the Day.* A tower built in 1400 by Sir Philip Courtenay, ancestor of the current owners, stands in the deer park. "Safari" rides (a tractor pulls a trailer) to see the 600 deer take place three times daily, and falconry displays are offered each day. The restaurant serves traditional English fare, and there's a farm shop and plant center. ⊠ *A379, Kenton* ☎ *01626/890243* ⊕ *www.powderham.co.uk* ⊠ *£9.50, deer park safari £3.50* ⊗ *Apr.–mid-July, Sept., and Oct., Sun.–Fri. 11–4:30; mid-July–Aug., Sun.–Fri. 11–5:30.*

⑤ **Royal Albert Memorial Museum.** This museum houses natural-history displays, superb Exeter silverware, and the work of some West Country artists. There is also an excellent international gallery and a fine archaeological section. The property is undergoing a major refurbishment and will reopen in late 2011. ⊠ *Queen St.* ☎ *01392/665858* ⊕ *www. rammuseum.org.uk* ⊠ *Free* ⊗ *Mon.–Sat. 10–5.*

WORTH NOTING

⑧ **Custom House.** Exeter's historic waterfront on the River Exe was the center of the city's medieval wool industry, and the Custom House, built in 1682 on the quay, attests to the city's prosperity. Victorian warehouses flank the city's earliest surviving brick building. ⊠ *The Quay.*

③ Guildhall. Just behind the Close, this is said to be the oldest municipal building in the country still in use. The current hall, with its Renaissance portico, dates from 1330, although a guildhall has occupied this site since at least 1160. Its timber-braced roof, one of the earliest in England, dates from about 1460. The building is frequently closed for civic functions—call to check. ⊠ *High St.* ☎ *01392/665500* ☒ *Free* ☉ *Weekdays 11–1 and 2–4:30, Sat. 10:30–12:30.*

② Mol's Coffee House. With its half-timber facade bearing the coat of arms of Elizabeth I, this building (now a gift shop), on the corner of Cathedral Close, is redolent of bygone times. It is said that Sir Francis Drake met his admirals here to plan strategy against the Spanish Armada in 1588, though this now seems unlikely. ⊠ *1 Cathedral Close.*

⑦ Quay House. This late-17th-century stone warehouse houses the Heritage Centre, with documents on the city's maritime history and an audiovisual display. ⊠ *The Quay* ☎ *01392/271611* ☒ *Free* ☉ *Apr.–Oct., daily 10–5; Nov.–Mar., weekends 11–4.*

QUICK BITES

At the **Prospect Inn** (⊠ *The Quay* ☎ *01392/273152*) you can contemplate the quayside comings and goings over a pint of real ale and a hot or cold meal. The nautical theme comes through in pictures and the ship's wheel hanging from the ceiling.

④ Rougemont Gardens. These gardens behind the Royal Albert Memorial Museum were laid out at the end of the 18th century. The land was once part of the defensive ditch of Rougemont Castle, built in 1068 by decree of William the Conqueror. The gardens contain the original Norman gatehouse and the remains of the Roman city wall, the latter forming part of the ancient castle's outer wall; nothing else remains of the castle. ⊠ *Off Queen St.*

⑥ Underground Passages. Exeter's Underground Passages, which once served as conduits for fresh water, are the only medieval vaulted passages open to the public in Britain. They date to the mid-14th century, although some were enlarged by the Victorians. An exhibition and video precede the 40-minute guided tour. Many of the passages are narrow and low: be prepared to stoop. Children under 5 are not permitted. ⊠ *2 Paris St.* ☎ *01392/665887* ⊕ *www.exeter.gov.uk* ☒ *£5* ☉ *June–Sept. and school vacations, Mon.–Sat. 9:30–5:30, Sun. 10:30–4; Oct.–May, Tues.–Fri. 11:30–5:30, Sat. 9:30–5:30, Sun. 11:30–4; last tours 1 hr before closing.*

WHERE TO EAT

£   ✕ **Ask.** This outpost of an Italian chain has secured an enviable site in a

ITALIAN   part-medieval, part-Georgian building opposite the cathedral. There are three dining areas. The large-windowed rooms offer superb views across the Close, the back room is older and has more atmosphere, and the courtyard is perfect for warm days. Although the food is unadventurous, with a generous choice of pizzas and pastas, everything is prepared to high standards, including good antipasti and salads. ⊠ *5 Cathedral Close* ☎ *01392/427127* ⊕ *www.askrestaurants.com* ▭ *AE, MC, V.*

£ ✕ **Herbie's.** A mellow stop, this friendly vegetarian bistro with wood
VEGETARIAN floors and simple tables is ideal for unwinding over leisurely conversa-
★ tion. You can snack on pita bread with hummus, or tackle the spicy
vegetable satay or spinach-and-mushroom lasagna. All the wines and
the superb ice cream are organic. ✉ *15 North St.* ☎ *01392/258473*
▬ *MC, V* ⊗ *Closed Sun. No dinner Mon.*

££££ ✕ **Michael Caines Restaurant.** Perfectly located within the Cathedral Close,
MODERN BRITISH this ultrachic restaurant is in the centuries-old building that is now the
★ Abode Exeter. Run by master chef Michael Caines (of Gidleigh Park
fame), the kitchen serves eclectic contemporary fare such as beef fillet
with celeriac puree or slow-poached Brixham brill with stir-fried *mange-
tout* (snow peas), shiitake mushrooms, and lemongrass foam. Alternatively, a more relaxed (and more affordable) café-bar next door serves
meals all day, including good fixed-price lunches; there's live jazz on alternate Friday evenings. The hotel's beautifully designed bedrooms have
the same clean-line style. ✉ *Cathedral Yard* ☎ *01392/223638* ⊕ *www.
michaelcaines.com* ▬ *AE, DC, MC, V* ⊗ *Restaurant closed Sun.*

£ ✕ **Ship Inn.** Here you can lift a tankard of stout in the very rooms where
BRITISH Sir Francis Drake and Sir Walter Raleigh enjoyed their ale. Drake, in
fact, once wrote, "Next to mine own shippe, I do most love that old
'Shippe' in Exon." The pub dishes out casual bar fare, from curries to
sausage and mash, either in the bar or the more secluded upstairs restaurant (lunchtime only). ✉ *St. Martin's La.* ☎ *01392/272040* ▬ *MC, V.*

WHERE TO STAY

££–£££ ⌂ **Abode Exeter.** The hotel's old name, the Royal Clarence, still appears
outside; it was built under that name in 1769, reputedly as the first inn
in England to be described as a "hotel." The Abode chain has transformed the property into an upscale boutique hotel that retains its
ancient lines while offering thoroughly contemporary rooms, though
the central location may be better than what the hotel delivers. On
the ground floor, two contrasting restaurants—formal and casual—
by noted chef Michael Caines are equally chic. **Pros:** superb location;
superior bedrooms are very comfortable. **Cons:** no lounge; some rooms
are small and viewless; no parking. ✉ *Cathedral Yard* ☎ *01392/319955*
⊕ *www.abodehotels.co.uk* ⌫ *53 rooms* ⌂ *In-room: a/c, safe, DVD,
Internet, Wi-Fi (some). In-hotel: 2 restaurants, room service, bar, pool,
gym, spa, Internet terminal, Wi-Fi hotspot* ▬ *MC, V* ⍣ *BP.*

££ ⌂ **Raffles.** A 10-minute walk from the center, this quirky B&B in a quiet
neighborhood makes an ideal base for a night or two in town. The owners, who are also antiques dealers, have adorned the Victorian building
with period furnishings, fascinating artwork, and a trove of objets that
invite lingering over. There's no sense of clutter, however; rooms are
scrupulously clean, and the organic breakfasts are superb. **Pros:** peaceful location; antique style. **Cons:** not very central for restaurants and
sights. ✉ *11 Blackall Rd.* ☎ *01392/270200* ⊕ *www.raffles-exeter.co.uk*
⌫ *6 rooms* ⌂ *In-room: no a/c, no phone, Internet. In-hotel: parking
(free), some pets allowed* ▬ *MC, V* ⍣ *BP.*

££ ⌂ **St. Olaves Court Hotel.** In a hushed enclave in an unattractive part
of Exeter's center, this hotel occupies a Georgian house with a walled
garden. A privileged but unfussy air prevails, with an old-fashioned

5

elegance in the spacious, pastel-color bedrooms. Ideal for fine dining, the first-rate Treasury Restaurant provides a sedate setting, and the bar menu is a cheaper lunchtime option. Nearby shops are lackluster, but the cathedral is only a few minutes away. **Pros:** intimate and refined atmosphere; secluded location in city center. **Cons:** some facilities are dated; some rooms small with no view. ⊠ *Mary Arches St.* ☎ *01392/217736* ⊕ *www.olaves.co.uk* ↬ *13 rooms, 2 suites* ♿ *In-room: no a/c, Wi-Fi (some). In-hotel: restaurant, bar, Wi-Fi hotspot, parking (free)* ☰ *MC, V.*

£ ⛳ **White Hart.** Guests have been welcomed to this inn since the 15th century, and it is said that Oliver Cromwell stabled his horses here. Beyond the lovely cobbled entrance, the main building retains all the trappings of a period inn—beams, stone walls, courtyard—but there are 40 more modern bedrooms in a separate wing. The hotel has a casual bar-restaurant where you can order such dishes as slow-cooked gammon, curries, and char-grills. **Pros:** plenty of atmosphere; friendly service. **Cons:** worn-down in places; modern wing bland and charmless. ⊠ *66 South St.* ☎ *01392/279897* ⊕ *www.whitehartpubexeter.co.uk* ↬ *55 rooms* ♿ *In-room: no a/c, Wi-Fi. In-hotel: restaurant, bar, Wi-Fi hotspot, parking (free)* ☰ *AE, MC, V* ⦿ *BP.*

NIGHTLIFE AND THE ARTS

Among the best known of the West Country's festivals, the **Exeter Festival** (☎ *01392/265200* ⊕ *www.exeter.gov.uk/festival*) mixes musical and theater events over two weeks in June/July and again in October/November. The **Exeter Festival of South West Food and Drink** (⊕ *www.exeterfoodanddrinkfestival.co.uk*) showcases local producers, chefs, and their gastronomic specialties, taking place in Rougemont Gardens and Northernhay Gardens in mid-April. Live music is staged in the evenings. Some of London's best companies often stage plays at the **Northcott Theatre** (⊠ *Stocker Rd.* ☎ *01392/493493* ⊕ *www.exeternorthcott.co.uk*).

SHOPPING

Many of Exeter's most interesting shops are along Gandy Street, off the main High Street drag, with several good food and clothes outlets. Exeter was the silver-assay office for the West Country, and the earliest example of Exeter silver (now a museum piece) dates from 1218; Victorian pieces are still sold. The Exeter assay mark is three castles. **Bruford's of Exeter** (⊠ *17 The Guildhall Centre, Queen St.* ☎ *01392/254901*) stocks antique jewelry and silver.

SPORTS AND THE OUTDOORS

Saddles and Paddles (⊠ *4 Kings Wharf, the Quay* ☎ *01392/424241*) rents bikes, kayaks, and canoes and is handily placed for a 7-mi route along the scenic Exeter Canal Trail, which follows the River Exe and the Exeter Ship Canal.

TOPSHAM

4 mi southeast of Exeter on B3182.

This town full of narrow streets and hidden courtyards was once a bustling port, and it remains rich in 18th-century houses and inns.

EXPLORING

Occupying a 17th-century Dutch-style merchant's house beside the river, the **Topsham Museum** has period-furnished rooms and displays on local and maritime history. One room has memorabilia belonging to the late actress Vivien Leigh. ⊠ *25 The Strand* ☎ *01392/873244* ☑ *Free* ⊙ *Apr.–July, Sept., and Oct., Mon., Wed., and weekends 2–5; Aug., Mon., Wed., Thurs., and weekends 2–5.*

★ The 16-sided, nearly circular **A la Ronde**, surely one of the most unusual houses in England, was built in 1798 by two cousins inspired by the Church of San Vitale in Ravenna, Italy. Among the 18th- and 19th-century curiosities here is an elaborate display of feathers and shells. The house is 5 mi south of Topsham. ⊠ *Summer La., on A376 near Exmouth* ☎ *01395/265514* ⊕ *www.nationaltrust.org.uk* ☑ *£6./0* ⊙ *Mid-Mar.–June, Sept., and Oct., Sat.–Wed. 11–5; July and Aug,. Fri.–Wed. 11–5; last admission at 4.*

**EN
ROUTE**
The **Jurassic Coast** (⊕ *www.jurassiccoast.com*), from Exmouth to Studland Bay in Dorset, 95 mi to the east, has been designated a World Heritage Site because of the rich geological record of ancient rocks and fossils exposed here. The reddish, grass-topped cliffs of the region are punctuated by quiet seaside resorts such as Budleigh Salterton, Sidmouth, and Seaton. *For more information about the Jurassic Coast, see Lyme Regis in Chapter 4.*

HONITON

20 mi east of Topsham, 20 mi east of Exeter.

Handsome Georgian houses line Honiton's long High Street. Modern storefronts have intruded, but the original facades remain at second-floor level. For 300 years the town was known for lace making, and the industry was revived when Queen Victoria selected the fabric for her wedding veil in 1840. Lace has not been made here commercially since the early 20th century, but individuals keep up the craft.

ESSENTIALS

Visitor Information Honiton (⊠ *Lace Walk Car Park, Dowell St.* ☎ *01404/43716* ⊕ *www.visithoniton.com*).

EXPLORING

After viewing the glorious collection of lace at **Allhallows Museum**—in what is claimed to be the town's oldest building—it's worth delving into the antiques shops where prized early examples are sold. ⊠ *High St.* ☎ *01404/44966* ⊕ *www.honitonmuseum.co.uk* ☑ *£2* ⊙ *Easter–Sept., weekdays 9:30–4:30, Sat. 9:30–1; Oct., weekdays 9:30–3:30, Sat. 9:30–12:30.*

WHERE TO EAT AND STAY

££   ✕ **The Holt.** For a satisfying lunch or dinner, try this pub and restaurant at
MODERN BRITISH   the bottom of High Street. Downstairs a vibrant, chattery pub with soft
orange walls serves fine Otter real ales; the buzz wafts upstairs, where
you can dine on such dishes as smoked pigeon, grilled bream with spiced
courgette (squash) fritter, and onion tarte tatin with wild mushrooms
and fennel. ✉ *178 High St.* ☎ *01404/47707* ⊕ *www.theholt-honiton.*
com ☐ *MC, V* ⊗ *Closed Sun. and Mon.*

££££   🏨 **Combe House.** Rolling parkland surrounds this luxurious Elizabethan
★   manor house. From the imposing Great Hall, with its huge, open fireplace, to the spacious, individually decorated bedrooms, the emphasis
is on country-house style that unites antiques and modern comfort. The
fixed-price restaurant prepares such sophisticated creations as Moroccan spiced quail with salted lemon couscous and eggplant puree, and
roast rabbit with bacon and wild mushrooms. You can fish on a 1½-mi
stretch of the River Otter and explore Gittisham, just west of Honiton, once described as "the ideal English village" by Prince Charles.
A two-night minimum stay is required on weekends. **Pros:** beautiful
rural surroundings; romantic ambience; attentive but informal staff.
Cons: rather remote. ✉ *Off A30, Gittisham* ☎ *01404/540400* ⊕ *www.*
thishotel.com ⤴ *13 rooms, 2 suites, 1 cottage* ⚒ *In-room: no a/c,*
Internet, Wi-Fi (some). In-hotel: restaurant, Wi-Fi hotspot, some pets
allowed ☐ *MC, V* �📶 *BP.*

SHOPPING

Honiton has several dozen fine antiques stores. The **Grove Antiques Centre**
(✉ *55 High St.* ☎ *01404/43377*) is a good stop for antiques of all kinds,
including art, furniture, and jewelry.

The Thames Valley

WINDSOR, HENLEY-ON-THAMES, OXFORD, BLENHEIM PALACE

WORD OF MOUTH

"At Windsor Castle, the free audioguide is very good; they also offer tours (free). If you arrive after opening time, expect a line. I spent the first hour around the grounds, plus seeing St George's Chapel. I watched the Changing of the Guard (40 minutes) and got in line for the Doll's House and State Apartments. So, allow 3 to 4 hours"

—yk

"Oxford's probably the most unsuitable city in Europe for hop-on, hop-off buses. Buses aren't allowed into most of the areas where there are interesting buildings. The official city walking tours are far, far better, and concentrate on the historic core, rather than the late Victorian suburbs."

—flanneruk

Updated by
Kate Hughes

Easy proximity to London made the Thames Valley enormously popular with the rich and powerful throughout the country's history. They built the lavish country estates and castles, including Windsor, that form the area's most popular tourist attractions today. Some of these, as well as Oxford with its university, are easy day trips from London.

Once an aquatic highway connecting London to the rest of England and the world, the River Thames was critical to the power of the city when the sun never set on the British Empire. By the 18th century the Thames was one of the world's busiest water systems, declining in commercial importance only when the 20th century brought other means of transportation to the forefront. Along its 215-mi course the river runs from the Cotswolds through London and on to where it pours into the sea in Essex. Traditionally, the area west of London is known as the Thames Valley, and the area to the east is called the Thames Gateway.

Anyone who wants to understand the mystique of the British monarchy should visit Windsor, home to the medieval and massive Windsor Castle. Farther upstream, the green quadrangles and graceful spires of Oxford are the hallmarks of one of the world's most famous universities. Within 10 mi of Oxford the storybook village of Woodstock and gracious Blenheim Palace, one of the grandest houses in England, are both well worth your time.

The railroads and motorways carrying traffic to and from London have turned much of this area into commuter territory, but you can still find timeless villages and miles of relaxing countryside. The stretches of the Thames near Marlow, Henley, and Sonning-on-Thames are lovely, with rowing clubs, piers, and sturdy waterside cottages and villas. It all conspires to make the Thames Valley a wonderful find, even for experienced travelers.

ORIENTATION AND PLANNING

GETTING ORIENTED

An ideal place to begin any exploration of the Thames Valley is the town of Windsor, about an hour's drive west of central London. From there you can follow the river to Marlow and to Henley-on-Thames, site of the famous regatta, and then make a counterclockwise sweep west to the area around Sonning-on-Thames, the countryside immortalized by Kenneth Grahame's *The Wind in the Willows*. To the north is Oxford, with its pubs, colleges, and museums; it can make a good base for exploring some of the area's charming towns and notable stately homes. If you're extending your itinerary, west of the region but nearby are both the Cotswolds and Stratford-upon-Avon.

TOP REASONS TO GO

Windsor Castle: The mystique of eight successive royal houses of the British monarchy permeates Windsor and its famous castle, where a fraction of the current Queen's vast wealth is displayed in heraldic splendor.

Mapledurham House: This is the house that inspired Toad Hall from *The Wind in the Willows;* you can picnic here on the grounds and drink in the views of the sleepy countryside.

Oxford: While scholars' noses are buried in their books, you get to sightsee among Oxford University's ancient stone buildings (look out for gargoyles around New College) and memorable museums. Try your luck at punting, too. You'll either proudly exhibit your balance and strength, or take a humiliating plunge into a slow-moving river.

Blenheim Palace: The only British historic home to be named a World Heritage Site has magnificent baroque architecture, stunning gardens and parkland, and remembrances of Winston Churchill. For a special treat, attend an outdoor summer concert.

A walk on the Thames Path. A stroll or hike is an ideal and peaceful way to see England's verdant riverside pastures and villages. This national trail is easily accessible, you don't need any special equipment, and you can walk as little or as long as you like. Marlow to Henley is a good stretch.

Windsor, Marlow, and Environs. Gorgeous Windsor has its imposing and battlemented castle, stone cottages, and tea shops, and nearby Eton is also charming. The meadows and villages around Marlow and Henley are lovely in summer when the flowers are in bloom. Mapledurham House near Sonning-on-Thames is an idyllic stop; you can take a boat here.

Oxford. Wonderfully walkable, this university town has one handsome, golden-stone building and museum after another to explore. Take a punt on the local waterways for a break. Oxford's good bars, pubs, and restaurants keep you going late at night as well.

Blenheim Palace to Althorp. So many grand manor houses, so little time: around the Thames Valley are many intriguing stops. Blenheim is a vast, ornate, extraordinary place that takes the better part of a day to see. Althorp, home of the late Princess Diana, seems almost small by comparison, although it's actually enormous.

THAMES VALLEY PLANNER

WHEN TO GO

High summer is lovely, but droves of visitors have the same effect on some travelers as bad weather. Consider visiting in late spring or early fall, when the weather is not too bad and the crowds have headed home. Book tickets and accommodations well in advance for Henley's Royal Regatta at the cusp of June and July or Ascot's Royal Meeting in mid-June. Visiting at Eton and the Oxford colleges is much more restricted during term time (generally September to late March and late April to mid-July). Most stately homes are open March through September or October only—call in advance if you're planning an itinerary. Avoid any driving in the London area during afternoon and morning rush hours.

PLANNING YOUR TIME

The major towns of the Thames Valley are easy to visit on a day trip from London. A train to Windsor, for example, takes about an hour, and you can fully explore Windsor and its environs in a day. Base yourself in Oxford for a couple of days, though, if you want to make a thorough exploration of the town and the surrounding countryside. To visit the great houses and the rural castles you'll need to either rent a car or join an organized tour.

GETTING HERE AND AROUND

BUS TRAVEL

Oxford and the area's main towns are convenient by bus from London, as is Windsor (although trains are faster), but St. Albans is best reached by train.

You can travel between the major towns by local bus, but it's complicated and can require changing more than once. For information, contact Traveline. If you want to see more than one town in this area in a day, it would be best to rent a car or join a tour.

Contacts Arriva (☎ 0871/200–2233 ⊕ www.arriva.co.uk). **First** (☎ 01344/782200 ⊕ www.firstgroup.com). **Megabus** (⊕ www.megabus.co.uk). **Oxford Bus Company** (☎ 01865/785400 ⊕ www.oxfordbus.co.uk). **Reading Buses** (☎ 0118/959–4000 ⊕ www.reading-buses.co.uk). **Stagecoach Oxford Tube** (☎ 01865/772250 ⊕ www.oxfordtube.com). **Traveline** (☎ 0871/200–2233 ⊕ www.traveline.org.uk).

CAR TRAVEL

Most towns in this area are within a one- or two-hour drive of central London—except during rush hour, of course. Although the roads are good, this wealthy section of the commuter belt has heavy traffic, even on the smaller roads. Parking in towns can be a problem, so expect to park in public parking lots near the outskirts of town centers.

TRAIN TRAVEL

Trains to Oxford (one hour) and the region depart from London's Paddington Station. Trains bound for Ascot (50 minutes) leave Waterloo on the half hour. Trains to St. Albans (20 minutes) leave from St. Pancras Station. A number of lines, including Chiltern and First Great Western, serve the area; National Rail Enquiries has information.

Contacts National Rail Enquiries (☎ 0845/748–4950 ⊕ www.nationalrail. co.uk).

RESTAURANTS

Londoners weekend here, and where they go, stellar restaurants follow. Bray (near Windsor), Marlow, and Great Milton (near Oxford) claim some excellent tables. Simple pub food, as well as classic French cuisine, can be enjoyed in waterside settings at many restaurants beside the Thames. Even in towns away from the river, well-heeled commuters

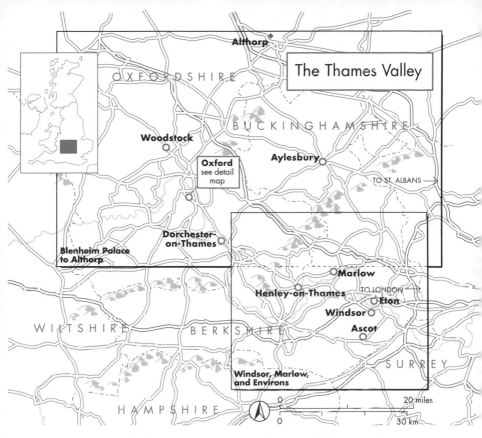

and Oxford professors support top-flight establishments. Reservations are strongly recommended, especially on weekends.

HOTELS

From converted country houses to refurbished Elizabethan inns, the region's accommodations are rich in history and distinctive in appeal. Many hotels cultivate traditional gardens and retain a sense of the past with impressive collections of antiques. Book ahead, particularly in summer; you're competing for rooms with many Londoners in search of a getaway.

WHAT IT COSTS IN POUNDS					
	£	££	£££	££££	£££££
Restaurants	under £10	£10–£14	£15–£19	£20–£25	over £25
Hotels	under £70	£70–£120	£121–£160	£161–£220	over £220

Restaurant prices are for a main course at dinner. Hotel prices are for two people in a standard double room in high season, including V.A.T., with no meals or, if indicated, CP (with Continental breakfast), BP (Breakfast Plan, with full breakfast), or MAP (Modified American Plan, with breakfast and dinner).

VISITOR INFORMATION

Contacts River Thames Alliance (⊕ www.visitthames.co.uk). Tourism Southeast (☎ 0238/062–5400 ⊕ www.visitsoutheastengland.com).

WINDSOR, MARLOW, AND ENVIRONS

Windsor Castle is one of the jewels of the area known as Royal Windsor, but a journey around this section of the Thames has other classic pleasures. The town of Eton holds the eponymous public school, Ascot has its famous racecourse, and Cliveden is a stately home turned into a grand hotel.

The stretch of the Thames Valley from Marlow to Sonning-on-Thames is enchanting. Walking through its fields and along its waterways, it's easy to see how it inspired Kenneth Grahame's classic 1908 children's book *The Wind in the Willows*. Whether by boat or on foot, you can discover some of the region's most delightful scenery here. On each bank are fine wooded hills, with spacious homes, greenhouses, flower beds, and neat lawns that stretch to the water's edge. Grahame wrote his book in Pangbourne, and his illustrator, E.H. Shepard, used the great house at Mapledurham as the model for Toad Hall. It all still has the power to inspire.

WINDSOR

21 mi west of London.

Only a small part of old Windsor—the settlement that grew up around the town's famous castle in the Middle Ages—has survived. The town isn't what it was in the time of Sir John Falstaff and the *Merry Wives of Windsor*, when it was famous for its convivial inns—in 1650, it had about 70 of them. Only a handful remain, with the others replaced, it seems, by endless tea shops. Windsor can feel overrun by tourists in summer, but even so, romantics will appreciate cobbled Church Lane and noble Queen Charlotte Street, opposite the castle entrance.

GETTING HERE AND AROUND

Fast Green Line buses leave from the Colonnades opposite London's Victoria Coach Station every half hour for the 70-minute trip to Windsor. National Express and First Group have frequent services from Heathrow Airport's Terminal 5; the journey takes less than an hour. First Group also offers regional bus services to small towns and villages near Windsor.

South West Trains travel from London Waterloo every 30 minutes, or you can catch a more frequent train from Paddington and change at Slough. The trip takes 40 minutes from Waterloo and 30 minutes from Paddington. If you're driving, take the M4 from London; journey time is around an hour. Park in one of the public lots near the edge of the town center.

TOURS   Orchard Poyle Carriage Rides offers 30-minute (£20) and one-hour (£40) horse-drawn carriage rides around the historic district. Tours leave from the Harte & Garter Hotel in central Windsor and tour the town and Windsor Great Park. City Sightseeing has hop-on, hop-off tours of Windsor and Eton, though it's easy to explore compact Windsor on foot; the price is £8.

TIMING

Windsor is at its best in the winter and fall when it's not as crowded with tour groups. In the summer it can be uncomfortably packed. Queen Elizabeth is in residence when her banner flies above the palace—everybody perks up a bit when that happens.

ESSENTIALS

Bus Contacts First (☎ *0175/352–4144* ⊕ *wwwfirstgroup.com*). **Green Line** (☎ *0844/801–7261* ⊕ *www.greenline.co.uk*). **National Express** (☎ *0871/781–8181* ⊕ *www.nationalexpress.com*).

Tour Information City Sightseeing (☎ *01708/866000* ⊕ *www.city-sightseeing. com*). **Orchard Poyle Carriage Rides** (☎ *01784/435983* ⊕ *www.orchardpoyle. co.uk*).

Visitor Information Windsor (✉ *Old Booking Hall, Windsor Royal Station, Thames St.* ☎ *01753/743900, 01753/743907 for accommodation* ⊕ *www. windsor.gov.uk*).

EXPLORING

Fodor's Choice
★ From William the Conqueror to Queen Victoria, the kings and queens of England added towers and wings to brooding, imposing **Windsor Castle,** visible for miles and now the largest inhabited castle in the world. Despite the multiplicity of hands involved in its design, the palace manages to have a unity of style and character. The most impressive view of Windsor Castle is from the A332 road, coming into town from the south. Admission includes an audio guide and, if you wish, a guided tour of the castle precincts. Entrance lines can be long in season and you're likely to spend at least half a day here, so come early.

William the Conqueror began work on the castle in the 11th century, and Edward III modified and extended it in the mid-1300s. One of Edward's largest contributions was the enormous and distinctive **Round Tower.** Later, between 1824 and 1837, George IV transformed the still essentially medieval castle into the fortified royal palace you see today. Most of England's kings and queens have demonstrated their undying attachment to the castle, the only royal residence in continuous use by the Royal Family since the Middle Ages.

As you enter the castle, **Henry VIII's gateway** leads uphill into the wide castle precincts, where you are free to wander. Across from the entrance is the exquisite **St. George's Chapel** (closed Sunday). Here lie 10 of the kings of England, including Henry VI, Charles I, and Henry VIII (Jane Seymour is the only one of his six wives buried here). One of the noblest buildings in England, the chapel was built in the Perpendicular style popular in the 15th and 16th centuries, with elegant stained-glass windows, a high, vaulted ceiling, and intricately carved choir stalls. The colorful heraldic banners of the Knights of the Garter—the oldest British Order of Chivalry, founded by Edward III in 1348—hang in the choir. The ceremony in which the knights are installed as members

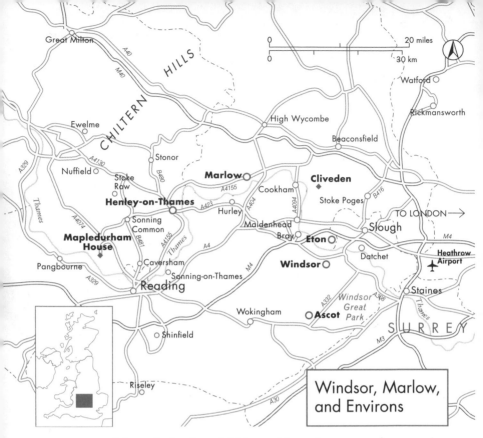

Windsor, Marlow,
and Environs

of the order has been held here with much pageantry for more than five centuries.

The **North Terrace** provides especially good views across the Thames to Eton College, perhaps the most famous of Britain's exclusive "public" boys' schools. From the terrace, you enter the **State Apartments,** which are open to the public most days, except when being used by the Queen (check in advance). Queen Elizabeth uses the castle far more than any of her predecessors did, as a sort of country weekend home.

■**TIP**→ **To see the castle come magnificently alive, check out the Changing of the Guard, which takes place at 11 AM Monday to Saturday from April through July and on alternate weekdays and Saturday from August through March.** Confirm the exact schedule before traveling to Windsor. When the Queen is in town, the guard and a regimental band parade through town to the castle gate; when she is away, a drum-and-fife band takes over.

Although a fire in 1992 gutted some of the State Apartments, hardly any works of art were lost. Phenomenal repair work brought to new life the **Grand Reception Room,** the **Green and Crimson Drawing Rooms,** and the **State and Octagonal Dining Rooms.** A green oak hammer-beam (a short horizontal roof beam that projects from the tops of walls for support) roof looms magnificently over the 600-year-old **St. George's Hall,** where the Queen gives state banquets. The State Apartments contain priceless furniture, including a magnificent Louis XVI bed and Gobelin tapestries; and paintings by Canaletto, Rubens, Van Dyck, Holbein, Dürer, and Bruegel. The tour's high points are the **Throne Room** and the **Waterloo Chamber,** where Sir Thomas Lawrence's portraits of Napoléon's victorious foes line the walls. You can also see arms and armor—look out for Henry VIII's ample suit. ■ **TIP**➜ A visit between October and March also includes the Semi-State rooms, the private apartments of George IV, resplendent with gilded ceilings.

☺ **Queen Mary's Dolls' House,** on display to the left of the entrance to the State Apartments, is a perfect miniature Georgian palace-within-a-palace, created in 1923. Electric lights glow, the doors all have tiny little keys, and a miniature library holds Lilliputian-size books especially written for the young Queen by famous authors of the 1920s. Five cars, including a Daimler and Rolls-Royce, stand at the ready. In the adjacent corridor are exquisite French couturier–designed costumes made for the two Jumeau dolls presented to the Princesses Elizabeth and Margaret by France in 1938. ⊠ *Castle Hill* ☎ *020/7766–7304 tickets, 01753/831118 recorded information* ⊕ *www.royalcollection.org.uk* ⊠ *£16 for Precincts, State Apartments, Gallery, St. George's Chapel, and Dolls' House; £8.50 when State Apartments are closed* ☉ *Mar.–Oct., daily 9:45–5:15, last admission at 4; Nov.–Feb., daily 9:45–4:15, last admission at 3.*

The **Jubilee Garden,** created in 2002, has a stone bandstand used for concerts on summer Sunday afternoons. The garden begins at the main gates and extends to St. George's Gate on Castle Hill.

Windsor Great Park (☎ *01753/860222* ⊕ *www.theroyallandscape.co.uk*), the remains of an ancient royal hunting forest, stretches for some 5,000 acres south of Windsor Castle. Much of it is open to the public and can be seen by car (parking charges apply; you can print maps from the Web site) or on foot, including its geographical focal points, the romantic 3-mi **Long Walk,** designed by Charles II to join castle and park, and **Virginia Water,** a 2-mi-long lake. A spectacular visitor center offers a good introduction to the surrounding landscape. The park contains one of Queen Victoria's most treasured residences, **Frogmore House** (☎ *020/7766–7305* ⊕ *www.royalcollection.org.uk* ⊠ *House, gardens £9.50 in May, £7 in Aug.* ☉ *May and Aug., selected days 10–5:30).* The sprawling white mansion is still a retreat for the Royal Family. The main horticultural delight of Windsor Great Park, the exquisite **Savill Garden** (⊠ *Wick La., Englefield Green, Egham* ☎ *01784/435544* ⊕ *www.theroyallandscape.co.uk* ⊠ *£8, £5.75 in winter* ☉ *Mar.–Oct., daily 10–6; Nov.–Feb., daily 10–4:30),* contains a lovely rose garden and a tremendous diversity of trees and shrubs. You need a car to get to Savill Garden; it's 4 mi from Windsor castle.

WHERE TO EAT
Bray, a tiny village 6 mi outside Windsor, is known for its restaurants more than anything else.

£££££ ✗ **Fat Duck.** One of the top restaurants in the country, and ranked by some reviewers among the best in the world, this extraordinary, discreet (there's no sign; look for the duck-inspired implements hanging outside) Bray establishment packs in fans of hyper-creative, hyper-expensive cuisine. Reserve a table two months in advance. Innovative chef Heston Blumenthal is famed for bizarre taste combinations—scrambled-egg-and-bacon ice cream, for example—and the laboratory-like kitchen in which this advocate of molecular gastronomy creates his dishes. The twelve items on the menu (£150) are never less than adventurous and include such dishes as jelly of quail; cream of crayfish with oak moss and truffle toast; and whisky wine gums. Like the food, the interior blends traditional and contemporary elements— modern art, exposed-brick walls, and ancient wooden beams. ⊠ *High St., Bray-on-Thames* ☎ *01628/580333* ⊕ *www.fatduck.co.uk* ⌕ *Reservations essential* ⊟ *AE, DC, MC, V* ☻ *Closed Mon. No dinner Sun.*

MODERN BRITISH
Fodor's Choice
★

> **TIME FOR A CUPPA**
>
> This is a tea-and-scones town, so having some in one of Windsor's many charming tearooms simply feels right. After taking in the castle and wandering the town's winding medieval lanes, a nice "cuppa," as the locals call it, is just perfect. **Crooked House of Windsor** (⊠ *51 High St.* ☎ *01753/857534*), with two tiny rooms in a 300-year-old house, is a traditional favorite for tea and plates of cakes and scones for £4–£7. It's open daily until 5.

£££ ✗ **Hinds Head.** The Fat Duck's esteemed chef Heston Blumenthal also owns this traditional pub across the road, where he sells less extreme dishes at more reasonable prices. The atmosphere and dress code are relaxed, and the look of the place is historic, with low beams, polished wood-panel walls, and brick fireplaces. A brilliant modern take on traditional English cuisine, the food includes oxtail-and-kidney pudding, and Aberdeenshire rump steak with bone-marrow sauce and triple-cooked fries. Bar snacks and sandwiches are available for weekday lunches as well. ⊠ *High St., Bray-on-Thames* ☎ *01628/626151* ⊕ *www. thehindsheadhotel.com* ⊟ *AE, MC, V* ☻ *No dinner Sun.*

MODERN BRITISH

£££ ✗ **Strok's Restaurant.** In Sir Christopher Wren's House Hotel—a mansion built in 1676 by the architect who designed St. Paul's Cathedral— Strok's offers an ever-changing modern British menu and a Thames-side wooden terrace that swells with crowds in summer. Dishes may include scallops with coriander jelly followed by leg of lamb with chickpea purée and ratatouille. ⊠ *Thames St. at Eton Bridge* ☎ *01753/861354* ⊕ *www.sirchristopherwren.co.uk* ⊟ *AE, MC, V.*

MODERN BRITISH

££ ✗ **Two Brewers.** Locals congregate in the two small, low-ceiling rooms of this 17th-century pub, right by the gates of Windsor Great Park. Children under 18 are not welcome inside (though they can be served at a few outdoor tables in season), but adults will find a suitable collection of wine, espresso, and local beer, plus an excellent little menu with dishes from salmon and lamb cutlets to salads. Reservations are essential on Sunday, when the pub serves a traditional lunchtime roast. Friday and Saturday are tapas nights. ⊠ *34 Park St.* ☎ *01753/855426* ⊟ *AE, MC, V* ☻ *No dinner Sun.*

BRITISH

WHERE TO STAY

££ 🏨 **Alma Lodge.** This friendly little bed-and-breakfast in an early-Victorian town house is just one of many that can be booked through the Windsor tourist office. Ornate ceilings and ornamental fireplaces are some of the house's original features, and each well-maintained room is decorated in an uncluttered Victorian style. **Pros:** very welcoming; beautiful fireplaces. **Cons:** few frills; can be too quiet for some. ⊠ *58 Alma Rd.* 🕾 *01753/855620* ⊕ *www.almalodge.co.uk* 🛏 *4 rooms* 🔥 *In-room: no a/c, no phone, Wi-Fi. In-hotel: parking (free)* 🖃 *MC, V* ⫼ *BP.*

££ 🏨 **Langton House.** A former residence for Queen Victoria's local gov-
🟢 ernment officials, this big Victorian mansion on a quiet, leafy road is a 10-minute walk from Windsor Castle. Rooms are spacious and unfussy, and the owner is eco-conscious. Guests have access to a small kitchen with refrigerator, toaster, microwave, and kettle. This place is very child-friendly, with supplies for babies; it also caters to vegans and vegetarians. **Pros:** soothing decor; family-friendly environment. **Cons:** not for those who prefer their privacy; a little out of town. ⊠ *46 Alma Rd.* 🕾 *01753/858299* ⊕ *www.langtonhouse.co.uk* 🛏 *4 rooms* 🔥 *In-room: no a/c, no phone, Wi-Fi. In-hotel: parking (free)* 🖃 *MC, V* ⫼ *BP.*

£££–££££ 🏨 **Mercure Castle Hotel.** You get an exceptional view of Windsor Castle's Changing of the Guard from this Georgian hotel, parts of which date back much further to its start in the 16th century as a coaching inn. In the older section guest rooms have gently tilting floors, whereas elsewhere it's smooth elegance, with tasteful fabrics in neutral tones juxtaposed against original architectural detail. The cozy lounges are perfect for afternoon tea. **Pros:** excellent location; wonderful afternoon tea. **Cons:** older rooms are small; you can get a good bump on the head from the low beams. ⊠ *High St.* 🕾 *01753/851577* ⊕ *www.mercure. com* 🛏 *108 rooms, 4 suites* 🔥 *In-room: a/c, Internet, Wi-Fi. In-hotel: restaurant, room service, bar, laundry service, Wi-Fi hotspot, parking (paid)* 🖃 *AE, DC, MC, V* ⫼ *BP.*

£££ 🏨 **Oakley Court.** A romantic getaway with plenty of pampering amenities, this Victorian-era Gothic mansion stands on landscaped grounds beside the Thames, 3 mi west of Windsor. Its bristling towers and spires have been used in several films, including *The Rocky Horror Picture Show* and *Dracula.* Note, however, that all the rooms, apart from the suites, are in modern wings and furnished in a standard style. Public rooms, however, retain their old-fashioned, wood-paneled, and clubby charm. The Dining Room restaurant (££££) serves Continental cuisine in plush surroundings. **Pros:** stunning mansion; tranquil riverside setting; friendly staff. **Cons:** many rooms in modern wings; river views cost more. ⊠ *Windsor Rd., Water Oakley* 🕾 *01753/609988* ⊕ *www. oakleycourt.co.uk* 🛏 *106 rooms, 12 suites* 🔥 *In-room: a/c, safe, Wi-Fi. In-hotel: restaurant, room service, bar, golf course, tennis courts, pool, gym, spa, laundry service, parking (free)* 🖃 *AE, DC, MC, V* ⫼ *BP.*

££££–£££££ 🏨 **Stoke Park Club.** On a 350-acre estate 4 mi northeast of Windsor, Stoke Park can make Windsor Castle, off in the distance, seem almost humble in comparison. Architect James Wyatt perfected this version of neoclassical grandeur when he built the house for the Penn family in 1791. Antiques, paintings, and original prints decorate the elegant

6

bedrooms, and the facilities are all about indulgence, from the famous golf course to the up-to-the-minute spa. The Park Restaurant (££££) serves traditional English cuisine. **Pros:** luxurious rooms; sweeping grounds; wonderful for antiques lovers. **Cons:** not for those lukewarm about golf; a bit stuffy. ⊠ *Park Rd., Stoke Poges* 🕾 *01753/717171* ⊕ *www.stokeparkclub.com* ↪ *49 rooms* ⸹ *In-room: a/c, Internet, Wi-Fi. In-hotel: 2 restaurants, bars, golf course, tennis courts, pool, gym, spa* ⦶ *BP*⊟ *AE, DC, MC, V.*

NIGHTLIFE AND THE ARTS

Windsor's **Theatre Royal** (⊠ *Thames St.* 🕾 *01753/853888*), where productions have been staged since 1910, is one of Britain's leading provincial theaters. It puts on plays and musicals year-round, including a pantomime for six weeks around Christmas.

Concerts, poetry readings, and children's events highlight the two-week **Windsor Festival** (🕾 *01753/740121* ⊕ *www.windsorfestival.com*), held in September, with events occasionally taking place in the castle. A similar festival is held over a weekend in March.

SPORTS AND THE OUTDOORS

From Easter to September, **John Logie Motorboats** (⊠ *Barry Ave.* 🕾 *07774/983809*) rents motorboats and rowboats by the half hour and hour.

SHOPPING

Most Windsor stores are open Sunday as well as the rest of the week; check out Peascod Street, opposite the castle, for a good selection of independent stores selling gifts, jewelry, toiletries, chocolates, and more. **Windsor Royal Station** (⊠ *5 Goswell Hill* 🕾 *01753/797070*), a collection of stores in a Victorian train station, includes Jaeger, Viyella, Hobbs, and arts-and-crafts stores.

ETON

23 mi west of London, linked by a footbridge across the Thames to Windsor.

Some observers may find it symbolic that almost opposite Windsor Castle—which embodies the continuity of the royal tradition—stands Eton, a school that for centuries has educated many future leaders of the country. With High Street, its single main street, leading from the river to the famous school, the old-fashioned town of Eton is much quieter than Windsor.

EXPLORING

★ The splendid redbrick Tudor-style buildings of **Eton College**, founded in 1440 by King Henry VI, border the north end of High Street; signs warn drivers of BOYS CROSSING. During the college semesters, the schoolboys dress in their distinctive pinstripe trousers, swallow-tail coats, and stiff collars (top hats have not been worn by the boys since the 1940s) to walk to class, and it's all terrifically photogenic. The Gothic **Chapel** rivals St. George's at Windsor in size and magnificence, and is both impressively austere and intimate. Beyond the cloisters are the school's playing fields where, according to the duke of Wellington, the Battle of

Waterloo was really won, since so many of his officers had learned discipline and strategy during their school days there. The **Museum of Eton Life** has displays on the school's history. ⊠ *Main entrance Brewhouse Yard* ☎ *01753/671177* ⊕ *www.etoncollege.com* ✉ *£6.20* ⊙ *Guided tours at 2 and 3:15: mid-Mar.–mid-Apr. and July–early Sept., daily; mid-Apr.–June and mid-Sept.–early Oct., Wed. and Fri.–Sun.*

WHERE TO EAT AND STAY

£££
BRITISH

✕ **Gilbey's Bar & Restaurant.** Just over the bridge from Windsor, this restaurant at the center of Eton's Antiques Row serves a fine, changing menu of imaginative fare, from spinach and cheese tart with sautéed mushroom salad to roasted pork belly with star anise. There's a fixed-price lunch and early dinner menu for £14.50. Well-priced French wines are a specialty, as are the savories—think British cheeses, fishcakes, and such—that you can order with afternoon tea. The conservatory, with its colorful scattering of cushions, is a particularly pleasant place to sit in fine weather. ⊠ *82–83 High St.* ☎ *01753/854921* ⊕ *www.gilbeygroup. com* ⊟ *AE, DC, MC, V.*

£££–££££

⊞ **Christopher Hotel.** Sister to Sir Christopher Wren's Hotel in Windsor, this former coaching inn on the main shopping street has spacious rooms in the main building as well as in the courtyard mews. Rooms have been renovated in a sleek, modern style; those in the courtyard have more privacy and space. Christopher's Bar and Grill focuses on classic English and American dishes, including hamburgers, rib-eye steaks, and braised lamb shank with mashed sweet potatoes. **Pros:** a nice mix of modern and historic; good restaurant. **Cons:** steep stairs and no elevator; restaurant can get booked up early. ⊠ *110 High St.* ☎ *01753/852359* ⊕ *www.thechristopher.co.uk* ⇋ *33 rooms* ⟁ *In-room: a/c (some), Internet, Wi-Fi. In-hotel: restaurant, room service, bar, Wi-Fi hotspot, parking (free), some pets allowed* ⊟ *AE, MC, V.*

ASCOT

8 mi southwest of Windsor, 28 mi southwest of London.

The posh town of Ascot (pronounced *as*-cut) has for centuries been famous for horse racing and for style. Queen Anne chose to have a racecourse here, and the first race meeting took place in 1711. The impressive show of millinery for which the Royal Meeting, or Royal Ascot, is also known was immortalized in *My Fair Lady,* in which osprey feathers and black-and-white silk roses transformed Eliza Doolittle into a grand lady. Betting on the races at England's most prestigious course is as important as dressing up; it's all part of the fun.

GETTING HERE AND AROUND

If you're driving, leave M4 at Junction 6 and take A332. Trains from London leave Waterloo Station every half hour, and the journey takes 50 minutes. The racecourse is a seven-minute walk from the train station.

EXPLORING

Ascot Racecourse (⊠ *A329* ☎ *0870/727–1234* ⊕ *www.ascot.co.uk*) continues to look gloriously upper class. The races run regularly throughout the year, and Royal Ascot takes place annually in mid-June.

■TIP→ Purchase tickets well in advance. Tickets for Royal Ascot generally go on sale from the previous November. Prices range from £17 for standing room on the heath to £66 for seats in the stands.

WHERE TO STAY

£££–££££ ⛆ **MacDonald Berystede Hotel & Spa.** With its turrets and half-timbering, this Victorian-era hotel is a magnificent neo-Gothic fantasy on 9 acres of countryside. The overall feeling is traditional, thanks to the patterned curtains and busy carpets. Most rooms have been renovated in a modern style though, and dark-brown and toffee shades predominate. Notable amenities are the luxurious spa, indoor pool, and high-tech gym. The Hyperion restaurant serves Modern British cuisine. **Pros:** lovely historic building; relaxing spa; all the modern conveniences. **Cons:** restaurant is a bit old-fashioned; most guest rooms are modern. ⊠ *Bagshot Rd.* ☎ *0844/879–9104* ⊕ *www.macdonaldhotels.co.uk/berystede* ⇗ *119 rooms, 10 suites* ⚭ *In-room: a/c, safe, Internet, Wi-Fi. In-hotel: restaurant, room service, bar, pool, gym, spa, laundry service, Wi-Fi hotspot, some pets allowed* ⊟ *AE, MC, V* ⓧⓞⓧ *BP.*

CLIVEDEN

8 mi northwest of Windsor, 16 mi north of Ascot, 26 mi west of London.

EXPLORING

Described by Queen Victoria as a "bijou of taste," **Cliveden** is a magnificent country mansion that has for more than 300 years lived up to its Georgian heritage as a bastion of aesthetic delights. The house, set in 376 acres of gardens and parkland above the River Thames, was rebuilt for the duke of Sutherland by Sir Charles Barry in 1861; the Astors, who purchased it in 1893, made it famous. In the 1920s and '30s the Cliveden Set met here at the strongly conservative (not to say fascist) salon presided over by Nancy Astor, who—though she was an American—was the first woman to sit in Parliament, in 1919. Cliveden now belongs to the National Trust, which leases it as a *very* exclusive hotel. The public can visit the spectacular grounds that run down to bluffs overlooking the Thames and, by timed ticket (£1) on a limited basis, three rooms in the house. ⊠ *Off A404, Taplow* ✛ *Near Maidenhead* ☎ *01628/605069, 01494/755562 recorded information* ⊕ *www.nationaltrust.org.uk* ✉ *Grounds £8, woodlands £3, house £1* ☉ *Grounds Apr.–Oct., daily 11–6; Nov. and Dec., daily 11–4. House Apr.–Oct., Thurs. and Sun. 3–5:30.*

WHERE TO STAY

£££££ ⛆ **Cliveden.** If you've ever wondered what it would feel like to be an
Fodor's Choice Edwardian grandee, splurge on a stay at this stately home, one of Brit-
★ ain's grandest hotels. Cliveden's opulent interior includes art such as John Singer Sargent's portrait of Nancy Astor (in the Great Hall), suits of armor, and a paneled staircase. The plush traditional bedrooms each bear the name of someone famous who has stayed here. Waldo's, one of three restaurants, serves excellent contemporary British and French cuisine. If your pocket doesn't rise to a night here, you can drop in for a luxurious afternoon tea (£30), but book ahead. **Pros:** like stepping back

in time; outstanding sense of luxury. Cons: can be rather stuffy; you might feel underdressed if you don't have designer duds. ✉ *Off A404 near Maidenhead, Taplow* ☎ *01628/668561* ⊕ *www.clivedenhouse. co.uk* ⇨ *38 rooms, 1 cottage* ⚬ *In-room: a/c (some), safe, Wi-Fi. In-hotel: 3 restaurants, room service, bar, tennis courts, pool, gym, spa, laundry service, some pets allowed* ☰ *AE, DC, MC, V* ◯ *BP.*

OUTDOORS

Cliveden Boathouse (✉ *Off A404 near Maidenhead, Taplow* ☎ *01628/ 668561*) at Cliveden hotel has two vintage boats and a vintage electric canoe that ply the Thames. The champagne sunset cruise (most days April through September at 5 and 6) is the most affordable at £45 per person; you can rent the boats, too.

MARLOW

7 mi west of Cliveden, 15 mi northwest of Windsor.

Just inside the Buckinghamshire border, Marlow and the surrounding area overflow with Thames-side prettiness. The unusual suspension bridge was built in the 1830s by William Tierney Clark, architect of the bridge linking Buda and Pest. Marlow has a number of striking old buildings, particularly the privately owned Georgian houses along Peter and West streets. In 1817 the Romantic poet Percy Bysshe Shelley stayed with friends at 67 West Street and then bought **Albion House** on the same street. His second wife, Mary, completed her Gothic novel *Frankenstein* here. **Marlow Place,** on Station Road, dates from 1721 and has been home to several princes.

Marlow hosts its own one-day regatta in mid-June. The town is a good base from which to join the Thames Path to Henley-on-Thames. On summer weekends, tourism can often overwhelm the town.

GETTING HERE AND AROUND

Hourly trains leave London from Paddington and involve a change at Maidenhead; the journey takes an hour. By car, leave M4 at Junction 8/9, following A404 and then A4155. From M40, join A404 at Junction 4.

ESSENTIALS

Visitor Information Marlow (✉ *31 High St.* ☎ *01628/483597*).

EXPLORING

Swan-Upping (☎ *01628/523030*), a traditional event that dates back 800 years, takes place in Marlow during the third week of July. By bizarre ancient laws, the Queen owns the country's swans, so each year swan-markers in skiffs start from Sunbury-on-Thames, catching the new cygnets and marking their beaks to establish ownership. The Queen's swan keeper, dressed in scarlet livery, presides over this colorful ceremony.

WHERE TO EAT AND STAY

££££ FRENCH ✕ **Vanilla Pod.** Discreet and intimate, this restaurant is a showcase for French-inspired cuisine by chef Michael Macdonald. Some of the best choices on the fixed-price menu are the cèpe (porcini mushroom) mousse with green beans and truffles, and the poached sea bass with lentils and

BOATING ALONG THE THAMES

One ideal way to see the Thames region is from the water. Water-based tours can range from 30 minutes to all day. Hobbs and Sons covers the Henley Reach (Easter–September) and also rents boats if you want to take the active approach. You can explore the Thames from Datchet, near Eton and Windstor, by the hour, day, or longer with a self-drive rental boat from Kris Cruisers (April–October). Salter's Steamers runs daily round-trip steamer cruises, mid-May to mid-September from Windsor, Oxford, Abingdon, Henley, Marlow, and Reading. Thames River Cruises conducts outings from Caversham Bridge in Reading, Easter through September. French Brothers operates river trips from the Promenade in Windsor, and from Runnymede going as far as Hampton Court.

The Environment Agency's Visit Thames Web site and telephone hotline provide information about boating, fishing, and walking the Thames.

CONTACTS AND RESOURCES
Environment Agency Visit Thames (☎ *0845/601–5336* ⊕ *www. visitthames.com*). **French Brothers** (✉ *The Promenade, Windsor* ☎ *01753/851900* ⊕ *www. boat-trips.co.uk*). **Hobbs and Sons** (✉ *Station Rd., Henley-on-Thames* ☎ *01491/572035* ⊕ *www.hobbs-of-henley.com*). **Kris Cruises** (✉ *Southlea Rd., Datchet* ☎ *01753/543930* ⊕ *www.kriscruisers.co.uk*). **Salter's Steamers** (✉ *Folly Bridge, Oxford* ☎ *01865/243421* ⊕ *www. salterssteamers.co.uk*). **Thames River Cruises** (✉ *Caversham Bridge, Reading* ☎ *0118/948–1088* ⊕ *www. thamesrivercruise.co.uk*).

bacon cream. For dessert, indulge in mango ravioli with ginger cream. The three-course £19.50 fixed-price lunch menu offers a fantastic bargain, and the seven-course *menu gourmand* for £50 is a tour de force. Vegetarians have a separate menu. ✉ *31 West St.* ☎ *01628/898101* ⊕ *www.thevanillapod.co.uk* ⌖ *Reservations essential* ☰ *AE, MC, V* ⊙ *Closed Sun. and Mon.*

£££–££££ 🏨 **Macdonald Compleat Angler.** Although fishing aficionados consider this luxurious 17th-century Thames-side inn the ideal place to stay, the place is stylish enough to attract those with no interest in casting a line. The name comes from Isaak Walton's 1653 masterpiece of angling advice and philosophy, which he wrote in this area. Rooms, traditional in style, are subtly decorated in earth tones, and many have views over the Thames. The hotel's two restaurants offer outstanding Modern British cooking with waterside views. A sunny conservatory serves afternoon tea. **Pros:** gorgeous rooms; great views of the Thames. **Cons:** nonanglers might find dinner conversation dull; need a car to get around. ✉ *Marlow Bridge, Bisham Rd.* ☎ *0844/879–9128* ⊕ *www.macdonaldhotels.co.uk/ compleatangler* 🛏 *61 rooms, 3 suites* ⌂ *In-room: a/c, safe, refrigerator, Internet, Wi-Fi. In-hotel: 2 restaurants, room service, bars, Wi-Fi hotspot, some pets allowed* ☰ *AE, MC, V* ⏀ *BP.*

HENLEY-ON-THAMES

7 mi southwest of Marlow, 8 mi north of Reading, 36 mi west of central London.

Henley's fame is based on one thing: rowing. The Henley Royal Regatta, held at the cusp of June and July on a long, straight stretch of the River Thames, has made the little riverside town famous throughout the world. Townspeople launched the Henley Regatta in 1839, initiating the Grand Challenge Cup, the most famous of its many trophies. The best amateur oarsmen from around the globe compete in crews of eight, four, or two, or as single scullers. For many spectators, however, the event is on par with Royal Ascot and Wimbledon.

The town is set in a broad valley between gentle hillsides. Henley's historic buildings, including half-timber Georgian cottages and inns (as well as one of Britain's oldest theaters, the Kenton), are all within a few minutes' walk. The river near Henley is alive with boats of every shape and size, from luxury cabin cruisers to tiny rowboats.

GETTING HERE AND AROUND

Frequent First Great Western trains depart for Henley from London Paddington; journey time is around an hour. If you're driving from London or from the west, leave M4 at Junction 8/9; follow A404(M) and then A4130 to Henley Bridge. From Marlow, Henley is a 7-mi drive southwest on A4155.

ESSENTIALS

Visitor Information Henley-on-Thames (✉ *Henley Town Hall, Market Pl.* ☎ *01491/578034* ⊕ *www.henley-on-thames.org*).

EXPLORING

The 16th century "checkerboard" tower of **St. Mary's Church** overlooks Henley's bridge on Hart Street. The adjacent, yellow-washed **Chantry House**, built in 1420, is one of England's few remaining merchant houses from the period. It is an unspoiled example of the rare timber-frame design, with upper floors jutting out. ✉ *Hart St.* ☎ *01491/577340* ☑ *Free* ☉ *By appointment.*

☼ The handsome **River & Rowing Museum** focuses not just on the history and sport of rowing but on the Thames and the town itself. One gallery interprets the Thames and its surroundings as the river flows from its source to the ocean; another explores Henley's history and the regatta. Galleries devoted to rowing display models and actual boats, from Greek triremes to lifeboats to sleek Olympic rowing boats. A *Wind in the Willows* exhibit evokes the settings of the famous children's book. ✉ *Mill Meadows* ☎ *01491/415600* ⊕ *www.rrm.co.uk* ☑ *£7.50* ☉ *May–Aug., daily 10–5:30; Sept.–Apr., daily 10–5.*

This section of the Thames inspired Kenneth Grahame's 1908 *The Wind in the Willows*, which began as a bedtime story for Grahame's son Alastair while the family lived at Pangbourne. Some of E. F. Shepard's illustrations are of specific sites along the river—none more fabled than

★ **Mapledurham House**, a redbrick Elizabethan mansion, bristling with tall chimneys, mullioned windows, and battlements. It became the inspiration for Shepard's vision of Toad Hall. The Eyston family, descendants of longtime owners of the estate, still lives at Mapledurham, and the house seems warm and friendly even with all the family portraits, magnificent oak staircases, and Tudor plasterwork ceilings. There's also a 15th-century working grain mill on the river. The house is 5 mi west of Sonning-on-Thames and 10 mi southwest of Henley-on-Thames. On summer weekends you can reach the house by a **Thames River Cruises** (☎ *0118/948–1088* ⊕ *www.thamesrivercruise.co.uk*) boat from Caversham Promenade in Reading. Departures are at 2 PM, and travel time is 45 minutes. You can linger at one of the seven rental cottages around the estate (from £335 a week). ⊠ *Off A074, Mapledurham* ☎ *0118/972–3350* ⊕ *www. mapledurham.co.uk* 🖭 *House and mill £6.75; house only, £4.25; grounds and mill £3.25* ⊗ *Easter–Sept., weekends and national holiday Mon. 2–5:30; Oct., Sun. 2–5:30.*

WALK THE CHILTERNS

Part of the Chiltern Hills is an **Area of Outstanding Beauty** (⊕ *www.chilternsaonb.org*), a nature reserve that stretches over 320 square mi, taking in chalk hills, valleys, forests, lakes, and pretty towns. Its springtime bluebell woods are famed, and its autumn colors are glorious. The distinctive chestnut-color birds soaring above you will be red kites. You'll likely drive in and out of the Chilterns as you explore, or you could walk part of the circular 124-mi Chiltern Way. A 13-mi section starts in Henley, runs north through the Hambleden Valley, and returns to Henley via the Assendons.

WHERE TO EAT AND STAY

£££
BRITISH ✕ **Crooked Billet.** The notice on the door of this cozy 17th-century country pub, offering an exchange of local, homegrown produce for lunch, tells you what you might expect inside. Local rabbit and free-range chicken may be served with wild garlic, field mushrooms, or barley butter; partridge with sloe gin; and British cheeses with homemade oatcakes. There's a garden for alfresco dining and regular music evenings. Foodies come from far and wide, so book ahead. Fixed-price lunches are another option. ⊠ *Newlands La., Stoke Row ⊹ 6 mi west of Henley-on-Thames, off B481* ☎ *01491/681048* ⊕ *www.thecrookedbillet. co.uk* ▭ *MC, V.*

££ 🖭 **Falaise House.** The rooms in this B&B, a Georgian town house in the center of Henley, are individually furnished in a sympathetic contemporary style, with a mixture of antique and modern decor (dark wood pieces as well as modern lamps, a mix of fabric and modern iron headboards, print drapes) that is soft and warm. There are luxurious Egyptian cotton sheets on the beds and crisp white linens on the breakfast tables, where the long menu lists choices from scrambled eggs with smoked salmon to eggs with ham and mushrooms. **Pros:** family-run; great breakfasts. **Cons:** some rooms face the main road; minimum two-night stay on summer weekends. ⊠ *37 Market Pl.* ☎ *01491/573388* ⊕ *www.falaisehouse.com* ↪ *6 rooms* ⌂ *In-room: no a/c, no phone, Internet, Wi-Fi. In-hotel: no kids under 12* ▭ *MC, V* ⦿ *BP.*

£££–££££ 🖭 **Hotel du Vin.** A sprawling brick brewery near the river has been transformed into a distinctively modern architectural showplace. Bedrooms have beige carpeting and whitewashed walls—other details and furnishings are tan, white, or black. The original brewery windows appear in strange places, and staircases are contorted to fit the space. Still, the minimalist ethic makes this hotel a pleasure. Wine gets special attention in the bar and bistro. **Pros:** striking decor; lovely river views from upper floors; good for oenophiles. **Cons:** won't thrill traditionalists; not everyone will like the stark black-and-white decor; there's a charge for parking. ⊠ *New St.* ☎ *01491/848400* ⊕ *www.hotelduvin.com* ☜ *43 rooms* ⌂ *In-room: a/c, refrigerator, DVD, Internet, Wi-Fi. In-hotel: restaurant, room service, bar, Wi-Fi hotspot* ☰ *AE, MC, V.*

NIGHTLIFE AND THE ARTS

A floating stage and spectacular musical events from classical to folk, as well as some art activities, draw a dress-code-abiding crowd to the upscale **Henley Festival** (☎ *01491/843404* ⊕ *www.henley-festival.co.uk*) during the week after the regatta in July. Book tickets ahead.

ROWING

Henley Royal Regatta (☎ *01491/572153* ⊕ *www.hrr.co.uk*), a series of rowing competitions that draws participants from many countries, takes place in late June and early July each year. Large tents are erected along both sides of the unique straight stretch of river here known as Henley Reach, and every surrounding field becomes a parking lot. There is plenty of space on the public towpath from which to watch the early stages of the races. You can also purchase a badge to enter the Regatta Enclosure; it's best to do this before the event. ■ TIP➔ **If you want to attend, book a room months in advance.** After all, 500,000 people, including members of the Royal Family, attend the event.

OXFORD

With arguably the most famous university in the world, Oxford has been a center of learning since 1167, with only the Sorbonne preceding it. It doesn't take more than a day or two to explore its winding medieval streets, photograph its ivy-covered stone buildings and ancient churches and libraries, and even take a punt down one of its placid waterways. The town center is compact and walkable, and at its heart is Oxford University. Alumni of this prestigious institution include 47 Nobel Prize winners, 25 British prime ministers (including former Prime Minister Tony Blair), and 28 foreign presidents (including former U.S. president Bill Clinton), along with poets, authors, and artists such as Percy Bysshe Shelley, Oscar Wilde, and W. H. Auden.

Oxford is 55 mi northwest of London, at the junction of the rivers Thames and Cherwell. The city is more interesting and more cosmopolitan than Cambridge, and although it's also bigger, its suburbs are not remotely interesting to visitors. The interest is all at the center, where the old town curls around the grand stone buildings, good restaurants, and historic pubs. Victorian writer Matthew Arnold described Oxford's "dreaming spires," a phrase that has become famous. Students rush past you on the sidewalks on the way to their exams, clad with marvelous antiquarian style in their requisite mortar caps, flowing dark gowns, stiff collars, and crisp white bow ties. ■TIP→ **In term time the city is awash with bikes. Watch your back when crossing roads; cycles are silent.**

GETTING HERE AND AROUND

Megabus, Oxford Bus Company, and Oxford Tube all have buses traveling from London 24 hours a day; the trip takes about one hour and 40 or 50 minutes. In London, Megabus departs from Victoria Coach Station, and Oxford Bus Company and Oxford Tube have pickup points near Victoria Train Station and Marble Arch Underground stations. Oxford Bus Company also offers round-trip shuttle service from Gatwick (£30) every hour and Heathrow (£22) every half hour. Most of the companies have multiple stops in Oxford, with Gloucester Green, the final stop, being the most convenient for most travelers. You can easily traverse the town center on foot, but the Oxford Bus Company offers a one-day ticket (£3.70) and seven-day (£14) passes for unlimited travel within Oxford.

Trains to Oxford depart from London's Paddington station for the one-hour trip. Oxford Station is just at the western edge of the historic town center on Botley Road.

To drive, take the M40 northwest from London. It's an hour's drive, except during rush hour when it can take twice as long. In-town parking is notoriously difficult, so use one of the five park-and-ride lots (free) and pay for the bus to the city. The Thornhill Park and Ride and the St. Clement's parking lot before the roundabout that leads to Magdalen Bridge are convenient for the M40.

TOURS   The Oxford Tourist Information Centre has information on the many guided walking tours of the city. The best way of gaining access to the collegiate buildings is to take the university and city tour, which leaves the Tourist Information Centre daily at 10:45 and 2. City Sightseeing offers hop-on, hop-off bus tours (£12) with 20 stops around Oxford; your ticket, purchased from the driver, is good for 24 hours.

TIMING

You can explore major sights in town in a day or so, but it takes more than a day to spend an hour in all of the key museums and absorb the scene at the colleges. Some colleges are open only in the afternoons during university terms. When the undergraduates are in residence, access is often restricted to the chapels, dining rooms, and libraries, too, and you are requested to refrain from picnicking in the quadrangles. All are closed certain days during exams, usually from mid-April to late June.

ESSENTIALS

Bus Contacts Megabus (⊕ www.megabus.com). **Oxford Bus Company** (☎ 01865/785400 ⊕ www.oxfordbus.co.uk). **Stagecoach Oxford Tube** (☎ 01865/772250 ⊕ www.oxfordtube.com).

Visitor and Tour Information City Sightseeing (☎ 01865/790522 ⊕ www.citysightseeingoxford.com). **Oxford Tourist Information Centre** (✉ 15/16 Broad St. ☎ 01865/252200 ⊕ www.visitoxford.org).

EXPLORING

Oxford University is not one easily identifiable campus, but a sprawling mixture of 38 colleges scattered around the city center, each with its own distinctive identity and focus. Oxford students live and study at their own college, and also use the centralized resources of the overarching university. The individual colleges are deeply competitive. Most of the grounds and magnificent dining halls and chapels are open to visitors, though the opening times (displayed at the entrance gates) vary greatly.

The **city center** of Oxford is bordered by High Street, St. Giles, and Longwall Street. Most of Oxford University's most famous buildings are within this area. **Jericho,** the neighborhood where many students live, is west of St. Giles, just outside the city center. Its narrow streets are lined with lovely cottages. The area north of the center around Banbury and Marston Ferry roads is called **Summertown,** and the area east of the center, along St. Clement's Street, is known as **St. Clement's.**

TOP ATTRACTIONS

❾ ★ **Ashmolean Museum.** Britain's oldest public museum, completely redesigned in 2009, displays its rich and varied collections from the Neolithic to the present day over five floors. Innovative galleries on the theme of "Crossing Cultures, Crossing Time" explore connections between the priceless Egyptian, Greek, Roman, Chinese, and Indian artifacts, and also display a superb art collection. Among the highlights are drawings by Raphael, the shell-encrusted mantle of Powhatan (father of Pocahontas), the lantern belonging to Guy Fawkes, and the Alfred Jewel. This ancient piece features a large semiprecious stone set in gold carved with the words AELFRED MEC HEHT GEWYRCAN, which translates from old English as "Alfred ordered me to be made." The piece dates from the reign of King Alfred the Great (ruled 871–899). ■ TIP➔ **There's too much to see in one visit. If you have time, dip in and out; it's free.** The Ashmolean Dining Room, Oxford's first rooftop restaurant (£££; also open in the evenings), is a good spot for refreshment. ✉ *Beaumont St.* ☎ *01865/278000* ⊕ *www.ashmolean.org* ✉ *Free* ☉ *Tues.–Sat. 10–5, Sun. noon–5.*

⓭ **Christ Church.** Built in 1546, the college of Christ Church is referred to by its members as "The House." This is the site of Oxford's largest quadrangle, Tom Quad, named after the huge bell (6¼ tons) that hangs in the Christopher Wren–designed gate tower and rings 101 times at five past nine every evening in honor of the original number of Christ Church scholars. The vaulted, 800-year-old chapel in one corner has been Oxford's cathedral since the time of Henry VIII. The college's medieval dining hall contains portraits of many famous alumni, including John Wesley, William Penn, and 13 of Britain's prime ministers. A reproduction of this room appears in the banquet scenes at Hogwarts School in the Harry Potter films. ■ TIP➔ **The hall is only open weekdays between 10 and 11:45 and 2:15 and 4.30 and weekends 2:15 to 4:30.** Lewis Carroll, author of *Alice in Wonderland,* was a teacher of mathematics here for many years; a shop opposite the meadows on St. Aldate's

6

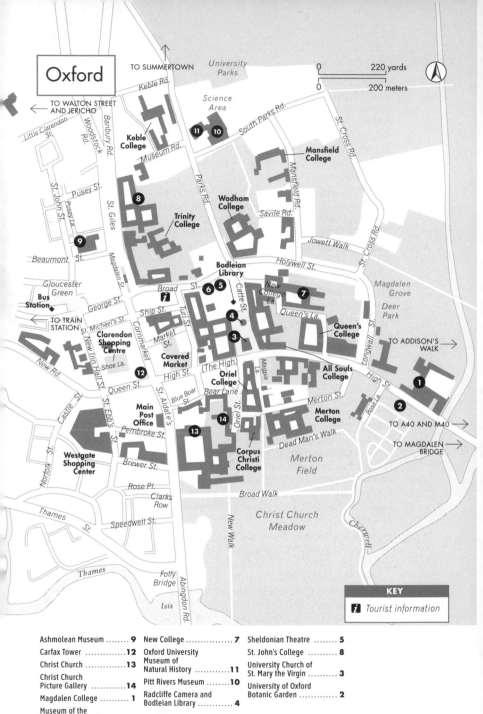

Oxford

TO SUMMERTOWN

University Parks

TO WALTON STREET AND JERICHO

Science Area

Keble Rd.

Little Clarendon St.

Woodstock Rd.

Banbury Rd.

St. John St.

Pusey St.

Pusey La.

St. Giles

Magdalen St.

Keble College

Museum Rd.

Parks Rd.

South Parks Rd.

St. Cross Rd.

Mansfield College

Mansfield Rd.

Wadham College

Savile Rd.

Jowett Walk

St. Cross Rd.

Trinity College

Beaumont St.

Gloucester Green

Bus Station

TO TRAIN STATION

George St.

St. Michael's St.

New Inn Hall St.

Clarendon Shopping Centre

Shoe La.

Cornmarket

Ship St.

Broad St.

Turl St.

Market St.

Covered Market

High St.

Bodleian Library

Catte St.

Holywell St.

New College La.

Queen's La.

New College La.

Queen's College

Magdalen Grove

Deer Park

TO ADDISON'S WALK

Longwall St.

High St.

(The High)

Oriel College

Magpie La.

Bear Lane

All Souls College

Oriel St.

Blue Boar St.

Corpus Christi College

Merton St.

Merton College

Dead Man's Walk

Merton Field

Main Post Office

St. Aldate's

St. Ebbe's

Pembroke St.

Brewer St.

Rose Pl.

Clarks Row

Speedwell St.

Westgate Shopping Center

Norfolk St.

Castle St.

Queen St.

New Rd.

Thames St.

Thames

Folly Bridge

Abingdon Rd.

New Walk

Broad Walk

Christ Church Meadow

Cherwell

Isis

TO A40 AND M40

TO MAGDALEN BRIDGE

0   220 yards
0   200 meters

KEY

🛈 Tourist information

sells Alice paraphernalia. ⊠ *St. Aldate's* ☎ *01865/276492* ⊕ *www.chch. ox.ac.uk* 🖽 *£6.30* ⊙ *Mon.–Sat. 9–5, Sun. 2–5.*

⑭ Christ Church Picture Gallery. This connoisseur's delight in Canterbury Quadrangle exhibits works by the Italian masters as well as Hals, Rubens, and Van Dyck. Drawings in the 2,000-strong collection are shown on a changing basis. ⊠ *Oriel Sq.* ☎ *01865/276172* ⊕ *www.chch. ox.ac.uk* 🖽 *£3* ⊙ *May–Sept., Mon.–Sat. 10:30–5, Sun. 2–5; Oct.–Apr., Mon.–Sat. 10:30–1 and 2–4:30, Sun. 2–4:30.*

❶ Magdalen College. Founded in 1458, with a handsome main quadrangle
★ and a supremely monastic air, Magdalen (pronounced *maud*-lin) is one of the most impressive of Oxford's colleges and attracts its most artistic students. Alumni include such diverse people as Cardinal Wolsey, P.G. Wodehouse, Edward Gibbon, Oscar Wilde, Dudley Moore, and retired U.S. Supreme Court Justice David Souter. The school's large, square tower is a famous local landmark. ■TIP➜ **A stroll around the Deer Park and along Addison's Walk is a good way to appreciate the place.** ⊠ *High St.* ☎ *01865/276000* ⊕ *www.magd.ox.ac.uk* 🖽 *£4* ⊙ *July–Sept., daily noon–6; Oct.–June, daily 1–6 or dusk.*

⑪ Oxford University Museum of Natural History. This highly decorative Vic-
Ⓒ torian Gothic creation of cast iron and glass, more a cathedral than a museum, is worth a visit for its architecture alone. Among the eclectic collections of entomology, geology, mineralogy, and zoology are the towering skeleton of a Tyrannosaurus rex and casts of a dodo's foot and head. There's plenty for children to explore and touch. The museum is adjacent to the Pitt Rivers Museum. ⊠ *Parks Rd.* ☎ *01865/272950* ⊕ *www.oum.ox.ac.uk* 🖽 *Free* ⊙ *Daily 10–5.*

⑩ Pitt Rivers Museum. More than half a million archaeological and anthropo-
Ⓒ logical items from around the globe, based on the collection bequeathed
Fodor'sChoice by Lieutenant-General Augustus Henry Lane Fox Pitt Rivers in 1884,
★ are crammed into glass cases and drawers. Items are organized thematically rather than geographically, an eccentric approach but actually thought-provoking. Labels are handwritten, and children are given flashlights to explore the farthest corners and spot the world's smallest dolly. Give yourself plenty of time to wander through the displays of shrunken heads, Hawaiian feather cloaks, masks, jewelry, amulets, canoes; the list is endless. Children will have a field day. ⊠ *S. Parks Rd.* ☎ *01865/270927* ⊕ *www.prm.ox.ac.uk* 🖽 *Free* ⊙ *Mon. noon–4:30, Tues.–Sun. 10–4:30.*

❹ Radcliffe Camera and Bodleian Library. A vast library, the round, domed Radcliffe Camera is Oxford's most famous building, built in 1737–49 by James Gibbs in Italian baroque style. It's usually surrounded by tourists with cameras trained at its golden-stone walls. The Camera (open to the public by tour only) contains part of the Bodleian Library's enormous collection, which was begun in 1602. Much like the Library of Congress in the United States, the Bodleian contains a copy of every book printed in Great Britain and grows by 4,000 books and leaflets a week. A new storage depot near Swindon, 27 mi to the southwest, has the capacity to house all but a million of the 9 million volumes. Take a tour to see the magnificent Duke Humfrey's Library, which was the

6

original chained library and completed in 1488, and to admire some of the ancient tomes (only dusted every 10 years). Other parts of the Bodleian—the Radcliffe Camera, Divinity School (a superbly vaulted room dating to 1462), and the 17th-century Convocation House where parliament sat during the Civil War—are also well worth visiting. Guides will show you the spots used for Hogwarts School in the Harry Potter films. ■TIP→ Tickets for the three to five tours daily are sold on a first-come, first-served basis (from 9 AM Mon.–Sat., from 11 AM Sun.), except for the extended tour, which can be prebooked. Audio tours don't require reservation and children under 11 are permitted on the audio tour only. Call ahead as tours are sometimes cancelled because of university functions. ⊠ *Broad St.* ☎ *01865/277224* ⊕ *www.www.bodleian.ox.ac.uk* ☑ *£1 (Divinity School only), audio tour £2.50; mini tour £4.50, standard tour £6.50; extended tour including Radcliffe Camera £13 (most Wed. and weekends; call ahead for times)* ☉ *Bodleian and Divinity School weekdays 9–5, Sat. 9–4:30, Sun. 11–5.*

8 St. John's College. One of Oxford's most attractive campuses, St. John's has seven quiet quadrangles surrounded by elaborately carved, cloisterlike buildings. You enter the first through a low wooden door. This college dates to 1555, when Sir Thomas White, a merchant, founded it. His heart is buried in the chapel (by tradition, students curse as they walk over it). The Canterbury Quad represented the first example of Italian Renaissance architecture in Oxford, and the Front Quad includes the buildings of the old St. Bernard's Monastery. St. John's is Oxford's wealthiest college, with an estimated endowment of half a billion dollars. ⊠ *St. Giles* ☎ *01865/277300* ⊕ *www.sjc.ox.ac.uk* ☑ *Free* ☉ *Daily 1–dusk.*

QUICK BITES
The **Eagle and Child pub** (⊠ *49 St. Giles* ☎ *01865/302925*) is a favorite not only for its good ales (try the local Old Hooky) and sense of history, but also for its literary associations. From the 1930s to the 1960s this was the meeting place of C. S. Lewis, J. R. R. Tolkien, and their circle of literary friends who called themselves the "Inklings." The pub is so close to St. John's College, and such a favorite of its students, that the college purchased it, although it remains open to the public.

5 Sheldonian Theatre. This fabulously ornate theater is where Oxford's impressive graduation ceremonies are held, conducted almost entirely in Latin. Dating to 1663, it was the first building designed by Sir Christopher Wren when he served as professor of astronomy. The D-shaped theater has pillars, balconies, and an elaborately painted ceiling. The stone pillars outside are topped by 18 massive stone heads, sculpted in the 1970s to replace originals destroyed by air pollution. ⊠ *Broad St.* ☎ *01865/277299* ⊕ *www.sheldon.ox.ac.uk* ☑ *£2.50* ☉ *Apr.–Oct., Mon.–Sat. 10–12:30 and 2–4:30; Nov.–Mar., Mon.–Sat. 10–12:30 and 2–3:30. Closed for 10 days at Christmas and Easter and for degree ceremonies and events.*

WORTH NOTING

 Carfax Tower. Passing through Carfax, the center of Oxford and where four roads meet, you can spot this tower. It's all that remains of St. Martin's Church, where Shakespeare stood as godfather for William Davenant, who himself became a playwright. Every 15 minutes, little mechanical "quarter boys" mark the passage of time on the tower front. ■ TIP→ **You can climb up the dark stairwell for a good view of the town center.** ✉ *Corner of Queen St. and Cornmarket* ☎ *01865/792653* 💷 *£2.20* 🕑 *Apr.–Sept., daily 10–5:30; Oct.–Mar., daily 10–dusk.*

 Museum of the History of Science. The Ashmolean, the world's oldest public museum, was originally housed in this 1638 building, which now holds scientific and mathematical instruments, from astrolabes to quadrants to medical equipment. The restored 18th-century chemical laboratory in the basement has the chalkboard Einstein used in a lecture on the theory of relativity. ✉ *Broad St.* ☎ *01865/277280* ⊕ *www.mhs. ox.ac.uk* 💷 *Free* 🕑 *Tues.–Fri. noon–5, Sat. 10–5, Sun. 2–5.*

⑦ New College. One of the university's best-known and oldest colleges (dating to 1379), New College stands alongside New College Lane, known for its Italianate Bridge of Sighs. Its grounds are big and enticing, with acres of soft green grass and pristinely maintained gardens. The college buildings, in ivory stone, are partly enclosed by the medieval city wall, and feature one of the city's best displays of Gothic gargoyles. Famous alumni include the actors Hugh Grant and Kate Beckinsale. ✉ *Holywell St.* ☎ *01865/279555* ⊕ *www.new.ox.ac.uk* 💷 *Easter–Sept. £2, Oct.–Easter free* 🕑 *Easter–Sept., daily 11–5; Oct.–Easter, daily 2–4.*

Rousham Park House and Garden. Fifteen mi north of Oxford and wonderfully uncommercialized, Rousham has an expansive 18th-century English landscape park as well as the austere, gray Dormer family mansion, built in 1635. The design of gardener William Kent (1685–1748) is preserved almost unaltered in the groves, meadows, and walled gardens. Longhorn cattle add an exotic touch to the English landscape. Tickets are sold on an honesty system through a vending machine. The house is only open to groups that book in advance, but the remarkable gardens are open all year. ■ TIP→ **There's no shop and no tearoom, so bring a picnic and plenty of water.** Children under 15 are not allowed, nor are dogs. ✉ *Off B4030, Rousham* ✛ *Near Steeple Aston* ☎ *01869/347110* ⊕ *www.rousham.org* 💷 *£5* 🕑 *Gardens daily 10–4:30.*

❸ University Church of St. Mary the Virgin. Seven hundred years' worth of funeral monuments crowd this church, including the tombstone of Amy Robsart, the wife of Robert Dudley, Elizabeth I's favorite. One pillar marks the site of Thomas Cranmer's trial under Queen Mary for his marital machinations on behalf of Henry VIII. ■ TIP→ **From the top of the church's 14th-century tower, you get a panoramic view of the city's skyline. It's worth the 127 steps.** The Vaults Café and Garden, a part of the church accessible from Radcliffe Square, serves generous portions of warm food—cafeteria style—under the room in which the charity Oxfam was founded. ✉ *High St.* ☎ *01865/279111* ⊕ *www.university-church.ox.ac.uk* 💷 *Church free, tower £3* 🕑 *Sept.–June, Mon.–Sat.*

9–5, Sun. noon–5; July and Aug., Mon.–Sat. 9–6, Sun. noon–6; last admission to tower 30 mins before closing.

② **University of Oxford Botanic Garden.** Founded in 1621 as a physic (healing) garden, this is the oldest of its kind in the British Isles. The compact but diverse garden displays 7,000 species from lilies to palms in greenhouses, a small walled garden, and special gardens (such as rock and bog gardens) outside the walled area. ⊠ *Rose La.* ☎ *01865/286690* ⊕ *www.botanic-garden.ox.ac.uk* ⊠ *£3.50* ⊙ *Mar., Apr., Sept., and Oct., daily 9–5; May–Aug., daily 9–6; Nov.–Feb., daily 9–4:30.*

WHERE TO EAT

The city's pubs offer more options for a quick bite.

£ ✕ **Big Bang.** Sausage and mash (mashed potatoes) is the theme of this
BRITISH friendly and buzzy little restaurant in the Jericho district, where the meat is ethically sourced from the local area. You're encouraged to mix and match, and could choose a carrot-and-swede (rutabaga) or a mustard-and-Stilton mash for the traditional Oxford sausages, or a rose-hue mash (beets give the color) to accompany the wild-mushroom-and-garlic sausages. Jazz nights take place every Tuesday; reservations are a good idea. ⊠ *124 Walton St.* ☎ *01865/511441* ⊕ *www.thebigbangrestaurants.co.uk* ▭ *No credit cards.*

£££ ✕ **Brasserie Blanc.** Raymond Blanc's sophisticated brasserie in the Jericho
FRENCH neighborhood, a hipper cousin of Le Manoir aux Quat' Saisons in Great
★ Milton, is one of the best places to eat in Oxford. Light-color walls, modern art, wood floors, and large windows keep the restaurant open and airy. The changing menu always lists innovative, visually stunning adaptations of bourgeois French fare, sometimes with Mediterranean or Asian influences. Try the steamed Loch Fyne mussels in a white-wine-and-cream sauce. The fixed-price menus (which start at £11.90 for lunch) are a good value. ⊠ *71–72 Walton St.* ☎ *01865/510999* ⊕ *www.brasserieblanc.com* ▭ *AE, MC, V.*

££ ✕ **Fishers.** Everything is remarkably fresh at what is widely viewed as
SEAFOOD the city's best seafood restaurant. Seafood is prepared with a European touch and frequently comes with butter, cream, and other sauces: smoked-salmon pasta with dill-cream sauce, for instance. Hot and cold shellfish platters are popular, as are the oysters, served either on ice or in a tempura batter. The interior has a casual nautical theme with wooden floors and tables, porthole windows, and red sails overhead. Bustling but relaxed, this place is often fully booked. Lunches are a very good value. ⊠ *36–37 St. Clement's St.* ☎ *01865/243003* ⊕ *www.fishers-restaurant.com* ▭ *MC, V.*

£££ ✕ **Gee's.** With its glass-and-steel framework, this former florist's shop
BRITISH just north of the town center makes a charming conservatory dining room. The constantly changing menu features locally raised meats and vegetables in modern versions of traditional English dishes, such as quail eggs and deviled kidneys, and sponge pudding desserts. ⊠ *61 Banbury Rd.* ☎ *01865/553540* ⊕ *www.gees-restaurant.co.uk* ▭ *AE, MC, V.*

£ ✕ **Grand Café.** Golden-hue tiles, towering columns, and antique marble
CAFÉ tables make this café both architecturally impressive and an excellent
spot for a light meal (sandwiches, salads, and some hot fare) or leisurely
drink. It's touristy and service can be slow, but this is still a pretty
spot for afternoon tea. At night it transforms into a popular cocktail
bar. ⊠ *84 High St.* ☎ *01865/204463* ⊕ *www.thegrandcafe.co.uk* ⊟ *AE,
MC, V.*

££££ ✕ **Le Manoir aux Quat' Saisons.** Standards are high at this 15th-century
FRENCH stone manor house, a hotel with one of the country's finest kitchens
Fodor'sChoice as well as a cooking school. Chef Raymond Blanc's epicurean touch
★ shows at every turn. Decide from among the innovative French creations (about £40 for a main course), such as braised Cornish brill with
scallops and wasabi, or try one of the fixed-price menus from £95 to
£125; a fixed-price lunch can be a good deal at £52.50. A stroll through
the hotel's herb and Japanese tea gardens is de rigueur; you may want
to linger for a night in one of the 32 luxurious rooms. The pretty town
of Great Milton is 7 mi southeast of Oxford. ⊠ *Church Rd., Great
Milton* ☎ *01844/278881* ⊕ *www.manoir.com* ⌕ *Reservations essential*
⊟ *AE, DC, MC, V.*

££ ✕ **Trout Inn.** More than a century ago, Lewis Carroll took three children
BRITISH on a Thames picnic. "We rowed up to Godstow, and had tea beside
a haystack," he told a friend at Christ Church; "I told them the fairy
tale of Alice's adventures in Wonderland." The haystacks are gone,
but you can stop at the creeper-covered Thames-side pub 2 mi north of
the city center for steaks, roasted chicken, and burgers as well as pastas, pizzas, and salads. There's a corner devoted to Carroll inside and
plenty of room for alfresco dining. The fictional Inspector Morse often
drank at the bar here. This place is at the heart of the tourist trail and
can get crowded, service may falter. ⊠ *195 Godstow Rd., Wolvercote*
☎ *01865/510930* ⊕ *www.thetroutoxford.co.uk* ⊟ *AE, MC, V.*

WHERE TO STAY

Oxford is pricey; for the cheapest lodging, contact the tourist information office for bed-and-breakfasts in locals' homes.

££ ⚏ **Brown's Guest House.** At the southern edge of central Oxford, this
redbrick Victorian house is a good bet in a town that has precious few
affordable guesthouses. Rooms are spacious, uncluttered, and simply
decorated; most rooms have two beds and lots of light. The breakfast
room is big and homey, and the food is good and hearty. One downside
is the 15-minute walk or a bus ride into the center. **Pros:** comfortable
rooms; friendly owners. **Cons:** a long walk to the center; some rooms
without private bathroom. ⊠ *281 Iffley Rd.* ☎ *01865/246822* ⊕ *www.
brownsguesthouse.co.uk* ⊷ *11 rooms, 6 with bath* ⌕ *In-room: no a/c,
no phone, Wi-Fi. In-hotel: parking (free)* ⊟ *MC, V* ⦿ *BP.*

££ ⚏ **Burlington House.** This Victorian guesthouse in Summertown, on the
outskirts of Oxford, shows flair in its decoration, breakfasts, and attentive, helpful service. Guest rooms are beautifully furnished in contemporary style in muted, neutral colors, and have flat-screen TVs with
Internet access. Homemade bread, preserves, yogurt, and Gruyère

omelets make breakfasts luxurious. **Pros:** friendly; superior breakfasts; double-glazed windows throughout. **Cons:** 10-minute bus ride to the center; main road location. ⊠ *374 Banbury Rd.* ☎ *01865/513513* ⊕ *www.burlington-house.co.uk* ⟿ *12 rooms* ⅔ *In-room: no a/c, DVD, Internet, Wi-Fi. In-hotel: parking (free), no kids under 12* ⊟ *MC, V* ⑩ *BP.*

£££–££££   ⊞ **Macdonald Randolph.** A 19th-century neo-Gothic landmark, the hotel faces both the Ashmolean and the Martyrs' Memorial. If their parents are feeling generous, undergraduates are treated to tea in the Morse Bar or dinner in the hotel restaurant. Rooms are large and elegantly designed in tones of coffee and cream; some have antique desks, and many have views of Oxford's spires. A tiled, vaulted spa with four treatment rooms is the latest pampering amenity. **Pros:** handy location; grand building. **Cons:** on a busy street; formality can be a bit daunting. ⊠ *Beaumont St.* ☎ *0844/879–9132* ⊕ *www.macdonaldhotels.co.uk/ randolph* ⟿ *151 rooms* ⅔ *In-room: a/c, Wi-Fi. In-hotel: restaurant, room service, bar, spa, laundry service, Wi-Fi hotspot, parking (paid), some pets allowed* ⊟ *AE, MC, V* ⑩ *BP.*

£££–££££   ⊞ **Malmaison Oxford Castle.** Inside a 19th-century prison, this high-concept boutique hotel was designed to remain sympathetic to the building's history. Guest rooms, modern in style and with pampering bathrooms, are divided into the old prison wings: A-Wing rooms are comfortably sized, C-Wing rooms include two semicircular suites. With its metal doors, exposed-brick walls, and clever embrace of its incarcerating past, this hotel is not for all. You half expect guests to come out and bang their spoons on the white metal railing if breakfast isn't served on time. But then, breakfast is always served on time. **Pros:** modern luxury; historic building; great bar and restaurant. **Cons:** prison life isn't for everyone; expensive parking. ⊠ *3 Oxford Castle* ☎ *01865/248432* ⊕ *www.malmaison.com* ⟿ *86 rooms, 8 suites* ⅔ *In-room: a/c, DVD, Internet, Wi-Fi. In-hotel: restaurant, room service, bar, laundry service, Wi-Fi hotspot, parking (paid)* ⊟ *AE, MC, V* ⑩ *BP.*

££   ⊞ **Newton House.** A handsome Victorian mansion just a five-minute walk from all of Oxford's action, the Newton is a sprawling, friendly place on three floors. Decent-size rooms are decorated in contemporary style with large-pattern wallpaper; some have original Victorian features. The breakfast is varied, with yogurt and croissants along with the usual eggs and bacon. This is one of the best deals in the city center, so book early. **Pros:** great breakfasts; parking lot. **Cons:** on a main road; no elevator. ⊠ *82 Abingdon Rd.* ☎ *01865/240561* ✎ *newton.house@ btinternet.com* ⟿ *11 rooms, 1 without bath* ⅔ *In-room: no a/c, Internet, Wi-Fi. In-hotel: parking (free)* ⊟ *AE, MC, V* ⑩ *BP.*

££££–£££££   ⊞ **Old Bank Hotel.** From its sleek lobby to the 20th-century British paintings on display and the modern furnishings in the guest rooms, this stately converted bank offers contemporary style in a city that favors the traditional. Oxford's most centrally located hotel also holds the busy contemporary Quod Bar and Grill, serving creative pastas and dishes such as duck confit. **Pros:** excellent location; great city views. **Cons:** standard rooms can be small; breakfast costs extra. ⊠ *92–94 High St.* ☎ *01865/799599* ⊕ *www.oldbank-hotel.co.uk* ⟿ *42 rooms* ⅔ *In-room:*

a/c, safe, DVD, Internet, Wi-Fi. In-hotel: restaurant, room service, bar, laundry service, Wi-Fi hotspot, parking (free) ⊟ *AE, MC, V.*

£££–££££ 🖼 **Old Parsonage.** A 17th-century gabled stone house in a small garden
★ next to St. Giles Church, this hotel provides a dignified escape from the surrounding city center. Dark red walls, eclectic art, and a crackling wood fire make the lobby a distinguished retreat. The fresh guest rooms are done in crisp white shades with bright splashes of color; bathrooms are marble. Memorable meals by the fire (or in the walled garden terrace in summer) keep people coming back. Afternoon teas with scones and clotted cream are excellent. **Pros:** interesting building; complimentary walking tours; great afternoon tea. **Cons:** pricey given what's on offer; bathrooms are small. ⊠ *1 Banbury Rd.* ☎ *01865/310210* ⊕ *www. oldparsonage-hotel.co.uk* 🛏 *26 rooms, 4 suites* ⚭ *In-room: a/c (some), safe, Internet, Wi-Fi. In-hotel: restaurant, room service, bar, laundry service, parking (free)* ⊟ *AE, MC, V.*

£££ 🖼 **Royal Oxford Hotel.** This hotel, a few steps from the train station, has simply furnished but bright, light, and modern rooms with contemporary furniture. Bathrooms are well equipped. Tea- and coffeemakers, and hospitality trays of chocolates, fruit, and cookies are welcome touches. **Pros:** comfortable rooms; good for train travelers. **Cons:** rooms are plain; not many amenities for the price. ⊠ *17 Park End St.* ☎ *01865/248432* ⊕ *www.royaloxfordhotel.co.uk* 🛏 *26 rooms* ⚭ *In-room: a/c, Internet, Wi-Fi. In-hotel: restaurant, room service, laundry service, Wi-Fi hotspot* ⊟ *AE, MC, V* ⦿ *BP.*

££ 🖼 **Tilbury Lodge.** What this modern house on the western outskirts of Oxford lacks in history, it makes up for in hospitality; the homemade tea and scones that greet you on arrival set the tone. Bedrooms are spotless and spacious, with plenty of light and no floral prints or clutter; and the ample breakfasts present plenty of choice—French toast and bacon, muffins, fresh fruit and yogurt, for example. A garden and conservatory are ideal for relaxing after a busy day. Walkers and cyclists are welcomed, and the bus stop to Oxford's center is a five-minute walk away. **Pros:** quiet location; free Wi-Fi; well-appointed bathrooms. **Cons:** away from the attractions of the city; not good for families with young kids. ⊠ *5 Tilbury La., Botley* ☎ *01865/862138* ⊕ *www.tilburylodge. com* 🛏 *8 rooms* ⚭ *In-room: no a/c, no phone, Wi-Fi. In-hotel: parking (free), no kids under 10* ⊟ *MC, V* ⦿ *BP.*

NIGHTLIFE AND THE ARTS

NIGHTLIFE AND PUBS

Nightlife in Oxford centers around student life, which in turn focuses on the local pubs, though you may find a few surprises, too. The popular Jericho area, around Walton Street north of the old city walls and within walking distance of the center of town, has good restaurants and pubs. **Freud** (⊠ *119 Walton St.* ☎ *01865/311171*), in a renovated neoclassical church, serves light meals and cocktails and offers nightly live jazz or funk. The **Kings Arms** (⊠ *40 Holywell St.* ☎ *01865/242369*), popular with students and fairly quiet during the day, carries excellent local brews as well as inexpensive pub grub.

Raoul's (✉ *32 Walton St.* ☎ *01865/553732*) is a trendy cocktail bar in the equally trendy Jericho neighborhood. The **Turf Tavern** (✉ *Bath Pl.* ☎ *01865/243235*), off Holywell Street, includes a higgledy-piggledy collection of little rooms and outdoor space good for a quiet drink and inexpensive pub food. The cozy **White Horse** (✉ *52 Broad St.* ☎ *01865/728318*), one of the city's oldest pubs, serves real ales and traditional food all day.

THE ARTS

Get into the spirit of the place by attending a concert or some theater; there are plenty of choices.

FESTIVALS AND CONCERTS

Choral music at the city's churches is a calming way to spend the early evening. Drop by weekdays during term time at 6 PM at Magdalen, New College (except Wednesday), or Christ Church (except Monday) to hear evensong.

The **Jacqueline Du Pre Music Building** (✉ *St. Hilda's College, Cowley Pl.* ☎ *01865/276821*), endowed with the city's best acoustics, showcases rising talent at recitals. **Music at Oxford** (☎ *01865/305305*), an acclaimed series of weekend classical concerts, takes place mid-September through June in such surroundings as Christ Church Cathedral and Sir Christopher Wren's Sheldonian Theatre. At the **Oxford Coffee Concerts** (✉ *Holywell Music Room, Holywell Rd.*), a program of Sunday morning chamber concerts, string quartets, piano trios, and soloists presents baroque and classical pieces in a 1748 hall. Reasonably priced tickets are available from the **Oxford Playhouse** (✉ *Beaumont St.* ☎ *01865/305305*).

Blenheim Palace (☎ *01993/811091* ⊕ *www.blenheimpalace.com*) in nearby Woodstock puts on marvelous classical and pop concerts in summer, sometimes combined with fireworks displays. ■ TIP→ **Pack a picnic of champagne, Kent strawberries, and fresh Henley cream, and head out for a true, elegant English summertime experience.**

THEATER

During term time, undergraduate productions are often given in the colleges or local halls. In summer, outdoor performances may take place in quadrangles or college gardens. Look for announcement posters and take a chance.

New Theatre (✉ *George St.* ☎ *0844/847–1585*), Oxford's main theater, stages popular shows, comedy acts, and musicals. **OFS Studio Theatre** (✉ *40 George St.* ☎ *01865/297170*), an alternative theater, showcases student productions, small-scale opera, and new musicals. The **Oxford Playhouse** (✉ *Beaumont St.* ☎ *01865/305305*) is a serious theater presenting classic and modern dramas as well as dance and music performances.

SPORTS AND THE OUTDOORS

BIKING

Bikes can be rented at **Summertown Cycles** (✉ *200–202 Banbury Rd.* ☎ *01865/316885*), north of the city center in Summertown.

PUNTING

Fodor's Choice ★ You may choose, like many an Oxford student, to spend a summer afternoon **punting**, while dangling your champagne bottle in the water to keep it cool. Punts—shallow-bottom boats that are poled slowly up the river—can be rented in several places, including at the foot of the Magdalen Bridge.

From mid-March through mid-October, **Cherwell Boathouse** (✉ *Bardwell Rd.* ☎ *01865/515978*), a punt station and restaurant a mile north of the heart of Oxford, will rent you a boat and, if you wish, someone (usually an Oxford student) to punt it. Rentals are £13–£15 per hour, £65–£75 per day. At the St. Aldates Road end of Folly Bridge, **Salter's Steamers** (☎ *01865/243421*) rents out punts and skiffs (rowboats) for £20 per hour, £60 per half day, and £100 per day. Its chauffeured punts are £60 per hour, booked in advance.

SPECTATOR SPORTS

At the end of May, during **Oxford's Eights Week**, men and women rowers from the university's colleges compete to be "Head of the River." Because the river is too narrow for teams of eight to race side by side, the boats set off, 13 at a time, one behind another. Each boat tries to catch and bump the one in front.

Oxford University Cricket Club (⊕ *www.cricketinthe parks.org.uk*) competes against leading county teams in late spring and summer and also, each summer, the major foreign teams visiting Britain. In the middle of the sprawling University Parks—itself worthy of a walk—the club's playing field is truly lovely.

SHOPPING

Small shops line High Street, Cornmarket, and Queen Street; the Clarendon and Westgate shopping centers, leading off them, have branches of several nationally known stores. **Alice's Shop** (✉ *83 St. Aldate's* ☎ *01865/723793*) sells all manner of *Alice in Wonderland* paraphernalia.

★ **Blackwell's** (✉ *48–51 Broad St.* ☎ *01865/792792*), family-owned and family-run since 1879, stocks an excellent selection of books. The **Covered Market** (✉ *Off High St.*), offering good food as well as clothes and more in its stalls, is a fine place for a cheap sandwich and a leisurely browse; the smell of pastries and coffee follows you from cobbler to jeweler to cheesemonger. **Scriptum Fine Stationery** (✉ *3 Turl St.* ☎ *01865/200042*) sells prints and secondhand books as well as leather-bound journals, quills, sealing wax, and handmade paper. **Shepherd & Woodward** (✉ *109–113 High St.* ☎ *01865/249491*), a traditional tailor, specializes in university gowns, ties, and scarves. The **University of Oxford Shop** (✉ *106 High St.* ☎ *01865/247414*), run by the university, sells authorized clothing, ceramics, and tea towels, all emblazoned with university crests.

BLENHEIM PALACE TO ALTHORP

The River Thames takes on a new graciousness as it flows along the borders of Oxfordshire for 71 mi; each league it increases in size and importance. Three tributaries swell the river as it passes through the landscape: the Windrush, the Evenlode, and the Cherwell. Tucked among the hills and dales are one of England's impressive stately homes, an Edenic village, and a former Rothschild estate. Closer to London in Hertfordshire is St. Albans, with its cathedral and Roman remains.

WOODSTOCK AND BLENHEIM PALACE

★ *8 mi northwest of Oxford on A44.*

Handsome 17th- and 18th-century houses line the trim streets of Woodstock, at the eastern edge of the Cotswolds. It's best known for nearby Blenheim Palace, and in the summer, tour buses clog the village's ancient streets. On a quiet fall or spring afternoon, however, Woodstock is a sublime experience: a mellowed 18th-century church and town hall mark the central square, and along its backstreets you can find flower-bedecked houses and quiet lanes right out of a 19th-century etching.

GETTING HERE AND AROUND

The public bus service S3 runs (usually every half hour) between Oxford and Woodstock and costs £3 one way.

ESSENTIALS

Visitor Information Woodstock (✉ *Oxfordshire Museum, Park St.* ☎ *01993/813276*).

EXPLORING

Fodor'sChoice
★
So grandiose is **Blenheim Palace** and so impressive are its articulations of splendor that it was named a World Heritage Site, the only historic house in Britain to receive the honor. Designed by Sir John Vanbrugh in the early 1700s in collaboration with Nicholas Hawksmoor, Blenheim was given by Queen Anne and the nation to General John Churchill, first duke of Marlborough, in gratitude for his military victories (including the Battle of Blenheim) against the French in 1704. The exterior is mind-boggling, with its huge columns, enormous pediments, and obelisks, all exemplars of English baroque. Inside, lavishness continues in monumental extremes: you can join a guided tour (free; good for the highlights) or walk through on your own. In most of the opulent rooms family portraits look down at sumptuous furniture, elaborate carpets, fine Chinese porcelain, and immense pieces of silver. Exquisite tapestries in the three state rooms illustrate the first duke's victories. ■ TIP→ When they are open, you can take a tour (bookable at the time of visit; £4.50) of the current duke's private apartments for a more intimate view of ducal life. For some visitors, however, the most memorable room is the small, low-ceiling chamber where Winston Churchill (his father was the younger brother of the then-duke) was born in 1874; he is buried in nearby Bladon.

Sir Winston wrote that the unique beauty of Blenheim lay in its perfect adaptation of English parkland to an Italian palace. Indeed, the 2,000

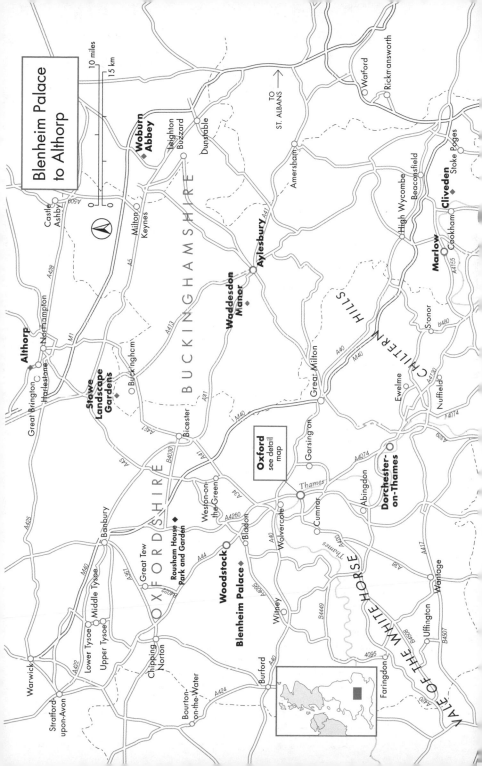

Blenheim Palace
to Althorp

10 miles
15 km

TO
ST. ALBANS

Woburn Abbey
Leighton Buzzard
Dunstable

Amersham

Watford
Rickmansworth

High Wycombe
Beaconsfield
Stoke Poges
Marlow
Cliveden
Cookham

Castle Ashby
A50

Milton Keynes

Aylesbury
A41

Waddesdon Manor

CHILTERN HILLS
M40

S'onor
B480

Nuffield
A4130

A4074

Althorp
Northampton
Great Brington
Harlestone

M1

Buckingham

Stowe Landscape Gardens

A413

BUCKINGHAMSHIRE
A41

Great Milton
M40

Ewelme

A329

Oxford
see detail map

Garsington

Dorchester-on-Thames
A4074

Abingdon

A425

Banbury

Bicester
A41
M40

Weston-on-the-Green

A34
A4260

Thames

Cumnor

Wantage
A417
A338

A425

Great Tew

Rousham House Park and Garden

Bladon

Wolvercote
A40

A4095

Warwick
Stratford-upon-Avon

Lower Tysoe
Middle Tysoe
Upper Tysoe

Chipping Norton

Woodstock
Blenheim Palace

Witney

Uffington
B4507

A417

A422
M40
A361

Bourton-on-the-Water

A424

Burford
A40

A4095

VALE OF THE WHITE HORSE

Faringdon
A420

A4449

OXFORDSHIRE

acres of grounds, the work of Capability Brown, 18th-century England's best-known landscape gardener, are arguably the best example of the "cunningly natural" park in the country. It's well worth a stroll. Tucked away here is the Temple of Diana, where Winston Churchill proposed to his future wife, Clementine. Blenheim's formal gardens include notable water terraces and an Italian garden with a mermaid fountain, all built in the 1920s.

The Pleasure Gardens, reached by a train that stops outside the main entrance to the palace, contain some child-pleasers: a butterfly house, notable 1-acre hedge maze, playground, and giant chess set. The herb-and-lavender garden is also delightful. In summer a miniature train runs every 30 minutes from 11 until 5, connecting the palace with the Pleasure Gardens. It's easy to spend half a day here. ⊠ *Off A4095, Woodstock* ☎ *0870/060–2080* ⊕ *www.blenheimpalace.com* ✉ *Palace, park, and gardens £18. Park and gardens £10.30* ☉ *Palace mid-Feb.– Oct., daily 10:30–4:45; Nov.–mid-Dec., Wed.–Sun. 10:30–4:45; park mid-Feb.–mid-Dec., daily 9–4:45.*

WHERE TO EAT AND STAY

££
BRITISH
Fodor's Choice
★

✕**Falkland Arms.** It's worth detouring a bit for this supremely appealing pub on the village green at Great Tew, about 8 mi northwest of Woodstock. The bar has impressive malt whiskies, and mugs and jugs hang from the beams. The small restaurant chalks up a traditional but creative menu, which includes such items as butternut squash risotto and Guinness-baked ham hock. A spiral stone staircase leads to five guest rooms (££), which have brass bedsteads or four-posters. Reservations are essential for both staying and eating here. ⊠ *19–21 The Green, <Great Tew, Chipping Norton* ☎ *01608/683653* ⊕ *www.falklandarms. org.uk* ⚄ *Reservations essential* ═ *AE, MC, V.*

£–££

🍴 **Blenheim Guest House & Tea Rooms.** Small and unassuming, this three-story guesthouse stands in the quiet village cul-de-sac that leads to the back gates of Blenheim Palace. You can still just make out the Victorian-era banner that says VIEWS AND POSTCARDS OF BLENHEIM. The guest rooms have modest period furnishings, with pretty sheer curtains, but the Marlborough room is unique—its bathroom offers a view of Blenheim. **Pros:** handy tearoom downstairs; bathroom views of Blenheim Palace. **Cons:** plain decor; floors are a bit creaky. ⊠ *17 Park St.* ☎ *01993/813814* ⊕ *www.theblenheim.com* ⭐ *6 rooms* ⚅ *In-room: no a/c. In-hotel: Wi-Fi hotspot* ═ *MC, V* ⊠| *BP.*

££££–£££££
★

🍴 **The Feathers.** Antique-bedecked guest rooms with floral prints and striped fabrics fill this stylish hotel in the heart of town. The inn was cobbled together from five 17th-century houses, and its elegant courtyard is favored for a summertime meal. In winter, log fires make the public rooms cozy. The seasonal menu and upscale dining room are worth the restaurant's hefty prices, though the bistro is a cheaper option. You might opt for sea bass with thyme gnocchi and truffle cappuccino, followed by saffron poached pear with rosewater ice. **Pros:** cozy lounges with fireplaces; great food. **Cons:** prices are high given what's on offer; minimum two-night stay on weekends in summer. ⊠ *Market St.* ☎ *01993/812291* ⊕ *www.feathers.co.uk* ⭐ *16 rooms, 4* *suites* ♿ *In-room: no a/c, Wi-Fi. In-hotel: 2 restaurants, room service, bar, laundry service* ⊟ *AE, DC, MC, V* |◎| *BP.*

£££–££££   📺 **Macdonald Bear.** Tudoresque wood paneling, beamed ceilings, wattle-and-daub walls, and blazing fireplaces in winter help define this as an archetypal English coaching inn. The guest rooms, overlooking either a quiet churchyard or the town square, have plenty of carved oak; the duplex suites would make a king feel at home, thanks to their timbered loft-balconies and gargantuan four-posters. Legend has it that the Bear is where Richard Burton finally popped the question to Elizabeth Taylor. **Pros:** true luxury; historic house. **Cons:** creaky floors; you can knock yourself silly on those old beams. ⊠ *Park St.* ☎ *0844/879–9143* ⊕ *www.macdonaldhotels.co.uk/bear* ⇆ *46 rooms, 8 suites* ♿ *In-room: a/c (some), Wi-Fi (some). In-hotel: restaurant, room service, bar, laundry service, Wi-Fi hotspot* ⊟ *AE, MC, V* |◎| *BP.*

▌EN
ROUTE

After taking in Blenheim Palace, stop by **Bladon,** 2 mi southeast of Woodstock on A4095 and 6 mi northwest of Oxford, to see the small, tree-lined churchyard that is the burial place of Sir Winston Churchill. His grave is all the more impressive for its simplicity.

DORCHESTER-ON-THAMES

6

16 mi southeast of Woodstock, 15 mi east of Uffington, 9 mi southeast of Oxford.

An important center in Saxon times, when it was the seat of a bishopric, Dorchester merits a visit chiefly because of its ancient abbey, but also because it's a charming little town. The main street, once a leg of the Roman road to Silchester, has timber houses, thatched cottages, ancient inns, and what must be the longest wisteria in the country (on the Old College building). Crossing the Thames at Day's Lock and turning left at Little Wittenham takes you on a bucolic and historic walk past the remains of the village's Iron Age settlements. The town is known for its pricey and alluring antiques shops.

GETTING HERE AND AROUND
Thames Travel runs a regular hourly bus service from Oxford (40 minutes). Drivers from Oxford should take A4074, which also connects with A4130 and Junction 8/9 of M4 for London.

ESSENTIALS
Bus Contacts Thames Travel (☎ *0871/200–2233* ⊕ *www.thames-travel.co.uk*).

EXPLORING
In addition to secluded cloisters and gardens, **Dorchester Abbey** has a spacious church (1170) with a rare lead baptismal font from the Norman period and two unique items from the 14th century: a sculptured stone Tree of Jesse window and a wall painting of the Crucifixion with an unusual cross design. The great tower was rebuilt in 1602, but incorporated the old 14th-century spiral staircase. ⊠ *Off A4074* ☎ *01865/340007* ⊕ *www.dorchester-abbey.org.uk* ▨ *Free* ⊙ *May–Sept., daily 8:30–7; Oct.–Apr., daily 8:30–dusk, except during services.*

OFF THE
BEATEN
PATH

Vale of the White Horse. Stretching up into the foothills of the Berkshire Downs between Swindon and Oxford is a wide fertile plain known as the Vale of the White Horse. Here, off B4507, cut into the turf of the hillside to expose the underlying chalk, is the 374-foot-long, 110-foot-high figure of a white horse, an important prehistoric site. Some historians believed that the figure might have been carved to commemorate King Alfred's victory over the Danes in 871, whereas others dated it to the Iron Age, around 750 BC. More current research suggests that it is at least 1,000 years older, created at the beginning of the second millennium BC. **Uffington Castle,** above the horse, is a prehistoric fort. English Heritage maintains these sites. To reach the Vale of the White Horse from Oxford (about 20 mi), follow A420, then B4508 to the village of Uffington.

WHERE TO STAY

££ 🏨 **George Hotel.** Overlooking Dorchester Abbey, this 500-year-old hotel was built as a coaching inn—there's an old coach parked outside—and it retains whitewashed walls, exposed beams, and fireplaces. Each room has an individual style and two have four-poster beds. Some rooms are furnished with genuine antiques, others with reproductions. Service is friendly and breakfasts are ample. **Pros:** lovely building; comfortable rooms. **Cons:** modern rooms are rather dull; small bathrooms. ⌂ 23 High St. ☎ 01865/340404 ⊕ www.thegeorgedorchester.co.uk ⥥ 17 rooms ⚒ In-room: no a/c, Wi-Fi. In-hotel: restaurant, room service, bar, laundry service, parking (free) ☰ AE, MC, V ⚏ BP.

AYLESBURY

22 mi east of Oxford, 46 mi northwest of London.

Aylesbury makes a good base for exploring the surrounding countryside, including stately homes and gardens. It's a pretty, historic place with a 13th-century church surrounded by small Tudor lanes and cottages. This market town has been associated with the Aylesbury duck since the 18th century, when flocks were walked 40 mi to the London markets. Children will appreciate a visit to the Roald Dahl's Children's Gallery on Church Street (open all year).

GETTING HERE AND AROUND

From London, Chiltern Railways runs frequent trains from Marylebone station (one hour). The town is easily accessible from Oxford by Arriva Bus 280, which runs every 30 minutes; travel time is 80 minutes. If you're driving from Oxford, take A40 and A418. From London, follow M1 and A41 and allow 90 minutes.

ESSENTIALS

Visitor Information Aylesbury (⌂ *King's Head Passage, off Market Sq.* ☎ *01296/330559*).

EXPLORING

Fodor's Choice
★

Many of the regal residences created by the Rothschild family throughout Europe are gone now, but **Waddesdon Manor** (now in the care of the National Trust) remains, a vision of the 19th century at its most sumptuous. G. H. Destailleur built the house in the 1880s for Baron

THAMES VALLEY HIKING AND BIKING

The Thames Valley is a great area to explore by foot or bike. It's not too hilly, and pubs and easily accessible lodgings dot the riverside and small towns. The Thames is almost completely free of car traffic along the Thames Path, a 184-mi national trail that traces the river from the London flood barrier to the river's source near Kemble, in the Cotswolds. The path follows towpaths from the outskirts of London, through Windsor, to Oxford and Lechlade.

Good public transportation In the region makes it possible to start and stop easily anywhere along this route. In summer the walking is fine and no special gear is necessary, but in winter the path often floods—check before you head out.

The Countryside Agency has been charting and preserving Thames paths for years, and through its Natural England branch it offers publications and information about them. For maps and advice, contact the National Trails Office or the Ramblers' Association. The Chiltern Conservation Board promotes walking in the Chilterns peaks.

Biking is perhaps the best way to see the Chilterns. Routes include the 99-mi Thames Valley Cycle Route from London to Oxford, the 200-mi Oxfordshire Cycleway around the county's countryside, and the 87-mi Ridgeway Path from Uffington that follows the Chilterns; the National Trails Office has information. The Thames Path also has plenty of biking opportunities.

CONTACTS AND RESOURCES
Chiltern Conservation Board (☎ 01844/355500 ⊕ www.chilternsaonb.org). **Chiltern Way** (☎ 01494/771250 ⊕ www.chilternsociety.org.uk). **National Trails Office** (☎ 01865/810224 ⊕ www.nationaltrail.co.uk). **Natural England** (☎ 0845/600–3078 ⊕ www.naturalengland.org.uk). **Ramblers' Association** (☎ 020/7339–8500 ⊕ www.ramblers.org.uk). **Sustrans (Thames Valley Cycle Route)** (☎ 0845/113–0065 ⊕ www.sustrans.org.uk).

Ferdinand de Rothschild in the style of a French château, with perfectly balanced turrets and towers and walls of creamy stone. Although intended only for summer weekend house parties, it was lovingly furnished over the course of 35 years with Savonnerie carpets, Sèvres porcelain, furniture made by Riesener for Marie Antoinette, and paintings by Guardi, Dutch and Flemish masters, Gainsborough, and Reynolds. An exquisite 21st-century broken porcelain chandelier by Ingo Maurer in the Blue Dining Room brings the collection up to date. The gardens are equally extraordinary, with an aviary, colorful plantings, and winding trails that provide panoramic views. In the restaurant you can dine on English or French fare and order excellent Rothschild wines if your pocketbook can take the hit. Admission prices are a bit higher on weekends. ■TIP➔ **Admission is by timed ticket; arrive early or book in advance.** ⊠ Waddesdon ✛ On A41 west of Aylesbury ☎ 01296/653226, 01296/653211 information line ⊕ www.waddesdon.org.uk 🎫 House and grounds £12–£13.50; grounds only, £5–£6.30 ۞ House Apr.–Oct., Wed.–Fri. and national holiday Mon. noon–4, weekends 11–4; gardens

Jan.–Mar., weekends 10–5; Apr.–Oct., Wed.–Sun. and national holiday Mon. 10–5.

★ A superb example of a Georgian garden, **Stowe Landscape Gardens** was created for the Temple family by the most famous gardeners of the 18th century. Capability Brown, Charles Bridgeman, and William Kent all worked on the land to create 980 acres of pleasing greenery in the valleys and meadows. More than 40 striking monuments, follies, and temples dot the landscape of lakes, rivers, and pleasant vistas; this is a historically important place, but it's not for those who want primarily a flower garden. Allow at least half a day if you want to explore the grounds. Stowe House, at its center, is now a fancy school with some magnificently restored rooms; it's closed to the public, apart from irregular tours throughout the year (call for dates and times). The gardens are about 3 mi northwest of Buckingham, which is 14 mi northwest of Aylesbury. ⊠ *Stowe Ave., off 422 Buckingham–Banbury Rd., Buckingham* ☎ *01280/822850, 01494/755568 information line, 01280/818166 house tours* ⊕ *www.nationaltrust.org.uk* ☒ *Gardens only, £6.80; house and gardens £10.70; house £4.40* ☺ *Mar.–Oct., Wed.–Sun. and national holiday Mon. 10:30–5:30; Nov.–Feb., weekends 10:30–4; last admission 90 mins before closing.*

WHERE TO STAY

££–£££ ⊡ **Five Arrows.** Fancifully patterned brick chimneys and purple gables decorate this baroque building next to the main entrance of Waddesdon Manor. Constructed to house the manor's workers, it now holds a hotel with traditional-style bedrooms. The delightful suites in the Courtyard Stables are big enough for families, or for couples who just want to stretch out a little. A fine restaurant and pub serves inspired modern fare with a Mediterranean twist; the wine list is excellent. The in-house "wine pub" is a regular award winner. **Pros:** charming historic building; lovely grounds. **Cons:** some rooms are small; on a busy main road. ⊠ *High St., Waddesdon* ☎ *01296/651727* ⊕ *www.waddesdon. org.uk/five_arrows* ↩ *9 rooms, 2 suites* ⚹ *In-room: no a/c, Internet, Wi-Fi. In-hotel: restaurant, bar* ⊟ *MC, V* ⫩*BP.*

££££–£££££ ⊡ **Hartwell House.** Part Jacobean, part Georgian, this magnificent stately home, now owned by the National Trust, offers formal luxury in an opulent countryside setting. The building is decorated with a masterful touch—crystal chandeliers, original oil paintings, and carved ceilings adorn the ornate public areas, and bedrooms with well-chosen antiques and comfortable beds are suitably grand. There are also guest rooms in the nearby Old Rectory. Some rooms have direct access to the gardens, which sprawl over 90 acres of landscaped parkland, perfect for strolls. This is the kind of place where you must dress to impress for dinner. **Pros:** truly elegant; soothing views of the gardens. **Cons:** atmosphere feels too formal; spa is open to the public. ⊠ *Oxford Rd. (A418)* ☎ *01296/747444* ⊕ *www.hartwell-house.com* ↩ *33 rooms, 13 suites* ⚹ *In-room: a/c (some), Internet, Wi-Fi. In-hotel: restaurant, room service, bar, tennis courts, pool, gym, spa, laundry service, some pets allowed, no kids under 4* ⊟ *AE, MC, V* ⫩*BP.*

ST. ALBANS

25 mi east of Aylesbury, 20 mi northwest of London.

A lively town on the outskirts of London, St. Albans is known for its historic cathedral, and it also holds reminders of a long history. From AD 50 to 440, the town then known as Verulamium was one of the largest communities in Roman Britain. You can explore this past in the Verulamium Museum and splendid Roman sites around the area. For activities more focused on the present, every Wednesday and Saturday the Market Place on St. Peter's Street bustles with traders from all over England, selling everything from fish and farm produce to clothing and CDs.

GETTING HERE AND AROUND

About 20 mi northwest of London, St. Albans is off the M1 and M25 highways, about an hour's drive from the center of the capital. First Capital Connect trains leave every half hour from London's St. Pancras Station, arriving in St. Albans in 30 minutes. The main train station is on Victoria Street, in the town center. A second station on the south side of town, St. Albans Abbey Station, serves smaller towns in the surrounding area. Bus service is not direct; take the train. Central St. Albans is small and walkable. There's a local bus service, but you're unlikely to need it. Taxis usually line up outside the train stations.

6

ESSENTIALS

Train Contacts First Capital Connect (☎ *0845/026–4700* 🌐 *www.firstcapitalconnect.co.uk*).

Visitor Information St. Albans (✉ *Town Hall, Market Pl.* ☎ *01727/864511* 🌐 *www.stalbans.gov.uk*).

EXPLORING

TOP ATTRACTIONS

Hatfield House. Six miles east of St. Albans, Hatfield House, an outstanding brick mansion surrounded by lovely formal gardens, stands as a testament to the magnificence of Jacobean architecture. Robert Cecil, earl of Salisbury, built Hatfield in 1611, and his descendants still live here. The interior, with its dark-wood paneling, lush tapestries, and Tudor and Jacobean portraits, reveals much about the era. Perhaps the finest feature is the ornate Grand Staircase, with carved wooden figures on the banisters. By the knot garden is the Old Palace (not open to the public), built around 1485, with its medieval brickwork; Elizabeth I lived here in her childhood. Thursday is the only day on which the East Garden, with topiaries, parterres, and rare plants, is open. The **Elizabethan Banquet** (☎ *01707/262055* 🌐 *www.hatfield-house.co.uk* 🎫 *£50* ⏲ *Fri. 7:30 PM–11 PM*) is a hearty five-course dinner accompanied by kitschy entertainment from King Henry VIII, Queen Elizabeth I, minstrels, and jokers. ✉ *Off A1 Hatfield* ☎ *01707/287010* 🌐 *www.hatfield-house.co.uk* 🎫 *House, gardens, and park £11.50 (£14.50 on Thurs., if you wish to see East Garden), gardens £6.50, park £3* ⏲ *Easter–Sept., mansion Wed.–Sun. and national holiday Mon. noon–4, west gardens Wed.–Sun. and national holiday Mon. 11–5 (daily in Aug.), East Garden Thurs. 11–5.*

St. Albans Cathedral. Medieval pilgrims came from far and wide to hilltop St. Albans Cathedral to honor its patron saint, a Roman soldier turned Christian martyr. Construction of the impressive, mainly Norman cathedral began in the early 11th century, but the nearly 300-foot-long nave dates from 1235. The tower is even more historic, and contains bricks from ancient Roman buildings. ⊠ *Holywell Hill at High St.* ☎ *01727/860780* ⊕ *www.stalbanscathedral.org.uk* ✉ *Donations welcome* ☉ *Daily 8:30–5:45; guided tours weekdays 11:30 and 2:30, Sat. 11:30 and 2, Sun. 2:30.*

☺ **Verulamium Museum.** With exhibits on everything from Roman food to burial practices, the Verulamium Museum, on the site of the ancient Roman city, explores life 2,000 years ago. The re-created Roman rooms contain colorful mosaics that are some of the finest in Britain. Every second weekend of the month, "Roman soldiers" invade the museum and demonstrate the skills of the Imperial Army. ⊠ *St. Michael's St.* ☎ *01727/751810* ⊕ *www.stalbansmuseums.org.uk* ✉ *£3.50* ☉ *Mon.– Sat. 10–5:30, Sun. 2–5:30.*

WORTH NOTING

Roman Theater. Imagination can take you back to AD 130 and to a Roman stage drama as you walk around the ruins of the Roman Theater, one of the few in this country. Next to the theater are the ruins of a Roman town house, shops, and a shrine. ⊠ *Bluehouse Hill* ☎ *01727/835035* ⊕ *www.romantheatre.co.uk* ✉ *£2.50* ☉ *Easter–Nov., daily 10–5; Dec.– Easter, daily 10–4.*

Shaw's Corner. From 1906 to his death in 1950, the famed Irish playwright George Bernard Shaw lived in the small village of Ayot St. Lawrence, 9 mi northeast of St. Albans. Today his small Edwardian home, Shaw's Corner, remains much as he left it. The most delightful curiosity is his little writing hut in the garden, which can be turned to face the sun. Take care when driving here; the access roads are very narrow. ⊠ *Off Hill Farm La., Ayot St. Lawrence* ☎ *01438/820307, 01438/829221 information line* ⊕ *www.nationaltrust.org.uk* ✉ *£5.50* ☉ *House mid-Mar.–Oct., Wed.–Sun. 1–5; gardens mid-Mar.–Oct., Wed.–Sun. noon–5:30.*

☺ **Verulamium Park.** Adjacent to the Verulamium Museum, this park contains the usual—playground, wading pool, lake—and the unusual— **Roman ruins** that include part of the Roman town hall and a hypocaust, a central-heating system. The hypocaust dates to AD 200 and included one of the first heated floors in Britain. Brick columns supported the floor, and hot air from a nearby fire was drawn underneath the floor to keep bathers warm. ⊠ *St. Michael's St.* ☎ *01727/751810* ⊕ *www. stalbansmuseums.org.uk* ✉ *Free* ☉ *Hypocaust Apr.–Sept., Mon.–Sat. 10–4:30, Sun. 2–4:30; Oct.–Mar., Mon.–Sat. 10–3:45, Sun. 2–3:45.*

WHERE TO EAT AND STAY

£   ✕ **Waffle House.** Indoors or outside, you can have a great budget meal at
BELGIAN   the 16th-century Kingsbury Watermill, near the Verulamium Museum. The organic flour for the high-quality, sweet and savory Belgian waffles comes from Redbournbury Watermill just north of the city; daily specials add variety. In the main dining room you can see the wheel churn

the water of the River Ver. Waffle House is open 10 to 5 in winter, to 6 in summer. ⊠ *Kingsbury Watermill, St. Michael's St.* ☏ *01727/853502* ⊕ *www.wafflehouse.co.uk* ⊟ *MC, V* ⊗ *No dinner.*

££
BRITISH

✕ **Ye Olde Fighting Cocks.** Some claim this is England's oldest pub, although that's a contentious category. Still, this octagonal building certainly looks suitably aged. The building was moved to this location in the 16th century, but the foundations date back to the 8th century. The small rooms with low ceilings make a cozy stop for a pint and good home-cooked food. Be prepared for crowds. ⊠ *16 Abbey Mill La.* ☏ *01727/869152* ⊟ *MC, V.*

£££–££££

▥ **St. Michael's Manor.** The Newling Ward family has owned this luxurious 16th-century manor house close to the center of St. Albans for three generations. The 5 acres of grounds, complete with a lake, add a sense of seclusion, and plush furniture helps make the antique- and painting-filled public areas inviting. The contemporary-style bedrooms are equipped with thoughtful extras like complimentary bottled water, fruit, and cookies. The conservatory restaurant (£££) serves Modern British cuisine with French touches. Champagne afternoon tea is a treat. Pros: spacious rooms; excellent food; beautiful grounds. Cons: a little too grand for some. ⊠ *Fishpool St.* ☏ *01727/864444* ⊕ *www. stmichaelsmanor.com* ⇥ *30 rooms* ♻ *In-room: a/c (some), DVD, Internet, Wi-Fi. In-hotel: restaurant, room service, bar, laundry service, Wi-Fi hotspot* ⊟ *AE, DC, MC, V* ▯◎▯ *BP.*

6

WOBURN ABBEY

30 mi west of St. Albans, 10 mi northeast of Aylesbury.

GETTING HERE AND AROUND

Woburn Abbey is easily accessible for drivers from M1 at Junction 12 or 13; a car is needed to tour the safari park. The nearest train station, Flitwick, is a 15-minute taxi ride away. Frequent trains connect with St Albans and London's King's Cross and St. Pancras station.

ESSENTIALS

Train Contacts First Capital Connect (☏ *0845/026–4700* ⊕ *www. firstcapitalconnect.co.uk).*

EXPLORING

♻ **Woburn Abbey** is the stately home as big business. Still the ancestral residence of the duke of Bedford, it houses countless Grand Tour treasures and old master paintings, including 20 stunning Canalettos that practically wallpaper the crimson dining salon, and excellent works by Gainsborough and Reynolds. The Palladian mansion contains a number of etchings by Queen Victoria, who left them behind after she stayed here. Outside, 10 species of deer roam grounds that include an antiques center and small restaurant. The adjacent **Woburn Safari Park** is a popular drive-through wildlife experience, home to big game from around the world. Jeep tours, walks with elephants, and other special packages are available. There are plenty of play areas, a boating lake with swan boats, and walkabouts with small animals such as wallabies. ■ TIP➔ **Allow at least half a day for the safari park. If you buy a joint ticket with the house, you can use it on another day.** ⊠ *A4012, off A5,*

Woburn ☎ Abbey 01525/290333, Safari Park 01525/290407 ⊕ www.
woburn.co.uk ⊠ House, gardens, and deer park £16.50, safari £18.50
in summer, £11 off-season; gardens and deer park only, £4 ⊙ House
Apr.–Sept., daily 11–4; Mar. and Oct., weekends 11–4. Safari Park
Mar.–Oct., daily 10–5; Nov. and Feb., weekends 11–3. Gardens and
deer park daily 10–5.

WHERE TO STAY

£££ ⊡ **The Inn at Woburn.** In the center of Woburn village, a small Georgian
town, this modern hotel has uncluttered and comfortable bedrooms.
Some rooms have beamed ceilings and skylights, and others have two
levels. Olivier's serves contemporary British cuisine with a Continental accent, and the pub is a snug place for a pint. ■ TIP➜ **Ask about**
packages that include entrance to Woburn Abbey and Safari Park. Pros:
close to Woburn Abbey; light-filled spaces. **Cons:** some decor lacks
character; small bathrooms. ⊠ *George St., Woburn ☎ 01525/290441*
⊕ *www.theinnatwoburn.com* ⟳ *50 rooms, 7 suites ⚹ In-room: no a/c,*
safe (some). In-hotel: restaurant, room service, bar, laundry service,
Wi-Fi hotspot, some pets allowed ⊟ *AE, DC, MC, V.*

ALTHORP

5 mi west of Northampton, 27 mi northwest of Woburn Abbey.

GETTING HERE AND AROUND

Signposted at Junction 16 of M1, Althorp is most easily reached by car.
However, if you ask the driver, Stagecoach bus 96 from Northampton's
train station will drop you here (Monday–Saturday). Buses run every
two hours.

ESSENTIALS

Train Contacts Stagecoach (☎ *01604/676060* ⊕ *www.stagecoachbus.com*).

EXPLORING

Deep in the heart of Northamptonshire sits **Althorp**, the ancestral home
of the Spencers, the family of Diana, Princess of Wales. Here, on a
tiny island within the estate park, is Diana's final resting place. Diana
and her siblings found the house too melancholy, calling it "Deadlock
Hall." What the house does have are rooms filled with Van Dycks,
Reynoldses, and Rubenses—all portraits of the Spencers going back 500
years—and an entry hall that architectural historian Nikolaus Pevsner
called "the noblest Georgian room in the country." To these attractions, Diana's brother, Earl Spencer, has added a visitor center devoted
to her, which includes her wedding dress, childhood memorabilia, and
an exhibition on her charitable work. A percentage of ticket income
is donated to the Diana Princess of Wales Memorial Fund. A literary
festival takes place here in mid-June. On the west side of the estate park
is Great Brington, the neighboring village where the church of **St. Mary**
the Virgin (⊙ *Daily noon–5*) holds the Spencer family crypt; it's best
reached by the designated path from Althorp. ⊠ *Rugby Rd., off A428*
☎ *01604/770107* ⊕ *www.althorp.com* ⊠ *£12.50 (£15, including 2nd*
floor of house) ⊙ July and Aug., daily 11–5.

Shakespeare Country

STRATFORD-UPON-AVON AND ENVIRONS

WORD OF MOUTH

"We went through Nash's House in Stratford-upon-Avon and it was fantastic . . . all beams, uneven floors at various levels, thick ancient doors, and well furnished with the things of those times. Late afternoon we saw Anne Hathaway's Cottage and its garden . . . even more beautiful than I had expected, especially the garden."

—moonrise

"If you are doing the Shakespeare properties and Warwick Castle and some similar sites, then by all means investigate the Great British Heritage Pass as it could save you big bucks—it's sold only to foreign tourists."

—PalenQ

Updated by
Kate Hughes

You get new insight into William Shakespeare when you visit the stretch of country where he was born and raised. The hills of sculpted farmland may look nothing like the forested countryside of the 16th century, but some sturdy Tudor houses that Shakespeare knew survive to this day. You can walk streets he might have traveled and cross streams where, as a child, he might have dangled his feet. There's beauty in this—and the possibility of tourist overkill.

Stratford-upon-Avon, with its carefully preserved Shakespeare sites and the theaters of the famed Royal Shakespeare Company, veers toward becoming "Shakespeare World." Still, it's a fascinating place, and there's much more to see—castles, churches, and countryside—in this famously lovely part of Britain.

Driving down Warwickshire's country lanes is one of the best ways to explore this area. Stop in at Charlecote, a grand Elizabethan manor house, and Baddesley Clinton, a superb example of late-medieval domestic architecture. Other treasure houses are Ragley Hall and Coughton Court, brimming with art and antiques; Compton Verney is a stately home that has been converted to an art gallery. Warwick Castle, a huge fortress, provides a glimpse into the country's turbulent history.

The price you pay for visiting Stratford is being caught among vast crowds of people, especially in peak season when the volume of visitors and the commercialization can be too much. If the hurly-burly bothers you, take a hint from the young Shakespeare. He often followed the Avon through quiet meadows and peaceful villages. You, too, can wander though a tranquil landscape and spend an afternoon picnicking in peace by a quiet river.

ORIENTATION AND PLANNING

GETTING ORIENTED

Busy Stratford-upon-Avon, the heart of this small region, is about 100 mi northwest of London. Tiny villages, some with Shakespearean connections, surround it, and the countryside beyond these hamlets is littered with stately "piles," as the British call the sprawling mansions built over the centuries. Many are open to the public, and each requires a few hours to explore. To the north lie two magnificent castles, Warwick and Kenilworth. The town of Warwick has much to offer besides its castle, and it's worth a visit.

Stratford-upon-Avon. The birthplace of Shakespeare, this bustling historic town is liberally dotted with 16th-century buildings the playwright

TOP REASONS TO GO

Shakespeare in Stratford: To see a play by Shakespeare in the town where he was born—and perhaps after you've visited his birthplace or other sites—is a magical experience. The Royal Shakespeare Company's productions are often outstanding.

A stroll to Anne Hathaway's Cottage: Taking the mile or so walk here from Stratford is as memorable as seeing the home of Shakespeare's wife. In spring and summer, flowers and soft green grass surround the path. The thatched cottage itself has rare period furniture and lush gardens.

Warwick Castle: Taking in the history—and some modern kitsch—at this sprawling medieval castle is a fun day out and great for the whole family. The castle is more than just the armory, great hall, and Tussauds waxworks. Expect year-round activities and events from jousting tournaments to demonstrations of falconry.

Kenilworth Castle: Exploring the substantial, red-stone ruins of Kenilworth helps you appreciate the great amount of history that took place here. Check out the castle's massive Norman keep as well as buildings constructed for a visit from Elizabeth I. Cromwell may have ravaged this fortress, but it still commands the tranquil countryside. This is a great place to picnic.

would recognize. Turn down the quieter old lanes for a more peaceful experience.

Around Shakespeare Country. Warwickshire—the county of which Stratford is the southern nexus—is a land of sleepy villages, thatch-roof cottages, and solitary farmhouses. Explore these as well as stately homes and sprawling Warwick Castle.

PLANNING

WHEN TO GO
The Shakespeare sights get very crowded on weekends and school vacations; Warwick Castle usually brims with visitors, so arrive early in the day to beat the rush. Some country properties fill up quickly on weekends, and most close in winter. Some stately homes have limited hours even in summer, and many close in winter.

PLANNING YOUR TIME
Stratford-upon-Avon is ideal for day visits from London or as a convenient base; depending on the depth of your love of Shakespeare, you probably won't need more than a day or two here. Warwick is small and can be explored in an hour or two. Castle lovers could spend half a day in the many lines at popular Warwick Castle. A drive through the villages along the area's country lanes is a pleasant way to spend a day; a stop at any of the stately homes (check hours, which can be limited) will take a couple of hours. You're also near the northern Cotswolds if you want to explore the countryside further.

GETTING HERE AND AROUND

BUS TRAVEL

The cheapest way to travel is by bus, and National Express serves the region from London's Victoria Coach Station; there's ample service to Stratford. Buses run from London's Heathrow and Gatwick airports to Coventry (change there for Warwick), and Stagecoach serves local routes throughout the Stratford, Birmingham, and Coventry areas. Megabus, a budget service booked online, runs double-decker buses from Victoria station in London to Birmingham and Coventry.

Contacts Megabus (⊕ www.megabus.co.uk). **National Express** (☎ 0871/781–8181 ⊕ www.nationalexpress.com). **Stagecoach** (☎ 01788/535555 or 0845/600–1314 ⊕ www.stagecoachbus.com).

CAR TRAVEL

Main roads provide easy access between towns, but one pleasure of this rural area is exploring the smaller "B" roads, which lead deep into the countryside, by car. Local public bus service is not sufficient for most sightseeing journeys, as buses are infrequent and unpredictable. Renting a car or taking a tour bus are the two best options, although trains go to all the major towns.

TRAIN TRAVEL

Stratford has good train service and can be seen as a day trip from London if your time is limited (a matinee is your best bet if you want to squeeze in a play). Chiltern Railways trains leave from London Marylebone station and also go to Warwick, and they offer a one-day (£30) or four-day (£45) Shakespeare Explorer ticket for the region. London Midland serves the area from Birmingham (about 40 mi from Stratford).

Contacts National Rail Enquiries (☎ 0845/748–4950 ⊕ www.nationalrail. co.uk). **Chiltern Railways** (☎ 0845/600–5165 ⊕ www.chilternrailways.co.uk). **London Midland** (☎ 0121/634–2040 ⊕ www.londonmidland.com).

RESTAURANTS

Stratford has many reasonably priced bistros and unpretentious eateries offering a broad choice of international fare. Warwick and Kenilworth both have good restaurant options.

HOTELS

Stratford and Warwick hold the highest concentration of lodgings in the area, from bed-and-breakfasts to hotels. Here you can find accommodations to fit every wallet. Because Stratford is *so* popular with theatergoers, book well ahead whenever possible. Most hotels offer discounted two- and three-day packages. Outside the towns, a number of top-notch country hotels guarantee discreet but attentive service—at fancy prices. At the other end of the scale, almost every village has an old inn with rooms at reasonable rates. If you're stuck, you can book a B&B through the local Tourist Information Centre.

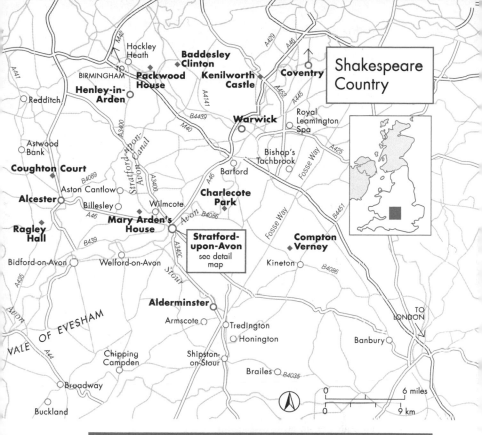

WHAT IT COSTS IN POUNDS					
	£	££	£££	££££	£££££
Restaurants	under £10	£10–£14	£15–£19	£20–£25	over £25
Hotels	under £70	£70–£120	£121–£160	£161–£220	over £220

Restaurant prices are for a main course at dinner. Hotel prices are for two people in a standard double room in high season, including V.A.T., with no meals or, if indicated, CP (with Continental breakfast), BP (Breakfast Plan, with full breakfast), or MAP (Modified American Plan, with breakfast and dinner).

VISITOR INFORMATION

Contacts Heart of England Tourist Board (⊕ *www.visittheheart.co.uk*). **Shakespeare Country** (☎ *0870/160–7930* ⊕ *www.shakespeare-country.co.uk*).

STRATFORD-UPON-AVON

Even under the weight of busloads of visitors, Stratford, on the banks of the slow-flowing River Avon, has somehow hung on to much of its ancient character and can, on a good day, still feel like an English market town. It doesn't take long to figure out who's the center of attention here. Born in a half-timber, early-16th-century building in the center of Stratford on April 23, 1564, Shakespeare died on April 23, 1616, his 52nd birthday, in a more imposing house at New Place. Although he spent much of his life in London, the world still associates him with "Shakespeare's Avon."

Here, in the years between his birth and 1587, he played as a young lad, attended grammar school, and married Anne Hathaway; and here he returned, as a prosperous man. You can see Shakespeare's whole life here: his birthplace on Henley Street; his burial place in Holy Trinity Church; Anne Hathaway's Cottage; the home of his mother, Mary Arden, at Wilmcote; New Place; and the neighboring Nash's House, home of Shakespeare's granddaughter.

Take Antonio's advice (*Twelfth Night*, act 3, scene 3) and "beguile the time, and feed your knowledge with viewing the town." By the 16th century Stratford was a prosperous market town with thriving guilds and industries. Half-timber houses from this era have been preserved, and they are set off by later architecture, such as the elegant Georgian storefronts on Bridge Street, with their 18th-century porticoes and arched doorways.

GETTING HERE AND AROUND

Stratford lies about 100 mi northwest of London; take M40 to Junction 15. The town is 37 mi southeast of Birmingham by A435 and A46 or by M40 to Junction 15.

Chiltern Railways serves the area from London's Marylebone Station. Five direct trains a day take just over two hours to reach Stratford; other trains require up to three changes. London Midland operates direct routes from Birmingham's Snow Hill station (journey time under an hour). From Stratford's train station at the edge of the town center on Alcester Road you can take a taxi or walk the short distance into town.

Stratford's center is small and easily walkable—it's unlikely you'd need to use the local bus service. City Sightseeing runs hop-on, hop-off guided tours of Stratford (£11.50), and you can combine the tour (about an hour with no stops) with entry to either three (£25) or five (£28.70) Shakespeare houses. In summer, the same company's Heart of Warwickshire tour includes Compton Verney, Charlecote Park, and Warwick (four trips on weekends in June and July, daily in August). The Stratford Town Walk runs all year and also offers ghost-theme walks and cruises. Note that at the time of this writing Stratford's tourist office was considering a move.

TIMING

If you have only a day here, arrive early and confine your visit to two or three Shakespeare Birthplace Trust properties, a few other town sights, a pub lunch, and a walk along the river, capped off by a stroll to the cottage of Anne Hathaway. If you don't like crowds, avoid visiting on weekends and school vacations, and take in the main Shakespeare shrines in the early morning to see them at their least frenetic. One high point of Stratford's calendar is the Shakespeare Birthday Celebrations, usually on the weekend nearest to April 23.

ESSENTIALS

Tour Information City Sightseeing (☎ 01789/412680 ⊕ www.city-sightseeing. com). **Stratford Town Walk** (☎ 01789/292478 ⊕ www.stratfordtownwalk.co.uk).

Visitor Information Stratford-upon-Avon (✉ 62 Henley St. ☎ 01789/264293 ⊕ www.stratford-upon-avon.co.uk).

EXPLORING

Most sights cluster around Henley Street (off the roundabout as you come in on the A3400 Birmingham road), High Street, and Waterside, which skirts the public gardens through which the River Avon flows. Bridge Street and Sheep Street (parallel to Bridge) are Stratford's main thoroughfares and the site of most banks, shops, and eating places. Bridgefoot, between the canal and the river, is next to Clopton Bridge—"a sumptuous new bridge and large of stone"—built in the 15th century by Sir Hugh Clopton, once lord mayor of London and one of Stratford's richest and most philanthropic residents.

The **Shakespeare Birthplace Trust** runs the main places of Shakespearean interest: Anne Hathaway's Cottage, Hall's Croft, Mary Arden's House, Nash's House and New Place, and Shakespeare's Birthplace. They have similar opening times. ■TIP➔ **You can buy a money-saving combination ticket to all five properties, or pay separate entry fees If you're visiting only one or two. Family tickets are an option, too.** Tickets for Hall's Croft and Nash's House and New Place are available only as a rather pricey (£12.50) joint ticket that includes the birthplace. You can check out special events at the properties, from talks about Tudor life to performances of Shakespeare's plays. ☎ 01789/204016 ⊕ www.shakespeare. org.uk ✆ Joint ticket to 5 properties £19; joint ticket to Shakespeare's Birthplace, Hall's Croft, and Nash's House–New Place £12.50.

TOP ATTRACTIONS

❻ Anne Hathaway's Cottage. The most picturesque of the Shakespeare Trust properties, on the western outskirts of Stratford, was the family home of the woman Shakespeare married in 1582. The "cottage," actually a substantial Tudor farmhouse, has latticed windows and a grand thatch roof. Inside is period furniture, including the settle where Shakespeare reputedly conducted his courtship, and a rare carved Elizabethan bed; outside is a garden planted in lush Victorian style with herbs and flowers. In a nearby field the **Shakespeare Tree Garden** has 40 trees mentioned in the playwright's works, a yew maze, and sculptures with Shakespearean themes. ■TIP➔ **The best way to get here is to walk, especially in late spring when the apple trees are in blossom.** There are two main footpaths, one via Greenhill Street by the railroad bridge, the other leaving from Holy Trinity Church up Old Town and Chestnut Walk. ✉ Cottage La., Shottery ☎ 01789/292100 ⊕ www.shakespeare.org.uk ✆ £7.50, Shakespeare Trust 5-property ticket £19 ☉ Apr.–Oct., daily 9–5; Nov.–Mar., daily 10–4; last entry 30 mins before closing.

❼ Holy Trinity Church. The burial place of William Shakespeare, this 13th-century church sits on the banks of the Avon, with a graceful avenue of lime trees framing its entrance. Shakespeare's final resting place is in

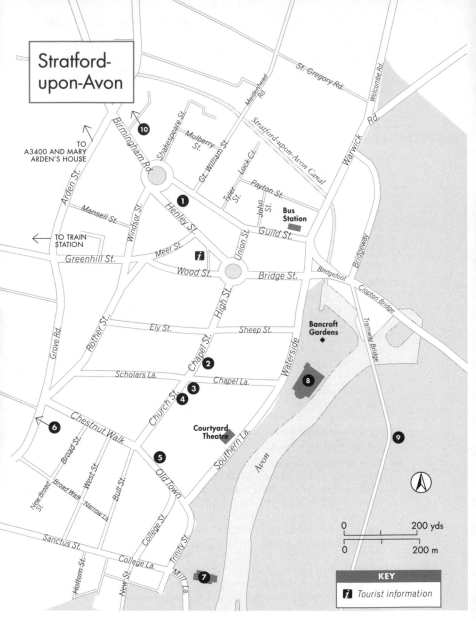

Stratford-upon-Avon

TO A3400 AND MARY ARDEN'S HOUSE

TO TRAIN STATION

Birmingham Rd.
Shakespeare St.
Mulberry St.
Gt. William St.
Maidenhead Rd.
St. Gregory Rd.
Welcombe Rd.
Stratford-upon-Avon Canal
Warwick Rd.
Arden St.
Mansell St.
Windsor St.
Henley St.
Tyler St.
Lock Cl.
John St.
Payton St.
Bus Station
Guild St.
Meer St.
Greenhill St.
Wood St.
Union St.
Bridge St.
Bridgefoot
Bridgeway
Clopton Bridge
High St.
Ely St.
Sheep St.
Chapel St.
Bancroft Gardens
Waterside
Tramway Bridge
Grove Rd.
Rother St.
Scholars La.
Chapel La.
Church St.
Chestnut Walk
Courtyard Theatre
Southern La.
Avon
Broad St.
West St.
Butt St.
Old Town
New Broad St.
Broad Walk
Narrow La.
College St.
Sanctus St.
Bottom St.
New St.
College La.
Trinity St.
Mill La.

KEY

🛈 Tourist information

0 — 200 yds
0 — 200 m

the chancel, rebuilt in 1465–91 in the late Perpendicular style. He was buried here not because he was a famed poet but because he was a lay rector of Stratford, owning a portion of the township tithes. On the north wall of the sanctuary, over the altar steps, is the famous marble bust created by Gerard Jansen in 1623, and thought to be a true likeness of Shakespeare. The bust offers a more human, even humorous, perspective when viewed from the side. Also in the chancel are the graves of Shakespeare's wife, Anne; his daughter Susanna; his son-in-law John Hall; and his granddaughter's husband, Thomas Nash. Nearby, the Parish Register is displayed, containing both Shakespeare's baptismal entry (1564) and his burial notice (1616). The church is trying to raise more than £3 million for restoration work. Its vicar warns that, without that work, all or part of the building will have to close within five years. ⊠ *Trinity St.* ⊕ *www.stratford-upon-avon.org* ⌨ *£1.50 for chancel* ⊙ *Mar. and Oct., Mon.–Sat. 9–5, Sun. 12:30–5; Apr.–Sept., Mon.–Sat. 8:30–6, Sun. 12:30–5; Nov.–Feb., Mon.–Sat. 9–4, Sun. 12:30–5; last admission 20 mins before closing.*

⑩ Mary Arden's House. A working farm, where food is grown using methods common in the 16th century, is the main attraction at Mary Arden's House (the childhood home of Shakespeare's mother) and Palmer's Farm. This bucolic stop is great for kids, who can see the lambs, listen as the farmers explain their work in the fields, and watch the cooks prepare food in the Tudor farmhouse kitchen. It all brings the past to life. There are crafts exhibits, a café, and a garden. The site is 3 mi northwest of Stratford; you need to walk or drive here, or else go with a tour. ⊠ *Off A3400, Wilmcote* ☎ *01789/293455* ⊕ *www.shakespeare. org.uk* ⌨ *£8.50, Shakespeare Trust 5-property ticket £19* ⊙ *Apr.–Oct. daily 10–5; last entry 30 mins before closing.*

❽ Royal Shakespeare Theatre. The Stratford home of the Royal Shakespeare Company (RSC), set amid gardens along the River Avon, has been closed for renovation since 2007 but will reopen for performances in February 2011. Highlights of the new theater are better sightlines, better seating, and better acoustics; a viewing tower and rooftop restaurant are other amenities. The company, which presents some of the world's finest productions of Shakespeare's plays, has existed since 1879. Until the new theater opens, performances are in the Courtyard Theatre up the street from the Royal Shakespeare Theatre. Shows are also staged in the Swan. *See Nightlife and the Arts for more information.* ⊠ *Waterside* ☎ *0844/800–1114 ticket hotline, 01789/403444 general information* ⊕ *www.rsc.org.uk.*

❶ Shakespeare's Birthplace. A half-timber house typical of its time, the playwright's birthplace is a much-visited shrine that has been altered and restored since he lived here. Entering through the modern visitor center, you are immersed in a good but basic introduction to Shakespeare through a "Life, Love, and Legacy" visual and audio exhibition; this can be crowded. You can see a First Folio and what is reputedly Shakespeare's signet ring, listen to the sounds of the Forest of Arden, and watch snippets of contemporary Shakespearean films. The house itself is across the garden from this large modern center. Colorful wall decorations and the furnishings in the actual house reflect comfortable, middle-class Elizabethan domestic life. Shakespeare's father, John, a glove maker and wool dealer, purchased the house; a reconstructed workshop shows the tools of the glover's trade. Mark Twain and Charles Dickens were earlier pilgrims here, and you can see the signatures of Thomas Carlyle and Walter Scott, scratched into Shakespeare's windowpanes. In the garden, actors present with excerpts from the plays. ⌧ *Henley St.* ☎ *01789/204016* ⊕ *www.shakespeare.org.uk* ✉ *£12.50, includes entry to Hall's Croft and Nash's House, 5-property ticket £19* ☉ *Nov.–Mar., daily 10–4; Apr.–June, Sept., and Oct., daily 9–5; July and Aug., daily 9–6; last entry 30 mins before closing.*

> ### SHAKESPEARE FOR SALE
>
> In 1847 two widowed ladies were maintaining Shakespeare's birthplace in a somewhat ramshackle state. With the approach of the tercentennial of the playwright's birth, and in response to a rumor that the building was to be purchased by P. T. Barnum and shipped across the Atlantic, the city shelled out £3,000 for the relic. It was tidied up and opened to a growing throng of Shakespeare devotees.

WORTH NOTING

❾ Butterfly Farm. Europe's largest displays of exotic butterflies, spiders, caterpillars, and insects from all over the world are housed in a tropical greenhouse, a two-minute walk past the Bridgefoot footbridge. You can watch as butterflies emerge from pupae or take look at the toxic black widow spider. ⌧ *Swan's Nest La.* ☎ *01789/299288* ⊕ *www.butterflyfarm.co.uk* ✉ *£5.95* ☉ *Apr.–Sept., daily 10–6; Oct.–Mar., daily 10–dusk.*

❸ Guild Chapel. This chapel is the noble centerpiece of Stratford's Guild buildings, including the Guildhall, the Grammar School, and the almshouses—all well known to Shakespeare. The ancient structure was rebuilt in the late Perpendicular style in the first half of the 15th century, thanks to the largesse of Stratford resident Hugh Clopton. Its otherwise plain interior includes fragments of a remarkable medieval fresco of the Last Judgment painted over in the 16th century and uncovered in a 20th-century reconstruction. The bell, also given by Sir Hugh, still rings as it did to tell Shakespeare the time of day. ⌧ *Chapel La. at Church St.* ☎ *01789/207111* ✉ *Free, donations welcome* ☉ *Daily 10–4.*

❹ Guildhall. Dating to 1416–18, the Guildhall is occupied by **King Edward's Grammar School,** which Shakespeare probably attended as a boy; it's still used as a school. On the first floor is the Guildhall proper, where traveling acting companies performed. Many historians believe that it was after seeing the troupe known as the Earl of Leicester's Men in 1587 that Shakespeare got the acting bug and set off for London. Upstairs is the classroom in which he is reputed to have learned "little Latin and less Greek." Visits are by prior arrangement only, usually on weekends during vacation time; contact the tourist information office. Immediately beyond the Guildhall on Church Street is a row of timber-and-daub almshouses, built for the poor in the early 15th century and still serving as housing for pensioners. ⌧ *Church St.*

❺ Hall's Croft. One of the finest surviving Jacobean (early-17th-century) town houses, this impressive residence has a delightful walled garden. Hall's Croft was the home of Shakespeare's elder daughter, Susanna, and her husband, Dr. John Hall, a physician who, by prescribing an herbal cure for scurvy, was well ahead of his time. His medical dispensary is on view along with the other rooms, all containing Jacobean furniture of heavy oak and some 17th-century portraits. ⊠ *Old Town* ☎ *01789/292107* ⊕ *www.shakespeare.org.uk* ⌧ *£12.50, includes admission to Shakespeare's Birthplace and New Place, 5-property ticket £19* ⊙ *Nov.–Mar., daily 11–4; Apr.–Oct., daily 10–5; last entry 30 mins before closing.*

❷ Nash's House and New Place. This is the home of Thomas Nash, who married Shakespeare's last direct descendant, his granddaughter Elizabeth Hall. The heavily restored house has been furnished in 17th-century style, and it also contains a local museum. In the gardens (note the Elizabethan knot garden) are the foundations of **New Place,** the house in which Shakespeare died in 1616. Built in 1483 "of brike and tymber" for a lord mayor of London, New Place was Stratford's grandest piece of real estate when Shakespeare bought it in 1597 for £60; it was torn down in 1759 by the Reverend Francis Gastrell, who was angry at the hordes of Shakespeare-related sightseers. The **Great Garden** of New Place, beyond the knot garden where archaeological work took place in 2010, has an ancient mulberry tree said to have been grown from a cutting from a tree Shakespeare planted. ⊠ *Chapel St.* ☎ *01789/292325* ⊕ *www.shakespeare.org.uk* ⌧ *£12.50, includes admission to Shakespeare's Birthplace and Hall's Croft, 5-property ticket £19* ⊙ *Nov.–Mar., daily 11–4; Apr.–Oct., daily 10–5; last entry 30 mins before closing.*

❙ QUICK BITES

Duck into the quaint **Hathaway Tea Rooms** (⊠ **19 High St.** ☎ **01789/ 292404**), above the shops on the busy High Street in a 17th-century building, for wonderful tea and scones. It can be packed in summer.

WHERE TO EAT

£
BRITISH
★

✕ **The Black Swan/The Dirty Duck.** The only pub in Britain to be licensed under two names (the more informal one came courtesy of American GIs who were stationed here during World War II), this is one of Stratford's most celebrated pubs—it has attracted actors since the 18th-century thespian David Garrick's days. A little veranda overlooks the theaters and the river here. Along with your pint of bitter, you can dig into English grill specialties as well as bar meals such as mussels and chips. Few people come for the food, which is mediocre: the real attraction is the ambience and the other customers. ⊠ *Waterside* ☎ *01789/297312* ▭ *AE, MC, V* ⊙ *No dinner Sun.*

££
MALAYSIAN

✕ **Georgetown Restaurant.** Small and somewhat eccentric, this restaurant serves exotic Malaysian cuisine from a menu divided to represent the country's diverse population. You can choose Malaysian Malay dishes, Malaysian Tamil Indian, or Malaysian Mandarin Chinese, and mix the options—perhaps starting with the Malay fried fish *ikan goreng,* and

7

moving on to the *rendang daging* dish of beef and coconut milk. The food is excellent, but portions tend to be small. Palm trees, gilded mirrors, and teak strike a colonial note. ⊠ *23 Sheep St.* 🕾 *01789/204445* ⊕ *www.georgetownrestaurants.co.uk* ⊟ *AE, MC, V.*

££   ✕ **Lambs of Sheep Street.** Sit downstairs to appreciate the hardwood
BRITISH floors and oak beams of this local epicurean favorite; upstairs, the look is a bit more contemporary. The updates of tried-and-true dishes include salmon cakes with wilted spinach, and Cotswold lamb shank with creamed potatoes. Desserts are fantastic here, and daily specials keep the menu seasonal. The two- and three-course fixed-price menus (£11.50 and £15) for lunch or pretheater dining on weekdays are good deals. ⊠ *12 Sheep St.* 🕾 *01789/292554* ⊕ *www.lambsrestaurant.co.uk* ⊰ *Reservations essential* ⊘ *Closed Sun. dinner* ⊟ *AE, MC, V.*

£££   ✕ **Malbec Petit Bistro.** Blending French and British styles seamlessly, this
BISTRO laid-back, sophisticated little restaurant has long drawn kudos for dishes such as its homemade pâté; Warwickshire lamb with peppers, onion purée, and thyme jus; and Cornish lemon sole with spinach and lobster sauce. You can dine in the informal main-floor space or in the cellar, with its flagstone floors and light oak tables. The constantly changing wine list is well chosen. Fixed-price lunches (two courses for £12) are a great deal. ⊠ *6 Union St.* 🕾 *01789/269106* ⊕ *www.malbecrestaurant. co.uk* ⊟ *AE, MC, V.*

££   ✕ **Old Town Restaurant.** Popular with theatergoers, this restaurant occu-
BRITISH pies a 16th-century building furnished with prints of the area. The fare, though reasonably priced, doesn't skimp on quality. On the daily-changing menu, chalked on a blackboard, are English specialties such as local sausages and pork with black pudding, along with seafood choices from seafood crepes to smoked haddock. Dairy-free and celiac menus are available, too. ⊠ *8 Church St.* 🕾 *01789/268822* ⊕ *www.oldtownrestaurant.co.uk* ⊰ *Reservations essential* ⊟ *AE, MC, V* ⊘ *Closed Mon.*

££   ✕ **Oppo.** Hearty, warming meals are offered at this informal, family-style
BRITISH restaurant in a 16th-century building on the main dining street near the theaters. The English and international dishes—chicken roasted with banana and served with curry sauce and basmati rice, for instance—win praise from the locals. There's a good range of lighter and vegetarian options as well. Make reservations a month ahead in summer. ⊠ *13 Sheep St.* 🕾 *01789/269980* ⊕ *www.theoppo.co.uk* ⊟ *MC, V.*

££   ✕ **Sorrento.** Family-run, this Italian restaurant takes a respectable, old-
ITALIAN fashioned approach to service. Upon arrival, guests can choose to sip an aperitif in the lounge before they're escorted to their tables for a silver-service, white-tablecloth meal. The menu of traditional favorites is cooked from family recipes, and includes smoked goose with Parmesan as a starter, followed by mains such as salmon and prawns in a cream-and-dill sauce, steak flambéed in brandy, and a pasta of the day. Pretheater dinners are a good value. ⊠ *8 Ely St.* 🕾 *01789/297999* ⊟ *AE, MC, V.*

££   ✕ **Thespian's Indian Restaurant.** A buzzing crowd of regulars frequents this
INDIAN casual Indian restaurant, drawn by its extensive menu of spicy dishes from the subcontinent and its friendly atmosphere. Choose from dishes

like the creamy lamb *saqi* (barbecued lamb simmered in coconut milk with ginger and mint), the tandooris, or fish specials. It's an excellent option when you're bored with meat and potatoes. ✉ *26 Sheep St.* ☎ *01789/267187* ▭ *AE, MC, V.*

££ ✕ **The Vintner.** The imaginative, bistro-inspired menu varies each day
BISTRO at this café and wine bar. Pork fillet with caper butter is a popular main course, as is the steak; a children's menu is available. To dine before curtain time, arrive early or make a reservation. The building, largely unaltered since the late 1400s, has lovely flagstone floors and oak beams. ✉ *5 Sheep St.* ☎ *01789/297259* ⊕ *www.the-vintner.co.uk* ▭ *AE, MC, V.*

WHERE TO STAY

The Ettington Park Hotel and the Fox & Goose, both near Alderminster, are excellent rural hotels a few miles from Stratford.

£££–££££ ⌂ **Arden Hotel.** All is up-to-the-minute in this redbrick boutique hotel right across the road from the Royal Shakespeare Theatre. Completely restyled in 2010, it offers everything you might expect in classic contemporary style. Bedrooms are spacious and discreet with splashes of greens, violets, and dark crimson; some have river views. The beds are all king-size, and marble bathrooms have roll-top baths and walk-in showers. The Champagne Bar and alfresco dining on the Terrace add to the attractions. **Pros:** convenient to the Shakespeare theater; crisp and modern style; large bathrooms. **Cons:** slightly impersonal; can be crowded. ✉ *Waterside* ☎ *01789/298682* ⊕ *www.theardenhotelstratford. com* ⌨ *45 rooms* ♿ *In-room: no a/c, safe, refrigerator, DVD, Wi-Fi. In-hotel: 2 restaurants, room service, bars, laundry service, Wi-Fi hotspot, parking (free)* ▭ *AE, MC, V* � *BP.*

££ ⌂ **Cherry Trees.** Although it's nothing fancy from the outside, this modern house offers three beautifully and individually furnished suites in a tranquil location near the river. Suites mix neutral tones with wood: the Garden Room has a four-poster bed and its own sitting room, and the other two rooms have their own conservatories. Breakfast presents many enticing choices (eggs Benedict, smoked salmon and eggs, and more) and is served in a sunny room overlooking the nearby Butterfly Farm. **Pros:** welcoming hosts; great breakfasts; convenient to in-town sights. **Cons:** too small for some. ✉ *Swan's Nest La.* ☎ *01789/292989* ⊕ *www.cherrytrees-stratford.co.uk* ⌨ *3 suites* ♿ *In-room: no a/c, no phone, Wi-Fi. In-hotel: parking (free)* ▭ *MC, V* � *BP.*

£ ⌂ **Heron Lodge.** Just a mile outside of Stratford town center, this B&B combines budget accommodation in a family home with high-quality service. Rooms are individually decorated in contemporary style. The hospitable owners David and Sarah Russon are serious about breakfast, offering pancakes, omelets, and more; locally sourced ingredients— from tea to jam and sausages—appear on the menu. You can also get a top-quality English breakfast. There's a bus stop near the house. **Pros:** welcoming and relaxing place; excellent service. **Cons:** outside of town. ✉ *260 Alcester Rd.* ☎ *01789/299169* ⊕ *www.heronlodge.com* ⌨ *5 rooms* ♿ *In-room: no a/c, no phone, Wi-Fi. In-hotel: parking (free), no kids under 5* ▭ *AE, MC, V* � *BP.*

7

££–£££ 🛏 **Holiday Inn Stratford-upon-Avon.** This good-value, modern chain hotel's best selling points are an excellent location in the center of the historic district, on the banks of the Avon, and views across the river and town center. It also has plenty of modern amenities. Rooms are large and full of light, but bathrooms are a bit of a squeeze. Children are welcomed enthusiastically and staff are friendly. Ask for rooms away from the elevators, as those can be a bit noisy. Package-tour groups spilling out of their buses add a steady background roar. **Pros:** good location; handy for families. **Cons:** modern and featureless; big and impersonal. ✉ *Bridgefoot* ☎ *0870/225–4701* ⊕ *www.holidayinn.com* 🛌 *251 rooms, 2 suites* ♿ *In-room: a/c, Wi-Fi. In-hotel: restaurant, room service, bar, pool, gym, parking (paid)* ⊟ *AE, MC, V* ⏚ *BP.*

££–£££ 🛏 **Legacy Falcon Hotel.** Licensed as an alehouse since 1640, this black-and-white timber-frame hotel in the center of town has an excellent location as well as a light, airy interior that looks out to a pleasant garden. The heavily beamed rooms in the older part are small and a bit more interesting, but the creaky, uneven antique floors might bother some. There's more space in the ordinary rooms in the modern extension. All guest rooms have neutral modern decor in shades of burgundy, brown, and taupe. Downstairs, the Oak Bar and Will's Restaurant have been sympathetically upgraded to keep their lovely, antique look. **Pros:** great location; old portion of the building is charming. **Cons:** some rooms in old part are a bit cramped; so-so restaurant. ✉ *Chapel St.* ☎ *0844/411–9005* ⊕ *www.legacy-hotels.co.uk* 🛌 *84 rooms* ♿ *In-room: no a/c, Wi-Fi. In-hotel: restaurant, room service, bars, laundry service, parking (free)* ⊟ *AE, MC, V* ⏚ *BP.*

£££ 🛏 **Macdonald Alveston Manor.** This redbrick Elizabethan manor house across the River Avon from central Stratford has plenty of historic details, as well as a modern spa. Rooms are comfortably sized, with faux antiques; a few Tudor-style rooms in the main building have four-poster beds, but those in the annex are of more modern design. Original fireplaces and paneling have been preserved in the comfortable lounges, where you can sip a cup of tea by a roaring fire. Legend says the grounds were the setting for the first production of *A Midsummer Night's Dream.* **Pros:** nice mix of historic and modern; good spa facilities; you can warm yourself by a fire in winter. **Cons:** modern rooms are less interesting; there's no elevator and lots of stairs. ✉ *Clopton Bridge* ☎ *0844/879–9138* ⊕ *www.macdonald-hotels.co.uk* 🛌 *110 rooms, 4 suites* ♿ *In-room: a/c, refrigerator, Internet, Wi-Fi. In-hotel: restaurant, room service, bar, pool, spa, laundry service, parking (free), some pets allowed* ⊟ *AE, DC, MC, V* ⏚ *BP.*

££££–£££££ 🛏 **Menzies Welcombe Hotel Spa & Golf Club.** With its mullioned bay windows, gables, and tall chimneys, this hotel in an 1886 neo-Jacobean-style building evokes the luxury of bygone days. You can relax in the clubby bar or on the Italianate terrace. Public rooms such as the Great Hall, with wood paneling and marble fireplace, complement the main-house guest rooms, which have faux-antique furnishings. Other rooms are in a new wing. The fancy Trevelyan Restaurant (jacket and tie required) relies on a French foundation to present British cuisine, and although the setting is not as formal as you might expect, the atmosphere certainly is.

The hotel is about a 10-minute drive from Stratford. **Pros:** great for golfers; good spa facilities; indoor pool. **Cons:** formal dining; atmosphere a bit stuffy. ⊠ *Warwick Rd.* ☎ *01789/295252* ⊕ *www.menzies-hotels. co.uk* ➷ *78 rooms* ⅋ *In-room: a/c (some), Internet, Wi-Fi. In-hotel: 2 restaurants, room service, bar, golf course, tennis court, pool, gym, spa, laundry service, parking (free)* ⊟ *AE, D, MC, V* ⦿*BP.*

£ ⛐ **Penryn House.** Traditional English prints and furnishings as well as some simple modern pieces fill the small but cheerful rooms here. The helpful proprietors, John and Heather Taylor, take pride in the hearty breakfast, and they always have options for vegetarians. The B&B is an easy walk from the city center, Anne Hathaway's Cottage, and the rail station. **Pros:** charming little place; great breakfasts. **Cons:** rooms are quite tiny; decor too 1980s pine and pastel for some. ⊠ *126 Alcester Rd.* ☎ *01789/293718* ⊕ *www.penrynguesthouse.co.uk* ➷ *8 rooms, 6 with bath* ⅋ *In-room: no a/c, no phone, Wi-Fi. In-hotel: laundry service, parking (free)* ⊟ *MC, V* ⦿*BP.*

££–£££ ⛐ **Shakespeare Hotel.** Built in the 1400s, this Elizabethan town house in
★ the heart of town is a vision right out of *The Merry Wives of Windsor*, with its five gables and long, stunning, black and-white half-timber facade. Its restaurant, bar, and lounge have blackened beams and a pleasantly aged look, and the intelligently modernized interiors provide a touch of luxury. Upstairs, rooms are named after Shakespeare's characters and the actors who have portrayed them. Hewn timbers carved with rose-and-thistle patterns decorate some of the rooms, which are furnished in greens, burgundies, and golds. Off-season deals are good. **Pros:** historic building; great lounge to relax in. **Cons:** prices are quite high for what's on offer; some very small bedrooms. ⊠ *Chapel St.* ☎ *01789/294997* ⊕ *www.mercure.com* ➷ *63 rooms, 10 suites* ⅋ *In-room: a/c, Internet, Wi-Fi. In-hotel: restaurant, room service, bar, laundry service, parking (paid), some pets allowed* ⊟ *AE, DC, MC, V.*

££–£££ ⛐ **The Stratford.** Although this modern hotel may lack the period charm of older hotels, its up-to-date facilities, spacious rooms, and ample grounds make it a good option for those for whom Tudor beamed ceilings are not that important. Rooms, all in polished oak with chocolate-and-beige color schemes, come in several shapes: some have four-poster beds, others are geared to the business traveler. You can use the leisure facilities, including an indoor pool, at a sister hotel, the Stratford Manor, 3 mi away. **Pros:** friendly; handy location; lots of modern conveniences. **Cons:** largely used as a conference hotel; rooms lack personality. ⊠ *Arden St.* ☎ *01789/271000* ⊕ *www.qhotels.co.uk* ➷ *102 rooms* ⅋ *In-room: a/c, Internet, Wi-Fi. In-hotel: restaurant, room service, bar, gym, laundry service, parking (free)* ⊟ *AE, DC, MC, V* ⦿*BP.*

£ ⛐ **Victoria Spa Lodge.** This good-value B&B lies 1½ mi outside town, within view of the Stratford Canal. The grand, clematis-draped building dates from 1837. Queen Victoria once stayed here before becoming queen, and you can even sleep in her room. Antiques fill the elegant and spacious lounge-breakfast room, and the white woodwork and lace tablecloths are set off to advantage by crimson damask walls. Guest rooms are individually decorated, and there's plenty of room for families. The nearby Park and Ride has bus service into town. **Pros:** beautiful

7

building; full of character; family friendly. **Cons:** away from the town center. ⊠ *Bishopton La., Bishopton* ☎ *01789/267985* ⊕ *www. victoriaspa.co.uk* ⊷ *7 rooms* ⚬ *In-room: no a/c, no phone, Wi-Fi. In-hotel: parking (free)* ☱ *MC, V* ⏏ *BP.*

££   ⊞ **White Swan.** Exposed beams, ★ low ceilings, and winding corridors make this cozy hotel a delight for those who like a little authenticity. It claims to be the oldest building in Stratford, and the look of the exterior (circa 1450) reinforces that

---

THE PUB'S THE THING

Take a break from Shakespeare. Having a pint of ale at the **White Swan**, on Rother Street, on a cool night when the fires are lighted and the mood is jovial, is a true English experience. You never know which direction the conversation will turn. Or stop by another of Stratford's pubs, such as the **Black Swan** (also known as the Dirty Duck), on Waterside.

---

boast. Each room is individually decorated, and although fabrics are not luxurious, admirable effort has been made to avoid traditional chintz. Heavy antiques mix with reproductions; some rooms have fireplaces, and some have four-poster beds. Bathrooms are tucked into what little space is available. ■ **TIP**→ **The popular pub, a traditional English boozer with ancient beams, attracts visitors and locals.** **Pros:** great for those who like ancient buildings; unique decor. **Cons:** some rooms are small; most bathrooms are even tinier. ⊠ *Rother St.* ☎ *01789/297022* ⊕ *www. pebblehotels.com* ⊷ *41 rooms* ⚬ *In-room: no a/c, Internet, Wi-Fi. In-hotel: restaurant, room service, parking (free)* ☱ *MC, V* ⏏ *BP.*

NIGHTLIFE AND THE ARTS

FESTIVALS

The **Shakespeare Birthday Celebrations** (☎ *01789/415536* ⊕ *www. shakespeare.org.uk*) take place on and around the weekend closest to April 23 (unless Easter occurs during that time). The events, spread over several days, include lectures, free concerts, processions, and impromptu performances.

THEATER

If you're suffering from a surfeit of Shakespeare, head for **Cox's Yard** (⊠ *Bridgefoot* ☎ *01789/404600, 0870/060–0100 ticket line* ⊕ *www. coxsyard.co.uk*), which hosts live music, comedy, and plays (for young children, too), as well as being a family pub and café.

Fodor's Choice   The **Royal Shakespeare Company** (⊠ *Waterside* ☎ *0844/800–1110 ticket* ★ *hotline, 01789/403444 general information* ⊕ *www.rsc.org.uk*) performs Shakespeare plays year-round in Stratford, as well as in other venues around Britain. Stratford's Royal Shakespeare Theatre is the home of the RSC, one of the finest repertory troupes in the world and long the backbone of the country's theatrical life. The company's stunningly renovated theater, with a stage remodeled on the lines of the original Globe Theater in London and showcasing some of the building's 1932 art deco features, opens in November 2010, but will not present performances for the public until February 2011. The Swan Theatre, part of the theater complex and built in the style of Shakespeare's Globe, stages plays by Shakespeare and contemporaries such as Christopher Marlowe and Ben Jonson. Take a trip up the viewing tower or a backstage tour, and make time for a meal in the rooftop restaurant. Until the main theater opens, performances take place in the 1,000-seat Courtyard Theatre on Southern Lane. Prices usually are £12 to £45. ■TIP→ **Book ahead through the RSC, as seats go fast, but day-of-performance and returned tickets are often available.** You can book tickets from London with Ticketmaster (☎ *0870/534–4444* ⊕ *www.ticketmaster.co.uk*), operating 24 hours a day.

SPORTS AND THE OUTDOORS

From Easter to October **Avon Boating** (⊠ *The Boatyard, Swan's Nest La.* ☎☎ *01789/267073*) rents boats and punts, and provides half-hour river excursions (£4.50) for a welcome escape from the crowds. A Venetian gondola can be rented for £45 per half hour. **Bancroft Cruises** (⊠ *Moathouse, Bridgefoot* ☎ *01789/269669*) runs regular 45-minute guided cruises daily (£5), departing from the Holiday Inn landing stage.

SHOPPING

Chain stores and shops sell tourist junk, but this is also a good place to shop for high-quality (and high-price) silver, jewelry, and china. There's an open **market** (great for bargains) every Friday in the Market Place at Greenhill and Meer streets. The **Antiques Centre** (⊠ *60 Ely St.*) contains 50 stalls displaying jewelry, silver, linens, porcelain, and memorabilia. **B&W Thornton** (⊠ *23 Henley St.* ☎ *01789/269405*), above Shakespeare's Birthplace, stocks Moorcroft pottery and glass. **Chaucer Head Bookshop** (⊠ *21 Chapel St.* ☎ *01789/415691*) is the best of Stratford's many secondhand bookshops. **Lakeland** (⊠ *4/5 Henley St.* ☎ *01789/262100*) sells a great range of kitchen and home wares. The **Shakespeare Bookshop** (⊠ *39 Henley St.* ☎ *01789/292176*), run by the Shakespeare Birthplace, carries Elizabethan plays, Tudor history books, children's books, and general paraphernalia.

AROUND SHAKESPEARE COUNTRY

This section of Warwickshire is marked by gentle hills, green fields, slow-moving rivers, quiet villages, and time-burnished halls, castles (Warwick and Kenilworth are the best examples, and well worth visiting), and churches. Historic houses such as Baddesley Clinton and Charlecote Court are another reason to explore. All the sights are close enough to Stratford-upon-Avon that you can easily use the town as a base if you wish.

HENLEY-IN-ARDEN

8 mi northwest of Stratford.

A brief drive out of Stratford will take you under the Stratford-upon-Avon Canal aqueduct to pretty Henley-in-Arden, whose wide main street is an architectural pageant of many periods. This area was once the Forest of Arden, where Shakespeare set one of his greatest comedies, *As You Like It.* Among the buildings to look for are the former Guildhall, dating from the 15th century, and the White Swan pub, built in the early 1600s. Near Henley-in Arden are two stately homes worth a stop, Packwood House and Baddesley Clinton.

GETTING HERE AND AROUND
The town is on the A3400. London Midland trains for Henley-in-Arden depart every hour from Stratford; the journey takes about 15 minutes. Train service from Birmingham takes about 40 minutes, and trains leave every hour. The town heritage center is not an official Tourist Information Centre but does have brochures; it's open Easter through October but is closed on Monday.

COUNTRY WALKS

The gentle countryside rewards exploration on foot. Ambitious walkers can try the 26-mi Arden Way loop (⊕ *www.ardenway.org*) that takes in Henley-in-Arden and the Forest of Arden. On the 3-mi walk from Stratford to Wilmcote and Mary Arden's House, you can see beautiful scenery. Parkland with trails surrounds stately homes such as Charlecote Park, Coughton Court, and Ragley Hall. Even Stratford can be the base for easy walks along the River Avon or on the path bordering the Stratford-upon-Avon Canal. Stratford's Tourist Information Centre has pamphlets with walks.

ESSENTIALS
Visitor Information Henley-in-Arden Heritage and Visitors Center (✉ *Joseph Hardy House, 150 High St.* ☎ *01564/795919* ⊕ *www.heritagehenley.org.uk*).

EXPLORING
Packwood House draws garden enthusiasts to its re-created 17th-century gardens, highlighted by an ambitious topiary Tudor garden in which yew trees depict Jesus' Sermon on the Mount. The house combines redbrick and half-timbering, and its tall chimneys are also typical of the period. Exquisite collections of 16th-century furniture and textiles in the interior's 20th-century version of Tudor architecture make this one of the area's finest historic houses open to the public. It's 5 mi north of Henley-in-Arden and 12 mi north of Stratford-upon-Avon. ✉ *Off B4439, 2 mi east of Hockley Heath* ☎ *01564/783294* ⊕ *www. nationaltrust.org.uk* 🎟 *£7.35, garden only £4.20, combined ticket with Baddesley Clinton £11.80* ☉ *House and garden mid-Feb.–July, Sept., and Oct., Wed.–Sun. 11–5; Aug., daily 11–5.*

★ **Baddesley Clinton** struck the eminent architectural historian Sir Nikolaus Pevsner as "the perfect late medieval manor house. The entrance side of grey stone, the small, creeper-clad Queen Anne brick bridge across the moat, the gateway with a porch higher than the roof and embattled—it could not be better." Set off a winding back road, this grand manor dating from the 15th century retains its great fireplaces, 17th-century paneling, and three priest holes (secret chambers for Roman Catholic priests, who were hidden by sympathizers when Catholicism was banned in the 16th and 17th centuries). The café is an idyllic spot. Admission to the house is by timed ticket; Baddesley Clinton is 2 mi east of Packwood House and 15 mi north of Stratford-upon-

Avon. ⊠ *Rising La., off A4141 near Chadwick End* ☎ *01564/783294* ⊕ *www.nationaltrust.org.uk* 🎫 *£8.40, garden only £4.20, combined ticket with Packwood House £11.80* ⊙ *House and grounds Feb.–July, Sept., and Oct., Wed.–Sun. 11–5; Aug., daily 11–5; Dec., Wed.–Sun. 11–4. Grounds also Nov., Wed.–Sun. 11–4.*

WARWICK

7½ mi southeast of Baddesley Clinton, 4 mi south of Kenilworth, 9 mi northeast of Stratford-upon-Avon.

Most famous for Warwick Castle—that vision out of the feudal ages—the town of Warwick (pronounced *war*-ick) is an interesting architectural mix of Georgian redbrick and Elizabethan half-timbering.

GETTING HERE AND AROUND
Frequent trains from London to Warwick leave London's Marylebone Station; travel time is about 90 minutes. National Express coaches make the same journey in three hours or more five times a day from Victoria Coach Station.

ESSENTIALS
Visitor Information Warwick (⊠ *Court House, Jury St.* ☎ *01926/492212* ⊕ *www.visitwarwick.co.uk*).

EXPLORING
Unattractive postwar development has spoiled much of Warwick's town center, but look for the 15th-century half-timber **Lord Leycester Hospital**, a home for old soldiers since the earl of Leicester dedicated it to that purpose in 1571. Within the complex are a chapel, an impressive beamed hall containing a small museum, and a fine courtyard with a wattle-and-daub balcony and 500-year-old gardens. Try a cream tea in the Brethren's Kitchen. ⊠ *High St.* ☎ *01926/491422* ⊕ *www.lordleycester.com* 🎫 *£4.90* ⊙ *Apr.–Sept., Tues.–Sun. 10–5; Oct.–Mar., Tues.–Sun. 10–4.*

★ Crowded with gilded, carved, and painted tombs, the **Beauchamp Chapel** of the **Collegiate Church of St. Mary** is the essence of late-medieval and Tudor chivalry—although it was built (1443–64) to honor the somewhat-less-than-chivalrous Richard Beauchamp, who consigned Joan of Arc to the flames. Alongside his impressive effigy in gilded bronze lie the fine tombs of Robert Dudley, earl of Leicester, adviser and favorite of Elizabeth I, and Leicester's brother Ambrose. The church's chancel, distinguished by its flying ribs, a feature unique to a parish church, houses the alabaster table tomb of Thomas Beauchamp and his wife; the adjacent tiny Dean's chapel has exquisite miniature fan vaulting. In the Norman crypt, look for the rare ducking stool (a chair in which people were tied for public punishment). There's a brass-rubbing center, and you can climb the tower in summer. It's a five-minute walk from Warwick Castle. ⊠ *Church St., Old Sq.* ☎ *01926/403940* ⊕ *www.saintmaryschurch.co.uk* 🎫 *£2 donation requested; tower £2.50* ⊙ *Apr.–Oct., daily 10–6; Nov.–Mar., daily 10–4:30.*

☺ Kids as well as adults appreciate the well thought-out **St. John's House**, a Jacobean building near the castle; beautiful gardens surround it. Inside are period costumes and scenes of domestic life, as well as a Victorian schoolroom and kitchen. ⊠ *Smith St.* ☎ *01926/412132* 🖾 *Free* ☉ *Apr.–Sept., Tues.–Sat. 10–5, Sun. 2:30–5; Oct.–Mar., Tues.–Sat. 10–5.*

☾ The vast bulk of medieval **Warwick Castle** rests on a cliff overlooking the
★ Avon—"the fairest monument of ancient and chivalrous splendor which yet remains uninjured by time," to use the words of Sir Walter Scott. Today the company that runs the Madame Tussauds wax museums owns the castle, and the exhibits and diversions can occupy a full day. Warwick is a great castle experience for kids, though it's pricey (there are family prices). Warwick's two soaring towers. bristling with battlements, can be seen for miles: the 147-foot-high Caesar's Tower, built in 1356, and the 128-foot-high Guy's Tower, built in 1380. The castle's most powerful commander was Richard Neville, earl of Warwick, known during the 15th-century Wars of the Roses as the Kingmaker. Warwick Castle's monumental walls enclose an impressive armory of medieval weapons, as well as state rooms with historic furnishings and paintings by Peter Paul Rubens, Anthony Van Dyck, and other old masters. Twelve rooms are devoted to an imaginative wax exhibition, "A Royal Weekend Party—1898." Another exhibit displays the sights and sounds of a great medieval household as it prepares for an important battle, while in the Princess Tower, preparations are under way for a fairy-tale wedding. At the Mill and Engine House, you can see the turning water mill and the engines used to generate electricity early in the 20th century. In the spooky dungeon exhibit, you can wander by wax re-creations of decaying bodies, chanting monks, executions, and "the labyrinth of lost souls"—a modern mirror maze. Elsewhere, falconry displays and rat-throwing (stuffed, not live) games add to the atmosphere. Below the castle, along the Avon, strutting peacocks patrol 60 acres of grounds elegantly landscaped by Capability Brown in the 18th century. ∎ **TIP→** **The castle is popular; arrive early to beat the crowds but expect some lines. If you book online, you can save on ticket prices.** Lavish medieval banquets (extra charge) and special events, including festivals, jousting tournaments, and a Christmas market, take place throughout the year, and plenty of food stalls serve lunches. ⊠ *Castle La. off Mill St.* ☎ *01926/495421, 08704/422000 24-hr information line* ⊕ *www.warwick-castle.co.uk* 🖾 *£17.95 without dungeon, £25.45 with dungeon. Parking £4–£6* ☉ *Apr.–Sept., daily 10–6; Oct.–Dec. and Jan.–Mar., daily 10–5.*

▌ QUICK
BITES

After a vigorous walk around the ramparts at Warwick Castle, you can drop by the cream-, crimson-, and gold-vaulted, 14th-century **Undercroft** (☎ *01926/495421*) for a spot of tea or a hot meal from the cafeteria.

WHERE TO EAT AND STAY

££   ╳ **The Art Kitchen.** You are encouraged to share the creative Thai dishes
THAI sold by "bytes" (small plates and larger portions) at this chic and contemporary restaurant. The green and red curries are favorites, especially the chicken or lamb Masaman curry; or try the prawn-and-coriander dumplings on lemongrass. Service is always courteous, and the art that peppers the walls is for sale. ⊠ *7 Swan St.* ☎ *01926/494303* ▤ *MC, V* ☉ *Closed Sun.*

££
BRITISH
✕ **Rose & Crown.** Stripped pine floorboards, red walls, big wooden tables, and solidly good food and drink set the tone at this contemporary gastro-pub with rooms on the town's main square; it's very popular with locals. The owners take pride in offering seasonal food that mixes British and international influences. Marinated anchovies and pickled quail eggs appear on the deli board; other options are salmon and sorrel fish cake with soft-boiled egg, and 28-day dry-aged Aberdeen rump steak and chips. Five moderately priced bedrooms provide simple but clean and modern lodging. ✉ *30 Market Pl.* ☎ *01926/411117* ▭ *MC, V.*

£–££
⊞ **Lord Leycester Hotel.** Built in 1726, this house with an appealing central location became a hotel in 1925, and signs of age and history abound. The hotel is due for refurbishment in 2011. Although some rooms have been upgraded, many need attention. That said, rooms are clean and pleasant enough, and the staff obliging. **Pros:** good price; great location. **Cons:** nothing fancy here; everything could use an update. ✉ *17 Jury St.* ☎ *01926/491481* ⊕ *www.lord-leycester.co.uk* ⇆ *49 rooms* ⬙ *In-room: no a/c, Internet, Wi-Fi. In-hotel: 2 restaurants, room service, bar, laundry service, parking (free)* ▭ *AE, MC, V* ◉ *BP.*

££££–£££££
⊞ **Mallory Court Hotel.** This elegant country-house hotel 6 mi southeast of Warwick makes a quiet, luxurious getaway; there's even a helipad. Mallory Court has 30 rooms but still manages to feel as if you're just visiting wealthy friends. The style in the comfortably designed bedrooms (some are in a separate building) is country chic, with clever touches of pattern and texture. One of the biggest attractions is the hotel restaurant (£££££), acclaimed for its exquisite French cuisine; the more casual brasserie is also good. You can use a nearby health club and also book spa treatments in your room. **Pros:** good for pampering; excellent restaurant. **Cons:** outside of town. ✉ *Harbury Lu., Bishops Tachbrook* ☎ *01926/330214* ⊕ *www.mallory.co.uk* ⇆ *30 rooms* ⬙ *In-room: no a/c, refrigerator, Internet, Wi-Fi. In-hotel: 2 restaurants, room service* ▭ *MC, V* ◉ *BP.*

7

KENILWORTH CASTLE

5 mi north of Warwick.

GETTING HERE AND AROUND

The local Stagecoach company offers services between Stratford on the 16 bus and Warwick on the X17 route The castle is a 1½ mi from the town center.

ESSENTIALS

Visitor Information Kenilworth (✉ *Kenilworth Library, 11 Smalley Pl.* ☎ *01926/748900* ⊕ *www.kenilworthweb.co.uk*).

EXPLORING

★ The sprawling, graceful red ruins of **Kenilworth Castle** loom over the green fields of Warwickshire, surrounded by the low grassy impression of what was once a lake that surrounded it completely. The top of the keep (central tower) has commanding views of the countryside, one good indication of why this was such a formidable fortress from 1120 until it was dismantled by Oliver Cromwell after the Civil War in the mid-17th century. Still intact are its keep, with 20-foot-thick walls; its great hall built by John of Gaunt in the 14th century; and its curtain walls, the low outer walls forming the castle's first line of defense. Even more than Warwick Castle, these ruins reflect English history. In 1326 King Edward II was imprisoned here and forced to renounce the throne, before he was transferred to Berkeley Castle and allegedly murdered with a red-hot poker. Here the ambitious Robert Dudley, earl of Leicester, one of Elizabeth I's favorites, entertained her four times, most notably in 1575 with 19 days of revelry. An exhibition in the restored gatehouse discusses the relationship between Leicester and Elizabeth, and a re-created Elizabethan garden with arbors and a fountain provides further interest for a visit for an hour or two. Sir Walter Scott's novel *Kenilworth* (1821) presented tales about the earl and Elizabeth, adding to a national fascination with the castle. This is a good place for a picnic and contemplation of the passage of time. The fine gift shop sells excellent replicas of tapestries and swords. ⊠ *Off A452, Kenilworth* ☎ *01926/852078* ⊕ *www.english-heritage.org.uk* ⊠ *£7.60* ☺ *Mar.–Oct., daily 10–5; Nov.–Feb., daily 10–4.*

WHERE TO EAT

£
BRITISH
✕ **Clarendon Arms.** A location close to Kenilworth Castle helps make this pub a good spot for lunch. You can order fine home-cooked food at the small bar downstairs. A larger, slightly pricier restaurant upstairs serves complete meals, from English roasts, steaks, and grills to more international fare. ⊠ *44 Castle Hill, Kenilworth* ☎ *01926/852017* ⊟ *AE, MC, V.*

££
FRENCH
✕ **Petit Gourmand.** Locals and those from farther afield are drawn to this relaxed, plush restaurant that has the look of an upscale modern French brasserie. The menu is a creative mixture of classic British dishes prepared with French flair. Seasonal and local produce and meats are well represented in dishes such as warm Severn & Wye smoked salmon, Scotch beef bourguignon with celeriac and potato *dauphinoise* (baked in milk, cream, and cheese), and free-range chicken served with your choice of sauce or butter. ⊠ *101 Warwick Rd., Kenilworth* ☎ *01926/864567* ⊟ *AE, MC, V* ☺ *Closed Sun. and Mon.*

COVENTRY

7 mi northeast of Warwick, 16 mi northeast of Stratford-upon-Avon.

Coventry, which thrived in medieval times as a center for the cloth and dyeing industries, is where, according to lore, a naked Lady Godiva allegedly rode through the streets in the 11th century to protest high taxes. In the 19th century the city became an industrial powerhouse, and the first British automobiles were manufactured here (the Coventry Transport Museum is a showcase for the now largely lost British auto industry). In World Wars I and II, Coventry was a center for weapons manufacturing, a fact that made it a favorite German target. On November 14, 1940, it suffered one of the worst air raids of the war: hundreds died, and the historic St. Michael's Cathedral was destroyed. Rapid postwar rebuilding was done in the cold architectural style of the

1950s and '60s, and Coventry is not a pretty town today, but it attracts history buffs and those who honor its past.

GETTING HERE AND AROUND

Virgin trains leave for Coventry every 20 minutes from London Euston station; it's a one-hour journey. Bus service from National Express and Megabus takes 2½ hours from Victoria Coach station.

If you're driving into town, use the city's hop-on, hop-off Park and Ride services. Park at the War Memorial Park off Kenilworth Road on the south side of town, or on the north side on Austin Drive, Courthouse Green. Park and Ride operates Monday to Saturday with frequent buses.

ESSENTIALS

Visitor Information Coventry (⊠ *St. Michael's Tower, Old Cathedral Ruins, Priory St.* ☎ *024/7622–5616* ⊕ *www.visitcoventry.org*).

EXPLORING

Before World War II, Coventry, like York and Canterbury, was virtually defined by its cathedral. After the war, to raise national morale, Sir Basil Spence was given the task of building a new cathedral. Wisely, he made no attempt to re-create the building that had been lost to German bombs. The striking, modern **Coventry Cathedral**, completed in 1962, stands beside the ruins of the blitzed St. Michael's, a powerful symbol of rebirth and reconciliation. Outside the sandstone building is Sir Jacob Epstein's *St. Michael Defeating the Devil*; the modern artworks inside include Graham Sutherland's stunning 70-foot-high tapestry *Christ in Glory* and unusual abstract stained glass. The visitor center in the undercroft shows a film about the cathedral; there's also a charred cross wired together from timbers from the bombed building. (⊠ *Priory Row* ☎ *024/7622–1200* ⊕ *www.coventrycathedral.org. uk* ✉ *Suggested cathedral donation £4.50, tower £2.50, visitor center £2* ☉ *Daily 9–5, services permitting.*

CHARLECOTE PARK

13 mi south of Coventry, 6 mi northeast of Stratford.

GETTING HERE AND AROUND

From Stratford by car take the B4086, or sign up there for City Sightseeing's Heart of Warwickshire tour *(see Straford-upon-Avon, above)*.

ESSENTIALS

Tour Information City Sightseeing (☎ *01789/412680* ⊕ *www.city-sightseeing. com*).

EXPLORING

A celebrated house in the village of Hampton Lucy, **Charlecote Park** was built in 1572 by Sir Thomas Lucy to entertain Queen Elizabeth I (in her honor, the house is shaped like the letter "E"). Shakespeare knew the house and may even have poached deer here. Standing at the edge of a glassy lake, the redbrick manor is striking and sprawling. It was renovated in neo-Elizabethan style by the Lucy family during the mid-19th century; a carved ebony bed is one of many spectacular pieces of furniture. The Tudor gatehouse is unchanged since Shakespeare's day, and a collection of carriages, a Victorian kitchen, and a small brewery occupy the outbuildings. Indulge in a game of croquet near the quirky, thatched, Victorian-era summer hut, or explore the deer park landscaped by Capability Brown. Interesting themed tours and walks take place in summer—call in advance to find out what's on offer. ⊠ *B4086, off A429, Hampton Lucy* ☎ *01789/470277* ⊕ *www.nationaltrust.org.uk* 🎫 *£8.15, grounds only £4.05* ⊗ *House Mar., Apr., and Oct., Fri.–Tues. noon–4:30; May–Sept., Fri.–Tues. 11–5; Nov. and Dec., weekends noon–4. Park and gardens daily 10–dusk.*

> **BARD'S REVENGE?**
>
> According to tradition, Shakespeare was caught poaching deer at Charlecote Park soon after his marriage and fled to London. Years later he supposedly retaliated by portraying Sir Thomas Lucy in *Henry IV, Part 2* and the *Merry Wives of Windsor* as the foolish Justice Shallow. Some historians doubt the reference, but Shakespeare does mention the "dozen white luces"—which figure in the Lucy coat of arms—and Shallow does tax Falstaff with killing his deer. Luce is another name for the pike fish.

COMPTON VERNEY

6 mi southeast of Charlecote Park.

GETTING HERE AND AROUND

From Stratford and Charlecote Park by car, take the B4086, or sign up in Stratford for City Sightseeing's Heart of Warwickshire tour *(see Straford-upon-Avon, above)*.

ESSENTIALS

Tour Information City Sightseeing (☎ *01789/412680* ⊕ *www.city-sightseeing.com*).

EXPLORING

A neoclassical country mansion remodeled in the 1760s by Robert Adam, **Compton Verney** has been repurposed by the Peter Moores Foundation as an art museum with more than 800 works. The house, set in 120 acres of parkland landscaped by Capability Brown, was decaying before the museum opened in 2004. The works of art are intriguingly varied and beautifully displayed in restored rooms: British folk art and portraits, textiles, Chinese pottery and bronzes, southern Italian art from 1600 to 1800, and German art from 1450 to 1600 are the main focus. Special exhibitions round out the program. ⊠ *Off B4086, near Kineton* ☎ *01926/645500* ⊕ *www.comptonverney.org.uk* 🎫 *£8; grounds £1* ⊗ *Late Mar.–mid-Dec., Tues.–Sun. and national holidays 11–5.*

ALDERMINSTER

5 mi south of Stratford-upon-Avon.

Alderminster is one of the most interesting of the so-called "Stour villages"—those places so characteristic of Shakespeare Country, strung along the winding route of the River Stour south of Stratford. The main street holds an unusual row of old stone cottages, and the church has a Norman nave and a tower dating from the 13th century. Although the interior of the church has been much restored, it's worth a peek for the carved faces between the arches and the old altar stone.

Other Stour villages include Honington, Shipston-on-Stour, and Tredington. A village green anchors Honington, where a lovely five-arched bridge crosses the river. Shipston, the largest of the group, is an old sheep-market town, its handsome batch of Georgian houses formerly owned by wealthy wool merchants. Tredington, an exquisite nutshell of a village, has an old stone church. These towns are close to northern Cotswolds towns such as Chipping Campden and Broadway.

GETTING HERE AND AROUND
Alderminster, on A3400, is very small. The Stagecoach bus service from Stratford-upon-Avon stops here throughout the day.

WHERE TO STAY

£££–££££   ⊡ **Ettington Park Hotel.** Victorian Gothic in style and with a modern wing, this mansion built on land owned by the Shirley family since the 12th century is a soothing retreat for theatergoers who don't want to cope with Stratford's crowds. Some of the individually decorated rooms have four-poster beds; rooms are grandly traditional in decor, and the fancier doubles are larger and cost more. The oak-paneled restaurant (££££) offers extremely good Modern British cuisine. For a break, take tea or a whisky in antique-filled public rooms or stroll on the 40-acre grounds, which contain the ruins of a 12th-century church. **Pros:** gorgeous building; spacious rooms; relaxing lounge. **Cons:** a bit too formal for some; well out of Stratford. ⊠ *Off A3400* ☎ *0845/072–7454* ⊕ *www. handpicked.co.uk* ⇦ *37 rooms, 11 suites* ☾ *In-room: a/c, safe, DVD, Wi-Fi. In-hotel: restaurant, room service, bar, tennis courts, pool, gym, bicycles, laundry service, Wi-Fi hotspot* ⊟ *AE, DC, MC, V* ⏐◯⏐ *BP.*

£–££   ⊡ **Fox & Goose.** A quirky style and fabulous fresh food make this place in the wee, unspoiled village of Armscote, 8 mi south of Stratford, more than just a pub with rooms. Everything is in place for relaxation: Victorian claw-foot tubs with candles, a DVD player, and a satisfying English breakfast served until noon. Rooms are themed around Clue (Cluedo in England) characters: Colonel Mustard's room is yellow, and Miss Scarlet's Boudoir is red and dimly lighted. The gastro-pub downstairs (££) serves a fusion menu and local ales. **Pros:** relaxing rooms; great restaurant. **Cons:** restaurant gets booked up; room decor can be bright and a bit quirky. ⊠ *Middle St., Armscote* ☎ *01608/682293* ⊕ *www. foxandgoosearmscote.co.uk* ⇦ *4 rooms* ☾ *In-room: no a/c, Wi-Fi. In-hotel: restaurant, bar* ⊟ *MC, V* ⏐◯⏐ *BP.*

ALCESTER

8 mi west of Stratford-upon-Avon.

The small market town of Alcester (pronounced *al*-ster) holds ancient buildings and Tudor houses. Search out the narrow **Butter Street,** off High Street, site of the 17th-century Churchill House, and on Malt Mill Lane (off Church Street) the **Old Malt House,** dating from 1500.

Two stately homes, Ragley Hall and Coughton Court, are a few miles from Alcester.

GETTING HERE AND AROUND

A car is needed to get here unless you find an organized tour that includes the stately homes.

EXPLORING

James Wyatt and other outstanding architects worked on **Ragley Hall**, a Palladian-style mansion with more than 100 rooms that hold architectural and decorative treasures. Outside you can explore parkland designed by Capability Brown in the 1750s and lovely gardens. The Great Hall has magnificent baroque plasterwork by James Gibbs, and there are portraits by Joshua Reynolds and Dutch masters, among others, as well as some striking 20th-century murals by Graham Rust. This is the ancestral home of the marquesses of Hertford, the third of whom figured in Thackeray's *Vanity Fair* and the fourth of whom collected many of the treasures in London's Wallace Collection. The gardens include the 2-mi Jerwood Foundation Sculpture Trail: look out for Antony Gormley's *Insider* and Elisabeth Frink's *Walking Man* pieces. Allow about three hours here to see everything. ■ TIP→ **Let the kids blow off energy in the adventure playground and picnic area.** The house is 2 mi southwest of Alcester. ⊠ *Off A435 and A46* ☎ *01789/762090* ⊕ *www. ragleyhall.com* ✉ *£8.50* ⊘ *House mid-Feb.–mid-July, Sept., and Oct., Sun. noon–4; Aug., Sun.–Fri. noon–4. Park mid-Feb.–mid-July, Sept., and Oct., weekends 10–6; Aug., daily 10–6. Call to confirm, as schedule may vary on particular wks.*

A grand Elizabethan manor house, **Coughton Court** (pronounced *Coat-un*) is the home of the Catholic Throckmorton family, as it has been since 1409. The impressive gatehouse, the centerpiece of a half-timber courtyard, contains a fine fan-vaulted ceiling and memorabilia, including the dress worn by Mary, Queen of Scots at her execution. There are double priest holes and a Gunpowder Plot exhibition, and you can wander in the excellent formal gardens (the roses are notable) and along a river and lake; allot an hour or so for a visit. The house is 2 mi north of Alcester and 8 mi northwest of Stratford. ⊠ *A435* ☎ *01789/400777* ⊕ *www.nationaltrust.org.uk* ✉ *£9.50, gardens only £5.80, parking £1* ⊘ *Mid-Mar.–June and Sept., Wed.–Sun. 11–5:30; July and Aug., Tues.– Sun. 11–5:30; Oct., Thurs.–Sun. 11–5.*

Bath and the Cotswolds

WORD OF MOUTH

"If you enjoy walking, then you can explore this delightful landscape by following some of the Cotswold Way, a public footpath that allows you to take in the breathtaking scenery of the Cotswolds. Village after village has its own individual feel, but each and every one is well worth a visit."

—lynbes1

"We'd heard that Bath was wonderful. I'd expected that the Roman Baths would be interesting—but it seemed that every inch of the city was exquisite. The architecture is simply gorgeous, as are the views from the river, and we walked and walked. Touring the Roman Baths—and every moment in Bath—far exceeded expectations."

—Songdoc

Updated
by Robert
Andrews

The rolling uplands of the Cotswold Hills represent the quintessence of rural England, as immortalized in countless books, paintings, and films. Here you can taste the glories of the old English village—its stone slate roofs, low-ceiling rooms, and gardens; the atmosphere is as thick as honey, and equally as sweet. On the edge of the Cotswolds is Bath, among the most alluring small cities in Europe.

The blissfully unspoiled Cotswolds, deservedly popular with visitors and convenient to London, occupies much of the county of Gloucestershire, in west-central England. It also takes in slices of neighboring Oxfordshire, Worcestershire, and Somerset. Together these make up a sweep of land stretching from Shakespeare Country in the north almost as far as the Bristol Channel in the south. On the edge of the area, three historic towns have absorbed, rather than compromised, the flavor of the Cotswolds: Bath, offering up "18th-century England in all its urban glory," to use a phrase by writer Nigel Nicolson; Regency-era Cheltenham, like Bath, a spa town with elegant architecture; and Gloucester, which holds an outstanding medieval cathedral and gives access to the ancient Forest of Dean, on the western edge of the area.

Bath rightly boasts of being the best-planned town in England. Although the Romans founded the city when they discovered here the only true hot springs in England, its popularity during the 17th and 18th centuries ensured its aesthetic immortality. Bath's fashionable period luckily coincided with one of Britain's most creative architectural eras, producing virtually an entire town of stylish buildings. Today people come to walk in the footsteps of Jane Austen, visit Bath Abbey and the excavated Roman baths, shop in an elegant setting, or have a modern spa experience at the stunning Thermae spa.

North of Bath are the Cotswolds—a region that more than one writer has called the very soul of England. Is it the pretty-as-a-picture villages with the perfectly clipped hedges? The mellow, centuries-old stone cottages festooned with honeysuckle? Whatever the reason, this idyllic region, which from medieval times grew prosperous on the wool trade, remains a vision of rural England. Here are time-defying churches, sleepy hamlets, and ancient farmsteads so sequestered that they seem to offer everyone the thrill of personal discovery. Hidden in sheltered valleys are fabled abodes—Sudeley Castle, Stanway House, and Snowshill Manor among them. The Cotswolds can hardly claim to be undiscovered, but, happily, the area's poetic appeal has survived the tour buses, crowds, and antiques shops.

TOP REASONS TO GO

Cotswold pubs: The classic pubs here press all the right buttons—low wooden beams, horse brasses, and inglenook fireplaces. Many pubs date back 300 years or more, but some have added smart dining areas. Most now offer tea and coffee, and also welcome children.

Perfect villages: With their stone cottages, Cotswold villages tend to be improbably picturesque; the hamlets of Upper and Lower Slaughter are among the most seductive. Part of the fun is to take almost any scenic lane or head for any evocatively named spot on the map.

Gloucester Cathedral: The Great East Window, Whispering Gallery, and cloisters are especially noteworthy in this ancient monument, one of the country's finest cathedrals. Look out, too, for the settings of scenes in the Harry Potter movies.

Hidcote Manor Gardens: In a region rich with imaginative garden displays, Hidcote lays good claim to eminence. Exotic shrubs from around the world and the famous "garden rooms" are the highlights of this Arts and Crafts masterpiece.

Roman Baths, Bath: Take a break from the town's Georgian elegance and return to its Roman days on a tour around this beautifully preserved bath complex, built around the country's only hot springs.

Shops in Cheltenham: The grand Regency terraces of Cheltenham make a wonderful setting for "country chic" boutiques, antiques shops, and gift stores that attract people from the entire region.

ORIENTATION AND PLANNING

8

GETTING ORIENTED

The region's major points of interest—Bath, the Cotswold Hills, and the Gloucester–Cheltenham axis—are one way to organize your explorations. Bath, in the southwestern corner of this area, is a good place to start; it can also be visited on a day out from London. The Cotswold Hills, about two hours west of London by car, cover some of southern England's most beautiful terrain. The area's small roads make for wonderful exploring, but public transportation is limited. To the west of the Cotswolds lie the cities of Gloucester and Cheltenham, a former spa town; beyond them, between the River Severn and the border of Wales, is the Forest of Dean. The road from Gloucester to Bath takes you by the castle at Berkeley.

Bath and Environs. With the Roman Baths—renovated and embellished in the 18th century—and the late-medieval Bath Abbey at its heart, Bath is one of the country's comeliest towns. You can also soak up its thriving cultural scene.

The Cotswolds. With a scattering of picture-postcard towns and villages separated by rolling dales and woods, the Cotswold Hills are rural England at its best. Nearby Cheltenham, with busy cafés and shops, provides a lively counterpoint.

Gloucester to the Forest of Dean. Sturdy Norman cathedrals dominate the towns of Gloucester and Tewkesbury. South of Gloucester, Berkeley Castle offers more medieval grandeur, and the Forest of Dean, to the west, offers a chance to stretch your legs.

PLANNING

WHEN TO GO

This area contains some of England's most popular destinations, and you would do well to avoid weekends in the busier areas of the Cotswolds. During the week, even in summer, you may hardly see a soul in the more remote spots. Bath is particularly congested in summer, when students flock to its language schools. On the other hand, Gloucester and Cheltenham are workaday places that can absorb many tour buses comfortably.

Book your room well ahead if you visit during the two weeks in May and June when the Bath International Music Festival hits town, or if you visit Cheltenham during the National Hunt Festival in mid-March. Note that the private properties of Hidcote Manor, Snowshill Manor, and Sudeley Castle close in winter. Hidcote Manor Garden is at its best in spring and fall, Bowood Gardens in May.

PLANNING YOUR TIME

Bath and Cheltenham are the most compelling towns in the region, and the obvious centers for an exploration of the Cotswolds Hills. Cheltenham is closer to the heart of the Cotswolds and is far less touristy, but has less immediate appeal. Bath is 29 mi from Cirencester in the southern Cotswolds, and 45 mi from Stow-in-the-Wold in the north.

It's also worth finding accommodation in the smaller Cotswold settlements, though overnight stops in this well-heeled area can be costly. Good choices include Cirencester, Stow-on-the-Wold, and Broadway. Gloucester is not such an attractive place for a stay, though it would make a feasible base for Tewkesbury to the north and Berkeley Castle to the south. If you have more time, consider a foray to the Forest of Dean, west of Gloucester.

You can get a taste of Bath and the Cotswolds in three hurried days; a weeklong visit gives you plenty of time for the slow wandering this small region deserves. Near Bath, it's an easy drive to Lacock and Castle Combe, two stately villages on the southern edge of the Cotswolds, and Winchcombe makes a good entry into the area from Cheltenham. At the heart of the Cotswolds, Stow-on-the-Wold and Broadway should on no account be missed. Within a short distance of these, Chipping Campden and Moreton-in-Marsh are less showy, with a more relaxed feel. Bourton-on-the-Water and Northleach are fairly low-key but still picturesque examples of the Cotswold hamlet, and Bibury, Owlpen, and Upper and Lower Slaughter are tiny settlements that can easily be appreciated on a brief passage. On the southern fringes of the area, Burford, Tetbury, and Cirencester have antiques and tea shops stores galore while avoiding the worst of the crowds.

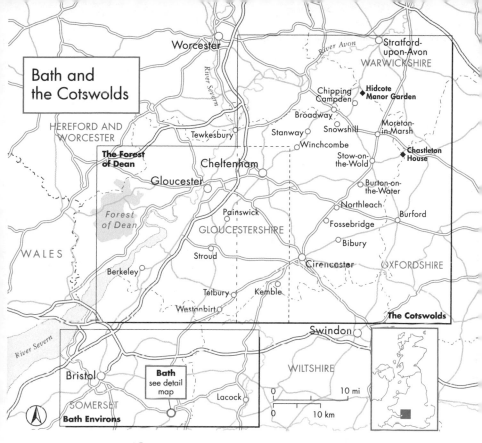

GETTING HERE AND AROUND

AIR TRAVEL

This area is about two hours from London; Bristol and Birmingham have the closest regional airports.

BUS TRAVEL

National Express buses head to the region from London's Victoria Coach Station. Megabus, a budget bus company, serves Cheltenham and Gloucester from London. It can take about three hours to get to Cheltenham, three to four hours to get to Bath. Bus service between some towns can be extremely limited. The First company covers the area around Bath. Stagecoach, Castleways, Johnson's Coaches, Swanbrook, and Pulhams operate in the Gloucestershire and Cotswolds regions. Traveline has information about public transportation.

Contacts Castleways (☎ 01242/602949 ⊕ www.castleways.co.uk).
First (☎ 0845/606 4446 ⊕ www.firstgroup.com). **Johnson's Coaches**
(☎ 01564/797070 ⊕ www.johnsonscoaches.co.uk). **Megabus** (☎ 0900/160-0900 premium-rate number ⊕ www.megabus.com). **National Express** (☎ 0871/781-8181 ⊕ www.nationalexpress.com). **Pulhams** (☎ 01451/820369 ⊕ www.pulhamscoaches.com). **Stagecoach** (☎ 01452/418630 ⊕ www.stagecoachbus.com). **Swanbrook** (☎ 01452/712386 ⊕ www.swanbrook.co.uk). **Traveline** (☎ 0871/200-2233 ⊕ www.traveline.org.uk).

CAR TRAVEL

A car is the best way to make a thorough tour of the area, given the limitations of public transportation. M4 is the main route west from London to Bath and southern Gloucestershire; expect about a two-hour drive. From Exit 18, take A46 south to Bath. From Exit 20, take M5 north to Gloucester (25 mi), Cheltenham, and Tewkesbury; from Exit 15, take A419 to A429 north to the Cotswolds. From London you can also take M40 and A40 to the Cotswolds, where a network of minor roads link the villages.

TRAIN TRAVEL

First Great Western trains serve the region from London's Paddington Station; First Great Western and CrossCountry trains connect Gloucester, Cheltenham, and Birmingham. Travel time from Paddington to Bath is about 90 minutes. Most trains to Cheltenham (two hours) and Gloucester (1¾ hours) involve a change at Swindon or Bristol. Train service within the Cotswold area is extremely limited, with Kemble (near Cirencester) and Moreton-in-Marsh being the most useful stops, both serviced by daily trains from London Paddington. A three-day or seven-day Heart of England Rover pass is valid for unlimited travel within the region.

Contacts National Rail Enquiries (☎ 0845/748–4950 ⊕ www.nationalrail. co.uk).

RESTAURANTS

Good restaurants dot the region, thanks to a steady flow of fine chefs seeking to cater to wealthy locals and waves of demanding visitors. The country's food revolution is in full evidence here. Restaurants have never had a problem with a fresh food supply: excellent regional produce, salmon from the rivers Severn and Wye, local lamb and pork, venison from the Forest of Dean, and pheasant, partridge, quail, and grouse in season. Also look for Gloucestershire Old Spot pork, bacon (try a delicious Old Spot bacon sandwich), and sausage on area menus.

HOTELS

The hotels of this region are among Britain's most highly rated—from bed-and-breakfasts in village homes and farmhouses to luxurious country-house hotels. Many hotels present themselves as deeply traditional rural retreats, but some have opted for a sleeker, fresher style, with boldly contemporary or minimalist furnishings. Spas are becoming increasingly popular at these hotels. Book ahead whenever possible and brace yourself for some high prices. B&Bs are a cheaper alternative to the fancier hotels, and most hotels offer two- and three-day packages. Note that most lodgings in Bath and many in the Cotswolds require a two-night minimum stay on weekends and holidays; rates are often higher on weekends. Hotels can front on heavily trafficked roads; ask for quiet rooms in the back.

There are numerous possibilities for renting a cottage in and around Bath and the Cotswolds, usually available by the week. Check out Manor Cottages or Jigsaw Holidays for a range of self-catering options.

Contacts Jigsaw Holidays (☎ 01242/252672 ⊕ www.jigsawholidays.co.uk). **Manor Cottages** (☎ 01993/824252 ⊕ www.manorcottages.co.uk).

WHAT IT COSTS IN POUNDS					
	£	££	£££	££££	£££££
Restaurants	under £10	£10–£14	£15–£19	£20–£25	over £25
Hotels	under £70	£70–£120	£121–£160	£161–£220	over £220

Restaurant prices are for a main course at dinner. Hotel prices are for two people in a standard double room in high season, including V.A.T., with no meals or, if indicated, CP (with Continental breakfast), BP (Breakfast Plan, with full breakfast), or MAP (Modified American Plan, with breakfast and dinner).

VISITOR INFORMATION

The South West Tourism Web site has information about the entire region; the Cotswold site is a government one that has a useful section on tourism. The major towns have Tourist Information Centres that provide advice and help with accommodations.

Contacts Cotswolds (⊕ *www.cotswold.gov.uk*). **Forest of Dean** (✆ *0845/838–8799* ⊕ *www.visitforestofdean.co.uk*). **South West Tourism** (⊕ *www. visitsouthwest.co.uk*).

BATH AND ENVIRONS

Anyone who listens to the local speech of Bath will note the inflections that herald the closeness of England's West Country. The city, however, has strong links with the Cotswold Hills stretching north, and the Georgian architecture and mellow stone that are such features of Bath recall the stone mansions and cottages of that region. The hinterland of the county of Somerset has plenty of gentle, green countryside.

BATH

★ *13 mi southeast of Bristol, 115 mi west of London.*

"I really believe I shall always be talking of Bath. Oh! who can ever be tired of Bath," enthuses Catherine Morland in Jane Austen's *Northanger Abbey,* and today plenty of people agree with these sentiments. In Bath, a UNESCO World Heritage Site, you are surrounded by magnificent 18th-century architecture, a lasting reminder of the vanished world described by Austen. In the 19th century the city lost its fashionable luster and slid into a refined gentility that is still palpable. Although the 20th century saw some slight harm from World War II bombing and slightly more from urban renewal, the damage was halted before it could ruin the city's Georgian elegance.

Bath is no museum, though: it's lively, with good dining and shopping, excellent art galleries and museums, the remarkable excavated Roman baths, and theater, music, and other performances all year. The Thermae Bath Spa allows you to take advantage of the hot springs that gave the city its fame. Many people rush through Bath in a day, but there's enough to do to merit an overnight stay—or more. In summer, the sheer volume of sightseers may hamper your progress on a stroll.

The Romans put Bath on the map in the 1st century, when they built a temple here, in honor of the goddess Minerva, and a sophisticated network of baths to make full use of the mineral springs that gush from the earth at a constant temperature of 116°F (46.5°C). ■ TIP→ **Don't miss the remains of these baths, one of the city's glories.** Visits by Queen Anne in 1702 and 1703 brought attention to the town, and soon 18th-century "people of quality" took it to heart. Assembly rooms, theaters, and pleasure gardens were built to entertain the rich and titled when they weren't busy attending the parties of Beau Nash (the city's master of ceremonies and chief social organizer, who helped increase Bath's popularity) and having their portraits painted by Gainsborough.

GETTING HERE AND AROUND

Frequent trains from Paddington and National Express buses from Victoria connect Bath with London. The bus and train stations are close to each other south of the center. By car from London, take M4 to Exit 18, from which A46 leads 10 mi south to Bath.

Drivers should note that parking is extremely limited within the city, and any car illegally parked is likely to be ticketed. Fees for towed cars can be hundreds of pounds. Public parking lots in the historic area fill up early, but the Park and Ride lots on the outskirts provide inexpensive shuttle service into the center, which is pleasant to stroll around.

TOURS   Free, two-hour walking tours of Bath are offered year-round by the Mayor of Bath's Honorary Guides. Individuals can just show up outside the main entrance to the Pump Room. Tours are Sunday through Friday at 10:30 and 2, Saturday at 10:30. There's also a tour at 7 PM Tuesday and Friday from May to September. The Jane Austen Centre arranges Jane-themed walking tours on weekends. City Sightseeing runs 50-minute guided tours of Bath on open-top buses year-round, leaving two to four times an hour from High Street, near the abbey. Tickets, valid for 24 hours, give a 10% reduction on entry to some of Bath's top attractions.

Mad Max Tours runs full-day tours from Bath through the Cotswolds, stopping at Tetbury, Upper Slaughter and Lower Slaughter, and either Bourton-on-the-Water or Stow-on-the-Wold. The departure point is the Glass House Shop on Orange Grove, near Bath Abbey, at 8:45. The company also has tours to Castle Combe, Lacock, Avebury, and Stonehenge.

TIMING

Schedule a visit to Bath during the week, as weekends see an influx of visitors. The city gets similarly crowded during its various festivals, though the added conviviality and cultural activity during these events are big draws in themselves.

ESSENTIALS

Visitor and Tour Information Bath (⊠ *Abbey Chambers, Abbey Churchyard* ☏ *0906/711–2000 [calls cost 50p per minute], +44844/847–5257 from abroad, 0844/847–5256 booking accommodation service* ⊕ *www.visitbath.co.uk*). **City Sightseeing** (☏ *01225/330444 in Bath* ⊕ *www.city-sightseeing.com*). **Mad Max Tours** (☏ *0799/050–5970* ⊕ *www.madmax.abel.co.uk*). **Mayor of Bath's Honorary Guides** (☏ *01225/477411* ⊕ *www.bathguides.org.uk*).

EXPLORING
TOP ATTRACTIONS

2 Bath Abbey. Dominating Bath's center, this 15th-century edifice of golden, glowing stone has a splendid west front, with carved figures of angels ascending ladders on either side. Notice, too, the miter, olive tree, and crown motif, a play on the name of the building's founder, Bishop Oliver King. More than 50 stained-glass windows fill about 80% of the building's wall space, giving the interior an impression of lightness. The abbey was built in the Perpendicular (English late-Gothic) style on the site of a Saxon abbey, and the nave and side aisles contain superb fan-vaulted ceilings. There are six services on Sunday, including Choral Evensong at 3:30. Forty-five-minute **tower tours**, allowing close-up views of the massive bells and panoramic cityscapes from the roof, take place most days; the 212 dizzying steps demand a level of fitness. The small, low-key **Heritage Vaults**, accessible from the abbey's south wall (the right-hand aisle), have an informative audiovisual presentation of the abbey's history, along with a reconstruction of the Norman cathedral that preceded it, some statuary, and a petition from 4th-century Bath that includes what is thought to be the first mention of the word Christian in Britain. ⊠ *Abbey Churchyard* ☎ *01225/422462* ⊕ *www. bathabbey.org* ✉ *Abbey £2.50 donation suggested, tower tours £5, Heritage Vaults free* ☉ *Abbey Apr.–Oct., Mon.–Sat. 9–6, Sun. 1–2:30 and 4:30–5:30; Nov.–Mar., Mon.–Sat. 9–4:30, Sun. 1–2:30 and 4:30–5:30. Tower tours Apr.–Oct., Mon.–Sat. 10–4 hourly; Nov. and Jan.–Mar., Mon.–Sat. 11, noon, and 2; call for Dec. hrs; Heritage Vaults Mon.–Sat. 10–4.*

9 Circus. John Wood designed the masterful Circus, a circle of curving, ★ perfectly proportioned Georgian houses interrupted just three times for intersecting streets. Wood died shortly after work on the Circus began; his son, the younger John Wood, completed the project. Notice the carved acorns atop the houses: Wood nurtured the myth that Prince Bladud founded Bath, ostensibly with the help of an errant pig rooting for acorns (this is one of a number of variations of Bladud's story), and the architect adopted the acorn motif in a number of places. A garden fills the center of the Circus. The painter Thomas Gainsborough (1727–88) lived at No. 17 from 1760 to 1774.

7 Fashion Museum and Assembly Rooms. In its role as the **Assembly Rooms,** ★ this neoclassical building was the leading center for social life in 18th-century Bath, with a schedule of dress balls, concerts, and choral nights. Jane Austen came here often, and it is here, in the Ballroom, that Catherine Morland has her first, disappointing encounter with Bath's beau monde in *Northanger Abbey;* the Octagon Room is the setting for an important encounter between Anne Elliot and Captain Wentworth in *Persuasion.* Built by John Wood the Younger in 1771, the building was badly damaged by wartime bombing in 1942 but was faithfully restored. Its stunning chandeliers are the 18th-century originals. Today the Assembly Rooms are well known for the entertaining **Fashion Museum,** displaying apparel from Jacobean times up to the present (audio guide included). You might see displays of pockets or punk fashions in changing exhibits. Throughout the year, classical concerts are given here,

8

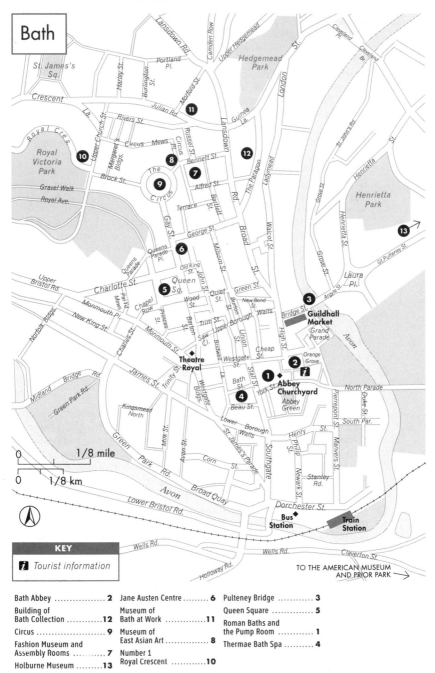

Bath

St. James's Sq.

Crescent

Royal Victoria Park

Hedgemead Park

Henrietta Park

Guildhall Market

Theatre Royal

Abbey Churchyard

Bus Station

Train Station

0   1/8 mile
0   1/8 km

TO THE AMERICAN MUSEUM AND PRIOR PARK →

KEY
i Tourist information

Bath Abbey **2**	Jane Austen Centre **6**	Pulteney Bridge **3**
Building of Bath Collection **12**	Museum of Bath at Work **11**	Queen Square **5**
Circus **9**	Museum of East Asian Art **8**	Roman Baths and the Pump Room **1**
Fashion Museum and Assembly Rooms **7**	Number 1 Royal Crescent **10**	Thermae Bath Spa **4**
Holburne Museum **13**		

just as they were in bygone days. ⊠ *Bennett St.* ☎ *01225/477173* ⊕ *www.museumofcostume.co.uk* ☎ *£7; combined ticket with Roman Baths, valid 7 days, £14.50* ☉ *Mar.–Oct., daily 10:30–6; Nov.–Feb., daily 10:30–4; last admission 1 hr before closing.*

⓭ ★ **Holburne Museum.** One of Bath's gems, this elegant 18th-century building houses a small but superb collection of 17th- and 18th-century decorative arts, ceramics, and silverware. Highlights include paintings by Gainsborough (*The Byam Family,* on indefinite loan) and George Stubbs (*Reverend Carter Thelwall and Family*), and Rachmaninoff's Steinway piano. In its original incarnation as the Sydney Hotel, the house was one of the pivots of Bath's high society, which came to perambulate in the pleasure gardens (Sydney Gardens) that still lie behind it. One visitor was Jane Austen, whose main Bath residence was No. 4 Sydney Place, a brief stroll across the road from the museum. At the time of this writing, the museum was closed for a major renovation scheduled to be finished in spring 2011. ⊠ *Great Pulteney St.* ☎ *01225/466669* ⊕ *www.bath.ac.uk/holburne* ☎ *£5.50* ☉ *Mid-Jan.–mid-Dec., Tues.–Sat. 10–5, Sun. and national holidays 11–5.*

JANE AUSTEN IN BATH

Though born and brought up in Hampshire, Jane Austen had close connections with Bath and lived here from 1801 to 1806. She wasn't overly fond of the place, peppering her letters with caustic comments about it (interspersed with gossip and effusions on bonnets and trimmings). Austen wrote her sister, Cassandra, that she left "with what happy feelings of escape." However, she is thought to have fallen in love here, and she received her only known offer of marriage while in Bath. Today Bath's 10-day Jane Austen Festival celebrates the writer each September.

8

❻ **Jane Austen Centre.** The one place in Bath that gives Austen any space provides a briefly diverting exhibition about the influence of Bath on her writings; *Northanger Abbey* and *Persuasion* are both set primarily in the city. There's a 15-minute introductory talk, and displays give a pictorial overview of life in Bath around 1800. The cozy Georgian house, a few doors up from where the writer lived in 1805 (one of several addresses she had in Bath), also includes the Austen-theme Regency Tea Rooms, open to the public. ■ **TIP➔ Buy tickets here for Jane Austen walking tours, which leave from the Abbey Churchyard at 11 on weekends and holidays (also at 4 on Friday and Saturday in July and August).** A tour ticket entitles you to a 20% reduction for entry to the exhibition. ⊠ *40 Gay St.* ☎ *01225/443000* ⊕ *www.janeausten.co.uk* ☎ *£6.95, tours £6* ☉ *Mid-Mar.–June and Sept.–early Nov., daily 9:45–5:30; July and Aug. Sun.–Wed. 9:45–5:30, Thurs.–Sat. 9:45–7; early Nov.–mid-Mar., Sun.–Fri. 11–4:30, Sat. 9:45–5:30.*

❿ Fodor'sChoice ★ **Number 1 Royal Crescent.** The majestic arc of the Royal Crescent, much used as a film location, is the crowning glory of Palladian architecture in Bath; Number 1 offers you a glimpse inside this splendor. The work of John Wood the Younger, the 30 houses fronted by 114 columns were laid out between 1767 and 1774. A house in the center is now the Royal Crescent Hotel. On the corner of Brock Street and the Royal Crescent,

Number 1 Royal Crescent has been turned into a museum and furnished as it might have been in the 18th century. The museum crystallizes a view of the English class system—upstairs is elegance, and downstairs is a kitchen display. ⊠ *Royal Crescent* ☎ *01225/428126* ⊕ *www.bath-preservation-trust.org.uk* ⊠ *£6* ⊙ *Mid-Feb.–late Oct., Tues.–Sun. and national holidays 10:30–5; late Oct.–mid-Dec., Tues.–Sun. 10:30–4; last admission 30 mins before closing.*

❸ Pulteney Bridge. Florence's Ponte Vecchio inspired this 18th-century span, one of the most famous landmarks in the city and the only work of Robert Adam in Bath. It's unique in Great Britain because shops line both sides of the bridge.

❺ Queen Square. Houses and the Francis Hotel surround the garden in the center of this small, peaceful square. An obelisk designed by the older John Wood and financed by Beau Nash celebrates the 1738 visit of Frederick, prince of Wales.

❶ Roman Baths and the Pump Room. The hot springs have drawn people here

Fodor's Choice
★

since prehistoric times, so it's quite appropriate to begin an exploration of Bath at this excellent museum on the site of the ancient city's temple complex and primary "watering hole." Here Roman patricians would gather to immerse themselves, drink the mineral waters, and socialize. With the departure of the Romans, the baths fell into disuse and were partially covered. When bathing again became fashionable at the end of the 18th century, this magnificent Georgian building was erected. Almost the entire Roman bath complex was rediscovered and excavated in the 19th century, and the museum displays relics that include a memorable mustachioed, Celtic-influenced Gorgon's head, fragments of colorful curses invoked by the Romans against their neighbors, and information about Roman bathing practices. The **Great Bath** is now roofless, and the statuary and pillars belong to the 19th century, but much remains from the original complex, and the steaming, somewhat murky waters are undeniably evocative. ■TIP➔ **There are free hourly tours of the baths, and in August you can take torch-lighted tours at night.** Adjacent to the Roman bath complex is the famed **Pump Room,** built in 1792–96, a rendezvous for members of 18th-century and 19th-century Bath society. Here Catherine Morland and Mrs. Allen "paraded up and down for an hour, looking at everybody and speaking to no one," to quote from Jane Austen's *Northanger Abbey.* Today you can take in the elegant space—or you can simply, for a small fee, taste the fairly vile mineral water. Charles Dickens described it as tasting like warm flatirons. ⊠ *Abbey Churchyard* ☎ *01225/477785* ⊕ *www.romanbaths.co.uk* ⊠ *Pump Room free, Roman Baths £11.50, £12.25 in July and Aug. with audio guide; combined ticket with Fashion Museum and Assembly Rooms (valid 7 days) £15* ⊙ *Mar.–June, Sept., and Oct., daily 9–6; July and Aug., daily 9 AM–10 PM; Nov.–Feb., daily 9:30–5:30; last admission 1 hr before closing.*

QUICK BITES

The quiet courtyard of two adjacent cafés, **Café René** and **Le Parisien** (⊠ *2 Shires Yard, off Broad St.* ☎ *01225/447147*), is handy for coffee or a lunchtime baguette. This is a prime spot for watching the locals go about their daily lives. You can linger in the **Pump Room** (⊠ *Abbey Churchyard*

A GOOD WALK IN BATH

For an hour-long stroll that takes in Bath's architectural showpieces, start in the traffic-free Abbey Churchyard, a lively piazza (often filled with musicians and street artists) dominated by Bath Abbey and the Roman Baths complex. Work your way east to Grand Parade and look out over flower-filled gardens and the River Avon, crossed by the graceful, Italianate Pulteney Bridge.

Stroll over the shop-lined bridge to gaze up the broad thoroughfare of Great Pulteney Street; then cross back over the bridge and head east up Bridge Street, turning right at High Street to follow up Broad Street and its northern extension, Lansdown Road. Turn left onto Bennett Street, passing the 18th-century Assembly Rooms and the Fashion Museum. Bennett Street ends at the Circus, an architectural tour de force compared by some to an inverted Colosseum.

The graceful arc of Bath's most dazzling terrace, the Royal Crescent, embraces a swath of green lawns at one end of Brock Street. Return to the Circus and walk south down Gay Street, which brings you past dignified Queen Square, with its obelisk, to the Theatre Royal. Wander east from here along tiny alleys packed with stores, galleries, and eating places, back to your starting point at Abbey Churchyard, where you could have a well-earned sit-down and tea at the Pump Room, or perhaps a soak in a pool at Thermae Bath Spa.

☎ *01225/444477*) **for morning coffee or afternoon tea after seeing the Roman Baths.**

❹ Thermae Bath Spa. The only place in Britain where you can bathe in natural hot-spring water, and in an open-air rooftop location as well, this striking complex designed by Nicholas Grimshaw consists of a Bath-stone building surrounded by a glass curtain wall. The only difficulty is in deciding where to spend more time—in the sleekly luxurious, light-filled Minerva Bath, with its curves and gentle currents, or in the smaller, open-air rooftop pool for the unique sensation of bathing with views of Bath's operatic skyline. Two 18th-century thermal baths, the Cross Bath and the Hot Bath, are back in use, too. End your session in the crisp third-floor café and restaurant. ■ TIP➔ **It's recommended that you book spa treatments ahead.** Towels, robes, and slippers are available for rent. Weekdays are the quietest time to visit. A separate, free **Visitor Centre** (April–October, Monday–Saturday 10–5, Sunday 10–4) opposite the entrance gives an overview of the project and provides audio guides (£2) for a brief tour of the exterior. ⊠ *Hot Bath St.* ☎ *0844/888–0844* ⊕ *www.thermaebathspa.com* ✆ £24 for 2 hrs, £34 for 4 hrs, £54 all day; extra charges for treatments ⊙ Daily 9 AM–10 PM; last entry at 7:30.

WORTH NOTING

American Museum in Britain. A Greek Revival (19th-century) mansion in a majestic setting on a hill southeast of the city holds the only museum of American decorative arts outside the United States. Rooms are furnished in historical styles, such as a 17th-century keeping room from

CLOSE UP

Bath's Georgian Architecture

Bath wouldn't be Bath without its distinctive 18th-century Georgian architecture, much of which was conceived by John Wood the Elder (1704–54), an antiquarian and architect. Wood saw Bath as a city destined for almost mythic greatness. Arriving in Bath in 1727, he sought an architectural style that would do justice to his concept, and found it in the Palladian style, made popular in Britain by Inigo Jones.

WHAT TO SEE
Wood created a harmonious city, building graceful terraces (row houses), crescents (curving rows of houses), and villas of the same golden local limestone used by the Romans. Influenced by nearby ancient stone circles as well as round Roman temples, Wood broke from convention in his design for Bath's Circus, a circle of houses broken only three times for intersecting streets.

After the death of Wood the Elder, John Wood the Younger (1728–82) carried out his father's plans for the Royal Crescent, an obtuse crescent of 30 interconnected houses. Today you can stop in at No. 1 Royal Crescent for a look at one of these homes—it's like eavesdropping on the 18th century. He also built the Assembly Rooms, now open to the public.

Massachusetts and a richly red New Orleans bedroom from the 1860s. Other galleries explore historical themes (the settlement of the West, the Civil War) or contain rugs and quilts, porcelain, and Shaker objects; a separate building is devoted to folk art. The parkland includes a reproduction of George Washington's garden at Mount Vernon. Take a bus headed to the University of Bath and get off at the Avenue, where signs point to the museum, half a mile away, or take a City Sightseeing bus. ⊠ *Claverton Manor, off A36, 2½ mi southeast of Bath* ☎ *01225/460503* ⊕ *www.americanmuseum.org* ✉ *Museum, special exhibitions, and grounds £8; special exhibitions and grounds £5.50* ⊙ *Mid-Mar.–July, Sept., and Oct., Tues.–Sun. and national holidays noon–5; Aug., daily noon–5; late Nov.–mid-Dec., Tues.–Sun. and national holidays noon–4:30.*

🟊 **Building of Bath Collection.** This absorbing museum in the Georgian Gothic–style Countess of Huntingdon's Chapel is an essential stop on any exploration of Bath, particularly for fans of Georgian architecture. It explains and illustrates the evolution of the city, with examples of everything from window design and wrought-iron railings to marquetry and other interior ornamentation. ⊠ *The Paragon* ☎ *01225/333895* ⊕ *www.bath-preservation-trust.org.uk* ✉ *£4* ⊙ *Mid-Feb.–Nov., Sat.–Mon. 10:30–5; last admission at 4:30.*

🟊 **Museum of Bath at Work.** The core of this industrial-history collection, which gives a novel perspective on the city, is an engineering works and fizzy drinks factory, relocated to this building. It once belonged to Bath entrepreneur Jonathan Bowler, who started his many businesses in 1872. The tour includes the original clanking machinery and offers glimpses into Bath's stone industry and cabinetmaking. ⊠ *Julian Rd.*

☎ *01225/318348* ⊕ *www.bathatwork.co.uk* ▨ *£5* ⊙ *Apr.–Oct., daily 10:30–5; Nov.–Mar., weekends 10:30–5; last admission at 4.*

8 **Museum of East Asian Art.** Intimate galleries on three floors finely display ancient and modern pieces, mostly from China but with other exhibits from Japan, Korea, and Southeast Asia. Highlights are a graphic 19th-century watercolor depicting the Chinese idea of hell, Chinese ivory figures, Buddhist objects, and Japanese lacquerware and prints. ⊠ *12 Bennett St.* ☎ *01225/464640* ⊕ *www.meaa.info* ▨ *£5* ⊙ *Tues.– Sat. 10–5, Sun. noon–5; last admission at 4:30.*

Prior Park. A vision to warm Jane Austen's heart, Bath's grandest house lies a mile or so southeast of the center, with splendid views over the Georgian townscape. Built around 1738 by John Wood the Elder of honey-color limestone, the Palladian mansion was the home of quarry owner and philanthropist Ralph Allen (1693–1764), whose guests included such luminaries as poet Alexander Pope and novelists Henry Fielding and Samuel Richardson. Today it is a Roman Catholic school and the interior is not open to the public, but you may wander through the beautiful grounds, designed by Capability Brown and embellished with a Palladian bridge and lake. A leisurely circuit of the park should take around an hour. ■ **TIP→ The parking here is only for people with disabilities: unless you relish the uphill trudge, take a taxi or bus from the center.** ⊠ *Ralph Allen Dr.* ☎ *01225/833422* ⊕ *www.nationaltrust.org. uk* ▨ *Grounds free* ⊙ *Mid-Feb.–Oct., Wed.–Mon. 11–5:30 or dusk; Nov.–late Dec. and Jan.–mid-Feb., weekends 11–5:30 or dusk; last admission 1 hr before closing.*

⊙ **Royal Victoria Park.** Originally designed as an arboretum, this tidy expanse of lawns and shady walks just west of the Royal Crescent provides the perfect setting for pleasant strolls and leisurely picnics. The park has a pond, an aviary, a **Botanic Garden,** and an adventure playground with plenty for kids. Hot-air balloon launches and open-air shows at festival time enliven the atmosphere. ⊠ *Upper Bristol Rd.* ▨ *Free* ⊙ *Daily 24 hrs.*

8

WHERE TO EAT

Among hotel restaurants, the Dower House in the Royal Crescent Hotel is outstanding; the Cavendish in Dukes Hotel and the Olive Tree in the Queensberry Hotel are noteworthy.

££
AMERICAN

✕ **Firehouse Rotisserie.** California comes to Bath. Tex-Mex, Pacific Rim, and creole influences are also evident on a menu that showcases dishes from the rotisserie and grill, such as spice-rubbed rib-eye steak with a fiery sauce, and crab and salmon cakes with roasted corn salsa. Brick-fired pizzas entice with creative toppings; try goat cheese, artichokes, and sun-dried tomatoes. Rustic decor, wooden floors and tables, and an easy, sociable vibe set the scene. ⊠ *2 John St.* ☎ *01225/482070* ⊕ *www. firehouserotisserie.co.uk* ▭ *AE, MC, V* ⊙ *Closed Sun.*

£££
MODERN BRITISH

✕ **Hole in the Wall.** Escape from Bath's busyness at this relaxed eatery serving sophisticated modern English fare in an 18th-century town house. At the bottom of a flight of stairs, the unfussy, stone-tile dining area—warmed by a generous open fire in winter—exudes calm and poise. (The piped-in music can be intrusive, however.) It's a great environment to indulge in such dishes as grilled fillet of mullet on stir-fried bok choy. While you wait for your order, nibble on the complimentary freshly baked bread. Lunches and pretheater meals are a good value. ⊠ *16 George St.* ☎ *01225/425242* ⊕ *www.theholeinthewall. co.uk* ⊟ *AE, MC, V.*

££   ✕ **Jamie's Italian.** Part of a chain owned by celebrity chef Jamie Oliver,
ITALIAN   this buzzing brasserie is a cheerful counterpoint to Bath's predominantly sedate tone. The dining areas, spread over two floors and including a rooftop terrace, have a contemporary, slightly industrial feel. Expect dishes typical of Oliver's straightforward Italian rustic style, such as bruschetta, lavish antipasti, garlicky prawn linguine, and beef carpaccio and arugula salad. Desserts include *affogato* (vanilla ice cream with espresso) and lemon ricotta cheesecake. There's always a line outside at busy times, but you can take advantage of the all-day service by coming during off-peak hours. ⊠ *10 Milsom Pl.* ☎ *01225/510051* ⊕ *www. jamieoliver.com* ⌲ *Reservations not accepted* ⊟ *MC, V.*

£   ✕ **Jazz Café.** Snack to a background of jazz classics in this cramped
ECLECTIC   but cozy café. Famous for its all-day breakfasts, the café is also a good spot for a quick lunch, with soups, salads, sandwiches, and fine vegetarian choices. Daily specials might include spicy beef chili, cassoulet, or Moroccan pork. Arrive early, as it closes at 6 PM (4 on Sunday). ⊠ *Kingsmead Sq.* ☎ *01225/329002* ⊕ *www.bathjazzcafe.co.uk* ⊟ *MC, V* ☻ *No dinner.*

£££   ✕ **No. 5 Restaurant.** An ideal spot for a light lunch or romantic dinner, this
FRENCH   airy bistro decorated with pretty plants and framed posters is just over Pulteney Bridge from the center of town. The menu changes daily but lists soups and such dishes as warm pigeon breast with cherry tomatoes, and rib of beef with buttered leeks and red wine jus. There's a good-value set-price lunch menu. ⊠ *5 Argyle St.* ☎ *01225/444499* ⊕ *www. no5restaurant.co.uk* ⊟ *AE, DC, MC, V* ☻ *Closed Mon. Apr.–Sept.*

££££   ✕ **Olive Tree.** A sleek space in the basement of the Queensberry Hotel
MODERN BRITISH   makes a calm, contemporary setting for top-notch English and Medi-
★   terranean dishes. The range of seductive, sophisticated choices includes sashimi of organic salmon for starters and such main courses as brochette of duck breast with buttery potatoes or steamed fillet of wild sea bass with fried eel, rice, ginger, and spring onion. Some dessert picks are dark chocolate fondant with malted milk and malted ice cream. Fixed-price menus are available at lunchtime. ⊠ *Russel St.* ☎ *01225/447928* ⊕ *www.thequeensberry.co.uk* ⊟ *AE, MC, V* ☻ *No lunch Mon.*

££   ✕ **Pump Room.** The 18th-century Pump Room, with views over the
BRITISH   Roman Baths, serves morning coffee, lunches of chicken, beef, and seafood dishes, and afternoon tea, often to music by a pianist or string trio. Its stately setting is the selling point rather than the food, but do sample the English cheese board and homemade Bath biscuits. It's open occasionally for fixed-price dinners (reservations are essential). Be prepared to wait in line for a table during the day. ⊠ *Abbey Churchyard* ☎ *01225/444477* ⊕ *www.romanbaths.co.uk* ⊟ *AE, MC, V* ☻ *No dinner except during Aug., Dec., and festivals.*

£   ✕ **Sally Lunn's.** Small and slightly twee, this tourist magnet near Bath
BRITISH   Abbey occupies the oldest house in Bath, dating to 1482. It's famous

for the Sally Lunn bun, actually a semisweet bread served here since 1680. You can choose from more than 40 sweet and savory toppings to accompany your bun, or turn it into a meal with such dishes as duck with sherry-and-ginger sauce. There's also an economical early-bird two-course evening menu. Daytime diners can view the small kitchen museum in the cellar (30p for nondining visitors). ⊠ *4 N. Parade Passage* ☎ *01225/461634* ⊕ *www.sallylunns.co.uk* ▭ *MC, V.*

££ ✕ **Strada.** The former home of Richard "Beau" Nash—the dictator of
ITALIAN fashion for mid-18th-century society in Bath—and his mistress Juliana Popjoy provides an elegant setting for this outpost of a reliable chain of Italian eateries. Modern wooden furnishings blend smoothly with the Georgian tone of the dining areas on two levels. Pizzas and pasta vie for space on the menu with classics like *saltimbocca di maiale* (fillet of pork in a sage-and-butter sauce). ⊠ *Beau Nash House, Saw Close* ☎ *01225/337753* ⊕ *www.strada.co.uk* ▭ *AE, MC, V.*

£££ ✕ **Tilleys Bistro.** This intimate, bow-windowed French eatery presents
FRENCH alluring meat and vegetarian dishes offered in small, medium, and large portions. Choices include medallions of pork *à la dijonnaise* (fried tenderloin and mushrooms in a brandy, cream, and mustard sauce), roasted *aubergine à la Tunisienne* (eggplant cooked with chick peas, dates, and apricots), and sautéed Gressingham duck breast. Pretheater meals are available weekdays between 6 and 7 PM. ⊠ *3 North Parade Passage* ☎ *01225/484200* ⊕ *www.tilleysbistro.co.uk* ▭ *MC, V* ☉ *No lunch Sun.*

WHERE TO STAY

££ ⊡ **Albany Guest House.** Homey and friendly, this Edwardian house close to the Royal Crescent has contemporary, simply furnished rooms. Most are decorated with neutral, beige, and cream colors. The attic room is the largest and best. Vegetarian and other dietary preferences are accommodated at breakfast, which may include tasty homemade vegetarian sausages. **Pros:** spotless rooms; convenient location; excellent breakfasts. **Cons:** some rooms are very small; limited parking. ⊠ *24 Crescent Gardens* ☎ *01225/313339* ⊕ *www.albanybath.co.uk* 🛏 *4 rooms* ♿ *In-room: no a/c, no phone, Wi-Fi. In-hotel: Wi-Fi hotspot, parking (free)* ▭ *AE, MC, V* ⏀ *BP.*

£££–££££ ⊡ **Bath Paradise House.** Don't be put off by the 10-minute uphill walk from the center of Bath—you'll be rewarded by a wonderful view of the city from the garden and upper stories of this Georgian guesthouse. Cool pastels and traditional furnishings decorate the rooms attractively, and there are open fires in winter and a lush garden for spring and summer. Rooms 3, 4, and 5 have the best views; Nos. 9, 11, and 12 open straight onto the garden. If the full English breakfast is too daunting, indulge in coffee and croissants in bed. **Pros:** great attention to detail; spectacular views from some rooms; gay-friendly vibe. **Cons:** uphill walk; books up far in advance. ⊠ *88 Holloway* ☎ *01225/317723* ⊕ *www.paradise-house.co.uk* 🛏 *11 rooms* ♿ *In-room: no a/c, DVD, Wi-Fi (some). In-hotel: bar, Internet terminal, Wi-Fi hotspot, parking (free)* ▭ *AE, MC, V* ⏀ *BP.*

8

££   **⁂ Cranleigh.** In a quiet location on the hill above the city center, this
Victorian guesthouse has wonderful views of the Avon Valley. Rooms,
including three with four-posters beds, are richly decorated. Large
breakfasts—pancakes with maple syrup, kippers, scrambled eggs
with smoked salmon, and vegetarian options—are served in the dining room, which overlooks the garden. There's a hot tub, costing £25
for two hours. The Cranleigh is a 30-minute walk from the center,
but you can take one of the frequent buses that stop nearby. **Pros:**
quiet rooms; period furnishings; many choices at breakfast. **Cons:** far
from center; along a busy road; steps to climb. ☒ *159 Newbridge Hill*
☎ *01225/310197* ⊕ *www.cranleighguesthouse.com* ⇩ *9 rooms* ⚮ *In-
room: no a/c, Wi-Fi. In-hotel: Internet terminal, parking (free), no kids
under 5* ⊟ *MC, V* ⦿ *BP.*

£££–££££   **⁂ Dukes Hotel.** True Georgian grandeur is evident in the refurbished
rooms of this Palladian-style mansion turned elegant small hotel.
Guest rooms are individually decorated in English-, French-, or Italian-inspired style, and some have elaborate plasterwork and large windows facing the street. The airy Cavendish Restaurant relies on locally
sourced and organic ingredients, and light lunches are served in the bar.
Pros: excellent central location; superb restaurant; friendly and helpful service. **Cons:** some rooms are small; steps to climb; slightly dated
decor. ☒ *Great Pulteney St. (entrance on Edward St.)* ☎ *01225/787960*
⊕ *www.dukesbath.co.uk* ⇩ *11 rooms, 6 suites* ⚮ *In-room: no a/c, Wi-Fi.
In-hotel: restaurant, bar, Internet terminal, Wi-Fi hotspot, some pets
allowed* ⊟ *AE, MC, V* ⦿ *BP.*

£££   **⁂ Harington's Hotel.** It's rare to find a compact hotel in the cobble-stone
heart of Bath, and this informal three-story lodging converted from
a group of Georgian town houses fits the bill nicely. Bedrooms aren't
spacious, there are no views from the windows, and the parking facilities can be tricky to find; however, the polite but friendly service and
the central location outweigh these minuses. The bar serves snacks all
day, and there's a bistro menu available until 8 PM. **Pros:** good breakfasts; helpful staff. **Cons:** occasional street noise from revelers; steps to
climb. ☒ *Queen St.* ☎ *01225/461728* ⊕ *www.haringtonshotel.co.uk*
⇩ *13 rooms* ⚮ *In-room: no a/c, Wi-Fi (some). In-hotel: bar, parking
(paid)* ⊟ *AE, MC, V* ⦿ *BP.*

££–£££   **⁂ Marlborough House.** A warm, informal welcome greets all who stay
at this Victorian establishment close to the Royal Crescent. Each room
charms with period furniture, fresh flowers, and antique beds, and
there's complimentary sherry for evening relaxation. Leisurely breakfasts are encouraged; choose from scones, yogurts, and savory omelets.
All the food is organic and vegetarian, and vegans and those with special
diets will find their needs amply supplied. **Pros:** obliging and helpful
hosts; immaculate rooms. **Cons:** some traffic noise; the walk to the
center is along a noisy road. ☒ *1 Marlborough La.* ☎ *01225/318175*
⊕ *www.marlborough-house.net* ⇩ *6 rooms* ⚮ *In-room: no a/c, Wi-Fi.
In-hotel: Wi-Fi hotspot, some pets allowed* ⊟ *MC, V* ⦿ *BP.*

£££–££££   **⁂ Queensberry Hotel.** Intimate and elegant, this boutique hotel in a resi-
Fodor's Choice   dential street near the Circus occupies three 1772 town houses built by
★   John Wood the Younger for the marquis of Queensberry. It's a perfect

marriage of chic sophistication, homey comforts, and attentive service. Renovations have preserved the Regency stucco ceilings and cornices and marble tile on the fireplaces, and each room is individually decorated in contemporary style. Four terraced gardens invite a summer aperitif, and downstairs is the excellent semiformal, understated Olive Tree restaurant. **Pros:** efficient service; tranquil ambience; valet parking. **Cons:** occasional street noise; no tea/coffee-making facilities in rooms. ⊠ *Russel St.* ☎ *01225/447928* ⊕ *www.thequeensberry.co.uk* ⇨ *26 rooms, 3 suites* ⚐ *In-room: no a/c, Wi-Fi (some). In-hotel: restaurant, bar, Internet terminal, Wi-Fi hotspot, parking (free)* ⊟ *AE, MC, V.*

££–£££ **Three Abbey Green.** Just steps away from Bath Abbey, a majestic plane tree dominates the gorgeous square that is home to this welcoming B&B. Parts of the building date from 1689, but contemporary design lightens the spacious, pastel-hue rooms. The Lord Nelson room is extra big, with a four-poster, separate sitting area, and handsome fireplace; there are also family rooms. The only downsides are Bath's perennial shortage of parking space—though parking lots are nearby—and the occasional noise at night. The hosts are ready with tips for visiting the city and beyond. Four apartments with kitchens are also available. **Pros:** superb location; airy rooms. **Cons:** some noise from pub goers; only one suite has a bathtub; no parking. ⊠ *3 Abbey Green* ☎ *01225/428558* ⊕ *www.threeabbeygreen.com* ⇨ *7 rooms* ⚐ *In-room: no a/c, Wi-Fi. In-hotel: Internet terminal* ⊟ *MC, V* ⍩ *BP.*

NIGHTLIFE AND THE ARTS

BARS AND PUBS The **Porter** (⊠ *2 Miles's Buildings, George St.* ☎ *01225/424104*), the city's only vegetarian pub, features nightly music and comedy performances in its grungy cellar bar. Pub aficionados will relish the friendly, unspoiled ambience of the **Raven** (⊠ *Queen St.* ☎ *01225/425045*), a great spot for a pint, with regular poetry readings, storytelling nights, and live music upstairs.

FESTIVALS **Bath Comedy Festival** (⊠ *Bath Festivals Box Office, 2 Church St., Abbey Green* ☎ *01225/463362* ⊕ *www.bathcomedyfestival.co.uk*) kicks off on April Fool's Day (April 1) for 11 days of comedy events at venues throughout the city.

★ The **Bath International Music Festival** (⊠ *Bath Festivals Box Office, 2 Church St., Abbey Green* ☎ *01225/463362* ⊕ *www.bathmusicfest.org. uk*), held for two weeks in May and June, presents concerts (classical, jazz, and world music), dance performances, and exhibitions in and around Bath, many in the Assembly Rooms and Bath Abbey.

The weeklong **Bath Literature Festival** (⊠ *Bath Festivals Box Office, 2 Church St., Abbey Green* ☎ *01225/463362* ⊕ *www.bathlitfest.org.uk*) in early March features readings and talks by writers, mostly in the 18th-century Guildhall on High Street.

The **Jane Austen Festival** (☎ *01225/443000* ⊕ *www.janeausten.co.uk/ festival*) celebrates the great writer with films, plays, walks, and talks over nine days in late September. It's a feast for Janeites.

THEATER The **Theatre Royal** (⊠ *Box Office, Saw Close* ☎ *01225/448844*), a gemlike Regency playhouse from 1805, has a year-round program that often includes pre- or post-London tours. You must reserve the best seats well in advance, but you can line up for same-day standby seats or standing room. Tours usually take place at 11 AM on the first Wednesday and the following Saturday of the month (booking not required). ■ TIP→ **Take care with your seat location—sight lines can be poor.**

SPORTS AND THE OUTDOORS

To explore the River Avon by rented punt or canoe, head for the **Bath Boating Station** (⊠ *Forester Rd.* ☎ *01225/312900*), behind the Holburne Museum. It's open Easter to September.

SHOPPING

Bath has excellent small, family-run, and specialty shops; many close on Sunday. The shopping district centers on Stall and Union streets (modern stores), Milsom Street (traditional stores), and Walcot Street (arts and crafts). Leading off these main streets are alleyways and passages lined with galleries and antiques shops.

For 18 days in late November and early December, the outdoor **Bath Christmas Market** (⊠ *Abbey Green, Abbey Gate St., and Kingston Parade* ☎ *01225/396417*) sells gift items—from handcrafted toys to candles, cards, and edible delights—in stalls around the abbey and Roman Baths.

★ **Bartlett Street Antiques Centre** (⊠ *Bartlett St.* ☎ *No phone*) has more than 50 showcases and stands selling every kind of antique imaginable, including silver, porcelain, and jewelry. **Bath Sweet Shop** (⊠ *8 North Parade Passage* ☎ *01225/428040*), the city's oldest candy store, boasts of stocking some 350 different varieties, including traditional licorice torpedoes, pear drops, and aniseed balls. Sugar-free treats are available. **Beaux Arts Ceramics** (⊠ *12–13 York St.* ☎ *01225/464850*) carries the work of prominent potters. The covered **Guildhall Market** (⊠ *Entrances on High St. and Grand Parade*), open Monday through Saturday 9 to 5, is the place for everything from jewelry and gifts to delicatessen food, secondhand books, bags, and batteries; there's a café, too. **Margaret's Buildings** (⊠ *Halfway between the Circus and Royal Crescent*) is a lane with gift shops and several stores selling secondhand and antiquarian books.

CASTLE COMBE

Fodor's Choice   *12 mi northeast of Bath, 5 mi northwest of Chippenham.*

★   This Wiltshire village lived a sleepy existence until 1962, when it was voted the "prettiest village" in England—without any of its inhabitants knowing that it had even been a contender. The village's magic is that it's so toylike, so delightfully all-of-a-piece: you can see almost the whole town at one glance from any one position. Castle Combe consists of little more than a brook, a pack bridge, a street (which is called the Street) of simple stone cottages, a market cross from the 13th century, and the Perpendicular-style church of St. Andrew. The grandest house in the village (on its outskirts) is the Upper Manor House, built in the 15th century by Sir John Fastolf and now the Manor House Hotel.

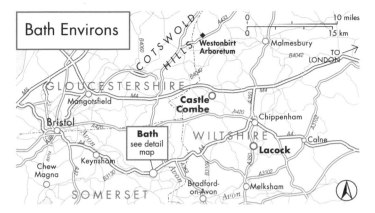

GETTING HERE AND AROUND

All buses from Bath to Castle Combe involve one or two changes and take 70 to 100 minutes, so it's best to drive or join a tour.

WHERE TO STAY

££££–£££££ ⊡ **Manor House Hotel**. This partly 14th-century manor house, outside the
★ village in a 23-acre park, is a baronial swirl of solid chimney stacks, carvings, and columns. Inside, a stone frieze depicts characters from Shakespeare's Falstaff plays, to commemorate the fact that Sir John Fastolf, thought to be the model for the character, was lord of this manor. Guest rooms—some in mews cottages—brim with antique character, and the secluded, landscaped setting is soothing, with green vistas on every side, though the village is only a few steps away. The golf course is excellent. The well-regarded Bybrook restaurant serves imaginative fixed-price meals. **Pros:** romantic getaway; rich historical setting; good golf course. **Cons:** occasional lapses in service; expensive restaurant. ⊠ *Castle Combe* ☎ *01249/782206* ⊕ *www.manorhouse.co.uk* ☎ *48 rooms* ⅋ *In-room: no a/c, Internet. In-hotel: restaurant, bar, golf course, tennis court, Internet terminal, Wi-Fi hotspot, some pets allowed* ⊟ *AE, DC, MC, V.*

LACOCK

Fodor's Choice *8 mi southeast of Castle Combe, 12 mi east of Bath.*
★
Owned by the National Trust, this lovely Wiltshire village is the victim of its own charm, its unspoiled gabled and stone-tile cottages drawing tour buses aplenty. Off-season, however, Lacock slips back into its profound slumber, the mellow stone and brick buildings little changed in 500 years and well worth a wander. Besides Lacock Abbey, there are a few antiques shops, the handsome church of St. Cyriac (built with money earned in the wool trade), a 14th-century tithe barn, and a scattering of pubs that serve bar meals in atmospheric surroundings.

GETTING HERE AND AROUND

All buses from Bath to Lacock involve a change and take 60 to 110 minutes, so it's best to drive or join a tour.

EXPLORING

Well-preserved **Lacock Abbey** reflects the fate of many religious establishments in England—a spiritual center became a home. The abbey, at the town's center, was founded in the 13th century and closed down during the dissolution of the monasteries in 1539, when its new owner, Sir William Sharington, demolished the church and converted the cloisters, sacristy, chapter house, and monastic quarters into a private dwelling. His last descendant, Mathilda Talbot, donated the property as well as Lacock itself to the National Trust in the 1940s. The abbey's grounds are also worth a wander, with a Victorian woodland garden and an 18th-century summerhouse. Harry Potter fans, take note: Lacock Abbey was used for some scenes at Hogwarts School in the film *Harry Potter and the Sorcerer's Stone.*

The **Fox Talbot Museum,** in a 16th-century barn at the gates of Lacock Abbey, illustrates the early history of photography with works by pioneers in the field and also exhibits contemporary artists. The museum commemorates the work of William Henry Fox Talbot (1800–77), who developed the first photographic negative at Lacock Abbey, showing an oriel window in his family home. ⊠ *Just east of A350* ☎ *01249/730459* ⊕ *www.nationaltrust.org.uk* ⊠ *Abbey, museum, gardens, and cloisters £10; museum, gardens, and cloisters £7.20* ⊙ *Abbey mid-Feb.–Oct., daily 11–5. Cloisters and gardens Jan.–mid-Feb. and early Nov.–mid-Dec., weekends 11–4; mid-Feb.–Oct., daily 11–5. Museum Jan.–mid-Feb. and early Nov.–mid-Dec., weekends 11–4; mid-Feb.–Oct., daily 11–5:30; last admission 30 mins before closing.*

WHERE TO EAT

£££ ✕ **Sign of the Angel.** An inn since the 15th century, this atmospheric res-
BRITISH taurant is known for its roasts, casseroles, and specialties like Stilton and walnut pâté. Don't pass up the homemade ice creams and sorbets. There are also somewhat cramped accommodations (£££)—some rooms are in comfortable older buildings, others are in a newer annex. ⊠ *6 Church St.* ☎ *01249/730230* ⊕ *www.lacock.co.uk* ⊟ *AE, DC, MC, V* ⊙ *Closed last wk of Dec.*

THE COTSWOLDS

The Thames rises among the limestone Cotswold Hills, a delightful cradle for that historic river. The Cotswolds are among England's best-preserved rural districts, and the quiet but lovely grays and ambers of the stone buildings here are truly unsurpassed. Much has been written about the area's age-mellowed towns, but the architecture of the villages actually differs little from that of villages elsewhere in England. Their distinction lies in their surroundings: the valleys are deep and rolling, and cozy hamlets appear to drip in foliage from church tower to garden gate. Beyond the town limits, you can explore, on foot or by car, the "high wild hills and rough uneven ways" that Shakespeare wrote about.

Over the centuries, quarries of honey-color stone have yielded building blocks for many Cotswold houses and churches and have transformed little towns into realms of gold. There's an elusive spirit about the Cotswolds, so make Chipping Campden, Moreton-in-Marsh, or Stow-on-the-Wold your headquarters and wander for a few days. Then ask yourself what the area is all about. Its secret seems shared by two things—sheep and stone. The combination isn't as strange as it may sound. These were once the great sheep-rearing areas of England, and during the peak of prosperity in the Middle Ages, Cotswold wool was in demand the world over. This made the local merchants rich, but many gave back to the Cotswolds by restoring old churches (the famous "wool churches" of the region) or building rows of almshouses, of limestone now seasoned to a glorious golden-gray.

Begin with Cheltenham—the largest town in the area and a gateway to the Cotswolds, but slightly outside the boundaries—then move on to the beauty spots in and around Winchcombe. Next are Sudeley Castle, Stanway House, and Snowshill Manor, among the most impressive houses of the region; the oversold village of Broadway; Chipping Campden—the Cotswold cognoscenti's favorite; and Hidcote Manor, one of the most spectacular gardens in England. Then circle back south, down through Moreton-in-Marsh, Stow-on-the-Wold, Upper Slaughter, Lower Slaughter, and Bourton-on-the-Water, and end with Bibury, Tetbury, and Owlpen. This is definitely a region where it pays to go off the beaten track to take a look at that village among the trees.

CHELTENHAM

50 mi north of Bath, 13 mi east of Gloucester, 99 mi west of London.

Although Cheltenham has acquired a reputation as snooty—the population (around 110,000) is generally well-heeled and conservative—it's also cosmopolitan. The town has excellent restaurants and bars, fashionable stores, and a thriving cultural life. Its primary claim to renown, however, is its architecture, rivaling Bath's in its Georgian elegance, with wide, tree-lined streets, crescents, and terraces with row houses, balconies, and iron railings.

Like Bath, Cheltenham owes part of its fame to mineral springs. By 1740 the first spa was built, and after a visit from George III and Queen Charlotte in 1788, the town dedicated itself to idleness and enjoyment. "A polka, parson-worshipping place"—in the words of resident Lord Tennyson—Cheltenham gained its reputation for snobbishness when stiff-collared Raj majordomos returned from India to find that the springs—the only purely natural alkaline waters in England—were the most effective cure for their "tropical ailments."

Great Regency architectural set pieces—Lansdown Crescent, Pittville Spa, and the Lower Assembly Rooms, among them—were built solely to adorn the town. The Rotunda building (1826) at the top of Montpellier Walk—now a bank—contains the spa's original "pump room," in which the mineral waters were on tap. More than 30 statues adorn the storefronts of Montpellier Walk. Wander past Imperial Square, with its ironwork balconies, past the ornate Neptune's Fountain, and along the Promenade. In spring and summer lush flower gardens enhance the town's buildings, attracting many visitors.

8

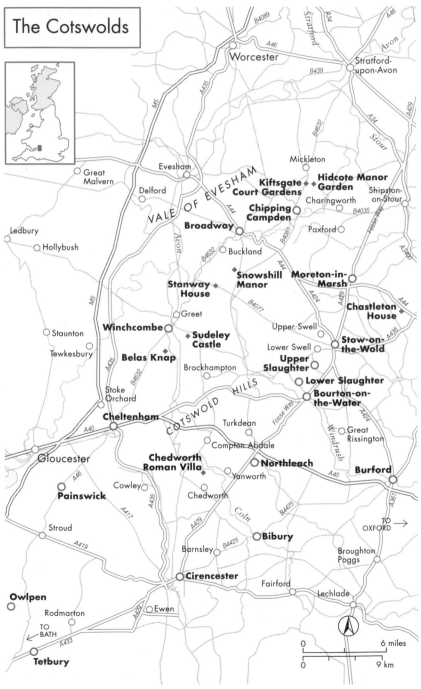

The Cotswolds

GETTING HERE AND AROUND

Trains from London Paddington and buses from London Victoria head to Cheltenham. The train station is west of the center, and the bus station is centrally located off Royal Well Road. Drivers should leave their vehicles in one of the numerous parking lots. The town center is easily negotiable on foot. Cheltenham's tourist office arranges walking tours (£4) of the town at 11:30 on Saturday April through October, also on Sunday in July and August.

FLOWERS AND FESTIVALS

Parts of the town may look like something out of a Gilbert and Sullivan stage set, but Cheltenham is the site of two of England's most progressive arts festivals—the Cheltenham Literature Festival and the town's music festival—as well as jazz and science fests.

ESSENTIALS

Visitor Information Cheltenham (⊠ *77 Promenade* ☎ *01242/522878* ⊕ *www.visitcheltenham.info*).

EXPLORING

From the 1880s onward, Cheltenham was at the forefront of the Arts and Crafts movement, and the **Cheltenham Art Gallery and Museum** contains fine displays of William Morris textiles, furniture by Charles Voysey, and wood and metal pieces by Ernest Gimson. Decorative arts, such as Chinese ceramics, are represented, and British artists, including Stanley Spencer and Vanessa Bell, make their mark in the art gallery. Other exhibits focus on local archaeology and history; one is devoted to Edward Wilson, who traveled with Robert Scott to the Antarctic on Scott's ill-fated 1912 expedition. ⊠ *Clarence St.* ☎ *01242/237431* ⊕ *www.cheltenhammuseum.org.uk* ⊠ *Free* ☉ *Apr.–Oct., daily 10–5 (11–5 1st Thurs. of month, 10–8 3rd Thurs. of month); Nov.–Mar., daily 10–4 (11–4 1st Thurs. of month, 10–8 3rd Thurs. of month).*

The grandest of the remaining spa buildings, the **Pittville Pump Room** is set amid parkland, a 20-minute walk from the town center. The classic Regency structure, built in the late 1820s, now serves mainly as a concert hall and a theatrical venue but still offers its musty mineral waters to the strong of stomach. ⊠ *E. Approach Dr., Pittville* ☎ *01242/523852* ⊕ *www.pittvillepumproom.org.uk* ⊠ *Free* ☉ *Mon.–Sat. 9–noon.*

WHERE TO EAT

££
FRENCH

✕ **Brasserie Blanc.** Housed in the former ballroom of Queen's Hotel, this offshoot of renowned chef Raymond Blanc's Manoir aux Quat' Saisons in Great Milton offers French provincial cooking in contemporary surroundings that harmonize well with the expansive Regency windows. The impressive menu takes in everything from Burgundian snails in garlic butter to grilled squid and courgettes. Among the lip-smacking desserts is flaming baked Alaska. ⊠ *The Promenade* ☎ *01242/266800* ⊕ *www.brasserieblanc.com* ⊟ *AE, MC, V.*

£££
MODERN FRENCH

✕ **Hotel du Vin.** Town movers and shakers have made the restaurant in the trendy Hotel du Vin a favorite dining spot. Casual but sophisticated, the basement-level bistro lies at the bottom of a grand staircase beneath an artful chandelier made of wine glasses. The numerous

8

bottles incorporated into the decor are a nod towards the formidable wine list. Don't be distracted from the French menu, which includes char-grilled rib-eye steak and butternut squash risotto. For dessert, dip into the lavender panna cotta with roast figs or lemon meringue pie. In fine weather, you can enjoy your lunch alfresco. ✉ *Parabola Rd., Montpellier* ☎ *01242/588450* ⊕ *www.hotelduvin.com* ▤ *AE, MC, V.*

£££££ 　✕ **Le Champignon Sauvage.** The relatively short, perfectly balanced menu
MODERN FRENCH 　at this well-established restaurant showcases the contemporary French
★ 　cooking of David Everitt-Matthias. Relax in a room with cream walls and modern art as you indulge in dishes such as pressed terrine of confit rabbit followed by Cinderford lamb. Desserts, including warm prune cake, are worth the calories; you can choose among many cheeses as well. Fixed-price menus at lunch (£25–£30) and dinner (£45–£64) help keep the cost down. ✉ *24 Suffolk Rd.* ☎ *01242/573449* ⊕ *www. lechampignonsauvage.co.uk* ▤ *AE, DC, MC, V* ☾ *Closed Sun., Mon., 3 wks in June, and 10 days in Dec. and Jan.*

££ 　✕ **Montpellier Wine Bar.** In Cheltenham's fashionable Montpellier shop-
BRITISH 　ping district, this busy, informal wine bar is a perfect place for a lunchtime snack or a full evening meal. The menu features such dishes as Gloucestershire Old Spot sausages and roast duck breast. Seating is on two floors—upstairs is casual and downstairs is more formal. Get in early for speedier service. ✉ *Bayshill Lodge, Montpellier St.* ☎ *01242/527774* ⊕ *www.montpellierwinebar.com* ▤ *AE, DC, MC, V.*

WHERE TO STAY

£££££ 　🏠 **Cowley Manor.** Good-bye, floral prints: this Georgian mansion on 55
acres brings country-house style into the 21st century with a mellow atmosphere and modern fabrics and furniture. Witty sculptures and lighting complement the public rooms, beds are huge and comfortable, and bathrooms are trendy, with glass walls and expansive showers. Half the rooms are in the house; the rest fill a transformed stable. There's a two-night minimum stay on weekends. The spa, set into the ground, looks like a work of art. Cowley Manor is 5 mi south of Cheltenham. **Pros:** beautiful grounds; family-friendly atmosphere; relaxed vibe. **Cons:** occasional poor soundproofing; food and service do not always justify the steep prices. ✉ *Off A435, Cowley* ☎ *01242/870900* ⊕ *www.cowleymanor.com* ⇴ *30 rooms* ♿ *In-room: DVD, Internet, Wi-Fi (some). In-hotel: restaurant, pools, gym, spa, Internet terminal, Wi-Fi hotspot* ▤ *AE, DC, MC, V* ⑩ *BP.*

££ 　🏠 **Hanover House.** This centrally located guest house dating from 1848
is brimming with character. The bright and airy rooms are enlivened by richly colored cushions and myriad books. Two, the Tennyson and the Elgar, have their own fireplaces. Delicious, locally sourced and organic breakfasts are taken overlooking the walled garden. **Pros:** convenient location; award-winning breakfasts. **Cons:** all guests share one large table at breakfast. ✉ *65 St. George's Rd.* ☎ *01242/541297* ⊕ *www. hanoverhouse.org* ⇴ *3 rooms* ♿ *In-room: no a/c, no phone, no TV, Wi-Fi. In-hotel: Wi-Fi hotspot, parking (free), no kids under 14* ▤ *No credit cards* ⑩ *BP.*

££ 　🏠 **Lypiatt House Hotel.** A short walk from central Cheltenham in the chic
Montpellier area, this splendid Victorian villa offers attentive service in

elegant surroundings. Guest rooms are mostly spacious and have chic bathrooms. The restful drawing room is done in deep pink, and the conservatory makes a good place for a drink. **Pros:** clean and elegant; capacious parking; excellent breakfasts. **Cons:** some steps to negotiate. ⊠ *Lypiatt Rd.* ☎ *01242/224994* ⊕ *www.lypiatt.co.uk* ⤳ *10 rooms* ♿ *In-room: no a/c, Wi-Fi. In-hotel: bar, laundry service, Wi-Fi hotspot, parking (free), no kids under 10* ⊟ *AE, MC, V* ⏐◎⏐ *BP.*

£££–££££ ▣ **Mercure Queen's Hotel.** Grandly dominating Imperial Gardens, this hotel in a classic Regency mansion has welcomed visitors to Cheltenham since 1838. Public areas and rooms leading off the stunning inner stairway are traditionally British (and rather old-fashioned) in style, and bedrooms are spacious and quiet. Top-floor rooms afford the best views. **Pros:** central location; grand style. **Cons:** old-fashioned feel; underwhelming breakfast. ⊠ *The Promenade* ☎ *01242/514754* ⊕ *www.mercure.com* ⤳ *79 rooms* ♿ *In-room: Internet, Wi-Fi (some). In-hotel: restaurant, bar, Internet terminal, Wi-Fi hotspot, parking (paid), some pets allowed* ⊟ *AE, DC, MC, V.*

NIGHTLIFE AND THE ARTS

The late-Victorian **Everyman Theatre** (⊠ *Regent St.* ☎ *01242/572573*) is an intimate venue for opera, dance, concerts, and plays. ■TIP→ **You can often catch pre– or post–West End productions here, at a fraction of big city prices.**

For information on the town's ambitious lineup of festivals, contact the **Festival Office** (⊠ *Cheltenham Town Hall, Imperial Sq.* ☎ *0844/576–8970* ⊕ *www.cheltenhamfestivals.com*). The **Cheltenham Jazz Festival**, held over a week in late April/early May, presents noted musicians.

★ The 10-day **Literature Festival** in October brings together world-renowned authors, actors, and critics for hundreds of readings and events. Cheltenham's famous **Music Festival,** in early to mid-July, highlights new compositions, often conducted by the composers, and classical pieces. The **Science Festival,** which takes place over five days in early June, attracts leading scientists and writers.

SPORTS

Important steeplechase races take place at **Cheltenham Racecourse** (⊠ *Prestbury Park* ☎ *0844/579–3003*), north of the town center. The Gold Cup awards crown the last day of the National Hunt Festival in mid-March.

SHOPPING

This is serious shopping territory. A stroll along Montpellier Walk and then along the flower-bedecked Promenade brings you to high-quality specialty stores and boutiques. A bubble-blowing Wishing Fish Clock, designed by Kit Williams, dominates the Regent Arcade, a modern shopping area behind the Promenade. A farmers' market enlivens the Promenade on the second and last Friday of the month, and local produce vendors set up stall there on the first Saturday of the month.

Cavendish House (⊠ *32–48 The Promenade* ☎ *01242/521300*) is a high-end department store with designer fashions. **Feva** (⊠ *20 Regent St.* ☎ *01242/222998*) sells eye-catching lines of clothes for women in

8

bright, splashy colors, as well as shoes, belts, and handbags. More-formal wear is sold on the upper floor. **Martin** (⊠ *19 The Promenade* ☎ *01242/522821*) carries a good stock of modern jewelry. **Q and C Militaria** (⊠ *22 Suffolk Rd.* ☎ *01242/519815*), a treasure trove for military buffs, offers badges and medals, breastplates, helmets, coats of arms, and books.

WINCHCOMBE

7 mi northeast of Cheltenham.

The sleepy, unspoiled village of Winchcombe (population 4,500), once the capital of the Anglo-Saxon kingdom of Mercia, has some attractive half-timber and stone houses, as well as a clutch of appealing old inns serving food. A good place to escape the crowds, it's near Sudeley Castle and is also the start of both the Warden's Way and Windrush Way walking trails.

GETTING HERE AND AROUND
Hourly Castleways buses take 20 minutes to get to Winchcombe from Cheltenham (no Sunday service). By car, take B4632, leading over the steep and panoramic Cleeve Hill.

ESSENTIALS
Visitor Information Winchcombe (⊠ *Town Hall, High St.* ☎ *01242/602925* ⊕ *www.visitcotswoldsandsevernvale.gov.uk*).

EXPLORING
Almost 40 outlandish gargoyles adorn the mid-15th-century Perpendicular-style **St. Peter's Church** (⊠ *Gloucester St.*), a typical Cotswold wool church.

★ One of the grand showpieces of the Cotswolds, **Sudeley Castle** was the home and burial place of Catherine Parr (1512–48), Henry VIII's sixth and last wife, who outlived him by one year. Here Catherine undertook, in her later years, the education of the ill-fated Lady Jane Grey and the future queen, Princess Elizabeth. Sudeley, for good reason, has been called a woman's castle. The term castle is misleading, though, for it looks more like a Tudor-era palace, with a peaceful air that belies its turbulent history. In the 17th century Charles I took refuge here, causing Oliver Cromwell's army to besiege the castle, leaving it in ruins until the Dent-Brocklehurst family stepped in with a 19th-century renovation.

The 14 acres of gardens, which include the spectacular roses of the Queen's Garden and a Tudor knot garden, are the setting for Shakespeare performances, concerts, and other events in summer. Inside the castle, however, visitors see only the West Wing, with the Long Room and temporary exhibitions that focus on such subjects as the Tudors, the Civil War, and the Victorians. The private apartments of Lord and Lady Ashcombe, where you can see paintings by Van Dyck, Rubens, Turner, and Reynolds, are viewable only on Connoisseur Tours on Tuesday, Wednesday, and Thursday (£12, including entry to the public rooms and a guidebook). The 11 cottages on the grounds are booked for a minimum of three-night stays. The castle is a mile southeast of

Winchcombe. ⊠ *Off B4632* ☎ *01242/602308* ⊕ *www.sudeleycastle. co.uk* ⊠ *£7.20* ☉ *Apr.–Oct., daily 10:30–5.*

A bracing 2-mi walk south of Winchcombe on the **Cotswold Way,** one of Britain's national walking trails, leads to the hilltop site of **Belas Knap,** a neolithic long barrow, or submerged burial chamber, above **Humblebee Wood.** ■ **TIP→ The site isn't much to see, but you hike next to and through one of the most enchanting natural domains in England, with views stretching over to Sudeley Castle.** If you have a car, take the scenic Humblebee Wood road down to the villages of Sevenhampton and Brockhampton.

A mile north of Winchcombe, at Greet, you can board a steam-hauled train of the **Gloucestershire and Warwickshire Railway,** which chugs its way along a 13-mi stretch at the foot of the Cotswolds between Toddington Station and Cheltenham Racecourse. The round-trip journey takes around 90 minutes. ⊠ *Greet* ☎ *01242/621405* ⊕ *www.gwsr.com* ⊠ *£10 round-trip* ☉ *Apr.–Sept., almost daily 10:30–5; Mar. and Oct.– Dec., weekends 10:30–5 (daily Dec. 22–31).*

WHERE TO EAT

££££
MODERN BRITISH

✕ **Wesley House.** Wooden beams and stone walls distinguish this 15th-century half-timber building, where the red-carpeted dining room makes a fine backdrop for superior Modern British dishes. The menu includes Hereford beef fillet with forest mushrooms and bordelaise sauce, and roast guinea fowl with tarragon sauce. Fixed-price lunch and evening menus are a good value. You can eat and drink less formally in the adjoining bar and grill, with a choice of pastas, steaks, and seafood. Upstairs, five small guest rooms (££) have twisted beams and sloping ceilings, including the Preacher's Room, where John Wesley used to stay. ⊠ *High St.* ☎ *01242/602366* ▤ *AE, MC, V* ☉ *No dinner Sun.*

BROADWAY

8 mi north of Winchcombe, 17 mi northeast of Cheltenham.

The Cotswold town to end all Cotswold towns, Broadway has become a favorite of day-trippers. William Morris first discovered the delights of this village, and J. M. Barrie, Vaughan Williams, and Edward Elgar soon followed. Today you may want to avoid Broadway in summer, when it's clogged with cars and buses. Named for its handsome, wide main street (well worth a stroll), the village includes the renowned Lygon Arms hotel and numerous antiques shops, tea parlors, and boutiques. Step off onto Broadway's back roads and alleys and you can discover any number of honey-color houses and colorful gardens.

GETTING HERE AND AROUND

Broadway can be reached by car via A44; drivers should park in one of the parking lots signposted from the main street. Johnson's Coaches connects the town with Stratford-upon-Avon, Chipping Campden, and Moreton-in-Marsh; Castleways connects Broadway with Winchcombe and Cheltenham. No services run on Sunday. You'll need a car to reach Broadway Tower, Stanway House, and Snowshill Manor.

ESSENTIALS
Visitor Information Broadway (⊠ *Russell Sq.* ☎ *01386/852937* ⊕ *www. beautifulbroadway.com*).

EXPLORING
Among the attractions of **Broadway Tower Country Park**, on the outskirts of town, is its **tower**, an 18th-century "folly" built by the sixth earl of Coventry and later used by William Morris as a retreat. Exhibits describe the tower's past and the local Arts and Crafts movement, and the view from the top takes in three counties. (The tower normally stays open longer than the advertised times in fine weather.) Peaceful countryside surrounds you on the nature trails and picnic grounds. ⊠ *Off A44* ☎ *01386/852390* ⊕ *www.broadwaytower.co.uk* ⊠ *Park free, tower £4.50* ⊙ *Tower Apr.–Oct., daily 10:30–5; Nov.–Mar., weekends 11–3.*

Ⓒ Snowshill, 3 mi south of Broadway and 13 mi northeast of Chelten-
★ ham, is one of the most unspoiled of all Cotswold villages. Snuggled beneath Oat Hill, with little room for expansion, the hamlet is centered around an old burial ground, the 19th-century St. Barnabas Church, and **Snowshill Manor**, a splendid 17th-century house that brims with the collections of Charles Paget Wade, gathered between 1919 and 1956. Over the door of the house is Wade's family motto, *Nequid pereat* ("Let nothing perish"). The rooms are bursting with Tibetan scrolls, spinners' tools, ship models, Persian lamps, and bric-a-brac. The Green Room displays 26 suits of Japanese samurai armor. Children love the place. Outside, an imaginative terraced garden provides an exquisite frame for the house. ■**TIP→ Admission is by timed tickets issued on a first-come, first-served basis, so arrive early in peak season.** ⊠ *Off A44, Snowshill* ☎ *01386/852410* ⊕ *www.nationaltrust.org.uk* ⊠ *£8.10; garden only, £4.40* ⊙ *House: mid-Mar.–Oct., Wed.–Sun. noon–5. Garden: mid-Mar.–Oct., Wed.–Sun. 11–5:30.*

★ **Stanway House**, a perfect Cotswold manor of glowing limestone in the small village of Stanway, dates from the Jacobean era. Its triple-gabled gatehouse is a Cotswold landmark, and towering windows dominate the house's Great Hall. They illuminate a 22-foot-long shuffleboard table from 1620 and an 18th-century bouncing exercise machine. The other well-worn rooms are adorned with family portraits, tattered tapestries, vintage armchairs, and, at times, Lord or Lady Neidpath themselves, the current owners. The partly restored baroque water garden has a fountain, built in 2004, that shoots up 300 feet. The tallest in Britain, it shoots at 2:45 and 4. To get to Stanway, about 5 mi south of Broadway, take B4632 south from town, turning left at B4077. ⊠ *Off B4077, Stanway* ☎ *01386/584469* ⊕ *www.stanwayfountain.co.uk* ⊠ *House and fountain £7; fountain only, £4.50* ⊙ *House and fountain: June–Aug., Tues. and Thurs. 2–5.*

WHERE TO EAT
£££   ✕**Russell's.** With a courtyard at the back and a patio at the front, this
MODERN BRITISH   chic "restaurant with rooms" is perfect for a light lunch at midday or a full meal in the evening. The restaurant, in a furniture factory once belonging to local designer George Russell, is modern and plush.

Menus concentrate on Modern British dishes, with such temptations as pizza with garlic, mushroom, artichoke, and spinach; corn-fed chicken with roasted new potatoes, Savoy cabbage, and honey-glazed parsnips; and panfried hake. There's also an outstanding cheese board. The seven boutique-style rooms upstairs (££–£££) are very sleek. ⊠ *20 High St.* ☎ *01386/853555* ⊕ *www.russellsofbroadway.co.uk* ☐ *AE, MC, V* ⊗ *No dinner Sun.*

SEEKING SHAKESPEARE

The country delights of the area lure you to linger, but keep in mind that in the northern part of the Cotswolds, you're less than 15 mi from Stratford-upon-Avon. It's easy to detour to visit the Shakespeare sights or even see a play at the Royal Shakespeare Theatre.

WHERE TO STAY

£££££ ★ **Buckland Manor.** As an alternative to the hustle and bustle of Broadway, you can splurge at this exceptional traditional country-house hotel 2 mi away in the idyllic hamlet of Buckland. The land was valued at £9 in the 11th-century Domesday Book, and the sprawling stone building dates back to Jacobean times. Public areas and guest rooms are plushly comfortable, with old paintings, fine rugs, and antiques everywhere. The gardens are well groomed and tranquil. The baronial restaurant (£££££, jacket and tie required) features largely traditional fare enhanced with modern trimmings. **Pros:** beautiful setting; elegant guest rooms; large bathrooms with high-quality toiletries. **Cons:** service can be spotty; some rooms are small; restaurant very formal. ⊠ *Off B4632, Buckland* ☎ *01386/852626* ⊕ *www.bucklandmanor.co.uk* ⟳ *13 rooms* ♻ *In-room: no a/c, Internet. In-hotel: restaurant, bar, tennis courts, no kids under 12* ☐ *AE, MC, V* ⦿ *BP.*

£££££ ★ **Dormy House Hotel.** Guest rooms in this converted 17th-century farmhouse overlook the Vale of Evesham from high on the Cotswolds ridge—one of the region's most celebrated vistas. Luxury rules at this establishment, where you can relax by a fireplace or play a game of croquet on the lawn. Modern furnishings blend comfortably with traditional pieces in the beamed bedrooms. Noted in the region, the restaurant (£37 fixed-price menu) has a superlative wine list. A more economical option is the beamed Barn Owl bar. The hotel is 2 mi north of Broadway. **Pros:** professional staff; well-equipped rooms; great location; good leisure facilities. **Cons:** slightly bland; standard rooms may be rather small and dark. ⊠ *Willersey Hill* ☎ *01386/852711* ⊕ *www.dormyhouse.co.uk* ⟳ *45 rooms* ♻ *In-room: no a/c, Internet (some), Wi-Fi (some). In-hotel: restaurant, bars, gym, golf course, Wi-Fi hotspot* ☐ *AE, DC, MC, V* ⦿ *BP.*

£££££ **Mill Hay House.** If the rose garden, trout-filled pond, and pet sheep at this 18th-century Queen Anne house aren't appealing enough, then the stone-flagged floors, leather sofas, and grandfather clocks should satisfy. Booking ahead is essential to secure one of the three beautiful, traditional-style pastel bedrooms at this B&B. Ask about discounted midweek and weekend packages. It's 1 mi from Broadway on Snowshill Road. **Pros:** delightful staff; beautifully landscaped gardens; gourmet breakfasts. **Cons:** books up quickly; no young children admitted.

8

⊠ *Snowshill Rd.* ☎ *01386/852498* ⊕ *www.millhay.co.uk* ⊷ *2 rooms, 1 suite* ₺ *In-room: no a/c, safe, refrigerator, Wi-Fi. In-hotel: Wi-Fi hotspot, no kids under 12* ⊟ *MC, V* ⦿ *BP.*

££   ⊡ **Old Stationhouse.** A 10-minute walk from Broadway, this former stationmaster's home sits on an acre of lawns and gardens. It has spacious, plainly furnished rooms with large beds (one's a four-poster). There's a comfortable lounge with games, books, and a piano for rainy days. Breakfast consists of homemade jams, cereals, and local produce. **Pros:** outside tourist scrum; airy rooms; welcoming and knowledgeable hosts. **Cons:** outside the village; lacks old-world ambience. ⊠ *Station Rd.* ☎ *01386/852659* ⊕ *www.oldstationhousebroadway.co.uk* ⊷ *6 rooms* ₺ *In-room: no a/c, no phone, refrigerator. In-hotel: Wi-Fi hotspot, parking (free)* ⊟ *MC, V* ⦿ *BP.*

££   ⊡ **The Olive Branch.** Right on the main drag, this 16th-century cottage has authentic period charm. It's strewn with antique knickknacks and black-and-white photos. The best feature is the lovely flagstone lounge with its inglenook fireplace. Guest rooms are clean and comfortable, and the garden has a grill for the use of guests. **Pros:** cottage character; tasty breakfasts; hospitable hosts. **Cons:** small bathrooms; narrow stairs; low ceilings. ⊠ *78 High St.* ☎ *01386/853440* ⊕ *www.theolivebranchbroadway.com* ⊷ *8 rooms* ₺ *In-room: no a/c, no phone, Wi-Fi (some). In-hotel: Wi-Fi hotspot, some pets allowed* ⊟ *AE, MC, V* ⦿ *BP.*

CHIPPING CAMPDEN

4 mi east of Broadway, 18 mi northeast of Cheltenham.

Undoubtedly one of the most beautiful towns in the area, Chipping Campden, with its population of about 2,500, is the Cotswolds in a microcosm. It has St. James, the region's most impressive church; frozen-in-time streets; a silk mill that was once the center of the Guild of Handicrafts; and pleasant, untouristy shops. One of the area's most seductive settings unfolds before you as you travel on B4081 through sublime English countryside and happen upon the town, tucked in a slight valley. North of town is lovely Hidcote Manor Garden. ■ **TIP**→ **Chipping Campden can easily be reached on foot along a level section of the Cotswold Way from Broadway Tower; the walk takes about 75 minutes.**

GETTING HERE AND AROUND

By car, Chipping Campden can be reached on minor roads from A44 or A429. There's a small car park in the center and spaces on the outskirts of the village. By bus, take Johnson's Coaches from Stratford-upon-Avon, Broadway, and Moreton-in-Marsh, or Pulhams Coaches from Bourton-on-the-Water and Cheltenham, changing at Moreton-in-Marsh (no Sunday service).

ESSENTIALS

Visitor Information Chipping Campden (⊠ *The Old Police Station, High St.* ☎ *01386/841206* ⊕ *www.chippingcampdenonline.org*).

EXPLORING

TOP ATTRACTIONS

Fodor's Choice **Hidcote Manor Garden.** Laid out around a Cotswold manor house, Hid-
★ cote Manor Garden is arguably the most interesting and attractive
large garden in Britain. Crowds are large at the height of the season,
but it's worthwhile anytime. A horticulturist from the United States,
Major Lawrence Johnstone, created the garden in 1907 in the Arts and
Crafts style. Johnstone was an imaginative gardener and avid traveler
who brought back specimens from all over the world. The formal part
of the garden is arranged in "rooms" separated by hedges and often
with fine topiary work and walls. Besides the variety of plants, what's
impressive are the different effects created, from calm open spaces to
areas packed with flowers. ■ TIP→ **Look out for one of Johnson's earliest
schemes, the red borders of dahlias, poppies, fuchsias, lobelias, and roses;
the tall hornbeam hedges; and the Bathing Pool garden, where the pool
is so wide there's scarcely space to walk.** The White Garden was probably the forerunner of the popular white gardens at Sissinghurst and
Glyndebourne. If you have time, explore tiny Hidcote Bartrim with its
thatched stone houses; it borders the garden and fills a storybook dell.
The garden is 4 mi northeast of Chipping Campden. ⊠ *Off B4081, Hidcote Bartrim* ☎ *01386/438333* ⊕ *www.nationaltrust.org.uk* ☜ *£8.60*
⊗ *Mid-Mar.–June and Sept., Mon.–Wed. and weekends 10–6; July and
Aug., daily 10–6; Oct., Mon.–Wed. and weekends 10–5; early Nov.–
mid-Dec., weekends noon–4; last admission 1 hr before closing.*

St. James. The soaring pinnacled tower of St. James, a prime example of
a Cotswold wool church (it was rebuilt in the 15th century with money
from wool merchants), announces the town from a distance; it's worth
stepping inside to see the lofty nave. The church recalls the old saying,
which became popular because of the vast numbers of houses of worship in the Cotswolds, "As sure as God's in Gloucestershire." ⊠ *Church
St.* ☎ *01386/841927* ⊕ *www.stjameschurchcampden.co.uk* ☜ *£1 donation suggested* ⊗ *Mar.–Oct., Mon.–Sat. 10–5, Sun. 2–6; Nov. and Feb.,
Mon.–Sat. 11–4, Sun. 2–4; Dec. and Jan., Mon.–Sat. 11–3, Sun. 2–3.*

WORTH NOTING

Court Barn Museum. Near the church of St. James, the museum occupies
an old agricultural building that has been smartly renovated to showcase the area's prominence in the fields of craft and design. You can
admire examples of silverware, bookbinding, printing, furniture, and
jewelry. Opposite the barn is an important row of almshouses dating
from the reign of King James I. ⊠ *Church St.* ☎ *01386/841951* ⊕ *www.
courtbarn.org.uk* ☜ *£3.75* ⊗ *Apr.–Sept., Tues.–Sat. 10:30–5:30, Sun.
11:30–5:30; Oct.–Mar., Tues.–Sat. 11–4, Sun. 11:30–4.*

Kiftsgate Court Gardens. While not so spectacular as Hidcote Manor
Garden, this intimate, privately owned garden, just a five-minute stroll
away, still captivates. It's skipped by the majority of visitors to Hidcote,
so you won't be jostled by the crowds. The interconnecting gardens
present harmonious arrays of color. Don't miss the prized Kiftsgate
rose, supposed to be the largest in England, flowering gloriously in
mid-July. ⊠ *Off B4081, Mickleton* ☎ *01386/438777* ⊕ *www.kiftsgate.*

8

CLOSE UP

Arts and Crafts in the Cotswolds

The Arts and Crafts movement flourished throughout Britain in the late 19th and early 20th centuries, but the Cotswolds are most closely associated with it. The godfather of the movement was designer William Morris (1834–96), whose home for the last 25 years of his life, Kelmscott Manor in Gloucestershire, became the headquarters of the school. A lecture by Morris, "The Beauty of Life," delivered in Birmingham in 1880, included the injunction that became the guiding principle of the movement: "Have nothing in your houses which you do not know to be useful or believe to be beautiful."

Driven by the belief that the spirit of medieval arts and crafts was being degraded and destroyed by the mass production and aggressive capitalism of the Victorian era, and aided by a dedicated core of artisans, Morris revolutionized the art of house design

and decoration. His work with textiles was particularly influential.

Many of Morris's followers were influenced by the Cotswold countryside, such as the designer and architect Charles Robert Ashbee, who transferred his Guild of Handicrafts from London to Chipping Campden in 1902. The village holds a small museum dedicated to local craftwork, including a permanent exhibition of pieces by the original group and those who followed in their wake. Their work can also be seen at Cheltenham's Art Gallery and Museum, and, in its original context, at Rodmarton Manor outside Tetbury—which Ashbee declared the finest application of the movement's ideals—and at Owlpen Manor. (Farther afield, Blackwell in the Lake District is a notable Arts and Crafts house.) To see the Arts and Crafts ethic applied to horticulture, visit Hidcote Manor Garden, near Chipping Campden.

co.uk 🖾 *£6.50* ☉ *Apr. and Sept., Mon., Wed., and Sun. 2–6; May–July, Sat.–Wed. noon–6; Aug., Sat.–Wed. 2–6.*

Market Hall. The broad High Street, lined with stone houses and shops, follows a captivating curve; in the center, on Market Street, is the Market Hall, a gabled Jacobean structure built by Sir Baptiste Hycks in 1627 "for the sale of local produce."

Silk Mill. In 1902 the Guild of Handicrafts took over the Silk Mill, and Arts and Crafts evangelist Charles Robert Ashbee (1863–1942) brought 150 acolytes here from London, including 50 guildsmen, to revive and practice such skills as cabinetmaking and bookbinding. The operation folded in 1920, but the refurbished building still houses an exhibition and the workshops of a silversmith, jeweler, and stone carver. ⊠ *Sheep St.* ☎ *No phone* 🖾 *Free* ☉ *Weekdays 9–5, Sat. 9–1.*

WHERE TO EAT

££   ✕ **Churchill Arms.** In this small country pub just outside Chipping Camp-
BRITISH   den, plain wooden tables and benches, a flagstone floor, and a roaring fire provide the backdrop for excellent food. Daily specials—grilled sea bass on a bed of spinach, and roasted chicken marinated in red wine— appear on the blackboard. If you feel like staying overnight, upstairs

are four traditionally furnished bedrooms (££). ⊠ *Off B4035, Paxford* ☎ *01386/594000* ⊕ *www.thechurchillarms.com* 🖃 *MC, V.*

££
BRITISH

✕ **Eight Bells.** Close to St. James Church, this traditional tavern has low beams, a flagstone floor, and a small courtyard. The long menu includes such enticing dishes as pigeon risotto, fillet of pork stuffed with apricots and chestnuts, and grilled sea bass. Fixed-price menus at lunchtime are easy on the wallet. Service is swift, and good local ales are dispensed. ⊠ *Church St.* ☎ *01386/840371* ⊕ *www.eightbellsinn.co.uk* 🖃 *MC, V.*

WHERE TO STAY

££

🏠 **Badgers Hall.** Expect a friendly welcome at this antique B&B above a tearoom just across from the Market Hall. The spacious, spotless rooms have beamed ceilings and exposed stonework. Guests are greeted with a cream tea on arrival, and the excellent breakfast will set you up for the day. Two nights is the minimum stay. **Pros:** atmospheric building; attentive hosts; delicious breakfasts. **Cons:** low ceilings; entrance is through tea shop. ⊠ *High St.* ☎ *01386/840839* ⊕ *www.badgershall.com* ⌁ *3 rooms* ⚲ *In-hotel: Wi-Fi hotspot, no kids under 10* 🖃 *MC, V* ⭕ *BP.*

££££–£££££

🏠 **Charingworth Manor.** Views of the countryside are limitless from this 14th-century manor house hotel just outside town. Mullioned windows and oak beams enhance the sitting room, and bedrooms have antique furniture. T.S. Eliot, a guest in the 1930s, used to enjoy walking the 50 acres of grounds. The fixed-price menus at the restaurant (£££££) include both traditional English and Mediterranean-inspired dishes such as local rack of lamb. The hotel is 3 mi east of Chipping Campden. **Pros:** helpful staff; peaceful setting; lots of amenities. **Cons:** pricey food; poor soundproofing in annex. ⊠ *Charingworth* ☎ *01386/593555* ⊕ *www.classiclodges.co.uk* ⌁ *23 rooms, 3 suites* ⚲ *In-room: no a/c, Wi-Fi, safe. In-hotel: restaurant, tennis court, pool, gym, Wi-Fi hotspot, some pets allowed* 🖃 *AE, DC, MC, V* ⭕ *BP.*

£££££

🏠 **Cotswold House.** This luxury hotel in the center of Chipping Campden injects contemporary design into a stately 18th-century manor house. From the swirling staircase in the entrance to the guest rooms studded with contemporary art and high-tech gadgetry, it's a winning formula. The lounges invite lingering, and the patio and spacious garden offer seclusion. The formal Juliana's Restaurant (£££££) and the livelier and cheaper Hicks' Brasserie (£££) both offer creative takes on English and Mediterranean dishes. Hicks' is open all day and is worth a stop even if you aren't staying here. **Pros:** faultless service; plenty of pampering; lovely garden. **Cons:** expensive for what you get; piped-in music in public rooms; guest rooms can be overheated. ⊠ *The Square* ☎ *01386/840330* ⊕ *www.cotswoldhouse.com* ⌁ *26 rooms, 4 suites* ⚲ *In-room: no a/c (some), refrigerator, DVD, Internet, Wi-Fi (some). In-hotel: 2 restaurants, bars, spa, Wi-Fi hotspot, some pets allowed, parking (free)* 🖃 *AE, MC, V* ⭕ *BP.*

£££

🏠 **Noel Arms Hotel.** Dating to the 14th century, Chipping Campden's oldest inn was built to accommodate foreign wool traders. Even though it has been enlarged, the building retains its exposed beams and stonework. Guest rooms—some in the 14th-century portion—are full of warm colors and dark oak furniture, and fully equipped with modern amenities. Breakfast can be taken in the flagstone conservatory. The

8

same owners run the nearby Cotswold House, and guests have access to its facilities. Pros: traditional character; friendly staff. Cons: some facilities are dated; rooms can be noisy and overheated. ⊠ *High St.* ☎ *01386/840317* ⊕ *www.noelarmshotel.com* ➳ *26 rooms* ♿ *In-room: no a/c. In-hotel: restaurant, bar, parking (free), some pets allowed* ☴ *AE, MC, V* �🍽 *BP.*

SHOPPING
At **Hart** (⊠ *The Silk Mill, Sheep St.* ☎ *01386/841100*), descendants of an original member of the Guild of Handicrafts specialize in fashioning lovely items from silver. **Martin Gotrel** (⊠ *Camperdene House, High St.* ☎ *01386/841360*) crafts fine traditional and contemporary jewelry.

MORETON-IN-MARSH

5 mi south of Chipping Campden, 18 mi northeast of Cheltenham, 5 mi north of Stow-on-the-Wold.

In Moreton-in-Marsh, the houses have been built not around a central square but along a street wide enough to accommodate a market. The village has fine views across the hills. One local landmark, St. David's Church, has a tower of honey-gold ashlar. This town of about 3,500 also possesses one of the last remaining curfew towers, dated 1633; curfew dates to the time of the Norman Conquest, when a bell was rung to "cover-fire" for the night against any invaders.

GETTING HERE AND AROUND
Moreton-in-Marsh is on the A429 north of Cirencester. Park along the main street or in the lot on Station Road. The town has a train station with daily connections to London Paddington. Pulhams buses arrive here from Cirencester (not on Sunday) or Cheltenham (not on Sunday in winter). There's also service to and from Stratford-upon-Avon, Stow-on-the-Wold, and Bourton-on-the-Water. For Sezincote, a car is necessary.

ESSENTIALS
Visitor Information Moreton-in-Marsh (⊠ *High St.* ☎ *01608/650881* ⊕ *www. cotswolds.info*).

EXPLORING
Supposed to be the largest street market in the Cotswolds, the **Tuesday Market** takes over the center of the main street between 8 and 2:30, with a mix of household goods, fruits and vegetables, and some arts-and-crafts and jewelry stalls. Check out this market, which is no newcomer: it was chartered in 1227.

It comes as somewhat of an architectural surprise to see the blue onion domes and miniature minarets of **Sezincote**, a mellow stone house and garden tucked into a valley near Moreton-in-Marsh. Created in the early 19th century, Sezincote (pronounced "see-zinct") was the vision of Sir Charles Cockerell, who made a fortune in the East India Company. He employed his architect brother, Samuel Pepys Cockerell, to "Indianize" the residence with Hindu and Muslim motifs. Note the peacock-tail arches surrounding the windows of the first floor. The exotic garden, Hindu temple folly, and Indian-style bridge were favorites of the future

Visiting Cotswold Gardens

Perhaps it's the sheer beauty of this area that has inspired the creation of so many superb gardens. Gardening is an English passion, and even nongardeners may be tempted by the choices large and small. The Arts and Crafts movement in Britain transformed not only interior design but also the world of gardening; at Hidcote Manor Garden, an influential, much-visited masterpiece of the style, hedges and walls set off vistas and surround distinct themed garden rooms. Rodmarton Manor also has a garden in this style.

In the Cotswolds, as elsewhere in England, gardens often complement a stately home and deserve as close a look as the house. At Sudeley Castle, the home of Catherine Parr (Henry VIII's last wife), you can explore the 19th-century Queen's Garden, beloved for its roses. Also large in scale but entirely different is Westonbirt National Arboretum, near Tetbury,

with its magnificent collection of trees. In contrast, the 18th-century Painswick Rococo Garden, with its Gothic screen and other intriguing structures, has a pleasant intimacy. Britain wouldn't be Britain without a touch of eccentricity, and in the Cotswolds the garden at the Indian-style manor of Sezincote, with its temple to a Hindu god, supplies a satisfying blend of the stately and the exotic.

Eager to see more? The **National Garden Scheme** (⊕ www.ngs.org.uk) publishes annual "yellow books" that list all gardens open throughout the country (£8.99). Bookstores sell these, too. Depending on your itinerary, buying a Great British Heritage Pass or joining the **National Trust** (⊕ www.nationaltrust.org.uk) may save you money on garden admissions. You can also contact Cheltenham's tourist office for information on garden tours in the Cotswolds.

8

George IV, who was inspired to create that Xanadu of Brighton, the Royal Pavilion. If you come in spring, glorious aconites and snowdrops greet you. Note that children are allowed indoors only at the owners' discretion. ⊠ *Off A44* ☎ *01386/700444* ⊕ *www.sezincote.co.uk* ⊠ *House and grounds £8, grounds £5* ⊙ *House May–Sept., Thurs., Fri., and national holidays 2:30–5:30; grounds Jan.–Nov., Thurs. and Fri. and national holidays 2–6 or dusk.*

WHERE TO EAT AND STAY

£ ✕ **Ask.** Two stone Cotswold cottages have been tastefully converted to ITALIAN form this warm, relaxed eating space in the center of Moreton. Part of a chain specializing in Italian standards, the restaurant has flagstone floors, modern art on the walls, and a menu that ranges from stone-baked pizzas to *pollo Marsala* (roast chicken with mushroom and wine sauce). Antipasti, salads, and espresso coffee complete the meal. ⊠ *High St.* ☎ *01608/651119* ⊕ *www.askcentral.co.uk* ⊟ *AE, MC, V.*

£££–££££ ⊡ **Manor House Hotel.** Secret passageways and a priest's hole testify to the age of this 16th-century building, set back from the main thoroughfare. Wing chairs and chintz-covered sofas and drapes adorn the public rooms, setting a traditional note. Bedrooms, revealing original stonework, mix stylish modern furnishings and fabrics with antiques.

The Mulberry restaurant serves an adventurous English menu. **Pros:** accommodating staff; historical ambience; top-notch toiletries. **Cons:** smallish rooms; some traffic noise in front rooms; occasionally malfunctioning plumbing and heating. ⊠ *High St.* ☎ *01608/650501* ⊕ *www. cotswold-inns-hotels.co.uk* ⟿ *35 rooms* ⟑ *In-room: safe (some), no a/c, Wi-Fi (some). In-hotel: restaurant, bar, Wi-Fi hotspot, some pets allowed* ⊟ *AE, DC, MC, V* ⫶⦶⫶ *BP.*

STOW-ON-THE-WOLD

5 mi south of Moreton-in-Marsh, 15 mi east of Cheltenham.

At an elevation of 800 feet, Stow is the highest town in the Cotswolds—"Stow-on-the-Wold, where the wind blows cold" is the age-old saying. Built around a wide square, Stow's imposing golden stone houses have been discreetly converted into high-quality antiques stores. The Square, as it is known, has a fascinating history. In the 18th century Daniel Defoe wrote that more than 20,000 sheep could be sold here on a busy day; such was the press of livestock that sheep runs, known as "tures," were used to control the sheep, and these narrow streets still run off the main square. Today pubs and cafés fill the area.

Also here are St. Edward's Church and the Kings Arms Old Posting House, its wide entrance still seeming to wait for the stagecoaches that used to stop here on their way to Cheltenham.

GETTING HERE AND AROUND

Stow-on-the-Wold is well connected by road (A429, A424, and A436) and bus (from Moreton-in-Marsh, Bourton-on-the-Water, Northleach, Cirencester, and Cheltenham). Parking is usually easy to find near the center. Chastleton House is only reachable by car.

ESSENTIALS

Visitor Information Stow-on-the-Wold (⊠ *12 Talbot Ct., off Sheep St.* ☎ *01451/870150* ⊕ *www.go-stow.co.uk*).

EXPLORING

★ **Chastleton House,** one of the most complete Jacobean properties in Britain, opts for a beguilingly lived-in appearance, taking advantage of almost 400 years' worth of furniture and trappings accumulated by many generations of the single family that owned it until 1991. The house was built between 1605 and 1612 for William Jones, a wealthy wool merchant, and has an appealing authenticity: bric-a-brac is strewn around, wood and pewter are unpolished, upholstery is uncleaned. The top floor is a glorious, barrel-vaulted long gallery, and throughout the house you can see exquisite plasterwork, paneling, and tapestries. The gardens include rotund topiaries and the first croquet lawn (the rules of croquet were codified here in 1865). ■ **TIP→ Admission is by timed ticket, so it's a good idea to call ahead to reserve.** Chastleton is 6 mi northeast of Stow, signposted off A436 between Stow and A44. ⊠ *Off A436, Moreton-in-Marsh* ☎ *01608/674981* ⊕ *www.nationaltrust.org.uk* ⊠ *£7.85* ☺ *Late Mar.–Sept., Wed.–Sat. 1–5; Oct., Wed.–Sat. 1–4.*

WHERE TO EAT AND STAY

£   ✕ **Queen's Head.** An excellent stopping-off spot for lunch or dinner,
BRITISH   this pub has a courtyard out back that's a quiet retreat on a summer day. The bench in front, under a climbing rose, makes a relaxing
spot for imbibing outdoor refreshment. Besides standard pub grub,
including ploughman's lunches, sandwiches, sausage and mash, and
chicken pie, there are daily specials such as lamb chops. ✉ *The Square*
☎ *01451/830563* 🖃 *MC, V.*

£–££   ⊡ **Number Nine.** Beyond the traditional stone-and-creeper exterior of
this former coaching inn—now a bed-and-breakfast—are unfussy, spacious bedrooms done in soothing white and pale colors. The inglenook
fireplace is a draw in winter, and wholesome breakfasts include poached
fruits and specialty breads. **Pros:** helpful and amiable hosts; excellent
breakfasts; attention to detail. **Cons:** not all bathrooms have showers;
low ceilings; steps to climb. ✉ *9 Park St.* ☎ *01451/870333* ⊕ *www.
number-nine.info* ⤳ *3 rooms* ♿ *In-room: no a/c, no phone, Wi-Fi. In-
hotel: Internet terminal* 🖃 *MC, V* ⊙ *BP.*

£££   ⊡ **Royalist Hotel.** Dating from the 10th century, this hostelry is jammed
with interesting features, including witches' marks on the beams, and
a tunnel to the church across the road. The owners have stylishly integrated designer bedrooms and the sleek 947AD restaurant (£££££). If the
elegant modern British dishes here don't appeal, the adjacent Eagle and
Child (££) offers a hearty brasserie-style menu from the same kitchen.
Pros: lots of character; large, comfortable suites. **Cons:** service occasionally dips; some rooms can be noisy and overheated. ✉ *Digbeth St.*
☎ *01451/830670* ⊕ *www.theroyalisthotel.com* ⤳ *12 rooms, 2 suites*
♿ *In-room: no a/c, Wi-Fi. In-hotel: restaurant, bars, Wi-Fi hotspot*
🖃 *AE, MC, V* ⊙ *BP.*

SHOPPING

Stow-on-the-Wold is the leading center for antiques stores in the
Cotswolds, with more than 40 dealers centered on the Square, Sheep
Street, and Church Street.

Duncan Baggott Antiques (✉ *Woolcomber House, Sheep St.* ☎ *01451/
830662*) displays fine old furniture, portraits and landscape paintings,
and garden statuary and ornaments. **Roger Lamb Antiques** (✉ *The Square*
☎ *01451/831371*) specializes in objets d'art and small pieces of furniture from the Georgian and Regency periods, with Regency "faux
bamboo," tea caddies, and antique needlework the particular fortes.
Head for **Talbot Galleries** (✉ *7 Talbot Ct.* ☎ *01451/832169*) if you're
interested in antique maps and prints.

BOURTON-ON-THE-WATER

*4 mi southwest of Stow-on-the-Wold, 12 mi northeast of
Cheltenham.*

Bourton-on-the-Water, off A429 on the eastern edge of the Cotswold
Hills, is deservedly famous as a classic Cotswold village. Like many others, it became wealthy in the Middle Ages because of wool. The little
River Windrush runs through Bourton, crossed by low stone bridges;
it's as pretty as it sounds. This village makes a good touring base and

8

CLOSE UP

Antiques and Markets in the Cotswolds

The Cotswolds contain one of the largest concentrations of art and antiques dealers outside London. The famous antiques shops here are, it is sometimes whispered, "temporary storerooms" for the great families of the region, filled with tole-ware, treen, faience firedogs, toby jugs, and silhouettes, plus country furniture, and ravishing 17th- to 19th-century furniture. The center of antiquing is Stow-on-the-Wold, in terms of volume of dealers. Other towns that have a number of antiques shops are Burford, Cirencester, Tetbury, and Moreton-in-Marsh. The Cotswolds have few of those "anything in this tray for £10" shops, however. For information about dealers and special events, contact the **Cotswold Antique Dealers' Association** (*CADA* ✉ *Broadwell*

House, Sheep St., Stow-on-the-Wold ☎ *07789/968319* ⊕ *www.cotswolds-antiques-art.com*), which represents more than 40 dealers in the area.

As across England, many towns in the region have market days, when you can purchase local produce (including special treats ranging from Cotswold cheeses to fruit juices), crafts, and items such as clothes, books, and toys. Attending a farmers' market or a general market is a great way to mingle with the locals and perhaps find a special treasure or a tasty treat. Head for Moreton-in-Marsh on Tuesday and Cirencester on Friday and some Saturdays; tourist information offices have information on market days, or check out **Country Markets** (⊕ *www.country-markets.co.uk*).

has a collection of quirky small museums, but in summer it can be overcrowded. A stroll through Bourton takes you past stone cottages, many converted to small stores and coffee shops.

GETTING HERE AND AROUND

Bourton-on-the-Water is served by Pulhams and Sons Coaches from Stow-on-the-Wold, Moreton-in-Marsh, Cirencester, and Cheltenham. By car, take A40 and A436 from Cheltenham. You may find parking in the center, but if not use the lot outside the village.

ESSENTIALS

Visitor Information Bourton-on-the-Water (✉ *Victoria St.* ☎ *01451/820211* ⊕ *www.bourtoninfo.com*).

EXPLORING

⏲ The **Cotswold Motoring Museum and Toy Collection**, housed in an old mill, contains more than 30 vintage motor vehicles and a collection of old advertising signs (supposedly the largest in Europe), as well as two caravans (trailers) from the 1920s, ancient bicycles, and children's toys. ✉ *Sherborne St.* ☎ *01451/821255* ⊕ *www.cotswold-motor-museum. co.uk* 🖃 *£4.10* ☾ *Mid-Feb.–early Dec., daily 10–6.*

⏲ The **Model Railway Exhibition** displays more than 40 British and Continental trains running on 500 square feet of scenic layout. There are plenty of trains and toys to buy in the shop. ✉ *Box Bush, High St.* ☎ *01451/820686* ⊕ *www.bourtonmodelrailway.co.uk* 🖃 *£2.50* ☾ *June–Aug., daily 11–5; Sept.–May, weekends 11–5 (call ahead in Jan.).*

An outdoor reproduction of Bourton, the **Model Village** was built in 1937 to a scale of one-ninth; you can walk through it. ⊠ *Old New Inn* 🕾 *01451/820467* ⊕ *www.theoldnewinn.co.uk* 🖃 *£3.50* ☉ *Late Mar.– Oct., daily 10–5:45; Nov.–late Mar., daily 10–3:45.*

WHERE TO STAY

££ 🔡 **Chester House Hotel.** Just steps from the River Windrush, this traditional stone building has been tastefully adapted with contemporary fittings and style. The open-plan bar and lounge area invites lingering on its comfy sofas. Guest rooms, in the main building or in the coach house, are modern, clean, and quiet. Across the road, the hotel operates The Croft, the pick of the places to eat in the village. **Pros:** friendly staff; stylish rooms. **Cons:** busy on weekends; coach house rooms overlook car park. ⊠ *Victoria St.* 🕾 *01451/820286* ⊕ *www.chesterhousehotel. com* 🛏 *22 rooms* ☖ *In-room: no a/c, Wi-Fi (some). In-hotel: restaurant, bar, Wi-Fi hotspot, parking (free), some pets allowed* ⊟ *AE, MC, V* ❑❑ *BP.*

SHOPPING

The **Cotswold Perfumery** carries many perfumes that are manufactured here, and also stocks perfume bottles and jewelry. You can exercise your olfactory skills in the Perfumed Garden, part of a prebooked factory tour that takes in the laboratory, compounding room, and bottling process. ⊠ *Victoria St.* 🕾 *01451/820698* 🖃 *Factory tour £5* ☉ *Mon.–Sat. 9:30–5:30, Sun. 10:30–5:30 (closes at 5 in winter).*

LOWER SLAUGHTER AND UPPER SLAUGHTER

Fodor's Choice *2 mi north of Bourton-on-the-Water, 15 mi east of Cheltenham.*

★ To see the quieter, more typical Cotswold villages, seek out the evocatively named Lower Slaughter and Upper Slaughter (the names have nothing to do with mass murder, but come from the Saxon word *sloh*, which means "a marshy place"). Lower Slaughter is one of the "water villages," with Slaughter Brook running down the center road of the town. Little stone footbridges cross the brook, and the town's resident gaggle of geese can often be seen paddling through the sparkling water. Lower and Upper Swell are two other quiet towns to explore.

EXPLORING

Connecting the two Slaughters is **Warden's Way** (⊕ *www.cotswoldsaonb. org.uk*), a mile-long pathway that begins in Upper Slaughter at the town-center parking lot and passes stone houses, green meadows, ancient trees, and a 19th-century corn mill with a waterwheel and brick chimney. Warden's Way continues south to Bourton-on-the-Water; the full walk from Winchcombe to Bourton is 14 mi. You can pick up an itinerary from Winchcombe's tourist office.

WHERE TO STAY

££££–£££££ 🔡 **Lords of the Manor Hotel.** A fishing stream winds through the rolling fields that surround this rambling 17th-century manor house with Victorian additions. It offers comfort and a warm welcome in a quintessential Cotswold village, with a choice of traditional bedrooms in the main house or more modern ones in the converted granary and barn.

Country-house chintzes and antiques set the style in the bedrooms and in the acclaimed restaurant, which has creative British-French fixed-price menus (£££££). Ask about midweek rates that include dinner. **Pros:** heavenly setting; seamless service; outstanding food. **Cons:** expensive extras; some rooms lack charm; two-night minimum stay on weekends. ⊠ *Upper Slaughter* ☎ *01451/820243* ⊕ *www.lordsofthemanor. com* 📮 *26 rooms* ὑ *In-room: no a/c, DVD. In-hotel: restaurant, bar, Wi-Fi hotspot* ☰ *AE, DC, MC, V* ◎ *BP.*

NORTHLEACH

7 mi southwest of Lower and Upper Slaughter, 14 mi southeast of Cheltenham.

Just off the Fosse Way (and bypassed by the busy A40), little Northleach—population around 2,000—has remained one of the least spoiled of Cotswold towns. Trim cottages, many with traditional stone-tile roofs, line the streets that converge on the spacious central square. By the 13th century Northleach had acquired substantial wealth thanks to the wool trade. The wool of the local Cotswold Lion sheep (so called because of their thick, manelike fleeces) was praised above all other by weavers in Flanders, to whom it was exported.

GETTING HERE AND AROUND

Pulhams and Sons Coaches links Northleach with Bourton-on-the-Water, and Swanbrook buses run from Cheltenham. It's an out-of-the-way village—signposted from A40 and A429—where you should be able to park near the central square and walk to the sights.

EXPLORING

The 15th-century church of **St. Peter and St. Paul,** with its soaring pillars and clerestory windows, contains notable memorial brasses, monuments to the merchants who endowed the church; each merchant has a wool sack and sheep at his feet. ⊠ *Mill End* ☎ *01451/860314* 🎟 *Free* ☼ *Apr.–Oct., daily 8–6; Nov.–Mar., daily 8–dusk.*

At **Keith Harding's World of Mechanical Music,** the diverting tour lets you hear pianolas, music boxes, and other mechanical instruments from times past. You can even listen to the maestros Grieg, Paderewski, Rachmaninov, and Gershwin on piano rolls. The shop stocks antique and modern music boxes and more. ⊠ *The Oak House, High St.* ☎ *01451/860181* ⊕ *www. mechanicalmusic.co.uk* 🎟 *£8* ☼ *Daily 10–5; last tour at 4.*

> ## COTSWOLD WALKS
>
> Short walks thread the gentle countryside and are a great way to appreciate the Cotswolds, an **Area of Outstanding National Beauty** (⊕ *www.cotswoldsaonb. org.uk*). Tourist information centers carry walking maps and have information about longer trails. You can also track the rivers on which many towns are built, following the **towpaths** that run near the water. The **Cotswold Way** (⊕ *www.nationaltrail.co.uk*), a 100-mi national trail between Bath and Chipping Campden, traces the ridge marking the edge of the Cotswolds and the Severn Valley and has incomparable views. You can walk just part of it.

WHERE TO EAT AND STAY

£££ ✕ **Wheatsheaf Inn.** This traditional pub has a cool, modern coffee
MODERN BRITISH lounge and adjoining restaurant specializing in Modern British fare.
On the menu you might such light dishes as Cornish mussels or wild
mushroom soup, and more substantial fare might include roast pork
loin with fennel, parsley, and cockles. The inn also offers nine stylish,
uncluttered bedrooms (££). ⊠ *West End* ☎ *01451/860244* ⊕ *www.
cotswoldswheatsheaf.com* ⊟ *AE, MC, V.*

££ 🖭 **Yew Tree Cottage.** For a peaceful stay in a traditional Cotswold cottage, you can't beat this guesthouse. Located in the hamlet of Turkdean,
a couple of miles northwest of Northleach, the house has spotless bedrooms overlooking an immaculate garden. In the morning you'll wake
to the sounds of sheep and birds and feast on breakfasts of homemade
breads, jams, and compotes using seasonal fruit. **Pros:** full of character;
charming hostess. **Cons:** a bit remote; dogs in the house. ⊠ *Turkdean*
☎ *01451/860222* ⊕ *www.bestcotswold.com* ⇦ *2 rooms* ⚴ *In-room: no
a/c, no phone, Wi-Fi. In-hotel: Internet terminal, Wi-Fi hotspot, some
pets allowed, no kids under 16* ⊟ *AE, MC, V* 🍽 *BP.*

BURFORD

*9 mi east of Northleach, 18 mi north of Swindon, 18 mi west of
Oxford.*

Burford's broad main street leads steeply down to a narrow bridge
across the River Windrush. The village served as a stagecoach stop for
centuries and has many historic inns; it's now a popular stop for tour
buses and seekers of antiques.

ESSENTIALS

Visitor Information Burford (⊠ *The Brewery, Sheep St.* ☎ *01993/823558*
⊕ *www.oxfordshirecotswolds.org*).

EXPLORING

Hidden away at the end of a lane at the bottom of High Street is the
splendid parish church of **St. John**, its interior a warren of arches, chapels, and shrines. The church was remodeled in the 15th century from
Norman beginnings. Among the monuments is one dedicated to Henry
VIII's barber, Edmund Harman, that depicts four Amazonian Indians;
it's said to be the first depiction of native people from the Americas in
Britain. Look also for the elaborate Tanfield monument and its poignant
widow's epitaph. ⊠ *Church Green* ☎ *01993/822275* 🎫 *Free* ☉ *Apr.–
Oct., daily 9–5; Nov.–Mar., daily 9–4.*

WHERE TO EAT AND STAY

£££ ✕ **The Angel at Burford.** Contemporary dishes you might see at the farm-
MODERN BRITISH house-style tables of this informal brasserie in a 16th-century coaching inn include salmon fillet with risotto or roast breast of pheasant
with honeyed parsnip mash. Upstairs, the three delightful guest rooms
(££) are furnished in different styles: Indian in rich reds, French with
wooden sleigh bed, or cool-blue contemporary Italian. ⊠ *14 Witney St.*
☎ *01993/822714* ⊕ *www.theangelatburford.co.uk* ⊟ *MC, V.*

8

££££ ⌂ **Burford House.** Family photographs, old books, and toys scattered throughout this 17th-century building make it feel more like home than a hotel. The richly decorated bedrooms, filled with antiques, come with freestanding baths and power showers. Intimate sitting rooms and a courtyard garden add to the charm. Lunch and afternoon tea are offered, and you can arrange evening meals on Thursday, Friday, and Saturday. **Pros:** welcoming ambience; lots of character; great dinners. **Cons:** housekeeping sometimes lapses; traffic noise in front rooms; no parking. ⊠ *99 High St.* ☎ *01993/823151* ⊕ *www.burford-house.co.uk* ⌐ *8 rooms* ⌂ *In-room: no a/c, DVD, Internet, Wi-Fi. In-hotel: restaurant, bar, Wi-Fi hotspot* ⊟ *AE, MC, V* ⎮⊚⎮ *BP.*

BIBURY

10 mi southwest of Burford, 6 mi northeast of Cirencester, 15 mi north of Swindon.

The tiny town of Bibury, with a population of less than 1,000, sits idyllically beside the little River Coln on B4425; it was famed Arts and Crafts designer William Morris's choice for Britain's most beautiful village. Fine old cottages, a river meadow, and the church of St. Mary's are some of the delights here.

EXPLORING

Arlington Row is a famously pretty and much-photographed group of 17th-century weavers' cottages made of stone.

☺ The remains of a mile of walls are what's left of **Chedworth Roman Villa,** one of the largest Roman villas in England, beautifully set in a wooded valley on the eastern fringe of the Cotswolds. Thirty-two rooms, including two complete bath suites, have been identified, and the colorful mosaics are some of the most complete in England. Audio guides are available, and the visitor center and museum give a detailed picture of Roman life in Britain. ■**TIP**➔ **Look carefully for the signs for the villa: from Bibury, go across A429 to Yanworth and Chedworth. The villa is also signposted from A40.** The site is 6 mi northwest of Bibury and 10 mi southeast of Cheltenham. ⊠ *Yanworth* ☎ *01242/890256* ⊕ *www. nationaltrust.org.uk* ⌐ *£6.30* ⊙ *Mid-Mar.–late Mar. and early Nov.– mid-Nov., Tues.–Sun. 10–4; late Mar.–Oct., Tues.–Sun. 10–5.*

QUICK BITES

For a fireside pint, a sandwich, or a hearty meal, the **Seven Tuns** (⊠ *Queen St., Chedworth* ☎ *01285/720242*) fits the bill—a traditional pub with a strong menu and outdoor seating. It sits just a short drive from the Roman villa, by a splashing stream and a handsome Perpendicular church.

WHERE TO STAY

£££–££££ ⌂ **Swan Hotel.** Crystal chandeliers and displays of plates and glassware adorn this mid-17th-century coaching inn on the banks of the River Coln. Guest rooms, all different though most are traditional in style, come with splendid modern bathrooms—Room 3 is dramatically tiled in black and white. The formal Gallery restaurant has fixed-price dinners, and there are also meals at the cheerful, cheaper Café Swan. **Pros:** idyllic spot; lovely rooms. **Cons:** busy with day-trippers on weekends;

restaurant can be disappointing. ✉ *Off B4425* ☎ *01285/740695* ⊕ *www.cotswold-inns-hotels.co.uk* ⤴ *18 rooms, 1 suites* & *In-room: no a/c, Wi-Fi. In-hotel: 2 restaurants, bar, Wi-Fi hotspot, some pets allowed* ⊟ *AE, MC, V* ⊚| *BP.*

CIRENCESTER

9 mi south of Chedworth, 14 mi southeast of Cheltenham.

Cirencester (pronounced sirensester) has been a hub of the Cotswolds since Roman times, when it was called Corinium; the town was second only to Londinium (London) in importance. It sits at the intersection of two major Roman roads, the Fosse Way and Ermin Street (today A429 and A417). In the Middle Ages Cirencester grew rich on wool, which funded its 15th-century parish church. Today this old market town is the area's largest, with a population of 19,000. It preserves many mellow stone buildings dating mainly from the 17th and 18th centuries, and bow-fronted shops that still have one foot in the past.

GETTING HERE AND AROUND

Cirencester has hourly bus service from Cheltenham, and less frequent service from Moreton-in-Marsh, Stow-on-the-Wold, Tetbury, and Gloucester. By road, the town can be accessed on A417, A419, and A429. Its compact center is easily walkable.

ESSENTIALS

Visitor Information Cirencester (✉ *Corinium Museum, Park St.* ☎ *01285/654180* ⊕ *www.cotswold.gov.uk*).

EXPLORING

At the top of Market Place is the magnificent Gothic parish church of **St. John the Baptist,** known as the cathedral of the "woolgothic" style. Its elaborate, three-tier, three-bay south porch, the largest in England, once served as the town hall. The chantry chapels and many coats of arms bear witness to the importance of the wool merchants as benefactors of the church. A rare example of a 15th-century wineglass pulpit sits in the nave. ✉ *Market Pl.* ☎ *01285/659317* 🎫 *Free, £3 donation suggested* ⊙ *Mon.–Sat. 10–5 (10–4 in winter), Sun. 2:15–5.*

★ Not much of the Roman town remains visible, but the **Corinium Museum** displays an outstanding collection of Roman artifacts, including jewelry and coins, as well as mosaic pavements and full-scale reconstructions of local Roman interiors. Spacious galleries explore the town's history in Roman and Anglo-Saxon times and in the 18th century; they include plenty of hands-on exhibits. ✉ *Park St.* ☎ *01285/655611* ⊕ *www.cotswold.gov.uk* 🎫 *£4.50* ⊙ *Mon.–Sat. 10–5, Sun. 2–5.*

WHERE TO EAT AND STAY

£££
ITALIAN
✕ **Barnsley House.** Fine dining in the Cotswolds doesn't get much better than at this honey-and-cream Georgian mansion, the former home of garden designer Rosemary Verey. Discreetly modernized, the building has jettisoned none of its charm. The well-tended gardens, overlooked by the dining room, continue to be an attraction. The menus reveal a strong Italian and Mediterranean influence in dishes like the classic *vincisgrassi* (baked pasta with Parma ham, porcini mushrooms, and

CLOSE UP

That Special Cotswold Stone

If there's one feature of the Cotswold landscape that sums up its special flavor, it's the oolitic limestone that is the area's primary building material. This stone can be seen in everything from drystone walls (whose total length in the region is said to equal or exceed that of the Great Wall of China) to snug cottages and manor houses. Even roof tiles are fashioned from the stone, contributing to a harmonious ensemble despite the different ages of the buildings.

Malleable when first quarried, and gradually hardening with age, the stone lends itself to every use. During the late-medieval heyday of the great churches funded by wool merchants, it was used to brilliant effect in the mullions, gargoyles, and other intricate decorations on ecclesiastical buildings. Some quarries are still

active, producing stone that is used mainly for restoration and repair purposes. The varying colors of the stone are caused by impurities in the rock. They include the honey hues of the northern reaches of the Cotswolds, and modulate to a more golden tone in the central area, with a paler hue in and around Bath.

Writer and commentator J.B. Priestley, however, wrote of Cotswold stone that "the truth is that it has no color that can be described. Even when the sun is obscured and the light is cold, these walls are still faintly warm and luminous, as if they knew the trick of keeping the lost sunlight of centuries glimmering about them." Walk or drive around Cotswold villages and towns for even a day, and you will know what he meant.

---

truffles). The desserts include such extravagances as clementine parfait with pistachio and citrus salad and panna cotta with blueberry compote. Chic, pricey rooms (£££££) are also available. ⊠ *B4425, 4 mi northeast of Cirencester, Barnsley* ☎ *01285/740000* ⊕ *www.barnsleyhouse.com* ⚑ *Reservations essential* ⊟ *AE, MC, V.*

£££ ✕**Wild Duck Inn.** The deep-red dining room of this Elizabethan inn 3
BRITISH mi southwest of Cirencester has an abundance of wood beams and oil portraits. Fresh fish is a strong suit here—try it in a beer batter—or sample such meat dishes as roast lamb. There's a garden for alfresco dining. Upstairs are 12 small but comfortable guest rooms (££–£££), traditionally furnished and most with four-posters. ⊠ *Off A429, Ewen* ☎ *01285/770310* ⊕ *www.thewildduckinn.co.uk* ⊟ *AE, MC, V.*

£ ⚏ **Ivy House.** Delicious breakfasts and friendly owners enhance a stay at this stone Victorian house, close to the center of town. The B&B's simple bedrooms, done up in pastels, are an excellent value, with double-glazed windows to block out traffic noise. Cyclists and walkers are welcomed. **Pros:** central location; child-friendly atmosphere. **Cons:** on a main road; two-night minimum stay on weekends in summer. ⊠ *2 Victoria Rd.* ☎ *01285/656626* ⊕ *www.ivyhousecotswolds.com* ⚑ *4 rooms* ⚐ *In-room: no a/c, no phone, Wi-Fi. In-hotel: parking (free)* ⊟ *MC, V* ⚏*BP.*

NIGHTLIFE AND THE ARTS

New Brewery Arts (✉ *Brewery Ct.* ☎ *01285/657181*) includes a theater, exhibition space, and a café.

SPORTS AND THE OUTDOORS

☺ You can indulge in water sports such as waterskiing and windsurfing at the **Cotswold Water Park,** 4 mi south of Cirencester. This group of 140 lakes covers 40 square mi and has multiple entrances. There's swimming May through September; the park also draws wildlife enthusiasts, walkers, cyclists, and kayakers. You pay individual charges for the activities, and you can rent equipment on-site. ✉ *Gateway Centre, B4696 (off A419), South Cerney* ☎ *01793/752413* ⊕ *www.waterpark. org* ✑ *Free* ☉ *Apr. and Sept., daily 9–7; May, daily 9–8; June–Aug., daily 9–9; Oct.–Mar., daily 9–5.*

SHOPPING

The **Corn Hall** (✉ *Market Place*) is the venue for a food market on Thursday, an antiques market on Friday, and a crafts market on Saturday. Every Monday and Friday, Cirencester's central **Market Place** is packed with stalls selling a motley assortment of goods, mainly household items but some local produce and crafts, too. A farmers' market takes place here every second and fourth Saturday of the month. **William H. Stokes** (✉ *6–8 Dollar St.* ☎ *01285/653907*) specializes in oak furniture from the 16th and 17th centuries.

PAINSWICK

16 mi northwest of Cirencester, 8 mi southwest of Cheltenham, 5 mi south of Gloucester.

An old Cotswold wool town of around 2,000 inhabitants, Painswick has become a chocolate-box picture of quaintness, attracting day-trippers and tour buses. But come during the week and you can discover the place in relative tranquillity. The huddled gray stone houses and inns date from as early as the 14th century and include a notable group from the Georgian era. The churchyard of St. Mary's is renowned for its table tombs and monuments and its 100 yew trees planted in 1792.

GETTING HERE AND AROUND

Painswick is on A46 between Stroud and Cheltenham, and is reachable from Gloucester on B4073. The village has hourly bus connections with Stroud (10 minutes), Cheltenham (30 minutes), and Gloucester (55 minutes), with reduced service on Sunday.

ESSENTIALS

Visitor Information Painswick (✉ *Town Hall, Victoria St.* ☎ *0750/351–6924* ⊕ *www.visitthecotswolds.org.uk*).

EXPLORING

The **Painswick Rococo Garden,** ½ mi north of town, is a delightful survivor from the exuberant rococo period of English garden design (1720–60). After 50 years in its original form, the 6-acre garden became overgrown with woodland. Beginning in 1984, after the rediscovery of a 1748 painting of the garden by Thomas Robins, the garden was restored. Now you can view the original architectural structures—such as the vaguely Gothic Eagle House and Exedra—and asymmetrical vistas. There are also a restaurant and a shop. ⊠ *B4073* ☎ *01452/813204* ⊕ *www.rococogarden.org.uk* ⊒ *£6* ☉ *Early Jan.–Oct., daily 11–6; last admission at 5.*

WHERE TO STAY

££ ★ ▥ **Cardynham House.** In the heart of the village, this 15th- to 16th-century former wool merchant's house, which retains its beamed ceilings, Jacobean staircase, and Elizabethan fireplace, has four-poster beds in almost all its rooms. The accommodations have creative themes such as the Medieval Garden, Dovecote, and Arabian Nights; one pricier option has a private pool. The adjoining restaurant serves simple English and European dishes. **Pros:** friendly welcome; heaps of character; abundant breakfast. **Cons:** some low ceilings; slightly worn around the edges. ⊠ *The Cross* ☎ *01452/814006, 01452/810030 restaurant* ⊕ *www.cardynham.co.uk* ⇆ *9 rooms* ♦ *In-room: no a/c, Internet. In-hotel: restaurant* ⊟ *AE, MC, V* ▯⦿▯ *BP.*

OWLPEN

★ *10 mi southwest of Painswick.*

Prince Charles described the beauty spot of Owlpen, an off-the-beaten-path hamlet, as "the epitome of the English village." First settled in Saxon days as Olla's Pen (meaning "valley"), the village centers on a church, a Tudor manor house, and pearl-gray stone cottages, all set against a hillside. A graceful grouping of tithe barns, garden buildings, and a gristmill softens the seignorial bearing of the manor house.

EXPLORING

The triple-gabled stone **Owlpen Manor** was built between 1450 and 1616, but was restored in the 1920s by local Arts and Crafts artisans, who also created some of the furnishings. Today Nicholas and Karin Mander live here with their family. Inside are oak chests fashioned by William Morris, family portraits, painted cloths from the Tudor and Stuart eras, and Queen Margaret's Room, said to be haunted by the spirit of Margaret of Anjou, wife of Henry VI, who visited here during the Wars of the Roses. You can also explore the terraced garden with its yew topiary, the envy of gardening masters. Note that the house will be closed for refurbishment until 2011 or 2012, but the gardens will remain open. ⊠ *Off B4066, near Uley* ☎ *01453/860261* ⊕ *www.owlpen.com* ⊒ *Gardens £4* ☉ *May–Sept., Mon., Wed., and Thurs. noon–5.*

TETBURY

6 mi southeast of Owlpen, 8 mi southwest of Cirencester, 12 mi south of Painswick.

Tetbury, with about 5,300 inhabitants, claims right royal connections. Indeed, the soaring spire of the church that presides over this Elizabethan market town is within sight of Highgrove House, the Prince of Wales's abode (not open to the public). The town is known as one of the area's antiques centers.

ESSENTIALS

Visitor Information Tetbury (✉ *33 Church St.* ☎ *01666/503552* ⊕ *www. visittetbury.co.uk*).

EXPLORING

In the center of the village, look for the eye-catching, white-painted stone **Market House** on Market Square, dating from 1655 and built up on rows of Tuscan pillars. Various markets are held here during the week.

The church of **St. Mary the Virgin** (✉ *Church St.* ☎ *01666/502333*), in 18th-century neo-Gothic style, has a galleried interior with pews.

QUICK BITES

Just steps from Market House, **Blue Zucchini** (✉ *7–9 Church St.* ☎ *01666/505852*) is a brasserie that makes a relaxed spot for coffee, light lunches, and afternoon tea. The interior has wooden floorboards and sofas, and you can dine alfresco at tables in the front and in the patio garden.

★ The 600-acre **Westonbirt National Arboretum**, 3 mi southwest of Tetbury (and about 10 mi north of Bath), contains one of the most extensive collections of trees and shrubs in Europe; it's a lovely place to spend an hour or two. The best times to come for color are in late spring, when the rhododendrons, azaleas, and magnolias are blooming, and in fall, when the maples come into their own. A gift shop, café, and restaurant are on the grounds. Open-air concerts take place in summer, and there are exhibitions throughout the year. ✉ *Off A433, near Tetbury* ☎ *01666/880220* ⊕ *www.forestry.gov.uk/westonbirt* 🎟 *£6 Jan. and Feb.; £8 Mar.–Nov.; Dec., free* ⊗ *Apr.–Nov., weekdays 9–8 or dusk, weekends 8–8 or dusk; Dec.–Mar., weekdays 9–5 or dusk, weekends 8–5 or dusk.*

One of the last English country houses constructed using traditional methods and materials, **Rodmarton Manor** (built 1909–29) is furnished with specially commissioned pieces in the Arts and Crafts style. Ernest Barnsley, a follower of William Morris, worked on the house and gardens. The notable gardens—wild, winter, sunken, and white—are divided into "rooms" bounded by hedges of holly, beech, and yew. The manor is 5 mi northeast of Tetbury. ✉ *Off A433, Rodmarton* ☎ *01285/841253* ⊕ *www.rodmarton-manor.co.uk* 🎟 *£8; garden only, £5* ⊗ *May–Sept., Wed., Sat., and national holidays 2–5.*

8

WHERE TO EAT AND STAY

££££   ✕ **The Chef's Table.** On Tetbury's Antiques Alley, this trendy eatery is a
MODERN BRITISH   blend of farmhouse kitchen and designer chic, with a few tables and
chairs next to an open kitchen. You can come for breakfast, snack
lunches, or more substantial fare such as wild mushroom risotto or crab
thermidor. Reserve ahead because of the limited dining space. If you
can't get a seat, however, do not despair—the downstairs delicatessen
supplies a lip-smacking range of cheeses, hams, and organic breads for
a takeout lunch. ✉ *49 Long St.* ☎ *01666/504466* ⊕ *www.thechefstable.
co.uk* ☰ *MC, V* ⊘ *Closed Sun. No dinner Mon. and Tues.*

£££££   🖫 **Calcot Manor.** Comfortable country-house furnishings in pale-hued
☾   rooms characterize this former farmhouse and the surrounding converted barns and stables. This is a family-friendly establishment with a
high-tech children's play area as well as the usual luxurious spa. Guest
rooms are airy and spacious; family suites have bunk beds in a separate
room and refrigerators. Dishes at the elegant Conservatory restaurant
(£££–££££) are a blend of traditional and modern elements, whereas the
Gumstool Inn provides more farmhouse-style fare; dinner is included in
the price on weekends and during the peak summer period. The hotel is
3 mi west of town. **Pros:** delightful rural setting; good choice of activities; children love it. **Cons:** most rooms are separate from main building;
patchy service. ✉ *A4135* ☎ *01666/890391* ⊕ *www.calcotmanor.co.uk*
📞 *26 rooms, 9 suites* ♿ *In-room: no a/c, safe, refrigerator, Wi-Fi. In-
hotel: 2 restaurants, bars, tennis courts, pool, gym, spa, Wi-Fi hotspot*
☰ *AE, DC, MC, V* ⎟◎⎟ *BP.*

SHOPPING

Tetbury is home to more than 30 antiques shops, some of which are
incorporated into small malls.

Highgrove Shop (✉ *10 Long St.* ☎ *01666/505666*) sells organic products
and gifts inspired by Prince Charles's interests. **House of Cheese** (✉ *13
Church St.* ☎ *01666/502865*) retails fine, farm-produced cheeses, all
wonderfully fresh and flavorsome. Pâtés, preserves, and chocolates
are other goodies at this tiny shop. **Long Street Antiques** (✉ *14 Long St.*
☎ *01666/500850*) houses more than 40 dealers specializing in everything from jewelry to oak and mahogany furniture.

GLOUCESTER TO THE FOREST OF DEAN

West of the Cotswolds a rather urbanized axis connects Gloucester
with Cheltenham. Despite their proximity on either side of the M5
motorway, the towns are very different; the down-to-earth Gloucester,
built around docks connected to the River Severn, contrasts with the
gentrified spa town of Cheltenham. North of Gloucester lies the riverside town of Tewkesbury with its imposing abbey; to the south, easily
accessible from M5, stands battlemented Berkeley Castle. Southwest of
Gloucester, the low-lying Forest of Dean (officially the Royal Forest of
Dean), once a private hunting ground of kings, is now a recreation area
for the public, with some of the country's most beautiful woodlands.

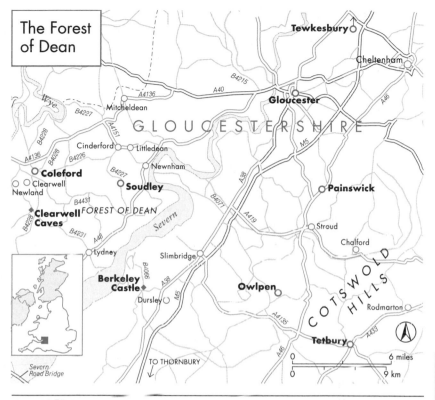

GLOUCESTER

13 mi southwest of Cheltenham, 56 mi south of Birmingham, 105 mi west of London.

Although much of the ancient heritage of this county seat has been lost to nondescript modern stores and offices, Gloucester (population about 111,000) has a number of worthwhile sights, most notably its cathedral.

GETTING HERE AND AROUND

Gloucester can be reached on trains from London Paddington, Bristol, Cheltenham, and Birmingham, and by bus on National Express and Megabus from London Victoria. The train and bus stations are close to each other near the center. The city is easily reached via the M5 motorway. Walking is the best way to tour the central sights—the dock area is 10 minutes southwest of the cathedral.

Between April and September, Gloucester Civic Trust organizes walking tours of the city (£3) that begin at 11:30 Monday to Saturday from St. Michael's Tower. There are also tours of the docks on most summer days, leaving from the Waterways Museum.

ESSENTIALS

Visitor and Tour Information Gloucester (✉ *28 Southgate St.*
☎ *01452/396572* ⊕ *www.thecityofgloucester.co.uk*). **Gloucester Civic Trust**
(☎ *01452/526955* ⊕ *www.gloucestercivictrust.org.uk*).

EXPLORING

★ Magnificent **Gloucester Cathedral**, with its soaring, elegant exterior, was
originally a Norman abbey church, consecrated in 1100. Reflecting
different periods, the cathedral mirrors perfectly the slow growth of
ecclesiastical taste and the development of the Perpendicular style. The
interior has largely been spared the sterilizing attentions of modern
architects and is almost completely Norman, with the massive pillars
of the nave left untouched since their completion. The fan-vaulted roof
of the 14th-century cloisters is the finest in Europe, and the cloisters
enclose a peaceful garden (used in the filming of *Harry Potter and the
Sorcerer's Stone*). ■ **TIP→ Don't miss the Whispering Gallery, which has a
permanent exhibition devoted to the splendid, 14th-century stained glass of
the Great East Window.** Tours of the tower (269 steps up) are also available. ✉ *Westgate St.* ☎ *01452/528095* ⊕ *www.gloucestercathedral.org.
uk* ✉ *£5 donation requested, photography permit £5. Tower tours £3,
exhibition £2* ☉ *Daily 7:30–6, except during services and special events.
Tower tours Apr.–Oct., Wed.–Fri. 2:30, Sat. and national holidays 1:30
and 2:30; also Mon. and Tues. at 2:30 during school vacations. Whispering Gallery Apr.–Oct., weekdays 10:30–4, Sat. 10:30–3:30.*

**▮ QUICK
BITES**

After a visit to the cathedral, drop in at Lily's Restaurant (✉ *5A College Ct.*
☎ *01452/307060* ☉ *Closed Sun.*) for a relaxed morning coffee, afternoon
cream tea, or lunch of quiche or shepherd's pie. The tearoom and restaurant is in a narrow alley just steps from the cathedral, opposite the Beatrix
Potter shop and museum.

The **Gloucester Folk Museum**, close to the cathedral, fills a row of fine
Tudor and Jacobean half-timber houses. Exhibits on the Civil War,
crafts, and domestic life illustrate the history of Gloucester and the
surrounding areas, and one room has a Toys and Childhood gallery.
✉ *99–103 Westgate St.* ☎ *01452/396868* ⊕ *www.gloucester.gov.uk*
✉ *Free* ☉ *Tues.–Sat. 10–5.*

The historic **Gloucester Docks**, a short walk from the cathedral along the
canal, still function but now cater mainly to pleasure craft. The vast
Victorian warehouses have been restored, and a few shops and cafés
added, reviving the area. One warehouse is now the Antiques Centre,
and others hold good museums.

ⓒ
Fodor's Choice
★

The **National Waterways Museum**, in a converted Victorian warehouse,
contains examples of canal houseboats, including gaily painted "canal
ware"—ornaments and utensils found on barges. The three stories are
full of the sounds and smells of the docks and canals around Gloucester, enhanced by interactive gizmos. From dredger buckets to full-
size vessels moored at the two quaysides, the imaginatively presented
exhibits explain the role of canals in the 18th and 19th centuries. You
can try "walking the wall," the boatmen's way of propelling barges
through tunnels with their feet. From the **pier** outside the National

Waterways Museum, boats leave for a 45-minute tour of the Gloucester Docks or all-day cruises that head as far north as Tewkesbury or south to the Severn Estuary at Sharpness. ⊠ *Llanthony Warehouse, Llanthony Rd., Gloucester Docks* ☎ *01452/318200* ⊕ *www.nwm.org. uk* ⊠ *£4.25* ⊙ *Apr.–June, Sept., and Oct., weekdays 11–4:30, weekends 10:30–4:30; July and Aug., daily 10:30–5; Nov.–Mar., daily 11–4; last admission 1 hr before closing.*

WHERE TO EAT

£ ✕ **Robert Raikes' House.** Named after the founder of the Sunday school
BRITISH movement, this magnificently restored timber-framed pub offers a wealth of snug corners with armchairs and fireplaces. There's also a huge courtyard for alfresco dining. Samuel Smith's beers and ciders are ingredients in such dishes as cider chicken, steak and ale pie, and shepherd's pie, and there's a good selection of puddings. ⊠ *36–38 Southgate St.* ☎ *01452/526685* ▭ *MC, V* ⊙ *No dinner Sun.*

SHOPPING

The locals say it's best to look in Cheltenham and buy in Gloucester, where prices are lower. The more than 140 dealers in Gloucester Quays at the **Antiques Centre** (⊠ *99A High Orchard St.* ☎ *01452/529716*) offer some good buys on items—clocks, silver, china, military collectibles, and more—in a five-floor Victorian warehouse by the Gloucester Docks.

Ⓒ The **Beatrix Potter Shop and Museum** (⊠ *9 College Ct.* ☎ *01452/422856*), next to the Cathedral Gate, is in the house that served as a model for the tailor's house in Potter's illustrated children's story *The Tailor of Gloucester*. The shop sells Potter-related items, and the small museum upstairs is dedicated to the author and her works.

TEWKESBURY

12 mi northeast of Gloucester.

Tewkesbury, an ancient town of black-and-white half-timber buildings, as well as some fine Georgian ones, sits by the rivers Avon and Severn. Its centerpiece is its imposing Norman abbey.

GETTING HERE AND AROUND

Tewkesbury can be reached by rail via the nearby station of Ashchurch, connected to the center by frequent local buses. There is also regular bus service from Cheltenham and Gloucester. The town is easily reached from M5. Parking can usually be found near the center.

ESSENTIALS

Visitor Information Tewkesbury (⊠ *100 Church St.* ☎ *01684/855040* ⊕ *www. visitcotswoldsandsevernvale.gov.uk*).

EXPLORING

The stonework in the Norman **Tewkesbury Abbey** has much in common with that of Gloucester Cathedral, but this church was built in the Romanesque (12th century) and Decorated Gothic (14th century) styles. Its exterior makes an impressive sight, with the largest Norman tower in the world—148 feet high and 46 feet square—and the 65-foot-high arch of the west front. Fourteen stout Norman pillars and

8

myriad gilded bosses on the roof of the nave and choir (best viewed through a mirror on wheels) grace the beautifully kept interior. Abbey tours take place on weekdays between Easter and late October, usually at 11 and 2. Tower tours should be booked in advance. ⊠ *Church St.* ☎ *01684/850959* ⊕ *www.tewkesburyabbey.org.uk* ⊠ *£5 donation, tower tours £5* ۞ *Easter–Oct., Mon.–Sat. 7:30–6, Sun. 7:30–7; Nov.– Easter, Mon.–Sat. 7:30–5:30, Sun. 7:30–7.*

WHERE TO EAT

££
MODERN BRITISH

✕ **Owens.** This half-timbered café and bistro welcomes you with a beamed and pillared dining room that is warmed by a fire in winter. The menu blends French and British influences; lamb breast with potatoes baked in milk and cream is one tasty dish, as is roast pollock with brown shrimp accompanied by a turnip and potato terrine. There's an agonizing choice of luscious desserts, among them orange syrup cake with cinnamon yogurt, and white chocolate panna cotta. Near the abbey, this place is also a good choice for morning coffee and afternoon tea. ⊠ *73 Church St.* ☎ *01684/292703* ⊕ *www.eatatowens.co.uk* ⊟ *MC, V* ۞ *Closed Mon. No dinner Sun.*

SOUDLEY

27 mi southwest of Tewkesbury, 15 mi west of Gloucester.

Soudley has a museum that provides a useful introduction to the surrounding forest.

EXPLORING

★ The ancient **Forest of Dean** (⊕ *www.visitforestofdean.co.uk*) covers much of the valley between the rivers Severn and Wye. Although the primordial forest has long since been cut down and replanted, the landscape here remains one of strange beauty, hiding in its folds and under its hills deposits of iron, silver, and coal that have been mined for thousands of years. Of the original forest established in 1016 by King Canute, 27,000 acres are preserved by the Forestry Commission. It's still a source of timber, but parking lots and picnic grounds have been created and eight nature trails marked. ■ TIP➔ **For a driving tour of the forest, head to Littledean, where signs direct you through the best of the forest.** To get to Littledean from Soudley, backtrack north on B4227, and turn east on A4151.

۞ The **Dean Heritage Centre,** in a restored mill in a wooded valley on the
★ forest's eastern edge, tells the history of the forest, with reconstructions of a forester's cottage, a waterwheel, and a "beam engine" (a primitive steam engine used to pump water from flooded coal mines). Other galleries show art with local themes as well as furniture, ornaments, and the like made from local oak. Also within the grounds is a smallholding (a small farm), with a couple of resident Gloucestershire Old Spot pigs, and a charcoal burner's hut. Craftspeople work in the outbuildings. ⊠ *B4227, near Cinderford* ☎ *01594/822170* ⊕ *www. deanheritagemuseum.com* ⊠ *£4.90* ۞ *Mar.–Oct., daily 10–5; Nov.– Feb., daily 10–4.*

COLEFORD

5 mi west of Soudley, 10 mi south of Ross-on-Wye.

The area around Coleford, a large village of more than 8,000 people, is a maze of moss-covered rocks, huge ferns, and ancient yew trees—a shady haven on a summer's day.

GETTING HERE AND AROUND

From Gloucester, you can reach Coleford on A40/A4136. Stagecoach buses 30 and 31 leave from Gloucester every hour, taking about an hour (reduced service on Sunday).

EXPLORING

A visit to the spectacular **Clearwell Caves**, 1½ mi south of Coleford, provides insight into the region's mining for iron and coal, which went on continuously from Roman times to 1945. Ocher (for paint pigments and cosmetics) is still mined here. ⊠ *Off B4228* ☎ *01594/832535* ⊕ *www.clearwellcaves.co.uk* ⊠ *£5.80, £7.50 Christmas Fantasy displays* ⊗ *Mid-Feb.–Oct., daily 10–5; late Nov.–late Dec., Sun.–Thurs. 10–5, Fri. 10–8.*

WHERE TO STAY

££ ⚐ **Tudor Farmhouse.** Despite its name, this former farmhouse has some sections dating to the 13th century. Polished oak staircases, mullioned windows, and a huge stone fireplace in the sitting room imbue the place with plenty of charm. Most of the traditionally styled bedrooms are in a converted barn, and two have four-poster beds. The restaurant (£££££) serves good-quality fare using seasonal ingredients; there's a cheaper bar menu. **Pros:** lovely setting; pleasant staff; good food. **Cons:** often booked with wedding parties; poor soundproofing in some rooms. ⊠ *High St., near Coleford, Clearwell* ☎ *01594/833046* ⊕ *www.tudorfarmhousehotel.co.uk* ⇆ *18 rooms, 2 suites* ♿ *In-room: no a/c, Wi-Fi. In-hotel: restaurant, some pets allowed* ⊟ *AE, MC, V* ⚭ *BP.*

SPORTS AND THE OUTDOORS

The densely wooded Forest of Dean is quite special for walking, with interesting villages and monastic ruins. There are easy walks out of Newland, around New Fancy (great view) and Mallards Pike Lake, and there's a slightly longer one (three hours) that takes in Wench Ford, Danby Lodge, and Blackpool Bridge. The area has picnic grounds, car parking, and, hidden away, old pubs where you can wet your whistle. For information on hiking in the Forest of Dean, contact the **Forestry Commission** (⊠ *Bank House, Bank St., Coleford* ☎ *01594/833057* ⊕ *www.forestry.gov.uk*).

BERKELEY CASTLE

17 mi southwest of Gloucester, 21 mi north of Bristol.

EXPLORING

★ **Berkeley Castle**, in the sleepy village of Berkeley (pronounced *bark*-ley), is perfectly preserved, down to its medieval turrets, and full of family treasures. It witnessed the murder of King Edward II in 1327—the cell in which it occurred can still be seen. Edward was betrayed by his

French consort, Queen Isabella, and her paramour, the earl of Mortimer. Roger De Berkeley, a Norman knight, began work on the castle in 1153, and it has remained in the family ever since. Magnificent furniture, tapestries, and pictures fill the state apartments, but even the ancient buttery and kitchen are interesting. The surrounding meadows, now the setting for pleasant Elizabethan gardens that include a tropical Butterfly House, were once flooded to make a formidable moat. Special events take place from Easter to November. ⊠ *Off A38, Berkeley* ☎ *01453/810332* ⊕ *www.berkeley-castle.com* ⊒ *£7.50; gardens only, £4; Butterfly House only, £2* ⊗ *House and gardens: Apr., May, early Sept., and Oct., Thurs., Sun., and national holidays 11–5:30; June–early Sept., Sun.–Thurs. 11–5:30; last admission at 4:30.*

WHERE TO STAY

££   ⬚ **Drakestone House.** Lovely and reasonably priced, this Cotswold Arts and Crafts house 3 mi east of Berkeley has wooden floors and beamed and plasterwork ceilings. Fine antiques and period furniture complement the architecture, and in the impressive garden clipped yew hedges surround an immaculate lawn and sunken pond. If you have a car, it's a good place to get away from it all. **Pros:** beautiful furnishings; secluded setting. **Cons:** no evening diversions nearby; hard to find. ⊠ *Off B4060, Stinchcombe, Dursley* ☎☎ *01453/542140* ⊕ *www.wolseylodges.com* ⟿ *3 rooms* ⌂ *In-room: no a/c, no phone, no TV, Wi-Fi. In-hotel: Wi-Fi hotspot, some pets allowed* ⊟ *No credit cards* ⎯⎯ *BP.*

££££–£££££   ⬚ **Thornbury Castle.** An impressive lodging, Thornbury has everything a
★   genuine 16th-century Tudor castle needs: huge fireplaces, moody paintings, mullioned windows, and a large garden. There's also plenty of history: Henry VIII, Anne Boleyn, and Mary Tudor all spent time here. The standards of comfort are famous, and the pampering touches in the "bedchambers" include complimentary decanters of sherry and well-appointed bathrooms. People come from all over to dine in the restaurant, where you'll find sophisticated fare such as loin of venison, quail, and duck. The hotel is 12 mi north of Bristol. **Pros:** grand medieval surroundings; sumptuous rooms. **Cons:** many steps to climb; village of Thornbury is dull. ⊠ *Castle St., off A38, Thornbury* ☎ *01454/281182* ⊕ *www.thornburycastle.co.uk* ⟿ *22 rooms, 5 suites* ⌂ *In-room: no a/c, Internet. In-hotel: restaurant, bar, some pets allowed* ⊟ *AE, DC, MC, V* ⎯⎯ *BP.*

The Welsh Borders

BIRMINGHAM, WORCESTER, HEREFORD, SHREWSBURY, CHESTER

WORD OF MOUTH

"I lived in Brindleyplace in Birmingham. This is a great area with loads of restaurants and is effectively canal central (narrowboat tours of the canal system are always available) for the country. Also worth a visit is the Ikon art gallery. For great cheap Indian food, check out the Balti Triangle."

—crellston

"Ludlow is a lovely town with many half-timber buildings and a good range of shops. Our next stop was Stokesay Castle, not far from Ludlow. This building dated from around 1291, with a half-timber gatehouse. We then drove to Shrewsbury, a pleasant and bustling town that has retained quite a few of its medieval buildings."

—GregY2

Updated by
Paul Cannon

Some of England's prettiest countryside lies along the 108-mi border with Wales, which stretches from the town of Chepstow on the Severn estuary in the south to the appealing walled city of Chester in the north. Much of the land along this border, in the counties of Herefordshire, Shropshire, and southern Cheshire, is remote and tranquil, a sublimely underexplored patch of England that rewards closer inspection.

Herefordshire, in the south, is a county of rich, rolling countryside and river valleys, gradually opening out in the high hills and plateaus of Shropshire. North of the Shropshire hills, the gentler Cheshire plain stretches toward Liverpool and Manchester. This is dairy country, dotted with small villages and market towns that have many of the 13th- and 14th-century black-and-white, half-timber buildings typical of northwestern England. These are the legacy of a forested countryside. (The Victorians, however, are responsible for the more recent fashion of painting these structures black and white.) In the market towns of Chester and Shrewsbury, the more elaborately decorated half-timber buildings are monuments to wealth, dating mostly from the early 17th century. More half-timbered structures are found in Ludlow, now a culinary center nestled in the lee of its majestic ruined castle.

Today's rural peace belies a turbulent past, when relations between the English and the Welsh were difficult. The 177-mi Offa's Dyke Path, a National Trail that runs near the border (two-thirds is in Wales), follows part of the 8th-century earthen wall built by King Offa as protection against Welsh raiders. A string of medieval castles also bears witness to this history.

In the 18th century, one small corner of Shropshire heralded the tumultuous birth of the Industrial Revolution. Here, in a wooded stretch of the Severn Gorge, the coke blast furnace was invented and the first iron bridge was erected (1779). You can get a sense of this history at the museums at Ironbridge Gorge.

The ramifications of that technological leap led to the growth of Britain's second-largest city, Birmingham, the capital of the Midlands. Birmingham has transcended its reputation as one of the country's least attractive cities. Its industrial center inspired the heavy metal sound of Black Sabbath and haunted JRR Tolkien enough for him to create the dark realm of Mordor in *The Lord of the Rings*. Today an imaginative makeover and active, varied cultural life, together with its historic architecture, are draws for anyone interested in modern urban Britain.

TOP REASONS TO GO

The city of Birmingham: The revamped city center shows off its superb art collections and cultural facilities, international cuisine, and renowned Jewellery Quarter amid full-bodied redbrick architecture, a link to Birmingham's industrial heritage.

Taste of the East: Spice up your life and sample the swath of Indian restaurants in and around Birmingham. After all, a curry is now regarded as a traditional English dish.

Half-timber architecture: Black-and-white half-timber houses are a mark of pride throughout the region; there are notable concentrations of buildings from medieval times to the Jacobean era in Chester, Shrewsbury, and Ludlow.

Walks on the Malverns: Take inspiration as composer Elgar did, as you stride across these hills and look across the fields and orchards to the Cotswolds in the east and misty Welsh mountains to the west.

Ironbridge Gorge: Recall the burgeoning of England's Industrial Revolution at the complex of museums within the shadow of this graceful bridge, the first of its kind in the world.

ORIENTATION AND PLANNING

ORIENTATION

The main eastern gateway to the region is bustling Birmingham, one of the best places in England for the performing arts, but many people visiting the region are seeking rural peace rather than urban action. The city of Worcester, to the south, is renowned for its proud cathedral and fine bone china. Farther south and west, along the lovely Malvern Hills, lie the peaceful spa town of Great Malvern and the prosperous agricultural city of Hereford. West of Birmingham is Bewdley, a terminus of the Severn Valley Railway, and beyond, the West Midlands—birthplace of modern British industry. In the western part of the region, hugged by the River Severn, the small city of Shrewsbury is near a cluster of excellent Ironbridge museums interpreting the region's industrial heritage. To its south lies Ludlow, an architectural and culinary hot spot; at the northwestern edge of the region is the ancient city of Chester, popular with visitors.

Birmingham. On the eastern edge of the region, Britain's second-largest city, once known as "the city of 1,001 trades," now recalls its past through excellent museums and a network of canals. Business sets the pace here, but so do an adventurous arts program, buzzing nightlife, and an excellent restaurant scene.

Worcester, Hereford, and Environs. This is a region of historic cathedral towns—Worcester and Hereford—and bucolic villages set amid rolling meadows and lush orchards. The backdrop to it all is the volcanic ridges of the Malvern Hills, where you'll find genteel Great Malvern and Ledbury.

9

Shrewsbury to Chester. The northern, most varied part of the region, studded with its characteristic half-timber buildings, embraces the World Heritage Site of Ironbridge Gorge, the Shropshire hills, and ancient Shrewsbury and Chester, as well as Ludlow with its gastronomic delights.

PLANNING

WHEN TO GO

Most attractions are open and the countryside is most appealing in the warmer weather between April and September. The open-air performances at Ludlow Castle take place at the end of June; the Three Choirs Festival, rotating from year to year among Worcester (2011), Hereford, and Gloucester, is held in mid-August; and the Autumn in Malvern Festival happens on weekends in October. Most rural sights have limited opening hours in winter. Even in the towns and cities, the majority of attractions close at 5.

PLANNING YOUR TIME

Birmingham makes a logical base if you're looking for cosmopolitan city life. The museums and sights will take you a full day to explore, and from here Worcester and Avoncroft to the south, as well as Dudley and Lichfield to the north, are feasible day trips.

It's easy to reach the countryside from the smaller cities of Hereford, Worcester, and Chester, but if you want to walk the hills, Ludlow is a good gateway for Wenlock Edge, as is Great Malvern or Ledbury for the Malvern Hills.

To the north of the region, Ironbridge Gorge and Chester demand a full day each. Ludlow and Shrewsbury take less time, though it would be a shame to leave Ludlow without sampling its fine food and dining. Shrewsbury makes a good central base, from which Chester and the north are easily reached. Once you've gone as far north as this, you might consider going on to Liverpool, if the Beatles and maritime history have any appeal, or to north Wales.

GETTING HERE AND AROUND

AIR TRAVEL

The region is served by Birmingham International Airport, 6 mi east of the city center, and the country's second-busiest airport. It has connections to all of Britain's major cities, and limited service to the United States.

Contacts Birmingham International Airport (✉ *A45, off Junction 6 of M42* ☏ *0870/733–5511* ⊕ *www.bhx.co.uk*).

BUS TRAVEL

National Express runs buses from London's Victoria Coach Station. You can reach Birmingham in less than three hours; Hereford, Shrewsbury, and Worcester take between four and five hours. It also operates services from London's Heathrow (2¾ hours) and Gatwick (four hours) airports to Birmingham.

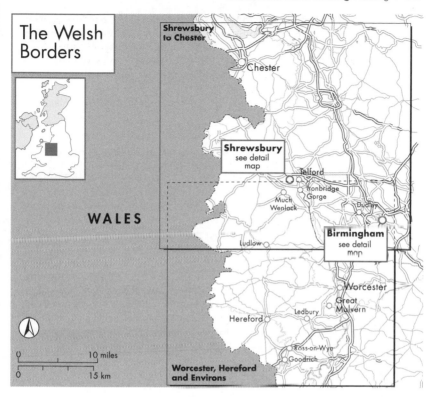

The Welsh Borders

Shrewsbury to Chester

Chester

Shrewsbury
see detail
map

Telford

Ironbridge
Gorge

Much
Wenlock

Dudley

WALES

Birmingham
see detail
map

Ludlow

Worcester

Great
Malvern

Ledbury

Hereford

Ross-on-Wye

Goodrich

0 ─── 10 miles
0 ─── 15 km

Worcester, Hereford and Environs

The First bus company has service between Birmingham, Worcester, Hereford, Kidderminster, and Ludlow.

Contacts First (☏ *0871/200–2233* ⊕ *www.firstgroup.com*). **National Express** (☏ *0871/781–8181* ⊕ *www.nationalexpress.com*).

CAR TRAVEL
Although all major towns are served by public transport, a car allows greater flexibility and the ability to get off the beaten track. To reach Birmingham (120 mi), Shrewsbury (150 mi), Ludlow (140 mi), and Chester (180 mi) from London, take M40 and keep on it until it becomes M42, or take M1/M6. M4 and then M5 from London take you to Worcester and Hereford in just under three hours. Driving can be difficult in the region's western reaches—especially in the hills and valleys west of Hereford, where steep, twisting roads often narrow down into mere trackways.

TRAIN TRAVEL
For travel to and between the main towns and cities, trains are more frequent and much quicker than the buses, though more expensive. From London, First Great Western and Arriva trains serve the region from Paddington Station, and Virgin, Central, and Silverlink trains leave from Euston (call National Rail Enquiries for information). Travel times are Paddington to Hereford, three hours, and Ludlow, 3¼ hours (both

changing at Newport); to Worcester, 2¼ hours; Euston to Birmingham, 1½ hours; Euston to Shrewsbury, with a change at Crewe or Birmingham, 2¾ hours; or to Chester, with a change at Crewe, 2¾ hours. West Midlands Day Ranger tickets (£16.80) and three- and seven-day Heart of England Rover tickets (£65.20 and £84.80) allow unlimited travel on trains throughout the region.

Contacts National Rail Enquiries (☎ *0845/748–4950* ⊕ *www.nationalrail. co.uk*).

RESTAURANTS

Birmingham has splendid international restaurants but is probably most famous for its Indian and Pakistani eateries; you'll find good choices both in the city center and out of town. The city has more Michelin-starred restaurants than any other British city outside of London and hosts the annual Taste of Birmingham Festival in July. In the rest of the area, casual spots dominate, though Ludlow is a culinary center.

HOTELS

The Welsh Borders are full of ancient inns and venerable Regency-style houses converted into hotels. Although some places are pricey, bargains can be found; Internet deals are always worth searching out. Birmingham's hotels, geared to the convention crowd and often booked up well in advance, are mostly bland and impersonal, but sophisticated; weekend rates may be heavily discounted.

WHAT IT COSTS IN POUNDS					
	£	££	£££	££££	£££££
Restaurants	under £10	£10–£14	£15–£19	£20–£25	over £25
Hotels	under £70	£70–£120	£121–£160	£161–£220	over £220

Restaurant prices are for a main course at dinner. Hotel prices are for two people in a standard double room in high season, including V.A.T., with no meals or, if indicated, CP (with Continental breakfast), BP (Breakfast Plan, with full breakfast), or MAP (Modified American Plan, with breakfast and dinner).

VISITOR INFORMATION

Traveline can field all general transportation inquiries. Local tourist offices can recommend day or half-day tours of the region and will have the names of registered Blue Badge guides. The Heart of England tourist board Web site covers Birmingham, the Black Country, Herefordshire, Ironbridge, and Worcestershire.

Contacts Heart of England Tourist Board (⊕ *www.visittheheart.co.uk*). **Traveline** (☎ *0871/200–2233* ⊕ *www.traveline.org.uk*).

BIRMINGHAM

The dynamic cultural life of Birmingham—the result of the museums, art galleries, theater, ballet, and symphony that thrive here—comes as a refreshing surprise. The city's visual appeal, thanks to heavy industry, German bombing during World War II, and some unfortunate late-20th-century civic architecture, may be less than instantly evident, but treasures and historic civic architecture remain. Creative redevelopment and public art are increasingly making areas more attractive, too. The redeveloped Bullring shopping center, part of which has a striking, curving facade of 15,000 aluminum disks, is one creation that has won praise.

Birmingham, with a metropolitan area population of 2.6 million, lies 25 mi north of Stratford and 120 mi northwest of London. "Brum," as it's known, is one of the country's most ethnically diverse urban areas, with nearly a third of its residents from minority groups. The city first flourished in the boom years of the 19th century's Industrial Revolution. Its inventive citizens accumulated enormous wealth, and at one time the city had some of the finest Victorian buildings in the country. It still has some of the most ravishingly beautiful Pre-Raphaelite paintings, on view in the Birmingham Museum and Art Gallery.

GETTING HERE AND AROUND

Bus 900 runs from the airport to the city center every 20 minutes; a taxi will cost you around £20. Try to avoid the city's convoluted road network. Drivers are often surprised that Birmingham's inner ring road twists through the city center. Parking in the center is free from 6 PM to 8 AM.

New Street train station is right in the center of the city, close to the Bullring shopping center. The bus station is at Oxford Street, a few minutes' walk from the Bullring.

Most of the central sights, which are well signposted, form a tight-knit group. The easiest way to get around the city is by foot, though you'll need a bus for the Barber Institute and Cadbury World, and a short metro (tram) trip for the Jewellery Quarter. A Daytripper ticket covering bus, train, and metro travel costs £5.20. The tourist information center, the best place to pick up a map, is close to public bus and rail stations. It has details of heritage walks.

TIMING

A full day gives you time to linger in the Jewellery Quarter and browse the art museums. Much of Birmingham is now pedestrian-friendly, the downtown shopping area transformed into arcades and buses-only streets. You can also explore restored canals and canal towpaths.

ESSENTIALS

Transportation Contacts Traveline (☎ *0870/200–2233* ⊕ *www.traveline.org. uk*).

Visitor Information Birmingham (✉ *The Rotunda, 150 New St.* ☎ *0844/888– 3883* ⊕ *www.visitbirmingham.com*).

EXPLORING

TOP ATTRACTIONS

❾ ★ Barber Institute of Fine Art. Part of the University of Birmingham, the museum has a small but astounding collection of European paintings, prints, drawings, and sculpture, including works by Bellini, Holbein, Poussin, Turner, Whistler, Degas, Monet, and van Gogh. The museum

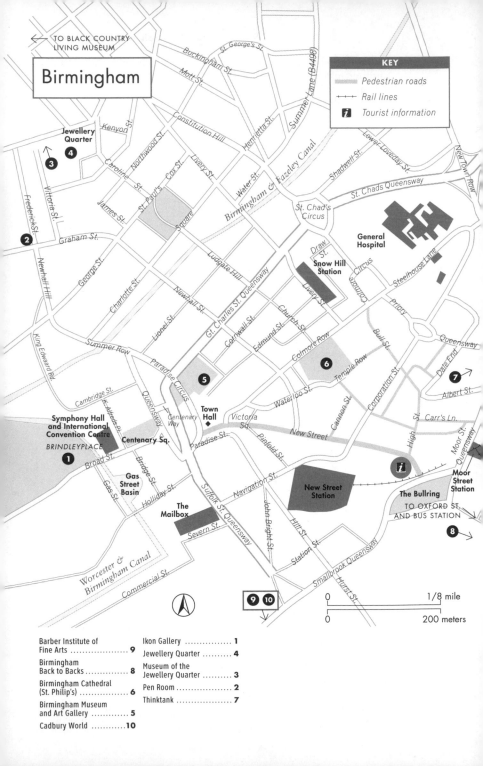

Birmingham

← TO BLACK COUNTRY LIVING MUSEUM

Jewellery Quarter **4**

3

2

Symphony Hall and International Convention Centre
BRINDLEYPLACE **1**

Centenary Sq.

Town Hall ◆

Victoria Sq.

Gas Street Basin

The Mailbox

Snow Hill Station

General Hospital

St. Chad's Circus

New Street Station

i

The Bullring
TO OXFORD ST. AND BUS STATION

Moor Street Station

7 →

8 →

9 **10** ↓

| 0 | | 1/8 mile |
| 0 | | 200 meters |

is 3 mi from the city center; to get here, take a train from New Street Station south to University Station, or Bus 61, 62, or 63 from the city center. ⊠ *Off Edgbaston Park Rd. near East Gate, Edgbaston* ☎ *0121/414–7333* ⊕ *www.barber.org.uk* ⬚ *Free* ☉ *Mon.–Sat. 10–5, Sun. noon–5.*

❽ Birmingham Back to Backs. Of the 20,000 courts of back-to-back houses (constructed around a courtyard and thus backing onto each other) built in the 19th century for the city's expanding working-class population, this is the only survivor. Three houses tell the stories of families, headed by a watchmaker, a locksmith, and a glassworker, who lived here between the 1840s and the 1930s. A few houses are available for overnight stays. Admission is by timed ticket, booked in advance; allow one hour for the tour and be prepared for steep stairs. The houses are closed the Tuesday after a national holiday. ⊠ *Hurst St., City Centre* ☎ *0121/666–7671* ⊕ *www.nationaltrust.co.uk* ⬚ *£5.15* ☉ *Feb.–Dec., Tues.–Sun. and national holidays 10–5.*

❺ Birmingham Museum and Art Gallery. Vast and impressive, this museum holds a magnificent collection of Victorian art and is known internationally for its works by the Pre-Raphaelites. All the big names are here—William Holman Hunt, John Everett Millais, and Dante Gabriel Rossetti—reflecting the enormous wealth of 19th-century Birmingham and the aesthetic taste of its industrialists. Galleries of metalwork, silver, and ceramics reveal some of the city's history, and works from the Renaissance, the Arts and Crafts movement, and the present day are also well represented. Also on view may be some of the Anglo-Saxon treasures (coins, helmets, and more) of the Staffordshire Hoard, discovered in 2009. Allow a couple of hours to visit, and consider a stop in the Edwardian Tea Room. ⊠ *Chamberlain Sq., City Centre* ☎ *0121/303–2834* ⊕ *www.bmag.org.uk* ⬚ *Free* ☉ *Mon.–Thurs. and Sat. 10–5, Fri. 10:30–5, Sun. 12:30–5.*

☾ Black Country Living Museum. It was in the town of Dudley, in the 17th ★ century, that coal was first used for smelting iron. The town became known as the capital of the Black Country, a term that arose from the resulting air pollution. The 26-acre Black Country Living Museum consists of an entire village made up of buildings from around the region, including a chain maker's workshop; a trap-works where animal snares were fashioned; his-and-hers hardware stores (pots and pans for women, tools and sacks for men); a druggist; and a general store where costumed women describe life in a poor industrial community in the 19th century. You can also sit on a hard bench and watch Charlie Chaplin in the 1920s cinema, peer into the depths of a mine, or ride on a barge through a tunnel to experience the canal travel of yesteryear. For sustenance there are two cafés, the 1930s-era Fried Fish Shop that serves fish-and-chips cooked in beef drippings, and the Bottle & Glass pub for ales and drinks. ■TIP➜ **To avoid the numerous school parties, visit on the weekend or during school vacations.** The museum, 3 mi from the M5, is best reached by car. Leave M5 at Junction 2 by A4123, and then take A4037 at Tipton. Trains from Birmingham New Street to Tipton Station take 16 minutes; buses from the train station run past the museum, which is 1 mi away. ⊠ *Tipton Rd., Dudley* ☎ *0121/557–9643*

9

Cruising Birmingham's Canals

With eight canals and 34 mi of waterways, Birmingham has more canals in its center than Venice. The city is at the heart of a system of waterways built during the Industrial Revolution to connect inland factories to rivers and seaports—by 1840 the canals extended more than 4,000 mi throughout the British Isles. These canals, which carried 9 million tons of cargo a year in the late 19th century and helped make the city an industrial powerhouse, have undergone extensive cleanup and renovation, and are now a tourist attraction.

A walk along the Birmingham Canal Main Line near the Gas Street Basin will bring you to modern shops, restaurants, and more developments such as Brindleyplace in one direction and the Mailbox in the other, and you can see the city from an attractive new perspective. Contact the city tourist offices for maps of pleasant walks along the towpaths and canal cruises on colorfully painted barges.

You can take an hour ride on a canal barge from **Sherborne Wharf** (✉ *Sherborne St., City Centre* ☎ *0121/455–6163* ⊕ *www.sherbornewharf.co.uk*). Trips leave daily April through October at 11:30, 1, 2:30, and 4, and on weekends the rest of the year, departing from the International Convention Centre Quayside.

⊕ *www.bclm.co.uk* ✍ *£12.95, barge trip £4.95, parking £1* ☉ *Mar.–Oct., daily 10–5; Nov.–Feb., Wed.–Sun. 10–4.*

❹ **Jewellery Quarter.** For more than two centuries, jewelers have worked in the district of Hockley, northwest of the city center; today around 200 manufacturing jewelers continue the tradition, producing more than a third of the jewelry made in Britain. ■TIP→ **The Jewellery Quarter is a great place to shop for jewelry. A free booklet from the tourist office gives you the lowdown on the area.** The city's Assay Office hallmarks 12 million items each year with the anchor symbol denoting Birmingham origin. The ornate green and gilded Chamberlain Clock, at the intersection of Vyse Street, Warstone Lane, and Frederick Street, marks the center of the district. Shops are closed on Sunday. The quarter is two stops along Metro Line 1 from Snow Hill station. ✉ *Hockley* ⊕ *www.the-quarter.com.*

OFF THE BEATEN PATH

Lichfield Cathedral. It's worth a detour (14 mi northeast of Birmingham on A38) to explore the only English cathedral with three spires. The sandstone building, beautifully sited by a tree-fringed pool, dates mainly from the 12th and 13th centuries, and the Lady Chapel glows with some 16th-century stained glass from the Cistercian abbey of Herkenrode, near Liège, in Belgium. Half-timber houses surround the peaceful grounds, and the town itself has Georgian buildings as well as the birthplace (now a museum) of lexicographer Dr. Samuel Johnson. Frequent trains from Birmingham New Street station take 35 minutes. ✉ *19A The Close, Lichfield* ☎ *01543/306100* ⊕ *www.lichfield-cathedral.org* ✍ *Suggested donation £4* ☉ *Daily 7:30–6:15; closes Sun. at 5 in winter.*

3 Museum of the Jewellery Quarter. The museum is built around the workshops of Smith & Pepper, a firm that operated here for more than 80 years until 1981; little has changed since the early 1900s. A factory tour (about an hour) and exhibits explain the history of the neighborhood and the jeweler's craft, and you can watch demonstrations of jewelry being made in the traditional way. ✉ *75–79 Vyse St., Jewellery Quarter* ☎ *0121/554–3598* ⊕ *www.bmag.org.uk* ✉ *Free* ⊙ *Tues.–Sat. and national holidays 11:30–4; last admission 1 hr before closing.*

7 Thinktank. This interactive museum in the state-of-the-art Millennium Point center allows you to explore science and the history of Birmingham over four floors of galleries. You can watch giant steam engines at work, explore deep space, program a robot to play the drums, and help perform a hip operation. The IMAX cinema and planetarium put on shows throughout the day. The museum is a 10-minute walk from Moor Street railway station. ✉ *Curzon St., Digbeth* ☎ *0121/202–2222* ⊕ *www.thinktank.ac* ✉ *£9; IMAX cinema £8, planetarium £2.45* ⊙ *Daily 10–5; last admission at 4.*

WORTH NOTING

6 Birmingham Cathedral. The early-18th-century Cathedral of St. Philip, a few blocks from Victoria Square, contains some lovely plasterwork in its elegant, gilded Georgian interior. The stained-glass windows behind the altar, designed by the Pre-Raphaelite Edward Burne-Jones (1833–98) and executed by William Morris (1834–96), glow with sensuous hues. ✉ *Colmore Row, City Centre* ☎ *0121/262–1840* ⊕ *www.birminghamcathedral.com* ✉ *Suggested donation £2* ⊙ *Daily 8:30–5.*

10 Cadbury World. The village of Bournville (4 mi south of the city center) contains this museum devoted to—what else?—chocolate. In 1879 the Quaker Cadbury brothers moved the family business from the city to this "factory in a garden." The museum traces the history of the cocoa bean and the Cadbury dynasty. The rain-forest walk, Cadabra ride, and exhibits may seem kitschy, and some are perhaps tired, but Cadbury World is extremely popular. You can watch (and smell) chocolates being made by hand, enjoy free samples, and then stock up from the cut-price shop. The restaurant has specialty chocolate cakes as well as lunches. ✉ *Off A38 (take train from New St. to Bournville Train Station), Bournville* ☎ *0845/450–3599* ⊕ *www.cadburyworld.co.uk* ✉ *£13.45* ⊙ *Feb.–Oct., daily; late Jan., Nov., and Dec., Tues.–Thurs. and weekends; times vary; reservations strongly advised, and essential at busy times.*

1 Ikon Gallery. Converted from a Victorian Gothic–style school, this gallery serves as the city's main venue for exhibitions of contemporary art from Britain and abroad. The bright, white interior is divided into comparatively small display areas, making the shows easily digestible. If you need fortifying, however, try the attached tapas bar. ✉ *1 Oozells Sq., Brindleyplace, City Centre* ☎ *0121/248–0708* ⊕ *www.ikon-gallery.co.uk* ✉ *Free* ⊙ *Tues.–Sun. and national holiday Mon. 11–6.*

9

QUICK BITES

The balcony of the redbrick **Malt House** (⊠ *75 King Edward's Rd.* ☎ *0121/633–4171*) is just the place to linger over a drink as you watch canal life go by.

❷ Pen Room. During the 19th century Birmingham was the hub of the world pen trade. This compact museum in a former factory illustrates that heyday through an overwhelming and decorative array of nibs, quills, fountain pens, inks, and all the paraphernalia of the pre-ballpoint era. You can try your hand at calligraphy and make your own nib. ⊠ *60 Frederick St., Jewellery Quarter* ☎ *0121/236–9834* ⊕ *www.penroom. co.uk* ⊠ *Free* ☉ *Mon.–Sat. 11–4, Sun. 1–4.*

WHERE TO EAT

£

CHINESE

✕ **Henry's.** A popular lunch spot, this traditional Cantonese restaurant on the edge of the Jewellery Quarter is a great place to stop during a shopping spree. The menu lists more than 170 items and also includes a good-value fixed-price menu and a Sunday buffet. The sizzling dishes, which arrive at your table on a metal plate, are a good choice. ⊠ *27 St. Paul's Sq., City Centre* ☎ *0121/200–1136* ⊕ *www.henrysrestaurant. co.uk* ⊟ *AE, MC, V.*

££

INDIAN

✕ **Itihaas.** Birmingham has some of the country's finest Indian restaurants, and this is one upbeat choice. The style is traditional and colonial; potted palms and portraits rub shoulders with antiques. Cooking concentrates on North Indian dishes, and some good choices are *koila murgh,* chicken marinated in yogurt and seared over charcoal, or *hara bara gosth,* a casserole of lamb cooked with garlic, chili, and spinach. The weekday lunchtime tapas menu is a deal at £8.95. ⊠ *18 Fleet St., City Centre* ☎ *0121/212–3383* ⊕ *www.itihaas.co.uk* ⊟ *AE, MC, V* ☉ *No lunch weekends.*

£££££

MODERN BRITISH

✕ **Love's.** Overlooking a spruced-up stretch of canal bobbing with barges, this contemporary eatery takes you on an imaginative journey through the British culinary landscape. Chef Steve Love accompanies his belly of Gloucestershire pork with pease pudding and cider jelly, while his wild black sea bream comes with smoked almond gnocchi. Many of the highlights appear between courses, with a well-chosen mango puree or leek and ginger foam with goat's cheese. The two-course lunch menu offers real value at £16.95; the tasting menu is £55. ⊠ *3 Canal Sq., City Centre* ☎ *0121/454–5151* ⊕ *www.loves-restaurant.co.uk* ⊟ *AE, MC, V* ☉ *Closed Sun. and Mon.*

£££

MODERN BRITISH

✕ **Opus.** The best seasonal ingredients are freshly prepared for discerning diners—anyone from ladies out on the town to intimate couples—enjoying this modern, light space. The accent is on local and British, so expect quince, pumpkins, wild mushrooms, and air-dried Cumbrian ham. Meat is free range and fish is wild caught. The weekday three-course fixed-price menu offer an excellent value at £18.50; you can also go the whole hog and treat yourself to a ringside seat at the chef's table, where five courses cost £75. ⊠ *54 Cornwall St., City Centre* ☎ *0121/200–2323* ⊕ *www.opusrestaurant.co.uk* ⊟ *AE, MC, V* ☉ *Closed Sun.*

££   ✕ **The Oriental.** Playful exoticism
ECLECTIC   epitomizes this Asian restaurant.
Silver-gray crushed velvet lines the
walls, red flowers paper the ceiling,
and the chairs come upholstered
with photographic portraits. The
food doesn't disappoint, and dishes
such as *rendang* chicken (slow-
cooked in spicy coconut sauce) and
*sambal (*scallops cooked in lemongrass, chilies, and shrimp paste)
reflect the Malaysian focus. Thai
curries and Chinese dishes are also
on the menu. A three-course banquet, at £22.95, is a good way to
sample all three cuisines. ⊠ *128–130*
Wharfside St., The Mailbox, City
Centre ☎ *0121/633–9988* ⊕ *www.*
theoriental.uk.com ⊟ *AE, MC, V.*

££££   ✕ **Simpsons.** Choose between the
FRENCH   conservatory with garden views or
Fodor's Choice   the inner dining space of this elegant
★   and gleaming Georgian villa known for French-influenced cuisine. Either
way, the light and immaculate surroundings and assured and welcoming service make it easy to savor specialties such as pavé of Aberdeenshire beef with slow-cooked ox cheek or pear tarte tatin with Roquefort
ice cream. There are four luxurious theme guest rooms for those who
wish to stray no farther, and a cooking school. It's a mile south of the
city center. ⊠ *20 Highfield Rd., Edgbaston* ☎ *0121/454–3434* ⊕ *www.*
simpsonsrestaurant.co.uk ⊟ *AE, MC, V* ☉ *No dinner Sun.*

££   ✕ **Thai Edge.** This elegant, contemporary eatery is perfectly at home
THAI   in fashionable Brindleyplace. Dishes such as *gaeng keow waan* (green
curry cooked in coconut milk with eggplant, lime leaves, and basil)
and sea bass in banana leaves are excellent. Lunches are a good value.
⊠ *7 Oozells Sq., City Centre* ☎ *0121/643–3993* ⊕ *www.thaiedge.co.uk*
⊟ *AE, MC, V.*

> **EAT BALTI IN BRUM**
>
> Birmingham is home to the Balti,
> a popular cuisine invented in the
> mid-1970s by the Pakistani com-
> munity. The food is cooked and
> brought to the table in a woklike
> dish and eaten with naan bread,
> not rice. Curry and other spices
> season the meat and vegetables.
> The more than 30 restaurants in
> the "Balti Triangle" of the Moseley
> and Sparkbrook districts include
> **Punjab Paradise** (⊠ *377 Lady-*
> *pool Rd.* ☎ *0121/499–4110*) and
> **Al Frash** (⊠ *186 Ladypool Rd.*
> ☎ *0121/753–3120* ⊕ *www.alfrash.*
> *com*). Buses 6, 12, 13, and 37 go
> to this area a few miles south of
> the center.

WHERE TO STAY

££–£££   ⛌ **City Inn.** This bustling hotel has an excellent central location near
the waterside nightlife scene. The crisp, modern bedrooms and bathrooms, though on the small side, are beautifully equipped and furnished in calm, neutral tones; all guest rooms come with iMacs. Floors
6 and 7 have the best views. Breakfast is included in the good weekend
deals. **Pros:** free Wi-Fi; windows open to catch the breeze. **Cons:** mostly
for business travelers. ⊠ *1 Brunswick Sq., Brindleyplace, City Centre*
☎ *0121/643–1003* ⊕ *www.cityinn.com* ⥥ *238 rooms* ♿ *In-room: a/c,*
DVD, Internet, Wi-Fi. In-hotel: restaurant, room service, gym, laundry
service, parking (paid) ⊟ *AE, DC, MC, V.*

9

££££   ⊡ **Hotel du Vin & Bistro.** A Victorian hospital in the city center got a makeover from a *très* hip chain but retains such original details as the ironwork double stairway and marble columns. Beyond the imposing redbrick exterior is an inner courtyard with a fountain and garden and an inviting billiard room. Bedrooms are sleek and contemporary, with huge, fluffy towels and white linens. The bistro is redolent of fin-de-siècle Paris, and in the Bubble Lounge, which has a walk-in cigar humidor, you can drown in more than 50 varieties of champagne. **Pros:** good for celebrity spotting; central location. **Cons:** no private parking; breakfast costs extra. ⊠ *25 Church St., City Centre* ☎ *0121/200–0600* ⊕ *www. hotelduvin.com* ⇆ *56 rooms, 10 suites* ᴧ *In-room: no a/c, Wi-Fi. In-hotel: restaurant, room service, bars, gym, spa, laundry service, parking (paid)* ⊟ *AE, MC, V.*

£££–££££   ⊡ **Macdonald Burlington Hotel.** Housed in one of the city's grand Victorian buildings, this traditional hotel's pedigree is confirmed by an impressive roll-call of prime ministers who have spent a night here. Guest rooms are decorated either with conservative dark woods and print fabrics or, for a slightly higher rate, in a modern, minimalist style using warm muted colors. Featuring organic ingredients, the menu at the sumptuous Berlioz restaurant includes Scottish steaks, oysters, and salmon. **Pros:** close to New Street station and shops; very good weekend rates. **Cons:** attracts a mainly business clientele. ⊠ *Burlington Arcade, 126 New St., City Centre* ☎ *0844/879–9019* ⊕ *www.burlingtonhotel. com* ⇆ *112 rooms* ᴧ *In-room: Wi-Fi, a/c. In-hotel: restaurant, room service, bar, gym, laundry service, parking (paid), some pets allowed* ⊟ *AE, DC, MC, V* ℉ *BP.*

££££   ⊡ **Malmaison.** Retail therapy is on your doorstep at this chic, up-to-the-minute hotel in the Mailbox shopping center. Large windows make the guest rooms light and airy by day, and there's subtle lighting by night. Furnishings are smoothly modern, in chocolate and cream colors. Bathrooms indulge you with tailor-made toiletries and soothing showers. A plush red carpet winds upstairs to the upbeat Brasserie, which concentrates on French cuisine. **Pros:** handy for shopping and dining; near canal-side attractions; good online specials. **Cons:** expensive parking (cheaper alternatives are close by); breakfast not included. ⊠ *1 Wharfside St., City Centre* ☎ *0121/246–5000* ⊕ *www.malmaison.com* ⇆ *189 rooms, 10 suites* ᴧ *In-room: a/c, Internet. In-hotel: restaurant, room service, bar, gym, spa, laundry service, Wi-Fi hotspot, parking (paid)* ⊟ *AE, DC, MC, V.*

££–£££
★   ⊡ **New Hall Hotel & Spa.** A tree-lined drive leads through 26 acres of gardens and open land to this moated, 12th-century manor house. Public rooms reflect the hotel's long history with touches such as the 16th-century oak paneling and Flemish glass, 18th-century chandeliers, and a stone fireplace from the 17th century. Guest rooms, most in a more modern section, are done in contemporary English country style with plain and print fabrics and marble-tile baths. Both the formal Bridge restaurant and the more relaxed Terrace Brasserie serve sophisticated English and French cuisine. The hotel is 7 mi northeast of the city center. **Pros:** historic building; beautiful grounds; plenty of sports facilities. **Cons:** a little difficult to locate; away from city center. ⊠ *Walmley Rd.,*

Sutton Coldfield ☎ *0121/378–2442* ⊕ *www.handpickedhotels.co.uk* ⇔ *49 rooms, 10 suites* ⚲ *In-room: no a/c (some), Wi-Fi. In-hotel: restaurant, room service, bar, golf course, tennis court, pool, gym, spa, laundry service, parking (free)* ⊟ *AE, MC, V* ⏀ *BP.*

£££–££££ ⚏ **Staying Cool.** The 19th and 20th floors of the Rotunda, an iconic office building from the middle of the last century, now contain spacious one- and two bedroom apartments, designed to the hilt in sleek '60s style. Each room features unique furnishings, designer kitchens, and all the latest gadgetry, but the real stars of the show are floor-to-ceiling windows that showcase every detail of the city's skyline. Organic breakfasts can be delivered. **Pros:** well-stocked kitchens; dreamy beds, free Wi-Fi. **Cons:** no designated parking. ⊠ *150 New St., City Centre* ☎ *0121/643–0815* ⊕ *www.stayingcool.com* ⇔ *15 apartments* ⚲ *In-room: no a/c, no phone, kitchen, refrigerator, Internet, Wi-Fi* ⊟ *AE, MC, V.*

££ ⚏ **Totel.** These large apartments, 1½ mi from Birmingham's center and off the main A456, make for a secluded and peaceful retreat. The large redbrick house, once a 19th-century private residence, now consists of one- and two-bedroom suites that are spacious and furnished in crisp, contemporary style. **Pros:** plenty of room; undisturbed by service staff; frequent buses to center. **Cons:** not in city center; no nearby shops or restaurants. ⊠ *Asquith House, 19 Portland Rd., Edgbaston* ☎ *0121/454–5282* ⊕ *www.toteluk.com* ⇔ *10 apartments* ⚲ *In-room: no a/c, kitchen, DVD, Wi-Fi. In-hotel: parking (free)* ⊟ *AE, MC, V* ⏀ *BP.*

NIGHTLIFE AND THE ARTS

NIGHTLIFE

The city's thriving nightlife scene is concentrated around Broad Street and Hurst Street, as well as the Brindleyplace and Mailbox areas.

Colorful **Asha's** (⊠ *12–22 Newhall St., City Centre* ☎ *0121/200–2767*), a bar and restaurant, has superb fresh fruit cocktails and Asian cuisine. **Bar Epernay** (⊠ *171 Wharfside St., City Centre* ☎ *0121/632–1430*), a champagne bar and brasserie in the Mailbox, has a revolving piano and a warming brazier, making it perfect for relaxing after a day's sightseeing. The **Jam House** (⊠ *3–5 St. Paul's Sq., Jewellery Quarter* ☎ *0121/200–3030*), an excellent drinking, dining, and dancing venue, benefits from nightly live entertainment—jazz, soul, or funk.

The spacious and high-domed **Old Joint Stock** (⊠ *4 Temple Row W, off Colmore Row, City Centre* ☎ *0121/200–1892*) serves good ales and pies, and there's a theater attached. The bar at the **Vaults** (⊠ *Newhall Pl., Newhall Hill, Jewellery Quarter* ☎ *0121/212–9837*) is perfect for an intimate drink. Another option is to reserve your own private, brick-vaulted booth, draw the curtain, adjust the music, and settle down.

THE ARTS

Birmingham's performing arts companies are well regarded throughout the country. Catch a performance if you can.

BALLET The **Birmingham Royal Ballet** (⊠ *Hurst St., City Centre* ☎ *0870/730–1234*), the second company of the Royal Ballet, is based at the Hippodrome Theatre, which also plays host to visiting companies such as the Welsh National Opera.

9

CONCERTS **Symphony Hall** (✉ *International Convention Centre, Broad St., City Centre* ☎ *0121/780–3333*) is the home of the distinguished City of Birmingham Symphony Orchestra and a venue for jazz, pop, and world as well as classical concerts. The **National Exhibition Centre** (✉ *M42, Junction 6, close to airport* ☎ *0844/338–8000*) promotes top names in rock and pop.

The splendidly refurbished neoclassical **Town Hall Birmingham** (✉ *Paradise St.* ☎ *0121/780–3333*) holds a wide range of events, including organ recitals, opera, and folk concerts.

THEATER   The **Alexandra Theatre** (✉ *Station St., City Centre* ☎ *0870/607–7533*) welcomes touring companies on their way to or from London's West End. The **Birmingham Repertory Theatre** (✉ *Centenary Sq., Broad St., City Centre* ☎ *0121/236–4455*), founded in 1913, is equally at home with modern or classical work as one of England's oldest and most esteemed theater companies.

FILM   The **Electric Cinema** (✉ *47–49 Station St., City Centre* ☎ *0121/643–7879*), the country's oldest working cinema if not the smartest, has sofas and waiter service to enhance the viewing experience at this individualistic art deco survivor.

SHOPPING

SHOPPING   The glass-roof **Bullring** (✉ *Between New St. and High St., City Centre*
CENTERS   ☎ *0121/632–1500*) has three floors of retail enticement, including two department stores, Debenhams and the stunningly curved Selfridges, covered with aluminum disks. Don't miss Selfridges' awesome Food Hall.

The **Mailbox** (✉ *150 Wharfside St., City Centre* ☎ *0121/632–1000*), once a Royal Mail sorting office, entices with trendy shops and designer outlets such as Harvey Nichols and Armani, restaurants, and hotels.

JEWELLERY   The **Jewellery Quarter** (✉ *Hockley* ☎ *0121/604–7700*) has more than
QUARTER   100 shops that sell and repair gold and silver handcrafted jewelry, clocks, and watches. The Information Centre at 120 Vyse Street provides information on artisans and retail outlets.

Crescent Silver (✉ *83–85 Spencer St., Jewellery Quarter* ☎ *0121/236–9006*) sells a range of interesting silver jewelry and gifts.

St. Paul's Gallery (✉ *94–108 Norwood St., Jewellery Quarter* ☎ *0121/236–5800*), an entertaining treasure trove, specializes in hand-signed fine-art prints of album covers, past and present.

WORCESTER, HEREFORD, AND ENVIRONS

In the arc of towns to the west of Birmingham and around the banks of the River Wye to the south, history and tradition rub up against deepest rural England. The cathedral towns of Worcester and Hereford make great bases from which to soak up the bucolic flavor of the Malvern Hills and Elgar country, or to view the spectacular swing of the Wye at Symonds Yat. En route, there's a taste of Georgian architecture at Bewdley.

WORCESTER

27 mi southwest of Birmingham, 118 mi northwest of London.

Worcester (pronounced *wuss*-ter), on the River Severn in the center of Worcestershire, is an ancient cathedral city proud of its history and in particular of its nickname, "the Faithful City," bestowed on the town for steadfast allegiance to the crown during the English Civil War. In that conflict between king and Parliament, two major battles were waged here. The second one, the decisive Battle of Worcester of 1651, resulted in the exile of the future Charles II.

Since the mid-18th century the town's name has become synonymous with fine bone china it once produced; Royal Worcester was purchased by Portmeirion Potteries in 2009. Despite unfortunate modernization in the 1960s, some of medieval Worcester remains. This ancient section forms a convenient and pleasant walking route around the great cathedral.

Southwest of Worcester lie the Malvern Hills, their long, low, purple profiles rising from the surrounding plain. These hills, great for walking, inspired much of the music of Sir Edward Elgar (1857–1934), who composed "Pomp and Circumstance." They also inspired his remark that "there is music in the air, music all around us."

GETTING HERE AND AROUND

Trains from London Paddington (2¼ hours) and Birmingham (one hour) arrive at the Foregate Street station, half a mile north of the city center. The bus station is close by on the Butts. First buses serve the local area. Worcester is just under three hours by car from London on M4 and then M5; a prettier but slower route is M40 to Oxford and then A44, which skirts the Cotswolds. Take care if you're driving on A44 west of Worcester, as there are frequent, sudden bends in the road.

Worcester itself is easily covered on foot; the city's mainly pedestrianized High Street runs through the center of town, from the cathedral to Foregate Street station.

ESSENTIALS

Bus Contact First (☎ 0871/200–2233 ⊕ www.firstgroup.com).

Visitor information Worcester (✉ The Guildhall, High St. ☎ 01905/726311 ⊕ www.visitworcester.com).

EXPLORING

TOP ATTRACTIONS

Commandery. Occupying a cluster of 15th-century half-timber buildings that later became the headquarters of the Royalist troops during the Battle of Worcester, the Commandery has a large exhibit about the English Civil War and a state-of-the-art audio guide that tells the story of the building. The magnificent, oak-beam Great Hall alone is worth a visit, but the museum's most interesting exhibit is a collection of grizzly paintings in what was once a medieval hospital. They include a rare depiction of Sir Thomas Beckett's martyrdom—rare because in 1538, Henry VIII had ordered the destruction of all such works. ✉ *Sidbury* ☎ *01905/361821* ⊕ *www.worcestercitymuseums.org.*

9

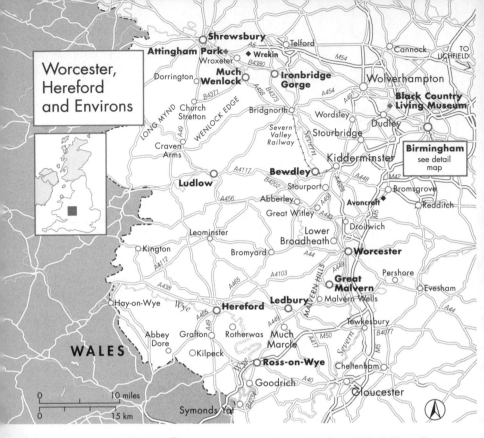

Worcester,
Hereford
and Environs

uk ✉ *£5.40* ⊙ *Easter–Oct., Mon.–Sat. 10–5, Sun. 1:30–5; Nov.–Easter, Mon.–Thurs. and Sat. 10–5, Sun. 1:30–5.*

★ **Worcester Cathedral.** There are few more quintessentially English sights than that of Worcester Cathedral, its towers overlooking the green expanse of the county cricket ground, and its majestic image reflected in the swift-flowing—and frequently flooding—waters of the River Severn. A cathedral has stood on this site since 680, and much of what remains dates from the 13th and 14th centuries. Notable exceptions are the Norman crypt (built in the 1080s), the largest in England, and the ambulatory, a cloister built around the east end. The most important tomb in the cathedral is that of King John (1167–1216), one of the country's least-admired monarchs, who alienated his barons and subjects through bad administration and heavy taxation and in 1215 was forced to sign that great charter of liberty, the Magna Carta. ■ **TIP→ Don't miss the beautiful decoration in the vaulted chantry chapel of Prince Arthur, Henry VII's elder son, whose body was brought to Worcester after his death at Ludlow in 1502.** The wealthy endowed the chantry chapels so priests could celebrate Masses there for the souls of the deceased. ⊠ *College Yard at High St.* ☎ *01905/732900* ⊕ *www.worcestercathedral.co.uk* ✉ *Donations welcome, tours £3* ⊙ *Daily 7:30–6, tours Apr.–Oct., Mon.–Sat. 11 and 2:30.*

Worcester Porcelain Museum. The world's largest collection of Worcester porcelain, bone china, and earthenware is displayed at this museum south of Worcester Cathedral. Tableware, dollhouse miniatures, and ornamental birds and animals are characteristically ornate, and the Victorian gallery presents pieces made on the Worcester site. ⊠ *Severn St.* ☎ *01905/21247* ⊕ *www.worcesterporcelainmuseum.org* ✎ *£5* ⊙ *Easter–Oct., Mon.–Sat. 10–5; Nov.–Easter, Tues.–Sat. 10:30–4.*

WORTH NOTING

Elgar Birthplace Museum. The composer Sir Edward Elgar was born in the village of Lower Broadheath—on B4204, 2 mi west of Worcester—in this tiny brick cottage. Set in a peaceful little garden, the museum contains personal memorabilia, and the Elgar Centre exhibits photographs, musical scores, and letters. ⊠ *Crown East La., Lower Broadheath* ☎ *01905/333224* ⊕ *www.elgarfoundation.org* ✎ *£6* ⊙ *Feb.–Dec., daily 11–5; last admission 45 mins before closing.*

Guildhall. Set back behind ornate iron railings, the 18th-century Guildhall has a facade dotted with gilded statues of Queen Anne, Charles I, and Charles II. Note the carving of Cromwell's head pinned up by the ears. In the Assembly Room on the second floor, impressive patrician portraits hang under a painted ceiling. ⊠ *High St.* ☎ *01905/723471* ✎ *Free* ⊙ *Weekdays 8:30–4:30, Sat. 8:30–4.*

OFF THE BEATEN PATH

Witley Court. About 10 mi northwest of Worcester is the romantic shell of an imposing stately home—a huge Italianate pile—that stood here before a fire in 1937. In contrast to this ruin, the tiny baroque parish church on the grounds is perfectly preserved. Inside are 10 colored windows and a ceiling painted by Antonio Bellucci. Witley Court's glorious gardens have been lovingly restored. One of the impressive fountains, the enormous Perseus and Andromeda, sends its jets skyward (April through October, weekdays at 11, noon, 2, 3, and 4, weekends on the hour from 11 to 4). ⊠ *A443, Great Witley* ☎ *01299/896636* ⊕ *www. english-heritage.org.uk* ✎ *£5.80* ⊙ *Apr., May, Sept., and Oct., daily 10–5; June–Aug., daily 10–6; Nov.–Mar., Wed.–Sun. 10–4.*

Worcester River Cruises. In summer, this company offers 45-minute river cruises daily on a 1926 launch, departing from South Quay. ⊠ *22 Britannia Rd.* ☎ *01905/611060.*

WHERE TO EAT

££
BRASSERIE
✕ **Fusion.** A 10-minute drive towards Pershore leads to this quirky brasserie known for its innovative marriage of indigenous ingredients and Italian cooking techniques. Chef Felice Tocchini wraps Cornish scallops in home-cured pancetta and tosses his house-made tagliatelle with pheasant ragout. More unequivocally local are the ales, including the flavorful Hobson's Best Bitter, brewed from Worcestershire hops. The eatery is in Hawbridge, a tiny village just off the B4084. ⊠ *Hawbridge* ☎ *01905/840647* ⊕ *www.fusionbrasserie.com* ☐ *AE, MC, V.*

£££
BRASSERIE
✕ **Glasshouse Brasserie.** Watch city life go by through all the windows—that is, if you can divert your attention from the offerings on your plate at this very contemporary and sleek brasserie. Striped blue-and-black banquettes complement the gray upholstered chairs and wood floor. Braised beef with horseradish potato, slow-roast pork belly with

9

Worcester apples, and sticky-toffee-pecan-and-date pudding are all winners. The restaurant is at the southern end of City Walls Road. ⊠ *Danesbury House, Sidbury* ☎ *01905/611120* ⊕ *www.theglasshouse. co.uk* ☰ *AE, MC, V* ⊘ *Closed Sun.*

££
CONTINENTAL
✕ **King Charles II.** A half-timber house in which Charles II hid after the Battle of Worcester is now an oak-paneled restaurant with lace table-cloths and a refreshing lack of matching chairs. The cuisine is mainly French and Italian, though royal portions of traditional English fare, including beef Wellington and Dover sole, are also served. ⊠ *29 New St.* ☎ *01905/22449* ⊕ *www.kingcharlesrestaurant.co.uk* ☰ *AE, MC, V* ⊘ *Closed Sun.*

WHERE TO STAY

£
★
🏠 **Manor Coach House.** Despite being close to the M5 motorway, this much-vaulted B&B on the northern periphery of Worcester offers a sense of tranquility. Terry and Sylvia Smith run their redbrick manor with eagle-eyed attention to detail without sacrificing warm hospitality. The rooms are light, spacious, and spotless. Combine all this with a superb breakfast and you can see why it's widely considered to be one of the country's finest guesthouses. **Pros:** flawless upkeep; unbeatable value; breakfast to die for. **Cons:** books up quickly. ⊠ *Hindlip La., Hindlip, Worcester* ☎ *01905/456457* ⊕ *www.manorcoachhouse.co.uk* 🛏 *5 rooms* ᯇ *In-room: no a/c, Wi-Fi. In-hotel: parking (free)* ☰ *AE, D, DC, MC, V.*

££
🏠 **Ye Olde Talbot Hotel.** This small hotel was originally a courtroom belonging to the cathedral, which stands close by. Modern extensions supplement the 16th-century building. The spacious bedrooms have double-glazed windows and are done in green, blue, and burgundy tones. Be sure to sample a cask ale in the Victorian bar. **Pros:** very central; all-morning breakfasts; power showers. **Cons:** no private parking; location on main road. ⊠ *Friar St.* ☎ *01905/235730* ⊕ *www. yeoldetalbot.com* 🛏 *29 rooms* ᯇ *In-room: no a/c, DVD, Wi-Fi. In-hotel: restaurant, room service, bar, laundry service, parking (paid)* ☰ *AE, MC, V* ⧀ *BP.*

NIGHTLIFE AND THE ARTS

Huntingdon Hall (⊠ *Crowngate* ☎ *01905/611427*), a 1773 Methodist chapel described by poet John Betjeman as "unique and irreplaceable," puts on a varied program of music, interspersed with theater and dance. The original pews are—thankfully—provided with cushions.

SHOPPING

★ **Bygones** (⊠ *3 College Precincts* ☎ *01905/23132*) sells antiques, finely crafted items, and small gifts in silver, glass, and porcelain. **G.R. Pratley** (⊠ *The Shambles* ☎ *01905/22678*) has tables piled high with glassware and fine china; it's closed Thursday afternoon.

GREAT MALVERN

7 mi south of Worcester.

Great Malvern feels a bit like a seaside resort, though instead of the ocean your eyes plunge into an expanse of green meadows rolling away

EATING WELL IN THE WELSH BORDERS

"The Malvern water," said John Wall in 1756, "is famous for containing nothing at all." The famously pure water is still bottled in the town and exported worldwide; it is said that the Queen never travels without it.

Outside Birmingham, this area is all rich farming country where, for centuries, the orchards have produced succulent fruit, especially apples and plums. Hereford cider, for example, is popular because it tastes much sweeter than the cider brewed farther south in Devon.

The meat and milk products, which come from the local red-and-white Hereford breed of cattle, are second to none. Cheshire cheese, one of the country's oldest cheeses, is noted for its rich, crumbly texture; blue-veined Shropshire cheese is more unusual and worth trying. Ludlow produces a formidable assortment of local meat products and is noted for its sausages.

In May the sheltered Vale of Evesham is the center for the asparagus crop.

into the Vale of Evesham. Off the A449, this attractive Victorian spa town's architecture has changed little since the mid-1800s. Its Winter Gardens complex with a theater, cinema, and gardens makes Great Malvern a good base for walks in the surrounding Malvern Hills.

GETTING HERE AND AROUND
To get here from Worcester will take 20 minutes or so by car. There are also frequent trains and buses run by First (15 minutes by train, one hour by bus). The 44B bus connects Worcester and Malverns via British Camp, a good spot to commence a walk in the hills.

ESSENTIALS
Bus Contact First (☎ 00781/200–2233 ⊕ www.firstgroup.com).

Visitor Information Great Malvern (✉ 21 Church St. ☎ 01684/892289 ⊕ www.malvernhills.gov.uk).

9

EXPLORING
The **Priory**, a solidly built early-Norman Benedictine abbey with later Perpendicular elements, dominates the steep streets downtown. The fine glass spans from the 15th century—including a magnificent east window and the vibrantly blue Magnificat window in the north transept—to the evocative Millennium Windows. There's a splendid set of misericords (the elaborately carved undersides of choir seats). ✉ *Church St.* ☎ *01684/561020* ⊕ *www.greatmalvernpriory.org.uk* ▨ *Free* ⊙ *Daily 9–5.*

During three days in mid-June, the agricultural **Three Counties Show** (☎ *01684/584900* ⊕ *www.threecounties.co.uk*) showcases rare animal breeds, equestrian events, competitions for the best cows, pigs, and sheep, and plenty of food.

WHERE TO STAY
£££–££££ ▥ **Cottage in the Wood.** On shady grounds, this family-run hotel sits high up the side of the Malvern Hills, with splendid views of the landscape. Country-house touches in the three buildings include floral prints and

white bedspreads; rooms with a view are equipped with binoculars. The mirrored restaurant, which has the best panorama, serves Modern British fare and offers more than 600 wines, among them many local vintages. **Pros:** family run; tremendous views; good food. **Cons:** three separate buildings; steep and narrow approach. ⊠ *Holywell Rd.* 🕾 *01684/588860* ⊕ *www.cottageinthewood.co.uk* ⇄ *30 rooms* ☖ *In-room: no a/c, Wi-Fi (some). In-hotel: restaurant, bar, some pets allowed* ☰ *AE, MC, V* �‖ *BP.*

£–££   🖭 **Sidney House.** In addition to having stunning views, this dignified early-19th-century bed-and-breakfast, run by a friendly husband-and-wife team, is near the town center. Rooms, done in pastel hues, are furnished with stripped-pine and period pieces. On a clear afternoon you can sit on the terrace and gaze out over the Vale of Evesham to the Cotswolds. **Pros:** great views; easy access to Malvern Hills. **Cons:** on busy road, so ask for room at the back. ⊠ *40 Worcester Rd.* 🕾 *01684/574994* ⊕ *www.sidneyhouse.co.uk* ⇄ *8 rooms* ☖ *In-room: no a/c, no phone. In-hotel: parking (free), some pets allowed* ☰ *MC, V* �‖ *BP.*

NIGHTLIFE AND THE ARTS

Malvern has links with Sir Edward Elgar as well as with George Bernard Shaw, who premiered many of his plays here. The **Autumn in Malvern Festival** (🕾 *01684/892277 or 01684/892289* ⊕ *www.malvernfestival. co.uk*) takes place on weekends throughout October and concentrates on classical music, including Elgar, as well as literary events.

LEDBURY

10 mi southwest of Great Malvern on A449.

Among the black-and-white half-timber buildings that make up the market town of Ledbury, take special note of two late-16th-century ones: the Feathers Hotel and the Talbot Inn. The cobbled Church Lane, almost hidden behind the 17th-century market house, is crowded with medieval half-timber buildings and leads to St. Michael's Church.

GETTING HERE AND AROUND

If you're driving, Ledbury is 25 minutes from Hereford via the A438, and 15 minutes from Great Malvern via the A449. There are local buses from both Hereford and Great Malvern, which has rail links with the rest of the country.

ESSENTIALS

Visitor Information Ledbury (⊠ *The Master's House, St. Katherine's* 🕾 *01531/636147* ⊕ *www.visitherefordshire.co.uk*).

EXPLORING

Ledbury Heritage Centre, in the old grammar school, traces the history of the building, town, railroad, and canal, mostly through local postcards. It also has displays on two literary celebrities linked to the area, John Masefield and Elizabeth Barrett Browning. ⊠ *Church La.* 🕾 *01531/636147* 🖾 *Free* ❍ *Easter–Oct., daily 10–4.*

★   Completed in 1820, **Eastnor Castle,** a turreted Norman Revival extravaganza on the eastern outskirts of Ledbury, includes some magnificent neo-Gothic salons designed by 19th-century architect Augustus Pugin. The Hervey-Bathurst family has restored other grand rooms, full of tapestries, gilt-framed paintings, Regency chandeliers, and Auntie's old armchairs and enormous sofas, making Eastnor a must-see for lovers of English interior decoration. In the Little Library, look out for the rare game of Life Pool, originally played on the billiards table. Eastnor hosts the innovative Big Chill arts festival each August. ⊠ *A438* ☎ *01531/633160* ⊕ *www. eastnorcastle.com* ⊠ *House and grounds £8.50; grounds only, £5.50* ⊘ *Mid-July and Aug., Sun.–Thurs. 11–4:30; June and Sept., Sun. and national holiday Mon. 11–4:30; last admission 30 mins before closing.*

Just outside the village of Much Marcle, 4 mi southwest of Ledbury, lies the beautiful 17th-century manor of **Hellens**, still in authentic condition. Part of the house dates from the 13th century and contains fine old-master paintings. The gloom and dust are part of the experience of visiting; candles illuminate the house, and central heating has been scorned. Take a walk in the gardens and, if you have time, also check out the 13th-century village church. ⊠ *½ mi east of A449, off B4024 and Monks Walk, Much Marcle* ☎ *01531/660504* ⊕ *www.hellensmanor.com* ⊠ *£5* ⊘ *Apr.–Sept., Wed., Thurs., Sun., and national holiday Mon. 2–5; tours at 2, 3, and 4.*

WHERE TO STAY

££–£££ ⬚ **Feathers Hotel.** You can't miss the striking black-and-white facade of this centrally located hostelry, which dates from the 16th century. Its interior has a satisfyingly antique flavor, with creaking staircases and ancient floorboards, and some rooms have four-posters. The hop-bedecked Fuggles Brasserie (named after a variety of hop) and the more formal Quills restaurant serve plenty of fresh fish, as well as lighter meals. **Pros:** guest rooms retain wooden beams; period feel; indoor heated pool. **Cons:** some guest rooms on the small side; some steps to climb. ⊠ *High St.* ☎ *01531/635266* ⊕ *www.feathers-ledbury.co.uk* ⬚ *22 rooms* ⬚ *In-room: no a/c, Wi-Fi. In-hotel: 2 restaurants, bar, pool, gym, some pets allowed* ⊟ *AE, MC, V* ⦿*BP.*

> ### WALKS AND DRIVES IN THE MALVERNS
>
> The Malvern Hills have climbs and walks of varying length and difficulty; the seasonal Malvern Hills Hopper bus gives useful access on weekends April through August. The best places to start are Great Malvern and Ledbury. The Elgar Route, a drive, extends for 45 mi and touches on Malvern and Worcester as it threads through the Malverns. The hilltop vistas across the countryside are spectacular Isolated hills rise up from the fairly flat plain. The area around Ross-on-Wye has ideal walks with scenic river views. For information on hiking the Malverns, contact the Malvern or Ross-on-Wye tourist office.

ROSS-ON-WYE

10 mi southwest of Ledbury.

Perched high above the River Wye in the Malvern Hills, Ross-on-Wye seems oblivious to modern-day intrusions and remains at heart a small market town. Its steep streets come alive on Thursday and Saturday—market days—but they're always a happy hunting ground for antiques. Nearby towns have sights from a castle to a scenic overlook on the river.

GETTING HERE AND AROUND

A449 connects Ross-on-Wye with Great Malvern and Ledbury, and M50 leads directly to Ross from Junction 8 of M5. Stagecoach buses run from Ledbury (30 minutes) and have frequent connections with Hereford (50 minutes) and Gloucester (45 minutes).

ESSENTIALS

Bus Contact Stagecoach (☎ *0871/200–2233* ⊕ *www.stagecoachbus.com*).

Visitor Information Ross-on-Wye (✉ *Swan House, Edde Cross St.* ☎ *01989/562768* ⊕ *www.visitherefordshire.co.uk*).

EXPLORING

Looming dramatically over the River Wye at Kerne Bridge, **Goodrich Castle** from the south looks like a fortress from the Rhineland amid the green fields; you quickly see its grimmer face from the battlements on its north side. Dating from the late 12th century, the red sandstone castle is surrounded by a deep moat carved out of solid rock, from which its walls appear to soar upward. Built to repel Welsh raiders, it was destroyed in the 17th century during the Civil War. The town of Goodrich is 3 mi south of Ross-on-Wye on the B4234. ✉ *Off A40, Goodrich* ☎ *01600/890538* ⊕ *www.english-heritage.org.uk* ☜ *£5.20, parking charge* ☉ *Mar.–June, Sept., and Oct., daily 10–5; July and Aug., daily 10–6; Nov.–Feb., Wed.–Sun. 10–4.*

Six miles south of Ross-on-Wye, outside the village of **Symonds Yat** ("gate"), the 473-foot-high Yat Rock commands superb views of the River Wye as it winds through a narrow gorge and swings around in a great 5-mi loop. It's best approached from the south on B4432, from which it's a short walk. A small ferry takes passengers across the river (80p).

SPORTS AND THE OUTDOORS

Symonds Yat Canoe Hire rents canoes and kayaks by the hour or for full days or more; it's a popular way to experience the River Wye. ✉ *The Leisure Park, Symonds Yat West* ☎ *01600/891069* ⊕ *www.canoehire.com*.

WHERE TO STAY

££–£££ 🏨 **Chase Hotel.** The public areas in this nicely renovated Georgian-style country-house hotel retain some original elements. Bedrooms in the main house are simply and comfortably furnished in pastels and print fabrics, and those in the newer wing are more modern. **Pros:** 11 acres of peaceful grounds; country-house appeal. **Cons:** conventional furnishings. ✉ *Gloucester Rd.* ☎ *01989/763161* ⊕ *www.chasehotel.co.uk* ⇥ *36 rooms* ⚘ *In-room: no a/c, Wi-Fi. In-hotel: restaurant, room service, bar, gym* ⊟ *AE, DC, MC, V* �🍴⚬⏐ *BP.*

HEREFORD

23 mi southwest of Worcester, 56 mi southwest of Birmingham, 54 mi northeast of Cardiff.

It's an important cathedral city, and the massive Norman building towers proudly over the River Wye. Before 1066 Hereford was the capital of the Anglo-Saxon kingdom of Mercia and, earlier still, the site of Roman, Celtic, and Iron Age settlements. Today people come primarily to see the cathedral but quickly discover the charms of this busy country town. Hereford is the center of a wealthy agricultural area known for its cider, fruit, and cattle—the white-faced Hereford breed has spread across the world.

GETTING HERE AND AROUND

The bus and train stations are about half a mile northeast of the center. A train from Birmingham will take around 1¾ hours. Traveling by car, take M50 at Junction 8 of M5, then A417 and A438 to Hereford. First buses cover the local area, and the city is compact enough to cover on foot.

ESSENTIALS

Visitor Information Hereford (⊠ *1 King St.* ☎ *01432/268430* ⊕ *www. visitherefordshire.co.uk).*

EXPLORING

TOP ATTRACTIONS

Hereford Cathedral. Built of local red sandstone, Hereford Cathedral retains a large central tower and some fine 11th-century Norman carvings but suffered considerable "restoration" in the 19th century. Inside, its greatest glories include a 12th-century chair, to the left of the high altar, one of the earliest pieces of furniture in the country and reputedly used by King Stephen, and some fine misericords. ⊠ *Cathedral Close* ☎ *01432/374200* ⊕ *www.herefordcathedral.org* ⊠ *Suggested donation £5, garden tours £5* ⊕ *Mon.–Sat. 9:15–5:30, Sun. 8–3:30; cathedral tours Apr.–Oct., Mon.–Sat. 11 and 2, garden tours Apr.–Oct., Wed. and Sat. at 3.*

★ **Mappa Mundi and Chained Library Exhibition.** This extraordinary double attraction includes the more than 20-square-foot parchment Mappa Mundi. Hereford's own picture of the medieval world shows the Earth as flat, with Jerusalem at its center. It's thought that the map was originally the central section of an altarpiece dating from 1290. The chained library contains some 1,500 books, among them an 8th-century copy of the Four Gospels. Chained libraries, in which books were attached to cupboards to discourage theft, are extremely rare: they date from medieval times, when books were as precious as gold. ⊠ *Cathedral Close* ☎ *01432/374219* ⊕ *www.herefordcathedral.org* ⊠ *£4.50* ⊕ *Apr.–late May, Sept., and Oct., Mon.–Sat. 10–5; late May–Aug., Mon.–Sat. 10–5, Sun. 11–4; Nov., Dec., Feb., and Mar., Mon.–Sat. 10–4; last admission 30 mins before closing.*

Old House. The half-timber Old House is a fine example of domestic Jacobean architecture, furnished in 17th-century style on three floors. You can see a kitchen, dining hall, parlor, and bedrooms. Look for the dog's door between the nursery and master bedroom. ⊠ *High Town* ☎ *01432/260694* ✉ *Free* ⊘ *Apr.–Sept., Tues.–Sat. 10–5, Sun. and national holiday Mon. 10–4; Oct.–Mar., Tues.–Sat. 10–5.*

WORTH NOTING

All Saints Church. On the west side of High Town, this 13th-century church contains superb canopied choir stalls and misericords, as well as unusual Queen Anne renovations in the south chapel. It also has an excellent coffee bar and restaurant. ⊠ *High St.* ☎ *01432/370414.*

Cider Museum. A farm cider house and a cooper's workshop have been re-created at the Cider Museum, where you can tour ancient cider cellars with huge oak vats. Cider brandy is made here, and the museum sells its own brand, along with other cider items. ⊠ *Pomona Pl. at Whitecross Rd.* ☎ *01432/354207* ⊕ *www.cidermuseum.co.uk* ✉ *£3.50* ⊘ *Apr.–Oct., Tues.–Sat. and national holiday Mon. 10–5; Nov.–Mar., Tues.–Sat. 11–3; last admission 1 hr before closing.*

WHERE TO EAT AND STAY

£
VEGETARIAN
★
✕ Café @ All Saints. Open 8 to 5 and a good spot for lunch, the western end and gallery of this community-minded church are given over to a coffee bar and restaurant, granting a rare opportunity to indulge body and spirit at one sitting. The imaginative vegetarian menu is worth every penny, but for something lighter, try the tasty sandwiches (roast mushroom and tofu, for example), salads, cakes, and local ice creams. Or come for breakfast or coffee—scrambled eggs and smoked salmon is one option. ⊠ *High St.* ☎ *01432/370415* ⊕ *www.cafeatallsaints.co.uk* ▤ *MC, V* ⊘ *Closed Sun. No dinner.*

££££
⌂ Castle House. These conjoined Georgian villas next to the moat (all that remains of Hereford Castle) offer luxury, a warm welcome, and good food. Delicate plasterwork graces the public areas. Spacious guest rooms vary in style, with yellow, cream, and red the preferred colors; each bedroom contains a decanter of local cider brandy. The excellent restaurant relies on locally sourced and regional fare, such as Hereford beef and Gloucester Old Spot pork; the bistro, with terrace, is open all day for light refreshment. **Pros:** close to cathedral; quiet setting; lovely garden. **Cons:** not cheap; some report slow service. ⊠ *Castle St.* ☎ *01432/356321* ⊕ *www.castlehse.co.uk* ⇌ *10 suites, 5 rooms* ⌂ *In-room: no a/c, safe, refrigerator, Internet. In-hotel: restaurant, room service, bar, Wi-Fi hotspot, parking (free), some pets allowed* ▤ *AE, MC, V* ⦿ *BP.*

£
⌂ Sink Green Farm. Benefits of staying on this informal working farm, which dates back to the 16th century, include views of the Wye Valley and use of the barbecue and outdoor hot tub in a summerhouse. Guest rooms in the stone farmhouse are prettily furnished with period pieces, and breakfasts, including local bacon and eggs, are taken at the communal dining table. The location is 3 mi southeast of the city. **Pros:** friendly and casual; lovely garden, river walks. **Cons:** car needed to get around. ⊠ *B4399, Rotherwas* ☎ *01432/870223* ⊕ *www.sinkgreenfarm. co.uk* ⇌ *4 rooms* ⌂ *In-room: no a/c, no phone, Wi-Fi. In-hotel: parking (free), some pets allowed* ▤ *No credit cards* ⦿ *BP.*

SHOPPING

Hereford has a market for livestock on Wednesday and for general retail on Saturday. The stores in **Capuchin Yard** (✉ *Off 29 Church St.*) display crafts, including handmade shoes and knitwear; other outlets sell haberdashery and ceramics.

BEWDLEY

14 mi north of Worcester, 3 mi west of Kidderminster.

In Bewdley, an exceptionally attractive Severn Valley town, tall, narrow-front Georgian buildings cluster around the river bridge. You can take a scenic train or boat ride from here to appreciate the rural landscape.

GETTING HERE AND AROUND

A half-hour drive from Worcester along the A449, Bewdley also connects with Kidderminster via the historic Severn Valley Railway. Buses to Kidderminster, caught outside the rail station, are considerably cheaper. The town itself can be easily explored on foot.

ESSENTIALS

Visitor Information Bewdley (✉ *Load St.* ☎ *01299/404740* 🌐 *www.visitworcestershire.org*).

EXPLORING

The 18th-century butchers' market, the Shambles, now holds **Bewdley Museum**, which documents local history, trades, and crafts with exhibits on rope making and clay-pipe making. Craftspeople working in wood, ceramics, stained glass, and textiles occupy the nearby workshops. ✉ *Load St.* ☎ *01299/403573* 🎫 *Free* ⏲ *Easter–Sept., daily 10–4:30; Oct., daily 11–4.*

Bewdley is the southern terminus of the **Severn Valley Railway**, a steam railroad running 16 mi north along the river to Bridgnorth, a lovely market town on a ridge above the Severn. The train stops at a handful of sleepy stations where time has apparently stood still since the age of steam. You can get off at any of these stations, picnic by the river, and walk to the next station to get a train back. Perching on a high sandstone ridge on the banks of the Severn, Bridgnorth has two distinct parts, High Town and Low Town, connected by a winding road, flights of steep steps, and—best of all—a cliff railroad. Even the tower of the Norman castle seems to suffer from vertigo, having a 17-degree list. ✉ *Railway Station* ☎ *01299/403816* 🌐 *www.svr.co.uk* 🎫 *£14 round-trip* ⏲ *Apr.–Sept., trains run daily; Oct.–Mar., weekends only.*

The **Stourport Steamer Co.** has short river trips, or you can take longer journeys as far as Worcester on Wednesday from the last week in July through August. Stourport is a few miles south of Bewdley. ✉ *6 Ash Grove, Stourport* ☎ *01299/871177 or 0786/046–8792* 🌐 *www.riverboathire.co.uk* 🎫 *£4–£12* ⏲ *Mar.–mid-July and Sept., Sun.; mid-July–Aug., daily.*

9

SHREWSBURY TO CHESTER

Rural Shropshire, one of the least populated English counties, is far removed from most people's preconceptions of the industrial Midlands. Within its spread are towns long famed for their beauty, such as Bridgnorth and Ludlow. Two important cities of the Welsh Border region, Shrewsbury and Chester, are both renowned for their medieval heritage and their wealth of half-timber buildings. The 6-mi stretch of the Ironbridge Gorge, however, gives you the chance to experience the cradle of the Industrial Revolution with none of the reeking smoke that gave this region west of Birmingham its name—the Black Country—during the mid-19th century. Now taken over by the Ironbridge Gorge Museum Trust, the bridge, the first in the world to be built of iron and opened in 1781, is the centerpiece of this vast museum complex.

SHREWSBURY

47 mi northwest of Dudley, 55 mi north of Hereford, 46 mi south of Chester, 48 mi northwest of Birmingham.

One of England's most important medieval towns, Shrewsbury (usually pronounced *shrose*-bury), the county seat of Shropshire, lies within a great horseshoe loop of the Severn. It has numerous 16th-century half-timber buildings—many built by well-to-do wool merchants—plus elegant ones from later periods. Today the town retains a romantic air (indeed, there are many bridal shops, along with churches), and it can be a lovely experience to stroll the Shrewsbury "shuts." These narrow alleys overhung with timbered gables lead off the central market square, which was designed to be closed off at night to protect local residents. You can also relax in Quarry Park on the river.

A good starting point for exploring the city is the small square between Fish Street and Butcher Row. These streets are little changed since medieval times, when some of them took their names from the principal trades carried on there, but Peacock Alley, Gullet Passage, and Grope Lane clearly got their names from somewhere else.

GETTING HERE AND AROUND

The train station is at the neck of the river that loops the center, a little farther out than the bus station on Raven Meadows. A direct train service runs here from Hereford (50 minutes) and Birmingham (one hour). If you're coming from London by car, take M40 and M42 north, then M6 and M54, which becomes A5 to Shrewsbury; it's 150 mi. The streets are full of twists, but it's small enough not to get lost. Walking tours of Shrewsbury depart daily from the tourist office at 2:30 from May through September and on Saturday the rest of the year (£4).

ESSENTIALS

Visitor Information Shrewsbury (✉ *Rowley's House, Barker St.* ☎ *01743/281200* ⊕ *www.visitshrewsbury.com*).

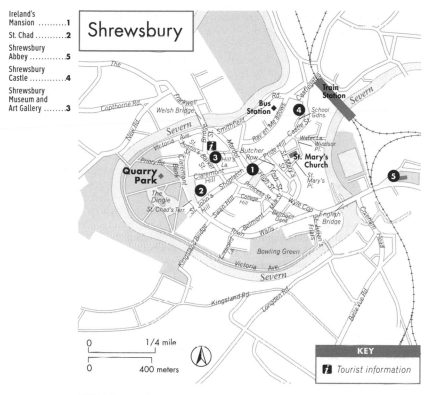

EXPLORING

TOP ATTRACTIONS

Attingham Park. Built in 1785 by George Steuart (architect of the church of St. Chad in Shrewsbury) for the first Lord Berwick, this elegant stone mansion has a three-story portico, with a pediment carried on four tall columns. The building overlooks a sweep of parkland, including a deer park landscaped by Humphrey Repton (1752–1818). Inside the house are painted ceilings and delicate plasterwork, a fine picture gallery designed by John Nash (1752–1835), and 19th-century Neapolitan furniture. Attingham Park is 4 mi southeast of Shrewsbury. ⊠ *B4380, off A5, Atcham* ☎ *01743/708162* ⊕ *www.nationaltrust.org.uk* ⊠ *£7.63, park and grounds only, £3.80* ☉ *House early Mar., weekends 1–4; mid-Mar.–Oct., Thurs.–Tues. 1–5:30, national holiday Mon. 11–5:30; last admission 1 hr before closing. Park and grounds mid-Feb.–Oct., daily 9–6; Nov.–mid-Feb., daily 9–5.*

② **St. Chad.** On a hilltop west of the town center, this church designed by George Steuart, the architect of Attingham Park, is one of England's most original ecclesiastical buildings. Completed in 1792, the round Georgian church is surmounted by a tower that is in turn square, octagonal, and circular—and finally topped by a dome. When being built, it provoked riots among townsfolk averse to its radical style. The interior has a fine Venetian east window and a brass Arts and Crafts pulpit. ⊠ *St. Chad's Terr.* ☎ *01743/365478* ✆ *Free* ⊙ *Apr.–Oct., daily 8–5; Nov.–Mar., daily 8–1.*

⑤ Shrewsbury Abbey. Now unbecomingly surrounded by busy roads, the abbey was founded in 1083 and later became a powerful Benedictine monastery. The abbey church has survived many vicissitudes and retains a 14th-century west window above a Norman doorway. A more recent addition is a memorial to the World War I poet, Wilfred Owen. To reach the abbey from the center, cross the river by the English Bridge. ⊠ *Abbey Church, Abbey Foregate* ☎ *01743/232723* ⊕ *www.shrewsburyabbey. com* ✆ *Donations welcome* ⊙ *Mon.–Sat. 10:30–3, Sun. 9:30–2:30.*

④ Shrewsbury Castle. Guarding the northern approaches to the town, the sandstone castle rises over the River Severn at the bottom of Pride Hill. Originally Norman, it was dismantled during the Civil War and later rebuilt by Thomas Telford, the Scottish engineer who designed many notable buildings and bridges in the early 19th century. The castle holds the **Shropshire Regimental Museum,** containing enough social history to engage the non–military buff. ■**TIP➜ The numerous benches in the gardens are good for a quiet sit-down.** ⊠ *Shrewsbury Castle, Castle Gates* ☎ *01743/358516* ⊕ *www.shrewsburymuseums.com* ✆ *£2.50* ⊙ *Mid-Feb.–May and mid-Sept.–Dec., Tues.–Sat. and national holiday Mon. 10:30–4; June–mid-Sept., Tues.–Sun. and bank holiday Mon. 10:30–5. Castle grounds Mon.–Sat. 9–5, Sun. 10:30–5.*

WORTH NOTING

① Ireland's Mansion. The cluster of restored half-timber buildings that link Fish Street with Market Square is known as Bear Steps; this mansion, built in 1575 with elaborate Jacobean timbering and richly decorated with quatrefoils, is the most notable. It's not open to the public.

③ Shrewsbury Museum and Art Gallery. The museum holds Shropshire pottery and ceramics, as well as items of local history and Roman finds, such as a unique silver mirror from nearby Wroxeter. A reconstructed 17th-century paneled bedroom showcases an elaborate four-poster bed (1593), enlivened with richly embroidered silk and velvet hangings. The Darwin Exhibition explores the life of Shrewsbury's famous son, Charles Darwin. ⊠ *Barker St.* ☎ *01743/361196* ⊕ *www. shrewsburymuseums.com* ✆ *Free* ⊙ *May–Sept., Mon.–Sat. 10–5, Sun. 10–4; Oct.–Apr., Mon.–Sat. 10–4.*

WHERE TO EAT

££
BRITISH
✕ **The Armoury.** This smartly converted warehouse on the Victoria Quay, whose arched windows overlook the river, is well stocked with books, prints, and curiosities, as well as good food, fine wines, and real ales. Among the appetizers are leek-and-Stilton quiche, while pot-roasted pheasant is a popular main course. Try bread-and-butter pudding with apricot sauce for dessert. Appetizing sandwiches—a lamb-and-yogurt tortilla, for example—are an alternative at lunch. ⊠ *Victoria Quay* ☎ *01743/340525* ⊕ *www.armoury-shrewsbury.co.uk* ▭ *AE, MC, V.*

££
BRITISH
✕ **Draper's Hall.** The dark-wood paneling, antique furniture, and intimate lighting of this 16th-century hall make it a distinctive dining spot

for up-to-date British cuisine. You might try the slow-roasted crispy duck with Cointreau; leave room for desserts such as meringue cake with berries and Chantilly cream. There are plenty of cheeses and salads, as well as good fish and vegetarian choices; special diets are accommodated. Another option is the lighter brasserie menu. ⊠ *10 St. Mary's Pl.* ☎ *01743/344679* ⊕ *www.drapershallrestaurant.co.uk* ▤ *AE, MC, V* ⊘ *No dinner Sun.*

££ ✕ **Mad Jack's.** Whether you eat in the sleek, dark-wood restaurant or
MODERN BRITISH the foliage-filled courtyard, you'll be tucking into good local and seasonal produce. Look out for the Shropshire lamb and, in winter, local venison sausages with Shropshire blue cheese mash. It's a good spot for plump sandwiches at lunchtime, or afternoon tea or cocktails later in the day. Four contemporary rooms are available should you wish to linger longer. ⊠ *15 St. Mary's St.* ☎ *01743/358870* ⊕ *www.madjacks. uk.com* ▤ *MC, V* ⊘ *No dinner Sun.*

WHERE TO STAY

££–£££ 🏨 **Albright Hussey Hotel.** Lovely gardens surround this Tudor manor house, originally the home of the Hussey family, which dates back to 1524. Black-and-white half-timbering combines with a later red-brick-and-stone extension. Beams, oak paneling, four-poster beds, and antiques enhance rooms in the original building, for which you should book well ahead; those in the extension are plainer. The hotel is 2½ mi north of Shrewsbury on A5228. **Pros:** friendly service; beautiful grounds. **Cons:** popular venue for weddings; books up for weekends. ⊠ *Ellesmere Rd.* ☎ *01939/290503* ⊕ *www.albrighthussey.co.uk* 🛏 *22 rooms, 4 suites* ♿ *In-room: no a/c, Wi-Fi. In-hotel: restaurant, room service, bar, laundry service, parking (free), some pets allowed* ▤ *AE, DC, MC, V* ⎮⊚⎮ *BP.*

££ 🏨 **The Lion Hotel.** The myriad corridors of this famous coaching inn in the heart of town creak with more than 600 years of history. Rooms are small and traditionally furnished, but the glorious lounge, with its high ceiling, oil paintings, and carved-stone fireplace, sets the Lion apart. Add to this the magnificent Adam Ballroom and you can see the appeal for former guests such as Charles Dickens, whose suite served as inspiration for *The Pickwick Papers.* **Pros:** historic appeal; good breakfasts. **Cons:** prone to wedding parties on weekends; smallish rooms. ⊠ *Wyle Cop* ☎ *01743/353107* ⊕ *www.thelionhotelshrewsbury.co.uk* 🛏 *59 rooms* ♿ *In-room: no a/c. In-hotel: restaurant, room service, bar, laundry service, Wi-Fi hotspot* ▤ *AE, MC, V* ⎮⊚⎮ *BP.*

£ 🏨 **Sandford House Hotel.** The Richards family runs this small Georgian hotel close to the river and the town center. Beautiful original decorative plasterwork is still in evidence; modern pine furnishes the bedrooms. Room 5 is seven-sided, with a beautiful molded ceiling, and there are eight modern rooms in the garden lodge. **Pros:** central location; good for people with disabilities; nice garden. **Cons:** some bedrooms face busy road; no parking. ⊠ *St. Julian Friars* ☎ *01743/343829* ⊕ *www. sandfordhouse.co.uk* 🛏 *18 rooms* ♿ *In-room: no a/c, no phone, Wi-Fi. In-hotel: Wi-Fi hotspot, some pets allowed* ▤ *AE, MC, V* ⎮⊚⎮ *BP.*

9

NIGHTLIFE AND THE ARTS

The **Theatre Severn** (✉ *Frankwell Quay* ☎ *01743/281281*) covers all the performance arts: music, both classical and popular; dance; and drama.

SHOPPING

The **Parade** (✉ *St. Mary's Pl.* ☎ *01743/343178*), just behind St. Mary's church, is a shopping center created from the neoclassical former Royal Infirmary, built in 1830. One of the most appealing malls in England, it has 25 attractive boutiques, a coffee shop, and a river terrace.

EN ROUTE If you head south of Shrewsbury on B4380 for around 5 mi, you can see, rising on the left, the **Wrekin**, a strange, wooded, conical, extinct volcano that is 1,335 feet high. The walk to the summit, which has panoramic views, is about 5 mi. A few miles farther on, you enter the wooded gorge of the River Severn.

MUCH WENLOCK

12 mi southeast of Shrewsbury.

Much Wenlock, a town on A458, is full of half-timber buildings, including a 16th-century guildhall. Nearby are popular places to walk; ask the tourist office for information.

GETTING HERE AND AROUND

The town is a half hour by car from Shrewsbury on A458, or you can take the Arriva bus service that runs hourly (35 minutes).

ESSENTIALS

Bus Contact Arriva (☎ *0871/200–2233* ⊕ *www.arrivabus.co.uk*).

Visitor Information Much Wenlock (✉ *The Museum, High St.* ☎ *01952/727679* ⊕ *www.muchwenlockguide.info*).

EXPLORING

The romantic ruins of Norman **Wenlock Priory**, with their elaborate decoration, are in a topiary garden. ✉ *High St.* ☎ *01952/727466* ⊕ *www.english-heritage.org.uk* 🎫 *£3.80* ⊙ *Late Mar.–Apr., Sept., and Oct., Wed.–Sun. and national holiday Mon. 10–5; May–Aug., daily 10–5; Nov.–Feb., Thurs.–Sun. 10–4.*

SPORTS AND THE OUTDOORS

The high escarpment of **Wenlock Edge** runs southwest from Much Wenlock and provides a splendid view. This is hiking country, and if a healthful walk sounds inviting, turn off B4371 through Church Stretton into Cardingmill Valley, or to the wide heather uplands on top of Long Mynd. You can park and set off on foot.

IRONBRIDGE GORGE

15 mi east of Shrewsbury, 28 mi northwest of Birmingham.

The River Severn and its tree-cloaked banks make an attractive backdrop to this cluster of villages; within a mile of the graceful span of the world's first iron bridge are a cluster of fascinating museums exploring

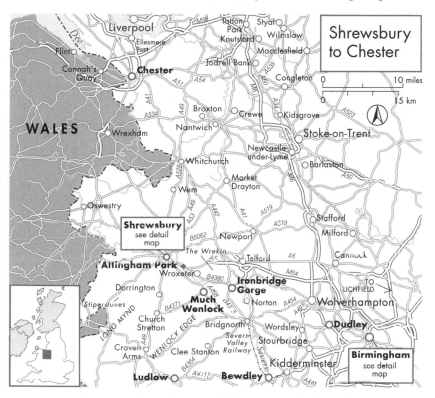

the area's industrial past and the reasons it has been described as the "cradle of the Industrial Revolution."

GETTING HERE AND AROUND

To drive here from Shrewsbury, take the A5 east, the A442 south, and then the A4169 west before following the brown signs for Ironbridge. On weekends and bank holidays from Easter to late October, the Gorge Shuttle Bus shuttles passengers between Ironbridge's museums; it's free of charge to museum passport holders.

ESSENTIALS

Visitor Information Ironbridge Visitor Information (✉ *The Toll House* ☎ *01952/884391* ⊕ *www.ironbridge.org.uk*).

EXPLORING

☾ The 10 sections of the **Ironbridge Gorge Museum**, spread over 6 square
★ mi, preserve the area's fascinating industrial history. ■ TIP➔ **Allow at least a full day to appreciate all the major sights, and perhaps to take a stroll around the famous iron bridge or hunt for Coalport china in the stores clustered near it.** On weekends and national holidays from April through October, a shuttle bus takes you between sites. The best starting point is the **Museum of the Gorge**, which has a good selection of literature and an audiovisual show on the gorge's history. In nearby Coalbrookdale, the **Museum of Iron** explains the production of iron and steel. You

can see the blast furnace built by Abraham Darby, who developed the original coke process in 1709. The adjacent **Enginuity** exhibition is a hands-on, feet-on, interactive exploration of engineering; it's good for kids. From here, drive the few miles along the river until the arches of the **Iron Bridge** come into view. Designed by T.F. Pritchard, smelted by Darby, and erected between 1777 and 1779, this graceful arch spanning the River Severn can best be seen—and photographed or painted—from the towpath, a riverside walk edged with wildflowers and shrubs. The tollhouse on the far side houses an exhibition on the bridge's history and restoration.

A mile farther along the river is the **Jackfield Tile Museum,** a repository of decorative tiles from the 19th and 20th centuries. Another half mile brings you to the **Coalport China Museum.** Exhibits show some of the factory's most beautiful wares, and craftspeople give demonstrations; visit the restrooms for the unique communal washbasins. Above Coalport is **Blists Hill Victorian Town,** where you can see old mines, furnaces, and a wrought-iron works. But the main draw is the re-creation of the "town" itself, with its doctor's office, bakery, grocer's, candle maker's, sawmill, printing shop, and candy store. At the entrance you can change some money for specially minted pennies and make purchases from the shops. Shopkeepers, the bank manager, and the doctor's wife are on hand to give you advice. If you don't fancy the refreshments at the Fried Fish shop, drop into the **New Inn** pub (in Blists Hill) for a traditional ale or ginger beer, and join in the sing-along around the piano at 1 and 3:30 (3 in winter), or tuck into a steak-and-kidney pudding from the butcher's next door. ⊠ *B4380, Ironbridge, Telford* ☎ *01952/884391* ⊕ *www.ironbridge.org.uk* 🎫 *£19.95* ☉ *Daily 10–5; Blists Hill Apr.–Oct., daily 10–5; Nov.–Mar., daily 10–4.*

WHERE TO EAT AND STAY

££££
MODERN BRITISH

✕ **Restaurant Severn.** This discreet eatery, set back from the main road in the center of Ironbridge, delivers fine quality food prepared with care and attention. Fixed-price dinner menus (around £25) of up-to-date English fare might feature wild mushroom soufflé, or duckling with damson plum compote; pear-and-almond tart rounds off the meal well. The warm yellow walls cast a glow on elegant surroundings. ⊠ *33 High St.* ☎ *01952/432233* ⊕ *www.restaurantseven.co.uk* ⊟ *AE, MC, V* ☉ *Closed Mon. and Tues. No dinner Sun.; no lunch Wed.–Sat.*

££

🛏 **Hundred House Hotel.** The low beams, stained glass, wood paneling, and patchwork cushions that greet you as you enter this Georgian inn set the tone for the whimsical guest rooms. Feel thoroughly cocooned by the antique beds, floral quilts, and lavender-scented sheets, and take a lulling sway on a velvet swing (many rooms have one). The excellent restaurant uses herbs and vegetables from the well-tended gardens. It's 3 mi from both Ironbridge and Bridgnorth. **Pros:** full of nooks and corners; good food. **Cons:** not for those who favor the plain and simple. ⊠ *A442, Norton* ☎ *01952/730353* ⊕ *www.hundredhouse.co.uk* ➪ *10 rooms* ♿ *In-room: no a/c, Wi-Fi. In-hotel: restaurant, bar, some pets allowed* ⊟ *MC, V* ⦿︎ *BP.*

££
★

🛏 **Library House.** At one time the village's library, this small guesthouse on the hillside near the Ironbridge museums (and a few steps from the bridge) has kept its attractive Victorian style while allowing for modern-day luxuries—a DVD library, for instance. Rooms are furnished with elegance, and service is warm without being obtrusive. **Pros:** welcoming hosts; good location; free parking passes for the town. **Cons:** not for families with young children. ⊠ *11 Severn Bank, Telford* ☎ *01952/432299* ⊕ *www.libraryhouse.com* ➳ *3 rooms* ⚲ *In-room: no a/c, no phone, DVD, Wi-Fi. In-hotel: bar, no kids under 12* ⊟ *MC, V* ¶⊚∣ *BP.*

LUDLOW

29 mi south of Shrewsbury, 24 mi north of Hereford.

Medieval, Georgian, and Victorian buildings jostle for attention in pretty Ludlow, which has a finer display of black-and-white half-timber buildings than even Shrewsbury. Dominating the center is the Church of St. Lawrence, its extravagant size a testimony to the town's prosperous wool trade. Cross the River Teme and climb Whitcliffe for a spectacular view of the church and the Norman castle.

Several outstanding restaurants have given the town of 10,000 a reputation as a culinary hot spot. Ludlow is now the national headquarters of the Slow Food movement, which focuses on food traditions and responsible production.

GETTING HERE AND AROUND

Ludlow has good train connections. From London Paddington, the journey time is 3¼ hours (changing at Newport), from Birmingham 1¾ hours, and from Shrewsbury 30 minutes. The train station is a 15-minute walk southwest to the center. Driving from London, take M40, M42, and then A448 to Kidderminster, A456, and A4117 to Ludlow. The town has good parking and is easily walkable.

ESSENTIALS

Visitor Information Ludlow (⊠ *Castle St.* ☎ *01584/875053* ⊕ *www.ludlow.org. uk*).

EXPLORING

The **Ludlow and the Marches Food Festival** (☎ *01584/873957* ⊕ *www. foodfestival.co.uk*) takes place over a weekend in mid-September and has demonstrations and tastings of local sausages, ale, and cider.

The "very perfection of decay," according to author Daniel Defoe, the ruins of the red sandstone **Ludlow Castle** date from 1085. No wonder the massive structure dwarfs the town: it served as a vital stronghold for centuries and was the seat of the Marcher Lords who ruled "the Marches," the local name for the border region. The two sons of Edward IV—the little princes of the Tower of London—spent time here before being dispatched to London and their death in 1483. Follow the terraced walk around the castle for a lovely view of the countryside. ⊠ *Castle Sq.* ☎ *01584/873355* ⊕ *www.ludlowcastle.com* ☜ *£4.50* ☉ *Jan. and Dec., weekends 10–4; Feb., Mar., Oct., and Nov., daily 10–4; Apr.–July and Sept., daily 10–5; Aug., daily 10–7; last admission 30 mins before closing.*

9

OFF THE
BEATEN
PATH

Stokesay Castle. This 13th-century fortified manor house built by a wealthy merchant is arguably the finest of its kind in England. Inside the main hall, the wooden cruck roof and timber staircase (a rare survival) demonstrate state-of-the-art building methods of the day. Outside, the cottage-style garden creates a bewitching backdrop for the magnificent Jacobean timber-frame gatehouse. ⊠ *Craven Arms ✛ Off A49 Shrewsbury road, 7 mi northwest of Ludlow* ☎ *01588/672544* ⊕ *www.english-heritage.org.uk* ⊠ *£5.20* ☉ *Mar. and Oct., Wed.–Sun. and national holidays 10–5; Apr.–Sept., daily 10–5; Nov.–Feb., Thurs.– Sun. 10–4.*

WHERE TO EAT

Ludlow is known for some pricier fine-dining establishments, but options from excellent tearooms to pubs and ethnic restaurants are also available.

££££
FRENCH

✕ **La Bécasse.** Dip into the past—the intimate building dates to 1349, the warm oak paneling merely to the 17th century—as you savor a fixed-price menu of French food that's bang up to the minute. Rose-color glass chargers on crisp white table linen signal the artistry with which dishes such as smoked pigeon with beetroot-infused spaghetti and horseradish-flavored ice cream are presented. Vegetarians are well served with a separate menu. Reservations are essential on weekends. ⊠ *17 Corve St.* ☎ *01584/872325* ⊕ *www.labecasse.co.uk* ⊟ *MC, V* ☉ *Closed Mon. No dinner Sun. No lunch Tues.*

££££
MODERN BRITISH

✕ **Mr. Underhill's.** Occupying a converted mill building beneath the castle, this secluded establishment looks onto the wooded River Teme. The restaurant is stylish, light, and informal. The superb Modern British, fixed-price menus (£50–£60) take advantage of fresh seasonal ingredients. For a main dish you might choose local venison with caper-and-raisin sauce, and for dessert, strawberry sponge cake with black-pepper ice cream. Book well ahead, especially on weekends; rooms and suites available should you want to make a night of it. ⊠ *Dinham Weir* ☎ *01584/874431* ⊕ *www.mr-underhills.co.uk* ⊟ *MC, V* ☉ *Closed Mon. and Tues. No lunch.*

WHERE TO STAY

£££–££££

🛏 **Dinham Hall.** This 1792 hotel near Ludlow Castle formerly served as a boys' dormitory for the local grammar school. The owners have successfully integrated modern amenities—including comfortable furniture and print fabrics—with the historic elements. The elegant dining room serves creative fixed-price meals. **Pros:** light and intimate; great views over walled garden; good restaurant. **Cons:** no Internet access; can be chilly in winter. ⊠ *Off Market Sq.* ☎ *01584/876464* ⊕ *www. dinhamhall.co.uk* ⊅ *10 rooms, 3 suites* ⅏ *In-room: no a/c. In-hotel: restaurant, room service, bar, laundry service, some pets allowed* ⊟ *MC, V* ⦿❘ *BP.*

£££–££££

🛏 **The Feathers.** Even if you're not staying here, take time to admire the extravagant half-timber facade of this hotel, described by the architectural historian Nicholas Pevsner as "that prodigy of timber-framed houses." The interior is equally impressive—dripping with ornate plaster ceilings, carved oak, paneling, beams, and creaking floors. Some guest rooms are done in modern style, but others preserve the antique look. **Pros:** ornate plasterwork; unpretentious feel. **Cons:** most guest rooms lack antique look. ⊠ *The Bull Ring* 🕾 *01584/875261* ⊕ *www. feathersatludlow.co.uk* 🔊 *40 rooms* 🕭 *In-room: no a/c. In-hotel: restaurant, room service, bar, laundry service, Wi-Fi hotspot, some pets allowed* ⊟ *AE, MC, V* 🍽 *BP.*

££ 🏠 **Timberstone.** The Read family has made a welcoming haven out of
☾ its rambling stone cottage in the Clee Hills. Rooms are furnished in neutral tones in a soothing, contemporary style; the Clay Room has its own veranda, and in summer the Garden Studio makes the perfect television-free retreat. Books and games abound, and reflexology treatment, a sauna, and evening meals are options if you wish to stay put. The owners have young children and are used to them. There's shuttle service to and from Ludlow, which is 5 mi away. **Pros:** relaxing and hospitable; geared to families; great food. **Cons:** out of center of Ludlow; twisty lanes. ⊠ *B4363, Clee Stanton* 🕾 *01584/823519* ⊕ *www. timberstoneludlow.co.uk* 🔊 *4 rooms* 🕭 *In-room: no a/c, no phone, no TV (some), Wi-Fi. In-hotel: some pets allowed* ⊟ *MC, V* 🍽 *BP.*

NIGHTLIFE AND THE ARTS

The two-week **Ludlow Festival** (🕾 *01584/872150* ⊕ *www.ludlowfestival. co.uk*), starting in late June, includes Shakespeare performed near the ruined castle, and opera, dance, and concerts around town.

CHESTER

75 mi north of Ludlow, 46 mi north of Shrewsbury.

Cheshire's thriving center is Chester, a city similar in some ways to Shrewsbury, though it has many more black-and-white half-timber buildings (some built in Georgian and Victorian times), and its medieval walls still stand.

Chester has been a prominent city since the late 1st century, when the Roman Empire expanded north to the banks of the River Dee. The original Roman town plan is still evident: the principal streets, Eastgate, Northgate, Watergate, and Bridge Street, lead out from the Cross—the site of the central area of the Roman fortress—to the four city gates, and the partly excavated remains of what is thought to have been the country's largest Roman amphitheater lie to the south of Chester's medieval castle.

History seems more tangible in Chester than in many other ancient cities. Much medieval architecture remains in the compact town center, and modern buildings have not been allowed to intrude. A negative result of this perfection is that Chester has become a favorite bus-tour destination, with gift shops, noise, and crowds.

GETTING HERE AND AROUND

There's a free shuttle bus to the center if you arrive by train, and buses pull up at Vicar's Lane in the center. Chester is 180 mi from London, and about 2¾ hours by train (change at Crewe). If you're driving and here for a day only, use the city's Park and Ride lots, as central parking lots fill quickly, especially in summer.

9

Guided walks leave the town hall daily at 10:30, and City Sightseeing operates daily tours of Chester in open-top buses from May to September.

ESSENTIALS

Visitor and Tour Information Chester (⊠ *Town Hall, Northgate St.* ✉ *Vicar's La.* ☎ *01244/402111* ⊕ *www.visitchester.com*). **City Sightseeing** (☎ *01244/381461* ⊕ *www.city-sightseeing.com*).

EXPLORING

TOP ATTRACTIONS

Chester Cathedral. Tradition has it that a church of some sort stood on the site of what is now Chester Cathedral in Roman times, but records indicate construction around AD 900. The earliest work traceable today, mainly in the north transept, is that of the 11th-century Benedictine abbey. After Henry VIII dissolved the monasteries in the 16th century, the abbey church became the cathedral church of the new diocese of Chester. The misericords in the choir stalls reveal intricately carved figures of people and animals, both real and mythical, and above is a gilded and colorful vaulted ceiling. In the small inner garden, a striking modern bronze statue depicts the woman of Samaria offering water to Jesus. ⊠ *St. Werburgh St., off Market Sq.* ☎ *01244/324756* ⊕ *www. chestercathedral.com* ⊠ *£4, includes audio guide* ⊙ *Mon.–Sat. 9–5, Sun. 12:30–4.*

City walls. The city walls, accessible from several points, provide splendid views of the city and its surroundings. The whole circuit is 2 mi, but if your time is short, climb the steps at Newgate and walk along toward Eastgate to see the great ornamental **Eastgate Clock,** erected to commemorate Queen Victoria's Diamond Jubilee in 1897. Lots of small shops near this part of the walls sell old books, old postcards, antiques, and jewelry. Where the **Bridge of Sighs** (named after the enclosed bridge in Venice that it closely resembles) crosses the canal, descend to street level and walk up Northgate Street into Market Square.

★ **Rows.** Chester's unique Rows, which originated in the 12th and 13th centuries, are essentially double rows of stores, one at street level and the other on the second floor with galleries overlooking the street. The Rows line the junction of the four streets in the old town. They have medieval crypts below them, and some reveal Roman foundations.

WORTH NOTING

ChesterBoat. This company runs excursions on the River Dee every 30 minutes daily (April through October) and hourly on weekends (November through March). Saturday evening cruises in summer feature discos. ⊠ *Boating Station, Souters La., The Groves* ☎ *01244/325394* ⊕ *www. chesterboat.co.uk.*

☼ **Chester Zoo.** Well-landscaped grounds and natural enclosures make the 80-acre zoo one of Britain's most popular, as well as the largest. Highlights include Chimpanzee Island, the jaguar enclosure, and the Islands in Danger tropical habitat. Baby animals are often on display. Eleven miles of paths wend through the zoo, and you can use the waterbus boats or the overhead train to tour the grounds. ⊠ *A41, 2 mi north of*

Chester ☎ *01244/380280* ⊕ *www.chesterzoo.org* ⚑ *Apr.–Oct. £16.90; Nov.–Mar. £13.60, bus £2, train £2* ☉ *Daily 10–dusk.*

Grosvenor Museum. Start a visit with a look at Roman Chester, particularly in the Roman Stones Gallery, which houses tombstones previously used to repair the walls; look out for the wounded barbarian. Then skip a few centuries to explore the period house for a tour from 1680 to the 1920s. ✉ *27 Grosvenor St.* ☎ *01244/402033* ⚑ *Free* ⊕ *www. grosvenormuseum.co.uk* ☉ *Mon.–Sat. 10:30–5, Sun. 1–4.*

WHERE TO EAT

£   ✕ **Albion.** You feel as if you're stepping back in time at this Victorian
BRITISH   pub; the posters, advertisements, flags, and curios tell you the idiosyncratic landlord keeps it as it would have been during World War I. The candlelit restaurant forms one of the three snug rooms and, unsurprisingly, serves up traditional fare such as corned beef hash, Staffordshire oatcakes, and gammon (thick-sliced ham) with pease pudding. You can stay overnight here as well. ✉ *Park St.* ☎ *01244/340345* ⊕ *www. albioninnchester.co.uk* ⊟ *No credit cards* ☉ *No dinner Sun.*

££   ✕ **Chez Jules.** Once a fire station, this bustling bistro is now unashamedly
BISTRO   French and rustic, with red-and-white-check tablecloths and a menu chalked up on the blackboard. Start perhaps with a tomato tarte tatin, and then follow with poached trout fillet with white wine–and–blue cheese sauce, or rabbit stew with truffle-infused dumplings. ✉ *71 Northgate St.* ☎ *01244/400014* ⊕ *www.chezjules.com* ⊟ *MC, V.*

£££££   ✕ **Simon Radley at the Chester Grosvenor.** Named for its noted chef, this
FRENCH   restaurant has a sophisticated panache. Expect the seasonal but not the usual: the cheekily named Carpetbagger is dry cured beef with rock oysters, truffles, and watercress, and Coffee is a chocolate cup with iced latte, espresso jelly, and coffee-bean brittle. There's a fixed-price dinner (£69) as well as a daily gastronomic menu (£80). The wine cellar has more than 1,000 bins. Reservations are essential on weekends, and children must be at least 12. ✉ *Chester Grosvenor Hotel, Eastgate St.* ☎ *01244/895618* ⊕ *www.chestergrosvenor.com* ⊟ *AE, DC, MC, V* ☉ *No dinner Mon. and Sun. Closed 1st 3 wks in Jan.*

WHERE TO STAY

££££–£££££   ▥ **Chester Grosvenor Hotel.** Handmade Italian furniture and French silk
★   furnishings fill this deluxe downtown hotel in a Tudor-style building. Molton Brown toiletries, CD and DVD players, and a luxury spa are among the pampering amenities. There are two restaurants, including the well-regarded Simon Radley at the Chester Grosvenor, and the intimate library is a perfect spot for afternoon tea. Breakfast is included in the weekend rates. **Pros:** pampering luxury; superb food; excellent service and facilities. **Cons:** no private parking. ✉ *Eastgate St.* ☎ *01244/324024* ⊕ *www.chestergrosvenor.com* ⇆ *66 rooms, 14 suites* ♿ *In-room: safe, Internet. In-hotel: 2 restaurants, room service, bar, gym, spa, laundry service, Wi-Fi hotspot* ⊟ *AE, DC, MC, V.*

££–£££   ▥ **Frogg Manor.** Leave the modern world behind, dance foxtrots after
★   dinner in the party room, and sleep in sumptuous tranquillity. Lavishly furnished with antiques, drapes, and ornaments (frogs in particular), this hotel makes its individualist statement and never fails its devotees.

9

Lady Guinevere is the only tree-house suite in the country, and the conservatory restaurant has a gourmet (£42) and set-price menu (£37). The hotel is 15 minutes' drive south of Chester. **Pros:** English eccentricity at its best; frills and furbelows. **Cons:** not for minimalists; outside town. ⊠ *A534, Nantwich Rd., Broxton* ☎ *01829/782629* ⊕ *www. froggmanorhotel.co.uk* ⌨ *8 rooms* ⌂ *In-room: no a/c, Wi-Fi. In-hotel: restaurant, bar, parking (free)* ☰ *AE, MC, V* ⏍ *CP.*

££££ ⌨ **Green Bough Hotel.** Chester's leafy outskirts are the setting for this memorable small hotel a mile from the town center. Furnished with antiques, including cast-iron and carved wooden beds, the individually designed guest rooms make luxurious and soothing retreats. The Olive Tree restaurant provides top-notch contemporary British fare in intimate surroundings. Head to the rooftop garden for a relaxing drink in summer. **Pros:** attentive service; well-designed rooms. **Cons:** no young children allowed. ⊠ *60 Hoole Rd.* ☎ *01244/326241* ⊕ *www. greenbough.co.uk* ⌨ *8 rooms, 7 suites* ⌂ *In-room: no a/c, DVD, Wi-Fi. In-hotel: restaurant, room service, bar, bicycles, laundry service, parking (free), no kids under 13* ☰ *AE, DC, MC, V* ⏍ *BP.*

£ ⌨ **Grove Villa.** The location of this family-run B&B, an early-19th-cen-
★ tury house on the banks of the River Dee, enhances its appeal. Add antique furniture and a sense of calm, and you are guaranteed a soothing stay. **Pros:** beautiful river location; breakfast around a communal table. **Cons:** cash or checks only; no Internet facilities. ⊠ *18 The Groves* ☎ *01244/349713* ⊕ *www.grovevillachester.com* ⌨ *3 rooms* ⌂ *In-room: no a/c, no phone. In-hotel: parking (free)* ☰ *No credit cards* ⏍ *BP.*

££ ⌨ **Recorder House.** This Georgian redbrick house has the perfect location right on the city wall and overlooking the River Dee. Meander through the picture-filled passages to find the rooms, the best of which have four-poster beds. Rooms are named after astrological signs, but the furnishings are straightforwardly traditional. The amiable hosts don't stint on breakfast choices: Parma ham and fresh pineapple, bacon-and-mushroom sandwich are but two of them. **Pros:** within easy reach of the center; excellent breakfasts. **Cons:** no elevator. ⊠ *19 City Walls* ☎ *01244/326580* ⊕ *www.recorderhotel.co.uk* ⌨ *11 rooms* ⌂ *In-room: no a/c, Wi-Fi. In-hotel: parking (free)* ☰ *AE, MC, V* ⏍ *BP.*

NIGHTLIFE AND THE ARTS

Oddfellows (⊠ *20 Lower Bridge St.* ☎ *01244/400001*) is the swankiest bar in town. Sip champagne cocktails or afternoon tea and admire the big wallpaper and big candelabra. You can dine (and stay) here, too.

SHOPPING

Chester has an **indoor market** in the Forum, near the Town Hall, every day except Sunday. Watergate Street hosts antiques shops with anything from ceramics to furniture. **Bluecoat Books** (⊠ *1 City Walls* ☎ *01244/318752*) specializes in travel, art, architecture, and history.

Lancashire and the Peaks

MANCHESTER, LIVERPOOL, AND THE PEAK DISTRICT

WORD OF MOUTH

"Liverpool is the home of the Beatles. Go into the Beatles Story at the Albert Dock. A 3D exhibition down at Pier Head is included in the ticket. It's where you would take the ferry across the Mersey, which you could do. The actual Cavern was pulled down—although there is a pub/club of the same name on the site."

—Hastobe_Katt

"I was very impressed with the Peak District. We spent a day in Buxton, which is a charming spa town. Our kids enjoyed Poole's Cavern there. (Derbyshire is known for its show caverns, and there are quite a few others to visit.)"

—Vttraveler

Updated by
Paul Cannon

For those looking for the postcard England of little villages, the northwest region of England might not appear at the top of a sightseeing list. Manchester, Britain's third-largest city, today bustles with redevelopment, and Liverpool is undergoing significant revitalization. However, the 200 years of smokestack industry that abated only in the 1980s have taken a toll on the east Lancashire landscape. The region does have some lovely scenery inland, in Derbyshire (pronounced Darbyshire)—notably the spectacular Peak District, a large national park at the southern end of the Pennine range.

Manchester and Liverpool, the economic engines that propelled Britain in the 18th and 19th centuries, are sloughing off their mid-20th-century decline and celebrating their rich industrial and maritime heritage in excellent museums—in imposing Victorian edifices, or, in Manchester's case, in strikingly modern buildings. The cities, each with a population of about 450,000, have reestablished themselves as centers of sporting and musical excellence, and as nightlife hot spots. Since 1962 the Manchester United, Everton, and Liverpool football (soccer in the United States) clubs have won everything worth winning in Britain and Europe. The Beatles launched the Mersey sound of the '60s; contemporary Manchester groups ride both British and U.S. airwaves. On the classical side of music, Manchester is also the home of Britain's oldest leading orchestra, the Hallé (founded in 1857)—just one legacy of 19th-century industrialists' investments in culture.

The Peak District is a wilder part of England, a region of crags that rear violently out of the plain. The Pennines, a line of hills that begins in the Peak District and runs as far north as Scotland, are sometimes called the "backbone of England." In this landscape of rocky outcrops and vaulting meadowland, you'll see nothing for miles but sheep, drystone (without mortar) walls, and farms, interrupted—spectacularly—by 19th-century villages and treasure houses. In and around this area are Victorian-era spas such as Buxton, pretty towns such as Bakewell, and magnificent houses such as Chatsworth, Hardwick Hall, and Haddon Hall.

The delight of the Peak District is being able to ramble for days in rugged countryside but still enjoy the pleasures of civilization.

TOP REASONS TO GO

The Beatles: Whether you want to relive the Fab Four's moments of glory, visit their haunts, see their childhood homes, or just buy a Beatles pencil sharpener, a magical mystery tour in Liverpool will provide it all.

Museums in Manchester and Liverpool: You don't need the excuse of rain to learn about these cities' industrial and maritime pasts. Take history lessons at the Museum of Science and Industry and the Imperial War Museum North in Manchester, and the Merseyside Maritime Museum in Liverpool. Then opt for art appreciation in the cities' galleries.

Manchester nightspots: Catch the city at night in any of its humming café-bars and pubs; strut your stuff, soak up the latest sounds, or just enjoy a good beer in a gloriously ornate Victorian-era pub.

Chatsworth House and Haddon Hall: Engage the past and imagine yourself as a country landowner roaming the great pile that is Chatsworth, or as a Tudor noble exercising in the paneled long gallery of the quintessentially English Haddon Hall. Haddon can take you a half day—Chatsworth a full day—to explore.

Walking in the Peak District: Even a short walk in Edale or High Peak reveals the rocky yet intimate scenery that is unique to the area—dales rubbing shoulders with moors, and drystone walls patterning the fields. Civilization, in the form of pubs and peaceful towns, is always close at hand; that's part of the pleasure.

ORIENTATION AND PLANNING

GETTING ORIENTED

Manchester lies at the heart of a tangle of motorways in the northwest of England, about a half hour across the Pennines from Yorkshire. It's 70 mi from the southern edge of the Lake District. The city spreads west toward the coast and the mouth of the River Mersey, where Liverpool is still centered on its port. For the Northwest's most dramatic scenery—indeed, its only real geological feature of interest—you must travel to the Peak District, a national park less than an hour's drive southeast of Manchester. England at its grandest and most ducal can be seen in the great houses of Derbyshire's Wye valley.

Manchester. The skies may be gray, but the vibrant city of Manchester is known for its modern urban design and its thriving music and club scenes. Great museums justify its status as the leading city of the Northwest.

Liverpool. Now in the midst of a postindustrial rebirth, this city is more than the Beatles. The imposing waterfront, the pair of cathedrals, and the grand architecture make this clear. But the museums don't forget to mention the city's place in rock-and-roll history.

10

The Peak District. Britain's first national park, the Peak District is studded with an array of stately homes, the most impressive being Chatsworth House. Dramatic moors, intimate dales, and limestone caverns invite exploration.

PLANNING

WHEN TO GO

Manchester has a reputation as one of the wettest cities in Britain, and visiting in summer won't guarantee fine weather. Nevertheless, wet or cold weather shouldn't spoil a visit because of the many indoor sights and cultural activities here and in Liverpool. Summer is the optimum time to see the Peak District, especially because traditional festivities take place in many villages at its start. The *only* time to see the great houses of Derbyshire's Wye Valley is from spring through fall.

PLANNING YOUR TIME

It's possible to see the main sights of Manchester or Liverpool in a day, but you'd have to take the museums at a gallop. In Manchester, the Museum of Science and Industry and the Imperial War Museum could easily absorb a day, as could the Albert Dock and Waterfront area of Liverpool, where the Beatles Story, Tate Liverpool, Merseyside Maritime, and International Slavery museums all vie for your attention. In Liverpool, an additional half day is needed to see the homes of John Lennon and Paul McCartney. The buzzing nightlife of each city demands at least an overnight stay. You can explore the Peak District on a day trip from Manchester in a pinch, but allow longer to visit the stately homes or to hike.

GETTING HERE AND AROUND

AIR TRAVEL

Both Manchester and Liverpool are well served by their international airports. Manchester, the third-largest airport in the country, has the greater number of flights, including some from the United States.

Airports Manchester Airport (☎ 0871/271–0711 ⊕ www.manchesterairport. co.uk). **Liverpool John Lennon Airport** (☎ 0871/521–8484 ⊕ www. liverpoolairport.com).

BUS TRAVEL

National Express buses serve the region from London's Victoria Coach Station. Average travel time to Manchester or Liverpool is five hours. To reach Matlock, Bakewell, and Buxton you can take a bus from London to Derby and change to the TransPeak bus service, though you might find it more convenient to travel first to Manchester.

Bus Contacts National Express (☎ 0871/781–8181 ⊕ www.nationalexpress. com). **TransPeak** (☎ 01733/712265 ⊕ www.transpeak.co.uk). **Traveline** (☎ 0871/200–2233 ⊕ www.traveline.org.uk).

CAR TRAVEL

If you're traveling by road, expect heavy traffic out of London on weekends. Travel time to Manchester or Liverpool from London via the M6 is 3 to 3½ hours. Although a car may not be an asset in touring the

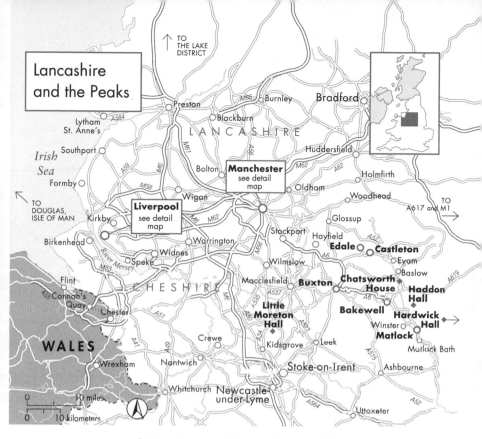

centers of Manchester and Liverpool, it is helpful in getting around the Peak District. Bus service there is quite good, but a car allows the most flexibility.

Roads within the region are generally very good. In Manchester and Liverpool, try to sightsee on foot to avoid parking problems. In the Peak District, park in signposted parking lots whenever possible. In summer, Peak District traffic is very heavy; watch out for speeding motorbikes, especially on the A6. In winter, know the weather forecast, as moorland roads can quickly become impassable.

TRAIN TRAVEL

Virgin Trains serves the region from London's Euston Station. Direct service to Manchester and Liverpool takes 2½ hours. There are trains between Manchester's Piccadilly Station and Liverpool's Lime Street every half hour during the day; the trip takes 50 minutes.

To reach Buxton, in the Peak District, from London, take the Manchester train; switch at Stockport. Local service—one train an hour—from Manchester to Buxton takes one hour. Call National Rail Enquiries for timetable information.

Train Contacts National Rail Enquiries (☎ 0845/748–4950 ⊕ www. nationalrail.co.uk).

TRANSPORTATION DISCOUNTS AND DEALS

A Wayfarer ticket (£9.20), which covers a day's travel on all forms of transport in Manchester and the Peak District, is a good deal. Contact National Rail Enquiries for information.

RESTAURANTS

Dining options in Manchester and Liverpool vary from smart cafés offering Modern British and Continental fare to excellent ethnic restaurants. Manchester has one of Britain's biggest Chinatowns, and locals also favor the 40-odd Bangladeshi, Pakistani, and Indian restaurants along Wilmslow Road in Rusholme, a mile south of the city center, known as Curry Mile.

One local dish that has survived is Bakewell pudding (*never* called "tart" in these areas, as its imitations are elsewhere in England). Served with custard or cream, the pudding—a pastry covered with jam and a thin layer of almond-flavor filling—is the joy of Bakewell. Another regional creation is Lancashire hot pot, a hearty meat stew.

HOTELS

Because the larger city-center hotels in Manchester and Liverpool rely on business travelers during the week, they may markedly reduce their rates on weekends. Smaller hotels and guesthouses abound in nearby suburbs, many just a short bus ride from downtown. The Manchester and Liverpool visitor centers operate room-booking services. Also worth investigating are serviced apartments, which are becoming more popular in the cities. The Peak District has inns, bed-and-breakfasts, and hotels, as well as a network of youth hostels. Local tourist offices have details; reserve well in advance for Easter and summer.

WHAT IT COSTS IN POUNDS				
£	££	£££	££££	£££££
Restaurants	under £10	£10–£14	£15–£19	£20–£25	over £25
Hotels	under £70	£70–£120	£121–£160	£161–£220	over £220

Restaurant prices are for a main course at dinner. Hotel prices are for two people in a standard double room in high season, including V.A.T., with no meals or, if indicated, CP (with Continental breakfast), BP (Breakfast Plan, with full breakfast), or MAP (Modified American Plan, with breakfast and dinner).

VISITOR INFORMATION

England's Northwest (⊕ *www.visitenglandsnorthwest.com*).

MANCHESTER

Today Manchester's center hums with the vibe of cutting-edge popular music and a swank café culture. The city's once-grim industrial landscape, redeveloped since the late 1980s, includes tidied-up canals, cotton mills transformed into loft apartments, and stylish contemporary architecture that has pushed the skyline ever higher. Beetham Tower, the second-tallest building in Britain after London's Canary Wharf, can't be overlooked. Bridgewater Hall and the Lowry, as well as the

Imperial War Museum North, are outstanding cultural facilities. Sure, it still rains here, but the rain-soaked streets are part of the city's charm, in a bleak, northern kind of way.

The now-defunct Haçienda Club marketed New Order to the world, and Manchester became the clubbing capital of England. Joy Division, Morrissey, Stone Roses, Happy Mondays, and Oasis rose to the top of the charts. The extraordinary success of the Manchester United football club (which now faces a stiff challenge from its newly rich neighbor, Manchester City, owing to a stupendous injection of cash from its oil-rich Middle Eastern owners) has kept the eyes of sports fans fixed firmly on Manchester.

GETTING HERE AND AROUND

Manchester Airport has many international flights, so you might not even have to travel through London. There are frequent trains from the airport to Piccadilly Railway Station (15–20 minutes) and buses to Piccadilly Gardens Bus Station (one hour). A taxi from the airport to Manchester city center costs between £18 and £20. For details about public transportation in Manchester, call the Greater Manchester Passenger Transport Executive (GMPTE) information line.

Driving to Manchester from London (3 to 3½ hours), take M1 north to M6, then the M62 east, which becomes M602 as it enters Greater Manchester. Trains from London's Euston Station drop passengers at the centrally located Piccadilly Railway Station. The journey takes 2½ hours. Chorlton Street Coach Station, a few hundred yards west of Piccadilly Railway Station, is the main bus station for regional and long-distance buses.

Most local buses leave from Piccadilly Gardens Bus Station, the hub of the urban bus network. Metroshuttle operates three free circular routes around the city center; service runs every 5 to 10 minutes Monday to Saturday 7 to 7 and Sunday 10 to 6.

Metrolink electric tram service runs through the city center and out to the suburbs. The Eccles extension has stops for the Lowry (Harbour City) and for the Manchester United Stadium (Old Trafford). Major extensions to the service will see routes added to Droylsden, Chorlton, Media City UK, and Oldham and Rochdale by 2012. Buy a ticket from the platform machine before you board. A £5.80 one-day tram and bus ticket is a good value.

Blue Badge Guides can arrange dozens of different tours of the city, and City Centre Cruises offers a three-hour Sunday lunch round-trip on a barge to the Manchester Ship Canal.

10

ORIENTATION

Manchester is compact enough that you can easily walk across the city center in 40 minutes, but buses and trams make it easy to navigate. Deansgate and Princess Street, the main thoroughfares, run roughly north–south and west–east; the lofty terra-cotta Victorian **Town Hall** sits in the middle, close to the visitor center and the fine **Manchester Art Gallery**. Dominating the skyline at the southern end of Deansgate is Manchester's newest and highest building, Beetham Tower, which houses a Hilton Hotel and marks the beginning of the **Castlefield Urban**

Heritage Park, with the Museum of Science and Industry and the canal system. The **Whitworth Art Gallery** is a bus ride from downtown; otherwise, all other central sights are within easy walking distance of the Town Hall. Take a Metrolink tram 2 mi south for the Salford Quays dockland area, with the **Lowry** and the **Imperial War Museum;** you can spend half a day or more in this area. ■TIP→ Keep in mind that the museums are both excellent and free.

ESSENTIALS

Transportation Contacts Greater Manchester Passenger Transport Executive (☎ *0161/244–1000 or 0871/200–2233* ⊕ *www.gmpte.com*). **Metrolink** (☎ *0161/205–2000* ⊕ *www.metrolink.co.uk*).

Visitor and Tour Information Blue Badge Guides (☎ *0161/440–0277*). **City Centre Cruises** (☎ *0161/902–0222* ⊕ *www.citycentrecruises.co.uk*). **Manchester Visitor Centre** (✉ *Town Hall Extension, Lloyd St., City Centre* ☎ *0871/222–8223* ⊕ *www.visitmanchester.com*).

EXPLORING

TOP ATTRACTIONS

❹ Castlefield Urban Heritage Park. Site of an early Roman fort, the district of Castlefield was later the center of the city's industrial boom, which resulted in the building of Britain's first modern canal in 1764 and the world's first railway station in 1830. What had become an urban wasteland has been beautifully restored into an urban park with canal-side walks, landscaped open spaces, and refurbished warehouses. The 7-acre site contains the reconstructed gate to the Roman fort of Mamucium, the buildings of the **Museum of Science and Industry,** and several of the city's hippest bars and restaurants. You can spend half a day here, including the museum. ✉ *Off Liverpool Rd., Castlefield.*

★ **Imperial War Museum North.** The thought-provoking exhibits in this striking, aluminum-clad building, which architect Daniel Libeskind described as representing three shards of an exploded globe, present the reasons for war and show its effects on society. Three Big Picture audiovisual shows envelop you in the sights and sounds of conflicts from 1914 to the present, and a storage system has select trays of objects to examine, including artifacts from the 2003 war in Iraq. A 100-foot viewing platform gives a bird's-eye view of the city. The museum is on the banks of the Manchester Ship Canal in Salford Quays, across the footbridge from the Lowry. It's a 10-minute (often breezy) walk from the Harbour City stop of the Metrolink tram. ✉ *Trafford Wharf Rd., Salford Quays* ☎ *0161/836–4000* ⊕ *www.iwm.org.uk* ✆ *Free* ☉ *Mar.–Oct., daily 10–6; Nov.–Feb., daily 10–5; last admission 30 mins before closing.*

The Lowry. This impressive arts center in Manchester's Salford Quays waterways occupies a dramatic modern building with a steel-gray metallic-and-glass exterior that reflects the light. L.S. Lowry (1887–1976) was a local artist, and one of the few who painted the industrial landscape. Galleries showcase Lowry's and other contemporary artists' work. The theater, Britain's largest outside London, presents an impressive lineup of touring companies. The nearest Metrolink tram

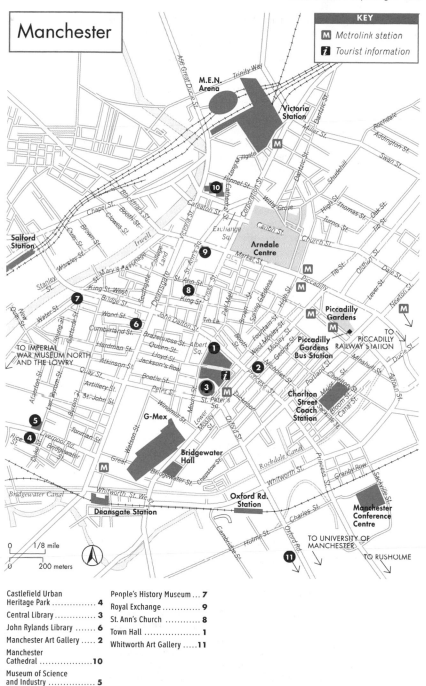

Manchester

KEY

M Metrolink station

ℹ️ Tourist information

stop is Harbour City, a 10-minute walk from the Lowry. ⊠ *Pier 8, Salford Quays* ☎ *0870/876–2001* ⊕ *www.thelowry.com* ⊠ *Free; prices vary for theater tickets and exhibitions; tours £3* ◯ *Building Sun. and Mon. 10–6, Tues.–Sat. 10–8, or last performance; galleries Sun.–Fri. 11–5, Sat. 10–5.*

❷ **Manchester Art Gallery.** Behind its impressive classical portico, this splen-
★ did museum presents its collections in both a Victorian and contemporary setting. Don't miss the outstanding examples of the vibrant paintings of the Pre-Raphaelites and their circle, notably Ford Madox Brown's masterpiece *Work* and Holman Hunt's *The Hireling Shepherd*. British artworks from the 18th century—*Cheetah and Stag with Two Indians* by George Stubbs, for instance—and the 20th century are also well represented. The Manchester Gallery illustrates the city's contribution to art, and the second-floor Craft and Design Gallery shows off the best of the decorative arts in ceramics, glass, metalwork, and furniture. ⊠ *Mosely St., City Centre* ☎ *0161/235–8888* ⊕ *www.manchestergalleries.org.uk* ⊠ *Free* ◯ *Tues.–Sun. and national holidays 10–5.*

❺ **Museum of Science and Industry.** The museum's five buildings, one of
Fodor'sChoice which is the world's oldest passenger rail station (1830), hold marvel-
★ ous collections relating to the city's industrial past and present. You can walk through a reconstructed Victorian sewer, be blasted by the heat and noise of working steam engines, see cotton looms whirring in action, and watch a planetarium show. The Air and Space Gallery fills a graceful cast-iron-and-glass building, constructed as a market hall in 1877. ■TIP➔ **Allow at least half a day to get the most out of all the sites, which are in the Castlefield Urban Heritage Park.** ⊠ *Liverpool Rd., main entrance on Lower Byrom St., Castlefield* ☎ *0161/832–2244* ⊕ *www.mosi.org.uk* ⊠ *Free, charges vary for special exhibitions; parking £3–£7, depending on time of day* ◯ *Daily 10–5.*

❼ **People's History Museum.** Not everyone in 19th-century Manchester
ⓒ owned a cotton mill or made a fortune on the trading floor. This refurbished and extended museum, reopened in 2009, recounts powerfully the struggles of working people in the city since the Industrial Revolution. It tells the story of the 1819 Peterloo Massacre and has an unrivaled collection of trade-union banners, tools, toys, utensils, and photographs, all illustrating the working lives and pastimes of the city's people. ⊠ *Left Bank, City Centre* ☎ *0161/838–9190* ⊕ *www.phm.org.uk* ⊠ *Free* ◯ *Daily 10–5.*

NEED A BREAK? The brick-vaulted, waterside **Mark Addy pub** (⊠ *Stanley St. off Bridge St., City Centre* ☎ *0161/832–4080*) is a good spot to have a drink and sample an excellent spread of pâtés and cheeses. The pub is named for the 19th-century boatman who rescued more than 50 people from the River Irwell.

❾ **Royal Exchange.** Throughout its commercial heyday, this was the city's most important building—the cotton market. Built with Victorian exuberance in 1874, the existing structure accommodated 7,000 traders. The building was refurbished and the giant glass-dome roof restored after damage by the 1996 IRA bombing. Visit to see the lunar module–inspired Royal Exchange Theatre, have a drink in the café, and browse

Manchester's History: Cottonopolis

Manchester's spectacular rise from a small town to the world's cotton capital—with the nickname Cottonopolis—in only 100 years began with the first steam-powered cotton mill, built in 1783. Dredging made the rivers Irwell and Mersey navigable to ship coal to the factories. The world's first passenger railway opened in 1830, and construction of the Manchester Ship Canal in 1894 provided the infrastructure for Manchester to dominate the industrial world. Check out ⊕ *www.industrialpowerhouse.co.uk* for information about seeing more of this industrial heritage.

A few people acquired great wealth, but factory hands worked under appalling conditions. Working-class discontent came to a head in 1819 in the Peterloo Massacre, when soldiers killed 11 workers at a protest meeting. The conditions under which factory hands worked were later recorded by Friedrich Engels (co-author with Karl Marx of the *Communist Manifesto*), who managed a cotton mill in the city. More formal political opposition to the government emerged in the shape of the Chartist movement (which campaigned for universal suffrage) and the Anti–Corn Law League (which opposed trade tariffs), forerunners of the British trade unions. From Victorian times until the 1960s, daily life for the average Mancunian was so oppressive that it bred the desire to escape, although most stayed put and endured the harsh conditions.

---

the crafts shop or the clothes outlets in the arcade. ⊠ *St. Ann's Sq., City Centre* ☎ *0161/834–3731* ⊕ *www.royalexchange.co.uk.*

① **Town Hall.** Manchester's imposing Town Hall, with its 280-foot-tall clock tower, speaks volumes about the city's 19th-century sense of self-importance. Alfred Waterhouse designed the Victorian Gothic building (1867–76); extensions were added just before World War II. Over the main entrance is a statue of Roman general Agricola, who founded Mamucium in AD 79. Above him are Henry III, Elizabeth I, and St. George, the patron saint of England. Murals of the city's history, painted between 1852 and 1865 by the Pre-Raphaelite Ford Madox Brown, decorate the Great Hall, with its emblazoned hammer-beam roof. Guided tours (twice a month) include the murals, but ask at the front desk: if the rooms aren't being used, you may be allowed to wander in. ⊠ *Albert Sq., public entrance on Lloyd St., City Centre* ☎ *0161/234–5000* ⊡ *Free; guided tours £6* ☉ *Mon.–Sat. 8:45–5; ask at tourist office about tour information.*

⑪ **Whitworth Art Gallery.** This University of Manchester–run art museum has strong collections of British watercolors, old-master drawings, and postimpressionist works, as well as wallpapers. The excellent textile gallery—befitting a city built on textile manufacture—demonstrates the meaning and power of clothing in such items as a 16th-century Spanish funeral cope, 18th-century babies' vests, and a modern-day Turkish circumcision suit. A good bistro and a gift shop are also here. To get to the museum, catch any southbound bus with a number in the 40s (except 47) on Oxford Road, or from St. Peter's Square or Piccadilly

10

Gardens. ✉ *Oxford Rd., University Quarter* ☎ *0161/275–7450* ⊕ *www.whitworth.manchester. ac.uk* 🎫 *Free* ⊘ *Mon.–Sat. 10–5, Sun. noon–4.*

WORTH NOTING

3 Central Library. The circular exterior of the city's main library, topped by a line of Doric columns and a massive Corinthian portico facing St. Peter's Square, is a major focus for Manchester's most prestigious civic quarter. Erected in 1930, it was at one time the biggest municipal library in the world. The glass-top reading room, inspired by the Pantheon, is worth seeing. The **Library Theatre** is part of the complex. ✉ *St. Peter's Sq., City Centre* ☎ *0161/234–1900* ⊘ *Mon.–Thurs. 9–8, Fri. and Sat. 9–5.*

CHINATOWN

The large red-and-gold Imperial Chinese Arch, erected in 1987, marks Manchester's Chinatown, one of the largest Chinese communities outside London. Bordered by Portland Street, Mosley Street, Princess Street, and Charlotte Street, the area buzzes on Sunday, when traders from all over the country stock up from the supermarkets, food stalls, herbalists, and gift shops. The restaurants offer excellent choices of authentic Cantonese cooking, so consider a stop here when your shopping energies run low.

6 John Rylands Library. Owned by the University of Manchester, this Gothic Revival masterpiece designed by Alfred Waterhouse was built by Enriqueta Augustina Rylands as a memorial to her husband, a cotton magnate. Constructed of red sandstone in the 1890s, the library resembles a cathedral and contains outstanding collections of illuminated manuscripts and personal papers of famous writers. Excellent exhibitions tell the story of the library. ✉ *150 Deansgate, City Centre* ☎ *0161/306–0555* ⊕ *www.library.manchester.ac.uk* ⊘ *Tues.–Sat. 10–5, Sun. and Mon. noon–5.*

10 Manchester Cathedral. The city's sandstone cathedral, set beside the River Irwell and originally a medieval parish church dating in part from the 15th century, is unusually broad for its length and has the widest medieval nave in Britain. Inside, angels with gilded instruments look down from the roof of the nave, and misericords (the undersides of choristers' seats) in the early-16th-century choir stalls reveal intriguing carvings. The octagonal chapter house dates from 1485. ✉ *Victoria St., Millennium Quarter* ☎ *0161/833–2220* ⊕ *www.manchestercathedral. org* 🎫 *Free, donations welcome* ⊘ *Weekdays 8:30–7, Sat. 8:30–5, Sun. 8:30–7:30.*

8 St. Ann's Church. Built in 1712 and sometimes wrongly attributed to Christopher Wren, St. Ann's is Manchester's oldest surviving classical building. The plain, elegant interior has a gallery supported by Tuscan columns, and light from the clear windows enhances the darkwood pews and chancel. ✉ *St. Ann's Sq., City Centre* ☎ *0161/834–0239* 🎫 *Free, donations welcome* ⊕ *www.stannsmanchester.com* ⊘ *Mon.– Sat. 9:45–4:45, Sun. 8:45–4:45 and 6–7:30.*

Urbis. The striking, glass-skinned triangle of a building known as Urbis has closed and will reopen as the National Football Museum in summer

2011; check the Web site for updates. Exhibits will include sacred memorabilia such as the ball from the 1966 World Cup Final and the signed shirts of legendary players such as Bobby Moore and Sir Stanley Matthews. There will also be interactive exhibits exploring soccer's role in British popular culture. Its restaurant and bar on the fifth floor, the Modern, remain open. ⊠ *Cathedral Gardens, Millennium Quarter* ☎ *0161/605–8200* ⊕ *www.urbis.org.uk.*

WHERE TO EAT

The city's dining scene, with everything from Indian (go to Rusholme) to Modern British fare, is lively. The Manchester Food & Drink Festival, held the first two weeks of October, showcases the city's chefs and regional products with special events. The city's pubs are also good options for lunch or dinner.

£ ✕ **Akbar's.** Locals line up for this big, bright, and buzzing contemporary
INDIAN restaurant just opposite the Museum of Science and Industry. If they're not tucking into sizzling, stir-fried Balti dishes (a don't-miss), they might be enjoying a mild and creamy korma, rogan josh (with tomatoes and coriander) or a sweet-and-sour dhansak dish (with pineapple and lentils)—all popular staples. Vegetarians have plenty of choices, too. Be prepared to wait at busy times. ⊠ *73–83 Liverpool Rd., Castlefield* ☎ *0161/834–8444* ⊕ *www.akbars.co.uk* ⚐ *Reservations not accepted* ▭ *MC, V.*

£ ✕ **Lal Haweli.** One of Rusholme's string of Indian restaurants, this bright
INDIAN and spacious establishment specializes in tandoori chicken and other Indian staples. What sets it apart are Nepalese offerings such as chicken sultani (with orange, pineapple, and chilies) and stir-fried Balti dishes from northern Pakistan. This mostly Asian (mainly Pakistani) area is full of bright neon signs and waiters trying to lure you into their restaurants. A mile south of the city center, it's easily accessible by Buses 41, 42, 43, 44, and 45, or a short taxi ride. ⊠ *68–72 Wilmslow Rd., Rusholme* ☎ *0161/248–9700* ▭ *AE, MC, V.*

££ ✕ **Mr. Thomas's Chophouse.** The city's oldest restaurant (1872) dishes out
BRITISH good old British favorites such as brown onion soup, steak-and-kidney pudding, Lancashire hot pot, and corned-beef hash to crowds of city types and shoppers. This hearty food is served in a Victorian-style room with a black-and-white-checked floor and green tiling. The wine list is exceptional. Mr. Sam's Chophouse in Chapel Walks serves similar fare. ⊠ *52 Cross St., City Centre* ☎ *0161/832–2245* ⊕ *tomsmanchester. thevictorianchophousecompany.com* ▭ *AE, MC, V.*

££ ✕ **Rosso.** Perched at the top of King Street, this popular new eatery
ITALIAN offers zingy Italian cuisine in the ornate, neoclassical interior of a Victorian building. Dishes such as a seafood *fritto misto* (dipped in batter and fried), spaghetti in squid ink with shellfish, and *coniglio al Barolo* (rabbit pot-roasted in Barolo wine with root vegetables) are all generously heaped and reasonably priced; but it's the grandiose domes, stained-glass windows, and buzzing atmosphere that steal the show. ⊠ *43 Spring Gardens, City Centre* ☎ *0161/832–1400* ⊕ *www. rossorestaurants.com* ▭ *AE, MC, V.*

10

££   ✕ **Sapporo Teppanyaki.** The emphasis is on riotous good fun at this mod-
JAPANESE   ern Japanese restaurant in Castlefield. Take your place around the chef's
iron griddle and the theater begins; once you've had potato fritters
tossed into your mouth and seen other morsels caught and balanced on
the chef's spatula, you can enjoy your choice of dishes such as yummy
teriyaki beef and sizzling scallops. For a quieter, lighter meal, take a
private table and peruse the sushi menu. Curiosity might tempt you
to try a Manchester roll, made of swordfish with Lancashire cheese
and crabmeat. ⊠ *91–93 Liverpool Rd., Castlefield* ☎ *0161/831–9888*
⊕ *www.sapporo.co.uk* ⊟ *AE, MC, V.*

£££   ✕ **Stock.** The Edwardian building that houses this buzzing Italian res-
ITALIAN   taurant was once the city's stock exchange—hence its name and grand
domed setting. Chef Enzo Mauro emphasizes the flavors of southern
Italy on a menu that might include fish and shellfish broth on a garlicky bruschetta or rump of lamb marinated in mint and chili. You can
accompany this with a fine-quality wine. Bonuses are a good-value
lunch deal, jazz on Friday, and occasional opera nights. ⊠ *4 Norfolk St.,
City Centre* ☎ *0161/839–6644* ⊕ *www.stockrestaurant.co.uk* ⊟ *AE,
MC, V* ☺ *Closed Sun.*

£££   ✕ **Sweet Mandarin.** Warm neon lighting and floor-to-ceiling windows
CHINESE   invite you into this contemporary Chinese restaurant from the hip
streets of the Northern Quarter. Deliciously simple family recipes have
earned it a growing reputation; locals flock to enjoy the famous salt and
pepper ribs, clay-pot chicken, Lily Kwok's curry, and crispy Szechuan
beef, all of which come on the banquet menu at £19.50 per head. On
the à la carte menu, try General Tse's sweet and sour chicken, named
after a late uncle said to have been almost militant in nurturing his cherished recipe. ⊠ *19 Copperas St., Northern Quarter* ☎ *0161/832–8848*
⊕ *www.sweetmandarin.com* ⊟ *AE, MC, V* ☺ *Closed Mon.*

WHERE TO STAY

£££–££££   ⊞ **Arora International.** The centrally located Arora International, opposite the Manchester Art Gallery, occupies one of the city's grand Victorian buildings. Its interior design, however, is minimalist modern.
Chunky contemporary upholstered furnishings fill the public areas and
guest rooms, where favored colors are beiges and muted reds and purples. Five rooms inspired by Cliff Richard songs contain artwork and
memorabilia from the singer's own collection. The luxurious bathrooms
have music speakers so you can listen to his tunes (or anyone else's, for
that matter). Each floor has its own cooking facilities. **Pros:** fun theme
rooms; historic building; good deals on weekends. **Cons:** no parking;
smallish rooms. ⊠ *18–24 Princess St., City Centre* ☎ *0161/236–8999*
⊕ *www.arorainternational.com* ↜ *141 rooms* ♨ *In-room: no a/c, safe,
refrigerator, Internet. In-hotel: restaurant, room service, bar, gym, laundry service, Wi-Fi hotspot* ⊟ *AE, DC, MC, V* ⍣ *BP, EP.*

££   ⊞ **Castlefield Hotel.** This popular modern hotel sits near the water's edge
in the Castlefield Basin, opposite the Museum of Science and Industry.
Public rooms are cheery and traditional; subdued tones help make the
bedrooms restful. Among the amenities—plentiful for a hotel in this
price range—are a gym with a range of exercise classes, an indoor

running track, and a dance studio. **Pros:** excellent leisure facilities; reasonable rates. **Cons:** rooms can feel stuffy; a bit far from downtown. ✉ *Liverpool Rd., Castlefield* ☎ *0161/832–7073* ⊕ *www.castlefield-hotel.co.uk* ⇥ *48 rooms* ☖ *In-room: no a/c, Wi-Fi. In-hotel: restaurant, room service, bar, pool, gym, laundry service, parking (paid)* ☰ *AE, MC, V* ⓉⓄⓁ *BP.*

£££££ ⚏ **Great John Street.** Once a Victorian schoolhouse, this plush boutique hotel next to the Granada TV studios now attracts well-heeled business executives, television stars, and anyone seeking something truly special. Duplex rooms have huge windows. Baroque furnishings, rich fabrics, and deep colors create a chic contrast with the original wooden flooring and exposed brick walls. Bathrooms, on a separate level, are equally spacious and luxurious. For some relaxation, unwind in the cozy Oyster Bar or head up to the rooftop garden with its outdoor hot tub. **Pros:** luxurious rooms; unique design; good online deals. **Cons:** valet parking is expensive; breakfast is extra. ✉ *Great John St., City Centre* ☎ *0161/831–3211* ⊕ *www.greatjohnstreet.co.uk* ⇥ *14 rooms, 16 suites* ☖ *In-room: a/c, DVD, Internet, Wi-Fi. In-hotel: room service, bar, gym, parking (paid)* ☰ *AE, MC, V.*

££££–£££££ ⚏ **The Lowry Hotel.** The strikingly modern design of this glass edifice exudes luxury and spaciousness. The clean-lined public areas and guest rooms are washed in soothing neutral tones, enlivened by brilliant splashes of color. Marble bathrooms and walk-in closets are nice touches. Classic British dishes are served in the elegant River Room restaurant. The hotel is next to the River Irwell across from the landmark Trinity Bridge designed by Santiago Calatrava. **Pros:** luxury at every turn; spacious rooms; good deals online. **Cons:** you feel swallowed up in the vast lobby; view of office blocks is less than inspiring. ✉ *50 Dearman's Pl., Chapel Wharf, City Centre* ☎ *0161/827–4000* ⊕ *www.thelowryhotel.com* ⇥ *157 rooms, 7 suites* ☖ *In-room: a/c, safe, DVD, Internet, Wi-Fi. In-hotel: restaurant, room service, bar, pool, gym, spa, laundry service, parking (paid)* ☰ *AE, DC, MC, V* ⓉⓄⓁ *BP.*

£££ ⚏ **The Midland Hotel.** The Edwardian splendor of the hotel's public rooms manages to shine through a contemporary makeover, evoking the days when this was the city's railroad station hotel. To get in the spirit, enjoy high tea in the grand lobby. Guest rooms, with huge photos of Manchester as headboards, are pleasant and light, with contemporary walnut furniture and dark-purple-and-cream furnishings. You're in the heart of the city, close to Town Hall and a Metrolink stop. **Pros:** central location; good restaurant; good for business travelers. **Cons:** impersonal feel; rooms facing road can be noisy. ✉ *Peter St., City Centre* ☎ *0161/236–3333* ⊕ *www.qhotels.co.uk* ⇥ *298 rooms, 14 suites* ☖ *In-room: a/c, safe, Internet, Wi-Fi. In-hotel: 2 restaurants, room service, bars, pool, gym, laundry service, parking (paid), some pets allowed* ☰ *AE, DC, MC, V* ⓉⓄⓁ *BP.*

£ ⚏ **The Ox.** Friendly and relaxed, this gastro pub with rooms is a real find for those who just want the basics. Guest rooms are simple, creamy cool and modern in style. The buzz-filled restaurant, decorated with local artwork, serves Modern British cuisine. Guest ales are on tap, complemented by a good selection of wines. The Ox is close to the Museum of

10

Science and Industry, at the southern end of the city center. **Pros:** friendly staff; bargain prices. **Cons:** breakfast not included; no-frills decor; noise from the bar reaches some of the rooms. ✉ *71 Liverpool Rd., Castlefield* ☎ *0161/839–7740* ⊕ *www.theox.co.uk* ⏱ *9 rooms* ♨ *In-room: no a/c. In-hotel: restaurant, bar* ▤ *MC, V.*

££   ⚃ **RoomZZZ.** Although the stylishly modern serviced apartments in this old cotton warehouse are all about self-contained autonomy bang in the center of town, the lobby and corridors have the jazzed-up feel of a boutique hotel. Corner rooms have huge windows with views of Chinatown; fifth-floor suites are playful mezzanines with gaping skylights. The hipness factor rises with the Mac and iPod (with docking station) in each apartment. Beds come with memory foam, evoking the hotel's name just as you drop off. **Pros:** maximum privacy but with staff on hand at all hours; on Chinatown's doorstep. **Cons:** some bathrooms offer little privacy. ✉ *36 Princess St., Chinatown* ☎ *0161/236–2121* ⊕ *www.roomzzz.co.uk* ⏱ *48 apartments* ♨ *In-room: a/c, safe (some), kitchen, refrigerator, Wi-Fi* ▤ *AE, DC, MC, V.*

£££–££££   ⚃ **Staying Cool.** A stay with this trendy chain, which has 11 serviced apartments in three locations across the city center, could mean a designer studio on the 30th floor of the Beetham Tower or a corner duplex in a converted dye works overlooking a stretch of Castlefield canal. Each apartment is decked out with Apple Macs, i-Pods, large plasma TVs, and distinctive flourishes such as purple diamond chairs or atmospheric Bola lights.**Pros:** high-tech gadgets; helpful staff; impressive range of options. **Cons:** some maintenance issues. ✉ *Worsley Street, 216 Box Works, Castlefield* ☎ *0161/832–4060* ⊕ *www.stayingcool.com* ⏱ *11 apartments* ♨ *In-room: a/c, kitchen, refrigerator, DVD, Wi-Fi* ▤ *AE, D, DC, MC, V.*

NIGHTLIFE AND THE ARTS

Manchester vies with London as Britain's capital of youth culture, but has vibrant nightlife and entertainment options for all ages. Spending time at a bar, pub, or club is definitely an essential part of any trip. For event listings, check out the free *Manchester Evening News* or *Manchester Metro News*, both widely available.

NIGHTLIFE
The action after dark centers on the Deansgate, Northern Quarter, and Gay Village areas.

CAFÉ-BARS AND PUBS
Barça (✉ *8–9 Catalan Sq., Castlefield* ☎ *0161/839–7099*) is a hip canalside bar-restaurant that has won awards for its interesting architecture. **Cloud 23** (✉ *Beetham Tower, 303 Deansgate, City Centre* ☎ *0161/870–1688*) in the Hilton has a stunning 360-degree view of the city that you'll pay for; but at 23 floors up, this swanky bar is not for the vertiginous. Book well ahead.

Dry Bar (✉ *28–30 Oldham St., Northern Quarter* ☎ *0161/236–9840*), the original café-bar in town, is still full of young people drinking and dancing. Whether you come to see or be seen, the **Living Room** (✉ *80 Deansgate, City Centre* ☎ *0161/832–0083*) is the city's top spot;

a pianist plays in the early evening. **Obsidian** (✉ *18–24 Princess St., City Centre* ☎ *0161/238–4348*) has a huge frosted-glass bar and great cocktails. **Tiger Tiger** (✉ *5–6 The Printworks, City Centre* ☎ *0161/385–8080*) is the place to go for a relaxed meal and to drink or dance.

Fodor's Choice The **Britons Protection** (✉ *50 Great Bridgewater St., Peter's Fields* ☎ *0161/236–5895*) is a relaxed pub with stained-glass windows, cozy back rooms, and a mural of the Peterloo Massacre. You can sample more than 230 whiskies and bourbons. **Dukes 92** (✉ *18 Castle St., Castlefield* ☎ *0161/839–8642*) has a perfect canal-side setting for a summer pub lunch or drink. **Peveril of the Peak** (✉ *127 Great Bridgewater St., Peter's Fields* ☎ *0161/236–6364*), a nifty Victorian pub with a green-tile exterior, draws a crush of locals to its tiny rooms. **Sinclair's Oyster Bar** (✉ *2 Cathedral Gates, Millennium Quarter* ☎ *0161/834–0430*), a half-timber pub built in the 17th century, specializes in fresh oyster dishes.

★ The **Gay Village**, which came to television in the British series *Queer as Folk*, has stylish bars and cafés along the Rochdale Canal; Canal Street is its heart. The area is not only the center of Manchester's good-size gay scene but also the nightlife center for the young and trendy. The chic **Manto** (✉ *46 Canal St., Gay Village* ☎ *0161/236–2667*) draws a mostly gay crowd to its split-level, postindustrial interior.

DANCE CLUBS
42nd Street (✉ *2 Bootle St., off Deansgate, City Centre* ☎ *0161/831–7108*) plays retro, indie, sing-along anthems, and classic rock. **Sankey's** (✉ *Beehive Mill, Jersey St., Ancoats* ☎ *0161/228–0863*) covers electro, techno, and hard-core music.

LIVE MUSIC
Band on the Wall (✉ *25 Swan St., Northern Quarter* ☎ *0161/834–1786*), a famous venue recently revamped, has a reputation for both established and pioneering music. Past performers include Joy Division, Simply Red, and Björk. **Manchester Apollo** (✉ *Stockport Rd., Ardwick Green* ☎ *0161/271–6921*) showcases live performances for all musical tastes. Major rock and pop stars appear at the **Manchester Evening News Arena** (✉ *21 Hunt's Bank, Hunt's Bank* ☎ *0844/847–8000*). The **Roadhouse** (✉ *8 Newton St., City Centre* ☎ *0161/237–9789*), an intimate band venue, also hosts funk and indie nights.

THE ARTS
PERFORMING ARTS VENUES
★ Dramatically modern **Bridgewater Hall** (✉ *Lower Mosley St., Peter's Fields* ☎ *0161/907–9000*) has concerts by Manchester's renowned Hallé Orchestra and hosts both classical music and a varied light-entertainment program. The **Lowry** (✉ *Pier 8, Salford Quays* ☎ *0870/787–5780*) contains two theaters and presents everything from musicals to dance and performance poetry. The **Opera House** (✉ *Quay St., City Centre* ☎ *0161/828–1700*) is a venue for West End musicals, opera, and classical ballet. The **Palace Theatre** (✉ *Oxford St., City Centre* ☎ *0844/245–6600*) presents large touring shows—major plays, ballet, and opera. **Royal Northern College of Music** (✉ *124 Oxford Rd., University Quarter* ☎ *0161/907–5555*) hosts classical and contemporary music concerts, jazz, and opera.

10

THEATER

Green Room (✉ *54–56 Whitworth St. W, City Centre* ☎ *0161/615–0500*) is an alternative space for theater, poetry, dance, and performance art. **Royal Exchange Theatre** (✉ *St. Ann's Sq., City Centre* ☎ *0161/833–9833*) serves as the city's main venue for innovative contemporary theater.

FOOTBALL

Football (soccer in the United States) is *the* reigning passion in Manchester. Locals support the local club, Manchester City, and glory seekers come from afar to root for Manchester United, based in neighboring Trafford. Matches for both clubs are usually sold out months in advance, though you have more of a chance with Manchester City. **Manchester City** (✉ *Rowsley St., SportCity* ☎ *0870/062–1894*) plays at the City of Manchester Stadium. At the **Manchester City Museum and Stadium Tours** (✉ *Rowsley St., SportCity* ☎ *0870/062–1894*) you can see club memorabilia, visit the players' changing rooms, and go down the tunnel to pitch side. Excluding match days, there are three tours daily Monday through Saturday, two on Sunday; admission is £9.50.

★ **Manchester United** (✉ *Sir Matt Busby Way, Trafford Wharf* ☎ *0161/868–8000*) has home matches at Old Trafford. You can take a trip to the Theatre of Dreams at the **Manchester United Museum and Tour** (✉ *Sir Matt Busby Way, Trafford Wharf* ☎ *0161/868–8000*), which tells the history of the football club. It's best to prebook the tour (not available on match days), which takes you behind the scenes, into the changing rooms and players' lounge, and down the tunnel. The museum is open daily 9:30 to 5; admission for the museum and tour is £12.50; for the museum only, £9. Take the tram to the Old Trafford stop and walk five minutes.

SHOPPING

The city is nothing if not fashion conscious; take your pick from glitzy department stores, huge retail outlets, designer shops, and idiosyncratic boutiques. Famous names are centered on Exchange Square, Deansgate, and King Street; the Northern Quarter provides style for younger trendsetters.

Afflecks Palace (✉ *52 Church St., Northern Quarter* ☎ *0161/839–0718*) attracts young Mancunians with four floors of bohemian glam, ethnic crafts and jewelry, and innovative gift ideas. **Barton Arcade** (✉ *51–63 Deansgate, City Centre* ☎ *No phone*) has specialty shopping inside a lovely Victorian arcade.

★ **Harvey Nichols** (✉ *21 New Cathedral St., City Centre* ☎ *0161/828–8888*), an outpost of London's chic luxury department store, is packed with designer goods and has an excellent second-floor restaurant and brasserie. The **Lowry Designer Outlet** (✉ *11 The Quays, Salford Quays* ☎ *0161/848–1850*), with 80 stores, has good discounts on top brands at stores such as Nike and Karen Millen. The **Manchester Craft and Design Centre** (✉ *17 Oak St., Northern Quarter* ☎ *0161/832–4274*) houses 18 workshop-cum-retail outlets. The world's largest **Marks & Spencer** (✉ *7 Market St., City Centre* ☎ *0161/831–7341*) department store offers its own brand of fashion and has an excellent food department. The **Triangle** (✉ *Millennium Quarter* ☎ *0161/834–8961*), a stylish mall in the Victorian Corn Exchange, has more than 30 stores, including independent designer shops.

Oldham Street, in the Northern Quarter, is littered with urban hip-hop boutiques and music shops.

LIVERPOOL

A city lined with one of the most famous waterfronts in England, celebrated around the world as the birthplace of the Beatles, and still the place to catch that "Ferry 'Cross the Mersey," Liverpool reversed a downturn in its fortunes with developments in the late 1980s, such as the impressively refurbished Albert Dock area and Tate Liverpool. Its stint as the European Union's Capital of Culture in 2008, when £3 billion was invested in the city, acted as a catalyst for further regeneration. UNESCO named six historic areas in the city center a World Heritage Site, in recognition of its maritime and mercantile achievements during the height of Britain's global influence. This heritage, together with the renowned attractions and a legacy of cultural vibrancy, now draw in an ever increasing number of visitors.

The 1960s produced Liverpool's most famous export—the Beatles. The group was one of hundreds that copied the rock and roll they heard from visiting American GIs and merchant seamen in the late 1950s, and one of many that played local venues such as the Cavern (demolished but rebuilt nearby). All four Beatles were born in Liverpool, but the group's success dates from the time they left for London. Nevertheless, the city has milked the group's Liverpool connections for all they are worth, with a multitude of local attractions such as Paul McCartney's and John Lennon's childhood homes.

GETTING HERE AND AROUND
Liverpool John Lennon Airport, about 8 mi southeast of the city, receives mostly domestic and European flights. The Airlink 500 bus service runs to the city center every 30 minutes, and a taxi to the center of Liverpool costs around £15.

Long-distance National Express buses, including service from London, use the Norton Street Coach Station, and local buses depart from Sir Thomas Street, Queen Square, and the Paradise Street Interchange. Traveline has information on long-distance and local routes. Train service on Virgin Trains from London's Euston Station takes 2½ hours.

If you're walking (which is easier than driving), you'll find the downtown sights well signposted. Take care when crossing the busy inner ring road separating the Albert Dock from the rest of the city. The circular C4 bus links Queen Square bus station with the Albert Dock (Gower Street stop).

TOURS Blue Badge Guides can arrange dozens of different tours, which can be booked through the tourist office. Cavern City Tours offers a Beatles Magical Mystery Tour of Liverpool, departing from the Albert Dock Visitor Centre. The two-hour bus tour, which costs £13.95, runs past

10

Penny Lane, Strawberry Field, and other mop-top landmarks. Liverpool Beatles Tours has personalized tours of Beatles sites. The oddly named Yellow Duckmarines runs daily tours on amphibious vehicles from World War II. The trips, which cost between £9.95 and £11.95, leave from the Gower Street bus stop in Albert Dock.

ORIENTATION

Liverpool has a fairly compact center, and you can see most of the city highlights on foot. The skyline helps with orientation: the Radio City tower on **Queen Square** marks the center of the city and is a stone's throw away from the '08 **Place,** which gives tourist information. The Liver Birds, on top of the **Royal Liver Building,** signal the waterfront and River Mersey. North of the Radio City tower lie Lime Street station and William Brown Street, a showcase boulevard of municipal buildings, including the outstanding **Walker Art Gallery** and **Liverpool World Museum.** The city's other museums and the **Beatles Story** are concentrated westward on the waterfront in the **Albert Dock** area, a 20-minute walk or five-minute bus ride away. The Museum of Liverpool is undergoing construction on nearby Mann Island, and is due to open during 2011. **Hope Street,** to the east of the center, connects the city's two cathedrals, both easily recognizable on the skyline. On nearby Berry Street the red, green, and gold **Chinese Arch,** the largest outside China, marks the small Chinatown area. ■ **TIP→** Allow extra time to visit the childhood homes of Paul McCartney and John Lennon (viewable only on a tour), as they lie outside the city center.

DISCOUNTS AND DEALS

If you're staying in Liverpool, you could make use of Your Ticket for Liverpool, a visitor card that gives free admission to selected sights, free bus travel in the city, and restaurant discounts over three consecutive days. It costs £24.99 and is available from tourist offices and online at ⊕ *www.yourticketforliverpool.com.*

ESSENTIALS

Bus Contacts Airlink 500 (☎ *0871/200–2233* ⊕ *www.arrivabus.co.uk*). **Traveline** (☎ *0871/200–2233* ⊕ *www.traveline.org.uk*).

Tour Contacts Blue Badge Guides (☎ *0796/451–5681 or 0791/865–5113*). **Cavern City Tours** (✉ *Mathew St., City Centre, Liverpool* ☎ *0151/236–9091* ⊕ *www.cavernclub.org*). **Liverpool Beatles Tours** (✉ *25 Victoria St., City Centre, Liverpool* ☎ *0151/281–7738* ⊕ *www.beatlestours.co.uk*). **YellowDuckmarines** (☎ *0151/708–7799* ⊕ *www.theyellowduckmarine.co.uk*).

Visitor Information Liverpool (✉ *'08 Place, 36–38 Whitechapel, City Centre* ☎ *0151/233–2008, 0151/233–2459, 0844/870–0123 for accommodations* ✉ *Anchor Courtyard, Albert Dock* ☎ *0151/707–0729* ✉ *Arrival Hall, South Terminal, John Lennon Airport* ☎ *0151/907–1057* ⊕ *www.visitliverpool.com*).

EXPLORING LIVERPOOL

TOP EXPERIENCE: BEATLES SIGHTS

Beatles Story. You can follow in the footsteps of the Fab Four at one of the more popular attractions in the Albert Dock complex. Entertaining scenes re-create stages in their career, from the enthusiastic early days in

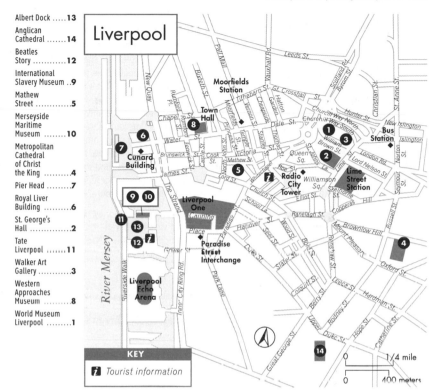

KEY

i *Tourist information*

Germany and the Cavern Club to the White Room, where "Imagine" seems to emanate from softly billowing curtains. Artifacts included are the glasses John Lennon wore when he composed "Imagine" and the blue felt bedspread used in the famous "Bed-in" in 1969. The "Going Solo" section follows the members' separate careers. ■ TIP→ **Avoid the crowds of July and August by visiting in the late afternoon.** You can purchase tickets, good for two days, online in advance. A shop sells everything from wallets to alarm clocks emblazoned with the Beatles logo. Admission to a second location at the new Mersey Ferries Terminal at Pier Head is included in the price: Fab4D, a 3D show with computer animation, and special exhibits are highlights. ⊠ *Britannia Vaults, Albert Dock, Waterfront* ☎ *0151/709–1963* ⊕ *www.beatlesstory.com* 🎫 *£12.95* ⊙ *Daily 9–7; last admission 2 hrs before closing.*

⑤ Mathew Street. It was at the Cavern on this street that Brian Epstein, the Beatles' manager, first heard the group in 1961. The Cavern had opened at No. 10 as a jazz venue in 1957, but beat groups, of whom the Beatles were clearly the most talented, had taken it over. Epstein became their manager a few months after first visiting the club, and within two years the group was the most talked-about phenomenon in music. The club was demolished in 1973; it was rebuilt a few yards from the original site. At No. 5 is the Cavern Pub, opened in 1994, with

CLOSE UP

Beatles Discovered . . . and Rediscovered

Brian Epstein was led to the Beatles in 1961 by a teenager who came into his record shop, NEMS (North End Music Stores) at 12–14 Whitechapel, and asked for a record by Tony Sheridan and the Beat Brothers. He couldn't find it in his catalog, but discovered that the backing band was the Beatles, a local group, playing at the nearby Cavern Club. Epstein heard the group, and the rest is history.

History lives on, though. If the Beatles Story, Mathew Street, Mendips, and 20 Forthlin Road can't sate your Beatlemania in Liverpool, you can add a guided tour of the essential and more off-the-beaten-path landmarks.

The faithful celebrate the Beatles' enduring appeal at the annual **International Beatle Week** (⊕ *www.cavernclub.org*), usually held the last week in August. It seems the entire city takes time out to dance, attend John and Yoko fancy-dress parties, listen to Beatles tribute bands from around the world, and more. The event includes concerts, a convention, flea markets, and more.

If you have the money, stay at—or at least visit the bar of—the Beatle-themed **Hard Day's Night Hotel** on Mathew Street. Yeah, yeah, yeah!

Beatles memorabilia and plenty of nostalgia. ■TIP➔ **At No. 31, check out the well-stocked Beatles Shop.**

QUICK
BITES

Not far from Mathew Street, Delifonseca (✉ *12 Stanley St., City Centre* ☎ *0151/255–0808*) **offers reviving coffee and cake, as well as excellent sandwiches and salads. You could also stock up on munchies from the capacious downstairs deli.**

Mendips. The National Trust (overseers of such landmarks as Blenheim Palace) maintains the 1930s middle-class, semidetached house that was the home of John Lennon from 1946 to 1963 and is a must-see for Beatles pilgrims. After his parents separated, John joined his aunt Mimi here; she gave him his first guitar but banished him to the porch, saying, "The guitar's all very well, John, but you'll never make a living out of it." The house can be seen only on a tour, for which you must book a seat on the minibus that connects the site with the Jurys Inn next to Albert Dock (mornings) or Speke Hall (afternoons). You can book online. ✉ *251 Menlove Ave., Woolton* ☎ *0844/800–4791 or 0151/427–7231* ⊕ *www.nationaltrust.org.uk* ✉ *£16.80, includes 20 Forthlin Road and Speke Hall gardens* ⊙ *Mid-Mar.–Oct., Wed.–Sun. and national holidays, 4 departures a day; early Mar. and Nov., Wed.–Sun., 3 departures a day. Call for times.*

20 Forthlin Road. From 1955 to 1964, Paul McCartney lived with his family in this modest 1950s council house (a building rented from the local government). A number of the Beatles' songs, including "Love Me Do" and "When I'm Sixty-Four," were written here. Inside is an exhibit of photographs of Paul taken by his brother, Mike McCartney. The house is viewable only on a tour, for which you must prebook a seat

on the minibus that connects the site with the Jurys Inn next to Albert
Dock (mornings) or Speke Hall (afternoons). You can book online. ✉ *20
Forthlin Rd., Allerton* ☎ *0844/800–4791 or 0151/427-7231* ⊕ *www.
nationaltrust.org.uk* ✍ *£16.80, includes Mendips and Speke Hall gardens* ☉ *Mid-Mar.–Oct., Wed.–Sun. and national holidays, 4 departures
a day; early Mar. and Nov., 3 departures a day. Call for times.*

TOP ATTRACTIONS

🄳 **Albert Dock.** To understand the city's prosperous maritime past, head for
★ waterfront Albert Dock, 7 acres of restored warehouses built in 1846.
Named after Queen Victoria's consort, Prince Albert, the dock provided
storage for silk, tea, and tobacco from the Far East until it was closed
in 1972. Rescued by the Merseyside Development Corporation, the fine
colonnaded brick warehouse buildings are England's largest heritage
attraction, containing the **Merseyside Maritime Museum,** the **International Slavery Museum, Tate Liverpool,** and the **Beatles Story.** Albert
Dock includes housing, shops, and plenty of restaurants as well as museums, though. When weather allows, sit at an outdoor café overlooking
the dock or take a boat trip through the docks and onto the river. Albert
Dock is part of the area known as **Liverpool's Historic Waterfront.**
■ **TIP**→ Much of the pedestrian area of the Albert Dock and Waterfront
area is cobblestone, so be sure to wear comfortable shoes. ✉ *Waterfront*
⊕ *www.albertdock.com.*

🄾 **International Slavery Museum.** On the third floor of the Maritime Museum,
this museum's three dynamic galleries recount the history of transatlantic slavery and trace its significance in contemporary society. "Life in
West Africa" reproduces a Nigerian Igbo compound, all the shackles
of slavery are shown in the "Enslavement" section, and many stories,
some never heard before, are told in "Legacies of Slavery." ✉ *Albert
Dock, Waterfront* ☎ *0151/478–4499* ⊕ *www.liverpoolmuseums.org.
uk* ✍ *Free* ☉ *Daily 10–5.*

🄿 **Merseyside Maritime Museum.** Part of the Albert Dock complex, this is a
☾ wonderful place to explore the role of the sea in the life of the city. The
Fodor's Choice museum captures the triumphs and tragedies of Liverpool's seafaring
★ history over five floors. Besides exhibits of maritime paintings, models,
ceramics, and ships in bottles, the main museum brings to life the ill-
fated stories of the *Titanic* and *Lusitania,* the Battle of the Atlantic, and
the city's role during World War II. The basement is home to Seized,
the Customs and Excise National Museum, which explores the heroes
and villains of the world of smuggling, together with the story of mass
emigration from the port in the 19th century. In summer full-size vessels
are on display. ✉ *Albert Dock, Waterfront* ☎ *0151/478–4499* ⊕ *www.
liverpoolmuseums.org.uk* ✍ *Free* ☉ *Daily 10–5.*

🄼 **Pier Head.** Here you can take a ferry across the River Mersey from Pierhead to Birkenhead and Seacombe and back. Boats leave regularly and
offer fine views of the city—a journey celebrated in "Ferry 'Cross the
Mersey," Gerry and the Pacemakers' 1964 hit song. It was from Pier
Head that 9 million British, Irish, and other European emigrants set
sail between 1830 and 1930 for new lives in the United States, Canada,
Australia, and Africa. The ferry terminal is now also home to a number

10

LIVERPOOL'S HISTORY: SHIPPING CENTER

Liverpool, on the east bank of the Mersey River estuary, at the point where it merges with the Irish Sea, developed from the 17th century through the slave trade. It became Britain's leading port for ferrying Africans to North America and for handling sugar, tobacco, rum, and cotton, which began to dominate the local economy after the abolition of the slave trade in 1807.

Because of its proximity to Ireland, the city was also the first port of call for those fleeing famine, poverty, and persecution in that country. Liverpool was often the last British port of call for thousands of mostly Jewish refugees fleeing Eastern Europe.

Many of the best-known liner companies were based in Liverpool, including Cunard and White Star, whose best-known vessel, the *Titanic,* was registered in Liverpool. The city was dealt an economic blow in 1894 with the opening of the Manchester Ship Canal, which allowed traders to bypass Liverpool and head to Manchester, 35 mi east. Britain's entry into the European Common Market saw more trade move from the west coast to the east, and the postwar growth of air travel diverted passengers from the sea. But as a sign of the city's revival, oceangoing liners returned to the city in 2008 after the building of a new cruise liner terminal at the Pier Head.

of Beatles Story attractions; you might want to make it the last stop on your Beatles tour, finishing the day off with a ferry trip. ■TIP→ **Take a short ferry ride or the longer cruise with commentary ("Scousers," as locals are known, are famous for their patter); the city views are worth the time and money.** ⊠ *Pier Head Ferry Terminal, Mersey Ferries, Waterfront* ☎ *0151/330–1444* ⊕ *www.merseyferries.co.uk* ⊠ *£2.30 round-trip, cruises £5.30* ⊙ *Ferries every 30 mins weekdays 7:30–9:30* AM *(Seacombe only) and 4:15–6:45; cruises hourly weekdays 10–3, weekends 10–6.*

6 **Royal Liver Building.** Best seen from the ferry, the 322-foot-tall Royal Liver (pronounced lie-ver) Building with its twin towers is topped by two 18-foot-high copper birds. They represent the mythical Liver Birds, the town symbol; local legend has it that if they fly away, Liverpool will cease to exist. For decades Liverpudlians looked to the Royal Liver Society for assistance—it was originally a burial club to which families paid contributions to ensure a decent send-off. ⊠ *Water St., Waterfront.*

11 **Tate Liverpool.** An offshoot of the London-based art galleries of the same name, the Liverpool museum, a handsome conversion of existing Albert Dock warehouses, was designed in the 1990s by the late James Stirling, one of Britain's leading 20th-century architects. Galleries display changing exhibits of challenging modern art. A free introductory tour begins daily at 12:30. The excellent shop sells art books, prints, and posters, and there's a children's art-play area and a dockside café-restaurant. ⊠ *The Colonnades, Albert Dock, Waterfront* ☎ *0151/702–7400* ⊕ *www.tate.org.uk* ⊠ *Free, charge for special exhibitions* ⊙ *Apr.–Sept., daily 10–5:50; Oct.–Mar., Tues.–Sun. and national holidays 10–5:50.*

❸ **Walker Art Gallery.** With a superb display of British art and some out-
Fodor'sChoice standing Italian and Flemish works, the Walker maintains its position
★ as one of the best British art collections outside London. Don't miss the
unrivaled collection of paintings by 18th-century Liverpudlian equestrian artist George Stubbs, and works by J. M. W. Turner, John Constable, Sir Edwin Henry Landseer, and the Pre-Raphaelites. Modern
artists are included, too—on display is one of David Hockney's typically Californian pool scenes. Other excellent exhibits showcase china,
silver, and furniture that once adorned the mansions of Liverpool's
industrial barons. The Tea Room holds center stage in the airy museum
lobby. ⊠ *William Brown St., City Centre* ☎ *0151/478–4199* ⊕ *www.
liverpoolmuseums.org.uk* ✉ *Free* ⊙ *Daily 10–5.*

❶ **World Museum Liverpool.** You can travel from the prehistoric to the space
ⓒ age through stunning displays in these state-of-the-art galleries. Ethnol-
ogy, the natural and physical sciences, and archaeology all get their due
on five floors. The World Cultures gallery colorfully illustrates the cosmopolitan history of the city. If the kids aren't grabbed by the monster
bugs in the Bug House or afternoon shows in the Treasure House Theatre and Planetarium, they'll find plenty to do in the hands-on centers.
⊠ *William Brown St.* ☎ *0151/478–4393* ⊕ *www.liverpoolmuseums.org.
uk* ✉ *Free* ⊙ *Daily 10–5.*

WORTH NOTING

⓮ **Anglican Cathedral.** The largest church in northern Britain overlooks the
city and the River Mersey. Built of local sandstone, the Gothic-style
cathedral was begun in 1903 by architect Giles Gilbert Scott; it was
finally finished in 1978. Take a look at the grand interior on your own or
experience the Great Space film and audio tour to help you appreciate the
building. The 331-foot-tall tower is a popular climb; two elevators and
108 steps take you to breathtaking views. View the Embroidery Gallery
on your way up. A refectory serves light meals and coffee. ⊠ *St. James's
Mount, City Centre* ☎ *0151/709–6271* ⊕ *www.liverpoolcathedral.org.
uk* ✉ *£3 suggested donation; combination ticket for tower, embroidery
exhibition, film, and audio tour £5 (valid for 2 days)* ⊙ *Daily 8–6. Tower
Mar.–Sept., Mon.–Sat. 10–4:30; Oct.–Feb., Mon.–Sat. 10–3:30. Film
and audio tour Mon.–Sat. 9–4, Sun. noon–2:30.*

10

Another Place. A hundred naked, life-size, cast-iron figures by sculptor
Antony Gormley stand proudly on the 2 mi of foreshore at Crosby
Beach, weathered by sand and sea. Unlike most other statues, you are
permitted to interact with these and even clothe them as you wish.
Check tide times before you go and be aware that it's not safe to walk
out to the farthest figures. The site is 6 mi north of Liverpool center; to get here, take the Merseyrail train to Waterloo from Moor-
fields station. A taxi will cost around £15. ⊠ *Mariners Rd., Crosby
Beach* ☎ *0151/237–3945, 0151/934–2967 for tide times* ⊕ *www.
visitsouthport.com* ✉ *Free.*

❹ **Metropolitan Cathedral of Christ the King.** Consecrated in 1967, this Roman
Catholic cathedral is a modernistic, funnel-like structure of concrete,
stone, and mosaic, topped with a glass lantern. Long, narrow, blue-glass
windows separate chapels, each with modern works of art. An earlier

design by classically inspired architect Edwin Lutyens was abandoned when World War II began (the current design is by Frederick Gibberd), but you can still take a look at Lutyen's vast brick-and-granite crypt and barrel-vaulted ceilings. ⊠ *Mount Pleasant, City Centre* ☎ *0151/709–9222* ⊕ *www.liverpoolmetrocathedral.org.uk* ⊠ *£3 suggested donation* ☉ *Mon.–Sat. 8–6, Sun. 8–5.*

❷ **St. George's Hall.** Built between 1839 and 1847, St. George's Hall is among the world's best Greek Revival buildings. When Queen Victoria visited Liverpool in 1851, she declared it "worthy of ancient Athens." Today the hall serves as a home for music festivals, concerts, and fairs. Self-guided tours tell the story of the building as a Crown court and cultural venue. ⊠ *Lime St., City Centre* ☎ *0151/225–6909* ☉ *Daily 10–5.*

Speke Hall and Gardens. This black-and-white mansion only 6 mi from downtown Liverpool is one of the best examples of half-timbering in Britain. Built around a cobbled courtyard, the great hall dates to 1490; an elaborate western bay with a vast chimneypiece was added in 1560. The house, owned by the National Trust, was heavily restored in the 19th century, though a Tudor priest hole and Jacobean plasterwork remain intact. Speke Hall is on the east side of the airport; the Airportxpress 500 bus drops you a pleasant 10-minute walk away. ⊠ *The Walk, Speke* ☎ *0151/427–7231* ⊕ *www.nationaltrust.org.uk* ⊠ *£7.63; gardens only, £4.54* ☉ *House mid-Mar.–Oct., Wed.–Sun. and national holidays 11–5; Nov.–early Dec., weekends 11–4:30. Gardens daily 11–5:30 or dusk. Last admission 30 mins before closing.*

❽ **Western Approaches Museum.** Be taken right back to the 1940s when you explore the warren of rooms under the city streets, once the top-secret headquarters for the Battle of the Atlantic during World War II. The lofty Operations Room, full of the state-of-the-art technology of the time, is especially evocative. ⊠ *1–3 Rumford St., off Chapel St., City Centre* ☎ *0151/227–2008* ⊕ *www.liverpoolwarmuseum.co.uk* ⊠ *£5.50* ☉ *Mar.–Oct., Mon.–Thurs. and Sat. 10:30–4:30.*

WHERE TO EAT

£££   ✗ **60 Hope Street.** The combination of a ground-floor restaurant and a
MODERN BRITISH   more informal basement bistro makes this a popular choice. A light, polished-wood floor and blue-and-cream walls help create an uncluttered backdrop for updated British dishes (roast sea bass comes with ricotta gnocchi, for example), but found only on British shores are fish in beer batter and the deep-fried jam sandwich with condensed-milk ice cream. ⊠ *60 Hope St., City Centre* ☎ *0151/707–6060* ⊕ *www.60hopestreet. com* ⊟ *AE, MC, V* ☉ *Closed Sun. No lunch Sat. in restaurant.*

£££   ✗ **Blue Bar and Grill.** Expect to rub shoulders with local celebrities in
BRITISH   this sophisticated modern restaurant and bar on the waterfront. The focal point is the beautiful Venetian crystal chandelier, a counterpoint to the original open brickwork, chunky furnishings, and plasma video monitors. Downstairs (less expensive) you can sample tapas, dim sum, and bruschetta; the fare in the upstairs gallery includes pork with pea purée and black pudding mash, and a large selection of meat and fish

steaks, accompanied by different sauces. ⊠ *Edward Pavilion, Albert Dock, Waterfront* ☎ *0151/702–5831* ⊟ *AE, MC, V.*

££ ✕ **Etsu.** Minimalist decor, friendly staff, and a polished Japanese menu
JAPANESE greet you at this inconspicuous street-corner locale just off the Strand (entrance on Brunswick Street). Along with the traditional sushi, noodle soups, and tempuras, all served with the freshest ingredients, are some witty East-meets-West creations, including sushi pizzas and tuna burgers made of rice blocks. The bento box meals provide great value at lunchtime in between museum visits. Make sure you try a shochu, a stronger version of sake, served neat or with oolong tea— though it's probably best enjoyed with dinner, not lunch. ⊠ *25 The Strand, City Centre* ☎ *0151/236–7530* ⊕ *www.etsu-restaurant.co.uk* ⊟ *AE, MC, V* ⊗ *Closed Mon. No lunch Wed. and weekends.*

£ ✕ **Everyman Bistro.** A cosmopolitan crowd can always be found at the
BRITISH simple wooden tables in the crypt of the Everyman Theatre. The hearty,
★ varied menu changes twice daily and might include lamb scouse (stew) with beetroot and red cabbage or smoked haddock with horseradish and pea-fish cakes, with apple-and-almond pudding for a notable dessert. Vegetarians have plenty of choices, and there are good soups, cheeses, and salads for lunch. ⊠ *5–9 Hope St., City Centre* ☎ *0151/708– 9545* ⊕ *www.everyman.co.uk* ⊟ *AE, MC, V* ⊗ *Closed Sun.*

££ ✕ **Side Door.** You'll often find couples enjoying a meal before a play or
BRITISH concert at this intimate and unpretentious bistro. The menu changes every week, but there is always plenty of fish, such as hake with rosemary potatoes or sea bass cannelloni with butternut squash. Sticky toffee pudding is a don't-miss dessert here. Pretheater fixed-price meals are good value, and service is attentive but unobtrusive. ⊠ *29a Hope St.* ☎ *0151/707–7888* ⊕ *www.thesidedoor.co.uk* ⊟ *MC, V* ⊗ *Closed Sun.*

£££ ✕ **Simply Heathcote's.** This chic contemporary restaurant, an outpost of
MODERN BRITISH chef Paul Heathcote's empire, has a curved glass front, cherry furnishings, and a granite floor. The menu has a local accent—lamb hot pot with pickled red cabbage, braised ox cheek (from the face) with horseradish foam, and bread-and-butter pudding—along with dishes from warmer climes. Vegetarians are well served, too. The restaurant is opposite the Royal Liver and Cunard buildings. ⊠ *25 The Strand, Waterfront* ☎ *0151/236–3536* ⊕ *www.heathcotes.co.uk* ⊟ *AE, MC, V.*

£ ✕ **Tate Café.** The Tate Liverpool's café-bar is a winner for daytime sus-
BRITISH tenance whether or not you're visiting the museum. Dockside seats are great on warm summer days, and you can choose from among the salads and open sandwiches including steak with Wirral watercress, as well as main dishes such as chicken breast with Savoy cabbage. Fruit scones with jam and cream also make an appearance. ⊠ *The Colonnades, Albert Dock, Waterfront* ☎ *0151/702–7581* ⊕ *www.tate.org.uk* ⊟ *MC, V* ⊗ *Closed Mon. in winter. No dinner.*

10

WHERE TO STAY

££–£££ ⊡ **Crowne Plaza Liverpool.** Many of the city's main sights are at the doorstep of this modern hotel on the waterfront next to the Royal Liver Building. A bright, bustling, glass atrium leads to well-equipped and spacious bedrooms, done in soothing colors. Family rooms have two double beds; children under 12 stay free and even get free meals in the Plaza Brasserie. **Pros:** on waterfront; friendly staff; plenty of activities. **Cons:** chain-hotel furnishings; guest-room windows cannot be opened. ⊠ *St. Nicholas Pl., Waterfront* ☎ *0151/243–8000* ⊕ *www.cpliverpool. com* ⌁ *159 rooms* ⏦ *In-room: a/c, Internet. In-hotel: 2 restaurants, room service, bar, pool, gym, laundry service, Wi-Fi hotspot, parking (paid)* ▭ *AE, DC, MC, V.*

£££–££££
Fodor's Choice
★

⌂ Hard Day's Night Hotel. "Everything seems to be right" since the marble-columned office block on the corner of Mathew Street was transformed into a hotel in homage to the Beatles. Their music is played in the public rooms and their photos (many original) loom large on the walls, but it's all done with finesse. A wide staircase spirals up from the humming brasserie and bar, the hub of the hotel, to sleek and luxurious guest rooms hung with original paintings. The unashamedly modern ambience, emboldened with bright orange, blue, and green fabrics, includes electronic gadgets that control everything. The moody red-and-black Hari's Bar is the place to see and be seen; Blakes restaurant provides the nourishment you need for your tour of Beatles sites. **Pros:** welcoming staff; sophisticated rooms; close to Beatles attractions. **Cons:** rumbling trains and street noise heard in some rooms; breakfast costs extra; no parking. ⊠ *Central Bldgs., N. John St., City Centre* ☎ *0151/236–1964* ⊕ *www.harddaysnighthotel.com* ⌁ *108 rooms, 2 suites* ⏦ *In-room: a/c, safe, Wi-Fi. In-hotel: restaurant, room service, bars, laundry service* ▭ *AE, DC, MC, V.*

£££
★

⌂ Hope Street Hotel. Liverpool's first boutique hotel is in a converted carriage warehouse built in the style of a Venetian palazzo. Hope Street Hotel puts the emphasis on traditional, natural materials and retains the exposed brickwork and cast-iron columns from the 1860s. A stunning oak staircase runs the height of the building. Light, elegant bedrooms are minimalist in style, with crisp white bed linens and custom-made walnut and cherry pieces; the rooms benefit from underfloor heating. The London Carriage Works restaurant concentrates on local and seasonal produce. **Pros:** beautiful design; plenty of space. **Cons:** service can be inconsistent; parking difficult to find; rooms face a busy street. ⊠ *40 Hope St., City Centre* ☎ *0151/709–3000* ⊕ *www.hopestreethotel. co.uk* ⌁ *41 rooms, 7 suites* ⏦ *In-room: no a/c, DVD, Internet. In-hotel: restaurant, room service, bars, laundry service, Wi-Fi hotspot, parking (paid)* ▭ *AE, MC, V.*

£

⌂ Liverpool Youth Hostel. This hostel a few minutes' walk from Albert Dock really should change its name, because it offers modest hotel standards for bargain prices. The smart rooms (for two, three, four, or six people) are fully carpeted, with private bathrooms and heated towel rails. **Pros:** breakfast included; plenty of parking. **Cons:** far from the center; limited number of double rooms. ⊠ *25 Tabley St., off Wapping, Waterfront* ☎ *0870/770–5924* ⊕ *www.yha.org.uk* ⌁ *100 beds* ⏦ *In-room: no a/c, no TV. In-hotel: restaurant, laundry facilities, Internet terminal, Wi-Fi hotspot* ▭ *MC, V* ⦿ *BP.*

££££

⌂ Malmaison. The only purpose-built hotel in this chic chain—most are in recycled older buildings— combines extreme glamour with sleek industrial modernity and a great sense of space. It's a five-minute walk north of the Liver Building and right on the waterfront, so request a riverside room with a view. Guest rooms, though not large, favor plum and orange and rich textures; walk-in "wet rooms" have a shower and a tub. Public areas are transformed in the evening when chairs change their livery and candlelight abounds, and a cocktail in the Plum Bar is an almost theatrical experience. Pros: buzzy atmosphere; rich decor. Cons: dim lighting in guest rooms; no parking; views to the back are disappointing. ☒ *Princes Dock Waterfront* ☎ *0151/229–5000* ⊕ *www. malmaison.com* ⤳ *128 rooms, 2 suites* ⟳ *In-room: a/c, safe, refrigerator, DVD, Internet, Wi-Fi. In-hotel: restaurant, room service, bar, gym, laundry service* ▤ *AE, MC, V.*

££–£££ ⊡ **Premier Apartments.** These recently built apartments in Liverpool's glossy Garden Quarter in the heart of downtown have everything you need for an independent stay—including groceries, which can be delivered to your door. Spacious and airy apartments have either one or two bedrooms and are furnished in cheerful contemporary style. Lime Street station is a five-minute walk away. Pros: great for travelers who don't need hotel services; plenty of room; breakfast delivered every morning (extra charge). Cons: more expensive on weekends; limited parking. ☒ *11 Hatton Gardens, City Centre* ☎ *0151/227–9467 or 0845/070–0907* ⊕ *www.premierapartments.com* ⤳ *62 apartments* ⟳ *In-room: no a/c, kitchen, Internet, Wi-Fi. In-hotel: laundry facilities, laundry service, parking (paid)* ▤ *AE, MC, V.*

££–£££ ⊡ **Staybridge Apartments.** These up-to-the-minute and well-fitted apart-
★ ments close to the Liverpool Echo Arena make for a great stay on the waterfront. Rooms are filled with light and contain compact kitchens, modern-style furnishings, and spare sofa beds. You can have breakfast (included in the price) with other guests, or stock up on food from the on-site shop. Reception, available 24 hours, is friendly and helpful. Pros: upbeat atmosphere; complimentary receptions on weekday evenings; public spaces for socializing. Cons: limited parking; no nice views. ☒ *21 Keel Wharf, Waterfront* ☎ *0151/703–9700* ⊕ *www.staybridge.co.uk* ⤳ *132 apartments* ⟳ *In-room: a/c, kitchen, refrigerator, Internet, Wi-Fi. In-hotel: gym, laundry facilities, laundry service, parking (paid)* ▤ *AE, MC, V* ⟦◎⟧ *BP.*

10

NIGHTLIFE AND THE ARTS

NIGHTLIFE

The many bars, clubs, and pubs of Liverpool are an experience in themselves, from the trendy to the traditional.

Fodor's Choice **Alma de Cuba** (☒ *Seel St., City Centre* ☎ *0151/702–7394*), a church trans-
★ formed into a luxurious bar, uses a huge mirrored altar and hundreds of dripping candles to great effect. **Baby Cream** (☒ *Atlantic Pavilion, Albert Dock, Waterfront* ☎ *0151/707–1004*) is known for its weekend DJs. The ladies can pamper themselves in the glitzy black powder room. The **Cavern Club** (☒ *8–10 Mathew St., City Centre* ☎ *0151/236–1965*) draws many on the Beatles trail, some of whom don't realize it's not the original spot—that was demolished years ago. The **Cavern Pub** (☒ *5 Mathew St., City Centre* ☎ *0151/236–4041*) merits a stop for nostalgia's

sake; here are recorded the names of the groups and artists who played in the Cavern Club between 1957 and 1973. Opposite Philharmonic Hall, the **Philharmonic** (✉ *36 Hope St., City Centre* ☎ *0151/707–2837*) is a Victorian-era extravaganza decorated in colorful marble. Make sure to check out the ornate loos (toilets). **Ye Cracke** (✉ *13 Rice St., off Hope St., City Centre* ☎ *0151/709–4171*), one of the city's oldest pubs, was much visited by John Lennon in the 1960s.

THE ARTS
FILM
The **FACT Centre** (✉ *88 Wood St., City Centre* ☎ *0151/707–4444*) of the Foundation for Art and Creative Technology shows art-house and independent films on three screens; galleries display experimental film, video, and new media.

PERFORMING ARTS VENUES
The well-regarded Royal Liverpool Philharmonic Orchestra plays its ★ concert season at **Philharmonic Hall** (✉ *Hope St., City Centre* ☎ *0151/709–3789*). The venue also hosts contemporary music, jazz, and world concerts, and shows classic films.

Bluecoat (✉ *School La., City Centre* ☎ *0151/702–5324*) features contemporary visual and performing arts. The **Liverpool Arena and Convention Centre** (✉ *Monarch's Quay, Waterfront* ☎ *0844/800–0400*) hosts large-scale concerts and exhibitions. The **Liverpool Empire** (✉ *Lime St., City Centre* ☎ *0844/847–2525*) presents major ballet, opera, drama, and musical performances.

THEATER
Everyman Theatre (✉ *5–9 Hope St., City Centre* ☎ *0151/709–4776*) focuses on works by British playwrights as well as experimental productions from around the world. **Royal Court Theatre** (✉ *1 Roe St., City Centre* ☎ *0870/787–1866*), an art deco building, is one of the city's most appealing sites for stand-up comedy and theater.

SPORTS AND THE OUTDOORS

FOOTBALL
Football (soccer) matches are played on weekends and, increasingly, weekdays. Tickets for Liverpool are sold out months in advance, but you should have more luck with Everton.

Liverpool (☎ *0844/844–0844*), one of England's top clubs, plays at Anfield, 2 mi north of the city center. The **Liverpool Museum and Stadium Tour** (✉ *Anfield Rd., Anfield* ☎ *0151/260–6677* 🎫 *£10* ☉ *Daily 10–3*) takes you into the dressing rooms and down the tunnel, and gives you a sense of match day. There are no tours on match days. **Everton** (☎ *0870/442–1878*), now reestablishing its historic competitiveness, plays at Goodison Park, about ½ mi north of Anfield.

HORSE RACING
Britain's most famous horse race, the Grand National steeplechase, has ★ been run at Liverpool's **Aintree Racecourse** (✉ *Ormskirk Rd., Aintree* ☎ *0844/579–3001*) almost every year since 1839. The race is held in March or April; book well ahead. Admission on most race days is £18.

SHOPPING

Circa 1900 (✉ *11–13 Holts Arcade, India Buildings, Water St., City Centre* ☎ *0151/236–1282*) specializes in authentic art nouveau and art deco pieces, from ceramics and glass to furniture. **From Me to You** (✉ *Cavern Walks, Mathew St., City Centre* ☎ *0151/227–1963*) may stock the mop-top knickknack of your dreams. **Liverpool One** (✉ *Off Paradise St., City Centre* ☎ *0151/232–3100*), the city's latest and largest shopping complex, has more than 160 stores, including John Lewis. **Metquarter** (✉ *35 Whitechapel, City Centre* ☎ *0151/224–2390*), with more than 40 stores, is the place for designer names and the latest fashions. The **Stanley Dock Sunday Market** (✉ *Great Howard St. and Regent Rd., City Centre*) operates each Sunday, selling bric-a-brac, clothes, and toys. The **Walker Art Gallery** (✉ *William Brown St., City Centre* ☎ *0151/478–4199*) has a small lobby shop with high-quality glassware, ceramics, and jewelry by local designers.

THE PEAK DISTRICT

Heading southeast, away from the urban congestion of Manchester and Liverpool, it's not far to the southernmost contortions of the Pennine Hills. Here, about an hour from Manchester, sheltered in a great natural bowl, is the spa town of Buxton: at an elevation of more than 1,000 feet, it's the second-highest town in England. Buxton makes a convenient base for exploring the 540 square mi of the Peak District, Britain's oldest and, some say, most beautiful—national park. About 38,000 people live in the towns throughout the park.

"Peak" is perhaps misleading; despite being a hilly area, it contains only gentle rises that don't reach much higher than 2,000 feet. Yet a trip around destinations such as Bakewell, Matlock, Castleton, and Edale, and the grand estates of Chatsworth House, Haddon Hall, and Hardwick Hall involves negotiating fairly perilous country roads, each of which repays the effort with enchanting views. Outdoor activities are popular in the Peaks, particularly caving (or "potholing"), walking, and hiking. Bring all-weather clothing and waterproof shoes.

10

BUXTON

25 mi southeast of Manchester.

Buxton makes a good base for Peak District excursions, but it has its own attractions as well. The town's spa days left a notable legacy of 18th- and 19th-century buildings, parks, and open spaces that give the town an air of faded grandeur. The Romans arrived in AD 79 and named Buxton Aquae Arnemetiae, loosely translated as "Waters of the Goddess of the Grove," suggesting they considered this area in the Derbyshire hills special. The mineral springs, which emerge from 3,500 to 5,000 feet below ground at a constant 82°F, were believed to cure assorted ailments; in the 18th century the town became established as a popular spa, a minor rival to Bath. You can still drink water from the ancient St. Anne's Well, and it's also sold throughout Britain.

GETTING HERE AND AROUND

Both the National Express and TransPeak bus services from Manchester stop at Buxton. There are departures every two to three hours from Manchester's Chorlton Street Bus Station. If you're driving from Manchester, take A6 southeast to Buxton. The journey takes one hour. The hourly train from Manchester to Buxton takes an hour.

ESSENTIALS

Bus Contacts GMPTE information line (☎ *0161/244–1000 or 0871/200– 2233* ⊕ *www.gmpte.com*). **National Express** (☎ *0871/781–8181* ⊕ *www. nationalexpress.com*). **TransPeak** (☎ *01733/712265* ⊕ *www.transpeak.co.uk*).

Visitor Information Buxton (✉ *Pavilion Gardens, St. John's Rd.* ☎ *01298/25106* ⊕ *www.visitpeakdistrict.com*).

EXPLORING

TOP ATTRACTIONS

Crescent. A good place to start exploring is the Crescent on the northwest side of the Slopes park (the town hall is on the opposite side); almost all out-of-town roads lead toward this central green with its curving semicircle of buildings. The three former hotels that make up the Georgian-era Crescent, with its arches, Doric colonnades, and 378 windows, were built in 1780 by fashionable architect John Carr for the fifth duke of Devonshire (of nearby Chatsworth House). The thermal baths at the end of the Crescent now house a shopping center.

OFF THE BEATEN PATH

Little Moreton Hall. The epitome of "magpie" black-and-white half-timber buildings, Little Moreton Hall, in the words of Olive Cook's *The English Country House,* "exaggerates and exalts the typical and humble medieval timber-framed dwelling, making of it a bizarre, unforgettable phenomenon." Covered with zigzags, crosses, and lozenge shapes crafted of timber and daub, the house was built by the Moreton family between 1450 and 1580. The long gallery and colorful Tudor-era wall paintings are spectacular, and the staggered lavatories are intriguing. Little Moreton Hall lies to the west of the Peak District; to get here from Liverpool, take the M6 to the A534 east to Congleton. The house is 20 mi southwest of Buxton. (✉ *A34, Congleton* ☎ *01260/272018* ⊕ *www. nationaltrust.org.uk* 🎫 *£6.35 Mar.–Nov., £3.30 Dec.* ☯ *Early–mid-Mar. and mid-Nov.–late Nov., weekends 11–4; late Mar.–early Nov., Wed.–Sun. and national holidays 11–5; early to mid-Dec., ground fl. only, weekends 11–4.*

Pavilion Gardens. Surrounded by 25 acres of pretty gardens, the Pavilion, with its ornate iron-and-glass roof, was originally a concert hall and ballroom. Erected in the 1870s, it remains a lively place that hosts fairs, events, and farmers' markets, and also has a plant-filled conservatory, two cafés, and a restaurant. The Pavilion is adjacent to the Crescent and the Slopes on the west; the tourist office is here, too, with a food and crafts shop. (✉ *Pavilion Gardens* ☎ *01298/23114* ⊕ *www. paviliongardens.co.uk.*

WORTH NOTING

Buxton Museum and Art Gallery. The museum, on the eastern side of the Slopes, contains a collection of Blue John stone, a semiprecious mineral found only in the Peak District. It also displays local archaeological finds and pieces made from Derbyshire black marble, and there's a small art gallery. ⊠ *Terrace Rd.* ☎ *01298/24658* ⊕ *www.derbyshire.gov.uk/ leisure* ▣ *Free* ☉ *Tues.–Fri. 9:30–5:30, Sat. 9:30–5, Sun. and national holidays (Apr.–Sept. only) 10:30–5.*

Devonshire Royal Hospital. This impressive 18th-century building, behind the Crescent, was originally designed by John Carr as a stable with room for 110 horses. In 1859 the circular area for exercising horses was covered with a massive 156-foot-wide slate-color dome—bigger than that of St. Paul's Cathedral in London—and incorporated into a hospital. The University of Derby has taken over the building and, when school is in session, runs an informal bistro open during the day and a restaurant serving excellent lunches (weekdays) and dinners (Thursday).

Poole's Cavern. The Peak District's extraordinary geology is revealed close to Buxton at this large limestone cave far beneath the 100 wooded acres of Buxton Country Park. The cave was inhabited in prehistoric times and contains, in addition to the standard stalactites and stalagmites, the source of the River Wye, which flows through Buxton. ⊠ *Green La.* ☎ *01298/26978* ⊕ *www.poolescavern.co.uk* ▣ *£8, including 50-min guided tour. Park and visitor center free* ☉ *Daily 9:30–5. Tours every 20 mins.*

WHERE TO EAT AND STAY

££ ✕ **Columbine**. The husband-and-wife team behind Columbine always go

BRITISH for local ingredients and flavors, no matter if the dishes are traditional, such as pork tenderloin with poached pear in mild Stilton sauce, or more retro, like duckling with oranges and Grand Marnier. The cozy venue, with upstairs and downstairs seating, is a good spot for pre- and post-theater meals. ⊠ *7 Hall Bank* ☎ *01298/78752* ▤ *MC, V* ☉ *Closed Sun. Closed Tues. Nov.–Apr. No lunch Aug.–June.*

££ ⊞ **Buxton's Victorian Guesthouse.** One of a terrace (a group of row houses)

★ built by the duke of Devonshire in 1860, this handsomely decorated house stands a stone's throw away from the Opera House. Victorian and Edwardian antiques and prints furnish the individually decorated rooms. Breakfasts, with options including oatcakes and kippers as well as the usual eggs, are taken in the dining room. **Pros:** peaceful location on Pavilion Gardens; family suite available. **Cons:** many stairs to climb; surcharge for credit cards. ⊠ *3A Broad Walk* ☎ *01298/78759* ⊕ *www. buxtonvictorian.co.uk* ⇝ *7 rooms, 1 suite* ♿ *In-room: no a/c, no phone. In-hotel: parking (free), no kids under 4* ▤ *AE, MC, V* ⫶◯⫶ *BP.*

££–£££ ⊞ **Old Hall**. In a refurbished 16th-century building, this hotel overlooks the Opera House. The individually decorated rooms are furnished in a mixture of period and modern styles. One room in the oldest section, Mary's Bower, retains its original ceiling moldings. The Cockerel Bar is popular with theatergoers, who stoke up on its hearty dishes; there's a more formal restaurant as well. **Pros:** unpretentious atmosphere; good dining choices. **Cons:** conventional furnishings; no private parking.

10

⊠ *The Square* ☎ *01298/22841* ⊕ *www.oldhallhotelbuxton.co.uk* ⇆ *38 rooms* ♿ *In-room: no a/c. In-hotel: restaurant, room service, bar, Wi-Fi hotspot, some pets allowed* ⊟ *AE, MC, V* ⏍ *BP.*

££ ⌴ **Stoneridge.** Built of stone, this Edwardian B&B close to the Opera House has been richly restored. Bedrooms are done in brown and cream and furnished with modern pieces. Hearty breakfasts include fresh fruit, omelets, and potato scones; packed lunches, afternoon teas, and three-course evening meals can be provided on request. **Pros:** excellent food choices; secluded and tranquil garden. **Cons:** no tubs in bathrooms; credit cards not accepted. ⊠ *9 Park Rd.* ☎ *01298/26120* ⊕ *www. stoneridge.co.uk* ⇆ *4 rooms* ♿ *In-room: no a/c, no phone, Wi-Fi. In-hotel: parking (free), some pets allowed, no kids under 5* ⊟ *No credit cards* ⏍ *BP.*

NIGHTLIFE AND THE ARTS

★ **Buxton Opera House** (⊠ *Water St.* ☎ *0845/127–2190*), bedecked with carved cupids, presents excellent theater, ballet, and jazz performances year-round; in late February it also hosts the annual Four-Four Time festival of world, jazz, blues, and folk music.

The renowned **Buxton Festival** (⊠ *Festival Office, The Square* ☎ *01298/ 70395* ⊕ *www.buxtonfestival.co.uk*), held for two weeks during mid-July each year, includes opera, drama, and concerts.

SHOPPING

Buxton has many kinds of stores, especially around Spring Gardens, the main shopping street. Stores in the beautifully tiled **Cavendish Arcade** (⊠ *The Crescent*), on the site of the old thermal baths, sell antiques, jewelry, fashions, and leather goods in stylish surroundings. A **market**, selling mainly food and clothes, is held in Buxton every Tuesday and Saturday.

▌**EN
ROUTE**

As you head southeast from Buxton on the A6, you pass through the spectacular valleys of Ashwood Dale, Wyedale, and Monsal Dale before reaching Bakewell.

BAKEWELL

12 mi southeast of Buxton, 32 mi northeast of Little Moreton Hall.

In Bakewell, a medieval bridge crosses the winding River Wye in five graceful arches, and the 9th-century Saxon cross that stands outside the parish church reveals the town's great age. Narrow streets and houses built out of the local gray-brown stone also make the town extremely appealing. Ceaseless traffic through the streets can take the shine off— though there's respite down on the quiet riverside paths.

This market town is the commercial hub of the Peak District, for locals and visitors. The crowds are really substantial on market day (Monday), attended by area farmers; a similarly popular traditional agricultural show takes place the first week of August. For a self-guided hour-long stroll, pick up a map at the tourist office, where the town trail begins. A small exhibition upstairs explains the landscape of the Peak District. Worth exploring nearby are two distinguished houses: Haddon Hall and Chatsworth.

CLOSE UP

Stoke-on-Trent: The Potteries

The area known as the Potteries, about 55 mi southeast of Liverpool, is still the center of Britain's ceramics industry, though production is increasingly being transferred overseas. The novels of Arnold Bennett (1867–1931), including *Anna of the Five Towns,* realistically describe life in the area as an "architecture of ovens and chimneys" with an atmosphere "as black as mud." There are, in fact, six towns, now administered as "the city of Stoke-on-Trent." Famous names such as Wedgwood, Royal Doulton, Spode, and Coalport carry on, though they were taken over by other companies in 2009.

The most famous manufacturer, Josiah Wedgwood, established his pottery works at Etruria, near Burslem, in 1759, and created the cream-color ware (creamware), which so pleased Queen Charlotte that in 1762 she appointed him royal supplier of dinnerware. Perhaps Wedgwood's best-known innovation was his blue jasperware, decorated with white cameo figures by the British artist John Flaxman. More recent innovators include the very collectible Clarice Cliff, who strove to brighten plain whiteware in the 1920s with her colorful geometric and floral designs, notably the bold crocus pattern. Also bold and colorful were the classic art deco pieces of Susie Cooper. Four museums evocatively portray the history of this area, and there's still plenty of shopping to be done, including good prices for seconds.

Ceramica occupies an ornate former town hall and uses displays, videos, and interactive technology to explore the area's history, the process of creating china, and some noted companies. In Bizarreland (the name comes from Clarice Cliff's art deco designs), kids can dig for relics from the past and take a virtual ride over the Potteries. A shop sells local wares. ⊠ *Market Pl., Burslem* ☎ *01782/832001* ⊕ *www.ceramicauk.com* ✉ *£4.10* ⊙ *Tues.–Sat. 10:30–4:30.*

The **Gladstone Pottery Museum**, the city's only remaining Victorian pottery factory, contains examples of the old bottle kilns, surrounded by original workshops where you can watch the traditional skills of throwing, casting, and decorating. The Flushed with Pride galleries tell the story of the toilet from the 1840s onward. ⊠ *Uttoxeter Rd., Longton* ☎ *01782/237777* ⊕ *www.stokemuseums.org.uk* ✉ *£5.95* ⊙ *Daily 10–5; last admission at 4.*

The modern **Potteries Museum and Art Gallery** displays a 5,000-piece ceramic collection of international repute, and is recognized worldwide for its unique Staffordshire pottery. ⊠ *Bethesda St., Hanley* ☎ *01782/232323* ⊕ *www.stoke.gov.uk* ✉ *Free* ⊙ *Mar.–Oct., Mon.–Sat. 10–5, Sun. 2–5; Nov.–Feb., Mon.–Sat. 10–4, Sun. 1–4.*

At the **Wedgwood Museum and Visitor Centre** you can learn about the history of Wedgwood, and see samples of its ware. Look out for portrait medallions, cauliflower ware and the innovative black basalt—the hedgehog bulb pot is a charming example. The visitor center has craft demonstrations and also displays Doulton and Minton ware. Both the museum and visitor center have shops where you can buy firsts and seconds. ⊠ *Off A5035, Barlaston* ☎ *01782/371900* ⊕ *www.wedgwoodmuseum.org.uk* ✉ *£9.50 joint ticket, £6 museum only* ⊙ *Weekdays 9–5, weekends 10–5.*

10

GETTING HERE AND AROUND

National Express and TransPeak offer bus services from Manchester's Chorlton Street Bus Station to Bakewell. By car, Bakewell is a one-hour, 30-minute drive southeast on the A6 from Manchester.

ESSENTIALS

Visitor Information Bakewell (✉ *Old Market Hall, Bridge St.* ☎ *01629/816558* ⊕ *www.visitpeakdistrict.com*).

EXPLORING

Fodor'sChoice
★   Stately house scholar Hugo Montgomery-Massingberd has called **Haddon Hall**, a romantic, storybook medieval manor set along the River

---

PRIDE AND CHATSWORTH

You may recognize the exterior and parkland of Chatsworth as Pemberley, home of Mr. Darcy, in the 2005 film version of *Pride and Prejudice*. It was Hollywood exaggeration to give him one of England's grandest country mansions, but no matter. The film also has some enticing views of the Peak District. The interior of the house is revealed in the 2008 film *The Duchess* with Keira Knightley.

Wye 2 mi southeast of Bakewell, "the *beau idéal* of the English country house." Unlike other trophy homes that are marble Palladian monuments to a European grand tour, Haddon Hall remains quintessentially English in appearance, bristling with crenellations and stepped roofs and landscaped with rose gardens.

The house, built between 1180 and 1565, passed into the ownership of the dukes of Rutland and remained largely unaltered until the early 20th century, when the ninth duke undertook a superlative restoration. This revealed a series of early decorative 15th-century frescoes in the chapel. The finest of the intricate plasterwork and wooden paneling is best seen in the superb Long Gallery on the first floor. Baking is still done in the bread ovens in the well-preserved Tudor kitchen. Here, too, is the unique collection of Gothic dole cupboards, some original to the house, which would have been filled with food and placed outside for those in need. The wider world saw the hall in *Jane Eyre* (both Franco Zeffirelli's 1996 version and the BBC's 2006 version), *Pride and Prejudice* with Keira Knightley (2005), and *The Other Boleyn Girl* (2008). ✉ *A6* ☎ *01629/812855* ⊕ *www.haddonhall.co.uk* ✉ *£8.95, parking £1.50* ☉ *May–Sept., daily noon–5; Apr. and Oct., Sat.–Mon. noon–5; last admission 1 hr before closing.*

⟳
★   Glorious parkland leads to **Chatsworth House**, ancestral home of the dukes of Devonshire and one of England's greatest country houses. The vast expanse of greenery, grazed by deer and sheep, sets off the Palladian-style elegance of "the Palace of the Peak." Originally an Elizabethan house, Chatsworth was conceived on a monumental scale. It was altered over several generations starting in 1686, and the architecture now has a hodgepodge look, though the Palladian facade remains splendid. The house is surrounded by woods, elaborate gardens, greenhouses, rock gardens, and the most famous water cascade in the kingdom—all designed by two great landscape artists, Capability Brown and, in the 19th century, Joseph Paxton, an engineer as well as a brilliant gardener. The gravity-fed Emperor Fountain can shoot as high as 300 feet. Perennially popular with children, the farmyard area has milking

demonstrations at 3 and an adventure playground. ■TIP➜ **Plan on at least a half day to explore the grounds; avoid Sunday if you prefer not to be with the heaviest crowds.**

Although death duties have taken a toll on the interior grandeur, as duke after duke has been forced to sell off treasures to keep the place going, there is more than enough to look at. Inside are intricate carvings, Van Dyck portraits, superb furniture, and a few fabulous rooms, including the Sculpture Gallery, the library, and the Blue Drawing Room, where you can see two of the most famous portraits in Britain, Sir Joshua Reynolds's *Georgiana, Duchess of Devonshire, and Her Baby,* and John Singer Sargent's enormous *Acheson Sisters.* Chatsworth is 4 mi northeast of Bakewell. ⊠ *Off B6012* ☎ *01246/582204* ⊕ *www.chatsworth. org* ✉ *House, gardens, and farmyard £15.50 (book online and save 10%); house and gardens £11.50; gardens only, £7.50; farmyard and adventure playground £5.25; parking £2* ۞ *Mid-Mar.–late Dec., house daily 11–5:30, gardens daily 11–6, farmyard and adventure playground daily 10:30–5:30; last admission 1 hr before closing.*

WHERE TO EAT AND STAY

£££
BRITISH
✕**Devonshire Arms.** This stone 18th-century coaching inn, which counts Charles Dickens as one of its many famous visitors, is divided into a cozy bar area and a modern brasserie, both serving great homemade fare. Typical dishes include Chatsworth shoulder of lamb with potato curry, and rice pudding with raisins and orange marmalade. There's an excellent snack menu, too. The inn is 2 mi south of Chatsworth and also has eight bedrooms. ⊠ *B6012, Beeley* ☎ *01629/733259* ⊕ *www. devonshirebeeley.co.uk* ▭ *AE, MC, V.*

£££££
BRITISH
★
✕**Fischer's.** The Fischer family bought this stately Edwardian manor on the edge of the Chatsworth estate, north of Bakewell, to house their restaurant. Intimate and formal, the restaurant takes pride in using high-quality local products; on the fixed-price menus you'll find wild venison, Derbyshire pork and lamb, and Yorkshire rhubarb, all presented with care and aplomb. If you can't decide, there's a six-course tasting menu of specialty dishes (£63). With 11 elegant bedrooms here as well, you might consider staying the night. Sunday dinner is for overnight guests only. ⊠ *Baslow Hall, Calver Rd., Baslow* ☎ *01246/583259* ⊕ *www. fischers-baslowhall.co.uk* ▭ *AE, MC, V.*

£
BRITISH
✕**The Old Original Bakewell Pudding Shop.** Given the plethora of local rivals, it takes a bold establishment to claim its Bakewell puddings as "original," but there's certainly nothing wrong with those served here, eaten hot with custard or cream. The oak-beam dining room also turns out commendable main courses of Yorkshireman (batter pudding with meat and vegetables) and steak-and-ale pie. ⊠ *The Square* ☎ *01629/812193* ⊕ *www.bakewellpuddingshop.co.uk* ▭ *MC, V.*

££
★
▥**Haddon House Farm.** This may be a working farm, but there's nothing workaday about the fresh and imaginatively designed rooms (with themes such as Monet and Shakespeare) that the Nicholls husband-and-wife team created. Even the bathrooms are special, with tiles hand-painted with insects and bamboo. The peaceful valley location, lovely antiques, and bouquets of flowers all contribute to a relaxing stay. Breakfasts are taken casually around the kitchen table. The location

10

on the A6 lies between Haddon Hall and Bakewell. **Pros:** charming and obliging hosts; outdoor hot tub (extra fee); easily accessible by bus. **Cons:** no credit cards; no single rooms. ⊠ *Haddon Rd.* ☎ *01629/814024* ⊕ *www.greatplace.co.uk* ⊅ *4 rooms* △ *In-room: no a/c, no phone, Wi-Fi. In-hotel: parking (free), no kids under 5* ⊟ *No credit cards* ⊙ *BP.*

SPORTS AND THE OUTDOORS

Dragon Balloons (⊠ *Mam House Farm, Hope Valley, Castleton* ☎ *01433/623007* ⊕ *www. dragonballoon.co.uk*) fly over Chatsworth House and Haddon Hall and surroundings in a hot-air balloon from the Bakewell Showground. The hour-long morning or evening flights cost from £137.

> ### BAKEWELL PUDDING
>
> Bakewell is the source of Bakewell pudding, said to have been created inadvertently when, sometime in the 19th century, a cook at the town's Rutland Arms Hotel (which is still in business) dropped some rich cake mixture over jam tarts and baked it. Every local bakery and tearoom claims an original recipe, so it's easy to spend a gustatory afternoon tasting rival puddings.

MATLOCK

5 mi south of Haddon Hall, 8 mi southeast of Bakewell.

In the heart of the Derbyshire Dales, Matlock and its near neighbor Matlock Bath are former spa towns compressed into a narrow gorge on the River Derwent. Some surviving Regency buildings in Matlock testify to its former importance, although it's less impressive an ensemble than that presented by Buxton. The surroundings, however, are particularly beautiful.

GETTING HERE AND AROUND

Matlock is served by National Express and TransPeak buses from Manchester's Chorlton Street Bus Station. The town is about a one-hour, 40-minute drive southeast on the A6 from Manchester.

ESSENTIALS

Visitor Information Matlock (⊠ *Crown Sq.* ☎ *01629/583388* ⊕ *www. visitpeakdistrict.com*).

EXPLORING

The **Matlock River Illuminations,** a flotilla of lighted boats shimmering after dark along the still waters of the river, takes place on weekends September through late October.

☾ At Matlock Bath, 2 mi south of Matlock, river and valley views unfold from the curving line of buildings that makes up the village. Aside from riverside strolls, the major attraction is the cable-car ride across the River Derwent that takes you to the **Heights of Abraham Country Park and Caverns** on the crags above, with a visitor center and café. The all-inclusive ticket allows access to the woodland walks and nature trails of the 60-acre park, as well as entry to a cavern and a guided descent into an old lead mine, where workers toiled by candlelight. ⊠ *A6, Matlock Bath* ☎ *01629/582365* ⊕ *www.heightsofabraham.com*

CLOSE UP

Well Dressing

Unique to the Peak District is the custom of well dressing, when certain wells or springs are decorated with elaborate pictures made of flowers. Frames up to 4 feet wide and 6 feet high, covered with a base of clay, are filled with a colorful mosaic of seeds, grasses, berries, and moss as well as flowers and flower petals, a process that involves a team of workers and takes about a week to complete. Although the designs usually incorporate religious themes such as biblical stories, they are a Christian veneer over an ancient pagan celebration of the water's life-giving powers. The well dressing and blessing ceremony, usually accompanied by a brass band, heralds the start of several days of festivities.

Of the 70 or so towns and villages that continue this summertime tradition, Tissington (May), south of Matlock; Bakewell (early July); and, near Chatsworth, Eyam (late August) are among the most popular. Check with local tourist offices for Information.

£11.50 ☉ Cable car and visitor center mid-Feb.–late Feb. and Oct., daily 10–4:30; early to mid-Mar., weekends 10–4:30; late Mar.–Sept., daily 10–5 (and later in summer).

OFF THE BEATEN PATH

Hardwick Hall. Few houses in England evoke the late Elizabethan era as vividly as Hardwick Hall, a beautiful stone mansion and treasure trove. The facade glitters with myriad windows, making it easy to see why the house came to be known as "Hardwick Hall, more glass than wall." ■ TIP→ Choose a sunny day to see the rooms and their treasures at their best. The vast state apartments well befit their original chatelaine, Bess of Hardwick. By marrying a succession of four rich husbands, she had become second only to Queen Elizabeth in her wealth when work on this house began. She took possession in 1597, and four years later made an inventory of the important rooms and their contents—furniture, tapestries, and embroideries. The wonder is that these items still remain here. Unique patchwork hangings, probably made from clerical copes and altar frontals taken from monasteries and abbeys, grace the entrance hall, and superb 16th- and 17th-century tapestries cover the walls of the main staircase and first-floor High Great Chamber. The collection of Elizabethan embroideries—table carpets, cushions, bed hangings, and pillowcases—is second to none. There are also fine examples of plasterwork, painted friezes, and ornamental chimneypieces. Outside, you can visit the walled gardens. Hardwick Hall is 10 mi east of Matlock. Access is signposted from Junction 29 of the M1 motorway. ⊠ *Doe Lea, Chesterfield* ☎ *01246/850430* ⊕ *www.nationaltrust.org. uk* ☜ *£9.50; gardens only, £4.80; parking £2* ☉ *House mid-Mar.–Oct., Wed.–Sun. and national holidays, noon–4:30; Dec., weekends noon–3. Gardens mid-Mar.–Oct., Wed.–Sun. and national holidays noon–4:30; Dec. weekends 11–3; last admission 30 mins before closing. Grounds daily 8–dusk.*

10

WHERE TO STAY

££ 🖼 **Dower House.** This charming 16th-century stone house sitting at the head of the pretty village of Winster, about 6 mi west of Matlock, has all you expect from a small country-house stay. Mullioned windows throw plenty of light into warmly furnished and spacious rooms, and the beamed dining room focuses on a wood fire. Courteous hosts prepare scrumptious breakfasts and, should you want, packed lunches, and the lovely walled garden is a perfect spot for relaxation. **Pros:** country house character; very peaceful; beautifully furnished. **Cons:** no credit cards; minimum two-night stay on weekends; not easily accessible without a car. ⊠ *Main St., Winster* ☎ *01629/650931* ⊕ *www. thedowerhousewinster.com* 🔄 *4 rooms* ♿ *In-room: no a/c. In-hotel: no kids under 12* ▭ *No credit cards* ⏀ *BP.*

SPORTS AND THE OUTDOORS

One of the major trails in the Peak District, **High Peak Trail** runs for 17 mi from Cromford (south of Matlock Bath) to Dowlow, following the route of an old railroad. For information, guidebooks, guide services, and maps, contact any Peak District National Park Office.

Red House Stables (⊠ *Old Rd., Darley Dale, Matlock* ☎ *01629/733–583* ⊕ *www.workingcarriages.com*) arranges carriage trips through the local countryside. An hour-long ride costs £30.

CASTLETON

24 mi northwest of Matlock, 10 mi northwest of Chatsworth, 9 mi northeast of Buxton.

The area around Castleton, in Hope Valley, contains the most famous manifestations of the geology of the Peak District. A number of caves and mines are open to the public, including some former lead mines and Blue John mines (amethystine spar; the unusual name is a corruption of the French *bleu-jaune* (meaning "blue yellow"). The limestone caverns attract many people, which means that pretty Castleton shows a certain commercialization. Summer brings the crowds, many of whom poke around in the numerous shops displaying Blue John jewelry and wares.

GETTING HERE AND AROUND

Hope Rail Station, 1.5 mi from the center of Castleton, is served by the Manchester–Sheffield railroad line. By car, Castleton is a one-hour drive southeast on the A6 from Manchester.

ESSENTIALS

Visitor Information Castleton (⊠ *Castle St.* ☎ *01433/620679* ⊕ *www. visitpeakdistrict.com*).

EXPLORING

In 1176 Henry II added the square tower to the Norman **Peveril Castle**, whose ruins occupy a dramatic crag above the town. The castle has superb views—from here you can still clearly see a curving section of the medieval defensive earthworks in the town center below. Peveril Castle is protected on its west side by a 230-foot-deep gorge formed by a collapsed cave. Park in the town center, from which it's a steep climb up. ⊠ *Market Pl., A1687* ☎ *01433/620613* ⊕ *www.english-heritage. org.uk* ✎ *£3.90* ☉ *Apr.–June, Sept., and Oct., daily 10–5; July and Aug., daily 10–6; Nov.–Mar., Thurs.–Mon. 10–4.*

Caves riddle the entire town and the surrounding area, and in the massive **Peak Cavern**—reputedly Derbyshire's largest natural cave—rope making has been done on a great ropewalk for more than 400 years. You can still see the remains of the 17th-century rope makers' village. ⊠ *Off Goosehill* ☎ *01433/620285* ⊕ *www.devilsarse.com* ✎ *£7.75; £13 joint ticket with Speedwell Cavern* ☉ *Apr.–Oct., daily 10–5; Nov.– Mar., weekends 10–5, call ahead for weekday hrs.*

The area's most exciting cavern by far is **Speedwell Cavern**, where 105 slippery steps lead down to old lead-mine tunnels, blasted out by 19th-century miners. Here you transfer to a small boat for the claustrophobic ¼-mi chug through an illuminated access tunnel to the cavern itself. At this point you're 600 feet underground, in the deepest public-access cave in Britain, with views farther down to the so-called Bottomless Pit, a water-filled cavern. A shop on-site sells items made of the Blue John mineral. Speedwell Cavern is at the bottom of Winnats Pass, 1 mi west of Castleton. ⊠ *Winnats Pass* ☎ *01433/620512* ⊕ *www. speedwellcavern.co.uk* ✎ *£8.25; £13 joint ticket with Peak Cavern; parking £2* ☉ *Daily 10–5; last tour 1 hr before closing.*

WHERE TO STAY

£ ⬚ **Bargate Cottage.** Dating to 1650, this cottage at the top of Market Place below the castle is one of Castleton's B&B treasures. The kindly owners scatter teddy bears with abandon, and the cutesy oak-beam rooms incorporate the necessary facilities. Breakfast is served at one table, with bonhomie and hiking advice on tap. **Pros:** peaceful location; great breakfasts. **Cons:** small rooms; no credit cards. ⊠ *Market Pl.* ☎ *01433/620201* ⊕ *www.bargatecottage.co.uk* ↪ *3 rooms* ⚑ *In-room: no a/c. In-hotel: no kids under 12* ⊟ *No credit cards* ⦿| *BP.*

££ ⬚ **Underleigh House.** Peaceful is the word for the location of this creeper-clad cottage and barn at the end of a lane in lovely walking country. The big lounge has a fireplace, and the flagstone entrance hall has one big table for breakfasts (expect local specialties such as fruit compotes, oatcakes, and black pudding). There are games for rainy days, and books, sweets, and flowers in the tidy modern bedrooms. Hope is 1 mi east of Castleton on A617. **Pros:** superb views; ample breakfasts. **Cons:** minimum stays on weekends; surcharge for credit cards. ⊠ *Off Edale Rd., Hope* ☎ *01433/621372* ⊕ *www.underleighhouse.co.uk* ↪ *3 rooms, 2 suites* ⚑ *In-room: no a/c, DVD. In-hotel: parking (free), some pets allowed, no kids under 12* ⊟ *MC, V* ⦿| *BP.*

EN ROUTE Heading northwest to Edale, the most spectacular driving route is over **Winnats Pass**, through a narrow, boulder-strewn valley. Beyond are the tops of Mam Tor (where there's a lookout point) and the hamlet of Barber Booth, after which you run into Edale.

10

EDALE

5 mi northwest of Castleton.

At Edale, an extremely popular hiking center, you're truly in the Peak District wilds. This sleepy, straggling village, in the shadow of Mam Tor and Lose Hill and the moorlands of the high plateau known as Kinder Scout (2,088 feet), lies among some of the most breathtaking scenery in Derbyshire. England can show little wilder scenery than Kinder Scout, with its ragged edges of grit stone and its interminable leagues of heather and peat. Late summer brings a covering of reddish purple as the heather flowers, and in late fall or early winter the moors seem to brood under low clouds.

GETTING HERE AND AROUND

Edale Rail Station has service to Manchester and Sheffield. By car, Edale is a one-hour drive southeast on the A6 from Manchester.

ESSENTIALS

Visitor Information Moorlands Centre (⊠ *Fieldhead* ☎ *01433/670207* ⊕ *www.visitpeakdistrict.com*).

EXPLORING

The **Old Nag's Head** (☎ *01433/670291*), a pub at the top of the village, has marked the official start of the Pennine Way since 1965. Call in at the Hiker's Bar, sit by the fire, and tuck into hearty bar meals and hot toddies. On Monday and Tuesday in winter, when this pub is closed, the Ramblers' Inn, at the other end of the village, is open.

In the village, the Edale **National Park Information Centre** has maps, guides, and information on all the walks in the area. There's limited accommodation in the village (all B&B-style), but the information center can provide a list or point you toward the local youth hostel. ⊠ *Fieldhead* ☎ *01433/670207* ⊕ *www.peakdistrict.com* ⊗ *Apr.–Oct., daily 9:30–5; Nov.–Mar., weekdays 10–3:30, weekends 9:30–4:30.*

SPORTS AND THE OUTDOORS

Edale is the starting point of the 250-mi-long **Pennine Way** (⊕ *www.nationaltrail.co.uk*), which crosses Kinder Scout. If you plan to attempt this, seek local advice first, because bad weather can make the walk treacherous. However, several much shorter routes into the Edale Valley, like the 8-mi route west to Hayfield, give you a taste.

The Lake District

WINDERMERE, GRASMERE, KENDAL, KESWICK

WORD OF MOUTH

"I loved Beatrix Potter's Hill Top farm and the solicitor's offices in town (Hawkshead) that were her husband's firm's; they are now a gallery of rotating illustrations from the books. We also thought Wordsworth's Dove Cottage in Grasmere was interesting, primarily for an excellent commentary."

—Cathinjoetown

"Kendal is considered the gateway to the southern lakes. The rule of thumb is that the northern Lake District (including Keswick) has the wilder, more dramatic scenery, while the southern area is more chocolate-box pretty. Ambleside is also a possibility in the south. My favorite way to stay in the Lakes is a farm bed-and-breakfast."

—Morgana

Updated by
Julius Honnor

"Let nature be your teacher." Wordsworth's ideal comes true in this popular region of jagged mountains, waterfalls, wooded valleys, and stone-built villages. No mountains in Britain give a greater impression of majesty; deeper and bluer lakes can be found, but none that fit so readily into the surrounding scene.

In 1951 the Lake District National Park was created here from parts of the counties of Cumberland, Westmorland, and Lancashire. The Lake District is a contour map come to life, covering an area of approximately 885 square mi and holding 16 major lakes and countless smaller stretches of water. You can cross it by car in about an hour, though that would be a shame: this is an area meant to be walked. The mountains are not high by international standards—Scafell Pike, England's highest peak, is only 3,210 feet above sea level—but they can be tricky to climb. In spring, many of the higher summits remain snowcapped long after the weather below has turned mild.

The poets Wordsworth and Coleridge, and other English writers, found the Lake District an inspiring setting for their work, and outdoors enthusiasts have followed ever since, to walk, go boating, or just relax and take in the views. Other literary figures who made their homes in the Lake District include Thomas De Quincey, John Ruskin, and later, the children's writers Beatrix Potter and Arthur Ransome. Seeing the homes and other sights associated with these writers can occupy part of a trip.

This area can be one of Britain's most appealing reservoirs of calm, though in summer the lakeside towns, however appealing, can lose their charm when cars and tour buses clog the narrow streets. Similarly, the walks and hiking trails that crisscross the region seem less inviting when you share them with a crowd. Despite the challenges of popularity, the Lake District has managed tourism and the landscape in a manner that retains the character of the villages and the natural environment. Explore beyond Windermere and Keswick to discover little farming communities eking out a living from the occasionally harsh conditions.

Today, too, a new generation of hotel and restaurant owners is making more creative use of the edible and other assets of the Lakeland fells, and chic modern or foodie-oriented establishments are springing up next to traditional tearooms and chintz-filled inns.

Off-season visits can be a real treat. All those inns and bed-and-breakfasts that turn away crowds in summer are eager for business the rest of the year (and their rates drop accordingly). It's not an easy task to find a succession of sunny days in the Lake District—some malicious statisticians allot to it about 250 rainy days a year—but when the sun breaks through and brightens the surfaces of the lakes, it is an away-from-it-all place to remember.

11

TOP REASONS TO GO

Hiking the trails: Whether it's a demanding trek up England's highest mountain, or a gentle wander around a tarn (a small mountain lake), walking is the number one pleasure and the way to see the Lake District at its rugged and spectacular best. Even in summer, there are fantastic opportunities to escape the crowds.

Mucking around in boats: There's nowhere better for renting a small boat or taking a cruise on a vintage boat and discovering the pleasures of bobbing around on the water. You'll get a different perspective on the mountains, too. The Coniston Boating Centre and Derwentwater Marina near Keswick are possible places to start.

Wordsworth's daffodils and literary landscapes: The Lake District has a rich literary history, in the children's books of Beatrix Potter such as *The Tale of Peter Rabbit*, in the writings of John Ruskin, and in the poems of Wordsworth, which resonate more deeply after you've seen his flowers dancing in the breeze. Stop at any of the writers' homes to enrich your experience.

Pints and pubs: Cumbria has some great microbreweries, and a pint of real ale in one of the region's atmospheric rural inns, such as the Drunken Duck near Hawkshead, may never taste as good as after a long hard day up a mountain.

Sunrise at Castlerigg. The stone circle at Castlerigg, in a natural hollow ringed by peaks, is a reminder of the region's ancient history. Blencathra and other mountains provide an awesome backdrop for the 38 stones. Sunrise is magical.

ORIENTATION AND PLANNING

GETTING ORIENTED

The Lake District is in northwest England, some 70 mi north of the industrial belt along the River Mersey that stretches from Liverpool to Manchester, and south of Scotland. The major gateway from the south is Kendal, and from the north, Penrith. Both are on the M6 motorway. Main-line trains stop at Oxenholme, near Kendal, with a branch linking Oxenholme to Kendal and Windermere. Windermere, in the south, is the most obvious starting point and has plenty of man-made attractions—museums, cafés, and gift shops. But the farther (and higher) you can get from the southern towns, the more you'll appreciate the area's spectacular landscapes. The Lake District National Park breaks into two reasonably distinct sections: the gentler, rolling south and the craggier, wilder north.

The Southern Lakes. The southern lakes and valleys contain the park's most popular, and thus most overcrowded in summer, destinations, incorporating the largest body of water, Windermere, as well as most of the quintessential Lakeland towns and villages: Bowness, Ambleside, Grasmere, Elterwater, Coniston, and Hawkshead. To the east and west of this cluster of habitation, the valleys and fells climb to some beautiful upland country.

Penrith and the Northern Lakes. In the north, the landscape opens out across the bleaker fells to reveal challenging, spectacular walking country. Here, in the northern lakes, south of Keswick and Cockermouth, you have the best chance to get away from the crowds.

LAKE DISTRICT PLANNER

WHEN TO GO

The Lake District is one of the rainiest areas in Britain, but June, July, and August hold the best hope of fine weather and are the time for all the major festivals. You will, however, be sharing the lakes with thousands of other people. If you must travel at this time, turn up early at popular museums and attractions, and expect to work to find parking. April and May, as well as September and October, are alternatives. Later and earlier in the year there will be even more space and freedom, but many attractions close, and from December to March, snow on high ground may preclude serious hill-walking without heavy-duty equipment.

PLANNING YOUR TIME

You could spend months tramping the hills, valleys, and fells of the Lake District, or, in three days, you could drive through the major towns and villages. The key is not to do too much in too short a time. If you are traveling by public transportation, many places will be off-limits. As a base, Windermere has the best transport links, but it can be crowded and it has less character than some of the smaller towns. Ambleside and Keswick also have plenty of sleeping and eating options; for a more intimate version of village life, try Coniston, Hawkshead, or Grasmere. Keep in mind that the northern and western lakes have the most dramatic scenery and offer the best opportunity to escape the summertime hordes.

The Lake District is compact but is not a place to hurry. Allow plenty of time for walking: paths can be steep and rocky, and in any case you'll want to stop frequently to look at the great views. A good day's walking with a picnic can be done from nearly anywhere. Driving brings its own speed inhibitors, from sheep on the roads to slow tractors.

You're likely to be based down near lake level, but try to experience the hills, too. If you're short of time, a drive over one of the high passes such as Hardknott, Honister, or Kirkstone will give you a glimpse of the enormity of the landscape.

GETTING HERE AND AROUND

AIR TRAVEL

Manchester Airport has its own rail station with direct service to Carlisle, Windermere, and Barrow-in-Furness. Manchester is 70 mi from the southern part of the Lake District.

Contact Manchester Airport (✉ *Near Junctions 5 and 6 of M56* ☎ *08712/710711* ⊕ *www.manchesterairport.co.uk*).

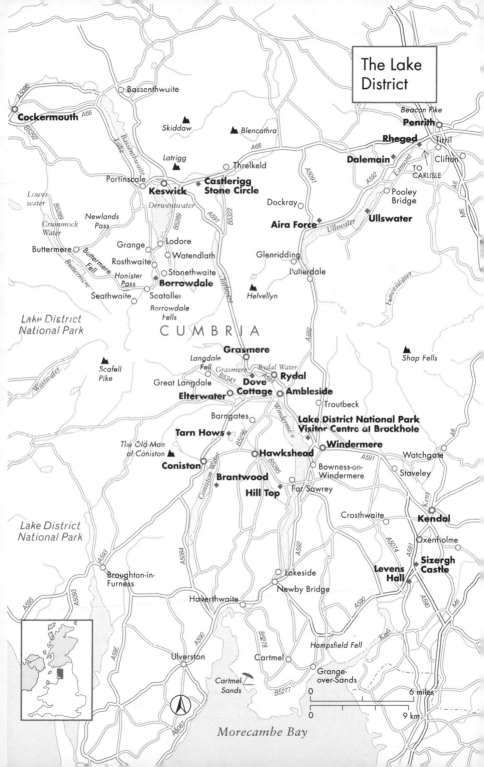

BOAT TRAVEL

Whether you rent a boat or take a ride on a modern launch or vintage vessels, getting out on the water is a fun (and often useful) way to see the Lake District. Windermere, Coniston Water, and Derwentwater all have boat rental facilities.

BUS TRAVEL

National Express serves the region from London's Victoria Coach Station and from Manchester's Chorlton Street Station. Average travel time to Kendal is just over seven hours from London; to Windermere, 7½ hours; and to Keswick, 8¼ hours. From Manchester there's one bus a day to Windermere via Ambleside, Grasmere, and Keswick. There's direct bus service to the Lake District from Carlisle, Lancaster, and York. Traveline handles public transportation inquiries.

Stagecoach in Cumbria provides local service between Lakeland towns and through the valleys and high passes. Contact Traveline for an up-to-date timetable. Bus service between main tourist centers is fairly frequent on weekdays, but much reduced on weekends and bank holidays. Don't count on reaching the more remote parts of the area by bus. Off-the-beaten-track touring requires a car or strong legs. A one-week Cumbria Goldrider ticket (£23.50), available on the bus, is valid on all routes. Explorer tickets (£9.75) are valid for a day on all routes.

Contacts National Express (🖷 08717/818178 ⊕ www.nationalexpress.com). **Traveline** (🖷 0871/200–2233 ⊕ www.traveline.org.uk).

CAR TRAVEL

A car is almost essential in the Lake District; bus service is limited and trains can get you to the edge of the national park but no farther. You can rent cars in Penrith and Kendal. Roads within the region are generally good, although minor routes and mountain passes can be steep and narrow. Warning signs are often posted if snow or ice has made a road impassable; check local weather forecasts in winter before heading out. In July and August and during the long public holiday weekends, expect heavy traffic. The Lake District has plenty of parking lots; use them to avoid blocking narrow lanes.

To reach the Lake District by car from London, take M1 north to M6, getting off either at Junction 36 and joining A590/A591 west (around the Kendal bypass to Windermere) or at Junction 40, joining A66 direct to Keswick and the northern lakes region. Travel time to Kendal is about four to five hours, to Keswick five to six hours. Expect heavy traffic out of London on weekends.

TRAIN TRAVEL

There are direct trains from Manchester and Manchester airport to Windermere. For schedule information, call National Rail Enquiries. Two train companies serve the region from London's Euston Station: take a Virgin or Northern Rail train bound for Carlisle, Edinburgh, or Glasgow and change at Oxenholme for the branch line service to Kendal and Windermere. Average travel time to Windermere (including the change) is 4½ hours. If you're heading for Keswick, you can either take the train to Windermere and continue from there by Stagecoach bus (Bus 554/555/556; 70 minutes), or stay on the main London–Carlisle train to Penrith Station (four hours), from which Stagecoach buses (Bus X5) also run to Keswick (45 minutes). Direct trains from Manchester depart for Windermere five times daily (travel time two hours). First North Western runs a local service from Windermere and Barrow-in-Furness to Manchester Airport. National Rail can handle all questions about trains.

Train connections are good around the edges of the Lake District, but you must take the bus or drive to reach the central Lakeland region, and they are reduced, or nonexistent, on Sunday.

Contacts National Rail Enquiries (☎ *0845/748–4950* ⊕ *www.nationalrail. co.uk*). **Northern Rail** (☎ *0845/000–0125* ⊕ *www.northernrail.org*). **Virgin Trains** (☎ *0845/722–2333* ⊕ *www.virgintrains.co.uk*).

NATIONAL PARK

The Lake District National Park head office (and main visitor center) is at Brockhole, north of Windermere. It's closed November through mid-February. Helpful regional national-park information centers sell books and maps, book accommodations, and provide walking advice.

Contacts Lake District National Park (✉ *Brockhole, A591, Ambleside Rd., near Windermere* ☎ *015394/46601* ⊕ *www.lake-district.gov.uk*). **Keswick** (✉ *Moot Hall, Main St.* ☎ *017687/72645*). **Ullswater** (✉ *Beckside Car Park, Glenridding* ☎ *017684/82414*).

TOURS

Mountain Goat and Lakes Supertours provide minibus sightseeing tours with skilled local guides. Half- and full-day tours, some of which really get off the beaten track, depart from Bowness, Windermere, Ambleside, and Grasmere.

Walks range from gentle, literary-oriented strolls to challenging ridge hikes. The Lake District National Park or tourist information centers can put you in touch with qualified guides. Blue Badge Guides can provide experts on the area. English Lakeland Ramblers organizes single-base and inn-to-inn guided tours of the Lake District. Lake District Walker offers guide day hikes for different abilities. Go Higher will take you on challenging routes and provides technical gear and courses on mountaineering skills.

Contacts Blue Badge Guides (☎ *020/7403–1115* ⊕ *www.blue-badge.org. uk*). **English Lakeland Ramblers** (✉ *18 Stuyvesant Oval, #1A, New York, NY* ☎ *01229/587382, 212/505–1020 or 800/724–8801 in U.S.* ⊕ *www.ramblers. com*). **Go Higher** (✉ *High Dyon Side, Distington* ☎ *01946/830476* ⊕ *www. gohigher.co.uk*). **Lake District Walker** (☎ *01900/822448* ⊕ *www.lakedistrict walker.co.uk*). **Lakes Supertours** (✉ *1 High St., Windermere* ☎ *015394/42751* ⊕ *www.lakes-supertours.co.uk*). **Mountain Goat** (✉ *Victoria St., Windermere* ☎ *015394/45161* ⊕ *www.mountain-goat.com*).

RESTAURANTS

Lakeland restaurants increasingly reflect a growing British awareness of good food. Local sourcing and international influences are common, and even old Cumberland favorites are being creatively reinvented. Pub dining in the Lake District can be excellent—the hearty fare often makes use of local ingredients such as Herdwick lamb, and real ales are a good accompaniment. If you're going walking, ask your hotel or B&B about making you a packed lunch. Some local delicatessens also offer this service.

HOTELS

Your choices include everything from small country inns to grand lakeside hotels; many hotels offer the option of paying a higher price that includes dinner as well as breakfast. The regional mainstay is the bed-and-breakfast, from the house on Main Street to isolated farmhouses. Most country hotels and B&Bs gladly cater to hikers and can provide on-the-spot information.

Wherever you stay, book well in advance for summer visits, especially those in late July and August. In winter many accommodations close for a month or two. On weekends and in summer it may be hard to find places willing to take bookings for a single night. Internet access in the Lakes is improving, and an increasing number of hotels and cafés offer Wi-Fi access.

WHAT IT COSTS IN POUNDS					
	£	££	£££	££££	£££££
Restaurants	under £10	£10–£14	£15–£19	£20–£25	over £25
Hotels	under £70	£70–£120	£121–£160	£161–£220	over £220

Restaurant prices are for a main course at dinner. Hotel prices are for two people in a standard double room in high season, including V.A.T., with no meals or, if indicated, CP (with Continental breakfast), BP (Breakfast Plan, with full breakfast), or MAP (Modified American Plan, with breakfast and dinner).

VISITOR INFORMATION
Contacts Cumbria Tourism (✉ *Windermere Rd., Staveley, Kendal* ☎ *015398/22222* ⊕ *www.golakes.co.uk*).

THE SOUTHERN LAKES

Among the many attractions here are the small resort towns clustered around Windermere, England's largest lake, and the area's hideaway valleys, rugged walking centers, and monuments rich in literary associations. This is the easiest part of the Lake District to reach, with Kendal, the largest town, just a short distance from the M6 motorway. An obvious route from Kendal takes in Windermere, the area's natural touring center, before moving north through Ambleside and Rydal Water to Grasmere. Some of the loveliest Lakeland scenery is to be found by then turning south, through Elterwater, Hawkshead, and Coniston.

KENDAL

70 mi north of Manchester.

The southern gateway to the Lake District is the "Auld Gray Town" of Kendal, outside the national park and less touristy than the towns to the north. You may want to stay closer to the action, but the town has some worthwhile sights. Nearby hills frame Kendal's gray stone houses and provide some delightful walks; you can also explore the ruins of Kendal Castle. ■ TIP➔ **Pack a slab of Kendal mint cake, the local peppermint candy that all British walkers and climbers swear by to provide them with energy. It's on sale in town gift shops and around the region.**

The town's motto, "Wool Is My Bread," refers to its importance as a textile center in northern England before the Industrial Revolution. It was known for manufacturing woolen cloth, especially Kendal Green, which archers favored. Away from the main road are quiet courtyards and winding medieval streets known as "ginnels." Wool merchants used these for easy access to the River Kent.

GETTING HERE AND AROUND

Kendal is just off the M6, about 70 mi north of Manchester. It has train service via a branch line from Oxenholme, and National Express bus service from London as well. It's the largest town in the area but is still plenty small enough to walk around.

ESSENTIALS

Visitor Information Kendal (✉ *Town Hall, Highgate* ☎ *01539/725758*).

EXPLORING

★ One of the region's finest art galleries, **Abbot Hall**, occupies a Palladian-style Georgian mansion built in 1759. In the permanent collection are works by Victorian artist and critic John Ruskin, who lived near Coniston, and by 18th-century portrait painter George Romney, who worked (and died) in Kendal. The gallery also owns some good contemporary British art and mounts a changing calendar of high-profile, often fascinating exhibitions of 20th- and 21st-century art. There's an excellent café. Abbot Hall is on the River Kent, next to the parish church; the Museum of Lakeland Life, with exhibits on blacksmithing and wheelwrighting and a wonderful re-creation of a period pharmacy, is in the former stable block of the hall, on the same site. ✉ *Off Highgate* ☎ *01539/722464* ⊕ *www.abbothall.org.uk* 💷 *£5.75, £7.50 combined ticket with Museum of Lakeland Life* ۞ *Apr.–Oct., Mon.–Sat. 10:30–5; Nov., Dec., and mid-Jan.–Mar., Mon.–Sat. 10:30–4.*

★ **Levens Hall**, a handsome Elizabethan house and the home of the Bagot family, is famous for its topiary garden, probably the most distinctive in the world. Laid out in 1694, the garden retains its original design, and the yew and beech hedges, cut into complex shapes that resemble enormous chess pieces, rise among a profusion of flowers. The house contains a stunning medieval hall with oak paneling, ornate plasterwork, Jacobean furniture, and Cordova goat-leather wallpaper. You can easily spend a couple of hours here admiring the place or getting lost in the living willow labyrinth. There's a play area for children. Levens Hall is 4 mi south of Kendal. ✉ *Off A590, Levens* ☎ *015395/60321* ⊕ *www.levenshall.co.uk* 💷 *£11; gardens only, £8* ۞ *Apr.–mid-Oct., Sun.–Thurs.; house noon–4:30, last admission at 4, gardens 10–5.*

Sizergh Castle, one of the Lake District's finest fortified houses, has a 58-foot-tall defensive peel tower that dates from 1340, when Scottish raids were feared. It has been the home of the Strickland family for more than 760 years. Expanded in Elizabethan times, the castle includes outstanding oak-paneled interiors with intricately carved chimneypieces and oak furniture. The estate has a rock garden with a large collection of ferns, two lakes, and an ancient woodland; there are good walks here, too. Sizergh is 3½ mi south of Kendal. ⊠ *Off A591, Sizergh* 🕾 *015395/60070* ⊕ *www.nationaltrust.org.uk* 🖃 *£7.15; gardens only, £4.65* ⊙ *Castle mid-Mar.–Oct., Sun.–Thurs. 1–5 (also noon–1 by guided tour); gardens mid-Mar.–Oct., Sun.–Thurs. 11–5.*

WHERE TO EAT AND STAY

The Brewery Arts Centre has other good dining options in Kendal, including the Grain Store restaurant and the theatrical Warehouse Café.

££ ✕ **The New Moon.** Small but sleek, this restaurant decorated in tones
MODERN BRITISH of warm off-white and pale, earthy brown has won a good local reputation for high-quality dishes. The vegetarian selections are always worthwhile, and the sometimes adventurous Modern British cooking shows Mediterranean flourishes. Damson plum and pork sausages come with mashed potatoes and a red wine jus, and the Lancashire cheese soufflé arrives on a bed of leek and potato cakes. Lunch and the fixed-price early dinner (5:30–7 weekdays) are especially good values. ⊠ *129 Highgate* 🕾 *01539/729254* ⊕ *www.newmoonrestaurant.co.uk* 🖃 *MC, V* ⊙ *Closed Sun. and Mon.*

£ ✕ **Waterside Wholefoods Café.** In summer, grab one of the outdoor
VEGETARIAN picnic tables overlooking the River Kent and order from the delicious, filling vegetarian menu of soups, buckwheat burgers, curried green lentil pie, salads, and cakes and scones. ⊠ *2 Kent View, Waterside* 🕾 *01539/729743* ⊕ *www.watersidewholefood.co.uk* 🖃 *MC, V* ⊙ *Closed Sun. No dinner.*

££ 🖭 **Beech House.** Old-fashioned qualities combine with modern luxuries such as heated bathroom floors in this comfortable, ivy-clad town house a five-minute walk up the hill from the center of town in a conservation area. Rooms are individually designed but share a contemporary feel. There's a well-stocked shared refrigerator. A full English breakfast includes local bacon, honey-glazed sausages, and pancakes. **Pros:** stylish, homey rooms; locally made toiletries; private parking. **Cons:** steep walk up the hill to get here; two-night minimum on weekends; double beds only, so not best best for kids; Kendal is outside the national park. ⊠ *40 Greenside* 🕾 *01539/720385* ⊕ *www.beechhouse-kendal.co.uk* ⇥ *6 rooms* ♿ *In-room: no a/c, DVD, Wi-Fi. In-hotel: Wi-Fi hotspot* 🖃 *MC, V* ¶⊙| *BP.*

NIGHTLIFE AND THE ARTS

★ The **Brewery Arts Centre**, a contemporary complex in a converted brewery, includes an art gallery, theater, cinemas, and workshop spaces. It gives Kendal a good, artsy vibe. The Grain Store, overlooking lovely gardens, serves lunch and dinner, the Warehouse Café offers savory crepes and occasional live performances, and Vats Bar has good beer and wine. In November the Mountain Film Festival presents productions aimed at climbers and walkers. ⊠ *Highgate* 🕾 *01539/725133* 🖃 *Free, except for special exhibitions* ⊙ *Mon.–Sat. 9 AM–11 PM.*

SHOPPING

Kendal has a pleasant mix of chains, factory outlet stores, specialty shops, and traditional markets. The most interesting stores are tucked away in the quiet lanes and courtyards around Market Place, Finkle Street, and Stramongate. There's been a **market** in Kendal since 1189, and outdoor market stalls still line the center of town along Stramongate and Market Place every Wednesday and Saturday.

Henry Roberts Bookshop (⊠ *7 Stramongate* ☎ *01539/720425*), in Kendal's oldest house (a 16th-century cottage), stocks a superb selection of regional books. **K Village** (⊠ *20 Stricklandgate* ☎ *01539/732363*), an outlet shopping center, sells some brand names at a discount: look for clothing, shoes, china, and more. The **Kentdale Rambler** (⊠ *34 Market Pl.* ☎ *01539/729188*) is the best local store for walking boots and equipment, maps, and guides, including Wainwright's Lakeland guides. **Peter Hall & Son** (⊠ *Danes Rd., Staveley* ☎ *01539/821633*), a woodcraft workshop 5 mi north of Kendal along A591, sells ornamental bowls and gifts.

> ### WAINWRIGHT'S GUIDES
>
> Alfred Wainwright, an accountant, became one of travel writing's most famous authors. First published in the 1950s and '60s, his handwritten, illustrated guides have sold more than 2 million copies; these classics are still sold in area bookstores. The gruff Wainwright seemed to want the hills to himself, yet he lovingly created 49 books that continue to introduce people to the Lakeland mountains.

WINDERMERE AND BOWNESS-ON-WINDERMERE

10 mi northwest of Kendal.

For a natural touring base for the southern half of the Lake District, you don't need to look much farther than Windermere, though it does get crowded in summer. The resort became popular in the Victorian era when the arrival of the railway made the remote and rugged area accessible. Wordsworth and Ruskin opposed the railway, fearing an influx of tourists would ruin the tranquil place. Sure enough, the railway terminus in 1847 brought with it Victorian day-trippers, and the original hamlet of Birthwaite was subsumed by the new town of Windermere, named after the lake.

The town has continued to flourish, despite being a mile or so from the water; the development now spreads to envelop the slate-gray lakeside village of Bowness-on-Windermere. Bowness is the more attractive, but they are so close it doesn't matter where you stay.

GETTING HERE AND AROUND

Windermere is easily reached by car, less than a half hour off the M6. There's also a train station at the eastern edge of town; change at Oxenholme for the branch line to Kendal and Windermere.

Bus 599, leaving every 20 minutes in summer (hourly the rest of the year) from outside Windermere train station, links the town with Bowness.

ESSENTIALS

Visitor Information Windermere (✉ *Victoria St.* ☎ *015394/46499*).

EXPLORING

TOP ATTRACTIONS

Fodor's Choice ★ **Blackwell.** From 1898 to 1900, architect Mackay Hugh Baillie Scott (1865–1945) designed Blackwell, a quintessential Arts and Crafts house with carved paneling, delicate plasterwork, and a startling sense of light and space. Originally a retreat for a Manchester brewery owner, the house is a refined mix of modern style and the local vernacular. Lime-washed walls and sloping slate roofs make it fit elegantly into the landscape above Windermere, and the artful integration of decorative features into stained glass, stonework, friezes, and wrought iron gives the house a sleekly contemporary feel. Rooms showcase works from different periods that embody Arts and Crafts ideals, and top-notch exhibitions display contemporary art and crafts, as well as sculptures. Accessibility is wonderful here: nothing is roped off and you can even play the piano. Peruse the shop and try the honey-roast ham in the excellent tearoom. ✉ *B5360, Windermere* ☎ *015394/46139* 🌐 *www.blackwell.org.uk* 🎫 *£6.50* ⏲ *Apr.–Oct., daily 10:30–5; Nov., Dec., and mid-Jan.–Mar., daily 10:30–4.*

★ **Lakes Aquarium.** On the quayside at the southern end of Windermere, this excellent aquarium has wildlife and waterside exhibits that focus mostly on the region. The highlight is an underwater tunnel walk along a re-created lake bed, complete with diving ducks, though the piranhas and the bumblebee poison arrow frogs also have their fans. Friendly staff are eager to talk about the exhibits. **■ TIP→ You can take a boat to Lakeside from Bowness (buy a combined Cruise and Aquarium ticket) or drive here.** ✉ *C5062, Lakeside* ☎ *015394/30153* 🌐 *www.lakesaquarium.co.uk* 🎫 *£8.95* ⏲ *Apr.–Oct., daily 9–6; Nov.–Mar., daily 9–5.*

OFF THE BEATEN PATH

Orrest Head. To escape the traffic and have a view of Windermere, set out on foot and follow the signs to the left of the Windermere Hotel (across from the train station) to Orrest Head. The shady, uphill path winds through Elleray Wood, and after a 20-minute hike you arrive at a rocky little summit (784 feet) with a panoramic view that encompasses the Yorkshire fells, Morecambe Bay, and the beautiful Troutbeck Valley (up which walks can be extended), toward the high passes to the north.

★ **Windermere.** No sights in Windermere or Bowness compete with that of Windermere itself. At 11 mi long, 1½ mi wide, and 200 feet deep, the lake is England's largest and stretches from Newby Bridge almost to Ambleside, filling a rocky gorge between steep, thickly wooded hills. The cold waters are superb for fishing, especially for Windermere char, a rare lake trout. In summer, steamers and pleasure craft travel the lake, and a trip across the island-studded waters, particularly the round-trip from Bowness to Ambleside or down to Lakeside, is wonderful. Although the lake's marinas and piers have some charm, you can bypass the busier stretches of shoreline (in summer they can be packed solid) by walking beyond the boathouses. Here, from among the pine trees, are fine views across the lake. The **car ferry,** which also carries pedestrians, crosses from Ferry Nab on the Bowness side of the lake to reach Far Sawrey and the road to Hawkshead. A ferry has been running this route since the 15th century. ☎ *01228/227653* ⊠ *Car ferry £3.50 cars, 50p foot passengers* ☉ *Ferries every 20 mins Mon.–Sat. 6:50 AM–9:50 PM, Sun. 9:10 AM–9:50 PM; Nov.–Mar. until 8:50 PM.*

WORTH NOTING

☉ **Lakeside & Haverthwaite Railway Company.** Vintage steam trains run on the 4-mi branch line between Lakeside and Haverthwaite along the lake's southern tip; you can add on a lake cruise. Departures from Lakeside coincide with ferry arrivals from Bowness and Ambleside; you can also depart from Haverthwaite. ☎ *015395/31594* ⊕ *www. lakesiderailway.co.uk* ⊠ *£5.90* ☉ *Apr.–Oct., daily 10:30–6.*

> **ARTS AND CRAFTS TRAIL**
>
> The Arts and Crafts movement of the late 19th century flourished in the Lake District, inspired by the landscape as well as the writings of John Ruskin, who lived here. The search for meaningful style produced many artistic gems in the area's houses, churches, and hotels. At Blackwell you can purchase an Arts and Crafts Trail map and explore the best of them. Blackwell's Web site, ⊕ *www. blackwell.org.uk,* has extensive information about trail sites.

☉ **Lake District National Park Visitor Centre at Brockhole.** Brockhole, a lakeside 19th-century mansion with 30 acres of terraced gardens sloping down to the water, serves as the park's official visitor center and has exhibits about the local ecology, flora, and fauna. It's a good stop at the start of your visit. The gardens, designed in the Arts and Crafts style by Thomas Mawson, are at their best in spring, when daffodils cover the lawns and azaleas burst into bloom. Among the park activities are lectures, guided walks, and demonstrations of traditional crafts such as drystone wall building. Some programs are geared to children, who appreciate the adventure playground here. You can also try the croquet lawn. The bookstore carries hiking guides and maps, and you can picnic here or eat at the café-restaurant. Bus 555/556 goes to the visitor center from the Windermere train station; the center is 3 mi north of Windermere. **Windermere Lake Cruises** (☎ *015394/43360* ⊕ *www. windermere-lakecruises.co.uk*) runs a seasonal ferry service to the center from Waterhead in Ambleside. ⊠ *A591, Ambleside Rd., Windermere* ☎ *015394/46601* ⊕ *www.lake-district.gov.uk* ⊠ *Free; parking £2.50 for 2 hrs, £4 for 4 hrs, £6 full day, £2 out of season* ☉ *Mid-Feb.–Oct., daily 10–5. Gardens daily dawn to dusk.*

Windermere Lake Cruises. This company employs modern launches and vintage cruisers year-round between Ambleside, Bowness, Brockhole, and Lakeside. Ticket prices vary; a Freedom of the Lake ticket gives unlimited travel on any of the ferries for 24 or 48 hours (£12/£14.50). ☎ *015394/73360* ⊕ *www.windermere-lakecruises.co.uk.*

☉ **The World of Beatrix Potter.** A touristy attraction aimed at kids interprets the author's 23 tales with three-dimensional scenes of Peter Rabbit and more. Skip it if you can and visit Potter's former home at Hill Top and the Beatrix Potter Gallery in Hawkshead. ⊠ *The Old Laundry, Crag Brow, Bowness-on-Windermere* ☎ *015394/88444* ⊕ *www.hop-*

skip-jump.com ⌨ *£6.75* ⊙ *Easter–Sept., daily 10–5:30; Oct.–Easter, daily 10–4:30.*

WHERE TO EAT

££
BRITISH
✕ **Angel Inn.** Up the steep slope from the water's edge in Bowness, this spacious, stylish pub serves good home-cooked fare as well as a fine collection of beers that includes its own Hawkshead brew. Specials, chalked on a board, might be grilled sole with crushed crab and char-grilled steak with thyme-roasted tomatoes. Leather sofas and open fires make the Angel a cozy place; service is low-key and friendly, and the decoration is bright, minimal, and contemporary, with wooden floors and off-white walls. Thirteen comfortable, good-value bedrooms complete the picture. ⊠ *Helm Rd., Bowness-on-Windermere* ☎ *015394/44080* ⊕ *www.the-angelinn.com* ⊟ *MC, V.*

£££
MODERN BRITISH
✕ **Jerichos at the Waverley.** The town's most stylish restaurant occupies an 1870 Victorian building near the center of town and has 10 smart bedrooms upstairs; staying here means you'll also get a high-quality breakfast. An open kitchen, bare wood, stone, and candles give the place a contemporary look and make for a sophisticated evening out. Choices from the brief, frequently changing Modern British menu might include pigeon on grilled black pudding, sea bass on roasted red peppers, and roast lamb on smoked-butter mashed potato. ⊠ *College Rd., Windermere* ☎ *015394/42522* ⊕ *www.jerichos.co.uk* ⊟ *MC, V* ⊙ *No lunch. Closed Thurs., last 2 wks of Nov., and 1st wk of Dec.*

££
BRITISH
✕ **Lazy Daisy's.** Wooden floors, a big window onto the main street, displays of hops, and the smell of homemade bread: it's a Lakeland kitchen with a contemporary twist, but friendly and cozy. Try the daily roast, slow cooked with herbs, or great sandwiches such as melted Brie, bacon, and tomato, and homemade soup. Good all day are cakes such as "lumpy bumpy"—a caloric mix of peanuts, sugar, and chocolate. This coffee shop opens for breakfast and serves a full dinner menu, and there's Wi-Fi, too. ⊠ *31–33 Crescent Rd., Windermere* ☎ *015394/43877* ⊕ *www.lazydaisyslakelandkitchen.co.uk* ⊟ *MC, V.*

£
MEDITERRANEAN
★
✕ **Lucy4 at the Porthole.** Tapas with a Lakeland twist are the specialty at this cheerful bistro and wine bar: Latin tunes and friendly service make it a laid-back place to spend an evening. You can have fun combining dishes from the complex menu. The wine list is extensive, and you should leave room for dessert. The patio is ideal for alfresco dining. ⊠ *3 Ash St., Bowness-on-Windermere* ☎ *015394/42793* ⊕ *www.lucysofambleside.co.uk* ⊟ *MC, V* ⊙ *No lunch weekdays.*

££
BRITISH
★
✕ **The Queen's Head Hotel.** A high-quality pub but one with few pretensions, this 17th-century inn north of Windermere is renowned for innovative pub food such as *bobotie* (a curried South African dish with minced lamb, almonds, and apricots). It's also noted for real ales served from what was once an Elizabethan four-poster bed. The intimate dining rooms have oak beams, flagged floors, and log fires. Lunches can be less hearty than the excellent evening meals. If you want to stay overnight, seven of the 15 guest rooms have four-posters, and all offer colorful fabrics and splendid views. ⊠ *A592, Troutbeck* ☎ *015394/32174* ⊕ *www.queensheadhotel.com* ⊟ *MC, V.*

WHERE TO STAY

££ ⊡ **1 Park Road.** On a quiet street, this fine example of a new breed of upmarket boutique B&Bs has spacious guest rooms with carefully chosen fabrics and contemporary touches such as iPod docking stations. Stained glass, books, and a piano help give the place a cultured air. Breakfast options include local sausages, fresh fruit, and kedgeree (a mixture of fish, rice, and eggs); dinner is also available on Friday and Saturday. **Pros:** welcoming and stylish; good-size family room; good food, wine, and beer. **Cons:** a 15-minute walk to the lake. ⊠ *1 Park Rd., Windermere* ☎ *015394/42107* ⊕ *www.1parkroad.com* ⇆ *6 rooms* ♿ *In-room: no a/c, no phone, DVD, Wi-Fi. In-hotel: restaurant, Wi-Fi hotspot* ⊟ *MC, V* ⎸◎⎸ *BP.*

£ ⊡ **Archway Guesthouse.** A chef and a restaurant manager make a fine team running this excellent little guesthouse in a Victorian building near the train station. Rooms are simple but comfortable, with metal-frame beds and neutral tones, and the many superior breakfast options include smoked haddock, pancakes, and omelets. **Pros:** great value; uncluttered sitting area; friendly service **Cons:** not as much space as you might find in more expensive places. ⊠ *13 College Rd., Windermere* ☎ *015394/45613* ⊕ *www.the-archway.co.uk* ⇆ *4 rooms* ♿ *In-room: no a/c, no phone, DVD, Wi-Fi. In hotel: Wi-Fi, parking (free)* ⊟ *MC, V* ⎸◎⎸ *BP.*

£££££ ⊡ **Gilpin Lodge.** Hidden in 22 acres of grounds with meandering paths
★ and five resident llamas, this family-run, rambling country-house hotel 2 mi east of Windermere pampers its guests in a low-key way. The hotel, in a converted 1901 house with two modern wings, has plush but understated public rooms furnished with comfy sofas and rugs and warmed by log fires. Bedrooms embody contemporary rustic chic, and most have sitting areas; six garden suites have outdoor hot tubs. Therapists provide spa treatments in your room. The superb restaurant (reservations essential; five-course fixed-price menu £52) serves imaginative modern dishes. You can use a well-equipped nearby health club, and the hotel helps arrange outdoor activities. If you're with a group, you can rent the exclusive-use Lake House (six bedrooms plus a pool). **Pros:** high-class but laid-back pampering with a smile; notable food; a policy of no weddings or conferences. **Cons:** location is beautiful, but it's a little out of the way if you want to eat out; expensive. ⊠ *Crook Rd., off B5284, Bowness-on-Windermere* ☎ *015394/88818* ⊕ *www. gilpinlodge.co.uk* ⇆ *14 rooms, 6 suites* ♿ *In-room: no a/c, safe. In-hotel: restaurant, room service, bars, Internet terminal, no kids under 7* ⊟ *AE, DC, MC, V* ⎸◎⎸ *BP, MAP.*

££ ⊡ **Ivy Bank.** One of Windermere's smarter bed-and-breakfasts, Ivy Bank is in a quiet, leafy part of town. The guest rooms have handsome wooden furniture and views over the rooftops. The owner is a qualified masseuse and aromatherapist and offers treatments to guests. You can use the local health club for free. **Pros:** bike storage; near good walks. **Cons:** no bathtub in most rooms (shower only). ⊠ *Holly Rd., Windermere* ☎ *015394/42601* ⊕ *www.ivy-bank.co.uk* ⇆ *5 rooms* ♿ *In-room: no a/c, no phone, DVD (some), Wi-Fi. In-hotel: Wi-Fi hotspot* ⊟ *MC, V* ⎸◎⎸ *BP.*

££££££ ⊡ **Miller Howe.** Location, lake views, and superb service help set this
Fodor's Choice luxurious Edwardian country-house hotel apart. The sumptuous guest
★ rooms have been given an Arts and Crafts–inspired makeover, with
William Morris wallpaper, fresh flowers, and contemporary art bright-
ening the individually decorated rooms. Some have lake views, so ask;
or you can relax in the conservatory and look at Windermere. The
Modern British restaurant (££££; open by reservation to nonguests)
serves sophisticated fare, and the hotel arranges activities from archery
to pony trekking. **Pros:** more than 5 acres of grounds; great lake views;
staff that take care of the little extras. **Cons:** sometimes closes for a
couple of weeks in winter. ⊠ *Rayrigg Rd., Bowness-on-Windermere*
☎ *015394/42536* 🖷 *015394/45664* ⊕ *www.millerhowe.com* ⟳ *15
rooms* ⚒ *In-room: no a/c. In-hotel: restaurant, Wi-Fi hotspot, some
pets allowed, no kids under 8* ☰ *AE, MC, V* ⦿ *MAP.*

££££ ⊡ **The Punch Bowl.** Under the same management as the celebrated
★ Drunken Duck Inn near Hawkshead, this outstanding inn and restaurant is a pleasantly modern retreat in the peaceful Lyth Valley, between
Windermere and Kendal. The bright, airy bedrooms have high oak-beam
ceilings and chic fabric designs and big baths. Health and beauty treatments are available if you book in advance. Sleek and slate-floored, the
bar serves fine real ales, and you can sample good locally sourced dishes
in the bright, contemporary restaurant. The pub has taken over duties
from the local post office, so you can even post a letter here. **Pros:** con-
temporary-yet-relaxed design will make you look at beer and Lakeland
lodgings in a new light; excellent food. **Cons:** a little way from the area's
main sights. ⊠ *Off A5074, Crosthwaite, Lyth Valley* ☎ *015395/68237*
⊕ *www.the-punchbowl.co.uk* ⟳ *9 rooms* ⚒ *In-room: no a/c, Wi-Fi
(some). In-hotel: restaurant, Wi-Fi hotspot* ☰ *AE, MC, V* ⦿ *BP.*

££££££ ⊡ **The Samling.** On its own sculpture-dotted 67 acres above Windermere,
★ this place oozes exclusivity from every carefully fashioned corner. Wordsworth used to come here to pay his rent. Today the hotel is favored by
the rich and famous, but it avoids the snobbishness sometimes found
in such establishments. Rooms are elegantly traditional though not
fussy, and have pretty wallpapers, muted colors, fireplaces, slate-floor
bathrooms, and roll-top baths. Service is a good mix of professional
and friendly, and the lake views are fantastic. The well-regarded restaurant (£55 fixed-price dinner menu) specializes in creative local fare;
it's open to nonguests for dinner, afternoon tea, and Sunday lunch (call
ahead). **Pros:** you'll feel like a star, and may sit next to one at breakfast, too. **Cons:** you'll likely miss the steep turn off the road the first
time you arrive; the exclusivity doesn't come cheap. ⊠ *Ambleside Rd.,
Windermere* ☎ *015394/31922* ⊕ *www.thesamling.com* ⟳ *11 suites*
⚒ *In-room: no a/c, DVD, Internet. In-hotel: restaurant, Wi-Fi hotspot*
☰ *AE, D, MC, V* ⦿ *BP.*

SPORTS AND THE OUTDOORS

Windermere Cycle Hire (⊠ *Railway Station, Windermere* ☎ *015394/44544*)
rents a variety of bikes from £5 per hour or £16 per day, and is right
next to the train station.

Windermere Lake Holidays (✉ *Mereside, Ferry Nab, Bowness-on-Windermere* ☎ *015394/43415*) rents boats, from small sailboats to houseboats.

SHOPPING

The best selection of shops is at the Bowness end of Windermere, on Lake Road and around Queen's Square: clothing stores, crafts shops, and souvenir stores of all kinds. At **Lakeland Jewellers** (✉ *Crag Brow, Bowness-on-Windermere* ☎ *015394/42992*) the local experts set semiprecious stones in necklaces and brooches.

> **STAY ON A FARM**
>
> The Cumbrian Web site, ⊕ *www.luxuryinafarm.co.uk*, is a good place to start checking out farm stays, whether B&B-style or self-catering (with kitchen); ⊕ *www.golakes.co.uk* has a wider selection of less luxurious options. Prices can be reasonable, but you'll need a car for most.

More? **The Artisan Baker,** between Kendal and Windermere, is the place to stop for mouthwatering, award-winning bread, cakes, and sandwiches. It also brews fine coffee, ✉ *Mill Yard, Staveley* ☎ *015398/22297*.

AMBLESIDE

7 mi northwest of Windermere.

Unlike Kendal and Windermere, Ambleside seems almost part of the hills and fells. Its buildings, mainly of local stone and many built in the traditional style that forgoes the use of mortar in the outer walls, blend perfectly into their setting. The small town sits at the northern end of Windermere along A591, making it a popular center for Lake District excursions. It has a better choice of restaurants than Windermere or Bowness, and the numerous outdoor shops are handy for fell walkers. Ambleside does, however, suffer from overcrowding in high season. Wednesday, when the local market takes place, is particularly busy.

GETTING HERE AND AROUND

An easy drive along A591 from Windermere, Ambleside can also be reached by ferry.

ESSENTIALS

Visitor Information Ambleside (✉ *Central Bldgs., Market Cross, Rydal Rd.* ☎ *015394/32582*).

EXPLORING

Bridge House, a tiny 17th-century stone former apple store, perches on an arched stone bridge that spans Stone Beck. It may have been built here to avoid land tax. This much-photographed building holds a National Trust shop and information center. ✉ *Rydal Rd.* ☎ *015394/35599* 🏷 *Free* ☉ *Easter–Oct., daily 10–5.*

QUICK BITES

Cozy Sheila's Cottage (✉ *The Slack* ☎ *015394/33079*), serving great home-made cakes and desserts, is a good place to gather the strength for a walk or to relax after one by the fire. Try a good-value afternoon tea with tea bread or, for full calorie replenishment, go for a hot chocolate loaded with cream.

The **Armitt Museum**, a fine local-history gallery and library, explores Ambleside's past and its surroundings through the eyes of local people such as William Wordsworth, Thomas De Quincey, Robert Southey, John Ruskin, and Beatrix Potter. You can study Beatrix Potter's natural-history watercolors or watch a Victorian lantern slide show. ⊠ *Rydal Rd.* ☎ *015394/31212* ⊕ *www.armitt.com* ⌦ *£2.50* ⊙ *Mon.–Sat. 10–5; last admission at 4:30.*

Windermere Lake Cruises (☎ *015394/43360* ⊕ *www.windermere-lakecruises.co.uk*) has year-round service between Ambleside, Bowness, Brockhole, and Lakeside. It's a pleasant way to experience the lake.

WHERE TO EAT

££ ✕ **Fellinis.** Styling themselves "Vegeterranean" to reflect Mediterranean
VEGETARIAN culinary influence, Fellinis is Cumbria's newest foodie destination. Upstairs a studio cinema shows art-house releases, while downstairs the restaurant rustles up sumptuous concoctions for a sophisticated crowd. The menu's imaginative dishes might start with Roquefort cheesecake and continue with portobello mushroom, mozzarella, beet, and lentil cartouche (cooked and served in paper). A large, open, rectangular dining room has soft seating, bold patterns, and oversize lamp shades, and a chill, jazzy sound track plays. White tablecloths, contemporary art, and fresh flowers enhance the modern sensibility. The same management runs nearby Zefferelli's—another cinema with a jazz bar and Italian food. Good-value combined cinema and dinner tickets can be used at either venue. ⊠ *Church St.* ☎ *01539/433845* ⊕ *www. fellinisambleside.com* ⊟ *MC, V* ⊙ *Closed Mon. in low season.*

££ ✕ **Glass House.** A converted medieval mill with a working waterwheel
MODERN BRITISH is an atmospheric setting for this restaurant serving Modern Brit-
★ ish cuisine. Look for an international twist in dishes such as chicken salad with poached egg and maple-glazed pancetta or braised lamb with dauphinoise potatoes. You can have an elegant dinner or just sip a cappuccino in the courtyard. There's a well-priced early-evening menu (two courses £15) weekdays from 6:30 to 7:30. ⊠ *Rydal Rd.* ☎ *015394/32137* *wwww.theglasshouserestaurant.co.uk* ⋈ *Reservations essential* ⊟ *MC, V.*

£££ ✕ **Lucy's on a Plate.** This informal café by day, restaurant by night is the
BRITISH perfect spot to relax, whether with mushroom stroganoff for lunch, a
★ chocolate almond torte for afternoon tea, or grilled char for dinner by candlelight. One room has scrubbed pine tables; a conservatory provides additional seating. Lucy's is famous for its puddings (desserts), and on the first Wednesday of every month the "up the duff" pudding night includes a menu with at least 30 choices. A nearby delicatessen sells high-class Cumbrian foods: sticky toffee pudding, farm cheeses, Cumberland sausage, jams, chutneys, and biscuits. Lucy's growing empire now includes cooking courses as well as a wine bar on nearby St. Mary's Lane: Lucy4. ⊠ *Church St.* ☎ *015394/31191* ⊕ *www.lucysofambleside. co.uk* ⊟ *MC, V.*

WHERE TO STAY

£ ▦ **3 Cambridge Villas.** Ambleside has a lot of inexpensive B&Bs, many clumped along the western end of the town, but it's hard to find a more welcoming spot than this lofty Victorian house right in the center, with hosts who know a thing or two about local walks. They'll also supply a packed lunch if you plan to be out exploring all day. Although space is at a premium, the rooms are pleasantly decorated with prints and wood furniture. **Pros:** especially good value for single travelers; warm family welcome; central. **Cons:** some rooms are a little cramped; can occasionally be noisy. ✉ *3 Church St.* ☎ *015394/32307* ⊕ *www.3cambridgevillas.co.uk* ↪ *7 rooms, 5 with bath* ⚲ *In-room: no a/c, no phone, Wi-Fi. In-hotel: Wi-Fi hotspot* ⊟ *MC, V* ⍐ *BP.*

££ ▦ **The Old Vicarage.** A quiet edge of Ambleside's old center is the peaceful
★ setting for this excellent-value B&B in a large Victorian former vicarage. Rooms are furnished in traditional English country style, with floral and print fabrics and dark-wood furniture; some are well equipped for families. Ask for a room in the new wing if you prefer a more modern room. A log fire and great breakfasts help make this a good deal even without the swimming pool. **Pros:** friendly welcome; indoor heated pool. **Cons:** some rooms are on the plain side of stylish; cuddly owls won't be to everybody's taste. ✉ *Vicarage Rd.* ☎ *015394/33364* ⊕ *www. oldvicarageambleside.co.uk* ↪ *15 rooms* ⚲ *In-room: no a/c, DVD, Wi-Fi. In-hotel: pool* ⊟ *MC, V* ⍐ *BP.*

SPORTS AND THE OUTDOORS

The fine walks in the vicinity include routes north to Rydal Mount or southeast over Wansfell to Troutbeck. Each walk will take up to a half day, there and back. Ferries from Bowness-on-Windermere dock at Ambleside's harbor, called Waterhead. ■ **TIP→ You can rent rowboats at the harbor for an hour or two to escape the crowds and get a different view of the area.**

Biketreks (✉ *Rydal Rd.* ☎ *015394/31245*), a good source for bike rentals, charges £20 per day.

> **LAKELAND LINGO**
>
> If someone tells you to walk along the "beck" to the "force" and then climb the "fell" to the "tarn," you've just been told to hike along the stream or river (beck) to the waterfall (force) before climbing the hill or mountain (fell) to reach a small mountain lake (tarn). Also, keep in mind that town or place names in the Lake District can be the same as the name of the lake on which the town stands. For example, Windermere is both the town and the lake itself—a "mere" is a lake in Old English.

RYDAL

1 mi northwest of Ambleside.

The village of Rydal, on the small glacial lake called Rydal Water, is rich with Wordsworthian associations.

EXPLORING

One famous beauty spot linked with Wordsworth is **Dora's Field**, below Rydal Mount next to the church of St. Mary's (where you can still see the poet's pew). In spring the field is awash in yellow daffodils, planted by William Wordsworth and his wife in memory of their beloved daughter Dora, who died in 1847.

If there's one poet associated with the Lake District, it is Wordsworth, who made his home at **Rydal Mount** from 1813 until his death. Wordsworth and his family moved to these grand surroundings when he was nearing the height of his career, and his descendants still live here, surrounded by his furniture, books, and portraits. You can see the study in which he worked, the family dining room, and the 4½-acre garden, laid out by the poet himself, that gave him so much pleasure. ■ TIP➜ **Surrounding Rydal Mount and the areas around Dove Cottage and Grasmere are many footpaths where Wordsworth wandered. His favorite can be found on the hill past White Moss Common and the River Rothay.** Spend an hour or two walking the paths and you may understand why the great poet composed most of his verse in the open air. A tearoom in the former saddlery provides cakes and drinks. ⊠ *A591* ☎ *015394/33002* ⊕ *www. rydalmount.co.uk* 🎫 *£6; garden only, £4* ☉ *Mar.–Oct., daily 9:30–5; Nov., Dec., and Feb., Wed.–Sun. 11–4.*

GRASMERE

3 mi north of Rydal, 4 mi northwest of Ambleside.

Lovely Grasmere, on a tiny, wood-fringed lake, is made up of crooked lanes in which Westmorland slate–built cottages hold shops and galleries. The village is a focal point for literary and landscape associations because this area was the adopted heartland of the Romantic poets, notably Wordsworth and Coleridge. The Vale of Grasmere has changed over the years, but many features Wordsworth wrote about are still visible. Wordsworth lived on the town's outskirts for almost 50 years and described the area as "the loveliest spot that man hath ever known."

EXPLORING

Wordsworth, his wife Mary, his sister Dorothy, and four of his children are buried in the churchyard of **St. Oswald's**, which is on the River Rothay. The poet planted eight of the yew trees here. As you leave the churchyard, stop at the Gingerbread Shop, in a tiny cottage, for a special local treat.

★ William Wordsworth lived in **Dove Cottage** from 1799 to 1808, a prolific and happy time for the poet. During this time he wrote some of his most famous works, including "Ode: Intimations of Immortality" and *The Prelude*; Wordsworth was also married here. Built in the early 17th century as an inn, this tiny, dim, and, in some places, dank, house is beautifully preserved, with an oak-paneled hall and floors of Westmorland slate. It first opened to the public in 1891 and remains as it was when Wordsworth lived here with his sister, Dorothy, and wife, Mary. Bedrooms and living areas contain much of Wordsworth's furniture and many personal belongings. Coleridge was a frequent visitor, as was Thomas De Quincey, best known for his 1822 autobiographical

CLOSE UP

11

Poetry, Prose, and the Lakes

The Lake District's beauty has whetted the creativity of many a famous poet and artist over the centuries. Here's a quick rundown of some of the writers inspired by the area's vistas.

William Wordsworth (1770–1850), one of the first English Romantics, redefined poetry by replacing the mannered style of his predecessors with a more conversational style. Many of his greatest works, such as *The Prelude*, draw directly from his experiences in the Lake District, where he spent the first 20 and last 50 years of his life. Wordsworth and his work had an enormous effect on Coleridge, Keats, Shelley, Byron, and countless other writers. Explore his homes in Rydal and Grasmere, among other sites.

John Ruskin (1819–1900), writer, art critic, and early conservationist, was an impassioned champion of new ways of seeing. He defended contemporary artists such as William Turner and the Pre-Raphaelites. His five-volume masterwork, *Modern Painters,* changed the role of the art critic from that of approver or naysayer to that of interpreter. Stop by Coniston to see his home and the Ruskin Museum.

Thomas De Quincey (1785–1859) wrote essays whose impressionistic style influenced many 19th-century writers, including Poe and Baudelaire. His most famous work, *Confessions of an English Opium-Eater* (1822), is an imaginative memoir of his young life, which indeed included opium addiction. He settled in Grasmere in 1809.

Beatrix Potter (1866–1943) never had a formal education; instead, she spent her childhood studying nature. Her love of the outdoors, and Lakeland scenery in particular, influenced her delightfully illustrated children's books, including *The Tale of Peter Rabbit* and *The Tale of Jemima Puddle-Duck*. Potter also became a noted conservationist who donated land to the National Trust. The story of her life was made into the 2006 film *Miss Potter,* starring Renée Zellweger and Ewan McGregor. Today you can visit Hill Top, the writer-artist's home in Hawkshead.

---

masterpiece *Confessions of an English Opium-Eater*. De Quincey moved in after the Wordsworths left. You visit the house on a timed guided tour, and the ticket includes admission to the spacious, modern **Wordsworth Museum and Art Gallery,** which documents the poet's life and the literary contributions of Wordsworth and the Lake Poets. Besides seeing the poet's original manuscripts, you can hear his poems read aloud on headphones. Books, manuscripts, and artwork capture the spirit of the Romantic movement. The museum includes space for major art exhibitions. The **Jerwood Centre,** open to researchers by appointment, houses 50,000 letters, first editions, and manuscripts. Afternoon tea is served at **Villa Colombina.** ⊠ *A591, 1 mi south of Grasmere* ☎ *015394/35544* ⊕ *www.wordsworth.org.uk* ⊡ *£7.50* ⊙ *Mar.–Nov., daily 9:30–5:30; Dec. and Feb., daily 9:30–4:30.*

QUICK BITES

Heidi's (⊠ *Red Lion Sq.* ☎ *015394/35248*) is a bustling, cozy little café and deli lined with jars of locally made jams and chutneys. Bang in the center of Grasmere, it's great for coffee and a delicious homemade pastry or flapjack (bars made with syrup, butter, and oats).

WHERE TO EAT

££ ✕ **The Jumble Room.** This small, stone-built restaurant, dating to the
BRITISH   18th century, was Grasmere's first shop and is a friendly, fashion-
★   able, and colorful place, with children's books, bold animal paintings,
fans, and hanging lamps. A dedicated local fan base means the place
always buzzes, and the owners' enthusiasm is contagious. The food is
an eclectic mix of international and traditional British: excellent fish-
and-chips and beefsteak appear on the menu with crab and cucumber
soup and Catalan fish stew with paprika and almonds. Lunches are
lighter and cheaper, with good soups and homemade puddings. Note:
hours can change frequently. ⊠ *Langdale Rd.* ☎ *015394/35188* ⊕ *www.*
thejumbleroom.co.uk ☰ *MC, V* ⊗ *Closed Mon. and Tues. Closed Sun.*
evening and Wed. Dec.–Easter.

£££ ✕ **Tweedies Bar.** Attached to the Dale Lodge Hotel, Tweedies is one of
BRITISH   the region's best gastro-pubs and attracts many locals as well as visitors.
★   Delicious updated British food such as slow-roasted pork belly with
caramelized apple and duck with apricots and parsnip puree is served
in a smart, cozy, wood-filled contemporary pub with mellow music
and a fireplace. Several of Cumbria's best beers are on tap alongside a
good selection of world beers; you can also try a number of real ales.
⊠ *Langdale Rd.* ☎ *15394/35300* ⊕ *www.tweediesbargrasmere.co.uk*
☰ *MC, V.*

WHERE TO STAY

££ ⊡ **Banerigg House.** You don't have to spend a fortune to find appealing
★   lakeside lodgings in Grasmere. This cozy, early-20th-century house, ¾
mi south of the village on A591, has unfussy, well-appointed rooms,
most with lake views. Games and books fill the guest lounge. The B&B
·   is walker-friendly, which means you get hiking advice from the owners,
drying facilities, and a roaring fire when needed. **Pros:** very welcoming.
hosts; good value for single rooms; canoes available. **Cons:** a little out of
town; the house has an awkward, and potentially dangerous, turn onto
the road. ⊠ *Lake Rd.* ☎ *015394/35204* ⊕ *www.banerigguesthouse.*
co.uk ⊲ *6 rooms, 5 with bath* ⚴ *In-room: no a/c, no phone, no TV,*
Wi-Fi. In-hotel: parking (free) ☰ *No credit cards* ⎮◯⎮ *BP.*

£££ ⊡ **Harwood Hotel.** A romantically decorated hotel, the small but sumptuous Harwood has a distinctly feminine sensibility, with floral wallpaper,
curly steel lamps, and painted woodwork. State-of-the-art contemporary touches such as TVs in the bathrooms and under-floor heating add
extra luxury, and two rooms have private terraces. Dig into a generous
and tasty breakfast downstairs in Heidi's Café. **Pros:** colorful, fantastic
bathrooms with whirlpool tubs; warm welcome. **Cons:** not good for
families; so pristine you may worry about your muddy boots. ⊠ *Red*
Lion Sq. ☎ *015394/35248* ⊕ *www.harwoodhotel.co.uk* ⊲ *6 rooms*
⚴ *In-room: no a/c, no phone, Internet. In-hotel: restaurant, no kids*
under 18 ☰ *MC, V* ⎮◯⎮ *BP.*

£££££ ⊡ **Moss Grove.** A Victorian building in the heart of Grasmere, Moss
Grove has been refurbished impressively, with an emphasis on its environmental credentials. Private hot tubs, balconies, luxurious duck-down
duvets, and flat-screen TVs appear along with reclaimed stained glass,
old timbers, and organic clay paints. Spacious and luxurious yet chicly

informal and a long way from quaint, this hotel adds a newly hip angle to upscale Lake District accommodation. For a special treat, request the champagne truffles on arrival. **Pros:** plenty of room; huge chunky furniture; modern design with a conscience. **Cons:** tight parking; not the place for a big fry-up breakfast. ⊠ *Red Lion Sq.* ☎ *015394/35251* ⊕ *www.mossgrove.com* ⇆ *11 rooms* ⚲ *In-room: no a/c, DVD, Internet (some). In-hotel: some pets allowed* ⊟ *AE, D, DC, MC, V* ⦿ *BP.*

SPORTS AND THE OUTDOORS

The most panoramic views of lake and village are from the south of Grasmere, from the bare slopes of **Loughrigg Terrace**, reached along a well-signposted track on the western side of the lake. It's less than an hour's walk, though your stroll can be extended by continuing around Rydal Water, passing Rydal Mount and Dove Cottage before returning to Grasmere, a 4-mi (three-hour) walk in total.

SHOPPING

★ The smells wafting across the churchyard draw many people to the **Grasmere Gingerbread Shop** (⊠ *Church Cottage* ☎ *015394/35428*). Since 1854 Sarah Nelson's gingerbread has been sold from this cramped 17th-century cottage, which was once the village school. The delicious treats, still made from a secret recipe, are available in attractive tins for the journey home or to eat right away.

ELTERWATER

2½ mi south of Grasmere, 4 mi west of Ambleside.

The delightful village of Elterwater, at the eastern end of the Great Langdale Valley on B5343, is a good stop for hikers. It's barely more than a cluster of houses around a village green, but from here you can choose from a selection of excellent circular walks.

WHERE TO EAT AND STAY

££ ✕ **Britannia Inn.** At this family-owned, 500-year-old pub, restaurant, BRITISH and inn in the heart of superb walking country, antiques, comfortable chairs, and prints and oil paintings furnish the cozy, beamed public rooms. You can relax with a bar meal and Cumbrian ale on the terrace while taking in the village green and the rolling scenery beyond. The hearty traditional British food—from grilled Hawkshead trout to chicken, ham, and leek pie—is popular with locals, as are the many ales and whiskies. It's mainly a traditional pub, though the nine smallish guest rooms are more modern in style, with new pine furniture. Ask about discounts for midweek stays. ⊠ *B5343* ☎ *015394/37210* ⊕ *www. britinn.net* ⊟ *MC, V.*

££ ⬚ **Old Dungeon Ghyll Hotel.** There's no more comforting stop after a day
★ outdoors than the Hiker's Bar of this 300-year-old hotel at the head of the Great Langdale Valley. The stone floor and wooden beams echo to the clatter of hikers' boots, and the roaring, smoky fire rapidly dries out wet walking gear. Thick slabs of flapjack (dense bar cookies) from behind the bar will get you up the surrounding Langdale Pikes, as will the hearty, good-value homemade soup. Guest rooms are decorated with traditional patterned carpets and flowered bed linens, though the hotel

exudes a rougher version of Lakeland life far away from Beatrix Potter quaintness. You can include dinner in the rate. **Pros:** ideally situated for walking; spectacular views all around. **Cons:** no-nonsense approach leaves little room for frippery or elegance and won't be to everyone's taste. ⊠ *Off B5343, Great Langdale* ☎ *015394/37272* ⊕ *www.odg. co.uk* ⇋ *13 rooms, 8 with bath* ⬩ *In-room: no a/c, no phone, no TV. In-hotel: restaurant, bars, Wi-Fi hotspot* ⊟ *AE, MC, V* ⚄ *BP.*

SPORTS AND THE OUTDOORS
There are access points to Langdale Fell from several spots along B5343, the main road; look for information boards at local parking places. You can also stroll up the river valley or embark on more energetic hikes to Stickle Tarn or to one of the summits of the Langdale Pikes. Beyond the Old Dungeon Ghyll Hotel, the Great Langdale valley splits in two around a hill known as the Band—a path up its spine has particularly good views back down over the valley and can be continued to the summit of Scafell Pike.

CONISTON

5 mi south of Elterwater.

This small lake resort and boating center attracts climbers to the steep peak of the **Old Man of Coniston** (2,635 feet), which towers above the slate-roof houses. It also has sites related to John Ruskin. Quieter than Windermere, Coniston is a good introduction to the pastoral and watery charms of the area, though the small town itself can get crowded in summer.

ESSENTIALS
Visitor Information Coniston (⊠ *Ruskin Ave.* ☎ *015394/41533* ⊕ *www. conistontic.org*).

EXPLORING
Coniston Water, the lake on which Coniston stands, came to prominence in the 1930s when Arthur Ransome made it the setting for *Swallows and Amazons,* one of a series of novels about a group of children and their adventures. The lake is about 5 mi long, a tempting stretch that drew boat and car racer Donald Campbell here in 1959 to set a water-speed record of 260 MPH. He was killed when trying to beat it in 1967. His body and the wreckage of *Bluebird K7* were retrieved from the lake in 2001. Campbell is buried in St. Andrew's church in Coniston, and a stone memorial on the village green commemorates him.

The **Ruskin Museum** holds fascinating and thought-provoking manuscripts, personal items, and watercolors by John Ruskin that illuminate his thinking and influence. There is also a focus on Donald Campbell; the tailfin of his *Bluebird K7,* dragged up from Coniston Water, is here, and a reconstruction project is under way. A new Bluebird wing has been built to house the speedboat. Good local-interest exhibits include copper mining, geology, lace, and more. ⊠ *Yewdale Rd.* ☎ *015394/41164* ⊕ *www.ruskinmuseum.com* 🖭 *£4.50* ⊙ *Mid-Mar.–mid-Nov., daily 10–5:30; mid-Nov.–mid-Mar., Wed.–Sun. 10:30–3:30.*

★ **Brantwood,** on the eastern shore of Coniston Water, was the cherished home of John Ruskin (1819–1900), the noted Victorian artist, writer, critic, and social reformer, after 1872. The rambling, white, 18th-century house (with Victorian alterations) is on a 250-acre estate that stretches high above the lake. Here, alongside mementos such as his mahogany desk, are Ruskin's own paintings, drawings, and books. On display is art that this great connoisseur collected, and in cerebral corners such as the Ideas Room visitors are encouraged to think about meaning and change. A video on Ruskin's life shows the lasting influence of his thoughts, and the **Severn Studio** has rotating art exhibitions. Ruskin himself laid out the extensive grounds; take time to explore the gardens and woodland walks. Brantwood hosts a series of classical concerts on some Saturdays as well as talks, guided walks, and study days. ■ TIP➜ It's an easy drive to Brantwood from Coniston, but it's pleasant to travel here by ferry across the lake, via either the Coniston Launch or the *Gondola,* a 19th-century steam yacht. Both depart from Coniston Pier through the summer. ✉ *Off B5285* ☎ *015394/41396* ⊕ *www.brantwood.org.uk* 🎫 *£6.30; gardens only, £4.50* ⊘ *Mid-Mar.–mid-Nov., daily 11–5:30; mid-Nov.–mid-Mar., Wed.–Sun. 11–4:30.*

Coniston Launch (☎ *017687/75753* ⊕ *www.conistonlaunch.co.uk*) connects Coniston Pier with Ruskin's home at Brantwood, offering hourly service (£8.90 hop-on, hop-off all-day ticket around the northern lake, with more extensive routes mid-March through November) on its wooden *Ruskin* and *Ransome* launches, which run on a solar–electric power system. Thematic sightseeing tours are also available.

Steam Yacht *Gondola* (☎ *015394/41288* ⊕ *www.nationaltrust.org.uk*) runs the National Trust's luxurious Victorian steam yacht (originally launched in 1859 and restored in the 1970s) between Coniston Pier, Brantwood, and Park-a-Moor at the south end of Coniston Water, daily from April through October (£7 round-trip). A stop at Monk Coniston jetty connects to the footpaths through the Monk Coniston Estate, linking Coniston Water to the beauty spot of **Tarn Hows.**

WHERE TO EAT

££ × **Black Bull Inn.** Attached to the Coniston Brewing Company, whose BRITISH ales are on tap here, the Black Bull is an old-fashioned pub in the heart of the village: a little gruff but a good pick for simple, hearty food and exemplary beer. Old photos of Donald Campbell's boat *Bluebird* decorate the walls, and there are wooden beams and benches. The menu lists daily specials as well as sandwiches for lunch or shrimp from Morecambe Bay. ✉ *Coppermines Rd.* ☎ *015394/41335* ⊕ *www. conistonbrewery.com* 🍴 *MC, V.*

£ × **Jumping Jenny's.** Named after Ruskin's beloved boat, the wood-BRITISH beamed tearoom at Brantwood occupies the converted coach house. It has an open log fire and mountain views, and serves morning coffee, lunch (sophisticated soups, pastas, sandwiches, and salads), and afternoon tea with homemade cakes. You can sit on the terrace in season. ✉ *Off B5285* ☎ *015394/41715* ⊕ *www.jumpingjenny.com* 🍴 *MC, V* ⊘ *Closed Mon. and Tues. Also closed Wed.–Fri. in Jan. No dinner.*

WALKING IN THE LAKE DISTRICT

You can choose gentle rambles near the most popular towns and villages or challenging hikes and climbs up some of England's most impressive peaks. Information boards at parking lots throughout the region point out the possibilities.

British mountaineering began in the Lake District, with its notable hikes: the famous Old Man of Coniston, the Langdale Pikes, Scafell Pike (England's highest peak), Skiddaw, and Helvellyn are all popular, though these require experience, energy, and proper hiking boots and clothing. The Cumbria Way (70 mi) crosses the Lake District, starting at the market town of Ulverston and finishing at Carlisle. The Coast-to-Coast Walk (190 mi) runs from St. Bees on the Irish Sea through the Lake District and across the Yorkshire Dales and the North York Moors; it ends at Robin Hood's Bay at the edge of the North Sea in Yorkshire. Guidebooks to these and other Lakeland walks are available in local bookstores—check out Alfred Wainwright's classic guides.

For short walks, consult the tourist information centers: those at Ambleside, Cockermouth, Grasmere, Kendal, Keswick, and Windermere provide maps and advice. The other main sources of information are the Lake District National Park information centers. Cumbria Tourism's Web site, *www.golakes.co.uk*, is helpful for planning. Several climbing organizations offer guided hikes as well as technical rock climbing.

WHERE TO STAY

££ ⊡ **Bank Ground Farm.** Used by Arthur Ransome as the model for the setting for *Swallows and Amazons,* Bank Ground is beautifully situated on the eastern shore of Coniston Water, opposite the village of Coniston on the western shore. It's a proper, old-fashioned, working farm, though some traditionally decorated rooms have a few contemporary elements such as stylish large-pattern wallpaper and oversize pillows. Cottages with kitchens are a good option for longer stays, and there's a guest lounge with an open fire. The tearoom is open to the public on weekends from Easter to October. **Pros:** stunning lake views; homey; traditional welcome. **Cons:** a fair walk from the village; no Internet access. ⊠ *Lake Rd., Coniston* ☎ *015394/41264* ⊕ *www.bankground. com* ⌨ *7 rooms, 5 cottages* ⚏ *In-room: no a/c, no phone, no TV. In-hotel: kitchen (some), parking (free)* ⏃ *BP.*

£ ⊡ **Beech Tree Guest House.** This Victorian stone house with friendly own-
★ ers and a garden is within walking distance of the town center. The individually furnished rooms, some of which look out over an ancient beech tree, are done in a country theme, and breakfast is hearty and vegetarian. There's a TV in the sitting room. **Pros:** cozy, family atmosphere; excellent breakfast. **Cons:** not for those wanting all the mod cons; no meat with breakfast. ⊠ *Yewdale Rd.* ☎ *015394/413717* ⌨ *8 rooms, 4 with bath* ⚏ *In-room: no a/c, no TV. In-hotel: some pets allowed* ⊟ *No credit cards* ⏃ *BP.*

££ ⊡ **Yew Tree Farm.** Homemade cakes on arrival set the scene for this friendly, working farm B&B 5 mi north of Coniston toward Skelwith

11

Bridge. Once owned by Beatrix Potter, and later used in filming the story of her life, Yew Tree Farm is nestled in some especially attractive hills, and it retains some of Potter's original furnishings. Guests have free access to a local health club. All this means that it's very popular, and you'll need to book in advance. Pros: pretty location; bacon from the farm for breakfast; two rooms have four-poster beds. Cons: not in town; often booked up far in advance; no small children unless you book whole house. ✉ *A593* ☎ *015394/41433* ⊕ *www.yewtree-farm. com* 🛏 *3 rooms* ♿ *In-room: no a/c, no phone, no TV, Wi-Fi. In-hotel: some pets allowed* 🍴 *MC, V* 🍽 *BP.*

SPORTS AND THE OUTDOORS

Steep tracks lead up from the village to the **Old Man of Coniston.** The trail starts near the Sun Hotel on Brow Hill and goes past an old copper mine to the peak, which you can reach in about two hours. It's one of the Lake District's most satisfying—not too arduous but high enough to feel a real sense of accomplishment and get some fantastic views (west to the sea, south to Morecambe Bay, and east to Windermere). Experienced hikers include the peak in a seven-hour circular walk from the village, also taking in the dramatic heights and ridges of Swirl How and Wetherlam.

★ **Coniston Boating Centre** (✉ *Lake Rd.* ☎ *015394/41366*), open 10–4:30 daily, can help you get out on the water. You can rent launches, canoes, kayaks, and wooden rowboats, or even take a sailing lesson. A picnic area and café are near the center, too.

HAWKSHEAD

3 mi east of Coniston.

In the Vale of Esthwaite, this small market town, with a pleasing hodge-podge of tiny squares, cobbled lanes, and whitewashed houses (and a pedestrianized center), is perhaps the Lake District's most picturesque village. There's a good deal more history here than in most local villages, however. The Hawkshead Courthouse, just outside town, was built by the monks of Furness Abbey in the 15th century. Hawkshead later derived much wealth from the wool trade, which flourished here in the 17th and 18th centuries.

As a thriving market center, Hawkshead could afford to maintain the **Hawkshead Grammar School,** at which William Wordsworth was a pupil from 1779 to 1787; he carved his name on a desk inside, now on display. In the village, Ann Tyson's House claims the honor of having provided the young William with lodgings. The twin draws of Wordsworth and Beatrix Potter—apart from her home, Hill Top, there's a Potter gallery—conspire to make Hawkshead crowded year-round.

GETTING HERE AND AROUND

Hawkshead is east of Coniston on B5285 and south of Ambleside via B5286. An alternative route is to cross Windermere via the car ferry from Ferry Nab, south of Bowness. Local buses link the village to others nearby.

ESSENTIALS
Visitor Information Hawkshead
(✉ *Main St.* ☎ *015394/36946* ⊕ *www. hawksheadtouristinfo.org.uk*).

EXPLORING

🔄 The **Beatrix Potter Gallery**, in the solicitor's offices formerly used by Potter's husband, displays an annually changing selection of the artist-writer's original watercolors and drawings, as well as information on her interests as a naturalist. Potter was a conservationist and an early supporter of the National Trust. The house looks almost as it would have in her day. Admission is by timed ticket. ✉ *Main St.* ☎ *015394/36355* ⊕ *www.nationaltrust.org.uk* ☜ *£4.20* ⊗ *Mid-Feb.–mid-Mar., Sat.–Thurs. 11–3:30; mid-Mar.–May, Sept., and Oct., Sat.–Thurs. 11–5; June–Aug., Sat.–Thurs. 10:30–5.*

> ### LAKE DISTRICT BIKING
>
> Cycling along the numerous bicycle paths and quiet forest roads in Cumbria is pleasurable and safe. Some flat paths are beside the lakes, but the best routes involve plenty of ups and downs. The Cumbria Cycle Way circles the county, and for local excursions guided bike tours are often available, starting at about £25 per day. Contact local tourist offices or bike-rental places for details on cycle routes.

Hill Top was the home of children's author and illustrator Beatrix Potter (1866–1943), most famous for her *Peter Rabbit* stories. The house looks much the same as when Potter bequeathed it to the National Trust, and fans will recognize details such as the porch and garden gate, old kitchen range, Victorian dollhouse, and four-poster bed, which were depicted in the book illustrations. ■TIP➜ **Admission to this often-crowded spot is by timed ticket; book in advance and avoid visiting during summer weekends and school vacations.** Hill Top lies 2 mi south of Hawkshead by car or foot, though you can also approach via the car ferry from Bowness-on-Windermere. ✉ *Off B5285, Near Sawrey* ☎ *015394/36269* ⊕ *www.nationaltrust.org.uk* ☜ *£6.20, gardens free when house closed* ⊗ *House mid-Feb.–Mar., Sat.–Thurs. 11–3:30; Apr., May, Sept., and Oct., Sat.–Thurs. 10:30–4:30; June–Aug., Sat.–Thurs. 10–4:30. Gardens and shop mid-Feb.–Mar., daily 10:45–4; Apr.–Oct., daily 10–5; Nov. and Dec., daily 10–4.*

Two miles northwest of the village (follow signs on B5285) is one of the Lake District's most celebrated beauty spots, **Tarn Hows**, a tree-lined lake. Scenic overlooks let you drink it all in, or you can take an hour to putter along the paths. A free National Trust bus runs here from Hawkshead and Coniston (Easter–October, Sunday only).

WHERE TO STAY

££–£££
Fodor's Choice
★

🔆 **Drunken Duck Inn.** After four centuries, this friendly old coaching inn remains an outstanding place for both food and lodging. Bedrooms—bright, chic, contemporary, and exceptionally comfortable—make good use of natural materials and have wonderful views of the Langdale Pikes. The price includes afternoon tea and breakfast. Nestle into the cozy bar with oak settles and order a tasty real ale from the Duck's Barngsate Brewery. There's an open fire, and hops hang over the bar. The two dining spaces have dark-wood furniture and hunting prints; halibut with

11

What's Real About Real Ale?

The English can be passionate about their drink, as the growing interest in real ale shows. It differs from other ales by the use of natural ingredients and the fact that it is matured by fermentation in the barrel from which the ale is served. The process doesn't use carbon dioxide, so pure taste wins out over fizz.

The **Directory of U.K. Real Ale Breweries** (⊕ www.quaffale.org.uk) lists 28 operating real-ale breweries in Cumbria, of which the Coniston Brewing Company, Barngates Brewery (at the Drunken Duck Inn), and Hawkshead (in Staveley, between Kendal and Windermere) are three of the best. Most real ales are caramel in color and hoppy, malty, and slightly bitter to taste. A pint of ale is the usual quantity to be consumed, though a half is acceptable; you can also find it in bottles.

Most pubs in the Lake District offer some sort of local brew—the better ones take enormous pride in their careful tending of the beer, from barrel to glass. Interested in the subject, or just in the taste? Check out the Web site of the **Campaign for Real Ale** (⊕ www.camra.org.uk).

---

chorizo and balsamic jus is typical of the Modern British fare; lunch is less formal. The inn is 2½ mi from both Ambleside and Hawkshead. **Pros:** superchic rural style; excellent dining and drinking. **Cons:** hunting paraphernalia may put you off your beer; can feel isolated. ⊠ *Off B5286, Barngates* ☎ *015394/36347* ⊕ *www.drunkenduckinn.co.uk* ⇋ *16 rooms* ⚭ *In-room: no a/c, Wi-Fi. In-hotel: restaurant, bar* ⊟ *AE, MC, V* ⏐◯⏐ *BP, MAP.*

££ ⋒ **Yewfield.** With the laid-back friendliness of a B&B but with most of the style of a fancier country-house hotel, this is a very good value for the money—especially if you can get one of the rooms with a great view across the valley from the front of the house. The 19th-century Gothic house, between Hawkshead and Tarn Hows, has a large lounge and sits on 30 acres of land. Breakfast is wholesome and vegetarian. Check out the good discounts for longer stays. **Pros:** a great out-of-the-way location; garden; apartments a convenient option for week-long stays. **Cons:** laid-back service can occasionally be too relaxed; not good for families with young kids. ⊠ *Hawkshead Hill* ☎ *015394/36765* ☎ *015394/36096* ⊕ *www.yewfield.co.uk* ⇋ *10 rooms, 2 apartments* ⚭ *In-room: no a/c, DVD, Wi-Fi (some). In-hotel: bar, Wi-Fi hotspot, no kids under 9* ⊟ *MC, V* ☉ *Closed Dec. and Jan.* ⏐◯⏐ *BP.*

PENRITH AND THE NORTHERN LAKES

The scenery of the northern lakes is considerably more dramatic—some would say bleaker—than much of the landscape to the south, a change that becomes apparent on your way north from Kendal to Penrith. Your easiest approach is a 30-mi drive on the A6 that takes you through the wild and desolate Shap Fells, which rise to a height of 1,304 feet. This is one of the most notorious moorland crossings in the country: even in summer it's a lonely place to be, and in winter snow on the road can be dangerous. From Penrith the road leads to Ullswater, possibly the grandest of all the lakes; then there's a winding route west past Keswick, south through the marvelous Borrowdale Valley, and on to Cockermouth. Outside the main towns such as Keswick, it can be easier to escape the summer crowds in the northern lakes.

PENRITH

30 mi north of Kendal.

The red-sandstone town of Penrith was the capital of Cumbria, part of the Scottish kingdom of Strathclyde in the 9th and 10th centuries. It was rather neglected after the Normans arrived, and the Scots sacked it on several occasions. Penrith has been a thriving market town for centuries; the market still takes place on Tuesday, and it continues to be known for good shopping.

The tourist information center, in the Penrith Museum, has information about the historic town trail, which takes you through narrow byways to the plague stone on King Street, where food was left for the stricken, to St. Andrew's churchyard and its 1,000-year-old "hog back" tombstones (stones carved as stylized "houses of the dead"), and finally to the ruins of Penrith Castle.

GETTING HERE AND AROUND
Penrith is just off the M6, 30 mi north of Kendal and 100 mi north of Manchester. Both the M6 and the alternative A6 cross the Pennines spectacularly at Shap Fells. From Windermere, you can reach Penrith by going over the Kirkstone Pass to Ullswater. There are some direct trains from Euston Station in London to Penrith; sometimes it's necessary to change.

ESSENTIALS
Visitor Information Penrith (⊠ *Penrith Museum, Middlegate* ☎ *01768/867466* ⊕ *www.visiteden.co.uk*).

EXPLORING
The evocative remains of the 15th-century redbrick **Penrith Castle** stand high above a steep, now-dry moat. Home of the maligned Richard, duke of Gloucester (later Richard III), who was responsible for keeping peace along the border, it was one of England's first lines of defense against the Scots. By the Civil War the castle was in ruins, and the townsfolk used some of the fallen stones to build their houses. The ruins stand across from the town's train station. ⊠ *Off Castlegate* ☎ *No phone* ⊕ *www.english-heritage.org.uk* ⊠ *Free* ☉ *June–Sept., daily 7:30 AM–9 PM; Oct.–May, daily 7:30–4:30.*

The **Penrith Museum**, in a 16th-century building that served as a school from 1670 to the 1970s, contains displays on the history of the Eden Valley, including Roman pottery and a medieval cauldron. The Penrith Tourist Information Centre is here. ⊠ *Robinson's School, Middlegate* ☎ *01768/212228* ⊕ *www.eden.gov.uk* ⊠ *Free* ☉ *Apr.–Oct., Mon.–Sat. 10–5, Sun. 1–4:45; Nov.–Mar., Mon.–Sat. 10–5.*

⟳ **Rheged**, the name of the Celtic kingdom of Cumbria, is the theme of this grass-covered visitor center with activities for kids and some interesting free exhibits about the history, culture, and other aspects of the Lake District. Its centerpiece, a large-format cinema (fee), shows 50-minute 3-D movies such as *"Dinosaurs Alive!"* and *"Fly Me To The Moon."* Shops showcase Cumbrian produce and crafts, and the Rheged Café and Café Pod and Taste Food Bar all offer drinks and light meals. Rheged is 2 mi southwest of Penrith and 1 mi west of Junction 40 on the M6. ⊠ *A66* ☎ *01768/868000* ⊕ *www.rheged.com* ☒ *Free, movie £4.95* ⊙ *Daily 10–5:30.*

Home of the Hasell family since 1679, **Dalemain**, 3 mi southwest of Penrith, began with a 12th-century peel tower built to protect the occupants from raiding Scots, and is now a delightful hodgepodge of architectural styles. An imposing Georgian facade of local pink sandstone encompasses a medieval hall and extensions from the 16th through the 18th century. Inside are a magnificent oak staircase, furniture dating from the mid-17th century, a Chinese drawing room, a 16th-century room with intricate plasterwork, and many fine paintings, including masterpieces by Van Dyck. The gardens are worth a look, too, and deer roam the estate. ⊠ *A592* ☎ *01768/486450* ⊕ *www.dalemain.com* ☒ *£9; gardens only, £6* ⊙ *House Apr.–Sept., Sun.–Thurs. 11:15–4; Oct., Sun.–Thurs. 11:15–3. Gardens Apr.–Oct., Sun.–Thurs. 10:30–5; Nov.–mid-Dec., Feb., and Mar., Sun.–Thurs. 11–4.*

WHERE TO EAT AND STAY

££ ✕ **George and Dragon.** Just south of Penrith, this freshly updated pub
BRITISH owned by the nearby Lowther estate makes good use of the estate's resources for its tasty traditional organic dishes, such as venison pie and chips. Other local suppliers are mapped out on the menu: sausages come from up the Eden valley, brown trout from the River Lowther. The inn is also a well-tended spot for a pint of local beer, with handsome slate floors and hanging hops. Bonnie Prince Charlie was once involved in a battle here, and the remains of 12 Scottish rebels were discovered in the pub's back garden. For an overnight stay, choose from 10 smart, individually designed guest rooms that catch the eye with bold contemporary patterns, black-and-white photos, and some furnishings from the Lowther family's collection; there's a spacious family room, too. ⊠ *A6, Clifton* ☎ *01768/865381* ⊕ *www.georgeanddragonclifton. co.uk* ⊟ *MC, V* ⊙ *No lunch Mon.*

£ ✕ **No. 15.** A laid-back, spacious contemporary gallery and café with a
CAFÉ large range of teas and coffees also serves light meals such as homemade soups and quiches and great cakes and desserts. Wi-Fi can be used for 30 minutes for £2, and there's monthly live music in the evening. ⊠ *15 Victoria Rd.* ☎ *01768/867453* ⊟ *MC, V.*

££ ☷ **Brooklands.** Pristinely refurbished in soothing tones, this Victorian terraced house is one of a cluster of B&Bs on Portland Place, a short walk north of Penrith's center. The welcome is friendly, the breakfast is hearty (salmon fish cakes and omelets are among the options), and rooms are bright and simple, with some patterned wallpaper and heavy, luxurious fabrics. Purples and browns predominate, and one room has a four-poster. **Pros:** well-looked-after B&B; bathrobes in room; fancy toiletries. **Cons:** Penrith is outside the national park and a drive from the spectacular Lakeland scenery. ⊠ *2 Portland Pl.* ☎ *01768/863395* ⊕ *www.brooklandsguesthouse.com* ➾ *8 rooms* ⚭ *In-room: no a/c, refrigerator, Wi-Fi. In-hotel: Wi-Fi hotspot* ⊟ *MC, V* ⍥ *BP.*

SHOPPING

Penrith is a diverting place to shop, with its narrow streets and arcades chockablock with family-run specialty shops—look for the free guide to the best of them. Major shopping areas include Devonshire Arcade, with its brand-name stores; the pedestrian-only Angel Lane and Little Dockray; and Angel Square. The stalls of the outdoor **market** line Dockray, Corn Market, and Market Square every Tuesday and sell fine local produce and original crafts.

The excellent **Bluebell Bookshop** (⊠ *8 Angel La.* ☎ *01768/866660*) sometimes hosts special events and readings. **James & John Graham of Penrith Ltd.** (⊠ *Market Sq.* ☎ *01768/862281*) has a great bakery and a well-stocked delicatessen that specializes in cheese and local products. The **Toffee Shop** (⊠ *7 Brunswick Rd.* ☎ *01768/862008*), where the Queen buys her toffee, may also have England's best fudge.

ULLSWATER

3 mi southwest of Dalemain, 6 mi southwest of Penrith.

Hemmed in by towering hills, Ullswater, the region's second-largest lake, is one of the least developed, drawing people for its calm waters and good access to the mountain slopes of Helvellyn. The A592 winds along the lake's pastoral western shore, through the adjacent hamlets of **Glenridding** and **Patterdale** at the southern end. Lakeside strolls, great views, tea shops, and rowboat rentals provide the full Lakeland experience.

ESSENTIALS

Visitor Information Ullswater (⊠ *Main Car Park, Glenridding* ☎ *017684/82414*).

EXPLORING

Ullswater Steamers (☎ *017684/82229* ⊕ *www.ullswater-steamers.co.uk*) sends its antique vessels, including an oil-burning, 19th-century steamer, the length of Ullswater between Glenridding in the south and Pooley Bridge in the north; it's a pleasant tour and combines well with a lakeside walk. The service operates 363 days a year from the pier at Glenridding. A one-way trip the full length of the lake is £7.80, or you can do any three stages for £10.70.

At **Aira Force** (⊠ *Off A592, 5 mi north of Patterdale*) a spectacular 65-foot waterfall pounds under a stone bridge and through a wooded ravine to feed into Ullswater. From the parking lot (£3.50–£5.50 fee, depending on how long you stay), it's a 10-minute walk to the falls, with more serious walks on Gowbarrow Fell and to the village of Dockray beyond. Bring sturdy shoes in wet weather. Just above Aira Force in the woods of Gowbarrow Park is the spot where, in 1802, William Wordsworth's sister Dorothy observed daffodils that, as she wrote," tossed and reeled and danced and seemed as if they verily laughed with the wind that blew upon them." Two years later Wordsworth transformed his sister's words into the famous poem "I Wandered Lonely as a Cloud." And two centuries later, national park wardens patrol Gowbarrow Park in season to prevent tourists from picking the few remaining daffodils.

★ West of Ullswater's southern end, the brooding presence of **Helvellyn** (3,118 feet), one of the Lake District's most formidable mountains, recalls the region's fundamental character. It's an arduous climb to the top, especially via the challenging ridge known as Striding Edge, and the ascent shouldn't be attempted in poor weather or by inexperienced hikers. Signposted paths to the peak run from the road between Glenridding and Patterdale and pass by **Red Tarn**, at 2,356 feet the highest small mountain lake in the region.

WHERE TO STAY

£££   **Howtown Hotel.** Near the end of the road down the isolated eastern side of Ullswater, this gloriously quiet, welcoming, family-run hotel is low-key and low-tech, though the Ullswater Steamer connects it to the outside world. Cut flowers, antiques, and stuffed deer heads decorate the steadfastly old-fashioned interior, and there are fireplaces and views over the lake from some rooms. The restaurant, open to nonguests, serves hearty Lakeland fare, and good take-out lunches are available. Howtown is popular, so book ahead. **Pros:** exceptionally quiet; spectacular location; dinner included in price. **Cons:** not for those who must be plugged in; a bit remote. ⊠ *4 mi south of Pooley Bridge* ☎ *017684/86514* ⊕ *www.howtown-hotel.com* ⇗ *12 rooms* ♿ *In-room: no a/c, no phone, no TV. In-hotel: restaurant, bars, some pets allowed, no kids under 7* ☰ *No credit cards* ☉ *Closed Nov.–Mar.* ⅢⅠ *MAP.*

££££–£££££   **Sharrow Bay.** Sublime views and exceptional service and cuisine add
★   distinction to this country-house hotel on the shores of Ullswater. Salons with oil paintings and fringed lamp shades represent classic Lakeland style. The traditional bedrooms are plushly opulent, although those in the Edwardian Gatehouse and in the Bank House, an Elizabethan farmhouse about 1½ mi away, are somewhat simpler. Your sophisticated dinner (reservations essential, £70 fixed-price menu) might include roast salmon on scallop risotto or venison with sweet-potato confit; choose a wine from the excellent list and leave room for sticky toffee pudding, which the hotel claims to have invented here. Be sure to request the lake-view dining room. Afternoon tea is another option (£19). **Pros:** great views across Ullswater; pretty garden. **Cons:** not for the faint of wallet; too floral for some tastes; some distance from other facilities. ⊠ *Howtown Rd., Pooley Bridge* ☎ *017684/86301* ⊕ *www.sharrowbay.co.uk* ⇗ *16 rooms, 8 suites* ♿ *In-room: no a/c (some). In-hotel: 2 restaurants, bars, Wi-Fi hotspot, no kids under 13* ☰ *AE, MC, V* ⅢⅠ *MAP.*

KESWICK

14 mi west of Ullswater.

The great mountains of Skiddaw and Blencathra brood over the gray slate houses of Keswick (pronounced *kezz*-ick), on the scenic shores of Derwentwater. The town is a natural base for exploring the rounded, heather-clad Skiddaw range to the north, and the hidden valleys of

Borrowdale and Buttermere (the latter reached by stunning Honister Pass) take you into the rugged heart of the Lake District. Nearby, five beautiful lakes are set among the three highest mountain ranges in England. The tourist information center here has regional information and is the place to get fishing permits for Derwentwater and Bassenthwaite.

Keswick's narrow, cobbled streets have a grittier charm compared to the refined Victorian elegance of Grasmere or Ambleside. However, it is the best spot in the Lake District to purchase mountaineering gear and outdoor clothing. There are also many hotels, guesthouses, restaurants, and pubs, making it a good base.

GETTING HERE AND AROUND

It's easily reached along A66 from Penrith, though you can get to Keswick more scenically via Grasmere in the south. Buses run from the train station in Penrith to Keswick. The town center is pedestrianized.

■ TIP→ Because traffic congestion can be horrendous in summer, and parking is difficult in the higher valleys, consider leaving your car in Keswick. The open-top Borrowdale bus service between Keswick and Seatoller (to the south) runs frequently, and the Honister Rambler minibus is perfect for walkers aiming for the high fells of the central lakes; it makes stops from Keswick to Buttermere. The Keswick Launch service on Derwentwater links to many walks as well as the Borrowdale bus service.

ESSENTIALS

Visitor Information Keswick (⊠ *Moot Hall, Market Sq.* ☎ *017687/72645* ⊕ *www.keswick.org*).

EXPLORING

★ To understand why **Derwentwater** is considered one of England's finest lakes, take a short walk from Keswick's town center to the lakeshore and past the jetty, and follow the **Friar's Crag** path, about a 15-minute level walk from the center. This pine-tree-fringed peninsula is a favorite vantage point, with its view of the lake, the ring of mountains, and many tiny islands. Ahead, crags line the **Jaws of Borrowdale** and overhang a mountain ravine—a scene that looks as if it emerged from a Romantic painting.

For the best lake views, take a wooden-launch cruise with **Keswick-on-Derwentwater Launch Co.** (☎ *017687/72263* ⊕ *www.keswick-launch.co.uk*) around Derwentwater. Between late March and November, cruises set off every hour in each direction from a dock at the shore; there is also a limited winter timetable. You can also rent a rowboat here. Buy a hop-on, hop-off Around the Lake ticket (£8.80) and take advantage of the seven landing stages around the lake that provide access to hiking trails, such as the two-hour climb up and down Cat Bells, a celebrated lookout point on the western shore of Derwentwater.

Borrowdale's long connection with graphite is celebrated at the entertaining **Cumberland Pencil Museum.** Legend has it that shepherds found graphite on Seathwaite Fell after a storm uprooted trees in the 16th century. The Derwent company still makes pencils here, and the museum contains the world's longest pencil, an item produced for World War II spies that contains a rolled-up map, and displays about graphite mining

Festivals and Folk Sports

With everything from rushbearing to Westmorland wrestling to traditional music, the Lake District hosts some of Britain's most unusual country festivals as well as some excellent but more typical ones.

MAJOR EVENTS

Major festivals include the Keswick Film Festival (February), Words by the Water (a literary festival in Keswick, March), Keswick Jazz Festival (May), Cockermouth and Keswick carnivals (June), Ambleside rushbearing (August) and sports (July), Grasmere rushbearing (August) and sports (August), and Lake District Summer Music (regionwide, in August)—but some sort of event or festival happens somewhere during most weeks throughout the year.

SPECIAL ACTIVITIES

Rushbearing dates back to medieval times, when rushes covered church floors; today processions of flower-bedecked children and adults bring rushes to churches in a number of villages. Folk sports, often the highlights at local festivals, include Cumberland and Westmorland wrestling, in which the opponents must maintain a grip around each other's body. Fell running, a sort of cross-country run where the route goes roughly straight up and down a mountain, is also popular.

A calendar of events is available at tourist information centers or on the Cumbria Tourism Web site, ⊕ *www. golakes.co.uk.*

---

and pencil making. There's a café and quizzes for kids. ⊠ *Southey Works* ☎ *017687/73626* ⊕ *www.pencilmuseum.co.uk* ⊠ *£3.25* ☉ *Daily 9:30–5; last admission at 4.*

★ A Neolithic monument about 100 feet in diameter, the **Castlerigg Stone Circle** (⊠ *Off A66, 4 mi east of Keswick*) lies in a brooding natural hollow called St. John's Vale, ringed by magnificent peaks and ranged by sheep. The 38 stones aren't large, but the site makes them particularly impressive. Wordsworth described them as "a dismal cirque of Druid stones upon a forlorn moor." A marked route leads to a 200-foot-long path through a pasture. You can visit at any time, no charge.

WHERE TO EAT

£   ✕ **Café Bar 26.** A metropolitan bar in the rural Lake District, where cozy
BRITISH   tearooms are more the norm, Café Bar 26 has Wi-Fi, wooden beams, mellow brick-color walls, candlelight, and live music every Saturday. The wine list is on the short side, but there are good nibbles at night, though no dinner. During the day light lunches are served, including tuna on roasted vegetables, linguine with sun-dried tomatoes, and Caesar salad. The three bedrooms upstairs are an excellent value for an overnight. ⊠ *26 Lake Rd.* ☎ *017687/80863* ⊠ *www.cafebar26.co.uk* ⊟ *MC, V* ☉ *No dinner.*

£   ✕ **Lakeland Pedlar.** Colorful and cheerful, this café and bike shop serves
VEGETARIAN   inspired international vegetarian and vegan cuisine such as spanakopita (Greek spinach pie) and chickpea tagine, and a filling, homemade soup. You can check out the fresh juices, espresso, and homemade cakes, and

hearty breakfasts are a specialty. Admire the fells (or the parking lot) from the outdoor tables, or take food with you for the trail. ✉ *Henderson's Yard, Bell Close* ☎ *017687/74492* *www.lakelandpedlar.co.uk* ▭ *MC, V* ⊙ *Closed Wed. No dinner Sept.–June.*

£££ BRITISH ✕ **Morrels**. One of the town's better eating places has cinematically themed art and wooden floors that give a contemporary edge to the bar and dining area. Updated British fare is the specialty at this mellow restaurant: a vegetable-and-lime fricassee complements the halibut, and duck breast comes with root vegetable mash and ginger sauce. A couple of equally stylish apartments upstairs are available for short-term rentals. ✉ *34 Lake Rd.* ☎ *017687/72666* 🌐 *www.morrels.co.uk* ▭ *MC, V* ⊙ *Closed Mon.*

£ CAFÉ ★ ✕ **Square Orange Café Bar**. Young locals and windblown walkers gather here for excellent coffee, tea, cordials, and some serious hot chocolate; cakes, paninis, and tapas are served as well. Music is laid-back, the walls have paintings and photos, and there are games, pizza (some days and nights), and snacks, and pints of local beer for long rainy days or cold winter nights. ✉ *20 St. John's St.* ☎ *017687/73888* *www.thesquareorange.co.uk* ▭ *MC, V.*

WHERE TO STAY

£–££ **Ferndene**. Exceptionally friendly, this spotless B&B has a warm, family atmosphere and is carefully tended by its kind owners. Comfortable rooms are decorated in neutral tones, breakfast is hearty, and there's always plenty of local advice on walking and local sights when you want it. Good-size family rooms have views over the mountains of Blencathra and Skiddaw, and you are a 10-minute walk from the lake. **Pros:** family-focused; good value; bicycle storage. **Cons:** can't compete with stylishness of more expensive lodgings. ✉ *6 St. John's Terr.* ☎ *017687/74612* 🌐 *www.ferndene-keswick.co.uk* *7 rooms, 4 with bath* *In-room: Wi-Fi. In-hotel: Wi-Fi hotspot* ▭ *MC, V* *BP.*

£££–££££ ★ **Highfield Hotel**. Slightly austere-looking on the outside but exceptionally friendly within, this family-run Victorian hotel overlooks the lawns of Hope Park and has lodging with great character, including turret rooms and a former chapel that holds a four-poster. Smaller rooms downstairs are simpler and less impressive. The balconies of the common areas have superb valley views, and some rooms look out to Derwentwater or Skiddaw. The well-regarded restaurant's daily-changing fixed-price menu (£29.50 or £42.50) uses local ingredients. A four-course dinner is included in the room rate, adding value. Check out the fine wine list and 25 whiskies in the bar. **Pros:** good service and food; great views. **Cons:** some small downstairs bedrooms; meal plan may not appeal to those who want to dine around. ✉ *The Heads* ☎ *017687/72508* 🌐 *www.highfieldkeswick.co.uk* *18 rooms* *In-room: no a/c, DVD. In-hotel: restaurant, bar, Internet terminal* ▭ *AE, MC, V* ⊙ *Closed Jan.–mid-Feb.* *MAP.*

££ **Howe Keld**. In a town that overflows with B&Bs, this comfortable town house–hotel combines local touches with contemporary flair and pampering touches. Pristinely redesigned and refurbished rooms have cherry, elm, oak, or slate floors, natural carpets using local wool, and bespoke wooden furniture by local craftsman Danny Frost. The style is streamlined and neutral and the beds are top-notch, with pocket-sprung mattresses and goose-down pillows and duvets. High-quality breakfasts might include home-baked bread and pancakes and meaty Cumbrian fry-ups. **Pros:** freshly renovated; famously good breakfasts; good ecological practices; one room accessible for people with disabilities. **Cons:** a short distance from the heart of town; backs onto a busy road. ✉ *5–7 The Heads* ☏ *017687/72417* ⊕ *www.howekeld.co.uk* ⛵ *14 rooms* ⛄ *In-room: no a/c, no phone. In-hotel: restaurant, bar, Wi-Fi hotspot, some pets allowed* ⊟ *MC, V* ⊗ *Closed Jan.* ⦿ *BP.*

NIGHTLIFE AND THE ARTS

The **Keswick Film Club** (☏ *017687/72398*) has an excellent festival in February and a program of international and classic films, screened at the old redbrick Alhambra Cinema on St. John's Street and at the Theatre by the Lake. The popular **Keswick Jazz Festival** (☏ *017687/74411*), held each May, consists of four days of music. Reservations are taken as early as before Christmas.

The company at the **Theatre by the Lake** (✉ *Lake Rd.* ☏ *017687/74411*) presents classic and contemporary productions year-round. Touring music and dance companies also perform. The Keswick Music Society season runs from September through January, and the Words on the Water literary festival takes place in March.

SPORTS AND THE OUTDOORS

BIKING **Keswick Mountain Bike Centre** (✉ *Southey Hill* ☏ *017687/75202*) rents bikes and provides information on trails; it also stocks accessories and clothing. Guided tours can be arranged with advance notice.

WATER SPORTS **Derwentwater Marina** (✉ *Portinscale* ☏ *017687/72912*) offers boat rentals in all shapes and sizes, and instruction in canoeing, sailing, windsurfing, and rowing as well as in other water-related activities such as ghyll scrambling—the fine art of walking up a steep Lakeland stream. A two-day sailing or windsurfing course costs £175. The marina is open year-round but has shorter hours November through February.

SHOPPING

Keswick has a good choice of bookstores, crafts shops, and wool-clothing stores tucked away in its cobbled streets, as well as excellent outdoor shops. Keswick's **market** is held Saturday.

George Fisher (✉ *2 Borrowdale Rd.* ☏ *017687/72178*), the area's largest and best outdoor equipment store, sells sportswear, travel books, and maps. Daily weather information is posted in the window. **Needle Sports** (✉ *56 Main St.* ☏ *017687/72227*) supplies equipment for mountaineering and for rock and ice climbing. The **Northern Lights Gallery** (✉ *22 St. John's St.* ☏ *01768/775402*) carries a good selection of contemporary paintings, photography, sculpture, jewelry, and ceramics by around 80 local artists. **Thomasons** (✉ *8–10 Station St.* ☏ *017687/80169*), a butcher and delicatessen, sells some very good meat pies—just the thing for putting in your pocket before you climb a Lakeland fell.

EN ROUTE The most scenic route from Keswick, B5289 south, runs along the eastern edge of Derwentwater, past turnoffs to natural attractions such as Ashness Bridge, the idyllic tarn of Watendlath, the Lodore Falls (best in wet weather), and the precariously balanced Bowder Stone. Farther south is the tiny village of **Grange,** a walking center at the head of Borrowdale, where there's a riverside café.

BORROWDALE

Fodor'sChoice *7 mi south of Keswick.*

★ South of Keswick and its lake lies the valley of Borrowdale, whose varied landscape of green valley floor and surrounding crags has long been considered one of the region's most magnificent treasures. **Rosthwaite,** a tranquil farming village, and **Seatoller,** the southernmost settlement, are the two main centers (both are accessible by bus from Keswick), though they are little more than clusters of aged buildings surrounded by glorious countryside.

GETTING HERE AND AROUND
The valley is south of Keswick on B5289. The Borrowdale bus service between Keswick and Seatoller runs frequently.

EXPLORING
The steep **Borrowdale Fells** rise up dramatically behind Seatoller. Get out and walk whenever inspiration strikes. Trails are well signposted, or you can pick up maps and any gear in Keswick.

England's highest mountain, the 3,210-foot **Scafell Pike** (pronounced *scar*-fell) is visible from Seatoller. One route up the mountain, for experienced walkers, is from the hamlet of Seathwaite, a mile south of Seatoller.

WHERE TO STAY
££££ ⊡ **Hazel Bank Country House.** Hikers and others of a less energetic bent appreciate the comforts of this stately, carefully restored Victorian home, which retains original elements such as the stained-glass windows. Immaculate, spacious bedrooms are done in a faux-Victorian theme, and some have four-posters and window seats. All rooms, including the sitting area, have inspiring views across the carpetlike lawns to the Borrowdale Valley and the central Lakeland peaks. Four-course dinners in the restaurant (£30) focus on local ingredients prepared with Modern British flair. **Pros:** serene location; immaculate gardens; packed lunches made on request. **Cons:** some distance from a lake; not for families with younger children. ⊠ *Off B5289, Rosthwaite* ☎ *017687/77248* ⊕ *www.hazelbankhotel.co.uk* ⟋ *8 rooms, 1 cottage* ♨ *In-room: no a/c. In-hotel: restaurant, bar, Internet terminal, no kids under 12* ⊟ *MC, V* ⍓ *BP, MAP.*

££ ⊡ **The Langstrath Country Inn.** Set in the tranquil hamlet of Stonethwaite at the top of Borrowdale, the Langstrath was originally built as a miner's cottage in the 16th century but has expanded. A perfect base for walks, it has spacious, unfussy rooms (some with wood beams) with stunning views out to the surrounding countryside and hills. Food in the bar downstairs is sourced locally, and there are Cumbrian cask-conditioned beers and a well-chosen wine list. **Pros:** great walks right out the door and up the Langstrath Valley; wonderfully peaceful. **Cons:** little or no choice of other places to eat nearby. ⊠ *Stonethwaite* ☎ *017687/77239*

⊕ *www.thelangstrath.com* ⇆ *8 rooms* ⚐ *In-room: no a/c, no phone, Wi-Fi. In-hotel: restaurant, bar* ▤ *MC, V* ⊗ *Closed Mon. late Mar.–Oct. and Sun. night–Wed. Nov.–mid-Dec. and Jan.–late Mar.* ⍥ *BP.*

Beyond Seatoller, B5289 turns westward through **Honister Pass** (1,176 feet) and Buttermere Fell. Boulders line the road, which is one of the most dramatic in the region; at times it channels through soaring rock canyons. The road sweeps down from the pass to the village of Buttermere, sandwiched between Buttermere (the lake) and Crummock Water at the foot of high, craggy fells. Just beyond the pass toward Buttermere, Syke House Farm sells fantastic ice cream made from the milk of its Ayrshire herd.

COCKERMOUTH

14 mi northwest of Seatoller.

This small but bustling town, at the confluence of the rivers Derwent and Cocker, has a maze of narrow streets that are a delight to wander. It's a bit off the usual tourist path, and a bit bohemian. The ruined 13th-century castle is open only on special occasions. Cockermouth was one of the places most affected in the Lake District floods of 2009, but conditions are generally back to normal.

GETTING HERE AND AROUND

The most straightforward access to the town is along the busy A66 from Penrith. For a more scenic, roundabout route, head over the Whinlatter or Honister passes from Keswick.

ESSENTIALS

Visitor Information Cockermouth (✉ *The Town Hall, Market St.* ☎ *01900/822634*).

EXPLORING

At **Jennings Brewery,** you can learn how real ales are made on a tour that includes the history of the company and allows you to see inside the huge fermentation casks, which hold up to 150 barrels of beer. It finishes up in the bar for some tastes of the finished product. There are one or two tours a day (more in summer), but no Sunday tours November through February. ✉ *Castle Brewery* ☎ *0845/129–7190* ⊕ *www.jenningsbrewery.co.uk* ⌑ *£6 tour* ⊗ *Shop Sept.–June, weekdays 9–5, Sat. 10–4; July and Aug., weekdays 9–5, weekends 10–4.*

From late June through July, the **Cockermouth Summer Festival** (⊕ *www.cockermouth.org.uk*) presents art, music, and theater in town.

Cockermouth was the birthplace of William Wordsworth (and his sister Dorothy), whose childhood home, **Wordsworth House**, is an 18th-century town house. The restored house looks close to what the poet would have known. You see it complete with clutter, costumed interpreters, and period cooking in the kitchen. Live harpsichord recitals take place regularly. Wordsworth's father is buried in the All Saints' churchyard, and the church has a stained-glass window in memory of the poet. ✉ *Main St.* ☎ *01900/824805* ⊕ *www.nationaltrust.org.uk* ⌑ *£6.20* ⊗ *Mid-Mar.–Oct., Sat.–Wed. and some Thurs. 11–5; last admission at 4.*

★ **Castlegate House Gallery,** one of the region's best galleries, displays and sells an outstanding collection of works, many by Cumbrian artists. Changing exhibitions focus on paintings, sculpture, glass, ceramics, and jewelry. ⊠ *Castlegate* ☎ *01900/822149* ⊕ *www.castlegatehouse. co.uk* ⊙ *Mar.–Dec., Fri., Sat., and Mon. 10:30–5.*

WHERE TO EAT AND STAY

££ ✕ **Bitter End.** Flocked floral wallpaper, old lamps, an open fire, and a
BRITISH handsome wooden floor set the tone at this appealing pub attached to Cumbria's smallest brewery, whose beers it sells. In contrast to big brother Jennings nearby, this outfit is homey and intimate, serving big, tasty portions of traditional British food such as lamb cobbler and fish-and-chips. ⊠ *15 Kirkgate* ☎ *01900/828993* ⊕ *www.bitterend.co.uk* ▤ *MC, V.*

£££ ✕ **Quince & Medlar.** Sophisticated and imaginative vegetarian cuisine,
VEGETARIAN served by candlelight, is the specialty at this refined, wood-paneled
★ Georgian town house. Diners are offered a drink in the sitting room before being called to their table; you choose from at least six main courses, such as smoked Cumberland cheese and mushroom roulade, all served with seasonal vegetables. Desserts are delicious, especially the lemon-and-almond sponge. ⊠ *13 Castlegate* ☎ *01900/823579* ⊕ *www. quinceandmedlar.co.uk* ▤ *MC, V* ⊙ *Closed Sun. and Mon. No lunch.*

£ ⊞ **Six Castlegate.** After a day of exploring, relax in stylish accommodation in an elegant B&B in a Grade 2–listed (considered to be of special architectural or historic interest) Georgian town house. The spacious rooms, named after local mountains, are decorated in pale, natural tones and have good views, generous showers, and big, comfortable beds. Breakfasts entice with local ingredients. You can use the pool and parking lot at the nearby leisure center. **Pros:** modern facilities and antique style blend nicely; near galleries and attractions; exceptional value for money. **Cons:** some road noise in some rooms. ⊠ *6 Castlegate* ☎ *01900/826786* ⊕ *www.sixcastlegate.co.uk* ⤳ *6 rooms* ⌂ *In-room: no a/c, DVD (some), Wi-Fi. In-hotel: Wi-Fi* ▤ *MC, V* ⦿ *BP.*

East Anglia

CAMBRIDGE, BURY ST. EDMUNDS, NORWICH, LINCOLN

WORD OF MOUTH

"Try and visit King's College Chapel in Cambridge; it's only open at certain times. We were there on a Sunday morning and heard the choir singing. The sun shining through the stained glass and the whole atmosphere of the massive church was amazing."

—KayF

"What about going to East Anglia? You would need a car, but Suffolk has villages just as chocolate-box pretty as the Cotswolds. It is Constable country, after all. Lavenham is unique. Norfolk has Norwich and several picturesque seaside villages."

—MissPrism

Updated by
Jack Jewers

One of those beautiful English inconsistencies, East Anglia
has no spectacular mountains or rivers to disturb the storied, quiet land, full of rural delights. Occupying an area of
southeastern England that bulges out into the North Sea, its
counties of Essex, Norfolk, Suffolk, Lincolnshire, and Cambridgeshire feel cut off from the central routes and pulse of
the country.

In times past, East Anglia was one of the most important centers of
power in Northern Europe. The towns of Colchester and Lincoln were
major Roman settlements, and the medieval wool trade brought huge
prosperity to the higgledy-piggledy streets of tiny Lavenham. Thanks
to its relative lack of thoroughfares and canals, however, East Anglia
was mercifully untouched by the Industrial Revolution. The area is
rich in idyllic, quintessentially English villages: sleepy, sylvan settlements in the midst of otherwise deserted lowlands. Even the towns
feel small and manageable; the biggest city, Norwich, has a population
of just 125,000. Cambridge, with its ancient university, is the area's
most famous draw. East Anglia also boasts four of the country's greatest stately homes: Holkham Hall, Blickling Hall, Houghton Hall, and
Sandringham—where the Queen spends Christmas. There are incomparable cathedrals, at Ely and Lincoln particularly, and one of the finest
Gothic buildings in Europe, King's College Chapel.

And yet, despite all of these treasures, the real joy of exploring East
Anglia is making your own discoveries. Spend a couple of days exploring the hidden byways of the Fens, or just taking in the subtle beauties
of the many England-like-it-looks-in-the-movies villages. If you find
yourself driving down a small country lane and an old church or mysterious, ivy-covered ruin peeks out from behind the trees, give in to your
curiosity and look inside. Such hidden places are East Anglia's best-kept
secret. There are real treasures to be found within those walls.

ORIENTATION AND PLANNING

GETTING ORIENTED

For purposes of sightseeing, East Anglia can be divided into distinct
areas: the central area surrounding the ancient university city of Cambridge and including Ely, with its magnificent cathedral rising out of
the flatlands, and the towns of inland Suffolk; the southeast, taking
in the ancient Roman town of Colchester and sweeping upward along
the Suffolk Heritage Coast; and the northeast, with the region's capital, Norwich, the waterways of the Broads, and the beaches and salt
marshes of the North Norfolk coast. Farther north, in Lincolnshire, are

12

TOP REASONS TO GO

Cambridge: A walk though the colleges is grand, but the best views of the university's colleges and immaculate lawns (and some famous bridges) are from a punt on the river. Try not to let your pole get stuck in the mud.

Constable country: In the area where Constable grew up, you can walk or row downstream from the pastel-shaded village of Dedham straight into the setting of one of the English landscape painter's masterpieces at Flatford Mill.

Grand houses: When the Queen's not in residence, you can visit the Royal Family's holiday home of Sandringham. If that's out of bounds, other options, including Holkham Hall and Burghley House, are just as spectacular.

Lincoln's old center: The ancient center of the city has a vast, soaring cathedral, a proper rampart-ringed castle, and winding medieval streets lined with small shops, restaurants, and cafés.

Wild North Sea coast: North Norfolk has enormous sandy beaches (great for walking) and opportunities to see seals and birdlife, especially on the salt marshes around Blakeney.

Lavenham: This medieval town is the most comely of the tight-knit cluster of places that did well from the wool trade: nearby are Sudbury and Long Melford. All have perhaps the region's most memorable architecture, including timber-frame houses gnarled into crookedness by age.

the city of Lincoln, landmarked by its tall, fluted cathedral towers, and the historic town of Stamford.

Cambridge. The home of the famous university may be East Anglia's liveliest town, but it's also refreshingly free of noise and traffic. The city center is perfect for ambling around the ancient colleges, museums, and King's College Chapel, one of England's greatest monuments.

Ely to Bury St. Edmunds. The villages within a short drive of Cambridge remain largely unspoiled. Ely's lofty cathedral dominates the surrounding flatlands, and Sudbury, Long Melford, Lavenham, and Bury St. Edmunds preserve their rich historical flavor.

Colchester and the Suffolk Coast. North of Colchester, with its Roman and Norman remains, and Dedham, the center of Constable Country, the Suffolk Coast includes such atmospheric seaside towns as Woodbridge and Aldeburgh.

Norwich to North Norfolk. Sights in Norwich include its soaring cathedral and sturdy castle. To the north and west you'll find the stately homes of Blickling Hall, Houghton Hall, and Sandringham and a string of quiet coastal resorts such as Blakeney and Wells-next-the-Sea.

Stamford and Lincoln. On the western fringes of East Anglia, Lincoln is worth visiting for its Norman cathedral, whereas Stamford is best known for Burghley House, an impressive Elizabethan mansion.

PLANNING

WHEN TO GO

Summer and late spring are the best times to visit East Anglia. Late fall and winter can be cold, windy, and rainy, though this is England's driest region and crisp, frosty days here are beautiful. To escape crowds, avoid the popular Norfolk Broads in late July and August. The Aldeburgh Festival of Music and the Arts, one of the biggest events on the British classical music calendar, takes place in June.

PLANNING YOUR TIME

Cambridge is the region's most interesting city, and you should allow two or three days to absorb its various sights. You could easily use the city as a base for exploring Ely, Bury St. Edmunds, Lavenham, Long Melford, and Sudbury, although you will also find accommodations in these towns. The Suffolk Coast offers enticing overnight stops in such small towns as Dedham and Aldeburgh. In the northern part of the region, Norwich makes a good place to stop for the night, and has enough sights to keep you interested for a day. If you're here to see the coast, you'd do better staying in villages such as Blakeney or Wells. Allow a full day for seeing large houses such as Blickling Hall, near Norwich, and Burghley House, outside Stamford. Lincoln, notable for its cathedral, and Stamford are west and north of Norfolk if you want to work them into an itinerary.

GETTING HERE AND AROUND

AIR TRAVEL

Norwich International Airport serves a limited number of domestic and international destinations, though not the United States. The vast majority of travelers to the region, however, arrive by train, car, or bus.

Airport Norwich International Airport (✉ *Amsterdam Way, A140, Norwich* ☏ *0844/748-0112* ⊕ *www.norwichinternational.com*).

BUS TRAVEL

National Express buses serve the region from London's Victoria Coach Station. Average travel times are three hours to Cambridge, two hours (with one transfer) to Colchester, 2½ hours to Bury St. Edmunds, five hours (with one transfer) to Norwich, and four hours to Lincoln.

Long-distance buses are useful for reaching the region and traveling between its major centers, but for smaller hops, local buses are best. Local First and Stagecoach buses cover the Cambridge, Lincolnshire, and Norwich areas. Information about local Norfolk service and county service is available from the Norfolk Bus Information Centre. Traveline can answer public transportation questions.

A FirstDay ticket from First for a day's unlimited bus travel around Norwich and the Norfolk coast costs £12 for a single or £25 for two adults and two children. A FirstWeek pass, good for seven days, costs £27 (no family version available). There are also various local passes that cost between £2 and £16.

Bus Contacts First (☏ *0845/602-0121* ⊕ *www.firstgroup.com*). **National Express** (☏ *0845/600-7245* ⊕ *www.nationalexpresseastanglia.com*). **Norfolk**

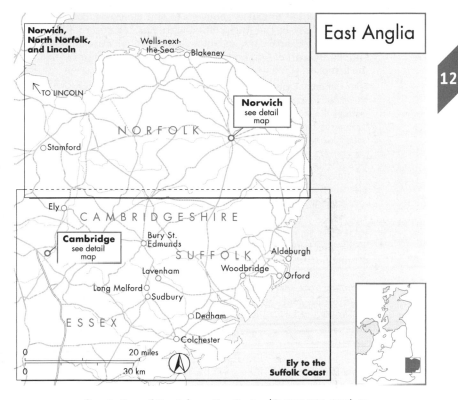

East Anglia

Norwich, North Norfolk, and Lincoln

Wells-next-the-Sea — Blakeney

TO LINCOLN

Norwich
see detail map

N O R F O L K

Stamford

Ely

C A M B R I D G E S H I R E

Cambridge
see detail map

Bury St. Edmunds

S U F F O L K

Aldeburgh

Lavenham

Woodbridge

Orford

Long Melford
Sudbury

E S S E X

Dedham

Colchester

0 — 20 miles
0 — 30 km

Ely to the
Suffolk Coast

12

County Council Bus Information Centre (☎ 0845/300–6116). **Stage-coach** (☎ 01223/423578 ⊕ www.stagecoachbus.com/cambridge). **Traveline** (☎ 0871/200–2233 ⊕ www.traveline.org.uk).

CAR TRAVEL

If you're driving from London, Cambridge (54 mi) is off M11. At Exit 9, M11 connects with A11 to Norwich (114 mi); A14 off A11 goes to Bury St. Edmunds. A12 from London goes through east Suffolk via Colchester and Ipswich. For Lincoln (131 mi), take A1 via Huntingdon, Peterborough, and Grantham to A46 at Newark-on-Trent. A more scenic alternative is to leave A1 at Grantham and take A607 to Lincoln.

East Anglia has few fast main roads besides those mentioned above. Once off the A roads, traveling within the region often means taking country lanes that have many twists and turns, and going even just a few miles can take much longer than you think.

TRAIN TRAVEL

The entire region is well served by trains from London's Liverpool Street, King's Cross, and St. Pancras stations. The quality and convenience of these services varies enormously, however. Cambridge trains leave from King's Cross and Liverpool Street, take around one hour, and cost just under £20. On the other hand, getting to Lincoln from St. Pancras entails at least two transfers, takes two to three hours, and costs around £55 to £80. A good way to save money on local trains in East Anglia is to buy an Anglia Plus Ranger Pass. It costs £13.50 for one day or £27 for three days, and allows unlimited rail travel in Norfolk, Suffolk, and part of Cambridgeshire. National Rail Enquiries should be the first place you try for timetable and fare information.

Train Contacts East Midlands Trains (☎ 0845/712–5678 ⊕ www.east-midlandstrains.co.uk). **First Capital Connect** (☎ 0845/026–4700 ⊕ www. firstcapitalconnect.co.uk). **National Express** (☎ 0845/600–7245 ⊕ www.nation-alexpresseastanglia.com). **National Rail Enquiries** (☎ 0845/748–4950 ⊕ www. nationalrail.co.uk).

RESTAURANTS
In summer the coast gets so packed with people that reservations are essential at restaurants. Getting something to eat at other than regular mealtime hours is not always possible in small towns; look for cafés if you want a mid-morning or after-lunch snack.

HOTELS
The region is full of centuries-old, half-timber inns with rooms full of roaring fires and cozy bars. Bed-and-breakfasts are a good option in pricey Cambridge. It's always busy in Cambridge and along the coast in summer, so reserve well in advance.

WHAT IT COSTS IN POUNDS				
	£	££	£££	££££	£££££
Restaurants	under £10	£10–£14	£15–£19	£20–£25	over £25
Hotels	under £70	£70–£120	£121–£160	£161–£220	over £220

Restaurant prices are for a main course at dinner. Hotel prices are for two people in a standard double room in high season, including V.A.T., with no meals or, if indicated, CP (with Continental breakfast), BP (Breakfast Plan, with full breakfast), or MAP (Modified American Plan, with breakfast and dinner).

VISITOR INFORMATION
Broads Authority (✉ Dragonfly House, 2 Gilders Way, Norwich ☎ 01603/610734 ⊕ www.broads-authority.gov.uk). **East of England Tourism** (✉ Dettingen House, Dettingen Way, Bury St. Edmunds ☎ 01284/727470 ⊕ www. visiteastofengland.com).

CAMBRIDGE

With the spires of its university buildings framed by towering trees and expansive meadows, its medieval streets and passages enhanced by gardens and riverbanks, the city of Cambridge is among the loveliest in England. The city predates the Roman occupation of Britain, but there's confusion over exactly how the university was founded. The most widely accepted story is that it was established in 1209 by a pair of scholars from Oxford, who left their university in protest over the wrongful execution of a colleague for murder.

Today Cambridge embodies a certain genteel, intellectual, and sometimes anachronistically idealized image of Englishness. Think William Wordsworth, Thackeray, Byron, Tennyson, E. M. Forster, and C. S. Lewis. The exquisite King's College choir defines the traditional English Christmas, when the *Festival of Nine Lessons and Carols* is broadcast live on Christmas Eve. On top of all this tradition and history, Cambridge remains a lively city and an extraordinary center of learning and research where innovation and discovery still happen behind its ancient walls.

Keep in mind there is no recognizable campus: the scattered colleges *are* the university. The town reveals itself only slowly, filled with tiny gardens, ancient courtyards, imposing classic buildings, alleyways that lead past medieval churches, and wisteria-hung facades. Perhaps the best views are from the Backs, the green parkland that extends along the River Cam behind several colleges. This sweeping openness, a result of the larger size of the colleges and from the lack of industrialization in the city center, is what distinguishes Cambridge from Oxford.

GETTING HERE AND AROUND

Good bus (three hours) and train (one hour) services connect London and Cambridge. The train station is a mile or so southeast of the center and is connected by the frequent Citi 3 bus service, run by Stagecoach, to Emmanuel Street, which is just around the corner from the long-distance bus terminus on Drummer Street. If you're driving, don't attempt to venture very far into the center—parking is scarce and pricey. The center is amenable to explorations on foot, or you could join the throng by renting a bicycle.

Stagecoach sells Dayrider (£3.50) tickets for all-day bus travel within Cambridge, and Megarider tickets (£11) for seven days of travel within the city. You can extend these to cover the whole county for a few extra pounds.

City Sightseeing operates open-top bus tours of Cambridge—the Backs, the colleges, the Imperial War Museum in Duxford, and the Grafton shopping center. Tours can be joined at marked bus stops in the city. Tickets are £12. Also ask the tourist office about tours.

TIMING

During the summer and over the Easter and Christmas holidays, Cambridge is devoid of students, its heart and soul. To see the city in full swing, visit from October through June. In summer there are arts and music festivals, notably the Strawberry Fair and the Arts Festival (both June) and the Folk Festival (late July to early August). The May Bumps, intercollegiate boat races, are, confusingly, held the first week of June. This is also the month when students celebrate the end of exam season, so expect to encounter some boisterous nightlife.

ESSENTIALS

Bus Contacts First (☎ 0845/602–0121 ⊕ www.firstgroup.com). **Stagecoach** (☎ 01223/423578 ⊕ www.stagecoachbus.com/cambridge).

Visitor and Tour Information Cambridge (✉ Wheeler St. ☎ 0871/226–8006, 44/1223/464732 from abroad ⊕ www.visitcambridge.org). **Cambridge**

University (☏ 01223/337733 ⊕ www.cam.ac.uk). **City Sightseeing** (✉ Cambridge train station, Station Rd. ☏ 01223/423578 ⊕ www.city-sightseeing.com).

EXPLORING

Exploring the city means, in large part, exploring the university. Each of the 25 oldest colleges is built around a series of courts, or quadrangles, framing manicured, velvety lawns. Because students and fellows (faculty) live and work in these courts, access is sometimes restricted, (and at *all* times you are asked not to picnic in the quadrangles.

Visitors are not normally allowed into college buildings other than chapels, dining halls, and some libraries; some colleges charge admission for certain buildings. The university's Web site (⊕ *www.cam.ac.uk*) has information about the colleges and related institutions. Public visiting hours vary from college to college, depending on the time of year, and it's best to call or to check with the city tourist office. Colleges close to visitors during the main exam time, late May to mid-June. Term time (when classes are in session) means roughly October to December, January to March, and April to June; summer term, or vacation, runs from July to September.

■TIP➜ **When the colleges are open, the best way to gain access is to join a walking tour led by an official Blue Badge guide—many areas are off-limits unless you do.** The two-hour tours (£11) leave up to four times daily from the city tourist office. The other traditional view of the colleges is gained from a punt—the boats propelled by pole on the River Cam.

TOP ATTRACTIONS

OFF THE BEATEN PATH

★ **Audley End House and Gardens.** A famous example of early-17th-century architecture, Audley End was once owned by Charles II, who bought it as a convenient place to break his journey on the way to the Newmarket races. Although the palatial building was remodeled in the 18th and 19th centuries, the Jacobean style is still on display in the magnificent Great Hall. You can walk in the park, landscaped by Capability Brown in the 18th century, and the fine Victorian gardens. Two newer exhibits focus on the lives of domestic servants in the late 19th century. The Service Wing lets you look "below stairs" at the kitchen, scullery (where fish were descaled and chickens were plucked) game larder (where pheasants, partridges, and rabbits were hung), while the Stables give kids the chance to see old saddles and tack and don Victorian riding costumes. The house is in Saffron Waldon, 14 mi south of Cambridge. ✉ B1383 ☏ 01799/522842 ⊕ *www.english-heritage.org. uk* ⚐ *£11.90, gardens and Service Wing exhibit only £8.30* ⊙ *House: Apr.–Sept., Wed.–Fri. and Sun., 11–5, Sat. 11–2:30; Oct., Wed.–Sun. 11–4. Gardens and Service Wing: Apr.–Sept., Wed.–Sun.10–6; Oct., 10–5; Nov.–late Dec. and early Feb., weekends 10–4; late Feb., Wed.– Sun. 10–4; Mar., Wed.–Sun. 10–5.*

❷ **Christ's College.** To see the way a college has grown over the centuries you could not do better than visit here. The main gateway bears the enormous coat of arms of its patroness, Lady Margaret Beaufort, mother of Henry VII, who established the institution in 1505. It leads into a fine

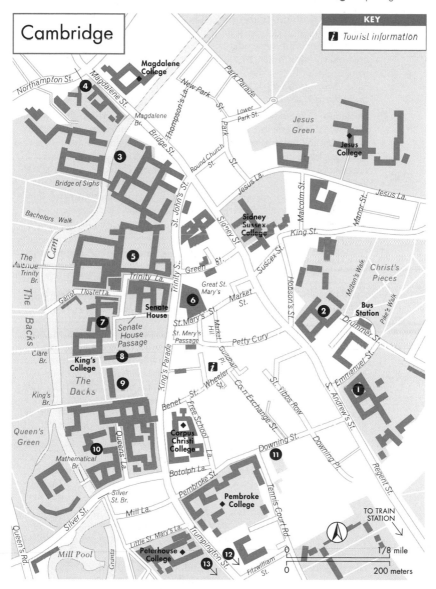

Cambridge

KEY

i Tourist information

12

courtyard, with the chapel framed by an ancient magnolia. In the dining hall hang portraits of John Milton and Charles Darwin, two of the college's more famous students. You next walk past a fellows' building credited to Inigo Jones, to the spacious garden (once the haunt of Milton), and finally to a modern ziggurat-like confection from the 1960s. ☎ *St. Andrew's St.* ☎ *01223/334900* ⊕ *www.christs.cam.ac.uk* ⊙ *Term time, daily 9:30–dusk; out of term, daily 9:30–noon.*

❶ **Emmanuel College.** The master hand of architect Christopher Wren (1632–1723) is evident throughout much of Cambridge, particularly at Emmanuel, built on the site of a Dominican friary, where he designed the chapel and colonnade. A stained-glass window in the chapel has a likeness of John Harvard, founder of Harvard University, who studied here. The college, founded in 1584, was an early center of Puritan learning; a number of the Pilgrims were Emmanuel alumni, and they remembered their alma mater in naming Cambridge, Massachusetts. ✉ *St. Andrew's St.* ☎ *01223/334200* ⊕ *www.emma.cam.ac.uk* ⊙ *Daily 9–6, except exam period.*

❸ **Fitzwilliam Museum.** In a Classical Revival building renowned for its grand Corinthian portico, the Fitzwilliam, founded by the seventh viscount Fitzwilliam of Merrion in 1816, has one of Britain's most outstanding collections of art and antiquities. Highlights include two large Titians, an extensive collection of French Impressionist painting, and many paintings by Matisse and Picasso. The opulent interior displays its treasures to marvelous effect, from Egyptian pieces such as inch-high figurines and painted coffins to sculptures from the Chinese Han dynasty of the 3rd century BC. Besides its archaeological collections, the Fitzwilliam contains English Staffordshire and other pottery, as well as a fascinating room of armor and muskets. Guided tours beginning at 2:30 PM on Saturday cost £3.50; you can buy tickets that day or in advance from the Tourism Office. ✉ *Trumpington St.* ☎ *01223/332900* ⊕ *www. fitzmuseum.cam.ac.uk* ✐ *Free* ⊙ *Tues.–Sat. 10–5, Sun. noon–5.*

FodorśChoice
★

❻ **Great St. Mary's.** Known as the "university church," Great St. Mary's has its origins in the 11th century, although the current building dates from 1478. The main reason to visit is to climb the 113-foot tower, which has a superb view over the colleges and marketplace. Also here is the **Michaelhouse Centre**, a small café, gallery, and performing arts venue, where free lunchtime concerts are occasionally held. ✉ *Market Hill, King's Parade* ☎ *01223/741716* ⊕ *www.gsm.cam.ac.uk* ✐ *Free, tower £2.50* ⊙ *May–Aug., Mon.–Sat. 9:30–5, Sun. 12:30–5; Sept.–Apr., Mon.–Sat. 9:30–4, Sun. 12:30–4.*

**OFF THE
BEATEN
PATH**

Imperial War Museum Duxford. The buildings and grounds of this former airfield, now Europe's leading aviation museum, house a remarkable collection of 180 aircraft from Europe and the United States. It's effectively a complex of several museums under one banner, and the ticket price covers admission to everything, save for occasional special events. The **Land Warfare Hall** features tanks and other military vehicles. The **American Air Museum**, housed in a striking Norman Foster–designed building, honors the 30,000 Americans who were killed in action flying from Britain during World War II. It contains the largest display of

12

American fighter planes outside the United States. (Duxford itself was the headquarters of the American 78th Fighter Group.) **AirSpace** contains a vast array of military and civil aircraft in a 3-acre hangar. Directly underneath is the **Airborne Assault Museum,** which chronicles the history of airborne forces, such as the British Parachute Regiment, which played a pivotal role in the Normandy Landings. There are also hangars where you can watch restoration work on World War II planes and exhibitions on maritime warfare and the Battle of Britain. On a handful of dates every summer and fall, the Imperial War Museum holds very popular air shows, some featuring historic war-

> **A GIFT FOR SCIENCE**
>
> For centuries Cambridge has been among the country's greatest universities, rivaled only by Oxford. Since the time of its most famous alumnus, Sir Isaac Newton, it has outshone Oxford in the natural sciences. The university has taken advantage of this prestige, sharing its research facilities with high-tech industries. Surrounded by technology companies, Cambridge has been dubbed "Silicon Fen," a comparison to California's Silicon Valley. The prosperity brought by these businesses is evident around the city.

planes. Check in advance for dates and ticket prices. ☒ *A505, Duxford* ☎ *01223/835000* ⊕ *duxford.iwm.org.uk* ☒ *£16.50* ☉ *Mid-Mar.–mid-Oct., daily 10–6; late Oct.–mid-Mar., daily 10–4. Last admission 1 hr before closing.*

⑨ King's College. Founded in 1441 by Henry VI, King's College's most famous landmark is its late-15th-century chapel. Other architecture of note is the neo-Gothic Porters' Lodge, facing King's Parade, which was a relatively recent addition in the 1830s, and the classical Gibbs building. ■ ❘❘P➔ **Follow the college's Back Lawn down to the river, from where the panorama of college and chapel is one of the university's most photographed views.** Past students of King's College include the novelist E. M. Forster, the economist John Maynard Keynes, and the World War I poet Rupert Brooke. ☒ *King's Parade* ☎ *01223/331100* ⊕ *www.kings. cam.ac.uk* ☒ *£5, includes chapel* ☉ *Term time, weekdays 9:30–3:30, Sat. 9:30–3:15, Sun. 1:15–2:15; out of term, Mon.–Sat. 9:30–4:30, Sun. 10–5.*

⑧ King's College Chapel. Based on Sainte-Chapelle, the 13th-century royal chapel in Paris, this house of worship is the final, perhaps most glorious flowering of Perpendicular Gothic in Britain. Henry VI, the king after whom the college is named, oversaw the work. This was the last period before the classical architecture of the ancient Greeks and Romans, then being rediscovered by the Italians, began to make its influence felt in Northern Europe. From the outside, the most prominent features are the massive flying buttresses and the fingerlike spires that line the length of the building. Inside, the most obvious impression is of great space—the chapel has been described as "the noblest barn in Europe"—and of light flooding in from its huge windows. The brilliantly colored bosses (carved panels at the intersections of the roof ribs) are particularly intense, although hard to see without binoculars. An exhibition in the chantries, or side chapels, explains more about

Fodor's Choice
★

the chapel's construction. Behind the altar is *The Adoration of the Magi,* an enormous painting by Peter Paul Rubens. Every Christmas Eve a festival of carols sung by the chapel's famous choir is broadcast worldwide from here. A small number of tickets to this service are available for the general public, but competition is fierce. To try your luck, join the line at the college's main front entrance early—doors open at 7 AM. ⊠ *King's Parade* ☎ *01223/331212* ⊕ *www.kings.cam.ac.uk* ✉ *£5, includes college and grounds* ☉ *Term time, weekdays 9:30–3:30, Sat. 9:30–3:15, Sun. 1:15–2:15; out of term, Mon.–Sat. 9:30–4:30, Sun. 10–5; hrs vary, so call ahead.*

▌**QUICK BITES** The 600-year-old **Pickerel Inn** (⊠ *30 Magdalene St.* ☎ *01223/355068*), one of the city's oldest pubs, makes for a good stop for a soothing afternoon pint of real ale or lager and a bowl of potato wedges. Watch for the low beams.

🔟 **Queens' College.** One of the most eye-catching colleges is Queens', named after Margaret, queen of Henry VI, and Elizabeth, queen of Edward IV. Founded in 1448, the college is tucked away on Queens' Lane, next to the wide lawns that lead down from King's College to the Backs. The secluded "cloister court" looks untouched since its completion in the 1540s. Queens' masterpiece is the **Mathematical Bridge,** the original version of which is said to have been built without any fastenings. The current bridge (1902) is securely bolted. ⊠ *Queens' La.* ☎ *01223/335511* ⊕ *www.quns.cam.ac.uk* ✉ *£2.50* ☉ *Mid-Mar.–mid-May, daily 10–4:30; June–early Oct., daily 10–4:30; early Oct.–late Oct., weekdays 2–4, weekends 10–4:30; Nov.–mid-Mar., daily 2–4.*

3 **St. John's College.** Two mythical beasts called "yales," with the bodies of antelopes and heads of goats, hold up the coat of arms and guard the gateway of Cambridge's second-largest college. St. John's was founded in 1511 by Henry VII's mother, Lady Margaret Beaufort. Its structures lie on two sites: from the main entrance, walk to the left through the courts to the 1831 **"Bridge of Sighs,"** whose only resemblance to its Venetian counterpart is its covering. The windowed, covered stone bridge reaches across the Cam to the mock-Gothic New Court (1825), nicknamed "the wedding cake." If you walk through to the riverbank, you can stroll along the Backs and photograph the elegant bridge. ⊠ *St. John's St.* ☎ *01223/338600* ⊕ *www.joh.cam.ac.uk* ✉ *£3* ☉ *Mar.–Oct., daily 10–5:30; Nov.–Feb., weekends only, hrs vary.*

5 **Trinity College.** Founded in 1546 by Henry VIII, Trinity replaced a 14th-century educational foundation and is the largest college in either Cambridge or Oxford, with nearly 700 undergraduates. Many of the buildings match its size, not least its 17th-century "great court." Here the massive gatehouse holds "Great Tom," a giant clock that strikes each hour with high and low notes. The college's greatest masterpiece is Christopher Wren's **library,** colonnaded and seemingly constructed with as much light as stone. Here you can see A. A. Milne's handwritten manuscript of *The House at Pooh Corner.* Alumni include Sir Isaac Newton, William Thackeray, Lords George Byron, Alfred Tennyson, Thomas Macaulay, and 31 Nobel Prize winners. ⊠ *St. John's*

CAMBRIDGE'S ARCHITECTURAL DETAILS

Cambridge is made up of 31 separate colleges, many of them with historic and beautiful buildings. Here are some with features that architecture buffs won't want to miss.

Founded in 1352, the beautiful and serene **Corpus Christi College is the longest** continuously inhabited college quadrangle in Cambridge (☎ *King's Parade* ☎ *01223/338000* ⊕ *www.corpus.cam.ac.uk).*

Jesus College (☎ *Jesus La.* ☎ *01223/339339* ⊕ *www.jesus.cam. ac.uk*) incorporates the old cloisters from the nunnery of St. Radegund, which existed before the college was founded in 1496. The Victorian restoration of the adjacent chapel building includes some Pre-Raphaelite stained-glass windows and ceiling designs by William Morris.

Magdalene College (☎ *Magdalene St.* ☎ *01223/332100* ⊕ *www.magd. cam.ac.uk*), confusingly pronounced

"*maud*-lin," was a lodging for Benedictine monks for more than 100 years before the college was founded in 1542. In the second court, the college's Pepys Library contains the books and desk of the famed 17th-century diarist Samuel Pepys.

Pembroke College (☎ *Trumpington St.* ☎ *01223/338100* ⊕ *www. pem.cam.ac.uk*) has some buildings dating from the 14th century in its first court, next to which Christopher Wren's chapel—his first major commission, completed in 1665—looks like a distinctly modern intrusion by comparison.

Peterhouse College (☎ *Trumpington St.* ☎ *01223/338200* ⊕ *www.pet. cam.ac.uk*) is the university's oldest college. Parts of the dining hall date from 1290, although the hall is most notable for powerful, 19th-century stained glass by William Morris and his contemporaries.

12

St. ☎ *01223/338400* ⊕ *www.trin.cam.ac.uk* ✉ *£1* ☉ *College and chapel daily 10–4, except exam period and event days; library weekdays noon–2, Sat. in term time 10:30–12:30; hall weekdays 3–5, except during services and rehearsals.*

WORTH NOTING

❹ **Kettle's Yard.** Originally a private house owned by a former curator of London's Tate galleries, Kettle's Yard contains a fine collection of 20th-century art, sculpture, furniture, and decorative arts, including works by Henry Moore, Barbara Hepworth, and Henri Gaudier-Brzeska. One gallery shows changing exhibitions of modern art and crafts, and weekly concerts and lectures attract an eclectic mix of enthusiasts. Ring the bell for admission. ✉ *Castle St.* ☎ *01223/748100* ⊕ *www.kettlesyard.co.uk* ✉ *Free* ☉ *House early Apr.–Sept., Tues.–Sun. 1:30–4:30; Oct.–early Apr., Tues.–Sun. 2–4. Gallery Tues.–Sun. 11:30–5.*

⓫ **Museum of Archaeology and Anthropology.** The university maintains some fine museums in its research halls on Downing Street—the wonder is that they are not better known to visitors. Geological collections at the Sedgwick Museum and the exhibits at the Zoological Museum are extensive, but be sure to see the Museum of Archaeology and Anthropology, which houses a superb collection of ethnographic objects brought back by early explorers, including members of Captain Cook's pioneering voyages to the Pacific. At this writing, the archaeological galleries were undergoing major renovation work. They were slated to reopen at the end of 2010, but call ahead to make sure. ✉ *Downing St.* ☎ *01223/333516* ⊕ *maa.cam.ac.uk* 🎫 *Free* 🕙 *Tues.–Sat. 10:30–4:30.*

❼ Trinity Hall. The green parkland of the Backs is best appreciated from Trinity's 14th-century neighboring college, Trinity Hall, where you can sit on a wall by the river and watch students in punts maneuver under the ancient ornamental bridges of Clare and King's. Access to the river is down Trinity Lane, off Trinity Street. The **Senate House** (✉ *King's Parade*), which stands between Clare College and Trinity Hall, is not part of a particular college. A classical building of the 1720s, it's used for graduation ceremonies and other events. There is no official public access, but if the gate is open, you can wander into the court. ✉ *Trinity La.* ☎ *01223/332500* ⊕ *www.trinhall.cam.ac.uk* 🕙 *Daily 9:15–noon and 2–5:30, except exam period and summer term.*

⓬ University Botanic Gardens. Laid out in 1846, these gardens contain rare specimens, conservatories, and a rock garden. They are a five-minute walk from the Fitzwilliam Museum. ✉ *Cory Lodge, Bateman St.* ☎ *01223/336265* ⊕ *www.botanic.cam.ac.uk* 🎫 *£4* 🕙 *Feb., Mar., and Oct., daily 10–5; Apr.–Sept., daily 10–6; Nov.–Jan., daily 10–4. Conservatories close ½ hr before gardens.*

WHERE TO EAT

££   ✗ **Fitzbillies.** Usually filled with visiting parents, Fitzbillies is rightly
CAFÉ   famous for its exceptionally sticky Chelsea buns (a sweet bun flavored with currants, lemon peel, and spices). If you don't want to sit down, the bakery next door has the same range of pastries to take away. It also serves filling and tasty lunches, and more formal evening meals, with dishes such as lamb noisettes (small, round boneless cuts) and sirloin steak. ✉ *52 Trumpington St.* ☎ *01223/352500* ⊕ *www.fitzbillies.co.uk* 🖃 *AE, MC, V* 🕙 *No dinner Sun.*

££   ✗ **Loch Fyne.** Part of a midsize Scottish chain that harvests oysters and
SEAFOOD   runs seafood restaurants, this airy, casual place across the street from the Fitzwilliam Museum is open for breakfast, lunch, and dinner. The oysters and other seafood are deservedly popular—mussels and salmon are fresh and well prepared, and line-caught tuna is served with a mint-and-caper salsa. ✉ *37 Trumpington St.* ☎ *01223/362433* ⊕ *www. lochfyne.com* 🖃 *AE, MC, V.*

£££££   ✗ **Midsummer House.** An elegant restaurant beside the River Cam on the
FRENCH   edge of Midsummer Common, this gray-brick building has a comfort-
★   able conservatory and a handful of tables in a lush secluded garden under fruit trees. Fixed-price menus for lunch and dinner offer innovative French and Mediterranean dishes. Choices might include braised turbot or roast venison. ✉ *Midsummer Common* ☎ *01223/369299* ⊕ *www.midsummerhouse.co.uk* ⚑ *Reservations essential* 🖃 *AE, MC, V* 🕙 *Closed Sun. and Mon. No lunch Tues.*

EATING WELL IN EAST ANGLIA

Farmland and the rivers and sea provide ample bounty for the table in East Anglia. Look for area specialties, such as duckling, Norfolk black turkey, hare, and partridge, on menus around the region. In Norwich, there's no escaping the hot, bright-yellow Colman's mustard, which is perfect smeared gingerly on some sausage and mash. A traditional cure for sore feet involves soaking them hot water mixed with a few teaspoons of powdered mustard. Among the culinary treats from the sea is samphire, a delicious plant that grows in the salt marshes along the North Norfolk and Suffolk coasts. The long coastline also provides tasty Cromer crabs and Yarmouth bloaters (a kind of smoked herring), whereas the Essex coast near Colchester has been producing oysters since Roman times. Brancaster and Stiffkey mussels, Sheringham lobster, and Thornham oysters are all seafood highlights worth indulging in while visiting North Norfolk. Eel, a delicacy in the Fens, is served smoked or jellied. Maldon sea salt is another famous local product. Sample fresh fish-and-chips on the Suffolk coast, especially in Aldeburgh, where local creations have gained national recognition.

For liquid refreshment, Adnams, Greene King, and Tolly Cobbold are major ale producers, and a pint of Suffolk cider is usually a good accompaniment to the local food. There's an equally venerable, though lesser know, tradition of wine making in the region. The Romans first introduced vines to Britain, and they took especially well here. Today East Anglia has more than 40 vineyards; check wine lists in local restaurants.

12

££ ╳**The Oak.** This charming, intimate restaurant has fast become a local
BRITISH favorite. The location near a busy intersection is unpromising, but the friendliness of the staff and classic bistro food more than make up for it. Typical mains could include smoked haddock with bubble and squeak (a traditional dish made of fried potatoes and onion), or rib-eye steak with fries. Ask to be seated in the lovely walled garden if the weather's fine. ⊠ *6 Lensfield Rd.* ☎ *01223/323361* ⊕ *www.theoakbistro.co.uk* ⊟ *AE, MC, V.*

£££££ ╳**Restaurant 22.** Pretty stained-glass windows separate this sophisticated
BRITISH little restaurant from the busy Chesterton Road. The setting, in a terrace of houses, is low-key, but the food is creative and eye-catching. The fixed-price menu changes monthly and features dishes such as sea bass fillet with lemony roast potatoes, or pork belly with black pudding. ⊠ *22 Chesterton Rd.* ☎ *01223/351880* ⊕ *www.restaurant22. co.uk* ⊟ *AE, MC, V* ⊘ *Closed Sun. and Mon. No lunch.*

££ ╳**River Bar & Kitchen.** Fashionable and stylish, this waterfront eatery
MODERN BRITISH designed by Terence Conran focuses on contemporary food with the occasional Eastern influence, such as spicy lamb samosas with mint-and-cucumber dip and Moroccan tagine. Light lunches are served between noon and 3, and cocktails are what most people come in for in the evening. Dinner service begins at 6:30. ⊠ *Quayside, off Bridge St.* ☎ *01223/307030* ⊕ *www.riverbarkitchen.com* ⚓ *Reservations essential* ⊟ *AE, MC, V* ⊘ *Closed Sun and Mon. (except bank holidays).*

£££   ✕ **Three Horseshoes.** This early-19th-century pub-restaurant in a thatched
ITALIAN   cottage has an elegant dining space in the conservatory, and more infor-
★   mal tables in the airy bar area. The tempting, beautifully presented,
and carefully sourced dishes are modern Italian with a British slant.
Appetizers include lentil soup with dried mushrooms, and among the
main courses is a tasty *fritto misto di mare* (mixed seafood platter).
The wine list is enormous and predominantly Italian, but there are also
some good New World choices. It's 5 mi west of Cambridge, about a
10-minute taxi ride. ⊠ *High St., Madingley* ☎ *01954/210221* ⊕ *www.*
threehorseshoesmadingley.co.uk ▤ *MC, V.*

WHERE TO STAY

There aren't many hotels downtown. For more (and cheaper) options,
consider one of the numerous guesthouses on the arterial roads and in
the suburbs. These average around £30 to £70 per person per night and
can be booked through the tourist information center.

££   ⛳ **Ashley Hotel.** This small establishment near the center of Cambridge
was converted from two adjacent Victorian houses. The bedrooms
won't win any interior design prizes, but they are a good value. Take
advantage of the restaurant and bar at the nearby Arundel House Hotel
at 53 Chesterton Road, where you check in. **Pros:** cheerful staff; free
parking. **Cons:** tiny bathrooms; plain rooms; off-site check-in. ⊠ *74*
Chesterton Rd. ☎ *01223/350059* ⊕ *www.arundelhousehotels.co.uk/*
ashleyhotel.html ⇆ *16 rooms* ⚐ *In-room: no a/c. In-hotel: parking*
(free) ▤ *AE, DC, MC, V* ⦿I *BP.*

£   ⛳ **Cityroomz.** Very much a bargain-basement option, this motel-like
lodging outside the train station has small bedrooms with wood floors,
white walls, and futon beds. Most double rooms have bunk beds. The
sparsely furnished spaces are for those who want a cheap, clean place
to sleep. **Pros:** helpful staff. **Cons:** minuscule rooms; can be noisy;
reserved parking very limited. ⊠ *Station Rd.* ☎ *01223/304050* ⊕ *www.*
cityroomz.com ⇆ *25 rooms* ⚐ *In-room: no a/c, no phone. In-hotel:*
parking (free) ▤ *MC, V* ⦿I *CP.*

££–£££   ⛳ **De Vere University Arms Hotel.** The 19th-century De Vere is well placed
in the city center, with comfortable, traditionally furnished guest rooms.
Many have views of Parker's Piece, the green backing the hotel, although
you pay slightly more for these; Parker's Bar also overlooks the greenery.
The lounge serves afternoon tea by the fireplace. You can use a nearby
swimming pool and a health club 2 mi away. **Pros:** good location; tasty
food; some rooms have Playstations. **Cons:** small rooms; needs refurbishment. ⊠ *Regent St.* ☎ *01223/351241* ⊕ *www.devere-hotels.com*
⇆ *117 rooms, 2 suites* ⚐ *In-room: safe, Internet. In-hotel: restaurant,*
room service, bars, Wi-Fi hotspot, parking (paid), some pets allowed
▤ *AE, DC, MC, V.*

££££–£££££   ⛳ **Doubletree by Hilton.** Many of the rooms have views of the water at this
modern establishment that makes the most of its peaceful riverside location. The gardens, conservatories, and bar also overlook the Cam. The
hotel is set among the colleges on 3 acres of private grounds. Although
the architecture exhibits a brutal use of concrete, the rooms are more

12

stylish. Ask about lower-price packages. **Pros:** very central position; good facilities; spacious rooms. **Cons:** occasionally poor service; disappointing breakfasts. ⊠ *Granta Pl. and Mill La.* ☎ *01223/259988* ⊕ *www.doubletreebyhilton.co.uk* ↪ *118 rooms, 4 suites* ⚹ *In-room: no a/c (some), refrigerator, Wi-Fi. In-hotel: restaurant, room service, bar, pool, gym, parking (paid)* ⊟ *AE, MC, V.*

££–£££ ⌦ **Duxford Lodge.** A short drive from the Imperial War Museum in Duxford, this family-run hotel sits off the main road between Cambridge and Saffron Walden. Bedrooms are spacious and individually designed, with warm tones of pink or buttermilk. Summer is the best time to stay here, as the ground-floor rooms open out directly onto the lovely, well-maintained garden. Some rooms also have four-poster beds. Le Paradis serves excellent modern European cuisine. **Pros:** feels off the beaten path; good food. **Cons:** need a car to get around; prices go up air show weekends. ⊠ *Ickleton Rd., Duxford* ☎ *01223/836444* ⊕ *www. duxfordlodgehotel.co.uk* ↪ *11 rooms* ⚹ *In-room: no a/c (some), Wi-Fi. In-hotel: restaurant* ⊟ *MC, V.*

££££–£££££ ⌦ **Hotel Felix.** This contemporary hotel has spacious bedrooms with stylish modern furnishings in neutral colors. The main part of the building is a converted Victorian mansion; today it contains some bedrooms as well as the sophisticated Graffiti restaurant and bar, serving Mediterranean food. You can use a health club and spa in the center of the city. **Pros:** up-to-the-minute furnishings; quiet location; easy to reach from motorway. **Cons:** impersonal feel; spotty service; can be noisy; 3 mi from center. ⊠ *Whitehouse La., off Huntingdon Rd.* ☎ *01223/277977* ⊕ *www.hotelfelix.co.uk* ↪ *52 rooms* ⚹ *In-room: no a/c, safe, refrigerator, Wi-Fi. In-hotel: restaurant, room service, bar, laundry service, parking (free), some pets allowed* ⊟ *AE, MC, V* ⎮◎⎮ *CP.*

££–£££ ⌦ **Regent Hotel.** A rare smaller hotel in downtown Cambridge, this handsome Georgian town house looks across Parker's Piece, a tree-lined park, through wooden sash windows. The cozy licensed bar has an open fire; bedrooms are a little more anonymous but are decorated in pale modern tones, and all have bathtubs. **Pros:** good view from top rooms; close to bars and restaurants. **Cons:** no parking; a tad scruffy; disappointing breakfasts. ⊠ *41 Regent St.* ☎ *01223/351470* ⊕ *www. regenthotel.co.uk* ↪ *22 rooms* ⚹ *In-room: a/c, Wi-Fi. In-hotel: bar* ⊟ *AE, DC, MC, V.*

NIGHTLIFE AND THE ARTS

NIGHTLIFE

The city's pubs provide the mainstay of Cambridge's nightlife and shouldn't be missed. The **Eagle** (⊠ *8 Benet St.* ☎ *01223/505020*), first among equals, is a 16th-century coaching inn with several bars and a cobbled courtyard that's lost none of its old-time character. It's extremely busy on weekends. **Fort St. George** (⊠ *Midsummer Common* ☎ *01223/354327*), which overlooks the university boathouses, gets the honors for riverside views. The **Free Press** (⊠ *7 Prospect Row* ☎ *01223/368337*) is a small, mobile phone–free pub, attracting a student rowing clientele.

THE ARTS

CONCERTS Cambridge supports its own symphony orchestra, and regular musical events are held in many colleges, especially those with large chapels. During regular terms, **King's College Chapel** (☎ *01223/331212*) has even-song services Monday through Saturday at 5:30, Sunday at 3:30. The **Corn Exchange** (✉ *Wheeler St.* ☎ *01223/357851*), beautifully restored, presents concerts (classical and rock), stand-up comedy, musicals, opera, and ballet.

The **Cambridge Folk Festival** (☎ *01223/357851* ⊕ *www.cambridge-folkfestival.co.uk*), spread over a weekend in late July or early August at Cherry Hinton Hall, attracts major international folk singers and groups.

THEATER The **ADC Theatre** (✉ *Park St.* ☎ *01223/300085* ⊕ *www.adctheatre. com*) hosts mainly student and fringe theater productions, including the famous Cambridge Footlights revue, training ground for much comic talent since the 1960s. The **Arts Theatre** (✉ *6 St. Edward's Passage* ☎ *01223/503333* ⊕ *www.cambridgeartstheatre.com*), the city's main repertory theater, was built by economist John Maynard Keynes in 1936 and supports a full program of plays and concerts. It also has a good ground-floor bar and two restaurants.

SPORTS AND THE OUTDOORS

BIKING

It's fun to explore by bike. **City Cycle Hire** (✉ *61 Newnham Rd.* ☎ *01223/365629*) charges super-cheap rates of £10 per day and £20 for a week. Advance reservations are essential in July and August.

PUNTING

You can rent punts at several places, notably at Silver Street Bridge–Mill Lane, at Magdalene Bridge, and from outside the Rat and Parrot pub on Thompson's Lane on Jesus Green. Hourly rental costs £15 to £20. Chauffeured punting on the River Cam is also possible at most rental places. Around £12 per head is the usual rate, and your chauffeur will likely be a Cambridge student. **Scudamore's Punting Co.** (✉ *Mill La. and Quayside* ☎ *01223/359750* ⊕ *www.scudamores.com*) rents chauffeured and self-drive punts. It also offers various tour packages, ranging from a punt-and-walk **Ghost Tour** for £17.50 to a more extravagant **Evening Champagne Punt Tour** for £225.

SHOPPING

Cambridge is a main shopping area for a wide region, and it has all the usual chain stores, many in the Grafton Centre and Lion's Yard shopping precincts. More interesting are the specialty shops found among the colleges in the center of Cambridge, especially in and around Rose Crescent and King's Parade. Bookshops, including antiquarian stores, are Cambridge's pride and joy.

All Saints Garden Art & Craft Market (✉ *Trinity St.* ⊕ *www.cambridge-art-craft.co.uk*) displays the wares of local artists outdoors on Saturday. It's also open Friday from June to August and Wednesday to Friday

Punting on the Cam

To punt is to maneuver a flat-bottom, wooden, gondolalike boat—in this case, through the shallow River Cam along the verdant Backs behind the colleges of Cambridge. One benefit of this popular activity is that you get a better view of the ivy-covered walls from the water. Mastery of the sport lies in your ability to control a 15-foot pole, used to propel the punt. With a bottle of wine, some food, and a few friends, you may find yourself saying things such as, "It doesn't get any better than this." One piece of advice: if your pole gets stuck, let go. You can use the smaller paddle to go back and retrieve it. Hang on to a stuck punt for too long and you'll probably fall in with it.

The lazier-at-heart may prefer chauffeured punting, with food supplied. Students from Cambridge often do the work, and you get a fairly informative spiel on the colleges. For a romantic evening trip, there are illuminated punts.

One university punting society once published a useful "Bluffer's Guide to Punting" featuring detailed instructions and tips on how to master the art. It can be found online at ⊕ *duramecho.com/Misc/HowToPunt.html.*

12

in December (weather permitting). **Ryder & Amies** (✉ *22 King's Parade* ☎ *01223/350371* ⊕ *www.ryderamies.co.uk*) carries official university wear and even straw boaters.

BOOKS **Cambridge University Press bookshop** (✉ *1 Trinity St.* ☎ *01223/333333* ⊕ *www.cambridge.org/uk/bookshop*) stands on one of the oldest bookstore sites in Britain; books have been sold here since at least 1581. Three-story **Galloway & Porter** (✉ *30 Sidney St.* ☎ *01223/367876* ⊕ *www.gallowayandporter.co.uk*) has an extensive collection of new and secondhand books. **G. David** (✉ *16 St. Edward's Passage* ☎ *01223/354619*), near the Arts Theatre, sells antiquarian books. The **Haunted Bookshop** (✉ *9 St. Edward's Passage* ☎ *01223/312913* ⊕ *www.sarahkeybooks.co.uk*) carries a great selection of old, illustrated books and British classics. **Heffer's** (✉ *20 Trinity St.* ☎ *01223/568568* ⊕ *bookshop.blackwell.co.uk*) stocks many rare and imported books, and boasts a particularly extensive arts section.

ELY TO BURY ST. EDMUNDS

This central area of towns and villages within easy reach of Cambridge is testament to the amazing changeability of the English landscape. The town of Ely is set in an eerie, flat, and apparently endless fenland, or marsh. Only a few miles south and east into Suffolk, however, all this changes to pastoral landscapes of gently undulating hills, and clusters of villages including pretty Sudbury and Lavenham.

ELY

16 mi north of Cambridge.

Known for its magnificent cathedral, Ely is the "capital" of the fens, the center of what used to be a separate county called the Isle of Ely (literally "island of eels"). Until the land was drained in the 17th century, Ely was surrounded by treacherous marshland, which inhabitants crossed wearing stilts. Today Wicken Fen, a nature reserve 9 mi southeast of town (off A1123), preserves the sole remaining example of fenland in an undrained state.

Enveloped by fields of wheat, sugar beets, and carrots, Ely is a small, dense town that fails to live up to the high expectations created by its big attraction, its cathedral. The shopping area and market square lie to the north and lead down to the riverside, and the medieval buildings of the cathedral grounds and the King's School (which trains cathedral choristers) spread out to the south and west. Ely's most famous resident was Oliver Cromwell, whose house is now a museum.

GETTING HERE AND AROUND
The 9 and X9 buses leave twice an hour from the Drummer Street bus station in Cambridge. The journey to Ely takes about 45 minutes. To drive there from Cambridge, simply take the A10 road going north out of the city. Ely is quite small, so find somewhere to park and walk to the center. Trains from Cambridge to Ely leave three times an hour and take 15 minutes.

ESSENTIALS
Visitor Information Ely (✉ *Oliver Cromwell's House, 29 St. Mary's St.* ☎ *01353/662062* ⊕ *visitely.eastcambs.gov.uk*).

EXPLORING
★ Known affectionately as the Ship of the Fens, **Ely Cathedral** can be seen for miles, towering above the flat landscape on one of the few ridges in the fens. In 1083 the Normans began work on the cathedral, which stands on the site of a Benedictine monastery founded by the Anglo-Saxon princess Etheldreda in 673. In the center of the cathedral you see a marvel of medieval construction—the unique octagonal **Lantern Tower**, a sort of stained-glass skylight of colossal proportions, built to replace the central tower that collapsed in 1322. Tours of the tower are daily between April and October and on weekends between November and March. The cathedral is also notable for its 248-foot-long **nave**, with its simple Norman arches and Victorian painted ceiling. Much of the decorative carving of the 14th-century **Lady Chapel** was defaced during the Reformation (mostly by knocking off the heads of the statuary), but enough traces remain to show its original beauty. The fan-vaulted, carved ceiling remains intact, as it was too high for the iconoclasts to reach. Guided tours begin daily at 10:45, 1, and 2, with an additional tour at 3 on weekends and also weekdays between April and October. ■**TIP→ Always call ahead about tours, as they are run by volunteers and subject to change.** The cathedral houses a superior **Stained Glass Museum** (☎ *01353/660347* ⊕ *www.stainedglassmuseum. com* ▣ *£3.50* ☉ *Easter–Oct., weekdays 10:30–5, Sat. 10:30–5:30,*

Sun. noon–6; Nov.–Easter, Mon.–Sat. 10:30–5, Sun. noon–4:30), up a flight of 12 steps. Exhibits trace the history of stained glass from medieval to modern times. ⊠ *The Gallery* ☎ *01353/667735* ⊕ *www.cathedral.ely.anglican.org* ▭ *£6, free on Sun. Tower tours £4, £6 on Sun. Tower tour and Stained Glass Museum £8* ⊙ *May–Oct., daily 7–7; Nov.–Apr., Mon.–Sat. 7:30–6, Sun. 7:30–5.*

Oliver Cromwell's House, a half-timber medieval building, stands in the shadows of Ely Cathedral. During the 10 years he lived here, Cromwell was leading the rebellious Roundheads in their eventually victorious struggle against King Charles I in the English Civil War. The house contains an exhibit about its former occupant. It's also the site of Ely's tourist information center. ⊠ *29 St. Mary's St.* ☎ *01353/662062* ▭ *£4.40* ⊙ *Apr.–Oct., daily 10–5; Nov.–Mar., weekdays 11–4, Sat. 10–5, Sun. 11–4.*

> ## DRAINING EAST ANGLIA
>
> Large areas of East Anglia were originally barely inhabited, swampy marshes. Drainage of the wetlands by the creation of waterways was carried out most energetically in the 17th and 18th centuries. The process was far from smooth. Locals, whose fishing rights were threatened, sometimes destroyed the work. Also, as the marshland dried out, it shrank and sank, requiring pumps to stop renewed flooding. Hundreds of windmills were used to pump water away; some of them can still be seen today.

WHERE TO EAT AND STAY

£££
BRITISH
★
✕ **Old Fire Engine House.** Scrubbed pine tables fill the main dining room of this converted fire station near the cathedral. Another room, used only for overflow, has an open fireplace and a polished wood floor, and also serves as an art gallery. Among the English dishes are traditional fenland recipes such as pike baked in white wine, as well as eel pie and game in season. Desserts include syllabub, a traditional dish made from cream, sugar, and wine. ⊠ *25 St. Mary's St.* ☎ *01353/662582* ⊕ *www.theoldfireenginehouse.co.uk* ▭ *MC, V* ⊙ *Closed 2 wks at Christmas. No dinner Sun.*

££
▦ **Cathedral House.** Run by Jenny and Robin Farndale, this Georgian house makes a pleasant overnight stop in Ely. The cozy bedrooms have antique furniture and coffeemakers, and an oriel window and handsome staircase are original features. In the back is a walled garden filled with flowers. **Pros:** heaps of character; steps from the cathedral; free parking. **Cons:** small bathrooms; on a busy road. ⊠ *17 St. Mary's St.* ☎ *01353/662124* ⊕ *www.cathedralhouse.co.uk* ↝ *3 rooms, 1 cottage* ⚲ *In-room: no a/c. In-hotel: parking (free)* ▭ *No credit cards* ⏉ *BP.*

SUDBURY

32 mi southeast of Ely, 16 mi south of Bury St. Edmunds, 14 mi northwest of Colchester.

An early silk-weaving industry (still in existence, on a smaller scale) as well as the wool trade brought prosperity to Sudbury, which has three fine Perpendicular Gothic churches and some half-timber houses.

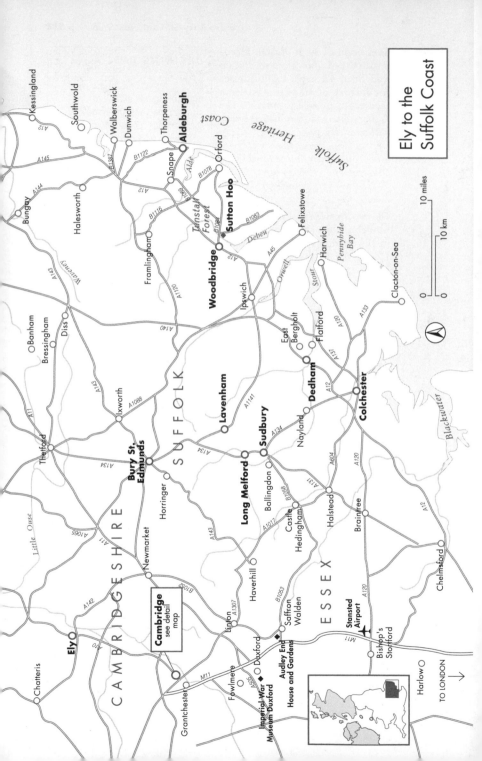

Ely to the
Suffolk Coast

10 miles

10 km

Suffolk Heritage Coast

Kessingland
Southwold
Walberswick
Dunwich
Thorpeness
Aldeburgh
Orford
Snape
Bungay
Halesworth
Framlingham
Woodbridge
Sutton Hoo
Tunstall Forest
Felixstowe
Harwich
Pennyhide Bay
Clacton-on-Sea
Banham
Bressingham
Diss
Ixworth
Lavenham
Ipswich
East Bergholt
Flatford
Dedham
Thetford
Bury St. Edmunds
Horringer
Long Melford
Sudbury
Nayland
Colchester
Ballingdon
Castle Hedingham
Halstead
Braintree
Chelmsford
Newmarket
Haverhill
Saffron Walden
Stansted Airport
Bishop's Stortford
Harlow
Ely
Chatteris
Linton
Duxford
Imperial War Museum Duxford
Audley End House and Gardens
Fowlmere
Grantchester
Cambridge
see detail map

SUFFOLK
ESSEX
CAMBRIDGESHIRE

Little Ouse
Blackwater
Alde
Deben
Orwell
Stour
Waveney

TO LONDON

A12 A140 A143 A134 A1088 A11 A142 M11 A120 A133 A137 A131 A604 A130 A1017 B1058 B1063 A1307 A1120 A1094 A1078 A1083 B1084 B1069 B1116 B1122 B1387 A145 A144 A146 A47

Today this town of 20,000 is the largest in this part of the Stour Valley. In Charles Dickens's first novel, *The Pickwick Papers*, Sudbury was the model for the fictional Eatanswill, where Mr. Pickwick stands for Parliament.

ESSENTIALS

Visitor Information Sudbury (✉ *Town Hall, Market Hill* ☎ *01787/881320* ⊕ *www.southandheartofsuffolk.org.uk*).

EXPLORING

Thomas Gainsborough, one of the greatest English portrait and landscape painters, was born here in 1727; a **statue of Gainsborough** holding his palette stands on Market Hill.

The birthplace and family home of Thomas Gainsborough (1727–88), **Gainsborough's House**, contains many paintings and drawings by the artist and his contemporaries. Although it presents a Georgian facade, with touches of the 18th-century neo-Gothic style, the building is essentially Tudor. The walled garden has a mulberry tree planted in 1620 and a printmaking workshop. The entrance is through the café and shop on Weavers Lane. ✉ *46 Gainsborough St.* ☎ *01787/372958* ⊕ *www. gainsborough.org* ☞ *£4.50, free Tues. 1–5* ☉ *Mon.–Sat. 10–5.*

LONG MELFORD

2 mi north of Sudbury, 14 mi south of Bury St. Edmunds.

It's easy to see how this village got its name, especially if you walk the full length of its 2-mi-long main street, which gradually broadens to include green squares and trees and finally opens into the large triangular green on the hill. Long Melford grew rich on its wool trade in the 15th century, and the town's buildings are an appealing mix, mostly Tudor half-timber or Georgian. Many house antiques shops. Away from the main road, Long Melford returns to its resolutely late-medieval roots.

GETTING HERE AND AROUND

Long Melford is just off the main A134. If you're driving from Sudbury, take the smaller B1064; it's much quicker than it looks on the map. There are several bus connections with Sudbury, Bury St. Edmonds, Colchester, and Ipswich. The nearest train station is in Sudbury.

EXPLORING

The largely 15th-century **Holy Trinity Church**, founded by the rich clothiers of Long Melford, stands on a hill at the north end of the village. Close up, the delicate flint flush-work (shaped flints set into a pattern) and huge Perpendicular Gothic windows that take up most of the church's walls have great impact, especially because the nave is 150 feet long. The Clopton Chapel, with an ornate ceiling, predates the rest of the church by 150 years. The beautiful Lady Chapel has an unusual cloister; the stone on the wall in the corner is an ancient multiplication table, used when the chapel served as a school in the 17th and 18th centuries. ✉ *Main St.* ☎ *01787/310845* ⊕ *www.stedmundsbury.anglican.org/ longmelford* ☉ *Apr.–Oct., daily 10–6; Nov.–Mar., daily 10–5.*

Melford Hall, distinguished from the outside by its turrets and topiaries, is an Elizabethan house with its original banqueting hall, a fair number of 18th-century additions, and pleasant gardens. Much of the porcelain and other fine pieces here come from the *Santissima Trinidad,* a ship loaded with gifts from the emperor of China and bound for Spain that was captured by one of the house's owners in the 18th century. Children's writer Beatrix Potter, who was related to the owners, visited the house often; there's a small collection of Potter memorabilia. ⊠ *Off A134* ☏ *01787/376395* ⊕ *www.nationaltrust.org.uk* ⊡ *£6.30* ☉ *Early Apr., Wed.–Mon. 1:30–5; mid-Apr. and Oct., weekends 1:30–5; May–Sept., Wed.–Sun. 1:30–5.*

ⓒ   A wide moat surrounds **Kentwell Hall,** a redbrick Tudor manor house with tall chimneys and domed turrets. Built between 1520 and 1550, it was heavily restored inside after a fire in the early 19th century. On some weekends from mid-April through September, costumed "servants" and "farmworkers" perform reenactments of Tudor life or life during World War II. There's also an organic farm with rare-breed farm animals. The house is a half mile north of Long Melford Green. Call ahead, as hours sometimes vary—charming though it is, this place has a frustrating habit of not sticking to its advertised opening times. It's closed to the public in June. ⊠ *Off A134* ☏ *01787/310207* ⊕ *www. kentwell.co.uk* ⊡ *£9.40, £6.60 farm and garden only* ☉ *Late Mar.– mid-Apr. and mid-July–early Sept., daily 11–5; late Apr.–mid-May and early Sept.–late Sept., Sun.–Wed. 11–5; early June, Mon.–Wed. 11–5; call ahead for dates in Oct.*

WHERE TO STAY

££–£££   ⌦ **The Bull.** This half-timber Elizabethan building reveals its long history with stone-flagged floors, bowed and twisted oak beams, and heavy antique furniture. Creature comforts offset the smallish size of the bedrooms, which retain their original character—some are crooked, with sloping floors. The restaurant is very good. **Pros:** historic atmosphere; comfortable bedrooms; friendly staff. **Cons:** booked with wedding parties in summer. ⊠ *Hall St.* ☏ *01787/378494* ⊕ *www.thebull-hotel.com* ⇥ *25 rooms* ♿ *In-room: DVD, no a/c. In-hotel: restaurant, bar* ⊟ *AE, MC, V* ⦿ *MAP.*

LAVENHAM

4 mi northeast of Long Melford, 10 mi southeast of Bury St. Edmunds.

Virtually unchanged since the height of its wealth in the 15th and 16th centuries, Lavenham is one of the most perfectly preserved examples of a Tudor village in England. The weavers' and wool merchants' houses occupy not just one show street but most of the town. The houses are timber-frame in black oak, the main posts looking as if they could last another 400 years, though their walls are often no longer entirely perpendicular to the ground. The town has many examples of Suffolk pink buildings, in hues from pale pink to apricot, and many of these house small galleries selling paintings and crafts.

12

GETTING HERE AND AROUND

Lavenham is on the A1141 and B1071. Take the latter if possible, as it's a prettier drive. There are hourly buses from Sudbury and Bury St. Edmunds and slightly less frequent buses from Colchester and Ipswich. The nearest train station is in Sudbury.

ESSENTIALS

Visitor Information Lavenham (✉ *Lady St.* ☎ *01787/248207* ⊕ *www. southandheartofsuffolk.org.uk*).

EXPLORING

The grand 15th-century Perpendicular **Church of St. Peter and St. Paul** (✉ *Church St.* ☎ *01787/247244*), set apart from the village on a hill, was built with wool money by cloth merchant Thomas Spring between 1480 and 1520. The height of its tower (141 feet) was meant to surpass those of the neighboring churches—and perhaps to impress rival towns. The rest of the church is perfectly proportioned, with intricately carved wood.

The timber-frame **Guildhall of Corpus Christi** (1529) dominates Market Place, a square with barely a foot in the present. Upstairs is a rather dull exhibition on the Wool Trade, although looking around the building itself is worth the admission charge. ✉ *Market Pl.* ☎ *01787/247646* ⊕ *www.nationaltrust.org.uk* ⬚ *£4.30* ☉ *Early Mar.–late Mar., Wed.– Sun. 11–4; Apr.–early Nov., daily 11–5; early Nov.–late Nov., weekends 11–4.*

Little Hall, a timber-frame former wool merchant's house, shows the building's progress from its creation in the 14th century to its subsequent "modernization" through the 17th century and has a beautiful garden. ✉ *Market Pl.* ☎ *01787/247019* ⊕ *www.littlehall.org.uk* ⬚ *£3* ☉ *Easter–Oct., Wed., Thurs., and weekends 2–5:30, bank holidays 11–5:30.*

QUICK BITES

In a haphazardly leaning old house, the **Tickled Pink Tea Room** (✉ *17 High St.* ☎ *01787/248438*) serves fresh cakes and coffee as well as soup and sandwiches.

WHERE TO EAT

££££
CONTINENTAL
★

✕ **Great House.** The town's finest "restaurant with rooms" occupies a 15th-century building on the medieval market square. Run by Régis and Martine Crépy, the dining room serves European fare with a French touch. The five spacious bedrooms have sloping floors, beamed ceilings, well-appointed bathrooms, and antique furnishings. ✉ *Market Pl.* ☎ *01787/247431* ⊕ *www.greathouse.co.uk* ▭ *MC, V* ☉ *Closed Mon. and Jan. No dinner Sun. No lunch Tues.*

££
INDIAN
Fodor's Choice
★

✕ **Memsaab.** In a town ready to burst with cream teas, it's a bit of a surprise to find an Indian restaurant, let alone such an exceptional one. Among the classics one would expect from a curry house—from mild kormas to spicy madrasas and jalfrezies (traditional curries made with chili and tomato)—are some finely executed specialties, including Nizami chicken (a fiery dish prepared with yogurt and fresh ginger) and duck *bhujon* (a fusion dish made with orange and Madeira sauce). The menu also contains regional specialties from Goa and Hyderabad.

⊠ *2 Church St.* ☎ *01787/249431* ⊕ *www.memsaaboflavenham.co.uk* ⊟ *MC, V.*

WHERE TO STAY

£££ ⊡ **Guinea House.** Still a private home 600 years after it was built, Guinea House is a good option for travelers seeking something a little more authentic than your average B&B. Rooms have exceptionally comfortable beds and modern bathrooms. Bill and Gillian Delucy are warm hosts with an encyclopedic knowledge of the area, and are happy to help with planning day trips and booking restaurants for evening meals. Gillian's breakfasts are hearty and filling, although you have to be precise about when you want them. There's no obvious sign or number on the outside of Guinea House; it's the bright-pink building on the corner of Bolton Street and Lower Road. **Pros:** quiet central location; intimate feel; one-of-a-kind atmosphere. **Cons:** Hobbit-sized doorways; no common areas; credit card payment must be arranged in advance. ⊠ *16 Bolton St.* ☎ *01787/249046* ⊕ *www.guineahouse.co.uk* ➦ *2 rooms* ᕫ *In-room: no a/c, no phone* ⦿ *BP.*

£££–££££ ⊡ **Lavenham Priory.** You can immerse yourself in Lavenham's Tudor history at this luxurious B&B in a sprawling house that dates in part to the 13th century. The great hall, sitting room, and 3 acres of gardens are great places to relax, and a walled herb garden is the scene for evening drinks in warm weather. Prints and wood furnishings fill the bedrooms; each has oak floors and timber ceilings, and some have four-posters. **Pros:** historic ambience; charming rooms; lovely garden. **Cons:** sloping floors are difficult for those with mobility problems; no locks on room doors; service can be surly. ⊠ *Water St.* ☎ *01787/247404* ⊕ *www.lavenhampriory.co.uk* ➦ *5 rooms, 1 suite* ᕫ *In-room: no a/c, no phone, Wi-Fi. In-hotel: bar, Wi-Fi hotspot, no kids under 10* ⊟ *MC, V* ⦿ *BP.*

££££–£££££ ⊡ **Swan Hotel.** This half-timber 14th-century lodging has aging beams, rambling public rooms, and roaring fireplaces. Along corridors so low that cushions are strategically placed on beams, most of the individually styled bedrooms have rich oak cabinets and original wood paneling. Bathrooms have been fashioned around ancient timbers and hidden rooms. The bar, which is a popular local meeting place, is full of memorabilia from the days when this was a favorite pub of American airmen stationed here during World War II. One wall is entirely covered with autographs and messages from the vets who loved this place, while another is a memorial to those who didn't return home. **Pros:** lovely building; atmospheric rooms. **Cons:** indifferent service; creaky floors; steps to climb. ⊠ *High St.* ☎ *01787/247477* ⊕ *www. theswanatlavenham.co.uk* ➦ *47 rooms, 2 suites* ᕫ *In-room: no a/c, refrigerator, DVD, Internet. In-hotel: restaurant, bar, Wi-Fi hotspot, some pets allowed* ⊟ *AE, MC, V.*

BURY ST. EDMUNDS

★ *10 mi north of Lavenham, 28 mi east of Cambridge.*

The Georgian streetscape helps make the town one of the area's prettiest, and the nearby Greene King Westgate Brewery adds the smell of sweet hops to the air. Robert Adam designed the town hall in 1774.

Bury St. Edmunds owes its name, and indeed its existence, to Edmund, the last king of East Anglia and medieval patron saint of England, who was hacked to death by marauding Danes in 869. He was subsequently canonized, and his shrine attracted pilgrims, settlement, and commerce. In the 11th century the erection of a great Norman abbey (now only ruins) confirmed the town's importance as a religious center. The tourist office has a leaflet about the ruins and can arrange a guided tour.

GETTING HERE AND AROUND

The 11 bus from Cambridge's Drummer Street bus station takes about an hour to reach Bury St. Edmunds. By car, the town is a short drive from either Lavenham or Cambridge. Trains from Cambridge to Bury St. Edmunds leave once or twice an hour and take 40 minutes.

ESSENTIALS

Visitor Information Bury St. Edmunds (✉ *6 Angel Hill* ☎ *01284/764667* ⊕ *www.stedmundsbury.gov.uk*).

EXPLORING

A walk along **Angel Hill** is a journey through the history of Bury St. Edmunds. Along one side, the Abbey Gate, cathedral, Norman Gate Tower, and St. Mary's church make up a continuous display of medieval architecture. Elegant Georgian houses line Angel Hill on the side opposite St. Mary's Church; these include the Athenaeum, an 18th-century social and cultural meeting place that has a fine Adam-style ballroom.

Originally three churches stood within the walls of the Abbey of St. Edmunds, but only two have survived, including **St. Mary's**, built in the 15th century. It has a blue-and-gold embossed "wagon" (barrel-shape) roof over the choir. Mary Tudor, Henry VIII's sister and queen of France, is buried here. ✉ *Angel Hill at Honey Hill* ☎ *01284/754680* ⊕ *www.stmarystpeter.net* ۞ *Daily 10–4; call to confirm.*

St. Edmundsbury Cathedral dates from the 15th century, but the brilliant paint on its ceiling and the gleaming stained-glass windows are the result of 19th-century restoration by the architect Sir Gilbert Scott. Don't miss the memorial (near the altar) to an event in 1214, when the barons of England took an oath here to force King John to grant the Magna Carta. The cathedral's original Abbey Gate was destroyed in a riot, and it was rebuilt in the 14th century with defense in mind—you can see the arrow slits. Guided tours are available every day except Sunday during the summer months. There's no need to prebook. ■**TIP**➔ **After your visit, stop by the modest café filled with locals.** ✉ *Angel Hill* ☎ *01284/748726* ⊕ *www.stedscathedral.co.uk* ▨ *Free, suggested donation £3* ۞ *Daily 8:30–6.*

The **Abbey Ruins and Botanical Gardens** are all that remain of the Abbey of Bury St. Edmunds, which fell during Henry VIII's dissolution of the monasteries. The Benedictine abbey's enormous scale is evident in the surviving Norman Gate Tower on Angel Hill; besides this, only the fortified Abbot's Bridge over the River Lark and a few ruins remain.

> **A HALF-PINT PUB?**
>
> While you're in Bury St. Edmunds, pop in for a pint of the local Greene King ale at the **Nutshell** (⊠ 17 The Traverse ☎ 01284/764867), which claims to be Britain's smallest pub, measuring just 16 feet by 7½ feet.

There are explanatory plaques amid the ruins, which are now the site of the Abbey Botanical Gardens, with roses, elegant hedges, and rare trees, including a Chinese tree of heaven planted in the 1830s. There's also an aviary, a putting green, and a children's play area on-site. ⊠ *Angel Hill* ☲ *Free* ⊘ *Mon.–Sat. 7:30 AM–dusk, Sun. 9 AM–dusk.*

The 12th-century **Moyse's Hall**, probably the oldest building in East Anglia, is a rare surviving example of a Norman house. The rooms hold local history and archaeological collections. One macabre display relates to the Red Barn murder, a local case that gained notoriety in a 19th-century play. ⊠ *Cornhill* ☎ *01284/757160* ⊕ *www.stedmundsbury. gov.uk* ☲ *£3* ⊘ *Daily 10–5; last entry 4.*

WHERE TO EAT

£   ✕ **Harriet's Café Tearooms.** In an elegant dining room, Harriet's brings
CAFÉ   back the tearooms of yesteryear. Munch on a savory sandwich or have a full cream tea while listening to hits from the 1940s. ⊠ *57 Cornhill Bldgs.* ☎ *01284/756256* ⊕ *www.harrietscafetearooms.co.uk* ☰ *MC, V* ⊘ *No dinner.*

£££   ✕ **Maison Bleue.** This stylish French restaurant, with the same owners
FRENCH   as the Great House in nearby Lavenham, specializes in locally caught seafood and serves some tasty meat dishes, too. The seafood depends on the day's catch, but grilled sole and roast cod are always available, as are cheeses imported from Paris. ⊠ *31 Churchgate St.* ☎ *01284/760623* ⊕ *www.maisonbleue.co.uk* ⌕ *Reservations essential* ☰ *AE, MC, V* ⊘ *Closed Sun., Mon., Jan., and 2 wks in summer.*

WHERE TO STAY

£££££   ⌂ **Ickworth Hotel.** You can live like nobility in the east wing of the Itali-
⟳   anate Ickworth House, a National Trust property with 1,800 acres of
★   grounds 5 mi southwest of Bury St. Edmunds. (If it's too pricey, you can just visit the grounds and see the fine art in the west wing for £7.90.) The splendid public rooms have stylish 1950s and '60s furniture and striking modern art. This look extends to most bedrooms, though some still have luxe period furnishings. The rows of tiny wellies in the porch attest to the hotel's emphasis on being family-friendly. Children are catered to with a free day-care room (for kids under 6) and a game center. Adults can dine in the more formal Frederick's restaurant and the casual Conservatory Restaurant. **Pros:** gorgeous grounds; relaxed atmosphere; family-friendly vibe. **Cons:** inconsistent service; some rooms are small. ⊠ *Off A143, Horringer* ☎ *01284/735350* ⊕ *www.ickworthhotel.*

co.uk ☞ 24 rooms, 11 apartments ♿ In-room: no a/c, kitchen (some), DVD, Wi-Fi. In-hotel: 2 restaurants, room service, bar, tennis court, pool, spa, bicycles, laundry service, some pets allowed ☰ AE, DC, MC, V ⍢ BP.

£££ ☷ **Ounce House.** Small and friendly, this Victorian B&B has a great
★ deal of charm. Print fabrics and wooden furniture adorn the generous and stylish guest rooms. You can unwind in the antique-filled drawing room and library, and have a drink from the honor bar. The house is a three-minute walk from the abbey ruins. **Pros:** spotlessly clean; spacious and comfortable rooms; generous breakfasts. **Cons:** fussy decor; booked up far in advance. ✉ *Northgate St.* ☎ *01284/761779* ⊕ *www. ouncehouse.co.uk ☞ 4 rooms ♿ In-room: no a/c, Internet. In-hotel: bar ☰ AE, MC, V ⍢ BP.*

NIGHTLIFE AND THE ARTS

The **Theatre Royal**, which presents touring shows, was built in 1819 and is a perfect example of Regency design. Guided tours in spring and summer can be booked at the box office. ✉ *Westgate St.* ☎ *01284/769505* ⊕ *www.theatreroyal.org.*

COLCHESTER AND THE SUFFOLK COAST

Although nobody quite knows for certain, Colchester claims to be the oldest town on record in Britain. Whether it is really the oldest is open to argument, but its long history (dating back to the Iron Age) make Colchester well worth visiting. The town also serves as a traditional base for exploring Constable Country, that quintessentially English rural landscape on the borders of Suffolk and Essex made famous by the early-19th-century painter John Constable. This area runs north and west of Colchester along the valley of the River Stour.

The 40-mi Suffolk Heritage Coast, which wanders northward from Felixstowe up to Kessingland, is one of the most unspoiled shorelines in the country. The lower part of the coast is the most impressive; try to avoid the area between Lowestoft and Great Yarmouth, a region of run-down beach resorts.

COLCHESTER

59 mi northeast of London, 47 mi southeast of Cambridge, 68 mi south of Norwich.

Evidence of Colchester's four centuries of Roman history is visible everywhere in this ancient town. The Roman walls still stand, together with a Norman castle, a Victorian town hall, and Dutch-style houses built by refugee weavers from the Low Countries in the late 16th century. Archaeological research indicates a settlement at the head of the Colne estuary at least as early as 1100 BC. Two thousand years ago it was the domain of Cunobelin (Shakespeare's Cymbeline), who was king of the Catuvellauni. On Cunobelin's death, the Romans invaded in AD 43. The emperor Claudius made it the first Roman colony in Britain, renaming the town *Colonia Victricensis,* the Colony of Victory. The settlement was burned during the failed revolt in AD 60 by Boudicca, queen of the Iceni. The English Civil War saw further conflict in Colchester, as the city endured a three-month siege in 1648 before the Royalist forces surrendered. Colchester has always had a strategic importance and still has a military base; a tattoo (military spectacle) is held in even-numbered years.

GETTING HERE AND AROUND

Drivers should take the A12 from London or the A134 from Bury St. Edmunds. Of Colchester's two train stations, Colchester North, half a mile north of the center, is for trains from London. The bus station is more central. Most of the sights can be visited on foot.

The tourism office offers walking tours around Colchester; tickets are £3. From April through September and for a week in late October, City Sightseeing operates hour-long hop-on, hop-off bus tours of the town for £7.50. They depart from the castle.

QUEEN BOUDICCA

After King Prasutagus died around AD 60, his wife, Boudicca, became queen of the Iceni kingdom, which covered roughly the same area as modern-day Norfolk. Alas, the occupying Romans annexed Iceni. They flogged Boudicca and raped her daughters; in revenge the queen led an uprising, destroying first Roman Colchester, then London and St. Albans. By the time Boudicca met with the army of the Roman governor, Suetonius, her army outnumbered the occupiers. The queen, however, was defeated. With her flowing red hair and her chariot, the warrior queen has become something of a national symbol of Britain.

ESSENTIALS

Visitor and Tour Information City Sightseeing (☎ 01206/252472 ⊕ www. city-sightseeing.com). **Colchester** (✉ 1 Queen St. ☎ 01206/282920 ⊕ www. visitcolchester.com).

EXPLORING

Colchester was important enough for the Romans to build massive fortifications around it, and the **Roman Walls**, dating largely from the reign of Emperor Vespasian (AD 69–79), can still be seen, especially along Balkerne Hill (to the west of the town center), with its splendid Balkerne Gate.

Near the castle, the remains of a 3,000-seat **Roman amphitheater** (✉ Maidenburgh St.) are visible. The curve of the foundations is outlined in the paving stones of the roadway, and parts of the walls and floor have been preserved in a building, where they can be viewed alongside an image of how the amphitheater would have looked.

☯ The castle built by William the Conqueror between 1076 and 1125, reusing brick and tiles from the ruins of the Roman town, is today the superb **Colchester Castle Museum**. All that remains is the keep, the largest the Normans built. The castle was constructed over the foundations of the huge Roman Temple of Claudius, and in the vaults you can descend through 1,000 years of history. Among the items on show in the museum are the beautifully carved tombstones of Facilis and Longinus, two Roman soldiers. ✉ Castle Park ☎ 01206/282939

12

⊕ *www.colchestermuseums.org.uk* ⌦ *£5.70, guided tours £2* ⊙ *Mon.–Sat. 10–5, Sun. 11–5; last admission 4:30.*

The excellent interactive **Hollytrees Museum**, in a Georgian mansion near the castle, tells the story of the daily lives of local people. There are chances to create a silhouette portrait or play with Victorian toys, and there are occasional children's events, such as puppet making. ⊠ *Castle Park, High St.* ☎ *01206/282940* ⊕ *www.colchestermuseums.org.uk* ⌦ *Free* ⊙ *Mon.–Sat. 10–5, Sun. 11–5.*

The narrow medieval streets behind the Town Hall, off High Street, are called the **Dutch Quarter**, because refugee weavers from the Low Countries settled here in the 16th century, when Colchester was the center of a thriving cloth trade.

WHERE TO EAT

££
BRITISH

✕ **The Lemon Tree.** Jazz evenings in the cellar enhance the atmosphere at this popular restaurant. Well-presented dishes such as seared salmon or lamb shank with parsnip puree are served in a building that incorporates part of the original Roman city wall. Set-price lunches and dinners are good values. ⊠ *48 St. Johns St.* ☎ *01206/767337* ⊕ *www.the-lemon-tree.com* ⊟ *AE, MC, V* ⊙ *Closed Sun.*

DEDHAM

Fodor'sChoice
★

8 mi northeast of Colchester, off A12 on B1029.

Dedham is the heart of Constable Country. Here gentle hills and the cornfields of Dedham Vale, set under the district's delicate, pale skies, inspired John Constable (1776–1837) to paint some of his most celebrated canvases. He went to school in Dedham, a picture-book village that did well from the wool trade in the 15th and 16th centuries and has retained a well-off air ever since. The 15th-century church looms large over handsomely sturdy, pastel-color houses.

GETTING HERE AND AROUND

From main the A12, Dedham is easily reached by car via the B1029. Public transportation is extremely limited, but Constable Coaches runs the 87 bus a handful of times a day from Colchester (no service on Sunday). There is no nearby train station.

Bus Contacts Constable Coaches (☎ *01473/823243* ⊕ *www.constablecoachesltd.co.uk).*

EXPLORING

Two miles northeast of Dedham, off A12, the Constable trail continues in **East Bergholt**, where Constable was born in 1776. Most of the village is modern and rather unattractive, but if you arrive from Flatford Mill, you'll see the older part—including **St. Mary-the-Virgin** (⊠ *Flatford Rd.* ☎ *01206/298932* ⊙ *Daily; hrs vary but usually 10–5* ⌦ *Free*), one of the most remarkable churches in the region. It was painted by Constable, but that's least among the reasons that make it worth a visit. The church was started just before the Reformation; the doors underneath the ruined archways outside (remnants of a much older church) contain a coded message left by Catholic sympathizers of the time. The striking interior is full of little treasures, including an ancient wall painting of the Virgin Mary in one of the rear chapels, a 14th-century chest, and an extraordinary series of florid memorial stones on the nave wall opposite the main entrance.

From Dedham, on the banks of the River Stour, you can rent a rowboat from the **Boathouse Restaurant** (⊠ *Mill La.* ☏ *01206/323153* ⊕ *www.dedhamboathouse.com* ⌨ *£12 per hr* ☉ *Easter–Sept., daily 10–5*). It's an idyllic way to travel the 2 mi downriver to **Flatford**, where you can see Flatford Mill, one of the two water mills owned by Constable's father.

> **CONSTABLE'S FAME**
>
> Constable's landscape paintings may be popular today, but *The Hay Wain*, now in London's National Gallery, did not sell after the Royal Academy displayed it. The artist sold only 20 paintings in England during his lifetime. He was elected to the Royal Academy with a majority of one vote at age 52.

The National Trust owns Flatford Mill and the houses around it, including the thatched 16th-century **Bridge Cottage**, on the north bank of the Stour, which has a shop and an exhibition about Constable's life. You can also rent rowboats from here. ⊠ *Off B1070, East Bergholt* ☏ *01206/298260* ⊕ *www.nationaltrust.org.uk* ⌨ *Free, guided tours £2.50* ☉ *Jan. and Feb., weekends 11–3:30; Mar., Wed.–Sun. 11–4; Apr., daily 11–5; May–Sept., daily 10:30–5:30; Oct., daily 11–4; Nov. and Dec., Wed.–Sun. 11–3:30. Guided tours Apr.–Oct., daily at 11:30, 1:30, and 2:30.*

Near Flatford Mill is the 16th-century **Willy Lott's House**, which is instantly recognizable from Constable's painting *The Hay Wain* (1821). Although the house itself is not open to the public, the road is a public thoroughfare, so you don't have to buy a ticket to see the famous—and completely unchanged—view for yourself. Just stand across from the two trees on the far bank, with the mill on your right, and look upstream. ■**TIP**→ **The display board on the outside wall of the mill contains a handy reproduction of** *The Hay Wain* **to help you compose your own photo.**

WHERE TO EAT

££££
BRITISH
★ ✕ **Le Talbooth.** A longtime favorite, this sophisticated restaurant in a Tudor house is idyllically set beside the River Stour. There are floodlighted terraces where food and drinks are served in summer and where jazz and steel bands play on summer Sunday nights. Inside, original beams, leaded-glass windows, and a brick fireplace add to the sense of age. The superb British fare at lunch and dinner may include loin of venison, local sea bass, or duck breast. This company owns the local hotels Maison Talbooth and Milsoms. ⊠ *Gun Hill* ☏ *01206/323150* ⊕ *www.milsomhotels.com/letalbooth* ⌨ *Reservations essential* ▭ *AE, DC, MC, V* ☉ *No dinner Sun. Nov.–May.*

£
BRITISH ✕ **Marlborough Head.** This friendly, 300-year-old pub across from Constable's school in Dedham serves traditional bar food with a flourish. Dishes such as venison pie and Lincolnshire sausages share the menu with fish-and-chips, pizzas, and burgers. There are also rooms available

(one with a four-poster bed) for £52–£100 per night, depending on the season. ✉ *Mill La.* ☎ *01206/323250* ⊕ *www.marlborough-head. co.uk* ▤ *MC, V.*

WOODBRIDGE

12

18 mi northeast of Dedham.

One of the first good ports of call on the Suffolk Heritage Coast, Woodbridge, off A12, is a town whose upper reaches center on a fine old market square, site of the 16th-century Shire Hall. Woodbridge is at its best around its old quayside, where boatbuilding has been carried out since the 16th century. The most prominent building is a white-clapboard mill, which dates from the 18th century and is powered by the tides.

ESSENTIALS

Visitor Information Woodbridge (✉ *The Station* ☎ *01394/382240* ⊕ *www. suffolkcoastal.gov.uk/tourism/tics*).

EXPLORING

The visitor center at **Sutton Hoo** helps interpret one of Britain's most significant Anglo-Saxon archaeological sites. In 1938 a local archaeologist excavated a series of earth mounds and discovered a 7th-century burial ship, probably that of King Raedwald of East Anglia. A replica of the 40-oar, 90-foot-long ship stands in the visitor center, which has artifacts and displays about Anglo-Saxon society. Trails around the 245-acre site explore the area along the River Deben. ✉ *Signposted on the B1083, 2 mi east of Woodbridge* ☎ *01394/389700* ⊕ *www.nationaltrust.org.uk* ▦ *£5.90* ◷ *Mid-Mar.–early Apr., Wed.–Sun. 10:30–5; early Apr.–Oct., daily 10:30–5; Nov.–early Mar., weekends 11–4.*

WHERE TO STAY

£££   ££££

★

⊡ **Crown and Castle.** Artsy, laid-back, and genuinely friendly, this little gem sits in an 18th-century building in the village of Orford, 10 mi east of Woodbridge. Many rooms have bathrooms with sunflower-size showerheads worth asking for. The garden rooms are spacious. The Trinity Bistro, run by food writer Ruth Watson, focuses on Modern British fare, including fresh fish and local Butley oysters. In warm weather the outdoor terrace is a great place for grandstand views of Orford Castle. **Pros:** warm service; good restaurant. **Cons:** need a car to get around. ✉ *Market Hill, Orford* ☎ *01394/450205* ⊕ *www.crownandcastle.co.uk* ⌑ *19 rooms* ⌂ *In-room: no a/c, DVD (some). In-hotel: restaurant, bar, some pets allowed, parking (paid)* ▤ *MC, V* ⑽ *BP.*

£££–££££

Fodor's Choice

★

⊡ **Seckford Hall.** The sense of history at this delightfully old-school hotel comes from more than just the magnificent Tudor architecture. Several pieces of furniture are castoffs from Buckingham Palace (King Edward VII died on one of the chairs in the drawing room) and one of the beds was supposedly slept in by Elizabeth I. Bedrooms are large and comfortable, with recently renovated bathrooms (some have whirlpool baths). The landscaped grounds are perfect for a stroll to admire the roses or the duck-filled lake. The main restaurant specializes in local lobster; for cheaper meals, grab a table in the Club House. Ask about the secret passage and the fabulously Bacchanalian ghost. **Pros:** antique charm; lovely setting; great atmosphere. **Cons:** no elevator; creaky old beds; fussy service in restaurant. ⊠ *Off the A12 outside Woodbridge* ☎ *01394/385678* ⊕ *www.seckford.co.uk* ⟳ *32 rooms* ⟳ *In-room: no a/c, Internet. In-hotel: 2 restaurants, room service, bar, pool, gym, spa, laundry service, some pets allowed* ⊟ *AE, DC, MC, V* ⦿ *BP.*

ALDEBURGH

15 mi northeast of Woodbridge, 41 mi northeast of Colchester.

Aldeburgh (pronounced orl-bruh) is a quiet seaside resort, except in June, when the town fills up with people attending the noted Aldeburgh Festival. Its beach is backed by a promenade lined with candy-color dwellings. Twentieth-century composer Benjamin Britten lived here for some time—he was born in the busy port of Lowestoft, 30 mi to the north. Britten grew interested in the story of Aldeburgh's native son, the poet George Crabbe (1754–1832), and turned his life story into *Peter Grimes,* a celebrated opera that perfectly captures the atmosphere of the Suffolk coast.

ESSENTIALS

Visitor Information Aldeburgh (⊠ *High St.* ☎ *01728/453637* ⊕ *www. suffolkcoastal.gov.uk/tourism/tics*).

EXPLORING

The Elizabethan **Moot Hall**, built of flint and timber, stood in the center of a thriving 16th-century town when first erected. Now it's just a few steps from the beach, a mute witness to the erosive powers of the North Sea. It's the home of the Aldeburgh Museum, a low-key collection that includes finds from an Anglo-Saxon ship burial. ⊠ *Market Cross Pl., Sea Front* ☎ *01728/454666* ⊕ *www.aldeburghmuseum.org.uk* ⊠ *£1* ☉ *Easter–Apr., weekends 2:30–5; May, Sept., and Oct., daily 2:30–5; June–Aug., daily noon–5.*

WHERE TO EAT AND STAY

£
BRITISH
✕ **Fish and Chip Shop.** When frying time approaches, Aldeburgh's most celebrated fish-and-chip shop always has a long line of eager customers, especially in summer. Popularity ensures a high turnover, so you know the fish is always fresh. The batter melts in your mouth, and the chips are satisfyingly chunky. Upstairs you can bring your own wine or beer and sit at tables. For the full experience, join a line for the paper-wrapped version. The deep-fried delicacies are equally good at the **Golden Galleon**, on the same road and run by the same team. ⊠ *226 High St.* ☎ *01728/452250* ⊟ *No credit cards.*

££
MODERN BRITISH
Fodor'sChoice
★
✕ **The Lighthouse.** An excellent value, this low-key brasserie with tightly packed wooden tables relies exclusively on local products. The menu focuses on seafood, including oysters and Cromer crabs. All the contemporary British dishes are imaginatively prepared. Desserts, such as the chocolate-and–Grand Marnier fudge cake, are particularly good. ⊠ *77 High St.* ☎ *01728/453377* ⊕ *www.lighthouserestaurant.co.uk* ⊟ *MC, V.*

£££–££££
▣ **Brudenell.** A top-to-bottom renovation in 2010 gave this seaside hotel a fresh, contemporary feel. The best possible use is made of the lovely

sea views; front-facing rooms open up onto magnificent vistas, and the restaurant (specializing, of course, in seafood) has a large terrace for alfresco dining in summer. The staff makes it easy for guests to relax. The White Lion hotel, dating to 1563, is the Brudenell's historic sister property. **Pros:** beautiful setting; pleasant staff; spacious rooms. **Cons:** some beds are small; limited parking. ⊠ *The Parade* ☎ *01728/452071* ⊕ *www.brudenellhotel.co.uk* ⇆ *42 rooms* ♿ *In-room: no a/c, Wi-Fi. In-hotel: restaurant, room service, bar, Wi-Fi hotspot, some pets allowed* ⊟ *AE, MC, V* ⊘ *BP.*

12

NIGHTLIFE AND THE ARTS

★ East Anglia's most important arts festival, and one of the best known in Great Britain, is the **Aldeburgh Festival** (☎ *01728/687110* ⊕ *www. aldeburgh.co.uk*). It's held for two weeks in June in the small village of Snape, 5 mi west of Aldeburgh. Founded by Benjamin Britten, the festival concentrates on music but includes related exhibitions, poetry readings, and even walks. A less hectic calendar of events continues through the year.

It's well worth a stop to take in the peaceful River Alde location of the **Snape Maltings** cultural center. It includes art galleries and crafts shops in distinctive large brick buildings once used to malt barley. You can pause at the tea shop or the Plough & Sail pub. Snape Maltings has special events year-round, such as the Britten Festival in October. Leisurely river cruises (£6) leave from the Quayside during high tide. ⊠ *Snape* ⚓ *Near Saxmundham* ☎ *01728/688303* ⊕ *www.snapemaltings.co.uk* ⊙ *Daily 10–5.*

NORWICH TO NORTH NORFOLK

Norwich, unofficial capital of East Anglia, is dominated by the 15th-century spire of its impressive cathedral. Norfolk's continuing isolation from the rest of the country, and its unspoiled landscape and architecture—largely bypassed by the Industrial Revolution—have proved to be a draw. Many of the flint-knapped (decorated with broken flint) houses in North Norfolk's newly trendy villages are now weekend or holiday homes. Windmills, churches, and waterways are the area's chief defining characteristics. A few miles inland from the Norfolk coast, the Broads begin, a national park made up of a network of shallow, reed-bordered lakes, many linked by wide rivers. Boating and fishing are great lures; rent a boat for a day or a week and the waterside pubs, churches, villages, and nature reserves are all within easy reach.

NORWICH

63 mi northeast of Cambridge.

It used to be said that Norwich had a pub for each day of the year and a church in which to repent for every Sunday. Although this is no longer true, real ales and steeples (including that of its grand cathedral) are still much in evidence in this pleasant city of 130,000. The University of East Anglia brings a cosmopolitan touch, including a lively arts scene, to an otherwise remote urban area. It's a good base from which to explore the Norfolk Broads and the coast.

Established by the Saxons because of its prime trading position on the rivers Yare and Wensum, the town sits in the triangle between the two waterways. The inner beltway follows the line of the old city wall, much of which is still visible. It's worth walking or driving around after dark to see the floodlit buildings. By the time of the Norman Conquest, Norwich was one of the largest towns in England, although much was destroyed by the Normans to create a new town. You can see the old flint buildings as you walk down the medieval streets and alleyways. Despite some industrial sites and many modern shopping centers, the town remains engaging.

GETTING HERE AND AROUND

There are regular bus and train connections from London; the trip takes about three hours. The bus and train stations are a 10-minute walk from the center. If you're driving, leave your car in any of the numerous lots scattered around the center.

City Sightseeing operates 45-minute open-top bus tours of Norwich, leaving hourly from Theatre Street. Tours cost £8.

ESSENTIALS

Visitor and Tour Information City Sightseeing (⊠ *Theatre St., across from Theatre Royal* ☎ *01263/587005* ⊕ *www.city-sightseeing.com*). **Norwich** (⊠ *The Forum, Millennium Plain* ☎ *01603/213999* ⊕ *www.visitnorwich.co.uk*).

EXPLORING
TOP ATTRACTIONS

★ **Blickling Hall.** Behind the wrought-iron entrance gate to Blickling Hall, two mighty yew hedges form a magnificent frame for this perfectly symmetrical Jacobean masterpiece. The redbrick mansion, 15 mi north of Norwich, has towers and chimneys, baroque Dutch gables, and, in the center, a three-story timber clock tower. The grounds include a formal flower garden and parkland with woods that conceal a temple, an orangery, and a pyramid. Blickling belonged to a succession of historic figures, including Sir John Fastolf, the model for Shakespeare's Falstaff; Anne Boleyn's family; and finally, Lord Lothian, ambassador to the United States at the outbreak of the Second World War. The Long Gallery (127 feet) has an intricate plasterwork ceiling with Jacobean emblems. Most of the interior is handsome but somewhat austere, although a sumptuous tapestry of Peter the Great at the Battle of Poltawa hangs in its own room. ⊠ *B1354, Blickling* ☎ *01263/738030* ⊕ *www.nationaltrust.org.uk* ⏴ *£10.25; gardens only, £7* ⊗ *House late Feb.–mid-July, early Sept., and Oct., Wed.–Sun. 11–5; mid-July–early Sept., Wed.–Mon. 11–5. Gardens Nov.–late Feb., Thurs.–Sun. 11–4; late Feb.–Oct., daily 10:15–5:15.*

❺ **Norwich Castle.** The decorated stone facing of this castle, now a museum on the hill in the center of the city, makes it look like a children's-book illustration. The castle is Norman (1130), but a stone keep replaced the original wooden bailey (wall). The thick walls and other defenses attest to its military function. Interactive displays explore topics from ancient Egypt to life in Norman times. You can even try out a copy of

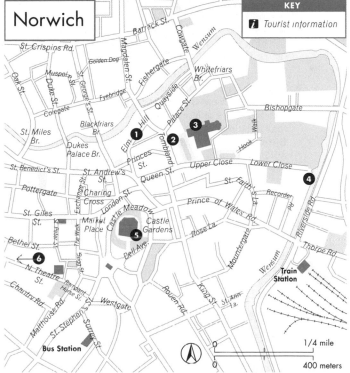

Queen Boudicca's chariot to relive her attack on Roman Colchester. The art section includes a gallery devoted to the Norwich School of painters who, like John Constable, focused on the everyday landscape and seascape. Daily tours explore the castle's battlements or dungeons. ✉ *Castle Meadow* ☎ *01603/495897* ⊕ *www.museums.norfolk.gov.uk* 🖾 *Gallery, museum, and castle £6.20 (£1 last hr before closing); special exhibitions £3.30; tours of battlements or dungeons £2* ⊗ *Oct.–June, weekdays 10–4:30, Sat. 10–5, Sun. 1–5; July–Sept., Mon.–Sat. 10–5, Sun. 1–5.*

❸ **Norwich Cathedral.** The grandest example of Norman architecture in
★ Norwich has the second-largest monastic cloisters in Britain (only Salisbury's are bigger). Although its 315-foot-tall spire is visible from everywhere in the city, you cannot see the building itself until you pass through St. Ethelbert's Gate. The cathedral was begun in 1096 by Herbert de Losinga, who had come from Normandy in 1091 to be its first bishop; his splendid tomb is by the high altar. The remarkable length of the nave is immediately impressive; the similarly striking height of the vaulted ceiling makes it a strain to study the delightful colored bosses, which illustrate Bible stories with great vigor and detail. (Binoculars are handy.) The grave of Norfolk-born nurse Edith Cavell, the British World War I heroine shot by the Germans in 1915, is at the east end of

the cathedral. There's also a small medieval-style herb garden, plus a restaurant and coffee shop. There are guided tours Monday to Saturday at 10:45, 12:30, and 2:15. ■TIP→ **Norwich Cathedral's Web site has two excellent interactive guides, including clickable maps.** ⊠ *62 The Close* ☎ *01603/218300* ⊕ *www.cathedral.org.uk* ⊡ *Free* ⊙ *Daily 7:30–6; call ahead to check, as times can vary. Herb garden Tues.–Thurs. 9–5.*

⑥ Sainsbury Centre for the Visual Arts. A hangarlike building designed by Norman Foster on the University of East Anglia campus holds the collection of the Sainsbury family, owners of a supermarket chain. It includes a remarkable quantity of tribal art and 20th-century works, especially art nouveau, and has pieces by Pablo Picasso and Alberto Giacometti. Rotating exhibitions include big-name photography and art shows. Buses 22, 25, 26, and 27 run from downtown Norwich to the university. ⊠ *Earlham Rd.* ☎ *01603/593199* ⊕ *www.scva.org.uk* ⊡ *Free; special exhibits vary* ⊙ *Tues. and Thurs.–Sun. 10–5, Wed. 10–8.*

WORTH NOTING

❶ Elm Hill. Off Tombland, this neighborhood is a cobbled and pleasing mixture of Tudor and Georgian houses that hold gift shops and tearooms.

❹ Pulls Ferry. The Cathedral Close (grounds) is one of the most idyllic places in Norwich; past the mixture of medieval and Georgian houses, a path leads down to the ancient water gate, Pulls Ferry.

❷ Tombland. Narrow lanes and alleys that used to be the main streets of medieval Norwich lead away from the market and end at Tombland by the cathedral. Neither a graveyard nor a plague pit, Tombland was the site of the Anglo-Saxon trading place, now a busy thoroughfare.

WHERE TO EAT AND STAY

£
BRITISH
╳ **Adam and Eve.** Said to be Norwich's oldest pub, this place dates back to 1249. From noon until 7, the kitchen serves such hearty pub staples as chicken-and-ham pie or cheese-and-ale soup from the short but solid bar menu. Theakston's and Adnams beer are available on tap, as is Aspall's cider. ⊠ *Bishopsgate* ☎ *01603/667423* ⊕ *www.adamandevenorwich.co.uk* ⊟ *MC, V.*

£
BRITISH
★
╳ **Britons Arms.** A converted pub, this cozy, thatched café and eatery has famously good homemade cakes as well as some pies and tarts. The 15th-century building has low ceilings, a garden in summer, and an open fire in winter. ⊠ *9 Elm Hill* ☎ *01603/623367* ⊟ *No credit cards* ⊙ *Closed Sun.*

£–££
BELGIAN
╳ **Waffle House.** The perfect antidote to all those heavy English breakfasts, this is the kind of place where walking through the door is enough to make you salivate with anticipation. It's waffles, waffles, and more waffles on the menu, although the selection shows imagination. Breakfast choices include such savory concoctions as smoked salmon waffles; later in the day you can order waffles topped with anything from tuna salad to guacamole and salsa. Or you could skip to dessert and waffles topped with pecan and butterscotch, banoffee sauce (a mix of banana and toffee), or maple syrup. ⊠ *39 St. Giles St.* ☎ *01603/612790* ⊕ *www.wafflehouse.co.uk* ⊟ *MC, V.*

CLOSE UP

Experiencing Norfolk's Broads

For many people, the joy of East Anglia is its desolate landscapes and isolated beaches. Of these, the Broads (expanded rivers) of Norfolk are the most dramatic. The water in the marshes and dikes reflects the arching sky, whose cloudscapes are ever-changing, stretching toward seemingly infinite horizons. The sunsets are to be treasured.

The reed-bordered **Norfolk Broads** (⊕ www.broads-authority.gov.uk) make a gentle landscape of canals and lakes that are ideal for boating and are alive with birds and animals. Touring by car isn't really an option if you want to see something of the Broads, because much of this area of shallow lakes linked by wide rivers is inaccessible by road. However, there are boat tours through the 150 mi of

waterways. There's also an extensive network of bicycle paths.

Explore the Broads by bicycle with **Broadland Cycle Hire** (⊠ The Rhond, Hoverton ☎ 07887/480331 ⊕ www. norfolkbroadscycling.co.uk), 8 mi northeast of Norwich. Rentals (£14 per day) are available from Easter through October and during school vacations. The company can recommend routes 7 to 20 mi from their base.

Broads Tours (☎ 01603/782207 Wroxham, 01692/670711 Potter Heigham ⊕ www.broads.co.uk), based at the quaysides in Wroxham, 7 mi northeast of Norwich, and Potter Heigham, 15 mi northeast of Norwich, offers day cruises in the Broads as well as half-day and full-day launch rental (lessons included).

12

£££–££££   ☷ **Dunston Hall Hotel & Country Club.** Gables and tall chimneys give this redbrick mansion built in 1859 an Elizabethan look. Extensive modern additions have transformed a country house into a luxurious retreat. The peaceful landscaped gardens and woodland are ideal for relaxing after a day's sightseeing. If you seek a sense of the past, ask for a four-poster bedroom or one of the small attic bedrooms with original low-beamed ceilings. The hotel is 4 mi south of the city center, on the A140. **Pros:** beautiful setting; friendly and efficient service; good for golfers. **Cons:** some rooms need renovation; food is mediocre and pricey. ⊠ Ips-wich Rd. ☎ 01508/470444 ⊕ www.devere-hotels.com ⇆ 157 rooms, 12 suites, 1 penthouse ♿ In-room: no a/c (some), Internet. In-hotel: 2 restaurants, room service, bars, golf course, tennis courts, pool, gym, spa, laundry service ⊟ AE, DC, MC, V ℄ BP.

NIGHTLIFE AND THE ARTS

The **King of Hearts** (⊠ 7–15 Fye Bridge St. ☎ 01603/766129 ⊕ www. kingofhearts.org.uk), a restored 15th-century merchant's house, serves as a small arts center that presents chamber and jazz concerts, sto-rytelling sessions, and poetry readings. It also has a good café. The **Maddermarket Theatre** (⊠ St. John's Alley ☎ 01603/620917 ⊕ www. maddermarket.co.uk), patterned after Elizabethan theaters, has been the base of amateur and community theater in Norwich since 1911. **Norwich Arts Centre** (⊠ St. Benedict's St. ☎ 01603/660352 ⊕ www.

norwichartscentre.co.uk) puts on an eclectic program of live music, dance, and comedy. Its café has free Internet access.

Norwich Playhouse (⊠ *Gun Wharf, St. George's St.* ☎ *01603/598598* ⊕ *www.norwichplayhouse.org.uk*), a professional repertory group, performs everything from Shakespeare to world premieres of new plays. Norwich's biggest and best-known theater, the **Theatre Royal** (⊠ *Theatre St.* ☎ *01603/630000* ⊕ *www.theatreroyalnorwich.co.uk*) hosts touring companies staging musicals, ballet, opera, and plays.

SPORTS AND THE OUTDOORS

Traffic on the River Yare is now mostly for pleasure rather than commerce, and a summer trip with **City Boats** (⊠ *Highcraft Marina, Griffin La.* ☎ *01603/701701* ⊕ *www.cityboats.co.uk*) gives a fresh perspective on Norwich. Longer trips are available down the rivers Wensum and Yare to the nearer Broads.

SHOPPING

The medieval lanes of Norwich, around Elm Hill and Tombland, contain the best antiques, book, and crafts stores. The **Mustard Shop** (⊠ *15 Royal Arcade* ☎ *01603/627889*) pays homage to Colman's Mustard, a company founded in Norwich in the early 19th century; it sells collectibles and more than 15 varieties of mustard. **Norwich Market** (⊠ *Market Pl., Gentleman's Walk* ☎ *01603/213537* ⊕ *www.norwich-market.co.uk*), the city's main outdoor market, is open daily; it sells everything from jewelry to clothes and food and has been the heart of the city for 900 years.The **Tombland Antiques Centre** (⊠ *14 Tombland* ☎ *01603/619129*), opposite the cathedral, is an old house crammed full of shops.

BLAKENEY

28 mi northwest of Norwich.

The Norfolk coast begins to feel wild and remote near Blakeney, 14 mi west of Cromer. Driving the coast road from Cromer, you pass marshes, sandbanks, and coves, as well as villages. Blakeney is one of the most appealing, with harbors for small fishing boats and yachts. Once a bustling port town exporting corn and salt, it enjoys a quiet existence today, and a reputation for wildlife viewing at Blakeney Point.

EXPLORING

Blakeney Point, 1,000 acres of grassy dunes, is home to nesting terns and about 500 common and gray seals. You can walk 3½ mi from Cley Beach to get here, but a boat trip from Blakeney or Morston Quay is fun and educational. An information center and a tearoom at Morston Quay open according to tides and weather. **Bishop's Boats** (⊠ *Ticket Office Blakeney Quay, opposite junction with High St.* ☎ *01263/740753* ⊕ *www.norfolksealtrips.co.uk*) runs one- or two-hour trips daily between February and October from Morston Quay and Blakeney harbor for £8 per person. ⊠ *A149* ☎ *01263/740241* ⊕ *www. nationaltrust.org.uk* ✍ *Free.*

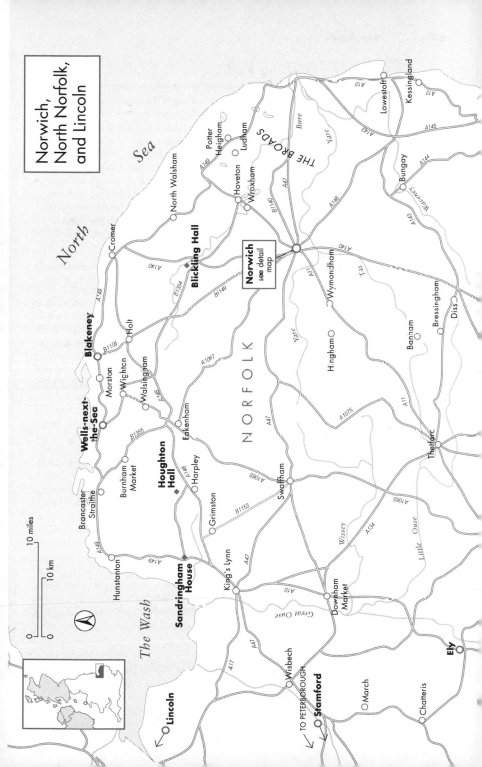

Norwich, North Norfolk, and Lincoln

North Sea

THE BROADS

NORFOLK

The Wash

North Walsham
Cromer
Blakeney
Wells-next-the-Sea
Morston
Wighton
Walsingham
Holt
Blickling Hall
Potter Heigham
Ludham
Hoveton
Wroxham
Lowestoft
Kessingland
Bungay
Diss
Bressingham
Banham
Wymondham
Norwich see detail map
Hingham
Eakenham
Swaffham
Thetford
Houghton Hall
Harpley
Burnham Market
Brancaster Staithe
Hunstanton
Sandringham House
King's Lynn
Grimston
Downham Market
Wisbech
Stamford
March
Chatteris
Ely
Lincoln
TO PETERBOROUGH

10 miles
10 km

A149 A148 A140 B1354 B1149 A1067 B1355 A148 B1153 A47 A10 A17 A47 A1065 A134 A11 A143 A146 A140 A11 A144 A145 A12 B1140 B1150 A149 B1156 A1065 Wissey Little Ouse Great Ouse Yare Bure Yare Waveney Tas

CLOSE UP · Popular Walking Paths

East Anglia is a walker's dream, especially if a relatively flat trail appeals to you. The long-distance footpath known as the Peddars Way follows the line of a pre-Roman road, running from near Thetford through heathland, pine forests, and arable fields, and on through rolling chalk lands to the Norfolk coast near Hunstanton. The Norfolk Coastal Path then continues eastward along the coast, joining at Cromer with the delightfully varied Weaver's Way, which passes through medieval weaving villages and deeply rural parts of the Norfolk Broads on its 56-mi route from Cromer to Great Yarmouth. Anyone interested in birds should carry binoculars and a field guide, as both of these routes have abundant avian life—both local and migratory. Tourist information centers and the regional Web site ⊕ *www. visiteastofengland.com* have further details.

WHERE TO EAT AND STAY

£
SEAFOOD

✕ **Anchor Inn.** This delightful little gastro-pub in Morston, 1½ mi west of Blakeney, has a cozy, coastal atmosphere. The menu doesn't consist solely of seafood, but why would you order anything else when the local catch is this good? Platters of mussels and oysters are popular, and prawns are served the way purists like them—in a pint glass, shells on, with a twist of lemon and a pot of homemade mayo. The tasty fish-and-chips draws crowds. ⊠ *22 The Street, Morston* ☎ *01263/741392* ▤ *MC, V.*

£££
MODERN BRITISH

✕ **White Horse at Blakeney.** Fine food is the draw at this former coaching inn. Goat's-cheese parcels, smoked eel, and roast pork tenderloin appear on the menu, along with pub classics such as ploughman's lunch and cod-and-chips. You can dine in the bar, an airy conservatory, or the more intimate Long Room. There are also a few simply furnished guest rooms with sea views that are worth the extra pence. ⊠ *4 High St.* ☎ *01263/740574* ⊕ *www.blakeneywhitehorse.co.uk* ▤ *MC, V.*

£££–££££
★

▦ **Byfords.** In a market town 5 mi southeast of Blakeney, Byfords epitomizes the increasing trendiness of North Norfolk. The self-styled "Posh B&B" rooms are stylish and comfortable, with Egyptian cotton linens, modern sound systems, and fresh flowers. Seven rooms are in an annex, and the rest are in the main building. The busy café by day turns into a restaurant offering Mediterranean and English fare in the evening. There's also a superb delicatessen—excellent for preparing a picnic. Booking on Saturday requires a stay of at least two nights. **Pros:** plush rooms; amiable staff; relaxed atmosphere. **Cons:** gets busy on weekends; service occasionally slow. ⊠ *1–3 Shirehall Plain, Holt* ☎ *01263/711400* ⊕ *www.byfords.org.uk* ⟿ *16 rooms* ⋄ *In-room: no a/c, DVD. In-hotel: restaurant* ▤ *MC, V* ❍ *BP.*

SPORTS AND THE OUTDOORS

Temples Seal Watching Trips (☎ *01263/740791* ⊕ *www.sealtrips.co.uk*) organizes two-hour boat trips out to Blakeney Point, where you can watch seals in their natural environment. Tours cost £8 for adults; there are usually two or three daily departures in high season. The ticket office is located in the Anchor Inn in Morston, 1½ mi west of Blakeney.

WELLS-NEXT-THE-SEA

10 mi west of Blakeney, 34 mi northwest of Norwich.

A quiet base from which to explore other nearby towns, the harbor town of Wells-next-the-Sea and the nearby coastline remain untouched, with many excellent places for bird-watching and walking on the sandy beaches of Holkham Bay, near Holkham Hall. Today the town is a mile from the sea, but in Tudor times, when it was closer to the ocean, it served as one of the main ports of East Anglia. The remains of a medieval priory point to the town's past as a major pilgrimage destination in the Middle Ages. Along the nearby beach a narrow-gauge steam train makes the short journey to Walsingham between Easter and October.

12

GETTING HERE AND AROUND

Wells-next-the-Sea is on the main A149 coastal road, but can also be reached via the B1105 from Fakenham. The nearest train station is about 16 mi away in Sheringham. There are regular buses from Sheringham, Fakenham, King's Lynn, and Norwich.

ESSENTIALS

Visitor Information Wells-next-the-Sea (⊠ *Staithe St.* ☎ *01328/711885* ⊕ *www.wells-guide.co.uk).*

EXPLORING

Fodor's Choice
★

The Palladian **Holkham Hall**, one of the most splendid mansions in Britain, is the seat of the Coke family, the earls of Leicester. In the late 18th century, Thomas Coke went on a grand tour of the Continent, returning with art treasures and determined to build a house according to the new Italian ideas. Centered by a grand staircase and modeled after the Baths of Diocletian, the 60-foot-tall Marble Hall (mostly alabaster, in fact), may be the most spectacular room in Britain. Beyond are salons filled with works from Coke's collection of masterpieces, including paintings by Gainsborough, Van Dyck, Rubens, and Raphael. Surrounding the house is parkland landscaped by Capability Brown in 1762. You'd be hard-pressed to walk through it without spotting several deer. A good way to see the grounds is a half-hour-long lake cruise. The original walled kitchen gardens have been restored and once again provide produce for the estate. The **Bygones Museum,** in the old stable block, has more than 5,000 items on display, from gramophones to fire engines. ⊠ *Off A149* ☎ *01328/710227* ⊕ *www.holkham.co.uk* ⚑ *Hall £9, museum £4, combined ticket £11; lake cruise £3.50; grounds free* ☉ *Hall Apr.–Oct., Sun., Mon., and Thurs. noon–4. Museum Apr.–Oct., daily 10–5. Walled gardens Apr.–Oct., daily noon–4. Park Apr.–Sept., Mon.–Sat. 7–7; Oct., Mon., Wed., Fri., and Sat. 7–7, Tues. and Thurs. 9:30–7; Jan.–Mar., Mon., Wed., and Fri. 7–7, Tues. and Thurs. 9:30–7.*

WHERE TO STAY

£££–££££
☕
Fodor's Choice
★

⛫ **Victoria at Holkham.** A colorful, whimsical hideaway, this hotel on the Holkham Hall estate is managed by the earl of Leicester's family. The atmosphere is more laid-back and family-friendly than the austere exterior suggests. Inside, shabby-chic decor contrasts with a young and sophisticated vibe. Bedrooms are on the small side, but comfortable, with elegant, handmade furniture and modern bathrooms. Most romantic is the Raj Room, with its claw-foot tub and ornate, precipitously tall (if somewhat creaky) bed. The hotel restaurant is one of the finest in the region, with an emphasis on modern European cuisine. The dune-backed Holkham Beach (where the final scene of *Shakespeare in Love* was filmed) is a few minutes away; show your room key to avoid the fee. **Pros:** original character; excellent location; outstanding food. **Cons:** extremely busy in summer; no elevator. ☒ *Park Rd., Holkham* ☎ *01328/711008* ⊕ *www.holkham.co.uk/victoria* ⤷ *9 rooms, 1 suite, 4 self-contained lodges*⟡ *In-room: no a/c (some), DVD. In-hotel: restaurant, room service, bar* ⊟ MC, V ⦿ CP.

SPORTS AND THE OUTDOORS
On Yer Bike Cycle Hire (☒ *The Laurels, Nutwood Farm, Wighton* ☎ *01328/820719* ⊕ *www.norfolkcyclehire.co.uk*) will deliver and collect bikes; rentals are £13 per day. Reservations are required.

HOUGHTON HALL

14 mi southwest of Wells-next-the-Sea, 35 mi northwest of Norwich.

GETTING HERE AND AROUND
Houghton Hall is in the tiny hamlet of Houghton, which is just outside Harpley, on the A148 between King's Lynn and Fakenham.

EXPLORING
Houghton Hall, a grand Palladian pile built by the first British prime minister, Sir Robert Walpole, in the 1720s, has been carefully restored by its current owner, the seventh marquess of Cholmondeley. The double-height Stone Hall and the sumptuous rooms reveal designer William Kent's preference for gilt, plush fabrics, stucco, and elaborate carvings. The Common Parlour, one of the original family rooms, is elegant but far simpler. Stroll in the 5-acre walled garden. ☒ *Off A148, near Harpley* ☎ *01485/528569* ⊕ *www.houghtonhall.com* ⊠ *£8.80; park and grounds only, £6* ☉ *House Apr.–Sept., Wed., Thurs., Sun., and bank holidays 1:30–5 (last admission 4:30); grounds Apr.–Sept., Wed., Thurs., Sun., and bank holidays 11–5:30.*

SANDRINGHAM HOUSE

8 mi west of Houghton Hall, 20 mi southwest of Wells-next-the-Sea, 43 mi northwest of Norwich.

GETTING HERE AND AROUND
Sandringham is just off the B1440, between Dersingham and Hillington.

EXPLORING
Not far from the old-fashioned seaside resort of Hunstanton, **Sandringham House** is where the Royal Family traditionally spends Christmas. The redbrick Victorian mansion was clearly designed for enormous country-house parties, with a ballroom, billiard room, and bowling alley, as well as a shooting lodge on the grounds. The house and gardens close when the Queen is in residence, but the woodlands, nature trails, and museum of royal memorabilia in the old stables remain

open, as does the church, medieval but in heavy Victorian disguise. Tours access most rooms but steer clear of personal effects of current royals. ✉ *Sandringham* ☎ *01553/612908* ⊕ *www.sandringhamestate. co.uk* ✉ *House, gardens, and museum £10, gardens and museum £8.50* ⊙ *House and museum mid-Apr.–late July and early Aug.–early Nov., daily 11–5 (last admission 3:30). Gardens daily 10:30–4.*

12

STAMFORD AND LINCOLN

The fens of northern Cambridgeshire pass imperceptibly into the three divisions of Lincolnshire: Holland, Kesteven, and Lindsey are parts of the county, divided administratively. Holland borders the Isle of Ely and the Soke of Peterborough. This marshland spreads far and wide south of the Wash. The chief attractions are two towns: Stamford, to the southwest, and Lincoln, with its magnificent cathedral.

STAMFORD

48 mi northwest of Cambridge

Serene, honey-hued Stamford, on a hillside overlooking the River Welland, has a well-preserved center, in part because in 1967 it was designated England's first conservation area. This unspoiled town, which grew rich from the medieval wool and cloth trades, has a delightful, harmonious mixture of Georgian and medieval architecture.

ESSENTIALS

Visitor Information Stamford (✉ *Stamford Tourist Information Centre, St. Mary's St.* ☎ *01780/755611* ⊕ *www.southwestlincs.com*).

EXPLORING

★ **Burghley House**, an architectural masterpiece that many consider the grandest house of the first Elizabethan age, is celebrated for its roofscape bristling with pepper-pot chimneys and slate-roof towers. It was built between 1565 and 1587 to the design of William Cecil, first Baron Burghley, when he was Elizabeth I's high treasurer; his descendants still occupy the house. The interior was remodeled in the late 17th century with treasures from Europe. The house contains 18 sumptuous rooms, with carvings by Grinling Gibbons and ceiling paintings by Antonio Verrio (including the dramatic Heaven Room and the Hell Staircase), as well as innumerable paintings and priceless porcelain. You can tour on your own or join a free 80-minute guided tour beginning daily at 3:30. In the 18th century Capability Brown landscaped the grounds (where deer roam and open-air concerts are staged in summer), dug the lake, and added the Gothic Revival orangery, where today you can take tea or lunch. In early September Burghley is host to the international Burghley Horse Trials. The house is a mile southeast of Stamford. ✉ *Off A1* ☎ *01780/752451* ⊕ *www.burghley.co.uk* ✉ *House and gardens £11.80; gardens only, £6.70* ⊙ *Easter–late Oct., Sat.–Thurs. 11–5.*

LINCOLN

★ *53 mi north of Stamford, 93 mi northwest of Cambridge, 97 mi northwest of Norwich.*

Celts, Romans, and Danes all had important settlements here, but it was the Normans who gave Lincoln its medieval stature after William the Conqueror founded Lincoln Castle as a stronghold in 1068. Four years later William appointed Bishop Remigius to run the huge diocese stretching from the Humber to the Thames, resulting in the construction of Lincoln Cathedral, the third largest in England after York Minster and St. Paul's. Since medieval times Lincoln's status has declined. However, its somewhat remote location (there are no major motorways or railways nearby) has helped preserve its traditional character.

The cathedral is on the aptly named Steep Hill; to its south, narrow medieval streets cling to the hillside. Jew's House, on the Strait, dating from the early 12th century, is one of several well-preserved domestic buildings in this area. The name is almost as old as the house itself—it refers to a former resident, Belaset of Wallingford, a Jewish woman who was murdered by a mob in 1290, the same year the Jews were expelled from England. The River Witham flows unobtrusively under the incongruously named High Bridge, a low, vaulted Norman bridge topped by timber-frame houses from the 16th century. West from here you can rent boats, or, in summer, go on a river cruise.

GETTING HERE AND AROUND
There are direct buses (four hours) from London, but most rail journeys (two to four hours) involve changing trains. The bus and train stations are south of the center, and it's a steep walk uphill to the cathedral and castle. You can avoid the climb by taking the Walk & Ride electric bus service from the stop on St. Mary's Street. Purchase tickets on board. Drivers will find parking lots around the bus and train stations and in the center at The Lawn and Westgate.

ESSENTIALS
Visitor Information Lincoln (✉ *9 Castle Hill* ☎ *01522/545458* ⊕ *www.lincoln. gov.uk*).

EXPLORING
★ Lincoln's crowning glory, the great **Cathedral of St. Mary**, was for hundreds of years the tallest building in Europe, but this magnificent medieval building is now among the least known of European cathedrals. The Norman bishop Remigius began work in 1072. The Romanesque church he built was irremediably damaged, first by fire, then by earthquake, but you can still see parts of the ancient structure at the west front. The next great phase of building, initiated by Bishop Hugh of Avalon, is mainly 13th century in character. The west front, topped by two strikingly tall towers, gives tremendous breadth to the entrance. It is best seen from the 14th-century Exchequer Gate arch in front of the cathedral, or from the castle battlements beyond.

Inside, a breathtaking impression of space and unity belies the many centuries of building and rebuilding. The 13th-century stained-glass window at the north end of the transept, known as the Dean's Eye,

12

is one of the earliest traceried windows, whereas its opposite number at the south end shows a 14th-century sophistication in its interlaced designs. ■ TIP→ Look for the Lincoln Imp on the pillar nearest St. Hugh's shrine; according to legend, an angel turned this creature to stone. Through a door on the north side is the chapter house, a 10-sided building that sometimes housed the medieval Parliament of England during the reigns of Edward I and Edward II. The chapter house is connected to the 13th-century cloister, notable for its amusing ceiling bosses. The cathedral library, a restrained building by Christopher Wren, was built onto the north side of the cloisters after the original library collapsed. Tours of the cathedral roof and tower are fascinating, but no children under 14 are allowed. Call or check Web site for all tour times. ⊠ *Minster Yard* ☎ *01522/561600* ⊕ *www.lincolncathedral.com* 🖾 *£5* ☉ *Late June–Aug., weekdays 7:15 AM–8 PM, weekends 7:15–6; Sept.–mid-June, Mon.–Sat. 7:15–6, Sun. 7:15–5.*

QUICK BITES

After climbing Steep Hill, you'll need at least one of the 23 different teas or 15 coffees available at Pimento (⊠ 27 *Steep Hill* ☎ *01522/544880*). Choose a cake or snack to go along with your pick-me-up.

The **Minster Yard**, which surrounds the cathedral on three sides, contains buildings of different periods, including graceful Georgian architecture. A statue of Alfred, Lord Tennyson, who was born in Lincolnshire, stands on the green near the chapter house.

The **Medieval Bishop's Palace**, on the south side of Minster Yard, has exhibits about the former administrative center of the diocese, plus a garden and working vineyard. ⊠ *Minster Yard* ☎ *01522/527468* ⊕ *www.english-heritage.org.uk* 🖾 *£4.20* ☉ *Apr.–Oct., daily 10–5; Nov.–Mar., Thurs.–Mon. 10–4.*

♺ **Lincoln Castle,** facing the cathedral across Exchequer Gate, was built on two great mounds by William the Conqueror in 1068, incorporating part of the remains of Roman garrison walls. The castle was a military base until the 17th century, after which it operated as a prison. In the extraordinary prison chapel you can see the cagelike stalls in which Victorian convicts listened to sermons. ■ TIP→ One of the four surviving copies of the Magna Carta, signed by King John at Runnymede in 1215, is on display in the same building. ⊠ *Castle Hill* ☎ *01522/511068* ⊕ *www.lincolnshire.gov. uk/lincolncastle* 🖾 *£4.10* ☉ *Apr. and Sept., daily 10–5; May–Aug., daily 10–6; Oct.–Mar., daily 10–4; last entry 1 hr before closing.*

♺ The **Collection** is made up of the **Usher Gallery,** an art gallery with paintings by Turner, Lowry, and Hitchens as well as some more contemporary works, and the modern **Archaeology Collection** next door, an interactive museum with local artifacts spanning 3,000 years of history. At this writing the Collection was closed for renovations; it was due to reopen in late 2010. ⊠ *Danes Terrace* ☎ *01522/550990* ⊕ *www. thecollection.lincoln.museum* 🖾 *Free* ☉ *Daily 10–4.*

WHERE TO EAT AND STAY

££
BRITISH

✕ **Brown's Pie Shop.** More than you might imagine from the modest name, Brown's Pie Shop serves the best of traditional British cuisine: succulent beef, great desserts, and some very good, freshly made savory pies.

There are also fish specials and a small selection of vegetarian dishes. This restaurant, close to the cathedral, serves an economical early-evening menu. ⊠ *33 Steep Hill* ☎ *01522/527330* ⊕ *www.brownspieshop. co.uk* ⊟ *MC, V.*

££–£££   ☷ **Bailhouse & Mews.** In a 14th-century baronial hall near the cathedral, the welcoming Bailhouse & Mews has four-poster beds in some rooms and plenty of antique features, such as flagstones and wooden beams. The gardens have a small swimming pool and a stone chapel, and you can help yourself to tea or coffee at any time from the kitchen. The hotel also has three self-catering cottages and one house available. **Pros:** good value; views of cathedral and castle; convenient parking. **Cons:** some street noise; unstaffed at night; some find security cameras off-putting. ⊠ *34 Bailgate* ☎ *01522/541000* ⊕ *www.bailhouse.co.uk* ➷ *10 rooms, 3 cottages, 1 house* ⌂ *In-room: no a/c, DVD (some), Wi-Fi. In-hotel: bar, pool* ⊟ *AE, MC, V* ⊺⊙⊺ *BP.*

££–£££   ☷ **White Hart.** Luxuriously furnished with a wealth of antiques, among
   ★   them some fine clocks and china, the establishment has been a hotel for 600 years. Bedrooms are individually decorated in traditional style, and many are outfitted with antiques. Hardwoods such as walnut and mahogany abound. **Pros:** excellent location; blend of period and modern furnishings. **Cons:** slow service; overpriced food. ⊠ *Bailgate* ☎ *01522/526222* ⊕ *www.whitehart-lincoln.co.uk* ➷ *39 rooms, 11 suites* ⌂ *In-room: no a/c, Internet. In-hotel: restaurant, room service, bar, laundry service, Wi-Fi hotspot, some pets allowed* ⊟ *AE, MC, V* ⊺⊙⊺ *BP.*

SHOPPING

The best stores are on Bailgate, Steep Hill, and the medieval streets leading directly down from the cathedral and castle. Just off Steep Hill, the **Cheese Society** (⊠ *1 St. Martin's La.* ☎ *01522/511003*) has a great selection of English and French cheeses and an attached café. **Cobb Hall Craft Centre** (⊠ *St. Paul's La. off Bailgate* ☎ *No phone*), a small mall of crafts shops and workshops, sells clocks, candles, and ornaments. Steep Hill has good bookstores, antiques shops, and crafts and art galleries, including **Harding House Galleries** (⊠ *Steep Hill* ☎ *01522/523537*).

Yorkshire

LEEDS, HAWORTH, YORK, WHITBY, CASTLE HOWARD

WORD OF MOUTH

"Many consider the Minster worth the trip to York alone. The city is very compact and walkable, and a walk around the city walls is a must—there will be loads of places you'll want to stop off and explore. The (free) National Railway Museum is superb, even for people who 'don't like trains.' "

—Morgana

"From Castle Howard, head north and explore the North Yorkshire Moors, as you won't need a full day at CH. The drive from Pickering over the moors to Whitby is spectacular, or you can take the steam railway which more or less follows the same route, Pickering to Whitby."

—Cathinjoetown

Updated
by Christi
Daugherty

A hauntingly beautiful region, Yorkshire is known for its wide-open spaces and dramatic landscapes. The hills of the moors and dales glow pink with heather in summer, and turn black with it in winter. Hearty fishing villages and ruined monasteries cling to the edges of cliffs in one of England's last remaining wildernesses.

Some of the region's biggest attractions are the result of human endeavor: the towering cathedral in medieval York; Castle Howard, a baroque masterpiece near York; and the old haunts of the Brontë sisters in the hillside town of Haworth.

The most rugged land is the North York Moors, a vast, lonely area free of fences, and dotted with fluffy sheep that wander at will in summer. (It is said that if the grazing sheep ever disappeared, the ancient forests would return.) Between the bleak moors and the rocky Pennine hills lie lush, green valleys known as the Yorkshire Dales, where the high rainfall produces luxuriant vegetation, swift rivers, sparkling streams, and waterfalls. The villages here, immortalized in the books of the Brontës and the late veterinarian Alf Wight (1916–95)—who wrote under the name James Herriot—are wonderfully peaceful, bursting into life only in summer as hundreds of hikers (or "ramblers" as they're known in England) appear over the hills.

The area is not all green fields and perfect villages—there's also a gritty, urban aspect to Yorkshire, whose manufacturing towns changed the course of British history. In West Yorkshire, once down-at-the-heels Leeds has remade itself with trendy restaurants and cafés, and its buzzing music industry and nightlife scene.

ORIENTATION AND PLANNING

GETTING ORIENTED

Yorkshire is the largest English region to explore (its fiercely proud inhabitants would say it's the only English region *worth* exploring). The industrial heartland is West Yorkshire, with the cities of Leeds and Bradford. What the tourist office likes to call Brontë Country—basically Haworth, home of the Brontë family—is just to the northwest, and northward spread the hills, valleys, and villages of the Yorkshire Dales. To the east is the ancient city of York, with its famous cathedral.

Along the coast, Yorkshire reveals itself as a seaside vacation destination, although never one that will win prizes for summerlike weather. But fine beaches and a fascinating history await you in the resort of Scarborough, the former whaling port of Whitby, and Robin Hood's Bay—a cliff-top, onetime smuggler's haunt. Finally, you can strike

TOP REASONS TO GO

York Minster: The largest Gothic cathedral in England helps make York one of the country's most visited towns. The building's history is told in its crypt, brilliantly converted into a museum.

North York Moors: There's enough space for walkers to experience isolation amid the heather-covered hills that glow crimson and purple in late summer and early fall.

Rievaulx Abbey: Heading down the tiny lane that leads to the ruins of one of the great Cistercian abbeys only serves to make it all the more dramatic when its soaring arches appear out of the trees.

Whitby: This bustling coastal town inspired Bram Stoker to write *Dracula.* At night, its gloomy clifftop church and skeletal abbey ruins loom over Whitby dramatically.

Robin Hood's Bay: Test your balance on the steep roads of this seaside village set in a ravine, and then breathe easy on the miles of outstanding beach.

Haworth: Looking as if it were carved from stone, this picture-perfect hillside town in the Dales is a lovely place to learn about the Brontë sisters.

13

inland to the North York Moors National Park. Isolated stone villages, moorland walks, and Rievaulx Abbey are within easy reach.

West Yorkshire and Brontë Country. Rocky and bleak, this windswept stretch of country makes sense of all those tragedies penned by the Brontë sisters in prettily gloomy Haworth. Leeds is a reviving former industrial center worth a stop.

The Yorkshire Dales. This mountainous region, a bit off the beaten track, has windswept moors and valleys that offer extraordinary views. Gorgeous villages like Bolton Abbey and Grassington are well worth exploring.

York. Still wrapped up in its medieval city walls, this beautifully preserved city makes the perfect introduction to Yorkshire. Its towering Minster and crooked little streets entrance history buffs.

York Environs. This rural region holds the exquisite Victorian spa town, Harrogate, as well as charming villages like Knaresborough, tucked away in a steep valley. Baroque Castle Howard is also near York.

The North Yorkshire Coast. Along this part of the coast, tiny fishing villages cling to the cliffs where the earth rushes down to meet the cold sea. Scarborough and adorable Robin Hood's Bay make ideal getaways.

The North Yorkshire Moors. A short drive north from York, these heather-covered hills are a perfect place to wander. Hutton-le-Hole and Helmsley are pleasant towns, and the ruins of Rievaulx Abbey are nearby.

PLANNING

WHEN TO GO

To see the heather at its lushest, visit in summer (but despite the season, be prepared for some chilly days). It's also the best time for the coast, when colorful regattas and arts festivals are under way. York Minster makes a splendid focal point for the prestigious York Early Music Festival in early July. Spring and fall bring their own rewards: far fewer crowds and crisp, clear days, although there's an increased risk of rain and fog. The harsh winter is hard to call: with snow and bright days, the coast, moors, and dales are beautiful, but storms and blizzards set in quickly. The moorland roads become impassable, and villages can be cut off entirely. In winter, stick to York and the main towns.

PLANNING YOUR TIME

Yorkshire is a vast region; it's difficult to explore in a short amount of time. If you're in a hurry, you could visit York or Leeds as a day trip from London; the fastest trains take just two hours. But proper exploration—especially of the countryside—requires time and effort. In a few days you could explore York and some highlights such as Castle Howard and Studley Royal. You'd need the better part of a week to take in the small towns, abandoned abbeys, and inspiring moors and coast. It's well worth it: this is the path less traveled. The Yorkshire Pass (⊕ www.yorkshirepass.co.uk), good for 1, 2, 3, or 6 days, can save you money on more than 70 attractions.

GETTING HERE AND AROUND

AIR TRAVEL

Leeds Bradford Airport, 8 mi northwest of Leeds, has frequent flights from other cities in England and Europe. Look for cheap fares from London on BMI Baby, Easyjet, or British Airways. Another good choice for this region is Manchester Airport, about 40 mi southwest of Leeds. This larger airport is well served by domestic and international carriers.

Airports Leeds Bradford International Airport (✉ A658, Yeadon ☎ 0871/288–2288 ⊕ www.lbia.co.uk). **Manchester Airport** (✉ Near Junctions 5 and 6 of M56 ☎ 0871/271–0711 ⊕ www.manairport.co.uk).

BUS TRAVEL

National Express and Megabus both have numerous daily departures from London's Victoria Coach Station to major cities in Yorkshire. Average travel times are 4¼ hours to Leeds, six hours to York, and eight hours to Scarborough. Once you're in the region, local bus companies take over the routes. There are Metro buses from Leeds and Bradford into the more remote parts of the Yorkshire Dales. Other companies are Harrogate & District for services to Ripon, Harrogate, and Leeds; Yorkshire Coastliner for Castle Howard, Scarborough, Whitby, Malton, and Leeds; and Arriva for Whitby, Scarborough, and Middlesbrough. In York the main local bus operator is First. Traveline has route information.

Bus Contacts Arriva (☎ 0844/800–4411 ⊕ www.arriva.co.uk). **First** (☎ 0845/604–5460 ⊕ www.firstgroup.com). **Harrogate & District** (☎ 01423/566061 ⊕ www.harrogatebus.co.uk). **Megabus** (☎ 0900/160–0900

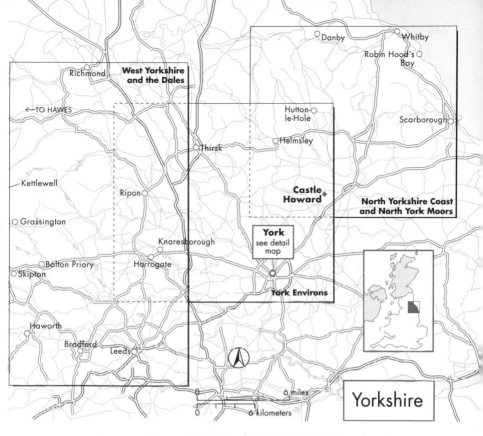

Yorkshire

⊕ www.megabus.co.uk). **Metroline** (☎ 0113/245–7676 ⊕ www.wymetro. com). **National Express** (☎ 0871/781–8181 ⊕ www.nationalexpress.com). **Traveline** (☎ 0870/608–2608 ⊕ www.traveline.org.uk). **Yorkshire Coastliner** (☎ 01653/692556 ⊕ www.yorkshirecoastliner.co.uk).

CAR TRAVEL

If you're driving, the M1 is the principal route north from London. This major thoroughfare gets you to Leeds in about two hours. For York (193 mi) and the Scarborough areas, stay on M1 to Leeds (189 mi), and then take A64. For the Yorkshire Dales, take M1 to Leeds, then A660 to A65 north and west to Skipton. For the North York Moors, take either B1363 north from York to Helmsley, or the A64 through Malton to Whitby. The trans-Pennine motorway, the M62, between Liverpool and Hull, crosses the bottom of this region. North of Leeds, A1 is the major north–south road, although narrow stretches, roadwork, and heavy traffic make this route slow going at times.

Some of the steep, narrow roads in the countryside off the main routes are difficult drives and can be perilous (or closed altogether) in winter. Main roads often closed by snowdrifts are the moorland A169 and the coast-and-moor A171. If you plan to drive in the dales or moors in winter, check the weather forecast in advance.

TRAIN TRAVEL

East Coast trains travel to Leeds and York from London's King's Cross station. Average travel times from King's Cross are 2½ hours to Leeds and two hours to York. Contact National Rail for train times, and to find out if any discounted Rover tickets are available for your journey.

Train Contacts East Coast (☎ 0845/722–5111 ⊕ www.eastcoast.co.uk). **National Rail Enquiries** (☎ 0845/748–4950 ⊕ www.nationalrail.co.uk).

RESTAURANTS

Generally speaking, Yorkshire is not known for its cuisine, and bacon-based breakfasts and lunches of pork pies do tend to pale fairly quickly. Luckily, in the larger towns and cities, particularly in Leeds, a foodie culture of sorts has developed. Indian eateries (called "curry restaurants") are very good in northern cities. Out in the countryside, pubs are your best bet for dining. Many offer excellent home-cooked food and locally produced meat (especially lamb) and vegetables. Roast beef dinners generally come with Yorkshire pudding, the tasty, light bread that is called a popover in the United States and Canada. It's generally served with lots of gravy. Be sure to sample local cheeses, especially Wensleydale, which has a delicate flavor and honeyed aftertaste.

HOTELS

Traditional hotels are limited primarily to major towns and cities; those in the country tend to be guesthouses. Many of the better guesthouses are at the edge of town, but some proprietors will pick you up at the main station if you're relying on public transportation—verify before booking. Rooms fill quickly at seaside resorts in July and August, and some places in the moors and dales close in winter. Always call ahead to make sure a hotel is open and has space available.

WHAT IT COSTS IN POUNDS					
	£	££	£££	££££	£££££
Restaurants	under £10	£10–£14	£15–£19	£20–£25	over £25
Hotels	under £70	£70–£120	£121–£160	£161–£220	over £220

Restaurant prices are for a main course at dinner. Hotel prices are for two people in a standard double room in high season, including V.A.T., with no meals or, if indicated, CP (with Continental breakfast), BP (Breakfast Plan, with full breakfast), or MAP (Modified American Plan, with breakfast and dinner).

VISITOR INFORMATION

Contact Yorkshire Tourist Board (☎ 01904/707961 ⊕ www.yorkshire.com).

WEST YORKSHIRE AND BRONTË COUNTRY

The busy city of Leeds provides an obvious starting point for a tour of West Yorkshire. From here you can strike out for the traditional wool towns, such as Saltaire, a UNESCO-protected gem, and the Magna museum at Rotherham, which draws long lines for its surprisingly interesting exploration of steel. But the main thrust of many visits to West

Yorkshire is to the west of Leeds, where the gaunt hills north of the Calder Valley and south of the River Aire form the district immortalized by the mournful writings of the Brontë sisters. Haworth, an otherwise gray village, might have faded into obscurity were it not for the magnetism of the literary sisters. Every summer, thousands toil up the steep main street to visit their hometown, but to truly understand their writing you need to go farther afield to the ruined farm of Top Withins, which is by legend, if not fact, Wuthering Heights.

13

LEEDS

43 mi northeast of Manchester, 25 mi southwest of York.

One of the cultural centers of the north, Leeds has successfully transformed itself. Its Victorian buildings have been polished and restored, its old factories and warehouses converted into pricey loft housing and modern offices. Everywhere are cafés with outdoor tables defying the northern weather, sleek bars, modern hotels, and upscale restaurants. Leeds University keeps the town young and hip, supporting the city's good music shops and funky clothing and jewelry boutiques.

GETTING HERE AND AROUND

Leeds Bradford Airport, 8 mi northwest of the city, is the main gateway to this part of the country. National Express and Megabus have frequent buses here from London's Victoria Coach Station. The journey takes about four hours. East Coast trains depart from London's King's Cross Station to Leeds Station about every 30 minutes during the week. The trip takes about 2½ hours. Leeds Station is in the middle of central Leeds and usually has a line of taxis waiting out front.

A city of nearly half a million people, Leeds has an efficient local bus service. Most visitors will never use it, as most sights are in the easily walkable downtown.

ESSENTIALS

Visitor Information Leeds (✉ *Leeds City Station* ☎ *0113/242–5242* ⊕ *www. visitleeds.co.uk*).

EXPLORING
TOP ATTRACTIONS

The Calls. East of Granary Wharf, the Calls has converted riverfront warehouses into snazzy bars and restaurants that enliven the cobbled streets and quayside. This is definitely the area to wander at lunchtime and when you're craving an afternoon coffee.

City Square. One of the city's best examples of Victorian architecture is City Square, right in front of the train station. Busy streets surround the traffic-free oasis where benches make a good place to get your bearings as you take in the 19th-century statues. On the east side is the 18th-century Mill Hill Chapel.

★ **Harewood House.** The home of the earl of Harewood, a cousin of the Queen, Harewood House (pronounced *har*-wood) is a spectacular neoclassical mansion, built in 1759 by John Carr of York. Highlights include Robert Adam interiors, important paintings and ceramics, and a large, ravishingly beautiful collection of Chippendale furniture

(Chippendale was born in nearby Otley), notably the magnificent State Bed. The Old Kitchen and Below Stairs exhibition illustrates life from the servants' point of view. Capability Brown designed the handsome grounds, and Charles Barry created a notable Italian garden with fountains in the 1840s. Also here are a bird garden with 120 rare and endangered species, a playground, and a butterfly house. The house is 7 mi north of Leeds; you can take Harrogate & District Bus 36. ■ TIP→ Ticket prices are discounted in spring and fall. ⊠ *Junction of A61 and A659, Harewood* ☎ *0113/218–1010* ⊕ *www.harewood.org* ⊠ *£13* ⊗ *House Apr.–Oct., daily noon–4. Gardens Apr.–Oct., daily 10–6; Feb. and Mar., weekends 10–4.*

★   **Leeds Art Gallery.** Next door to the Victorian Town Hall, the recently renovated Leeds Art Gallery is Yorkshire's most impressive art museum, with a strong core collection of works by Courbet, Sisley, Constable, Crome, and the internationally acclaimed Yorkshire sculptor Henry Moore, who studied at the Leeds School of Art. The graceful statue on the steps outside the gallery is Moore's *Reclining Woman.* More works by Moore are at the adjacent **Henry Moore Institute,** which also has regular exhibitions of modern sculpture. The **Craft Centre and Design Gallery,** also in the museum, exhibits and sells fine contemporary crafts. ⊠ *The Headrow* ☎ *0113/247–8256* ⊕ *www.leeds. gov.uk/artgallery* ⊠ *Free* ⊗ *Mon., Tues., and Thurs.–Sat. 10–5, Wed. noon–5, Sun. 1–5.*

QUICK BITES Step down to the cozy, book-lined **New Conservatory** (⊠ *The Albions, Albion Pl., off Briggate* ☎ *0113/246–1853*) for fresh sandwiches, wraps, and cakes. You can also sit and relax with a cup of tea or coffee.

WORTH NOTING

Granary Wharf. Once the center of Leeds' decayed industrial area, two adjacent neighborhoods along the River Aire are now a trendy area of pricey loft apartments, chic bars, and pleasant cafés. Granary Wharf, in the Canal Basin, reached via the Dark Arches where the River Aire flows under City Station, is a good place to go exploring design and crafts shops, music shops, and a regular festival market.

ⓒ   **Royal Armouries.** Much of the legendary arms and armor originally collected in the Tower of London fills the Royal Armouries, which occupies a redeveloped 13-acre dockland site, a 15-minute walk from the city center. Five theme galleries—War, Tournament, Self-Defense, Hunting, and Arms and Armor of the Orient—trace the history of weaponry. The state-of-the-art building is stunningly designed: expect a full-size elephant in armor, warriors on horseback, and floor-to-ceiling tents, as well as spirited interactive displays and live demonstrations. Shoot a crossbow, direct operations on a battlefield, experience a Wild West gunfight or an Elizabethan joust: it's your choice. ⊠ *Armouries Dr., off M1 or M621* ☎ *0113/220–1999* ⊕ *www.armouries.org.uk* ⊠ *Free* ⊗ *Daily 10–5.*

Temple Newsam. The Leeds City Council uses Temple Newsam, a huge Elizabethan and Jacobean building, to display its impressive collections of furniture, paintings, and ceramics. The house was the birthplace in

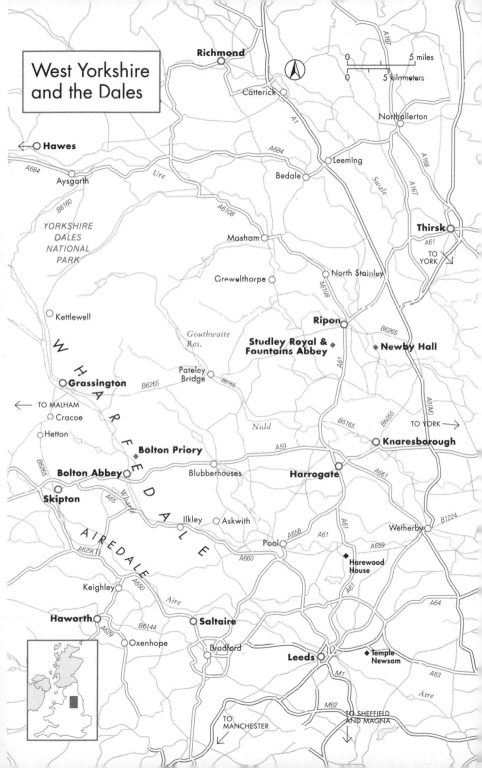

1545 of Lord Darnley, the doomed husband of Mary, Queen of Scots. Surrounding the house is a public park with rose gardens, greenhouses, and miles of woodland walks, all laid out by Capability Brown in 1762. Temple Newsam is 4 mi east of Leeds on A63; Buses 18, 40, 88, and 163–165 leave from Leeds Central Bus Station every 30 minutes and stop at the Irwin Arms, a 10-minute walk from the site. ⊠ *Off Selby Rd.* ☎ *0113/264–5535* ⊕ *www.leeds.gov.uk/templenewsam* 🏛 *House £3.50, farm £3, joint ticket £5.60; parking £4* ☉ *Apr.–Oct., Tues.–Sun. and national holiday Mon. 10:30–5; Nov.–Mar., Tues.–Sun. and national holiday Mon. 10:30–4. Last admission 45 mins before closing.*

OFF THE BEATEN⟳ PATH

Magna. A 45-minute drive south from Leeds to Rotherham brings you squarely in view of Yorkshire's industrial past, embodied by a former steelworks that houses Magna, a widely respected science museum. Smoke, flames, and sparking electricity bring one of the original six arc furnaces roaring to life in a sound-and-light show. Steelworkers lost their jobs in the 1970s and '80s when the British coal and steel industries collapsed, and a permanent exhibit explores what happened to those workers afterward. Four pavilions engagingly illustrate the use of fire, earth, air, and water in the production of steel. ⊠ *Junction 33 or 34 off M1, Sheffield Rd., Rotherham* ☎ *01709/720002* ⊕ *www. visitmagna.co.uk* 🎫 *£10* ☉ *Daily 10–5.*

WHERE TO EAT

£££
MODERN BRITISH

✗ **Anthony's.** The chef in this intimate basement restaurant takes a lot of chances, and the results are hugely rewarding to lovers of daring food. Main courses change daily but can include Moroccan-spiced scallops with apricots and cocoa, or sautéed John Dory with whelks and chorizo. These unusual combinations work well in the formal setting. Other Anthony's outposts are a lunch spot at Flannels on Vicar Lane, a larger restaurant in the Corn Exchange, and a patisserie in the Victoria Quarter shopping arcade. ⊠ *19 Boar La.* ☎ *0113/245–5922* ⊕ *www. anthonysrestaurant.co.uk* 🗃 *AE, DC, MC, V* ☉ *Closed Sun. and Mon.*

£££
MODERN BRITISH

✗ **Brasserie Forty 4.** Within the elegant 44 The Calls Hotel, the Brasserie is one of the city's best restaurants. The atmosphere, like the menu, is modern and upscale, but not snobby. The dining room has exposed stone walls and arched windows overlooking the canal. In the summer there's a balcony for alfresco dining. The often-changing menu usually features appetizers like crabmeat and corn fritters or smoked salmon and smoked trout with potato salad. Elegant main courses include Yorkshire duck breast served with bok choy or venison steak with cassoulet. For dessert try the chocolate fondue with marshmallows and fruit. Book in advance. ⊠ *42–44 The Calls* ☎ *0113/234–3232* ⊕ *www. brasserie44.com* 🗃 *AE, DC, MC, V.*

££
MODERN BRITISH

✗ **Fourth Floor Restaurant.** If the Harvey Nichols department store has been a roaring success, it's partly because of the lure of this swank eatery, a standout for both food and dramatic, high-tech design. The well-crafted Modern British menu changes several times a week, but is sure to have stylish takes on dishes such as risotto with shrimp, nutmeg, and lemon, organic rack of lamb with baby leeks, and the freshest lemon sole. ⊠ *Harvey Nichols, 107–111 Briggate* ☎ *0113/204–8000* 🗃 *AE, DC, MC, V* ☉ *No dinner Sun. and Mon.*

£ ✕ **Salts.** This attractive deli is done in proper Victorian style: the walls are
DELI lined with wooden shelves, stacked high with sparkling bottles and colorful cans. The affordable menu is classic British deli food using locally
produced meats and vegetables. Locals stop by for salads (chicken and
avocado, tomato, or arugula and blue cheese), quiches, and made-to-
order sandwiches. It's open early for breakfast weekdays. There's plenty
of seating at rustic wooden tables in a comfortable dining room flooded
with light from the tall windows. ⊠ *14 Swinegate* ☎ *0113/243–2323*
⊕ *www.saltsdeli.co.uk* ⊟ *MC, V* ☺ *Closed Sun.*

£ ✕ **Whitelocks.** The city's oldest pub, dating from 1715, is tucked away
BRITISH in an alley in the city center. It's been known for years for traditional
pub food, including bangers and mash, meat pies, and real ale. The
long, narrow bar has all the trappings of the Victorian era—stained
glass, etched mirrors, copper-top tables, and red-plush banquettes. Service is brisk and friendly, and during the day the emphasis is more on
food than drink. ⊠ *Turks Head Yard, off Briggate* ☎ *0113/245–3950*
⊟ *AE, MC, V.*

WHERE TO STAY

££££–£££££ 🏨 **42 The Calls.** This high-tech, high-concept hotel in the trendy waterfront area was once a grain mill, and each room shows creative flair but
retains such original elements as exposed beams and atmospheric brickwork. The amenities are up-to-the-minute, including in-room music
players. Some rooms even come with fishing rods (bring your own
bait). **Pros:** laid-back vibe; luxurious rooms; clever use of space. **Cons:**
some find it too trendy; rather pricey. ⊠ *42 The Calls* ☎ *0113/244–0099*
⊕ *www.theetoncollection.com* ⇆ *41 rooms* ⚐ *In-room: no a/c, refrigerator, Wi-Fi. In-hotel: restaurant, room service, bar, some pets allowed*
⊟ *AE, DC, MC, V* ⚏ *BP.*

£££–££££ 🏨 **Malmaison.** Passengers who used this building as a tram and bus termi-
★ nal could hardly have envisioned its rebirth as a chic hotel exuding contemporary class and comfort. Guest rooms have color themes of subtle
tones—plum, charcoal, and ocher—and are beautifully outfitted with
velvet pillows and floor-to-ceiling windows. The dark-panel brasserie
concentrates on French food with a Mediterranean twist. **Pros:** beautiful design; spacious rooms; comfortable beds. **Cons:** restaurant is often
booked up; overly trendy. ⊠ *1 Swinegate* ☎ *0113/398–1000* ⊕ *www.
malmaison.com* ⇆ *100 rooms* ⚐ *In-room: no a/c, Wi-Fi. In-hotel: restaurant, bar, gym, spa, laundry service* ⊟ *AE, DC, MC, V* ⚏ *BP.*

£££–££££ 🏨 **Quebecs.** The grand Leeds and County Liberal Club may have changed
its identity when it became a boutique hotel, but the building has lost
none of its Victorian verve. The sweeping oak staircase, lighted by tall
stained-glass windows, leads up to classy bedrooms of different shapes
and sizes, all sympathetically decorated in muted colors. The paneled
Oak Room, an unusual circular design, is a must for a drink. Lower
weekend rates include breakfast. **Pros:** gorgeous building; spacious
rooms; great bar. **Cons:** a bit too formal; some rooms are better than
others. ⊠ *9 Quebec St.* ☎ *0113/244–8989* ⊕ *www.theetoncollection.
com* ⇆ *45 rooms, 6 suites* ⚐ *In-room: no a/c, safe, refrigerator, Internet.
In-hotel: restaurant, room service, bar* ⊟ *AE, DC, MC, V* ⚏ *BP.*

13

NIGHTLIFE AND THE ARTS
NIGHTLIFE
At fashionable café-bars all over Leeds, you can grab a bite or sip cappuccino or designer beer until late into the night. There's no shortage of clubs, either; Leeds has one of the best party scenes outside London. **Bar Norman** (⌂ *36 Call La.* ☎ *0113/234–3988*) has won the local in-crowd with its weird and wonderful design, including curved walls. Japanese food and music are other draws. **Cuban Heels** (⌂ *The Arches, 28–30 Assembly St.* ☎ *0113/234–6115*) kicks out salsa sounds most nights. **Mojo** (⌂ *18 Merrion St.* ☎ *0113/244–6387*) is a real rock-and-roll bar, with the music and the look to match. Around for 300 years, **The Ship** (⌂ *71A Briggate* ☎ *0113/246–8031*) is a friendly place to stop in for a quick drink or a tasty pub lunch.

THE ARTS
Opera North, a leading provincial opera company, has its home in Leeds at the **Grand Theatre** (⌂ *46 New Briggate* ☎ *0113/222–6222*); the opulent auditorium is modeled on that of La Scala. Opera North also plays for free each summer at Temple Newsam.

The Victorian **Town Hall** (⌂ *The Headrow* ☎ *0113/224–3801*) hosts an international concert season (October through May) that attracts top performers and conductors. In September it is the site of the fourth and final stage of the prestigious Leeds International Piano Competition.

The ultramodern **West Yorkshire Playhouse** (⌂ *Playhouse Sq., Quarry Hill* ☎ *0113/213–7700*) was built on the slope of an old quarry. Its adaptable staging makes it eminently suitable for new and classic productions.

SHOPPING
★ For upscale items for the home, visit the shops inside the historic **Corn Exchange** (⌂ *Call La.* ☎ *0113/234–0363*). The circular structure is also a good place to grab a coffee or stop for lunch. The city has some excellent markets, notably **Kirkgate Market** (⌂ *34 George St.* ☎ *0113/214–5162* ☉ *Closed Wed. morning and Sun.*), an Edwardian beauty that's the largest in the north of England. The glistening **Victoria Quarter** (⌂ *Briggate* ☎ *0113/245–5333*), with its 70 stores, epitomizes fin-de-siècle style and 21st-century chic. It's on Briggate Street, one of the city's best shopping strips.

SALTAIRE

12 mi east of Leeds, 8 mi east of Haworth.

GETTING HERE AND AROUND
Saltaire is 4 mi north of Bradford, an old wool-market town. There are regular bus and train services to Saltaire from Bradford. Drivers should take A650 to Shipley and follow the signs.

ESSENTIALS
Visitor Information Saltaire Tourist Information Center (⌂ *2 Victoria Rd., Saltaire* ☎ *01274/774993* ⊕ *www.saltaire-village.co.uk*).

EXPLORING

★ A UNESCO World Heritage Site, the former model town of **Saltaire** was built in the mid-19th century by textile magnate Sir Titus Salt, who was trying to create the ideal industrial world. When he decided to relocate his factories from the dark mills of Bradford to the countryside, he hoped to create a beautiful environment in which his workers would be happy. The Italianate town is remarkably well preserved, its former mills and houses now turned into shops, restaurants, and galleries. Salt's Mill, built in 1853, resembles a palazzo and was the largest factory in the world when it was built. Today it holds an art gallery and crafts and furniture shops. One-hour guided tours (£3.75) depart weekends at 2 PM from the **tourist information center** (⊠ *2 Victoria Rd., Saltaire* ☎ *01274/599887* ⊕ *www.saltaire-village.info*). The **1853 Gallery** (⊠ *Salt's Mill, Victoria Rd.* ☎ *01274/531163* 🖾 *Free* ☉ *Daily 10–6*) holds a remarkable exhibition of 400 works by Bradford-born artist David Hockney. There are two restaurants on-site.

OFF THE BEATEN PATH

Most travelers go to Bradford, 10 mi west of Leeds, for the museums, particularly the renowned **National Media Museum**, which traces the history of photographic media. It's a huge and hugely entertaining place, with five galleries displaying the world's first photographic negative, the latest digital imaging, and everything between. ∎ TIP→ **The museum's popularity with children means you should come early or late in the day if you want to see the displays in peace.** ⊠ *Pictureville, Prince's Way* ☎ *01274/202030 or 0870/701–0200* ⊕ *www.nationalmediamuseum. org.uk* 🖾 *Free* ☉ *Tues.–Sun. and bank holidays 10–6.*

HAWORTH: HEART OF BRONTË COUNTRY

★ *8 mi west of Saltaire, 10 mi northwest of Bradford, 4 mi southwest of Keighley.*

Whatever Haworth might have been in the past, today it is Brontë country. This old stone-built village on the edge of the Yorkshire Moors long ago gave up its own personality and allowed itself to be taken over by the doomed sisters, their mournful books, and their millions of fans. In 1820, when Anne, Emily, and Charlotte were very young, their father moved them and their other three siblings away from their old home in Bradford to Haworth. The sisters—Emily (author of *Wuthering Heights*, 1847), Charlotte (*Jane Eyre*, 1847), and Anne (*The Tenant of Wildfell Hall*, 1848) were all affected by the stark, dramatic countryside. These days it seems that every building they ever glanced at has been turned into a memorial, shop, or museum.

GETTING HERE AND AROUND

To reach Haworth by bus or train, buy a Metro Day Rover for bus and rail (£6.20) and take the Metro train from Leeds train station to Keighley. There are about three hourly. From Keighley, take the Keighley & Worth Valley Railway for the trip to Haworth (weekends only; £7 round-trip), or Keighley and District Bus 663, 664, or 665 (Monday–Saturday, every 20 minutes; Sunday, every half hour). From Bradford station, Interchange buses run every half hour to Keighley. By car, Haworth is an easy drive 3 mi south on A629 from Keighley;

it's well signposted, and there's plenty of cheap parking in town. The Haworth Visitor Center has information about accommodations, maps, books on the Brontës, and inexpensive leaflets to help you find your way to such outlying *Wuthering Heights* sites as Ponden Hall (Thrushcross Grange) and Ponden Kirk (Penistone Crag).

ESSENTIALS

Visitor Information Haworth Visitor Center (✉ *2–4 West La.* ☎ *01535/642329*).

EXPLORING

Haworth's steep, cobbled **Main Street** has changed little in outward appearance since the early 19th century, but today acts as a funnel for the people who crowd into the points of interest: the **Black Bull** pub, where the reprobate Branwell, the Brontës' only brother, drank himself into an early grave; the **post office** from which Charlotte, Emily, and Anne sent their manuscripts to their London publishers; and the **church,** with its gloomy graveyard (Charlotte and Emily are buried inside the church; Anne is buried in Scarborough).

The best of the Brontë sights in Haworth is the **Brontë Parsonage Museum.** In the somber Georgian house in which the sisters grew up, it displays original furniture (some bought by Charlotte after the success of *Jane Eyre*), portraits, and books. The Brontës moved to this simple house when the Reverend Patrick Brontë was appointed to the local church, but tragedy soon struck—his wife, Maria, and their two eldest children died within five years. They were done in, along with hundreds of others, by water wells tainted by seepage from the neighboring graveyard. The museum explains the family's tragic life story and makes it real with a strong collection of enchanting mementos of the four children, including tiny books they made when they were still very young, Charlotte's wedding bonnet and the sisters' spidery, youthful graffiti on the nursery wall. Branwell painted several of the portraits on display. ✉ *Church St.* ☎ *01535/642323* ⊕ *www.bronte.info* 🎟 *£6.50* ☉ *Apr.– Sept., daily 10–5:30; Oct.–Mar., daily 11–5; last admission 30 mins before closing.*

If you have the time, you can pack a lunch and walk an hour or so along a field path, a lane, and a moorland track to the lovely, isolated waterfall that has, inevitably, been renamed the **Brontë Waterfall**. It was a favorite of the sisters, who wrote about it in poems and letters.

Top Withins, a ruined, gloomy house on a bleak hilltop farm 3 mi from Haworth, is often taken to be the inspiration for Heathcliff's gloomy mansion, Wuthering Heights. Brontë scholars say it probably isn't; the ruins never looked the way the book describes them. Still, it's an inspirational walk across the moors. There and back from Haworth is a two-hour walk. ■TIP➜ **If you've read** *Wuthering Heights,* **you don't need to be reminded to wear sturdy shoes and protective clothing.**

Haworth is on the **Keighley & Worth Valley Railway,** a gorgeous 5-mi-long branch line along which steam engines run between Keighley (4 mi northeast of Haworth) and Oxenhope. On special days, family fairs en route add to the fun. The **Museum of Rail Travel** (🎟 *£2* ☉ *Daily 11–4*), at Ingrow along the line, exhibits vintage train cars. ✉ *Railway Station, Keighley* ☎ *01535/645214* ⊕ *www.kwvr.co.uk* 🎟 *£9.40* round-trip, £14 Day Rover ticket ☉ Sept.–June, weekends; July and Aug., daily; call for schedules.

WHERE TO EAT AND STAY

£££ ✕ **Weavers**. Although Weavers is
BRITISH known primarily as a restaurant, upstairs there are a few chintz-filled rooms with antique French beds. The restaurant serves traditional, organic Yorkshire fare like slow-cooked Yorkshire lamb with lentils, organic pork with crushed potatoes, or breast of Yorkshire duck with rhubarb and ginger, all served with home-baked bread. ⊠ 15 West La. ☎ 01535/643822 ⊕ www.weaversmallhotel.co.uk ⊟ AE, DC, MC, V ☉ Closed Sun. and Mon. No lunch Tues. or Sat.

£ ⊡ **Aitches**. This intimate 19th-century stone house is close to the Brontë Parsonage. The guest rooms are modern, with pine pieces and colorful quilts and drapes. A fixed-price meal in the elegant small restaurant, available to guests only, might include local pork cutlet with Stilton crumble followed by a bread-and-butter pudding. **Pros:** intimate building; friendly staff. **Cons:** the rustic decor won't appeal to everyone. ⊠ 11 West La. ☎ 01535/642501 ⊕ www.aitches.co.uk ⟋ 5 rooms ☊ In-room: no a/c, no phone. In-hotel: restaurant ⊟ MC, V ⓞ⎮ BP.

££–£££ ⊡ **Ashmount Country House**. This charming stone building at the top of the hill was once home to the Brontë sisters' physician, Dr. Amos Ingham. Today it's a peaceful hideaway a short walk from the Parsonage and surrounded by gardens with sweeping views over the valley. Spacious and sunny rooms are cheerfully decorated with fluffy floral comforters. Some have four-posters, others have whirlpool tubs. The owners are friendly and helpful, the atmosphere is relaxed, and breakfasts are delicious. **Pros:** lovely old building; ideal location; great views. **Cons:** books up in advance; it's one of the priciest places in town. ⊠ Mytholmes La. ☎ 01535/646726 ⊕ www.ashmounthaworth. co.uk ⟋ 8 rooms ☊ In-room: no a/c, no phone, Wi-Fi. In-hotel: Wi-Fi hotspot ⊟ MC, V ⓞ⎮ BP.

> ### LANDSCAPE AS MUSE
>
> The rugged Yorkshire Moors helped inspire Emily Brontë's 1847 *Wuthering Heights*; if ever a work of fiction grew out of the landscape in which its author lived, it was surely this. "My sister Emily loved the moors," wrote Charlotte. "Flowers brighter than the rose bloomed in the blackest of the heath for her; out of a sullen hollow in a livid hillside her mind could make an Eden. She found in the bleak solitude many and dear delights; and not the least and best loved was liberty."

13

THE YORKSHIRE DALES

The western equivalent of the North York Moors, the Yorkshire Dales are just as beautiful and nearly as wild. The word dale comes from the Viking word for valley, which gives you an indication that, although the moors have steep hills, the dales are more rugged, with sharper, higher hills culminating in the mountains Pen-y-ghent, Ingleborough, and Whernside. These river valleys fall south and east from the Pennines, and beyond Skipton they present an almost wholly rural aspect. Ruined priories, narrow roads, drystone walls made without mortar, and babbling rivers make for a quintessentially English landscape, full of paths and trails to explore.

BOLTON ABBEY

12 mi north of Haworth, 24 mi northwest of Leeds.

A leafy, picturesque village amid the rolling hills of the Yorkshire Dales, Bolton Abbey is a famously attractive town with a stone church and evocative priory ruins. Much of the area is still technically owned by the duke of Devonshire, who has a huge estate nearby—a lingering remnant of the country's feudal past.

GETTING HERE AND AROUND

Bolton Abbey, off the A59 between Skipton and Harrogate, is best reached by car. Buses are infrequent, but you can take the 74 from Ilkley, or the 883, 884, or 850 from Skipton, Shipley, or Bradford.

EXPLORING

★ Some of the loveliest Wharfedale scenery comes into view around **Bolton Priory,** the ruins of an Augustinian priory, which sits on a grassy embankment inside a great curve of the River Wharfe. The priory is just a short walk or drive from the village of Bolton Abbey. You can wander through the 13th-century ruins or visit the priory church. The duke of Devonshire owns the Bolton Abbey estate, including the ruins. John Ruskin, the Victorian art critic, rated it the most beautiful of all English ruins. Close to Bolton Priory, surrounded by romantic woodland scenery, the River Wharfe plunges between a narrow chasm in the rocks (called the Strid) before reaching **Barden Tower,** a medieval hunting lodge. This lodge is now a ruin and can be visited just as easily as Bolton Priory, in whose grounds it stands. ⊠ *B6160, off A59* ☎ *01756/718009* ⊕ *www.boltonabbey.com* ✉ *Free, parking £6* ☉ *Daily 9–dusk.*

You can ride the scenic 4-mi **Embsay & Bolton Abbey Steam Railway** (☎ *01756/710614, 01756/795189 recorded timetable*), which has a station in Bolton Abbey.

WHERE TO STAY

££££ **Devonshire Arms.** Originally an 18th-century coaching inn, and still
★ belonging to the dukes of Devonshire, this luxurious country-house hotel is near the River Wharfe, an easy walk from Bolton Abbey. The bedrooms are tastefully decorated with antiques and memorabilia from the family home, Chatsworth House in Derbyshire. Downstairs, the Burlington restaurant has earned numerous awards. Its fixed-price menu (£60) uses game and fish from the estate. The brasserie serves more modestly priced fare. There's a lovely spa with an indoor swimming pool where you can work off that dinner. **Pros:** one of the region's best hotels; real manor-house style. **Cons:** you pay for all that charm; you need a car to get here. ⊠ *Bolton Abbey, Skipton* ☎ *01756/710441* ⊕ *www.thedevonshirearms.co.uk* ✍ *37 rooms, 3 suites* ⚓ *In-room: no a/c, Internet. In-hotel: 2 restaurants, bars, tennis court, pool, gym, spa, some pets allowed* ▭ *AE, DC, MC, V* ⦿ *BP.*

SKIPTON

6 mi west of Bolton Abbey, 12 mi north of Haworth, 22 mi west of Harrogate.

Skipton in Airedale, capital of the limestone district of Craven, is a typical Dales market town with as many farmers as visitors milling in the streets. There are markets Monday, Wednesday, Friday, and Saturday, and shops selling local produce predominate.

GETTING HERE AND AROUND

Skipton is off A59 and A65 at the edge of the Yorkshire Dales. From Leeds, First Leeds buses run regularly to Skipton. Dales buses depart regularly from Harrogate and Keighley. There are regular trains from Leeds and Bradford; the journey takes about 40 minutes.

ESSENTIALS

Visitor Information Skipton (⊠ *35 Coach St.* ☎ *01756/792809* ⊕ *www. skiptononline.co.uk).*

EXPLORING

★ **Skipton Castle,** built by the Normans in 1090 and unaltered since the 17th century, is one of the best-preserved of English medieval castles. After the Battle of Marston Moor during the Civil War, it remained the only Royalist stronghold in the north of England. So sturdy was the squat little fortification with its rounded battlements (in places the walls are 12 feet thick) that Oliver Cromwell ordered that the roof be removed, as it had survived one bombardment after another during a three-year siege. When the castle's owner, Lady Anne Clifford, later asked if she could replace the roof, he allowed her do so, as long as it was not strong enough to withstand cannon fire. Today the buildings are marvelously complete, and in the central courtyard a yew tree, planted more than 300 years ago by Lady Anne herself, flourishes. ⊠ *High St.* ☎ *01756/792442* ⊕ *www.skiptoncastle.co.uk* ☑ *£6.20* ⊗ *Mar.–Sept., Mon.–Sat. 10–6, Sun. noon–6; Oct.–Feb., Mon.–Sat. 10–4, Sun. noon–4.*

WHERE TO EAT

£££ ✕ **Angel Inn.** Diners at the Angel clog the hidden-away hamlet of Hetton
BRITISH with their vehicles, such is the attraction of this place with its casual brasserie and more formal restaurant. Roasted lamb and duck are specialties in the restaurant. The ancient stone barn across the road has five well-equipped guest rooms decorated in unfussy country styles. The inn is 5 mi north of Skipton. ⊠ *Off B6265, Hetton* ☎ *01756/730263* ⊕ *www.angelhetton.co.uk* ⊟ *AE, DC, MC, V.*

GRASSINGTON

10 mi north of Skipton, 14 mi northwest of Ilkley, 25 mi west of Ripon.

A small, stone village built around an ancient cobbled marketplace, Grassington makes a good base for exploring Upper Wharfedale. The Dales Way footpath passes through the village, and there's a mix of guesthouses, stores, pubs, and cafés. In summer it becomes overwhelmed

HIKING IN MALHAM

Avid summer hikers descend in droves on Malham to tour the remarkable limestone formations Malham Cove and Gordale Scar, and Malham Tarn. The three sites are on a circular walk of 8 mi that takes most people four to five hours. Those with less time should cut out the tarn (a small lake): a circular walk from the village to the limestone formations Malham Cove and Gordale Scar can be completed in just over two hours.

Malham's **National Park Centre** (☎ *01969/652380* ⊕ *www.yorkshiredales.org.uk* ☉ *Apr.–Oct., daily 10–5; Nov.–Mar., Fri.–Sun. 10–4*) has displays and will give you ideas of what to do locally and in Yorkshire Dales National Park. You can get a list of bed-and-breakfast and pub accommodations, too.

Malham Cove, a huge, 300-foot-high natural rock amphitheater, is a mile north of the village and provides the easiest local walk. Following the path up to the top is a brutal climb, though rewarded by magnificent views.

At **Gordale Scar,** a deep natural chasm between overhanging limestone cliffs, the white waters of a moorland stream plunge 300 feet. It's a mile northeast of Malham by a lovely riverside path.

A walk of more than 3 mi leads north from Malham to **Malham Tarn,** an attractive lake in windswept isolation. There's a nature reserve on the west bank and an easy-to-follow trail on the east bank. Malham is 10 mi west of Grassington: take B6265 south 2 mi through Cracoe, then branch west onto the minor road past Hetton and Calton. Malham is also 12 mi northwest of Skipton, off A65.

by day-trippers and walkers. There are plenty of local walks, however, and if you're prepared to make a day of it, you can soon leave the crowds behind.

EXPLORING

The **National Park Centre** has guidebooks, maps, and bus schedules to help you enjoy a day in the Yorkshire Dales National Park. ⊠ *Colvend, Hebdon Rd.* ☎ *01756/752774* ⊕ *www.yorkshiredales.org.uk* ☉ *Apr.– Oct., daily 10–5; Nov.–Mar., Wed. and Fri.–Sun. 10–4.*

WHERE TO EAT AND STAY

££ ✕ **Devonshire Hotel.** This traditional inn makes a comfortable rural dining spot, with its oak-paneled dining room aglow with flickering candles. Local lamb, beef, and dishes such as creamy fish pie appear on the menu alongside pasta and other options. There are also seven beautifully decorated rooms with a mix of antiques and modern furniture. ⊠ *Main St.* ☎ *01756/752525* ▭ *MC, V.*

BRITISH

HAWES

28 mi north of Grassington.

The best time to visit the so-called cheesiest town in Yorkshire is on Tuesday, when farmers crowd into town for the weekly market. Hawes is the business center for Wensleydale's traditional cheese making. Crumbly, white Wensleydale cheese has been made in the valley for centuries, and it is sold in local stores and at the market. Allow yourself time to wander the cobbled side streets, some of which are filled with antiques shops and tearooms.

EXPLORING

The **Wensleydale Creamery Visitor Centre,** in a working dairy farm, includes a museum that tells the story of the famed local cheese so beloved by the cartoon characters Wallace and Gromit. You can watch production (best seen between 10 and 2) from the viewing gallery, and then taste (and buy) the output in the shop. A restaurant on-site has plenty of cheese samples as well, such as smoked, with ginger, or with apple pie. ⊠ *Gayle La.* ☎ *01969/667664* ⊕ *www.wensleydale.co.uk* ▣ *Museum £2.50* ⊙ *Mon.–Sat. 9:30–5:30, Sun. 10–4:30.*

The Yorkshire Dales National Park Information Centre in the old train station contains the **Dales Countryside Museum,** which gives a picture of Dales life in past centuries. A traditional rope-making shop here also welcomes visitors. ⊠ *Station Yard* ☎ *01969/666210* ⊕ *www. yorkshiredales.org.uk* ▣ *Museum £3* ⊙ *Daily 10–5.*

RICHMOND

22 mi northeast of Hawes, 25 mi northwest of Ripon.

Richmond tucks itself into a curve above the foaming River Swale, with a network of narrow Georgian streets and terraces opening onto a large cobbled marketplace. Despite appearances, it would be a mistake to date the town to the 18th century. The Normans swept in during the late 11th century, determined to subdue the local population and establish their rule in the north. This they did by building a mighty castle, around which the town grew, and throughout the Middle Ages Richmond was effectively a garrison town.

GETTING HERE AND AROUND

Trains run to Richmond from Darlington every 30 minutes or so; the journey takes half an hour. By car, Richmond is on the rural B6274— follow signs off A1.

ESSENTIALS

Visitor Information Richmond (⊠ *Friary Gardens, Victoria Rd.* ☎ *01748/850252* ⊕ *www.yorkshiredales.org*).

EXPLORING

The immense keep of Norman **Richmond Castle** towers above the river, providing excellent views of the countryside. Built around 1071 by Alan Rufus, first earl of Richmond, it was used as a prison for William "the Lion" of Scotland 100 years later. The castle retains its thick curtain wall and chapel, and a great hall that has been restored to its medieval splendor; even the 14th-century graffiti remains. There's a heritage garden, and a path along the river leads to the ruins of golden-stone Easby Abbey. One historical note: when Henry Tudor (son of Edmund Tudor, earl of Richmond) became Henry VII in 1485, he began calling his palace in southwest London by the name Richmond after his family seat in Richmond. The name gradually came to be used to describe that area of London. ☎ *01748/822493* ⊕ *www.english-heritage.org.uk* 🎫 *£4.50* ⊙ *Apr.–Sept., daily 10–6; Oct.–Mar., Thurs.–Mon. 10–4.*

The tiny Georgian **Theatre Royal**, a jewel box built in 1788, retains original features such as the wooden seating from the days of the 18th-century Shakespearean actor David Garrick. The museum holds scenery dating from 1836. There are hourly tours of the theater every weekday between 10 and 4. ⊠ *Victoria Rd.* ☎ *01748/823710, 01748/825252 box office* ⊕ *www.georgiantheatreroyal.co.uk* 🎫 *Museum £2.50 suggested donation* ⊙ *Museum mid-Feb.–Dec., Mon.–Sat. 10–4:30.*

WHERE TO EAT AND STAY

££
BRITISH
✕ **Black Bull.** Over the years the Black Bull has grown from a small place popular with locals to a sprawling operation that attracts visitors from throughout the area. The menu is broad and varied in the main dining room, where the French-influenced British cuisine includes breaded flounder with prawn sauce, rack of venison with cassis jus, and roasted duck with bitter orange sauce. Less fussy food (sausages and mash, Brie sandwiches) is served in the pub. The friendly staff doesn't mind if you just want a drink. ⊠ *Back La., Moulton* ☎ *01325/377289* ⊕ *www.blackbullmoulton.com* ▤ *MC, V* ⊙ *No dinner Sun.*

£££
🏨 **Frenchgate Hotel.** This three-story Georgian town house on a quiet cobbled street has a secluded walled garden for summer days. The bright and welcoming interior is furnished with some flair. Public rooms hark back to the 17th century, but the decorative mice (symbol of local craftsman Mousey Thompson) hidden in the woodwork are more recent. Works by area artists fill the hotel, and the spacious bedrooms are subtly decorated in soothing cream and taupe. Some bathrooms have deep roll-top baths. The in-house restaurant creates tasty French fare and is popular with locals. **Pros:** lovely gardens; quiet neighborhood. **Cons:** restaurant can be a bit noisy; not a lot of amenities. ⊠ *59–61 Frenchgate* ☎ *01748/822087* ⊕ *www.thefrenchgate.co.uk* 🛏 *11 rooms* ⅍ *In-room: no a/c. In-hotel: restaurant, bar* ▤ *MC, V* ⦿ *BP.*

£££
🏨 **Millgate House.** This 18th-century house in the center of Richmond has been beautifully restored, as you'll note from the elegant dining room and lounge. The bedrooms are spacious havens in creams and whites. All have views of the town or the extraordinary gardens, which have won Royal Horticultural Society awards. Big claw-foot tubs lure you into the bathrooms—some of which have their own fireplaces. Breakfasts here win raves for their variety and freshness. In addition to the five rooms, there are two self-catering apartments. **Pros:** in the middle of town; grand historic house. **Cons:** rooms can be a bit chilly; not the bargain it once was. ⊠ *Millgate* ☎ *01748/823571* ⊕ *www.millgatehouse.com* 🛏 *5 rooms, 2 apartments.* ⅍ *In-room: no a/c, no phone, kitchen (some)* ▤ *MC, V* ⦿ *BP.*

YORK

It would be unthinkable to visit North Yorkshire without first visiting the historic cathedral city of York. Much of the city's medieval and 18th-century architecture has survived, making this city a delight to explore. ■ TIP→ The city is one of the most popular short-stay destinations in Britain, and only two hours by train from London's King's Cross Station.

Named "Eboracum" by the Romans, York was the military capital of Roman Britain, and traces of garrison buildings survive throughout the city. After the Roman Empire collapsed in the 5th century, the Saxons built "Eoforwic" upon the ruins of a fort, but were soon defeated by Vikings who called the town "Jorvik" and used it as a base from which to subjugate the countryside. The Normans came in the 11th century and emulated the Vikings by using the town as a military base. It was during Norman times that the foundations of York Minster, the largest medieval cathedral in England, were laid. The only changes the 19th century brought were large houses, built mostly on the outskirts of the city center.

13

GETTING HERE AND AROUND
If you're driving, take the M1 north from London. Stay on it to Leeds, and then take the A64 to York; York is 25 mi northeast of Leeds. The journey should take around three hours. National Express and Megabus have motor coaches departing from London's Victoria Coach Station every hour. The journey takes 4½ hours. National Express trains run from London's King's Cross Station about every 30 minutes during the week. The trip takes about two hours. York Station, just outside the city walls, has a line of taxis out front to take you to your hotel. If you don't have bags, the walk to town takes eight minutes.

York's city center is mostly closed to traffic and is very walkable. The old center is a compact, dense web of narrow streets and tiny medieval alleys called "snickleways." These provide shortcuts across the city center, but they're not on maps, so you never quite know where you'll end up, which in York is often a pleasant surprise.

TOURS   City Sightseeing runs frequent bus tours of York that stop at the Castle Museum, the Shambles, and Jorvik. You can get on and off as often as you please. York Association of Voluntary Guides arranges short walking tours around the city, which depart daily at 10:15. There are additional tours at 2:15 April through October and at 6:45 July and August. The tours are free, but tips are appreciated.

TIMING
In July and August tourists choke the narrow streets and form long lines at the Minster. April, May, June, and September are less crowded, but the weather can be unpredictable. April is also the time to see the embankments beneath the city walls filled with the pale gold ripple of daffodils.

ESSENTIALS
Tour Information City Sightseeing (☎ 01904/655585 ⊕ www.citysightseeing. co.uk). **York Association of Voluntary Guides** (✉ De Grey Rooms, Exhibition Sq. ☎ 01904/640780).

Visitor Information York (✉ 1 Museum St. ☎ 01904/550099 ⊕ www.visityork. org ✉ York Train Station ☎ 01904/621756).

EXPLORING

TOP ATTRACTIONS

❶ ★ City walls. York's almost 3 mi of ancient stone walls are among the best-preserved in England. A walk on the narrow paved path along the top leads you through 1,900 years of history, from the time the earthen ramparts were raised by the Romans and York's Viking kings to repel raiders, to their fortification by the Normans, to their current colorful landscaping by the city council. The walls are crossed periodically by York's distinctive "bars," or fortified gates: the portcullis on Monk's Bar on Goodramgate is still in working order, and Walmgate Bar in the east is the only gate in England with an intact barbican. It also has scars from the cannon balls hurled at it during the Civil War. Bootham Bar in Exhibition Square was the defensive bastion for the north road, and Micklegate Bar, in the city's southwest corner, was traditionally the monarch's entrance. For a small fee you can explore all of these gates. To access the path and the lookout towers, find a staircase at one of the many breaks in the walls. ⌸ *Free* ⊙ *Daily 8* AM–*dusk.*

❾ ☺ Dig. This venture from the people behind the Jorvik Viking Centre is a great way to get young people inspired about history and archaeology. It's an ongoing archaeological dig in and beneath an old church; kids, supervised by knowledgeable experts, help with the work. After your dig, record your findings and head to the lab to learn what archaeological finds discovered on the site reveal about how people lived in the past. It's an educational, fun, fascinating way to spend a couple of hours. ⊠ *St. Saviour's Church, St. Saviourgate* ☎ *01904/543403* ⊕ *www.vikingjorvik.com* ⌸ *£5.50; joint admission to Jorvik Viking Centre £13* ⊙ *Apr.–Oct., daily 10–5; Nov.–Mar., daily 10–4.*

❻ Guildhall. The mid-15th-century guildhall, by the River Ouse, was a meeting place for the city's powerful guilds. It was also used for mystery plays (medieval dramas based on biblical stories and the lives of saints). Restoration after World War II bombing damage has given it something of its erstwhile glory. The guildhall is behind the 18th-century Mansion House; you can visit it when no function is in progress. ⊠ *St. Helen's Sq.* ☎ *01904/613161* ⌸ *Free* ⊙ *May–Oct., weekdays 9–5, Sat. 10–5, Sun. 2–5; Nov.–Apr., weekdays 9–5.*

❿ ☺ Jorvik Viking Centre. This kid-focused exhibition re-creates a 10th-century Viking village. A mixture of museum and carnival ride, it requires you to "travel through time." You climb into a Disney-esque machine that propels you above straw huts and mannequins in Viking garb. Commentary is provided in 10 languages (click on the British flag to hear it in English). Kids will get a lot out of it, but adults are unlikely to learn anything new. A small collection of Viking-era artifacts is on display at the end of the ride. ⊠ *Coppergate* ☎ *01904/643211, 01904/543403 advance booking* ⊕ *www.vikingjorvik.com* ⌸ *£9; joint admission to Dig £13* ⊙ *Apr.–Oct., daily 10–5; Nov.–Mar., daily 10–4.*

❼ ☺ National Railway Museum. For train-lovers one and all: here Britain's national collection of locomotives forms part of a massive train museum. Among the exhibits are gleaming giants of the steam era, including the *Mallard*, holder of the world speed record for a steam engine (126 MPH).

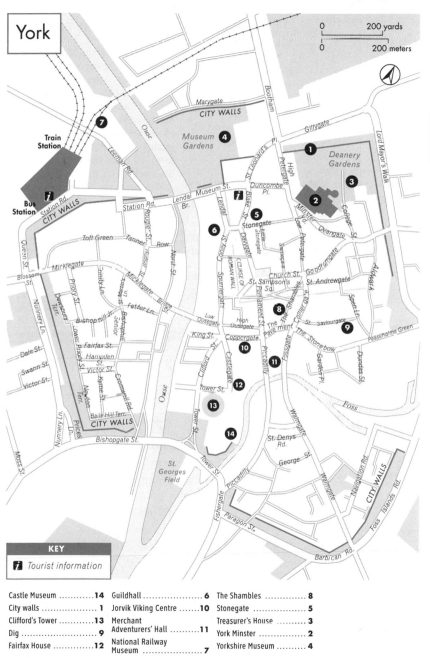

York

0 — 200 yards
0 — 200 meters

13

Train Station

Bus Station

KEY

Tourist information

Passenger cars used by Queen Victoria are on display, as well as the only Japanese bullet train to be seen outside Japan. You can clamber aboard the trains, some of which are started up regularly to keep the engines working. ✉ *Leeman Rd.* ☎ *01904/621261, 01904/686286 information line* ⊕ *www.nrm.org. uk* ✉ *Museum free* ⊙ *Daily 10–6.*

⑧　The Shambles. York's best-preserved medieval street has half-timber stores and houses with overhangs so massive you could almost reach across the street from one second-floor window to another. Once the city's street of butchers (meat hooks are still fastened outside some of the doors), today it's filled with touristy shops of scant interest to most visitors. Still, it's beautiful to walk down for the atmosphere.

> **WHERE ARE THE GATES?**
>
> The Viking conquerors of northern England held the region for more than a century and made York their capital. Gate was the Viking word for "street," hence the street names such as Goodramgate and Micklegate. Adding to the confusion, the city's entrances, or gates, are called "bars," from an Old English term. As local tour guides like to say, "In York, our streets are called gates, our gates are called bars, and our bars are called pubs."

⑤　Stonegate. This narrow, pedestrian-only street of Tudor and 18th-century storefronts and courtyards retains considerable charm. It has been in daily use for almost 2,000 years, since first being paved in Roman times. Today it's lined with jewelry stores, knickknack shops, tea shops, and ancient pubs. A passage just off Stonegate, at 52A, leads to the remnants of a 12th-century Norman stone house attached to a more recent structure. You can see the old Norman wall and window. Look out for the little red devil that once announced a printer's shop. ■**TIP→ Keep an eye out throughout the area for similar tiny statues that once acted as signs for businesses.** At the intersection of Stonegate and High Petergate, Minerva lounges on a stack of books. She once advertised a bookseller.

┌ NEED A BREAK?　At the opposite end of Stonegate from the Minster, **Betty's** (✉ *6–8 Helen's Sq., off Stonegate* ☎ *01904/659142*) has been a York institution since 1912. This tea-and-cakes salon in an attractive art nouveau building is more beloved for its history and ambience than for its so-so food. Still, it's a piece of history, and a good place to take a rest. There's always a line out front, so expect a short wait for a table.

② **York Minster.** Focal point of the city, this vast cathedral is the largest
Fodor's Choice Gothic church in England and attracts almost as many visitors as Lon-
★ don's Westminster Abbey. Inside, the effect created by its soaring pillars and lofty vaulted ceilings is almost overpowering. Come with binoculars if you wish to study the dazzling 128 stained-glass windows. Glowing with deep wine reds and cobalt blues, they are bested only by those in Chartres Cathedral in France. Mere statistics cannot convey the scale of the building; however, the central towers are 184 feet high, and the church is 534 feet long, 249 feet across its transepts, and 90 feet from floor to roof. Contributing to the cold, crushing splendor are the ornamentation of the 14th-century nave; the east window, one of the greatest

TOURS OF HAUNTED YORK

Given its storied history, dark streets, and atmospheric buildings, it's no surprise that York feels like it could be haunted. What might startle you is that York *is* haunted, at least according to the Ghost Research Foundation International. Because of York's 500 recorded cases of ghostly encounters, the foundation has determined that it is the most haunted city in England, and one of the most haunted in the world.

Not everybody believes in earthbound spirits, but it seems that just about every tour company does. Here are a few options, should you choose to explore the towns spookier side.

Ghost Creeper (☎ *07947/325239* ⊕ *www.ghostdetective.com*) runs "bloodcurdling" tours every night from July through Halloween, starting at 7:30 PM outside the Jorvik Viking Centre. Tickets are £4 per person.

Ghost Hunt (☎ *01904/608700* ⊕ *www.ghosthunt.co.uk*) guides take a slightly tongue-in-cheek approach to the ghouls. The tours start at 7:30 PM nightly in the Shambles and cost £5 per person.

Ghost Trail of York (☎ *01904/633276* ⊕ *www.ghosttrail. co.uk*) explores the city's spectral species. It takes a straightforward approach to ghosts—telling you what other people have heard or seen, and what they have seen themselves. The hour-long tours commence at 7:30 PM by the Minster and cost £4 per person.

The Original Ghost Walk of York (☎ *017947/603159* ⊕ *www. theoriginalghostwalkofyork.co.uk*), a longtimer among the tour groups, presents the city's ghost tales as fascinating unexplained mysteries. The tours depart at 8 PM from in front of the King's Arms Pub on Ouse Bridge and cost £4.50 per person.

13

pieces of medieval glazing in the world; the north transept's **Five Sisters** windows, five tall lancets of frosted 13th-century glass; the enormous choir screen portraying somewhat whimsical images of every king of England from William the Conqueror to Henry VI; and the imposing tracery of the **Rose Window,** commemorating the marriage of Henry VII and Elizabeth of York in 1486 (the event that ended the Wars of the Roses and began the Tudor dynasty). Don't miss the exquisite 13th-century **Chapter House** and the **Undercroft, Treasury, and Crypt.** Finds during the latest renovation date back to Roman times, and include a Saxon child's coffin. After exploring the interior, you might take the 275 winding steps to the roof of the great **Central Tower** (strictly for those with a head for heights), not only for the close-up view of the cathedral's detailed carving but for a panorama of York and the surrounding moors. ■ TIP➔ **Attending Evensong here is a memorable experience.** ⊠ *Duncombe Pl.* ☎ *01904/557216* ⊕ *www.yorkminster.org* ☎ *Minster £8; Central Tower £4* ☉ *Apr.–Oct., Mon.–Sat. 9–5, Sun. noon–3:45; Nov.–Mar., Mon.–Sat. 9:30–4:45, Sun. noon–3:45.*

WORTH NOTING

⑭ Castle Museum. A former 18th-century debtors' prison, this quirky museum of everyday items presents detailed exhibitions and recreations, including a Victorian street complete with crafts shops and a working water mill, as well as notable domestic, costume, and arms and armor displays. One treasure is the Coppergate Helmet, a 1,200-year-old Anglo-Saxon helmet discovered during excavations of the city; it's one of only three such objects found. You can also visit the cell where Dick Turpin, the 18th-century highwayman and folk hero, spent the night before his execution. ⊠ *Clifford St.* ☎ *01904/687687* ⊕ *www.yorkcastlemuseum.org.uk* ⊠ *£8* ⊘ *Daily 9:30–5.*

> ### A WALK IN YORK
>
> York is a fine city for walking, especially along the walls embracing the old center. Start at the Minster and head down the medieval lane, Stonegate, which is lined with shops and leads directly to Betty's tea shop. From there you can swing right to find antiques shops, or left for more modern shops, and eventually the shopping area known as the Shambles, and the remains of the old castle. At any point, climb the steps to the top of the city walls for perspective on where you are in town. The Ouse River, by the way, is more like an undeveloped canal, hidden away by buildings.

⑬ Clifford's Tower. Apart from the city walls, this rather battered-looking keep is all that remains of the old York castle. The stone tower, which sits on a grassy mound surrounded by a parking lot, dates from the mid-12th century. The Norman version that preceded it was infamously destroyed in 1190, when more than 150 Jews locked themselves inside with no food or water to protect themselves from a violent mob. In the end, they committed mass suicide by setting their own prison aflame. These days the tower's future is threatened, as the city has approved the construction of a shopping center around it. ⊠ *Tower St.* ☎ *01904/646940* ⊕ *www.cliffordstower. com* ⊠ *£3* ⊘ *Apr.–June and Sept., daily 10–6; July and Aug., daily 9:30–7; Oct.–Mar., daily 10–4.*

⑫ Fairfax House. This 1762 Georgian town house is a museum of decorative arts. The house is beautifully decorated with period furniture, crystal chandeliers, and silk wallpaper. ⊠ *Castlegate* ☎ *01904/655543* ⊕ *www. fairfaxhouse.co.uk* ⊠ *£5.40* ⊘ *Feb.–Dec., Mon.–Thurs. and Sat. 11–5, Sun. 1:30–5; last admission 4:30; Fri., guided tours 11 and 2.*

⑪ Merchant Adventurers' Hall. Built between 1357 and 1368 by a wealthy medieval guild, this is the largest half-timber hall in York. Portraits, silver, and furniture are on display, and the house itself is much of the attraction. A riverfront garden lies behind the hall. On most Saturdays antiques fairs are held inside the building. ⊠ *Fossgate* ☎ *01904/654818* ⊕ *www.theyorkcompany.co.uk* ⊠ *£5* ⊘ *Apr.–Sept., Mon.–Thurs. 9–5, Fri. and Sat. 9–3:30, Sun. noon–4; Oct.–Mar., Mon.–Sat. 9–3:30; closed 1st wk in Dec.*

❸ Treasurer's House. Surprises await inside this large 17th-century house, the home from 1897 to 1930 of industrialist Frank Green. With a fine eye for texture, decoration, and pattern, Green created period rooms—including a medieval great hall—as a showcase for his collection of antique furniture. Delft tiles decorate the kitchen, copies of medieval stenciling cover the vibrant Red Room, and 17th-century stump work adorns the Tapestry Room. ⊠ *Minster Yard* ☎ *01904/624247* ⊕ *www.nationaltrust.org.uk* ⌨ *House and garden £5.40; £6.55 with cellar tour* ☉ *Apr.–Oct., Sat.–Thurs. 11–5; last admission 30 mins before closing.*

❹ Yorkshire Museum. The natural and archaeological history of the county, including material on the Roman, Anglo-Saxon, and Viking aspects of York, is the focus of this museum. After a £2 million refurbishment in 2010, the museum is now divided into themed galleries focusing on the different time periods. On display in the solid, Doric-style building is the 15th-century Middleham Jewel, a pendant gleaming with a large sapphire. The museum lies just outside the walled city, through Bootham Bar (one of York's old gates), on the site of the medieval St. Mary's Abbey. ⊠ *Museum Gardens, Museum St.* ☎ *01904/687687* ⊕ *www. yorkshiremuseum.org.uk* ⌨ *£6* ☉ *Daily 10–5.*

13

WHERE TO EAT

££££
BRITISH
★

✕ **Blue Bicycle.** One of York's best restaurants is in a building that once served as a brothel. Downstairs are intimate walled booths, and at street level is a lively room lighted with candles. The menu changes with the seasons and concentrates on local beef and seafood. Typical dishes include seared salmon with spiced cauliflower and spinach croquettes; panfried bass with potatoes, peas, and pancetta; and fillet of beef with twice-roasted potatoes. The wine list is good, and the service couldn't be friendlier. The restaurant has launched a small guesthouse—a handful of luxury rooms in a mews nearby, called Blue Rooms. ⊠ *34 Fossgate* ☎ *01904/673990* ⊕ *www.thebluebicycle.com* ⌨ *Reservations essential* ☐ *MC, V.*

££
MODERN BRITISH

✕ **Café Concerto.** Music is the theme at this relaxed, intimate bistro in sight of York Minster. The kitchen serves updated versions of British classics. Dinner favorites include braised lamb shank with caramelized onion mash, panfried pork fillet with a Madeira cream sauce, or sirloin steak with field mushrooms and roast potatoes. Lunch is mostly salads and sandwiches, and you can always pop in for tea and cake. ⊠ *21 High Petergate* ☎ *01904/610478* ⊕ *www.cafeconcerto.biz* ☐ *No credit cards.*

£££
MODERN BRITISH

✕ **Melton's.** Once a private house, this unpretentious restaurant has local art on the walls, but you'll more likely be watching the open kitchen. The excellent seasonal menus are highly imaginative with modern English and European fare, such as Yorkshire trout with almonds, lemon, and capers, or local duck with five spices. Melton's is a 10-minute walk from York Minster. ⊠ *7 Scarcroft Rd.* ☎ *01904/634341* ⊕ *www. meltonsrestaurant.co.uk* ⌨ *Reservations essential* ☐ *MC, V* ☉ *Closed 3 wks at Christmas, and 1 wk in Aug. No lunch Mon. No dinner Sun.*

£
BRITISH

✕ **Spurriergate Centre.** Churches are not just for services, as this 15th-century house of worship proves. Resurrected as a cafeteria, St. Michael's is a favorite spot for travelers and mothers with strollers to refuel spiritually as well as gastronomically. You may end up eating bean-and-cabbage hot pot on the spot where John Wesley prayed in 1768. Don't pass up the cream scones. ⊠ *Spurriergate* ☎ *01904/629393* ⊕ *www. thespurriergatecentre.com* ⊘ *Closed Sun. No dinner.*

WHERE TO STAY

££   🏠 **Dairy Guest House**. Victorian stained glass, fine woodwork, and intricate plaster cornices are original features of this former dairy near the city walls. Bedrooms, done in pleasant pastels, come with books and games, and the imaginative breakfasts can accommodate vegetarians and vegans. The flower-filled internal courtyard is lovely. **Pros:** great breakfast; interesting building. **Cons:** a bit of a walk to the center; few amenities. ⊠ *3 Scarcroft Rd.* ☎ *01904/639367* ⊕ *www.dairyguesthouse. co.uk* ⌁ *5 rooms* ☖ *In-room: no a/c, no phone. In-hotel: some pets allowed* ⊟ *MC, V* ⑩| *BP.*

£££–££££   🏠 **Grange Hotel**. Built in the early 19th century as a home for high-ranking clergy from York Minster, the Grange is now a luxury boutique ★   hotel. The decor in the public rooms is reminiscent of a grand country home, and bedrooms are all open and airy. Look for lovely period details like fireplaces. **Pros:** spacious rooms; lovely decor. **Cons:** can feel a bit fussy. ⊠ *1 Clifton* ☎ *01904/644744* ⊕ *www.grangehotel.co.uk* ⌁ *30 rooms* ☖ *In-room: no a/c, refrigerator, Wi-Fi. In-hotel: restaurant, bar, gym, parking (free)* ⊟ *AE, MC, V* ⑩| *BP.*

££   🏠 **The Hazelwood**. Close to York Minster, this tall Victorian town house stands in a peaceful cul-de-sac, away from the hustle and bustle. Reds and golds dominate bedrooms furnished with rich fabrics and handsome traditional wood pieces. The memorable breakfasts include black pudding, Danish pastries, and local sausages. **Pros:** quiet neighborhood; lovely building. **Cons:** not much privacy; few amenities. ⊠ *24–25 Portland St.* ☎ *01904/626548* ⊕ *www.thehazelwoodyork.com* ⌁ *14 rooms* ☖ *In-room: no a/c, no phone. In-hotel: parking (free), no kids under 8* ⊟ *MC, V* ⑩| *BP.*

££££–£££££   🏠 **Hotel Du Vin**. Oliver Twist would have been pleasantly surprised by what's become of this 19th-century orphanage. Converted into a swanky hotel, it still has the original brick walls and arched doorways, but now filling the rooms are leather furnishings, impressive pieces of art, and lots of flickering candles. Rooms are spacious and very quiet; some are on two levels, with the bathrooms upstairs. Most have claw-foot tubs and showers big enough for two. The in-house restaurant specializes in buttery French cuisine. Workers are helpful and jovial. There's a two-night minimum stay on weekends. **Pros:** makes great use of the space; jovial staff; comfortable beds. **Cons:** minimum stay on weekends. ⊠ *89 The Mount* ☎ *01904/557350* ⊕ *www.hotelduvin.com* ⌁ *44 rooms* ☖ *In-room: safe, refrigerator, Internet. In-hotel: restaurant, room service, bar, parking (free)* ⊟ *AE, DC, MC, V* ⑩| *BP.*

££££–£££££   🏠 **Middlethorpe Hall & Spa**. This splendidly restored 18th-century mansion, about 1½ mi from the city center, was the sometime home of ★   the traveler and diarist Lady Mary Wortley Montagu (1689–1762). Antiques, paintings, and fresh flowers fill the traditionally decorated rooms, some in cottage-style accommodations around an 18th-century

13

courtyard. The extensive grounds include a lake and elaborate gardens that are currently being restored. The British menu of the formal wood-paneled restaurant changes seasonally, but always has more than a hint of luxury—like the hotel itself. Pros: traditional splendor; gorgeous grounds. Cons: some rooms are getting a bit worn; has an old-fashioned approach. ⊠ *Bishopthorpe Rd.* ☎ *01904/641241* ⊕ *www.middlethorpe. com* ⌑ *23 rooms, 8 suites* ⟁ *In-room: no a/c, Internet. In-hotel: restaurant, bar, pool, gym, spa, laundry service, parking (free), no kids under 8* ⊟ *AE, MC, V* ⦿ *CP.*

£££–££££ ⊡ **Mount Royale Hotel.** In a quiet country house in the upscale residential part of west York, this hotel offers excellent service that is both professional and friendly. Outside near the pool, discover orange, lemon, and fig trees mingling with the sprays of flowers in the pristine English garden. Rooms are spacious and decorated simply with subtle colors; four have walk-in closets and verandas that lead to the garden. ∎TIP➔ **The Mediterranean restaurant, One19 The Mount, is one of York's most popular; if you drive, expect to fight for parking.** Pros: country-club feel; lovely pool and garden. Cons: well outside the town center. ⊠ *117–119 The Mount* ☎ *01904/628856* ⊕ *www.mountroyale.co.uk* ⌑ *23 rooms* ⟁ *In room. no a/c, Wi-Fi. In-hotel: restaurant, room service, bar, pool, laundry service* ⊟ *AE, DC, MC, V* ⦿ *BP.*

NIGHTLIFE AND THE ARTS

NIGHTLIFE

York is full of historic pubs where you can while away an hour over a pint. The **Black Swan** (⊠ *Peasholme Green* ☎ *01904/686911*) is the city's oldest pub, in a 16th-century Tudor building. It's said to be haunted by a young girl who sits by the fireplace. The **Old White Swan** (⊠ *Goodramgate* ☎ *01904/540911*) is vast, spreading across five medieval, half-timbered buildings on busy Goodramgate. It's known for good pub lunches and its ghosts—it claims to have more than the Black Swan. The **Snickleway Inn** (⊠ *Goodramgate* ☎ *01904/656138*) is in a 15th-century building with open fireplaces and a real sense of history.

THE ARTS

The **Early Music Festival** (☎ *01904/658338 festival office, 01904/621756 Tourist Information Centre* ⊕ *www.ncem.co.uk*), featuring pre-18th-century music, is held each July. The **Viking Festival** (⊠ *Jorvik, Coppergate* ☎ *01904/543402* ⊕ *www.vikingjorvik.com*) takes place each February. The celebrations, including a parade and long-ship regatta, end with the Jorvik Viking combat reenactment, when Norsemen confront their Anglo-Saxon enemies.

In a lovely 18th-century building, the **York Theatre Royal** (⊠ *St. Leonard's Pl.* ☎ *01904/623568*) presents plays, music, poetry readings, and art exhibitions.

SHOPPING

Stonegate is the city's main shopping street. Winding down from the Minster toward the river, it's lined with a mix of unique shops and boutiques. Other good shopping streets include Petergate, which has mostly chain stores. The Shambles is another prime shopping area, with an eclectic mix of mostly local stores. The **Minster Gate Bookshop** (✉ *8 Minster Gate* ☎ *01904/621812*) sells secondhand books, old maps, and prints. **Mulberry Hall** (✉ *Stonegate* ☎ *01904/620736*) is a sales center for all the famous names in fine bone china and crystal. It also has a neat café. The **York Antiques Centre** (✉ *2 Lendal* ☎ *01904/641445*) has 25 shops selling antiques, bric-a-brac, books, and jewelry.

YORK ENVIRONS

West and north of York a number of sights make easy, appealing day trips from the city: the spa town of Harrogate, atmospheric Knaresborough, the ruins of Fountain Abbey, the market town of Ripon and nearby Newby Hall, and Thirsk, with its James Herriot connection. If you're heading northwest from York to Harrogate, you might take the less direct B1224 across Marston Moor, where, in 1644, Oliver Cromwell won a decisive victory over the Royalists during the Civil War. A few miles beyond, at Wetherby, you can cut northwest along the A661 to Harrogate. Also nearby, northeast of York, is Castle Howard, a magnificent stately home.

HARROGATE

★ *21 mi west of York, 11 mi south of Ripon, 16 mi north of Leeds.*

During the Regency and early-Victorian periods, it became fashionable for the noble and wealthy to retire to a spa to "take the waters" for relaxation. In Yorkshire the trend reached its grandest heights in Harrogate, an elegant town that flourished during the 19th century. Today the Regency buildings, parks, and spas built during that time make Harrogate an absorbing getaway.

GETTING HERE AND AROUND

Northern Rail trains from York leave every hour or so, and the journey takes about 30 minutes. There are no direct trains from London. National Express buses leave from York every hour most days; the journey takes about 40 minutes. By car, Harrogate is off A59, and is well marked. It's a walkable town, so you can park in one of its central parking lots and explore on foot.

Within and around Harrogate, the Transdev bus company provides area services, but the town itself is easily walkable and taxis are plentiful.

ESSENTIALS

Visitor Information Harrogate (✉ *Royal Baths, Crescent Rd.* ☎ *0845/389–3223* ⊕ *www.harrogate.gov.uk*).

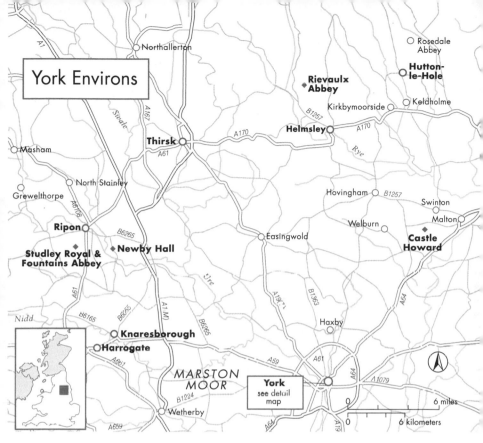

EXPLORING

The **Royal Pump Room Museum** is in the octagonal structure built in 1842 over the original sulfur well that brought great prosperity to the town. You can still drink the evil-smelling (and nasty-tasting) spa waters here. The museum displays some equipment of spa days gone by, alongside a rather eccentric collection of fine 19th-century china, clothes, and bicycles. ⊠ *Crown Pl.* ☎ *01423/556188* ⊕ *www.harrogate.gov.uk* 🎫 *£3* ⊗ *Apr.–Oct., Mon.–Sat. 10–5, Sun. 2–5; Nov.–Mar., Mon.–Sat. 10–4, Sun. 2–4.*

★ The exotic and fully restored **Turkish Baths** (1897) allow you to experience what brought so many Victorians to Harrogate. After changing into your bathing suit, you can relax on luxurious lounge chairs in the stunning mosaic-tile warming room. Move on to increasingly hot sauna rooms, and then soak up eucalyptus mist in the steam room before braving the icy plunge pool. You can also book a massage or facial. Open hours are divided into women-only, men-only, and couples-only nights, so book in advance. ⊠ *Parliament St.* ☎ *01423/556746* ⊕ *www. harrogate.gov.uk/turkishbaths* 🎫 *£12.50–£18 per bath and sauna session* ⊗ *Daily; call for schedules.*

At the edge of the town center, the 200-acre grassy parkland known as the **Stray** is a riot of color in spring. It contains many of the mineral springs that first made Harrogate famous.

The **Valley Gardens,** southwest of the town center, include a boating lake, tennis courts, and a little café.

WHERE TO EAT AND STAY

£ ✕ **Betty's.** The celebrated Yorkshire tearoom began life in Harrogate in
CAFÉ the 1920s, when Swiss restaurateur Frederic Belmont brought his Alpine specialties to England. The elegant surroundings have changed little since then, the cakes, pastries, and teas not at all. A pianist plays nightly. ⊠ *1 Parliament St.* ☎ *01423/502746* ⊕ *www.bettys.co.uk* ⊟ *MC, V.*

££ ⊡ **Balmoral Hotel.** Luxurious contemporary furnishings and antique pieces, patterned wallpapers, and colorful ornaments fill this mock-Tudor edifice. The recently renovated bedrooms have traditional furnishings in mahogany and walnut, and some have oak four-poster beds all frilled and draped. The Harrogate Grille restaurant looks like a gentlemen's club, with leather seats, and has a high-quality contemporary British menu. Guests have access to a nearby health club. **Pros:** spacious rooms; attractive restaurant. **Cons:** a bit old-fashioned; very formal atmosphere. ⊠ *Franklin Mt.* ☎ *01423/508208* ⊕ *www.balmoralhotel. co.uk* ⇘ *17 rooms, 3 suites* ⌕ *In-room: no a/c. In-hotel: restaurant, bar, some pets allowed, Wi-Fi hotspot* ⊟ *AE, MC, V* ⊡ *BP.*

£££ ⊡ **Hotel du Vin.** Tired of chintz? This hip hotel chain has taken over eight Georgian houses, using stripped-wood floors, clubby leather armchairs, and a purple billiard table to set the tone. Bedrooms, clean-lined and modern, are done in beige and cream tones. The pampering bathrooms are a nice touch, with deep tubs and spacious showers. The bar is a serious place to drink good wine, and the popular bistro offers French-influenced takes on classics like roasted lamb and rib-eye steaks. **Pros:** relaxed lounge; wonderful wine list; modern vibe. **Cons:** a bit battered around the edges; the bar can take over the lounge. ⊠ *Prospect Pl.* ☎ *01423/856800* ⊕ *www.hotelduvin.com* ⇘ *35 rooms, 8 suites* ⌕ *In-room: no a/c, safe, Internet. In-hotel: restaurant, bar, gym, Wi-Fi hotspot* ⊟ *AE, MC, V.*

NIGHTLIFE AND THE ARTS

★ Harrogate's annual **International Festival** (☎ *01423/562303* ⊕ *www. harrogate-festival.org.uk*) of ballet, music, contemporary dance, film, comedy, street theater, and more takes place during two weeks at the end of July and beginning of August.

KNARESBOROUGH

3 mi northeast of Harrogate, 17 mi west of York.

At the bottom of a precipitously deep rocky gorge along the River Nidd, the little town of Knaresborough couldn't be more photogenic. It's best seen from a train, crossing the high Victorian viaduct above. In summer you can rent a boat and paddle down the slow-moving river and wander the town's little marketplace, and year-round you can climb to the hilltop ruins of the castle where Richard II was imprisoned in 1399.

GETTING HERE AND AROUND

Northern Rail trains leave from Harrogate and York every hour or so, taking 12 and 20 minutes. Local Transdev buses travel here from nearby towns, but they are less frequent. By car, the village is on A59, and well sign-posted.

The village lies on a precipitous hill. The town is easily walkable, although it helps to be in good shape. There are clearly marked public parking areas.

EXPLORING

The touristy **Mother Shipton's Cave**, across the river from the main riverside attractions, is tucked in a pleasant park. The cave is, according to local lore, the birthplace of the titular 16th-century prophetess. Events supposedly foretold by her include the defeat of the Spanish Armada. The mineral-rich well beside her cave is famed for its ability to turn any object to stone in just a few hours. It's all good fun. ⊠ *Prophesy House, High Bridge* ☎ *01423/861600* ⊕ *www.mothershipton.co.uk* ⊠ *£6* ⊘ *Apr.–Oct., daily 10–5:30, last admission 5; Nov. and Feb.– Mar., weekends 10–4:30.*

13

RIPON

11 mi north of Harrogate, 24 mi northwest of York.

Ripon was thriving as early as the 9th century as an important market center. A relatively small church has been designated a cathedral since the mid-19th century, which makes Ripon, with only about 15,000 inhabitants, technically a city. Market day, Thursday, is probably the best day to stop by.

EXPLORING

★ **Studley Royal Water Garden & Fountains Abbey.** You can easily spend a day at this World Heritage Site, an 822-acre complex made up of an 18th-century water garden and deer park and the majestic ruins of medieval Fountains Abbey. Here a neoclassical vision of an ordered universe— with spectacular terraces, classical temples, and a grotto—blends with the glories of English Gothic architecture. The abbey, on the banks of the River Skell, was founded in 1132 and completed in the early 1500s. The Cistercian monks here, called "White Monks" for the color of their robes, devoted their lives to silence, prayer, and work. Of the surviving buildings, the lay brothers' echoing refectory and dormitory impresses most; the Gothic tower was a 16th-century addition. Fountains Mill, with sections dating back to 1140, displays reconstructed mill machinery (wool was the monks' large and profitable business). The 17th-century Fountains Hall, partially built with stones taken from the abbey, has an exhibition and video display. The water garden and Fountains Abbey is 9 mi northwest of Knaresborough, 4 mi southwest of Ripon. ⊠ *Off B6265* ☎ *01765/608888* ⊕ *www.fountainsabbey.org. uk* ⊠ *£8.50* ⊘ *Apr.–Sept., daily 10–5; Oct. and Mar., daily 10–4. Nov.– Jan., Sat.–Thurs. 10–4.*

Successive churches here were destroyed by the Vikings and the Normans, and the current **Ripon Cathedral**, dating from the 12th and 13th

Visiting Yorkshire's Monastic Past

Today the ruined abbeys at Fountains, Rievaulx, and Whitby are top attractions where you can learn about the religious and business worlds of the great monasteries of Yorkshire, and the political machinations that destroyed them. They serve as vivid reminders of what life was like in the Middle Ages.

THE FALL OF THE MONASTERIES
The sheer number of once richly decorated monastic buildings here is a testament to the power of the Catholic monks of medieval Yorkshire. They became some of the richest in Europe by virtue of the international wool trade that they conducted, with

the help of lay workers, from their vast religious estates. The buildings lie mostly in romantic ruins, a result of the dissolution of the monasteries during the 16th century, part of Henry VIII's struggle with the Catholic church over finances and his divorce request (the rejection of which he perceived as a calculated way to deny him a male heir). Henry's break with Rome was made official in 1534 with the Act of Supremacy, which made him head of the Church of England. By 1540 no monasteries or abbeys remained; the king confiscated all their property, distributed the lands, and destroyed or gave away many buildings.

centuries, is notable for its finely carved choir stalls. The Saxon crypt (AD 672), now an empty series of chambers, housed sacred relics. ⊠ *Minster Rd.* ☎ *01765/602072* ⊕ *www.riponcathedral.org.uk* ⊠ *£3 donation requested* ⊙ *Daily 8–5.*

☺ An early-18th-century house redecorated later in the same century by Robert Adam for his patron William Weddell, **Newby Hall** contains fine decorative art of its period, particularly ornamental plasterwork and Chippendale furniture. The domed Sculpture Hall with Roman works, and the Tapestry Hall, with its priceless Gobelin tapestries, are gorgeous; both are Adams designs. The 25 acres of gardens are justifiably famous; a double herbaceous border, which runs down to the river, separates garden "rooms," each flowering during a different season. A miniature railroad, playground, and pedal boats amuse kids. The house is 5 mi southeast of Ripon. ⊠ *Skelton-on-Ure* ☎ *0845/450–4068* ⊕ *www.newbyhall.co.uk* ⊠ *£12; gardens only, £8.50* ⊙ *Apr.–Sept., Tues.–Sun. and national holiday Mon., house noon–5, grounds 11–5:30; last admission 30 mins before closing.*

WHERE TO EAT AND STAY

£££ ✕ **Perk Up.** This attractive eatery on the market square started as a
BRITISH coffee shop—the owner couldn't find a good cup in Ripon. It then expanded to a café, and now to a respected restaurant. During the day it offers good sandwiches on fresh-baked bread. At night it offers gourmet takes on classic British dishes using local meats and produce. The menu changes constantly, but usually includes dishes such as sea bass with tempura prawns, wild partridge with roast asparagus, or chowder with smoked haddock, lobster, and clams. The atmosphere is informal and

friendly. ⊠ *43 Market Place South* ☎ *01765/698888* ⊕ *www.perkup. co.uk* ☰ *MC, V* ☺ *Closed Sun. and Mon.*

££££–£££££   🏨 **Swinton Park.** The Cunliffe-Lister family operates part of its ancestral castle—a stately pile rebuilt in the 18th and 19th centuries with battlements and a turret—as a hotel. The plush public rooms give you space to relax, and the traditionally decorated bedrooms are named and themed after towns in Yorkshire. About 200 acres of parkland near Yorkshire Dales National Park guarantee seclusion and abundant outdoor pursuits. Chef-author Rosemary Shrager has a cooking school on the grounds. Masham is 8 mi north of Ripon and 35 mi north of Leeds and York. **Pros:** eye-popping castle; gorgeous rooms. **Cons:** some rooms have better views than others; atmosphere is very formal. ⊠ *Off A1, Swinton Park, Masham* ☎ *01765/680900* ⊕ *www.swintonpark.com* ⇨ *26 rooms, 4 suites* ⚲ *In-room: no a/c, Internet. In-hotel: restaurant, gym, bicycles, some pets allowed* ☰ *AE, DC, MC, V* ⦿ *BP.*

THIRSK

13 mi north of Newby Hall, 23 mi north of York.

This busy market town on the western edge of the moors was once a thriving stopover on the main east–west route from the dales to the coast. Today it's a busy, affluent farm town. Lovely Georgian houses abound, and the cobbled medieval Market Place is handsome; Saturday and Monday are market days. Thirsk is best known as the place where veterinarian Alf Wight (who wrote about his experiences under the name James Herriot) had his practice.

EXPLORING

☺   The popular **World of James Herriot,** in the author's actual office, recreates the operating room and the living spaces of the 1940s and '50s; it also displays veterinary artifacts. The interactive displays upstairs appeal to kids and adults alike. ⊠ *23 Kirkgate* ☎ *01845/524234* ⊕ *www.worldofjamesherriot.org* ⊑ *£6* ☺ *Apr.–Oct., daily 10–5; Nov.– Mar., daily 11–4; last admission 1 hr before closing.*

CASTLE HOWARD

15 mi northeast of York, 14 mi southeast of Rievaulx Abbey, 12 mi southeast of Helmsley.

GETTING HERE AND AROUND

There is no easy public transportation to Castle Howard, which is well outside any town and several miles off any public road. The nearest train stop is Malton, and you can take a taxi from there; check www.yorkshiretravel.net for more information. By car, follow signs off A64.

EXPLORING

Fodor's Choice   Standing serene among the Howardian Hills to the west of Malton, ★   **Castle Howard** is an opulent, stately home whose magnificent profile is punctuated by stone chimneys and a graceful central dome. Many people know it best as Brideshead, the home of the Flyte family in Evelyn Waugh's tale of aristocratic woe, *Brideshead Revisited,* because much of

13

the 1981 TV series was filmed here. The house was designed by Sir John Vanbrugh (1664–1726) for the Howard family. Considering its many theatrical, even flamboyant features, it seems fitting that Vanbrugh was praised more as a playwright than an architect (he also had careers as a soldier and adventurer). This was Vanbrugh's first building design; his self-assurance knowing no bounds, he went on to create Blenheim Palace, the Versailles of England.

The audacity of the great baroque house is startling, proclaiming the wealth and importance of the Howards. This was the first private residence in Britain built with a stone dome. A magnificent central hallway spanned by a hand-painted (in the 20th century) ceiling dwarfs all visitors, and there is no shortage of grandeur: vast family portraits, delicate marble fireplaces, immense and fading tapestries, huge pieces of Victorian silver on polished tables, and a great many marble busts. Outside, the stunning neoclassical landscape of carefully arranged woods, lakes, bridges, and obelisks led Horace Walpole, the 18th-century connoisseur, to comment that a pheasant at Castle Howard lives better than most dukes elsewhere. The grounds sprawl for miles, and hidden away among the hills and lakes (there's even a fanciful playground for children) are the Temple of the Four Winds and the Mausoleum, whose magnificence caused Walpole to quip that all who view it would wish to be buried alive. Hourly tours, included in the admission price, fill you in on more background and history. ⊠ *Off A64 and B1257, Coneysthorpe* ☎ *01653/648333* ⊕ *www.castlehoward.co.uk* ☒ *£12.50; gardens only, £8.50* ⊘ *House Mar.–Oct., daily 11–6; last admission 4. Grounds daily 10–6:30 or dusk; last admission 4:30.*

THE NORTH YORKSHIRE COAST

The North York Moors plummet down to the sea in spectacular cliffs that stretch down the coastline, creating a dramatic view of pink heather and white cliffs hundreds of feet above the dark sea. The red roofs of Robin Hood's Bay, the sharply curved bay at Whitby, and the gold-and-white buildings of Scarborough capture the imagination at first sight. Most coastal towns still support an active fishing industry, and every harbor offers fishing and leisure trips throughout summer. Beaches at Scarborough, Whitby, and Filey have patrolled areas: swim (in cold water) between the red-and-yellow flags, and don't swim when a red flag is flying. All the North Sea beaches are ideal for fossil hunting and seashell collecting.

SCARBOROUGH

34 mi northeast of York.

There is no Scarborough Fair, and historians are divided on whether there ever was one, but don't let that stop you from heading to this classic English seaside resort, where lemon-hued Victorian houses top cliffs overlooking the dark blue sea. The older, more genteel side of Scarborough is in the southern half of town, with carefully laid-out crescents and squares, the ruins of its castle, and views across Cayton Bay. The

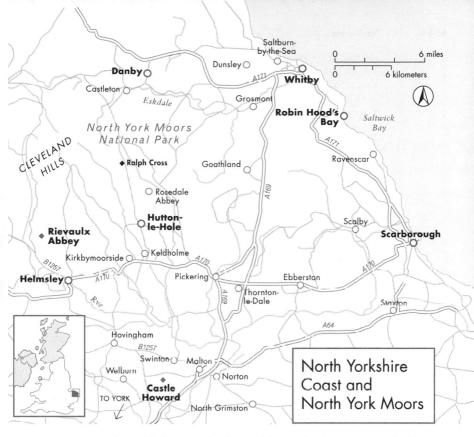

North Yorkshire
Coast and
North York Moors

northern side is a riot of tacky seaside arcades, ice-cream stands, bingo halls, and stores selling "rock" (luridly colored hard candy). The huddle of streets, alleyways, and red-roof cottages around the harbor gives an idea of what the town was like before the resort days.

GETTING HERE AND AROUND

Scarborough is rather difficult to reach by public transportation. Transpennine Express trains leave from York every hour or so; the journey takes just under an hour. The journey from Leeds by National Express bus takes about four hours. There are no direct trains from London, and a bus from London takes all day. By car, Scarborough is on the coastal A165 road.

ESSENTIALS

Train Information Transpennine Express (☎ 0845/600–1671 ⊕ www. tpexpress.co.uk).

Visitor Information Scarborough (✉ Unit 3, Pavilion House, Valley Bridge Rd. ☎ 01723/383636 ⊕ www.discoveryorkshirecoast.com).

EXPLORING

For nearly 900 years the rambling ruins of **Scarborough Castle** have dominated the northern headland. The Romans used the site as a signaling station in the 4th century, and archaeological digs have uncovered evidence that people lived here in the Bronze age. The current structure dates to 1136, when it was built by William de Gros to replace a wooden fort. Henry II later took the castle for himself because he believed it was impossible to invade. He was right: although the castle was repeatedly besieged, it was never taken by force. ■ TIP→ The castle has spectacular views across the North Bay and the shore gardens. ⊠ *Castle Rd.* ☎ *01723/372451* ⊕ *www.english-heritage.org.uk* ⊡ *£4.70* ⊗ *Apr.–Sept., daily 10–6; Oct.–Mar., Thurs.–Mon. 10–4.*

Most visitors to the little medieval church of **St. Mary** (⊠ *Castle Rd.* ☎ *01723/500541*) are attracted by the churchyard's most famous occupant: Anne, the youngest Brontë sister. She was taken to Scarborough from Haworth when suffering from tuberculosis in a futile effort to save her life by exposing her to the sea air. She died in 1849. The church is near the castle on the way into town.

> ### A SPA IS BORN
>
> In 1626 Elizabeth Farrow came upon a stream of acidic water running from a cliff south of Scarborough. This led to the town's establishment as a hugely popular spa on a par with Harrogate. By the 18th century, when icy sea bathing came into vogue, no beaches were busier than Scarborough's. Donkeys and horses drew wheeled cabins called bathing machines into the surf and anchored there. The city's prosperity manifested itself in the handsome Regency and early-Victorian residences and hotels you see today.

The extraordinary circular building that holds the **Rotunda Museum** was constructed in 1829 for William Smith of the Scarborough Philosophical Society to display his geological collection. It now contains important archaeological and local history collections, and changing temporary exhibits. ⊠ *Vernon Rd.* ☎ *01723/374753* ⊡ *£4.50* ⊗ *Tues.–Sun. 10–5.*

⟡ Recognizable by its white pyramids, **Scarborough Sea Life Centre** is a great—if expensive—way to entertain the kids for an afternoon. Fish, crabs, and stingrays are presented in an engaging way, with all the marine habitats native to Great Britain. ⊠ *Scalby Mills, North Bay* ☎ *01723/373414* ⊕ *www.sealifeeurope.com* ⊡ *£13* ⊗ *Mar.–Oct., daily 10–6; Nov.–Feb., daily 10–4; last admission 1 hr before closing.*

WHERE TO EAT AND STAY

£   ✕ **The Golden Grid.** Everyone has to have fish-and-chips at least once in
SEAFOOD   Scarborough, and this harbor-front spot is a classic of its kind. Choose an upstairs window table and tuck into freshly fried cod or haddock. ⊠ *4 Sandside* ☎ *01723/360922* ⊕ *www.goldengrid.co.uk* ⊟ *MC, V* ⊗ *No dinner Sun.–Thurs. Sept.–Mar.*

£££   ✕ **Lanterna Ristorante.** This unpretentious restaurant prides itself on *not*
ITALIAN   being modern. Instead it offers classic Italian dishes, including tender steak cooked with ham and cheese, and seafood chosen fresh off the boats in the harbor. Opt for seasonal specials using fresh vegetables, fish, and white truffles (October to January). ⊠ *33 Queen St.* ☎ *01723/363616* ⊕ *www.lanterna-ristorante.co.uk* ⊟ *MC, V* ⊗ *No lunch. Closed Sun. and 2 wks late Oct.*

££–£££   ⊡ **The Crown Spa.** The centerpiece of the Regency Esplanade, this 19th-century hotel overlooks South Bay and the castle headland. Built to accommodate fashionable visitors to Scarborough Spa, it has been considerably refurbished; rooms are modern and done in muted colors. Rates drop for some two-night stays. **Pros:** pure Victorian style; modern amenities. **Cons:** small bathrooms. ⊠ *The Esplanade* ☎ *01723/357426* ⊕ *www.crownspahotel.com* ⟿ *87 rooms* ♿ *In-room: no a/c, Wi-Fi. In-hotel: restaurant, bar, pool, gym, spa, some pets allowed* ⊟ *AE, MC, V* ⫿◯⫾ *BP.*

NIGHTLIFE AND THE ARTS

Scarborough is one of England's busy theater towns, especially for summer repertory, with most of the activity buzzing around the **Stephen Joseph Theatre** (⊠ *Westborough* ☎ *01723/370541*). It presents productions on two stages and also has a cinema, a restaurant, and a bar. The tourist office also has box-office details.

13

ROBIN HOOD'S BAY

★   *15 mi northwest of Scarborough.*

This tiny fishing village squeezed into a steep narrow ravine is absolutely adorable, from its name right down to its little red-roof cottages and cobbled roads. The village has no connection to the famous medieval outlaw, though. It was once a smuggling center that passed contraband up the streambed beneath the cottages, linked to one another by secret passages. The attraction here is the town itself, with its winding stone staircases that eventually wander off across the headland. ■**TIP→ Park in the pay lots at the top of the hill. Do not attempt to drive down the hill.**

EXPLORING

The **beach** is lovely, but mercurial—the tide rushes in quickly, so take care not to get cut off. Provided the tide is out, you can stroll for a couple of hours south from the town, along a rough stone shore full of rock pools, inlets, and sandy strands. A few stretches of sand are suitable for sunbathers. To the south, at the curiously named **Boggle Hole,** a ravine nestles an old water mill, now an atmospheric youth hostel (signs mark the way on the cliff-top path). Farther south is **Ravenscar,** a Victorian village that now consists of little more than a hotel, which can be reached by a hazardous but exhilarating path up the cliff. The walk back, along the cliff, is less tricky but no less energetic.

WHERE TO EAT AND STAY

£   ✕ **Bay Hotel.** The village's most favored pub is this friendly Victorian
SEAFOOD retreat, perfectly positioned at the bottom of the village. It sits on a rocky outcrop lapped by the sea, so there are nice views. The bar is festooned with oak and brass; in winter, a roaring fire warms all comers. Whitby scampi and savory meat pies are often on the menu. ⊠ *The Dock* ☎ *01947/880278* ⊟ *MC, V.*

£££–££££   ⊡ **Raven Hall Hotel.** This Georgian hotel with landscaped grounds offers unrivaled coastal views from the headland of Ravenscar, 3 mi southeast of Robin Hood's Bay. All rooms have lovely views, but the best ones look out over the bay. The hotel is known for its good sports facilities; the bar marks the traditional end of the punishing, long-distance Lyke-

Wake Walk. There are also skeet shooting and themed murder-mystery dinners and wine tastings. It's worth checking for dinner and B&B deals year-round. **Pros:** breathtaking coastal views; great for sports fanatics. **Cons:** a bit off the beaten track; need a car to get around. ⊠ *Ravenscar* ☎ *01723/870353* ⊕ *www.ravenhall.co.uk* ↝ *53 rooms* ⚐ *In-room: no a/c, Internet. In-hotel: restaurant, bar, golf course, tennis courts, pool, gym* ⊟ *AE, MC, V* ⌶◯⌶ *BP.*

SPORTS AND THE OUTDOORS

Several superb long-distance walks start at, finish in, or run through Robin Hood's Bay. The coastal part of **Cleveland Way** (⊕ *www. nationaltrail.co.uk*) runs north to Whitby and south to Scarborough. The village marks one end of the 190-mi **Coast-to-Coast Walk**; the other is at St. Bees Head on the Irish Sea. Walkers finish at the Bay Hotel, above the harbor. The trans-moor **Lyke-Wake Walk** (⊕ *www.lykewakewalk. co.uk*) finishes 3 mi away at Ravenscar. **Wellington Lodge** (⊠ *Staintondale* ☎ *01723/871234* ⊕ *www.llamatreks.co.uk*), 3 mi south of Ravenscar, schedules llama treks along the moors or the coast; you walk, and the llamas carry your lunch.

WHITBY

Fodor's Choice
★
7 mi northwest of Robin Hood's Bay, 20 mi northeast of Pickering.

A scenic seaside town with a Gothic edge, Whitby is a busy tourist hub, but it handles that fact so well you might not notice (except at dinnertime, when it's hard to get a seat in a restaurant). Whitby curves around its symmetrical harbor and winds its way up the cliffs. The glassy waters of the slow-moving River Esk cut through the town. Fine Georgian houses dominate the west side of the river (known as West Cliff), and across the swing bridge smaller 17th-century buildings mark the old town (known as East Cliff). Here cobbled Church Street is packed in summer with people exploring the shop-lined alleyways.

Whitby came to prominence as a whaling port. The first ships sailed from here to Greenland in the mid-18th century, captained by local men such as William Scoresby. Herman Melville paid tribute to this inventor of the crow's nest in *Moby Dick*. Whaling brought Whitby wealth, and shipbuilding made it famous: Captain James Cook (1728–79), explorer and navigator, sailed on his first ship from Whitby in 1747, and all four of his subsequent discovery vessels were built in the town.

GETTING HERE AND AROUND

A car is a must, as there are no direct buses or trains from London. National Express and Megabus have buses to the region, but you must change at least once, and the journey can take up to 10 hours. National Express trains from London's King's Cross Station go to Leeds, where you can change to a local train. The entire journey can take six hours.

Whitby has a very small town center, and it's easily walkable. The train station is in the town center, between its two cliffs. If you're looking for a taxi, they tend to line up outside the station.

ESSENTIALS
Visitor Information Whitby (✉ *Langbourne Rd.* ☎ *01947/602674* ⊕ *www. whitbyonline.co.uk*).

EXPLORING
On top of the East Cliff—reached by climbing 199 stone steps—the Gothic church of **St. Mary** overlooks the town, while it in turn is watched over by the gaunt ruins of Whitby Abbey. Bram Stoker lived in Whitby briefly and later said his stay inspired him to write *Dracula*. He was particularly struck by the image of pallbearers carrying coffins up the long stone staircase to St. Mary's spooky churchyard. The unusual-looking church with its ship's-deck roof, triple-decker pulpit, and enclosed box pews dates from the 12th century, although almost everything else you see today is the result of 19th- and 20th century renovations. The weather-beaten churchyard is filled with the crooked old gravestones of ancient mariners. ■ **TIP→ Rather than walking the 199 steps, you can drive to the hilltop and park in the abbey's large parking lot for a small fee.** ✉ *Church La., East Cliff* ☎ *01947/603421* ⚑ *Free, donation suggested* ☉ *Apr., daily 10–4; May–Aug., daily 10–5; Sept. and Oct., daily 10–3; Nov.–Mar., daily 10–2.*

★ The glorious ruins of **Whitby Abbey**, high on the East Cliff, dominate the area. The skeletal remains of the once grand church can even be seen from the hills of the moors miles away. St. Hilda founded the abbey in AD 657. It was one of very few founded by a woman, and operated with a mixed population of monks and nuns. Caedmon (died circa 670), the first identifiable poet of the English language, was a monk here. Sacked by the Vikings in the 9th century, the monastery was refounded in the 11th century and enlarged in the 13th century, from which point these ruins date. It flourished until Henry VIII destroyed it. The visitor center is excellent, with exhibits on Hilda and Bram Stoker, artifacts from the site, interactive displays on the medieval abbey, and a tea shop. ✉ *Abbey La., East Cliff* ☎ *01947/603568* ⊕ *www.english-heritage.org.uk* ⚑ *£5.80* ☉ *Apr.–Sept., daily 10–6; Oct.–Mar., Thurs.–Mon. 10–4.*

Filled with exhibits relating to the man and explorer, the **Captain Cook Memorial Museum** is in the 18th-century house belonging to ship owner John Walker. Cook lived here as an apprentice from 1746 to 1749. On display are mementos of his epic expeditions, including maps, diaries, and drawings. ✉ *Grape La.* ☎ *01947/601900* ⊕ *www.cookmuseumwhitby. co.uk* ⚑ *£4.50* ☉ *Apr.–Oct., daily 9:45–5; Mar., daily 11–3.*

Exhibits in the quirky **Whitby Museum** wander from local geology and natural history to archaeology, whaling, and trade routes in Asia. It's interesting for its old-fashioned approach—displays have handwritten cards. ✉ *St. Hilda's La., Pannett Park* ☎ *01947/602908* ⊕ *www.*

A LOCAL HAUNT

Locals know well that St. Mary's church is an eerie sight—at night it is chillingly illuminated. Kids like to stand in between the lights and the church, casting huge scary shadows that can be seen from the town below. In Bram Stoker's *Dracula*, the count claimed Lucy as his victim in the churchyard. Even though the tale is fiction, few linger up there after dark.

13

CLOSE UP

Whitby Jet

In the 19th century Whitby became famous around the western world for jet, a very hard, black form of natural carbon, found in thin seams along the coast here and worked into jewelry and ornaments. Known since prehistoric times and sometimes used to ward off the evil eye, it reached the peak of its popularity in the 1850s when 1,400 men and boys, supplied by 200 miners, made a good living in jewelry workshops all over the town.

The queen of Bavaria was impressed enough to order a chain more than 4 feet long. On the death of her husband, Queen Victoria introduced jet into court circles and set the fashion for mourning memorabilia.

You can see fine examples in the Whitby Museum on St. Hilda's Terrace and in the shop displays in the old town along Church Street and parallel to Sandgate. If you buy a piece, keep it shiny with baby oil.

whitbymuseum.org.uk ⌨ *£3* ⊘ *May–Sept., Mon.–Sat. 9:30–5:30, Sun. 2–5; Oct.–Apr., Tues. 10–1, Wed.–Sat. 10–4, Sun. 2–4.*

OFF THE BEATEN PATH

Goathland. This moorland village, 8 mi southwest of Whitby, has a cute 1865 train station that served as Hogsmeade Station for students arriving at the school of wizardry in the film *Harry Potter and the Sorcerer's Stone*. The 18-mi **North Yorkshire Moors Railway** (⊠ *Pickering Station, Park St., Pickering* ☎ *01751/472508, 01751/473535 recorded information* ⊕ *www.nymr.co.uk* ⌨ *£14.50 round-trip* ⊘ *Late Mar.–early Nov., daily; early Nov.–Feb., some weekends and holiday periods*), between Grosmont and Pickering, passes through neat towns and moorland. Steam-powered trains provide a great outing. Day passes are £16. You can also extend your journey to Whitby at certain times.

WHERE TO EAT

£££
SEAFOOD

✕ **Greens of Whitby.** One of the most highly rated restaurants in Whitby, Greens specializes in fresh local seafood served with a Continental flair. The restaurant is two eateries in one: downstairs a more casual bistro, upstairs a white-linen restaurant. The menu changes constantly, but downstairs grilled and fried seafood lead the way. Upstairs Whitby langoustines (large prawns) might be served in butter sauce, line-caught sea bass is served with sautéed potatoes and fennel, or Yorkshire lamb with red currant jus. ⊠ *13 Bridge St.* ☎ *01947/600284* ⊕ *www.greensofwhitby.com* ▤ *MC, V* ⊘ *No lunch Mon.–Thurs.*

££
SEAFOOD

✕ **Magpie Café.** Whitby is full of fish-and-chips places, but this is the one that draws the biggest crowd with a well-stocked menu that includes plaice, cod, and haddock along with grilled fish and meat platters. The food is good and fans say it's worth the wait, which can stretch to an hour on busy nights. ⊠ *14 Pier Rd.* ☎ *01947/602058* ⚲ *Reservations not accepted* ▤ *MC, V* ⊘ *Closed Jan.*

WHERE TO STAY

££ ⊡ **Broom House.** Tucked away in the tiny village of Egton Bridge, about 5 mi outside of Whitby, this two-story stone house sits beside a babbling brook at the base of forested hills. The rooms are decorated with impeccable taste, and all have plenty of space and peaceful views. Breakfasts are fresh and tasty. During the day you can wander through the orchard, and in the evening sit by the crackling fire. The restaurant serves Modern British cuisine using local produce. **Pros:** gorgeous setting; beautifully decorated rooms. **Cons:** far from Whitby; need a car to get around. ☒ *Broom House La., Egton Bridge* ☎ *01947/895279* ⊕ *www.egton-bridge.co.uk* ⇆ *10 rooms* ♿ *In-room: no a/c, no phone* ☐ *MC, V* ⦿ *BP.*

£££–££££ 🔲 **Dunsley Hall Hotel.** Built as the home of a shipping magnate, this family-run Victorian country-house hotel has 4 acres of gardens and grounds. Stained- and leaded-glass windows and plenty of wood paneling complement rich carpets, rocking chairs, and leather armchairs. Bedrooms are spacious, and the only intrusion is the occasional screech of a peacock. A new wing opened in 2007 added eight modern guest rooms. The hotel is 4 mi west of Whitby. **Pros:** acres and acres of gardens; spacious bedrooms. **Cons:** peacocks might wake you up early; modern rooms not as charming. ☒ *Dunsley* ☎ *01947/893437* ⊕ *www.dunsleyhall.com* ⇆ *26 rooms* ♿ *In-room: no a/c. In-hotel: restaurant, bar, tennis court, pool, gym* ☐ *AE, MC, V* ⦿ *BP.*

£ 🔲 **Shepherd's Purse.** This splendid little complex in the cobbled old town consists of boutique-style guest rooms, an organic café, and a health-food store. There are two less-expensive bedrooms above the stores and others in the galleried courtyard at the back. Although small, many rooms have four-poster or brass bedsteads; floors are wooden, the furniture is country style, and two rooms have balconies. **Pros:** quirky style; comfortable rooms. **Cons:** some rooms are quite small; no elevator. ☒ *95 Church St.* ☎ *01947/820228* ⇆ *9 rooms, 5 with bath* ♿ *In-room: no a/c, no phone. In-hotel: restaurant, some pets allowed* ☐ *MC, V.*

££ 🔲 **White Horse and Griffin.** When looking for the perfect inn, you want an old building with character, a roaring fire, and food to thrill. This 18th-century establishment, in which Charles Dickens once slept and railway pioneer George Stephenson lectured, fills the bill. The tidy rooms, done in an uncluttered traditional style, are warmly decorated in muted colors, and downstairs the cozy bistro serves a fine, changing menu with locally caught fish and game in season. **Pros:** lots of character; tasty food. **Cons:** old-fashioned style; few amenities. ☒ *Church St.* ☎ *01947/604857* ⊕ *www.whitehorseandgriffin.co.uk* ⇆ *10 rooms* ♿ *In-room: no a/c, no phone. In-hotel: restaurant, bar, some pets allowed* ☐ *MC, V* ⦿ *BP.*

NIGHTLIFE AND THE ARTS

★ The **Whitby Regatta** (⊕ *www.whitbyregatta.co.uk*), held each August, is a three-day jamboree of boat races, fair rides, lifeboat rescue displays, fireworks, and music. Music (but also traditional dance and storytelling) predominates during **Whitby Folk Week** (⊕ *www.whitbyfolk.co.uk*), usually held the week before the late-August bank holiday, when pubs, sidewalks, and halls become venues for more than 600 traditional folk events by British performers.

13

THE NORTH YORK MOORS

The North York Moors are a dramatic swath of high moorland starting 25 mi north of the city of York and stretching east to the coast and
west to the Cleveland Hills. Once covered in forest, of which a few
pockets survive, the landscape changed when the monks at Rievaulx
and Whitby abbeys began raising huge flocks of sheep in medieval
times. Over the course of centuries, the sheep have kept the moors
deforested, and still ensure that the pink heather on which they feed
spreads lushly across the hills. A series of isolated, medieval "standing
stones" that once acted as signposts on the paths between the abbeys
are now handy for hikers.

For more than four decades the area has been a national park, ensuring
the protection of the bleak moors and grassy valleys that shelter brown-
stone villages and hamlets. Minor roads and tracks crisscross the hills,
and there's no single, obvious route through the region. Perhaps the
most rewarding approach is west from the coast at Whitby, along the
Esk Valley to Danby, which is also accessible on the Esk Valley branch-
train line between Middlesbrough and Whitby. From Danby, minor
roads run south over the high moors reaching Hutton-le-Hole, beyond
which main roads lead to interesting towns on the moors' edge, such
as Helmsley. Completing the route in this direction leaves you with an
easy side trip to Castle Howard before returning to nearby York.

DANBY

15 mi west of Whitby.

The old stone village of Danby nestles in a green valley, just a short walk
from the tops of the moors. It's been settled since Viking times—Danby
means "village where the Danes lived"—and these days it bumbles
along in a semitouristed way. There's a pub, and a cozy bakery with a
tearoom, and if you bring hiking boots, within 10 minutes you can be
above the village looking down, surrounded by moorland.

GETTING HERE AND AROUND
To get here from Whitby, take A171 west and turn north for Danby after
12 mi, after which it's a 3-mi drive over Danby Low Moor to the village.

EXPLORING
In a house on the eastern outskirts of Danby, the North York Moors
National Park's **Moors Centre** will interest gardeners with its extensive
displays on the flora and fauna of the moors. Local arts and crafts, a tearoom, and a picnic area are also here. There's a beautiful play area for
kids as well as an indoor climbing wall. The summer Moorsbus operates from the center for the 30-minute journey south to Hutton-le-Hole.
⊠ *Danby Lodge* ☎ *01439/772737* ⊕ *www.visitnorthyorkshiremoors.
co.uk* ⊠ *Free; parking £2* ☉ *Jan. and Feb., weekends 11–4; Mar., Nov.,
and Dec., daily 11–4; Apr.–Oct., daily 10–5.*

**EN
ROUTE**

From Danby take the road due west for 2 mi to Castleton, and then turn
south over the top of the moors toward Hutton-le-Hole. The narrow
road offers magnificent views over North York Moors National Park,

especially at the old stone **Ralph Cross** (5 mi), which marks the park's highest point. Drive carefully: sheep-dodging is a necessary art.

HUTTON-LE-HOLE

13 mi south of Danby.

Similar to many other area villages, sleepy Hutton-le-Hole is a charming little place based around a wide village green, with fluffy sheep snoozing in the shade of stone cottages. Unfortunately, because of its frequent selection by guidebooks as *the* village to see in the area, it can be unbearably crowded in summer. You can always keep driving to either the charming nearby burg of Thorton-le-Dale or to the medieval market towns of Helmsley or Pickering.

13

EXPLORING

The excellent open-air **Ryedale Folk Museum** interprets life in the Dales from prehistory onward through craft demonstrations and 13 historic buildings, including a medieval kiln, 16th-century cottages, and a 19th-century blacksmith's shop. ☎ *01751/417367* ⊕ *www.ryedalefolkmuseum.co.uk* 🎫 *£5.50* ☉ *Early Mar.–Oct., daily 10–5:30; Nov.–Feb., daily 10–dusk; last admission 4:30.*

HELMSLEY

8 mi southwest of Hutton-le-Hole, 27 mi north of York.

The market town of Helmsley, with its flowering window boxes, stone cottages, arched bridges across streams, and churchyard, is the perfect place to spend a relaxing afternoon. You can while away a few hours lingering in its tea shops and tiny boutiques, and exploring the craggy ruins of its Norman castle (destroyed during the Civil War). Market day is Friday. Nearby are the impressive ruins of Rievaulx Abbey.

GETTING HERE AND AROUND

There is no train station in Helmsley, and it has no major bus service. The Moorsbus stops in Helmsley once a day during the summer. By car, Helmsley is on A170.

ESSENTIALS

Bus Information Moorsbus (☎ *01845/597000* ⊕ *www.northyorkmoors.org.uk*).

Visitor Information Helmsley (✉ *Town Hall, Market Pl.* ☎ *01439/770173* ⊕ *www.ryedale.gov.uk*).

EXPLORING

Fodor's Choice The perfect marriage of architecture and countryside, **Rievaulx** (pronounced ree-*voh*) Abbey has a dramatic setting 2 mi northwest of Helmsley; its sweeping arches soar at the precise point where a forested hillside rushes down to the River Rye. A French Cistercian sect founded this abbey in 1132, and though its monks led a life of isolation and silence, they were active in the wool business. By the end of the 13th century the abbey was massively wealthy, with hundreds of lay workers and farmland filling the valley. The evocative ruins give a good indication of how vast the abbey once was. Medieval mosaic tiling can still be seen here and there, and part of the symmetrical cloisters remains. The Chapter House retains the original shrine of the first abbot, William, by the entrance. By the time of Henry VIII the abbey had shrunk dramatically; only 20 or so monks lived here when the king's soldiers arrived to destroy the building in 1538. After that, the earl of Rutland owned Rievaulx, and he demolished what was left to the best of his ability. What remains is a beautiful ghost of the magnificent building that once stood here. The abbey is a 1½-hour walk northwest from Helmsley by signposted footpath, or 2 mi by vehicle. ⊠ *Off B1257* ☎ *01439/798228* ⊕ *www.english-heritage.org.uk* ⊠ *£5.30* ☉ *Apr.–Sept., daily 10–6; Oct., daily 10–5; Nov.–Mar., Thurs.–Mon. 10–4.*

OFF THE BEATEN PATH

Rievaulx Terrace and Temples. From Rievaulx Abbey it's a short walk or drive up to the hill where Rievaulx Terraces have a magnificent view of the abbey. The long, grassy walkway on the hillside ends at the remains of several Tuscan- and Ionic-style classical temples, once maintained by the earl of Rutland. If you must choose between the two, visit the abbey. ⊠ *Off B1257* ☎ *01439/798340* ⊕ *www.nationaltrust.org.uk* ⊠ *£4.75* ☉ *Late Mar.–Sept., daily 10:30–6; Oct., daily 10:30–5; last admission 1 hr before closing.*

WHERE TO STAY

£££–££££   🏨 **Black Swan.** A splendid base for exploring the area, this ivy-covered property sits on the edge of Helmsley's market square. The building is a hybrid—part 16th-century coaching inn, part Georgian house. Cozy rooms overlook either the square or the fine walled garden at the back. The restaurant serves traditional British and local dishes. **Pros:** ivy-covered charm; great location. **Cons:** decor is a bit old-fashioned; bathrooms need updating. ⊠ *Market Pl.* ☎ *01439/770466* ⊕ *www. blackswan-helmsley.co.uk* 🛏 *45 rooms* ♿ *In-room: no a/c. In-hotel: restaurant, bar, some pets allowed* ▤ *AE, DC, MC, V* ☯ *BP.*

££   🏨 **No. 54.** Tea and cakes provide a tasty welcome in this stone cottage just off market square. The light-filled rooms are decorated in creamy hues. Owner Lizzie Would knows everything about the area and is happy to help. She'll cook you a fine dinner for £25 if you book in advance. **Pros:** tea and cakes for everyone; comfy beds. **Cons:** small rooms; not much privacy. ⊠ *Bondgate* ☎ *01439/771533* ⊕ *www.no54. co.uk* 🛏 *3 rooms* ♿ *In-room: no a/c, no phone. In-hotel: some pets allowed* ▤ *No credit cards* ☯ *BP.*

SPORTS AND THE OUTDOORS

Helmsley, on the southern edge of the moors, is the starting point of the **Cleveland Way** (⊕ *www.nationaltrail.co.uk*), the long-distance moor-and-coastal footpath. Boots are donned at the old cross in the market square; it's 50 mi or so across the moors to the coast and then a similar distance south to Filey along the cliff tops. The footpath is 110 mi long and takes around nine days start to finish. The trail passes close to Rievaulx Abbey, a few miles outside town, and walking to Rievaulx is a good way to sample the trail. Maps are available at the tourist center in town, but the Rievaulx section is well signposted.

The Northeast

DURHAM, HADRIAN'S WALL,
LINDISFARNE ISLAND

WORD OF MOUTH

"My husband is from Newcastle and there are loads of picturesque castles to visit on the coast and around the Northeast. It is also easy to get to the Lake District from there (about 3 hours). This is prime farming territory—I'm sure you would love it and it is off the beaten path for many Americans."

—palatino82

"I'd favor Vindolanda over Birdoswald (which needn't detain you long, though you could walk a hundred yards along Hadrian's Wall to look for the good-luck symbol some builders left, which might shock some). Housesteads (walk up the hill alongside the Wall for views) and Vindolanda could each keep you enthralled for a couple of hours."

—PatrickLondon

www.fodors.com/community

Updated by
Jack Jewers

For many Britons, the words the Northeast provoke a vision of near-Siberian isolation. The truth is a revelation. For although there are wind-hammered, wide-open spaces and empty roads threading the wild high moorland, the Northeast also has simple fishing towns, small villages of remarkable charm, and historic abbeys and castles that are all the more romantic for their often ruinous state.

Even the remoteness can be relative. Suddenly, around the next bend of a country road, you may come across an imposing church, a tall monastery, or a gorgeous country house built by a Victorian-era millionaire. The value found in the shops and accommodations, the uncrowded beaches ideal for walking, and the friendliness of the people also add to the region's appeal. Still, outside of a few key sights, the Northeast is off the well-trodden tourist path.

Mainly composed of the two large counties of Durham and Northumberland, the Northeast includes English villages adjacent to the Scottish border area, renowned in ballads and romantic literature for feuds, raids, and battles. Fittingly, Durham Cathedral, the seat of bishops for nearly 800 years, has been described as "half church of God, half castle 'gainst the Scot." Hadrian's Wall, which marked the northern limit of the Roman Empire, stretches across prehistoric remains and moorland in this region. Not far north of Hadrian's Wall are some of the most interesting parts of Northumberland National Park. Steel, coal, railroads, and shipbuilding made prosperous towns such as Newcastle upon Tyne (now re-creating itself as a cultural center) and Darlington.

The region's 100 mi of largely undeveloped coast is one of the least visited and most dramatic shorelines in all Europe. Several outstanding castles perch on headlands and promontories along here, including Bamburgh, which according to legend was the site of Joyous Garde, the castle of Sir Lancelot du Lac.

ORIENTATION AND PLANNING

GETTING ORIENTED

The historic cathedral city of Durham, one of the region's top attractions, sits to the east of the wooded foothills of the Pennines mountain range, in the southern part of the region. Farther north, busy Newcastle straddles the region's main river, the muddy Tyne. West of Newcastle, the remains of Hadrian's Wall snake through rugged scenery. Head northwest of the wall for the wilderness of Northumberland National Park. Along the far northeastern coast, towering castles and misty islands punctuate the stunning, final miles of England's eastern shoreline.

TOP REASONS TO GO

Castles, castles, castles: Fought over for centuries by the Scots and the English, and prey to Viking raiders, the Northeast was one of the most heavily fortified regions in England.

Medieval Durham: A splendid Norman cathedral that dates back to the 11th century is just one of the city's charms. Take a stroll on its ancient winding streets or along the River Wear; this is a fairy-tale town hewn from stone.

Hadrian's Wall: The ancient Roman wall is a wonder for the wild countryside around it and the resiliency of its stones. For an awe-inspiring sense of history, nothing beats a hike along part of the Hadrian's Wall Path national trail or a ride on Hadrian's Cycleway.

Lindisfarne (Holy Island): Just getting to this historic island is an unusual experience; you drive across a causeway that floods at high tide. This remote spot includes the ruins of Lindisfarne Priory.

Alnwick Castle and Gardens: The inland seat of the dukes of Northumberland is fascinating with its formidable walls, luxurious interiors, and multimillion-dollar gardens.

14

Durham, Newcastle, and Environs. The historic city of Durham, set on a rocky spur, has a stunning castle and cathedral. South and west are scenic towns with castles and industrial heritage sites. Newcastle, to the north, is a sprawling metropolis with a lively regional arts scene.

Hadrian's Wall Country. England's wildest countryside is traversed by the remains of the wall that marked the northern border of the Roman Empire. Hexham is a useful base, and Housesteads Roman Fort is a key site. It's stunning country for walking or biking.

The Far Northeast Coast. In this dramatic landscape, rocky hillsides plunge into the sea. The ruins of castle towers such as Dunstanburgh and Bamburgh stand guard over windswept beaches, and Lindisfarne has a long religious history. Alnwick, inland, has spectacular gardens.

PLANNING

WHEN TO GO

The best time to see the Northeast is in summer. This ensures that the museums—and the roads—will be open, and you can take advantage of the countryside walks that are one of the region's greatest pleasures. Rough seas and inclement weather make it dangerous to swim at any of the beaches except in July and August; even then, don't expect warm water. At the end of June, Alnwick hosts its annual fair, with a medieval market, art shows, and concerts. The Durham Regatta also takes place in June. The Northumberland Traditional Music Festival runs over two weeks in October.

PLANNING YOUR TIME

If you're interested in exploring Hadrian's Wall and the Roman ruins, you will probably want to base yourself at a guesthouse in or around Hexham. From there you can easily take in Housesteads and the other local landmarks. It's worth taking a day trip to Durham to see its lovely ancient buildings, and Newcastle's museums are a favorite destination of art lovers. Make Newcastle a day trip, as the city's tourist offerings are limited. Romantics will want to spend a day or two driving up the coast to take in the incredible castle views.

GETTING HERE AND AROUND

AIR TRAVEL

Newcastle's airport (a 15-minute drive from the city center) has flights from British and European cities.

Contact Newcastle Airport (✉ *Off A696* ☎ *0871/882–1121* ⊕ *www. newcastleairport.com*).

BUS TRAVEL

National Express and Megabus (book online to avoid premium-line charges) travel to Durham and Newcastle and leave from London's Victoria Coach Station, but the journey takes between six and eight hours, much longer than by train. Connecting services to other parts of the region leave from those cities. Traveline has information.

The Explorer Northeast Pass (£8, one day) allows unlimited travel on most local bus and Metro train services in the region and is available from the bus driver or local bus or Metro stations.

Contacts Explorer Northeast Pass (⊕ *www.explorernortheast.co.uk*).**Megabus** (☎ *0900/160–0900* ⊕ *www.megabus.com/uk*). **National Express** (☎ *0871/781–8178* ⊕ *www.nationalexpress.com*). **Traveline** (☎ *0871/200–2233* ⊕ *www. traveline.org.uk*).

CAR TRAVEL

If you're headed to small villages, remote castles, or Hadrian's Wall, traveling by car is the best alternative. The A1 highway links London and Newcastle (five to six hours). The scenic route is the A697, which branches west off A1 north of Morpeth. For the coast, leave the A1 at Alnwick and follow the minor B1340 and B1339 for Craster, Seahouses, and Bamburgh. Holy Island is reached from the A1.

TRAIN TRAVEL

Within England, the train is still the best way to reach this region. East Coast runs the train service from London to the Northeast. The average travel times from London are 2½ hours to Darlington, and three hours to Durham and Newcastle. From Newcastle, you can catch local trains to Alnwick, Corbridge, Hexham, and Carlisle; these journeys take about a half hour. National Rail Enquiries has information.

Contacts East Coast (☎ *0845/722–5333* ⊕ *www.eastcoast.co.uk*). **National Rail Enquiries** (☎ *0845/748–4950* ⊕ *www.nationalrail.co.uk*).

RESTAURANTS

Make sure to sample fine local meats and produce. Look for restaurants that serve game from the Kielder Forest, local lamb from the hillsides, salmon and trout from the rivers, and shellfish, crab, and oysters from the coast. Outside the cities, the region lags somewhat behind other parts of England in terms of good places to eat, although there are special spots to be found. Aside from the ubiquitous chains, the best

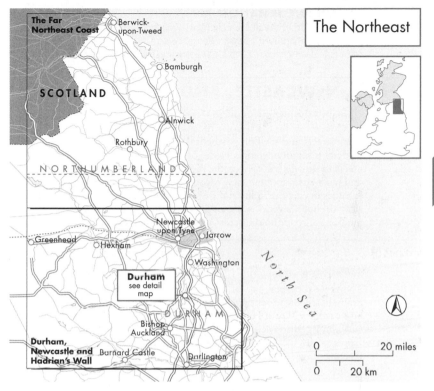

The Far
Northeast Coast

The Northeast

14

bets are often small country pubs that serve the traditional, hearty fare associated with the region. Don't wait until 9 PM to have dinner, though, or you may have a hard time finding a place that is still serving.

HOTELS

The large hotel chains don't have much of a presence in the Northeast, outside the few cities. Instead, you can expect to find country houses converted into welcoming hotels, old coaching inns that still greet guests after 300 years, and cozy bed-and-breakfasts convenient to hiking trails. Many budget accommodations close in winter.

WHAT IT COSTS IN POUNDS					
	£	££	£££	££££	£££££
Restaurants	under £10	£10–£14	£15–£19	£20–£25	over £25
Hotels	under £70	£70–£120	£121–£160	£161–£220	over £220

Restaurant prices are for a main course at dinner. Hotel prices are for two people in a standard double room in high season, including V.A.T., with no meals or, if indicated, CP (with Continental breakfast), BP (Breakfast Plan, with full breakfast), or MAP (Modified American Plan, with breakfast and dinner).

VISITOR INFORMATION
Contacts Hadrian's Wall Country (⊕ www.hadrians-wall.org). **Northumbria Regional Tourist Board** (✉ Stella House, Goldcrest Way, Newburn Riverside, Newcastle upon Tyne ☎ 01271/336182 ⊕ www.visitnorthumbria.com).

DURHAM, NEWCASTLE, AND ENVIRONS

Durham—the first major northeastern town on the main road up from London—is by far the region's most interesting historic city. Its cobblestone streets and towering cathedral make it a charming place to visit. The city is surrounded on all sides by scenic countryside, ruined castles, and isolated villages. Newcastle, though, is the region's biggest, liveliest, and most cosmopolitan city. Most other towns in the area made their fortunes during the Industrial Revolution and have since subsided into slow decline. Several, such as bustling Darlington, birthplace of the modern railroad, hold interesting relics of their 19th-century heyday.

DURHAM

250 mi north of London, 15 mi south of Newcastle.

The great medieval city of Durham, seat of County Durham, stands dramatically on a rocky spur, overlooking the countryside. Its cathedral and castle, a World Heritage Site, rise together on a wooded peninsula almost entirely encircled by the River Wear (rhymes with "beer"). For centuries these two ancient structures have dominated Durham—a thriving university town, the Northeast's equivalent of Oxford or Cambridge. Steep, narrow streets overlooked by perilously angled medieval houses and 18th-century town houses make for fun exploring. In the most attractive part of the city, near the Palace Green and along the river, people go boating, anglers cast their lines, and strollers walk along the shaded paths.

Despite the military advantages of its location, Durham was founded surprisingly late, probably in about the year 1000, growing up around a small Saxon church erected to house the remains of St. Cuthbert. It was the Normans, under William the Conqueror, who put Durham on the map, building the first defensive castle and beginning work on the cathedral. From here, Durham's prince-bishops, granted almost dictatorial local powers by William in 1072, kept a tight rein on the county, coining their own money and maintaining their own laws and courts; not until 1836 were these rights finally restored to the English Crown.

GETTING HERE AND AROUND

East Coast trains from London's King's Cross Station arrive at the centrally located Durham Station once an hour during the day. The journey takes about three hours. Trains from York arrive three to four times an hour; that journey takes roughly 50 minutes. A handful of National Express and Megabus buses make the seven-hour trip from London daily.

Between 10 and 4 on Monday through Saturday, cars are charged £2 (on top of parking charges) to enter the Palace Green area. You pay the charge at an automatic tollbooth on exiting. Bus 40 links parking lots and the train and bus stations with the cathedral.

ESSENTIALS

Visitor Information Durham (✉ *Millennium Pl.* ☎ *0191/384–3720* ⊕ www. thisisdurham.com).

EXPLORING

❷ Durham Castle. Facing the cathedral across Palace Green, the castle commands a strategic position above the River Wear. It has required many renovations and repairs through the ages because of less-than-stable foundations, but it remains an impressive pile. For almost 800 years the castle was the home of successive prince-bishops; from here they ruled large tracts of northern England and kept the Scots at bay. Henry VIII first curtailed the bishops' independence, although it wasn't until the 19th century that the prince-bishops finally had their powers annulled. They abandoned the castle, turning it over to University College, one of several colleges of the University of Durham (founded 1832), the oldest in England after Oxford and Cambridge. You can visit the castle only on a 45-minute guided tour—usually three times daily on weekdays during term time, more frequently during vacation periods (times vary, so call ahead). ✉ *Palace Green* ☎ *0191/334–3800* ⊕ *www.dur.ac.uk/university.college* ☞ *£5* ☾ *Call for guided tour hrs.*

QUICK BITES

Drop into the **Almshouses Café** (✉ *Palace Green* ☎ *0191/386–1054* ⊕ *www.the-almshouses.co.uk*), in an ancient almshouse between the cathedral and castle, for fat brownies or tasty cheesecake. These sweet treats are perfect with your tea.

---

❶ Durham Cathedral. A Norman masterpiece in the heart of the city, the cathedral is an amazing vision of solidity and strength, a far cry from the airy lightness of later, Gothic cathedrals. Construction began in about 1090, and the main body was finished in about 1150. The round arches of the nave and the deep zigzag patterns carved into them typify the heavy, gaunt style of Norman, or Romanesque, building. The technology of Durham, however, was revolutionary. This was the first European cathedral to be given a stone, rather than a wooden, roof. When you consider the means of construction available to its builders—the stones that form the ribs of the roof had to be hoisted by hand and set on a wooden structure, which was then knocked away—the achievement seems staggering.

The origins of the cathedral go back to the 10th century. In 995 monks brought to this site the remains of St. Cuthbert, which had been removed from the monastery at Lindisfarne after a Viking raid in 875. Soon the wealth attracted by Cuthbert's shrine paid for the construction of a cathedral. The bishop's throne here was claimed to be the loftiest in medieval Christendom; the miter of the bishop is the only one to be encircled by a coronet, and his coat of arms is the only one to be crossed with a sword as well as a crosier. **Cuthbert's shrine** lies surrounded by columns of local marble, with the saint's remains buried below a simple slab. An unobtrusive tomb at the west end of the cathedral, in the handsome, Moorish-influenced **Galilee Chapel,** is the final resting

Fodor's Choice
★

14

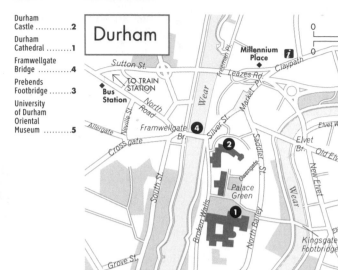

place of the **Venerable Bede,** an 8th-century Northumbrian monk whose contemporary account of the English people made him the country's first reliable historian. He died in Jarrow in 735, and his remains were placed here in 1020.

Upon entering the cathedral, note the 12th-century bronze **Sanctuary Knocker,** shaped like the head of a ferocious mythological beast, mounted on the massive northwestern door. By grasping the ring clenched in the animal's mouth, medieval felons could claim sanctuary; cathedral records show that 331 criminals sought this protection between 1464 and 1524. The current knocker is, in fact, a reproduction. The original is kept in the cathedral **Treasury,** along with ancient illuminated manuscripts, fragments of St. Cuthbert's oak coffin, and more church treasures well worth a look. You can view a film and an exhibit about building the cathedral, see the medieval monks' dormitory (now a library), and in good weather you can climb the **tower.** There's also a restaurant in the atmospheric undercroft, and a lovely shop. ⊠ *Palace Green* ☎ *0191/386–4266* ⊕ *www.durhamcathedral. co.uk* 🎫 *£5 donation requested; Treasury £2.50, tower £4, monks' dormitory £1, guided tours £4* ⊙ *Cathedral mid-June–early Sept., daily 7:30 AM–8 PM; early Sept.–mid-June, Mon.–Sat. 7:30–6, Sun. 7:45–5:30. (Prayer and services only until 9:30 Mon.–Sat., until 12:30 Sun.). Tower*

Apr.–late Sept., Mon.–Sat. 10–4; late Sept.–Mar., Mon.–Sat. 10–3. Treasury Mon.–Sat. 10–4:30, Sun. 2–4:30. Monks' dormitory Mon.–Sat. 10–4, Sun. 12:30–4. Choral evensong service Tues.–Sat. 5:15, Sun. 3:30. Guided tours Easter wk, July–Sept., and school holiday wks in May and Oct., Mon.–Sat. 10:30, 11, and 2:30.

❹ Framwellgate Bridge. If you follow the far side of the Wear north from Prebends Footbridge, you can recross the river at this 12th-century bridge. Many of the elegant town houses that line the narrow lanes back up to the cathedral now house departments of the University of Durham. ⊠ *Between Silver St. and Crossgate.*

❸ Prebends Footbridge. Delightful views are the reward of a short stroll along the River Wear's leafy banks, especially as you cross this footbridge, reached from the southern end of Palace Green. J.M.W. Turner reveled in the view from here and painted a celebrated scene of Durham from the bridge.

❺ University of Durham Oriental Museum. This museum, a 15-minute walk from the cathedral, displays fine art- and craftwork from all parts of Asia. Its collection of Chinese ceramics is notable, and don't miss the nearby 18-acre Botanic Gardens. ⊠ *Elvet Hill, off South Rd. (A1050)* ☎ *0191/334–5694* ⊕ *www.dur.ac.uk/oriental.museum* ⊠ *£1.50* ☉ *Weekdays 10–5, weekends noon–5.*

DURHAM'S REGATTA	

The pretty River Wear winds through Durham, curving beneath the cathedral and castle. In mid-June each year the city hosts the prestigious Durham Regatta, Britain's oldest rowing event. Three hundred racing crews compete in events, including races for single sculls and teams of eight.

14

WHERE TO EAT

£££
FRENCH
✕ **Bistro 21.** A few miles northwest of the center, Durham's most fashionable restaurant is in a superbly restored farmhouse. The eclectic, seasonal menu has a pronounced French accent. Look for such dishes as poached salmon and fillet steak with red wine sauce, as well as rich desserts. You can get here by taxi, or take Bus 43 to Durham Hospital and walk five minutes. ⊠ *Aykley Heads* ☎ *0191/384–4354* ⊕ *www.bistrotwentyone.co.uk* ⊟ *AE, DC, MC, V* ☉ *No dinner Sun.*

££
THAI
✕ **Numjai.** This Thai restaurant provides variety to the north's meat-and-vegetables diet. To top it all off, it has a lovely setting in the Milburngate shopping center. Its wraparound windows let you gaze out over your coconut green curry at the cathedral. ⊠ *19 Milburngate* ☎ *0191/386–2020* ⊕ *www.durham.thai-food-restaurants.co.uk* ⊟ *MC, V.*

££
BRITISH
✕ **Oldfields Restaurant.** At this convivial restaurant, cheerful raspberry-hue walls and unfussy walnut furnishings create a nicely laid-back vibe that complements the excellent food. Organic vegetables and free-range meat, sourced mostly from the surrounding region, are a specialty. The seasonal menu, featuring such dishes as roast chicken, mutton hotpot, and rabbit and crayfish pie, tends to be served with hearty root vegetables in the winter, and greens and beans in the summer. ⊠ *18 Clay Path* ☎ *0191/370–9595* ⊕ *www.oldfieldsrealfood.co.uk* ⊟ *MC, V.*

WHERE TO STAY

During college vacations (late March through April, July through September, and December), reasonably priced accommodations are available at the **University of Durham** (☎ 0191/334–2887 ⊕ www.dur.ac.uk/conferences), in Durham Castle, and in buildings throughout the city.

££   ⌂ **Georgian Town House.** At the top of a cobbled street overlooking the cathedral and castle, this family-run guesthouse has a location almost good enough to make you overlook the sometimes startling decor (such as burgundy curtains with lime green accents). Rooms are small and snug and have pleasant city views. Every bit of space is crowded with knickknacks, but the place is friendly and the breakfasts are big. **Pros:** great location; jovial owners; laid-back atmosphere. **Cons:** small rooms; odd design choices. ⊠ 11 Crossgate ☎ 0191/386–8070 ⊕ www.thegeorgiantownhouse.co.uk ➽ 8 rooms ♿ In-room: no a/c ⊟ No credit cards ☉ Closed last wk of Dec. ⍾○⍾ BP.

££   ⌂ **Seven Stars Inn.** Warm oranges and tartans in the public areas enhance the coziness of this good-value early-18th-century coaching inn. The simple bedrooms are done in creamy yellows and reds and have modern pine furniture. At the restaurant, tuck into such dishes as rib-eye steak with black pudding and bacon. The inn is 2 mi south of the city; Bus 56 from the city center takes 15 minutes and stops outside the inn. **Pros:** cozy lounge; reasonable rates. **Cons:** far from the center; on a main road; two-night minimum stay in high season. ⊠ High St. N, Shincliffe Village ☎ 0191/384–8454 ⊕ www.sevenstarsinn.co.uk ➽ 8 rooms ♿ In-room: no a/c, Wi-Fi. In-hotel: restaurant, some pets allowed ⊟ MC, V ⍾○⍾ BP.

£–££   ⌂ **Three Tuns Hotel.** In central Durham, this 16th-century inn has echoes of its solid country past. Some sections retain the old oak beams and fireplaces. The bedrooms are more contemporary, although antiques keep the historic feel going. Guests can use the indoor pool and health club at the nearby Swallow Royal County Hotel. Browns restaurant serves staples such as veal, steak, and salmon. **Pros:** nice mix of the old and the new; lots of atmosphere. **Cons:** it's a bit of a walk to use the pool and health club. ⊠ New Elvet ☎ 0191/386–4326 ⊕ www.swallowhotels.com ➽ 50 rooms ♿ In-room: no a/c. In-hotel: restaurant, bar, parking (free) ⊟ MC, V ⍾○⍾ BP.

NIGHTLIFE AND THE ARTS

Durham's nightlife is geared to university students. The **Hogshead** (⊠ 58 Saddler St. ☎ 0191/386–9550) pub is a true student haunt. The **Market Tavern** (⊠ 27 Market Pl. ☎ 0191/386–2069) draws fans of real ales.

UPSTAIRS, DOWNSTAIRS

Gorgeous Raby Castle acts as a living museum for castle life through the centuries. It's especially good at juxtaposing life as a servant with life as a lord. In the lord's dining room, rich red carpets and patterned silk wallpaper glow under a soaring, intricately carved ceiling. Downstairs, the servants had their meals in the bare, low-ceilinged medieval servants' hall, sitting at a rough pine table on hard wooden benches. Ouch!

SHOPPING

Bramwells Jewellers (✉ 24 *Elvet Bridge* ☎ 0191/386–8006) has its own store specialty, a pendant copy of the gold-and-silver cross of St. Cuthbert. The food and bric-a-brac stalls in **Durham Indoor Market** (✉ *Market Pl.* ☎ 0191/384–6153 ⊕ www.durhammarkets.co.uk), a Victorian arcade, are open Monday through Saturday 9 to 5. A farmers' market is held on the third Thursday of every month.

SPORTS AND THE OUTDOORS

Brown's Boat House (✉ *Elvet Bridge* ☎ 0191/386–3779) rents rowboats April through early November and offers short cruises all year.

BISHOP AUCKLAND

14

10 mi southwest of Durham.

For 700 years, between the 12th and 19th century, the powerful prince-bishops of Durham had their country residence in Auckland Castle, in the town of Bishop Auckland. When finally deprived of their powers in 1836, the bishops left Durham and made Bishop Auckland their official home. You can tour the house as well as nearby Raby Castle.

GETTING HERE AND AROUND

Bishop Auckland is just off the A1 motorway from London (260 mi) or Durham (13 mi). There's no direct train service here from London or Durham. However, you can take a train from either city to Darlington and change. The journey takes about three hours from London and one hour from Durham. National Express offers a regional bus service between Bishop Auckland and Durham. This trip takes about 30 minutes.

ESSENTIALS

Visitor Information Bishop Auckland (✉ *Town Hall, Market Pl.* ☎ *01388/604922* ⊕ www.thisisdurham.com).

EXPLORING

Arguably the greatest of the prince-bishops of Durham's properties is the episcopal palace of **Auckland Castle**, which you enter through an elaborate stone arch. Much of what you see today dates from the 16th century, although the limestone-and-marble chapel, with its dazzling stained-glass windows, was built in 1665 from the ruins of a 12th-century hall. ■ TIP→ Don't miss some of the palace's greatest treasures: paintings by the 17th-century Spanish artist Zurbarán of Jacob and his 12 sons. ✉ *Off Market Pl.* ☎ *01388/601627* ⊕ *www.auckland-castle.co.uk* 🎫 £4 ⊙ *Apr.–June and Sept., Mon. and Sun. 2–5; July and Aug., Mon. and Wed. 11–5, Sun. 2–5; park daily 7 AM–sunset.*

★ The stone battlements and turrets of moated **Raby Castle**, once the seat of the powerful Nevills and currently the home of the 11th baron Barnard, stand amid a 200-acre deer park and ornamental gardens. Charles Nevill supported Mary, Queen of Scots in the 1569 uprising against Elizabeth I; when the Rising of the North failed, the estate was confiscated. Dating mostly from the 14th century (using stone plundered from Barnard Castle) and renovated in the 18th and 19th centuries, the luxuriously furnished castle has displays of art and other

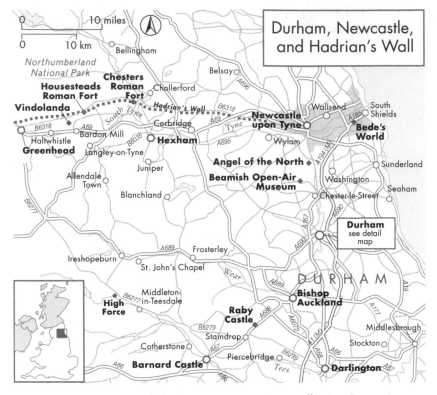

treasures, including an important Meissen collection. Rooms in wonderfully elaborate Gothic Revival, Regency, and Victorian styles are
open for viewing. Raby Castle is 7 mi southwest of Bishop Auckland, 19 mi southwest of Durham. ⊠ *A688, 1 mi north of Staindrop*
☎ *01833/660202* ⊕ *www.rabycastle.com* ⊠ *Castle, park, and gardens
£9.50, park and gardens £5* ☉ *May, June, and Sept., Sun.–Wed. 1–5
(park 11–5:30); July and Aug., Sun.–Fri. 1–5 (park 11–5:30). Also
open Sat. on bank holiday weekends.*

BARNARD CASTLE

14 mi south of Bishop Auckland, 25 mi southwest of Durham.

The handsome market town of Barnard Castle has sights of its own
and can also serve as a base for venturing into the Teesdale Valley to
the northwest. Its unusual butter-market hall (known locally as Market Cross), surmounted by an old fire-alarm bell, marks the junction
of the streets Thorngate, Newgate, and Market Place. Stores, pubs,
and cafés line these thoroughfares. In 1838 Charles Dickens stayed at
the **King's Head Inn** here while doing research for his novel *Nicholas
Nickleby*. The local tourist office has a free *In the Footsteps of Charles
Dickens* leaflet.

GETTING HERE AND AROUND

Barnard Castle is about a 20-minute drive from Bishop Auckland on A688. Bus 20 departs from Bishop Auckland at roughly 15 minutes past the hour; the trip to Barnard Castle takes an hour. The town is small, and walking is an easy way to explore.

ESSENTIALS

Visitor Information Barnard Castle (☒ *Woodleigh, Flatts Rd.* ☎ *01833/696356* ⊕ *www.teesdalediscovery.com*).

EXPLORING

The substantial ruins of **Barnard Castle**, which gave its name to the town, cling to an aerie overlooking the River Tees. Inside you can see parts of the 14th-century Great Hall and the cylindrical, 13th-century tower, built by the castle's original owners, the Anglo-Scottish Balliol family. It takes less than an hour to see it. ☒ *Off Galgate* ☎ *01833/638212* ⊕ *www.english-heritage.org.uk* ☜ *£4.20* ☉ *Apr.–Sept., daily 10–6; Oct.–Mar., weekends 10–4.*

14

★ The **Bowes Museum**, a vast French-inspired château a mile west of the town center, was built between 1862 and 1875 to house the art and artifacts accumulated by philanthropists John and Josephine Bowes. Highlights include paintings by Canaletto, El Greco, Francisco Goya, and François Boucher, and 18th-century French furniture. ■ **TIP→ Time your visit so you can see the extraordinary 18th-century life-size, mechanical silver swan in action. It sits on a stream of twisted glass and catches and swallows a silver fish every day at 2.** ☒ *Up Newgate, follow signs from town center* ☎ *01833/690606* ⊕ *www.thebowesmuseum.org.uk* ☜ *£6* ☉ *Daily 10–5.*

The Upper Teesdale Valley's elemental nature shows its most volatile aspect in the sprays of England's highest waterfall, the 72-foot **High Force**. From the roadside parking lot it's a 10-minute walk through woodland to the massive rocks over which the water tumbles. A precarious viewpoint puts you right above the falls, at their best in springtime after a rain. The waterfall is 15 mi northwest of Barnard Castle. ☒ *Off B6277* ☎ *01833/640209* ☜ *£1.50; parking £2* ☉ *Easter–Oct., daily 9:30–5; Nov.–Easter, open but unattended (honesty box for fee).*

WHERE TO EAT

£ ✕ **Market Place Teashop.** A nicely old-fashioned air pervades this 17th-
BRITISH century building on the main square. Waitresses clad in striped uniforms serve such dishes as lasagna and chicken-and-mushroom pie, as well as many vegetarian options. Afternoon tea comes in silver teapots. ☒ *29 Market Pl.* ☎ *01833/690110* ⊕ *www.teashop-barnard-castle.co.uk* ☐ *MC, V* ☉ *Closed Sun. except afternoons Apr.–Oct. No dinner.*

DARLINGTON

15 mi east of Barnard Castle, 21 mi south of Durham.

Still rooted in its 19th-century industrial past, the town of Darlington gained fame in 1825, when George Stephenson piloted his steam-powered *Locomotion* along newly laid tracks the few miles to nearby Stockton, thus kick-starting the railway age. Today it's a somewhat workaday place, although the Head of Steam museum is worth a visit, especially for families.

ESSENTIALS

Visitor Information Darlington (✉ *Dolphin Centre* ☎ *01325/388666* ⊕ *www. visitdarlington.net*).

EXPLORING

🌀 **Head of Steam: The Darlington Railway Centre and Museum** tells the story
★ of the early days of rail travel. It occupies the town's 1842 train station, a 20-minute walk from the town center. The interactive exhibits and big steam trains are great for kids, and antique engines and scale models help bring history to life. There's also a café and children's activity room. ✉ *North Rd. Station, Station Rd.* ☎ *01325/460532* ⊕ *www. darlington.gov.uk* ☜ *£5* ⊙ *Apr.–Sept., Tues.–Sun. 10–4; Oct.–Mar., Mon.–Thurs. 11–3:30.*

WHERE TO STAY

££–£££   🏨 **Hall Garth Hotel, Golf & Country Club.** Occupying a lovely early-19th-
BRITISH   century building, this hotel is surrounded by 67 acres of parkland, complete with lakes and woodlands, as well as a 9-hole golf course. At the edge of Darlington, it's a pleasant option even for nongolfers, with an indoor swimming pool and sauna, bucolic views, and lots of peaceful grounds to wander. The rooms have modern, tasteful decor, and the restaurant serves traditional British cuisine. **Pros:** pastoral setting; relaxing rooms; good golfing. **Cons:** rooms aren't as charming as the common areas. ✉ *Coatham Mundeville, Darlington* ☎ *0870/609–6131* ⊕ *www. foliohotels.com/hallgarth* ⟿ *51 rooms* & *In-room: no a/c, Wi-Fi. In-hotel: restaurant, bar, golf course, pool* ⊟ *AE, MC, V* ¶◎¶ *BP.*

BEAMISH OPEN-AIR MUSEUM

8 mi north of Durham, 8 mi south of Newcastle upon Tyne.

EXPLORING

★ The sprawling **Beamish Open-Air Museum** village, with buildings moved here from throughout the region, explores the way people in the Northeast lived and worked from the early 1800s to the early 1900s. A streetcar takes you around the site and to a reconstructed 1920s shopping street with a dentist's office, pub, and grocery store. Other attractions include a small manor house, a railroad station, and a coal mine. In summer, a steam train makes a short run. ■TIP➔ **Allow at least a half day if you come in summer, a couple of hours in winter.** ✉ *Off A693, between Chester-le-Street and Stanley* ☎ *0191/370–4000* ⊕ *www.beamish.org. uk* ☜ *£16 Apr.–Oct., £7.50–£10 Nov.–Mar.* ⊙ *Apr.–Oct., daily 10–5; Nov.–mid-Dec. and Jan.–Mar., Tues.–Thurs. and weekends 10–4; last admission 3.*

WHERE TO STAY

£££–££££   🏨 **Lumley Castle Hotel.** This is a real Norman castle, right down to the
Fodor'sChoice   dungeons and maze of dark flagstone corridors. Antiques, silks, and
★   deep, rich fabrics furnish all the sumptuous rooms, which are designed with clever touches such as a bathroom hidden behind a bookcase. The rooms in the courtyard annex are less expensive. You can join in the

merriment of the Friday and Saturday night Elizabethan banquets or dine in the Black Knight restaurant. The hotel is just east of town via the B1284. **Pros:** great for antiques lovers; delightful hidden rooms. **Cons:** it's easy to get lost down the winding corridors. ⊠ *Chester-le-Street* ☎ *0191/389–1111* ⊕ *www.lumleycastle.com* ⬎ *59 rooms* ♿ *In-room: no a/c, Wi-Fi. In-hotel: restaurant, bar, Wi-Fi hotspot* ▤ *AE, DC, MC, V.*

NEWCASTLE UPON TYNE

8 mi north of Beamish Open-Air Museum, 16 mi north of Durham.

Durham may have the glories of its castle, cathedral, and university, but the liveliest city of the Northeast is Newcastle, currently reinventing itself as a regional center for culture and modern architecture after years of decline. Settled since Roman times on the Tyne River, the city made its fortune twice—first by exporting coal and later by shipbuilding. As a 19th-century industrial center, Newcastle had few equals in Britain, showing off its wealth in grand Victorian buildings lining the broad streets. Some of these remain, particularly on Grey Street. The cluster of bridges (older and newer) crossing the Tyne is a quintessential city sight.

Much of the regeneration since the early 1990s has been based around the Gateshead Quays. Here the Baltic Centre for Contemporary Art and the pedestrian-only Millennium Bridge—the world's first tilting bridge, which opens and shuts like an eyelid—have risen from wasteland.

GETTING HERE AND AROUND

Newcastle Airport, a 15-minute drive from the city center, has flights from British and European cities. Metro trains connect to the center. The A1 highway links London and Newcastle (five to six hours).

East Coast trains from London's King Cross take about three hours. National Express and Megabus have service from London's Victoria Coach Station several times a day for the six- to eight-hour trip.

Newcastle has a good public transportation system. Its Metro light rail network is easy to use, well signposted, and has stops near most sights. Buses go all the places Metro doesn't reach.

ESSENTIALS

Visitor Information Newcastle upon Tyne (⊠ *8–9 Central Arcade, Market St.* ☎ *0191/277–8000* ⊕ *www.visitnewcastlegateshead.com).*

EXPLORING
TOP ATTRACTIONS

★ ***Angel of the North.*** If you're approaching Newcastle from the south, 8 mi from the city center, at the junction of A1(M) and A1 at Gateshead, stands England's largest—and one of its most popular—sculptures, the *Angel of the North.* Created by Antony Gormley in 1998, the rust-color steel sculpture is a sturdy, abstract human figure with airplane-like wings rather than arms. It stands 65 feet tall and has a horizontal wingspan of 175 feet. There's parking nearby, signposted on A167.

14

Baltic Centre for Contemporary Art. Formerly a grain warehouse and now the country's largest national gallery for contemporary art outside London, Baltic presents intriguing changing exhibitions. ⊠ *Gateshead Quays, South Shore Rd.* ☎ *0191/478–1810* ⊕ *www.balticmill.com* ⊠ *Free* ⊙ *Tues. 10:30–6, Wed.–Mon. 10–6.*

Ⓒ **Great North Museum.** This excellent new museum combines the collections of the University of Newcastle upon Tyne's Museum of Antiquities and the Shefton Museum of Greek Art and Archaeology, and also contains natural history exhibits from the Hancock Museum. The modern, £26 million facility contains an impressive collection of ancient archaeological finds, including remnants left behind by the Roman builders of Hadrian's Wall. It also holds superb ancient Greek artifacts, as well as a reconstruction of the 1st-century Temple of Mithras at Carrawburgh. This is a very kid-friendly museum, with a planetarium and an exhibit of live animals alongside dusty Victorian stuffed specimens. The museum is next to the University of Newcastle upon Tyne, just off the Great North Road, and five minutes from the Haymarket Metro station. ⊠ *Barras Bridge* ☎ *0191/222–6765* ⊕ *www.twmuseums.org.uk/ greatnorthmuseum* ⊠ *Free* ⊙ *Mon.–Sat. 10–5, Sun. 2–5.*

QUICK
BITES
The popular, 70-year-old art deco **Tyneside Coffee Rooms** (⊠ *10 Pilgrim St.* ☎ *0191/227–5520*), on the second floor above the Tyneside Cinema, makes an intriguing place to stop for teas, coffee, and a good, unfussy lunch. It's open daily.

★ **Laing Art Gallery.** The Northeast's finest art museum merits at least an hour's visit for its selection of British art. Some of the most extraordinary paintings are those by 19th-century local artist John Martin, who produced dramatic biblical landscapes. The Pre-Raphaelites are on show, too, and the Art on Tyneside exhibition traces 400 years of local arts, highlighting glassware, pottery, and engraving. ⊠ *Higham Pl. near John Dobson St.* ☎ *0191/232–7734* ⊕ *www.twmuseums.org. uk/laing* ⊠ *Free* ⊙ *Mon.–Sat. 10–5, Sun. 2–5.*

WORTH NOTING

Bede's World. Four miles east of Newcastle, this site holds substantial monastic ruins, a visitor center–museum, and the church of St. Paul, all reflecting the long tradition of religion and learning that began here in AD 681, when the first Saxon church was established on the site. The Venerable Bede, deemed to be England's earliest historian, moved into the monastery when he was 7 and remained until his death in AD 735. You can gain a sense of medieval life from the reconstructed farm buildings and the rare breeds of pigs and cattle on the 11-acre Anglo-Saxon farm. From the southern exit traffic circle at South Tyne tunnel, take A185 to South Shields and follow signs to St. Paul's Church and Jarrow Hall; or use Bus 526 or 527, or the Bede/Jarrow Metro stop (20-minute walk). ⊠ *Church Bank, Jarrow* ☎ *0191/489–2106* ⊕ *www. bedesworld.co.uk* ⊠ *£5.50* ⊙ *Mon.–Sat. 10–5, Sun. noon–5; last admission 1 hr before closing.*

Ⓒ **Discovery Museum.** Kids and history buffs will get the most out of the
★ Discovery Museum, which tells Newcastle's story. Reconstructed streets

and homes lead you from Roman times to the present day, and the Tyne galleries show off maritime and industrial achievements. *Turbinia* is a model of the 1897 ship that was the world's first to be powered by steam turbines. ⊠ *Blandford Sq.* ☎ *0191/232–6789* ⊕ *www.twmuseums.org. uk/discovery* ⊠ *Free* ☉ *Mon.–Sat. 10–5, Sun. 2–5.*

Segedunum Roman Fort, Baths and Museum. For a good introduction to Britain's Roman history, dip into this museum. It includes the remains of the substantial Roman fort of Segedunum, built around AD 125 as an eastern extension to Hadrian's Wall, and part of the original wall as well as a reproduction section. There's also a reconstructed Roman bath complex and an observation tower. It's near the Wallsend Metro station. ⊠ *Buddle St., Wallsend* ☎ *0191/236–9347* ⊕ *www.twmuseums.org.uk/ segedunum* ⊠ *£4.25* ☉ *Apr.–Oct., daily 10–5; Nov.–Mar., daily 10–3.*

Tyne Bridge. By the old quayside, this bridge (built in 1929) is the symbol of Newcastle, and is one of seven bridges spanning the river in the city.

WHERE TO EAT AND STAY

£££
MODERN BRITISH
★
✕ **Café 21.** A Newcastle classic, this sleek brasserie has been a favorite for business lunches and romantic dinners for years. Warm wood, leather banquettes, and crisp white table linens lend a polished look. The menu focuses on modern versions of classic British cuisine. Try the pot-roast pheasant with Calvados, apples, and cream, or the grilled lemon sole with new potatoes. Desserts such as custard tart with nutmeg ice cream are excellent. The three-course early-bird menu (£19.50; 5:30–7 and all evening Sunday) is a good way to try it all. ⊠ *Trinity Gardens, Quayside* ☎ *0191/222–0755* ⊕ *www.cafetwentyone.co.uk* ⊟ *AE, MC, V.*

££££–£££££
★
🛏 **Jesmond Dene House.** Occupying a sprawling 19th-century mansion in the northeastern part of the city, this hotel has been racking up accolades since opening in 2007. It's surrounded by lush gardens and filled with polished oak floors, huge windows, and wandering staircases. You can read the paper by the inglenook fireplace in the lounge or curl up on a firm bed in one of the spacious, modern guest rooms. The elegant restaurant has become a local favorite for its use of regional meat and produce. **Pros:** beautiful light-filled rooms; lovely gardens. **Cons:** the restaurant is popular, so you need to book in advance. ⊠ *Jesmond Dene Rd.* ☎ *0191/212–3000* ⊕ *www.jesmonddenehouse.co.uk* ⤺ *40 rooms* ♿ *In-room: a/c, Internet. In-hotel: restaurant, bar, pool, gym, spa* ⊟ *AE, MC, V* ☉❙ *BP.*

££££
🛏 **Malmaison.** Converted from an old riverside warehouse, this member of a glamorous, design-conscious chain sits right beside the pedestrian Millennium Bridge. Guest rooms, done in a modern style with clever rococo-esque touches of gilt and velvet, are spacious, and the huge beds are piled high with pillows. The discreet Mal restaurant presents modern French fare in a room overlooking the Tyne. **Pros:** interesting building; gorgeous restaurant; irresistible claw-foot tubs. **Cons:** bar and restaurant get very crowded. ⊠ *Quayside* ☎ *0191/245–5000* ⊕ *www. malmaison.com* ⤺ *116 rooms* ♿ *In-room: a/c, Wi-Fi. In-hotel: restaurant, room service, bar, gym, spa, laundry service, some pets allowed* ⊟ *AE, MC, V.*

14

££££££ ★ **Seaham Hall.** Byron married Annabella Milbanke in this foursquare mansion on a cliff top overlooking the sea in 1815; today the sumptuous contemporary interior filled with warm natural hues is a haven of luxury. Elegant bedrooms have their own fireplaces, original artwork, two-person baths, and exotic flowers. At the equally elegant restaurant (£££££), indulge in dishes such as loin of venison and root vegetables flavored with chocolate. Make some time for the excellent Serenity Spa, inspired by feng shui principles. Seaham is 15 mi south of the center of Newcastle, off A19. **Pros:** pampering rooms; full of atmosphere. **Cons:** far outside town; you'll have to dress up for dinner. ⊠ *Lord Byron's Walk, Seaham* ☎ *0191/516–1400* ⊕ *www.seaham-hall.com* ⇘ *19 suites* △ *In-room: a/c, Internet. In-hotel: restaurant, bar, pool, gym, spa* ⊟ *AE, MC, V* ⅃⊙⅃ *BP.*

NIGHTLIFE AND THE ARTS

★ **Offshore 44** (⊠ *40–44 Sandhill* ☎ *0191/261–0921*) is an old pub with a nautical theme. The upstairs terrace of the **Pitcher and Piano** (⊠ *108 Quayside* ☎ *0191/232–4110*), a popular pub with floor-to-ceiling windows, is the perfect viewing point for the Millennium Bridge.

★ The **Sage Gateshead** (⊠ *West St., Gateshead Quays* ☎ *0191/433–4661*) hosts concerts—jazz, world, pop, classical, folk, and rock—in a curving, modern building designed by Sir Norman Foster.

Theatre Royal (⊠ *Grey St.* ☎ *0844/811–2121*), the region's most established theater, has high-quality productions and is also a venue for opera and dance.

HADRIAN'S WALL COUNTRY

A formidable line of Roman fortifications, Hadrian's Wall was the Romans' most ambitious construction in Britain. The land through which the old wall wanders is wild and inhospitable in places, but that seems only to add to the powerful sense of history it evokes. Museums and information centers along the wall make it possible to learn as much as you want about the Roman era.

HADRIAN'S WALL

73 mi from Wallsend, north of Newcastle, to Bowness-on-Solway, beyond Carlisle.

ESSENTIALS

Visitor Information Hexham Tourism Information Centre (⊠ *Wentworth Car Park* ☎ *01434/652220* ⊕ *www.visitnortheastengland.com*). **Once Brewed National Park Visitor Centre** (⊠ *In Northumberland National Park, B6318, Once Brewed* ☎ *01434/344396* ⊕ *www.northumberland-national-park.org.uk* ☉ *Mid-Mar.–Nov., daily 9:30–5*).

EXPLORING

Fodor's Choice ★ Dedicated to the Roman god Terminus, the massive span of **Hadrian's Wall** once marked the northern frontier of the Roman Empire. Today remnants of the wall wander across pastures and hills, stretching 73 mi from Wallsend ("Wall's End," north of Newcastle) in the east, to Bowness-on-Solway in the west. Today, the wall is a World Heritage Site, and excavating, interpreting, repairing, and generally managing the Roman remains is a Northumbrian growth industry. ■TIP➔ At Chesters, Housesteads (the best-preserved fort), and Vindolanda, and at the Roman Army Museum near Greenhead, you get a good introduction to the life led by Roman soldiers on the frontier. In summer most sites sponsor talks, Roman drama, and festivals; local tourist offices and the sites have details.

At Emperor Hadrian's command, three legions of soldiers began

FAST WALL FACTS

■ No slaves were used to build the wall; it was built by skilled Roman masons with the labor of thousands of soldiers.

■ The wall was a multicultural military zone, with soldiers (and their families) coming from places such as Germany, Spain, and North Africa. Lively wall communities were made up of people with different languages and customs.

■ Only 5% of the Roman remains in the region around the wall have been excavated.

14

building the wall in AD 122, and finished it in four years. It was constructed after repeated invasions by troublesome Pictish tribes from what is now Scotland. During the Roman era it was the most heavily fortified wall in the world, with walls 15 feet high and 9 feet thick; behind it lay the vallum, a ditch about 20 feet wide and 10 feet deep. Spaced at 5-mi intervals along the wall were massive forts (such as those at Housesteads and Chesters), which could house up to 1,000 soldiers. Every mile was marked by a thick-walled milecastle (a fort that housed about 30 soldiers), and between each milecastle were two turrets, each lodging four men who kept watch. For more than 250 years the Roman army used the wall to control travel and trade and to fortify Roman Britain against the barbarians to the north.

During the Jacobite Rebellion of 1745, the English dismantled much of the Roman wall and used the stones to pave what is now the B6318 highway. The most substantial stretches of the remaining wall are between Housesteads and Birdoswald (west of Greenhead). Running through the southern edge of Northumberland National Park and along the sheer escarpment of Whin Sill, this section is also an area of dramatic natural beauty. The ancient ruins, rugged cliffs, dramatic vistas, and spreading pastures make it a good area for hiking. For information about the wall, check out ⊕ www.hadrians-wall.org.

A special **Hadrian's Wall Bus** (☎ 01434/322002 ⊕ www.hadrians-wall. org) offers day passes (£8) for service between Wallsend and Carlisle, stopping at Newcastle, Hexham, and the major Roman forts. The service runs daily from April to October and on Sunday throughout the year. ■TIP➔ Free travel for two kids is included in the price of a day pass on Mondays. Another bus runs daily from Wallsend to Bowness, and another from Hexham to Vindolanda (£3).

SPORTS AND THE OUTDOORS
BIKING
Hadrian's Cycleway (⊕ *www.cycle-routes.org/hadrianscycleway*), between Tynemouth and Whitehaven, follows the river Tyne from the east coast until Newcastle, before chasing the entire length of Hadrian's Wall. It then continues west to the Irish Sea. Maps and guides are available at the Tourist Information Centre in Newcastle or online. Bikes in the **Bike Shop** (✉ *16–17 St. Mary's, Hexham* ☎ *01434/601032*) cost £15 per day. **Purple Mountain Bike Centre** (✉ *Kielder Castle, Kielder* ☎ *01434/250532*) rents mountain bikes for £15 to £25 per day.

HIKING
Hadrian's Wall Path (☎ *01434/322022* ⊕ *www.nationaltrail.co.uk/ hadrianswall*), one of Britian's national trails, runs the entire 73-mi length of the wall. If you don't have time for it all, take one of the less challenging circular routes. One of the most scenic but also most rugged sections is the 12-mi western stretch between Sewingshields and Greenhead.

HEXHAM

22 mi west of Newcastle, 31 mi northwest of Durham.

The area around the busy market town of Hexham is a popular base for visiting Hadrian's Wall. Just a few miles from the most significant remains, it's a bustling working town, but it has enough historic buildings and winding medieval streets to warrant a stop in its own right. First settled in the 7th century, around a Benedictine monastery, Hexham later became a byword for monastic learning, famous for its book painting, sculpture, and singing.

GETTING HERE AND AROUND
No major bus companies travel to this region. East Coast trains take about three hours to travel from London's King Cross to Newcastle. From there, catch a local train. The A1 highway links London and the region (five to six hours).

Hexham is a small, walkable town. It has infrequent local bus service, but you're unlikely to need it. If you're driving, park in the lot by the tourism office and walk into town. The tourism office has free maps and will point you in the right direction.

ESSENTIALS
Visitor Information Hexham Tourism Information Centre (✉ *Wentworth Car Park* ☎ *01434/652220* ⊕ www.visitnortheastengland.com).

EXPLORING
★ Ancient **Hexham Abbey**, a site of Christian worship for more than 1,300 years, forms one side of the town's main square. Inside, you can climb the 35 worn stone "night stairs," which once led from the main part of the abbey to the canon's dormitory, to overlook the whole ensemble. Most of the current building dates from the 12th and 13th centuries, and much of the stone, including that of the Anglo-Saxon crypt, was taken from the Roman fort at Corbridge. Note the portraits on the 16th-century wooden rood screen and the four panels from a 15th-century

Dance of Death in the sanctuary. ✉ *Beaumont St.* ☎ *01434/602031*
⊕ *www.hexhamabbey.org.uk* ✉ *Requested donation £3* ⊙ *Daily 9:30–*
5. Crypt daily at 11 and 3:30.

Since 1239, Hexham's central **Market Place** has been the site of a weekly
market, now held each Tuesday. Crowded stalls are set out under the
long slate roof of the Shambles; other stalls, protected only by bright
awnings, take their chances with the weather.

Dating from 1330, Hexham's **Old Gaol**, across Market Place from the
abbey, houses fascinating exhibits about Border history. Photographs,
models, a house interior, and weapons tell the story of the "Middle
March," the medieval administrative area governed by a warden and
centered on Hexham. A glass elevator takes you to four floors, including the dungeon. ✉ *Hallgate* ☎ *01434/652439* ✉ *£3* ⊙ *Mar.–Oct., daily*
10–4:30; Nov. and Feb., Mon., Tues., and Sat. 10–4:30.

Chesters Roman Fort, a cavalry fort in a wooded valley on the banks
of the North Tyne River, was known as Cilurnum in Roman times,
when it protected the point where Hadrian's Wall crossed the river.
You approach the fort directly from the parking lot, and, although the
site cannot compete with Housesteads in setting, the recently renovated museum here holds a fascinating collection of Roman artifacts,
including statues of river and water gods, altars, milestones, iron tools,
weapons, and jewelry. The military bathhouse by the river is well preserved. The fort is 4 mi north of Hexham. ✉ *B6318, ½ mi southwest of*
Chollerford ☎ *01434/681379* ⊕ *www.english-heritage.org.uk* ✉ *£4.80*
⊙ *Apr.–Sept., daily 10–6; Oct.–Mar., daily 10–4.*

WHERE TO EAT AND STAY

££££ ✕ **Langley Castle.** Rescued from decline by a professor from the United
BRITISH States in the mid-1980s, this lavish 14th-century castle hotel with turrets
and battlements offers an elegant fine-dining experience. The baronial
dining room is romantic, with little candlelit alcoves draped in rich
fabric. Choose from an excellent menu (£34 prix fixe) of traditional
English dishes and game—perhaps the Barbary duck breast with caramelized orange compote, or the lamb rump with dauphinoise potatoes
and rosemary jus. It is 6 mi west of Hexham. ✉ *A686, Langley-on-Tyne*
☎ *01434/688888* ⊕ *www.langleycastle.com* ▭ *AE, DC, MC, V.*

£ ▦ **Dene House.** Peaceful and stone-built, this former farmhouse on 9
acres of lovely countryside has beamed ceilings and homey rooms with
pine pieces and colorful quilts. Breakfasts, taken in the cozy kitchen,
include homemade bread and preserves. The house is 4 mi south of
Hexham; follow signs for Dye House. **Pros:** tasty breakfasts; warm
atmosphere. **Cons:** not a lot of privacy. ✉ *B6303, Juniper, Hexham*
☎☎ *01434/673413* ⊕ *www.denehouse-hexham.co.uk* ✉ *3 rooms, 1*
with private bath ⚲ *In-room: no a/c, no phone, no TV. In-hotel: bar*
▭ *AE, MC, V* ⫿ *BP.*

££ ▦ **Montcoffer.** This charming guesthouse sits in cozy, whitewashed stables that were converted in 1999. Its three guest rooms are spacious,
with pine floors warmed with soft rugs, and comfortable beds covered
in thick white comforters and blankets. The knowledgeable owners can
suggest sights off the beaten track. Breakfasts, served in the attractive,

14

beamed dining room, are hearty, and vegetarians are well cared for. All rooms are on the ground floor and accessible to those with mobility problems. **Pros:** big rooms; helpful owners. **Cons:** it gets booked up early. ⊠ *Bardon Mill, Hexham* ☎ *01434/344138* ⊕ *www.montcoffer. co.uk* ◁ *3 rooms* ⚬ *In-room: no a/c, refrigerator* ☰ *No credit cards* ⊚| *BP.*

££ ☐ **Shieldhall Guesthouse.** A lovely 19th-century farmhouse and its origi-
★ nal outbuildings have been converted into this guesthouse about 15 mi northeast of Hexham. Surrounded by miles of rolling farmland, it's an ideal base if you want to explore remote stretches around Hadrian's Wall. Rooms are small but beautifully decorated, with draped fabric; bathrooms are big and modern. The friendly owners have a woodworking shop nearby where they make all the furniture in the house. Elegant dinners are served at the main house's large dining table with advance notice. **Pros:** lots of peace and quiet; dinners are exceptional. **Cons:** well outside town; need a car to get around. ⊠ *Off B6342, about 15 mi northeast of Hexham, Belsay* ☎ *01830/540387* ⊕ *www. shieldhallguesthouse.co.uk* ◁ *3 rooms* ⚬ *In-room: no a/c. In-hotel: res-taurant* ☰ *MC, V* ⊚| *BP.*

NIGHTLIFE AND THE ARTS

The **Queen's Hall Arts Centre** (⊠ *Beaumont St.* ☎ *01434/652477* ⊕ *www. queenshall.co.uk*) presents theater, dance, and art exhibitions. It also sponsors events such as June's jazz festival.

GREENHEAD

18 mi west of Hexham, 49 mi northwest of Durham.

Tiny Greenhead has the Roman Army Museum, an informative Hadrian's Wall site. Other important sites are nearby, too.

EXPLORING

The **Roman Army Museum**, at the garrison fort of Carvoran, near the village, makes an excellent introduction to Hadrian's Wall. Full-size models and excavations bring this remote outpost of the empire to life; authentic Roman graffiti adorn the walls of an excavated bar-racks. Opposite the museum, at Walltown Crags on the Pennine Way (one of Britain's long-distance national hiking trails), are 400 yards of the best-preserved section of the wall. ⊠ *Off B6318, 1 mi northeast of Greenhead* ☎ *01697/747485* ⊕ *www.vindolanda.com* ▱ *£4.50; joint ticket with Vindolanda £9* ⊙ *Mid-Feb.–Mar. and Oct., daily 10–5; Apr.–Sept., daily 10–6.*

Fodor'sChoice If you have time to visit only one Hadrian's Wall site, **Housesteads Roman**
★ **Fort**, Britain's most complete example of a Roman fort, is your best bet. It includes an interpretive center, views of long sections of the wall, the excavated 5-acre fort itself, and a small but interesting museum containing statues and other items uncovered at the fort. The steep, 10-minute walk up from the parking lot by B6318 to the site rewards the effort, especially for the sight of the wall disappearing over hills and crags into the distance. Excavations have revealed remains of gra-naries, gateways, barracks, a hospital, and the commandant's house.

The fort is 11 mi east of Greenhead, and about 35 mi from Durham. ✉ *B6318* ☎ *01434/344363* 🌐 *www.english-heritage.org.uk* 🎫 *£4.80* ⏲ *Apr.–Sept., daily 10–6; Oct.–Mar., daily 10–4.*

The great garrison fort of **Vindolanda**, 8 mi east of Greenhead, holds the remains of eight successive Roman forts and civilian settlements, which have provided intriguing information about daily life in a military compound. Most of the visible remains date from the 2nd and 3rd centuries, and excavations are always under way. A reconstructed Roman temple, house, and shop provide context, and the museum displays rare artifacts such as writing tablets. A full-size reproduction of a section of the wall gives a sense of its massiveness. ✉ *Near Bardon Mill* ☎ *01434/344277* 🌐 *www.vindolanda.com* 🎫 *£5.90; joint ticket with Roman Army Museum £9* ⏲ *Mid-Feb.–Mar. and Oct., daily 10–5; Apr.–Sept., daily 10–6; call to confirm times in winter. Last admission 45 mins before closing.*

In Northumberland National Park, **Once Brewed National Park Visitor Centre**, ½ mi north of Vindolanda, has informative displays about Hadrian's Wall and can advise about local walks. ✉ *B6318, Once Brewed* ☎ *01434/344396* 🌐 *www.northumberland national-park.org.uk* 🎫 *Free* ⏲ *Apr.–Oct., daily 9:30–5; Nov.–Mar., weekends 10–3.*

WHERE TO EAT AND STAY

££ BRITISH ★ ✕ **Milecastle Inn.** The snug traditional bar and restaurant of this remote, peaceful 17th-century pub make an excellent place to dine. Fine local meat goes into its famous pies; take your pick from rabbit, venison, and duckling. Two cottages (three-night minimum stay) are available for rent. The inn is on the north side of Haltwhistle on B6318. ✉ *Military Rd., Haltwhistle* ☎ *01434/321372* 🌐 *www.milecastle-inn.co.uk* 💳 *AE, MC, V.*

££ 🏨 **Holmhead Guest House.** This former farmhouse in open countryside is not only built *on* Hadrian's Wall but also *of* it. Stone arches and exposed beams add to the feeling of history. Rooms are small but comfortable, the beds covered with soft, white eiderdown. You can book a fixed-priced dinner that may include organic vegetables. There's also an apartment in a cottage (prices start at £265 per week) and eight hostel-style beds in a barn. **Pros:** perfect for history buffs; close to Hadrian's Wall. **Cons:** rooms are a bit of a squeeze; you need a car out here. ✉ *Off A69* ☎📠 *016977/47402* 🌐 *www.bandbhadrianswall.com* *4 rooms, 8 beds, 1 apartment* *In-room: no a/c, no TV. In-hotel: restaurant* 💳 *MC, V* 🍽 *BP.*

THE FAR NORTHEAST COAST

Extraordinary medieval fortresses and monasteries line the final 40 mi of the Northeast coast before England gives way to Scotland. Northumbria was an enclave where the flame of learning was kept alive during Europe's Dark Ages, most notably at Lindisfarne, home of saints and scholars. Castles abound, including the spectacularly sited Bamburgh and the desolate Dunstanburgh. The region also has some magnificent beaches, though because of the cold water and rough seas, they are far better for walking than swimming. The 3-mi walk from Seahouses to Bamburgh gives splendid views of the Farne Islands, and the 2-mi hike from Craster to Dunstanburgh Castle is unforgettable. A bit inland are a few other pretty towns and other castles.

ALNWICK

9 mi northeast of Rothbury, 30 mi north of Newcastle, 46 mi north of Durham.

Dominated by a grand castle, the little market town of Alnwick (pronounced *ahn*-ick) is the best base from which to explore the dramatic coast and countryside of northern Northumberland.

ESSENTIALS

Visitor Information Alnwick (⊠ *2 The Shambles* ☎ *01665/511333* ⊕ *www. visitalnwick.org.uk*).

EXPLORING

A weekly open-air market (every Saturday) has been held in Alnwick's cobbled **Market Place** for more than 800 years. Note the market cross, built on the base of an older cross; the town crier once made his proclamations from here. In the last week of June, this site is host to the **Alnwick Fair,** a festival noteworthy for the enthusiastic participation of locals in medieval costume.

Ⓒ ★ The grandly scaled **Alnwick Castle**, on the edge of the town center, is known for its gardens as well as the castle itself. This is still the home of the dukes of Northumberland, whose family, the regal Percys, dominated the Northeast for centuries. Known as "the Windsor of the North," it has been remodeled several times since Henry de Percy adapted the original Norman keep. Nowadays Alnwick is in favor as a set for films such as the first two Harry Potter movies (in the first, the castle grounds appear as the exterior of Hogwarts School in scenes such as the Quidditch match). In contrast with the cold, formidable exterior, the interior has all the opulence of the palatial home it still is. You see only 6 of the more than 150 rooms, but among the treasures are a galleried library, niches with larger-than-life-size marble statues, and Venetian-mosaic floors. Kids appreciate Knights' Quest, a mock training school for knights where they get to dress up and complete interactive challenges, and Dragon's Quest, a labyrinth designed to teach a bit of medieval history while providing a few harmless scares. The castle's extensive gardens (separate admission) include a modern, 260-foot-long stepped water cascade as well as ornamental gardens. ⊠ *Above junction of Narrowgate and Bailiffgate* ☎ *01665/510777* ⊕ *www.alnwickcastle. com* ⊠ *£12.50, combined ticket with gardens £20* ☉ *Late Mar.–late Oct., daily 11–5; last admission 4:15.*

★ A marvelous flight of fancy developed since 2000, the **Alnwick Garden** represents the vision of the duchess of Northumberland. Centering on modern terraced fountains by Belgian designers Jacques and Peter Wirtz, the still-expanding gardens include traditional features (shaded woodland walks, a rose garden) and funkier, kid-appealing elements such as a Poison Garden and a labyrinth of towering bamboo. It's also

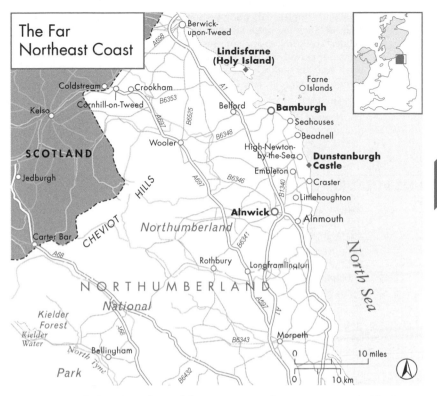

The Far
Northeast Coast

SCOTLAND

Berwick-upon-Tweed

Lindisfarne
(Holy Island)

Farne
Islands

Coldstream   Crookham

Cornhill-on-Tweed

Kelso

Belford   **Bamburgh**

Seahouses

Beadnell

Wooler

High-Newton-
by-the-Sea

**Dunstanburgh
Castle**

Jedburgh

Embleton

Craster

Littlehoughton

HILLS

Alnwick   Alnmouth

CHEVIOT

Northumberland

Carter Bar

Rothbury   Longframlington

NORTHUMBERLAND

Kielder
Forest

Kielder
Water

National

Bellingham

North Tyne

Morpeth

Park

North Sea

0   10 miles

0   10 km

14

the location of one of the area's most unique restaurants, the Treehouse. ⊠ *Denwick La.* ☎ *01665/511350* ⊕ *www.alnwickgarden.com* ⊠ *£9.50, combined ticket with Alnwick Castle £20* ☉ *Daily 10–dusk; last admission 45 mins before closing.*

WHERE TO EAT AND STAY

£££   ✕ **The Treehouse.** You don't have to visit Alnwick Garden to eat at this
BRITISH extraordinary restaurant set among the treetops on the grounds. Though at first glance the location may seem gimmicky, the food exceeds expectations, with a menu strong on British classics. Typical dishes include baked halibut with garlic mash, and pork Wellington with Stilton and walnuts. Lunch selections are more limited but offer good value, with no main dish exceeding £10; another option is just to have a drink at the bar. ⊠ *Alnwick Garden, Denwick La.* ☎ *01665/511852* ⊕ *www. alnwickgarden.com/eat* ⊟ *AE, MC, V* ☉ *No dinner Tues. and. Wed. No dinner Mon. Oct.–May.*

££–£££   🛏 **White Swan Hotel.** The surprise feature of this 18th-century coaching inn near the town square is that one lounge, the Olympic Suite, has been reconstructed with the paneling, stained glass, and mirrors of the *Olympic,* sister ship of the *Titanic.* It's used as a function room, but guests can take a look. The hotel was refurbished in 2007, and the rooms have a sleeker, more contemporary look, with pastel and neutral hues and simple, mahogany furniture; a few rooms have four-poster beds. ■TIP→ **You get a discount of about 5% on your room by booking online.** Pros: modern and comfortable rooms; relaxed restaurant. Cons: lost some period charm. ⊠ *Bondgate Within* ☎ *01665/602109* ⊕ *www. classiclodges.co.uk* ⤳ *57 rooms* ⌂ *In-room: no a/c, TV, DVD player. In-hotel: restaurant, bar, some pets allowed* ☰ *AE, MC, V* ⊙I *BP.*

SHOPPING

The **House of Hardy** (⊠ *A1* ☎ *01665/602771*), just outside Alnwick (from downtown, take A1 south to just beyond the traffic circle on the left, clearly marked), is one of Britain's finest stores for country sports. It has a worldwide reputation for handcrafted fishing tackle.

DUNSTANBURGH CASTLE

8 mi northeast of Alnwick.

GETTING HERE AND AROUND

The castle is 8 mi northeast of Alnwick, and is accessible only by footpaths from the villages of Craster or Embleton off the B1339 rural road. Follow the signs to the castle. To get here you'll need a car—there is no public transportation to or near the site.

EXPLORING

Perched romantically on a cliff 100 feet above the shore, the **Dunstanburgh Castle** ruins can be reached along a windy, mile-long coastal footpath that heads north from the tiny fishing village of Craster. Built in 1316 by the earl of Lancaster as a defense against the Scots (or perhaps as a symbol of Lancaster's deteriorating relationship with King Edward II), and later enlarged by John of Gaunt, the powerful duke of Lancaster who virtually ruled England in the late 14th century, the castle is known to many from the popular paintings by 19th-century artist J.M.W. Turner. Several handsome sandy bays indent the coastline immediately to the north. ■TIP→ **If you're making the hike from Craster, take time to sample the great kippers—salted and smoked herring—produced in smokehouses here and served in local pubs there.** ☎ *01665/576231* ⊕ *www.english-heritage.org.uk* ▣ *£3.80* ⊙ *Apr.–Sept., daily 10–5; Oct., daily 10–4; Nov.–Mar., Thurs.–Mon. 10–4.*

BAMBURGH

14 mi north of Alnwick.

Tiny Bamburgh has a splendid castle, and several beaches are a few minutes' walk away.

GETTING HERE AND AROUND

Bamburgh can be reached by car on B3140, B3141, or B3142. Arriva runs buses from Alnwick to Bamburgh every two hours at quarter to the hour. The nearest train station is in Chathill, about 7 mi away.

EXPLORING

Especially stunning when floodlighted at night, **Bamburgh Castle** dominates the coastal view for miles, set atop a great crag to the north of Seahouses and overlooking a magnificent sweep of sand and sea backed by high dunes. It was once believed to be the legendary Joyous Garde of Sir Lancelot du Lac, one of King Arthur's fabled knights. A fortification of some kind has stood here since the 6th century, but the Norman castle was damaged during the 15th century. Much of the castle—the home of the Armstrong family since 1894—was restored during the 18th and 19th centuries, including the Victorian Great Hall, although the great Norman keep (central tower) remains intact. Exhibits include armor, porcelain, jade, furniture, and paintings. Parts of the castle are now rented as apartments. ⊠ *Off B1340, 3 mi north of Seahouses, Bamburgh* ☎ *01668/214515* ⊕ *www.bamburghcastle.com* ⊡ *£7.50; parking £1* ⊙ *Late Feb.–Oct., daily 10–5, last admission 4 PM; Nov.–mid-Feb., weekends 11–4:30.*

	WALK AND BIKE

Wide vistas, quiet roads, and fresh air make hikes and bike rides appealing in the Northeast. Long-distance footpaths include the 90-mi Teesdale Way, which follows the River Tees through Barnard Castle and Middleton-in-Teesdale. Otherwise, the russet hills and dales of Northumberland National Park will please any serious walker. Bike routes to explore—in whole or in part—are the 220-mi Northumbria's Cycling Kingdom loop and the 81-mi Coast and Castles cycle route.

14

WHERE TO EAT AND STAY

££££   ✕ **Waren House.** Six acres of woodland surround this Georgian house on
BRITISH   a quiet bay between Bamburgh and Holy Island. The crisply elegant restaurant has romantic views of Holy Island when the trees are bare; two- to four-course fixed-price dinners might include loin of monkfish with smoked salmon and rosemary cream, pork tenderloin with black pudding, and baked lemon cheesecake. Public areas are furnished comfortably in period style, and there are guest rooms (£££–££££) if you want to linger overnight. ⊠ *B1342, Waren Mill, Bamburgh* ☎ *01668/214581* ⊕ *www.warenhousehotel.co.uk* ⊟ *AE, MC, V.*

££   🛏 **Lord Crewe Hotel & Restaurant.** This cozy, stone-walled inn with oak beams is in the heart of the village, close to Bamburgh Castle. Pine furnishings decorate the simple, modern guest rooms, and the food in the bar and in the restaurant, especially seafood dishes, is excellent. It's an ideal spot for lunch while you're touring the area. **Pros:** in the center of the village; good restaurant. **Cons:** pub can get quite crowded. ⊠ *Front St.* ☎ *01668/214243* ⊕ *www.lordcrewe.co.uk* ⇋ *18 rooms* ⚴ *In-room: no a/c. In-hotel: restaurant, bar, some pets allowed, no kids under 5* ⊟ *MC, V* ⊙ *Closed Dec. and Jan.* ⊚ *BP.*

LINDISFARNE (HOLY ISLAND)

★   *6 mi north of Bamburgh off the A1, north of Bamburgh, 22 mi north of Alnwick.*

Cradle of northern England's Christianity and home of St. Cuthbert, Lindisfarne (or Holy Island) has a religious history that dates from AD 635, when St. Aidan established a monastery here. Under its greatest abbot, the sainted Cuthbert, Lindisfarne became one of the foremost centers of learning in Christendom. Today you can explore the atmospheric ruined priory and a castle.

GETTING HERE AND AROUND

By car, the island is reached from the mainland via a long drive on a causeway that floods at high tide, so check when crossing is safe. The times, which change daily, are displayed at the causeway and printed in local newspapers. Traffic can be heavy; allow at least a half hour for your return trip. The only public transportation link to Holy Island is run by Perryman's Buses. Bus 477 has limited service (two buses a day in summer, and not every day) from Berwick-upon-Tweed railroad station to the island.

ESSENTIALS

Bus Contacts Perryman's Buses (☎ *01289/308719* ⊕ *www.perrymansbuses. co.uk*).

EXPLORING

In the year 875, Vikings destroyed the Lindisfarne community; only a few monks managed to escape, carrying with them Cuthbert's bones, which they reburied in Durham. The sandstone Norman ruins of **Lindisfarne Priory**, reestablished in the 11th century by monks from Durham, remain both impressive and beautiful. A museum here displays Anglo-Saxon carvings. ✉ *Lindisfarne* ☎ *01289/389200* ⊕ *www.english-heritage.org.uk* ✆ *£4.50* ⊙ *Feb. and Mar., daily 10–4; Apr.–Sept., daily 9:30–5; Oct., daily 9:30–4; Nov.–Jan., Mon. and weekends 10–2.*

Reached during low tide via a causeway from the mainland, **Lindisfarne Castle** appears to grow out of the rocky pinnacle on which it was built 400 years ago, looking for all the world like a fairy-tale illustration. In 1903 architect Sir Edwin Lutyens converted the former Tudor fort into a private home that retains the original's ancient features. Across several fields from the castle is a walled garden designed by Gertrude Jekyll. Call ahead for times, as these change with the tides. ✉ *Lindisfarne* ☎ *01289/389244* ⊕ *www.nationaltrust.org.uk* ✆ *£6; garden only, £1.30* ⊙ *Castle mid-Mar.–Oct., Tues.–Sun., call for hrs (generally 10–3 or noon–5); mid-Feb., daily 10–3; garden daily 10–dusk.*

Wales

WORD OF MOUTH

"Crickhowell is a pretty town perched between Table Mountain and the River Usk. We'd picked it for its proximity to Tintern Abby, Caerphilly Castle, and some good wulking in the area. That evening, trout were rising to a hatch on the river, and I would have sold my soul for a fly rod."

—Fra_Diavolo

"I vote for Conwy so you can walk the town walls in the evening after a day of exploring. Lots of choices for eats in Conwy. I spent a week there and found it very centrally located for exploring."

—irishface

Updated by
Roger Thomas

Known as the Land of the Song, Wales is also a land of mountain and flood, where wild peaks challenge the sky and waterfalls thunder down steep, rocky chasms. It is a land of gray-stone castles, ruined abbeys, male-voice choirs, and a handful of cities. Pockets of the southeast and northeast were heavily industrialized in the 19th century, largely with mining and steelmaking, but long stretches of the coast and the mountainous interior remain areas of unmarred beauty.

Small, self-contained Wales has three national parks (Snowdonia, including Snowdon, highest mountain in England and Wales; the Brecon Beacons; and the Pembrokeshire Coast) and five official Areas of Out-standing Natural Beauty (the Wye Valley, Gower Peninsula, Lln Peninsula, Isle of Anglesey, and Clwydian Range), as well as large tracts of unspoiled moor and mountain in Mid Wales, the least traveled part of the country. Riches of other sorts fill the country: medieval castles, seaside resorts, traditional market towns, the glorious Bodnant Garden and the National Botanic Garden, the stately houses of Powis and Plas Newydd, steam-powered trains running through Snowdonia and central Wales, and the cosmopolitan capital of Cardiff.

The 1941 film *How Green Was My Valley* depicted Wales as an industrial cauldron filled with coal mines. Although mining did take place in Wales, the picture was not accurate then and is certainly not accurate now. One of the glories of visiting Wales is the drive through beautiful countryside from south to north without passing through any large towns. On such a drive, it's easy to believe that Wales has a population of about 2.9 million but is home to 5.5 million sheep. The country's 750 mi of coast consists mainly of sandy beaches, grassy headlands, cliffs, and estuaries.

The Welsh are a Celtic race. When the Anglo-Saxons spread through Britain beginning around AD 500, they pushed the indigenous Celts farther back into their Welsh mountain strongholds. In fact, "Wales" comes from the Saxon word *Weallas,* which means "strangers," the name impertinently given by the new arrivals to the natives. The Welsh, however, have always called themselves Y *Cymry,* the companions. Not until the English king Edward I (1272–1307) waged a brutal campaign to conquer Wales was English supremacy established. Welsh hopes were finally crushed with the death in battle of Llywelyn ap Gruffudd, last native prince of Wales, in 1282.

Today Wales has achieved a measure of independence from its English neighbor. In a 1999 referendum, a narrow majority of the Welsh people voted for partial devolution for the country. Elections were held and the Welsh Assembly was born. Unlike the Scottish Parliament, the Welsh Assembly has no lawmaking powers, but it does have significant administrative responsibilities and considerable control over Welsh affairs.

TOP REASONS TO GO

Castle country: Wales is the "Land of Castles." With more than 400 historic sites, it has one of the highest concentrations of castles in Europe. They range from evocative ruins of the native Welsh princes, such as Criccieth Castle, and the fairy-tale Victorian extravaganza of Castell Coch to the huge, mighty fortresses of Caernarfon and Harlech.

Cardiff old and new: The capital of Wales is young and vibrant. Compare the stately architecture of Cardiff's neoclassical Civic Centre with the futuristic form of Wales Millennium Centre, the new arts complex on lively Cardiff Bay.

Coast and mountain walks: Hike along the coast at St. David's, one of the most magical sections of the long-distance Pembrokeshire Coast Path. Or take a hike to the top of Pen y Fan, the highest peak in the grassy Brecon Beacons National Park.

A ride on the rails: Wales has 13 mostly narrow-gauge railways that transport you at the more leisurely pace of a bygone era along scenic routes throughout the country. The rack-and-pinion Snowdon Mountain Railway takes you to the summit of the highest mountain in England and Wales.

Pump the pedals: Brecon is great for biking. From this attractive town country roads lead into the national park; mountain bikers can climb grassy trails and tracks up into the hills.

15

The Welsh Assembly is housed in a building on Cardiff Bay designed by the world-famous British architect Sir Richard Rogers.

The Welsh language continues to flourish. Although spoken by only a fifth of the population, it has a high profile within the country. Welsh-language schools are popular, there is a Welsh TV channel, and road signs are bilingual. Ironically, although in the 15th and 16th centuries the Tudor kings Henry VII and Henry VIII continued England's domination of the Welsh, principally by attempting to abolish the language, another Tudor monarch, Elizabeth I, ensured its survival by authorizing a Welsh translation of the Bible in 1588. Many older people say they owe their knowledge of Welsh to the Bible. You may see (and hear) Welsh throughout your travels, but everyone in Wales speaks English, too.

ORIENTATION AND PLANNING

GETTING ORIENTED

Wales has three main regions: North, Mid, and South. North Wales is a mixture of mountains, popular sandy beaches, and coastal hideaways. Although dominated by the rocky Snowdonia National Park, the north has a gentler, greener side along the border with England. Mid Wales is pure countryside, fringed on its western shores by the arc of Cardigan Bay. Here you'll find Wales's rural heartland, with mountain lakes, quiet roads, hill sheep farms, and traditional market towns. The south is the most varied, for its boundaries include everything from Wales's capital city, Cardiff, to unspoiled coastline, grassy mountains, and wooded valleys. It's a landscape of dramatic, sudden contrasts—within minutes of urban areas you can be among national parklands, moors, and mountains.

North Wales. Wales's most famous castles are found in its northern region. The cream of the crop is Caernarfon, a medieval palace dominating the waterfront on the Menai Strait. Conwy (castle and town) is popular, too. Snowdonia's mountains are a major draw, as is quirky Portmeirion, a faux-Italian village.

Mid Wales. The quietest part of Wales is home to scenic countryside, from rolling hills to more rugged mountains. Dolgellau is in the mountainous southern part of Snowdonia National Park. Hay-on-Wye is famous for its secondhand and antiquarian bookstores.

South Wales. Cardiff, the lively young capital city, is here, as are two very different national parks: the green, swooping hills of the Brecon Beacons and, in the far west, the sea cliffs, beaches, and estuaries of the Pembrokeshire Coast. Both are excellent for outdoor activities such as sailing, walking, and mountain biking,

PLANNING

WHEN TO GO
The weather in Wales, as in the rest of Britain, is a lottery. It can be warm in spring and cool in summer; come prepared for rain or shine. Generally speaking, southwest Wales enjoys a milder climate than elsewhere in Britain, thanks to the moderating effects of the sea. Spring and autumn can be surprisingly dry and sunny. Spring may arrive very early in Pembrokeshire, in the southwest. In contrast, mountainous areas like Snowdonia and the Brecon Beacons can be chilly at any time of the year. Book ahead for major festivals such as the literary Hay Festival, Brecon Jazz, Abergavenny Food Festival, and Llangollen's International Musical Eisteddfod.

PLANNING YOUR TIME
First-time visitors often try to cover too much ground in too little time. Wales is often perceived as a destination to be covered in just a few days. If you have limited time, base yourself in one region—North or South Wales, for example—and see the surrounding sights. From Cardiff, it's easy to visit the Wye Valley, Brecon Beacons, and the Gower Peninsula. Along the North Wales coast, Llandudno is a good base for Snowdonia and a sandy seashore. But many people return for a longer visit and get to know the country, its history, culture, and off-the-beaten-track locations.

The location of Wales lends itself to a border-hopping trip. Well-known locations like Bath (near South Wales) and Chester (near North Wales) are no more than an hour from the Welsh border, so it is easy to create an itinerary that combines both Wales and England.

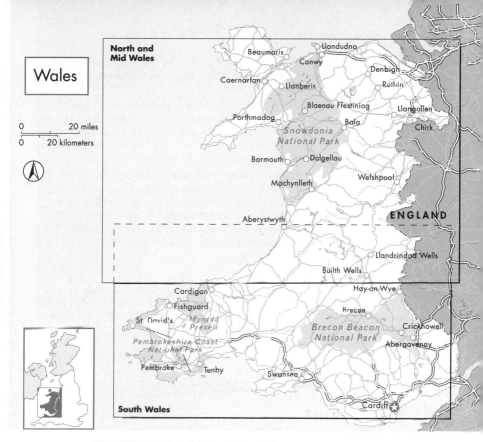

GETTING HERE AND AROUND

AIR TRAVEL

If you're arriving from the United States, London's Heathrow and Gatwick airports are usually your best options because of their large number of international flights. Heathrow (two hours) is slightly closer than Gatwick (2½ hours), but both have excellent motorway links with South Wales. For North Wales, the quickest access is via Manchester Airport, with a travel time of less than an hour to the Welsh border.

Cardiff International Airport, 19 mi from downtown Cardiff, is the only airport in Wales with international flights. These are mostly from Europe and Canada, however. A bus service runs from the airport to Cardiff's central train and bus stations.

Airports Cardiff International Airport (✉ *A4226, Rhoose* ☎ *01446/711111* ⊕ *www.cwlfly.com*). **Manchester Airport** (✉ *Near Junctions 5 and 6 of M56* ☎ *08712/710711* ⊕ *www.manchesterairport.co.uk*).

BUS TRAVEL

Most parts of Wales are accessible by bus. National Express buses arrive from London's Victoria Coach Station and also direct from London's Heathrow and Gatwick airports. The company also has routes into Wales from many major towns and cities in England and Scotland. Average travel times from London are 3½ hours to Cardiff, four hours to Swansea, 5½ hours to Aberystwyth, and 4½ hours to Llandudno. Regional buses fan out across Wales, but local timetables and connections can be complicated.

Wales's three national parks run summer bus services. The Snowdon Sherpa runs into and around Snowdonia and links with main rail and bus services. The Pembrokeshire Coastal Bus Service operates in the Pembrokeshire Coast National Park, and the Beacons Bus serves the Brecon Beacons National Park.

Bus Contacts Brecon Beacons National Park (✉ *Plas-y-Ffynnon, Cambrian Way, Brecon* ☎ *01874/624437* ⊕ *www.breconbeacons.org).* **National Express** (☎ *0871/781–8181* ⊕ *www.nationalexpress.com).* **Pembrokeshire Coast National Park** (✉ *Llannion Park, Pembroke Dock* ☎ *0845/345–7275* ⊕ *www.pcnpa.org.uk).* **Snowdonia National Park** (✉ *Penrhyndeudraeth* ☎ *01766/770274* ⊕ *www.eryri-npa.gov.uk).* **Traveline** (☎ *0871/200–2233* ⊕ *www.traveline-cymru.info).*

CAR TRAVEL

The easiest way to get around Wales is by car. In the rural areas—which constitute most of Wales—bus and train service can often be slow. If you don't want to rent a car at the airport, you can do so at major destinations like Cardiff or Swansea. Distances in miles may not be great in Wales, but getting around takes time because there are few major highways. There is no single fast route from north to south (the mountains discouraged that); A470 is good and scenic, and A487 runs along or near most of the coastline. Many smaller mountain roads are winding and difficult to maneuver, but they have magnificent views.

TRAIN TRAVEL

Travel time on the fast InterCity rail service from London's Paddington Station is about two hours to Cardiff and three hours to Swansea. InterCity trains also run between London's Euston Station and North Wales. Average travel times from Euston are 3¾ hours and five hours to Aberystwyth. Regional train service covers much of Wales. There are many scenic routes, such as the Cambrian Coast Railway, running 70 mi between Aberystwyth and Pwllheli, and the Heart of Wales line, linking Swansea and Craven Arms, near Shrewsbury.

Train Contacts National Rail Enquiries (☎ *0845/748–4950* ⊕ *www. nationalrail.co.uk).* **Regional & Intercity Railways** (☎ *0845/748–4950* ⊕ *www. thetrainline.com).* **Snowdon Mountain Railway** (✉ *Llanberis, Caernarfon* ☎ *0844/493–8120* ⊕ *www.snowdonrailway.co.uk).*

DISCOUNTS AND DEALS

For travel within Wales, ask about money-saving unlimited-travel tickets (such as Freedom of Wales Flexi Pass, North and Mid Wales Rover, and the South Wales Flexi Rover), which include the use of bus services. A discount card offering a 20% reduction on each of the narrow-gauge Great Little Trains of Wales is also available. It costs £10 and is valid for 12 months.

The Cadw/Welsh Historic Monuments Explorer Pass is good for unlimited admission to most of Wales's historic sites. The seven-day pass costs £17.50 (single adult), £29 (two adults), or £36 (family ticket); the three-day pass costs £11, £18, and £26, respectively. Passes are available at any site covered by the Cadw program. All national museums and galleries in Wales are free.

Discount Information Cadw/Welsh Historic Monuments (✉ *Plas Carew, Unit 5–7, Cefn Coed, Parc Nantgarw, Treforest* ☎ *01443/336000* ⊕ *www. cadw.wales.gov.uk*). **Flexi Pass information** (☎ *0845/606–1660* ⊕ *www. walesflexipass.co.uk*). **Great Little Trains of Wales** (✉ *Wharf Station, Tywyn* ☎ *01654/710472* ⊕ *www.greatlittletrainsofwales.co.uk*). **National Museums and Galleries of Wales** (⊕ *www.museumwales.ac.uk*).

TOURS

A good way to see Wales is by local tour bus; in summer there are day and half-day excursions to most parts of the country. In major resorts and cities, ask for details at a tourist information center or bus station.

The Wales Official Tourist Guide Association (WOTGA) uses only guides recognized by VisitWales and will create tailor-made tours. You can book a driver-guide or someone to accompany you as you drive.

Tour Information Wales Official Tourist Guide Association (☎ *01633/774796* ⊕ *www.walestourguides.com*).

RESTAURANTS

Today even many rural pubs are more interested in offering meals than serving pints of beer, so do consider them as a dining option. Don't overlook hotel restaurants in Wales; many, particularly those in country inns or hotels, are excellent. More and more restaurants are creating dishes using local produce—Welsh lamb, Welsh Black beef, Welsh cheeses, and seafood from the Welsh coast—that show off the best of the region's cuisine.

HOTELS

A 19th-century dictum, "I sleeps where I dines," still holds true in Wales, where good hotels and good restaurants often go together. Castles, country mansions, and even small railway stations are being transformed into interesting hotels and restaurants. Traditional inns with low, beamed ceilings, wood paneling, and fireplaces remain Wales's pride, but they, as well as farmhouse accommodations, tend to be off the beaten track. Cardiff and Swansea have some large chain hotels, and, for luxury, Wales has good country-house hotels. An added attraction is that prices are generally lower than they are for equivalent properties in the Cotswolds, Scotland, or southeast England.

WHAT IT COSTS IN POUNDS					
	£	££	£££	££££	£££££
Restaurants	under £10	£10–£14	£15–£19	£20–£25	over £25
Hotels	under £70	£70–£120	£121–£160	£161–£220	over £220

Restaurant prices are for a main course at dinner. Hotel prices are for two people in a standard double room in high season, including V.A.T., with no meals or, if indicated, CP (with Continental breakfast), BP (Breakfast Plan, with full breakfast), or MAP (Modified American Plan, with breakfast and dinner).

VISITOR INFORMATION

Contacts VisitWales Centre (☎ *08708/300306* ⊕ *www.visitwales.com*). **Wales in Style** (⊕ *www.walesinstyle.com*).

NORTH WALES

Wales masses all its savage splendor and fierce beauty in the north. Dominating the area is Snowdon, at 3,560 feet the highest peak in England and Wales. It is impossible to describe the magnificence of the view from the mountain on a clear day: to the northwest the Menai Strait, Anglesey, and beyond to the Irish Sea; to the south the mountains of Merionethshire, Harlech Castle, and the Cadair Idris mountain range; and all around towering masses of wild and barren rock. ■TIP→ **If you plan to ascend the peak by the Snowdon Mountain Railway, call ahead to check whether it is free from mist. You lose much when clouds encircle the monster's brow, as often happens.**

The peak gives its name to **Snowdonia National Park,** which extends southward all the way to Machynlleth in Mid Wales. The park consists of 840 square mi of rocky mountains, valleys clothed in oak woods, moorlands, lakes, and rivers, all guaranteeing natural beauty and, to a lesser extent, solitude. As in other British national parks, much of the land is privately owned, so inside the park are towns, villages, and farms. The park has become a popular climbing spot, and some fear that Snowdon itself is becoming worn away by the boots of walkers.

Along the sandy, north-facing coast, seaside resorts have attracted visitors for well over a century. Llandudno, the dignified "Queen of the North Wales coast," was built in Victorian times as a seaside watering hole. Nearby Conwy, with its medieval castle and town walls, deserves a look, as do other great North Wales castles such as Harlech and Caernarfon. There are two official Areas of Outstanding Beauty: the Isle of Anglesey (connected by bridge to the mainland), and the Llyn Peninsula, dotted with quieter small resorts and villages. Portmeirion, a mock-Italianate village, is a different kind of escape.

CHIRK AND THE CEIRIOG VALLEY

22 mi southwest of Chester, 60 mi southwest of Manchester.

Chirk, poised on the border between England and Wales, is a handy gateway to the Ceiriog Valley, a narrowing vale that penetrates the silent, green foothills of the lofty Berwyn Mountains.

GETTING HERE AND AROUND

Chirk is near the border of England and has handy rail links via Shrewsbury and Chester. But to make the most of the remote Ceiriog Valey you will need a car.

EXPLORING

The impressive medieval fortress of **Chirk Castle,** finished in its original form in 1310, has evolved into a grand home (albeit one with a medieval dungeon), complete with an 18th-century servants hall and interiors furnished in 16th- to 19th-century styles. Surrounding the castle are

beautiful formal gardens and parkland. ✉ *Off B4500* ☎ *01691/777701*
⊕ *www.nationaltrust.org.uk* ✉ *£9.60; garden and medieval tower only,*
£6.80 ◷ *Castle mid-Mar.–June, Wed.–Sun. 10–5; July and Aug., Tues.–*
Sun. 10–5; Sept and Oct., Wed.–Sun. 11–5; Nov., weekends 10–4.
Garden and tower mid-Mar.–June, Wed.–Sun. 11–5; July and Aug.,
Tues.–Sun. 11–5; Sept. and Oct., Wed.–Sun. 11–5.

West of Chirk is the **Vale of Ceiriog**, nicknamed Little Switzerland. Take
B4500 west 6 mi through the lovely valley to the village of Glyn Ceiriog,
at the foothills of the remote Berwyn Mountains. The area attracts pony
trekkers, walkers, and anglers.

WHERE TO STAY

£ ⚏ **Bron Heulog.** Carefully restored in period style as a guesthouse, this
former home of a Victorian politician boasts a peaceful location in Berwyn Mountains. It was built in 1861 and stands in an acre of gardens.
Fireplaces, high ceilings, and an oak staircase are original elements of
the large stone house. Rooms have showers only—no bathtubs. **Pros:**
all rooms have good views; self-catering option. **Cons:** no evening meal;
need a car to get around. ✉ *Waterfall St., off B4396, Llanrhaeadr ym*
Mochnant ☎ *01691/780521 www.bronheulog.co.uk* ⬎ *3 rooms ⟡ In-*
room: no a/c, no phone. In-hotel: laundry service ▤ *MC, V* ◉ *BP.*

EN
ROUTE
The peat-brown water of **Pistyll Rhaeadr**, the highest waterfall in Wales,
thunders down a 290-foot double cascade. To get here, take B4500
southwest from Glyn Ceiriog, and then its unnumbered continuation,
to reach Llanrhaeadr ym Mochnant, in the peaceful Tanat Valley. Here,
in 1588, the Bible was translated into Welsh, thus ensuring the survival of the language. Turn northwest and go 4 mi up the road to the
waterfall.

LLANGOLLEN

5 mi northwest of Chirk, 23 mi southwest of Chester.

Llangollen's setting in a deep valley carved by the River Dee gives it a
typically Welsh appearance. The bridge over the Dee, a 14th-century
stone structure, is named in a traditional Welsh folk song as one of the
"Seven Wonders of Wales." In July the very popular International Musical Eisteddfod brings crowds to town. For a particularly scenic drive in
this area, head for the Horseshoe Pass.

GETTING HERE AND AROUND

You'll need a car to get here, but once you arrive you can take a trip
on the Llangollen Railway. Along the Llangollen Canal longboat tours
head both west and east. The town itself is easy to explore on foot.

ESSENTIALS

Visitor Information Llangollen (✉ *Y Capel, Castle St.* ☎ *01978/860828*).

EXPLORING

Plas Newydd (not to be confused with the similarly named Isle of
Anglesey estate) was the home from 1778 to 1828 of Lady Eleanor
Butler and Sarah Ponsonby, the eccentric Ladies of Llangollen, who set
up a then-scandalous single-sex household, collected curios and magnificent wood carvings, and made it into a tourist attraction even during

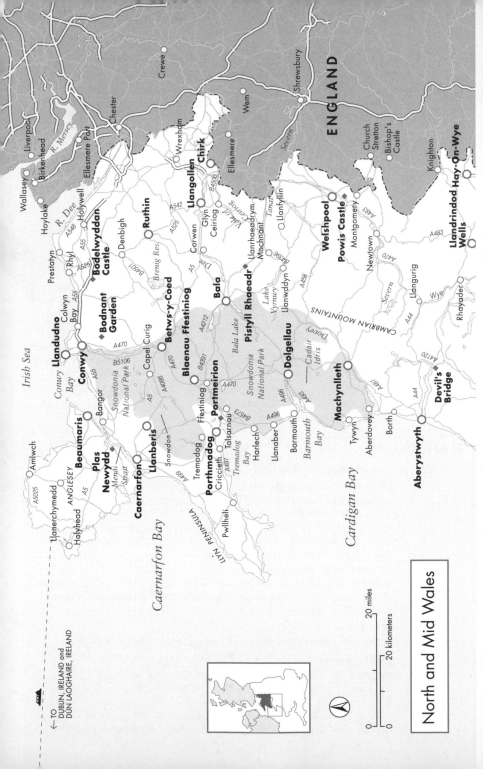

North and Mid Wales

CLOSE UP

All Aboard: Steam Railways in Wales

Wales is the best place in Britain for narrow-gauge steam railways, many of which wind through extraordinary landscapes. The Great Little Trains of Wales (⊕ www.greatlittletrainsofwales. co.uk) operate in spring, summer, and fall through the mountains of Snowdonia and central Wales (there are also a few lines in South Wales). The ride is just part of the fun; a good deal of history is associated with the old trains and train stations, some of which served industry before they became attractions for visitors. The Ffestiniog Railway, which links two British Rail lines at the old slate town of Blaenau Ffestiniog and Porthmadog, climbs the mountainside in Snowdonia National Park around an ascending loop. Snowdonia also has Britain's only alpine-style steam-rack railway, the Snowdon Mountain Railway, where little sloping boiler engines on a rack-and-pinion track push their trains 3,000 feet up from Llanberis to the summit of Snowdon.

15

their lifetimes. You can take tea there, as did Wordsworth and the Duke of Wellington, and stroll in the attractively terraced gardens. ⊠ *Hill St.* ☎ *01978/862834* ⊕ *www.denbighshire.gov.uk* 🎫 *£5.50* ☉ *Apr.–Oct., daily 10–5.*

From the **canal wharf** (☎ *01978/860702*) you can take a horse-drawn boat or a narrow boat (a slender barge) along the Llangollen Canal to the largest navigable aqueduct in the world at Pontcysyllte, a UNESCO-designated World Heritage Site.

☾ The **Llangollen Railway**, a restored standard-gauge steam line, runs for 7 mi along the scenic Dee Valley. The terminus is near the town's bridge. ☎ *01978/860979* ⊕ *www.llangollen-railway.co.uk* 🎫 *£10 round-trip* ☉ *Apr.–Oct., daily 10:30–5; Nov.–Mar., weekends, limited service.*

WHERE TO STAY

££ 🎦 **Cornerstones Guesthouse.** Made up of three 16th-century cottages with views over the River Dee, this lodging blends period charm with modern amenities. In the luxurious Red Lion River room you can lounge in the huge roll-top bathtub and gaze out over the River Dee. In the inglenook room you're treated to Welsh breakfasts made with local ingredients. **Pros:** spacious bedrooms; free passes for town parking lots. **Cons:** directly on the street; no garden. ⊠ *Regent St.* ☎ *01978/861569* ⊕ *www.cornerstones-guesthouse.co.uk* 🛏 *3 rooms, 2 suites* ☖ *In-room: no a/c, no phone, refrigerator, DVD, Wi-Fi. In-hotel: some pets allowed* 🍴 *AE, MC, V* 🍽 *BP.*

NIGHTLIFE AND THE ARTS

★ The six-day **International Musical Eisteddfod** (☎ *01978/862001* ⊕ *www. international-eisteddfod.co.uk*), held in early July, brings together amateur choirs and dancers—more than 12,000 participants in all—from all corners of the globe for a large, colorful folk-arts festival. The tradition of the *eisteddfod,* held throughout Wales, goes back to the 12th century. Originally gatherings of bards, the *eisteddfodau* of today are more like competitions or festivals.

SPORTS AND THE OUTDOORS

There are easy walks along the banks of the River Dee or along part of the **Offa's Dyke Path** (⊕ *www.offasdyke.demon.co.uk*), which passes through hills, river valleys, and lowlands. This 177-mi-long National Trail follows the line of an ancient earthen wall, still surviving in parts, which was built along the border with England in the 8th century by King Offa of Mercia to keep out Welsh raiders.

BALA

18 mi southwest of Llangollen.

The staunchly Welsh town of Bala makes a good base for exploring the eastern and southern sections of Snowdonia National Park as well as the gentler landscapes of borderland Wales. It stands at the head of Lln Tegid (Bala Lake), at 4 mi long the largest natural lake in Wales. This is a fine place for kayaking and windsurfing.

GETTING HERE AND AROUND

Rural bus service is infrequent and patchy, so you really need a car to explore the area. To get here from Llangollen, take the A5 to the A494.

ESSENTIALS

Visitor Information Bala (✉ *Pensarn Rd.* ☎ *01678/521021*).

EXPLORING

Ⓒ The scenic, narrow-gauge **Bala Lake Railway** (*Llanuwchllyn* ☎ *01678/ 540666* ⊕ *www.bala-lake-railway.co.uk*), one of the Great Little Trains of Wales, runs along Bala Lake's southern shore. The station in Llanuwchllyn has parking.

★ To experience Wales at its wildest, you can drive over **Bwlch y Groes** *(Pass of the Cross)*, the highest road in Wales, whose sweeping panoramas are breathtaking. To get here, take the narrow road south from Bala through Cwm Hirnant and over the mountain to Lake Vyrnwy. Turn right at the lake and drive for a mile on B4393 before heading west on the mountain road.

WHERE TO STAY

££ ⊡ **Cyfie Farm**. This refurbished, ivy-clad, 17th-century farmhouse sits in a tranquil area close to Lake Vyrnwy. Rooms have oak beams and log fireplaces. The luxurious suites, in converted barns and stables, offer all the sophistication of those in a top hotel. **Pros:** in-room fireplaces; outdoor hot tub; hosts are trained chefs. **Cons:** remote location; need a car to get around. ✉ *Off B4393, near Llanfyllin, Llanfihangel-yng-Ngwynfa* ☎ *01691/648451* ⊕ *www.cyfiefarm.co.uk* ☜*4 suites* ♿ *In-room: no a/c, no phone, DVD. In-hotel: no kids under 10, Wi-Fi hotspot* ☰ *AE, MC, V* ⓄⓁ *BP.*

£££ ⊡ **Lake Vyrnwy Hotel**. Awesome views of mountain-ringed Lake Vyrnwy
★ are just one asset of this country mansion on a 24,000-acre estate. For the ultimate sporting vacation you can fish, play tennis, watch birds, or take long hikes. Sailboats are also available. The less energetic can linger in the superb spa. Leather chairs, log fires, and antiques add luxury, and the bedrooms are full of pampering touches. The sophisticated

contemporary cuisine includes seasonal game and lamb from the estate's very own flock. **Pros:** perfect for outdoor pursuits; dramatic lakeside location; luxurious spa. **Cons:** too remote for some; no nearby sights. ✉ *Off B4393, Llanwddyn* ☎ *01691/870692* ⊕ *www.lakevyrnwy.com* ☞ *52 rooms* ⚹ *In-room: no a/c. In-hotel: restaurant, room service, bars, tennis court, gym, spa, water sports, bicycles, laundry service, Wi-Fi hotspot, some pets allowed* ☰ *AE, DC, MC, V* ✵⎮*BP.*

BLAENAU FFESTINIOG

22 mi northwest of Bala, 10 mi southwest of Betws-y-Coed.

Most of the world's roofing tiles used to come from this former "slate capital of North Wales," and commercial quarrying continues here. On the hillsides around the town is the evidence of decades of mining. The enterprises that attract attention nowadays, however, remain the old slate mines, which opened to the public in the 1970s. The narrow-gauge Ffestiniog Railway, which begins in Porthmadog, ends in the town, near the caverns.

ESSENTIALS

Visitor Information Blaenau Ffestiniog (✉ *High St.* ☎ *01766/830360*).

EXPLORING

At the **Llechwedd Slate Caverns,** you can take two trips: a tram ride through floodlighted tunnels where Victorian working conditions have been re-created, and a ride on Britain's deepest underground railway to a mine where you can walk by an eerie underground lake. Either tour gives a good idea of the difficult working conditions the miners endured. Above are a re-created Victorian village and slate-splitting demonstrations. ✉ *Off A470* ☎ *01766/830306* ⊕ *www.llechwedd-slate-caverns. co.uk* ⎮ *Tour £9.50, grounds free* ⊗ *Apr.–Sept., daily 10–5:15; Oct.– Mar., daily 10–4:15.*

PORTHMADOG

12 mi southwest of Blaenau Ffestiniog, 16 mi southeast of Caernarfon.

The little seaside town of Porthmadog, built as a harbor to export slate from Blaenau Ffestiniog, stands at the gateway to Llyn, an unspoiled peninsula of beaches, wildflowers, and country lanes. It's also near Harlech Castle. The location between Snowdonia and Llyn, as well as the good beaches nearby and the many attractions around town, make the town a lively place in summer.

GETTING HERE AND AROUND

Train buffs can get here on the mainline Cambrian Coast Railway, which runs along Cardigan Bay from Aberystwyth to Pwllheli; connect at Shrewsbury. When you arrive you can take a scenic trip on the town's charming "little railways." Porthmadog is a stop on the excellent Snowdon Sherpa bus service. The town itself is totally walkable and has good access to coastal trails.

ESSENTIALS

Visitor Information Porthmadog (⊠ *High St.* ☎ *01766/512981*).

EXPLORING

TOP ATTRACTIONS

Ⓒ **Ffestiniog Railway.** The oldest Welsh narrow-gauge line (founded in the early 19th century to carry slate), the Ffestiniog Railway, runs from a quayside terminus and continues through a wooded vale into the mountains. Its northern terminus is Blaenau Ffestiniog, where you can visit the slate caverns. ☎ *01766/516000* ⊕ *www.festrail.co.uk* ⊠ *£18.50 round-trip* ☯ *Apr.–Oct., daily, plus limited winter service; call for times.*

★ **Harlech Castle.** A wealth of legend, poetry, and song is conjured up by the 13th-century Harlech Castle, built by Edward I to help subdue the Welsh; it's now a UNESCO World Heritage Site. The castle, on a promontory, dominates the little coastal town of Harlech, 12 mi south of Porthmadog. Its mighty ruins, visible for miles and commanding wide views, are as dramatic as its history (though you have to imagine the sea, which has since receded). Harlech was occupied by Owain Glyndr from 1404 to 1408 during his revolt against the English. The music of Ceiriog's song *Men of Harlech* reflects the heroic defense of this castle in 1468 by Dafydd ap Eynion, who, summoned to surrender, replied: "I held a castle in France until every old woman in Wales heard of it, and I will hold a castle in Wales until every old woman in France hears of it!" Later in the 15th century the Lancastrians survived an eight-year siege during the Wars of the Roses here, and it was the last Welsh stronghold to fall in the 17th-century Civil War. ⊠ *Off B4573* ☎ *01443/336000* ⊕ *www.cadw.wales.gov.uk* ⊠ *£3.60* ☯ *Mar.–Oct., daily 9:30–5; Nov.–Feb., daily 10–4.*

Fodor's Choice **Portmeirion.** One not-to-be-missed site in North Wales is Portmeirion, ★ a tiny fantasy-Italianate village on a private peninsula surrounded by hills, which is said to be loosely modeled after Portofino. Begun in 1926 by architect Clough Williams-Ellis (1883–1978), the village has a hotel, restaurant, town hall, shops (selling books, gifts, and Portmeirion pottery), rental cottages, and woodland walks; beaches are nearby. Williams-Ellis called it his "light-opera approach to architecture," and the result is magical, though distinctly un-Welsh. Royalty, political figures, artists, and other celebrities have stayed here, and the cult 1967 TV series *The Prisoner* was filmed here. Portmeirion is a short trip east of Porthmadog. ⊠ *A487* ☎ *01766/772321* ⊕ *www.portmeirion-village. com* ⊠ *£8* ☯ *Daily 9:30–5:30.*

WORTH NOTING

Criccieth. In the Victorian seaside resort of Criccieth, a few miles west of Porthmadog on A497, a medieval castle with sweeping views crowns the headland. David Lloyd George, the prime minister of Britain from 1916 to 1922, grew up in Wales and lived here; a small museum in his childhood home honors him.

OFF THE BEATEN PATH

Nant Gwrtheyrn. This is a worthwhile stop—for awesome views of Caernarfon Bay as well as cultural information—if you're exploring the Llyn Peninsula. A former village for granite-quarry workers serves as the Welsh Language and Heritage Centre, offering Welsh-language classes

EATING WELL IN WALES

Talented chefs making use of the country's bountiful resources have put Wales firmly on the culinary map. Welsh Black beef and succulent Welsh lamb are world renowned, and the supply of fish and seafood (including mussels and oysters) from coasts and rivers is excellent. Organic products are available to restaurants and the public from specialty companies, farm shops, and farmers' markets.

Ty Nant Welsh spring water graces restaurant tables worldwide, and there are a few small vineyards producing nice whites scattered here and there in the south. There's even a Welsh whisky that has won awards at international tastings.

Cheese making has undergone a remarkable revival. You can try traditionally named cheeses such as Llanboidy and Caws Cenarth or an extra-mature cheddar called Black Bomber.

Contemporary cuisine has the buzz, but traditional dishes are worth seeking out. Cawl, for example, is a nourishing broth of lamb and vegetables, and laverbread is a distinctive-tasting pureed seaweed that's usually fried with eggs and bacon.

For information on high-quality Welsh food, check out the Web site **Wales—the True Taste** (⊕ www. walesthetruetaste.com).

and cultural courses (in Welsh). The chapel is a tourist information center and has modest historical exhibits, and a café serves good sandwiches and snacks. ⊠ Off B4417, Llithfaen ☎ 01758/750334 ⊕ www. nantgwrtheyrn.org ⊠ Free ☉ Apr.–Sept., daily 11–3.

Tremadog. North of Porthmadog is Tremadog, a handsome village that was the birthplace of T. E. Lawrence (1888–1935), better known as Lawrence of Arabia.

☉ **Welsh Highland Heritage Railway.** You can take a short rail ride, tour the engine sheds, and clamber in the cabs of the locomotives housed here. ⊠ Tremadog Rd., Porthmadog ☎ 01766/513402 ⊕ www.whr.co.uk ⊠ £6 ☉ Easter–Oct., daily 10:30–4.

WHERE TO EAT AND STAY

££££ ✕ **Castle Cottage.** Close to Harlech's mighty castle, this friendly "restau-
BRITISH rant with rooms" is a wonderful find. The emphasis is on the excep-
★ tional cuisine of chef-proprietor Glyn Roberts, who uses ingredients from lobster to Welsh lamb to create imaginative, beautifully presented contemporary dishes. There's a fixed-price dinner menu (£36.50), but no lunch. The hotel has three spacious modern rooms with four more in the annex, a former 16th-century coaching inn. ⊠ Near B4573, Harlech ☎ 01766/780479 ⊕ www.castlecottageharlech.co.uk ⊟ MC, V.

£££–££££ ▦ **Hotel Maes-y-Neuadd.** Eight acres of gardens and parkland create a
★ glorious setting for this luxurious country hotel in a manor house dating from the 14th century. Walls of local granite, oak-beam ceilings, and an inglenook fireplace add character; the updated bedrooms have different shapes and details but use prints and pastel fabrics. The restaurant's three-course, fixed-price (£35) menu of Welsh, English, and

French specialties uses herbs and vegetables grown in the hotel's own prolific walled garden to complement local meat, fish, and cheeses. The hotel is 3½ mi northeast of Harlech. **Pros:** magnificent location above Tremadog Bay; close to many attractions; historic house. **Cons:** on a narrow road; need a car to get around. ⊠ *Off B4573, Talsarnau* 🕾 *01766/780200* ⊕ *www.neuadd.com* 🖘 *15 rooms* ⚹ *In-room: no a/c, Wi-Fi. In-hotel: restaurant, room service, bar, laundry service, Wi-Fi hotspot, some pets allowed* 🖃 *MC, V* ⅏⅃ *BP.*

£££££   📺 **Hotel Portmeirion.** One of the most elegant and unusual places to stay
★   in Wales is also supremely relaxing. Clough Williams-Ellis built his Italianate fantasy village around this waterside Victorian mansion with a library and curved, colonnaded dining room. The hotel bedrooms are comfortable and richly decorated. Accommodation is also available in cottage suites around the village and in chic, minimalistic suites in Castell Deudraeth, a castellated 19th-century house. The restaurant, which has a fixed-price dinner menu (£39.50), highlights local foods with a sophisticated contemporary style. **Pros:** unique architecture; woodland walks; far-reaching estuary views. **Cons:** long walk from some rooms to dining room; grounds can be crowded with day-trippers; some rooms are a bit shabby. ⊠ *A487, Portmeirion* 🕾 *01766/770000* ⊕ *www.portmeirion-village.com* 🖘 *14 rooms in main hotel, 28 rooms in cottages, 11 suites in Castell Deudraeth* ⚹ *In-room: no a/c, Internet (some). In-hotel: restaurant, room service, bar, tennis court, pool, laundry service, Wi-Fi hotspot* 🖃 *AE, MC, V* ⅏⅃ *BP.*

BETWS-Y-COED

25 mi northeast of Porthmadog, 19 mi south of Llandudno.

The rivers Llugwy and Conwy meet at Betws-y-Coed, a popular resort village set among wooded hills with excellent views of Snowdonia. Busy in summer, the village has a good selection of hotels and crafts shops. The chief landmark here is the ornate iron Waterloo Bridge (1815) over the Conwy, designed by Thomas Telford (1757–1834), and the magnificent Bodnant Garden south of the town of Conwy makes a delightful excursion.

GETTING HERE AND AROUND

The town is easy to reach on the Conwy Valley Railway that runs from Llandudno to Blaenau Ffestiniog (part of the National Rail network). Betws-y-Coed is also a hub for the excellent Snowdon Sherpa bus service that covers most of Snowdonia's beauty spots, so it's feasible to explore this part of Wales without a car.

ESSENTIALS

Visitor Information Betws-y-Coed (⊠ *Royal Oak Stables* 🕾 *01690/710426*).

EXPLORING

On the western (A5) approach to Betws-y-Coed are the **Swallow Falls** (£1 admission charge), a famous North Wales beauty spot where the River Llugwy tumbles down through a wooded chasm.

WHERE TO EAT AND STAY

££
MODERN BRITISH
✕ **Ty Gwyn.** This 17th-century coaching inn overlooking Waterloo Bridge on the outskirts of Betws-y-Coed is a delight for lovers of antiques, old beams, and rustic, uneven floors. Fresh local produce is used in the good-value bar meals and full à la carte menu. Wild sea bass, king prawns, or roast rack of venison with wild mushroom risotto are good choices on the contemporary menu. ⊠ *A5* ☎ *01690/710383* ⊕ *www. tygwynhotel.co.uk* ⊟ *MC, V.*

££
⌨ **Aberconwy House.** This luxurious Victorian house has panoramic views over Betws-y-Coed and Snowdonia. Built in the 1870s, the bed-and-breakfast successfully combines period features and contemporary style. The bedrooms are well equipped and the owners are extremely hospitable. The village is only a 10-minute walk away. **Pros:** reasonable rates; great breakfasts. **Cons:** no bar; stairs to climb. ⊠ *Turn onto Lôn Muriau off A470, then Llanrwst* ☎ *01690/710202* ⊕ *www.aberconwy-house.co.uk* ⇨ *8 rooms* ♿ *In-room: no a/c, Wi-Fi* ⊟ *MC, V* ⏿ *BP.*

££
⌨ **Pengwern Country House.** In Victorian times this stone-and-slate country house on 2 acres of woodland was an artists' colony. Today the polished slate floors, beamed bedrooms, and traditional furnishings reflect the house's original charm. The house is about a mile south of Betws-y-Coed. **Pros:** scenic woodland location; wealth of Victorian features. **Cons:** close to main road; car essential to reach town. ⊠ *A5, Allt Dinas* ☎ *01690/710480* ⊕ *www.snowdoniaaccommodation.co.uk* ⇨ *3 rooms* ♿ *In-room: no a/c, no phone, no TV, Wi-Fi. In-hotel: Internet terminal, no kids under 13* ⊟ *MC, V* ⏿ *BP.*

£££–££££
⌨ **Tan-y-Foel Country House.** Hidden away on a wooded hillside outside Betws-y-Coed, this quiet, contemporary hideaway has views over the Conwy Valley and Snowdonia mountain range. The vibrant hues of the stylish interior contrast with the dark stone exterior, and some bedrooms have four-posters. Chef-owner Janet Pitman prepares exquisite food with French and Asian influences. **Pros:** strikingly contemporary decor; inventive cuisine; views over Conwy Valley to Snowdon. **Cons:** meals by arrangement only; too far to walk into town. ⊠ *Off A5, Capel Garmon* ☎ *01690/710507* ⊕ *www.tyfhotel.co.uk* ⇨ *6 rooms* ♿ *In-room: no a/c, DVD, Wi-Fi. In-hotel: restaurant, bar, no kids under 12* ⊟ *MC, V* ⏿ *BP.*

15

LLANBERIS

17 mi west of Betws-y-Coed, 7 mi southeast of Caernarfon.

Llanberis, like Betws-y-Coed, is a focal point for people visiting Snowdonia National Park.

GETTING HERE AND AROUND
Llanberis is accessible by bus. The most convenient service, targeted at visitors, is the Snowdon Sherpa bus route.

ESSENTIALS
Visitor Information Llanberis (⊠ *41b High St.* ☎ *01286/870765*).

EXPLORING

The town stands beside twin lakes at the foot of the rocky **Llanberis Pass**, which cuts through the highest mountains in the park and is lined with slabs popular with rock climbers. There are hiking trails from the top of the pass, but the going can be rough for the inexperienced. Ask for local advice before starting any ramble.

> **TRAINING FOR EVEREST**
>
> Lord Hunt, Sir Edmund Hillary, and their team used the rock-strewn slopes of Snowdonia to train for the first successful ascent of Mt. Everest in 1953. The Pen-y-Gwryd Hotel, a famous climbing inn just beyond the summit of Llanberis Pass, has memorabilia from those times.

☾ ★ Llanberis's most famous attraction is the rack-and-pinion **Snowdon Mountain Railway**, with some of its track at a thrillingly steep grade; the train terminates within 70 feet of the 3,560-foot-high summit. Snowdon, Yr Wyddfa in Welsh, is the highest peak south of Scotland and lies within the 840-square-mi national park. From May through September, weather permitting, trains go all the way to the summit; on a clear day you can see as far as the Wicklow Mountains in Ireland, about 90 mi away. In 1998 the National Trust bought the mountain, ensuring its long-term protection. ☎ *0870/458–0033* ⊕ *www.snowdonrailway. co.uk* ✉ *£25 round-trip* ⊙ *Mar.–Oct., daily; schedule depends on customer demand.*

Perched at the top of Snowdon is **Hafod Eryri**, the eco-friendly replacement for the previous visitor center (once described by Prince Charles as "the highest slum in Wales"). The new building has a curved granite roof and huge panoramic windows, and it blends beautifully into the rocky landscape. Inside there's a café and exhibitions about the mountain, its ecology, and its history.

On Lake Padarn in the Padarn Country Park, the old Dinorwig slate quarry serves as the **National Slate Museum**, dedicated to what was an important industry here: Welsh slate roofed many a building. The museum has quarry workshops and slate-splitting demonstrations, as well as restored worker housing, all of which convey the development of the industry and the challenges faced by those who worked in it. The narrow-gauge Llanberis Lake Railway runs from here. ✉ *A4086* ☎ *01286/870630* ⊕ *www.museumwales.ac.uk* ✉ *Free* ⊙ *Easter–Oct., daily 10–5; Nov.–Easter, Sun.–Fri. 10–4.*

CAERNARFON

7 mi northwest of Llanberis, 26 mi southwest of Llandudno.

The town of Caernarfon, which has a historic pedigree as a walled medieval settlement, has little to rival the considerable splendor of its castle. Don't miss the garrison church of St. Mary, built into the town walls.

GETTING HERE AND AROUND

The nearest railway station is at Bangor, 9 mi northeast. There is reasonably good local bus service, especially the Snowdon Sherpa. You can also travel into the mountains on the narrow-gauge Welsh Highland Railway.

ESSENTIALS

Visitor Information Caernarfon (⊠ *Oriel Pendeitsh, opposite castle entrance* ☎ *01286/672232).*

EXPLORING

★ Standing like a warning finger, the grim, majestic mass of **Caernarfon Castle**, "that most magnificent badge of our subjection," wrote Thomas Pennant (1726–98), looms over the waters of the River Seiont. It's a UNESCO World Heritage Site. Numerous bloody encounters were witnessed by these sullen walls, erected by Edward I in 1283 as a symbol of his determination to subdue the Welsh. The castle's towers, unlike those of Edward I's other castles, are polygonal and patterned with bands of different-color stone. In 1284 the monarch thought of a scheme to steal the Welsh throne. Knowing that the Welsh chieftains would accept no foreign prince, Edward promised to designate a ruler who could speak no word of English. His long-suffering queen, Eleanor of Castile, was dispatched to this cold stone fortress, where she gave birth to a son. Edward presented the infant to the assembled chieftains as their prince "who spoke no English, had been born on Welsh soil, and whose first words would be spoken in Welsh." The ruse worked, and on that day was created the first prince of Wales of English lineage. This tradition still holds: in July 1969, Elizabeth II presented Prince Charles to the people of Wales as their prince from this castle. In the Queen's Tower, a museum charts the history of the local regiment, the Royal Welsh Fusiliers. ⊠ *Castle Hill* ☎ *01286/677617* ⊕ *www.caernarfon.com* ☎ *£4.95* ☉ *Mar.–Oct., daily 9:30–5; Nov.–Feb., Mon.–Sat. 10–4, Sun. 11–4.*

☉ You can take a trip on a coal-fired steam locomotive at the **Welsh Highland Railway–Rheilffordd Eryri**, a narrow-gauge line that operates on the scenic route of an abandoned railway. The line is scheduled to extend to Porthmadog in 2011, linking with the Ffestiniog Railway. The terminus is on the quay near Caernarfon Castle. ⊠ *St. Helens Rd.* ☎ *01766/516000* ⊕ *www.welshhighlandrailway.net* ☎ *£28 round-trip* ☉ *Apr.–Oct., daily 10–4; Nov.–Mar., limited weekend service.*

WHERE TO STAY

££–£££ 🏠 **Meifod Country House.** Former home of the high sheriff of Caernarfon, this opulent Victorian house has polished tile floors, wood-burning fireplaces, and bedrooms with features such as Victorian claw-foot baths and chandeliers. The atmosphere is luxurious but unpretentious. The house stands on lush grounds less than 2 mi south of Caernarfon, making it a convenient base for exploring Snowdonia. **Pros:** authentic atmosphere; good food. **Cons:** often booked with wedding parties; not walking distance to town. ⊠ *Off A487, Bontnewydd* ☎ *01286/673351* ⊕ *www.meifodcountryhouse.co.uk* 🛏 *5 rooms* ♿ *In-room: no a/c. In-hotel: restaurant, room service, bars, tennis court, laundry service, Wi-Fi hotspot* ▭ *MC, V* ⏐○⏐ *BP.*

15

BEAUMARIS

13 mi northeast of Caernarfon.

Elegant Beaumaris is on the Isle of Anglesey, the largest island directly off the shore of Wales and England. It's linked to the mainland by the Britannia road and rail bridge and by Thomas Telford's remarkable chain suspension bridge, built in 1826 over the Menai Strait. Though its name means "beautiful marsh," Beaumaris has become a town of pretty cottages, Georgian houses, and bright shops.

GETTING HERE AND AROUND

The nearest main-line train station is in Bangor, 6 mi away on the mainland; bus service operates between the station and Beaumaris. Ferries and catamarans to Ireland leave from Holyhead, on the island's western side.

EXPLORING

The town dates from 1295, when Edward I commenced work on impressive **Beaumaris Castle**, the last and largest link in an "iron ring" of fortifications around North Wales built to contain the Welsh. Guarding the western approach to the Menai Strait, the unfinished castle (a World Heritage Site) is solid and symmetrical, with concentric lines of fortification, arrow slits, and a moat: a superb example of medieval defensive planning. ⊠ *Castle St.* ☎ *01248/810361* ⊕ *www.cadw.wales. gov.uk* ⊠ *£3.60* ⊙ *Apr.–Oct., daily 9–5; Nov.–Mar., Mon.–Sat. 9:30–4, Sun. 11–4.*

On Castle Street the **Tudor Rose**, a house dating from 1400, is an excellent example of Tudor timberwork.

To learn about the grim life of a Victorian prisoner, head to the old **gaol**, built in 1829 by Joseph Hansom (1803–82), who was also the designer of the Hansom cab. ⊠ *Steeple La.* ☎ *01248/810921* ⊠ *£3.50* ⊙ *Easter–Sept., daily 10:30–5.*

The 14th-century **Church of St. Mary and St. Nicholas,** opposite the gaol in Steeple Lane, houses the stone coffin of Princess Joan, daughter of King John (1167–1216) and wife of Welsh leader Llewelyn the Great.

OFF THE BEATEN PATH

Plas Newydd. Some historians rate this mansion on the Isle of Anglesey the finest house in Wales. Remodeled in the 18th century by James Wyatt (1747–1813) for the marquesses of Anglesey (who still live here), it stands on the Menai Strait about 7 mi southwest of Beaumaris (don't confuse it with the Plas Newydd at Llangollen). The interior has some fine 18th-century Gothic Revival decorations. In 1936–40 the society artist Rex Whistler (1905–44) painted the mural in the dining room. A museum commemorates the Battle of Waterloo, where the first marquess, Wellington's cavalry commander, lost his leg. The woodland walk and garden are worth exploring, and you can ask about boat trips on the strait. The views of Snowdonia are magnificent. ⊠ *Off A4080, southwest of Britannia Bridge, Llanfairpwll* ☎ *01248/715272* ⊕ *www. nationaltrust.org.uk* ⊠ *House £8.60; garden only, £6.40* ⊙ *House mid-Mar.–early Nov., Sat.–Wed. noon–5; last admission ½ hr before closing. Garden mid-Mar.–early Nov., Sat.–Wed. 11–5:30.*

WHERE TO EAT AND STAY

£££££ ✕ **Ye Olde Bull's Head.** Originally a coaching inn built in 1472, this small
BRITISH place is filled with history. Samuel Johnson and Charles Dickens were
both guests here. Eat in the stylish brasserie with its slate floors and oak
tables or the excellent oak-beam dining room dating from 1617. Contemporary dinner specialties (£38.50 fixed-price menu) include Welsh
beef fillet with braised oxtail; seafood dishes win praise, too. ⊠ *Castle
St.* ☎ *01248/810329* ⊕ *www.bullsheadinn.co.uk* ⊟ *AE, MC, V.*

££ ⊞ **Cleifiog.** This cozy gem of a Georgian house overlooks the Menai
★ Strait just a short stroll from Beaumaris Castle. Its charms include
wood-panel walls, limestone floors, and a magnificent staircase dating
from 1680. **Pros:** seafront location; close to town; interesting history.
Cons: minimum stay on weekends; a little claustrophobic for some.
⊠ *Townsend* ☎ *01248/811507* ⊕ *www.cleifiogbandb.co.uk* ⤤ *3 rooms*
⚘ *In-room: no a/c, no phone, DVD. In-hotel: Internet terminal, no kids
under 3* ⊟ *MC, V* ⊠ *BP.*

NIGHTLIFE AND THE ARTS

The **Beaumaris Festival** (☎ *01248/810415* ⊕ *www.beaumarisfestival.
com*) takes place annually in late May. The whole town is used as a
site for special concerts, dance performances, and plays.

15

CONWY

★ *23 mi east of Beaumaris, 48 mi northwest of Chester.*

The still-authentic medieval town of Conwy grew up around its castle
on the west bank of the River Conwy. A ring of ancient but well-preserved walls, built in the 13th century to protect the English merchants
who lived here, enclose the old town and add to the strong sense of history. It's well worth strolling the streets and walking on top of sections
of the wall, which has 21 towers. A walk on the walls rewards with
impressive views across huddled rooftops to the castle on the estuary,
with mountains in the distance.

GETTING HERE AND AROUND

The A55 expressway links Conwy into the central U.K. motorway system via the M56. The town is also on the North Wales coast rail route,
which ends at Holyhead on Anglesey. The town itself—surrounded by
its wonderfully preserved walls—is perfect for pedestrians.

ESSENTIALS

Visitor Information Conwy (⊠ *Castle Bldg.* ☎ *01492/592248*).

EXPLORING

Fodor'sChoice Of all Edward I's fortresses, **Conwy Castle**, a mighty, many-turreted
★ stronghold built between 1283 and 1287, preserves most convincingly
the spirit of medieval times. Along with Conwy's town walls, the castle
is a UNESCO World Heritage Site. The eight large round towers and tall
curtain wall, set on a rocky promontory, provide sweeping views of the
area and the town walls. Although the castle is roofless (and floorless in
places), you can read the signs, take a tour, or buy a guidebook to help
you visualize the Great Hall and other chambers. Narrow stairs lead
into towers such as the Chapel Tower. Conwy Castle can be approached

on foot by a dramatic suspension bridge completed in 1825; engineer Thomas Telford designed the bridge with turrets to blend in with the fortress's presence. ⊠ *Rose Hill St.* ☎ *01492/592358* ⊕ *www.cadw. wales.gov.uk* ✉ *£4.60; £6.85 joint ticket with Plas Mawr* ⊙ *Apr.–Oct., daily 9.30–5; Nov.–Mar., Mon.–Sat. 9:30–4, Sun. 11–4.*

What is said to be the **smallest house in Britain** (⊠ *Lower Gate St.* ☎ *01492/593484* ✉ *£0.75* ⊙ *Apr.– Oct., daily 10–4:30*) is furnished in mid-Victorian Welsh style. The house, which is 6 feet wide and 10 feet high, was reputedly last occupied in 1900 by a fisherman who was more than 6 feet tall.

Plas Mawr, a jewel in the heart of Conwy, is the best-preserved Elizabethan town house in Britain. Built in 1576 by Robert Wynn (who later became both a member of Parliament and sheriff of Caernarfonshire), this richly decorated house with its ornamental plasterwork gives a unique insight into the lives of the Tudor gentry and their servants. ⊠ *High St.* ☎ *01492/580167* ⊕ *www.cadw.wales.gov.uk* ✉ *£4.95; £6.85 joint ticket with Conwy Castle* ⊙ *Apr.–Sept., Tues.–Sun. 9–5; Oct., Tues.–Sun. 9:30–4.*

Built in the 14th century, **Aberconwy House** is the only surviving medieval merchant's house in Conwy. Each room in the restored building reflects different eras of its long history. ⊠ *Castle St.* ☎ *01492/592246* ⊕ *www. nationaltrust.org.uk* ✉ *£3* ⊙ *Mid-Mar.–Oct., Wed.–Mon. 11–5.*

Fodor's Choice
★

With a reputation as the finest garden in Wales, **Bodnant Garden** remains a pilgrimage spot for horticulturists from around the world. Laid out in 1875, the 87 acres are particularly famed for rhododendrons, camellias, and magnolias. ■ **TIP→** Visit in May to see the laburnum arch that forms a huge tunnel of golden blooms. The mountains of Snowdonia form a magnificent backdrop to the Italianate terraces, rock and rose gardens, and pinetum. The gardens are about 5 mi south of Conwy. ⊠ *Off A470, Tal-y-Cafn* ☎ *01492/650460* ⊕ *www.nationaltrust.org.uk* ✉ *£7.95* ⊙ *Mar.–Nov., daily 10–5.*

WHERE TO EAT AND STAY

££
MODERN BRITISH

✕ **Groes Inn.** Beamed ceilings, log fires, and rambling rooms abound at this old inn dating back to the 15th century. Eat in the restaurant or the more casual bar. The inventive menus make good use of local crab, plaice, pheasant, and game. ⊠ *B5106, Ty'n-y-Groes* ☎ *01492/650545* ⊕ *www.groesinn.com* ▭ *MC, V.*

CASTLE COUNTRY

More than 400 fortresses in Wales provide an inexhaustible supply of inspiration for any lover of history. These ancient strongholds, some of which were built by Edward I in the 13th century during his struggles with the rebellious Welsh, punctuate the landscape from south (Caerphilly) to north (Harlech, Beaumaris, Conwy), and include romantic ruins and well-preserved fortresses. To make the most of a visit, buy a guidebook or take a tour of a site so that you can best appreciate the remains of a distant era. The great North Wales castles, such as Caernarfon, are particularly famous; four are World Heritage Sites.

£££ ✕ **Le Gallois.** Just off the coast road 4 mi west of Conwy, this small and
MODERN BRITISH unpretentious restaurant is a culinary oasis. The chef-proprietor offers
a changing chalkboard menu using the best local produce. Dishes like
juicy scallops with a beurre blanc, Conwy crab au gratin, and local
lamb cooked pink with a mint-and-Madeira sauce are typical daily fare.
⊠ *Pant yr Afon, Penmaenmawr* ☎ *01492/623820* ⊟ *MC, V* ☼ *Closed
Mon.–Wed. No lunch.*

£££–££££ ⊞ **Castle Hotel.** Sitting snugly within Conwy's medieval walls, this former
coaching inn has wooden beams, old fireplaces, and plenty of antiques.
Illustrious former guests include William Wordsworth, Samuel Johnson, and Charlotte Brontë. The bedrooms are plushly luxurious, with
elaborate modern bathrooms. Dawson's Cuisine and Bar is decorated
with paintings of scenes from Shakespeare's plays, traded by distinguished Victorian artist John Dawson-Watson in return for lodgings.
Here you can enjoy excellent Modern British cuisine, such as salmon
on a creamy Conwy crab risotto. **Pros:** oozes history; in the heart of
medieval Conwy; good food. **Cons:** small rooms; noisy seagulls; narrow
town center streets. ⊠ *High St.* ☎ *01492/582800* ⊕ *www.castlewales.
co.uk* ⇦ *28 rooms* ♿ *In-room: no a/c, Wi-Fi. In-hotel: restaurant, bar,
some pets allowed* ⊟ *AE, MC, V* ❢❢ *BP.*

££–£££ ⊞ **Sychnant Pass House.** On a peaceful wooded hillside above Conwy,
this hotel has all the qualities of a country-house hotel but without
any unnecessary formality. The enthusiastic owners, Bre and Graham
Carrington-Sykes, provide a genuine welcome and good food with a
set-price dinner menu (£32.50). There are spacious sitting rooms with
big comfortable sofas and nicely furnished bedrooms, some with French
windows opening out onto an attractive decked terrace. The leisure
facilities are excellent. **Pros:** great indoor pool and hot tub; beautiful
grounds; unforced hospitality. **Cons:** pets allowed in rooms; far outside
Conwy. ⊠ *Sychnant Pass Rd.* ☎ *01492/596868* ⊕ *www.sychnant-pass-
house.co.uk* ⇦ *12 rooms* ♿ *In-room: no a/c, no phone, safe, refrigerator, DVD. In-hotel: restaurant, pool, gym, Wi-Fi hotspot, some pets
allowed* ⊟ *MC, V* ❢❢ *BP.*

15

LLANDUDNO

3 mi north of Conwy, 50 mi northwest of Chester.

This appealingly old-fashioned North Wales seaside resort has a wealth
of well-preserved Victorian architecture and an ornate amusement pier
with entertainments, shops, and places to eat. Attractively painted
hotels line the wide promenade, and the shopping streets behind also
look the part, thanks to their original canopied walkways. Llandudno
has the largest choice of lodging of any resort in Wales.

GETTING HERE AND AROUND

Llandudno is on the North Wales railway line, with fast access from
London and other major cities. By road, it is connected to the motorway
system via the A55 expressway. The scenic Conwy Valley rail line runs
via the popular mountain resort of Betws-y-Coed to Blaenau Ffestiniog.
It is also on the network covered by the convenient "hop-on, hop-off"
Snowdon Sherpa bus service.

ESSENTIALS
Visitor Information Llandudno (✉ *Mostyn St.* ☎ *01492/876413*).

EXPLORING

Llandudno has little in the way of garish arcades, preferring to stick to the faithful **Great Orme Tramway** (☎ *01492/879306* ⊕ *www. greatormetramway.co.uk* ✉ *£5.60 round-trip* ☉ *Late Mar.–late Oct., daily 10–6*) that climbs to the summit of the Great Orme headland above the resort.

Besides a tram, the town has an **aerial cable car** (☎ *01492/879306* ✉ *£7 round-trip* ☉ *Easter–Sept., daily 10–4:30*) to the top of the Great Orme. There's also a large, dry ski slope (with an artificial surface you can ski on year-round) and year-round toboggan run.

The prehistoric **Great Orme Mines** are at the summit of the Great Orme (*orme*, a Norse word meaning "sea monster"), with its views of the coast and mountains of Snowdonia. Copper was first mined here in the Bronze Age, and you can tour the ancient underground workings. ✉ *Great Orme* ☎ *01492/870447* ⊕ *www.greatormemines.info* ✉ *£6* ☉ *Mar.–Oct., daily 10–5.*

WHERE TO STAY

££££–£££££
★

Bodysgallen Hall. Tasteful antiques, comfortable chairs by cheery fires, pictures, and polished wood distinguish one of Wales's most luxurious country-house hotels. The part 17th-, part 18th-century building is set in walled gardens 2 mi out of town. Bedrooms in the house combine elegance and practicality; seekers of privacy may prefer the cottage suites scattered around the estate. The outstanding restaurant uses local ingredients in creative ways, such as roe deer with choucroute, truffled gnocchi and cauliflower, or pavé of turbot with mustard-glazed ham knuckle. **Pros:** superb spa and swimming pool; rare 17th-century knot garden; elegant dining. **Cons:** too formal for some; very expensive. ✉ *Off A470* ☎ *01492/584466* ⊕ *www.bodysgallen.com* ⇆ *15 rooms, 16 cottage suites* ⌕ *In-room: no a/c (some), DVD, Wi-Fi. In-hotel: restaurant, room service, bar, pool, gym, spa, laundry service, Internet terminal, Wi-Fi hotspot, some pets allowed, no kids under 6* ▤ *AE, MC, V* ⦿*BP.*

££

Bryn Derwen Hotel. Many hoteliers at British seaside resorts have not upgraded their accommodations and food, but this immaculate Victorian hotel exemplifies how it should be done. Fresh flowers, plush period furnishings in the public areas, and soothing, warm-hued bedrooms show the owners' attention to detail. Bryn Derwen offers truly excellent value for the price. **Pros:** on-site beauty salon; plenty of parking; close to the beach. **Cons:** no sea views; not child friendly. ✉ *34 Abbey Rd.* ☎ *01492/876804* ⊕ *www.bryn-derwen.co.uk* ⇆ *9 rooms* ⌕ *In-room: no a/c, no phone, DVD, Wi-Fi. In-hotel: restaurant, bar, no kids under 12* ▤ *MC, V* ⦿*BP.*

£££–££££

St. Tudno Hotel. From the outside, one of Britain's best small seaside hotels blends unobtrusively with its neighbors. But the interior contains opulently furnished guest rooms and public areas with plenty of print fabrics and chintz. It's perfectly situated on the seafront promenade overlooking the beach and the pier. The fine contemporary cuisine includes dishes such as hake with leek and rarebit glaze or venison with truffled Welsh honey glaze. **Pros:** ocean views; well-trained staff; tasty food. **Cons:** some rooms are snug; overly fussy decor; small pool. ⊠ *Promenade* ☎ *01492/874411* ⊕ *www. st-tudno.co.uk* ⇨ *18 rooms* ⚹ *In-room: no a/c (some). In-hotel: restaurant, room service, bar, pool, laundry service, Wi-Fi hotspot, some pets allowed* ☐ *AE, DC, MC, V* ⏷⦶ *BP.*

EN ROUTE

Inland from Rhyl, **Bodelwyddan Castle**, between Abergele and St. Asaph, is the Welsh home of London's National Portrait Gallery. Gardens, including a maze, aviary, and woodland walks, surround the Victorian castle. Galleries display Regency and Victorian portraits by artists such as John Singer Sargent, Thomas Lawrence, Dante Gabriel Rossetti, and Edwin Landseer. There are also hands-on galleries of Victorian amusements and inventions. ⊠ *Off A55, Bodelwyddan* ☎ *01745/584060* ⊕ *www.bodelwyddan-castle.co.uk* ⊠ *£6* ◔ *Jan.–Apr., weekends 10:30–4; May–mid-July and Sept., Sat.–Thurs. 10:30–5; mid-July–Aug., daily 10:30–5; Oct.–mid-Dec., weekends 10–5.*

> ## ADVENTURES IN WONDERLAND
>
> Llandudno was the summer home of the family of Dr. Liddell, the Oxford don and father of the immortal Alice, inspiration for Lewis Carroll's *Alice's Adventures in Wonderland.* The book's Walrus and the Carpenter may be based on two rocks on Llandudno's West Shore close to the now demolished Liddell home. A statue of the White Rabbit stands on the West Shore.

15

RUTHIN

33 mi southeast of Llandudno, 23 mi southwest of Chester.

Once a stronghold of Welsh hero Owain Glyndr (circa 1354–1416), Ruthin is a delightful market town with elegant shops, good inns, and a fascinating architectural mix of medieval, Tudor, and Georgian buildings. The town also hosts medieval-style banquets and has a crafts complex with displays of the artisans' creations.

EXPLORING

The 17th-century **Myddleton Arms** in the town square has seven Dutch-style dormer windows, known as the "eyes of Ruthin," set into its red-tile roof.

You can tour **Ruthin Gaol**, where from 1654 to 1916 thousands of prisoners were incarcerated, and learn about prison conditions over the centuries. ⊠ *Clwyd St.* ☎ *01824/708281* ⊕ *www.ruthingaol.co.uk* ⊠ *£3.50* ◔ *Feb.–Oct., daily 10–5.*

WHERE TO STAY

££ ⛹ **Eyarth Old Railway Station.** This Victorian railway station 2 mi south of Ruthin has been converted into an outstanding B&B. The modern bedrooms are spacious, with large windows looking out over the Vale of Clwyd. **Pros:** good base for exploring; secluded garden; extensive views. **Cons:** rooms a little dated. ⊠ *Off A525, Llanfair Dyffryn Clwyd* ☎ *01824/703643* ⊕ *www.eyarthstation.com* ⇨ *6 rooms* ⚹ *In-room: no* *a/c, no phone, no TV, Wi-Fi. In-hotel: bar, pool, Internet terminal, Wi-Fi hotspot, some pets allowed* ⊟ *MC, V* ⎮⊚⎮ *BP.*

££–£££   🖼 **manorhaus.** A Georgian town house in the heart of Ruthin has been converted into a simply stunning boutique hotel. Each entirely original room is a mini–art gallery, designed and decorated in collaboration with the artist whose work hangs on the walls. There's also a library, gallery, sauna, steam room, private cinema, and restaurant serving fresh, locally sourced food. **Pros:** cutting-edge design; art lover's paradise; trendy bistro. **Cons:** small rooms; limited parking. ⊠ *Well St.* ☎ *01824/704830* ⊕ *www.manorhaus.com* ⤳ *8 rooms* ⚲ *In-room: DVD, Wi-Fi. In-hotel: restaurant, bar, gym, spa* ⊟ *AE, MC, V* ⎮⊚⎮ *BP.*

MID WALES

Traditional market towns and country villages, small seaside resorts, quiet roads, and rolling landscapes filled with sheep farms, forests, and lakes make up Mid Wales, the country's green and rural heart. Because this is Wales's quietest vacation region, lodgings are scattered thinly. Outside of one or two large centers, Aberystwyth and Llandrindod Wells, accommodations are mainly country inns, small hotels, and farmhouses. This area also has some splendid country-house hotels.

Although green is the predominant color here, the landscape differs around the region. The borderlands with England are gentle and undulating, rising to the west into high, wild mountains. Farther north, around Dolgellau, mountainous scenery becomes even more pronounced in the southern section of the Snowdonia National Park. Mountains meet the sea along Cardigan Bay, a long coastline of headlands, peaceful sandy beaches, and beautiful estuaries that has long been a refuge from the crowd. In the 19th century Tennyson, Darwin, Shelley, and Ruskin came to this area to work and relax; today thousands more come to delight in the numerous antiquarian bookstores of Hay-on-Wye.

HAY-ON-WYE

★   *57 mi north of Cardiff, 25 mi north of Abergavenny.*

Bookshops and a mostly ruined castle dominate this town on the border of Wales and England. Hay is a lively place, especially on Sunday, when the rest of central Wales seems to be closed down. In 1961 Richard Booth established a small secondhand and antiquarian bookshop here. Other booksellers soon got in on the act, and bookshops now fill several houses, a movie theater, and a pub. At last count there were about 40 bookstores, all in a town of only 1,300 inhabitants. It's now the largest secondhand bookselling center in the world, and priceless 14th-century manuscripts rub spines with "job lots" selling for a few pounds. Hay also has antiques and crafts centers.

GETTING HERE AND AROUND

You'll need a car to get to Hay. Once you're there, parking is plentiful and everything is accessible by foot.

ESSENTIALS
Visitor Information Hay-on-Wye (✉ *Craft Centre* ☎ *01497/820144* ⊕ *www. hay-on-wye.co.uk/tourism*).

EXPLORING
★ Things buzz in early summer during the 10-day **Hay Festival** (☎ *0870/990– 1299* ⊕ *www.hayfestival.com*), a celebration of literature that attracts famous writers from all over the world.

QUICK BITES

After some browsing, stop off at the Granary (✉ *Broad St.* ☎ 01497/820790), a wood-beamed former grain store by the clock tower. The chalkboard menu lists soups, lamb-and-spinach curry, and cheese-and-garlic toasties (open, toasted sandwiches).

WHERE TO EAT AND STAY
£££
BRITISH
✗ **Old Black Lion.** A 17th-century coaching inn close to Hay's center is ideal for a lunch break while you're ransacking the bookshops. The oak beamed bar serves food, and the breakfasts are especially good. The restaurant's sophisticated cooking has an international flavor and emphasizes local meats and produce. You can even opt for an overnight stay in one of the country-style rooms. ✉ *Lion St.* ☎ *01497/820841* ⊕ *www. oldblacklion.co.uk* ⊟ *AE, MC, V.*

££££–£££££
⌂ **Llangoed Hall.** This magnificent Jacobean mansion on the banks of the River Wye was renovated by the late Bernard Ashley, husband of designer Laura Ashley. There are antiques everywhere, beautiful fabrics and furnishings, open fireplaces, a sweeping carved staircase, and a paneled library dating back to 1632. Bernard Ashley's personal collection of paintings adorns the walls. Savor main courses like grilled salmon fillet with saffron, crushed potatoes, and crayfish sauce on the fixed-price menu (£15 for four courses). **Pros:** exclusive fabric shop; private fishing on River Wye; wonderful art collection. **Cons:** very expensive; often filled with wedding parties; no attractions within walking distance. ✉ *Llyswen* ☎ *01874/754525* ⊕ *www.llangoedhall.com* 📞 *23 rooms* ⚒ *In-room: no a/c, DVD (some), Wi-Fi. In-hotel: restaurant, Wi-Fi hotspot, no kids under 8* ⊟ *AE, MC, V* ⍟ *BP.*

SHOPPING
Boz Books (✉ *13A Castle St.* ☎ *01497/821277*) specializes in 19th-century novels, including first editions of Dickens. A former movie theater houses the town's largest book outpost, the **Hay Cinema Bookshop** (✉ *Castle St.* ☎ *01497/820071* ⊕ *www.haycinemabookshop.co.uk*), which stocks 200,000 volumes on subjects from art to zoology at prices from 50p to £5,000.

LLANDRINDOD WELLS

27 mi north of Hay-on-Wye, 67 mi north of Cardiff.

Also known as Llandod, the old spa town of Llandrindod Wells preserves its Victorian look with turrets, cupolas, loggias, and balustrades everywhere. Cross over to South Crescent, passing the Glen Usk Hotel with its wrought-iron balustrade and the Victorian bandstand in the gardens opposite, and you reach Middleton Street, a Victorian thoroughfare. From there, head to Rock Park and the path that leads to the Pump Room. This historic building is now an alternative health center, but visitors can freely "take the waters."

GETTING HERE AND AROUND

On a branch-line rail route and with good bus service, Llandrindod makes a useful base for exploring the region. Follow in the tracks of the early spa-goers and hop on the Heart of Wales line that runs between Swansea to Shrewsbury. The town is about halfway along this scenic route. This Victorian town was built for promenading with wide streets and extensive parks.

> ### PLAYING DRESS-UP
>
> During Llandrindod Wells's **Victorian Festival** (☎ *01597/823441* ⊕ *www.victorianfestival.co.uk*), in late August, shop assistants, hotel staff, and anyone else who cares to join in wear period costume and enjoy "old-style" entertainment.

ESSENTIALS

Visitor Information Llandrindod Wells (⊠ *Temple St.* ☎ *01597/822600*).

EXPLORING

The **Radnorshire Museum**, in Memorial Gardens, presents the spa's development from Roman times and explains some Victorian "cures" in gruesome detail. ☎ *01597/824513* 🎫 *£1* ⊗ *Apr.–Sept., Tues.–Fri. 10–4, Sat. 10–5, Sun. 1–5; Oct.–Mar., Tues.–Fri. 10–4, Sat. 10–1*.

WHERE TO STAY

£ ⛳ **Brynhir Farm.** You get a warm welcome at this immaculate, cream-color farmhouse tucked into the hills on a 200-acre sheep-and-cattle farm. Country-style furnishings enhance the rooms. The farm is 2 mi from Llandrindod. **Pros:** bird-watcher's delight; serves homegrown Welsh lamb; extensive views. **Cons:** too rural for some; not walking distance to town. ⊠ *Chapel Rd., Howey* ☎ *01597/822425* ⊕ *www.brynhir.farm.btinternet.co.uk* ➟ *3 rooms* ☖ *In-room: no a/c, no phone. In-hotel: restaurant, Internet terminal, Wi-Fi hotspot, no kids under 6* ☰ *MC, V* ⎮⊙⎮ *BP.*

££ ⛳ **Guidfa House.** Friendly hosts Tony and Anne Millan run this stylish Georgian guesthouse with a welcoming log fire and bright, individually furnished bedrooms. Cordon Bleu–trained Anne prepares dinners (for guests only) from fresh local produce; the guinea fowl with apple brandy and mushroom sauce is delicious. **Pros:** good base for exploring; great wine list; romantic coach house suite. **Cons:** overlooks a road junction; far from Llandod. ⊠ *Crossgates, near Llandrindod Wells* ☎ *01597/851241* ⊕ *www.guidfa-house.co.uk* ➟ *6 rooms* ☖ *In-room: no a/c, no phone, DVD. In-hotel: restaurant, Wi-Fi hotspot, no kids under 10* ☰ *MC, V* ⎮⊙⎮ *BP.*

EN ROUTE From Llandrindod, take A4081/A470 to Rhayader, a good pony-trekking center and gateway town for the **Elan Valley**, Wales's Lake District. This 7-mi chain of lakes, winding between gray-green hills, was created in the 1890s by a system of dams designed to supply water to Birmingham, 73 mi to the east.

From the Elan Valley you can follow the narrow Cwmystwyth mountain road west to **Devil's Bridge**, a famous (and popular) beauty spot where three bridges set one on top of the other span a chasm over the raging River Mynach, before continuing on to Aberystwyth. You can also take the Vale of Rheidol Railway to this site from Aberystwyth.

ABERYSTWYTH

41 mi northwest of Llandrindod Wells via A44, 118 mi northwest of Cardiff.

Aberystwyth makes the best of several worlds as a seaside resort (complete with promenade and amusement pier) and a long-established university town that is home to the impressive National Library of Wales. It also has a small harbor and is a major shopping center for Mid Wales. More than 5,000 students expand the full-time population of 12,000. The town, midway along Cardigan Bay, came to prominence as a Victorian watering hole thanks to a curving beach set beneath a prominent headland. Aberystwyth is a good gateway for exploring Mid Wales: few towns in Wales present such varied scenery within their immediate neighborhood, from the Devil's Bridge to the green Rheidol Valley.

GETTING HERE AND AROUND
A resort that was born with the coming of the railways, Aberystwyth is easily reached by train. A cross-country line still runs from the main hub of Shrewsbury. Of interest to visitors is the Cambrian Coast line, which runs from Aberystwyth to Pwllheli on the Llyn Peninsula. This is one of Britain's great scenic rail routes, with views of coast and mountains. Another must is a trip on the narrow-gauge Vale of Rheidol Railway that runs into the mountains. If you're arriving by car, the scenic A470 connects to the A44. You won't need a car to get around town, as all the attractions are within easy walking distance.

TIMING
Aberystwyth is a busy resort and university town, so if you have specific accommodation in mind, it is advisable to book ahead.

ESSENTIALS
Visitor Information Aberystwyth (✉ *Terrace Rd.* ☎ *01970/612125*).

EXPLORING
TOP ATTRACTIONS
Constitution Hill. At the northern end of the beach promenade a zigzag cliff path–nature trail at Constitution Hill leads to a view from the hilltop. An enjoyable way to reach the summit of Constitution Hill is by the **Aberystwyth Cliff Railway** (☎ *01970/617642* ⊕ *www. aberystwythcliffrailway.co.uk* ✉ *£3.50 round-trip* ⊗ *Mar.–Oct., daily 10–5; call for winter hrs*), the longest electric cliff railway in Britain. Opened in 1896, it retains its Victorian look. At the 430-foot summit of Constitution Hill is the **Great Aberystwyth Camera Obscura** (☎ *01970/617642* ✉ *£1*), a modern version of a Victorian amusement: a massive 14-inch lens gives a bird's-eye view of the whole of Cardigan Bay and 26 Welsh mountain peaks. It has the same hours as the railway.

National Library of Wales. The massive, neoclassical National Library of Wales, on a hill amid the buildings of the modern University of Wales–Aberystwyth houses notable Welsh and other Celtic literary works

15

The Language of Cymru

Welsh, the native language of Wales (Cymru, in Welsh), is revered in the country, but it was not legally recognized in Britain until the 1960s. Today Welsh schoolchildren under 14 are required to take classes to learn the language, and Welsh is surviving more successfully than its Celtic cousin, Breton, which is spoken in northwestern France. Welsh may look daunting to pronounce, but it is a phonetic language; pronunciation is fairly easy once the alphabet is learned. Remember that "dd" is sounded like "th" in

they, "f" sounds like "v" in save, and "ff" is the equivalent of the English "f" in forest. The "ll" sound has no English equivalent; the closest match is the "cl" sound in "close."

Terms that crop up frequently in Welsh are *bach* or *fach* (small), *craig* or *graig* (rock), *cwm* (valley; pronounced cum), *dyffryn* (valley), *eglwys* (church), *glyn* (glen), *llyn* (lake), *mawr* or *fawr* (great, big), *mynydd* or *fynydd* (mountain, moorland), *pentre* (village, homestead), *plas* (hall, mansion), and *pont* or *bont* (bridge).

among its more than 4.5 million printed volumes. This self-described national treasure house also has enormous archives of maps, photographs, films, and sound recordings. ■TIP→ Material doesn't circulate, but the public can do research; many people pursue genealogical history here. The gallery has art shows, and exhibitions highlight Welsh and other subjects. ⊠ *Off Penglais Rd.* ☎ *01970/632800* ⊕ *www.llgc.org. uk* ⊠ *Free* ⊙ *Weekdays 9:30–6, Sat. 9:30–5.*

Ꙍ **Vale of Rheidol Railway.** At Aberystwyth Station you can hop on the narrow-gauge, steam-operated Vale of Rheidol Railway for an hour-long ride to the **Devil's Bridge,** where the rivers Rheidol and Mynach meet in a series of spectacular falls. Clamped between two rocky cliffs where a torrent of water pours unceasingly, this bridge well deserves its name—Pont y Gwr Drwg, or Bridge of the Evil One. There are actually three bridges (the oldest is 800 years old), and the walk down to the lowest bridge is magnificent but strictly for the sure-footed. ⊠ *Park Ave.* ☎ *01970/625819* ⊕ *www.rheidolrailway.co.uk* ⊠ *£14 round-trip* ⊙ *Easter–Oct.; call for schedule.*

WORTH NOTING

Castle. At the southern end of the bay near the New Promenade, the castle was built in 1277 and rebuilt in 1282 by Edward I. It was one of several strongholds to fall, in 1404, to the Welsh leader Owain Glyndr. Today it is a romantic ruin on a headland.

Ceredigion Museum. Housed in a flamboyant 1905 Edwardian theater, the Ceredigion Museum has fine collections related to folk history. Highlights include a reconstructed mud-walled cottage from 1850, exhibits from the building's music-hall past, and items illustrating the region's seafaring, lead-mining, and farming history. ⊠ *Terrace Rd.* ☎ *01970/633088* ⊕ *museum.ceredigion.gov.uk* ⊠ *Free* ⊙ *Apr.–Sept., Mon.–Sat. 10–5; Oct.–Mar., Mon.–Sat. noon–4:30.*

WHERE TO EAT AND STAY

££ ✗ **Gannets.** A simple, good-value bistro, Gannets specializes in hearty
BISTRO roasts and pies produced from locally supplied meat, fish, and game. Organically grown vegetables and a good French house wine are further draws for a university crowd. ⊠ *7 St. James's Sq.* ☎ *01970/617164* ⊟ *MC, V* ⊙ *Closed Sun.–Tues.*

££–£££ ⊡ **Gwesty Cymru.** This seafront Edwardian home makes the perfect guesthouse for the 21st century. The hotel makes abundant and stylish use of the natural materials of Wales, so there's plenty of slate and oak. There are also spectacular sea views, designer bathrooms, original paintings, and illuminated Welsh poetry. **Pros:** Welsh atmosphere; sea views. **Cons:** no guest lounge; tiny entrance hall; small restaurant. ⊠ *19 Marine Terr.* ☎ *01970/612252* ⊕ *www.gwestycymru.com* ⇆ *8 rooms* ♿ *In-room: no a/c, DVD, Wi-Fi. In-hotel: restaurant, bar* ⊟ *MC, V* ⊺⊙⏽ *BP.*

15

MACHYNLLETH

18 mi northeast of Aberystwyth.

Machynlleth, at the head of the beautiful Dovey Estuary, does not look like a typical Welsh country town. Its long and wide main street (Heol Maengwyn), lined with a mixed style of buildings from sober gray stone to well-proportioned Georgian, creates an atypical sense of openness and space. Machynlleth's busiest day is Wednesday, when the stalls of market traders fill the main street.

ESSENTIALS

Visitor Information Aberdyfi (⊠ *The Wharf Gardens* ☎ *01654/767321* ⊙ *Easter–Oct., daily 9:30–5:30).* ·

EXPLORING

At the **Owain Glyndŵr Centre,** a small exhibition celebrates Wales's last native leader, who established a Welsh parliament at Machynlleth in the early 15th century. ⊠ *End of Heol Maengwyn* ☎ *01654/702932* ⊕ *www.canolfanowainglyndwrcentre.org.uk* ⊡ *£2* ⊙ *Easter–Sept., Mon.–Sat. (and Sun. in summer) 10–4.*

In a former chapel that's now a cultural and performing-arts center is **Y Tabernacl Museum of Modern Art**, a superb gallery with permanent displays, including works by Welsh artist Kyffin Williams. ⊠ *Heol Penrallt* ☎ *01654/703355* ⊕ *www.momawales.org.uk* ⊡ *Free* ⊙ *Mon.–Sat. 10–4.*

♻ At the unique **Centre for Alternative Technology,** in an abandoned slate quarry in the forested hills just north of Machynlleth, a railway transports you to a futuristic village equipped with all things green: alternative energy sources (solar roofs, wood-chip boilers), organic gardens, and a vegetarian café. Interactive displays present practical ideas about renewable resources, and the store is full of inspirational books and eco-friendly products. ⊠ *Off A487* ☎ *01654/705950* ⊕ *www.cat.org. uk* ⊡ *£8.50* ⊙ *Late Mar.–mid-July and Sept.–Oct., daily 10–5:30; mid-July–Aug., daily 10–6; Jan.–late Mar. and Nov.–Dec., daily 10–dusk.*

WHERE TO STAY

££££ 🖭 **Llety Bodfor**. The delightful little sailing center of Aberdovey is perched at the mouth of the Dovey Estuary, west of Machynlleth. This contemporary Victorian town house has bright bedrooms that look out over Cardigan Bay. All were decorated by owner and interior designer Ann Hughes. The open-plan guest lounge–dining room has capacious leather sofas, a small bar, and a piano. You can even buy items of hotel decor that take your fancy at Seld Interiors, the on-site shop. **Pros:** stylish decor; sea views; great shopping. **Cons:** no evening meals; no parking. ⊠ *Bodfor Terrace, Aberdovey* 🕾 *01654/767475* ⊕ *www.lletybodfor.co.uk* ⟿ *8 rooms* △ *In-room: no a/c, DVD. In-hotel: bar* 🖃 *MC, V* ⫶❂⫶ *BP.*

£££££ 🖭 **Ynyshir Hall**. Idyllic gardens and grounds surround this supremely
★ luxurious Georgian mansion once owned by Queen Victoria. Inside, the place glows with jewel-like tones and vibrant paintings by the former owner, artist Rob Reen. Antiques and Welsh pottery fill the public areas; the pampering guest rooms, named after artists (Hogarth, Matisse, Goya), have antique beds. The outstanding contemporary cuisine in the candlelit restaurant uses local favorites, from wild salmon and venison to farmhouse cheeses. **Pros:** arty ambience; unabashed luxury; great food. **Cons:** very expensive; isolated location. ⊠ *Off A487, southwest of Machynlleth, Eglwysfach* 🕾 *01654/781209* ⊕ *www.ynyshirhall.co.uk* ⟿ *9 rooms* △ *In-room: no a/c. In-hotel: restaurant, room service, bar, laundry service, Internet terminal, Wi-Fi hotspot, no kids under 9* 🖃 *AE, DC, MC, V* ⫶❂⫶ *BP.*

OUTDOORS

The 128-mi **Glyndŵr's Way** (⊕ *www.glyndwrsway.org.uk*) walking route passes through Machynlleth before it turns east to climb above the Dovey with wonderful views north to Cadair Idris.

DOLGELLAU

16 mi north of Machynlleth, 34 mi northeast of Aberystwyth.

A solidly Welsh town with dark stone buildings and old coaching inns made of the local gray dolerite and slate, Dolgellau (pronounced dol-*geth*-lee) thrived with the wool trade until the mid-19th century. Sheep are still auctioned here, but now they're valued for meat rather than wool. Prosperity left striking architecture, with buildings of different eras side by side on crooked streets that are a pre-Norman legacy. The town trail booklet, sold in the tourist office on Eldon Square, tells the story. Dolgellau, in a valley, has long been a popular base for people eager to walk the surrounding countryside. Look down the streets or above the buildings, and you'll see mountains rising up in the distance.

The town became the center of the Welsh gold trade in the 19th century, when high-quality gold was discovered locally. A nugget of Dolgellau gold is used to make royal wedding rings. You can still try your luck and pan for gold in the Mawddach.

GETTING HERE AND AROUND

Dolgellau's nearest railway station is at Barmouth, about 10 mi away. The town is small and full of interesting nooks and crannies easily explored on foot. To discover the surrounding area you will need a car.

ESSENTIALS

Visitor Information Dolgellau (⊠ *Ty Meirion, Eldon Sq.* ☎ *01341/422888*).

EXPLORING

The **Museum of the Quakers**, in the town square, commemorates the area's strong links with the Quaker movement and the Quakers' emigration to the American colonies. ⊠ *Eldon Sq.* ☎ *01341/422888* ☞ *Free* ☉ *Easter–Oct., daily 9:30–5:30; Nov.–Easter, Thurs.–Mon. 9:30–4:30.*

The National Centre for Welsh Folk Music, **Ty Siamas**, is in the converted Victorian Market Hall and Assembly Rooms. It has a fascinating interactive folk music exhibition, performance auditorium, and café and bar. ⊠ *Neuadd Idris, Eldon Sq.* ☎ *01341/421800* ⊕ *www.tysiamas. com* ☞ *£3.95* ☉ *Easter–Sept., Wed.–Fri. 10–4, Sat. 10–1. Call for off-season hrs.*

To the south of Dolgellau rises the menacing bulk of **Cadair Idris** (2,927 feet); the name means "the Chair of Idris," though no one is completely sure who Idris was—probably a warrior bard. It is said that anyone sleeping for a night on a certain part of the mountain will awaken either a poet or a madman, or not at all.

15

WELSHPOOL

38 mi east of Dolgellau, 19 mi southwest of Shrewsbury.

The border town of Welshpool, "Trallwng" in Welsh, is famous as the home of Powis Castle, one of Mid Wales's greatest treasures, but it also has an appealing town center.

ESSENTIALS

Visitor Information Welshpool (⊠ *Vicarage Gardens Car Park, Church St.* ☎ *01938/552043*).

EXPLORING

★ Continuously occupied since the 13th century, **Powis Castle** is one of the most opulent residential castles in Britain, with gardens that are equally renowned. Its battlements rear high on a hilltop, and Italian- and French-influenced terraced gardens surround the castle. Below gigantic yew hedges, the grounds fall steeply down to wide lawns and neat Elizabethan gardens. The interior contains many treasures: Greek vases; paintings by Thomas Gainsborough, Joshua Reynolds, and George Romney; and the **Clive of India Museum,** with a good collection of Indian art. The tearoom is excellent. A timed-ticket system may be in effect on busy days. ⊠ *Off A483* ☎ *01938/551944* ⊕ *www. nationaltrust.org.uk* ☞ *£11.50; gardens only, £8.50* ☉ *Castle and museum Mar.–Oct., Thurs.–Mon. 1–5. Gardens Mar.–June and Sept. and Oct., Thurs.–Mon. 11–4:30; Nov., weekends 11–3:30, Thurs., Fri., and Mon. 11–5:30; July and Aug., Wed.–Mon. 11–5:30.*

The excellent **Powysland Museum**, in a converted warehouse on the banks of the Montgomery Canal, focuses on local history from the Stone Age to Victorian times. ✉ *Canal Wharf* ☎ *01938/554656* 🎟 *£1* ⏲ *May–Sept., Mon., Tues., Thurs., and Fri. 11–1 and 2–5, weekends 10–1 and 2–5; Oct.–Apr., Mon., Tues., Thurs., and Fri. 11–1 and 2–5, Sat. 11–2.*

SOUTH WALES

The most diverse of Wales's three regions, the south covers not only the immediate region around Cardiff and the border of Wales and England, but also the southwest as far as the rugged coastline of Pembrokeshire. The very different natures of its two national parks reveal South Wales's scenic variety. The Brecon Beacons National Park, a short drive north of Cardiff, is an area of high, grassy mountains, lakes, and craggy limestone gorges. In contrast, the Pembrokeshire Coast National Park holds one of Europe's finest stretches of coastal natural beauty, with mile after mile of spectacular sea cliffs, beaches, headlands, and coves. Other pieces of the complicated South Wales jigsaw include traditional farmlands, cosmopolitan urban areas, rolling border country, wooded vales, and the former industrial valleys where coal was mined in huge quantities during the 19th and early 20th centuries.

CARDIFF

20 mi southwest of the Second Severn Bridge, which carries the M4 motorway across the Severn Estuary into Wales.

Home to the Welsh Assembly and with a population of 306,000, Cardiff is financially, industrially, and commercially the most important city in Wales. It's also one of Europe's youngest and most vibrant capital cities, with an appealing blend of old and new. Attracting increasing numbers of tourists are its handsome Civic Centre, magnificent parklands, canopied shopping arcades, and a castle with abundant Victorian verve. These traditional sights stand alongside new landmarks like the Millennium Stadium and Cardiff Bay, a onetime coal-exporting hub that has undergone a dazzling regeneration. Here a dam across the Taff and Ely rivers has created a freshwater lake edged by 8 mi of prime waterfront, an area of promenades, shops, restaurants, attractions, and exciting modern buildings like the Wales Millennium Centre.

True to the Welsh tradition of vocal excellence, Cardiff is home base for Britain's adventurous and acclaimed Welsh National Opera. Cardiff is also the sporting center of Wales and the Welsh capital of rugby football. To hear crowds singing their support for the Welsh team is a stirring experience.

GETTING HERE AND AROUND

The capital is a major transportation hub with good connections to other parts of Wales and with England. A local rail network runs north into the South Wales valleys, and there are fast mainline rail and bus services to Swansea and southwest Wales. Cardiff is easily accessible by road, with the M4 motorway running to its doorstep. For walkers there are two Cardiffs: the established city center and the waterfront a mile or so to the south. Bus and rail links connect the two.

SeeWales offers day trips from Cardiff to destinations including Brecon Beacons National Park and the Gower Peninsula.

TIMING

If you don't like crowds, avoid Cardiff during international rugby tournaments or other major sporting events.

ESSENTIALS

Visitor and Tour Information Cardiff (✉ *The Old Library, The Hayes* ☎ *08701/211258* ⊕ *www.visitcardiff.com*). **SeeWales** (☎ *029/20–227227* ⊕ *www.seewales.com*).

EXPLORING

TOP ATTRACTIONS

Cardiff Bay. Panoramic bay views, promenades, shops, restaurants, museums, and prestigious buildings make Cardiff Bay well worth a visit. The revitalized dockland, 1 mi south of the city center, can be reached by bus, train, or taxi. The **Cardiff Bay Visitor Centre,** a cylindrical building known locally as "the Tube," tells the story of the transformation of the area. Next door is the timber Norwegian Seamen's Church where author Roald Dahl (whose children's books include *James and the Giant Peach* and *Charlie and the Chocolate Factory*) was baptized. It's now known as the **Norwegian Church Arts Centre** and houses a performance space, a gallery, and a café. North of the visitor center is the **National Assembly Debating Chamber,** a canopied glass structure designed by Richard Rogers that complements the neighboring modern buildings. Across the street the imposing Victorian **Pierhead** is home to a lively exhibition about Cardiff Bay.

❶ ★ Cardiff Castle. In Bute Park, one section of the city's hundreds of acres of parkland, is an unusual historic site, with Roman, Norman, and Victorian associations. Parts of the walls are Roman, the solid keep is Norman, and the whole complex was restored and transformed into a Victorian ego flight by the third marquess of Bute. He employed William Burges (1827–81), an architect obsessed by the Gothic period, and Burges transformed the castle into an extravaganza of medieval color and careful craftsmanship. It is the perfect expression of the anything-goes Victorian spirit. ✉ *Bute Park* ☎ *029/2087–8100* ⊕ *www.cardiffcastle.com* 🎟️ *£10.50; £13.50 with guided tour* ⏰ *Mar.–Oct., daily 9–5; Nov.–Feb., daily 9–4.*

QUICK
BITES

Café Minuet (✉ *42 Castle Arcade* ☎ *029/2034–1794* ⏰ *Mon.–Sat. 11–5*), in the Victorian shopping arcade opposite Cardiff Castle, has pale wood floors and checked tablecloths and serves tasty rustic Italian food like homemade soups, pasta, and pizzas. Service is prompt and friendly.

❺ ★ Castell Coch. Perched on a hillside is the Red Castle, a turreted Victorian vision. It was built (on the site of a medieval stronghold) in the 1870s, about the time that Ludwig II of Bavaria was creating his fairy-tale castles, and it could almost be one of them. The castle was another collaboration of the third marquess of Bute and William Burges, builders

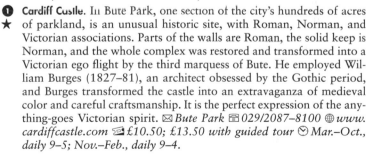

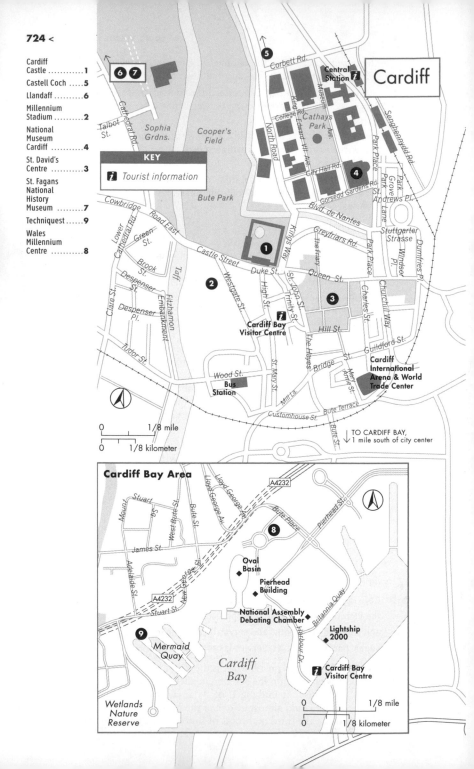

of Cardiff Castle. Burges created everything—architecture, furnishings, murals—in a remarkable exercise in Victorian-Gothic whimsy. ⊠ *A470, 4 mi north of Cardiff, Tongwynlais* ☏ *029/2081–0101* ⊕ *www.cadw. wales.gov.uk* ⌑ *£3.60* ☾ *Apr.–Oct., daily 9–5; Nov.–Mar., Mon.–Sat. 9:30–4, Sun. 11–4.*

Civic Centre. Two blocks north and east of Cardiff Castle is a well-designed complex of tree-lined avenues and Edwardian civic buildings with white Portland stone facades; Cathays Park is in the center. A Welsh dragon sits atop the domed City Hall, and inside the Marble Hall contains statues of Welsh heroes, including St. David, Henry Tudor, and Owain Glyndwr (although he razed Cardiff in 1404). Neoclassical law courts and university campus buildings are also here. ⊠ *Bordered by North Rd. on the west and Park Pl. on the east.*

❹ **National Museum Cardiff.** This splendid museum, next to City Hall, tells
Fodor'sChoice the story of Wales through its plants, rocks, archaeology, zoology,
★ art, and industry. The Evolution of Wales gallery gives a dazzling run through Wales's past using robotics and audiovisual effects. There's a fine collection of modern European art, including the largest collection of French impressionist and postimpressionist works in the country (don't miss *La Parisienne,* by Renoir). ■ **TIP→ Allow at least half a day at the museum.** ⊠ *Cathays Park* ☏ *029/2039–7951* ⊕ *www.museumwales. ac.uk* ⌑ *Free* ☾ *Tues.–Sun. 10–5.*

❸ **St. David's Centre.** South of the Civic Centre are the shopping and business areas of Cardiff. A large, modern shopping mall holds **St. David's Hall,** one of Europe's best concert halls, with outstanding acoustics. People come here for classical music, jazz, rock, ballet, and even snooker championships. Nearby is the **Cardiff International Arena,** a multipurpose center for exhibitions, concerts, and conferences. ⊠ *Queen St. and St. John St.*

OFF THE
BEATEN
PATH **Tintern Abbey.** When Wordsworth penned "Lines Written a Few Miles Above Tintern Abbey," he had no idea of all the people who would flock to Tintern to gaze at the abbey's substantial ruins. Remote and hauntingly beautiful as the site is, its appeal is diminished in summer because of crowds, so visit early or late in the day to best appreciate the complex stonework and tracery of the Gothic church. The abbey, 5 mi north of Chepstow and 30 mi northeast of Cardiff, is on the banks of the River Wye. ⊠ *A466, Tintern* ☏ *01291/689251* ⊕ *www.cadw. wales.gov.uk* ⌑ *£3.60* ☾ *Apr.–Oct., daily 9–5; Nov.–Mar., Mon.–Sat. 9:30–4, Sun. 11–4.*

WORTH NOTING

Caerphilly Castle. One of the most impressive fortresses in Wales was remarkable at the time of its construction in the 13th century. Built by an Anglo-Norman lord, the concentric fortification contained inner and outer defenses. More than 30 acres of grounds and a moat surround the castle, but Caerphilly is no longer on guard; some walls have toppled and others lean haphazardly. Exhibits in the gatehouse trace its turbulent history. The castle is 7 mi north of Cardiff. ⊠ *Access off A470–A468, Caerphilly* ☏ *029/2088–3143* ⊕ *www.cadw.wales.gov.uk* ⌑ *£3.60* ☾ *Apr.–Oct., daily 9:30–5; Nov.–Mar., Mon.–Sat. 9:30–4, Sun. 11–4.*

15

6 **Llandaff.** In a suburb that retains its village feeling, you can visit **Llandaff Cathedral,** which was repaired after serious bomb damage in World War II. The cathedral includes the work of a number of Pre-Raphaelites as well as *Christ in Majesty,* a 15-foot-tall aluminum figure by sculptor Jacob Epstein (1880–1959). From Cardiff, cross the River Taff and follow Cathedral Road for about 2 mi. Guided tours are available by arrangement. ☎ *029/2056–4554* ⊕ *www.llandaffcathedral.org.uk.*

2 **Millennium Stadium.** The modern, 72,000-seat stadium stands beside the River Taff on the site of the famous Cardiff Arms Park, the

> ### MALE-VOICE CHOIRS
>
> In a land of song, Wales is famous for its male choirs. Many were formed by quarry and mine workers, where singing songs and hymns reinforced community. The tradition continues, and attending anything from a choir rehearsal to a choral festival is well worthwhile. (Listen to Only Men Aloud, a popular updated version, too). Check with tourist boards or Web sites such as ⊕ *www. homecomingwales.com* or *www. malevoicechoir.net.*

spiritual home of Welsh rugby. The stadium's retractable roof enables it to be used for concerts and special events throughout the year, as well as for rugby. On a one-hour tour you can walk the players' tunnel and see the Royal Box, dressing rooms, pitch, and broadcasting suite. ⊠ *Entrance Gate 3, Westgate St.* ☎ *029/2082–2228* ⊕ *www. millenniumstadium.com* ⊠ *Tours £6.50* ☉ *Call for tour times.*

7 **St. Fagans National History Museum.** On 100 acres of gardens, this excellent open-air museum has farmhouses, cottages, shops, a school, chapels, St. Fagans castle (a 16th-century manor house), and terraced houses that celebrate Wales's rich rural culture and show the evolution of building styles. All but two of the structures were brought here from places around Wales. Galleries display clothing and articles from daily life. Special events highlight ancient rural festivals. The museum is accessible from Junction 33 on the M4. ⊠ *St. Fagans* ☎ *029/2057–3500* ⊕ *www.museumwales.ac.uk* ⊠ *Free* ☉ *Daily 10–5.*

9 **Techniquest.** A large science-discovery center on the waterfront, Techniquest has 160 interactive exhibits, a planetarium, and a science theater. ⊠ *Stuart St., Cardiff Bay* ☎ *029/2047–5475* ⊕ *www.techniquest.org* ⊠ *£7* ☉ *Weekdays 9:30–4:30, weekends 10–5.*

8 **Wales Millennium Centre.** This huge arts complex with a curving golden steel roof and purple slate walls is a world-class stage for full-scale ballet, opera, and musical performances. The center contains dance and recording studios, an orchestra hall, and a 1,900-seat auditorium. Seven leading Welsh cultural organizations make this their home base, including the Welsh National Opera Company and the Dance Company of Wales. There are shops, bars, and restaurants; one-hour tours are available. ⊠ *Cardiff Bay* ☎ *08700/402000* ⊕ *www.wmc.org.uk* ⊠ *Free. Tours £5.50* ☉ *Call to arrange tour.*

WHERE TO EAT

£££
MODERN BRITISH

✕ **Armless Dragon.** It's worth the five-minute drive from the city center to eat at this comfortable restaurant with a contemporary menu that changes daily. Dishes such as Brecon rabbit braised in port and root vegetables are created from seasonal, local ingredients. There are always excellent vegetarian options, too. ✉ *97 Wyverne Rd.* ☎ *029/2038–2357*⊕ *www. armlessdragon.co.uk* ▤ *AE, MC, V* ☺ *Closed Sun. and Mon.*

£
BRITISH

✕ **Harry Ramsden's.** You can dine on (reputedly) the world's most famous fish-and-chips in a chandeliered, 200-seat dining room with wonderful views across Cardiff Bay. If you like live music with your meal, call about sing-along evenings. ✉ *Landsea House, Stuart St.* ☎ *029/2046– 3334* ▤ *MC, V.*

£££
MODERN BRITISH
★

✕ **Le Gallois.** Its minimalist furnishings and varied menu help make this sophisticated restaurant, close to Sophia Gardens, one of the city's most popular. The cooking is European in style and takes advantage of local ingredients. Try the woodland pork belly with potatoes mashed with double cream and butter. A good-value fixed-price menu (£20 for three courses) is available at lunch. ✉ *8 Romilly Crescent* ☎ *029/2034–1264* ⊕ *www.legallois.co.uk* ▤ *MC, V* ☺ *Closed Sun. and Mon.*

££
ITALIAN

✕ **Valentino's.** With its cozily rustic decor and friendly Italian staff, this little restaurant simply drips with authenticity. In addition to the usual pizzas and pastas, there is an ever-changing selection of fresh, locally sourced meat and fish dishes. ✉ *5 Windsor Pl.* ☎ *029/2022–9697* ⊕ *www.valentinocardiff.co.uk* ▤ *AE, DC, MC, V* ☺ *Closed Sun.*

WHERE TO STAY

££–£££

▦ **Jolyons Hotel.** Every room has different interior design, fabrics, and antiques at this sumptuous little boutique hotel close to the Millennium Centre. All the beds are king-size, so you can spread out with the morning paper. The lively Bar Cwtch (which means "cuddle" or "cubbyhole" in Welsh) has a wood-burning stove (watch pizzas cook in the log fire). It's a great base for exploring the attractions of Cardiff Bay. **Pros:** bursting with character; comfortable bar; in the heart of Cardiff Bay. **Cons:** not near the city center. ✉ *Bute Crescent, Cardiff Bay* ☎ *029/2048–8775* ⊕ *www.jolyons.co.uk* ⤴ *6 rooms* ⌂ *In-room: no a/c, Wi-Fi. In-hotel: room service, bar, laundry service, Wi-Fi hotspot, no kids under 13* ▤ *AE, DC, MC, V* ⏀| *BP.*

££–£££

▦ **Maltsters.** This pub has spent a small fortune on renovating its superb bedrooms, which combine cool design and true comfort. They come equipped with state-of-the-art entertainment systems (you can even watch your plasma TV from your bath). The real ale remains at the downstairs bar, which is warm and welcoming and serves very good food. The hotel is just a mile from the city center in Llandaff, which has a village atmosphere. **Pros:** combines luxury and informality: great food. **Cons:** not a quiet retreat; on a busy road. ✉ *42 Cardiff Rd., Llandaff* ☎ *029/2033–3096* ⊕ *www.maltsterscardiff.co.uk* ⤴ *5 rooms* ⌂ *In-room: no a/c, DVD, Wi-Fi. In-hotel: restaurant, bar* ▤ *MC, V* ⏀| *BP.*

££–£££

▦ **Park Plaza.** At this award-winning hotel just off Cardiff's main shopping street, spacious rooms are individually designed in a clean-lined, uncluttered style with sumptuous fabrics. After a hard day of retail therapy, unwind in the luxury health club and enjoy the simple, locally

15

sourced food served in the restaurant. **Pros:** central location; excellent fitness center; stainless-steel pool. **Cons:** a bit corporate; lacks Welsh atmosphere. ☒ *Greyfriars Rd.* ☎ *029/2011–1111* ⊕ *www.parkplaza. com* ↩ *129 rooms* ☖ *In-room: safe, Wi-Fi. In-hotel: restaurant, room service, bar, pool, gym, spa, laundry service, Wi-Fi hotspot* ▤ *AE, MC, V* ⎮◯⎮ *BP.*

£££–££££ 🏨 **St. David's Hotel and Spa.** Natural light from a glass atrium floods this
★ up-to-the-minute luxury hotel along the waterfront. Every room, done in soothing neutral tones with sleek modern furniture, has a private balcony and views over Cardiff Bay. You can indulge in a hydrotherapy spa treatment or feast at the Tides restaurant, which specializes in modern French fare. Special promotional deals are often available. **Pros:** a bit like staying on a cruise ship; relaxing spa. **Cons:** entrance rather stark; not convenient to downtown. ☒ *Havannah St.* ☎ *029/2045–4045* ⊕ *st-davidshotelcardiff.co.uk* ↩ *132 rooms* ☖ *In-room: safe, DVD, Internet. In-hotel: restaurant, room service, pool, gym, spa, laundry service, Internet terminal, Wi-Fi hotspot* ▤ *AE, DC, MC, V.*

££ 🏨 **Town House.** Cosmopolitan in style, this immaculate guesthouse near the city center is considered Cardiff's best B&B. The elegant Victorian building retains many original features and has neat, well-equipped bedrooms. You can have traditional British or American breakfasts in the formal dining room. **Pros:** close to Cardiff Castle; near shops. **Cons:** rooms quite small; guests share a table at breakfast. ☒ *70 Cathedral Rd.* ☎ *029/2023–9399* ⊕ *www.thetownhousecardiff.co.uk* ↩ *8 rooms* ☖ *In-room: no a/c. In-hotel: bar, Wi-Fi hotspot, some pets allowed* ▤ *AE, MC, V* ⎮◯⎮ *BP.*

NIGHTLIFE AND THE ARTS

NIGHTLIFE Cardiff's clubs and pubs make for a lively nighttime scene. **Café Jazz** (☒ *21 St. Mary St.* ☎ *029/2038–7026*) presents live jazz five nights a week and has TV screens in the bar and restaurant so you can enjoy the on-stage action. **Clwb Ifor Bach** (☒ *Womanby St.* ☎ *029/2023–2199*), a distinctively Welsh club (its name means "Little Ivor's Club"), has three floors of eclectic music, from funk to folk to rock.

THE ARTS The city's big theaters present a full program of entertainment: drama and comedy, pop and the classics. The huge **Cardiff International Arena** (☒ *Mary Ann St.* ☎ *029/2022–4488*) showcases artists who can draw huge crowds, from Tom Jones to Bob Dylan. **St. David's Hall** (☒ *The Hayes* ☎ *029/2087–8444* ⊕ *www.stdavidshallcardiff.co.uk*), a popular venue, presents the Welsh Proms in July, attracting major international orchestras and soloists. It also stages rock, pop, jazz, and folk events.

New Theatre (☒ *Park Pl.* ☎ *029/2087–8889* ⊕ *www.newtheatrecardiff. co.uk*), a refurbished Edwardian playhouse, presents big names, including the Royal Shakespeare Company, the National Theatre, and the Northern Ballet.

Wales has one of Britain's four major opera companies, the outstanding **Welsh National Opera** (☒ *Wales Millennium Centre, Cardiff Bay* ☎ *029/2063–5000* ⊕ *www.wno.org.uk*). The company spends most of its time touring Wales and England.

SHOPPING

Canopied Victorian and Edwardian shopping arcades lined with specialty stores weave in and out of the city's modern shopping complexes. The **Cardiff Antiques Centre** (⊠ *Royal Arcade* ☎ *029/2039–8891*), in an 1856 arcade, is a good place to buy vintage jewelry. Cardiff's traditional **covered market** (⊠ *The Hayes* ☎ *029/2087–1214*) sells tempting fresh foods beneath its Victorian glass canopy. **Melin Tregwynt** (⊠ *26 Royal Arcade* ☎ *029/2022–4997* ⊕ *www.melintregwynt.co.uk*) is an elegant shop selling woolen clothing, bags, and cushions woven in an old Pembrokeshire mill.

ABERGAVENNY

28 mi north of Cardiff.

The market town of Abergavenny, near Brecon Beacons National Park, is a popular base for walkers and hikers. It also has a ruined castle and is near some notable industrial heritage sites, including the excellent Big Pit: National Coal Museum.

15

ESSENTIALS

Visitor Information Abergavenny (⊠ *Swan Meadow, Monmouth Rd.* ☎ *01873/853254*).

EXPLORING

The popular **Abergavenny Food Festival** (☎ *01873/851643* ⊕ *www. abergavennyfoodfestival.com*), held over a weekend in September, has lectures, demonstrations, and a food market. It's another sign of the growing interest in Welsh food.

Ruined **Abergavenny Castle**, built early in the 11th century, witnessed a tragic event on Christmas in 1176: the Norman knight William de Braose invited the neighboring Welsh chieftains to a feast and, in a crude attempt to gain control of the area, had them all slaughtered as they sat to dine. The Welsh retaliated and virtually demolished the castle. Most of what now remains dates from the 13th and 14th centuries. The castle's 19th-century hunting lodge houses the excellent museum with exhibits about area history. The re-creation of a Victorian Welsh farmhouse kitchen includes old utensils and butter molds. ⊠ *Castle Museum, Castle St.* ☎ *01873/854282* ☐ *Free* ☉ *Mar.–Oct., Mon.–Sat. 11–1 and 2–5, Sun. 2–5; Nov.–Feb., Mon.–Sat. 11–1 and 2–4.*

West of Abergavenny lie the valleys—the Rhondda is the most famous—so well described by Richard Llewellyn in his 1939 novel *How Green Was My Valley*. The slag heaps of the coal mines are green now, thanks to land reclamation plans. The area southwest of Abergavenny, around the former iron- and coal-mining town of Blaenavon, has been named a World Heritage Site by UNESCO; it provides a fascinating glimpse into Wales's industrial past. At the **Big Pit: National Coal Museum**, ex-miners take you underground on a tour of an authentic coal mine for a look at the hard life of the South Wales miner. You can also see the pithead baths and workshops. ⊠ *Off A4043, Blaenavon* ☎ *01495/790311* ⊕ *www.museumwales.ac.uk* ☐ *Free* ☉ *Feb.–Nov., daily 9:30–5; underground tours 10–3:30.*

Fodor's Choice
★

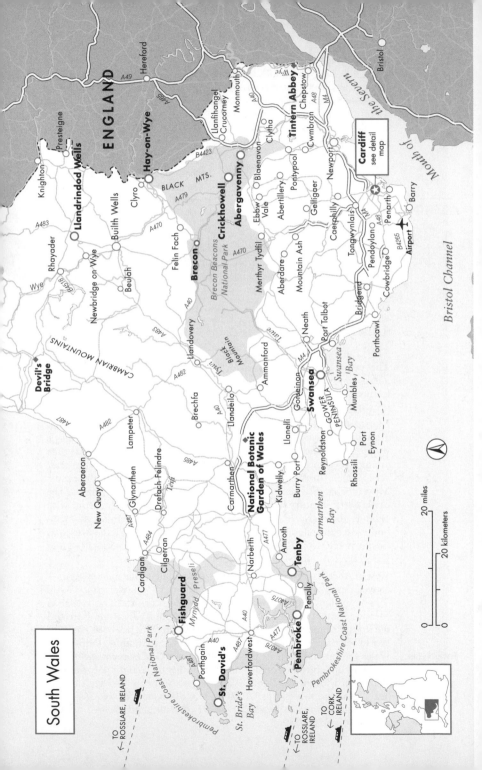

The **Blaenavon Ironworks,** dating from 1789, trace the entire process of iron production in that era. Well-preserved blast furnaces, a water-balance lift used to transport materials to higher ground, and a terraced row of workers' cottages show how the business operated. ⊠ *A4043, Blaenavon* ☎ *01495/792615* ⊕ *www.cadw. wales.gov.uk* ⊠ *Free* ⊙ *Apr.–Oct., daily 10–5; Nov.–Mar., Fri. and Sat. 9:30–4, Sun. 11–4.*

> ### LOVE SPOONS
>
> The rural Welsh custom of giving one's beloved a wooden spoon intricately hand carved with symbols of love dates from the mid-17th century. Motifs include hearts, flowers, doves, intertwined vines, and chain links. These days you don't have to make the effort yourself, because shops all over Wales sell them as souvenirs.

WHERE TO EAT AND STAY

££
MODERN BRITISH
✕ **Clytha Arms.** A converted house on the banks of the River Usk near Abergavenny serves imaginative modern food in a relaxed setting. Try the wild sea bass with crab-and-laver sauce. You can eat very cheaply in the bar (try the real ales) or pay a little more in the restaurant. ⊠ *Off B4598, Clytha* ☎ *01873/840206* ⊕ *www.clytha-arms.com* ⊟ *AE, MC, V* ⊙ *Closed Mon.*

£££
🛏 **Llansantfraed Court Hotel.** This grand country house dating from 1400 is set on 20 acres of well-tended grounds with a trout lake and views of the Brecon Beacons. The rooms are large and have four-poster beds. There's a log fire in the lounge, and the terrace is perfect for afternoon tea. The acclaimed restaurant is known for using organic meats. **Pros:** excellent food; peaceful setting; great for anglers. **Cons:** unexciting decor; out-of-the-way location. ⊠ *Old Raglan Rd., Clytha* ☎ *01873/840678* ⊕ *www.llch.co.uk* ⊠ *21 rooms* ⌕ *In-room: no a/c, Wi-Fi. In-hotel: restaurant, room service, bar, laundry service, Internet terminal, Wi-Fi hotspot, some pets allowed* ⊟ *AE, MC, V* ⊚*BP.*

15

CRICKHOWELL

5 mi northwest of Abergavenny.

If you take A40 northwest out of Abergavenny, you pass Sugar Loaf mountain and come to Crickhowell, a charming town on the banks of the River Usk with little shops, an ancient bridge, and a ruined castle.

ESSENTIALS

Visitor Information Crickhowell (⊠ *Beaufort St.* ☎ *01873/812105* ⊕ *www. crickhowellinfo.org.uk*).

EXPLORING

Tretower Court, 3 mi northwest of Crickhowell, is a splendid example of a fortified medieval manor house. Nearby, and part of the site, are the ruins of a Norman castle. ⊠ *A479* ☎ *01874/730279* ⊕ *www.cadw. wales.gov.uk* ⊠ *£3* ⊙ *Mar.–Oct., daily 10–5; Nov.–Apr., Fri. and Sat. 10–4, Sun. 11–4.*

WHERE TO STAY

££–£££ 🛏 **Bear Hotel.** In the middle of town, this coaching inn is full of character. The low-beamed bar, decorated with memorabilia from the days when stagecoaches stopped here, has a log fire in winter. Rooms in the hotel or in a modern addition in the former stable yard vary widely; the most luxurious have four-poster beds and antiques. The Bear serves creative contemporary cuisine, including excellent-value bar food. **Pros:** friendly bar; in the heart of Crickhowell; good food. **Cons:** some rooms overlook the road; rooms vary in size; can get busy on weekends. ⊠ *A40* ☎ *01873/810408* ⊕ *www.bearhotel.co.uk* 🛏 *35 rooms* ⟡ *In-room: no a/c, DVD, Wi-Fi. In-hotel: restaurant, room service, bar, laundry service, Wi-Fi hotspot, some pets allowed* ⊟ *AE, MC, V* 🍽 *BP.*

BRECON

14 mi northwest of Crickhowell, 19 mi northwest of Abergavenny, 41 mi north of Cardiff.

Brecon, a historic market town of narrow passageways, Georgian buildings, and pleasant riverside walks, is also the gateway to Brecon Beacons National Park. It's particularly appealing on market days (Tuesday and Friday). You may want to purchase a hand-carved wooden love spoon similar to those on display in the Brecknock Museum.

GETTING HERE AND AROUND

Brecon's nearest railway stations are at Merthyr Tydfil and Abergavenny (both about 19 mi away). Beacons Bus service runs to many parts of Brecon Beacons National Park. Brecon is a handsome town that is a joy to explore on foot—especially the riverside walk along the Promenade.

ESSENTIALS

Visitor Information Brecon (⊠ *Market Car Park* ☎ *01874/622485*).

EXPLORING

Cavernous **Brecon Cathedral** (☎ *01874/623857* ⊕ *www.breconcathedral. org.uk*), with a heritage center that traces its history, stands on the hill above the middle of town.

In the colonnaded Shire Hall built in 1842 is the **Brecknock Museum** (⊠ *Captain's Walk* ☎ *01874/624121*), with its artifacts from rural life, art exhibits, superb collection of carved love spoons, and perfectly preserved 19th-century assize court.

The military exhibits in the **South Wales Borderers' Museum** span centuries of conflict; some relate to battles in which this regiment participated. The Zulu Room recalls the Borderers' defense of Rorke's Drift in the Anglo-Zulu war of 1879, an action dramatized in the 1964 film *Zulu,* starring Michael Caine. ⊠ *The Barracks* ☎ *01874/613310* ⊕ *www.rrw. org.uk* 🏷 *£3* ☉ *Oct.–Mar., weekdays 10–5; Apr.–Sept., weekdays 10–5, Sat. 10–4.*

South of Brecon the skyline fills with mountains, and wild, windswept uplands stretch to the horizon in Brecon Beacons National Park. The **Brecon Beacons National Park Visitor Centre** on Mynydd Illtyd, a grassy stretch of upland west of A470, is an excellent source of information

HIKING AND BIKING IN WALES

Hiking and walking are the most popular outdoor activities in Wales, and a great way to see the country. Long-distance paths include the Pembrokeshire Coast Path (which runs all along the spectacular shores of southwest Wales), the south–north Offa's Dyke Path, based on the border between England and Wales established by King Offa in the 8th century, and the Glyndr Way, a 128-mi-long highland route that traverses Mid Wales from the border town of Knighton via Machynlleth to Welshpool. Signposted footpaths in Wales's forested areas are short and easy to follow. Dedicated enthusiasts might prefer the wide-open spaces of Brecon Beacons National Park or the mountains of Snowdonia.

Wales's reputation as both an on-road and off-road cycling mecca is well established. There's an amazing choice of scenic routes and terrain from challenging off-road tracks (⊕ *www.mtbwales.com* is for the serious cyclist) to long-distance road rides and gentle family trails; VisitWales has information to get you started.

CONTACTS AND RESOURCES
Cycling Wales (⊕ *www.cycling. visitwales.com*). **Offa's Dyke Centre** (☎ *01547/528753* ⊕ *www.offusdyke. demon.co.uk*). **Pembrokeshire Coast Path** (⊕ *www.nationaltrail. co.uk*). **Ramblers' Association in Wales** (☎ *029/2064–4308* ⊕ *www. ramblers.org.uk/wales*).

for activities within this 519-square-mi park. It also gives wonderful panoramic views across to Pen-y-fan, at 2,907 feet the highest peak in South Wales. If you plan to explore Wales's open moorlands on foot, come well equipped. Mist and rain can quickly descend, and the Beacons' summits are exposed to high winds. ⊠ *Off A470, Libanus, Brecon* ✚ *5½ mi southwest of Brecon* ☎ *01874/623366* ⊕ *www.breconbeacons. org* 🎫 *Free; fee for parking* ⊗ *Daily 9:30–5.*

WHERE TO EAT AND STAY

£ ✕ **Brecon Beacons National Park Visitor Centre Tea Room and Restaurant.** The
BISTRO spectacular view across the Beacons and homemade dishes make this a very popular spot. The parsnip-and-apple soup and the Welsh Black beef pie are among the good choices. You can indulge in a cream tea or fresh-baked cake, or just have coffee and enjoy the view. ⊠ *Off A470, Libanus, Brecon* ☎ *01874/624979* ⊕ *www.breconbeacons.org* 🗖 *MC, V* ⊗ *No dinner.*

£££ ✕ **Felin Fach Griffin.** Old and new blend perfectly in this modern country-
BRITISH style inn with old wood floors, comfy leather sofas, and terra-cotta–color stone walls hung with bright prints. The excellent menu makes use of fresh local produce, much of it coming from the Griffin's own organic garden. Try the wild venison with butternut squash, roasted carrots, and elderberries. Two-course lunches (£15.90) and dinners (£21) are great deals. ⊠ *A470, east of Brecon, Felin Fach* ☎ *01874/620111* ⊕ *www.eatdrinksleep.ltd.uk* 🗖 *MC, V.*

££ ⊞ **The Coach House.** This former coach house provides contemporary town-house lodging. The Welsh-speaking owners are a wealth of information on where to go and what to do in the Brecon Beacons. At the end of a hectic day's activities they offer relaxing holistic massages. Inventive Welsh breakfasts and evening meals are served in the small stylish restaurant. **Pros:** friendly hosts; central location. **Cons:** on a main road; garden is small. ⊠ *Orchard St.* ☏ *01874/620043* ⊕ *www. coachhousebrecon.co.uk* ⇆ *7 rooms* ⚴ *In-room: no a/c, safe, DVD, Wi-Fi. In-hotel: restaurant, room service, bar, Wi-Fi hotspot, no kids under 16* ⊟ *MC, V* ⑩ *BP.*

££   ⊞ **Felin Glais.** In the 17th century Felin Glais was a barn; enlarged but without losing its ancient character, it provides spacious and comfortable accommodations. The owners are extremely sociable, and many of their customers become friends. They are also enthusiastic about cooking (meals are available weekends for guests) and make good use of locally sourced produce. **Pros:** beautiful building; spacious rooms; good food. **Cons:** dogs allowed in rooms; communal dining table. ⊠ *Abersycir, near Brecon* ☏ *01874/623107* ⊕ *www.felinglais.co.uk* ⇆ *4 rooms* ⚴ *In-room: no a/c, no phone, refrigerator, DVD, Wi-Fi. In-hotel: restaurant, laundry service, Wi-Fi hotspot, some pets allowed* ⊟ *No credit cards* ⑩ *BP.*

NIGHTLIFE AND THE ARTS

Each summer the town hosts **Brecon Jazz** (☏ *0870/990–1299* ⊕ *www. breconjazz.co.uk*), an international jazz festival that attracts top performers.

Theatr Brycheiniog (⊠ *Canal Wharf* ☏ *01874/611622*), on the canal, is the town's impressive venue for the arts. It also has a gallery and waterfront bistro.

SPORTS AND THE OUTDOORS

Crickhowell Adventure Gear (⊠ *Ship St.* ☏ *01874/611586*), which also has a smaller shop in Crickhowell, sells outdoor gear such as clothes and climbing equipment.

Brecon is an ideal center for on- and off-road cycling. **Biped Cycles** (⊠ *10 Ship St.* ☏ *01874/622296* ⊕ *www.bipedcycles.co.uk*) will rent you the right bike and equipment to take to the hills.

SWANSEA

36 mi southwest of Brecon, 40 mi west of Cardiff.

Swansea, the birthplace of poet Dylan Thomas (1914–53), marks the end of the industrial region of South Wales. Despite some undistinguished postwar architecture, Wales's second-largest city (population 224,000) has a number of appealing sights, including the waterfront pedestrian Sail Bridge, which has a 300-foot-high mast.

GETTING HERE AND AROUND

There's an hourly rail service between Swansea and London's Paddington Station, and regular rail services from Swansea to the Midlands and north of England. The city has direct National Express coach services to the rest of Wales, London, and other U.K. cities. The city is best explored on foot; it takes only 10 minutes to walk from the shopping center to the beach.

ESSENTIALS

Visitor Information Swansea (✉ *Plymouth St.* ☎ *01792/468321* ⊕ *www. visitswanseabay.com*).

EXPLORING
TOP ATTRACTIONS

Dylan Thomas Centre. Situated on the banks of the Tawe close to the Maritime Quarter, the Dylan Thomas Centre is the National Literature Centre for Wales. The center houses a permanent Dylan Thomas exhibition, art gallery, restaurant, and café-bookshop, and hosts literary events such as the annual Dylan Thomas Festival. ■ TIP→ **Those interested in following in the poet's footsteps can buy a booklet that outlines the Dylan Thomas Trail around South Wales.** ⊠ *Somerset Pl.* ☎ *01792/463980* ⊕ *www.dylanthomas.com* ✉ *Free* ⊙ *Daily 10–4:30.*

★ **Gower Peninsula.** The 14-mi-long Gower Peninsula, only minutes away from Swansea's center, was the first part of Britain to be declared an area of Outstanding Natural Beauty. Its shores are a succession of sheltered sandy bays and awesome headlands. Actress Catherine Zeta-Jones was born here, in the Victorian seaside resort of Mumbles. ■ TIP→ **For the area's most breathtaking views, head to Rhossili on its western tip.**

Maritime Quarter. Swansea was extensively bombed during World War II, and its old dockland has reemerged as the splendid Maritime Quarter, a modern marina with attractive housing and shops and a seafront that commands views across the sweep of Swansea Bay.

☾ ★ **National Botanic Garden of Wales.** Opened in 2000, this sprawling, modern botanic garden celebrates conservation and education. It's based at Middleton Park, a 568-acre, 18th-century estate with seven lakes, cascades, fountains, and a Japanese garden. The garden's centerpiece is the Norman Foster–designed Great Glass House, the largest single-span greenhouse in the world, which blends into the curving landforms of the Tywi Valley. The greenhouse's interior landscape includes a 40-foot-deep ravine and thousands of plants from all the Mediterranean climates of the world. There's plenty to occupy a day here. The garden, 20 mi northwest of Swansea, is signposted off the main road between Swansea and Carmarthen. ⊠ *Off A48 or B4310, Llanarthne* ☎ *01558/668–7688* ⊕ *www.gardenofwales.org.uk* ✉ *£8* ⊙ *Apr.–Oct., daily 10–6; Nov.–Mar., daily 10–4:30.*

☾ **National Waterfront Museum.** Housed in a construction of steel, slate, and glass grafted onto a historic redbrick building, the National Waterfront Museum's galleries have 15 theme areas. State-of-the-art interactive technology and artifacts bring Welsh industrial and maritime history to a 21st-century audience. ⊠ *Oystermouth Rd., Maritime Quarter* ☎ *01792/638950* ⊕ *www.museumwales.ac.uk* ✉ *Free* ⊙ *Daily 10–5.*

WORTH NOTING

Covered market. Swansea's covered market, part of Quadrant Shopping Centre, is the best fresh-foods market in Wales. You can buy cockles from the Penclawdd beds on the nearby Gower Peninsula, and laverbread, that unique Welsh delicacy made from seaweed, which is usually served with bacon and eggs.

15

Egypt Centre. A substantial collection of ancient Egyptian artifacts is on display here, including bead necklaces from the time of Tutankhamen and the beautiful painted coffin of a Theban musician. ⊠ *University of Wales–Swansea, Singleton Park* ☎ *01792/295960* ⊕ *www.swansea. ac.uk/egypt* ☜ *Free* ☉ *Tues.–Sat. 10–4.*

Swansea Museum. Founded in 1841, this museum contains a quirky and eclectic collection that includes an Egyptian mummy, china, local archaeological exhibits, and the intriguing Cabinet of Curiosity, which holds artifacts from Swansea's past. The museum is close to the Maritime Quarter. ⊠ *Victoria Rd.* ☎ *01792/653763* ⊕ *www.swanseaheritage. net* ☜ *Free* ☉ *Tues.–Sun. 10–5.*

WHERE TO EAT AND STAY

£££ ✕ **La Braseria.** This lively, welcoming spot resembles a Spanish bodega
SPANISH (wine cellar), with its flamenco music, oak barrels, and whitewashed walls. Among the house specialties are sea bass in rock salt, roast suckling pig, and pheasant (in season, of course). There's a good choice of 140 Spanish and French wines. ⊠ *28 Wind St.* ☎ *01792/469683* ⊕ *www.labraseria.com* ☰ *AE, MC, V* ☉ *Closed Sun.*

£ ✕ **Verdi's.** This family-run Italian ice-cream parlor, café, and restaurant
ITALIAN sits right on the seafront. Every indoor and outdoor table has panoramic views of Swansea Bay. ⊠ *Knab Rock* ☎ *01792/369135* ⊕ *www.verdis-cafe.co.uk* ☰ *MC,V.*

££££–£££££ ⊞ **Fairyhill.** Luxuriously furnished public rooms, spacious bedrooms,
★ and 24 acres of wooded grounds make this 18th-century country house in the western part of the scenic Gower Peninsula a restful retreat. The restaurant is renowned for sophisticated cuisine and a well-chosen wine list. The fixed-price dinner menus (£35 for two courses, £45 for three) are hard to beat. **Pros:** peaceful surroundings; local seafood a specialty. **Cons:** difficult to find; restaurant always busy. ⊠ *Off B4295, 11 mi southwest of Swansea, Reynoldston* ☎ *01792/390139* ⊕ *www.fairyhill. net* ⊷ *8 rooms* ⟁ *In-room: no a/c, DVD, Wi-Fi. In-hotel: restaurant, bar, laundry service, Internet terminal, Wi-Fi hotspot, no kids under 8* ☰ *AE, MC, V* ⛾ *BP.*

£££–££££ ⊞ **Morgans.** This old Victorian Port Authority building in the Maritime Quarter has lost none of its period features: moldings, pillars, stained glass, and wood floors. The modern rooms, in both the main building and in the Town House across the road, are immaculate with crisp cotton sheets and drapes of satin, silk, and suede. The stylish restaurant serves dishes like panfried fillet of local sea bass with crushed-pea-and-potato cake and watercress sauce, and lighter treats at the café-bar. **Pros:** near the marina; short walk to shops; maritime flair. **Cons:** no outdoor space; busy bars; popular for weddings. ⊠ *Somerset Pl.* ☎ *01792/484848* ⊕ *www.morganshotel.co.uk* ⊷ *41 rooms* ⟁ *In-room: no a/c (some), DVD, Internet (some), Wi-Fi (some). In-hotel: restaurant, room service, bars, gym, laundry service, Internet terminal, Wi-Fi hotspot* ☰ *AE, MC, V.*

TENBY

53 mi west of Swansea.

Pastel-color Georgian houses cluster around a harbor in this seaside resort, where two golden sandy beaches stretch below the hotel-lined cliff top. Medieval Tenby's ancient town walls still stand, enclosing narrow streets and passageways full of shops, inns, and places to eat. From the harbor you can take a short boat trip to beautiful Caldey Island and visit the monastery, where monks make a famous perfume from the local plants.

GETTING HERE AND AROUND

Tenby is on the southwest Wales rail route from London's Paddington Station. You have to change trains at Swansea. The center of Tenby, a maze of narrow medieval streets, has parking restrictions. During the summer the downtown area is closed to traffic, so you'll have to park in more remote lots and take the park-and-ride shuttle buses.

15

TIMING

Tenby, Pembrokeshire's most popular seaside resort, is very busy in summer and on holiday weekends. During these times booking ahead is essential.

ESSENTIALS

Visitor Information Tenby (✉ *Unit 2, Upper Park Rd.* ☎ *01834/842402*).

EXPLORING

The ruins of a castle stand on a headland overlooking the sea, close to the informative **Tenby Museum and Art Gallery** (✉ *Castle Hill* ☎ *01834/842809* ⊕ *www.tenbymuseum.org.uk*), which recalls the town's maritime history and its growth as a fashionable resort.

The late-15th-century **Tudor Merchant's House**, in town, shows how a prosperous trader would have lived in the Tenby of old. ✉ *Quay Hill* ☎ *01834/842279* ⊕ *www.nationaltrust.org.uk* 🎫 *£3* ⊙ *Apr.–Oct., Sun.–Fri. 11–5.*

WHERE TO EAT AND STAY

£££
BRITISH
✗ **Plantagenet House.** Flickering candles, open fireplaces, exposed stone walls, and top-notch locally sourced food are hallmarks of this popular restaurant and bar. The setting is a beautiful 15th-century Merchant's House in the heart of Tenby. ✉ *Quay Hill* ☎ *01834/842350* ▭ *MC, V* ⊙ *Closed Jan.–mid-Feb.*

£
📷 **Ivy Bank Guest House.** This comfortable and immaculate Victorian house is just a five-minute stroll from the sea. The breakfast menu is extensive and the rooms are furnished with light flowery fabrics. **Pros:** reasonable rates; walled garden; close to sea. **Cons:** no parking lot; no sea views; a little dated. ✉ *Harding St., Tenby* ☎ *01834/842311* ⊕ *www.ivybanktenby.co.uk* 🛏 *5 rooms* ⋄ *In-room: no a/c, no phone. In-hotel: bar* ▭ *AE, MC, V* ⦿*BP.*

£££–££££
📷 **Penally Abbey.** Built on the site of a 6th-century abbey on 5 acres of lush forest overlooking Camarthen Bay, this dignified 18th-century house is awash with period details. Bedrooms in the house are furnished with antiques and four-poster beds, whereas those in the light and airy lodges have a touch of urban chic. The hotel is relaxed rather

than stuffy, but service is first-class. **Pros:** informal luxury; great views; friendly hosts. **Cons:** small pool; 2 mi from Tenby. ⊠ *Off A4139, 2 mi west of Tenby, Penally* ☎ *01834/843033* ⊕ *www.penally-abbey.com* ⇒ *17 rooms* ⚹ *In-room: no a/c, Wi-Fi. In-hotel: restaurant, bar, pool, Wi-Fi hotspot* ⊟ *AE, MC, V* ⍟⊙⍟ *BP.*

££££–£££££   ⌖ **St. Brides Spa Hotel.** Between Amroth and Tenby, this luxury hotel perches in a breathtaking location above Carmarthen Bay. Most of the superbly appointed rooms have stunning sea views, and there's a state-of-the-art spa with infinity pool, steam room, sauna, salt infusion room, and ice fountain. The restaurant specializes in locally sourced produce, seafood being a particular highlight. **Pros:** amazing view; wonderful spa; displays of contemporary Welsh art. **Cons:** steep walk up from beach; area lacks charm. ⊠ *Saundersfoot* ☎ *01834/812304* ⊕ *www. stbridesspahotel.com* ⇒ *35 rooms* ⚹ *In-room: no a/c, DVD, Internet (some), Wi-Fi (some). In-hotel: restaurant, room service, bar, pool, spa, laundry service, Wi-Fi hotspot* ⊟ *AE, DC, MC, V* ⍟⊙⍟ *BP.*

PEMBROKE

13 mi west of Tenby, 13 mi south of Haverfordwest.

In Pembroke you are entering the heart of Pembrokeshire, one of the most curious regions of Wales. All around are English names such as Deeplake, New Hedges, and Rudbaxton. Locals more often than not don't understand Welsh, and South Pembrokeshire is known as "Little England beyond Wales." History is responsible: in the 11th century the English conquered this region with the aid of the Normans, and the English and Normans intermarried and set about building castles.

ESSENTIALS
Visitor Information Pembroke (⊠ *Commons Rd.* ☎ *01437/776499*).

EXPLORING
One of the most magnificent Norman fortresses is massive **Pembroke Castle**, dating from 1190. Its walls remain stout, its gatehouse mighty, and the enormous cylindrical keep proved so impregnable to cannon fire in the Civil War that Cromwell's men had to starve out its Royalist defenders. You can climb the towers and walk the walls for fine views. This was the birthplace, in 1457, of Henry Tudor, who seized the throne of England as Henry VII in 1485, and whose son Henry VIII united Wales and England in 1536. ☎ *01646/684585* ⊕ *www.pembroke-castle. co.uk* ⊠ *£4.50* ⊙ *Apr.–Sept., daily 9:30–6; Oct. and Mar., daily 10–5; Nov.–Feb., daily 10–4.*

ST. DAVID'S

25 mi northwest of Pembroke, 16 mi southwest of Fishguard.

This tiny village holds what has been described as the holiest ground in Great Britain, the Cathedral of St. David and the shrine of the patron saint of Wales, who founded a monastic community here in the 6th century. The entire area around St. David's, steeped in sanctity and history, was a place of pilgrimage for many centuries, two journeys to St. David's equaling, in spiritual value, one to Rome. Here, on the savagely beautiful coastline, edged by the Pembrokeshire Coast Path, Pembrokeshire is at its unspoiled best. If you have a day to spare, the 6½-mi walk along the coastal path around the St. David's headland from St. Justinian to Caerfai Bay is magnificent. ■ TIP→ **Come in May and June to see the hedgerows and coastal path full of wildflowers.**

ESSENTIALS

Visitor Information St. David's Oriel y Parc (✉ *1 High St.* ☎ *01437/720392* ⊕ *www.orielyparc.co.uk*).

FISH WEEK

Pembrokeshire Fish Week takes place in late June and early July, celebrating all things fishy. Events include gourmet seafood evenings, mackerel barbecues, sea fishing, and kayak trips. For dates and locations, visit ⊕ *www. pembrokeshire.gov.uk/fishweek*.

EXPLORING

Unlike any other cathedral, the venerable 12th-century **St. David's Cathedral** (⊕ *www.stdavidscathedral.org.uk*) does not seek to dominate the surrounding countryside with its enormous mass; it is in a vast hollow. You must climb down 39 steps (called locally the Thirty-Nine Articles) to enter the cathedral. Its location helped protect the church from Viking raiders by hiding it from the view of invaders who came by sea. From the outside, purple-stone St. David's has a simple austerity that harmonizes with the beautiful windswept countryside, but the interior is more intricate. Treasures include the fan vaulting in Bishop Vaughan's Chapel, the delicate carving on the choir stalls, and the oaken roof over the nave. Across the brook are the ruins of the medieval **Bishop's Palace.** ☎ *01437/720517* ⊕ *www.cadw.wales.gov.uk* ☑ *£3* ☉ *Apr.–June, Sept., and Oct., daily 9–5; July and Aug., daily 9:30–6; Nov.–Mar., Mon.–Sat. 10–4, Sun. 11–4.*

St. David's Oriel y Parc (✉ *1 High St.* ☎ *01437/720392* ⊕ *www.orielyparc. co.uk* ☉ *Daily 9:30–5:30*) was built entirely using green technology. The 180-degree monopitch roof is aligned with the path of the sun and supported by conical pillars, and the building houses a visitor information center and gallery dedicated to the interpretation of landscape. The exhibits are drawn from the huge collection of art and artifacts at the National Museum Wales.

WHERE TO STAY

££££–£££££ ☒ **Warpool Court Hotel.** Overlooking a stunning stretch of coastline, this hotel sits on a bluff above St. Non's Bay. Many rooms have sea views; decorative tiles adorn public areas and some bedrooms. The building dates from the 1860s, when it housed St. David's Cathedral Choir School. The well-equipped hotel offers contemporary cuisine, with fish, including roast halibut and wild bass fillets, as a specialty; the dining room overlooks the water. **Pros:** on the coastal path; peaceful gardens; good food. **Cons:** unattractive entrance; expensive rates. ⊠ *Off Goat St.* ☎ *01437/720300* ⊕ *www.warpoolcourthotel.com* ⇆ *25 rooms* ⌂ *In-room: no a/c, Wi-Fi. In-hotel: restaurant, room service, bar, tennis court, pool, gym, laundry service, Internet terminal, Wi-Fi hotspot, some pets allowed* ▤ *AE, MC, V* ⍩ *BP.*

15

FISHGUARD

16 mi northeast of St. David's, 26 mi north of Pembroke.

Fishguard is a town of three parts. The ferry terminal at Goodwick across the waters of Fishguard Bay sees activity year-round as boats sail to Rosslare, Ireland, across the Irish Sea. Fishguard's main town stands on high ground just south of Goodwick, separating the modern port from its old harbor in the Lower Town, where gabled cottages are grouped around the quayside. The Lower Town was the setting for the 1973 film of Dylan Thomas's *Under Milkwood,* which starred Elizabeth Taylor and Welsh actor Richard Burton.

ESSENTIALS

Visitor Information Fishguard (⊠ *Town Hall, Market Sq.* ☎ *01437/776636*).

EXPLORING

The 100-foot-long **Last Invasion Tapestry,** on display in a gallery in the Town Hall, is modeled on the famous Bayeux Tapestry that celebrates the Norman invasion of 1066, but this work commemorates a far less successful assault. In 1797 a small French force, commanded by a U.S. citizen, landed near Fishguard. After some skirmishing the group was allegedly forced to surrender by local women. In 1997, 70 Fishguard women spent 40,000 hours stitching this impressive tapestry. ⊠ *Town Hall, Market Sq.* ☎ *01437/776639* ☜ *Free* ☉ *Apr.–Sept., Mon.–Wed., Fri., and Sat. 9:30–5, Thurs. 9:30–6:30; Oct.–Mar., Mon.–Wed., and Fri. 9:30–5, Thurs. 9:30–6:30, Sat. 9:30–1.*

UNDERSTANDING ENGLAND

English Architectural Styles

Books and Movies

Chronology

ENGLISH ARCHITECTURAL STYLES

In England you can see structures that go back to the dawn of history, such as the hauntingly mysterious circles of monoliths at Stonehenge or Avebury, or view the surviving remains of the Roman Empire preserved in Bath, Cirencester, and other towns. On the other hand, you can startle your eyes with the very current designs of contemporary architects in areas such as London's Docklands or the City. Knowing a few hallmarks of particular styles can enhance your enjoyment. Here, then, is a primer of a millennium of architectural styles.

Norman

Duke William of Normandy brought the solid Norman style to Britain when he invaded and conquered England in 1066, although William's predecessor, King Edward (the Confessor) used the style in the building of Westminster Abbey a little earlier, in 1042. Until around 1200 it was favored for buildings of any importance, and William's castles and churches soon dominated the countryside.

Norman towers tended to be hefty and square, arches were always round-top, and the vaulting was barrel shaped. Decoration was mostly geometrical, but within those limits, ornate. Norman motte-and-bailey castles had two connecting stockaded mounds, with the keep on the higher mound, and other buildings on the lower mound. *Best seen in the Tower of London and in the cathedrals of St. Albans, Ely, Gloucester, Durham, and Norwich, and at Tewkesbury Abbey.*

Gothic Early English

From 1130 to 1300, pointed arches began to supplant rounded ones, buttresses became heavier than the Norman variety, and windows lost their rounded tops to become more pointed and lancet shaped. Buildings climbed skyward and were less squat and heavy, with the soaring effect accentuated by steep roofs and spires. *Best seen in the cathedrals of York, Salisbury, Ely, Worcester, Wells (interior), and*

Canterbury (east end), and Westminster Abbey's Chapter House.

Decorated. From the late 1100s until around 1400, elegance and ornament became fully integrated into architectural design, rather than applied to the surface of a solid, basic form. Windows filled more of the walls and were divided into sections by carved mullions. Vaulting grew increasingly complex, with ribs and ornamented bosses proliferating; spires became even more pointed; arches took on the ogee shape, with its unique double curve. This style was one of England's greatest gifts to world architecture. *Best seen at the cathedrals of Wells, Lincoln, Exeter, Durham (east transept), and Ely (Lady Chapel and Octagon).*

Perpendicular. In later Gothic architecture, the emphasis on the vertical grew more pronounced, as shown in features such as slender pillars, huge expanses of glass, and superb fan vaulting resembling the formalized branches of frozen trees. Walls were divided by panels. One of the chief areas in which to see Perpendicular architecture is East Anglia, where towns that grew rich from the wool trade built magnificent churches in the style. Houses, too, began to reflect the prevailing taste. Perpendicular Gothic lasted for well over two centuries from its advent around 1330. *Best seen at St. George's Chapel in Windsor, Gloucester Cathedral (cloister), Henry VII's Chapel in Westminster Abbey, Bath Abbey, and King's College Chapel in Cambridge.*

Tudor

With the great period of cathedral building over, from 1500 to 1560 the nation's attention turned to the construction of spacious homes characterized by this latest fashionable architectural style. The rapidly expanding, newly rich middle class, created by the two Tudor Henrys (VII and VIII) to challenge the power of the aristocracy, built spacious manor houses, often on the foundations of pillaged monasteries. Thus began the era of the great stately homes. Brick replaced stone as the most popular medium, and plasterwork and carved wood displayed the elaborate motifs of the age.

Timber-frame and plaster buildings were also popular in this period for domestic and commercial use. Many "black-and-white" structures, as they are called, are copies made in later eras, but notable originals survive. (The Victorians are responsible for the fashion of painting half-timber buildings, of whatever era, black and white.) Wealthier individuals could afford to have the exposed wood beams carved or shaped; Little Moreton Hall, in Congleton near the Peak District, has wonderfully intricate patterns. Speke Hall in Liverpool is another notable example, and Shrewsbury and Ludlow in the Welsh Borders have many half-timber buildings in this style.

Another way the social climbers could make their mark, and ensure their place in the next world, was by building churches. Money earned in the wool trade continued to fund splendid parish churches. Some of the most magnificent are in Suffolk, Norfolk, and the Cotswolds *Domestic architecture is best seen at Hampton Court and St. James's Palace, London; for wool churches, Lavenham and Long Melford (though its tower is much later) in Suffolk, and Cirencester, Chipping Campden, Northleach, and Winchcombe in the Cotswolds.*

Renaissance Elizabethan

For a short period under Elizabeth I, 1560–1600, this development of Tudor style flourished as Italian influences began to seep into England, seen especially in symmetrical facades. The most notable example was Hardwick Hall in Derbyshire, built in the 1590s by Bess of Hardwick; the jingle that describes it goes "Hardwick Hall, more glass than wall." However grand the houses were, they were still on a human scale, warm and livable, built of a mellow amalgam of brick and stone. *Other great Elizabethan houses are Longleat in Wiltshire and Burghley House in Cambridgeshire.*

Jacobean

At the beginning of the 17th century, for the first 15 years of the reign of James I (the name Jacobean is taken from the Latin word for James, Jacobus), architecture did not change noticeably. Windows were still large in proportion to the wall surfaces. Gables, in the style of the Netherlands, were popular. Carved decoration in wood and plaster (especially the geometrical patterning called "strapwork," another element of Dutch origin, which resembled intertwined leather belts) remained exuberant, now even more so.

A change was on the way, though. Inigo Jones (1573–1652), the first great modern British architect, attempted to synthesize the architectural heritage of England with current Italian theories. Two of his finest remaining buildings—the Banqueting House in London and the Queen's House at Greenwich—epitomize his genius, which was to introduce to England the Italian-created Palladian style that would dominate England's architecture for centuries. It uses the classical Greek orders: Doric, Ionic, and Corinthian. The grand classical style that proved so monumentally effective under a hot Mediterranean sun was transformed in England, domesticated and tamed. Columns and pediments decorated the facades, and huge frescoes provided acres of color to interior walls and ceilings, all in the Italian manner.

Two quite distinct styles ran concurrently: the comfortably domestic and the purer classical in public buildings. They were finally fused by the talent of Christopher Wren. *Jacobean is best seen at the Bodleian Library, Oxford; Audley End, near Cambridge; Chastleton House, near Stow-on-the-Wold; Hatfield House, near St. Albans; and Emmanuel College, Cambridge.*

Wren and the English Baroque

The work of Sir Christopher Wren (1632–1723) constituted an architectural era all by itself. Not only was he one of the world's greatest architects, but he was also given an unparalleled opportunity in 1666 when the disastrous Great Fire of London wiped out the center of the capital, destroying no fewer than 89 churches and 13,200 houses. Although Wren's great scheme for a modern city center was rejected, he did build 52 churches in London, the greatest of which was St. Paul's, completed in just 35 years. The range of Wren's designs is extremely wide, from simple classical shapes to the extravagantly dramatic baroque. He was also at home with domestic architecture, where his combinations of brick and stone produced a warm, homey effect.

The influence of the Italian baroque can be seen in Sir John Vanbrugh's Blenheim Palace, where the facade echoes the piazza of St. Peter's in Rome, and at Vanbrugh's exuberant Castle Howard in Yorkshire.

Nicholas Hawksmoor, Wren's pupil, designed some notable London churches and also the baroque Mausoleum at Castle Howard. The baroque had only a brief heyday in England; by 1725 the Palladian style was firmly in favor and the vast pile of Blenheim was being mocked by trendsetters. *Wren's ecclesiastical architecture is best seen at St. Paul's Cathedral (baroque with classical touches) and his other remaining London churches, his domestic style at Hampton Court Palace, Kensington Palace, the Royal Hospital in Chelsea, and the Old Royal Naval College in Greenwich. English baroque is best seen at Blenheim Palace (Oxfordshire) and Castle Howard (Yorkshire).*

Palladian

In Britain this style is often referred to as Georgian, so called from the Hanoverian kings George I through IV, although it was introduced as early as Inigo Jones's time. During the 18th century, classical inspiration was thoroughly acclimatized.

Though they looked completely at home among the hills, lakes, and trees of the English countryside, Palladian buildings were derived from the Roman-inspired designs of the Italian architectural theorist Andrea Palladio (1508–80), with pillared porticoes, triangular pediments, and strictly balanced windows. In domestic architecture, this large-scale classicism was usually modified to quiet simplicity, preserving mathematical proportions of windows, doors, and the exactly calculated volume of room space, to create a feeling of balance and harmony.

The occasional departures from the classical manner at this time included the over-the-top Indian-style Royal Pavilion in Brighton, built for the prince regent (later George IV) by John Nash. The Regency style comes under the Palladian heading, though strictly speaking it lasted only for the few years of the actual Regency (1811–20).

Architects such as the brilliant Robert Adam, who was born in Scotland but also worked in England, handled the Palladian style with more freedom than their counterparts elsewhere in Europe, and the United States took its cue from the British. *Among the best Palladian examples are Regent's Park Terraces (London), the library at Kenwood (London), the Royal Crescent and other streets in Bath, Stourhead (Wiltshire), and Holkham Hall (Norfolk).*

Victorian

Elements of imaginative fantasy, already seen in the Palladian era, came to the fore during the long reign of Victoria (1837–1901). The country's vast profits made from the Industrial Revolution were spent lavishly. Civic building accelerated in all the major cities, with town halls modeled after medieval castles or French châteaux.

The Victorians plundered the past for styles, with Gothic, about which the scholarly Victorians were very knowledgeable, leading the field. The supreme examples here are the Houses of Parliament by Charles Barry and Augustus Pugin, and the Albert Memorial by George Gilbert Scott, both in London. (To distinguish between the Victorian variety and a version of the style that flourished in the late 1700s, the earlier one is commonly spelled "Gothick.") Among the other styles in the running was the attractively named, and self-explanatory, "Wrenaissance." *Other striking examples of Victorian architecture are Truro Cathedral, Manchester Town Hall, and Ironbridge.*

Edwardian

Toward the end of the Victorian era, in the late 1800s, architecture calmed down considerably, with a return to a solid sort of classicism, and even to a muted baroque. The Arts and Crafts movement, especially the work of William Morris (1834–96) and work inspired by Morris, produced simpler designs, sometimes returning to medieval models. In an age of increasing mechanization, craftsmanship was emphasized. Architectural elements incorporated stylized natural motifs. *Best seen in Buckingham Palace and the Admiralty Arch in London. Rodmarton Manor near Tetbury (the Cotswolds), and Blackwell in Windermere (the Lake District) are notable Arts and Crafts houses.*

Modern

A furious public debate has raged in Britain for years between traditionalists and the adherents of modernistic architecture. Britons tend to be strongly conservative when it comes to their environment. These arguments have been highlighted by the intervention of such notable figures as Prince Charles, who derides excessive modernism and who said, for instance, that the design for the Sainsbury Wing of the National Gallery in London's Trafalgar Square would be like "a monstrous carbuncle on the face of a much-loved and elegant friend."

One reason for the strength of this attitude is that the country suffered from much ill-conceived development after World War II, when large areas of city centers had to be rebuilt after the devastation caused by German bombs. Town planners and architects created badly built and worse-designed towers and shopping areas. Today, however, there is an increased readiness to embrace the new, as designers draw people into user-friendly, lighthearted buildings such as City Hall in London and the Sage Gateshead in Newcastle.

The situation created in the '50s and '60s is slowly being reversed. High-rise apartment blocks are being taken down and replaced by more humanly scaled housing. Commercial areas in a number of cities are slowly being rebuilt. The emphasis has gradually moved to planning, design, and construction that pays more attention to the needs of inhabitants. A healthier attitude also exists toward the conservation of old buildings. Happily, many that survived the wreckers' ball are being restored and put back to use.

Nowadays, a number of architectural styles prevail. A predominant one draws largely on the past, with nostalgic echoes of the country cottage, and leans heavily on variegated brickwork and close attention to decorative detail. Urban centers have buildings in the most innovative styles, which are exciting and ecologically sensitive, too, using light to more thoughtful effect. These new designs have turned many fatigued or declining areas, from Newcastle to Manchester, into destinations to see and be seen in.

In London, the Lloyd's of London tower in the City, by Sir Richard Rogers, designer of the Pompidou Center in Paris, began the trend toward modernism in the 1980s. The Millennium Dome, Rogers's tour de force, transformed the industrial blot of Greenwich peninsula; it closed but reopened in 2007 as O2, a performance venue. Sir Norman Foster's graceful Millennium Bridge became a landmark almost as soon as it opened. Foster's glassy masterpiece, City Hall, near Tower Bridge, has been knocked as a "glass testicle," but it is one of the boldest designs in London.

Skyscrapers in the City of London are the exception rather than the rule, although the regenerated space of the old Docklands has allowed more room for imagination, as at Canary Wharf. Other buildings, such as Barclays Bank with its jukebox dome, and Swiss Re's "Gherkin" at 30 St. Mary Axe, the latter by Foster and looking akin to a glittering carousel pole, have begun to push height limitations established because of the proximity of historic buildings.

Other centers of modern architectural innovation include Manchester, with the Imperial War Museum North by Daniel Libeskind. After the city center was bombed by the Irish Republican Army in 1996, Manchester received an impressive face-lift. Also in the north, Gateshead Quays is the spectacularly renovated industrial area around the River Tyne and Newcastle. The tilting Millennium Bridge in Newcastle is as dramatic as London's, and the city has opened the Baltic Centre for Contemporary Art, as well as the Sage, a curvaceous steel-and-glass music venue. Birmingham has the Selfridges department store, with its coat of shimmering disks, and Cornwall the Eden Project, the world's largest conservatories, which are set in a former china-clay pit and massed to make a giant glass crater.

Numerous cultural institutions, particularly in London, have undergone innovative renovations, in part to add visitor-friendly, interactive technology. The Royal Opera House, Tate Modern and Tate Britain, the Great Court at the British Museum, the Queen's Gallery, St. Pancras Station, and the Wellcome Wing at the Science Museum are among the noteworthy projects that have embraced the new, with a subtle emphasis on complementing the old. Anyone with an interest in architecture should visit the headquarters of the Royal Institute of British Architects (RIBA) in Portland Place, London, for exhibits on buildings great and small, new and old.

What's next? The approach of the 2012 Summer Olympics in London has prompted some ambitious building plans. Everyone's waiting for a swimming pool by world-renowned architect Zaha Hadid and the 1,016-foot "Shard" designed by Italian Renzo Piano—it will be the tallest building in London by 2012. *Among other buildings to see are Richmond House and the Clore Building at Tate Britain (in London), the campus of Sussex University (outside Brighton), the Royal Regatta Building (Henley), the Sainsbury Centre for the Visual Arts (Norwich), and the Lowry Centre (Manchester).*

BOOKS AND MOVIES

Fiction and Poetry

Many writers' names have become inextricably linked with the regions in which they set their books or plays. Hardy's Wessex, Daphne Du Maurier's Cornwall, Wordsworth's Lake District, Shakespeare's Arden, and Brontë Country in Yorkshire are now evocative catchphrases, treasured by local tourist boards. However hackneyed the tags may be, you *can* still get a heightened insight into an area through the eyes of authors of genius, even though they may have written a century or more ago. Here are a few works that may provide you with an understanding of their authors' loved territory.

Thomas Hardy's novels *The Mayor of Casterbridge, Tess of the d'Urbervilles,* and *Far from the Madding Crowd* (and indeed almost everything he wrote) are solidly based on his Wessex (Dorset) homeland. Daphne Du Maurier had a deep love of Cornwall from her childhood; *Frenchman's Creek, Jamaica Inn,* and *The King's General* all capture the county's Celtic mood. The wildness of Exmoor in Devon is captured in the historical novel *Lorna Doone* by R.D. Blackmore. The Brontë sisters' *Wuthering Heights, The Tenant of Wildfell Hall,* and *Jane Eyre* breathe the sharp air of the moors around the writers' Haworth home. William Wordsworth, who was born at Cockermouth in the Lake District, depicts the area's rugged beauty in many of his poems, especially the *Lyrical Ballads.*

Virginia Woolf's visits to Vita Sackville-West at her ancestral home of Knole, in Sevenoaks, inspired the novel *Orlando.* The stately home is now a National Trust property. American writer Henry James lived at Lamb House in Rye, also in East Sussex, as did E.F. Benson, whose delicious Lucia novels take place in a thinly disguised version of the town. Lamb House is a National Trust building.

A highly irreverent and very funny version of academic life, *Porterhouse Blue,* by Tom Sharpe, will guarantee that you look at Oxford and Cambridge with a totally different eye. Also irreverent is *England, England* by Julian Barnes, in which an entrepreneur takes over the Isle of Wight and establishes a theme park based on national clichés. John Fowles's *The French Lieutenant's Woman,* largely set in Lyme Regis, is full of local color about Dorset, and Laurie Lee's *Cider with Rosie* is a poignant reminiscence about Cotswold village life in the 1920s.

Mysteries are almost a way of life, partly because many of the best English mystery writers set their plots in their home territories. Modern whodunits by P.D. James and Ruth Rendell convey a fine sense of place, and Ellis Peters's Brother Cadfael stories re-create life in medieval Shrewsbury with a wealth of telling detail. Colin Dexter's Inspector Morse mysteries capture the flavor of Oxford's town and gown. There are also always the villages, vicarages, and scandals of Agatha Christie's "Miss Marple" books.

The fans of Arthurian legends can turn to some excellent, imaginative novels that not only tell the stories but also give fine descriptions of the countryside. Among them are *Sword at Sunset,* by Rosemary Sutcliffe, *The Once and Future King,* by T.H. White, and the four Merlin novels by Mary Stewart: *The Crystal Cave, The Hollow Hills, The Last Enchantment,* and *The Wicked Day.* Edward Rutherfurd's historical novels *Sarum, London,* and *The Forest* deal with British history with a grand sweep from the prehistoric past to the present.

The late James Herriot's veterinary surgeon books, among them *All Creatures Great and Small,* give evocative accounts of life in the Yorkshire Dales during much of the 20th century; the books were made into popular television shows.

An animal's close-to-the-earth viewpoint can reveal all kinds of countryside insights. *Watership Down,* a runaway best seller about rabbits, was written by Richard Adam in the early '70s. *The Wind in the Willows,* by Kenneth Grahame, gives a vivid impression of the Thames Valley almost 100 years ago that still holds largely true today. Devon, the northern part in particular, is the setting of Henry Williamson's *Tarka the Otter,* a beloved nature story published in the 1920s; many paths in the region are signposted as part of the Tarka Trail.

Nonfiction

Those interested in writers and the surroundings that influenced their works should look at *Bloom's Literary Guide to London,* by Donna Dailey, and *The Oxford Literary Guide to the British Isles,* edited by Dorothy Eagle and Hilary Carnell (now out of print). One author currently in vogue is Jane Austen: Janeites will want to read Maggie Lane's *Jane Austen's World* and Nigel Nicolson's wonderful *World of Jane Austen* (now out of print).

Good background books on English history are *The Oxford Illustrated History of Britain,* edited by Kenneth O. Morgan, and *The Story of England,* by Christopher Hibbert. *The Isles,* a long history by Norman Davies, challenges conventional Anglocentric assumptions. *The English: A Portrait of a People,* by Jeremy Paxman, examines the concept of Englishness in a changing world. Simon Schama's three-volume *History of Britain,* with handsome color illustrations, was written to accompany the BBC–History Channel television series. Peter Ackroyd's illustrated *London: A Biography* captures the city's energy and its quirks from prehistory to the present. Ronald Blythe's well-regarded *Akenfield: Portrait of an English Village,* written in the 1960s, gives a perceptive account of life in the English countryside.

The finest book on the country's stately homes is Nigel Nicolson's *Great Houses of Britain,* written for the National Trust

(now out of print). Also spectacular is the picture book *Great Houses of Britain and Wales,* by Hugh Montgomery-Massingberd. *The Buildings of England,* written by Nikolaus Pevsner but much updated since his death, is part of a multivolume series, organized by county. Pevsner's *Best Buildings of Britain* is a grand anthology with lush photographs. New Pevsner Architectural Guides continue to be published. For the golden era of Georgian architecture, check out John Summerson's definitive *Architecture in Britain 1530–1830.*

Simon Jenkins's *England's Thousand Best Churches,* with photographs, describes parish churches (not cathedrals) large and small. The same author's delightful *England's Thousand Best Houses* has pithy descriptions (and star ratings) of small and large houses open to the public. Mark Girouard's *Life in the English Country House* focuses on houses over the centuries, and *The Victorian Country House* (out of print) addresses the lifestyles of the rich and famous of the 19th century. For a scenic look at English villages, see *The Most Beautiful Villages of England,* by James Bentley, with ravishing photographs by Hugh Palmer.

Timothy Mowl's entertaining Historic Gardens series, with titles that focus on individual counties, is the gardening equivalent to Pevsner on buildings. The titles are more easily available in Britain, but check an online bookseller.

There are many delightful travel books about Britain. Bill Bryson's *Notes from a Small Island* is perennially popular, though it is becoming a bit dated. Few of today's authors have managed to top the wit and perception of Henry James's magisterial *English Hours.*

Movies

From *Wuthering Heights* to *Jane Eyre,* great classics of literature have been rendered into great classics of film. It's surprising to learn, however, how many of them were creations of Hollywood and not the British film industry (which had its heyday from the 1940s to the 1960s). From Laurence Olivier to Kenneth Branagh, noted director-actors have cross-pollinated the cinema in Britain and the United States.

Films can motivate travelers to visit specific locations and sights in a favorite film. VisitBritain (⊕ *www.visitbritain.com*) has recognized this by including movies on its Web site and producing "movie maps" with the locations for certain films such as the Harry Potter series.

A survey can begin with the dramas of Shakespeare: Olivier gave the world a memorable *Othello* and *Hamlet*, Orson Welles a moody *Macbeth,* and Branagh gave up mod versions of *Hamlet* and *Much Ado About Nothing.* Leonardo DiCaprio graced Australian Baz Luhrmann's contemporary version of *Romeo and Juliet.* Going behind the scenes, so to speak, Tom Stoppard created the Oscar winner *Shakespeare in Love.* Charles Dickens has also provided the foundation for film favorites: David Lean's immortal *Great Expectations,* George Cukor's *David Copperfield,* and *A Christmas Carol,* with Alastair Sim as Scrooge, top this list, which continues to grow with additions such as Douglas McGrath's *Nicholas Nickleby.*

McGrath's *Emma,* starring Gwyneth Paltrow, and Ang Lee's *Sense and Sensibility,* starring Emma Thompson and Kate Winslet, are just two of the recent film versions of Jane Austen's works. Keira Knightley had the role of Elizabeth Bennet in the latest *Pride and Prejudice* (2005). Anne Hathaway played Jane Austen herself in *Becoming Jane,* which imagines an early love affair for the novelist.

Harry Potter and the Sorcerer's Stone (in Britain, *Harry Potter and the Philosopher's Stone*), based on the wildly popular children's books by J.K. Rowling, was filmed in many British locations, including London, Gloucester, the Cotswolds, Northumbria, Yorkshire, and Scotland.

The second movie, *Harry Potter and the Chamber of Secrets,* used some of the same settings as the first. *Harry Potter and the Prisoner of Azkaban, Harry Potter and the Goblet of Fire, Harry Potter and the Order of the Phoenix,* and *Harry Potter and the Half-Blood Prince* are additional installments; *Harry Potter and the Deathly Hallows* will appear in late 2010.

Of the film versions of Agatha Christie's books, one is especially treasured: *Murder, She Said,* which starred the inimitable Margaret Rutherford. With its quiet English village setting, harpsichord score, and the dotty Miss Marple as portrayed by Rutherford, this must be the most English of all Christie films. (Miss Marple remains a fixture on public television, with new shows being produced.)

Lovers of opulence, spectacle, and history (or just juicy costume dramas) have choices that grow each year—including Robert Bolt's classic version of Sir Thomas More's life and death, *A Man for All Seasons.* His *Lady Caroline Lamb* is surely the most beautiful historical film ever made. Richard Harris made a stirring Lord Protector in *Cromwell,* and the miniseries on Queen Elizabeth I, starring Glenda Jackson, is a great BBC addition to a DVD library. Elizabeth's adversary came to breathless life in Vanessa Redgrave's rendition of *Mary, Queen of Scots,* certainly one of her finest performances. More recent and a chilling performance of tortuous times is Cate Blanchett as *Elizabeth*; 2007 saw the release of *The Golden Age,* a sequel.

The historical movies keep coming: Helen Mirren played a dignified Elizabeth II as she faces the dilemmas caused by the death of Princess Diana in the excellent *The Queen.* *Miss Potter,* with Renée Zellweger, explored the life of the beloved children's book writer and illustrator Beatrix Potter, who had a home in the Lake District. Keira Knightley starred in *The Duchess,* the story of Georgiana, duchess of Devonshire, a flamboyant 18th-century aristocrat, and Emily Blunt played the young Queen Victoria in *The Young Victoria* (2009). *Sherlock Holmes* (2009) with Robert Downey Jr. and *Robin Hood* (2010) with Russell Crowe gave these characters a new shot of cinematic life and showed some lovely British scenery. The television series *The Tudors* has won fans on both sides of the Atlantic.

Musicals? Near the top of anyone's list are four films set in England—three of them in Hollywood's England—that rank among the greatest musicals of all time: Walt Disney's *Mary Poppins,* George Cukor's *My Fair Lady,* Carol Reed's Oscar-winner *Oliver!,* and—yeah, yeah, yeah!—the Beatles' *A Hard Day's Night,* a British production.

If you're seeking a look at contemporary England, you might view *My Beautiful Laundrette,* about Asians in London, or *Secrets and Lies,* about a dysfunctional London family. Manchester's rocking music scene from the 1970s to early 1990s is the subject of the well-named *24 Hour Party People.* Mods, New Romantics, and Skinheads feature in *This Is England*, a sensitive tale of working-class life in the Midlands in the early 1980s.

Closer, adapted from Patrick Marber's play, takes a dark look at love in modern London. Woody Allen set his movies *Match Point* and *Scoop* in London; there are gorgeous shots of historic and modern locations in both.

You might lighten up with *The Full Monty,* about six former steelworkers in Sheffield who become strippers, or one of numerous romantic comedies: *Notting Hill,* with Julia Roberts and Hugh Grant; Hugh Grant again in *Four Weddings and a Funeral*; Gwyneth Paltrow in *Sliding Doors*; and Renée Zellweger (and Hugh Grant, again) in *Bridget Jones's Diary* and *Bridget Jones: The Edge of Reason.* *Calendar Girls,* filmed in rural Yorkshire, follows the true story of middle-aged women who raise money for charity with an (almost) bare-all calendar.

Quintessentially British are some comedies of the 1950s and '60s: Alec Guinness's *Kind Hearts and Coronets,* Peter Sellers's *The Mouse That Roared,* and Tony Richardson's Oscar winner and cinematic style setter, *Tom Jones,* starring Albert Finney, are best bets.

In 2001 American director Robert Altman took a biting look at the country's class system in *Gosford Park,* a country-house murder mystery set in the 1930s that stars mostly British actors, including Jeremy Northam and Maggie Smith. *Atonement* (2007), based on Ian McEwan's novel and starring Keira Knightley, also explores class tensions and depicts a small country estate between the world wars. A more staid, upstairs-downstairs look at the class system is the film of Kazuo Ishiguro's novel *The Remains of the Day,* featuring Anthony Hopkins as the stalwart butler, with Emma Thompson. Today some people's visions of turn-of-the-20th-century England have been captured by the Merchant and Ivory films, notably their *Howard's End,* which won many awards.

CHRONOLOGY

3000 BC First building of Stonehenge (later building 2100–1900 BC)

54 BC–AD 43 Julius Caesar's exploratory invasion of England. Romans conquer England, led by Emperor Claudius

60 Boudicca, a native British queen, razes the first Roman London (Londinium)

122–27 Emperor Hadrian completes the Roman conquest and builds a wall across the north to keep back the Scottish Picts

300–50 Height of Roman colonization, administered from such towns as Verulamium (St. Albans), Colchester, Lincoln, and York

410 Roman rule of Britain ends, after waves of invasion by Jutes, Angles, and Saxons

ca. 490 Possible period for the legendary King Arthur, who may have led resistance to Anglo-Saxon invaders

550–700 Seven Anglo-Saxon kingdoms emerge—Essex, Wessex, Sussex, Kent, Anglia, Mercia, and Northumbria—to become the core of English social and political organization for centuries

597 St. Augustine arrives in Canterbury to Christianize Britain

871–99 Alfred the Great, king of Wessex, unifies the English against Viking invaders, who are then confined to the Northeast

1040 Edward the Confessor moves his court to Westminster and founds Westminster Abbey

1066 William, duke of Normandy, invades, defeats King Harold at the Battle of Hastings, and is crowned William I at Westminster in December

1086 Domesday Book completed, a survey of all taxpayers in England, drawn up to assist administration of the realm

1167 Oxford University founded

1170 Thomas à Becket murdered in Canterbury; his shrine becomes center for international pilgrimage

1209 Cambridge University founded

1215 King John forced to sign Magna Carta at Runnymede. It promulgates basic principles of English law: no taxation except through Parliament, trial by jury, and property guarantees

1272–1307 Reign of Edward I, a great legislator; in 1282–83 he conquers Wales and reinforces his rule with a chain of massive castles

1337–1453 Edward III claims the French throne, starting the Hundred Years War. In spite of dramatic English victories—1346 at Crécy, 1356 at Poitiers, 1415 at Agincourt—the long war of attrition ends with the French driving the English out from everywhere but Calais, which finally falls in 1558

1348–49   The Black Death (bubonic plague) reduces the population of Britain from around 4.25 million to around 2.5 million; decades of social unrest follow

1399   Henry Bolingbroke (Henry IV) deposes and murders his cousin Richard II, beginning of the rivalry between houses of York and Lancaster

1402–10   The Welsh, led by Owain Glendŵr, rebel against English rule

1455–85   The Wars of the Roses; the York–Lancaster struggle erupts into civil war

1477   William Caxton prints first book in England

1485   Henry Tudor (Henry VII) defeats Richard III at the Battle of Bosworth and founds the Tudor dynasty; he suppresses private armies, develops administrative efficiency and royal absolutism

1530s   Under Henry VIII the Reformation takes hold; he dissolves the monasteries and finally demolishes medieval England. The land goes to wealthy merchant families, creating new gentry

1555   During the reign of papal supporter Mary I (reigned 1553–58), Protestant bishops Ridley and Latimer are burned in Oxford; in 1556 Archbishop Cranmer is burned

1558–1603   Reign of Elizabeth I: Protestantism reestablished; Drake, Raleigh, and other freebooters establish English claims in the West Indies and North America

1568   Mary, Queen of Scots, flees to England; in 1587 she is executed

1588   Spanish Armada fails to invade England

1603   James VI of Scotland, son of Mary, Queen of Scots and Lord Darnley, becomes James I of England

1605   Guy Fawkes and friends plot to blow up Parliament

1611   King James Authorized Version of the Bible published

1620   Pilgrims sail from Plymouth on the *Mayflower* and settle in what becomes New England

1629   Charles I dissolves Parliament, decides to rule alone

1642–49   Civil War between the Royalists and Parliamentarians (Cavaliers and Roundheads); the Parliamentarians win

1649   Charles I executed; England is a republic

1653   Oliver Cromwell becomes Lord Protector, establishing England's only dictatorship

1660   The Restoration: Charles II restored to the throne; accepts limits to royal power

1666   The Great Fire: London burns for three days; its medieval center is destroyed

1689 Accession of William III (of Orange) and his wife, Mary II, as joint monarchs; royal power further limited

1700s Under the first four Georges, the Industrial Revolution develops and with it Britain's domination of world trade

1707 Union of English and Scots parliaments under Queen Anne

1714 The German Hanoverians succeed to the throne; George I's deficiency in English leads to the establishment of a council of ministers, the beginning of the cabinet system of government

1715, 1745–46 Two Jacobite rebellions fail to restore the House of Stuart to the throne; in 1746 Charles Edward Stuart (Bonnie Prince Charlie) is decisively defeated at Culloden Moor in Scotland

1775–83 Britain loses the American colonies that become the United States

1795–1815 Britain and its allies defeat France in the Napoleonic Wars; in 1805, Admiral Lord Nelson is killed at Trafalgar; in 1815, Battle of Waterloo is fought

1801 Union with Ireland

1811–20 Prince Regent rules during his father's (George III) madness, the Regency period

1825 The Stockton to Darlington railway, the world's first passenger line with regular service, is established

1832 The Reform Bill extends the franchise, limiting the power of the great landowners

1837–1901 During the long reign of Victoria, Britain becomes the world's richest country, and the British Empire reaches its height

1887 Victoria celebrates her Golden Jubilee; in 1901 she dies, marking the end of an era

1914–18 World War I: fighting against Germany, Britain loses a whole generation, with 750,000 men killed in trench warfare alone; enormous debts and inept diplomacy in the postwar years undermine Britain's position as a world power

1919 Ireland declares independence from England; bloody Black-and-Tan struggle is one result

1936 Edward VIII abdicates to marry American divorcée Wallis Simpson

1939–45 World War II: Britain declares war on Germany when Germany invades Poland in September 1939. London badly damaged during the Blitz, September 1940–May 1941; Britain's economy shattered

1945 Labour wins a landslide victory; stays in power for six years, transforming Britain into a welfare state

1952 Queen Elizabeth II accedes to the throne

1973 Britain joins the European Economic Community after referendum

1975 Britain begins to pump North Sea oil

1981 Marriage of Prince Charles and Lady Diana Spencer

1982 Falklands regained in war with Argentina

1987 Conservatives under Margaret Thatcher win a third term in office

1992 Great Britain and European countries join to form one European Community (EC), whose name changed to European Union in 1993

1994 The Channel Tunnel opens a direct rail link between Britain and Europe

1996 The Prince and Princess of Wales receive a divorce

1997 "New Labour" comes to power, with Tony Blair as prime minister. Diana, Princess of Wales, dies at 36 in a car crash in Paris. She is buried at Althorp in Northamptonshire

2002 Queen Elizabeth celebrates her Golden Jubilee. Queen Elizabeth (the Queen Mother) and Princess Margaret die. Euro coins and notes enter circulation; Britain continues to ponder adopting the euro

2003 Britain joins U.S. and coalition forces in invading Iraq

2005 Prince Charles and Camilla Parker Bowles wed in a civil ceremony. The ban on the traditional sport of fox hunting with hounds is put into effect. Tony Blair is elected to a historic third term as prime minister. London wins the bid for the 2012 Olympics in July

2007 Gordon Brown becomes prime minister

2009 British economy suffers as part of the global recession; Brown and the Labour Party lose popularity; pressure for government reform increases during the parliamentary expense scandals, in which some members of Parliament are accused of misusing allowances and permitted expenses

2010 The general election in May fails to yield a majority in the House of Commons, producing the first "hung" parliament since 1974. The Conservative party, led by David Cameron, wins the greatest number of seats. He establishes a coalition with the Liberal Democrats, led by Nick Clegg.

Travel Smart England

WORD OF MOUTH

"We have found [tourist information offices] to be a great resource. . . . We have often made them our first stop upon arriving in a town. They have info and photos of lots of types of accommodation."

—taggie

"I would, however, recommend either buying or renting a Sat Nav. Driving on the other side of the road, reading a map, trying to enjoy the countryside, and not kill your travel companion is too much!"

—BKP

GETTING HERE AND AROUND

▌ AIR TRAVEL

The least expensive airfares to England are often priced for round-trip travel and must usually be purchased in advance. Airlines generally allow you to change your return date for a fee; most low-fare tickets, however, are nonrefundable.

Flying time to London is about 6½ hours from New York, 7½ hours from Chicago, 9½ hours from Dallas, 10 hours from Los Angeles, and 21½ hours from Sydney. From London, flights take an hour to Paris or Amsterdam, 1½ hours to cities in Switzerland or Luxembourg, and two hours to Rome.

If you're flying from England, plan to arrive at the airport two hours in advance for flights to Europe, three hours for the United States. Security at Gatwick and Heathrow airports is always fairly intense. Most people can expect to be patted down after they pass through metal detectors. Travelers are randomly searched again at the gate before transatlantic flights.

Airline Security Issues Transportation Security Administration (⊕ www.tsa.gov).

AIRPORTS

Most international flights to London arrive at either Heathrow Airport (LHR), 15 mi west of London, or at Gatwick Airport (LGW), 27 mi south of the capital. Most flights from the United States go to Heathrow, with Terminals 3, 4, and 5 handling transatlantic flights (British Airways uses Terminal 5). Gatwick is London's second gateway, serving many U.S. destinations. A third, much smaller airport, Stansted (STN), is 35 mi northeast of the city. It handles mainly European and domestic traffic. Luton Airport (LLA), 30 mi north of the city, is also quite small, and serves British and European destinations. Luton is the hub for the low-cost easyJet airline. Manchester (MAN) in northwest England handles some flights from the United States. Birmingham (BHX), in the Midlands, handles mainly European and British flights as well as flights from Chicago, Philadelphia, Newark, New York, and Orlando.

Heathrow and Gatwick are enormous and can seem like shopping malls. Both airports have bars and pubs, and dining options. Several hotels are connected to each airport, and both Gatwick and Heathrow are near dozens of hotels that run free shuttles to the airports. Heathrow has a Hotel Hoppa service that runs shuttles between the airport and around 20 nearby hotels for £4 each way. A free, subsidized local bus service operates between the Central Bus Station serving Terminals 1, 2, and 3 and nearby hotels. You can find out more at the Central Bus Station or at the Transport for London (TfL) Information Centre in the Underground station serving Terminals 1, 2, and 3. Yotel has budget pod hotels in both Heathrow and Gatwick with cabin-size rooms to be booked in advance in four-hour blocks (£25) or overnight (£98).

In comparison, other British airports have much more limited shopping, hotel, and dining options; a delay of a few hours can seem like years.

Airport Information Birmingham Airport (☎ 0844/576–6000 ⊕ www.bhx.com). **Gatwick Airport** (☎ 0844/335–1802 ⊕ www. gatwickairport.com). **Heathrow Airport** (☎ 0844/335–1801 ⊕ www.heathrowairport. com). **Luton Airport** (☎ 01582/405100 ⊕ www.london-luton.co.uk). **Manchester Airport** (☎ 0161/489–3000 or 0871/271–0711 ⊕ www.manchesterairport.co.uk). **Stansted Airport** (☎ 0844/355–1803 ⊕ www. stanstedairport.com).

GROUND TRANSPORTATION

London has excellent bus and train connections between its airports and downtown. The Transport for London Web site has helpful information, and airport Web sites have links to transportation services.

You can get discounts on many tickets if you book on the Internet.

Train service can be quick, but the downside (for trains from all airports) is that you must get yourself and your luggage to the train via a series of escalators and connecting trams. Airport link buses (generally National Express Airport buses) may ease the luggage factor and drop you closer to central hotels, but they're subject to London traffic, which can be horrendous. Taxis can be more convenient than buses, but prices can go through the roof. Airport Travel Line has additional transfer information and takes advance booking for transfers between airports and into London. The official sites for Gatwick, Heathrow, and Stansted are useful resources for transportation options.

FROM HEATHROW TO CENTRAL LONDON		
Travel Mode	Time	Cost
Taxi	1 hour+	£50+
Heathrow Express Train	15 min	£16.50 (£32 round trip) and £26 for first class
Underground	50 min	£4 one way (less with Oyster card)
National Express Bus	1 hour	£5 one way

Heathrow by Bus: National Express buses take one hour to reach the city center (Victoria) and cost from £5 one way and £10 round-trip. Buses leave frequently from 5:20 AM to 9:40 PM. National Express also operates other bus services between 5 AM and 9:30 PM that travel to Earls Court, Kensington, and Hammersmith in west London. Prices are from £5 one way, and the trip takes between 40 and 60 minutes depending on traffic. The National Express Hotel Hoppa service runs from all terminals to around 20 hotels near the airport (£4). Alternatively, nearly every hotel in London is served by the Hotel By Bus service. Fares to Central London average around £22. SkyShuttle also offers a minibus service between Heathrow and any London hotel. The N9 night bus runs every half hour from midnight to 5 AM to Trafalgar Square; it takes an hour and costs £4.

Heathrow by Train: The cheap, direct route into London is via the Piccadilly line of the Underground (London's extensive subway system, or "Tube"). Trains normally run every four to eight minutes from all terminals from early morning until just before midnight. The 50-minute trip into central London costs £4.50 one way and connects with other central Tube lines. The Heathrow Express train is comfortable and very convenient, if costly, speeding into London's Paddington Station in 15 minutes. Standard one-way tickets cost £16.50 (£32 round-trip) and £26 for first class. Book ahead (online is the cheapest option, at a counter or kiosk less so), as tickets are more expensive to buy on board. There's daily service from 5:10 AM (5:50 AM on Sunday) to 11:25 PM (10:50 PM on Sunday), with departures every 15 minutes. A less expensive option is the Heathrow Connect train, which stops at local stations between the airport and Paddington. Daily service is every half hour from 5:20 AM (6:05 AM on Sunday) to 11:20 PM (11:05 PM on Sunday). The journey takes about 30 minutes and costs £7.90 one way (£15.80 round-trip).

Gatwick by Bus: Hourly bus service runs from Gatwick's north and south terminals to Victoria Station with stops at Hooley, Coulsdon, Mitcham, Streatham, Stockwell, and Pimlico. The journey takes up to 90 minutes and costs £7.50 one way. Make sure you get on a direct bus not requiring a change; otherwise the journey could take hours. The easyBus service runs a service to west London (Earls Court) from as little as £2; the later the ticket is booked online, the higher the price (up to £10 on board).

Gatwick by Train: The fast, nonstop Gatwick Express leaves for Victoria Station every 15 minutes 5:15 AM–midnight. The 30-minute trip costs £15.20 one way,

£23 round-trip. Book in advance, as tickets cost more on board. The First Capital Connect rail company's nonexpress services are cheaper; trains runs regularly throughout the day until midnight to St. Pancras International, London Bridge, and Blackfriars stations; departures are every 15 to 30 minutes, and the journey takes almost one hour. Tickets are from £9 one way. You can also reach Gatwick by First Capital Connect coming from Brighton in the opposite direction. First Capital Connect service is on commuter trains, and during rush hour trains can be crowded, with little room for baggage and seats at a premium.

Stansted by Bus: Hourly service on National Express Airport bus A6 (24 hours a day) to Victoria Coach Station costs from £5 one way, £10 round-trip, and takes about one hour and 40 minutes. Stops include Golders Green, Finchley Road, St. John's Wood, Baker Street, Marble Arch, and Hyde Park Corner. The easyBus service to Victoria via Baker Street costs from £2.

Stansted by Train: The Stansted Express to Liverpool Street Station (with a stop at Tottenham Hale) runs every 15 minutes 5:30 AM–1:30 AM daily (12:30 PM on Saturday). The 45-minute trip costs £18 one way, £26.70 round-trip if booked online. Tickets cost more on board.

Luton by Bus and Train: A free airport shuttle runs from Luton Airport to the nearby Luton Airport Parkway Station, from which you can take a train or bus into London. From there, the First Capital Connect train service runs to St. Pancras, Farringdon, Blackfriars, and London Bridge. The journey takes about 40 minutes. Trains leave every 10 minutes or so from 5 AM until midnight. One-way tickets cost from £12 (off-peak). The Green Line 757 bus service from Luton to Victoria Station runs three times an hour, takes about 90 minutes, and costs £14 (£19 round-trip).

Heathrow, Gatwick, Stansted, and Luton by Taxi: This is an expensive and time-consuming option. The city's congestion charge (£8) will be added to the bill, you run the risk of getting stuck in traffic, and if you take a taxi from the stand, the price will be even more expensive (whereas a cab booked ahead is a set price). A taxi trip from Heathrow to Victoria, for example, can take more than an hour and cost more than £58. Checkercars offers cars from Gatwick, Heathrow, and Stansted for a flat fee—at this writing, the fee to Victoria Station is £47 from Heathrow, £98.50 from Gatwick, and £106 from Stansted, not including the congestion charge. Another option, if you have friends in the London area, is to have them book a reputable mini-cab firm to pick you up. The cost of a mini-cab from Heathrow to central London is approximately £45. Your hotel may also be able to recommend a car service.

TRANSFERS BETWEEN AIRPORTS

Allow at least two to three hours for an inter-airport transfer. The cheapest option—but most complicated—is public transport: from Gatwick to Stansted, for instance, you can catch the nonexpress commuter train from Gatwick to Victoria Station, take the Tube to Liverpool Street Station, then catch the train to Stansted from there. To get from Heathrow to Gatwick by public transport, take the Tube to King's Cross, then change to the Victoria Line, get to Victoria Station, and then take the commuter train to Gatwick.

The National Express Airport bus is the most direct option between Gatwick and Heathrow. Buses pick up passengers frequently from 5:20 AM to 11 PM from both airports, every hour from midnight to 5 AM. The trip takes around 75 minutes, and the fare is £19.50 one way. It's advisable to book tickets in advance. National Express buses between Stansted and Gatwick depart every hour and take around three hours. The adult one-way fare is £29.30. Some airlines may offer shuttle services as well—check with your airline before your journey.

Contacts **Airport Travel Line** (☏ 0871/200–2233 or 0870/574-7777). **Checkercars** (⊕ www.checkercars.com). **easyBus** (⊕ www.easybus.co.uk). **First Capital Connect** (⊕ www.firstcapitalconnect.co.uk). **Gatwick Express** (☏ 0845/850–1530 ⊕ www.gatwickexpress.com). **Green Line** (⊕ www.greenline.co.uk). **Heathrow Express** (☏ 0845/600–1515 ⊕ www.heathrowexpress.com). **Hotel By Bus Heathrow** (☏ 0845/850–1900 ⊕ www.hotelbybusheathrow.com). **National Express** (☏ 0870/580–8080 ⊕ www.nationalexpress.com). **SkyShuttle** (☏ 0845/481–9060 ⊕ www.skyshuttle.co.uk). **Stansted Express** (☏ 0845/850–0150 ⊕ www.stanstedexpress.co.uk). **Transport for London** (☏ 020/7222–1234 ⊕ www.tfl.gov.uk)

FLIGHTS

British Airways offers mostly nonstop flights from 19 U.S. cities to Heathrow, along with flights to Manchester and Birmingham. It offers myriad add-on options that help bring down ticket costs. In addition, it has a vast program of discount airfare–hotel packages. Britain-based Virgin Atlantic is a strong competitor in terms of packages. London is a very popular destination, so many U.S. carriers have flights and packages, too.

Because England is such a small country, internal air travel is much less important than it is in the United States. For trips of less than 200 mi, the train is often quicker, with rail stations more centrally located. Flying tends to cost more, but for longer trips air travel has a considerable time advantage (you need to factor in time to get to and from the airport, though).

British Airways operates shuttle services between Heathrow or Gatwick and Manchester. bmi/British Midland operates from Heathrow to Leeds and Manchester, as well as to Washington, D.C., Chicago, Las Vegas, and major cities in eastern Canada.

Low-cost airlines such as easyJet, bmi baby, and Ryanair offer flights within the United Kingdom as well as to cities in Ireland and continental Europe. Prices are low, but these airlines usually use satellite cities and fly out of smaller British airports such as Stansted and Luton (both near London). Check ⊕ www.cheapflights.com for price comparisons.

Major Airline Contacts American Airlines (☏ 800/433–7300, 020/7365–0777 in London ⊕ www.aa.com) to Heathrow, Gatwick, Manchester. **British Airways** (☏ 800/247–9297, 0844/493–0787 in U.K. ⊕ www.britishairways.com) to Heathrow. **Continental Airlines** (☏ 800/231–0856 for international reservations ⊕ www.continental.com) to Heathrow, Gatwick. **Delta Airlines** (☏ 800/221–1212 for U.S. reservations, 800/241–4141 for international reservations, 0845/600–0950 in U.K. ⊕ www.delta.com) to Gatwick. **United Airlines** (☏ 800/864–8331 for U.S. reservations, 800/538–2929 for international reservations, 0845/844–4777 in U.K. ⊕ www.united.com) to Heathrow. **US Airways** (☏ 800/428–4322 for U.S. and Canada reservations, 0845/600–3300 in U.K. ⊕ www.usairways.com) to Heathrow, Gatwick, Manchester. **Virgin Atlantic** (☏ 800/821–5438, 0844/209–7777 in U.K. ⊕ www.virgin-atlantic.com) to Heathrow, Gatwick.

Within England and to Europe bmi baby (☏ 0845/810110 from outside U.K., 0844/848–4888 in U.K. ⊕ www.bmibaby.com). **easyJet** (☏ 0870/600–0000 in U.K. ⊕ www.easyjet.com). **Ryanair** (☏ 353/1812–1212 Ireland office ⊕ www.ryanair.com).

PASSES

The Discover Europe Airpass from bmi is available on the airline's British and European flights. The pass is valid for up to 90 days and allows passengers to travel to a combination of European cities for reduced fares. The Visit Europe Pass from British Airways offers travelers a way to choose from the airline's and its partners' networks.

Air Pass Info bmi (☏ 800/788–0555, 020/8745–7321 in U.K. ⊕ www.flybmi.com). **British Airways** (☏ 800/247–9297, 0844/493–0787 in U.K. ⊕ www.britishairways.com). **FlightPass** (EuropebyAir ☏ 888/321–4737 ⊕ www.europebyair.com). **Premier**

Gateway/DER Air (☎ 800/777–8369 ⊕ www.premiergateway.com).

■ BOAT TRAVEL

Ferries, hovercraft, and Seacats (a kind of ferry) travel regular routes to France, Spain, Ireland, and Scandinavia. Hoverspeed provides fast travel to France and Belgium. P&O runs ferries between Belgium, Great Britain, Ireland, France, the Netherlands, and Spain. DFDS Seaways covers Denmark, Holland, Germany, Norway, Poland, and Sweden. Stena Line serves Ireland and the Netherlands.

Low-cost airlines and Eurotunnel (which lets you take a car to France on the train) have cut into ferry travel, but companies have responded by cutting fares and upgrading equipment.

For fares and schedules, contact companies directly. Traveler's checks (in pounds), cash, and major credit cards are accepted for payment. Prices vary; booking early ensures cheaper fares, but also ask about special deals. Seaview is a comprehensive online ferry- and cruise-booking portal for Great Britain and continental Europe. Ferry Cheap is a discount Web site.

Information DFDS Seaways (☎ 0871/522–9955 ⊕ www.dfdsseaways.co.uk). **Ferry Cheap** (⊕ www.ferrycheap.com). **Hoverspeed** (☎ 0870/164–2114 ⊕ www.hoverspeed.com). **P&O** (☎ 0871/664–5645 in U.K., 44 + 130/486–3000 in U.S. ⊕ www.poferries.com). **Seaview** (⊕ www.seaview.co.uk). **Stena Line** (☎ 0844/770–7070 ⊕ www.stenaline.co.uk).

TRANSATLANTIC AND OTHER CRUISES

Most cruise ships leave from southern England—particularly Southampton and Portsmouth. Some ships leave from Liverpool and Dover as well, or from Harwich, near London. Each cruise company has its own journeys and policies, so check their Web sites or contact a travel agent if you're interested in more information about cruising from England to Europe. *For information about cruising England's*

rivers, lakes, and canals, see Sports and the Outdoors in Essentials, below.

Cruise Lines Cunard Line (☎ 661/753–1000 or 800/728–6273 ⊕ www.cunard.com). **Holland America Line** (☎ 877/932–4259 ⊕ www.hollandamerica.com). **Norwegian Cruise Line** (☎ 305/436–4000 or 800/327–7030 ⊕ www.ncl.com). **Princess Cruises** (☎ 866/234–0292 ⊕ www.princess.com). **Royal Caribbean International** (☎ 305/539–6000 or 866/562–7625 ⊕ www.royalcaribbean.com).

■ BUS TRAVEL

Britain has a comprehensive bus (short-haul) and coach (the British term for long-distance buses) network that offers an inexpensive way of seeing England and Wales. National Express is the major coach operator, and Victoria Coach Station, near Victoria Station in central London, is the hub of the National Express network, serving over 1,000 destinations within Britain and Ireland and, via Eurolines, 500 in continental Europe. Tickets and information are available from any of the company's 2,000 agents nationwide, including offices at London's Heathrow and Gatwick airport coach stations.

Green Line is the next-largest national service, serving airports and major tourist towns.

A budget option on the long-distance bus travel scene, Megabus has double-decker buses that serve cities across Britain. (Note: Megabus does not accommodate wheelchairs, and the company limits luggage to one checked piece per person and one piece of hand luggage.) In London the company's buses depart from the Green Line bus stand at Victoria Station. Greyhound has launched low-cost, long-distance bus service to four southern England destinations, offering free Wi-Fi.

Coach tickets can be as low as half the price of a train ticket (even lower if you take advantage of special deals), and buses are just as comfortable as trains. For example, an Oxford Tube bus ticket from London to Oxford is £14, whereas a train ticket is £25. However, most bus services take twice as long as trains. All bus services forbid smoking, and National Express has onboard refreshments and toilets. There is only one class of service.

Double-decker buses make up many of the extensive networks of local bus services, run by private companies. Check with the local bus station or tourist information center for bus schedules. Most companies offer day or week Explorer or Rover unlimited-travel tickets, and those in popular tourist areas operate special scenic tours in summer. The top deck of a double-decker bus is a great place from which to view the countryside.

DISCOUNTS AND DEALS

National Express's Discount Coach Card for students, 16–26, is good for one year and qualifies you for 20% to 30% discounts off many fares. A similar card for the over-60s qualifies you for a 50% discount off-peak, 30% peak times. Apex tickets (advance-purchase tickets) save money on standard fares, and traveling midweek is cheaper than over weekends and holidays. Most companies offer a discount for children under 15.

FARES AND SCHEDULES

You can find schedules online, pick them up from tourist information offices, or get them by phone from the bus companies. Fares vary based on how close to the time of travel you book—Megabus tickets, for example, are cheaper if ordered in advance online.

PAYING

Tickets for National Express can be bought from the Victoria, Heathrow, or Gatwick coach stations, or by phone with a credit card, or via the National Express Web site, or from most British travel agencies. Reservations are advised. Tickets for Megabus must be purchased online in advance, or by phone (avoid this, as the surcharge is at least 60p per minute). Surcharges for tickets bought online in advance rarely rise above £5.

Most companies will accept MasterCard and Visa for advance purchases, but it's cash-only if you're purchasing your tickets on the bus on the day of travel.

RESERVATIONS

There are no surcharges for booking in advance; in fact, it's a much better idea, as busy routes and times can book up quickly. With most bus companies (National Express, Megabus, Green Line), if you pay in advance your receipt can be e-mailed to you, and your name is placed on a list given to the bus driver.

Bus Contacts Green Line (☎ *0844/801–7261* ⊕ *www.greenline.co.uk*). **Greyhound** (⊕ *www.greyhounduk.com*). **Megabus** (☎ *0900/160–0900* ⊕ *www.megabus.com*), 60p per minute for calls from landlines in U.K. **National Express** (☎ *0871/781–8181* ⊕ *www.nationalexpress.com*). **Victoria Coach Station** (✉ *164 Buckingham Palace Rd., London* ☎ *020/7730–3466* ⊕ *www.tfl.gov.uk/vcs*).

▌ CAR TRAVEL

With more than 50 million inhabitants in England and Wales, and a road system designed in part for horse-drawn carriages, Britain can be a challenging place in which to drive. That's even without considering that people drive on the left side of the road, most rental cars have standard transmissions, and the gearshift is on the wrong side entirely.

There's no reason to rent a car for a stay in London, since the city and its suburbs are well served by public transportation, and traffic is desperately congested. Here and in other major cities it's best to rely on public transportation.

Outside the cities, a car can be very handy. Many sights are not easily reached without one—castles, for example, are rarely connected to any public transportation system. Small villages might have only one or two buses a day pass through them. Driving between the tall hedgerows or on country roads is a truly English experience.

In England and Wales your own driver's license is acceptable. However, you may choose to get an International Driving Permit (IDP), which can be used only in conjunction with a valid driver's license and which translates your license into 10 languages. Check the AAA Web site for more info as well as for IDPs ($10) themselves. These permits are universally recognized, and having one in your wallet may save you a problem with the local authorities.

GASOLINE
Gasoline is called petrol in England and is sold by the liter. The price you see posted at a petrol station is the price of a liter, and there are about four liters in a U.S. gallon. Petrol is expensive; it was around £1.20 per liter, or $7 per U.S. gallon, at this writing. Supermarket pumps just outside city centers frequently offer the best prices. Unleaded petrol is predominant, denoted by green stickers on fuel pumps and pump lines. Premium and super premium are the two varieties, and most cars run on regular premium. Diesel is prevalent; be sure not to use it by mistake. Along busy motorways, most large stations are open 24 hours a day, seven days a week. In rural areas, hours can vary. Most service stations accept major credit cards, and most are self-service.

PARKING
Parking regulations are strictly enforced everywhere, so look out for signs that display the rules where you're thinking of parking. If there are no signs on a street, it's free to park there. However, many streets have centralized "pay and display" machines, in which you deposit the required money and get a ticket allowing you to park for a set period of time. You display that ticket in your windshield. (In London's City of Westminster, most machines have been replaced by a pay-by-phone scheme, which enables you to pay using a cell phone but requires pre-registration (⊕ *www.westminster.gov.uk*). In town centers your best bet is usually to park in a public car lot. Square blue street signs with a white P in the center direct you to the nearest lot.

If you park on the street, follow these basic rules: Do not park within 15 yards of an intersection. Do not park in bus lanes, on double yellow lines or on single yellow lines during parking meters' hours of operation. Park as close to the curb as possible. On "Red Routes"—busy roads with red lines painted on the street—you cannot park or stop to let a passenger out of the car. If you feel you have been issued a ticket in error, you can appeal. Information is given on the parking ticket.

RENTALS
Rental rates are generally reasonable, and insurance costs are lower than in most U.S. cities. If you want the car only for country trips, consider renting your car in a medium-size town in the area where you'll be traveling, and journeying there by train and picking up the car once you arrive. Rental rates are slightly cheaper out in the country, and you can avoid traversing London's notoriously complex road system. Rental rates vary widely, beginning at £25 a day and £160 a week for a midsize car, usually with manual transmission. Air-conditioning and unlimited mileage generally come with larger automatic transmission cars. As in the United States, prices are higher at times of heaviest use—summer and holidays. Car seats for children usually cost about £20 extra. Adding one extra driver is usually included in the original rental price. Most rental companies offer GPS (SatNavs in England) as an optional extra from around £8, and in some cases they are included on higher-cost vehicles.

Major car rental agencies are much the same in Britain as in the United States: Alamo, Avis, Budget, Enterprise, Hertz, and National all have offices in Britain, and you can reserve a car in advance on their Web sites. Europcar is another large company.

Companies may not rent cars to people who are under 23 or over 75.

ROAD CONDITIONS

There's a very good network of major highways (motorways) and divided high ways (dual carriageways) throughout most of England and Wales, although in remote areas (including parts of Wales), where unclassified roads join villages and are little more than glorified one-lane paths, travel is slower. Motorways (with the prefix M), shown in blue on most maps and road signs, are mainly two or three lanes in each direction. Other major roads (with the prefix A) are shown on maps in green and red. Sections of fast dual carriageways (with black-edged, thick outlines on maps) have both traffic lights and traffic circles; right turns are sometimes permitted. Turnoffs are often marked by highway numbers, rather than place names. An exit is called a junction in Britain.

The vast network of lesser roads, for the most part old coach and turnpike roads, might make your trip take twice the time but show you twice as much. Minor roads drawn in yellow or white on maps, the former prefixed by B, the latter unlettered and unnumbered, are the ancient lanes and byways, a way of discovering the real England. Some of these (the white roads, in the main) are pothole-filled switch-backs. Should you take one of these, be prepared to back up into a passing place if you meet an oncoming car.

ROADSIDE EMERGENCIES

On major highways emergency roadside telephone booths are positioned within walking-distance intervals. Contact your car-rental company (there should be an emergency assistance phone number on the car's paperwork), or call the police. You can also call the British Automobile Association toll-free. You can join and receive assistance from the AA or the RAC on the spot, but the charge is higher than a simple membership fee. If you are a member of AAA (the American Automobile Association), check before you travel; reciprocal agreements may give you free roadside aid.

Emergency Services Ambulance, fire, police (☎ *999*). **Automobile Association** (☎ *0800/887-7661* ⊕ *www.thcaa.com*). **RAC** (☎ *0800/197-7815* ⊕ *www.rac.co.uk*).

RULES OF THE ROAD

You must drive on the left side of the road. You may find it's easier than you expected, as the steering and mirrors on British cars are designed for driving on the left. You use the side mirrors much more this way. If you have a standard transmission car, you have to shift gears with your left hand. Give yourself time to adjust before leaving the rental-car lot. Seat belts are obligatory in the front and back seats. It is illegal to talk on a hand-held cell phone while driving.

Pick up a copy of the official Highway Code (£2.50) at a service station, newsstand, or bookstore, or check it out online by going to ⊕ *www.direct.gov.uk* and putting "Highway Code" in the search bar. Besides driving rules and illustrations of signs and road markings, this booklet contains information for motorcyclists, cyclists, and pedestrians.

Speed limits are complicated, and there are speed cameras everywhere. The speed limit (shown on circular red signs) is generally 30 MPH in towns, 40–60 MPH on two-lane highways, and 70 MPH on motorways. At traffic circles (called roundabouts), you turn clockwise; you will see signs before the roundabout that indicate where each exiting road is headed. As cars enter the circle, they must yield to those already in the circle. If you're taking an exit all the way around the circle, stay to the center until just before your own exit.

Pedestrians have the right-of-way on "zebra" crossings (black-and-white-stripe crosswalks between two orange-flashing globe lights). If there's a person waiting to cross the street, treat the crossing like a stop sign. The curb on each side of the zebra crossing has zigzag markings. It is illegal to park within zigzag areas or to pass a vehicle at a zebra crossing. At other crossings, pedestrians must yield to traffic, but they do have the right-of-way over traffic turning left.

Drunk-driving laws are strictly enforced. The legal limit is 80 milligrams of alcohol per 100 ml of blood, which means two units of alcohol—two glasses of wine, one pint of beer, or one glass of whisky—but amounts vary, depending on your weight or what you have eaten that day.

▌ TRAIN TRAVEL

Operated by private companies, the train system in Britain is extensive and useful, though less than perfect. Some regional trains are old, and virtually all lines suffer from occasional delays, schedule changes, and periodic engineering work that runs over schedule. Worst of all, you will pay quite a lot for all of that. Work is under way to improve the situation, and changes on some lines seem likely. All major cities and many small towns are served by trains, and despite the difficulties, rail travel is the most pleasant way to cover long distances.

On long-distance runs some rail lines have buffet cars; on others you can purchase snacks from a mobile snack cart. Most train companies now have "quiet cars" on trains, where mobile-phone use is forbidden (in theory, anyway) and conversation is meant to be kept at a low volume.

CLASSES

Most rail lines have first-class and second-class cars. In virtually all cases, second class is perfectly comfortable. First class generally is quieter and less crowded, has superior seating and tables, and marginally larger seats. First class usually costs two to three times the price of second class, though, so it's not always worth the cost. However, most train operators offer a Weekend First ticket. Available Saturday, Sunday, and holidays, these tickets are bought on the train and allow you to upgrade for as little as £5.

FARES AND SCHEDULES

The best way to find out which train to take, which station to catch the train, and what times trains travel to your destination is to call National Rail Enquiries. It's a helpful, comprehensive, free service that covers all the country's rail lines. National Rail will help you choose the best train, and then connect you with the ticket office for that train company; you can also use the Web site to book. A similar service is offered online by The Trainline, which provides train information and ticket booking for all rail services. The Man in Seat 61, a Web site, offers objective information along with booking facilities.

You can find timetables of rail services in Britain and some ferry services in the *Thomas Cook European Timetable,* issued monthly and available at travel agents and some bookstores in the United States.

Ticket prices are set on a sliding scale, and they cost more the closer you get to the day of travel. Book several weeks in advance and tickets can be half or one-third of what you might pay if you bought the ticket the same day you traveled. A journey from London to Cardiff will cost around £21 if purchased more than two weeks in advance, but if purchased on the day you travel, the ticket can cost more than £90. However, this is the case only for long-distance travel—journeys within commuting distance of city centers are sold at set prices, and those can be purchased on the day you expect to make your journey.

In all cases ticket prices are more expensive during rush hour, so, whether your journey will be short or long, travel after 9:30 AM, and before 4:30 PM or after 6:30 PM if you want the best prices.

▌TIP➔ **Ask the local tourist board about hotel and local transportation packages that include tickets to major events.**

Information National Rail Enquiries (☎ 0845/748–4950, 020/7278–5240 outside U.K. ⊕ www.nationalrail.co.uk). **The Man**

in Seat 61 (⊕ www.seat61.com). **Trainline** (☎ 0871/244–1545 ⊕ www.thetrainline.com).

PASSES

National Rail Enquiries has information about rail passes such as Rovers, which save you money on individual railroads.

If you plan to travel a lot by train in England and Wales, consider purchasing a BritRail Pass, which gives unlimited travel over the entire British rail network and can save you money. If you don't plan to cover many miles, you may come out ahead by buying individual tickets. You must buy your BritRail Pass before you leave home. They are available from most travel agents or from ACP Rail International, Flight Centre, or VisitBritain. Note that Eurail Passes are not honored in Britain and that the rates listed here are subject to change.

BritRail passes come in two basic varieties. The Classic pass allows travel on consecutive days, and the FlexiPass allows a number of travel days within a set period of time. The cost (in U.S. dollars) of a BritRail Consecutive Pass adult ticket for eight days is $375 standard and $559 first class; for 15 days, $559 standard and $839 first class. The cost of a BritRail FlexiPass adult ticket for four days' travel in two months is $315 standard and $495 first class; for eight days' travel in two months, $459 standard and $649 first class. Prices drop by about 25% for off-peak travel passes between October and March. Passes for students, seniors, and ages 16 to 25 are discounted, too.

Many travelers assume that rail passes guarantee them seats or sleeping accommodations on the trains they wish to ride. Not so. You need to book seats ahead even if you are using a rail pass, especially on trains that may be crowded, particularly in summer on popular routes.

Discount Passes ACP Rail International (☎ 866/938–7245 ⊕ www.acprail.com). **BritRail** (☎ 866/274–8724) ⊕ www.britrail.com). **Flight Centre** (☎ 0870/499–0040 ⊕ www.flightcentre.com). **VisitBritain**

(☎ 800/462–2748 in U.S., 0207/578–1000 in U.K. ⊕ www.visitbritainshop.com).

PAYING

Cash and credit cards are accepted by all train ticket offices; credit cards are accepted over the phone.

RESERVATIONS

Reserving your ticket in advance is recommended. Even a reservation 24 hours in advance can provide a substantial discount. Look into cheap day returns if you plan to travel a round-trip in one day.

CHANNEL TUNNEL

Short of flying, taking the Eurostar through the Channel Tunnel is the fastest way to cross the English Channel. Travel time is 35 minutes from Folkestone to Calais, 60 minutes from motorway to motorway, or two hours and 15 minutes from London's St. Pancras Station to Paris's Gare du Nord. It takes two hours to reach Midi Station in Brussels from London.

Early risers can easily take a day trip to Paris or an overnight if time is short. Book ahead, though, as Eurostar tickets increase in price the closer you get to your day of travel. If purchased in advance, round-trip tickets from London to Belgium or France cost around £125.

Channel Tunnel Car Transport Eurotunnel (☎ 0844/335–3535 in U.K., 070/223210 in Belgium, 08-10-63-03-04 in France ⊕ www.eurotunnel.com). **French Motorail/Rail Europe** (☎ 0844/848–4050 ⊕ www.raileurope.co.uk).

Channel Tunnel Passenger Service Eurostar (☎ 0843/218–6186 in U.K. ⊕ www.eurostar.co.uk). **Rail Europe** (☎ 800/622–8600 in U.S., 0844/848–4064 in U.K. for inquiries and credit-card bookings ⊕ www.raileurope.com).

ESSENTIALS

∎ ACCOMMODATIONS

Hotels, bed-and-breakfasts, or small country houses—there's a style and price to suit most travelers. The lodgings listed are the best options we've found in each price category. Wherever you stay, make reservations well in advance: England is popular. (*For additional descriptions of kinds of lodgings, see the England Lodging Primer in Chapter 1.*)

Properties are assigned price categories based on a range that includes the cost of the least expensive standard double room in high season (excluding holidays) and the most expensive. Lodgings are indicated in the text by ⌶. Unless otherwise noted, all lodgings listed have a private bathroom, a room phone, and a television.

We always list the facilities that are available—but we don't specify whether they cost extra: when pricing accommodations, always ask what's included and what costs extra. Throughout Britain, lodging prices often include breakfast of some kind, but this is generally not the case in London.

CATEGORY	LONDON	ELSEWHERE
£	under £80	under £70
££	£80–£140	£70–£120
£££	£141–£200	£121–£160
££££	£201–£300	£161–£220
£££££	over £300	over £220

Prices are for two people in a standard double room in high season, including V.A.T., and are given in pounds.

∎TIP➔ Assume that hotels operate on the European Plan (**EP**, no meals) unless we specify that they use the Breakfast Plan (**BP**, with full breakfast), Continental Plan (**CP**, Continental breakfast), or Modified American Plan (**MAP**, breakfast and dinner).

APARTMENT AND HOUSE RENTALS

If you deal directly with local agents, get a recommendation from someone who has used the company. Unlike with hotels, there's no accredited system for apartment-rental standards. *Also see Chapter 2 for London rental resources.*

BED-AND-BREAKFASTS

B&Bs can be a good budget option, and will also help you meet the locals.

Reservation Services Bed & Breakfast.com (☎ 512/322–2710 or 800/462–2632 ⊕ www.bedandbreakfast.com). **Bed & Breakfast (GB)** (☎ 800/454–8704, 0208/956–2390 in U.K. ⊕ www.bedbreak.com). **The Bed and Breakfast Club** (☎ 0870/803–4414 ⊕ www.thebedandbreakfastclub.co.uk). **Host & Guest Service** (☎ 020/7385–9922 in U.K. ⊕ www.host-guest.co.uk). **Wolsey Lodges** (☎ 01473/822058, 01473/827500 for brochure ⊕ www.wolseylodges.com).

COTTAGES

Contacts Classic Cottages (☎ 0132/655–5555 ⊕ www.classic.co.uk). **Luxury Cottages Direct** (☎ 02920/212491 ⊕ www.luxury-cottages.co.uk). **National Trust** (☎ 0844/800–2070 ⊕ www.nationaltrustcottages.co.uk). **Rural Retreats** (☎ 01386/701177 ⊕ www.ruralretreats.co.uk). **VisitBritain** (⊕ www.visitbritain.us).

FARMHOUSES

Contacts Farm & Cottage Holidays UK (☎ 0123/745–9888 ⊕ www.holidaycottages.co.uk). **Farm Stay UK** (☎ 024/7669–6909 ⊕ www.farmstayuk.co.uk). **VisitBritain** (⊕ www.visitbritain.us).

HISTORIC BUILDINGS

Contacts Celtic Castles (☎ 0142/223–3200 ⊕ www.celticcastles.com). **English Heritage** (☎ 0870/333–1181 ⊕ www.english-heritage.org.uk). **Landmark Trust** (☎ 01628/825925 ⊕ www.landmarktrust.org.uk). **National Trust** (☎ 0162/882–5925 ⊕ www.nationaltrustcottages.co.uk). **Portmeirion**

Online Booking Resources

Contacts		
The Apartment Service	0208/944–1444	www.apartmentservice.com
At Home Abroad	212/421–9165	www.athomeabroadinc.com
Barclay International Group	516/364–0064 or 800/845–6636	www.barclayweb.com
English Country Cottages	0845/268–0785	www.english-country-cottages.co.uk
In the English Manner	01559/371600 or 800/422–0799	www.english-manner.co.uk
Interhome	800/882–6864	www.interhome.us
National Trust	0844/800–2070	www.nationaltrustcottages.co.uk
Suzanne B. Cohen & Associates	207/622–0743	www.villaeurope.com
Vacation Rentals By Owner (VRBO)	201/767–9393 or 800/876–4319	www.vrbo.com
Villanet	877/255–4366 or 206/417–3444	www.rentavilla.com
Villas International	415/499–9490 or 800/221–2260	www.villasintl.com

Cottages (☎ 01766/770000 ⊕ www.portmeirion-village.com). **Rural Retreats** (☎ 01386/701177 ⊕ www.ruralretreats.co.uk). **Stately Holiday Cottages** (☎ 01638/674756 ⊕ www.statelyholidaycottages.co.uk). **Unique Home Stays** (☎ 01637/881942 ⊕ ww.uniquehomestays.com). **Vivat Trust** (☎ 01981/550753 from U.S., 0845/090–0194 from U.K. ⊕ www.vivat.org.uk).

HOME EXCHANGES

With a direct home exchange you stay in someone else's home while they stay in yours. Some outfits also deal with vacation homes, so you're not actually staying in someone's full-time residence, just their vacant weekend place. There are several exchange clubs to choose from. Home Exchange.com offers a one-year membership for $99.95, HomeLink International costs $115 for an annual Web membership which includes a directory listing, and Intervac U.S. offers international membership for $99.

If you're interested in home exchange but don't feel like sharing, some home-exchange directories list rentals, too.

Exchange Clubs Home Exchange.com (☎ 800/877–8723 ⊕ www.homeexchange.com). **HomeLink International** (☎ 800/638–3841 ⊕ www.homelink.org). **Intervac U.S.** (☎ 800/756–4663 ⊕ www.intervacus.com).

HOTELS

Most hotels have rooms with "en suite" bathrooms—as private bathrooms are called—although some older ones may have only washbasins; in this case, showers and bathtubs (and toilets) are usually down the hall. When you book a room in the mid-to-lower price categories, confirm your request for a room with en suite facilities. Especially in London, rooms and bathrooms may be smaller than what you find in the United States.

Besides familiar international chains, England has some local chains that are worth a look; they provide rooms from the less expensive (Travelodge, basic but bargain, and Premier Inn are the most widespread; Jurys Inns offer good value in city centers) to the trendy (ABode, Hotel du Vin, Malmaison).

LOCAL DOS AND TABOOS

CUSTOMS OF THE COUNTRY

In general, British and American rules of etiquette are much the same. Differences are subtle. British people find Americans' bluntness somewhat startling from time to time, but are charmed by their friendliness.

British people tend to take politeness extremely seriously. They say "thank you" at every stage of a financial transaction, but are less likely to offer a "God bless you" should a stranger sneeze.

The famous British stiff upper lip is more relaxed these days, but on social occasions it's best to observe what the others do, and go with the flow. If you're visiting a family home, a gift of flowers is welcome, as is a bottle of wine.

GREETINGS

Older British people will shake hands on greeting old friends or acquaintances; female friends may greet each other with a kiss on the cheek. In Britain, you can never say "please," "thank you," or "sorry" too often; to thank your host, a phone call or thank-you card does nicely. E-mail thank-yous are fine for younger hosts.

SIGHTSEEING

As in the United States, in public places it is considered polite to give up your seat to an elderly person, to a pregnant woman, or to a parent struggling with children and bags. Jaywalking is not illegal in England and everybody does it. However, since driving is on the left in England, the traffic flow may be confusing; use caution.

British people used to take waiting in line (called queuing) incredibly seriously, but, especially in London bus queues, line discipline is breaking down. Nevertheless, many still highly value patience, and will turn on "queue jumpers" who try to cut in line. Complaining while waiting in line is considered wimpy. Enduring the wait with good humor is considered a sign of strong moral character.

The single thing you can do that will most mark you as a tourist—and an impolite one—is fail to observe the written and spoken rule that, on virtually all escalators but especially those in Tube stations, you stand on the right side of the escalator and leave room for people to walk past you on the left.

OUT ON THE TOWN

Etiquette in restaurants is much the same as in any major U.S. city. In restaurants you hail a waiter by saying, "Excuse me..." as one passes by, or by trying to catch his eye by politely signaling with subtle hand signals. It is common to have drinks before dinner, and wine with dinner. Friends and co-workers frequently gather in pubs, but you don't have to drink alcohol—some people in the pub drink juice or sodas. Nonetheless, drunkenness can be common in major cities after 10 PM.

You're generally expected to dress "smart casual" for the theater (suits or nice jackets for men, skirts or nice slacks for women), and those going to nightclubs will dress just the same here as they would in New York or Chicago—the flashier the better. Pubs are very casual places, however.

Smoking is forbidden in all public places, including bars and restaurants.

DOING BUSINESS

Punctuality is of prime importance; if you anticipate a late arrival, call ahead. For business dinners, if you proffered the invitation, it's usually assumed that you will pick up the tab. If you're the visitor, however, it's good form for the host to pay the bill. Alternatively, play it safe and offer to split the check.

Local Chains **ABode** (⊕ www.abodehotels. co.uk). **Hotel du Vin** (⊕ www.hotelduvin. com). **Jurys Inn** (☏ 0870/410–0800 ⊕ www. jurysinn.com). **Malmaison** (☏ 0845/365– 4247 ⊕ www.malmaison.com). **Premier Inn** (☏ 0871/527–8000, 1582/567890 outside U.K. ⊕ www.premierinn.com). **Travelodge** (⊕ www. travelodge.co.uk).

HOTEL GRADING SYSTEM

Hotels, guesthouses, inns, and B&Bs in the United Kingdom are all graded from one to five stars by the tourism board, VisitBritain. Basically, the more stars a property has, the more facilities it has, and the facilities will be of a higher standard. It's a fairly good reflection of lodging from small B&Bs up to palatial hotels. The most luxurious hotels will have five stars; a simple, clean, acceptable hostelry will have one star.

DISCOUNTS AND DEALS

Hotel rates in major cities tend to be cheapest on weekends, whereas rural hotels are cheapest on weeknights. The lowest occupancy is between November and April, so hotels lower their prices substantially during these months. Web sites of chains are worth checking for discounts.

In larger cities and in some towns, certain universities offer their residence halls to paying vacationers between terms. The facilities available are usually compact single sleeping units that share bath facilities, and they can be rented on a nightly basis. You can check with local tourist boards for information.

Travelodge can have deep-discount online sales (some so deep you may want to use the room to rest in for a few hours if you don't want to drive immediately). Lastminute.com offers deals on hotel rooms all over the United Kingdom. VisitLondon.com, London's official Web site, has some good deals. LondonTown.com's London Information Centre provides free maps, tourist information, and last-minute hotel bookings in the city, with savings

WORD OF MOUTH

Did the resort look as good in real life as it did in the photos? Did you sleep like a baby, or were the walls paper thin? Did you get your money's worth? Rate hotels and write your own reviews in Travel Ratings or start a discussion about your favorite places in Travel Talk on www. fodors.com. Your comments might even appear in our books. Yes, you, too, can be a correspondent!

of up to 50%. Its kiosk in Leicester Square is open daily 10 AM–6 PM.

Local Resources Lastminute.com (⊕ www. lastminute.com). **LondonTown.com's London Information Centre** (✉ Leicester Sq. ☏ 0207/437–4370 ⊕ www. LondonInformationCentre.com).

▌ COMMUNICATIONS

INTERNET

If you're traveling with a laptop, carry a spare battery and adapter. If you expect to have to use dial-up, get a telephone cord that's compatible with a British phone jack; these are available in Britain at airports and electronics stores. Wi-Fi is increasingly available in hotels, and broadband coverage is widespread in cities. Generally speaking, the pricier the hotel, the more likely you are to find Wi-Fi there. Wireless access is relatively rare in cafés and coffee shops compared to the United States, but its popularity there is growing.

Contacts Cybercafes (⊕ www.cybercafes. com). **Wi-Fi Freespot** (⊕ www.wififreespot.com).

PHONES

British Telecom runs the telephone service in Great Britain and is generally reliable. All calls (including local calls) made within the United Kingdom are charged according to the time of day. The standard rate applies weekdays 7 AM to 7 PM; a cheaper rate is in effect weekdays 7 PM to 7 AM and all day on weekends, when it's even cheaper. A local call before 6 PM costs 20p for three minutes; this doubles to 40p for the same from a pay phone. A daytime call to the United States will cost 24p a minute on a regular phone (weekends are cheaper), 80p on a pay phone.

A word of warning: 0870 numbers are *not* toll-free numbers in Britain; in fact, numbers beginning with this or the 0871, 0844, or 0845 prefixes cost extra to call. The amount varies and is usually relatively small—except for numbers with the premium-rate 0905 prefix, which cost an eye-watering £1 per minute when dialed from within the country—but can be excessive when dialed from outside Britain.

CALLING ENGLAND

The country code for Great Britain (and thus England) is 44. When dialing an English number from abroad, drop the initial 0 from before the local area code. For example, let's say you're calling Buckingham Palace—020/7839–1377—from the United States. First, dial 011 (the international access code), then 44 (Great Britain's country code), then 20 (London's center-city code—without its initial 0), then the remainder of the number.

CALLING WITHIN ENGLAND

For all calls within England (and Britain), dial the area code (which usually begins with 01, except in London), followed by the telephone number.

There are three types of pay phones: those that accept (a) only coins, (b) only British Telecom (BT) phone cards, or (c) BT phone cards and credit cards. Most coin-operated phones take 10p, 20p, 50p, and £1 coins. Insert the coins *before* dialing (minimum charge is 20p). The indicator panel shows how much money is left; add more whenever you like. If there is no answer, replace the receiver and your money will be returned.

For pay and other phones, if you hear a repeated single tone after dialing, the line is busy; a continuous tone means the number didn't work.

There are several different directory-assistance providers. For information anywhere in Britain, try dialing 118–888 or 118–118; you'll need to know the town and the street (or at least the neighborhood) of the person or organization for which you're requesting information. For the operator, dial 100. For genuine emergencies, dial 999.

CALLING OUTSIDE ENGLAND

For direct overseas dialing from England (and Britain), dial 00, then the country code, area code, and number. For the international operator, credit card, or collect calls, dial 155; for international directory assistance, dial 118505. The country code for the United States is 1.

Access Codes AT&T Direct (☎ *In the U.K., there are AT&T access numbers to dial the U.S. using two different phone types: 0500/890011 British Telecom, 0800/890–0011 AT&T).* **MCI WorldPhone** (☎ *0800/279–5088 in the U.K. for the U.S. via MCI).* **Sprint International Access** (☎ *0800/890877).*

CALLING CARDS

Public card phones operate with special cards that you can buy from post offices or newsstands. Ideal for longer calls, the cards are composed of units of 10p, and come in values of £3, £5, £10, and more. To use a card phone, lift the receiver, insert your card, and dial the number. An indicator panel shows the number of units used. At the end of your call the card will be returned. Where credit cards are taken, slide the card through, as indicated.

MOBILE PHONES

Any cell phone can be used in Europe if it's tri-band, quad-band, or GSM. Travelers should ask their cell-phone company if their phone fits in this category and make sure it is activated for international calling before leaving their home country. Roaming fees can be steep, however: $1 a minute is considered reasonable. And overseas you normally pay the toll charges for incoming calls. It's almost always cheaper to send a text message than to make a call, since text messages have a low set fee (often less than 25¢).

If you just want to make local calls, consider buying a new SIM card once you're in England (note that your provider may have to unlock your phone for you to use a different SIM card) and a prepaid service plan in the destination. You'll then have a local number and can make local calls at local rates. If your trip is extensive, you could simply buy a new cell phone in your destination.

You can rent a cell phone from most major car-rental agencies in England. Some upscale hotels now provide loaner cell phones to their guests. Beware, however, of the per-minute rates charged.

Contacts Cellular Abroad (☎ 800/287–5072 ⊕ www.cellularabroad.com). **Mobal** (☎ 888/888–9162 ⊕ www.mobalrental.com). **Planet Fone** (☎ 888/988–4777 ⊕ www.planetfone.com). **Renta Mobile Phone** (☎ 020/7353–7705 ⊕ www.rent-mobile-phone.com).

▎CUSTOMS AND DUTIES

You're always allowed to bring goods of a certain value back home without having to pay any duty or import tax. But there's a limit on the amount of tobacco and liquor you can bring back duty-free, and some countries have separate limits for perfumes; for exact figures, check with your customs department. The values of so-called "duty-free" goods are included in these amounts. When you shop abroad, save all your receipts, as customs inspectors may ask to see them as well as the items you purchased. If the total value of your goods is more than the duty-free limit, you'll have to pay a tax (most often a flat percentage) on the value of everything beyond that limit.

Fresh meats, plants and vegetables, controlled drugs, and firearms (including replicas) and ammunition may not be brought into the United Kingdom, nor can dairy products from non-EU countries. Pets

from the United States or Canada with the proper documentation may be brought into the country without quarantine under the U.K. Pet Travel Scheme (PETS). The process takes about six months to complete and involves detailed steps.

You will face no customs formalities if you enter Scotland or Wales from any other part of the United Kingdom.

Information in England HM Revenue and Customs (☎ 0845/010–9000 ⊕ www.hmrc.gov.uk). **Pet Travel Scheme** (☎ 0870/241–1710 ⊕ www.defra.gov.uk/wildlife-pets/pets/travel/pets/contacts.htm).

U.S. Information U.S. Customs and Border Protection (⊕ www.cbp.gov).

▎EATING OUT

The stereotypical notion of English meals as parades of roast beef, overcooked vegetables, and stodgy puddings (desserts) is gradually being replaced—particularly in London, other major cities, and some country hot spots—with an evolving picture of the country as foodie territory. From trendy gastro-pubs to the see-and-be-seen dining shrines, England is becoming known for a global palate.

In general, restaurant prices are high. If you're watching your budget, seek out pubs and ethnic restaurants.

CATEGORY	LONDON	ELSEWHERE
£	under £10	under £10
££	£10–£16	£10–£14
£££	£17–£23	£15–£19
££££	£24–£32	£20–£25
£££££	over £32	over £25

All prices are per person in pounds for a main course at dinner.

DISCOUNTS AND DEALS

Eating out in England's big cities in particular can be expensive, but you can do it cheaply. Try local cafés, more popularly known as "caffs," where heaping plates of English comfort food (bacon sandwiches and stuffed baked potatoes, for example) are served. England has plenty of the big names in fast food, as well as smaller places selling sandwiches, fish-and-chips, burgers, falafel, kebabs, and the like. For a local touch, check out curry houses; Indian food is popular throughout the country. Marks & Spencer, Sainsbury's, Tesco, and Waitrose are chain supermarkets with outlets throughout the country. They're good choices for groceries, premade sandwiches, or picnic fixings.

MEALS AND MEALTIMES

Cafés serving the traditional English breakfast (called a "fry-up") of eggs, bacon, sausage, beans, half a grilled tomato, and strong tea are often the cheapest—and most authentic—places for breakfast. For lighter morning fare (or for real brewed coffee), try the Continental-style sandwich bars and coffee shops—the Pret-a-Manger chain being one of the largest—offering croissants and other pastries.

At lunch you can grab a sandwich between sights, pop into the local pub, or sit down in a restaurant. Dinner, too, has no set rules, but a three-course meal is standard in most midrange or high-end restaurants. Pre- or post-theater menus, offering two or three courses for a set price, are usually a good value.

Note that most pubs do not have any waitstaff and that you are expected to go to the bar, order a beverage and your meal, and inform them of your table number. Also, in cities many pubs do not serve food after 3 PM, so they're usually a better lunch option than dinner.

On Sunday, for pure Englishness, a traditional roast beef, pork, or lamb dinner still tops the list. Its typical accompaniment is Yorkshire pudding—a savory soufflé-like batter of eggs, milk, and flour oven-baked until crisp, then topped with a rich, dark gravy. Shepherd's pie, a classic pub dish, is made with diced or minced lamb and a mashed-potato topping, and "bangers and mash" are English sausages with mashed potatoes and onion gravy.

In the pubs, you'll also find a ploughman's lunch—crusty bread, English cheese (perhaps cheddar, blue Stilton, crumbly Cheshire, or smooth red Leicester), and pickles, or small pies with fillings such as steak and kidney or leek and chicken. And there's also fish-and-chips, usually made from cod or haddock deep-fried in a crispy batter and served with thick french fries. Take time for afternoon tea—whether with scones (with cream and jam, called a "cream tea") and pastries or just a hot cup of Assam—at least once on your stay; it's a civilized respite.

Breakfast is generally served between 7:30 and 9, lunch between noon and 2, dinner or supper between 7:30 and 9:30, sometimes earlier, seldom later except in large cities. These days tea is rarely a proper meal anymore (it was once served between 4:30 and 6), and tea shops are often open all day in touristy areas (they're not found at all in nontouristy places). So you can have a cup and pastry or sandwich whenever you feel you need it. Sunday roasts at pubs last from 11 AM or noon to 3 PM.

Smoking is banned in pubs, clubs, and restaurants throughout Britain.

PAYING

Credit cards are widely accepted in restaurants, but not in pubs, which generally still require cash (although a growing minority are taking plastic). Be sure that you don't double-pay a service charge. Many restaurants exclude service charges from the printed menu (which the law obliges them to display outside), and then add 10% to 15% to the check. Others will stamp SERVICE NOT INCLUDED along the bottom of the bill, in which case you should add 10% to 15%. Cash is always appreciated, as it is more likely to go to the specific waiter, while tips on credit cards may go into a general pool.

PUBS

A common misconception among visitors to England is that pubs are bars. Pubs are also gathering places, conversation zones, even restaurants. In many pubs the social interaction is as important as the alcohol. Pubs are, generally speaking, where people go to meet their friends and catch up on one another's lives. In small towns pubs act almost as town halls. Some people in a pub drink soft drinks, tea, or coffee, rather than beer, and cocktails are usually in short supply. Even if you don't drink alcohol, go to a pub and have an orange juice or a soda, relax, and meet the locals. Traditionally pub hours are 11–11, with last orders called about 20 minutes before closing time, but pubs can choose to stay open until midnight or 1 AM, or later.

Though to travelers it may appear that there's a pub on almost every corner, in fact pubs are something of an endangered species, closing at a rate of 39 a week (as of February 2010), with independent, non-chain pubs at particular risk.

Most pubs tend to be child-friendly, but others have restricted hours for children. If a pub serves food, it will generally allow children in during the day with adults. Some pubs are stricter than others, though, and will not admit anyone younger than 18. Some will allow children in during the day, but only until 6 PM. If you're in doubt, ask the bartender. Family-friendly pubs tend to be packed with kids, parents, and all of their accoutrements, so you can just use your common sense. Some even have children's play areas with jungle gyms and toys.

RESERVATIONS AND DRESS

Regardless of where you are, it's a good idea to make a reservation if you can. We mention them specifically only when reservations are essential or when they are not accepted. For popular restaurants, book as far ahead as you can (often 30 days), and reconfirm as soon as you arrive. (Large parties should always call ahead to check the reservations policy.) We mention dress only when men are required to wear a jacket or a jacket and tie.

Online reservation services aren't as popular in England as in the United States,

WORD OF MOUTH
Was the service stellar or not up to snuff? Did the food give you shivers of delight or leave you cold? Did the prices and portions make you happy or sad? Rate restaurants and write your own reviews in Travel Ratings or start a discussion about your favorite places in Travel Talk on www.fodors.com. Your comments might even appear in our books. Yes, you, too, can be a correspondent!

but Toptable and Square Meal have a fair number of listings in England.

Contact Square Meal (⊕ *www.squaremeal.co.uk*). **Toptable** (⊕ *www.toptable.co.uk*).

WINES, BEER, AND SPIRITS

Although hundreds of varieties of beer are brewed around the country, the traditional brew is known as bitter and is not carbonated; it's usually served at room temperature. Fizzy American-style beer is called lager. There are also plenty of other potations: stouts like Guinness and Murphy's are thick, pitch-black brews you'll either love or hate; ciders, made from apples, are an alcoholic drink in Britain (Bulmer's and Strongbow are the names to remember); shandies (oddly) are a low-alcohol mix of lager and lemon soda. Real ales, which have a natural second fermentation in the cask, have a shorter shelf life (so many are brewed locally) but special flavor; these are worth seeking out. Generally the selection and quality of cocktails is higher in a wine bar or café than in a pub. The legal drinking age is 18.

▌ECOTOURISM

Ecotourism is an emerging trend in the United Kingdom. The Shetland Environmental Agency Ltd. runs the Green Tourism Business Scheme (GTBS), a program that evaluates sites and lodgings in England, Scotland, and Wales and gives them a gold, silver, or bronze rating according to their sustainability. You can find a list of green hotels, B&Bs, apartments, and other properties on the GTBS Web site. Also check out the VisitBritain Web site, which has information and tips about green travel in Britain.

Contact Green Tourism Business Scheme (☎ *01738/632162* ⊕ *www.green-business. co.uk*). **VisitBritain** (⊕ *www.visitbritain.us*).

■ ELECTRICITY

The electrical current in Great Britain is 220–240 volts (in line with the rest of Europe), 50 cycles alternating current (AC); wall outlets take three-pin plugs, and shaver sockets take two round, oversize prongs. British bathrooms are not permitted to have 220–240 volt outlets in them. Blackouts and brownouts are rare and are usually fixed in a few hours.

Consider making a small investment in a universal adapter, which has several types of plugs in one lightweight, compact unit. Most laptops and mobile phone chargers are dual voltage (i.e., they operate equally well on 110 and 220 volts), so require only an adapter. These days the same is true of small appliances such as hair dryers. Always check labels and manufacturer instructions. Don't use 110-volt outlets marked FOR SHAVERS ONLY for high-wattage appliances such as hair dryers.

Contacts Steve Kropla's Help for World Travelers (⊕ *www.kropla.com*). **Walkabout Travel Gear** (⊕ *www.walkabouttravelgear. com*).

■ EMERGENCIES

If you need to report an emergency, dial 999 for police, fire, or ambulance. Be prepared to give the telephone number you're calling from. You can get 24-hour treatment in Accident and Emergency at British hospitals, although you should expect to wait hours for treatment. Prescriptions are valid only if made out by doctors registered in the United Kingdom.

Although England has a subsidized National Health Service, free at the point of service for British residents, foreign visitors are expected to pay for any treatment they receive. Expect to receive a bill after you return home. Check with your health-insurance company to make sure you're covered. Some British hospitals now require a credit card or other payment before they'll offer treatment.

U.S. Embassies American Embassy (✉ *24 Grosvenor Sq., London* ☎ *020/7499– 9000* ⊕ *www.usembassy.org.uk*). **U.S. Passport Unit** (✉ *55 Upper Brook St., London* ☎ *0207/370–3777*).

General Emergency Contacts Ambulance, fire, police (☎ *999*).

■ HEALTH

SPECIFIC ISSUES IN ENGLAND

If you take prescription drugs, keep a supply in your carry-on luggage and make a list of all your prescriptions to keep on file at home while you are abroad. You will not be able to renew a U.S. prescription at a pharmacy in Britain. Prescriptions are accepted only if issued by a U.K.-registered physician.

OVER-THE-COUNTER REMEDIES

Over-the-counter medications in England are similar to those in the United States, with a few significant differences. Medications are sold in boxes rather than bottles, and are sold in small amounts—usually no more than 24 pills. There may also be fewer brands. All headache medicine is usually filed under the "painkillers." You can buy generic ibuprofen or a popular European brand of ibuprofen, Nurofen. Tylenol is not sold in the United Kingdom, but its main ingredient, acetaminophen, is—bit it's called paracetomol.

Among sinus and allergy medicines, Claritin is the main option here; it's the same brand sold in the United States. Some medicines are pretty much the same as brands sold in the United States—instead of Nyquil cold medicine, there's Night

Nurse. The most popular over-the-counter cough medicine is Benylin.

Drugstores are generally called pharmacies, but sometimes referred to as chemists' shops. The biggest drugstore chain in the country is Boots, which has outlets everywhere, except for the smallest towns. If you're in a rural area, look for shops marked with a sign of a green cross.

If you can't find what you want, ask at the counter; many over-the-counter medicines are kept behind the register.

SHOTS AND MEDICATIONS
No special shots are required or suggested for England.

Health Warnings National Centers for Disease Control & Prevention (*CDC* ☎ *800/232-1616 international travelers' health line* ⊕ *wwwnc.cdc.gov/travel*). **World Health Organization** (*WHO* ⊕ *www.who.int*).

▌HOURS OF OPERATION

Most banks are open weekdays from 9:30 until 3:30 or 4:30. Some have Thursday evening hours, and a few are open Saturday morning. Normal office hours for most businesses are weekdays 9 to 5.

The major national museums and galleries are open daily from 9 until 6, including lunchtime, but have shorter hours on Sunday. Regional museums are usually closed Monday and have shorter hours in winter. In London many museums are open late one evening a week.

Independently owned pharmacies are generally open Monday through Saturday 9:30 to 5:30, although in larger cities some stay open until 10 PM; local newspapers list which pharmacies are open late.

Usual retail business hours are Monday through Saturday 9 to 5:30, Sunday noon to 4. Outside the main centers most shops close at 1 PM once a week, often Wednesday or Thursday. In small villages many also close for lunch and do not open on Sunday at all. In large cities—especially London—department stores stay open late (usually until 7:30 or 8) one night a

week, usually Thursday. On national holidays most stores are closed, and over the Christmas holidays most restaurants are closed as well.

HOLIDAYS
Holidays are January 1, New Year's Day; Good Friday and Easter Monday; May Day (first Monday in May); spring and summer bank holidays (last Monday in May and August, respectively); December 25, Christmas Day; and December 26, Boxing Day (day after Christmas). If these holidays fall on a weekend, the holiday is observed on the following Monday. During the Christmas holidays many restaurants, as well as museums and other attractions, may close for at least a week—call to verify hours. Book hotels for Christmas travel well in advance, and check whether the hotel restaurant will be open.

▌MAIL

Stamps can be bought from post offices (open weekdays 9 to 5:30, Saturday 9 to noon), from stamp machines outside post offices, and from news dealers' stores and newsstands. Mailboxes, known as post or letter boxes, are painted bright red. Allow seven days for a letter to reach the United States and about 10 days to two weeks to Australia or New Zealand by airmail. Surface mail service can take up to four or five weeks. The useful Royal Mail Web site has information on everything from buying stamps to finding a post office.

Airmail letters up to 10 grams (0.35 ounce) to North America cost 62p; postcards cost 62p. Letters within Britain are 39p for first class, 30p for second class. Rates for envelopes larger than 353 mm (13.9 inches) long, 250 mm (9.84 inches) wide, and 25 mm (1 inch) deep are higher. All rates are subject to change.

Contact Royal Mail (⊕ *www.royalmail.com*).

SHIPPING PACKAGES

Most department stores and retail outlets can ship your goods home. You should check your insurance for coverage of possible damage. Private delivery companies such as Federal Express and DHL offer two-day delivery service to the United States, but you'll pay a considerable amount for the privilege.

Express Services DHL (☎ 0844/248–0844 ⊕ www.dhl.co.uk). **Federal Express** (☎ 0845/607–0809 ⊕ www.fedex.com). **Parcelforce** (☎ 0844/800–4466 ⊕ www.parcelforce.co.uk).

■ MONEY

No doubt about it, prices in England can seem high because of the exchange rate. The rate has improved during the ongoing recession, though: between this and the increased availability of deals, the country has become more affordable. London remains one of the most expensive cities in the world. However, for every yin there's a yang, and travelers can get breaks: staying in bed-and-breakfasts or renting a city apartment brings down lodging costs, and national museums are free. The chart below gives some ideas of the prices you can expect to pay for day-to-day life.

ITEM	AVERAGE COST
Cup of Coffee	£1.50–£3
Glass of Wine	£3.50 in a pub or wine bar, £5.50 or more in a restaurant
Glass of Beer	£2.70 or more
Sandwich	£3.50
One-Mile Taxi Ride in London	£4.60–£8.60
Museum Admission	National museums free; others £5–£10

Prices throughout this guide are given for adults. Substantially reduced fees—generally referred to as "concessions" throughout Great Britain—are almost always available for children, students, and senior citizens.

■ TIP→ Banks never have every foreign currency on hand, and it may take as long as a week to order. If you're planning to exchange funds before leaving home, don't wait until the last minute.

ATMS AND BANKS

Make sure before leaving home that your credit and debit cards have been programmed for ATM use abroad—ATMs in England and Wales accept PINs of four or fewer digits only; if your PIN is longer, ask about changing it. If you know your PIN as a word, learn the numerical equivalent, since most keypads in England show numbers only, not letters. Most ATMs are on both the Cirrus and Plus networks. ATMs are available at most main-street banks, large supermarkets such as Sainsbury's and Tesco's, some Tube stops in London, and many rail stations. Major banks include Barclays, HSBC, and NatWest.

Your own bank will probably charge a fee for using ATMs abroad; the foreign bank you use may also charge a fee. (Check with your bank to see if they have a better rate with particular foreign banks.) Nevertheless, you'll usually get a better rate of exchange at an ATM than you will at a currency-exchange office or even when changing money in a bank. And extracting funds as you need them is a safer option than carrying around a large amount of cash.

CREDIT CARDS

Throughout this guide the following abbreviations are used: **AE**, American Express; **DC**, Diners Club; **MC**, MasterCard; and **V**, Visa.

The Discover card is not accepted throughout Britain. Other major credit cards, except Diners Club, are accepted virtually everywhere in Britain; however, you're expected to know and use your pin number for all transactions—even for credit cards, so it's a good idea to do some quick memorization for whichever card you intend to use in England.

Inform your credit-card company before you travel, especially if you're going abroad and don't travel internationally very often. Otherwise, the credit-card company might put a hold on your card owing to unusual activity. Record all your credit-card numbers in a safe place. Both MasterCard and Visa have general numbers you can call (collect if you're abroad) if your card is lost, but you're better off calling the number of your issuing bank, since MasterCard and Visa usually just transfer you to your bank; your bank's number is usually printed on your card.

If you plan to use your credit card for cash advances, you'll need to apply for a PIN at least two weeks before your trip. Although it's usually cheaper (and safer) to use a credit card abroad for large purchases (so you can cancel payments or be reimbursed if there's a problem), note that some credit-card companies *and* the banks that issue them add substantial percentages to all foreign transactions, whether they're in a foreign currency or not. Check on these fees before leaving home.

Reporting Lost Cards American Express (☎ 01273/696933 in U.K., 336/393–1111 collect from abroad ⊕ www.americanexpress. com). **Diners Club** (☎ 0870/190–0011 in U.K., 303/799–1504 collect from abroad ⊕ www.dinersclub.com). **MasterCard** (☎ 0800/964767 in U.K., 636/722–7111 collect from abroad ⊕ www.mastercard.com). **Visa** (☎ 0800/891725 in U.K., 410/581–9994 collect from abroad ⊕ www.visa.com).

CURRENCY AND EXCHANGE

The unit of currency in Great Britain is the pound sterling (£), divided into 100 pence (p). The bills (called notes in Britain) are 50, 20, 10, and 5 pounds. Coins are £2, £1, 50p, 20p, 10p, 5p, 2p, and 1p. If you are traveling beyond England and Wales, note that Scotland and the Channel Islands have their own bills, and the Channel Islands their own coins, too. Scottish bills are accepted in the rest of Britain, but you cannot use Channel Islands currency outside the islands.

At the time of this writing, the exchange rate was about U.S. $1.59 to £1.

British post offices exchange currency with no fee, and at decent rates.

■**TIP➜** Even if a currency-exchange booth has a sign promising no commission, rest assured that there's some kind of huge, hidden fee. And as for rates, you're almost always better off getting foreign currency at an ATM or exchanging money at a bank.

Currency Conversion Google (⊕ www. google.com). **Oanda.com** (⊕ www.oanda.com). **XE.com** (⊕ www.xe.com).

■ PACKING

England can be cool, damp, and overcast, even in summer. You'll want a heavy coat for winter and a lightweight coat or warm jacket for summer. There's no time of year when a raincoat or umbrella won't come in handy. For the cities, pack as you would for an American city: coats and ties for expensive restaurants and nightspots, casual clothes elsewhere. Jeans are popular in England and are perfectly acceptable for sightseeing and informal dining. For women, ordinary street dress is acceptable everywhere. If you plan to stay in budget hotels, take your own soap. It's also a good idea to take a washcloth. Pack insect repellent if you plan to hike.

■ PASSPORTS

U.S. citizens need only a valid passport to enter Great Britain for stays of up to six months. Travelers should be prepared to show sufficient funds to support and accommodate themselves while in Britain (credit cards will usually suffice for this) and to show a return or onward ticket. If you're within six months of your passport's expiration date, renew it before you leave—nearly expired passports are not strictly banned, but they make immigration officials anxious, and may cause you problems. Health certificates are not required.

■ RESTROOMS

Public restrooms are sparse in England, although most big cities maintain public facilities that are clean and modern. If there is an attendant, which is rare, you are expected to pay admission (usually 30p). Train stations and department stores have public restrooms that occasionally charge a small fee, usually 30p. Most pubs, restaurants, and even fast-food chains reserve their bathrooms for customer use only. Hotels and museums are usually a good place to find clean, free facilities. On the road, gas-station facilities are usually clean and free.

Find a Loo The Bathroom Diaries (⊕ *www. thebathroomdiaries.com*).

■ SAFETY

England has a low incidence of violent crime. However, petty crime, mostly in urban areas, is on the rise, and tourists can be the target.

Use common sense. When in a city center, if you're paying at a shop or a restaurant, never put your wallet down or let your bag out of your hand. When sitting on a chair in a public place, keep your purse on your lap or between your feet. Always use the bag hooks in public toilet stalls.

Don't wear expensive jewelry or watches. Store your passport in the hotel safe; use your driver's license for identification, although you'll never be asked for it. Don't leave anything in your car.

Although scams do occur in Britain, they are not pervasive. Do, however, watch out for pickpockets, particularly in London. They often work in pairs, one distracting you in some way. Always take a licensed black taxi or call a car service (sometimes called minicabs) recommended by your hotel. Avoid using minicab services offered by drivers who approach you on the street. In most cases they will overcharge you. Always buy theater tickets from a reputable dealer. If you are driving in from a British port, beware of thieves

posing as customs officials. The thieves stop travelers after they have followed them from the port. Then they flag them down and "confiscate illegal goods."

If you're getting money out of an ATM, beware of someone bumping into you to distract you. You may want to use ATMs inside banks rather than those outside them. In London scams are most common at ATMs on Oxford Street and around Piccadilly Circus.

In recent years there have been a few terrorist incidents in England, usually on public transportation. While traveling, don't leave any bags unattended, as they may be viewed as a security risk and taken away by the authorities. If bags are taken away, they will be destroyed. If you see an unattended bag on the train, bus, or Tube, find a worker and report it, but do not touch the bag yourself. Never hesitate to get off a Tube, train, or bus if you feel unsafe.

■TIP➔ **Distribute your cash, credit cards, IDs, and other valuables between a deep front pocket, an inside jacket or vest pocket, and a hidden money pouch. Don't reach for the money pouch once you're in public.**

General Information and Warnings Trans-portation Security Administration (*TSA* ⊕ *www.tsa.gov*). **U.K. Foreign & Commonwealth Office** (⊕ *www.fco.gov.uk/travel*). **U.S. Department of State** (⊕ *www.travel.state. gov*).

■ SIGHTSEEING PASSES

DISCOUNT PASSES

If you plan to visit castles, gardens, and historic houses during your stay in England and Wales, look into discount passes or organization memberships that can provide significant savings. Just be sure to match what the pass or membership offers against your itinerary to see if it's worthwhile.

The National Trust, English Heritage, and the Historic Houses Association each encompass hundreds of properties.

English Heritage's Overseas Visitors Pass costs £20 for a seven-day pass and £24.50 for a 14-day pass for one adult. You can order it in advance by phone or online, or get the order form online and then submit it by fax or mail. If you are traveling within 21 days, you can purchase the pass at a participating property in England. The National Trust Touring Pass, for overseas visitors, must be purchased in advance of a visit; it is sold online or by phone but not at the properties. A seven-day pass is £21; a 14-day pass is £26.

VisitBritain's Great British Heritage Pass is £45 for four days, £65 for one week, and £85 for 15 days, and includes more than 500 properties belonging to English Heritage and the National Trust. The pass is sold online and at major tourist information centers in Britain. Family passes are available, too.

Annual membership in the National Trust (through the Royal Oak Foundation, the U.S. affiliate) is $55 a year, versus £48 if you join in Britain. English Heritage membership is £44, and the Historic Houses Association is £38. Memberships entitle you to free entry to properties.

For London Pass information, see Chapter 2. For passes specifically for Wales, see Chapter 15.

Information English Heritage (☎ 0870/333–1181 ⊕ www.english-heritage.org.uk). **Great British Heritage Pass** (☎ 0870/242–9988, 0166/448–5020 from U.S. ⊕ www.britishheritagepass.com). **Historic Houses Association** (☎ 01464/896–688 ⊕ www.hha.org.uk). **National Trust** (☎ 0844/800–1895 ⊕ www.nationaltrust.org.uk). **Royal Oak Foundation** (☎ 212/480–2889 or 800/913–6565 ⊕ www.royal-oak.org).

▌ SPORTS AND THE OUTDOORS

In addition to the associations listed below, VisitBritain and local Tourist Information Centres can recommend places to enjoy your favorite sport.

BIKING

The national body promoting cycle touring is the Cyclists' Touring Club (CTC; £35 a year). Members get free advice and route information, a B&B handbook, and a magazine. The CTC and VisitBritain publish a free guide, "Britain for Cyclists." Both the CTC and VisitBritain provide lists of travel agencies specializing in cycling vacations.

Contacts Cyclists' Touring Club (☎ 01483/283337 ⊕ www.ctc.org.uk). **Visit-Britain** (⊕ www.visitbritain.us).

BOATING

Boating can be a leisurely way to explore the English landscape, ranging from bucolic rivers to industrial canals, from a unique perspective. For boat-rental operators along Britain's several hundred miles of historic canals and waterways, from the Norfolk Broads to the Lake District, contact the Association of Pleasure Craft Operators or Waterway Holidays. British Waterways has maps and other information. Waterway Holidays arranges boat accommodations from traditional narrow boats (small, slender barges) to wide-beam canal boats, motorboats, and sailboats; Waterways UK has both brochures and a reservation service online.

Contacts Association of Pleasure Craft Operators (☎ 0844/800–9575 ⊕ www.apco.org.uk). **British Waterways** (☎ 01923/201120 ⊕ www.waterscape.com). **Waterway Holidays** (☎ 01252/796400 ⊕ www.waterwaysholidays.com). **Waterways UK** (☎ 01952/796400 ⊕ www.waterways-uk.com).

GOLF

Invented in Scotland, golf is a beloved pastime all over England. Some courses take advantage of spectacular natural settings, from the ocean to mountain backdrops. Most courses are reserved for club members and adhere to strict rules of protocol and dress. However, many famous courses can be used by visiting golfers if they reserve well in advance. In addition, numerous public courses are open to anyone, though reservations are advised for these as well. Package tours with companies such as Golf International and Owenoak International Golf Travel allow visitors into usually exclusive clubs. For further information on courses, fees, and locations, try the Web sites UK Golf Guide or English Golf Courses.

Contacts English Golf Courses (⊕ *www. englishgolf-courses.co.uk*). **Golf International** (☎ *212/986–9176 or 800/833–1389 in U.S.* ⊕ *www.golfinternational.com*). **Owenoak International Golf Travel** (☎ *203/854–9000 or 800/426–4498 in U.S.* ⊕ *www.owenoak. com*). **UK Golf Guide** (⊕ *www.uk-golf.com*).

WALKING

Walking and hiking, from the slowest ramble to a mountainside climb requiring technical equipment, are enormously popular in England. For information about stunning National Trails visit ⊕ *www. nationaltrail.co.uk*. The Ramblers, a well-known charitable organization that promotes walking and care of footpaths, publishes a magazine and a yearbook full of resources, and a list of B&Bs within 2 mi of selected long-distance footpaths; its Web site is extensive. Some of the best maps for walking are the Explorer Maps, published by the Ordnance Survey; check out ⊕ *www.ordnancesurvey.co.uk*.

Contacts Long Distance Walkers Association (☎ *01753/866685* ⊕ *www.ldwa.org. uk*). **Natural England** (☎ *0845/600–3078* ⊕ *www.naturalengland.gov.uk*). **The Ramblers** (☎ *020/7339–8500* ⊕ *www.ramblers.org.uk*).

■ TAXES

An air passenger duty of £10 Economy (£20 First and Club class) per person traveling within the EU and £40 Economy (£80 First and Club class) per person traveling outside the EU is included in the price of your ticket, although the government has announced plans to replace this with a per-flight duty.

The British sales tax (V.A.T., Value Added Tax) is 17.5%. As of this writing, it is due to increase to 20% in 2011. The tax is almost always included in quoted prices in shops, hotels, and restaurants. The most common exception is at high-end hotels, where prices often exclude V.A.T. Be sure to verify whether the room price includes V.A.T. Outside of hotels and rental-car agencies, which have specific additional taxes, there is no other sales tax in England.

Most travelers from outside the EU can get a V.A.T. refund by either the Retail Export or the more cumbersome Direct Export method. Refunds apply for V.A.T. only on goods being taken out of Britain, and purchases must exceed a minimum limit (check with the store—generally £50–£100). Many large stores provide V.A.T.–refund services, but only if you request it; they will handle the paperwork. For the Retail Export method, you must ask the store to complete Form V.A.T. 407 (you must have identification—passports are best), to be given to customs at your last port of departure. Have the form stamped like any customs form by customs officials when you leave the country or, if you're visiting several European Union countries, when you leave the EU. Be ready to show customs officials what you've bought; budget extra time at the airport for this. After you're through passport control, take the form to a refund-service counter for an on-the-spot refund (if the retailer has an agreement with the firm running the counter; ask the store when you make your purchase), or mail it back to the store or a refund service from the airport or after you arrive home. The refund will be forwarded to you in about eight weeks, minus a service charge, either in the form of a credit to your charge card or as a British check, which American banks charge you to convert.

With the Direct Export method, the goods are mailed directly to your home; you must have a Form V.A.T. 407 certified by customs, police, or a notary public when you get home and then sent back to the store, which will refund your money. For inquiries, call the local Customs and

Excise office listed in the telephone directory. Remember, V.A.T. refunds can't be processed after you arrive back home.

Another option is a refund service, which processes refunds for most shops. Global Refund is a Europe-wide service with 225,000 affiliated stores and more than 700 refund counters at major airports and border crossings. Its refund form, called a Tax Free Check, is the most common across the European continent. The service issues refunds in the form of cash, check, or credit-card adjustment. The latter is useful for small purchases as the cost of cashing a foreign-currency check may exceed the amount of the refund.

V.A.T. Refunds Global Refund (☎ 866/706–6090, 0800–321–1111 in U.K. ⊕ www.globalrefund.com). **HM Revenue and Customs** (☎ 0845/010–9000 ⊕ www.hmrc.gov.uk).

▌ TIME

England sets its clocks by Greenwich Mean Time, five hours ahead of the U.S. East Coast. British summer time (GMT plus one hour) generally coincides with American daylight saving time adjustments.

Time Zones Timeanddate.com (⊕ www.timeanddate.com/worldclock).

▌ TIPPING

Tipping is done in Britain just as in the United States, but at a lower level than you would back home. Tipping more can look like you're showing off. Do not tip theater ushers or bar staff in pubs—although you can always offer to buy the latter a drink. There's no need to tip at clubs (it's acceptable at posher establishments, though) unless you're being served at your table. Rounding up to the nearest pound or 50p is appreciated.

TIPPING GUIDELINES FOR ENGLAND	
Bartender	£1–£2 per round of drinks, depending on the number of drinks, except in pubs where tipping is not the custom
Bellhop	£1 per bag, depending on the level of the hotel
Hotel Concierge	£5 or more, if he or she performs a service for you
Hotel Doorman	£1 if he helps you get a cab
Hotel Maid	It's extremely rare for hotel maids to be tipped; £1 or £2 would be generous.
Hotel Room-Service Waiter	Nothing, if a service charge is added to the bill
Porter at Airport or Train Station	£1 per bag
Skycap at Airport	£1 per bag checked
Taxi Driver	10p per pound of the fare, then round up to nearest pound
Tour Guide	Tipping optional: £1 or £2 is generous.
Waiter	10%–15%, with 15% being the norm at high-end London restaurants; nothing additional if a service charge is added to the bill, unless you want to reward particularly good service. Check your bill carefully, or ask. Tips in cash preferred.
Other	Restroom attendants in more expensive restaurants expect some small change or £1. Tip coat-check personnel £1 unless there is a fee, then nothing. Hairdressers and barbers get 10%–15%.

▌ TOURS

Visiting London on a fully escorted tour can feel a bit unnecessary because of its extensive public transport and wide network of taxicabs. There are many tour companies offering day tours to the city's sights highlights, and getting around is fairly easy. However, there can be cost advantages to booking all-inclusive trips.

If you're planning to travel beyond London, packaged tours can be very useful, particularly for those who don't want to rent a car or take trains and strike out on their own. Because many sights are off the beaten track and not accessible by public transportation—particularly castles, great houses, and small villages—tour groups make the country accessible to all. There are a few downsides to escorted tours: rooms in castles and medieval houses tend to be small and can feel overrun when tour groups roll in.

Dozens of companies offer fully guided tours in Britain. Most of these are full packages including hotels, all food, and transportation costs in one flat fee. Because each tour company has different specialties, do a bit of research—either on your own or through a travel agent—before booking. You'll want to know about the hotels you'll be staying in, how big your group is likely to be, precisely how your days will be structured, and who the other people are likely to be.

Among the most reliable tour companies, two U.S.-based companies—Trafalgar Tours and Globus & Cosmos Tours—specialize in moderately priced trips that feature plenty of sights but not much in the way of five-star hotels. Both offer fairly comprehensive, two-week tours within Britain, as well as shorter, less wide-ranging trip options. Tauck is another well-established company. At the high end of the price scale is Abercrombie & Kent, known for luxurious tours that include everything from castle hotels to journeys on vintage railways.

Contacts Abercrombie & Kent (☎ 800/554–7016 ⊕ www.abercrombiekent.com). **Globus & Cosmos Tours** (☎ 866/785–8581 Globus, 800/276–1241 Cosmos ⊕ www.globusandcosmos.com). **Tauck** (☎ 800/788–7885 ⊕ www.tauck.com). **Trafalgar Tours** (☎ 866/544–4434 ⊕ www.trafalgartours.com).

SPECIAL-INTEREST TOURS

CULINARY

Britain's foodie culture is increasingly rich and thriving. Gourmet on Tour, a U.S.-based tour company, offers vacations dominated by cooking, eating, and fine wine.

Contacts Gourmet on Tour (☎ 646/461–6088, 0207/558–8796 in U.K. ⊕ www.gourmetontour.com).

GARDENS

England is a land of garden lovers, and its gardens are varied and impressive. Adderley and Flora are British companies; the American tour companies Coopersmiths and Lynott Tours also offer tours of gardens around Britain. The Web site ⊕ *www.gardenvisit.com* is a useful reference site.

Contacts Adderley Travel Ltd. (☎ 01953/606906 ⊕ www.adderleytravel.com). **Coopersmiths** (☎ 415/669–1914 ⊕ www.coopersmiths.com). **Flora Garden Tours** (☎ 01366/328946 ⊕ www.flora-garden-tours.co.uk). **Lynott Tours** (☎ 800/221–2474 ⊕ www.lynotttours.com).

HEALTH

You can relax with yoga- and spa-based holidays throughout the United Kingdom. Lotus Journeys offers some good options.

Contact Lotus Journeys (☎ 0845/170–1747 ⊕ www.lotusjourneys.com).

HIKING AND WALKING

For those who prefer to spend their vacations on the move, Adventureline will keep you on your bike, on your feet, or swinging from hillsides. Country Walkers and England Lakeland Ramblers, based in the United States, have guided walks in Britain.

Contacts Adventureline (☎ 01209/820847 ⊕ www.adventureline.co.uk). **Country Walkers** (☎ 800/464–9255 ⊕ www.countrywalkers.com). **England Lakeland Ramblers** (☎ 800/724–8801 ⊕ www.ramblers.com).

HISTORY

England is rich in history and culture, to the point where it has developed what is known as the "heritage industry." Inscape offers tours (four days or less) oriented toward fine art and architecture, with knowledgeable academics as leaders. Classic England specializes in private tours to castles, cathedrals and areas of historic interest.

Contacts **Classic England** (☎ *01277/841651*, 🖷 *866/464–7389* ⊕ *www.classic-england. com*). **Inscape** (☎ *020/724–8801* ⊕ *www. inscapetours.co.uk*).

■ VISITOR INFORMATION

ONLINE TRAVEL TOOLS

ALL ABOUT ENGLAND

Enjoy England (⊕ *www.enjoyengland. com*), part of VisitBritain, includes a handy list of local Tourist Information Centres. All of England's regions, along with most major towns and cities, have their own dedicated tourism Web sites providing useful information. VisitBritain (⊕ *www.visitbritain.us*), the official visitor Web site, focuses on information most helpful to England bound U.S. travelers, from practical information to money-saving deals; you can even find out about movie locations. Visit London (⊕ *www.visitlondon.com*) is packed with information and can help you book your accommodations.

GARDENS

The National Gardens Scheme opens exceptional gardens attached to private houses and private garden squares to the public on selected weekends.

Contact **National Gardens Scheme** (⊕ *www. ngs.org.uk*).

HISTORIC SITES

The British monarchy has an official Web site with practical information about visiting royal homes and more. English Heritage, the National Trust, and VisitBritain all offer discount passes (*see Sightseeing Passes for more information*).

Contacts **The British Monarchy** (⊕ *www. royal.gov.uk*). **English Heritage** (⊕ *www. english-heritage.org.uk*). **National Trust** (⊕ *www.nationaltrust.org.uk*).

MUSEUMS AND THE ARTS

The London Theatre Guide, created by the Society of London Theatre, presents what's on and sells tickets. Their half-price ticket booths, tkts, located in London's Leicester Square and Brent Cross Shopping Centre, offer same-day bargains. Culture 24 is a nonprofit, partly government-funded site packed with information about publicly funded museums (including special exhibits), art galleries, and historic sights.

Contacts **Culture 24** (☎ *01273/623266* ⊕ *www.culture24.org.uk*). **London Theatre Guide** (⊕ *www.officiallondontheatre.co.uk*). **tkts** (⊕ *www.tkts.co.uk*).

VISITOR INFORMATION OFFICES

In many towns there are local and regional tourist information centers; many have Web sites. Offices offer services from discounts for local attractions, to visitor guides, maps, parking information, accommodation advice, and, in several locations, a booking service for local B&Bs.

The Britain and London Visitor Centre (open weekdays 9:30 to 6:30, weekends 10 to 4) provides details about travel, accommodations, and entertainment for London and Britain, but you must visit in person.

In London Britain and London Visitor Centre (✉ *1 Regent St., Piccadilly Circus* 🖷 *No phone* ⊕ *www.visitbritain.com*).

In the U.S. VisitBritain (☎ *212/986–2200 or 800/462–2748* ⊕ *www.visitbritain.us*).

INDEX

PHOTO CREDITS

10, *Ellen Isaacs/age fotostock.* 11 (left), *Walter Bibikow/viestiphoto.com.* 11 (right), *Blaine Harrington/age fotostock.* 12, *Walter Bibikow/viestiphoto.com.* 13 (left), *danilo donadoni/Marka/age fotostock.* 13 (right), *Bramwellslocker / Alamy.* 16 (left), *Visit London.* 16 (top center), *British Tourist Authority.* 16 (bottom center), *Bryce Newell/Shutterstock.* 16 (top right), *Adalberto Ríos Lanz/age fotostock.* 16 (bottom right), *Eduardo Ripoll/age fotostock.* 17 (top left), *Jose Moya/age footstock.* 17 (bottom left), *British Tourists Authority.* 17 (top center), *Ant Clausen/Shuterstock.* 17 (bottom center), *David Hughes/Shutterstock.* 17 (right), *Kevin Eaves/Shutterstock.* 18, *Homer Sykes/Alamy.* 19, *Ian Goodrick/Alamy.* 20, *Walter Bibikow/viestiphoto.com.* 21 (left), *Nikreates/Alamy.* 21 (right), *Jesús Rodríguez/age footstock.* 22, *David Noble Photography/Alamy.* 23 (left), *Cotswolds Photo Library/Alamy.* 23 (right), *Barbara Opitz/Bildarchiv Monheim/age fotostock.* 24, *Charles A. Blakeslee/age fotostock.* 25, *Walter Bibikow/viestiphoto.com.* 26, *britainonview/Martin Brent.* 28, *Walter Bibikow/viestiphoto.com.* 30, *Pat Behnke / Alamy.* 31, *Joe Viesti/viestiphoto.com.* 32, *David Hoffman Photo Library / Alamy.*

ABOUT OUR WRITERS

Longtime contributor Robert Andrews loves warm beer and soggy moors, but hates shopping malls and the sort of weather when you're not sure if it's raining—all of which he found in abundance while updating the South, West Country, and Bath and the Cotswolds chapters. He writes and revises other guidebooks and has penned his own guide to Devon and Cornwall.

Paul Cannon spent his youth following in JRR Tolkien's footsteps, traipsing around the Welsh Borders in search of its secret spots. He likes nothing better than a ramble in the hills of his native Worcestershire. Today he divides his time between Britain and Spain, working for Spanish television and contributing to Fodor's England and Spain guides. Paul covers the Welsh Borders and Lancashire and the Peaks chapters.

Texan by birth and Anglophile at heart, Christi Daugherty has lived in (and written about) England for nearly a decade. Her Fodor's territory included Where to Stay in London and chapters on the Southeast and Yorkshire. She has written and edited guidebooks to Ireland and Paris.

Freelance writer Kiki Deere has written for the *Rough Guides* and *Time Out*. Her work appears in the shopping, nightlife and arts, and pubs sections of the London chapter.

Jan Fuscoe is a Londoner by birth and loves everything about the city, particularly the East End. She works as a freelance editor and travel writer for such publications as the *Guardian*, *Times*, and *Independent* newspapers. Jan updated the Bloomsbury and Legal London, City, and South Bank sections of London.

Julius Honnor lives in London, but his Fodor's beat included rural spots in the Lake District, where he has observed chic new hotels and restaurants popping up alongside more traditional places. His work for other guidebooks has taken him around the globe.

Writer and editor Kate Hughes acquired a liking for the big city when she studied classical literature in Liverpool. Having since indulged her penchant for the country and landed gentry by getting a master's in garden history, she feels qualified to pass judgment on matters both urban and rural. She is responsible for the Thames Valley and Shakespeare Country chapters.

A Londoner since public transportation was cheap, Jack Jewers has directed films for the BBC and reviewed pubs for *Time Out;* he writes a popular blog called *The Red Pants of Justice*. He updated the East Anglia and Northeast chapters as well as several London neighborhoods.

Michelle Rosenberg, a freelance writer, published author, and mother of two gorgeous gals, loves being a tourist in her own city and spends most of her time (and money) at Charing Cross bookstore Foyles. She updated sections of London including Westminster and Royal London and Covent Garden and Soho.

Ellin Stein has written for publications on both sides of the Atlantic, including the *New York Times*, the *Times of London*, and *InStyle*. She has lived in London for 15 years and is married to a native. For this edition, Ellin updated Travel Smart England and the London chapter Planner.

Always hoping to entertain—and surprise—his readers, Fodor's contributor Roger Thomas spends almost every minute tracking down the latest and the best of Wales. He has to: he's editor of *A View of Wales* magazine.

By day, Londoner and Shoalin kung fu enthusiast Alex Wijeratna works as a global hunger activist for ActionAid; by night he hunts down the capital's best food. With his English/Sri Lankan roots, Alex knows that the real flavor of London is found in its ethnic diversity. Alex updated the Where to Eat section of London.